The World Encyclopedia of Food

The World Encyclopedia of Food

L. Patrick Coyle

Photographs by Bobbi Mapstone

Drawings by Shoshonah Dubiner

and Erika Oller

Facts On File, Inc.
460 Park Avenue South
New York, N.Y. 10016

The World Encyclopedia of Food

Library of Congress Cataloging in Publication Data

Coyle, L Patrick.
The world encyclopedia of food.

Includes index.
1. Food—Dictionaries. I. Title.
TX349.C69 641'.03'21 80-23123
ISBN 0-87196-417-1

Printed in the United States of America
10 9 8 7 6 5 4 3 2 1

Permissions

Grateful acknowledgment is made to all authors, publishers and copyright holders for permission to quote from the following copyrighted material:

Excerpt, as quoted in David Ogilvy, *Confessions of an Advertising Man.* Copyright © 1963 by David Ogilvy Trustee. Reprinted with the permission of Atheneum Publishers.

Excerpt from *Yarbrough Mountain* by Karl Kopp. Copyright © 1977 by Karl Kopp. Reprinted by permission.

Excerpts from "The Selling of H_2O" from *Consumer Reports,* Vol. 45, No. 9 (September 1980) pp. 531-538. Copyright 1980 by the Consumers Union of the United States, Inc., Mount Vernon, NY 10550. Reprinted by permission from *Consumer Reports,* September 1980.

Excerpt from *The Complete Book of Fruits and Vegetables* by F. Bianchini and F. Corbetta. Copyright © 1975 by F. Bianchini and F. Corbetta. Reprinted by permission of Crown Publishers, Inc., New York.

Excerpt from *Meetings with Remarkable Men* by G. I. Gurdjieff. Copyright © 1963 by Editions Janus. Reprinted by permission of the publisher, E. P. Dutton, Inc., and of Triangle Editions, Inc., New York.

Excerpts from *Verses from 1929 On* by Ogden Nash. Copyright © 1941, 1942 by The Curtis Publishing Co. First appeared in the *Saturday Evening Post.* Reprinted by permission of Little, Brown & Co., Boston.

Excerpt from *Dictionary of Foods* by Gaylord Hauser and Ragnar Berg. Copyright © 1970 by Benedict Lust Publications. Reprinted by permission.

Excerpt from the jacket copy of *The Day of St. Anthony's Fire* by John Fuller. Copyright © 1968 by the Macmillan Publishing Co., Inc. Reprinted by permission of the Macmillan Publishing Co., Inc., New York.

Excerpts from *Eating in America: A History* by Waverley Root and Richard de Rochemont. Copyright © 1976 by Waverley Root and Richard de Rochemont. Reprinted by permission of William Morrow and Co., Inc., New York.

Excerpt from *The Coffee Lover's Companion* by Norman Kolpas. Copyright © 1977 by Norman Kolpas. Reprinted by permission of Perigee Books, New York.

Excerpt from Henry Miller, *The Colossus of Maroussi.* Copyright 1941 by Henry Miller. Reprinted by permission of New Directions Publishing Corporation, New York.

Excerpt from *Mushrooms: Wild and Edible* by Vincent Marteka. Copyright © 1980 by Vincent Marteka. Reprinted by permission of W. W. Norton & Co., Inc., New York.

Excerpt from *A Dictionary of Gastronomy* by Andre L. Simon and Robin Howe. Text and photographs copyright © 1970 by Rainbird Reference Books Ltd. Reprinted by permission of The Overlook Press, Lewis Hollow Road, Woodstock, New York 12498.

Excerpts from *The Man-Eating Myth: Anthropology & Anthropophagy* by W. Arens. Copyright © 1979 by Oxford University Press, Inc., New York. Reprinted by permission.

Excerpt from *The Food of Italy* by Waverley Root. Copyright © 1977 by Waverley Root. Reprinted by permission.

Excerpt from "The History of Herbs: A Fondness Even in Folksongs" by Waverley Root from *The Los Angeles Times,* February 26, 1981, Part VIII, p. 29. Copyright © 1981 by Waverley Root. Reprinted by permission.

Excerpt from *Grossman's Guide to Wines, Beers and Spirits,* 6th Revised Edition by Harold J. Grossman, revised by Harriet Lembeck. Copyright © 1977 by Charles Scribner's Sons. Reprinted with the permission of Charles Scribner's Sons, New York.

Excerpt from "Laid Back in Lau" by Herb Payson from *Sail,* Vol. 11, No. 3 (March 1980), pp. 97-101. Copyright © 1980 by *Sail* magazine, Boston. Reprinted by permission.

Excerpt from *The Greek Passion* by Nikos Kazantzakis. Copyright © 1954 by Nikos Kazantzakis. Reprinted by permission of Simon & Schuster, New York.

Excerpts from *Food: An Authoritative and Visual History and Dictionary of the Foods of the World* by Waverley Root. Copyright 1980 by Waverley Root. Reprinted by permission of Simon & Schuster, New York, a Division of Gulf & Western Corporation.

The information in the chart entitled "Nutritive Value of Foods," pp. 432-475, was derived from information in the U.S. Department of Agriculture's *Home and Garden Bulletin,* No. 72, dated September 1978. The information in the chart entitled "The Sodium Content of Foods," pp. 618-636, was derived from information in the U.S. Department of Agriculture's *Home and Garden Bulletin,* No. 233, dated 1980.

The author of this book has attempted to obtain permission to include some previously published materials here from the owners of copyrights in all such materials. If, in any instance, passages from other works are included here without acknowledgment, it is because the author has been unsuccessful in contacting the copyright owners. The author wishes to apologize for any inconvenience such omissions may cause, and will gladly make any corrections that might be necessary in future editions.

To Frances and Pat Coyle, whose collaboration made all the difference in the world.

Contents

List of Color Plates

Acknowledgments

Many people contributed to this undertaking. Heading the list is Donald Carroll, who provided entree to the project, and helped to shape it. I wish to single out for special thanks Bobbi Mapstone, who managed production of all the graphics, and who offered moral support and encouragement as needed. For contributions to the writing, I am grateful to Dr. Karl Kopp, especially on the subject of wine, and to Leslie P. Coyle, Sr. Sara Eichhorn's expert research assistance was indispensable to the project. For typing portions of the manuscript, I wish to thank Frances G. Coyle, as well as Irene March-Davison of Marina Secretarial. Discussions with James F. Coyle were very helpful in the early planning of the graphics. Michael Warshaw furnished much needed logistical support.

The following persons and organizations were generous with their time and/or facilities in support of the photography: Englehart Orchard, Escondido, Calif.; Steven Spangler, Exotica Seed Co., Vista, Calif.; Golden West Meats, Santa Monica, Calif.; Charmers Market Restaurant, Santa Monica, Calif.; Pioneer Boulangerie, Santa Monica, Calif.; Los Angeles Honey Co., Los Angeles, Calif.; Rancho Arnaz, Ojai, Calif.; Halls Apricot Farm, Ojai, Calif.; Rancho Sisquoc Flood Ranch Co., Santa Maria, Calif.; Magoo's Nut Shop, Los Angeles, Calif.; the New Zealand Consulate General, Los Angeles, Calif.; One Life Health Food, Santa Monica, Calif.; and Alan Daviau, who deserves special thanks.

The following were generous with their time and/or facilities in support of the drawings: Dr. R. Drewes of the California Academy of Sciences, Dr. Frank Baugh of Pierce College, Dr. R.A. Frey of Kansas State University, Elaine Zorbas of the Pasadena Public Library and Joan DeFato of the Los Angeles County Arboretum in Arcadia.

Introduction

This volume was written for the general reader, a non-specialist who needs quick, basic information about specific foods or beverages. It is meant to be comprehensive, however, and thus might be useful to an expert outside his or her narrow field. Modes of preparation are touched upon to characterize the way a particular item is usually treated. Although cooking is not dealt with as a subject, many cooking terms are defined.

The one-volume format demands brief treatment of most topics. An article, on the average, contains 125 words. Priority has been given to identification (including the scientific name), description, and discussions of where and how an item is eaten or drunk and what it tastes like. Where possible, the text has been enlivened with historical, cultural and literary material.

The great majority of items in this book are individual fruits, grains, vegetables, animals, fishes and the like. Prepared foods, dishes and cooking styles are largely excluded. Exceptions are such prepared foods as sausage, cheese, wine, bread and sauces because they seem to constitute separate and distinct foods in themselves, apart from their ingredients. Where there was a fine distinction between a dish and a food, I opted for inclusion.

Apart from specific foods and beverages, articles have been devoted to broad topics such as meat, vegetables, cereal and fish and to selected components of food such as fat, vitamins and gum. Components have also been treated in tabular form, most prominently, sodium and other nutritive elements of food. Throughout, an effort has been made to be descriptive rather than prescriptive.

Readers should find this volume easy to read. There are more than 400 illustrations accompanying the text. Articles are arranged alphabetically. Words appearing within an article in **bold face type** are the subject of separate articles. Generous use has been made of cross references, and, to increase access, an extensive index has been provided. The index does not repeat the main listings, but does include secondary references to other topics within each article, taxonomic terms, proper names, and some geographic references.

This volume is a work of secondary research. Consequently, the author is deeply indebted to other writers in the field, past and present. A selected bibliography has been appended. Furthermore, many people helped in the preparation of this work. Their efforts have been recognized in the preceding acknowledgments.

The World Encyclopedia of Food

A

AARDVARK

Also ANTBEAR, CAPE ANTEATER. An anteater, *Orycteropus capensis*, found everywhere in Africa south of the Sahara, the aardvark is eaten mainly in tropical Africa. The name in Afrikaans, a South African dialect of Dutch, means earth pig, but the animal more resembles a bear with its strong fore-paws and sharp claws, which it uses to tear apart the high, solid African anthills. A similarly named beast, the aardwolf *(Proteles lalandi)*, preys on the white ant, or termite. It is found throughout Africa, south of the Sahara but is eaten mainly by the natives of South Africa. It looks have been described as something between a hyena and a civet.

AARFUGL

This is a game bird from Norway, small, with black feathers and highly prized for the table by Norwegian hunters. The usual style of preparation is to braise and dress it with sour cream.

ABALONE

A mollusk much like the sea snail, but with a flat oval shell, abalone is found throughout the Pacific basin, and is highly prized as a food, particularly in China and Japan.

The shell, though a dull brown on the outside, has a lustrous inner surface that is a major source of commercial mother-of-pearl. It rarely exceeds 30 inches in circumference, and is usually less than 20.

The abalone clings to rocks with its muscular foot, and it is this central muscle that is good to eat. When separated from the shell and cleaned, it looks like a large **scallop** and has round, firm, white flesh. It is approximately two to four inches wide and three to four inches thick.

Southern California is a center of abalone production in the United States. There it is generally eaten fresh. To avoid toughness, cooking must be brief. For other palates, abalone may be dried, salted or canned. It is cured before canning, and may be eaten straightaway or added to a salad or soup. It gives a strong clamlike flavor to chowder. In Japan it is known as *awabi*, in Australia as muttonfish and in South America as *loco*.

ABERTAM

This is a hard, Czechoslovakian goat's milk cheese from the Carlsbad region of Bohemia.

ABINSI GRAPE

A woody vine, *Vitis pallida*, of West Africa bears these edible berries. Sold locally, abinsi grapes are eaten raw or in soups.

ABLETTE

Also called ablet, bleak and blay, this is a shiny, silvery, little freshwater fish, *Alburnus lucidus* of the carp family *(Cyprinidae)*, found in European rivers and streams. The ablette is only four or five inches long, and its flesh is white and rather insipid. The usual table preparation is frying.

The ablette's scales are lined with a silvery pigment used in the manufacture of artificial pearls.

See also: **Bleak.**

ABRICOCK

See **Apricot.**

ABRICOTINE

This is an apricot liqueur with a brandy base, which is usually proofed at between 60 and 70. It is made in France at Enghien-les-Bains. The center of the kernel as well as the fresh pulp of apricots are used in its flavoring.

ABRONIA

A plant common in California, and other western states, abronia *(Abronia fragrans)* has starchy roots that can be made into flour. It is used for baking or porridge.

ABSINTHE

A liqueur with a lurid reputation, absinthe was banned from France, the United States, and many other countries before World War I. The offending ingredient was wormwood oil, a bitter and allegedly habit-forming distillation of the wormwood plant *(Artemesia absinthium).* It was combined in an elixir with other aromatic plants such as star-anise, balm-mint, **hyssop** and **fennel.** Yet the potent effect was also attributable to a high alcohol content: 138 proof.

Henri-Louis Pernod acquired the formula in 1797 and in later years the name Pernod became synonomous with absinthe. Present-day Pernod is an anise-flavored liqueur of 90 proof, somewhat reminiscent of absinthe, but lacking wormwood.

Canadian poet John Glassco, who sampled absinthe in Luxembourg in 1928, wrote his impressions in *Memoirs of Montparnasse:*

> *The clean sharp taste was so far superior to the sickly licorice flavor of legal French Pernod that I understood the still rankling fury of the French at having that miserable drink substituted for the real thing in the interest of public morality. The effect also was as gentle and insidious as a drug: in five minutes the world was bathed in a fine emotional haze unlike anything resulting from other forms of alcohol.*

It was served in an unusual way. Cold water was dripped from the top half of a special two-part glass, through a cube of sugar, into the bottom half, which contained a jigger of absinthe. The resulting mixture was a cloudy green.

ABSINTHIUM

See **Wormwood.**

ABUTILON

This is also called Indian mallow and *Bencao de deus*, Portuguese for "blessing of god." It is a large genus of the mallow family *(Mallaceae)* with over sixty species. Abutilons are widely grown around the world in tropical climates. They are eaten as vegetables in India and South America. Their leaves taste somewhat like spinach when boiled, but with a sour taste. *A. Indicum* is the most popular species in India. *A. esculentum* is the most popular species in Brazil, where the flowers are cooked with meat.

Abutilons are attractive plants with lobed leaves and showy, bell-shaped flowers. In Europe they are cultivated not for food, but solely for their beautiful appearance.

ACACIA

Also MIMOSA, WATTLE. Here is a large genus of shrubs and trees of the mimosa family. Many of them yield pods and seeds that can be dried or milled into flour for breadmaking. Included in these are the prairie acacia, of the southern United States and Mexico; the giraffe acacia or camel thorn *(Acacia giraffae)* of South Africa; the umbrella acacia of Australia, and the seyal acacia or gum arabic tree *(A. seyal)* of eastern Africa.

Others yield such useful products as **catechu** *(A. catechu)*, gum arabic *(A. verek, A. arabica, A. vera)* and tannin *(A. decurrens, A. molissima).*

In France the yellow and white flowers of the acacia shrub are used to make fritters or as an ingredient in homemade liqueur.

ACANTHUS

This is the genus *Acanthus*, family *Acanthaceae*, of perhaps 20 species, a perennial, prickly herb with spiny, bracted flowers that grows in the Mediterranean region. When harvested early, leaves are used for salads.

Mature acanthus leaves are so decorative, graceful and elegantly shaped that ancient Greek sculptors used them as models for the Corinthian style of column capitals.

ACARNE

See **Bream.**

ACCENT

See **Monosodium Glutamate.**

ACCOUB

This is a kind of thistle of the aster family *Carduaceae*, widely grown in the Mediterranean region and in parts of the Middle East. Highly prized for the table because of its unusual falvor, somewhere between asparagus and globe artichoke, it has another virtue—the whole plant can be eaten.

The flower buds, plucked well before flowering, may be prepared as artichoke hearts. The shoots, if no longer than five or six inches, may be prepared like asparagus and the roots like salsify.

ACELINE

This is the French name for a fish, caught and eaten in Europe, that rather resembles the common perch. It may be prepared for table as perch and is a well regarded food in France.

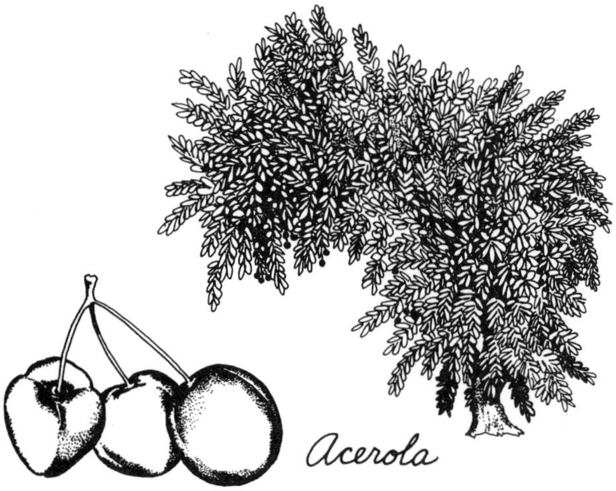

ACEROLA

This is a shrub-like tree *Malpighia glabra*, family *Malpighiaceae* that grows to about 12 feet, indigenous to tropical and subtropical regions of America. Its fruit, called a cherry, is ½ to 1 inch in diameter, thin-skinned, reddish yellow to deep red. Its flesh roughly matches its skin color, and it has three large seeds. It is a good source of Vitamin C, containing 1 to 4 percent ascorbic acid. Although acerola fruit looks like a cherry, its flavor varies. When raw it compares to a tart strawberry; when cooked it compares to a crabapple.

Chopped raw acerola bits can be used to liven up a salad, but its widest commercial use is as a juice. This is used to flavor salads, preserves and gelatin desserts and to add vitamin C. It has become an important cash export for Puerto Rico.

ACETABULA

This name is applied to two genera, *Acetabula vulgaris* and *A. sulcata*, of delicate green algae having broad cupolas resembling mushrooms. *Vulgaris* changes color from bright red in spring to orange-yellow in autumn, while *sulcata* remains steadily dark brown. Both are of the family *Cladaceae*, native to subtropical and tropical ocean regions. They are a highly prized food delicacy.

Table preparation should be similar to other fungi, such as mushrooms or chanterelles.

ACETOMEL

This is a sweet-sour syrup popular as a relish in France and Italy. It is a half-and-half mixture of honey and vinegar. In addition to being a relish, acetomel finds wide use preserving fruits, such as pears, peaches and grapes.

The special Italian name for such preserved fruit is *aceto-dolce*, or "vinegar-sweet."

ACHAR

Also ACHARD. This is a popular pickling relish from the Indian archipelago, which is also used in the West Indies. It consists of palm cabbage and tender bamboo shoots, sometimes with other fruits and vegetables added, all pickled and highly spiced.

If expense is no consideration, saffron may be included to add appetizing color.

ACHE DES MARAIS

See **Celery Seed.**

ACHILLEA

Also YARROW, SNEEZEWORT. These are highly aromatic herbs of the North Temperate Zone. They are found mainly in the Old World and belong to the thistle or aster family *Carduaceae*. Usually achillea have divided leaves and small heads of ray and tubular flowers with flattened achenes. *Achillea millefolium* is called "yarrow" and *A. ptarmica* is called "sneezewort."

Yarrow leaves can be made into an alcoholic drink by fermentation; or a mash of crushed leaves and sugar may be drunk fresh as a soft drink. In bygone days its leaves were used to flavor beer and made into a form of tea. Sneezewort leaves, finely chopped and added in small quantities, improves any green salad or *sauce vert*.

Sneezewort leaves, dried and ground into powder and sniffed up the nostrils, make one sneeze. This was considered a very healthful reaction when sniffing snuff was popular.

ACHIOTE

See **Annatto.**

ACHIRA

See **Tous-les-Mois.**

ACHOCHA

An herbaceous vine, *Cyclanthera pedata*, produces this cucumberlike vegetable in Central and South America. The fruit has prickly skin and reaches a length of two inches.

ACIDOPHILUS CHEESE

See **Yogurt Cheese.**

ACIDOPHILUS MILK

Whole cow's milk is fermented by adding the *Lacto bacillus acidophilus* bacteria to produce this. Many persons cannot drink milk because their digestive systems do not contain an enzyme called lactase, which splits lactose, a hard to digest milk sugar, into two more digestible sugars, glucose and galactose. The *L. acidophilus* in the milk converts lactose to lactic acid. In this process milk develops a sour, tart taste, which many persons find unpalatable.

In 1975 a team of research scientists at North Carolina State University developed a way to make acidophilus milk without losing the normal sweet taste. It is called "Sweet Acidophilus Milk." This milk apparently can be tolerated by persons with lactase deficiencies. However, Sweet Acidophilus Milk must be refrigerated from the time the dormant bacillus is added until it is consumed. Heating above 110°F (43.3C) will destroy the bacteria.

Therapeutic properties attributed to acidophilus milk do not appear to be sustained by clear scientific evidence, but many users are enthusiastic boosters. It may restore intestinal flora depopulated by our use of antibiotics. Pragmatic consumers feel that this milk helps regulate bowel movements and restore digestive balance. One pint to one quart per day is frequently recommended as a suitable regimen.

ACKAWAI NUTMEG

This fruit of a South American tree *(Acrodiclidium camara)* can be used as a spice in place of nutmeg. It is found from the Guianas to Brazil.

ACKEE

A tropical fruit that, though native to Africa, is basic to the diet of Jamaicans, ackee was apparently brought to the West Indies on slaveships. Captain Bligh, of *Mutiny on the Bounty* fame, first brought samples to England. His name is enshrined in its scientific designation, *Blighia sapida*. The fruit is poisonous until ripe. When ready for plucking, the pod is bright red. It cracks open naturally to reveal creamy white flesh and black seeds.

Though abundant on other islands of the area, it is readily eaten only in Jamaica, where it is something of a national dish. When cooked, it looks and tastes like scrambled eggs, and is frequently eaten with salt cod.

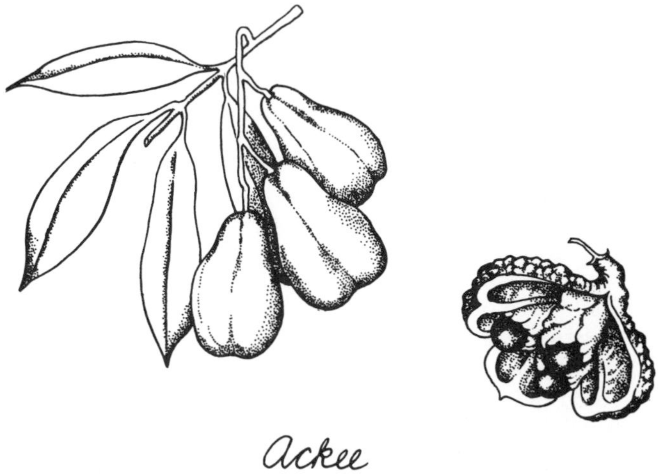

ackee

ACORN

Francis Bacon wrote that acorns were good until bread was found. They are the fruit of the oak tree, and some types of these small, brown nuts are edible. There is evidence that prehistoric humans used them as food. Classical references to them as food abound, but today in Northern Europe and the United States they serve mainly as food for pigs. In times of famine, however, they were ground as flour in place of grain, or used as a coffee substitute.

In Southern Europe and parts of North Africa, sweet acorns of the holm *(Quercus ilex)* are prepared and eaten like chestnuts. They have a sweet, nutty flavor, and are cylindrical in shape.

See also: **Chestnut.**

ACORN BARNACLE

Also ACORN SHELLS, RACK BARNACLE, ACORN-FISH, TURBAN SHELL. An immobile, marine crustacean found in rocky ocean-shore waters throughout the world, acorn barnacle is of the order *Ciripedia*, family *Balanidae*, species *Balanus*. In the larval state, these barnacles are free-swimming, but in the adult state they are firmly attached to rocks and must be pried loose. Their shells are rough on the surface and conical with a wide variation in size. The largest are the *Balanus nubilus* found on the Pacific Coast of America, some measuring almost a foot in diameter. They are much smaller on the Atlantic Coast and in other parts of the world.

The *Balanus* varieties are the most highly prized as food. They have delicate flesh and may be prepared for eating according to most recipes for crab.

ACORN SQUASH

A small winter squash of the gourd family, genus *Cucurbita*, it is dark green and fluted, somewhat resembling an acorn in shape. Pre-Columbian natives of South and Central America cultivated and ate acorn squash as a staple diet item. Later, in North America, the Algonquian Indians introduced the European settlers of Massachusetts to what they called *askoot*—a squash. The colonists gladly accepted the nourishing food but bobtailed the name into "squash." Back in the motherland, the English also gladly accepted the new food, but they decided to call it "marrow."

Being a vine-ripened variety, acorn squash has a hard rind and seeds that are discarded. Only the soft, yellow-orange flesh is eaten. This flesh is rather bland, so it is usually sugared, buttered or seasoned after boiling or baking. Another use is as a filling for pies. A pound of acorn squash should yield a cup of cooked squash.

ACOUCHY

Also SURINAM RABBIT. This is a rodent, *Myoprocta acouchy*, a small species of agouti, slightly smaller than a rabbit or a guinea pig. It is native to the West Indies and South America and is an herbivorous, diurnal wild animal.

Among gastronomes, acouchy might be prepared like suckling pig, or it might simply be stewed in a pot with other savory ingredients.

See also: **Agouti, Guinea Pig.**

ACQUA DI FIRENZE

In English, this is also called "Water of Florence." It is an Italian aperitif wine, from Florence, and is made with spices and lemon peel.

ACQUETTE

Two types of this liqueur or cordial are popular in northern Italy and southern France, the silver and the gold. The silver is distilled from alcohol flavored with cloves, nutmeg and cinnamon; and the gold from alcohol flavored with angelica, cloves, cinnamon, lemon peel and daucus of Crete. Silver and gold leaf are added for coloring.

ACTEPHILA

This is a shrub, *Actephila excelsa*, of tropical Asia whose flowers and leaves are used to make a palatable and nutritious beverage.

ACTINELLA

The flower tops of this aromatic herb, *Actinella odorata*, are used to produce a beverage consumed locally in the southwestern United States.

ACTINIA

See **Sea Anemone.**

ACTINIDIA

See **Kiwi Fruit.**

ADALAH

Also QUEENSLAND HALIBUT. This is a flatfish of the Indian and Pacific Oceans but is fished most intensively off the east and north coasts of Australia. The adalah *(Psettodes erumei)* is a popular food fish where it is plentiful. It reaches a length of up to 25 inches and a weight of up to 20 pounds. It is relatively thick bodied. Unlike many flatfish it may live to a great extent in midwater, rather than lying on the bottom. A closely related species, *P. blecheri*, is plentiful along the west coast of Africa and is exploited there for food.

ADAM'S APPLE

See **Lime.**

ADANE

Also ADANA. This is a species of sturgeon fished from the Po River in northern Italy. Its caviar has been declared excellent. While the flesh is usually eaten cooked, much is prepared by smoking and is as highly regarded as the caviar.

ADDAX

Here is a white antelope of the Sahara Desert whose meat and skin are highly prized by people from Senegambia and Algeria eastward to the Sudan. The addax *(Addax nasomaculatus)* is heavily built, standing a little more than three feet high at the shoulder but weighing up to 260 pounds. It is not a swift runner and is said to be heading for extinction under the onslaught of improved firearms and mobile hunting techniques.

ADE

This is a popular drink made from fruit juice (usually citrus) and sugar, which may or may not be mixed with water. Examples are orangeade, lemonade, grapeade and others. There are commercial products called ades, which are made with artificial flavoring and coloring.

Though most ades are made up as soft drinks, they readily lend themselves to additions of alcoholic beverages. Wines, liqueurs and liquors add a fillip for more adventurous palates. Distribution and consumption of ades is worldwide.

ADLAY

Also ADLAI. This grain plant has soft-hulled seeds and is of the genus *Coixlacryma-jobi mayuen.* It is a variety of the grain **Job's Tears,** which has hard, pearly white, capsulelike seeds.

Adlay is an important food plant in the Philipines, Japan and Southeast Asia. It is ground into flour, a process made easier by its soft hull, and used for the usual purposes.

ADRAGANTE

See **Tragacanth.**

ADVOCAAT

A Dutch liqueur, much like eggnog, bottled at 30 proof, *Advocaat* is creamy and smooth and contains brandy, eggs and sugar. It is sometimes called "egg brandy."

ADZUKI BEAN

This small, red, annual and bushy bean, *Phaseolus angularis,* is grown in Japan and China. It is a popular and important, staple food, particularly in Japan. There it is eaten as a fresh vegetable. It is also dried, ground and made into flour for cakes and confectionery.

Adzuki beans also have ceremonial significance as ingredients in dishes prepared to celebrate the emperor's birthday. They also appear in many other festival dishes like bean jam and *Yokan.* The latter may be served on black lacquer plates with a ceremony pleasing to the eye as well as to the palate, or even to the artistic soul. Adzuki beans may now be found in some American supermarkets.

AEOLANTHUS

A perennial herb, *Aeolanthus heliotropoides,* of tropical Africa, it is used to flavor various dishes, especially soups.

AERATED BREAD

This bread is made by a patented process that produces a light loaf, yet dispenses with the normal leavening agents, such as yeast and baking powder. Flour, salt and water charged with carbon dioxide are mixed together in kneading machines inside a closed chamber. The resulting mixture goes directly to the ovens and is leavened by the release of the gas during baking. The process was patented in 1856 by John Dauglish, an English chemist, at a time when the baking industry was coming under close scrutiny. Eliza Acton's *The English Bread Book,* published in 1857, described shocking conditions in London bakeries. The premises were often vermin infested, dough was adulterated with potato and alum, and kneading was done by hand. This guaranteed a liberal admixture of sweat to the dough. Dr. Daulglish's process had many virtues: bypassing fermentation, it cut preparation time by hours; dough was mixed untouched by human hands, and was therefore much cleaner; it made alum unnecessary; it gave reliable and uniform results; and it made working conditions safer, since flour dust is unhealthy to breathe, and can explode under certain circumstances.

Although aerated bread achieved some popularity in London, it did little to change the industry, which, 50 years later, was still very backward. Aerated bread did not catch on in the United States because, according to one authority, the taste seemed flat to the American palate.

See also: **Bread.**

AFRICAN ARROWROOT

A plant of the canna family, *Canna bidentata,* it has starchy roots that yield a flour used for baking or cooking as porridge or gruel. This variety is native to Africa, but there are also Queensland, Brazilian and West Indian varieties.

See also: **Arrowroot.**

AFRICAN HORNED CUCUMBER

Also METULIFERUS CUCUMBER. The spiny, red fruit of an African species, *Cucumis metuliferus,* it is three to five inches long at maturity, and is used in salads.

AFRICAN OLIVE

A tropical tree, *Vitex cienkowskii,* of the verbena family native to Africa produces this olivelike fruit. It is highly esteemed locally.

AFRICAN SPANGLETOP

The seeds of this African or Australian plant, *Leptochloa capillacea,* are used as a famine food. Apart from that it is an important fodder.

Agar-agar

AFRICAN SUNPLANT

This is a tropical African shrub, *Solanum duplosinuatum*, whose yellow, bitter fruit is used to make soups.

AFRICAN UNONA

An African tree, *Unona undulata*, of the *Anonaceae* order produces this aromatic, slightly acrid fruit, which is used as a condiment.

AGAMI

Also TRUMPETER. The agami may be any of several long-legged, long-necked, wading birds of South America of the genus *Psophia*, especially, *P. crepitans* of Guiana and Brazil. As wild birds, they are forest dwellers but are very gregarious and are easily tamed. Their loud, screeching cry causes Brazilians to domesticate them and place them among the poultry in the barnyard as guards.

Agami flesh, when young, is said to be delicate and may be prepared as any other game fowl or, as in South America, braised and served with boiled rice and fried pimientos.

AGAR-AGAR

A tasteless, odorless gelatinous substance, agar-agar is made from red seaweed, *Gelidium sp.*, which is common off the coasts of Japan, China and other Asian countries, such as Sri Lanka, and off the Atlantic and Pacific coasts of the United States. It is known by a variety of names including *kanten* (Japanese), Chinese moss, Ceylon moss, Chinese isinglass, Japanese isinglass, etc. The seaweed is eaten fresh in Japan, but its derivative, agar-agar, is used to thicken gelatin desserts, jellies and soups. A major application in the United States is as a stabilizer in ice cream, in which the agar-agar absorbs or binds some of the water to prevent it from freezing into grainy crystals, thus keeping the ice cream smooth and creamy. Agar-agar is more effective than many other gelatins in that respect because it can absorb up to 200 times its volume of water. In powdered form it may be taken as a bulk food for relief of constipation. It is also a popular culture medium for bacteriological experiments.

Agar-agar is marketed in several forms, in sticks called square kanten, in masses like fine hair called slender kanten, and in powdered form. The bird's nests in **bird's nest** soup are made up of the gelatinous saliva of the Salangane swallow, which feeds on red seaweed.

AGARIC

See **Mushroom.**

AGASTACHE

This Mexican plant, *Agastache neomexicana*, of the giant hyssop genus is a perennial, and its leaves are used as a flavoring herb.

AGATI

Also SCARLET WISTARIA TREE. An ornamental tree, *Sesbania grandiflora*, it is native to tropical Asia but transplanted to south Florida and the West Indies. In southeast Asia its flowers are used in salads and as potherbs. They are also enjoyed boiled or fried.

AGAVE

See **Maguey.**

AGONE D'ISTRIA

Also AGONE, AGONI and AGON. This is a small, flat fish found in the freshwater Italian lakes of Como and Garda. Some Italians call the *agone* by the name *sardina*, probably because it resembles its salt-water cousin, the sardine, in size and taste.

Preparation for eating usually follows recipes for sardines. It may be salted, dried or cooked in oil and then marinated in vinegar.

AGOU

Also NEGROES SAGOU. This is a plant, grown in various parts of Africa, which provides grain that resembles small-grain millet. It may be cooked like rice, ground into flour to make cakes or made into a kind of porridge.

AGOUTI

A rodent, *Dasyprocta aguti*, of the cavy, or guinea pig, family native to the West Indies and South America, it is an herbivorous, diurnal, wild animal about the size of a rabbit, but whose flesh has a stronger taste. Its pelt is brownish or grizzled with barred hair in several alternating dark and light bands, blackish blue or brown at the base and yellowish at the tip. The agouti is a swift runner whose hind legs are particularly well developed.

Agouti is prepared like suckling pig, or it may simply be boiled in a pot with other savory ingredients.

AGRAFA

This is a popular, high quality cheese made in Greece. Some gastronomes consider it to be the equal of French Gruyere, which it resembles in flavor and texture. *Agrafa* has this important difference, it is made not from cow's milk but from fresh ewe's milk.

AGRAZ

Also AGRAS, GRANULATED ALMOND MILK. This is an iced, sweet soft drink invented and popular in Algeria. Its ingredients are sweet, crushed almonds, verjuice, water and sugar. The resulting liquid is strained and served about half frozen.

Agraz has found acceptance in Europe where sophisticated palates have discovered that a dash of kirsch adds an interesting fillip.

AGRIMONY

Also AGRIMONIA. The agrimony plants form a small genus of the rose family *Rosaceae* and grow mostly in north temperate regions. Their leaves are featherlike, their fruit bristly and flowers yellow. The European agrimony *(Agrimonia eupatoria)* may be the most widespread species. There are others: the hemp agrimony *(Eupatorium cannabinum)* and the water agrimony,often called bur marigold. Wafer ash is another name for agrimony bark. Leaves of the European agrimony are used for making a tea, once thought to have medicinal qualities.

AGRODOLCE SAUCE

This Italian sweet-and-sour sauce has been served since Roman times. It consists of brown sugar, currants or raisins, chocolate, candied peel, garlic, bay leaves, capers and vinegar, plus the juice of the meat it is to accompany. It is used with rabbit, hare, wild boar, venison and other braised meat. A fish variation contains chopped tomatoes, herbs and sometimes pine nuts.

See also: **Sauce.**

AGUARDIENTE

In Spanish, this is a generic term for distilled liquor, akin to the *eau de vie* of France. The literal translation would be "firewater." It is used most often to refer to strong, raw liquor distilled from wine (or grapes) or molasses and bottled without aging or rectifying. In Puerto Rico, rum fresh from the still is called *aguardiente* before it is barreled for aging. The term is used in Spain and in most Latin American countries.

See also: **Brandy, Eau de Vie, Rum.**

AGUGLIE

Also AGUGLIA, GARFISH, GARPIKE. Aguglie is a long, bony fish *(Belonidae)* with a needlelike beak found in Italian waters of the Mediterranean Sea. Not too meaty, aguglie have been referred to as "floating pincushions."

They can be prepared for the table by frying or baking and serving in a tomato and onion sauce. However, the most popular way is to make them into soup.

See also: **Gar, Pike.**

AGUNCATE

See **Avocado.**

AHOLEAHOLE

A small, food fish, *Kuhlia sandvicensis*, found only around the Hawaiian Islands, it is slender and silvery and reaches a length of about 12 inches. It frequents reefs and sunken wrecks. Though mainly a marine fish, it can adapt to freshwater. Hawaiians have a high regard for its flesh; they fish for it at night with baited hooks and nets.

AIGRE DE CEDRE

See **Citron.**

AIGUEBELLE

A strong French liqueur of the Chartreuse type. Distilled in the Rhone Valley, it comes in two shades, green and yellow. The yellow variety is sweeter.

AINAWE

See **Greenling.**

AIOLI

Also AIOLLI, AILLOLI. A sauce of southern France, very much like **mayonnaise,** but containing a lot of pounded, pressed garlic, plus other seasonings. The basic ingredients are olive oil, egg yolks and garlic; but the recipe, as well as the seasonings, varies from region to region. The original of this sauce is believed to be *ali-oli*, a Spanish garlic sauce, which dates back at least to the 11th century. Aioli is eaten with poached fish, salt cod, potatoes, eggs, snails and is added to bouillabaisse.

See also: **Sauce.**

AISY, CENDRE D'

This is a cow's milk cheese from Burgundy in France. It is aged in ashes of grapevines, whence comes its name and appearance—"ashen"—*cendre* being the French word for that look. These cheeses are reputed to be at their best from October to July.

AJI

See **Chili.**

AJINOMOTO

See **Monosodium Glutamate.**

AJMUD

An herb of the same genus as caraway, ajmud *(Carum roxburghiana)* is found in India and Indochina. The seeds are used as a flavoring agent.

AKAKA

A perennial herb of the onion family, akaka *(Allium akaka)* is native to Iran, and grows in other parts of temperate Asia. It has strongly odorous bulbs that are used much like onions.

AKALA

Also AKELA, AKALA BERRY. This is an upright shrub, *Rubus macraei*, that grows in the Hawaiian Islands. Akala bushes vary in appearance; some are climbing creepers, some are spiny, some smooth; but they all produce purplish or orange berries. These are large, sometimes as much as two inches in diameter, juicy, with small seeds, and they taste like raspberries or strawberries. There is some variation in taste, too; some are slightly bitter, while most are sweet, delicate and well-flavored.

AKEBIA QUINATA

Also AKEBIA LOBATA, AKEBI. These are two species of hardy, twining shrubs of the family *Lardizabalaceae*, native to temperate East Asia, having purple-brown flowers. *A. quinata* produces valuable oily seeds, and the long vines are used in basket weaving. In Japan, China and Korea, *A. lobat*, or *A. trifoliata*, is a climbing shrub with edible fruit that is dark purple with black seeds. This fruit is about the size of a small banana and, though rather insipid, is widely eaten in China and Japan. These plants are cultivated in America but only as ornamentals.

AKEE

See **Ackee.**

AKU

See **Tuna Fish.**

AKVAVIT

See **Aquavit.**

ALANCHA

See **Sardine.**

ALASCH

See **Kummel.**

ALASKA BLACKFISH

Related to the pike, the Alaska blackfish *(Dallia pectoralis)* lives in brooks, lakes and marshes and can reputedly survive being frozen into the ice. This fish's range includes the coastal regions of Alaska, the rivers of the Arctic coast and parts of Siberia. It rarely exceeds eight inches in length and is not much used for food nowadays, although in former times it was resorted to as nourishment for humans and dogs.

ALBACORE

See **Tuna Fish.**

ALBATROSS

The definition includes any of several web-footed sea birds related to the petrels of the genus *Diomedea* and allied genera. Most familiar of the species are the wandering albatross *(D. albatrus)* chiefly white and short-tailed, the dusky, black-footed albatross *(D. nigripes)*, the Layson Albatross *(D. immutibilis)* and the yellow-nosed albatross *(Thalassogeron chlorohynchos)*.

These are the largest of sea birds. They inhabit the southern oceans and the northern Pacific up to about 30° of latitude. Albatross eat mainly fish and squid, but have been known to soar gracefully over ships far at sea for days on end feeding on garbage thrown overboard.

The albatross is the well-known gooney bird, plague of American aviators in the South Pacific during World War II. Gooneys fell in love with landing strips on Wake Island, Guam and other places. Clouds of these clumsy, slow-moving birds on and over the strips endangered flight activities for the mechanical birds.

An albatross is easy to catch with a baited line and, despite the Ancient Mariner's stricture not to harm the bird that made the wind to blow, they have served as food, particularly when young. They should be prepared like young duck.

ALBERGE

See **Peach.**

ALBERT SAUCE

English hot horseradish sauce, which is served with beef or smoked trout. Its ingredients are cream, butter, breadcrumbs, horseradish, mustard and vinegar. Alternatively, it can be made with **bechamel sauce,** horseradish and cream.

See also: **Sauce.**

ALBUMIN

Also ALBUMEN. This could be any one of a class of proteins found in many substances. Examples include milk, muscle tissue, egg white and other animal and vegetable tissues. It is an important constituent of human blood serum. Albumin contains nearly 2 percent of sulphur.

Albumin is valuable in nutrition. Two good and appetizing sources are coddled eggs and rare beef, both rich in soluble, easy-to-digest albumin.

Applying heat to albumin causes coagulation and has a clarifying effect on liquids, a useful quality for cooking and sugar refining.

Confectionery is now made with albumin instead of with egg whites for whisk-up paste, marshmallow, licorice and meringue products. It replaces whole eggs in commercial cake and biscuit making and egg whites in commercial almond paste.

ALBURN

See **Bleak.**

ALCHERMES

See **Alkermes.**

ALCOHOL

Alcoholic beverages contain ethyl alcohol, a product of the reaction of yeast with sugar called **fermentation.** For high-proof spirits the alcohol is further refined and concentrated by **distillation.** This involves heating the fermented mash and condensing alcohol from the resulting vapor. In its pure state, ethyl alcohol is a clear, colorless liquid with a mild, pleasant odor but a pungent taste. It is highly volatile and burns with a pale blue flame.

Alcohol is the intoxicating element in all beers, wines and liquors with the possible exception of **absinthe.** Beers and table wines contain 14 percent alcohol or less, because at that point fermentation is halted by the presence of so much alcohol. Wines with a higher alcoholic content—some run as high as 23 percent—are called "fortified" wines, because alcohol has been added to them. They normally keep better than wines with the low alcoholic content.

Alcohol is high in calories and is metabolized as sugar, but it has little or no nutritive value. An ounce of 100 proof liquor usually contains 100 calories.

Alcohol depresses the central nervous system and acts swiftly to slow reflexes and release social inhibitions. Initially, it induces excitement, gaiety and talkitiveness—if the social atmosphere is conducive. As more is drunk, the depressive effects predominate, ending in sleep, if enough is taken.

It is an addictive substance. Prolonged use in some cases leads to habituation and dependence. Many writers have chronicled drinkers' struggles against alcohol. Most notable in this century were Jack London in *John Barleycorn*, and Malcolm Lowery in his novel, *Under the Volcano.* Lowery, writing his own epitaph, summed up his experience in this bit of humorous doggerel:

Malcolm Lowery
Late of the Bowery
His prose was flowery
And often glowery
He lived, nightly, and drank, daily,
And died playing the ukulele.

ALDER

Also ALNUS. This is the genus *Alnus* of 30 species of shrubs or trees, the alders, of the birch family *Betulaceae.* They grow usually in moist ground, creeks and river bottoms in the North Temperate Zone and in the Andes Mountains of South America. The fruit is woody and conelike, while the leaves are toothed. In the fall, the leaves turn a bright reddish yellow forming a brilliant dash of color in the landscape.

A bitter juice can be extracted from the fruit, which has been used to flavor bitters and vermouth.

ALE

A fermented drink, much like **beer,** but more bitter to the taste and heavier. It originated in Northern Europe, in countries where little wine was produced. Until the 19th century, it was brewed from malted barley alone, but then hops were added, as in beer, so that the difference between the two lies in the fermentation process. Historically, it has been popular in England and remains so today, while in other countries the distinction between beer and ale has all but disappeared.

Shakespeare sang its praises, perhaps most characteristically in *Henry V*, who moaned, "I would give all my fame for a pot of ale and safety."

ALECOST

Also COSTMARY, BALSAMITA, MINT GERANIUM, BALSAM HERB and MACE. Alecost *(Chrysanthemum balsamita)* of the family *Compositae* is a pot herb and salad plant whose minty flavor goes well with soups, game, poultry and veal. Infusing the leaves in boiling water produces a spicy, aromatic tea. Poultices of dampened leaves are thought to relieve the pain of bee stings. This plant flourishes throughout the Middle East, southern Europe and England.

Another definition of costmary is this: A dish of eggs, sugar and rose water mixed with cream and herb juices and baked in butter in a shallow dish; and another: A village feast on Shrove Tuesday.

ALEGAR

This is a malt vinegar made from sour ale. It is used for flavoring, pickling and cooking where malty flavor will enhance palatability. Although produced in both England and America, it has become a favorite accompaniment of fish and chips in England.

ALEMTEJO

For this soft, cylindrical cheese made in the province of Alemtejo, Portugal, warm ewe's milk is curdled with an extract of flowers of a certain thistle. Goat's milk is often added. It comes in three sizes: two ounces, one pound and four pounds. Ripening takes several weeks, and the taste is strong.

ALEWIFE

A small North American fish, *Pomolobus pseudoharengus*, of the *Clupeidae* family, which includes herring, shad and sardines, the alewife was an important food fish

Alfalfa sprouts

alewife

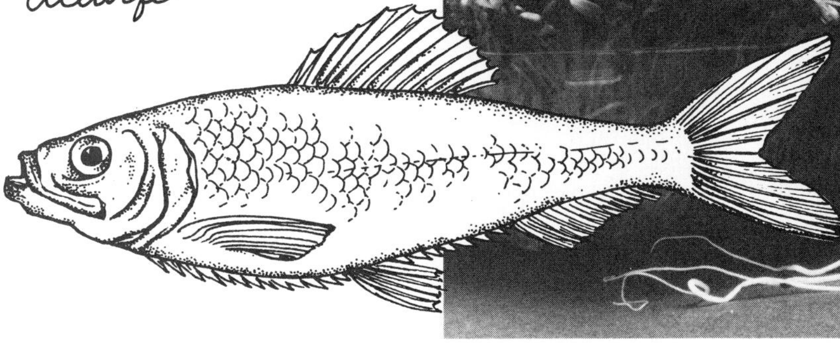

for the early settlers of New England. Today it is largely exported, after salting, to the West Indies and is used in North America mainly as a pan-fish and as bait.

In spring the alewife spawns in ponds and quiet rivers of eastern North America between Newfoundland and Chesapeake Bay, and then spends the rest of its life in the sea in large schools. Some have invaded the Great Lakes from the North Atlantic and have become landlocked.

The alewife grows to about a foot in length and has a dark green back with bright silver sides and belly. It tastes best when lightly fried and garnished with parsley, salt and lemon. It is known by other names: sawbelly, grayback, gaspereau, skipjack and branch herring. "Alewife" is probably derived from a Native American language.

ALEXANDERS

Also HORSE PARSLEY. This herbaceous plant, *Smyrnium olusatrum*, is native to the Mediterranean region, but grows from the Caucasus to the Canary Islands. It is strongly aromatic, and the leaves may be used as a substitute for parsley. Alexanders attains a height of from two to four feet; it grows wild in the south of France and in Britain, especially in cool shady places. It was much cultivated formerly, especially for its stalks and roots but was gradually displaced by celery. Alexanders is a valuable vegetable, but much neglected nowadays.

ALFALFA

Also LUCERNE. This is the species *Medicago sativa*, family *Leguminosae*, subfamily *Faboideae*, and is one of the most important leguminous forage plants. It is cultivated widely through the world's temperate zones. Human consumption has been increasing since its recognition and promotion as a diet supplement. The taste is mild and pleasant, and the odor is attractive. Harvested at the late bud or early bloom stage and properly cured, alfalfa contains 17 to 24 percent protein and certain vitamins and minerals along with carbohydrates and fat. In addition, the bluish purple, cloverlike flowers of the alfalfa plant furnish beekeepers with hundreds of tons of honey.

ALFONCINO

A beautiful rose-red fish, *Beryx splendens*, is found in the northern parts of both the Atlantic and Pacific Oceans but fished commercially mainly off the coast of Portugal. It reaches a length of 25 inches. A related species, *B. decadactylus*, is an orange color and inhabits the European Atlantic coast, the Mediterranean and as far south as the bulge of Africa. Both fish have a deep body and large head and eyes. Both also frequent fairly deep water, so that, although the quality of their flesh is rated excellent, they are not often seen in fish markets.

ALGAE

Also ALGA. Algae are a primary division of the phylum *Thallophyta*, comprising the classes blue green algae *(Cyanphyceae)*, brown algae *(Phaeophyceae)*, and red algae *(Rhodophyceae)*. These classes include almost all seaweeds, such as rock weed, sea moss, sea lettuce and others. They also number allied freshwater and nonaquatic forms like pond scums, fallen stars and stoneworts.

Algae have a vast range in size, from giant kelp plants, whose stems extend up to 600 feet, to the tiny cells that color red snow. Fresh and salt water bodies all over the world may and do harbor growths of algae.

These water plants are eaten many places in the world. In Scotland, seaweeds of several varieties are food items. In America, kelp is a staple in health food stores for fiber and vitamin C. In a pinch in Finland, the Lapp herdsmen can consume lichens and moss. The Japanese have long used algae of the *Laminaria* genus to make the *kombu* and *kantu* gelatins used in preparing jellies, soups and sauces. Kelp has a medical function, being used to treat goiter and obesity. It is also a source of algin, used in processed foods, ice cream, jellies, pharmaceuticals, cosmetics and lotions. Diatoms *(Bacillarieae)* are used as a dietary fiber source.

See also: **Fungus, Kelp.**

ALGARROBA

See **Mesquite.**

ALGERIAN WINES

See **Wines, North African.**

ALICANTE BOUSCHET

This grape variety produces a semidry red table wine high in alcohol content and rich in tannin. Alicante Bouschet wine is grown most commonly in Algeria, Morocco and Tunisia and is often used in blending with other red wine grapes, particularly the **Gamay, Cabernet** and **Pinot.**

See also: **Wine Grapes.**

ALICANTE WINE

A red dessert wine, sweet and with a high alcohol content, this comes from the Alicante region of Spain, in Murcia on the eastern Mediterranean coast. The basic grape in this region is the Moscatel, rich in sugar, which makes a deeply colored, fortified wine of up to 18 percent alcohol.

ALIGOTE WINE

A dry white wine made from the Aligote grape derives from ancient vines planted and still cultivated in Burgundy. Bourgogne-Aligote is perhaps the best representative of this wine, although a Russian table wine called "Aligote" is grown in Moldavia (near the Rumanian border) and in the Crimea.

See also: **Burgundy Wines.**

ALIMENTARY PASTE

See **Pasta.**

ALKANET

Also BUGLOSS, PUCCOON, BLOODROOT. This is a European shrub, *Alkanna tinctoria*, of the family *Boraginaceae*, with funnel-shaped flowers and pitted or wrinkled nutlets and an important root. From this root comes a red coloring substance, alkannin, used to color tinctures, cosmetics, fats, cheese, essences and beverages. Under the name "Henna," it is also used to color human hair.

See also: **Borage, Bugloss.**

ALKEKENGI

See **Ground Cherry.**

ALKERMES

Two liqueurs are called by this name, one French and one Italian; both are red. The French variety is sweet and colored by small scarlet grain insects of the Cochineal genus, famous for their red dye. The Italian is prepared from a base of alcohol, sugar syrup and orange-blossom water, with cloves, cinnamon and vanilla added for flavor.

ALLARIA

Also JACK-BY-THE-HEDGE, DONKEY FOOT, GARLIC MUSTARD, SAUCE ALONE. This strong, garlic-scented plant, a native of Europe and Asia, of the genus *Alium*, family *Alliaceae*, is common now in the United States and eastern Canada. It is used as a salad herb or for flavoring, though its popularity has declined.

ALLEMANDE SAUCE

The classic *veloute* sauce, reduced by half, and enriched with egg yolks and cream. It is light in color, and sometimes called *sauce parisienne*, or *sauce blonde.*

It is served with fish, eggs and chicken and is the basis for many creamed dishes.

See also: **Sauce.**

ALLGAUER EMMENTALER

See **Allgauer Rundkase.**

ALLGAUER RUNDKASE

Also ALLGAUER EMMENTALER. Named for the Alpine district of Allgau in southwestern Bavaria, it is a type of Swiss cheese from 5 to 5¾ inches thick, usually weighing from 150 to 175 pounds.

See also: **Swiss Cheese.**

ALLIARIA

See **Allaria.**

ALLICE

See **Shad.**

ALLIGATOR

See **Crocodile.**

ALLIGATOR PEAR

See **Avocado.**

ALLSPICE

Also BAYBERRY, JAMAICA PEPPER, PIMENTO. This aromatic spice is obtained from a single source, the berry of a West Indian tree, *Pimenta officinalis*, or *Eugenia pimenta*. It is not a mixture of several spices, as one might suppose from the name. Allspice gained its name by seeming to combine the fragrance of three spices, cinnamon, nutmeg and clove. Some authorities add a fourth, ginger.

The allspice tree grows particularly well in Jamaica, which produces most of the world's supply. There it is called bayberry. The fruit is allowed to grow to full size, but it is picked unripe and then dried in the sun. After drying, the berries are pea-sized and brown. At this point they are usually ground to powder for use in medicine and cookery, but whole berries can be purchased for grinding at home. The latter practice is recommended for maximum freshness and aroma. If allowed to mature, the berries have a sweet, highly scented taste but are very hot.

The allspice tree is a member of the myrtle family, and is closely related to the clove and bay rum trees. In local cooking, crushed leaves are often added to the berries for seasoning, and occasionally bay rum leaves and berries (malagueta peppers) are substituted for allspice.

Allspice is particularly popular in Sweden and Finland. Elsewhere it is most often added to sausages, pickles, marinating liquids, fish dishes and tomato-juice cocktails. In French, allspice is called *toute epice*, which is an exact translation. Confusingly, the term *toute epice* is also used for another spice, nigella.

ALMOND

Among edible nuts, the almond is second only to the **walnut** in popularity and length of cultivation. It is produced by a peachlike tree, *Prunus amygdalus*, as the pit of a leathery fruit. The eaten nut is actually the seed within the pit.

There are two main categories among many varieties: sweet and bitter almonds, the sweet being what the consumer normally understands as almond. The bitter are used mainly as a source of flavoring and of an oil that goes into cosmetics and pharmaceuticals.

It is thought that almond trees originated in Russia, China and Japan. They were introduced into the Mediterranean area—probably by Phoenicians—centuries before Christ. The tree is mentioned in the Bible, Aaron's rod being an almond branch. The ancient Romans much appreciated almonds, calling them "Greek nuts." The tree favors arid, rocky soil, and its cultivation spread all over the Mediterranean area, including Italy, Spain, Sardinia, Morocco and

Almonds: shelled and unshelled

Sicily. In France, almonds have been cultivated since the 14th century, and in England since the 16th. They were introduced into California in mid-19th century, and their cultivation has become a large industry there.

In some places almonds are harvested while they are green, the shells soft and the outer coverings tender. They may be eaten fresh, or preserved in *eau de vie* as a delicacy.

The almond seed is nutritious, consisting of about 50 percent oil and 15 percent protein with significant amounts of vitamin B1, iron, calcium and phosphorus. The best California almonds have thin, light-colored shells called paper shells, which are easily opened with the fingers. But shell strength ranges through semisoft to hard, which requires the aid of a hammer or fancy nutcracker to open. Almonds are eaten raw, frequently salted as an accompaniment to cocktails, but also candied, in nougats and macaroons, and in cakes, other desserts and sauces.

Two of the finest almonds are Spanish: the Jordan and the Valencia. The Jordan is plump and long, while the Valencia is plump at one end and pointed at the other. The choicest almonds are salted and eaten whole; those of irregular shape are made into paste and butters.

Oil of sweet—as opposed to bitter—almonds is high in protein and low in carbohydrates, and in Spain and Portugal is preferred in the kitchen for frying fish and vegetables.

The oil of bitter almond, which is used to flavor almond extract and liqueurs, is more often than not taken from the pits of apricots, peaches and prunes, which have a higher oil yield than the almond itself.

ALMOND, EARTH

See **Chufa.**

ALMONDETTE

The seeds of a tropical tree, *Buchanania lanzan*, native to India and Malaysia, almondettes are used in making candy and other confections.

ALMOND EXTRACT

Also ALMOND ESSENCE. A flavoring solution obtained from adding alcohol to macerated bitter almond kernels, almond extract is used in making cakes, puddings, ice cream and many pastries. Manufacture and use is world-wide, except in Moslem areas.

See also: **Almond.**

ALMOND PASTE

See **Marzipan.**

ALMOND SYRUP

This nonalcoholic flavoring solution is obtained from a mixture of ground sweet and bitter almond kernels (usually 10 parts sweet to three parts bitter) emulsified in barley syrup. Apricot or peach kernels may be substituted for the bitter almonds and a syrup of orange-flower water and sugar used in place of barley syrup. Almond syrup is widely made and consumed by bakeries, pastry shops, soda fountains and many home cooks.

ALMORTA

See **Vetch.**

ALOCASIA

Also APE, PAI, TARO. This is an Asian root vegetable closely related to the more widely cultivated **Taro** *(Colocasia esculenta).* Alocasia *(Alocasia macrorrhiza)* roots are starchy and nutritious, though considered inferior to the *Colocasia* species. Both plants are known as elephant's ear because of their wide, green fronds.

ALOE

Also ALOES. This is a large genus of succulent plants of over 200 species of the lily family *Liliaceae* mainly from South Africa. The aloe is such an attractive and useful plant that it is cultivated worldwide out of doors in tropic and subtropic regions and in a protected environment in cooler climates. Its basal, leathery leaves and spigate, showy flowers make it a sturdy, exotic ornamental. It also has numerous medicinal, flavoring and cosmetic uses.

In Biblical times, aloe *(Aguilaria agallocha),* a fragrant East Indian tree, provided an incense comparable to frankincense and myrrh.

The bitter tasting juice from the leaves, called "aloes," is used for flavoring for fernets and bitters and for homemade wines and cordials. In England it was used to discourage nailbiting among children. Probably the most widely used species is the *Aloe vera.* The crystal clear leaf juice, thick enough to be termed a gel, is used for many kinds of skin burns, as a shampoo, as an unguent for skin massage and relaxing muscles and, diluted, as a laxative and general aid to digestion.

The aloe is closely related to the maguey, which is called the "American aloe," and from it comes the Mexican national drink, tequila.

See also: **Maguey.**

ALOXE-CORTON

Perhaps the finest red wine from the Cote de Beaune in Burgundy. Brighter in color than the Burgundy wines from the nearby Cote de Nuits, it is a lively vintage, "worthy of a gourmet's table." *Corton* comes from the Latin *curtis,* or "garden," of the Emperor Otho *(curtis Othonis).* The commune of Aloxe-Corton lies slightly north of Beaune along the noted Burgundian "slopes of gold" (Cote d'Or). The vineyards that produce this excellent dry red wine date from before the time of Charlemagne (in the eighth century), and later were partially owned by the dukes of Burgundy and the kings of France. A vineyard, or *clos,* bears the name *Le Clos du Roy,* or "the king's vineyard," in this neighborhood today. Aloxe-Corton wine is best drunk when aged at least five years. It is smooth, delicate but full-bodied.

See also: **Burgundy Wines.**

ALPACA

A four-footed ruminant, *Auchenia pacos,* with long, fine and wooly hair, domesticated in the northern Andean countries of South America, it is related to the llama and the guanaco *(Lama guanicoe)* and allied to the camel family, but it is smaller and has no hump.

Peruvians and others in the Andes highlands raise alpaca for their valuable wool. Since these beasts are slow breeders and growers like their cousins the camels, it is not economical to use them for slaughter. When their wool-producing days are over, though, they do end up in the cooking pot.

ALPES

See **Bel Paese.**

ALPHEUS

Also ALPHEE. With its slightly compressed body, this saltwater crustacean looks like a crayfish and tastes like one. It does not have quite the delicate quality of the spiny lobster, for one, but it is widely fished and well received at table. Its habitat is vast and varied and includes the coasts of Europe, Asia, Australia and America. Alpheus should be prepared for eating like lobster or crayfish.

ALPIN

Also CLERIMBERT. A variant of **Mont d'Or** cheese, it is made in the Alpine region of France, usually of cow's milk, with the occasional addition of goat's milk. It most often measures 3 to 4 inches in diameter by 2½ inches thick.

ALQUE

See **Auk.**

ALSACE, MUSCAT D'

This is both a white dessert and ceremonial wine from Alsace and a famous grape variety. Muscat d'Alsace is distinguished from other Muscat dessert wines by being less overpoweringly sweet, more faithful to the natural grape, "fruity" taste and by having a fresh and aromatic bouquet.

ALSTROEMERIA

Also LILY OF THE INCAS, PERUVIAN LILY. A genus of tuberous-rooted herbs native to tropical and temperate South America, it generally reaches a height of three to four feet and has small-leaved stems and lilylike flowers. The food value lies in the tuberous roots. A Chilean variety, *A. pulchra*, produces in its rhizomes a starch resembling arrowroot. The genus was named for the Swiss botanist, Claude Alstroemer.

ALTAR WINE

Also SACRAMENTAL WINE. Wine is used in rituals of many Western religions. The Roman Catholic Church requires wine used in the Eucharist ceremony be pure grape juice, naturally fermented with a maximum alcohol content of 12 percent. Jewish ritual, guided by rabbinical law, requires pure and natural wine. Red or white wine is acceptable, but soured wine is not.

ALTENBURGER

Also ALTENBURGER ZIEGENKASE. A rather soft German cheese made from goat's milk, it originated in central Germany, especially near Thuringen. It measures eight inches in diameter by two thick and usually weighs about two pounds.

ALUM

The two double salts, *potassium aluminum phosphate* and *ammonium aluminum sulphate*, are usually called common or ordinary alum. In its crystalized state common alum has a sweetish-sourish taste and is colorless and odorless. It has a variety of uses. As an ingredient in baking powder it finds its widest food use, but it is also used to give crispness to pickles and maraschino cherries and to harden gelatin. Alum's medical uses are as an astringent, a styptic and an emetic. Other uses are for waterproofing fabrics, sizing paper, purifying water, and manufacturing paints, matches, dyes and deodorants.

Alum can be a dangerous substance. Ingestion of 30 grams (1 ounce) has killed adult humans. Concentrated solutions have caused breakdown of gum tissues, kidney damage and fatal intestinal bleeding. Alum is illegal as an adulterant but is legal for use in baking powder. In pickles and cherries, the amount usually left in the packaged product amounts to less than .2 percent. Formerly common alum was used in preparing confectionery and patisserie, but this practice is now illegal.

AMANITA

See **Orange Amanita.**

AMARACUS

See **Cretan Dittany.**

AMARETTO

This is an Italian liqueur whose almond flavor comes from apricot stones. It is bottled at from 48 to 56 proof.

AMBARELLA

Also OTAHEITE APPLE. A tropical fruit native to the Society Islands, it is now widely grown in the other tropical areas including Florida, the West Indies and West Africa. The ambarella grows on an erect tree, *Spondias cytherea*, which attains a height of 60 feet. The fruit is pear- or egg-shaped, two to three inches long. Its skin is thin, but tough, and has an orange red color. The pulp is yellow, with a firm, juicy texture, and a nearly acid flavor reminiscent of pineapple. Bad specimens may have an unpleasantly resinous flavor. The fruit is eaten raw and also considered excellent for jellies, marmalades, preserves and pickles. It is in season during June and July.

Another variety, which grows on Java and other islands of the East Indies, is called amboina berry. It is red, one to two inches long and grows on a shrub. It is eaten either raw or cooked.

AMBER FISH

Also AMBERJACK. This may be any of numerous tropical or subtropical fish of the genus *Seriola*, family *Carangidea*, some of which are good food. *S. grandis* ranges in the waters off Australia and New Zealand, and *S. capensis* in the South Atlantic off South Africa. The Western Atlantic from New Jersey to Brazil is home to *S. lalandi*, and *S. dumerili* lives in the Mediterranean, tropical Atlantic, West Indies and the Gulf of Mexico. Probably the finest food fish of this genus, however, is found off California and Baja California in Mexico, *S. dorsales*, commonly called yellowtail.

The average weight of the yellowtail is six to ten pounds but it does grow larger, sometimes up to 100 pounds. Smaller species of the *Seriola* genus are called madre gala, coronado, common amber, madamoiselle and lemon fish. These fish are easily identified by the amber or yellowish color of their tails. Amberjack may be prepared for table just like cod, halibut or other large fish that can be cut into steaks.

See also: **Yellowtail.**

AMBERGRIS

This morbid substance, somewhat like wax, comes from the alimentary canal of a whale. Sometimes it is found floating on tropic seas. It contains the sterol, ambrain. Ambergris is extremely valuable and is used in making perfume.

Long ago ambergris was thought to be an aphrodisiac by many persons including James Boswell, English biographer, and Brillat-Savarin, great French culinary writer. Their invigorated feeling may have resulted from the sterol.

Modern day athletes, such as shotputters, discus throwers and football players, are said to ingest steroids containing sterols that are laboratory-produced in order to put on weight and muscle. It seems from recent medical reports that ingesting steroids will increase weight and muscle, but will produce an effect opposite to an aphrodisiac.

AMBERJACK

See **Amber Fish.**

AMBERT

This cylindrical, cow's milk cheese made in central France is a type of Roquefort, but differs from others in that salt is mixed with the curd instead of being rubbed on the surface. Ambert is best during the winter season. Curing requires at least three months.

AMBOINESE COLEUS

Also SPANISH THYME, INDIAN BORAGE. The aromatic shoots of this tropical plant, *Coleus amboinicus*, are used to season meat dishes in Malaysia and Indonesia.

AMBRETTE

Also ABELMUSK, ABELMOSK, AMBER SEED, MUSK SEED, OKRA. Ambrette *(Abelmoschus moschatus)*, of the mallow family, is a tall, bushy plant indigenous to tropical Asia and the East and West Indies. Musk-flavored seeds of this plant are used in perfumery and for flavoring beverages including coffee, particularly in India. *A. esculenthus* is the vegetable **okra** popular in the southeastern United States and a key ingredient in gumbo. *Ambrette* is also the name of a French dessert pear which has a musky odor.

AMBROSIA

Also RAGWEED, MEXICAN TEA. Aside from the mythical "food of the gods," there is a real family of ambrosia plants, the *Ambrosiaceae*. They form a small genus of herbs, mostly American, which are known popularly as ragweeds. Apart from giving us hay fever, several ambrosia plants serve as worm purges. Examples are wormseed *(Chenopodium botyrs)*; Mexican tea or epazote *(C. ambrosioides)*, which is also a good antiflatulent and is used by Mexicans to season bean dishes; European wormwood *(Ambrosia pauciflora)*, and levant wormseed, which contains the drug santonica.

As to modern food, the name "ambrosia" has been applied to an American dish, a fruit compote covered with shredded coconut and whipped cream. Commercially, the name has been misapplied to various products attempting to cash in on the "food of the gods" of Homeric legend.

See also: **Mexican Tea, Wormwood.**

AMELANCHIER

See **Juneberry.**

AMERICAN CHEDDAR

A hard cow's milk cheese, it is like traditional English cheddar, but made from pasteurized milk. It is available in a wide range of firmness and of taste, from mild to very sharp. Various shapes, sizes and varieties have distinctive names, such as daisies, flats, longhorns, Tillamook, twins, Vermont, Wisconsin and young America.

See also: **Colby, Coon, Herkimer.**

AMERICAN CHEESE

This term is loosely applied to two different sorts of cheese made in the United States, a processed cheese of the cheddar type, and American cheddar cheese, which is far and away the most popular natural cheese produced in the United States. For more information on these two types look under **Processed Cheese** and **American Cheddar.**

A huge variety of cheeses are made in America that do not come under the rubric "American cheese." They are called by their traditional names, such as "Brie," "Camembert," "Limburger" and "Swiss." For more information, look under these traditional names. Where the product made in the United States differs from the original, it will be noted.

Certain cheeses originated in the United States, and they are discussed under the specific names.

See also: **Brick Cheese, Monterey Cheese, Poona.**

AMERICAN CRESS

See **Barbarea.**

AMERICAN PARTRIDGE

See **Partridge.**

AMERICAN QUAIL

See **Partridge.**

AMERICAN SEA ROCKET

The leaves of this North American seashore herb, *Cakile edentula*, may be eaten in salads. This is seldom done, but the plant is considered a good standby in case of scarcity.

AMERICAN SHAD

See **Shad.**

AMERICAN WIDGEON

See **Baldpate.**

AMER PICON

This bitter French aperitif tastes of burnt orange and is made by redistilling brandy laced with orange peel, then adding an infusion of bark, roots and herbs. It runs as high as 80 proof and is frequently mixed with grenadine or cassis along with plain or carbonated water.

AMMODAUCUS

Also ZEUS' CARROT. The seeds of this perennial plant, *Ammodaucus leucotricus*, are used as a condiment in sauces. *Ammodaucus* is found in Sahara oases, the upper valley of the Nile and in Mauretania.

AMMOPERDRIX

Also AMMAPERDRIX. This partridge was probably indigenous to North Africa but is now found in Israel, Iran and India. Occasionally it appears in the south of France. These are related to European partridges *(Perdix alectoris)* and allied genera, all stout-bodied, gallinaecous, game birds. American cousins of ammoperdrix are ruffed grouse and bob white. They are delicate and appetizing to eat and should be prepared for table like any other small game birds.

See also: **Grouse, Quail.**

AMOMUM

See **Cardamom.**

AMONTILLADO

See **Sherry.**

AMOROSO

See **Sherry.**

ANACARD

This locally popular vinegar made from the fruit of the cashew tree, *Anacardium occidentale* of the sumac family, is naturalized world-wide in warm regions. In Brazil, when the kidney-shaped fruit has been harvested and the cashew nuts separated, the remaining pulp is fermented and made into a tasty vinegar.

ANADONTA

Also ANADON, ANADONTE, BARNACLE. This is a fresh water mollusk, *Anadonta cygnea*, of somewhat inferior taste, gathered and eaten like mussels mainly in Italy and southern France. It is found in ponds and has a large, thin shell, up to eight inches in length. A variety called *berncle* ("Barnacle") is much smaller and is found in running fresh water, streams and rivers. It is prepared like mussels.

See also: **Barnacle.**

ANATTO

See **Annatto.**

ANCHOVETA

This variety of anchovy, *Engraulis ringens*, found in the coastal waters of Peru constitutes an inportant economic resource for that country. Smaller than the European anchovy, it swarms in tremendous numbers in the Humboldt Current, which flows up from the Antarctic regions past Peru. The *anchoveta* is responsible for attracting the flocks of birds whose droppings form guano, the nitrate deposits on the Guanape Islands off Peru.

More recently, however, this benefit has been surpassed by its direct contribution to the food supply as fresh fish. It is also exploited for oil and fish meal.

See also: **Anchovy.**

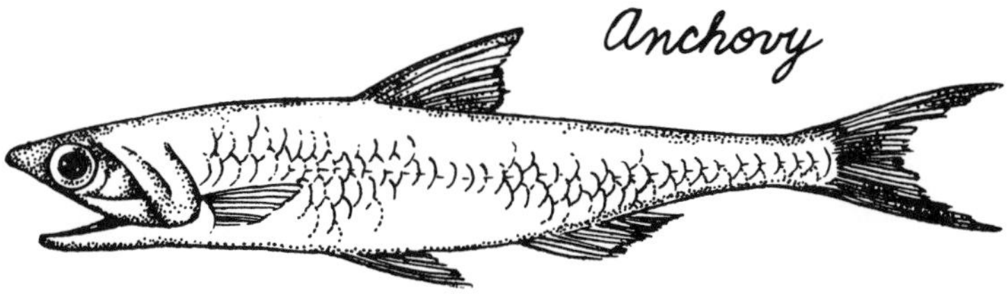

ANCHOVY

A small, fine-tasting fish of the herring family, the anchovy is used more as a garnish or flavoring ingredient than as a main dish. The best known is the European anchovy *(Engraulis encrasicholus)*, which is native to the Mediterranean and the English Channel, but ranges as far north as Norway. Its colors are dark on top and greyish silver on the sides. It averages four to five inches in length, and may be recognized by the deep cleft of its mouth and its gills, which are larger than those of the herring. Its fresh flavor is excellent, more pronounced than that of sardines, but still delicate. However, most people encounter the fish in preserved form—fillets pickled in brine, oil or other liquid—and there the flavor is powerfully developed. The latter are generally served as hors d'oeuvre, antipasto, smorgasbord and as a garnish for cutlets of one sort or another.

The taste of anchovies is said to sharpen the appetite and to enhance the flavors of other foods. Accordingly, anchovies are made into butters and pastes that serve as the basis for a wide variety of sauces. This type of preparation goes back to the ancient Romans, who used anchovies as a basis for their all-purpose seasoning, **garum.** The *aphye*—believed to be the anchovy—was the preferred fish of the ancient Greeks.

A smaller variety, called the California anchovy *(E. mordax)*, is native to the Pacific coast of North America. Anchovies were once most plentiful in the Mediterranean, but water pollution there has practically eliminated them as a commercial catch.

ANCHOVY PEAR

This russet-colored fruit grows on an ornamental West Indian tree, *Grias cauliflora*, of the family *Lecythidaceae*, that reaches from 30 to 50 feet high. The fruit is usually pickled, is slightly larger than a hen's egg and tastes like a mango.

See also: **Mango.**

ANCIEN IMPERIAL

A French cheese from the Normandy region, ancien imperial is eaten either fresh or cured. It is very soft and creamy but prepared and cured in the Neufchatel manner. Packaged in two-inch squares, the fresh cheese is called *petit carre* and the cured *carre affine*.

See also: **Neufchatel.**

ANDERSON WOLFBERRY

A variety of box thorn, the Anderson wolfberry *(Lycium andersonii)* is indigenous to Arizona and California. It is a woody shrub whose berries are eaten fresh or dried. They are sometimes used to flavor soups.

ANDRACHNE

The edible fruit of an evergreen tree, *Arbutus andrachne*, is found in southeast Europe and Asia Minor. It is an orange berry closely related to the **arbutus berry.**

ANDROCYMBIUM

This plant, *Androcymbium punctatum*, is used as a condiment by the Tauregs of North Africa.

ANESADO

See **Anisette.**

ANETH

Also ANETHUM. A plant related to fennel, dill and anise, its leaves and oil-bearing seeds were highly regarded in classical antiquity as a vegetable, tonic and flavoring agent. Just what the ancients meant by aneth has not been clearly identified botanically; they did, however, distinguish between aneth and dill *(Anethum graveolens)*, fennel or anise, as do modern confectioners and bakers who use aneth to flavor candy and baked goods, to which it gives a distinctive taste. They often refer to dill as sweet aneth; and *aneth* is the French word for dill. In England, aneth leaves are an accepted ingredient of pickling solutions.

The ancient Egyptians, Hebrews and Greeks ate aneth leaves as a vegetable. They believed it to have fortifying qualities and medicinal properties. Roman naturalists described aneth as being a plant halfway between fennel and anise. They too ate it as a vegetable and as a seasoner and used it as a medicine. Gladiators, especially, swore by the strengthing properties of aneth, and added aneth oil to their food at every meal. Pliny hailed it as a builder of virility. This belief survives as folklore in Flanders where a bride may hide aneth seeds in her shoes as a charm to insure that conjugal life gets off to a good start. Medicinally, aneth was best known as a carminative, whose powers are described in the following jingle:

> *Aneth drives out the winds, reduces every ill,*
> *And flattens swollen bellies, leaving them calm and still.*

It has a good reputation for curing hiccoughs, and was used as an antidote during World War I by the French Army, which suffered an epidemic of hiccoughs after an outbreak of Spanish influenza.

ANGELFISH

Also MONKFISH, BUTTERFLY FISH, PADDLEFISH, SPADEFISH, SCALARE, ANGE DE MER. The term "angelfish" covers a multitude of species. It includes the shark *(Squatina squatina)* of the northeast Atlantic and the Mediterranean Sea and a similar species, *S. dumeril*, found on the Atlantic coast of North America. They are characterized by broad, winglike pectoral fins. They have no commercial importance today, but in earlier times the skin was used as ornamental shagreen or leather. Some anglers deliberately seek them out. The pectoral fins are edible, and are prepared like skate or ray. The American variety is known as the monkfish. In France, the fish is called *ange de mer.*

The black or gray angelfish *(Pomocanthus arcuatus)* is an excellent food fish of the western Atlantic, found from New England to Brazil. It is an extremely deep-bodied fish, which is black with yellow bars when young and a chalky gray when an adult. It reaches a length of two feet. The yellow or blue angelfish *(Angelichthys ciliaris)* abounds in the warm waters off Florida, Bermuda and the West Indies. They are also called butterfly fish and have a blue and gold body, long blue streamers and electric blue eyelids. They may be fileted for the table like plaice or flounder.

The spadefish *(Chaetodipterus faber)* is a deep-bodied, spiny-finned food fish of the western Atlantic from Cape Cod to Cuba. Also known as paddle fish, it may be prepared like other flat fish.

The *scalare (Pterothyllum scalare)* is a small tropical fish from the rivers of South America whose laterally compressed body has black and silver stripes and large spiky fins. Because of its small size and striking beauty, *scalare* is more prized as an ornamental in aquariums than as a food fish. It is most plentiful in the Amazon basin.

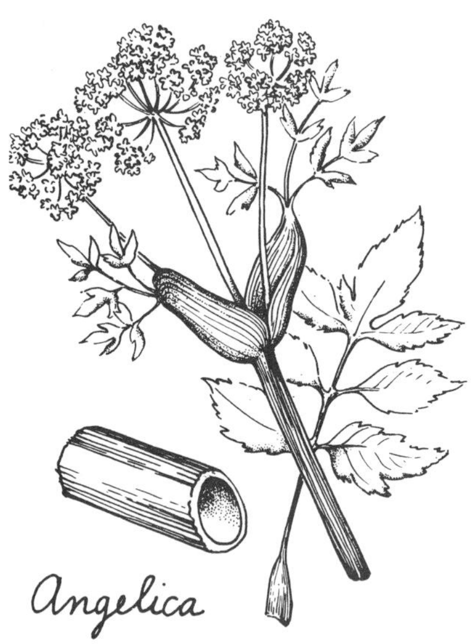

ANGELICA

This aromatic herb *(Angelica archangelica)* acquired its reverential title in earlier times when it was believed to confer protection against plague, hence the name *herba angelica* or *archangelica*, herb of the angels. Nowadays it is employed chiefly to flavor vermouth and such liqueurs as **Chartreuse** and **Benedictine.**

It is a biennial plant, native to the Alps, but grown in many European countries and in the United States. There are more than 50 varieties in addition to the main one. Reaching a height of four to five feet, angelica is cultivated for its roots and stalk, which are used as a seasoning and as a medicine. In France the stalks are candied and figure in cake decorations, while in Lapland the roots are ground and used as a substitute for bread.

ANGLER

Also LOTTE DE MER. Member of a small family of marine fish *Lophiidae*, the anglerfish *(Lophius piscatorius)* is found off the coasts of many European countries from the Barents Sea to North Africa, and in the Mediterranean and Black Seas. The name angler derives from its feeding habits. It lies on the bottom, half buried, waving the fleshy lobe at the end of its first dorsal ray to lure small fish into its open mouth. It is an extremely ugly fish, with an enormous, broad, depressed head and a large mouth. It reaches a maximum length of about five feet. Despite the wastage represented by the head, it is a moderately important food fish because of its relatively slender but muscular body.

Along most of the Italian coast, it is known as the *rana piscatrice*, and is thought to be a trash fish whose highest destiny is chowder or stew. But in Venice, where it is called *coda di rospo*, it is deliciously broiled, fried or poached. The flesh of the tail is said to be reminiscent of scampi in texture. In France, the angler is a celebrated ingredient of Marseilles bouillabaisse.

The American angler or goosefish *(L. americanus)* is found from the Newfoundland coast south to the Caribbean. In the latter place it is served as chowder, in a stew with small fish. The tail, which is compared to lobster in taste, may be broiled and garnished with lime or lemon juice.

ANGOBERT

See **Pear.**

ANGOLAN PLUM

A pulpy fruit, *Chrysobalanus orbicularus*, native to Africa, it has an insipid taste and in other ways is similar to the **coco plum.**

ANGOSTURA BARK

Bark of a tree, *Galipea cusparia*, that grows wild in the vicinity of the Orinoco River in Venezuela. Its extract contains a volatile oil, angosturin, which has an exceedingly bitter taste. Venezuelan natives used it as an antimalarial agent and as a laxative. Commercially it is used in tonics and as a flavoring ingredient in beverage bitters. Surprisingly, the celebrated flavoring bitters Angostura Bitters does not contain extract of angostura bark, but does take its name from the same place, a Venezuelan city formerly named Angostura. The city's name was changed in 1846 to Ciudad Bolivar.

See also: **Bitters.**

ANGURIA

Also WEST INDIAN GHERKIN, BUR GOURD, GOOSEBERRY GOURD. The fruit of this running herb, *Cucumis anguria*, reaches a length of only two inches at maturity. It is oval or oblong, resembling a small cucumber, and is eaten boiled or made into pickles. This is not the commercial gherkin, which is an immature cucumber. This plant is of cultivated origin, deriving perhaps from an African species, *C. longipes*.

ANIS

See **Anisette.**

ANISE

The seeds of this annual plant have a powerful licorice flavor, and have been used for centuries to spice pastry, confections and liqueurs. Anise *(Pimpinella anisum)*, native to several Mediterranean countries, is a member of the parsley family. Often

confused with dill, anise leaves are used as potherbs, in salads or as garnishes.

It is the essential oil of aniseed that is extracted by distillation for the anise-flavored liqueurs popular in Mediterranean countries. The oil precipitates when water is added, thus imparting the characteristic cloudy color to the drinks. The names vary, depending on the country, but include *pastis* (France), *ouzo* (Greece) and *raki* (Turkey). See also under the specific names of liqueurs.

Star-anise *(Illicium anisatum)*, a member of the magnolia family, is native to the Far East, but has a similar flavor. The name derives from its star-shaped fruit consisting of eight parts, each containing a seed. In China it is highly regarded for its therapeutic properties, but in the West it is used much like aniseed.

ANISEED

See **Anise.**

ANISETTE

Also ANIS, ANESADO. These are three liqueurs made from aniseed, and have a flavor reminiscent of liquorice. Anisette is one of the sweetest of French liqueurs. It incorporates some other herbs as flavoring, is clear in color and is bottled at about 50 to 60 proof. *Anis* is made in Spain and Latin America, and runs 78 to 96 proof. *Anesado* is made in Italy and the United States at 90 proof.

ANISINA

See **Anisette.**

ANJOU WINES

See **Loire Wines.**

ANNAM PLUM

Also MADAGASCAR PLUM. The edible fruit of a small tree, *Flacourtia indica*, it is native to the tropics of eastern Asia. The fruit is a translucent blackish-red, round and about one-half inch in diameter. It has a tart but pleasant flavor and is used medicinally. The flower clusters are eaten as a vegetable or in salads.

ANNATTO

Also ACHIOTE. Annatto is an orange red food dye obtained from a tree, *Bixia orellana*, native to South and Central America and the West Indies. The tree bears a reddish fruit, which has little taste, but contains the annatto seed or *achiote*, as it is called in Spanish. The coloring is contained in the pulp surrounding the seed. The seed itself is crushed and packaged as a condiment in Latin America and India. The powder has a rusty red color and a delicate flavor. It imparts a deep golden, orange color to dishes it flavors. *Achiote* is especially popular in the Yucatan where they make chicken *pibil*, a dish consisting of chicken parts marinated in a sauce containing it. After cooking, the chicken has a pungent flavor and bright red color.

At one time, American Indians used annatto to color their bodies. Nowadays it is used to color butter, margarine and candy. In England, both red cheshire and leicester cheese are colored with annatto.

ANNONA

See **Bullock's Heart.**

ANOA

A small water buffalo found wild in the Celebes and the Philippines, the anoa *(Anoa depressicornis)* rarely stands higher than 41 inches at the shoulder, as opposed to 70 for the water buffalo. Its flesh is tender and well flavored. People hunt them for their hides as well. Consequently, anoas have become rare.

ANON

Anon is an excellent food fish of the genus *Gadus*, a variety of haddock and a cousin of the cod. The white, flaky flesh may be prepared for table like haddock or whiting. It may not be quite as tasty as haddock for some. The main habitat of anon seems to be the English Channel, especially the southern end, where they are very prolific and very welcome.

See also: **Burbot, Cod, Cusk, Haddock, Hake, Pollack, Whiting.**

ANONA DEL MONTE

This fruit of a small tree, *Annona testudina*, is closely related to the soursop, and resembles the **posh te.** It is native to Honduras and Guatamala. The pulp is aromatic and very juicy.

ANSERINE

See **Goosefoot.**

ANT

Also TERMITE. Insects of the genus *Formica* are usually black or red in color but also include termites or white ants, which are social insects, living together in colonies like true ants. Ants and termites are generally not considered food in developed countries, if one excepts the chocolate-covered ants occasionally sold in exotic food stores to tempt the impulse buyer of joke items. Among the native populations of Latin America, Africa and Asia they are widely enjoyed as food, and must be considered a valuable source of protein. Following are a few examples:

Latin America. In Mexico, honey ants, like big yellow currants, are obligatory fare at country weddings. In Colombia, the *culon* ("big bottom") ant is captured in the spring and fried in oil. A similar ant is gathered from coffee trees around Bogota and either roasted or fried and served as cocktail hors d'oeuvres. The Jivaro headhunters of Peru and Ecuador eat parasol ants raw, while the Jicaques of Central America prefer to stew theirs. Indians of the Amazon and of Honduras first pull off the wings, heads and legs of white ants, then eat the bodies toasted.

Africa. Pygmies eat ants dried, roasted or raw, even the small common or picnic ant. Termites, or white ants, are a special delicacy of Zanzibar, Malawi and Zimbabwe. Termites *(Macrotermes goliath)* swarm in mounds as large as 12 feet high and 30 feet in diameter. Fried termites contain three times as much protein as T-bone steak, and research is being conducted toward creating a food staple out of them. In Malawi and Zimbabwe they are relished sun-dried by the spoonful. In Zanzibar, they are made into a white ant "pie," consisting of termites ground together with sugar and banana flour to form a kind of honey-nougat paste. In Swaziland, swarming termites are drowned, sun-dried and roasted.

India. The Indians make a red ant chutney, in which the ants are ground into a paste together with salt and chilis, then baked. It is eaten with alcoholic drinks, or curries, and is said to have a sharp clean taste.

ANT BEAR

See **Aardvark.**

ANTELOPE

Also ELAND, ADDAX, IZARD, GAZELLE, PRONGHORN, BLACK BUCK and other names. Antelope is a general name for any four-footed, ruminant mammal of a group *Antelopinae* in the family *Bovidae.* They more closely resemble deer than oxen, with light graceful bodies, slender legs, up-jutting horns and great speed afoot. Sizes vary greatly from the cowlike eland down to miniature species only a foot high. Their habitat is generally the temperate zones of Asia, Europe and, especially, Africa. The pronghorn, found in America, is not a true antelope.

In America in the 1870s, while railroads were expanding across the Great Plains, antelope steaks—along with buffalo steaks, oysters on the half shell, quail and fresh trout—were a leading menu item in Union Pacific dining cars. The price of a meal was seventy-five cents.

Older antelope are preferred over younger ones for the table because they have more taste. They may be prepared for eating the same ways as venison.

See also: **Gazelle.**

ANYU

See **Ysano.**

AOSO

Also SHIROSO. This is an annual herb, *Perilla arguta,* native to Japan. Its flower clusters are eaten after salting.

AOUDAD

Also BEARDED ARGALI. A wild sheep, *Ammotragus lervia,* inhabiting the Saharan mountains of North Africa. Shyness and a rugged habitat have made the aoudad a difficult animal to stalk, but this protection is vanishing due to the increased range, accuracy and killing power of modern firearms. Its numbers appear to be diminishing.

Some scholars think the aoudad may be the chamois referred to in the Old Testament. The males have luxuriant beards, and they are sometimes called bearded argali to distinguish them from a closely related species, the argali *(Ovis ammon).* The aoudad is hunted and eaten by local inhabitants, and not much is known about how it is prepared.

See also: **Argali.**

APE

See **Alocasia.**

APERITIF

The name refers to an alcoholic drink taken before meals to stimulate the appetite. The name comes from a Latin word meaning "opening," in the sense of to begin a meal or to "break the ice" conversationally. Originally, an aperitif was held to be more or less bitter, strongly alcoholic, and medicinally flavored with herbs, such as **anise, wormwood,** various **bitters** or quinine. The high alcohol content was thought necessary to dissolve the essences of the drink, which in such aperitifs as **anisette** and **absinthe** go cloudy when mixed with water. The high percentage of alcohol counteracts any beneficent value of the herbs. The French have a saying that an aperitif of this nature "opens the appetite with a skeleton key." Today, *un aperitif* means any drink—usually wine—that precedes a meal, especially **port, sherry, champagne, vermouth** or **Dubonnet.**

APHRODISIAC

Many foods and drinks are reputed to have the power to increase sexual capacity or desire. This may include such collateral benefits as reducing inhibitions, toning the sexual organs, overcoming weariness and intensifying orgasm. Most of those discussed below are also listed elsewhere under alphabetical order for their food value.

Absinthe. Oil of **wormwood,** the operative ingredient, is alleged to have an immediate aphrodisiac effect on both men and women. In the liqueur, it combines with the disinhibiting influence of alcohol. On the other hand, large doses or prolonged use are deemed destructive to sexual potency.

Alcohol. It increases sexual desire by suppressing inhibitions, but frequently hinders performance.

Basil. It is a popular belief in Italy that eating large quantities of this herb increases the size of the penis. There seems to be no scientific evidence to support this, although the oil in basil may irritate the urethra causing a state of semierection, thus seeming to enlarge the organ.

Betel Nuts. Millions of Asians habitually chew the areca nut wrapped in a betel leaf. The two contain several mild stimulants, but there seems to be nothing that directly affects the sexual organs. Any aphrodisiacal effect would stem from the general alertness and mood elevation produced by moderate use.

Black Tea. This is a common variety of tea *(Camellia thea)*, but taken in highly concentrated form, as a thick syrup, which is prepared by boiling several ounces of tea leaves in a gallon of water for hours. Tea contains caffeine and other stimulants, but in China, India and Japan it is believed that a few drops of this syrup can stimulate the libido (as well as the central nervous system).

Capsicum. Pepper plants, including the familiar Cayenne pepper, heat up the mouth. By extension, it is believed, they also heat up the urethral canal as oils pass out of the body, thus stimulating sexual excitement.

Cubeb. Asians use cubeb berries as a flavoring ingredient. The berries stimulate the mucous membranes, and are supposed to be helpful in rousing the male organ and in maintaining an erection.

Damiano. Essence of this shrub is used as a flavoring in a Mexican liqueur of the same name. An infusion of the leaves, which provides more of the essence, has a soothing effect. Over a period of time, taken in moderation, it is believed to have a tonic effect on the sexual organs.

Fugu. Some Japanese live dangerously in sampling the testicular fluid of this poisonous puffer fish. It can incite passion, or poison you. The difficulty in predicting the outcome leads to many deaths each year in Japan.

Garlic. A generally healthy food, garlic receives some credit in Asia for promoting sexual vigor. Some Indian men go so far as to anoint themselves with a garlic salve to assure a powerful erection. One wonders how stimulating the odor would be to a garlicless partner.

Guarana. The basis of a popular soft drink in Brazil, guarana seeds contain caffeine and are thought to be otherwise sexually stimulating, although what they possess to accomplish this has not been determined.

Kava Kava. An intoxicating beverage made from the roots of the *piper methysticum* shrub on many South Pacific Islands, it is said to produce a tingling in the genitals, which many find enhancing to sexual pleasure.

Kola Nuts. A major source of flavoring and caffeine in cola drinks, these nuts are chewed by some natives of Sierra Leone to boost sexual energy.

Licorice Root. An infusion prepared from either the fresh or dried root of the plant *Glycyrrhiza glabra* is believed to enhance sexual performance.

Nutmeg. The common spice, nutmeg, is chewed by Yemenites to increase their virility, yet how it does so is unclear. More than a few grams per day can be harmful to health, and may produce hallucinations.

Pumpkin Seeds. Fortified with phosphorus, these seeds are believed to be beneficial to the prostate gland.

Sarsaparilla. Long known as a flavoring agent, sarsaparilla is also a commercial source of testosterone, the male hormone. As a source of this hormone, however, an infusion of sarsaparilla root may not be too efficient, since testosterone is destroyed by digestive juices. Moreover, although testosterone therapy has been found useful in increasing the size of the penis and in overcoming impotence, selfdosing could result in the body's ceasing its own secretion of the hormone.

Saw Palmetto. The berries of this tree, which is common in the southeastern United States, are believed to tone glandular tissue and increase sperm production. They combine well with **damiano.**

Vanilla. This is the plant that yields the famous flavoring extract. Its pods, when chewed, produce an erotic effect through mild irritation of the urethral canal. Those who handle vanilla pods in their work develop skin irritations, so frequent use of them as a sex drug would seem to be unwise.

Wild Mint. Since ancient times, tea made from wild mint leaves has been considered erotically stimulating. The same was true of thyme and rosemary.

API

Also LADY APPLE. A small, rather flat apple with color ranging from creamy yellow to deep crimson, it is aromatic, firm and juicy. The fruit has a long recorded history, starting in the first century A.D. The Etruscans developed this delicious fruit and named it for the horticulturist responsible, a farmer named Apis. This may have been a respectful nickname favorably comparing his industriousness to that of the social bee *Apis mellifera.* The French faithfully maintain his name and fame to this day.

The English version, lady apple, may be a tribute to its petite size and sweetness. In colonial times, it was deemed a special treat at Christmas. Dedicated apple eaters recommend that Lady Apples be eaten unpeeled because the skin is especially delicious.

See also: **Azarole.**

APOLLINARIS WATER

This effervescent, alkaline mineral water is drawn from natural sources in the Ahr Valley of West Germany. It has a relatively high sodium content (114 mg. per 8-ounce serving), plus calcium and magnesium. In a taste rating sponsored by the Consumers Union in 1980, the following comments were made about Apollinaris' flavor: mildly sour, mildly astringent, mild soapy flavor, distinctly salty, distinctly bitter.

See also: **Mineral Water.**

APONOGETON´

Also CAPE POND WEED, CAPE ASPARAGUS, WATER HAWTHORNE. A family of aquatic herbs, *Aponogetonaceae*, native mostly to Europe, whose flat, oblong, often skeletonized leaves and small flowers float upon the water's surface like water lilies.

One species, cape asparagus *(A. distachyus)* has been cultivated for many years in Montpellier, France. Its young shoots are eaten as a delicacy. It originated in Cape Town, South Africa. In the United States, this plant is known as cape pond weed or water hawthorne.

APPENZELLER

This is cow's milk cheese, made in both full-fat and skim versions, from the canton of Appenzell, Switzerland. It is also made in St. Gall, Zurich and Thurgovia, as well as in the German districts of Bavaria and Baden. The whole milk curd is soaked in cider or white wine for several days and has a delicate flavor. The skim milk type, called *rass*, has a pungent flavor, and is left in the cider or white wine for a month or more. It resembles Swiss, and comes in 20-pound wheels.

APPETITOST

Also APPETOST. A Danish cheese made from sour buttermilk with caraway seeds added, it is smooth and mellow. A small amount is made in the United States, but most is imported.

APPLE

Easily the most familiar and best-liked fruit of the temperate zones, the apple has innumerable varieties within the genus *Malus*. It is a pome, a type of fruit having a core with parchmentlike walls that contains several seeds. (Pears and quinces are also pomes.) The apple tree is the most widely cultivated tree in the rose family. It attains a height of 30 to 35 feet, branches profusely and has a scaly ash-brown bark. It is strongly resistant to drought and freezing weather, preferring a cool, humid climate.

The apple is a small fruit—yellow, green or red in color—with firm flesh and a sweet, slightly tart flavor. The shape is generally round, with some species tending to be longer and narrower, and others wider and slightly flattened at the ends. It is said to have had its origin in Central Asia and the Caucasus, but cultivation preceded the dawn of history. It was well known to the ancient Egyptians, Hebrews, Greeks and Romans. One Roman, writing in the fourth century A.D., described 37 varieties of apple. It was imported into North America at the beginning of the 17th century, and a little later to South Africa and Australia. At the present time there are thousands of varieties worldwide.

Apples are grouped in various ways: by time of ripening (summer, autumn, winter); by size, color or flavor, and by use (eating, cooking, cider, drying). The apple is a prized table fruit, but also makes excellent jelly, preserves, apple butter and compotes. Eating apples are sweet and fragrant, red, yellow, or occasionally pale green, as in the case of some early summer varieties. Cooking apples are tart and acid and usually large and green; the tartness is due to the presence of tannin. Apple's high pectin content assures a firm jelly consistency in the jams and preserves.

Before 1850, cider, including pear and peach, was the national drink of the United States. The cider of those days had an alcoholic content of from 1 to 8 percent; and partly due to pressure from temperance groups, it was displaced in popularity by coffee. Cider apples are also used to make apple brandy (applejack), which is especially popular in France, with its world-famous **calvados** brandy.

The food value of the apple is high. It contains about 10 percent carbohydrate (mostly glucose and fructose), ample quantities of vitamins C and B, and several minerals, including calcium, iron, phosphorus and potassium. The apple is a notable thirst-quencher, with about 85 percent water. Underripe apples, however, should not be eaten raw. The large amounts of starch make them difficult to digest. Cooking makes them easily digestible, since it converts the starch to sugar. The medicinal and therapeutic properties of the apple are the subject of legend.

The Red Delicious is the world's leading apple variety, and together with the Golden Delicious, accounts for about one-fifth of the U.S. crop. McIntosh (dark red or green) are next in importance, followed by Winesaps (dark red), Jonathans (blood red), Rome Beauties (yellow with red stripes) and Staymans (red with yellow stripes). Popular cooking apples are the soft-skinned Gravensteins, used for applesauce; the crisp tart Greening, a favorite in apple pie, and the sweet Golden Grimes. Washington leads the United States in apple production, followed by California, New York, Virginia, Michigan and Pennsylvania.

The best known English varieties are Cox's Orange Pippin, in season from September to Christmas; the Golden Delicious and the Blenheim Orange. Australians greatly prize the Granny Smith, a green apple whose lineage is traced back to an elderly widow who discovered a wild apple tree growing on her farm in Queensland. For fresh eating, the French revere the *Reinette grise;* the *Reine des reinettes* (large, yellow streaked with red); the *Reinette franche* (medium size, yellowish green) and the *Calvilles*, which are conical rather than round, and come in red and yellow varieties.

The American folk hero, Johnny Appleseed, was a real person, not a legend. A nurseryman surnamed Chapman, born in Leominster, Massachusetts in 1775, he was nicknamed Appleseed from his practice of collecting appleseeds from cider mills, putting them up in little paper bags, and giving them to everyone he met who was going West. Later on, he took to the road himself, and for forty years wandered Ohio, Indiana, Illinois and Iowa planting seeds in likely spots. Despite the ravages of time, many of the trees he planted still bear fruit.

APPLE BUTTER

Also called apple sauce, or apple jam, this is a thick sauce made from sliced apples slowly boiled down in cider or apple juice and thickened by evaporation. It must be stirred from time to time, flavored with cloves, allspice and cinnamon and stewed until it becomes a dark brown jam. Just enough juice should be left to keep it soft and buttery. Indeed, it makes an excellent substitute for butter.

Apple butter was a long-time favorite in Germany, and immigrants brought the treasured recipe to America where it became a standard ingredient in Pennsylvania Dutch cooking.

APPLEJACK

Also APPLE BRANDY, JERSEY LIGHTNING. This is a brandy distilled from fermented apple juice, i.e., hard cider. It is aged in oak barrels a minimum of two years and is sold as straight brandy at 100 proof or as a blend at 80 proof. The term "Jersey Lightning" justly recognizes the potency of applejack and its first commercial source in America, the distillery that an immigrant Scot, William Laird, established in New Jersey around 1698.

American troops participating in the Normandy landings of World War II found themselves in applejack country, which there is called **calvados.**

The English have different definitions for applejack. It is a pastry containing sliced apples; or it may be apple dumplings.

See also: **Apple Juice, Cider.**

APPLE JUICE

Juice from apples that have been washed, crushed and pressed, it is separated from the pulp by filtering, and may be bottled with or without clarification. Its vitamin content is not impaired by this processing.

Apple juice becomes sweet cider when enough fermentation is allowed to take place, but not enough to use up all the sugar. It becomes hard cider when fermentation continues until the sugar is used up, leaving a liquid with a sour taste and an alcohol content of about 8 percent.

In the United States, bottled, unsweetened apple juice is far more popular than sweet or hard cider.

See also: **Applejack, Cider.**

APPLE ROSE

The hips of this plant, *Rosa villosa*, are used to make preserves, sauces and beverages. It is a source of rosehoney. It is found from western Europe to Iran, and was known to the ancient Romans, who made it into rose wine. In Bavaria and Austria, apple rose leaves are used to make an herb tea called *Deutscher tee*.

APRICOT

A small, round or oblong fruit, orange-yellow in color, which grows best in temperate climates, the apricot is sweet and juicy and contains a single stone. It is a versatile food in that it may be enjoyed raw, cooked, dried or canned. In flavor and texture, the apricot is often compared to the peach. As a fresh fruit it is considered somewhat inferior to the latter, but, dried or preserved, the apricot outshines the peach due to its stronger flavor, which seems to improve in cooking and preserving. In the northern hemisphere, apricots ripen in June, July and August. Fresh apricots should be plump, firm and uniform in color, except for rosy highlights. No more than 10 percent of the world crop is eaten fresh, however. The rest is canned in syrup, as jam or dried or frozen.

The apricot tree, which attains a height of 13 to 25 feet, is native to North China, growing wild in the hills around Peking. Although the Chinese cultivated it as early as 2200 B.C., opinions differ as to when it arrived in the West. The scientific name is *Prunus armeniaca*, which suggests to some scholars that the apricot came to Europe through Armenia, brought by Pompey's soldiers who campaigned there in the first century B.C. A second theory maintains that the apricot was cultivated in the Hanging Gardens

Apricots

of Babylon and that the term *armeniaca* derives from the Babylonian-Assyrian name for the fruit, *armanu*. In any case, the apricot was known and appreciated by the ancient Romans, but disappeared from Europe with the collapse of the Roman Empire, and did not reappear until after the Crusades. The Arab sphere of influence must be excepted from this generalization, particularly Spain, where the moors cultivated them extensively around Granada. The apricot reached England in the early 16th century and North America most probably in the 18th century, brought to California by the Spanish mission fathers.

Today commercial cultivation of apricots is widespread. Spain is the leading producer, followed by the United States and France. In the United States, California produces more than any other state. As a fresh fruit, California's apricots are rivaled only by those of France's Loire Valley, which include the succulent musk apricot.

Though sweet, apricots contain only 6 to 7 percent usable sugars, which is less than the sugar content of apples. They are high in potassium, iron and vitamin A.

Apricots are featured in the cuisines of some Middle Eastern countries, where lamb is the most important meat. In Iran, the taste of apricot is believed to be the perfect complement of lamb, and the two are often cooked together. Throughout Moslem countries, a form of dried apricot, called *kamraddin*, is made. A puree of apricot is thinly spread on metal trays or canvas and dried in the sun, then chewed as a snack or mixed with water and used to make sherbet. Diluted *kamraddin* is often used to break the fast at sundown during the Ramadan, because it is not only refreshing and sweet, but soothing to the digestion after a day spent without food or water.

The apricot is closely related to the **almond** *(P. amygdalus)*. Both are succulent fruits with nut-like kernels. The kernels of apricots may be sweet or bitter, depending on the variety, and some people eat them as they would almonds. The bitter varieties, however, contain amygdalin, which is poisonous and should not be eaten. Apricot kernels are commercially valuable as a source of almond oil, which is used to flavor extracts and liqueurs, such as *amaretto*.

APRICOT BRANDY

There are two distinct products that are called apricot brandy. One, such as **Barack Palinka,** of Hungary, is distilled from a mash consisting of the juice, pulp and kernel of fresh apricots. It is dry to the taste and is bottled at 80 to 100 proof. The second is a cordial, consisting of a brandy base (distilled from grapes), sweetened and flavored with dried apricots. It is bottled at 60 to 70 proof, and may bear such trade names as **Abricotine** or Apry.

APRICOT LIQUEUR

An apricot-flavored, sweetened after-dinner drink of 60 to 70 proof, it contains certain beneficial and essential oils regarded as natural digestives. Trade names are **Abricotine** and Apry.

Liqueurs are also used in cooking and baking, to flavor ice cream and ices, in making sauces and in desserts.

APRON

This freshwater fish of Europe reaches a length of no more than six inches. It is, nevertheless, highly esteemed by gastronomes. Only two species are known, and they are found in the Rhine and Danube Rivers. The sweet, delicate flesh of the apron comes in an ugly body that is covered by rough scales and features a flattened head, protruding snout and extra large gill slits. It is prepared like perch.

AQUAVIT

Also AKVAVIT. This clear, usually colorless alcoholic drink is distilled from many sources: grain, potatoes, wine or even sawdust. The ancient Romans called it *aqua vitae*, "water of life." Latter day Romans have other versions, *aquavite de genianza*, flavored with gentian, and *aquavite de ginepro*, flavored with juniper. The French follow the ancient Romans with *eau de vie*. Ancient Celts called it *usquebaugh*, which was later shortened to **"whisky."** Scandinavians call it aquavit or akvavit and frequently flavor it with caraway seeds. It is the Scandinavian national drink.

Aquavit is never aged, merely filtered, reduced in proof and stored in glass-lined vats or bottled immediately. In Norway, Sweden and Denmark, similar methods are used in making aquavit, but the Danish akvavit, made from potatoes, is recognized by Scandinavians as the best. All of these versions are about 86 proof.

The Swedes have an interesting ritual for downing their before-meal aquavit. Starting with a bottle frozen in a block of ice, they fill jigger glasses brimful and, after the toast, toss the contents down in one gulp. It is said to be an old Scandinavian custom at formal gatherings to drink as many toasts as there are buttons on the men's dress vests.

See also: **Eau De Vie.**

AQUA VITAE

See **Aquavit.**

AQUAVITE DE GENZIANA

See **Aquavit.**

AQUAVITE DI GINEPRO

See **Aquavit.**

AQUIBOQUIL

This sweet, pulpy fruit of an evergreen vine, *Lardizabala biternata*, is native to Chile and Peru. The *aquiboquil* has a dark purple color, a pleasant taste and attains a length of three inches. The fruit is sold only locally.

ARABIAN TEA

See **Khat.**

ARACA

The fruit of a small tree, *Psidium guineense*, native to tropical America, it is similar to guava, but smaller. The pulp when ripe is usually yellow, while the guava is red. The plant is widely diffused in southern Europe, including such places as Andalusia, Sicily, Provence, the Cote d'Azur and Madeira.

The taste of *araca* is a little too resinous and bittersweet to have much appeal raw. Instead, the juice of the fruit is used to make jelly or paste. The leaves and fruit are also used medicinally in Madeira as a cure for diarrhea because of the high tannin content.

See also: **Guava.**

ARAK

Also BATAVIAN ARAK. This light-bodied but highly aromatic rum is produced in Java but usually blended and bottled in the Netherlands. Its distinct, brandylike flavor is due to the mixture of molasses, river water and red Javanese rice cakes used to make up the mash for distillation. A wild, uncultured yeast, *Myces vodermanni* is also used in fermentation and adds a special quality to the taste. *Arak* is distilled in and around Djakarta, where it is aged for three to four years. Then it is shipped to the Netherlands for further aging of four to six years and blending and bottling. Although usually drunk neat in the East Indies, the Dutch mix it with fruit juices. It is popular in Scandanavia as the main ingredient of **Swedish punsch.**

ARAPAIMA

Also PAICHE, PIRARUCU. A freshwater fish, *Arapaima gigas*, of tropical South America, this is thought to be the largest freshwater fish in the world. It reaches a length of 13 feet or more, and a weight of around 450 pounds. The arapaima is abundant in the Amazon River and in smaller rivers of Guyana, Brazil and Peru. It is a valuable food fish, and the quality of its flesh is rated very high, so much so that overfishing has produced alarming depletions in the Amazon River. Restrictions have been placed on landing fish under three feet long. It is prepared in a variety of ways including, in Brazil, the sun-drying of its flesh in long strips.

The arapaima is a member of the *Osteoglossidae* family whose edible members include the *Heterotis niloticus* of the upper Nile and the rivers of Chad, Niger, Senegal and Gambia. It rarely exceeds three feet in length. The *arawana (Osteoglossum bicirrhosum)* of the same areas in South America has a maximum length of a little more than three feet. A relative, the spotted barramundi *(Scleropages leichardti)* of tropical Australia, is considered good eating and fine sport for fly fishermen.

ARBOIS

Here is a wine from the slopes of the French Jura (the mountain region between France and Switzerland) in the basin of the **Rhone.** Arbois is the birthplace of Louis Pasteur, who owned a vineyard here and worked on his study of fermentation. The wines of Arbois are chiefly red and rose—from the Ploussard, Trousseau, and Pinot Noir grapes—though a good *Arbois Mousseux* (semisparkling wine) is produced also. These wines are full-bodied, lively and rich in color and taste.

ARBUTUS BERRY

Also ARBUTE. The round, red, edible fruit of the strawberry tree, *Arbutus unedo*, is native to the Medi-

terranean area. The tree is evergreen and shrublike, reaching a height of 18 to 22 feet. The berry is attractive in appearance and looks much like a strawberry, down to the warty-textured skin, but it has neither the taste nor the yielding texture of the strawberry. When ripe, it is sweet, rather tasteless, sometimes unpleasantly sour, and grainy in consistency. Occasionally, a few raw arbutus berries are served in a mixed fruit salad, chiefly as ornaments. Cooked, they are made into preserves and, in Spain and Italy, used in candy. Wines and liquors are made from them in Spain and Italy; the French make a liqueur called *creme d'arbouse*.

The arbutus was well known in Classical Antiquity, and several writers—including Theophrastus, Theocritus, Virgil, Ovid and Pliny—left descriptions or commented on it. It has been widely transplanted to such places as the Southern United States, Mexico, the Canary Islands and County Kerry, Ireland.

ARCA

See **Arch.**

ARCH

Also ARCH, ARCHE, ARK SHELL. A genus, *Arca*, of marine bivalve mollusks with dark, boxlike shells, they are found on the coasts of France, and though not highly prized for taste, they may be eaten raw or cooked like mussels.

ARCHANGELICA

See **Angelica.**

ARCHERFISH

A small fish of the Indian and Pacific Oceans considered to be a good food fish, especially in Thailand, the archerfish *(Toxotes jaculator)* feeds mainly on insects, which it captures in a remarkable way. It spits drops of water at them, knocking them off their leaf, branch or web and into the water where it pounces. Taking aim with its eyes below the water's surface, the archerfish is extremely accurate at distances up to three feet and has been known to hit its target at a distance of 10 feet.

ARECA NUT

See **Betel Nut.**

ARENGA PALM

Also SUGAR PALM. A species of palm tree *Arenga pinnata*, which grows wild and is cultivated in Malaysia and other parts of tropical Asia, the arenga palm has pendant, branching spadices and large, berrylike fruits. The male spadices are tapped and the sap collected for conversion into sugar or toddy. Sap is converted to sugar by evaporation. Simple heat of the sun or boiling will produce a brownish sugar. Natural fermentation will produce palm wine or toddy.

ARGALI

This is a large wild sheep, *ovis ammon*, that ranges in the mountains of northeast Asia. The outstanding characteristic of male argali is their magnificent sets of horns. Sometimes the American Big Horn sheep is mistakenly called "argali." Another cousin, the **aoudad** of the Saharan mountains in North Africa, is mistakenly called "bearded argali."

ARGENTEUIL

See **Asparagus.**

ARGENTINE

Any of several small marine fishes belonging to the family *Argentinidae*, they are found worldwide in tropical and temperate seas. One of the largest is the Atlantic argentine *(Argentina silus)*, which reaches a length of 22 inches. It is found on both sides of the Atlantic and is considered only mediocre eating, its flesh being rather soft and insipid. A Mediterranean variety is eaten fried, in chowder, or in bouillabaisse.

ARGUA

A tropical fruit, *Pouteria arguacoepsium*, of the same genus as the sapote and the ti-es, the *argua* is native to Colombia and highly esteemed locally. It is pear-shaped and yellow in color.

ARGUS PHEASANT

Also TRAGOPAN, HORNED PHEASANT. This bird may be any one of several East-Indian pheasants, genus *Argusianus*, family *Phasianidae*, found in Java and Sumatra, which are closely related to the peacock. Their brilliant plumage, with its numerous "eyes" also resembles that of a peacock. However, the male crimson tragopan, or horned pheasant, *(Tragopan satyrus)* carries on its head two brightly colored wattles with a pair of fleshy, hornlike protuberances.

Argus pheasant should be prepared for table just as any other pheasant.

See also: **Peafowl.**

ARIA

Also WHITE BEAM, CHESS APPLE. Fruit of a northern European tree, *Sorbus aria*, it is scarlet, round and about one-half inch in diameter. Aria is used to make brandy and vinegar.

ARLES SAUSAGE

A large sausage of the **saucisson** type, it is made all over the south of France but originated in Arles. Its chief ingredient is lean pork, with a little beef. Both are chopped fine and mixed with pepper, garlic cloves, paprika and a pinch of saltpeter. Peppercorns and a little red wine are also added. After being encased, they are smoked for about a month. Arles sausage is usually sliced cold and eaten raw as an hors d'oeuvre, but chunks of this sausage are sometimes added to soups and stews.

See also: **Sausage.**

ARMADILLO

This small, burrowing mammal is native to Texas and parts of Central and South America. Its body and head are encased in segmented, shelllike armor. The armadillo is toothless and feeds chiefly on fruit, roots, insects and plants. Some species can roll up into a compact ball when attacked.

There are various species, some attaining a length of up to three feet. The larger varieties inhabit South America. For example, the three-banded armadillo *(Tolypeutes trincinctus)* is highly esteemed there as food. The kind eaten in Texas is the nine-banded armadillo *(Dasypus novemcinctus)*. It is considered edible but far from delicious. The flesh has a musky taste and thus must be abundantly spiced and/or cooked with a strong wine. Baked armadillo is stuffed with a mixture of chopped potatoes, cabbage, carrots, apple slices and various spices, put in the oven for 30 minutes and served in its shell. A sausage made from armadillo meat was once popular in Texas. The meat is also used to make both a clear and a thick soup.

ARMAGNAC

A French brandy, distilled from wine, Armagnac is generally considered to be second only to **cognac** in quality. Like cognac, Armagnac is smooth on the palate, but its aroma is drier and more pungent than cognac's. For this reason some persons prefer the Armagnac without challenging the statement that the best cognacs have a little more finesse and breed than the best Armagnacs.

Armagnac is produced predominantly in the department of Gers, which includes most of the old province of Gascony. Trade in Armagnac centers in the city of Condom, which is southeast of Bordeaux. In making the wine for distillation into Armagnac, only white grapes are used, including the Saint-Emilion (Ugni Blanc), Folle Blanche and the hybrid Baco 22A. Three quality grades are produced: *grands*, *fins* and *petits armagnacs*. If a bottle is simply labeled "Armagnac," this means the contents are a blend of brandies from two or three major producing regions: Bas-Armagnac, Tenareze and Haut-Armagnac. If brandy from only one region is used, the source will be divulged on the label.

Although distillation in Cognac utilized the traditional batch process with separate redistillation, armagnac is distilled and redistilled in a continuous process. It is aged in black oak casks from the Monlezun Forest. It is often bottled at 10 years old, but age-labeling requirements are similar to cognac's, including such designations as three stars, VSOP, etc.

ARMAVIR

This Russian cheese made from whole ewe's milk is soured by the addition of sour buttermilk or whey. It originated in the western Caucasus and resembles **hand cheese.**

ARNAUTEN

See **Travnik.**

ARRACACHA

Also ARRACACH, ARRACACIA, APIO, PERUVIAN CARROT. A South American plant, *Arracacia xanthorrhiza*, with thick, edible, farinaceous rootstocks, it is cultivated in the Andes Mountains from Venezuela to Bolivia. It grows best at altitudes of 7,000 to 8,000 feet.

Flour is made from the roots and baked into bread or flatcakes. The roots may also be treated like yams or potatoes, being served baked, fried or in soups and stews. Arracacha is an important food crop. Peruvian carrot is somewhat of a misnomer since arracacha is not a carrot, and its country of origin is believed to be Colombia.

ARRACK

Arrack is a strong alcoholic drink distilled from various saps or liquids in Asia, especially in the Far and Middle East. The words means "sweat" or "sap" in Arabic, and so arrack may originally have been made from the sap of the coconut palm. Another origin of its name may have to do with the areca nut, or **betel nut,** which yields an Indian version of the drink. In Lebanon and Syria, arrack is a milky-white grape brandy strongly flavored with **anise.** It is almost always cut with water and is drunk ceremoniously or with traditionally heavy meals. In the Far East, arrack is distilled from rice, molasses, fermented coconut milk, and palm sap.

See also: **Anisette, Arak, Ouzo, Raki.**

ARRAYAN

The edible fruit of a small evergreen tree, *Eugenia foliosa*, arrayan is found in Ecuador and other countries of western South America, such as Chile. The arrayan has dark purple skin and a white pulp of delicate texture. The taste is subacidic and pleasant. The fruit is usually eaten raw.

ARROPE

See **Wine and Liquor Terms.**

ARROWHEAD WATER

This mountain spring water is sold in plastic containers as bulk drinking water, especially in the Southern California area. It has a relatively low mineral content. A 1980 Consumers Union sensory panel rated the taste of Arrowhead Mountain Spring Water as very good, with the following qualifying comment: mild plastic flavor.

See also: **Mineral Water.**

ARROWROOT

The roots of a West Indian plant, *Maranta arundinacea*, are dried and ground to produce this fine, powdery starch or flour. Arrowroot is native to Brazil and the Guianas, but its cultivation spread to the West Indies before the arrival of Europeans, who quickly saw its value and transplanted it to many other tropical regions of the world. It is now also produced in significant quantities in India, Australia, Southeast Asia and southern Africa.

The term "arrowroot" has expanded to cover a multitude of similar starches from a variety of plants, most of them tropical. The starches may be extracted from the rhizome, rootstock, corm, tuber or stems. These other arrowroot plants include the genus *Zamia*, fernlike plants represented in the United States by the **coontie,** and the comfortroot; the genus *Canna*, which provides tulema arrowroot; the genus *Musa*, another West Indian arrowroot; the yam genus *Dioscorea*, many members of which are cultivated for the starch in their tubers; East Indian arrowroot *(Curucma angustifolia)*, which is a member of the same family as ginger; otaheite arrowroot, which comes from a palm, *Tacca pinnatifida*, found throughout the South Pacific Islands, and Brazilian arrowroot from the cassava *(Manihot succulenta)*, which also gives us **tapioca.**

Arrowroot is similar to tapioca in its easy digestibility when mixed with water, and in its composition, which is about 85 percent carbohydrate. For these reasons, it was long thought to be particularly suitable for invalids, the aged and young children. Nowadays, however, it is mostly used as a thickener in soups, gravies, sauces, puddings and other desserts. It is good for thickening clear liquids because it does not cause clouding.

One nontropical source of arrowroot is spotted arum *(Arum maculatum)*, a plant growing in temperate climates, which is identified under a variety of colorful names such as cuckoopoint, wake robin and Lords and Ladies (England); Jack-in-the-Pulpit, green dragon, skunk cabbage and sweet flag (U.S.); and calf's foot, oxtongue and hare's bread (France). When young, this plant produces highly toxic red berries and also secretes a sap that is irritating to the mucous membranes. Once the toxins are removed through a series of boilings, however, the rootstalk proves highly nutritious. Flour from the rootstalk has been used to make bread, and was the basis of portland arrowroot, a product that used to be commercially important in Great Britain. So-called British arrowroot is a potato starch, which has been used to adulterate more expensive arrowroot.

The name "arrowroot" has inspired some fanciful etymologies. One says the name derives from the West Indian practice of treating wounds from poisoned arrows with extracts of the root. Another says some varieties of arrowroot were used to poison arrows. The *Zamia* genus, for example, contains strychnine and the alkaloid curarine, a constituent of curare arrow poisoning. The most probable source is the native American word, *araruta*, meaning "flour root," whose English approximation is arrowroot.

Artichokes

ARTICHOKE

Of the several vegetables called artichoke, the French or globe artichoke *(Cynara scolymus)* is considered the true artichoke. Other types, namely, the Jerusalem, Japanese, Chinese and Indian, are not related botanically, and will be discussed under separate headings.

The artichoke plant is cultivated for its edible flowers, or heads, which are picked before they blossom. They are usually dark green, but can also be bluish, violet, brown or even red, depending on the subvariety. The head varies in size from tiny to an average market size of three to five inches in diameter. It resembles a thistle, with thick, stiff leaves, which overlap and, in some species, are tipped with thorns. Inside the dense covering of leaves is the *fond* or heart, which is surmounted by a fine, hairlike growth called the choke. If permitted to mature the choke would become a flower. It is not edible. The edible portions are the base of each leaf, and the heart.

The plant originated in North Africa, but grows well in all temperate areas of the world. Artichokes have been cultivated for centuries, and were a popular vegetable in ancient Greece and Rome. Pliny, the Roman naturalist and writer, did not like them however. He wondered why people would pay good money for mere thistles. Some authorities maintain that the artichoke referred to in classical writings was actually its close relative, the **cardoon.**

In Renaissance times, the artichoke gained the reputation of being an aphrodisiac, and was not thought to be proper food for young ladies. Yet Catherine de Medici, a noble young lady flouting convention, is credited with introducing artichokes into France when she became queen in the 16th century.

Artichokes have been a common and inexpensive vegetable throughout Europe since the 17th century despite the short growing season, which lasts from June to September. In contrast, the artichoke was uncommon and thought to be a luxury in the United States until about 40 years ago. Nowadays California produces about 70 million pounds, and has a year-round growing season. Despite this, per capita European consumption far exceeds American.

The manner of eating artichokes provoked the observation that there seems to be more of the artichoke after eating than before. After being boiled, the head is served as a separate dish, either hot or cold. Each leaf is stripped off with the fingers, dipped into sauce or melted butter and scraped clean of soft flesh at the base with the lower teeth. Where before there was a neatly closed head, there remains a pile of scraped leaves. When completely stripped, the heart is cut up and eaten with a fork.

Tiny artichokes, gathered late in the season, are preserved in olive oil, and eaten as hor d'oeuvres.

See also: **Crosne, Jerusalem Artichoke.**

ARTOCARPUS

See **Breadfruit.**

ARUM MACULATUM

Also CUCKOOPINT, PORTLAND ARROWROOT, LORD'S AND LADIES, WAKE ROBIN, WILD GINGER. This species of small herb, *Arum maculatum*, native to Europe and Asia, has heart-shaped leaves and a large spathe. The name is applied to several allied species. Both leaves and roots may be eaten, and their marked acidity has given rise to such common names as wild ginger, and pepper cabbage, which is a translation of the French *chou poivre*. But from the rhizomes, or roots, come the most important foodstuff, a starch, similar to **sago** that is made into flour and meal. *Arum maculatum* has poisonous properties, and one must boil it before it is eaten.

ASADERO

Also OAXACA. A white, whole milk cheese, asadero originated in the Mexican state of Oaxaca, although much of it is now made in the state of Jalisco. To prepare the cheese, the curd is heated, then cut, braided or kneaded into loaves that vary in size from eight ounces to 11 pounds. This cheese melts easily, which earned it the name *asadero*, which means "fit for roasting."

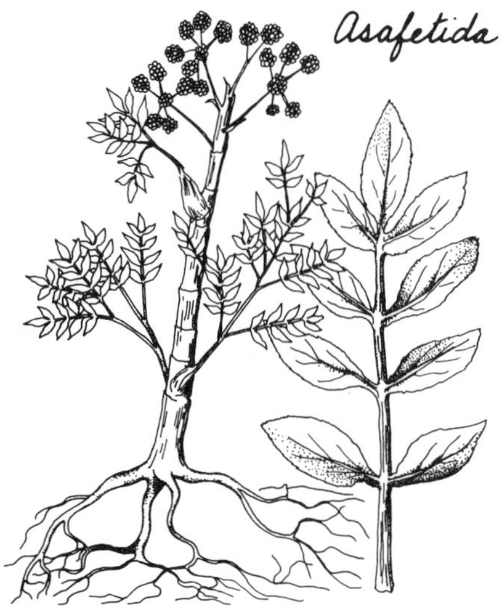

ASAFETIDA

Also HING. Resin from the asafetida plant *(Ferula foetida)* achieved popularity in classical antiquity as a flavoring ingredient, but nowadays is only used as such with any frequency in the Asian countries of its origin, such as Iran, Afghanistan and India. The plant is a member of the same family as parsley and carrots, and it grows to heights of five or six feet, taking four years to mature. The most striking characteristic of the resin, as far as Westerners go, is its offensive odor, which has been described as "putrid," and "onions or garlic unbearably intensified." This did not seem to deter ancient Romans, nor does it modern Asians, who collect pearly white sap from an incision made in the root of the plant. The sap quickly turns pink, then reddish brown. It is used as nearly liquid resin or in powdered form.

The name *asafoetida* derives from a latinization of the Persian word for gum or mastic, *asa*, and the Latin word for stinking, *foetida*. It came into favor in Rome at the time of Nero as a replacement for **silphium,** a highly popular and expensive herb that Romans imported from North Africa. It was quickly hailed as a panacea for such ailments as anemia, worm infestation and stomach gas, and as a calmative in cases of hysteria and other nervous afflictions. But it was most prized as a condiment, and as such was often combined with other powerfully aromatic foods like cheese, onions, leeks and garlic. It was often added to fish dishes, though it is now impossible to say in what amount. Nowadays it is occasionally used in French cooking. A microscopic amount of the resin added to a fish dish is said to give an indescribable but pleasant taste to the whole. It is greatly admired in Iran, Afghanistan and India, where it is called *hing*. It may be eaten as a fresh vegetable, where the interior of the stem is considered the best part. The resin is used to flavor curries, meatballs and pickles.

ASAM

See **Tamarind.**

A SANTE NAPA VALLEY WATER

This is bottled, sparkling mineral water drawn from a geyser in the Napa Valley, California. Some of the minerals are removed before bottling, so that it has a relatively modest 645 ppm of total dissolved solids. Sodium content is 46 mg. per eight-ounce glass.

A 1980 Consumers Union sensory panel rated the taste of this water as good, with the following qualifying comments: mildly bitter, mildly sour, mild bitter aftertaste, mild soapy flavor, mildly salty, mild soapy aroma.

See also: **Mineral Water.**

ASCORBIC ACID

See **Vitamin.**

ASH CAKE

Also ASH BREAD, HOECAKE. A traditional American food, which the original white settlers learned how to make from the Native Americans. It is made from cornmeal. Native Americans from the Eastern Seaboard all the way to the Southwest, including the Navahos, made this bread and ate it as a staple part of their diet. It was especially popular in the East and mid-South.

Ashcake is made of cornmeal mixed with water, shaped into a cake, wrapped in cabbage leaves and baked in hot ashes. Corn pone came from corn meal and water shaped into a flat, broad cake and baked in an oven. With hoecake, the oven wasn't necessary. It could be made by adding salt to the cornmeal dough and baking the flat cake on a hoe over an open fire.

See also: **Corn, Cornmeal.**

ASH GOURD

See **Chinese Watermelon.**

ASH TREE

This may be any tree of the genus, *Fraxinus*, family *Oleaceae*, which are valuable both as shade and as timber trees. Their bark is thin and furrowed; their branchlets are ash-colored; their fruit is a winged seed called a "key." Ashwood is best known in America as raw material for baseball bats, but the tree does have a tradition of use as food.

In early English times, the keys were pickled. After twice boiling and twice draining, the keys, while still hot, were covered with spicy, boiling vinegar. After cooling, they could be eaten to enliven drab meals.

The French make something called *frenette*, or ash drink, which is deemed both healthy and economical. Starting with ash leaves, they make a sort of spiked lemonade of low alcohol content and low cost. The tender young shoots of this tree make delicious salad material.

ASIAGO

A hard Italian cheese made from cow's milk in the northern provinces of Carnia, Venetia, Trentino and Lombardy, asiago is a member of the **grana** group of cheese. When young, i.e., aged four to 10 months, it is mild-flavored and makes a good table cheese. When aged 12 to 20 months, however, it is more suitable for grating because the texture becomes hard and the flavor and aroma very strong. Asiago is made from partly skimmed milk, and in earlier times was a pecorino, or sheep's milk cheese. In Italy, cheeses are round and flat, weighing from 16 to 22 pounds.

In the United States, Asiago is made in three categories, fresh, medium and old. The fresh, which as a soft texture, is aged from two to four months; the medium for at least six months, and the old for more than a year.

ASIN

Also WATER CHEESE. This is an Italian sour milk cheese whose curd is soft and buttery with a few large eyes, and whose flavor is very mild. It is made in the mountains of northern Italy. Fresh cow's milk is allowed to curdle without the aid of rennet, and the curd is washed in warm water, a process that guarantees a higher moisture content, lower acidity, and a softer, more open texture. Asin is ripened with the aid of surface mold, which also turns the rind yellow. Curing takes one to two months.

Cheeses are round and flat, measuring eight inches across by six thick, and weigh 14 pounds. Popular as a dessert cheese, asin goes well with honey and fruit. Another version of asin, called *salmistra*, is aged for three to five months in brine, and has a stronger flavor.

ASP

A slender, large-mouthed fish, *Aspius aspius*, found in European and Asian rivers from the Baltic to the Caspian Sea. It reaches a length of four feet, but rarely exceeds 20 pounds in weight. The asp is a commercial fish of some consequence in the Baltic Sea region, and is also popular with anglers who take it on a spinner or with bait. Its coloring is green brown above and silver white below. The asp is a member of the carp family and is showing signs of depletion in European rivers.

ASPARAGUS

A spring vegetable, asparagus *(Asparagus officinalis)* seems to enjoy universal popularity through the Northern Temperate Zone. Two varieties are generally recognized, white and green. The difference between the two is basically one of cultivation rather than botany. A white asparagus has been planted eight to 10 inches below ground and gathered as soon as the tip breaks the surface. Having been protected from the sun's rays throughout its entire growth, it emerges blanched. The white is reputed to be more tender and delicate than the green, which has had the benefit of the sun during its growth. The green is said to have a stronger flavor. A good deal of white asparagus is canned, while most of the green is sold fresh.

The asparagus we eat is the immature sprout or spear. If allowed to mature, the plant produces a fernlike leaf which is not edible. Moreover, if allowed to grow beyond six to nine inches, the stalk becomes woody and tough. It is a member of the lily family, along with onions, leeks and garlic, although its flavor is far more delicate than that of its relatives. Gourmets sometimes prefer a variety of wild asparagus, *A. acutifolius,* whose tiny branches often end in thorns. It is more aromatic and has a stronger flavor.

The asparagus plant prefers sandy soil, and in the wild state is found along coast lines and river banks. Although its origins are obscure, it appears to be native to the Russian steppes. The ancient Greeks liked wild asparagus. So did the Egyptians, as evidenced by pictures in royal tombs. The Romans were apparently the first to cultivate it. Julius Caesar praised the asparagus of Lombardy, liking it boiled and served with butter, still a popular way of preparing it. Ravenna asparagus was noted for its large size and fine flavor, a gastronomic tradition that continues to the present.

Asparagus dropped out of sight during the Middle Ages. It reappeared during the Renaissance in Tuscany, and began its climb back to popularity by becoming a staple item at the table of King Louis XIV of France during the 17th century. It became known in England about the same time by the popular name of sparrowgrass. Argentueil in France produced the best asparagus and remains famous today for the white variety. Throughout history, many people have considered asparagus to be an aphrodisiac because of its shape, and thus not fit food for women.

Asparagus has little nutritive value, consisting of about 94 percent water by weight. It has vitamins A and B, about 1 percent protein, 6 to 7 percent carbohydrates, and no fat; 3½ ounces amount to 52 calories.

Since it usually grows in sandy soil, it must be washed carefully, removing all grit from the tips. A simple way of cooking is to tie together a small bundle of spears with string, and stand them endwise in water with the tips above the surface of the water. This cooks the stalks without ruining the appearance of the tips. Cooking is brief, no more than 15 to 20 minutes. This brevity has led to a popular phrase in Italian: "Quicker than you can cook asparagus," which is roughly equivalent to the English phrase, "Quicker than you can say Jack Robinson."

Asparagus

ASPARAGUS BEAN

Also YARD-LONG BEAN. An edible bean, native to South America, whose pods routinely reach a length of two to three feet, asparagus beans are eaten when young and fresh as green beans. Although the asparagus bean *(Vigna sesquipedalis)* is widely grown in Europe and the United States, it has achieved limited popularity as food, principally in the southern United States, where it is known as the "blackeyed bean," and with Italians and Chinese. The asparagus bean is related to the cowpea, which is popularly known as the "blackeyed pea."

The plant itself is quite ornamental, with climbing stalks that reach nine to 12 feet in height, and with beautiful, violet blue flowers. The pods are picked unripe, boiled, drained and served as green beans, sauteed in butter and garlic and seasoned with lemon juice or stewed with tomato sauce. The beans themselves are red or yellow brown, resembling kidney beans, and in Texas they are dried, soaked before cooking and served with pork dishes. The flavor is unusual but not a valid reason for their lack of popularity.

See also: **Bean.**

ASPARAGUS BUSH

This is a woody plant, *Dracaena manni*, of tropical Africa whose young shoots are consumed like asparagus.

ASPARAGUS LETTUCE

Also PAMIR LETTUCE. This is *Lactuca sativa angustana*, a variety of romaine lettuce that forms no head but is grown for its thick edible stem. To prepare for eating, stems are boiled for one-half hour, then drained. The tough outer cover is removed and the tender inside flesh eaten with melted butter.

ASPARAGUS PEA

Also GOA BEAN, MANILA BEAN, PRINCESS BEAN, WINGED BEAN. This is a south European plant, *Lotus tetragonolobus*, with twiggy branches, pale blue flowers and thin, green pods. The plant grows about 18 inches high, and the pods should be picked before they exceed two inches in length lest they become stringy. Plucked young, however, and simmered in very little water for 10 minutes or so, they make excellent eating. The name is rather a mystery since they neither look nor taste like asparagus.

ASPERULA

Also ASPERULE, WOODRUFF. Here is a small, sweetly scented, Old World herb, *Asperula odorata*, with China-blue flowers and pale green leaves. The leaves are a staple seasoning herb in Austrian cookery. When dried, the leaves smell like hay and used to be infused to make a medicinal tea. Nowadays, the plant is used to flavor wines, candy, other confections, liqueurs and punches.

ASPHODEL

Also JACOB'S ROD. An Old World plant with bulbous roots, the asphodel *(Asphodeline lutea)* is a member of the lily family. It was widely cultivated in classical antiquity from the Mediterranean region to the Caucasus. A common article of diet for the ancient Greeks and Romans, it was eaten much like potatoes are today.

ASPIC

See **Gelatin.**

ASS

See **Donkey.**

ASSAM TEA

A black tea named for a state in northeast India, it grows there and in Pakistan at relatively low altitudes. It is an extra robust variety, full-bodied with a malty taste and a cloudy amber color. The lower grades tend to be bitter. Assam tea is famous for its pungent taste.

See also: **Tea.**

ASTI

This is a wine from the Piemontese region of Asti, in northern Italy. Although Asti lends its name to a hearty dry red **Barbera,** the major grape of Piedmont, it is more widely known for its *spumante*, a sparkling wine grown in the manner of **champagne.** Asti Spumante is a sweet, white, frothy wine produced from the Yellow Muscat (or Muscat di Canelli) grape. Like champagne, it is fermented a second time in the bottle—but the wine is then transferred to large closed vats *(cuves)*, where it is filtered and clarified. The concentration of carbonic gas makes this wine similar to champagne in type, but the different vinestock and soil yield a vintage that is mellower, sweeter and less austere than the great French wine.

ASTRAGALUS

Also MILK VETCH. A large genus of the pea family, it contains certain species that are sources of gum **tragacanth,** most notably *A. gummifer.* The pods of another variety are roasted and ground for use as a coffee substitute, or they may be pickled and used in salads like capers.

See also: **Vetch.**

ASTRODERME

Also FEI AERMICA. Astroderme is an odd looking marine fish, spotted black against yellow pink on the back and sides with a silver-spotted belly. Considered a sort of trash fish, it is used mainly in soups and bouillabaisse along the French Mediterranean coast, its principal habitat.

ASTROLOMA

Also CRANBERRY HEATH, AUSTRALIAN CRANBERRY. A low shrub, *Astroloma humifusum*, it bears green, sweet, edible berries. There are two species native to Australia, and the fruit is much liked locally.

ATAMASCO LILY

A member of the zephyr lily genus, the atamasco lily *(Zephyranthes atamasco)* is native to the southeastern United States. Its bulbous roots are cooked and eaten.

ATHERINE

Also SMELT and SILVERSIDES. Atherine *(Atherina presbyter)* is a fresh and salt water fish, small, spiny-finned, with silver banded sides. It is a school fish which is netted by thousands, whose firm flesh and delicate flavor make it a popular food item. Varieties of atherine are found widely in temperate zones living in the seas and going up rivers to spawn or living in landlocked lakes. Preparation for table is usually by frying in deep fat, although recipes for small bass are suitable. A true smelt has a smell of cucumber. Atherine smells like a fish.

See also: **Silverside, Smelt.**

ATKAFISH

Also ATKA MACKEREL. This is *Pleurogramus monoptergius*, a mackerellike marine food fish found in waters off the Alaskan coast and the Aleutian Islands. Atkafish average about 18 inches in length, weigh two to three pounds, and have typical mackerel vertical stripes on their sides. Sometimes these stripes may be almost black.

This fish is named for one of the two tribes of Eskimo linguistic stock, the Atka, which inhabits the Aleutian chain. Preparation for table is similar to that for mackerel.

See also: **Mackerel.**

ATLANTIC COD

See **Cod.**

ATRIPLEX

See **Orach.**

ATTAR OF ROSES

Also ATAR, OTTO, ROSE EXTRACT, ROSE WATER and OTTAR. Attar of roses is a fragrant volatile oil distilled from fresh rose petals and water. The Damask rose *(Rosa damascina)* furnishes most of these petals. The finest petals formerly came from the famous rose gardens of Bulgaria, where attar of roses originated. The principal odor-producing ingredients in attar are geraniol and citronellol.

Attar is used in many foods like candies, cakes and confections both for its delightful aroma and its subtle flavor. Rose water is an important ingredient in the Balkan dish, *Rahat Lokum*, and among Arabs it is a necessity in their haute cuisine. It is also a prime ingredient in Turkish Delight. In Egypt and the Balkans, rose petal jam is popular and is believed to be a mild aphrodisiac.

See also: **Rose, Rose Apple, Rose Hips.**

AUBERGINE

See **Eggplant.**

AUBRYA

This woody plant, *Aubrya gabonensis*, is native to Africa where a beverage called *stouton* is prepared from its fruit.

AUK

Also ALQUE, ALKA and ALKE. The auk is any sea bird of the family *Alcidae* of divers and swimmers. Specific species are the great auk *(Plautus impennis)*, now extinct, the razor billed auk *(Alca torda)* and the little auk *(Alle alle)*, commonly called dovekie or little dove. Auks breed in colder regions of the Northern Hemisphere, but are also found on the coasts of Scotland, England and France. They nest and lay eggs on rocky ledges, in crevices of seaside cliffs or in burrows. The little auk, only about 15 inches high when full grown, is a relatively good flyer and so is able to nest in almost inaccessible places.

Auks are not harvested commercially but are eagerly pursued and netted by fishermen who have to come to their cold, remote habitat to fish. Their flesh and fat are highly prized for eating. Eggs laid by auks are pointed and do not easily roll out of crude nests or off rocky ledges.

AUROCHS

The wild ox of Europe, *Bos primigenius*, which is believed to be one of the ancestors of modern domestic cattle, the aurochs was also found in North Africa and southwestern Asia. It became extinct about 1627 but was "reconstructed" in the 1920s by the atavistic back-breeding of domestic cattle that still possessed characteristics of the aurochs.

The aurochs somewhat resembled the American bison, but was heavier in the pelvic area and had a lighter thorax and less shaggy head and neck. Its domestication occurred as far back as 2500 B.C. in Egypt and Mesopotamia. Julius Caesar referred to it in his writings, and it was brought into England by the Anglo-Saxons who bred it with the smaller Celtic shorthorn. The term "aurochs" is used also to refer to the European bison.

See also: **Bison.**

AURORA SAUCE

This Danish sauce is based on **bechamel sauce** or **mornay sauce** but colored and flavored by tomato puree and a little butter. It is usually served with fish.

See also: **Sauce.**

AUSTRALIAN DROPGRASS

Seeds of this perennial plant, *Sporobolus pallidus*, are milled into flower, mixed with water and baked into cakes. It is found in Queensland.

AUSTRALIAN GAULTHERIA

Also WAXBERRY. An erect, evergreen shrub, *Gaultheria hispida*, it is native to Australia, where its white fruit is eaten locally.

AUSTRALIAN GOOSEBERRY

This is the fruit of a small, climbing shrub, *Muehlenbeckia adpressa*, of the wire plant genus, native to Australia. The white berries resemble gooseberries. They are used to make pies, puddings and confectionery in Australia.

AUVERNAT WINE

Auvernat is a heady, bright red wine from the Auvergne region of France in the vicinity of Orleans. In the time of Louis XIV, Auvernat was frequently mixed with lighter, paler **Loire wines** to obtain roses that were sold under the name of "*Ermitage*," touted and declaimed in literature by the poet Boileau.

AVA

See **Kava.**

AVELLAN

See **Hazelnut.**

AVERIN

See **Cloudberry.**

AVOCADELLA

See **Zapallito de Tronco.**

AVOCADO

Also ALLIGATOR PEAR. The heavy, usually large fruit of a tree, *Persea americanus*, the avocado is native to Central and South America. It has a tough skin, a buttery pulp and a large stone at the center. The pulp is greenish yellow, while the skin ranges from yellow through bright green to dark purple. Avocados have a bland taste, which some persons describe as nutlike. They may weigh as much as three or four pounds.

The name "avocado" is an approximation of *ahuacatl*, an Aztec word. Mexican Spanish comes closer to it with *aguacate*, whereas in South America, with other linguistic influence at work, the fruit is called *palta*. No one is certain how the name "alligator pear" came about. Some avocados are pear-shaped, although others are round or long oval. Some varieties grow best in tropical areas, where alligators can be expected to lurk. Also, the skin of certain varieties—most notably the California fuerte—have a rough surface, suggesting an alligator's skin. The term is going out of use.

The fruit was first described for Europeans in 1519 by Martin Fernandez de Enciso in his book, *Suma de Geografia*. For the next 400 years, the avocado made little impression on North Americans or Europeans, although it remained an inexpensive everyday dish in many Latin American countries. It began to take hold in the United States after 1900 when it was planted commercially in Florida and then in California. The avocado has been increasing in popularity ever since. Europe all but ignored the avocado until the late 1960s and early 1970s when Israel began to market them on the Continent. Israel is the third largest exporter of avocados after California and South Africa. Of the three basic types, the West Indian, the Guatemalan and the Mexican, the last is the hardiest and is preferred in California, where it is plentiful from January through April.

Avocado

For a fruit, the avocado is unusually nutritious. By the same token, it is quite fattening. It contains about 60 percent water—less than most fruits—and about 30 percent unsaturated fat. There are appreciable amounts of protein and starch, plus vitamins A through K, but virtually no sugar or acid. In the market, select avocados for immediate use that are just beginning to soften. Very firm ones can be ripened at home by placing them in a sunny spot. Avocados bruise easily, and bruised ones should be avoided because bruises affect the quality of the flesh.

The avocado is served sliced in salads or by itself, halved, with dressing or lemon juice. It is a good sandwich filling, and with a blender it may be combined in soups. After cutting, avocados turn dark and unappealing if allowed to stand. To avoid this, place the pit in the dish with the slices, or sprinkle lemon juice on them.

AVOCET

Also AVOSET, AVOCETTE. The name includes any of several wading shorebirds of the family *Grallatores*, with long legs, webbed feet and slender, upcurving bills. An avocet's body is about the size of a pigeon and has beautiful pied plumage. The habitat of *Avocet americana* is the western and southern coastal regions, where it is becoming scarce. In Europe, the Poitou region of France seems to be favored.

The flesh is delicate but has a fishy taste, probably reflecting its diet, which consists mainly of small fish, worms and aquatic insects. It may be prepared for the table like teal.

See also: **Baldpate, Mallard, Pintail, Teal.**

AXOLOTL

This name refers to any member of the genus

Ambystoma of salamanders living in mountain lakes in Mexico and the western United States. Axolotl is an Aztec word meaning "servant of water." Though *A. tigrinum* usually lives its life as a larva, nature provides a capability, when its pond dries, of losing gills and fins while starting to breathe air at the water surface. By the time its water habitat has evaporated, it has become an adult, terrestrial salamander. Both as a larva and as a salamander, axolotl is an esteemed food in Mexico. It may be prepared like frogs.

AYAPANA

This is a Brazilian plant, *Eupatorium ayapana*, whose leaves, when dried and infused like tea, make a strong, aromatic drink used as a laxative and a soporific. Leaves may also be dried and ground, making a condiment. This plant grows wild in tropical regions of South America and Asia where it finds great acceptance and is even cultivated. Twelve or so leaves are sufficient in a six-pot teapot. Ayapana makes a good nog as it blends well with egg yolk and cream.

AYGREEN

Also HEN-AND-CHICKENS, OLD MAN-AND-WOMAN, HOUSELEEK. A common European succulent, *Sempervivum tectorum*, it grows prolifically on old walls and roofs and in many gardens as an herb and vegetable. It is attractive and tenacious, with pink flowers and leaves clustered in a basal rosette.

AYLESBURY

See **Duck.**

AYU

One of the most important and popular freshwater food fishes of Japan, the ayu *(Plecoglossus altivelis)* is a migratory fish, resembling the smelt in appearance. It breeds in freshwater, passes the winter in the sea, then returns to spawn. There are also landlocked varieties in Lake Biwa. The ayu is fished extensively with fish traps and nets, but an unusual traditional method involves the use of cormorants. The **cormorant** is a voracious sea bird which is trained to catch migrating ayu. The fisherman fits a metal ring around its throat. The cormorant is tethered to the boat, then dispatched to catch an ayu, which it is prevented from swallowing by the metal ring. The fisherman retrieves the fish from the bird's maw. Later, he removes the metal ring and rewards the bird with a lesser fish.

The ayu is well known in other northern Pacific countries, such as Taiwan, Korea and China. A good-sized ayu is about 12 inches long.

AZAROLE

Also NEOPOLITAN MEDLAR, LADY APPLE. The *azarole (Crataegus azarolus)* is a fruit of the Mediterranean area, which, though of little commercial importance, is delicious eaten fresh. Botanically, it is related to the hawthorn bush. It is grown chiefly in Algeria, Spain, Italy and southern France. The fruit is round, a little larger than a cherry and has an acid sugary taste. On the northern fringes of its growing area, the fruit never fully matures and is eaten only in jams and preserves.

Three varieties are cultivated; the scarlet *azarole*, with sweet, red pulp; pear *azarole*, whose taste is more tart; and the hedgerow *azarole.* Candy and liqueur are also made from the *azarole.*

AZUKI

See **Adzuki Bean.**

B

BABACO

Also PAPAYA DE MICO. This fruit of a small tropical tree, *Carica pentagona*, is closely related to **papaya.** It is found in lowland areas of Central and South America and is eaten locally.

BABASSU NUT OIL

The gigantic wild palm, *Orbignya speciosa*, a tree growing in northeastern Brazil, produces a hard-shelled nut yielding an oil used to make soap. The nuts and oil are also edible and they resemble coconuts and coconut oil in aroma and taste. Natives in the natural habitat of the tree eat them.

Babassu trees, slow growing and slow bearing, are mostly cultivated as ornamentals in the tropics and subtropics. Commercial harvesting of nuts for soap oil appears to depend on whether prices are high enough to reward the effort required.

BABIROUSSA

Also spelled BABIRUSA and BABIRUSSA. This large wild pig, *Babirussa babirussa*, is found in the East Indies. It likes a swampy forest habitat but it can be domesticated. The male has tusks that are very large and recurved, coming out through the lips. These striking tusks distinguish babiroussa from other wild pigs. Its flesh is highly regarded in the Celebes Islands and the Malay Archipelago.

See also: **Wild Pig.**

BABOONROOT

Baboonroot is a South African plant, *Babiana plicata*, whose corms are cooked and eaten as vegetables.

BABY MARROW

See **Zucchini.**

BACALAO

See **Cod.**

BACALHEU

See **Cod.**

BACCAUREA

Several species of this tropical fruit, *Baccaureas spp.*, of Southeast Asia, are eaten raw, cooked or used in preserves.

BACHANG MANGO

This acidic tasting fruit of the tree *Mangifera feotida* is found in Malaysia and Indonesia. It is steeped in lime water or syrup before eating. Sometimes it is mixed with hot peppers, soya and fish to make a dish called *sambal.*

BACKSTEINER

This is a German cheese that is similar to **Limburger** and **Romadur** but smaller and cured for a briefer period. Made from partly skimmed milk, *backsteiner* means "brick," from its bricklike shape, but is not like **brick cheese** made in the United States. It averages 20 to 25 percent protein.

BACON

The cured, smoked meat from the sides, back, belly and breast of pigs, bacon today serves more as a condiment than as a basic food. This was not always so, for bacon is one of the oldest meats and for centuries was a staple for the poor and working classes.

Bacon must have been a familiar item to ancient Greeks, because Aesop mentions it in his fable of the town mouse and the country mouse, which dates

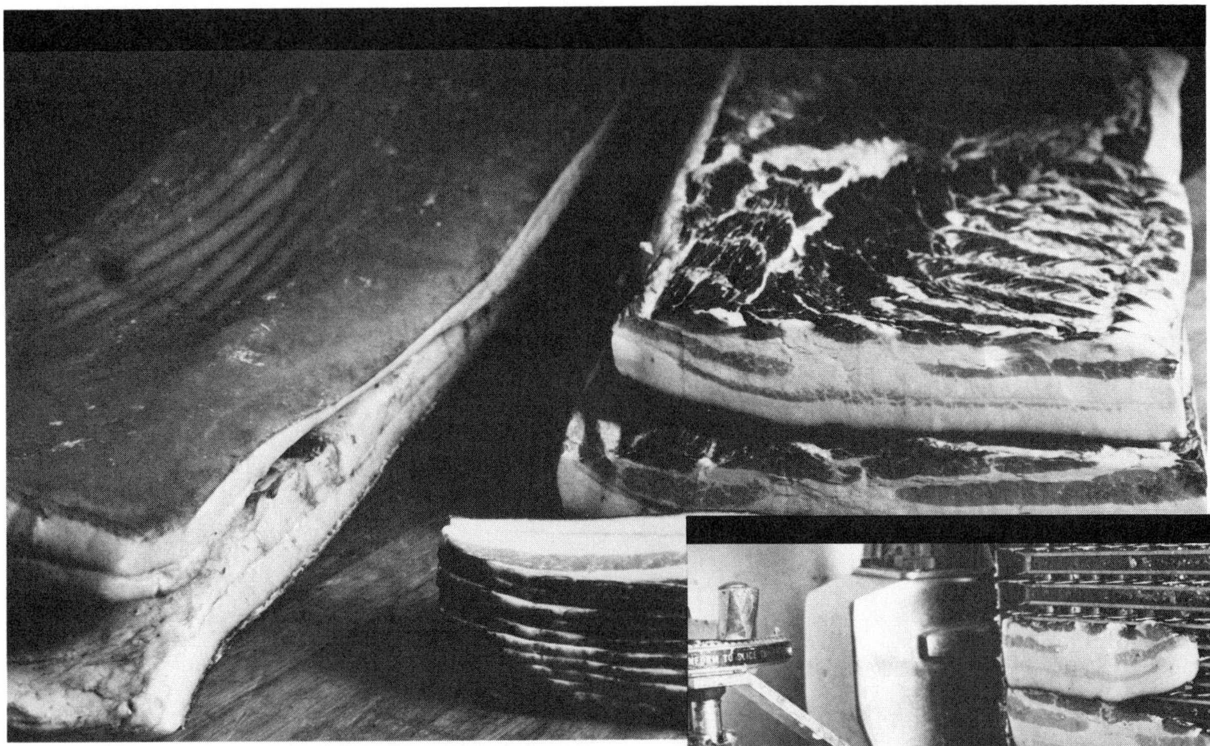
Bacon: Slab appears on the left; slices on the right

Bacon slicing machine

from 550 B.C. The country mouse says, "Better beans and bacon in peace, then cakes and ale in fear." By the first century A.D., the heyday of the Roman Empire, bacon had become a basic item issued to the poor through the Roman dole of "bread and circuses" fame. The finest Roman bacon came from the hogs of Lucania whose diet was mostly acorns from the oak forests of the region. But France, then the province of Gaul, also exported bacon and spiced meats to Rome.

The word "bacon" came to English from French, where it was the general word for pork in medieval times. Bacon was the poor man's meat of that era, except in France where, perhaps because of long tradition, pork products were held in high esteem, and a particular gastronomic highlight was the *repas baconique*, in which every course was based on some pork product. Today the French word for bacon is *lard*, the same as our word for pig fat.

In Britain, beans and bacon is one of the oldest dishes, and along with bread, cheese and beer, served as the staple diet for working people from the early Middle Ages until the end of the 19th century. According to legend, the phrase, "Bring home the bacon," dates from Norman times in England where at the monastery of Dunmow a flitch of bacon was offered as a prize to any man who could swear before the church that for a year and a day he had not quarreled with his wife nor wished himself single.

In America, bacon was popular from the beginning and survives today as a condiment for breakfast eggs, salads and the like. Canadian bacon is a different cut of meat entirely, being boned loin of pork, which has been cured and smoked. Danish bacon is cured differently than the U.S. variety, and is too salty for some tastes. German bacon, or *speck*, and Irish bacon are more heavily smoked than the U.S. product, and the Irish includes portions of the loin as well as the side.

Pigs bred specially for bacon are longer and

leaner than those bread for ham. Bacon is cut from the carcass after the spareribs have been removed and is available either lean or fat. Quality varies according to the age of the animal, the breed, its feeding and the way the bacon was cured. Generally, the leaner the bacon, the more it costs. Meat from the breast is considered best.

In the market, the lean part should be tender and red, while the fat should be firm and a clear white. Although most consumers purchase bacon already sliced in the market, it is also available in slabs. The cheaper forms of bacon, such as chunks, squares or ends serve quite well as flavoring agents.

Sliced bacon is perishable, and keeps well for a week, or at the most two weeks in the refrigerator, providing it is well wrapped. Freezing should be avoided as it dehydrates bacon and makes it hard. According to some authorities, it also increases the chances of rancidity.

BACORETA

See **Tuna Fish.**

BACURU PARY

Fruit of a tropical tree, *Rheedia macrophylla*, native to Brazil. It is yellow, has a good subacid taste and is used to make jam.

BADDERLOCKS

Also MURLIN, HONEYWARE ,HENWARE. This is a large black seaweed, *Alaria esculenta*, regularly eaten as a vegetable in the Faroe Islands and northern British Isles.

BADGER

A strong, fur bearing animal, weighing up to 45 pounds, of the family *Mustelidae*, the badger has heavy claws on its forefeet, powerful jaws and anal scent glands. Badgers are great burrowers both to find foods, plants and rodents, and to make their homes. They are nocturnals and, when attacked, are formidable fighters. There are six genera, of which the honey badger *(Mellivora capensis)* is not one, it being correctly labeled a ratel, a related group.

Badgers inhabit a large part of the world. The American species, *Taxidea taxis*, found in open, dry regions of the West, is a solitary; the Eurasian species, *Meles meles*, is gregarious; the ferret species, *Melogale* and *Helictus*, also called tree badger, inhabits China, Burma and Java; the hog species, *Aretonyx collaris*, also called sand badger, is found in Southeast Asia; the Malayan stink species, *Mydaus javaniensis*, and the Palaman stink species, *Mydaus marchei*, complete the list.

Badgers have commercial value. Besides being trapped for sale to zoos or pet shops, their fur is used to make brushes and as a trim for clothing. Before 1850, when such activities were outlawed, badger baiting was a sport in England. A badger put into a barrel and presumably lying on its side, fiercely defended itself from attacking dogs.

Badger meat is rich and flavorful, although rarely eaten. It is said to taste somewhat like young pig, and can be cured like bacon. In England, on occasion, it is roasted whole over an open fire.

BADIAN ANISE

See **Anise.**

BAEL FRUIT

See **Bengal Quince.**

BAGEL

This is a Jewish bread that has been described as an unsweetened doughnut with rigor mortis. Firm and crusty, and often sprinkled with caraway or sesame seeds, it is frequently eaten with cream cheese and smoked salmon.

BAGOZZO

Also BRESCIANO. An Italian cheese of the Parmesan type, with a hard, yellow body and a sharp flavor, *Bagozzo* is smaller than **Reggiano** or **Parmesan.** Its outside is usually red. It is made near Brescia.

BAGRE SAPO

This catfish, *Rhamdia sapo*, of rivers and lakes of central South America, is considered a food fish of moderate importance in the area. It rarely exceeds a length of 16 inches. Its flesh is described as white and firm.

BAKCHOI

See **Pakchoi.**

BAKERS' CHEESE

A skim milk cheese, used in commercial baking products, this is much like **cottage cheese** but has a more acid taste and a softer, smoother texture. It is used in cheesecakes and pastry fillings and is seldom offered for retail sale.

Rennet is added to pasteurized cow's milk, and the resulting curd is drained of whey either in large bags, or in a continuous centrifuge. The cheese is packed in polythylene-lined cans, and in this form it can be kept for months in cold storage. It may be salted or unsalted.

BAKING POWDER

A compound of simple chemicals is used as a leavening agent in cakes, quick breads and some puddings. It consists of an alkali, usually bicarbonate of soda; a starch or flour, often cornstarch, and an acid, either cream of tartar, calcium acid phosphate or sodium aluminum sulfate. The acid acts on the alkali to produce carbon dioxide gas, which causes the dough or batter to rise. The starch is an inert ingredient that serves to slow down the process by coating the other chemicals. That way the carbon dioxide gas is not all released immediately upon contact with moisture; some is retained to be released during the heating.

Baking powder was invented in mid-19th century as a convenient substitute for yeast, which was homemade and generally unpredictable, especially in cold weather. Yeast was often kept in the kitchen in the form of "starter," i.e., part of the last batch of bread dough in which yeast was already working. This practice continues for homemade sourdough bread and biscuits. At the end of the 18th century it was discovered that wood ashes could release carbon dioxide gas in dough, and the pearl ash industry boomed. In 1792 America decimated its forests to export 8,000 tons of pearl ash to Europe.

The next improvement was baking soda (bicarbonate of soda) which the cook could combine with buttermilk or sour milk to get the desired reaction. With sweet milk, a cook added some cream of tartar. Baking soda was also called "saleratus." This arrangement was soon superseded by commercial preparations. Preston & Merrill of Boston produced the first commercial baking powder. There are basically three kinds of baking powder.

SAS-Phosphate is double acting, i.e., a small amount of gas is released when liquid is added to the dry ingredients, but a larger amount is released when the mixture is heated. *Tartarate* reacts almost immediately when the liquid is added to the dry ingredients. *Phosphate* is another double-acting powder. Various salts and minerals are left in the bread as a result of the chemical reaction, but in negligible amounts.

In adding baking powder, it is important to sift it thoroughly, and follow the recipe carefully as regards the amount needed. Too much of any raising agent spoils both the texture and the flavour of a cake. Baking powder should be kept in an air-tight container to avoid having its action dissipated by ambient moisture.

BAKING SODA

See **Bicarbonate of Soda.**

BAKLAVA

A sweet Greek dessert or breakfast pastry made with *filo* (very thin, leaf-like dough), honey, sugar and chopped walnuts, baklava is best when prepared a day or two before it is eaten. The mixture of buttered *filo*, cinnamon and walnuts is first baked and then—when still hot—is drenched with a sauce of boiled honey, water, sugar and lemon juice.

BAKUPARI

This orange yellow, tough-skinned fruit of a Brazilian tree, *Rheedia braziliensis*, is much liked in its local habitat. The pulp is white and is used to make jam.

BALACHAN

Also BALACHONG, BLACHAN. A flavorful condiment from Thailand, balachan is found in Burmese and Malayan cuisines as well. The ingredients are small shrimps, small fishes and spices. This mixture is allowed to ferment in a heap under the hot sun, then washed and pounded with salt and left to dry in the sun. The end product, according to some gastronomes, is "the caviar of the Far East." They have held their noses, eaten and learned to relish it. There is another school of thought that says, "Balachan is relished by lovers of decomposed cheese."

BALANE

See **Acorn Barnacle.**

BALAOU

A small fish with a French name, resembling the sardine, balaou is found in abundance in West Indian waters. The flesh of this fish is very delicate, appetizing and easy to digest. It should be prepared for table according to recipes for sardines.

BALDPATE

Also AMERICAN WIDGEON. This migrant duck, *Mareca americana*, ranges widely over the western United States and Canada, down to Central America. It follows the seasons, going north in spring and south in autumn. Widgeons are midway in size between teals, and mallards. They have a patch of white feathers on their heads, which makes them look bald. They are equally at home on fresh or salt water.

Widgeons are one of the group called dabbling ducks, who do not dive for food but feed in shallow waters, on mud flats, and often seize food from just surfaced diving ducks. Their nests are built on dry ground that is hollowed slightly, of twigs, grass and down. The mother does the incubating.

These birds, like many others, flock to government-sponsored game refuges located along their flyways. These refuges help to prevent over-hunting. Widgeons should be prepared for the table just like other wild duck.

See also: **Duck, Mallard, Pintail, Teal.**

BALLYHOO

A species of half beak *(Hemiramphus brasiliensis)* of the tropical Atlantic, ballyhoo is a schooling fish that reaches a maximum length of 18 inches. It is closely related to the **flying fish** and is able to skitter along the surface of the water. Its lower jaw is prolonged into a sharp beak, hence the name. The ballyhoo is found off the coast of West Africa as well as that of Brazil, and as far north a New England. It is caught in seine nets for human consumption.

BALL TREE

See **Bengal Quince.**

BALM

Also LEMON BALM, GARDEN BALM, BALM MINT. A lemon-scented member of the mint family, balm *(Melissa officinalis)* was once highly regarded as a medicinal herb—balm tea was thought to promote longevity—but today serves as a minor culinary herb, an ingredient in perfumes and as a flavoring for liqueurs. It is a great favorite with bees, and its scientific name derives from the Greek for honey, *melissa.*

It is a prolific plant that grows to a height of one or two feet and has pale yellow flowers and heart-shaped leaves. Native to Europe, it is a common garden plant, which also grows wild in North America. The leaves can be used to flavor white wines and summer beverages and can give a distinctive taste to soups, sauces, stuffings and salads.

Balm's essential oils are believed to be slightly sedative and to aid digestion, which is perhaps why they found their way into such after dinner liqueurs as Chartreuse and Benedictine.

BALSAM PEAR

See **Bitter Melon.**

BALSAMROOT

The term covers several species of ornamental herbs, including Puget balsamroot *(Balsamorhiza deltoidea)* and Oregon sunflower *(B. sagittata)*, the starchy taproots of which are cooked and eaten as vegetables.

BAMBARRA GROUNDNUT

This seed of a creeping, annual plant, *Voandzeia subterranea*, is native to West Africa. The name derives from the Bambarra district of Mali. Like the peanut, the bambarra groundnut is encased in a pod, which is buried in the ground. It is not as rich in oil as the peanut, however, and therefore is cultivated mainly for the rich starch and protein content of the seed.

Bambarra seeds are most popular in Zambia and Madagascar where, before cooking, they are soaked, split and pounded. They come in an assortment of colors, red, white, black or mottled. Crops are consumed locally.

Bamboo

Bamboo shoots

BAMBELLE

See **Carp.**

BAMBOO

Edible portions of the bamboo plant (family *Bambusoideae)* include sprouts, shoots, leaves, fruit heart and bamboo sugar, which is obtained from the sectional joints. It is a staple vegetable in many Asian countries, as well as a source of wood and bamboo sheaths, which are used in plaiting hats and sandals. It has more than 200 species. Bamboo is native to Southeast Asia, but grows well in all tropical areas and many temperate ones.

It is a subfamily of the grasses, and is characterized by phenomenal growth. Some species of bamboo are capable of growing more than a foot in length in 24 hours. Moreover the growth is unceasing, unlike most plants, which require a resting period some time during their growing season. A peculiarity of the life cycle is that every 33 or 66 years, depending on the species, every bamboo plant in a given area will simultaneously bloom, bear fruit and then die. This can be a disaster in certain Asian countries where bamboo is the only dependable source of cheap wood. Members of the bamboo family vary in size anywhere from dwarfs of six inches to giants rising 120 feet in the air that have stalks eight inches in diameter.

The first and most tender food yielded by the bamboo is the sprout. It is sent up from an underground root system and is gathered as soon as it breaks the surface of the ground. If allowed to mature a little, sprouts become shoots, which are ivory colored and covered by a tough sheath. Two types are sold fresh in Asian markets, winter and spring. The winter type is softer, lighter in color, tastier, and therefore more expensive. The spring type tends to be dark and slightly woody. Shoots of the larger species may be several inches thick, and may have to be banked, much in the manner of asparagus, to extend their length. As a basic preparation, shoots are boiled in salted water until tender. Their taste has often been compared to asparagus, and, indeed, they may be served in any way suitable to asparagus. In Japan, they are frequently eaten alone. In China, they are most often added to more complex dishes, such as soups or stews. Canned or bottled shoots are the forms most familiar to Westerners. Canned shoots have been cooked previously, sometimes with salt, sometimes without. Pickled sprouts are often used to prepare *achard*, a hot condiment popular in Southeast Asia and India.

Bamboo foliage is most often used as cattle fodder, although some tender young leaves are eaten. Heart of bamboo is the sap-soaked pith and is very sweet. Bamboo sugar is a residue that gathers within the joints. It is also called *tabasheer* and is esteemed as a medicine in the East Indies. The plants final production, its fruit, is pear-shaped and consists of separate seeds, much like the kernels on a corn cob. The Japanese consider it a delicacy.

BAMBOO TEA

This type of Chinese black tea comes packaged in bamboo leaves that are tied off in rounded sections to define serving portions. The taste is strong and bitter. Two sections are used to brew the average pot of tea.

See also: **Tea.**

BAMBUSA

A large, carplike fish, *Elopicthys bambusa*, of the Amur River and some larger rivers in China, the bambusa often attains lengths of more than six feet, and is a commercially valuable food fish. Fishermen catch the bambusa in floating nets and seines, but the largest fish are seldom landed because they leap over or break through the nets.

BANANA

The sweet and nourishing fruit of the tropical plant *Musa sapientia*, the banana is believed to be native to Southeast Asia. Its cultivation is of such antiquity that, according to Hindu legend, the banana was the forbidden fruit of the Garden of Eden. After the fall, Adam and Eve covered their nakedness with a banana leaf, an ample garment indeed. Before acquiring the name *banana*, which derived from a particular tribe in Africa, the fruit was known as the "apple of paradise" and "Adam's fig." One species common to India, *Musa paradisiaca*, acknowledges this legend in its scientific name.

Cultivation of the banana spread throughout Asia and Oceania before recorded history. Ancient Greeks heard of bananas from soldiers of Alexander the Great who encountered them campaigning in India in the third century B.C. Arabs brought their cultivation to Africa in the seventh century. Banana shoots were introduced into the New World by Spanish colonists in 1516.

There are two general types of banana, the small, sweet fruit type, with red or yellow skin, which is recognized in temperate as well as tropical areas, and a vegetable type, or plantain, which is starchy but not sweet, and always eaten cooked. It is unusual outside of tropical areas. *Musa paradisiaca* is of this second type, which will be discussed more fully in a separate article. (See **Plantain.**)

Although the banana plant has a treelike appearance, it is botanically classified as an herb. The plant reaches heights of up to 20 feet, but its "trunk" consists entirely of tightly wrapped, overlapping leave sheaths. The top consists of an open crown of leaves, which can be as much as ten feet long and 20 inches wide. Fruit grows from the crown on single stem, which can hold up to 300 bananas growing in rows or "hands." Bunches containing seven to 12 hands are considered ideal for commercial transport. A plant produces a single bunch of fruit, and is then cut down, to be replaced by another tree from the same plant in 10 to 12 months. The banana is considered the most prolific known food plant and its fruit one of the most life sustaining, containing about 20 percent assimilable sugars. It is also high in vitamins A, B, C and B_2, with appreciable amounts of iron, phosphorus, potassium and calcium.

Bananas were little known in the United States before 1870, yet today Americans eat more bananas than any other fruit. This fact is largely due to their prolific cultivation in Central America and improved technology in transportation, particularly refrigeration. In the tropics, the red and the tiny "lady-finger" bananas are highly esteemed yet are rarely seen elsewhere because they do not travel well. The American market is dominated by the Cavendish, which supplanted the Gros Michel in 1962 because of its stronger stems, and superior resistance to disease. In Europe, the one most often seen in the Canary Island banana, which is smaller and sweeter than the Cavendish. Although the Caribbean area is the most prolific exporter of bananas, Africa is the most prolific producer, but it consumes 90 percent of its output.

Bananas are most often eaten raw, and should not be refrigerated, the ideal storage temperature being 55-65°F (13°–18°C). Black spots on the skin are an indication of ripeness, not spoilage. Apart from food, the banana plant has other uses. The leaves are used as roofing materials in the tropics and contain a fiber that can be made into cloth or paper. Another variety, *Musa textilis*, bears no fruit but is the source of manila hemp, which is made into rope.

BANBURY

This small, round English cheese is soft and rich in texture. Made near the town of Banbury in Oxfordshire, it was very popular early in the 19th century.

BANCANA

The fruit of a small Malaysian tree, *Garcinia bancana*, it is closely related to the **mangosteen** and is eaten locally.

BANCHA

A Japanese green tea of the cheapest grade, bancha has a mild taste and a light green color. It consists of the tougher leaves and stems of the tea plant.

See also: **Tea.**

B & B

This French liqueur is a mixture of Benedictine, a plant liqueur, and brandy. It is somewhat drier than the original Benedictine and is bottled at 86 proof.

BANDED KNIFEFISH

A freshwater fish, *Gymnotus carapo*, of Central America and eastern South America, it is closely related to the **electric eel.** It is edible and fished with some intensity throughout its range. Reaching up to two feet in length, it has a thin, eellike shape and a long anal fin that runs from its blunt head to its sharply pointed tail. Like its relative the electric eel, the knifefish develops considerable voltage that it uses both as a guidance system (it is nearly blind and a night hunter) and to stun its prey. Its coloring is pale gray with numerous mottled blue-green markings and dark bands.

BANDFISH

A South American freshwater fish of the knifefish family *(Rhamphichthyidae)*, it is shaped somewhat like an eel, except that its body tapers to a point at the tail, and it possesses a long, trunklike snout with a small mouth. As with other knifefish, the bandfish *(R. rostratus)* is highly regarded as food. It reaches a length of up to 54 inches and is found in streams and rivers of the Guianas and Brazil.

BANDICOOT

This is a small, furry mammal *(Peramelidae* family) hunted and eaten by Australian aborigines. Several species are found in Australia, Tasmania, New Guinea and adjacent islands. Bandicoots are ground-dwelling marsupials found in open plains, thick grass along the banks of swamps and rivers, thick scrub and forests. A large adult may be as much as 22 inches long. They eat a mixed diet.

BANGER

See **Sausage.**

BANILLES

Also BANILLE, BANILLOES. These are small pods, thin and tapering, which yield a sweet, fragrant juice. The pods come from a plant, *Vanilla pompona*, similar to the vanilla. After their pod juice has been extracted, dried and crystallized, it is used as a substitute for vanilla flavoring and in the manufacture of chocolate and other confectionary.

BANNOCK

This primitive form of unleavened bread is traditional in Scotland and the northern English counties. The bannock is made from oatmeal, barley, maslin (a mixture of barley, oats and rye), rarely wheat (food for the wealthy in former times), and in dire circumstances, flour made from dried peas and beans.

According to superstition bannock dough must be kneaded from right to left, as the reverse is unlucky. The dough is then formed into a flat oval and baked on the open hearth or on a griddle over the open fire, first one side and then the other.

The Scottish word "bannock" derives from the Latin *panicum*, a type of **millet** popular in ancient Rome among the poor as the chief ingredient of *pulmentum*, a gruel. The bannock is typical of unleavened hearth bread found in many ancient European and Mediterranean cultures. It was in general use throughout the British Isles in the time of King Alfred the Great (846–899 A.D.). Until the present century, bannocks were made for all festive occasions in Scotland.

Varieties include the Selkirk bannock, a fruit cake; the Pitcaithly bannock, a festive shortbread; the Aran bannock, a mixture of flour and maize shortened with butter; and the Sauty bannock, made of oatmeal, eggs, milk and golden syrup.

See also: **Bread.**

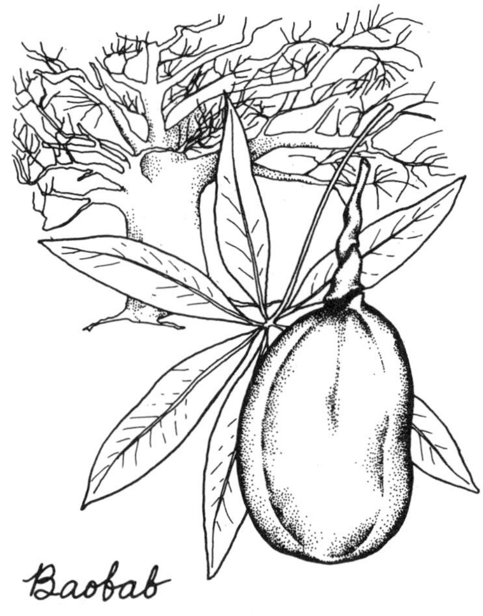

BANTAM

A very small, domestic fowl with decorative plumage and feathered legs and feet, it is thought to come from a community in Java called Bantam. The name has been broadened to include any dwarf breed that may be a miniature of a larger breed like Brahma Bantam or Cochin Bantam. The flesh of this fowl is fine, with delicate flavor and resembles chicken. It may be cooked just like chicken. Bantam eggs are thought to be superior to chicken eggs but are barely half the size.

See also: **Chicken.**

BANYULS

Banyuls is a wine from the Languedoc area of Banyuls in southern France. This region is noted for its mellow red wine—from the Grenache grape—grown in vineyards that overlook the Mediterranean Sea. The wine is dark red or brick-colored and is "warm" with a special *rancio* (or "old") taste dear to Catalonian palates. When allowed to age, the Banyuls wine acquires a rich golden-purple hue.

BAOBAB

This curious looking African tree, *Adansonia digitalis*, is a veritable storehouse of useful products, including food, drink, soap, medicine, fiber and even shelter. Though native to Africa, it is found in other tropical areas, such as Madagascar, southern Florida and Australia, where it is known as the bottle tree. The trunk of the baobab grows to very great thickness—a circumference of 75 feet has been recorded—but seldom reaches more than 30 feet in height. It earned the name "bottle" because its thick trunk slopes inward toward the crown—much like the shoulders of a bottle. Top-heavy branches sprout out of the crown and bow down to the ground, providing a tent of greenery around the trunk. It grows quickly and is long-lived.

The tree is known primarily for its gourd-like fruit, which is called monkey bread because of the monkey's predilection for it. It is kidney-shaped and grows up to 15 inches long. The fruit is brown yellow and has a downy surface. Below that a hard shell encloses cells of juicy, fibrous pulp that is acidic in flavor, and mealy in texture. The juice is made into a popular, refreshing drink. The pulp is dried and added to various dishes to give them a tart flavor. Soap is made from spoiled fruit. An infusion of the leaves and bark reputedly has pain-killing and fever-reducing qualities. The leaves are also dried, reduced to powder and used as a seasoner called *lalo*, or as a thickener for soups, sauces and gravies. The baobab is called the cream of tartar tree in South Africa because the seeds of the fruit are made into a crude baking powder. They are also eaten roasted or ground and used as a spice.

The bark of the baobab tree is soft and spongy, and chunks can be easily ripped away using an iron-tipped cane. Water is wrung from the bark as from a damp towel. Animals not only eat the leaves but chew the bark for moisture. Africans make rope and cloth from fiber obtained from the bark. If the tree is burnt, the ashes, which contain chlorides, can be used as a salt substitute.

Without doing permanent damage to the tree, African families have been known to hollow living spaces out of the living wood of the trunks. The tree is virtually indestructible.

BAR

See **Catfish.**

BARACK PALINKA

This Hungarian apricot brandy is not a sweet liqueur, or a grape brandy flavored with apricots, but a true brandy distilled from a mash of fresh apricot juice, pulp and pits. It is made in the manner of other fruit brandies, i.e., the mash is allowed to ferment for about six weeks, then is twice distilled in pot stills. Unlike many other fruit brandies, however, Barack Palinka is not a white alcohol. It is aged in wood, a process that gives it a golden brown color. Proof of the final distillation is fairly low (100), so as to retain much of the aroma and flavor of the fruit. It is unsweetened and generally bottled at 80 to 100 proof. The center of Barack Palinka production is Kecskemet in the south of Hungary.

See also: **Brandy.**

BARBADOS CHERRY

Fruit of a shrub, *Malpighia glabra*, this is found in Texas, the West Indies and northern South America. The fruit is red, juicy and about three-eighths inch in diameter. It is used to make jellies and preserves.

BARBADOS CREAM

Also CREME DES BARBADES. Here is a heavy, sweet French liqueur spiced with mace, cinnamon and cloves, and flavored with citrus peels. It has a brandy base.

BARBADOS GOOSEBERRY

Also BLADE APPLE, LEAFY CACTUS, LEMON VINE. This is the yellow, olive-sized, edible fruit of *Pereskia aculeata*, family *Cactaceae*, a West Indian cactus plant. Unusual for a cactus, this plant has trailing branches and many leaves. The fruit is well liked in the West Indies, and small quantities are imported in America.

BARBAREA

Also ROCKET, YELLOW ROCKET, WINTER CRESS, AMERICAN CRESS, HERB OF ST. BARBARA. This is a tiny genus of herbs of the mustard family, *Brassicaceae*, genus *Cruciferae* that grow wild as roadside weeds and are also raised commercially and as garden potherbs. They have an almost endless number of common names.

B. vulgaris has smooth, shining, dark green leaves, yellow flowers and an erect angular stem. It is sometimes considered a noxious weed.

B. verna may be cultivated for its leaves as salad, seasoning and garnishes despite its common name, scurvy grass.

These cresses are North Temperate Zone plants with some, like water cress and winter cress, needing a damp habitat. They are fast growers. Salad leaves may be harvested after only two months, and they continue growing in severe winter weather if afforded some protection.

Barbarea are considered antiscorbutic.

See also: **Rocket.**

BARBARIN

See **Mullet.**

BARBARY FIG

See **Prickly Pear.**

BARBECUE SAUCE

This American basting sauce is used in grilling meat. Recipes vary, but generally it is highly seasoned and contains such things as tomato puree, gravy, chutney, horseradish, onion juice, mustard, paprika, garlic powder, chili, sugar, plus plenty of Worcestershire Sauce and vinegar.

See also: **Sauce.**

BARBEL

This is a freshwater fish, several species of which are found in British and European rivers. All are distinguished by four whiskerlike barbels attached to the upper jaw, two near the point of the snout and two near the corners of the mouth. The common barbel, *Barbus vulgaris*, averages from 12 to 18 inches in length, although large specimens, taken from the Loire River, have measured up to three feet, and weighed as much as 18 pounds. Barbels are also found in African and Asian rivers, where they commonly attain a much larger size. The barbel belongs to the carp family.

The barbel is not a highly regarded food fish, tending to be coarse in texture, insipid in taste, and rather too bony for easy eating. The soft roe, however, is considered a delicacy. On the other hand, the hard roe is said to be poisonous.

In France, the barbel is most often poached and served with a sauce, such as white, Hollandaise or butter sauce. It may also be braised, baked or roasted.

BARBERA

A dry red wine from Piedmont, northern Italy, it makes up roughly half of the wine produced in that region. Barbera derives its name from its vine, which is often used in the production of other quality red wines. The Barbera vine is especially hardy. It has adapted well to other areas of the world, particularly in northern California, where a good quality Barbera is produced by several local growers.

BARBER EEL

This is a marine catfish, *Plotosus lineatus*, with an eellike appearance found in coastal waters of the Red Sea and the Indian Ocean in reefs, harbors and estuaries. It reaches its greatest length along the coast of East Africa, where specimens 29 inches long have been caught. The flesh of the barber eel has excellent flavor and is considered a delicacy. It must be handled with care however, because the barbed spines of its pectoral and dorsal fins can inflict painful wounds.

BARBEREY

Also FROMAGE DE TROYES. Named for a village near Troyes, France, Barberey is a soft cheese resembling **Camembert.** Milk is coagulated with rennet while still warm, then the curd is molded for 24 hours. It is usually allowed to ripen for about three weeks. The best season is from November to May, but in the summer it is often sold without ripening. Customary size in 5¼ inches in diameter by 1½ inches thick.

BARBERRY

This includes any shrub of the genus *Barberis.* Eastern Asia supplies most of the ornamental species. Europe sent the common barberry *(B. vulgaris)* to the United States where it grows in mountainous regions of Oregon and the Alleghanies. It grows in most continental uplands of the world. In Oregon, barberry is called "Oregon Grape" and has been chosen as the official flower of the state.

As a food, barberries are used in pastry, as flavoring and even to make a wine. As medicine, barberries are used to aid digestion by increasing bile secretion, to reduce fevers, to relieve some urinary ailments and as an astringent.

Barberries have a sinister side, too. They host a fungus that attacks and kills growing wheat. This is the wheat black stem rust.

Barberries vary in taste from tart, acid, and sour that must be cooked and used sparingly, to milder species that may be eaten raw.

BARBIER

See **Sucker.**

BARCELONA NUT

See **Hazelnut.**

BARDOLINO

A light dry Italian red wine from the Veneto region around Venice, it is less dry and robust than the darker, more regal **Barolo.** Bardolino, nevertheless, is more suitable than Barolo for a wide variety of foods. It is especially apt, for example, with veal or pasta. Bardolino is made from a mixture of vines, but in particular the Molinara (or Rosara), the Corvina Veronese, and the Negrera. It is ready for consumption almost immediately after fermentation but—like most red wine—improves if aged for two or three years.

BARFI

A fudgelike candy, popular in northern India, it is often flavored with almonds or pistachio nuts and colored accordingly. A variety colored green, white and saffron is nicknamed "National Flag."

BAR-LE-DUC

A town of northwestern France produces these famous currant preserves. This confection is often called Bar-Le-Duc jelly, a misleading term, since the product consists of whole berries, carefully pierced and seeded by hand so as to retain the original shape, then preserved in a clear, white syrup. The process is said to have been created by one Perrin Lamothe, a 14-century cellarer to Robert, duke of the old province of Lorraine. Although originally made only with red or white currants, it now also uses strawberries, gooseberries and raspberries.

The preserves are also referred to as *confiture de groseille* and Lorraine jelly. They are marketed in small jars at fancy prices.

BARLEY

Barley *(Hordeum vulgare)* is a hardy and versatile cereal grain that has adapted well to different climates from Norway to the Equator and different altitudes from sea level to 15,000 feet. It is believed to be the first grain cultivated. Although there are hundreds of species, they can be divided into three groups by the number of rows of kernels on a sprig: two, four or six; and into three groups by the nature of the hulls: loosely attached, tightly attached, or no hulls at all. Certain types are associated with specialized uses, e.g., two-rowed varieties are used in the preparation of malt for brewing beer. Other varieties are ground into flour for making barley bread, and "pearl" barley is made into soups. The hull typology is useful in tracing the origin of barley strains. For example, hullless barley originated in the mountains of China, while the hulled varieties are thought to have their origin either in southwestern Asia, or the highlands of Ethiopia.

The chief modern uses of barley are animal fodder, the manufacture of beer and whisky, milling of flour for bread, and the preparation of some soups. The Soviet Union is the leading producer of barley with an annual crop of about 25 million tons. It is followed by Great Britain, France and the United States at 10 million tons each, then by Canada and other countries.

The food value of barley is similar to that of wheat, but it has two disadvantages as regards the latter: barley has less protein and much less gluten, which makes it unsuitable for making porous, light bread. Its advantages are adaptability to harsher climates, and greater resistance to spoilage. Much of the dark bread of northern and central Europe and Russia is made from barley with the addition of hard wheat to lighten it. Still, it retains the characteristic heaviness of barley bread. The flat, unleavened breads of North Africa and the Middle East, such as pita bread, are made from barley. Porridge is another common use for barley in Europe, North Africa and the Middle East.

In ancient times, barley reigned supreme from prehistory down to the Roman Empire, when wheat began to make some inroads due to its superiority in breadmaking. It was the mainstay for Hebrews, Egyptians and Greeks, who employed it in the secret rites of Demeter and of the oracle at Delphi. Fumes of burning laurel and barley were used to induce a trance in the Pythoness, the priestess who delivered the oracles. Sprigs of barley were a frequent motif on ancient coins and appeared on statues, plaited into the hair of the goddess Ceres. After the fall of Rome barley regained primacy in Europe, and retained it until the 16th century on the continent and the 17th century in England.

The term "barleycorn" has an antique flavor today since John Barleycorn stands as an old-fashioned symbol of beer and liquor. In earlier times, however, it was a standard measure of length. In 1324 an English royal decree standardized the inch as being equal to three barleycorns (grains) from the center of the ear laid end to end. The same decree specified that the longest normal foot was equal to 39 barleycorns. In 1888 the U.S. shoe industry accepted this standard, which established size 13 (39 barleycorns) as the largest regularly manufactured shoe.

See also: **Barley Meal, Barley Sugar, Barley Water, Malt, Pearl Barley.**

BARLEY MEAL

This is barley ground into a wholemeal flour, the form in which barley is usually sold for breadmaking and manufacturing. Barley meal is darker in color than wheat meal, which accounts for the darker color of barley breads. The Scots use it to make porridge and gruel.

BARLEY SUGAR

Barley sugar is a candy made formerly from boiled sugar combined with barley water and lemon juice. Nowadays it is made with synthetic flavoring. In finished form, it was an amber-colored, twisted stick. In British slang, barley sugar also means twisting a person's arm painfully behind his back.

BARLEY WATER

Barley water is a preparation of pearl barley, boiled in water and flavored with lemon juice. It is considered a nourishing dietary supplement for invalids or infants and may be given plain or stirred into milk.

BARLEY WINE

This term has been used in various epochs to denote a strong beer or ale, which today is more likely to be called a malt liquor. The ancient Babylonians, Sumerians and Egyptians made barley wine, which contained as much as 12 percent alcohol. It was sweet and aromatic. According to Athenaeus, the Greek grammarian and rhetorician, "those who drank this beer were so pleased with it that they sang and danced, and did everything like men drunk with wine."

The term was used in medieval England for strong ale, and it still occasionally appears as a poetic alternative to **malt liquor.** Brews referred to as barley wine are usually made without hops and so technically are ales.

BARM

Also BREWER'S YEAST. Barm is the brown, frothy scum that forms on top of beer or other malt liquors during fermentation. Less often it is used to refer to the scum on fermenting wine. During the Middle Ages and until the 19th century, barm obtained from breweries, and from winemaking operations in season, was used to leaven bread. The quality varied, however. Barm tended to be unstable and not as vigorous as the compressed yeast, which supplanted it as a leavening agent in the 19th century. Moreover, barm is said to impart a slightly bitter taste to the bread. Brewer's yeast has also been used as a dietary supplement because of its high protein and vitamin content. A traditional Irish yeast cake is called *barm brack.*

The word "barm" derives from the Anglo Saxon word for yeast, *beorma.* The British slang term "barmy" and its varient, "balmy," meaning silly or idiotic, is said to come from "barm."

See also: **Yeast.**

BARNACLE

The barnacle is a relative of the lobster. Although it looks more like a mollusk with its hard shell and manner of clinging to objects, it is a marine crustacean. Many species of barnacle are edible, the most familiar, perhaps, being the goose barnacle *(Lepas anatifera).* It is most often encountered clinging to intertidal rocks, to which it seems permanently cemented. Yet, when covered by water the barnacle releases part of its shell to feed. This operation has been described as keeping its head firmly attached to the rock and whisking food into its mouth with its feet, which resemble a curl of hair. Its food is plankton and other barnacle larvae.

The name "barnacle" derives from a supposed relationship between *Lepas anatifera* and the barnack, or European barnacle goose *(Anser bernicla).* Medieval observers saw a resemblance between the shape of the crustacean's mantle and that of the goose's beak. They concluded that the goose grew out of the barnacle. They envisioned tiny geese curled up inside

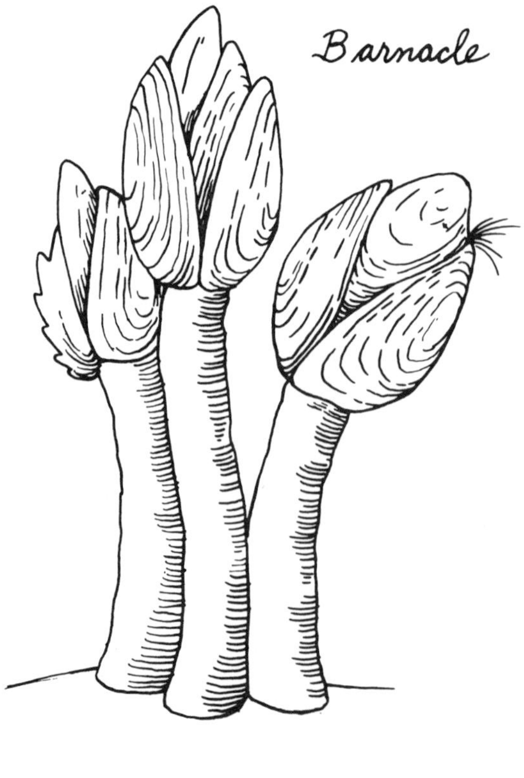

crustaceans' shells, and naturally applied the name of the goose to the shellfish. It was later extended to other species of barnacle. Goose barnacles are eaten all along the French coast, and in some parts of Italy and Spain. They are preferred raw and very fresh, and may be accompanied by chopped onions, thin slices of buttered rye bread or a vinaigrette sauce. Larger barnacles are better cooked, like mussels, or grilled with butter.

Other edible species include the acorn barnacle, which the French call *balane* and consider the most delicate in taste; and the Pacific barnacle *(Balanus psittacus)*, which is perhaps the world's largest, on the coast of Chile reaching a size of nine inches by three inches. It is much liked there, and is similar to large barnacles eaten by the native Americans of the Pacific Northwest. Even the traveling barnacles, which are regarded as a nuisance when attached to the bottom of a ship, can be made into a passable shrimp-flavored soup when boiled in the shell and strained.

BARNACLE GOOSE

This species of European wild goose, *Anser bernicla*, breeds in the Arctic but is found in Ireland, England and France during the winter months. It is related to other wild geese, such as the brant and the graylag. Though edible, it is not fat and succulent like the domestic bird, but tough, stringy and strongly flavored.

Its name is rooted in legend. In medieval times it was thought to hatch out of a barnacle shell or out of the shelllike fruit of a tree that resembled a barnacle. On the other hand, these may have been attempts to explain its Celtic name, *bairneach*, which sounds so much like barnacle. *Bairneach* means "bare-necked."

Barnacle goose may be prepared in any way suitable for other wild geese.

BAROLO

"The king of Italian wines" is so called because of its popularity with the 19th-century rulers of the House of Savoy. Barolo is grown and produced in a small area in the Langhe district, a region of hills around Alba in Piedmont, northern Italy. It is the product of a grape called Nebbiolo, a vine already under cultivation around 1300 A.D. It is an excellent wine *da arrosto*—with grilled or roast meats. It is strong, with a 13 to 14 percent alcohol content, robust, rich and fiery. Barolo requires a long aging process, even though the name can be applied after three years in the casks, when the wine turns a beautiful orange red. Connoisseurs advise that a bottle of Barolo should be opened at least one hour before consumption.

BARRACOUTA

See **Snoek.**

BARRACUDA

Any one of several voracious, pikelike carnivorous fishes, of the genus *Sphyraena*, family *Sphyraenidea*, bears this name. Barracuda live in tropical and subtropical seas. Most are excellent food fishes, while some species are regarded as toxic. A great game fish, sometimes growing to six feet in length, 30 inches around, and 100 pounds in weight, it will attack almost any living thing in the sea, including humans. The barracuda's teeth have cutting edges on both sides, and these, combined with their powerful jaws, can sever the body of a much larger fish. They are often called the "Tiger of the Sea."

Barracuda, while not an important food fish, are popular, particularly in California. Their long, slender bodies and firm flesh lend themselves to steaking. They are also excellent when smoked.

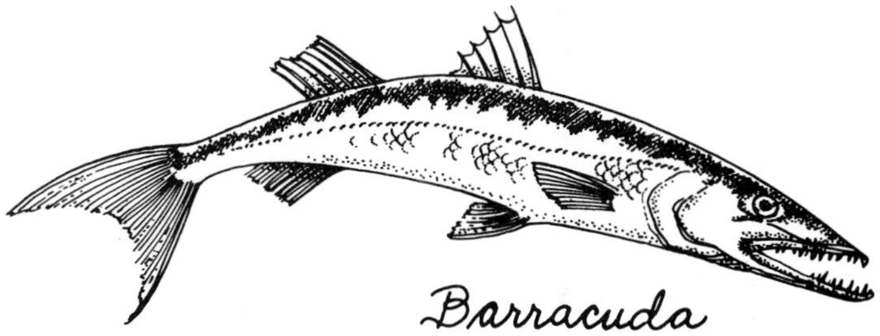

BARRACUTA

Also KATONKEL, SERRA. A large fish, *Scomberomorus commerson*, of the mackerel family found in the Indian and Pacific Oceans and widely valued as a food fish. Larger specimens measure upwards of seven feet long, and can weigh as much as 130 pounds, although those caught commercially average 25 pounds. The fish move seasonally with changes in water temperature, and at various times are abundant in the Red Sea, and the East African coast. Farther east, they move between the coasts of China and Japan and south to Australian waters.

The barracuta is extremely important as a commercial fish, as well as being popular with anglers. It has a long body, pointed snout and a line that bisects the side horizontally. Its color is deep blue on the back and silver below with the wavy vertical lines typical of mackerels. It is closely related to the kingfish, the Spanish mackerel and the painted mackerel and may be prepared in any way suitable for these fish.

See also: **Kingfish, Mackerel.**

BARRED-FACE SPINE CHEEK

This is a food fish of Australian waters, so called because it has a sharp spine immediately beneath the eye. Although it rarely exceeds 17 inches in the length, the spine cheek *(Scolopsis temporalis)* is widely used for food along the Queensland coast and the Great Barrier Reef. This fish is related to the snapper family *(Lutjanidae)*.

BARRED SURFPERCH

A favorite catch of Southern California anglers, the barred surfperch *(Amphistichus argenteus)* is found from Bodega Bay to Baja California. Its body coloring is light, marked with dark bars and spots; it weighs from one to three pounds and is up to 17 inches long. It is generally caught in the surfline of sandy beaches. The barred surfperch has a delicious light flavor and is caught year round.

BARSAC

This strong sweet white wine comes from a tiny township of the same name near Bordeaux in western France. The name *Barsac* is usually coupled with that of **Sauternes.** The vineyards of these two districts lie adjacent to each other and combine to produce some of the world's best sweet Sauternes. The grapes harvested are the same—chiefly of the Semillon variety—and the elaborate, careful process in harvesting is identical. The label "Sauternes-Barsac" is usually found on the best of these vintages.

See also: **Bordeaux Wines.**

BARTABELLES

See **Partridge.**

BARTLETT WATER

A sparkling mineral water bottled in Visalia, California, Bartlett's is spring water with carbonation added. It is relatively high in mineral content (1950 ppm. of total dissolved solids) and naturally alkaline. A 1980 Consumers Union sensory panel rated the taste of this water as fair, with the following qualifying comments: mildly bitter, mildly sour, mild bitter aftertaste, mild soapy flavor, soapy mouthfeel, mildly salty, mild salty aftertaste, mild sweet aftertaste.

See also: **Mineral Water.**

BASELLA

Also CEYLON SPINACH, INDIAN SPINACH, MALABAR NIGHTSHADE. A trailing vine, native to tropical Africa or Southeast Asia, this is eaten as a potherb or spinach substitute. Some varieties furnish edible tubers and purple dye.

The most common variety, *Basella alba*, grows to some 30 feet long, and has large, fleshy, green leaves that resemble spinach. It is cultivated in France where it is eaten both in salads and as a cooked green. Basella leaves become quite mucilaginous when cooked. It was introduced into the United States as a spinach substitute in hot weather. Its season follows that of spinach, i.e., from July to frost.

BASIL

Also SWEET BASIL. An aromatic annual plant, whose leaves are highly regarded as a seasoning, sweet basil *(Ocimum basilicum)* is native to India but widely cultivated in warm areas throughout the world.

It was the chief seasoning of the ancient Greeks, who nominated it "king of herbs." It was well liked in the Middle Ages, and romantic legends about it abound. In the *Decameron*, Boccacio relates a story in which the heroine, Isabella, waters with her tears a pot of basil in which her lover's head is buried.

The plant, which has large heart-shaped leaves and white tubular flowers, varies in size from three to 18 inches. When fresh, the leaves have a clovelike flavor and smell, and have a special affinity to tomatoes. When dried, their taste is more like curry. In addition to tomatoes, it is used to season soups, steaks, duck, spaghetti sauce and cheeses.

See also: **Aphrodisiac.**

BASKING SHARK

A huge but harmless fish that used to be fished extensively in the North Atlantic for its liver oil and as a source of fish meal, the basking shark *(Cetorhinus maximus)* is the second largest fish known, with specimens exceeding six tons in weight and measuring up to 34 feet long. The name derives from its custom of swimming sluggishly on the surface of the sea, apparently basking in the sun. It lives on plankton. Small boats have been upset by basking sharks, but these occurrences seem to have been accidental. The basking shark is found worldwide, but the fishing of it seems to have lapsed almost completely due to competing sources of fish meal and vitamin A.

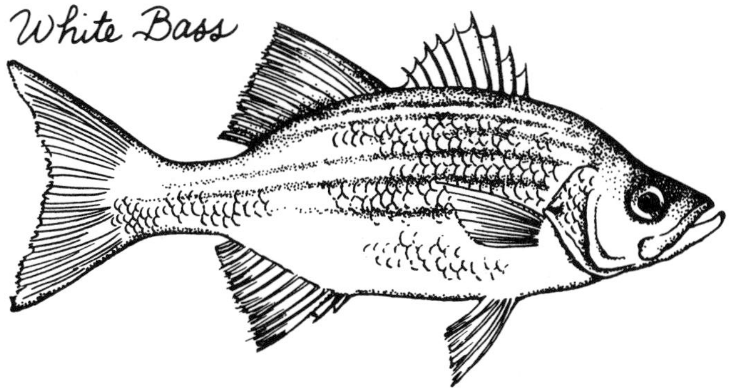

BASS

The name is given to several kinds of fish with spiny dorsal fins. They are considered both good game and good eating fishes. The word bass comes from the Old English "byrst," meaning bristle, and referring to the spines. It is similar to the Dutch *baers*, the French *bar* and the German *Barsch*, which are sometimes applied, somewhat confusingly, to both bass and perch. The many different fish going under the name bass include both fresh and saltwater varieties, such as the following:

Sea bass. An excellent food fish of the Mediterranean Sea, with firm white flesh, called by the French *loup de mer* or "sea wolf." It acquired the name "wolf" on account of its voracious eating habits, and was first called thus by the ancient Romans, who greatly prized it. It often ascends rivers to live in brackish or fresh water, and gourmets claim to be able to distinguish by taste between those living in fresh and saltwater habitats. In France, the sea bass is often grilled over a fire of fennel twigs.

A similar fish is the striped sea bass *(Dicentrarchus punctatus)*, found off the Atlantic coasts of England and France. It is stronger in taste and oilier than the Mediterranean variety and resembles salmon enough to be called salmon dace, sea salmon and white salmon in England. The flesh is firm, lean and rather bony. It can be cooked in any way appropriate to salmon.

American saltwater bass of the Atlantic coast include the sea bass, or white perch *(Morone americana)*, which like the *loup* mounts rivers and is the best eating; the striped bass, or "rockfish," which attains weights of 75 pounds and was a staple for the Pilgrims; the channel bass, or red drum *(Sciaenops ocellatus)*, small specimens of which are fine eating (10 pounds or less), and the black sea bass, or blackfish *(Centropristes striatus)*, which averages one to two pounds, and is the least good of the four to eat.

On the Pacific Coast, the California white sea bass is large, often reaching a weight of 50 to 100 pounds, and the Pacific black sea bass, or jewfish *(Stereolepis gigas)* is a veritable giant, sometimes tipping the scales at 500 pounds. Stone bass is a deepwater perch of the tropical Atlantic.

Freshwater bass. The best known both as a game and table fish is the small-mouth black bass *(Micropterus dolomieu)* of U.S. lakes and rivers. Almost equally well known is the large mouth black bass *(M. salmoides)*. The small-mouth runs from ½ to five pounds, and the large-mouth from two to eight. They are not fished commercially, and thus are rarely seen in markets. The white bass *(Roccus chrysops)*, of the Great Lakes and upper Mississippi, are marketed fresh and usually weigh one or two pounds. The calico or yellow bass *(Pomoxis sparoides)* inhabits the same waters but is a much smaller fish, averaging less than ½ pound in weight. It is an excellent food fish.

BASSWOOD

Also LINDEN, LIME TREE. This is not the citrus tree, but a genus of large, decorative trees with yellow flowers and heart-shaped leaves. The American variety, *Tilia americana*, is called basswood. The European varieties, especially *Tilia cordata*, are called linden in Great Britain and Germany.

Lindens are native to the North Temperate Zone, and have been put to use mainly as shade trees to line city boulevards. Their yellow flowers, however, may be infused to make a sort of tea, which, according to tradition, is effective against nervous headaches and hysteria. In France, the scented flowers are used in cooking and in green salads. During World War I, linden leaves were used as famine food in Poland. The trees are important bee plants, producing a fine-tasting honey.

See also: **Lime.**

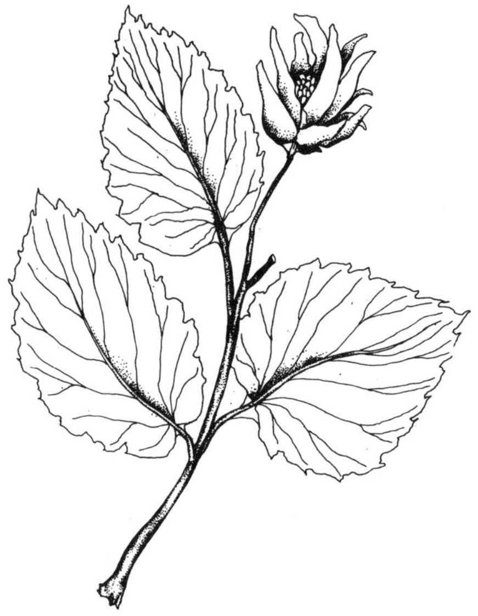

BAT

This is a nocturnal, flying mammal, the numerous species of which belong to the order *Chiroptera.* They are more abundant and larger in warm countries. Caves are a favored abode. The Carlsbad Caverns in New Mexico harbor thousands of these creatures. Their presence predates history, as their remains have been found from the Eocene Period. Most live on insects; the so-called flying foxes live on fruit; and a few suck the blood of other animals.

In China, and some other Oriental countries, the meat of bats is considered a delicacy. Bats can be reservoirs for rabies, however, and those flying in daylight or otherwise behaving abnormally should be avoided. Fruit bats are baked in Samoa in an underground oven, or *umu*, or fried with salt, pepper and onions.

BATARDE SAUCE

A butter sauce, somewhat like **allemande sauce,** it consists of a roux mixed with boiling salt water, an egg yolk and a half pint of butter. It may be sharpened with a few drops of lemon juice. Batarde is served with boiled fish or vegetables.

See also: **Sauce.**

BATARD MONTRACHET

See **Montrachet.**

BATAVIAN ARAK

See **Arak.**

BATAW

See **Lablab Bean.**

BATEIFUN

See **Tuberous Rush.**

BATTELMATT

A cow's milk cheese made in Switzerland and northern Italy. It is of the Swiss type, but softer and smaller, the wheels measuring 18 to 24 inches across and weighing 40 to 80 pounds. The flavor is closer to **Tilsiter** than to Swiss, and the eyes are smaller. It ripens rapidly, the aging period lasting three to four months and has a high moisture content.

BAUDEN

See **Koppen.**

BAYBERRY

See **Allspice.**

BAY LEAF

A favorite potherb, and part of the classic *bouquet garni*, bay leaf comes from the sweet bay, or laurel tree *(Laurus nobilis)*, an evergreen that grows wild in the Mediterranean area.

It is the stuff of ancient legend, Ovid telling us that the nymph Daphne was transformed into a laurel tree to escape the attentions of the god Apollo, who then adopted the tree as his own. Since then, the laurel has symbolized kings, nobility and high honor. Laurel wreaths were awarded to victorious warriors, and winners in the Olympic Games. Even today, a person who is awarded a Nobel prize is called a laureate, after the ancient custom. In medieval times, the death of a bay tree was considered an omen of royal disaster. In *Richard II*, Shakespeare refers to that belief in these lines, "Tis though the King is dead; we will not stay, the Bay trees in our country are all wither'd."

Although naturalized worldwide, bay trees grow best in warm climates, reaching a height of 60 feet in some cases. They are common in the Far East, and notable cultivations are found in the Canary Islands, Central America and the southern United States.

Bay leaves are strongly aromatic and must be used with discretion. They taste best fresh but preserve their flavor well when dried. They improve

the flavor of practically any dish, including soups, stews, fish, game, salads and meats. They are de rigueur in pickling solutions.

BEACH PLUM

Also SHORE PLUM. A wild variety of plum *(Prunus maritima)*, it grows on the sandy seashore of the eastern United States from Maine to Delaware. Often reaching 10 feet in height, the plant is straggling but decorative, with pointed oval leaves.

The fruit ranges in color from yellow to deep purple. It measures from one-half to one inch in diameter when fully ripe and in that state may be eaten raw. The pulp is sweet and juicy with a pleasant tang, but the skin remains uncomfortably sour. Often, however, the fruit is too tart or bitter to eat raw but makes an excellent jelly or preserve. The taste of beach plum preserve goes well with roast pork or poultry.

BEACH STRAWBERRY

See **Chiloe Strawberry.**

BEAMING

See **Scallop.**

BEAN

The name is given to certain edible seeds that are smooth to the touch, and high in protein. Along with peas and lentils, beans belong to the family of legumes, plants whose fruits grow in pods, several at a time in a single row. These plants may grow erect or take the form of trailing vines, and they are bewilderingly profuse in their many varieties. Historically, three types have been of outstanding importance as food: the soybean *(Glycine max)*, the haricot, or kidney bean *(Phaseolus vulgaris)*, and the broad or fava bean *(Vicia faba)*. Cultivation of these beans began in prehistory, and each originated in a different part of the world.

The soybean is native to China and has been under cultivation for at least 4,000 years. Today the United States is the largest producer and exporter of soybeans. With 40 percent protein and 21 percent oil, the soybean is a major source for industrial use and for animal and human consumption. This last use is less important in the United States than in other major producing countries, such as Brazil, the People's Republic of China and Indonesia. Other important food beans of the Far East are the cowpea, and the mung, gram, rice and adzuki beans, all of the genus *Vigna*.

The haricot bean *(Phaseolus vulgaris)* is of American origin, and there is evidence to suggest that its cultivation goes back 7,000 years. The word "haricot" derives from the Aztec word, *ayacotl*. This bean is the most versatile of all in respect to shape of plant, color and shape of pod and color and shape of bean. The most familiar to Americans is the kidney bean, which, when green, is known as the string brean, but other well known varieties include the black bean of Latin America, the lima bean, the pigeon pea, the black-eyed pea and the pinto bean.

The haricot was unknown in Europe until the

16th century but after that began its encroachment on the territory of the broad or fava bean, which hitherto had been the only bean in the diet of Europeans and Middle Easterners. The broad bean, so named because of its broad, plump shape, was cultivated in the Stone Age, and in historic times was a staple food in ancient Egypt, Greece and Rome. In the Middle Ages, it was daily fare for European peasantry. Throughout history it has played a role in certain rituals. For example, in the ancient pagan festival of Saturnalia, the master of revels was chosen by drawing beans, and when this festival was incorporated into the Christian calender as Twelfth Night, the title of king (or queen) fell to the person who received a piece of holiday cake with a fava bean baked into it.

For culinary purposes, beans can be classified by whether they are eaten fresh or dried. Those eaten fresh are string, lima and broad, while those eaten dry are lima, navy, kidney, pinto, cowpeas and soybeans.

See also: **Broad Bean, Kidney Bean, Soybean.**

BEAN SPROUTS

Although practically any bean can be germinated, it is usually the sprouts of mung or soy beans that are featured in Asian cooking. Mung beans are tiny and green, and generally soaked for several hours before being placed in cans for sprouting. In the course of four days, they are held at a constant temperature of 65°F (18°C), sprinkled with water every six hours, and increase in bulk fivefold. A typical mung sprout is one to two inches long, tender, and rich in vitamin C. To retain its food value, it should be cooked only briefly, i.e., two minutes boiling or lightly fried in butter and oil. Bean sprouts are also delicious raw in salads.

See also: **Mung Bean, Soybean.**

BEAN VINE

Also WILD BEAN. This seed of a twining plant, *Phaseolus polytachysus*, is found in the east and southern United States. The beans are dried, then eaten after boiling. It is well liked in its natural habitat.

Varieties of bean sprouts

BEAR

This large, stout, furry quadruped of the *Ursidae* family, though edible, is eaten with increasing rarity these days due to reduced numbers and restrictive hunting laws. There are numerous species, including the brown or black bear of Europe and Asia *(Ursus arctos)*, the American black bear *(Ursus americanus)* and the polar bear of the Arctic regions *(Ursus maritimus)*. With few exceptions, they inhabit temperate or arctic zones. Bears are carnivorous, but subsist much of the time on insects, fruits and roots.

In colonial days, bears were very numerous in North America and were an important item of diet for natives and European settlers alike. Bear meat was an original ingredient of mince pie. Bear fat was the standard cooking fat in the colonial kitchen, and was indispensable for authentic Boston Baked Beans. In 1869, Alexandre Dumas wrote in his *Le Grand Dictionnaire de Cuisine:*

> *Bear meat is now eaten everywhere in Europe. From the most ancient times, the front paws have been regarded as the most delicate morsel. The Chinese esteem them highly. In Germany, where the meat of the bear cub is much sought after, the front paws are a delicacy reserved for the very rich.*

Smoked bear hams were available in the Paris of his day, and could be purchased in London and New York up until the outbreak of World War II.

Bear meat is classed as venison, and only the fillet, steaks, hams and paws are eaten. The most desirable of all is cub meat, because the older animals tend to be tough, and their meat must be marinated for at least three days before cooking. In the United States, it is possible to contract trichinosis by eating undercooked bear meat. Some authorities liken it to beef and others to pork, but the Arctic explorer Nansen and his colleagues ate bear meat (especially paws) every day for many months without tiring of it. They singled out breast of polar bear cub as especially good.

Nowadays only in Russia is bear served with any regularity. There the meat is marinated for four or five days in a solution of red wine, vinegar, salt and pepper, sugar, mustard, flour, carrots and small onions. Cooking includes simmering for several hours and then braising. It is served with potatoes and strong vodka.

A traditional Chinese recipe for bear paw involves coating the claw with clean clay, then baking it in an oven. When the clay is removed, it takes the hair with it. The paw is simmered until the gamy smell dissipates, then shredded chicken and ham are added, plus a little sherry, and the simmering continues until the paw is very soft. It is sliced thinly like ham and served with gravy.

BEARBERRY

Red fruit of a creeping shrub, *Arctostaphylos uvi-ursi*, found in the colder regions of Europe, northern Asia and North America, the berry has a shriveled appearance and an interesting taste. The plant has white or pink flowers and bright green leaves, which are used medicinally and, in Sweden, for tanning.

BEARNAISE SAUCE

This is merely **Hollandaise sauce** spiced with reduced wine, wine vinegar and herbs. It is served with fillet of beef or grilled red meat, but also with fish, chicken or eggs. Usually shallots and tarragon are boiled in the wine and wine vinegar, which is then thickened with egg yolk and butter. Stock from the meat or fish course is added to the mixture, and the whole thing thickened by a liaison of cream and egg.

It should be kept and served slightly warm, because if heated too much the sauce will curdle. The herb-vinegar taste is strong and the sauce must be handled discreetly.

See also: **Sauce.**

BEAR'S GARLIC

See **Ramsons.**

BEAUJOLAIS

This red wine from the Gamay grape is produced in the region of Beaujolais in southern Burgundy, between Macon and Lyons. Beaujolais is perhaps the most popular red wine in France, providing most of the wine (when it is not Algerian) served in pitchers and carafes. "Three rivers flow into Lyons—the Rhone, the Saone and the Beaujolais."

The Beaujolais wine district (32 miles long and between seven and 10 miles wide) does, however, produce much red wine of exceptional quality. The Gamay grape, which elsewhere makes a wine of great volume but of only moderate quality, flourishes in the hot sun of this region and in the freshness of the two rivers.

One of the heaviest and best known of the Beaujolais is made in the township of Moulin-a-Vent. The Beaujolais of Fleurie is lighter and fruitier with a slight perfume appropriate to the name, which means "flowery." Beaujolais reds are generally lighter, more delicate and not as deeply colored as the red wine of northern Burgundy, which is almost exclusively produced from the more aristocratic Pinot grape.

See also: **Burgundy Wines.**

BEAUNE

The appelation includes wine from the vineyards in and near this ancient Burgundian city. The Cote de Beaune is a 16-mile strip of land covered by vineyards that extends south from the equally famous wine-growing region of **Nuits-St.-Georges** to the wine area of **Mercurey.** Some of the best white Burgundy wines come from the Cote de Beaune, including the **Meursault** and **Montrachet.** One fine red wine of Beaune is Le Corton (from the Latin *curtis*, meaning "estate" or "garden"), which, with its bright color, is the smoothest of the red Burgundies. ("A Corton under five years of age is not worth drinking.")

It was near Beaune in 775 that Charlemagne donated his vineyard to the Abbey of Saulieu. A white wine, Le Corton Charlemagne, honors him today. Beaune the city is noted not only as a wine center since before the tenth century but also for its famous *Hospice:* two buildings—The Hotel Dieu and the Hospice de la Charite—founded as a home for the aged and ill in 1443 by Nicolas Rolin, a tax collector and chancellor of Burgundy. To this day the Hospice maintains a vineyard of some 180 acres, and is the site of an annual wine auction, the *Vente des Vins des Hospices,* held on the third Sunday of November. The auction has been called "the world's greatest charity sale." Its proceeds are used to preserve the institution.

The wine of Beaune was especially admired by Rabelais, in his *Gargantua and Pantagruel:*

> *. . . and Panurge cried out, "By God, this is the wine of Beaune, and the best that ever I tasted, and may a hundred and six devils run away with me if it isn't! How grand it would be to have a neck six feet long, so as to taste it longer . . ."*

BEAVER

Beaver is a member of the rodent family that lives on land as well as in water, and generally reaches a length of from 2½ to 4 feet. The American beaver *(Castor canadensis)* formed part of the native American diet at the time European settlers arrived. Beaver pelts quickly became a standard item of commerce, but the flesh was not considered very palatable by Americans, except perhaps for the tail, which accounts for about one-third of the animal's length. In the 18th century, an Englishman, traveling in Canada, likened the taste of beaver tail to fat pork sandwiched between layers of finnan haddock. In more recent times, Eugene Walter, writing in *American Cooking: Southern Style,* reported this description of beaver meat: "Very dark meat, very mild and tasty. You parboil it a little, then roast it."

The European beaver *(Castor fiber),* which is smaller than the American species, is now found only in Germany, France and Scandanavia. American food writer Waverly Root dined on domesticated beaver in France in 1957, and commented as follows:

> *Not . . . particularly dark in color, rather the contrary. It offered, unpleasantly, little resistance to the teeth. It impressed me as resembling rather flavorless rabbit. I ate it roasted, but felt it would have been better stewed, with high seasoning.*

The Germans relish *Biberschwanz,* as they call the tail, frying it in hot fat after first simmering it and dipping it into a batter of egg and breadcrumbs. Beaver tail is also a favorite Lenten dish in Poland.

When preparing a beaver carcass, it is recommended that great care be taken not to cut the musk gland, which would cause the flesh to be permeated with a strong aroma. Castoreum, a resin obtained from the musk, is used in perfumery.

BEAVERBREAD SCURFPEA

A rootplant, *Psoralea castorea,* closely related to the **breadroot,** beaverbread scurfpea is indigenous to the central United States and northern Mexico. The starchy roots are dried, ground to flour and used to make bread, porridge or gruel.

BECASSE

See **Woodcock.**

BECASSE DE MER

See **Mullet.**

BECCAFICO

See **Garden Warbler.**

BECHAMEL SAUCE

A white sauce, and one of the basic French sauces, it was named after and supposedly created for Louis de Bechamel, Marquis de Nointel, a financier and lord steward at the court of Louis XIV. It was frequently served at his banquets.

It consists of milk or cream thickened with a roux of butter and flour. Bechamel comes in various thicknesses and is a basic building block for many other sauces, hence it is seldom used as such. With the addition of grated cheese, it becomes *mornay* sauce; with cream and egg yolks, *sauce a la creme,* etc.

See also: **Sauce.**

BECHE-DE-MER

See **Sea Cucumber.**

BEDAGOSA

Ground seeds of this variety of cassia, probably *Cassia occidentalis*, known also as coffee senna, make a type of synthetic coffee often used in Europe to adulterate natural coffee. The cassia family includes about 500 leguminous trees and shrubs, many used for medicinal purposes.

See also: **Cassia.**

BEDSTRAW

See **Cleavers.**

BEE BALM

Also OSWEGO TEA. A variety of horsemint, bee balm *(Monarda didyma)* is a perennial herb native to eastern North America. The leaves are used as a flavoring agent and as a condiment. They have a minty flavor. The dried leaves are used to make an infusion called Oswego tea.

BEECH LEAVES

The English of Buckinghamshire traditionally make a cordial or noyau of beech leaves. They are first steeped in gin for six days, then strained and cooked with sugar, brandy and water. This mixture is bottled together with some bitter almonds for flavoring.

BEECHNUT

Also BEECHMAST. The small, triangular fruit of the beech tree (genus *Fagus)*, beechnuts were in wide use in prehistoric times, as their presence in Swiss and English archeological sites attests. They were made into a sort of meal for bread, or pressed for their oil. Both Pliny and Theophrastus praised beechnuts for their sweetness.

Beechnuts grow in pairs inside of a prickly burr. The kernel is tender and sweet to the taste. The flavor has been described as midway between a hazelnut and a chestnut. They are usually roasted before eating to dispel a slight astringency present in the taste of the raw nut.

The nuts, or "mast," as the nutmeats are sometimes called, can be pressed for their edible oil, which is considered nearly on a par with olive oil for taste and cooking qualities. Beechnuts are eaten plain or salted and used to flavor confections. More often, they are fed to animals. Their small size and the difficulties of gathering, cleaning and preparing beechnuts has hindered their commercial production and consequently their popularity as human food.

BEEF

Meat of any adult bovine, whether ox, bull, steer or cow, is called beef. The best beef comes from steers, castrated when young, and specially fattened for the market on grain in feed lots. In the United States, they are generally slaughtered at the age of 18 months or a little less. Elsewhere they are customarily allowed to reach the age of two years or more. An exception to this is the *chianina* steer of Italy, a fast-growing breed, which is slaughtered at between 15 and 17 months.

Beef from cows is comparatively rare. Age for age cow meat is more tender than steer meat, but it is unusual for a cow to be slaughtered while it is still reproductive, i.e., up to at least eight years. Then the meat becomes tough. Meat from sterile cows of beef cattle is considered very fine by some connoisseurs, and the meat of nearly mature heifers almost comparable. Other experts contend that while young cow meat may be more tender, it is seldom, if ever, juicy or fine flavored.

Meat from bulls, oxen and cows over six years of age is less tender and considered fit only for such dishes as stews, ragout, goulashes and sauerbratens. Baby beef comes from steers and heifers aged four to 18 months (i.e. too old to be veal, too young to be beef). The threshhold for **veal** is much lower in Europe (14 weeks or so) than in the United States (up to 12 months). Baby beef is thought to be less desirable than veal, but does afford consumers small, high-quality cuts.

Most of today's beef cattle are descended from the aurochs, the wild bull of Europe, now extinct. It was domesticated as early as 2,500 B.C. in Mesopotamia and Egypt. This animal was held in great awe by the earliest organized societies, and by some was installed as chief god associated with fertility. A prime test of manhood was matching wits against the bull, which is still the case in some Mediterranean countries. The aurochs was brought to England before A.D. 500 and bred with the smaller Celtic shorthorn. The most important cattle breeds in the United States are of British origin, and they include the shorthorn, the Hereford, the Abderdeen-Angus and the Galloway. Others, of different origin, include the Brahman (from India), the Africander (from Africa), the Charolais (from France), and those developed in the United States: Beefmaster, Braford, Brangus, Cattalo, Charbrais and Santa Gertrudis.

It is not surprising that the most important beef breeds originated in England, since the idea of raising

A typical beef feed lot

cattle expressly for meat was a comparatively recent invention of the British upper class. In the 18th century, Englishmen Robert Bakewell and later Charles Colling, working on the theory that "like produces like," inbred selected animals to emphasize blocky bodies set on short legs. In 1795, Colling produced a bull of the then unheard-of size of 3,024 pounds. It was called the Durham. In the winter, the Durham was fed on turnips, a recent innovation due largely to the efforts of Viscount "Turnip" Townshend, who had introduced improved strains of turnip from Holland to serve as winter fodder for British cattle. Durhams were introduced early on into the United States, and were there known as shorthorns. Hereford were imported into the United States in 1817, and eventually became the mainstay of ranching in the old West due to their ability to thrive exclusively on range grass. They replaced longhorn cattle, of Spanish origin, known for their tough flesh. The Aberdeen-Angus were first brought to the United States in 1873, and bred to longhorns, the result of which, though not so heavy as the shorthorn or Hereford, became the most numerous breed in the East and the South. Galloways, Scottish in origin and hornless, first arrived in about 1860. Brahmans, or zebu, were brought to the United States for their special qualities: they thrive on sparse vegetation, require no shade, and are resistant to heat, drought and certain insect pests. Most of them are concentrated in an area within a few hundred miles of the Gulf of Mexico, where intense heat is a factor. They were crossed

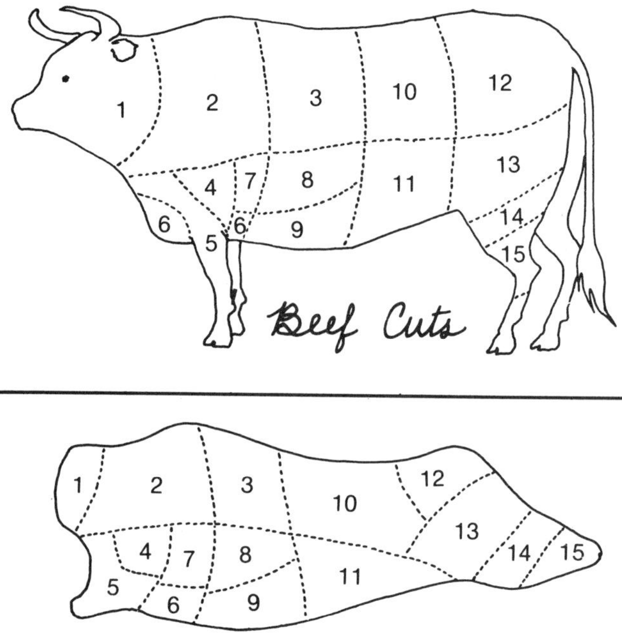

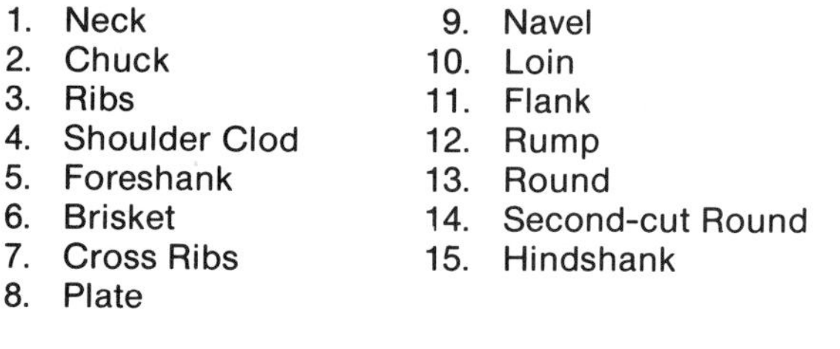

1. Neck
2. Chuck
3. Ribs
4. Shoulder Clod
5. Foreshank
6. Brisket
7. Cross Ribs
8. Plate
9. Navel
10. Loin
11. Flank
12. Rump
13. Round
14. Second-cut Round
15. Hindshank

with the shorthorn, which produced offspring, the Santa Gertrudis, with the looks of a shorthorn and the adaptive qualities of the Brahman.

A unique breed of beef cattle, which has not been imported to the United States, is the *chianina* of Tuscany, Italy. It is distinguished by being the oldest, heaviest (4,000 pounds) and tallest cow in the world. Pure white in color, it resembles the Indian buffalo, with the important difference that the buffalo is raised for its milk, while the *chianina* cow has barely enough milk for its own calves. The breed, which was raised by the ancient Romans, has remained virtually unchanged for 3,000 years.

Beef, especially steak, is far and away America's favorite meat. As one writer put it, "In America, steak is to meat what Cadillac is to cars." This applies only to muscle meat, really, and perhaps to one kind of organ meat, liver. The rest of the animal, such as the head, tongue, eyes, brains, feet, tail, heart, lungs, spleen, stomach (tripe), udder, **sweetbreads,** pancreas, kidneys and testicles are not so popular. (They will be discussed at length under **Variety Meats,** and a few under separate headings.)

The United States, with more than 122 million head of cattle is the world's leading producer of beef. (India has more than 200 million head but, given the taboo against cow slaughter, virtually no beef industry at all.) Yet, the United States's per capita consumption, at 116 pounds per year (1973 figures), is not the world's highest. That honor goes to Argentina with 137 pounds per year. Other countries with high per capita beef consumption are New Zealand with 105 pounds, Canada with 93 pounds, Australia with 90 pounds, France with 65 pounds, Belgium and Luxembourg with 63 pounds, West Germany with 55 pounds and the United Kingdom with 54. The United States figure is more than twice what it was in 1925 and is still climbing, despite a rise in beef prices of more than 550 percent during the interval.

In the market, lean beef is a brilliant red, and the fat is nearly white. The best cuts have the lean flecked with fat, a condition called marbling. The meat should be firm to the touch. Beef is graded according to U.S. government criteria in the following categories: Prime, Choice, Good, Standard and Commercial. Prime is exceptionally fine and tender beef from an animal nine to 18 months old. It rarely appears in food stores, but is sold directly to a few restaurants, hotels and clubs. The grades Choice through Standard are found in retail stores.

A carcass is first divided into wholesale cuts, namely, round, rump, loin, flank, short loin, plate, rib, brisket, chuck and shank. The tender and more expensive cuts come from the round, loins and ribs. Specifically, top round, side of round and bottom round, all inside parts of the leg, come from the round; sirloin steaks come from the loin; center cut (called *Chateaubriand* by the French), T-bone steak, porterhouse steak, shell steak, club steak and top loin steak come from the tenderloin; and standing rib roast, rib steak, boneless rib steak and rib-eye roast of steak come from the ribs.

Appropriate cooking methods for tender cuts are broiling or pan-broiling, roasting and frying. The other parts of the carcass produce less tender cuts, which must be pot-roasted, braised, simmered or stewed, all moist methods of cooking. The foregoing are American cuts. See the accompanying charts for an illustration of these cuts, plus a comparison with British and French cuts of beef.

Following is the nutritional value of a U.S. Choice grade T-bone steak: 14.7 percent protein, 37.1 percent fat, .008 percent calcium, .135 percent phosphorus, .0022 percent iron, .065 percent sodium, .355 percent potassium, thiamine .006 percent, riboflavin .00013 percent, niacin .0035 percent; 70 international units of vitamin A per 3½ ounces (100 grams), plus water and traces of other substances.

Beefalo

BEEFALO

Also CATALO, CATTALO. This hybrid beef animal was bred by crossing the domestic Polled Angus with the American bison. Charles Goodnight, a Texas frontiersman, developed the catalo in the mid-19th century. He preferred bison meat to beef and, in this hybrid, sought to combine good flavor with adaptation to drought conditions and resistance to certain diseases and pests, such as heel flies. The resultant catalo retained a good beef configuration.

More recent breeding experiments have produced the beefalo, which is three-eighths bison and five-eighths beef. This too has a good beef configuration and grows very large. Unlike most hybrids, it is able to reproduce and has become a registered breed.

BEEF-BREAD

See **Sweetbreads.**

BEEF EXTRACT

Also BEEF ESSENCE. The soluble parts of lean beef—mainly juices and mineral salts—are reduced by boiling and evaporation to a concentrated liquid or paste. During the process, fibrous portions are strained out and fat is removed to prevent the product from being vulnerable to rancidity. It is marketed as a bottled liquid, a paste or as cubes.

Beef extract is used to flavor meat dishes or as a substitute for beef stock in preparing sauces or soups. It may also be used to prepare beef tea, an infusion given to invalids and infants who are unable to take solid food.

BEEF JUICE

This includes blood and other juices obtained from lean beef that is raw or has been lightly cooked either by boiling or broiling. The liquid may be extracted using a meat juice press or by scraping the meat with a knife, then squeezing the resulting pulp.

Beef juice is usually put to immediate use and served hot. Commercial products are evaporated by using a vacuum process.

BEEFSTEAK FUNGUS

Also LIVER FISTULA. A large edible mushroom, *Fistulina hepatica*, grows on living tree trunks—especially oaks and chestnuts—in North America, the British Isles and Europe. The French term, *langue de boeuf* or "beef tongue," is a little more descriptive in that the cap of this fungus, when young, has a broad, velvety, reddish surface reminiscent of beef tongue.

Its flesh is fibrous, and when cooked it bears a distinct resemblance to meat. The flavor, however, is slightly acrid with a fruity aroma. When older, the surface color turns dull crimson or liver-brown. The flesh is red-streaked and yields a red juice when cut.

Before being cooked, it should be sliced across the grain and soaked in salt water. After that, it may be broiled, stewed or added to soups. The cap, usually two to six inches across, reaches a maximum of 16 inches in breadth.

See also: **Mushroom.**

BEEF TEA

This hot drink consists of the soluble parts of lean beef—mainly juices and mineral salts—in water. In former times, this was prepared at home by cubing lean beef and boiling it in water until the soluble portions had been extracted, straining out the fibers and then serving what amounted to a very hot, concentrated broth. Nowadays, if used at all, it would be prepared from commercial extract, such as beef cubes.

BEE GRUB

In Thailand, the larvae of honey bees fed on honey and pollen are considered a delicacy. They may be fried or used as an ingredient in curry. Another way of preparing them is to marinate them in coconut cream containing pepper, sliced onions and citrus leaves. They are then wrapped in linen, steamed and served over rice.

BEER

An effervescent, alcoholic drink, beer is made from fermented barleymalt and **hops.** Sometimes referred to as "liquid bread," it is a nutritious beverage and a favorite thirst quencher.

Archeological evidence suggests that large scale beer brewing goes back at least six thousand years. Clay tablets from the Mesopotamian area detail recipes for 18 different kinds of beer. Refined methods of producing modern beer took shape in England and Europe in the Middle Ages when monasteries began to dominate beer production. Master brewer-monks experimented with different strains of barley and different sources of water. One of their most famous products was "brown October ale" from the English town of Burton on the river Trent, the waters of which were highly prized for their clear and sparkling quality. Burton-on-Trent is still an important brewing center.

Beer in America. Dutch colonists established the first brewery in the New World, and some of the founding fathers of the United States were brewers or tavernkeepers, e.g., Samuel Adams. Early Americans were famed as hard drinkers, so beer, with its low alcohol level, was considered much as present-day soft drinks are. Not all agreed on this point. Washington Irving wrote, "They who drink beer will think beer."

Yet many were taken by surprise when the Prohibition Amendment of 1919 was applied to beer, and America became a nation of home brewers. According to government figures, more than 700,000,000 gallons of beer were produced at home in 1929.

Modern Brewing. Barley of uniform quality is selected and allowed to soak in cold water for at least 40 hours. It is then spread on the floor of a malt house to germinate for about 26 hours. When it loses its firmness and becomes crumbly, it is roasted. The roasting changes it to malt.

The malt is ground, and the resulting grist is turned into mash, called "wort," by mixing with hot water. Hops are added to the wort and the mixture boiled to impart the characteristic hops flavor and to convert the starch in the malt to fermentable sugar. Yeast is then added and fermentation takes place. The shorter the fermentation, the sweeter the brew and the lower its alcoholic content. After fermentation, the beer must be aged before it is ready for marketing.

English beers are fermented with the yeast near the top of the liquor. Two types are popular, bitter and mild. Bitter is pale and dry, highly hopped and made from lightly cured malt. Mild has some sugar added and is made from highly cured malt. Thus it is sweeter and darker. It has a lower hop rate and consequently a malty taste.

German and American beers tend to be bottom fermented, using the lager process that originated in Germany. It involves slower fermentation at very low temperatures and produces a light beer of low alcoholic content.

Beer is the generic term for fermented barley beverages, such as **ale** and **porter.** The latter two are produced as beer, but with the addition of black malt, which gives them darker color.

Maxwell Bodenheim, an artist and celebrity of the 1920s, sums up the popular attitude to beer with the following: "He drinks beer, a habit no more bacchanalian than taking enemas."

BEEREN AUSLESE

See **Wines, German.**

BEESTINGS

This is the first milk given by a cow after delivery of a calf. Its flavor is different from that of later milk, and it has a thick yellow consistency rather like egg yolk. It is not sold but is frequently given away in rural areas. It is used to prepare custards, cakes, puddings and tarts in England after being diluted by three to four times its volume of plain milk.

See also: **Milk.**

BEET

Also BEETROOT, RED BEET. The name covers several varieties of plant with edible leaves and a thick, fleshy root belonging to the genus *Beta.* The one most commonly eaten at table is the red beet *(B. vulgaris* var. *rapa* form *rubra).* Other well known varieties, all descended from a common wild ancestor, are the **chard,** the sugar beet (see also: **Sugar**) and the mangel wurzel.

The beet plant is native to the Mediterranean area and was well known to the ancient Romans, who at first appreciated it for its leafy tops. It is assumed that this early form more closely resembled chard, which is still grown for tops only. As the Romans entered the Christian era, however, mention began to be made of the root of the beet, which some epicures claimed to be a vegetable superior to the cabbage. One form appreciated by both ancient and modern epicures are the tiny beets attached to new leaves, which are obtained when thinning the plants in the spring. These can be made into a delicious salad.

The red beet is on the small side as root vegetables go, averaging one to three inches in diameter when harvested. Round roots predominate among red beets, but there are also varieties with flat to roundish roots and some with long roots extending up to 12 inches. The beet plant is a cool-season biennial, producing roots one year and seeds the next. It has a high tolerance for salty soil and is often grown in areas reclaimed from the sea. Yet it adapts easily to different climatic conditions, provided there are no prolonged periods of intense heat.

The red beet is a nutritious food. Cooked, the root consists of about 10 percent carbohydrate (mainly sucrose)—very high for a vegetable—and about 2 percent good quality protein. It also contains minerals such as iron and calcium. Beet greens are a good source of vitamin A and C, riboflavin and iron. Red beets deliver about 46 calories per 3½ ounces (100 grams), about twice the average for other vegetables.

Red beets are usually marketed already cooked, at least in the United States, where nearly two-thirds of beets are eaten canned. They may be plain, pickled or spiced and may be prepared whole, sliced, diced, quartered or cut julienne style. If purchased fresh, however, they should be neither cut nor peeled before cooking because this will result in the nutrients and color being leached from them.

The sugar beet *(B. vulgaris)* has a long, white tapering root. Though long known to have a high sugar content, the beet came into prominence as a source of sugar during the 18th century when France's sugar supply (from the Antilles) was cut off by the anti-Napoleonic blockade. Napoleon ordered 70,000

Beets

acres to be planted in beets, and a French financier, Benjamin Delessert, built a refinery in the Passy section of Paris to process them. Production lapsed after the war, but development of the white Silesian beet in the 1880s gave further impetus to the sugar beet industry. Using a new process, production today accounts for about one third the world's supply of refined sugar.

The mangel wurzel is a large, coarse variety of beet, usually yellowish in color. Though edible, it is not appetizing and therefore is used mainly for winter cattle feed.

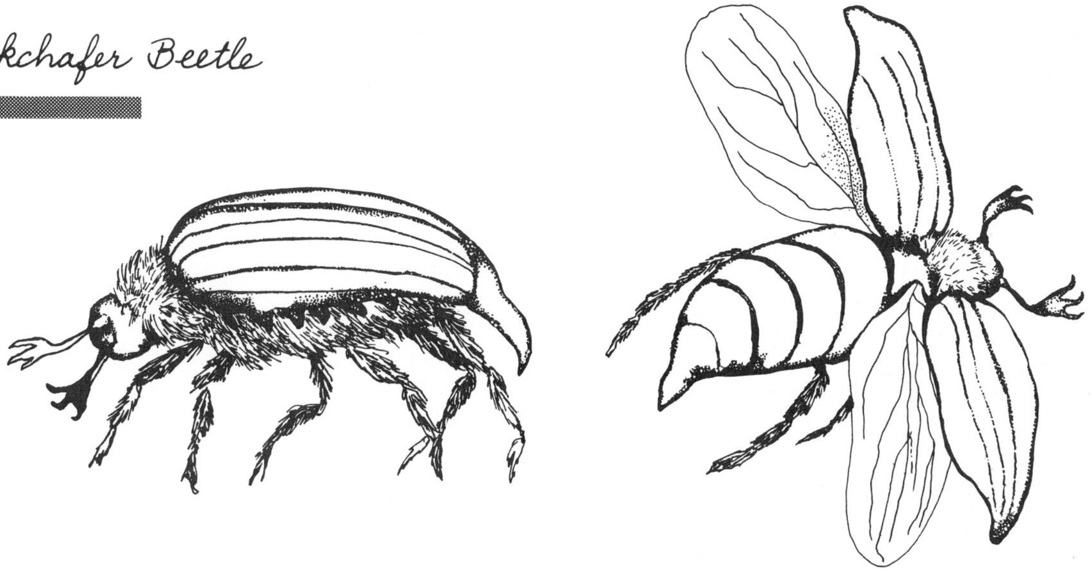

Cockchafer Beetle

BEETLES

Notorious insect pests to most Westerners, beetles are commonly eaten—both as grubs (larvae) and adults—in the Far East, the Pacific Islands and in the Caribbean. France, noted for its daring and adaptable cuisine, is the only Western European country to experiment much with beetle recipes. Edible varieties include various kinds of water beetles, the cockchafer (both adult and grub), the longhorn borer grub, the longhorn grub and the palmworm, which is a snout beetle grub.

In the French West Indies, palmworms are rolled in a mixture of breadcrumbs and spices, and then charcoal roasted. The Vietnamese dip these grubs into **nuoc-mam** sauce and fry them in lard, or roll them in flour and fry them in butter. The Japanese gather grubs of the longhorn beetle, preferring those feeding on figs, then marinate them in soy sauce and broil them.

The cockchafer *(Melontha melontha)* is a large, scarab-type beetle of Europe. To make cockchafer soup *(Soupe de hanneton)*, the French remove the heads and wings from adult beetles, then pound the remains in a mortar (or blend them electrically), sieve them into hot bouillon. The grubs are marinated in vinegar for several hours, then dipped in batter and fried in butter. Grubs are also baked in parchment envelopes, after being rolled in a mixture of breadcrumbs and flour.

Samoans think nothing of popping the grub of the longhorn borer into their mouth raw. They consider roasted grubs delicious too, particularly after the larvae have been fed for a day on coconut shavings.

Adult water beetles are regarded as a special delicacy in Southeast Asia and China, and are believed to relieve symptoms of diarrhea. Basic preparation includes removing the head, legs, wings and hard wing covers. The Vietnamese roast them and serve with *nuoc-mam* sauce. In China they are fried in oil and salt and eaten like nuts. Indonesians serve them as a relish with curry.

In Laos, water beetles are steamed, then marinated in shrimp sauce and eaten as hand food. The taste has been compared to **gorgonzola.** The Laotians also make a vegetable dip by pounding together boiled shrimp and water beetles, then mixing the paste with lime juice, garlic and pepper.

BEGONIA

This herbaceous plant of the *Begoniacae* family, with showy, red, white or pink flowers has more than 1,000 species. The fresh, young leaves of some varieties are occasionally added to green salads or cooked as a vegetable. In France, the leaves are treated like **sorrel.**

BELEMBE

Unlike other members of its genus, the belembe *(Xanthosoma braziliense)* is cultivated for its young, unfolded leaves, which are used as spinach or in stews and soups. It is indigenous to tropical America and grown mainly in the West Indies. Other *Xanthosomae*, such as yautia and blue taro, are prized for their tuberous roots.

BELGIAN ENDIVE

See **Chicory.**

BELLE-ISLE CRESS

See **Barbarea.**

BELLELAY

Also, TETE DE MOINE, MONK'S HEAD. A blue-veined cheese resembling **Gorgonzola,** it takes its name from the Abbey of Bellelay in the canton of Berne, Switzerland. Although originated by the monks, Bellelay is now made by dairies in the district and has a delicate flavor, milder than most monastery cheeses. In firmness it is somewhere between **Limburger** and **Swiss cheese** but has a buttery consistency and can be spread on bread. It is cured for 12 months at a low temperature so that no eyes develop. A whole milk cheese, Bellelay typically measures about seven inches in diameter and weighs from nine to 15 pounds. In cold storage it will keep for three or four years.

BELLWORT

This herbaceous plant, *Uvularia sessilifolia*, with green yellow, bell-shaped flowers is indigenous to the eastern United States. Its shoots are tasty and make a palatable asparagus substitute. Its rhizomes may also be cooked and eaten as vegetables. Bellwort is, as a rule, eaten only in emergencies.

BEL PAESE

The particular Italian cheese was first made in Melzo, Lombardy, in 1920. By extension the term is used to refer to a group of Italian cheeses that have much in common: a soft, creamy texture; sweet, mild taste and a brief period of ripening, employing surface bacteria. This type of cheese has been made for at least 80 years in Italy, and is available all over the country.

Cheeses in the Bel Paese group include *Bella Alpina*, *Bella Milano*, *Bel Piano Lombardo*, *Bel Piemonte*, *Fior d'Alpe*, *Konigkase*, *Savoia* and *Vittoria*. Non-Italian cheeses of this type are *Fleur des alpes* and *Shonland.* In Germany and Canada, this type of cheese is known as butter cheese. An excellent Bel Paese-type cheese is made in the United States, but because of trademark restrictions, it is marketed under various tradenames.

Bel Paese is produced from whole cow's milk. During curing, surface slime is allowed to grow on the cheese for three weeks, then cheeses are washed and wrapped in tinfoil for a further holding period of three to six weeks. They generally weigh from four to five pounds and measure six inches in diameter.

Bel Paese is basically a table cheese that goes well with fruit and red wine. However, because of its texture it is an excellent melting cheese and, in a pinch, can be substituted for mozzarella in pasta dishes.

BENEDICTINE

The formula for this highly aromatic liqueur was devised by Benedictine monks in 1510, which makes it the oldest liqueur still being produced. It is also probably the best known. Benedictine is a very sweet after-dinner cordial with a fine cognac base, utilizing some 27 different herbs and peels as flavoring.

Originally it was developed as an elixir or restorative for the monks when they were tired or ill. The Benedictine distillery, which is no longer connected with any religious order, stands on the spot where the liqueur was first produced in the Norman abbey in Fecamp, France. The formula came into commercial hands after the French Revolution when the abbey was razed and the order disbanded. Production was begun again in 1863 on the basis of the original recipe, which was, and remains today, a closely guarded secret. Every effort was made to reproduce the original elixir, which, since then, has successfully resisted many attempts at imitation.

The bottle has a distinctive shape, and the label bears the initials "D.O.M.," meaning "To God, most good, most great." Benedictine is 86 proof. To make it somewhat drier, it is often mixed with an equal amount of brandy, a practice which led the company to produce a second liqueur called **"B & B".**

BENGAL CHESTNUT

A type of woody grass, *Melocalamus compactiflorus*, it is native to Bangladesh and Burma. Its large, mealy and edible seeds resemble chestnuts and are eaten roasted or dried and ground for flour.

BENGAL GAMBOGE

The cherry-sized, yellow fruit of an Indian tree, *Garcinia ventulosa*, Bengal gamboge flourishes in Malaysia and the Philippines. It is eaten fresh in the immediate vicinity.

BENGAL QUINCE

Also BALL TREE, BAEL FRUIT, GOLDEN APPLE. The Bengal quince is a citrus fruit, *Aegle marmelos*, of India. It somewhat resembles the true quince in appearance, being round to pear-shaped, three to four inches in diameter and having a gray to green yellow rind. Unlike the quince, however, it can be eaten fresh when ripe. It has a fragrant aroma and deliciously sweet taste. It is sometimes harvested half-ripe, when the taste is astringent, to be used in preserves.

The Bengal quince tree is important in Hindu ritual, being sacred to Siva. Its cultivation is encouraged, and Hindus are forbidden to uproot it or cut it down. According to tradition, a Hindu who dies in its shade is granted immediate salvation.

BENNE

Here is another name for the sesame plant whose seeds are an important source of cooking oil and are also used as a flavoring agent.

See also: **Sesame.**

BENNET

Also HERB BENNET. This ornamental herb, *Geum urbanum*, was once used as a flavoring agent and potherb. It is sometimes mistakenly called "pimpernel."

BENZOATE OF SODA

Also SODIUM BENZOATE. A salt of benzoic acid is used commercially as a food preservative, especially with such acidic foods as apple cider, soft drinks and fruit cocktails. It is a white crystalline powder with a slightly sweet, astringent taste.

For commercial use benzoic acid is synthesized from coal tar, but it occurs naturally in fruits such as cranberries. Other sources include the East Indian tree, *Styrax benzoin*, whose resinous juice yields benzoic acid when subjected to heat, and the tolu tree of South America whose balsam is treated similarly.

BERCY SAUCE

This is basic *veloute* sauce flavored with fish stock, seasoned with white wine, shallots, parsley and butter. It is used with fish.

See also: **Sauce.**

BERGAMOT

A citrus fruit, *Citrus bergamia*, cultivated for the valuable essential oil of its rind, the bergamot is believed to be a mutant or hybrid of the sour orange. If the latter is true, however, the other parent is not known. The first one was discovered growing in Calabria, Italy in the 17th century. It was in an orchard, yet no one had planted it.

Bergamot

The bergamot is inedible fresh, its flavor being closer to the lemon than the orange. It is pear-shaped, and its essential oil is the basis of several perfumes. The oil is extracted from its highly scented peel, which is also used in confectionary and preserves. Calabria remains its chief producer.

BERGAMOT PEAR

See **Pear.**

BERGKASE

Several cheeses, generally of the Swiss type, are grouped under this name. They are made in the Alpine regions of Switzerland, Italy, Austria and France. Each is described under its own name, but the list includes the following: **Battelmatt, Fontina, Montasio, Piora** and Wallis. **Vacherin,** a soft cheese of Fribourg, Switzerland, is also classed as a Bergkase.

BERGQUARA

This cheese, resembling **Gouda,** has been made in Sweden since the 18th century.

BERMUDA CHUB

This sizeable sea chub *(Kyphosus sectatrix)* is found on both sides of the middle Atlantic and is most plentiful in the Caribbean. It reaches a length of up to 30 inches and is esteemed as both food and game.

The bermuda chub has a deep, slender body, a small round head and an overall dull, gray coloring relieved by narrow lengthwise stripes and yellow marks on the head. It is closely related to the silver drummer *(K. sydneyanus)* of Australia whose flesh is edible but judged to be of poor quality.

BERNARDE

This Italian cheese made with whole cow's milk is combined with 10 percent goat's milk for flavor. It is colored by saffron and rubbed with salt until 2 to 3 percent is absorbed. Curing takes about two months.

BERRY

See **Fruit;** also articles on individual berries.

BERRY SUGAR

This white sugar with very fine crystals (0.5 mm in diameter) is called superfine in the United States and caster (or castor) in Great Britain. It dissolves faster than coarser varieties and is therefore popular at table for use over cereals and fruit and in making puddings and cakes.

See also: **Sugar.**

BERRY WINE

See **Fruit Wine.**

BESUGA DE LAREDO

See **Gilthead.**

BETEL NUT

Also ARECA NUT. This is the seed of the betel palm *(Areca catechu)*, a tall slender tree of tropical Asia, which is also known as the areca palm. The ripe seed is slightly larger than a chestnut, with an orangish outer covering and white meat. Betel nut is chewed by millions of Asians, much as a Westerner might chew tobacco or chewing gum. The nut meat is wrapped in the leaf of the betel pepper *(Piper betle)* and seasoned with a pinch of lime.

The betel nut is said to sweeten the breath, strengthen the gum and promote digestion, and it has an active ingredient that acts as a mild stimulant and produces a sense of well-being. On the negative side, it produces a copious flow of red saliva that stains the teeth and gums. It is not unusual for a habitual chewer to be toothless by the age of 25. Betel has an acrid odor and astringent taste.

The nut is sometimes used as a dentifrice. It is reduced to powder by first burning it to charcoal and then pulverizing it. Sri Lanka and Malaysia are the areas of most intense use, but it is widely chewed in India too.

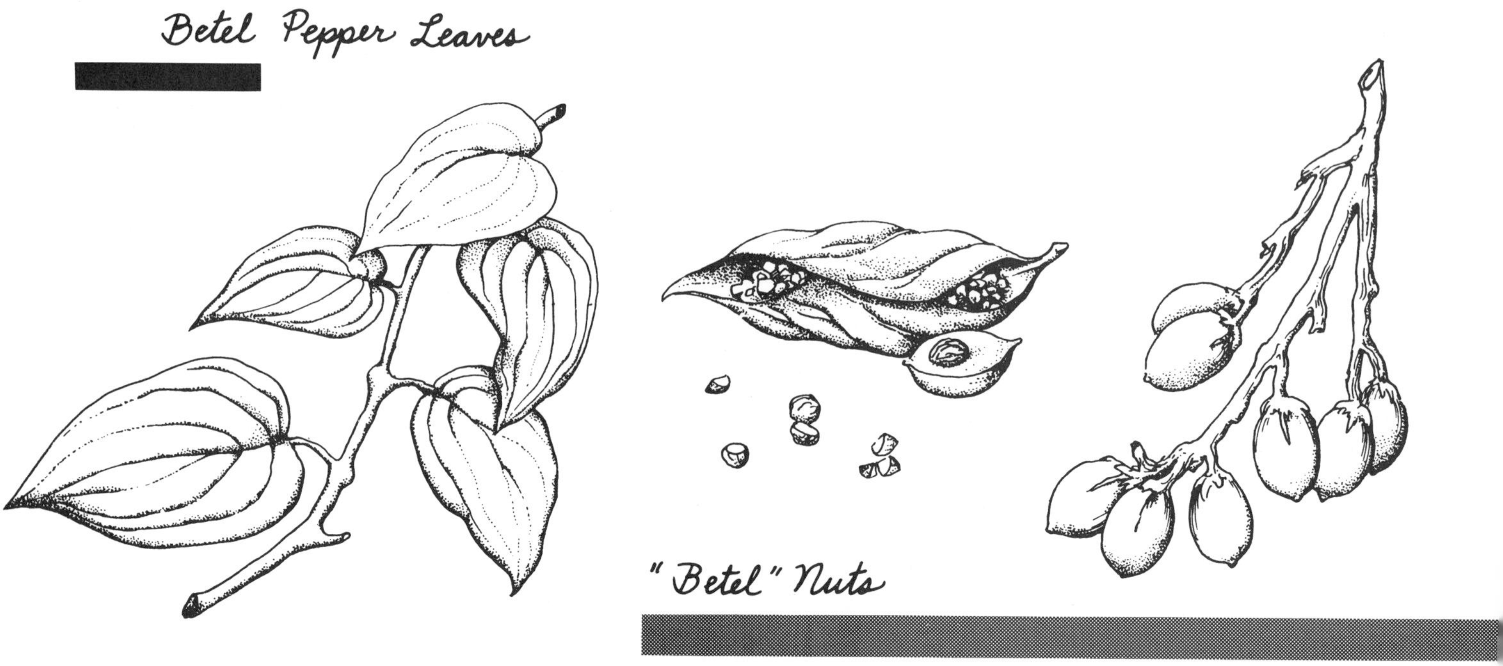

BETONY

The dried leaves and flowers of this herb, *Stachys officinalis*, were used to make a medicinal tea that had a mint flavor. Its name derives from that of a tribe of ancient Gaul, the Vettones. The Romans believed betony to have the power of warding off serpents. Because of its odor, they would supposedly refuse to cross a barrier made of its twigs. Betony is rarely cultivated now, though it grows wild in the woods of North American and Europe. It was also sometimes used to dye wool a dark yellow.

BGUG-PANIR

Also DARALAG. This Armenian cheese is made from partly or entirely skimmed ewe's milk, which is coagulated by rennet and flavored with herbs and salt.

BIANCHETTI

See **Whitebait.**

BIB

Also POUTING. A common European marine fish of the cod family, the bib *(Trisopterus luscus)* inhabits inshore waters and is frequently caught by anglers. It is abundant from Sweden south to the Mediterranean. Though edible, it is not important commercially. The bib reaches a length of 16 inches. It is bronze above with light bars and is silver green below.

BIBB LETTUCE

See **Lettuce.**

BICARBONATE OF SODA

Also BAKING SODA, SODIUM BICARBONATE. A kitchen chemical sold in the form of a white, granular powder, it is an alkali that combines readily with acid to produce carbon dioxide gas. It is a basic ingredient of baking powder, where it is mixed with dry acid crystals. Combined in dough with water and heated, the powder releases carbon dioxide gas, which has a leavening effect on the dough. A similar effect can be achieved by combining baking powder with sour milk or buttermilk. If added to the water used to cook some vegetables, bicarbonate of soda will help retain bright colors in the vegetables. This used to be common practice, but is rarely done nowadays because it was found that bicarbonate of soda destroys the vitamin C contained in the vegetables.

Bicarbonate of soda is also used in carbonated drinks. In medicine, it is used as an alkali or antiacid. It may also be used to absorb unpleasant odors in refrigerators and cooking pots.

See also: **Baking Powder.**

BIDENS

A perennial herb, *Bidens bigelovii*, indigenous to the American Southwest and northern Mexico, its flower tops are made into a thirst-quenching beverage.

BIGARADE SAUCE

A rich sauce served with duck and named after the bigarade or bitter orange *(Citrus aurantium)*, it consists of duck stock or gravy reduced and thickened with a roux of butter and flour and flavored by the rind of bitter oranges, a squeeze of lemon juice and sugar. It is sometimes thickened with arrowroot or duck's liver.

See also: **Sauce.**

BIGHORN SHEEP

This wild sheep, *Ovis canadensis*, of western North America, is found in mountainous areas, particularly the Rocky Mountains. With its massive spiral horns it somewhat resembles the Asian **argali.** The bighorn sheep stands a little over three feet in height and is tawny yellow color in summer and gray brown in winter, with white underbelly and buttocks.

It is avidly sought as a game trophy by hunters who have managed over the past century and a half to reduce its numbers from approximately two million to around 7,000. Today it is found mainly in the vicinity of Yellowstone Park and areas directly north. During the summer its flesh is considered quite a delicacy, although it is tough and tasteless in other seasons. It may be prepared like mutton.

BIGNAY

See **Chinese Laurel.**

BIGOLOT

See **Rollot.**

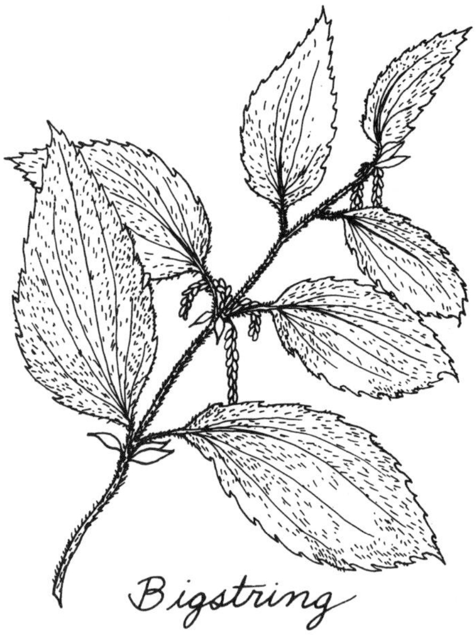

BIGSTRING

Also STINGING NETTLE. A perennial herb, *Urtica dioica*, found in both Europe and Asia, its young tops and stems may be boiled and eaten as spinach or added to soup. It is considered a useful emergency food plant.

BILBERRY

See **Huckleberry.**

BILIMBI

See **Carambola, Cucumber Tree.**

BILTONG

These strips of dried lean meat, usually cut from the rumps of antelopes, buffaloes and elephants are a South African delicacy, sold in butcher shops throughout the country. The word comes from the Africaans, *bil* or "rump," the source, and *tong* or "tongue," the shape.

The meat is dried in the sun or, more properly, in the rafters of drafty sheds until it has a leathery consistency. It is said to retain its flavor and food value for years. Described as tasty but a little coarse, biltong is grated or cut into thin pieces and eaten raw or used as a sandwich filling.

BINNY

This large, edible fish, *Barbus bynni*, of the Nile River, belongs to the barbel family.

BINUCAO

The acid fruit of a small Indian tree, *Garcinia binucao*, is found in Malaysia, Indonesia and the Philippines. It is related to the **mangosteen.** Binucao is lemon-yellow with a rather flattened shape, about one to two inches in diameter. It is a frequent accompaniment to fish dishes.

BIRCH BEER

Birch beer may be either a clear, effervescent North American beverage made from fermented sap of the sweet or black birch tree *(Betula lenta)*, or a nonalcoholic soft drink flavored with oil of birch or oil of wintergreen. A large birch tree, when tapped in spring, can yield from four to six quarts of sap in a day. Birch beer is made with honey or sugar and yeast, and ferments in about a week. "Bottle the beer and cap it tightly," writes Euell Gibbons.

> *Store in a dark place, and serve it ice cold before meals after the weather gets hot. It has a reputation for stimulating the appetite. More than a glass or two at a time is likely to stimulate other things, for this beer has a kick like a mule.*

In New England a popular nonalcoholic drink similar to root beer in taste, although colorless and not dark, is sometimes marketed as "Birch Beer." Birch twigs can also be used to make an herb tea. The sweet birch grows in the eastern part of the United States. It is delicate and slender, reaching eighty feet in height.

BIRCH SUGAR

A crude sugar from the evaporated sap of the sweet birch tree *(Betula lenta)*, it was once made in Scotland, Scandanavia and the United States much in the manner of **maple sugar.** The young twigs and bark of this tree are a major source of oil of wintergreen.

BIRD CHERRY

Name given to several varieties of wild fruit trees, *Prunus padus*, which prefer hardy northern climes. One U.S. variety, *P. serotina*, bears fruit that has an interesting, acid taste much like the famous sour morello cherry *(P. acida)*. It is used to flavor rum, brandy and liqueurs.

See also: **Cherry.**

BIRD'S-FOOT TREFOIL

See **Lotus.**

BIRD'S NEST

The edible nest of the salangane swallow is highly esteemed by gourmets, particularly in China, when served in tiny porcelain cups as soup. Such nests are small, about one-half ounce each after cleaning. The species of swallow that builds them is limited, and nesting areas, the Malay Archipelago, Java and the coast of Annam, are difficult to reach. Harvesting the nests from the sea caves is an arduous, dangerous effort. Bird's nest soup is commensurately expensive.

These nests are not made of twigs or mud like most but are built up in layers by the mother swallow using her own saliva, which becomes a thick, viscous, glutinous liquid before mating season. Prior to cooking, the nests are washed in successive hot water baths, kneaded with nut oil and washed once more in hot water. Any remaining litter from the birds is carefully picked out.

The clean nests are cooked in a duck stock for half an hour. Cooking causes the nests to disintegrate into thin gelatinous strings releasing the bird saliva that held them together to give the soup its prized flavor. A one-half ounce nest will flavor ten to twelve ounces of soup stock.

BIRK WINE

Wine made from the sap of the birch tree in Scotland; "birk" is northern English dialect for birch. Raisins, almonds and crude tartar are added to the wine.

BISCUIT

In American usage the name refers to a kind of small hotbread, tender and flaky, and generally raised with baking powder or soda. The biscuit was developed by American colonists and consists basically of flour, shortening and milk. The comparatively large amount of shortening in the recipe produces the flaky texture. Like pie crust, biscuit dough should not be kneaded much after mixing to avoid toughness. This rule has often been violated, as evidenced in the line from a comic song: "Oh, the biscuits in the Army, they say they're mighty fine. One rolled off the table and killed a pal o' mine." The basic dough is unsweetened, and the basic shape of the baked biscuit is round. The formula may be enriched with sugar and more shortening to make sweetbreads. Flavorings added to the basic dough include caraway seeds, cheese, cinnamon, honey, jam, lemon, orange, raisins, shrimp, sour cream and tomato.

The word "biscuit" comes from the French *biscuit* and means "twice cooked." It was a term applied to traveling rations, such as ships's biscuit, which were cooked twice to drive out all moisture and to enhance their keeping qualities. Such bread was unleavened and also known as hard tack. (For more on this see: **Knackebrod.**)

The nearest thing the English have to the American biscuit is the scone, which is often triangular in shape and is eaten hot with tea. The term "biscuit" in England is a general one that covers both the **cookie,** its sweetened form, and the **cracker,** its unsweetened form.

See also: **Bread, Roll.**

BISCUITROOT

The native Americans of the Pacific Northwest ate this rootplant as a vegetable or converted it into flour to make bread. It was known to them as *cowas* or *conse*, depending on the tribe, and the name "biscuitroot" first came to light in the report of Lewis and Clark, who encountered it on their expedition of 1804–1806.

The name "biscuitroot" is applied to several different plants, and they in turn are often confused with the **breadroot.** This ambiguity is reflected in biscuitroot's scientific name, *Peucadanum ambiguum*. When young, fresh biscuitroot has a parsleylike flavor; the mature plant tastes more like celery. At this stage, the root is more white and brittle and is easily made into flour. The native Americans also made a sort of celery soup from it or a pudding sweetened with buffalo berries.

BISHOP'S ELDER

See **Goutweed.**

BISON

A humped, oxlike creature, the bison in North America went in one century from being the most populous of wild mammals to near extinction. *Bison americanus* dwelt in huge herds in open country, especially the Great Plains, in numbers estimated at 60 million at the time America was settled.

A quadruped, the bison has forequarters that are massive and shaggy, short horns curving upward and tapering hindquarters. Its appearance caused Cortez, the first European to set eyes on a American bison, to call them "humpbacked cows" when he viewed them in Montezuma's private zoo in 1521. Other Europeans called them oxen, and later on the English dubbed them "buffalo," a name that stuck.

The bison was the economic mainstay of several native American tribes. For them the animal was a source of food, fuel, shelter, clothes, weapons, thread, utensils and grease. The European began to prey on the bison first for its tongue, then its hides, then its meat and then simply to exterminate the beasts as a means of getting rid of the Native Americans who were dependent on them. When the railroads spread West, they hired professional hunters to speed this process along and to make sure the bison didn't interfere with the trains.

By 1900 there were no wild bison left, apart from a small herd in Yellowstone park and one near Lake Athabasca in Canada. In recent years, the bison has rebounded somewhat under the protection of the federal government, which maintains a herd numbering 12,000 in wildlife refuges. When the herd is thinned, bison meat becomes available in certain markets, though the meat is from older animals and therefore strong-tasting and tough.

Meat from the young bison has been compared favorably with beef. The taste is said to be slightly sweeter and the texture more tender with no gaminess. In the mid-19th century, the American bison was crossed with European cattle to produce the cattalo, a hybrid that was resistant to disease, not disturbed by heel flies, which plagued the Great Plains, matured quickly and had a good beef configuration.

The original "jerky," now made from beef, came originally from the buffalo. The plains tribes cut wide slices of meat and hung them in the sun folded over poles until they were brown and hard. The word derives from the Spanish *charqui*, which in turn derives from a South American word for dried strips and slices of meat. Another Native American way of preserving bison meat was called *pemmican*, a mixture of dried meat, which had been pounded to powder, bone-marrow fat, dried berries and dried vegetables. It is a portable, high-energy food especially useful to travelers.

Bison

The European bison *(Bison bonasus)* came to grief much earlier than its American cousin. It was an important food animal during prehistoric times and still ranged over most of temperate Europe in the times of the ancient Greeks. Unlike the American bison, it inhabited woods, and as these diminished with the spread of civilization, the bison dwindled finally to a few hundred head. The final surviving herd lives in the Polish forest of Bialowieza and numbers about 400. It was wiped out in World War II, and reconstituted from zoo animals. There appear to be no prospect that the European bison will become a source of marketable meat. The name "bison" is also applied to the **aurochs.**

The only commercial sources of bison meat are in the United States, where its production prospers mildly due to curiosity about the taste of meat that was once the staple of the Native Americans. The parts considered choice are the hump and tongue.

See also: **Buffalo.**

BISQUE

See **Soup.**

BISTOLA DE ROCA

See **Forkbeard.**

BISTORT

Also SNAKEROOT, SNAKEWEED. Bistort is a perennial plant of Europe, Asia and North America. Its S-shaped roots were once eaten because of their farinaceous and astringent qualities. Bistort *(Polygonum bistorta)* reaches a height of two feet, and has spikes of pink or white flowers. Russian Samoyeds used the roots as a bread substitute, baking them on hot coals. They were also used in traditional Easter puddings in England. The young leaves of an alpine variety, *Polygonum viviparum*, are eaten in salads.

Snakeroot is one of the five kinds of herbs mentioned in the Jewish agricultural tractates of the Misrah to be used at Passover, the others being field lettuce, peppermint, wild cherry and dandelion.

BITTER APPLE

See **Colocynth.**

BITTER ASH

See **Bitters.**

Bitter melon

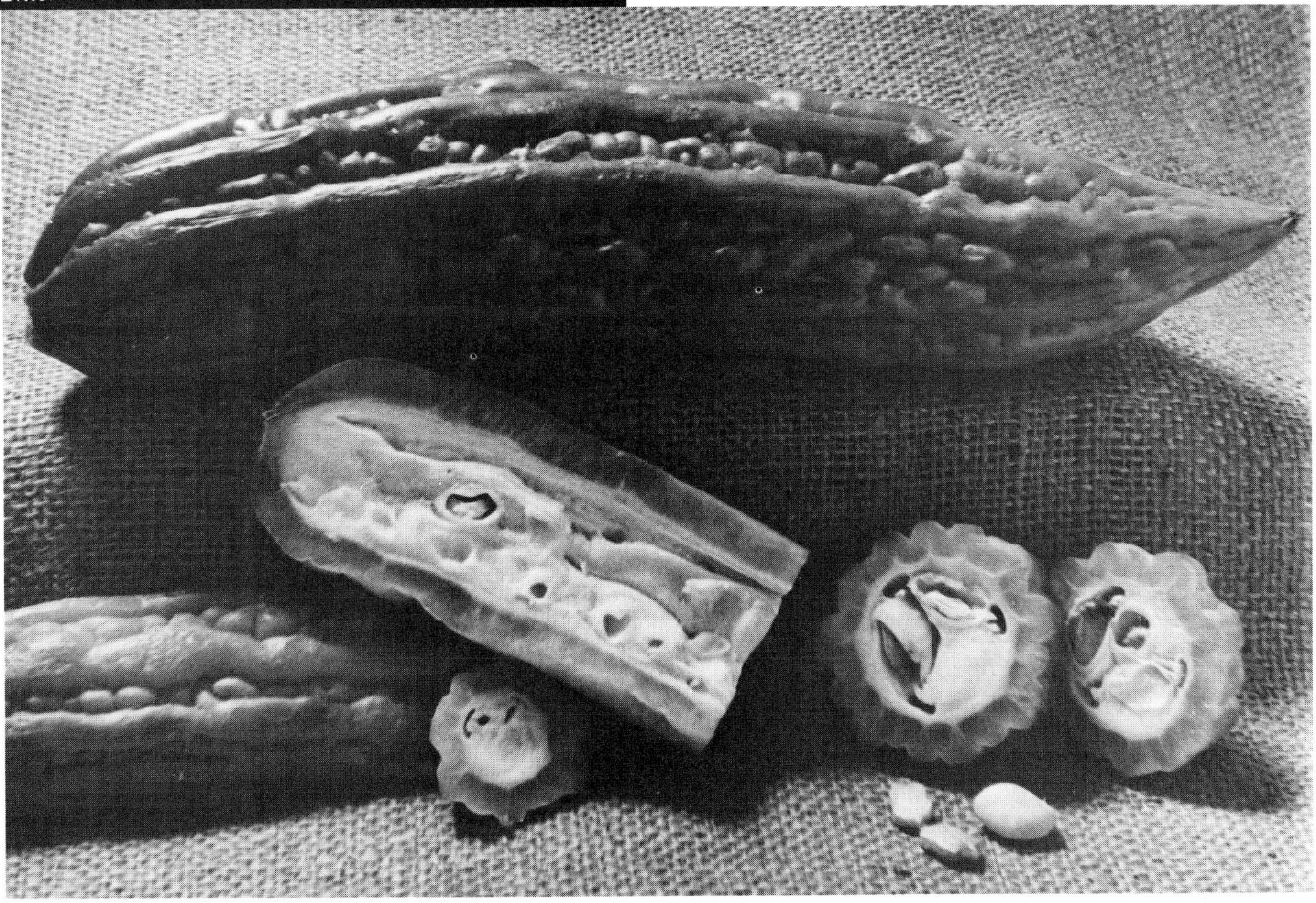

BITTER CUCUMBER

See **Colocynth.**

BITTER GOURD

See **Colocynth.**

BITTER MELON

Also called BALSAM PEAR. Described variously as a melon, a fruit and a vegetable, it has a cucumber-like shape with an irregular surface. Its name describes its taste—bitter—not unlike quinine. Chinese cooks, who probably know it best, use bitter melon mostly in soups and braised dishes.

BITTERN

The bittern *(Botaurus stellaris)* is a wading bird of nocturnal habits that looks like a heron. It is not much eaten now, but was once held in high favor by the gourmets of the 14th through 17th centuries, fetching three times the price of chicken. It was featured at a banquet celebrating the first marriage of King Henry IV of England in 1399. The spur on its claw was valued as a toothpick. The taste of its flesh was compared to that of hare, and it was usually prepared by roasting with ginger and pepper.

Its thunderous cry seemed to have apocalyptic overtones to the English poet Henry Kirk White, who wrote in 1803 this vision of England's ruin:

> *Where now is Britain?*
> *Even as the savage sits upon the stone that marks*
> *where stood her capitols,*
> *And heard the bittern booming in the weeds,*
> *He shrinks from the dismaying solitude.*

The North American species is the *Botaurus lentiginosa.*

BITTERROOT

A plant of the purslane family native to the Pacific Northwest, the bitteroot *(Lewisia rediviva)* has a nutritious root shaped like a forked radish or a short carrot. It is fleshy and succulent and was highly esteemed as food by native Americans of the region, who made a kind of bread from it. Its range extends from northern California north to British Columbia and east to the Rocky Mountains.

The first Europeans to depend on it to any extent were members of the Lewis and Clark Expedition. When they first ate it, they found it lived up to its name. Then they learned to peel it before cooking, and it ceased to be bitter. Since Captain Lewis was the first man to collect the specimen and report on it, his name figures in the taxonomic term.

The bitterroot's two-inch pink blossom is the state flower of Montana, and a river and mountain range in that state bear its name.

BITTERS

This term is used for two different products: beverage bitters and flavoring bitters. Both are aromatic liquors consisting of an alcoholic base to which are added essences and distillates of bitter herbs, fruits, flowers, leaves, barks, roots or stems. Typical of these are gentian, orange rind, quassia, quinine, myrrh, cinchona bark, cascarilla, calamus and angostura bark.

Beverage bitters are usually taken undiluted or with a little water or club soda just before a meal as an aperitif or just after as a digestif. They are said to have tonic and stomachic properties and are supposed to stimulate the appetite or aid digestion. Well known beverage bitters are **Fernet Branca** and **Campari.**

The second class of bitters may also be taken as a stomachic or for other medicinal purpose. More often they are used a drop or two at a time in cocktails to add flavor, tang or smoothness. They are also used to flavor food, such as soups, gravies, sauces, puddings and pies. Well-known flavoring bitters are Angostura, Underberg's and Peychaud's.

Perhaps the most famous is Angostura, a product of Trinidad. It contains no angostura bark, but takes its name from the town of Angostura, Venezuela, whose name was changed to Ciudad Bolivar in 1846. Like other proprietary bitters, Angostura is based on a secret formula, containing gentian, "harmless vegetable flavoring extractives and vegetable coloring matter," plus 45 percent alcohol. It was formulated by an English Army surgeon in 1830.

BITTO

An Italian cheese of the Swiss type, bitto can be made from cow's milk, goat's milk or a combination of the two. The milk can also be used whole or skimmed, depending on the intended use. The whole-milk version is used when not fully cured as table cheese, while the skimmed version is fully cured, then grated for use as a condiment.

Bitto is semicooked with small eyes and generally weighs between 35 and 75 pounds. It is made in Friuli and Lombardy.

See also: **Cooked Cheese.**

BIWA

See **Loquat.**

BLACK AMUR

A large carplike fish, *Mylopharyngodon piceus,* found in the Amur River as well as in other large rivers of China and Taiwan, it has a very dark cylindrical body with large, prominent scales. The black amur attains lengths of up to three feet and is caught in numbers substantial enough to be of great economic importance in China.

BLACK-BARRED GARFISH

Also NEEDLEFISH, CANDLEFISH. A member of the halfbeak family *(Ecocoetidae)* found in African, Asian and Australian waters, it is called black-barred garfish in Australia and needlefish or candlefish in South Africa. The species is *Hemiramphus far*, and it reaches a maximum length of 26 inches. As is typical of the family, *H. far's* lower jaw is prolonged to form a sharp-pointed beak. It is a light green brown above with dark blotches and silvery sides. This fish is good to eat, and it runs in large, surface swimming schools that are fished at night under lights, using seines or dipnets.

BLACKBERRY

Also BRAMBLE. The small, edible, dark purple or black berry of the rambling shrub *Rubus fruticosis* and a close relative of the **raspberry,** the blackberry grows wild in temperate regions throughout the Northern Hemisphere. It is cultivated extensively in the United States and to a lesser extent in Great Britain, yet in most areas the wild variety is preferred. Fanciers claim that the latter is sweeter and less tart than the cultivated variety. Wild blackberries are rough, prickly shrubs, hence the story of the man seeking blackberries "who jumped into a bramble bush and scratched both his eyes out."

Formerly, blackberries were used to make dark blue or purple dyes. Nicolas Culpeper, a 17th-century English writer on astrology and medicine, recommended that blackberries be boiled with lye to make a solution that "maketh the hair black." The tips of the dried young leaves were used to make a tisane.

In English literature, the blackberry has been used to symbolize abundance and, by extension, fecklessness. In Shakespeare's *Henry IV*, Part I, Sir John Falstaff says,

> *What, upon compulsion? Zounds, an I were at the strappado, or all the racks in the world, I would not tell you on compulsion. Give you a reason on compulsion! if reasons were as plentiful as blackberries, I would give no man a reason upon compulsion, I.*

It was this very plenty, perhaps, that caused Elizabeth Barrett Browning to use this image of blackberries in her poem *Aurora Leigh:*

> *Earth's crammed with heaven,*
> *And every common bush afire with God;*
> *And only he who sees takes off his shoes;*
> *The rest sit round and pluck blackberries.*

The American poet Walt Whitman, on the other hand, saw in the blackberry a sublime work of God. In the poem "Song of Myself," he wrote, "And the running blackberry would adorn the parlors of heaven. . . ."

Depending on the local species or variety, blackberries may ripen in early, middle or late summer and on into the fall. They contain about 10 percent carbohydrate, mostly fructose, but have a tartly refreshing taste. They also have a higher content (than most other fruit) of vitamin B1 and calcium. Blackberries, especially in Britain and the United States, are eaten raw, alone or with cream and sugar. They are also baked into pies or made into jams, preserves, syrups. It is in the cooked form or in liqueur, brandy or cordial that they are preferred in Europe.

BLACKBERRY BRANDY

This liquor is produced from a mash of fresh blackberries in such countries as Switzerland, France and Germany, where it is known as *Brombeergeist*. Distilled at a fairly low proof to preserve the fruit flavor and aroma, it is colorless unless aged in wood or darkened by the addition of juice. Proof is from 80 to 100. A similar product sold in the United States is blackberry-flavored brandy, which is a mixture of brandy (distilled from grapes), blackberry flavoring and sugar.

BLACKBERRY CORDIAL OR LIQUEUR

A medium heavy, sweet liqueur flavored by, and usually distilled from, blackberries, it sometimes has a small amount of red wine added to it. Two of the best known are the Polish *Jerzynowka*, and the German *Kroatzbeere*, which reputedly has a bouquet of wild blackberries and is not too sweet.

Sixty proof is usual.

BLACKBIRD

The name applies to any of several different species whose males are mostly or entirely black. One is the common thrush of England *(Turdus merula)* or merle. Several birds in America fit this description, the rusty blackbird, the grackle and the cowbird.

Blackbirds are used as food in Corsica and the Mediterranean littoral, both European and African. The meat is aromatic and slightly bitter and is more palatable in the fall. Though hardly a common dish, blackbirds can be baked in pies, just as in the old nursery rhyme. Montagne gives a splendid recipe in *Larousse Gastronomique*, but even the most determined cook must pale at plucking and boning two dozen of these tiny creatures for the few ounces of meat that would result.

BLACK BREAM

See **Luderick.**

BLACK BRYONY

A wild plant of England, Europe and Western Asia, black bryony *(Tamus communis)* is a member of the gourd family. It young shoots are edible after boiling for a few hours in salted water. They are served hot with butter, or cold with oil and vinegar. This is the way they are prepared in England. On the continent, they were eaten in Rome at the time of Apicius (first century A.D.), but not apparently since. The plant bears bright red berries, which are used to make certain drugs but are reputedly poisonous to eat.

BLACK CARROWAY

A perennial African herb, *Pimpinella saxifraga,* whose seeds are used as a condiment, it is closely related to **anise.**

BLACKCOCK

Also BLACK GROUSE. A game bird, *Tetrao tetrix,* it is common in the north of England and in the highland districts of North and Central Europe. The male of the species has plumage of a deep, glossy black with white tail feathers. It is called blackcock, and the female is named grayhen. The adult male

will weigh about four pounds in season from October to December and the female half that.

Blackcock is related to the **capercaillie** and red **grouse** but is not nearly as popular as food, though similar in taste. It is generally roasted or made into a casserole or a pie. The bird is called *coq de bruyere* in France, and a related species, *Lyrurus mlokosiewiczi*, is found in the Caucasus Mountains.

BLACK CUMIN

Also NUTMEG FLOWER, ROMAN CORIANDER. Not to be confused to **cumin,** this plant, *Nigella sativa*, is a wild herb of the Mediterranean area and western Asia. Its seeds are used in India as a spice, but in the West, especially England, it is grown as a decorative herb.

Black Cumin has bright blue flowers one to 1½ inches across and feathery, fennellike foliage. It is a member of the *Renunculus* family. Its seeds grow in groups of three to seven in follicles and may be used as a substitute for pepper.

BLACK-EYED PEA

See **Cowpea.**

BLACKFISH

Also TAUTOG. The name applies to many dark-colored fish on both sides of the Atlantic and in the Pacific Ocean. It may, for example, be used for sea bass, or the female salmon immediately after spawning. In the United States, however, it usually refers to a dark green black fish of the eastern seaboard, originally called *tautog* by the native Americans, meaning "sheep's head."

The tautog *(Tautoga onitis)*, or oyster fish, may be found from Maine to South Carolina and is a fine food fish with delicate white flesh. It averages two to three pounds in weight, but it can go as high as 20 pounds and reach a length of three feet. It is in season from April to October and may be prepared in any way suitable for **pompano.**

The English call the *Centrolophus niger* blackfish. It resembles the **perch.** In the Pacific area, the Alaskan freshwater food fish *Dallia pectoralis* is called blackfish. It can live after being frozen in ice for long periods. Blackfish include the Australian fish *Girella simplex*, which resembles the **blenny.**

BLACK FOREST WATER

A naturally sparkling mineral water bottled in West Germany, it has a relatively high mineral content (905 ppm. of total dissolved solids) and a relatively high sodium content (39 mg. per 8-ounce glass). A 1980 Consumers Union sensory panel rated the taste of this water as fair, with the following qualifying comments: mildly bitter, mild bitter aftertaste, mild chemical flavor, mild manure aroma, mild soapy flavor.

See also: **Mineral water.**

BLACK GAMBOGE

Fruit of a Malaysian tree, *Garcinia nigro-lineata*, related to the **mangosteen,** black gamboge is a sweet, agreeable fruit, oval in shape, up to an inch and a half long, with orange skin. A similar species is the small-leaved gamboge *(G. parviflora)* whose yellow, cherry-sized fruit is mixed with hot peppers, fish and soya to make a popular dish. Both these species are consumed in the area of cultivation.

BLACK GRAM

Also URD BEAN. A species of bean closely related to the **mung bean,** the black gram *(Vigna mungo)* is native to tropical Asia. It produces fewer seeds than the mung bean; they are also smaller, darker and oblong in shape. Nevertheless, the black gram is highly regarded as food. The beans may be boiled and eaten whole or ground into meal and baked into bread. The whole cooked beans are also shaped into spiced balls. In India, black gram meal is also shaped into very thin wafers or pancakes and fried in oil until very crisp. They are called *pappadoms.*

BLACK GROUPER

One of the largest of the west Atlantic groupers, the black grouper *(Mycteroperca bonaci)* can weigh as much as 180 pounds but averages around 50. The black grouper is a thick-bodied fish and rarely exceeds four feet in length. It is found from New England to Brazil, including the Caribbean and the Gulf of Mexico. It is esteemed both as a food and sport fish. Coloring varies from pale to dark reddish gray with regular black blotches.

See also: **Grouper.**

BLACK GROUSE

See **Blackcock.**

BLACK HAW

Also STAGBUSH. Black haw is the blue black fruit of either of two trees, the *Cratageus douglasii* of the Pacific coast and Midwest or the *Viburnam prunifolium*, of the East Coast of the United States. The fruit is small—up to one-half inch across—sweet and juicy. *Viburnam prunifolium* is better after the first frost. They are used principally in making jellies.

BLACK PUDDING

See **Blood Sausage.**

BLACK SAPOTE

This popular fruit, *Diospyros digyna*, of the persimmon type is native to Mexico and Central America but has been naturalized in tropical Asia. The fruit is olive green and becomes nearly black when ripe. It measures about four inches in diameter. The pulp is chocolate brown, very soft, and, when eaten fresh, it is usually seasoned with lime or orange juice.

BLACK SEA BREAM

Also OLD WIFE. An edible sea bream found in the Atlantic from the Canary Islands and North Africa to the British Isles and Norway, the old wife *(Spondyliosoma cantharus)* has an overall dark gray to black coloration. It is a rather small fish, weighing about three pounds at most and reaching a length of about 12 inches. It is popular with anglers but not commercially exploited.

BLACK-SPINED SHAD

A migratory fish of the Caspian Sea, *Caspialosa kessleri* is an important food fish of the region. It is a predator that reaches a maximum length of about 20 inches. Spending most of its life in the marine environment, it moves to fresh water to spawn, mainly in the Volga estuary. Most of the commercial catch is landed there.

BLACKSTRAP

See **Molasses.**

BLACK TREE FUNGUS

Also CLOUD EAR, TREE EAR, WOOD EAR. Tree ears, a type of fungus or mushroom, are staple ingredients of Chinese cooking. Two species are the wood ear and the cloud ear, which grow on trees in China. A similar species, called Jew's ear *(Auricularia auricula)* is found in the United States and generally grows on the branches and trunks of the elder tree. This American variety is more properly called the ear of Judas, who, according to legend, hanged himself from an elder. By stretching it a bit, these fungi, with their flat, wrinkled and thin fruiting bodies, can be said to resemble ears. The wood ear is brown and when fresh has a rubbery consistency. It shrinks when dry and becomes brittle. The cloud ear is larger, with one side black and the other silver. The dried form has a withered, gnarled, tightly closed look and when soaked in water expands fivefold. It then becomes soft and slightly crisp.

In Chinese cuisine, tree ears are thought of as a texture food and used in soups and vegetable dishes. They are a staple ingredient of Szechuan hot-and-sour soup, for example. Yet, they have also long had a reputation among the Chinese as a longevity tonic. This belief was recently substantiated by a study published in the *New England Journal of Medicine*, which said the fungus may slow the tendency of the blood to clot, thus lowering the likelihood of death due to heart disease and stroke.

BLADDER

The bladder is a membraneous bag or sac that functions internally in animals to hold secretions, such as gall or urine. The pig's bladder is occasionally used in cooking, especially in France. For example, Rouen duckling is placed in a pig's bladder and poached for 45 minutes in veal stock. It is not eaten in this dish, however. The only way bladder is eaten is as sausage casing.

BLANC DE BLANC

See **Champagne.**

BLANCMANGE

A sweet dessert, consisting of milk, flour, gelatin, sugar and usually some flavoring, it is cooked in a mold and served cold. Blancmange has a long history. It originated in France where the name means "white food." The medieval version would be scarcely recognizable today, consisting of rice boiled in almond milk until soft, then mixed with white meat of chicken seasoned with sugar and salt, then cooked until thick. It was garnished with whole almonds and anise seeds. In the 17th century it might have referred to calf's foot or other jellies made from white meat.

French gastronomic writer Grimod de la Reyniere claimed that blancmange originated in Languedoc, and the secret of making it was lost in the French Revolution. However, in the early 19th century, it was served, along with 13 other desserts, by Thomas Jefferson at formal White House dinners.

Andre Simon and Robin Howe, in their *Dictionary of Gastronomy*, deplored the blancmange made in modern Britain. They wrote:

> *This is a sweet pudding which has sunk very low indeed in Britain . . . According to Grimod de la Reyniere the dish was difficult to make and, in fact, he doubted whether anyone would make the true recipe correctly. . . . What he would have said of the modern British blancmange would probably beggar description.*

BLANQUETTE DE LIMOUX

Blanquette de Limoux is a sparkling and fruity white wine from the upper valley of the Aude, near the French Pyrenees. Made from the Mauzac and Clairette grapes, it was granted an *appellation controlee* in 1938. It is noted for its lively sparkle and elegant flavor.

See also: **Burgundy Wines; Wines, French.**

BLEAK

Also ABLETTE, ALBURN. A small river fish of Europe that belongs to the carp family, the bleak *(Alburnus lucidus)* has white skin and silvery scales. It averages four to six inches in length.

More popular in the Middle Ages than it is now, the bleak has a bland taste and is usually fried, although many prepare it as they would a **sprat.** The silver pigment in its scales was used in France in the manufacture of artificial pearls.

BLENNY

The name includes several species of small fish living in both fresh and salt waters that belong to the *Blenniidae* family. They are four to six inches long, round-bodied, scaleless and somewhat resemble a small eel. Fresh water blennies abound in Europe, while salt water ones are plentiful along the American and Canadian shores of Puget Sound. However, they are found on most rocky coasts of the world's temperate zones. Blennies vary their appearance by adopting protective coloration.

The flesh of these fish is white and has a good flavor, though it is rather soft in texture. Cooked quickly in butter, it is delicious. It may also be fried or used in fish stew.

The male crested blenny plays a large role in reproduction. In late winter and early spring, the female lays eggs in little balls among the shoreside stones, then the male curls around the egg ball and protects it until hatching time.

BLEU CHEESE

See **Blue Cheese.**

BLEWIT

Also BLUET, BLUE LEG, MASKED TRICHOLOMA. An edible wild mushroom, *Tricholoma personatum*, of North America, the British Isles and Europe, the blewit rivals the **field mushroom** in pleasant aroma and flavor. It is a sturdy mushroom three inches high and five inches across the cap that grows in grassy pastures and meadows and is identified by its violet gray cap and blue gills. It fruits in late autumn.

Blewit is often cooked in stews or with onions since the taste is said to resemble tripe. According to one source, mushroom fanciers cultivate the blewit by burying a few caps in a compost pile or a pit of old leaves. The spores permeate the pile and bring up a crop every autumn.

A related species, the wood blewit *(Tricholoma nudum)* sprouts in late autumn woodlands and is considered by connoisseurs to be the equal of the common blewit in flavor.

See also: **Mushroom.**

BLOATERS

See **Herring.**

BLOOD

The fluid, usually red, that circulates in the heart, veins and arteries of many animals is according to Goethe, "a juice of the rarest quality." Ancient nomads and some modern pastoral peoples would heartily second Goethe's opinion, since blood was and is a staple item in their diet. As a food, blood is rich in protein and minerals, especially potassium and phosphorus, and contains some fat and small amounts of vitamins A and B.

It was a particularly attractive food for the Mongol hordes of central Asia, since it required no transport and could be drunk fresh, which was convenient because fuel was scarce. In the 13th century, Marco Polo told how each Mongol horseman on a 10-day journey brought a string of 18 horses and mares, which allowed for frequent changes of mount and the withdrawing of about one half a pint of blood every tenth day from each animal. It was enough to sustain the rider without weakening the horse.

The Irish in the vicinity of Cork still eat an ancient dish of coagulated milk and blood called *drisheen*. A 17th-century French traveler described how the Irish peasants "bled their cows and boiled the blood with some of the milk and butter that came from the beast; and this with a mixture of savory herbs is one of their most delicious dishes."

In modern Tanzania, the pastoral Masai tribe drink the fresh blood of their cattle. Using a special arrow, they tap the jugular vein of the animal, stopping the hole with a plug after the blood is drained off. If slaughtered, a thousand-pound steer yields 30 to 40 pounds of blood.

In the West, blood has come increasingly under a food taboo. As recently as the 19th century, proper ladies might visit the slaughterhouse periodically to drink animal blood as a tonic. Today drinking blood invokes images of Count Dracula or of cannibals. The use of blood does survive in certain forms, however.

Pig and sheep blood are used to make **blood sausage,** and rabbit, hare, goose and chicken bloods are used to thicken dishes called civets, or blood stews. The Chinese prepare a chicken blood soup and the French an unusual shad-head, blood and red wine soup. When using blood as a thickener, it is well to remember that blood coagulates at 158 degrees F. (70°C), so as not to curdle it inadvertently.

BLOOD PUDDING

See **Blood Sausage.**

BLOOD SAUSAGE

Also BLACK PUDDING, BLOOD PUDDING. This is a sausage whose basic ingredients are pork, pig's blood, spices and onions. Variations of it are made in almost every European country, the British Isles and the United States. Its many names include *blutwurst* (German), *boudin noir* (French), *drisheen* (Irish), *morcilla asturiana* (Spanish), *palten* (Russian), and *veripalttu* (Finnish). According to one authority, blood sausage originated in ancient Phoenicia (now Lebanon), a specialty of the hog butchers of Tyre, and has come down to us over the centuries relatively unchanged. Many illuminated manuscripts of the Middle Ages show pictures of the winter pig killing and the preparation of blood sausages. It remains popular today, particularly in France and the north of England.

Blood sausages can be made from the blood of other animals, such as beef or sheep or even wild animals including fowls, rabbits and deer. They are generally considered to be inferior to sausage made from pork.

Pig fat is diced and mixed with finely chopped lean pork, herbs and spices, hog blood and onions, then stuffed into casings. The latter are usually 1½ inches wide and 18 inches long. The ends are often tied together so that the sausage assumes a horseshoe shape. The casing may be beef or hog gut or increasingly, nowadays, plastic. Blood is brushed over the outside of the casing, giving it the characteristic black color. The sausage is then boiled. In France, the ingredients sometimes include chestnuts, apples, cream or spinach. In the British Isles, oatmeal and liver are often added.

On the European continent, blood sausages are cooked by simmering in stock and are served with cooked dried beans. Slices of blood sausage are fried in England and Ireland and served with bacon and potato. The latter dish is a traditional Sunday breakfast in Ireland. In France, blood sausage is diced and sauteed with apples.

See also: **Sausage.**

BLOODWORT

See **Sorrel.**

BLUEBACK SALMON

See **Salmon.**

Blueberries

BLUEBERRY

The name applies to a variety of blue black berries produced by shrubs of the *Vaccinium* genus, most of which are native to North America. The blueberry and the **huckleberry** are thought by some to be identical and the names interchangeable, yet there are valid distinctions between the two groups of berries. The blueberry has many tiny seeds, which are hardly noticeable when you eat them, whereas the huckleberry has ten large, bony ones. The blueberry is cultivated, while the huckleberry is not, and it is larger and sweeter.

Blueberries are eaten fresh in season, which is from early June to the end of August, and are popular canned in preserves and jams or as filling for pies and puddings. Approximately three-quarters of the American crop is grown commercially, all from native stock, and harvested by machine. Cultivated blueberries are larger and sweeter than the wild variety. The latter is harvested by hand, using the cranberry rake, or scoop. Its tart and distinctly fruity flavor is said to make a better pie filling than the more insipid cultivated berry.

An attractive quality of the blueberry is its penchant for swampy, arid or peaty soils that would otherwise be unsuitable for agriculture. The shrubs are generally divided into "low" and "high" types in relation to the ground and include the dryland blueberry *(V. ashei)*, cultivated in the dry soils of Georgia and Florida; the lowbush blueberry *(V. lamarckii)*, which grows on dry hillsides in Maine, other New England states and in Michigan and Minnesota; the evergreen blueberry *(V. ovatum)* of the Northwest, which grows wild and whose twigs have ornamental value; and the highbush blueberries *(V. australe* and *V. corymbosum)*, which favor swampy ground and provide most of the cultivated plants. These last reach six to eight feet in height and are cultivated extensively in New Jersey, Michigan, North Carolina and Washington.

Blueberries grow in clusters, which facilitates the picking. For this reason they were transplanted to Europe where the blueberry's closest native relative is the bilberry, which grows singly. Certain American varieties of blueberry are called bilberry, particularly in Canada. In Europe, the blueberry grows most plentifully in Spain, where it is called *arandano.*

Assorted blue cheeses

BLUE CHEESE

Also BLEU CHEESE, FROMAGE BLEU, FROMAGE PERSILLE. This is a term used to characterize Roquefort-type cheeses made from goat or cow's milk outside of France. Similar cheeses made inside France are called *bleu.* There are more than 50 of them worldwide that are based on the great French Roquefort, a sheep's milk cheese whose origin antedates the Christian era. Roquefort's distinguishing characteristic is the use of *penicillium* mold during the curing period, a technique that causes blue green veins to grow in the curd, giving it a mottled, marbled appearance and a pungent flavor. Perhaps more important for the success of the cheese are the existence near Roquefort of natural limestone caves whose temperature, humidity and wind conditions are perfect for the promotion of mold growth. A myth about the origin of Roquefort states that a shepherd left his lunch, containing a piece of cheese, in a cave. For one reason or another, it was several weeks before he returned. By this time, blue mold had ripened the cheese. Instead of throwing it away (perhaps he was very hungry), he ate it and made a great discovery. Much of the success of blue cheese making depends on approximating the atmospheric conditions naturally occuring in the Roquefort caves. French law restricts the name *Roquefort* to sheep's milk cheese made in the Roquefort area.

In France, blue cheeses include *bleu d'Auvergne*, *laguiole*, *gex*, *Mont Cenis*, *sassenage*, *septmoncel* and *St. Flour*.

The best known blue cheeses outside France are the English **Stilton,** and the Italian **Gorgonzola.** Blue cheese was not made successfully in the United States until 1918, but now forms an important part of cheese production. Much blue cheese is also imported from Argentina, Canada, Denmark, France, Finland and Sweden.

In general terms, blue cheese is made as follows. Fresh whole milk is set with rennet. Blue mold powder and salt are added to the curd while it is still in the vat, or just before hooping. After hooping, the cheese is pierced with many holes to facilitate mold growth, and it is placed in a curing room that approximates the conditions of the Roquefort caves. This stage of curing takes three months, and during the period, the surface of the cheese is kept clean of bacteria and mold by scraping. Cheeses are then wrapped in tinfoil or parchment, and kept at a temperature of 40°F (4.4°C) for another two or three months before shipping.

BLUE CHESHIRE CHEESE

See **Cheshire Cheese.**

BLUE COD

Also BUFFALO COD. This is a large, ocean food fish, *Ophiodon elongatus*, caught in the North Pacific and around New Zealand where it is usually smoked or salted.

BLUE DORSET

Also BLUE VINNY. This hard white cheese, from Dorset County, England, has a horizontal streak of blue mold running through it. The regularity of the blue veining is unusual, since most other blue cheeses, such as **Stilton,** have irregular veining that produces a marbling effect. Dorset cheese is made from skimmed cow's milk, as a rule on farms, though some is manufactured in Sherborne. The paste is firm and chalk white.

Blue Dorset is also known as "blue vinny," after an old word of the West of England, "vinew," which means moldy. This cheese is increasingly difficult to obtain, except locally, and is reputed not to travel well.

See also: **Blue Cheese.**

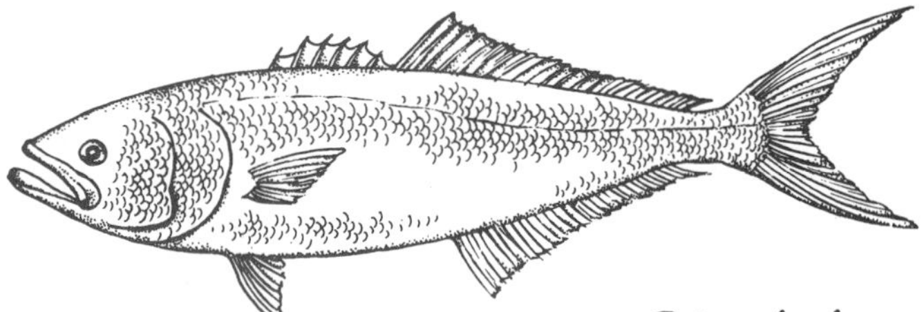

Bluefish

BLUEFISH

Also SKIPJACK. A game fish, *Pomatomus saltatrix*, found in warm waters around the world, bluefish is especially plentiful off the Atlantic Coast of the United States. Depending on the season, it will be found in large schools from Maine to the Carolinas or off the coast of Florida and in the Gulf of Mexico. The bluefish, a member of the seabass family, resembles a mackerel in shape and averages from four to six pounds in weight and 18 inches in length. On rare occasions, large specimens in the 20 to 50 pound range are caught.

Bluefishing is considered great sport. The bluefish has been nicknamed "bulldog of the ocean" and is thought to be the gamest fish for its size in the world. It is the most voracious fish of the Atlantic seaboard, wreaking havoc on shoals of smaller fish.

It gained its name from the dark blue green color of its upper skin and the delicate bluish tint of its flesh. The latter is firm, lean and sweet, and highly regarded as seafood. It may be broiled, baked, stuffed or poached. Bluefish filets are prepared like filet of sole or flounder.

Bluefish is known also as skipjack or skip mackerel owing to its frequent leaps above the surface of the sea. In South Africa, it is called "elf" and in Australia, "tailor."

BLUEGILL

Also called bluegill bream or bluegill sunfish, this is a common sunfish *(Lepomis machrocherus)* found in the Great Lakes and much of the southeastern United States including the Mississippi River and its tributaries. Bluegill are good eating and usually of a handy size for pan frying.

These fish are so hardy, so lively when on the hook and so good to eat that they are widely stocked in reservoirs and artificial lakes. They do have one amusing local name: Pumpkinseed.

See also: **Bream, Sunfish.**

BLUE GROPER

Also GIANT PIGFISH. A well-known Australian sport fish, the blue groper *(Achoerodus gouldi)* can weigh as much as 80 pounds and be more than four feet long. Smaller specimens are much more palatable than larger ones, whose flesh tends to be coarse and tasteless. The blue groper is a member of the wrasse family, living close inshore in caves and under rocky overhangs. Males and females have distinct color patterns, with males being purple brown with orange lines, and the females a dull brick red.

BLUE LEG

See **Blewit.**

BLUEMOUTH

Also BLACKBELLY, ROSEMOUTH. Bluemouth is a European scorpionfish, *Helicolenus dactylopterus,* relished as food in Mediterranean countries. It is found on both sides of the Atlantic and from Norway to Madeira as well as in the Mediterranean Sea. Only in the latter area does it enjoy any acceptance as food. The bluemouth reaches a length of 18 inches and as an adult is found in deep water. This fish has a rosy back and sides with blue mouth and gill covers. There are large spines in its dorsal fin and around its head.

BLUET

See **Blewit.**

BLUE VINNY

See **Dorset Cheese.**

BLUEWOOD CONDALIA

A wild shrub, *Condalia obovata,* of Texas, its fruits make a good jelly.

BOAR

See **Wild Pig.**

BOARFISH

A small fish with a protruding snout, the boarfish *(Capros aper)* is found in the Mediterranean and the North Atlantic. Specimens vary in color depending on the depth at which they are caught: deep water—brick red; shallow water—pale straw. Their taste is mediocre, and they are used mainly in stews and soups.

BOB WHITE

See **Quail.**

BOCKWURST

A small sausage much resembling the frankfurter but prepared differently, the bockwurst contains both veal and pork in a ratio of three to one, plus eggs, milk and onions. It is seasoned with leeks, parsley, clove and pepper. These ingredients are stuffed into casings and sold uncured, as opposed to the **frankfurter,** which is usually smoked.

Bockwurst spoils easily and must be refrigerated. It is usually prepared by first boiling, then browning in a frying pan. Bockwurst is often added to bean dishes or served as breakfast sausage. After thorough cooking, it may be allowed to cool, then be served cold, with mustard. In former times, it was traditional to serve bockwurst only in the spring when bock beer came on the market.

See also: **Sausage.**

BOGUE

Also BOCE, BOGA, BOOPS, BOX. A fish, *Box boops,* of the Mediterranean Sea, its flesh varies in taste, depending on where it is caught. It is reputedly best in the area of Malta. The bogue has a yellow back, silver belly, and measures up to 14 inches long. There are two species, the common bogue and the bogue saupe. It is used in fish stews, such as bouillabaise and matelote, or may be fried, baked or poached.

BOJERI

Fruit of a tropical American tree, *Mimusops bojeri,* it is round to oval, about the size of a small plum and has a sweet flavor.

BOKCHOY

See **Pakchoi.**

BOKSER

See **Carob.**

BOLETE

Also CEPE. Boletes are a group of edible mushrooms. The most famous among them is the king bolete, which is known also as *cepe, steinpilz* and *porcino.* The king bolete grows wild under pine or other evergreen trees, and has been described by one enthusiast as, "with the possible exception of the **morel . . .** the finest-tasting mushroom known to humankind." The king bolete *(Boletus edulis)* is a large mushroom with a cap shaped like a hamburger bun and a thick club-shaped stem, often bulblike at the base. Specimens usually measure three to six inches across, and reach four to seven inches in height. Larger specimens reach a weight of five pounds. The color of the cap ranges from brown to red brown and the stem from white to pale brown. The flesh is solid and white. Unlike the **field mushroom,** the king bolete does not have gills under the cap but a spongy layer peppered with hundreds of tiny holes. Boletes are native to Central and Northern Europe and certain parts of North America, particularly the Pacific Northwest.

The king bolete was well known to the ancient Greeks and Romans, the name deriving from the Greek term *bolites*, which covered all mushrooms. The bolete was not the Romans' favorite, however. That honor was reserved for the Caesar's mushroom, or **orange amanita.** Romans referred to the king boletes as the *suilli*, or hog fungi, because they had observed that swine were fond of it. Martial, a Roman writer of the first century A.D., complained in an epigram that at a banquet a rival was offered a plate of Caesar's mushrooms, while he had to content himself with the king bolete.

The king bolete is excellent fresh, usually sauteed in butter. The flavor is said to combine sweetness and nuttiness. The texture is crunchy. After being cooked, they may be preserved by canning, pickling or freezing. Boletes also dry well, the process distilling the mushroom's flavor. This is usually accomplished by putting them out in the sun, the small caps dried whole, and the larger caps cut into thin slices.

Other edible boletes include the granulated bolete, the painted bolete, the admirable bolete, the orange bolete and the birch bolete. Some boletes are poisonous, e.g., the red-pored bolete *(Boletus subvelutipes)*. Boletes to be avoided have one or all of the following characteristics: red pores, stain blue, bitter taste.

See also: **Mushroom.**

BOLOGNA SAUSAGE

A large sausage that takes its name from the city of Bologna, Italy, where it originated, it is now made all over the world, but the best still comes from Bologna. There are two kinds, beef bologna and ham bologna. Beef is the more common of the two and consists of both beef and pork, at a ratio of about five to two, with a third of the pork fat, plus some veal trimmings and salt, sage, cayenne, ground black pepper and a pinch of saltpeter. The meat is minced, mixed with the other ingredients and stuffed into casings, after which it is cooked and smoked. Casings vary in width from two to six inches.

One of the largest in the United States is the Lebanon bologna, made in Eastern Pennsylvania by the Pennsylvania Dutch. It is done up in cheesecloth and has a strong, sweet flavor. Ham bologna consists of diced bits of lean pork shoulder and shoulder butt. Kosher bologna is all beef.

Bologna is rarely cooked, but usually served cold in slices. It is a favorite lunch meat in the United States. It is occasionally substituted for ham in baked beans.

See also: **Sausage.**

BOMBAY DUCK

Also BUMMALO FISH. This Indian relish is made from the dried, salted flesh of a saltwater lizard fish called bummalo *(Harpodon nehereus)*. This long, thin, nearly transparent fish is also eaten fresh and has a pleasant taste. However, the dried fish is impregnated with **asafetida,** a plant resin with a strong odor which many Westerners find offensive. The dried fish has no resemblance to a duck, and the name is said to be a corruption of the Indian word for the fish, *bombil*.

Bombay duck is used chiefly to flavor curry, but in earlier times it was used by travelers going into the interior of the subcontinent as a convenience food while on the road.

BONDART

See **Bondon.**

BONDE

See **Bondon.**

BONDON

Also BONDE, BONDART. This small, soft French cheese is made from whole ewe or cow's milk in the Normandy region. It is salted and somewhat resembles neufchatel but is usually eaten fresh. One version is ripened with the aid of *Penicillium candidum* mold. Cheese is produced in small loaves or cylinders.

BONDOST

This Swedish cow's milk cheese, often flavored with either **cumin** or **caraway** seeds, has been made in the United States for the past four decades. Either raw or pasteurized milk is used, and the finished product is small and round, weighing from two to three pounds. Minimum curing is six to eight weeks, but if a more pronounced flavor is desired, it should be left two or three weeks longer.

BONE

A hard substance composed of calcium salts and cartilage, it makes up the skeletons of mammals, birds and fishes. The interior cavities are filled with *marrow*, a fatty substance, and the surface is covered with a membrane called *periosteum*. Bones are boiled in water and seasoning to make stocks for soups and sauces. Beef and fowl bones have a lot of cartilage that produces gelatinous material. These, together with the other juices extracted by boiling, can be reduced further to make a meat jelly, which can be kept indefinitely. Bone marrow contributes much to the nutritious quality and flavor of stock, but it may also be eaten as a separate dish, as in deviled bones. Fish bones are boiled to produce a stock called *fumet*, which is used in fish soups and sauces.

See also: **Bone Marrow, Soup, Sauce.**

BONEFISH

Also LADYFISH. A game fish noted for its magnificent fighting qualities, the bonefish *(Albula vulpes)* is found worldwide in tropical seas. It does not grow particularly large—maximums of three feet and 20 pounds. It is much appreciated by anglers, nonetheless. The bonefish is particularly plentiful off Florida and the Bahamas, on the African coast, off Hawaii and in warm Australian waters.

Its flesh is palatable but rated only mediocre in flavor. The bonefish has a long, slender body with a small mouth and projecting snout. It is silvery overall, with a green blue back.

BONE MARROW

This fatty, nutritious tissue fills the cavities of hollow bones. The long bones of beef are particularly rich in marrow. It is flavorful and gelatinous and an important ingredient of the stocks used in French cooking to prepare soups and sauces. These stocks are made by boiling the bones for a long time in seasoned water to extract the marrow and other juices and to dissolve the cartilage clinging to the bone. When reduced still further by boiling, this broth makes a meat jelly. Fowl bones are also used for this purpose.

Bone marrow used to be prepared as an appetizer. Bones were cut into two-inch lengths, the ends stopped with dough and then boiled for a couple of hours. They were then set on napkins on plates, and the marrow extracted with long, thin marrow spoons. It was usually spread on toast with salt and pepper. An Italian variation of this is *ossobucco*, or stewed veal shins. Marrow, extracted raw and then cooked by boiling, poaching or frying, can be made into marrow balls for soups or used as a spread for canapes.

Marrow is easily digestible. The Latin poet Horace (65 B.C. to 8 A.D.) mentioned that dried marrow and liver was a popular aphrodisiac.

BONGO

Also BROAD-HORNED ANTELOPE. This is an African species found from Sierra Leone to Kenya. Unlike the eland, which it much resembles, the bongo *(Boocerus eurycreus)* inhabits dense, humid forests. It is a bright chestnut red on back and sides and is marked by vertical white stripes and black belly. It is hunted for meat and hides.

BONITO

The name includes several medium-size fish of the mackerel family. They are larger than a mackerel and smaller than a tuna, with an average length of 18 to 36 inches, weighing an average of six to 10 pounds. Bonito *(Sarda sarda)* travel in schools and are a good game fish. The Mediterranean Sea and warmer waters of the Atlantic and Pacific Oceans are their habitat. Bonito are fierce, fast swimmers who live on other fish.

While not as good to eat as mackerel or tuna, many persons find bonito quite palatable. It can be prepared the same way as tuna.

BONNIEBROOK SPRING WATER

This bulk, uncarbonated drinking water is bottled in plastic containers in the United States. It is relatively low in mineral content. A 1980 Consumers Union sensory panel rated the taste of this water as fair, with the following qualifications: mildly bitter, mildly astringent, mild chemical flavor, stale, old flavor.

See also: **Mineral Water.**

BOOPS

See **Bogue.**

BOQUERON

A variety of small sardine *(Sardinella allecia)*, it resembles an anchovy. It is commonly served as an hor d'oeuvre in Spain and cooked in a characteristic way. A slit is made above the tail of one fish, and the tails of two or three others slipped through it. They are dipped in flour, spread out like a fan and fried in hot oil.

BORAGE

An aromatic herb unfamiliar to most Americans, borage *(Borrago officinalis)* is a wild flower of the Mediterranean area, with vivid blue flowers and bristly hairs on the leaves and stalk.

The flowers are sometimes candied, but the plant is cultivated or gathered chiefly for the leaves,

which smell like cucumbers and taste somewhat like oysters. Their aroma adds interest to wine cups and summer beverages. The leaves must be finely chopped for salads, though, because the hairy texture is unpleasant. Their flavor goes well with yogurt and cream cheese. In Europe, the less tender leaves are often cooked as a vegetable like spinach.

In the 16th century it had a reputation for making people happy and was a favorite flavoring base for liqueurs.

BORASSUS

See **Palm Sugar.**

BORBONIA

Also RED BAY, SWEET BAY. A small tree, *Persea borbonia*, related to the avocado, its dried leaves are used as a condiment, to stuff roast chicken and other fowls, to flavor soups and in crab gumbo. It is native to the southern and southeastern United States.

BORDEAUX WINES

These internationally famous wines are grown in the vicinity of Bordeaux, on the Garonne in southwestern France. Bordeaux wines have been cherished from antiquity and are practically synonymous with the English word **"claret."** Vineyards abound on both banks of the Garonne and the Dordogne, which joins the Garonne about fifteen miles north of Bordeaux, and along the wide tidal estuary of these two rivers—the Gironde, in the rich plain of the **Medoc** east of the city, and near the forest of the Landes. The Bordeaux region is warmed by the Gulf Stream. Consequently, it is blessed by brief, mild winters and long, temperate summers. Its fertile gravelly soil, deposited for centuries by the three great rivers, is perfect for drainage and for deep root formation of the vines.

Bordeaux (ancient *Burdigala)* was the capital of the Roman province of Aquitania Secunda. Its wines were among the greatest in the empire and flourished in spite of the decree of Domitian in 92 A.D. that all Gallic vines should be uprooted. Domitian's reason for this policy was ostensibly to remedy a grave shortage of wheat in the empire. The provincial wine growers thought otherwise. "Eat me down to the roots," was the message of several anonymous pamphlets delivered to the emperor, "I shall still bear enough grapes for libations to be poured on the day that Caesar is slain!" Four years later Domitian was assassinated, and the decree was rescinded. For three hundred years in the Middle Ages, Aquitaine and its major city of Bordeaux belonged to the British—the beginning of the English trade in *"Claret."* Richard the Lion-Hearted was born in Bordeaux, and the troubadours who flocked to the London court of his mother—the beautiful Eleanor of Aquitaine—sang the praises of their southern wine along with those of the new English queen.

The best wine of Bordeaux today is usually ascribed to the reds—of Medoc and **St. Emilion.** But elegant dry white wines, sparkling wines and sweet dessert wines are justly famed as well. The Bordeaux wine-growing region contains five main districts—**Graves,** Medoc, **Pomerol,** St. Emilion and **Sauternes.** Another district, **Entre-Deux-Mers,** which lies between the Garonne and the Dordogne, is important for its clear and refreshing white wine. The tidewater plain of the Medoc, on the left banks of the Garonne and the Gironde, yields numerous "great growths" *(grands crus)* of dry red wine, while both white and red wine of superior quality is grown in the region of Graves south and east of the city. In the seventeenth and eighteenth centuries the red Graves was known to the English as *"Claret."* Today a dry white Graves outproduces the red wine grown here. From the left (or southern) bank of the Garonne comes the princely, semisweet white wine of Sauternes and **Barsac.** St. Emilion and Pomerol, on the right bank of the Dordogne, produce numerous outstanding red wines.

Unlike Burgundy, where vineyards are owned by many separate individuals, the Bordeaux wine region is typified by large *chateaux*, which are owned by single companies or syndicates. The names of these *chateaux*, or large wine-growing estates, grace the labels of Bordeaux wine sold throughout the world: *Chateau Haut-Brion*, *Chateau Lafite-Rothschild*, *Chateau Margaux*, *Chateau Latour*—all from Graves and the Medoc; *Chateau d'Yquem*—from Sauternes-Barsac; and *Chateau Ausone*—from St. Emilion—named for the Roman vintner-poet Ausonius, a native of Bordeaux. The American name "*Cadillac*" derives from a subdistrict that makes an excellent white wine and is indicative of the nobility and prestige of the grapes grown in this important part of the world.

See also: **Burgundy Wines.**

BORDELAISE SAUCE

Here is a French sauce based on red wine that has been seasoned with chopped shallot, thyme, bay leaf, salt and peppercorns, then much reduced. It is mixed with meat glaze and butter, then reduced again. It is garnished with diced bone marrow and parsley. Bordelaise is used with grilled meats, such as steak, hamburgers and kidneys.

See also: **Sauce.**

BORDEN POLAR SPRING WATER

A still spring water, bottled in plastic containers for bulk drinking in the United States, it is relatively low in mineral content. A 1980 Consumers Union sensory panel rated the taste of this water as poor, with the following qualifications: mildly bitter, distinctly plastic flavor, mild manure aroma.

See also: **Mineral Water.**

BORECOLE

See **Kale.**

BORELLI

This is a small, buffalo's milk cheese made in Italy.

BORNEO JAMBOSA

The dark purple fruit comes from a tree, *Syzygium polycephalum*, found in India, Java and Borneo. The fruit is a berry which attains a diameter of 1½ inches and is highly esteemed locally for making jellies.

BORSCHT

See **Soup.**

BOSTON BROWN BREAD

A popular New England bread, made from rye, whole wheat flours and cornmeal, it is dark brown, moist and sweetened with molasses. It is cooked in a tin can to give it the characteristic round shape. The preferred method of cooking is steaming, although this may be combined with baking.

Boston brown bread is served piping hot with butter, and is the traditional accompaniment to the celebrated Boston Baked beans, a dish the colonists in Massachusetts learned to make from the native Americans. According to Waverly Root and Richard de Rochemont in their well written book, *Eating in America:*

> *The Boston dish is basically the same as the Indian one. As for the brown bread that accompanies baked beans so perfectly, it is made today with a mixture of flours, but it still includes cornmeal, the only one the Indians possessed; and when properly made it is* steamed, *the way the Indians cooked it.*

See also: **Bread.**

BOTARGO

Also BOTTARGA, BOTTERIGO. This relish is made from the salted roes of the Mediterranean gray mullet or tuna fish. Sardinians have developed botargo as one of their special condiments, but it is also popular in Greece and Turkey. In centuries past, botargo was a common dish in England, or so it can be inferred from the following quote taken from the *Diary* of Samuel Pepys for June 6, 1661, "We stayed talking and singing and drinking great draughts of claret, and eating botargo and bread and butter till twelve at night." The English way of preparing it was to mix it with fish blood, salt and lemon juice. This has been described as a kind of sausage.

Botargo has a flavor all its own, and is sometimes described grandiloquently as "red caviar." The Greeks especially are skilled at trapping the mullet in August, its spawning time. The females are led into fish pens, speared and immediately gutted for their roe, which is cleaned, soaked in brine and dried in the sun. The dried roe may be eaten on bread, or it is coated with beeswax to preserve it. In the latter form, it is rich and thick as caramel, and may stick to the teeth and roof of the mouth. It is sliced and eaten on bread or toast or often scrambled into eggs.

BOTOKO PLUM

See **Annam Plum.**

BOTTLE GOURD

Also CALABASH GOURD. The bottle-shaped fruit of a long-running vine, *Lagenaria siceraria*, is indigenous to the Old World tropics. When young, these gourds can be eaten as vegetables and are excellent baked or boiled and mashed with butter. At maturity they can reach a length of three feet, and they assume the shape of a large decanter. The shell is smooth and hard when ripe, and the fruit may be hollowed out and used as a vessel for liquids. In the past, the bottle gourd made a good gunpowder flask. The plant is also known as the white-flowered gourd or the trumpet gourd.

BOUDANNE

A cow's milk cheese made in France, it is round, measuring eight inches wide by three deep, and takes two or three months to mature.

BOUDIN BLANC

This French white sausage is made from the white meat of chicken or sometimes pork or veal. The meat is minced and mixed with eggs, breadcrumbs, pepper, onions, parsley and chives. In the case of pork, both lean and fat are used, occasionally supplemented by butter or fat goose liver. The mixture is stuffed into casings about 1½ inches wide by 12 inches long. The sausages are boiled before being sold. Boudin blanc is grilled or broiled and often served with mashed potatoes.

See also: **Sausage.**

BOUILLABAISSE

A fish stew that originated in Marseilles, it is made with many local variations the entire length of the French Riviera. The classic bouillabaisse is supposed to have at least six different kinds of fish—tender as well as firm-fleshed—tomatoes and olive oil, plus such seasonings as thyme, garlic, fennel and especially saffron. Some recipes include crustacea, such as spiny lobster, and shellfish.

Some authorities assert that true bouillabaisse can be made only on the shores of the Mediterranean because fish essential to the recipe exist nowhere else. These include the rascasse (hogfish), the lotte (anglerfish), the merlan (resembling whiting or hake) and the daurade (John Dory). Others claim that the essence of bouillabaisse is its variability, and what is important is not the identity of the fish but their absolute freshness. One exception is the rascasse, which is essential because it acts as a catalyst, bringing out the delicate flavors of the other fish. For the rest, substitutes include eel, grouper, Pacific spiny lobster, sea bass and codfish.

A *fumet* is made from the fish heads and used to cook the stew. In it are placed the tomatoes, olive oil, saffron and other seasonings, the firm-textured fish and, 10 minutes later, the tender fish. The whole is cooked at a fast boil for no more than 15 to 20 minutes. The fish are removed from the liquid and served on a separate plate. The soup is poured into a bowl over slices of dry french bread called *marettes*. The stew is usually accompanied by a special hot sauce called *rouille*, which looks like red mustard and has a creamy texture. It is made by crushing garlic and red pepper together with bread crumbs, olive oil and fish bouillon.

The English poet and novelist, William Makepeace Thackeray, wrote a poem about a bouillabaisse he ate in Terre's Tavern in Paris:

This Bouillabaisse a noble dish is—
A sort of soup, or broth, or brew,
Or hotchpotch or all sorts of fishes,
That Greenwich never could outdo;
Green herbs, red peppers, mussels, saffron,
Soles, onions, garlic, roach and dace;
All these you eat at Terre's tavern
In that one dish of Bouillabaisse.

BOURGAIN

A soft, unsalted cheese of the Neufchatel type, Bourgain is made in France from cow's milk and, because of its perishable nature, is consumed locally and not exported.

BOURGUEIL

A fresh, fruity red wine grown southwest of Tours, along the Loire in France, Bourgueil resembles the wine of nearby Chinon. It is made from the same grape—the Cabernet Franc—and has a slight raspberry flavor and bouquet. It can—and should—be drunk when it is tender and young.

See also: **Loire Wines.**

BOURGUIGNONNE SAUCE

A French sauce served with meat, eggs, fish and poultry, it is a variation of **bordelaise sauce** and is based on red wine, which is cooked with chopped shallots, parsley, bay leaves and mushroom trimmings. It is then strained and thickened with a butter and flour paste.

See also: **Sauce.**

BOURRACHE

See **Borage.**

BOUZY WINE

A famous dry red "still" wine from the vineyards of **Champagne** in France, Bouzy wine is typically robust and has a special fruity flavor similar to the great red wines of southern Burgundy. Like the **Sillery wine** from the same district, it should be drunk when cooled and when slightly aged. Bouzy is marketed by individual growers in the region, since it does not require the special blending used in the production of sparkling white champagnes. Its quality varies, therefore, from vineyard to vineyard in a single year. The name has no connection, as some have conjectured, with the word "booze" which stems from an Anglo Saxon verb meaning "to boast."

See also: **Burgundy Wines.**

BOVRIL

See **Beef Extract.**

BOWFIN

Also BOWFISH. A small freshwater fish of the eastern United States, the bowfish *(Amia calva)* has a dark green back and voracious eating habits. It is found in the Great Lakes, the Mississippi River and other waters of the Mississippi Valley.

The bowfish has a long narrow fin on its back and rounded tail fins. It is a living fossil, the remaining member of a family of fishes that flourished more than 130 million years ago. It is known locally by many names, including the blackfish, the mudfish, the grindle, the dogfish, the lake lawyer, the marsh fish, the coupique and the willow pike. It frequents deeper waters by day.

The bowfish feeds at night in marshy areas and boggy places and may be taken there with a spear or by hand if fishing by lantern. The flesh of fresh bowfin is soft and pasty and not considered appetizing. Salted or smoked, however, it is thought to be a delicacy and compared to finnan haddie.

BOX CHEESE

Firm box and soft box are two different German cheeses, the former being more important commercially. Depending on the locality, it is also known as *Hohenberg*, *Mondsee* and *Weihenstephan*. The firm variety is made with whole cow's milk and colored with saffron. Its mild and piquant flavor, frequently enhanced by caraway seeds, is similar to American **brick cheese.** Cheeses weigh between one and four pounds.

The soft variety is made from partly skimmed milk, and likewise colored with saffron. It is often called *Hohenheimer* cheese after the small village of Hohenheim where it is made. *Fromage de boite*, a soft cheese of this type, is made in Doubs, France, during the fall.

BOXFISH

See **Trunkfish.**

BOYSENBERRY

A hybrid berry, obtained by crossing the blackberry, raspberry and loganberry, it is large, purple in color and has fewer seeds than its parents. It tastes somewhat like a raspberry. The boysenberry is named after the American botanist and horticulturist, Rudolph Boysen, who developed the hybrid in 1923. Like the raspberry and blackberry, the boysenberry is of the genus *Rubus*. It is eaten fresh or used in preserves, and is prepared like the **loganberry.**

BRA

This Italian cheese takes its name from the town of Bra in Piedmont, where it was originally made by nomads. It is hard, nearly white, and has a sharp flavor, which is slightly salty due to immersion in brine. Bra has a compact texture and is made from partly skimmed cow's milk. Its average weight is 12 pounds. *Bra* is also the name of a small, soft, creamy cheese of more recent origin, which is made around Turin.

BRACKEN

Also BRAKE, FIDDLEHEAD FERN. The young fronds, rhizomes and even shoots of certain ferns have been eaten since prehistoric times. This is true of North America's most common fern, the bracken or pasture brake *(Pteris aquilina)*, which is also distributed worldwide.

The young fronds are snapped off while still in the fiddlehead stage, i.e., curled up in a form resembling the shape of a fiddlehead. They are tied in small bundles, boiled in salted water and served with bacon fat or butter. The taste is distinctive, like a cross between asparagus and mushrooms. It is well liked in the Far East. The underground roots, or rhizomes, are also eaten, although in Europe only in times of famine. The roots are boiled until tender, then served cold with an oil and vinegar dressing. In the Canary Islands, a type of bread called *goflo* is made from powdered bracken roots and barley meal. *Hortus III* warns that, although the fronds and roots have been eaten for centuries, they are now known to be carcinogenic.

The fiddlehead or cinnamon fern *(Osmunda cinnamomea)* is a wild delicacy especially popular in Maine. It is a hardy fern growing on river banks. Native Americans taught settlers to collect the young budding stems and fiddlehead fronds. They are washed and cooked like broccoli and served with hollandaise sauce, or cold with a vinaigrette dressing. The taste is reminiscent of broccoli, asparagus and artichokes. They are also available canned.

BRAINS

Brains are the central mass of nerve tissue located in the head of a vertebrate, controlling the body, senses and mental functions. Most commonly eaten as food are those of beef cattle, calves, sheep and pigs. The English prefer sheep brains, while in the United States calf brains are thought best. Brains are classed as one of the **variety meats.**

Although delectable and nutritious, brains are not a popular food, at least in the United States. Many people are put off by the idea of eating a brain, and many who try it object to the consistency, which is very tender, and even dislike the taste, although it is bland, even neutral. A beef brain contains about the same amount of protein as a T-bone steak and about one-fourth the fat.

Brains are highly perishable. If they are not to be cooked the same day as purchased, they should be parboiled or blanched to avoid spoilage. First, however, they are usually soaked in salted water for several hours, washed well and then cleaned of membrane and blood clots. Blanching is done in a court bouillon with vinegar or in salted water and vinegar. They are then placed in ice water, allowed to cool and carefully dried.

Brains are prepared in a variety of ways, usually in a simple manner. A favorite in France is to dip them in egg batter and bread crumbs and fry them. They are then sliced, arranged in rings and stuffed with chopped cooked spinach. Blanched brains may be cubed, mixed in a batter of egg and chopped spinach and fried. The French also prepare brain croquettes, or creamed brains with bechamel sauce, which is used to fill vol-au-vent pastry shells. Norwegians are fond of brain dumplings, and in Germany brain soup is made. A Mexican delicacy is brain tacos, made usually from sheep or lamb brains.

Perhaps the most exotic brain dish was that served by the Roman Emperor Heliogabalus—ostrich brains garnished with tiny gold nuggets.

See also: **Variety Meats.**

BRAKE

See **Bracken.**

BRAMBLE

See **Blackberry.**

BRAN

This is the skin or outer husk of grains, such as wheat, oats and rye. Wheat bran is removed from the berry in milling white flour. This byproduct may be fed to cattle, used in breakfast food or as an additive to white flour.

Wheat bran is composed largely of indigestible cellulose whose passage through the alimentary tract promotes regular bowel movements. Whole, unsifted wheat flour contains all of the bran, and is known also as Graham flour, after Dr. Sylvester Graham, a food researcher of the 19th century. Dr. Graham crusaded against white bread, which was the prevailing symbol of good living. He advocated eating bread made from coarse, unsifted flour, principally for the laxative effect of the bran. The same effect can be obtained by eating breakfast food with bran added. It should be used with care, however, since bran irritates many people's intestines.

See also: **Bread, Wheat.**

BRANCINO

A fish caught in the Adriatic Sea, highly thought of in Venice, the brancino resembles a perch or perch pike. It is usually poached in white wine stock and served hot with sauce genovese, or it may be fried or served in aspic.

BRAND

Also BRANDKASE. A hand cheese made in Germany from sour milk curd is ripened in beer kegs. Sometimes it is moistened with beer during ripening. A typical cheese weighs five ounces.

BRANDEWIN

See **Liquor.**

BRANDY

This alcoholic liquor is distilled from wine or from a fermented mash of fruit. The name comes from the earlier "brandywine," which was adapted from the Dutch *brandewijn*, meaning "burnt wine." Brandy is of fairly recent invention, dating from the 16th century. According to tradition, a Dutch shipmaster was involved in transporting wine from La Rochelle, a port on the Charente River in France. To reduce the bulk of his cargo, he hit upon the idea of removing most of the water from the wine, retaining just the "spirit" of it in the form of a concentrate. On arriving in Holland he expected to reconstitute it by adding water, but his friends tasted it and liked it as it was. They named the new product *brandewijn*.

To qualify as such, a brandy must be suitably aged in wood. The first brandy was made in France, and the finest brandy continues to be made there in the Cognac region. Following an ancient tradition, the wine is twice distilled in the venerable pot still, or alembic, and aged in oak casks. Coming from the still, the spirits are colorless and have a sharp, but fruity, coppery bouquet and taste from the copper stills. After aging in oak, the taste mellows, and the color turns a beautiful amber. Cognac in the cask consists of 70 percent alcohol. Before bottling, the strength is reduced by dilution and blending to from 40 to 43 percent. Only brandies from this region may be called *cognac*. (For more information, see: **Cognac.)**

The word "brandy," however, has no geographical limitation and therefore should be qualified to indicate its origin, such as French brandy, American brandy, Greek brandy, etc. The finest are tied to a region, such as cognac or **Armagnac,** another fine French brandy. Almost all American brandy comes from California, distilled from wines of the state. The preferred grapes for brandy are Thompson Seedless and Flame Tokay. Instead of the pot still, the more modern patent still is used, but, as in France, California brandy is aged in white oak casks. Brandy in appreciable quantities are also made in Germany, Greece (See: **Metaxas),** Israel, Italy (See: **Grappa),** Mexico, Peru (See: **Pisco),** Portugal and Spain. Much Spanish brandy has a characteristic sherry taste.

An inferior brandy is made from the pomace, i.e., the grape skins, seeds and stems left over from pressing the wine. Pomace is called *marc* (silent *c*) in French and the distillate is known as *eau de vie de marc*. It has a strawlike, woody taste, which some find irresistible, although many would not dignify it with the name "brandy."

Fruit brandies are divided into three categories: those made from apples and pears, such as calvados; those made from such stone fruits as cherries, plums and apricots, such as kirsch, and those made from such berries as raspberries, strawberries, blackberries and elderberries, such as framboise.

The categories are arranged in descending order of quantity produced and alcoholic content. By a quirk of U.S. law, fruit brandies may not be labeled as such, but instead are called by specific name, e.g., kirsch may not be labeled cherry brandy, but is known simply as kirsch or kirschwasser; slivovitz may not be labeled plum brandy, but simply slivovitz and so on. This is because under the law something labeled brandy must be made from grapes. Fruit-flavored brandies made in the United States are just that—a grape brandy alcoholic base flavored with fruit syrup.

Early in brandy's history, Dr. Samuel Johnson set the tone for brandy drinking when he remarked, "Claret is the liquor for boys; port for men; but he who aspires to be a hero must drink brandy."

BRANDY SAUCE

Here is a dessert sauce used in the United States and Great Britain mainly on puddings and mince pie. Brandy sauce is a **hard sauce** based on powdered sugar and butter, flavored with brandy. It is served cold with the hot dessert.

See also: **Sauce.**

BRANNVIN

See **Aquavit.**

BRANT

A small, wild goose of Europe and North America with dark plumage, it has a good, but gamy, flavor. It rarely reaches the table.

BRANZA DE BRAILA

See **Teleme.**

BRATWURST

See **Sausage.**

BRAUNSCHWEIGER

See **Liverwurst.**

BRAWN

Cubed meat that has been boiled, seasoned and molded in its own gelatin, brawn is served cold with mustard sauce. Brawn is similar to **headcheese,** a type of sausage. It is a traditional English dish made from boar's head, cow or calf's head or a leg of lamb. These are favored because they produce a thick gelatinous broth upon being boiled. The ingredients are simmered until the meat leaves the bone easily. The meat is then chopped, spiced and pressed and placed in a mold. The stock is poured over it and jellies upon cooling. The mold is often square to facilitate slicing the brawn.

BRAZILIAN APPLE

The edible fruit of a Brazilian shrub, *Solanum agrarium*, the Brazilian apple is eaten only when ripe.

BRAZILIAN CHERRY

See **Surinam Cherry.**

BRAZILIAN PINE

Also PARANA PINE. The seeds of this tree, *Araucaria braziliensis*, are edible and are used like other pine nuts or pinones. This species is found in Brazil, Paraguay and Argentina and is consumed in the area of cultivation.

BRAZIL NUT

Also PARANUT, CREAM NUT. This large, popular nut has a taste similar to almond or coconut. It is the fruit of an immense jungle tree, *Bertholletia excelsa*, that grows in the Amazon River Valley. Brazil is the largest producer, but other sources are Venezuela, Peru, Ecuador and the Guianas.

The tree carries the nuts in a woody capsule, which resembles a large coconut. Inside, a dozen to two dozen nuts are arranged in regular tiers. Each nut is encased in a very hard, brown, three-cornered shell. When a capsule is ripe, it crashes to the ground, sometimes from heights of 100 to 130 feet. Most nuts are gathered in January, sun dried, washed and exported in the shell.

The nut is called *castanha* ("chestnut") in Brazil. Locally the oil is used for lighting and cooking. It does not store well, however, and quickly goes rancid. They are called "American chestnuts" in France.

Brazil nuts may be eaten alone, salted, as a snack, either whole or cut into chips. They have a high caloric content, and the flavor goes well in cakes and cookies.

Brazil Nut

BREAD

In its most basic form, bread is a flour and water mixture which has been baked into a loaf or pancake. The earliest bread was unleavened. It came into use more than 10,000 years ago, shortly after Neolithic man adopted an agricultural way of life. Its modern descendants are such flatbreads as the Mexican *tortilla*, the Indian *chupatty*, the Chinese *pao ping* and the Hebrew *matzo.* Leavened bread is a more recent discovery, attributed to the ancient Egyptians, who learned to use wild yeast to lighten bread and to ferment beer. Leavened bread flourishes today in countless forms, most of which are variations on the basic formula of flour, water, salt and a leavening agent.

It was the cultivation of cereals—barley, millet, wheat—that converted our prehistoric ancestors from nomadic hunters to sedentary farmers. They first used the grain to make a porridge consisting of grain, roasted for digestibility, and water. This porridge, baked perhaps by accident on a hearthstone, became the first unleavened bread, but for leavened bread, a grain with a high gluten content, such as wheat or rye, is required. Gluten is a protein substance found in cereal grains. It becomes very sticky when ground into flour and mixed with water. This stickiness enables it to retain the gas released by the working of the yeast in the dough, thus lightening the whole mass. Heating changes the texture of gluten from sticky to elastic, a quality that enables a baked loaf to retain its shape.

The Egyptians, then, first put the two essential elements together—high-gluten wheat flour and yeast—to produce a lighter bread. This first leavened bread was **sourdough bread,** which utilized a wild

Bread dough, in a small commercial bakery

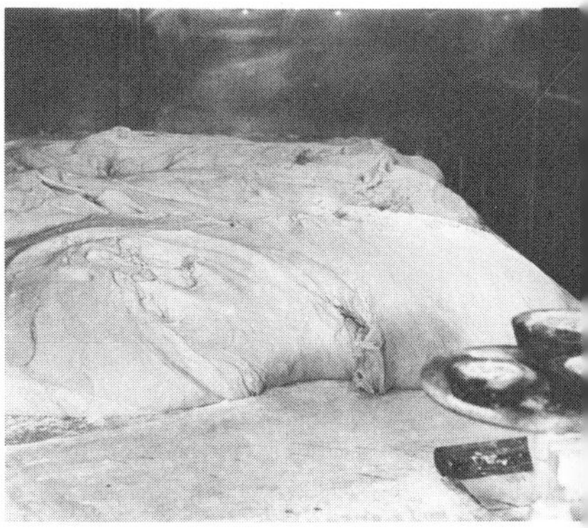

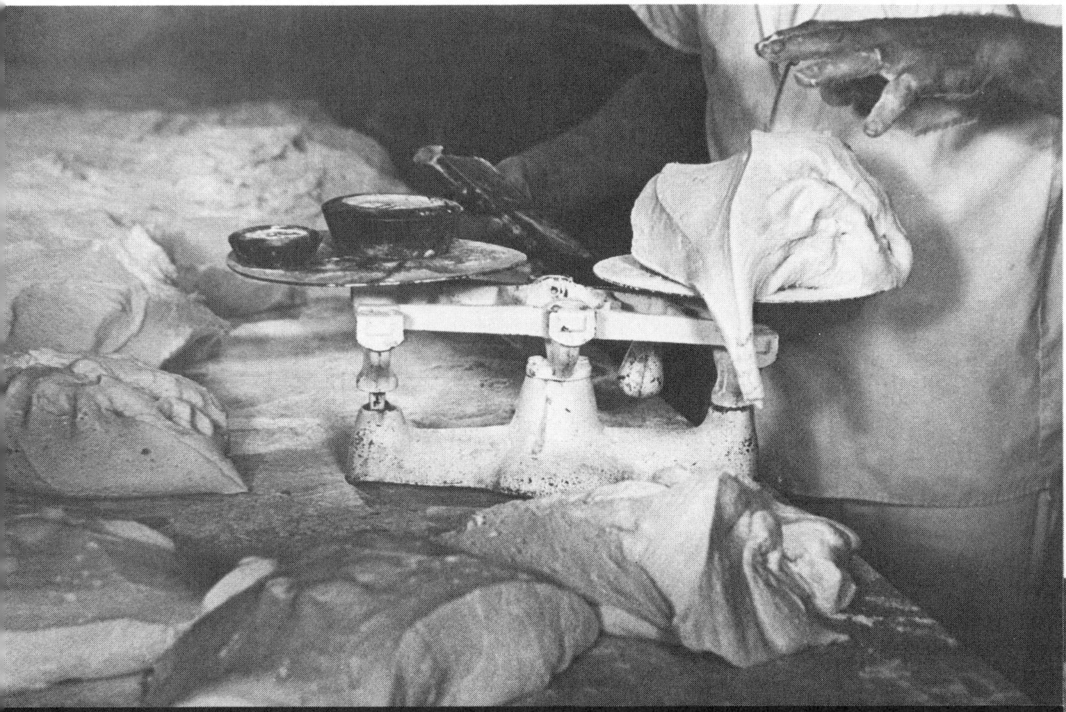

Weighing dough before baking

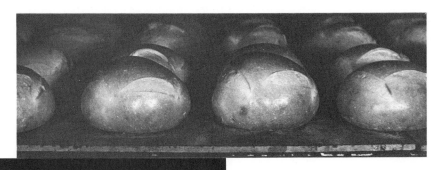

Shaping bread dough into loaves

Baked loaves of bread, still in the oven

strain of yeast that was kept alive and working between breadmaking sessions in a piece of leftover dough. It was used to start the next batch of dough fermenting and imparted a characteristic sour taste to the finished loaf. This represented a considerable advance over previous breads, yet, according to Adrian Bailey in *The Blessings of Bread:*

> *By some accounts, the bread of the Egyptians was pretty awful. For one thing it was gritty, because the grain contained particles of sand from the desert, and flecks of mica and limestone from the grinding stones and sickles . . . They greatly enjoyed their bread nevertheless. Not for nothing did the Greeks call them* artophagoi—*the bread eaters . . . It was* ta *[sourdough bread], barley beer and onions that built the Pyramid at Giza.*

The Egyptians passed on their knowledge of breadmaking to the Greeks, who improved on it and, in turn, passed it on to the Romans. Invention of the rotary mill improved the quality of the flour, and much emphasis was placed, especially among the wealthier classes, on the whiteness of the flour. This is understandable, given the impurities noted in Egyptian bread, but it led to the adulteration of flour with chalk, a practice that persisted for centuries. Chalk was later supplemented by other substances, most notably alum. The Romans invented the first form of dried yeast—wheat bran soaked in wine, then dried in the sun. Baking became a tremendous industry in Rome, some bakeries producing 50,000 to 100,000 loaves a day. Varieties included *cappadocia*, the finest bread made of the best flour, oil, salt and milk; *artoplites*, a molded bread for refined persons, and *autopyron* (self-baked), a coarse, solid loaf made of bran mixed with a little flour. Much bread was distributed free through the *annona*, or dole system, which was immortalized in the phrase, "bread and circuses," the Roman policy for domestic peace.

The Romans spread the art of making leavened bread throughout Northern Europe, yet after the fall of Rome things backslid a bit. During the Middle Ages, the average peasant had to get along on unleavened flat bread like the Scottish oatcake, the French *fougasse* and the English ashcake. The last has been described as a small, round flat loaf, so dense that a knife point couldn't penetrate it and would slip off its surface. It had to be broken in half with the hand, and contained mainly barley, beans, acorns and perhaps some wheat and rye flours. At the next level, the standard flour was made from a mixture of wheat and rye grains called *maslin. Maslin*'s rye content had the disadvantage of being vulnerable to attack by a fungus called ergot, which could and did periodically cause widespread poisonings. When consumed, the contaminated rye produced a spectacular syndrome known as "St. Anthony's fire," which contemporary opinion held to be the work of the devil. (See also **Rye.**) Moneyed city folk, who could afford to demand the finest white bread, had to put up with such adulterants as alum, ammonium carbonate, magnesium carbonate, zinc sulphate, plaster of Paris, pipe clay, bone ash, slaked lime and powdered flint.

The next leap in bread-making technology occurred in the mid-19th century with the development in Hungary of the steel roller mill, which could produce any amount of white flour completely free of wheat germ and bran, the ingredients that kept flour dark. Coinciding with the tremendous burgeoning of wheat production from the American and Canadian plains, this enabled the masses to have their fill, cheaply, of the sort of bread that had always been preferred by the rich: light, white bread. Moreover, automation of the baking industry since 1900 ensures a purer, cleaner bread, unsullied by the sweat and dirt from the hands of the baker who used to knead the dough. This has culminated in the present-day profusion of tasteless, spongy white bread, which is presliced and has long shelf life.

Just as white bread came into the reach of the masses, however, its nutritional value was challenged by Dr. Sylvester Graham, a Presbyterian minister, who maintained that bran was essential to health. (See: **Graham Bread.**) Dr. Graham made his objections before the discovery of vitamins, but a host of subsequent critics have pointed out that removing the germ from wheat removes most of its vitamin content (mainly B and E), not to mention its calcium, iron and phosphorus. This was followed by the advent of "enriched bread," i.e., bread made with flour containing additives, such as vitamin B-1, nicotinic acid, iron, riboflavin, calcium and phosphorus. This would seem to involve a lot of wasted motion, that is, first taking these elements out, then replacing them. The point is, however, that if they are removed, the flour becomes white, and the public demands white bread.

The demand for all things natural boomed in the 1960s and 1970s, bringing a profusion of whole-grain breads to the supermarket shelves. However, the label on the bread should be read carefully to ascertain what has been added to or subtracted from the product in question. White bread accounts for about 82 percent of all bread produced in the United States.

Quick breads are those leavened by an agent other than yeast, such as **baking powder.** This type of bread does not require a fermentation period, but may be baked as soon as the dough is mixed.

See also: **Flour, Yeast.**

BREADFRUIT

Breadfruit is a staple food in many tropical areas of the world, taking the place of such temperate zone starches as potatoes and cereals. More a vegetable than a fruit, it is the product of a sturdy, broad-leaved tree, *Artocarpus communis*, which easily attains heights of 60 feet.

According to tradition, a large breadfruit tree can produce enough food to sustain a good-sized family for a year. The fruit resembles a green melon—ranging up to eight inches in diameter and 10 pounds in weight—with a rough, warty skin. Inside, the pulp is white, starchy and fibrous, rather like grainy bread. This is true of breadfruit that are picked before they are fully mature, which is usually the case.

Although English navigator/pirate William Dampier was the first European to record an encounter with breadfruit in 1667, it was Captain Cook's first voyage to Tahiti that brought breadfruit forcefully to the attention of British merchants and planters who were looking for a cheap source of food for the slave labor that tended their Caribbean sugarcane fields. In 1787, the Crown dispatched Captain William Bligh of the ship *Bounty* on an ill-fated voyage to Tahiti. Bligh, who had been a lieutenant of Cook's, was to gather a thousand breadfruit saplings and transport them alive and in good condition to the West Indies. The voyage out took longer than expected, as did the gathering of trees. On the way back, an exasperated crew mutinied when Bligh cut their water ration to keep the trees alive. The mutineers tossed the trees overboard, and set Bligh and other officers adrift in open boats. In a remarkable feat of seamanship, Bligh managed to reach Portuguese Timor. In 1793, "Breadfruit Bligh," as he was known by then, successfully brought a load of breadfruit trees to Port Royal, Jamaica. Breadfruit was duely transplanted on Jamaica, St. Vincent and other islands, but never attained the anticipated popularity among the native workers, who preferred plantain as a starch and continue to do so today. Bligh continued his career as a transplanter by bringing rubber trees from Brazil to the Malay states.

The breadfruit tree is a relative of the mulberry, and is probably native to Malaysia. Fossil remains of breadfruit from the Eocene era have been found near Leipzig, East Germany, an indication of the extent of the Tropical Zone. Other parts of the tree are useful, such as the bark, which can be made into cloth and paper; the leaves, which serve to roof dwellings and wrap food; the wood, which is made into canoes and furniture, and the sap, a latexlike substance used as glue.

If boiled or baked, breadfruit's taste is minimal and bland, although some writers have detected faint overtones of artichoke or olives. If the fruit is allowed to ripen, it turns yellow or brown and feels like a ripe banana. The ripe fruit is usually baked as a dessert, and reputedly tastes like sweet potato. In some areas, such as the Marquesas Islands, the unripe pulp is sun-dried reduced to powder and stored for a year or more in watertight pits, where it tends to ferment, assuming the appearance of soft cheese. It is baked like the fresh fruit.

BREADNUT

A tree of the mulberry family, native to Mexico, Central America and the West Indies, it is grown for its seeds, which are boiled, ground into flour and made into bread. Particularly well known is the Jamaican breadnut.

The breadnut tree *(Brosimum alicastrum)* reaches 100 feet in height. The fruit is round, yellow and averages one inch in diameter. This tree was the one most often cultivated by the ancient Mayans.

BREADROOT

Also INDIAN TURNIP, PRAIRIE APPLE, PRAIRIE POTATO, POMME BLANCHE. This herbaceous plant of western and southern United States has a large, turnip-shaped root that is rich in starch. It was a favorite food of the Sioux and was eaten by Lewis and Clark on their exploratory expedition of 1804–1806. Breadroot *(Psoralea esculenta)* is perennial and leguminous. The root can be ground into flour for making cakes and bread. A closely related plant, the Utah breadroot *(P. mephitica)*, can be employed similarly.

BREAD SAUCE

A thick sauce served with game in England, it consists of white, crustless breadcrumbs cooked in milk and flavored with mace, onions and cloves. Butter, cream and seasonings are added, and the sauce is served hot.

See also: **Sauce.**

BREAD WINE

A beverage resembling the Russian *kvass*, it is made with brown bread, sugar and water. It is kept in a warm place until it ferments.

BREAKFAST FOOD

Also BREAKFAST CEREAL. A dry product manufactured from cereal grains, such as corn, wheat, oats and rice, it is eaten for breakfast with milk and sugar. The term is also applied to older hot cereals, such as oatmeal, porridge and mush.

Dry cereals were invented in the mid-19th century in the United States and popularized around the end of that century as a health food. It is ironic that in the past two decades they have been attacked as being deficient in food value, in effect, being unhealthy. The charge of "empty calories" has led some manufacturers—but by no means all—to add vitamins and minerals to their products. All of them have the merit of leading the buyer to consume milk, a primary food.

The largest producer of breakfast cereals is the Kellogg company of Battle Creek, Michigan. Dr. John Harvey Kellogg, director of the Battle Creek Sanatorium, a kind of health resort, invented his first cereal in the 1870s. It was called Granose. Later he went on to develop Kellogg's Toasted Corn Flakes, which revolutionized America's breakfast habits and remains the biggest seller today. A patient of Dr. Kellogg's, Charles W. Post, was inspired by his example to invent Grapenut Flakes, and later Post Toasties. Dr. Kellogg's original theory was that people needed to chew dry, brittle food to keep their teeth in shape.

Breakfast foods were popularized through intensive use of advertising and today represent a billion-dollar industry, with more than 100 competing types of breakfast cereal. Some of the better known are Shredded Wheat, Puffed Wheat, Puffed Rice and Total.

BREAM

This name is applied to numerous fish of two different families. The European fresh water bream *(Abramis brama)* is of the carp *(Cyprinidae)* family with narrow deep body, spiny fins and arched back. An allied genus in America is called golden shiner. Various fresh water sunfishes of the genus *(Lepomis)* are called breams as well.

Salt water breams are of the family *Sparidae* and are called sea breams. They are related to grunts, snappers, porgies, scup and sheepheads and are widely found in the oceans. A common European species is *Pagellus centrodontus.* The rose fish *(Sebastes marinus)* is also a bream.

European freshwater bream are not well fleshed and do not yield much eatable food. In contrast, the sea breams yield much more food per fish, and many are fished commercially. They are excellent eating whether prepared in stews, fried, sauteed, baked, steaked or any other way.

See also: **Bluegill.**

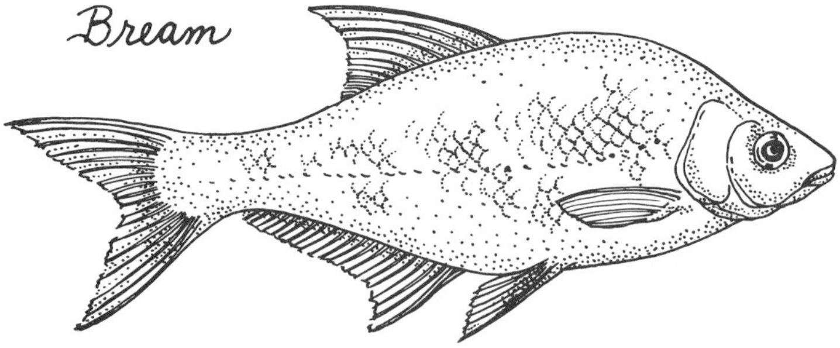

BRESCIANO

See **Bagozzo.**

BRET

See **Turbot.**

BRICKBAT CHEESE

An English cheese made in Wiltshire from fresh cow's milk with some cream added, its manufacture dates from the 18th century. After curing, it is said to last for as long as a year.

BRICK CHEESE

This cheese originated in Wisconsin, and thus is one of the few truly American cheeses. The taste is reminiscent of both **cheddar cheese** and **limburger,** although not quite so sharp as the former nor as strong as the latter. It is sweet and mild, yet pungent. The body is semisoft but elastic, with many small, round or irregular eyes. Bricks are used to press whey out of the curd—and this may account for the name—but the final shape is also bricklike.

Raw or pasteurized whole cow's milk is used. Curing takes two to three months. A typical five-pound brick measures 10 by five by three inches. Brick cheese slices without crumbling and is popular in sandwiches.

BRICK TEA

This traditional Chinese product consists of tea leaf and tea dust compressed into small bricks or slabs. These are scored by indented lines into small, easily separated squares which expand in the cup or pot when covered with boiling water. Alternatively, the brick may be rubbed into a fine powder and mixed with milk, butter, salt and herbs to form a smooth, oily, brown liquid resembling cocoa. It is most popular in Tibet, parts of Central Asia and Siberia.

See also: **Tea.**

BRIDONNES

Fruit of a tree, *Garcinia indica*, of tropical Asia, which has a pleasant acid flavor, it is closely related to the **mangosteen** and is often cultivated. Bridonnes is eaten raw or made into a jelly or syrup.

BRIE

A soft, French cow's milk cheese that originated centuries ago in the district of La Brie in the French Department of Seine-et-Marne, Brie is a celebrated cheese. In the 15th century, it was a favorite with Charles d'Orleans, father of Louis XII. In 1848, Talleyrand took it with him to the Congress of Vienna, where it won the title, "King of Cheeses," in a competition with 60 others from participating countries.

Brie, like **camembert,** is ripened by molds, bacteria and probably yeast that grow on the surface of the cheese. It has a very pronounced odor and a delicately sharp taste. It has no rind, but in ripening develops a reddish crust with traces of white. The interior should be pale yellow and creamy, but not runny.

Melun, Coulombiers and Meaux are centers of production in the department, and quality varies depending on whether the milk used is whole, partly skimmed or skimmed. The best is reputed to be *Brie de Meaux*, which is full fat, and in season from November to May. Brie is also made elsewhere in France and in other countries, including the United States.

Three sizes are customary, large (16-inch diameter, six pounds); medium (12-inch diameter, three pounds), and small (five-to-eight-inch diameter, one pound).

Brie is perishable and must be refrigerated, although it should be removed from the refrigerator at least three hours before serving.

BRIE DE MELUN

See **Melun.**

BRIER

Several species of this woody or herbaceous vine, *Smilax*, have edible rootstocks. These include golden brier *(S. auriculata)* and Beyrich's brier *(S. beyrichii)* of eastern North America; saw greenbrier *(S. bonanox)* and laurel brier *(S. laurifolia)* of the Southeast, and the long-stalked greenbrier *(S. pseudo-china)* of the eastern United States and the West Indies. The roots are typically dried and ground into flour for bread-making, or into meal for porridge or gruel.

BRILL

This European flatfish, *Rhombus laevis*, is considered second only to the **turbot** in gastronomic excellence. The brill is a bottom dweller, with both eyes placed on its upper (left) side, which is brownish in color. Its underside is white. The brill tends to be much smaller and more oval in shape than the turbot and has smooth scales. It seldom exceeds 16 inches in length. The Atlantic brill is considered the best of several species, but the Mediterranean brill also has good flavor. The flesh is light and firm, and is at its best from April to August. Brill is often baked whole or filleted, and then it may be prepared according to any one of three score different recipes.

Essentially a cold water fish, the Atlantic brill is not found in North American waters, barred from migrating by the warm waters of the Gulf Stream. A quite similar fish, however, is the petrale *(Eupsetta*

Brie

Brioche

jordani), which is often called a brill. It is a good food fish, with an average market weight of between three and eight pounds. This latter fish sometimes appears on restaurant menus masquerading as "Dover sole." The brill in Scotland is known as the "bonnet fleuk," and in the west of England as kike, and bret. The French word for brill is *barbue*.

BRINE

This solution of salt and water is used to preserve or pickle foods. It may be a matter of preserving the color or fruit while they are being prepared for cooking, in which case the solution is a simple one. In order to pickle vegetables or fish, sugar, herbs and spices are sometimes added, and in the case of meat, saltpeter, which helps preserve the desired red color.

BRINSEN

See **Brinza.**

BRINZA

Also BRINSEN, LIPTAUER, BRYNDZA. This soft Hungarian cheese is made from ewe's milk. It has a sharp, salty flavor and a buttery texture. It originated in Liptow province, northern Hungary, but is made in many villages of the Carpathian Mountains of Hungary and Czechoslovakia. The curd is prepared daily by herdsmen and collected weekly by the factory, where it is salted, cured and packed in casks and jars. This gives it a pickled quality. It is known by many local names including *Landoch*, *Zips*, *Siebenburger*, *Neusohl*, *Altsohl*, *Klencz* and *Ftinoporino*.

BRIOCHE

A light-textured roll made from yeast dough enriched with butter and eggs, the brioche is French in origin, but has been naturalized in other countries. The brioche is slightly sweet and may be considered either a rich bread or a plain cake. By adjusting the amount of sugar in the recipe, it may be used as a casing for either sweet or savory fillings. Typically, the French might breakfast on a brioche, served hot with butter and a cup of *cafe au lait*. The brioche is usually formed in the shape of a roll with a small topknot *(brioche a tete)*, but the crown shape is also common *(brioche en couronne)* as is the *brioche mousselline*, a small column, somewhat resembling a chef's hat.

The French have been making brioches for centuries, and they disagree on the origin of the word. Some authorities maintain that the bread was first made in the district of *Brie*, which is famous for its cheese. In former times, it is said, cheese was used in the recipe for the brioche. Other authorities suggest that the word comes from two old French words, *bris* (meaning to break) and *hocher* (to stir) run together as brioche. Brioche in the figurative sense means "blunder" in French, usage stemming from a custom among musicians of assessing a fine against a colleague who played out of tune. The money was then spent on brioches.

See also: **Bread.**

BRIOLER

See **Westphalia Sour-Milk Cheese.**

BRIONNE

See **Chayote.**

BRISKET

A cut of meat from the breast of an animal, usually beef or mutton, brisket in Europe is a rib cut, including half the breast bone and parts of five ribs. In the United States it starts higher up and includes part of the shoulder. In beef, the meat consists of layers of lean and fat. It is often salted and pressed for corn beef. For salt or fresh, moist methods of cooking are appropriate, such as boiling, braising or stewing. Brisket makes an economical roast, with the upper part (toward the shoulder) leaner than the lower part.

BRIZECON

See **Reblochon.**

BROAD BEAN

Also FAVA BEAN, WINDSOR BEAN. This broad plump bean, native to the Mediterranean basin, has been eaten throughout Europe and the Middle East since prehistoric times. The broad bean *(Vicia faba)* somewhat resembles the **lima bean,** but is rounder in shape. The pod is long, tough and has an interior lining with a thick, loose texture. When half grown, the broad bean is sometimes eaten in the pod like snow peas. These beans have a fine taste and are prepared in a number of ways. They may be pureed, served with a sauce or creamed. They mature in the summer months and are a frequent accompaniment to ham or bacon. They are also dried or frozen.

In Italy, this bean is called *fava*. It was well known to ancient Romans as well as to other ancient peoples of the Mediterranean area. It was a staple food, yet had a certain aristocratic aura about it, since the noble Roman house of Fabius took its name from this bean. Beans were used as voting tokens in elections, and the phrase "abstain from beans" meant keep out of politics. Despite their popularity, they were considered unlucky. The Romans connected them with death, and the priests of Jupiter were forbidden to touch them or even mention them. The Greeks had religious reservations against them too and thought them harmful to the vision. A strange illness among Mediterranean people, called favism, is associated with broad beans. It is a hemolytic disorder brought on by eating the beans or by inhaling their scent, particularly if they are grown on marshy ground. Favism is believed to afflict only those with a hereditary predisposition to it, like an allergy.

This bean was the only common bean known in Europe before the discovery of the New World, and was a staple of the peasantry during the Middle Ages. It is still widely grown in Europe, and is particularly popular in England. The older varieties of broad bean did not adapt well to the New World, although New World beans of the *Phaseolus* genus (kidney, lima, etc.) were readily naturalized in Europe. Only recently has the broad bean gained some foothold in the United States, where it is known as the fava bean.

The fresh beans are about 85 percent water, with 5 percent protein and 4 percent carbohydrate, and contain about 40 calories per 3½ ounces (100 grams). In dried form, they consist of 21 percent protein, 53 percent carbohydrate, and 3 percent fat and contain 332 calories per 3½ ounces (100 grams).

See also: **Kidney Bean.**

Broad bean
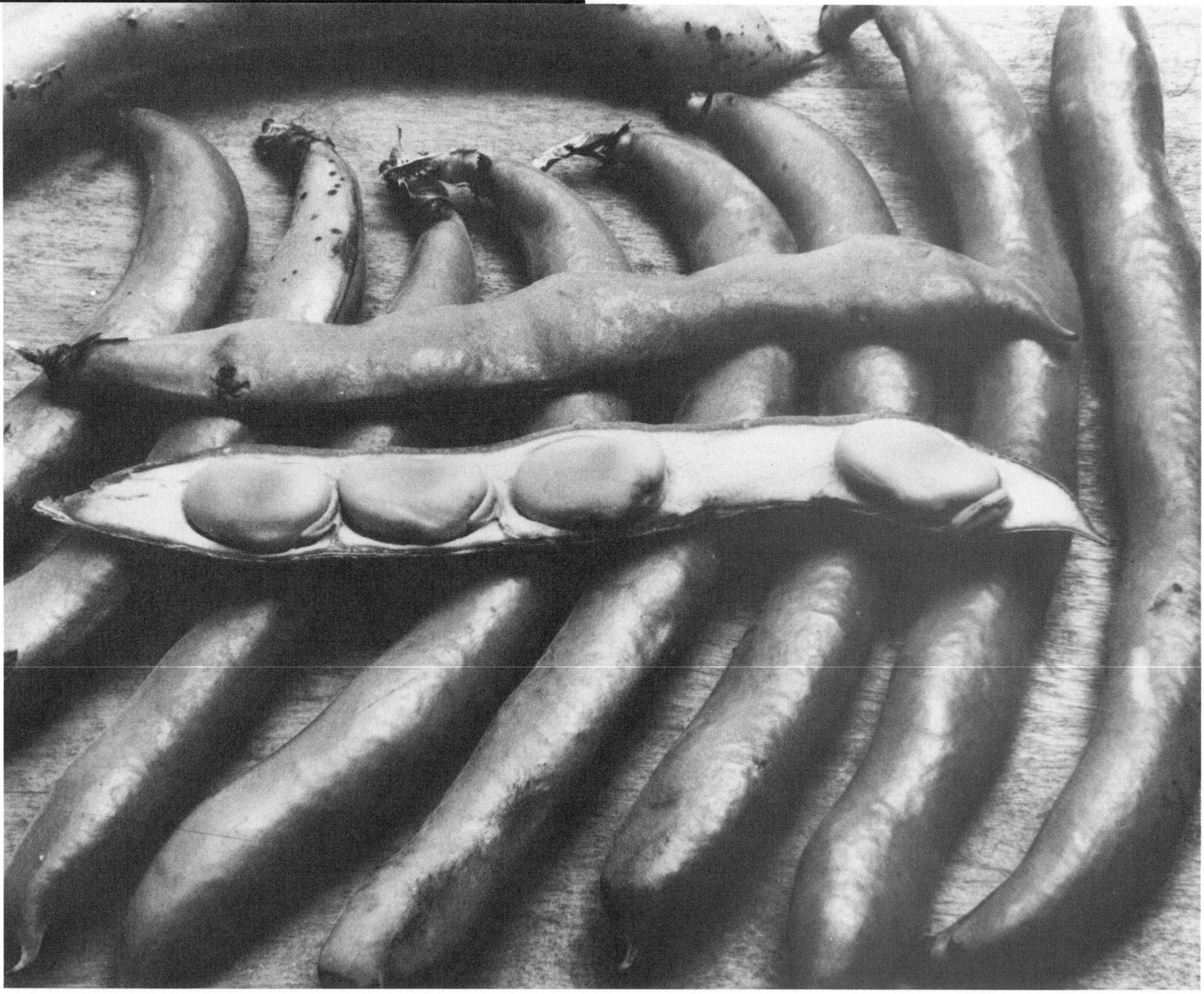

BROCCIO

Also BROUSE. Two cheeses are called *broccio.* The first is a whey cheese like **ricotta.** Fresh and sour whey are mixed and brought to a near boil. Coagulum rises to the surface (it is chiefly albumin) and is skimmed off and drained. The cheese must be eaten very soon because it will only keep for a day or two. Salting improves the keeping qualities.

The second is a creamy, sour milk cheese made from goat or ewe's milk in Corsica. It has a slightly salty, delicate flavor and is in season from April to November. Broccio is used to prepare such Corsican delicacies as *falulella,* a cheesecake, and *fidene,* a special cake.

BROCCOLI

This member of the cabbage family was a favorite with ancient Romans, its name deriving from the Latin, *bracchium,* meaning arm or branch. Drusas, son of the Emperor Tiberius, is said to have provoked his father's ire by overeating boiled broccoli, a minor vice, it would seem, since broccoli is highly esteemed for its food value.

Many varieties are available, mostly conforming to two types: the sprouting, or Italian type, and the heading type. The former, sometimes known as Calabrese, has a thick green stalk, growing to about two feet in height, and culminating in a branching head of bud clusters. The latter somewhat resembles the **cauliflower.**

The heads are usually dark green, but can range from white through dark purple. To ensure freshness, the buds should be tightly closed, and the stalk easy to pierce with a fingernail.

The stalk, buds and leaves are all edible. Broccoli is usually boiled, and served with butter or a hollandaise sauce. To speed cooking, the stalk can be split in two. It has a medium strong flavor and a strong odor when being cooked. This can be controlled somewhat by adding a piece of bread to the cooking water.

BROOKLIME

Also WATER PIMPERNEL. An herbaceous plant that grows wild in damp places in various parts of Europe and temperate Asia, brooklime *(Veronica becabunga)* is also known as water pimpernel. It resembles watercress in appearance and taste and may be substituted for it in salads. Its leaves and stems also make a passable spinach.

BROOK TROUT

See **Char.**

BROOM

A flowering shrub native to Europe but naturalized in the United States, broom *(Cytisus scoparius)* is sought for its leaves and buds, which are pickled in vinegar and salt and used as capers.

BROTH

See **Soup.**

BROTOLA DE ROCA

See **Blenny.**

BROUSE

See **Broccio.**

BROWN-BANDED CATSHARK

This Australian catshark, *Hemiscyllium punctatum*, is considered to be an excellent food fish. It frequents inshore shallows and off-shore banks of south Queensland to the Torres Straits and of the Northern Territory. Young specimens are banded, but adults are a uniform reddish brown or fawn. Large fish reach a length of 3½ feet. The flesh is well flavored and firm.

BROWN BUTTER SAUCE

Butter is flavored with herbs, capers or lemon and cooked until it bubbles. It is served hot with broiled meat, fish, cabbage, broccoli and asparagus.

See also: **Sauce.**

BROWN FUNGUS

See **Black Tree Fungus.**

BROWN SAUCE

See **Espagnole Sauce.**

BRUGNON

A peach hybrid that resembles a red plum or an apricot. It is grown in France and is propagated by cuttings rather than by seed. It tastes somewhat like a nectarine and the term "brugnon" is often used for nectarine as well as this fruit. The brugnon is sweet, but tart, and makes a good dessert fruit. It is in season from late July to late August.

BRUSH CHERRY

Also RED MYRTLE. Edible berry of an Australian tree, *Syzygium paniculatum*, brush cherry has been planted in Florida and California. The fruit varies in color from rose to purple and is used to make jellies.

BRUSSELS SPROUTS

These are miniature cabbages that sprout from a long stalk, which is topped by a canopy of leaves. Each sprout measures from one-half inch to an inch and one-half in diameter. The plant is named for the capital of Belgium, where it originated in the 13th century.

The sprouts have neither a heart, like the common cabbage, nor an edible bud, like the cauliflower. Instead, each has a mass of concave leaves closely and compactly wrapped around one another.

The smaller the head, the more delicate the flavor. The larger heads have a more cabbagy taste. The best specimens are bright green and firm to the touch. They are a good source of vitamins A and C, and are in season from September through January. The usual methods of cooking are boiling or steaming.

BRYNDZA

See **Brinza.**

BRYONIA

Also BRYONY. About ten species of this climbing, ornamental vine are grown in Europe and western Asia. Two of them have tuberous roots that have been used to make flavoring bitters. They are the white bryony *(Bryonia alba)* and the red bryony *(B. dioica)*. Both plants have berries, which are not eaten.

BUAL

See **Madeira.**

BUCKEYE

Also HORSE CHESTNUT. This hardy tree of North America, southeastern Europe and eastern Asia bears a starchy, edible seed fruit. Three species of buckeye are most suitable: the European horse chestnut *(Aesculus hippocastanum)*, the California buckeye *(A. californica)* and the red buckeye *(A. pavia)*. The seeds can be made into a very nutritious flour, but first must be treated to remove tannin and glucosides. They are first boiled and then macerated before being milled. The flour has been used to make bread, but apparently only native Americans have eaten horse chestnut flour with any regularity.

BUCKSHORN PLANTAIN

Also CROWFOOT PLANTAIN. A variety of plantain *(Plantago coronopus)* found originally in Europe, Asia and North Africa, it is now also found in Australia and New Zealand. Its leaves may be eaten in salads.

BUCKWHEAT

Buckwheat is an herbaceous plant which, though not a true cereal, produces a grainlike fruit that looks, tastes and acts like a cereal and is accepted as such on the gastronomic level. Its scientific designation, *Fagopyrum*, gives a clue to its appearance. *Fagus* means beech tree, and *pyrum* means cereal. Grains of buckwheat look like tiny beechnuts. The English term "buckwheat" derives from the German, *buchweizen*, meaning "beechwheat."

Buckwheat originated in Asia, specifically in a wide area between Lake Baikal in Siberia and Manchuria. The two most widely grown species are

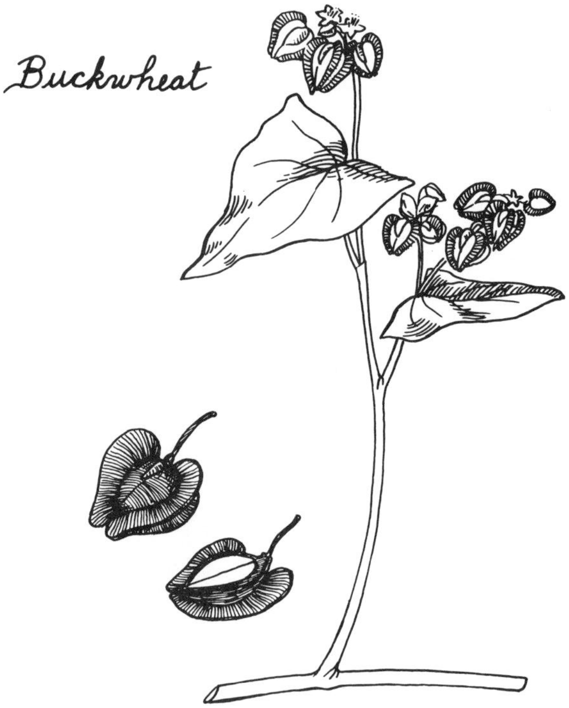

common buckwheat *(Fagopyrum esculentum)* and tartar buckwheat *(Fagopyrum tataricum)*. Cultivation of buckwheat spread to China, Japan and India early on, but it was not until the late Middle Ages that buckwheat made its appearance in Europe. Its cultivation in northern and eastern Europe is generally attributed to Tartars, while in Western and southern Europe the Moors are given credit.

The French, Italian and Spanish all call it saracen wheat, "saracen" being the general term for Arabs or all Moslems during the time of the Crusades. Another explanation for this terminology is buckwheat's dark color, recalling the darker complexion of the Moors. At any rate, there is no evidence that ancient Greeks and Romans knew about buckwheat, and there is no mention of it in Europe until the mid-15th century.

Buckwheat is at home in cold, damp, windy climates. It is used more as animal fodder than human food, except in certain areas of harsh climate, where buckwheat does better than other grains. These areas include Finland, regions of France, such as lower Normandy, Brittany and the Massif Central (Central Plateau), Styria in Austria and the South Tyrol area, which includes parts of Austria and northern Italy. In the United States, it is greatly appreciated by the Pennsylvania Dutch, who admire its heavy, coarse, rib-sticking qualities.

Buckwheat has been most successful in noodles and pancakes. The ubiquitous *soba* of Japan are buckwheat noodles, as are the Tyrolean or black noodles, which have an admixture of rye. Buckwheat griddle cakes, which also contain wheat middlings, are very popular in the United States, especially with butter and maple syrup. Little Finnish pancakes, large crepes of Brittany, and sweet *bourriolles* of the French Auvergne also rely on buckwheat as a main ingredient. *Kasha*, or buckwheat groats, are a staple food in eastern Europe. They are cooked and served like rice. Buckwheat is occasionally used to make bread, but the loaf produced tends to be dry, crumbly and tasteless. Bees are greatly attracted to buckwheat's pink and white blossoms, and buckwheat honey is a standard item in health-food stores.

BUFFALO

This type of ox *(Bubalus buffelus)*—larger and less docile than the common ox—is found in hot, swampy areas of Asia and Africa. The buffalo was first domesticated in India, then its use spread to Malaysia, Indonesia, the Philippines, Africa and elsewhere. It is also common in Italy. Buffalo have massive, curved horns and splayed feet, adapted to wading. They are used as draft animals, and their milk is good to drink. It also makes excellent cheese and a type of butter, called *ghee* in India.

Buffalo live chiefly on aquatic grass and plants. Their flesh is beeflike, but tougher, and is rarely eaten. It has a sweet taste. In Africa, there are wild species, which are larger than domesticated buffalo and quite savage. An example is the cape buffalo *(Bubalus caffer)*, which is found in South Africa.

The name "buffalo" is often applied, in error, to the American bison, which is an unrelated animal.

See also: **Bison.**

BUFFALO BERRY

This fruit of a thorny shrub, *Shepherdia argentea*, native to the American Midwest is especially plentiful in the Dakotas, Minnesota and Kansas. The plant reaches a height of 18 feet and has silvery leaves. Its fruit is red or yellow, about one-quarter inch across and round. It has a tart but pleasant flavor. A closely related, but smaller, species, *S. canadensis*, produces a similar berry, whose taste is insipid.

The buffalo berry was a great favorite with native Americans. They served them as preserves with buffalo meat, or dried with starchy dishes—much as one would raisins—to sweeten and flavor them. George Catlin, an American artist who visited the Mandan tribe in the 1830s, left this description of one dish:

> *[It] . . . was filled with a kind of paste or pudding, made of the flour of the "pomme blanche" [See* **Biscuitroot]**, *as the French call it, a delicious turnip of the prairie, finely flavored with the buffalo berries, which are collected in great quantities in this country, and used with divers dishes in cooking, as we in civilized countries use dried currants, which they very much resemble.*

Buffalo berries are cultivated today to make preserves, tarts, pies and jellies. Because of their hardiness, they are also grown as an ornamental hedge plant. They are also called soapberries, Nebraska currants and rabbit berries.

BUFFALO COD

See **Blue Cod.**

BUFFALO CURRANT

Two species of American currant are known by this name, one of the Midwest, *Ribes odoratum*, and one of the West, *R. aureum*. The plants are similar in appearance, growing to six feet tall and having bright yellow flowers and black berries. *Ribes odoratum* is the one usually grown for its fruit, and *R. aureum* for its ornamental value. *R. odoratum* has a distinctive odor, which pleases some people and offends others. The fruit is at its best when made into jams, jellies or pies. *R. aureum* is also known as golden currant or Missouri currant.

BUFFALO FISH

The humpbacked appearance of this large, widely eaten, freshwater fish, *Megastomatobus cyprinella*, of the Mississippi Valley accounts for its name. There are three main varieties: the common, or big-mouthed; the small-mouthed and the black buffalo fish. It is caught in large rivers, shallow lakes and even bayous and may reach a weight of 50 pounds and a length of three feet. The flesh of the larger varieties is quite coarse. It is usually taken in the three to five pound size, and in this case the flesh is much finer as well as wholesome and nutritious.

Buffalo fish is a member of the **sucker** family. It may be baked, poached or sauteed and is good smoked.

BUFFALO THORN

Also CAPE THORN. A small tree of the jujube genus, *Ziziphus mucronata*, indigenous to tropical and southern Africa, its datelike fruit is yellow to reddish brown and three-quarter inch across. Though edible, it is not considered very palatable. The plant is also used medicinally and its seeds are made into rosary beads, used to count repeated prayers, especially in the Catholic Church.

BUFFEL-HEADED DUCK

This is a wild duck, *Anas bucephala*, of North America. The fullness of its feathers makes its head appear abnormally large. It has a short, blue bill and looks like the canvas back. It is smaller, though, and not nearly as good to eat. The taste of its flesh varies, depending on the type of fish it feeds on. It is prepared as other wild duck.

BUGLOSS

Also ALKANET, ANCHUSA. The Bugloss *(Anchusa officinalis)* is a small European shrub, with thick leaves and bright blue flowers. The flowers may be eaten as salad. Leaves may be eaten when prepared as spinach.

In the British Isles, the common name for *anchusa* is ox tongue. In France, there is a legend that King Louis XIII enjoyed these flowers as salad and regarded them as a tonic.

See also: **Alkanet.**

BULBOUS CHERVIL

See **Chervil.**

BULGUR

Also BULGHUR. A type of cracked wheat favored by the ancient Persians, it is still a staple food in the Middle East. In Turkey, it is often used in place of rice for pilaf. It may be mixed with raisins, peas or pine nuts and used to stuff baby lamb or chicken. Bulgur and nuts, or bulgur and lamb meat, are cooked in olive oil and used to stuff eggplant. It is a major ingredient of ***kibbeh*** in Syria and Lebanon.

Bulgur is also made in the United States. It is a specially processed wheat product. Made of partly debranned, parboiled wheat, it is used either whole or cracked like rice, in soups, main dishes and desserts. It is a popular product in health-food stores.

BULLACE

A type of plum, *Prunus insititia*, it is not often cultivated but is found in the wild state in England, southern Europe, North Africa and Asia Minor. The fruit is usually blue black, but there are yellow green varieties. The bullace is closely related to the **sloe,** but is larger and more palatable raw. It is also closely related to the damson, but rounder and without its pleasant, rough taste.

In some parts of the United States, bullace is synonymous with damson. In northern regions, the bullace is left on the tree until after the first frost in order to sweeten the taste. It is sweeter in warmer regions, but even so, is most often used in jams, jellies and pies. It also cans well and is used to flavor liqueurs, such as bullace gin.

The term, spelled *"bullis,"* is used in the American South for a wild purple grape, which is juicy but high in tannin. It is used for jams and jellies. Bullace is also the name of an ocean fish, *Larimus fasciatus*, of the same region. In the Caribbean, bullace plum is another name for the ***ginep.***

BULLHEAD

See **Catfish.**

BULLNUT

Also BIG BUD HICKORY, MOCKERNUT. The fruit of a variety of hickory tree, *Carya tomentosa*, it is found in the eastern United States from Massachusetts to Florida and west to Texas. The tree reaches a height of 90 feet. Its nuts are oblong and rounded. They are eaten in the area of cultivation.

See also: **Hickory Nut.**

BULLOCK'S HEART

Also CUSTARD APPLE. A sweet, pulpy fruit of the American tropics, bullock's heart *(Annona reticulata)*

belongs to the same genus as the cherimoya, soursop and sweetsop. All of these are referred to in one place or another as the "custard apple" because of the soft sweetness of their flesh. The bullock's heart is one of the largest of the group and has been widely transplanted in tropical Asia. The fruit is generally heart-shaped and has smooth, reddish brown skin with hexagonal markings. It may measure up to five inches across, and weigh eight to 10 pounds. It is usually the size of a small **pineapple** which it resembles. The pulp is soft, yellowish and sweet, but insipid to the taste.

On his first visit to the New World, Columbus was presented with bullock's heart, which he had never seen before. It is still rarely seen by dwellers of temperate zones, because it does not travel well. Some bullock's heart from California, Florida and the West Indies is exported to Europe. In France, it is usually served raw, peeled and sliced, and perhaps steeped in white wine. It may also be fried in batter.

BULLOO

Also EMU APPLE. This fruit of an Australian tree, *Owenia adicula*, is eaten in some parts of the country. It has a reddish color and a refreshingly acid flavor.

BULRUSH

See **Cattail.**

BULUNGU

The fruit of an African tree, *Cararium edule*, it resembles a plum and is violet in color.

BUN

A small leavened bread, roll or cake, it may be round, square or oblong. In the United States buns are usually unsweetened and used to encase such traditional sandwiches as the hamburger and the hot dog. Buns in Britain, however, are usually sweetened and come in many varieties, often named after places, such as London, Bath and Chelsea.

These sweetcakes have a venerable history, which some authorities trace back to ancient Egypt and Greece. Among the Egyptians it was traditional to offer small round cakes to the goddess of the moon. They were marked on top with a sign representing the horns of an ox. This bun may be the remote ancestor of the hot cross bun, which the English consume in great numbers at Easter. On the other hand, its origin may have been with the Anglo Saxons who honored the name day of their goddess, Eastre, in the spring with an offering of heavily spiced buns. Christianity later assimilated this custom, but updated the marking on the bun by making it a cross, a Christian symbol. The word "bun" itself is believed to derive from the Greeks, who made a small, sacred cake, which they called the *bous* (ox), whose accusative form, *boun*, survived as bun. The Romans too had their sacred buns, which they sold outside temples; the crosslike markings on these buns are believed simply to have facilitated their even division.

English hot cross buns are eaten on Good Friday. Traditionally, the cross is believed to ward off evil. For centuries it was the custom to retain a hot cross bun all year long, hanging it from the ceiling as a lucky charm. Cross buns are large circular cakes, often containing currants, raisins or peel. On Good Friday morning in many English towns they are hawked in the streets.

The Bath bun is also a sweet, yeast cake, which contains candied peel, but it has an irregular shape and is sugar-coated on top. This bun came to the fore in the 18th century when the city of Bath was a very fashionable spa frequented by the likes of Beau Brummel and the Prince Regent. The Bath bun shared its popularity with the Sally Lunn, a teacake in muffin style, which also originated in Bath. It is said that its creator, Sally Lunn, owned a tea shop in the city. Other authorities doubt that she ever existed, and maintain the teacake came across the Channel from France where it was called the *solimeme.* This bears a remarkable resemblance to the Sally Lunn.

The Chelsea bun is square and closely resembles the American cinnamon roll. In Scotland, the black bun and the currant bun are rich fruit cakes. A round loaf of plain bread is called "bun" in Northern Ireland.

See also: **Bread.**

BUNCHOSA

This fruit of a small tree, *Bunchosia armeniaca*, of the Andean region is sometimes eaten. The bunchosa is round, one to two inches in diameter and has a single seed and greenish skin. The white or cream-colored pulp has a sweet taste.

BUNTING

The term is used for several species of wading birds of the genus *Emberiza* that belongs to the finch family. These birds are found in marshes in many parts of the world and include the common bunting, the snow bunting and the rice bunting or **reedbird.** In Europe, their flesh, though gamy, is considered gourmet fare.

BUPHTHALMUM

This Vietnamese plant, *Buphthalmum olaraceum,* of the oxeye genus has young, aromatic leaves that are dried and used as a condiment, especially with fish.

BURBOT

In Europe it may be either of two fresh water fishes, genus *Lota lota,* which are allied to the cod. In America the species is *Lota maculosa,* but it is ordinarily called eelpout or ling. It inhabits the Great Lakes, northern New England and the Canadian lakes.

Burbot is not a large factor in commercial fishing but is taken mainly by sport fishermen. It is excellent food, however, and may be prepared like cod. The French serve it stuffed and prepared *a la creole.* They also prepare the liver by poaching as one would soft fish roe.

See also: **Cod Burbot.**

BURDOCK

Also GOBO. A weedy plant with large leaves and burrs, burdock *(Arctium lappa)* grows wild in Europe and North America. With the exception of the burrs, all parts of the plant are edible, yet it has received wide acceptance only in Scotland and Japan, where it is assiduously cultivated. Spring shoots are cooked like asparagus; the mature stalk is peeled and boiled in salted water, and then served with a dressing. It has a starchy consistency like potatoes, but is not so nourishing; young, fresh leaves are added to salads, and tender young roots are peeled, sliced and boiled.

Through careful cultivation, the Japanese have improved the plant. The root, which they call *gobo,* is longer, smoother and more refined. It is harvested after only two or three months in the ground, before it branches and becomes woody. They use *gobo* as an all-purpose seasoner, and it often appears on sukiyaki.

In earlier times in the West, burdock had a great reputation as a medicinal plant. Poultices were made of it to reduce swellings from the stings of wasps and bees. Internally, an infusion of burdock was considered curative in cases of gout and diabetes. In Scotland it was used to prepare burdock ale and burdock wine. Burdock burrs are sometimes called bachelor buttons.

BURGALL

See **Cunner.**

BURGOS CHEESE

This popular Spanish cheese originating from the province of Burgos is prepared from ewe's milk and has a soft texture.

BURGUNDY CHEESE

Also FROMAGE DE BOURGOGNE. A soft, white, French cheese, it is produced in loaves weighing four pounds.

BURGUNDY WINES

One of the most famous wine-growing regions of France and therefore of the world, it is the home of **Chablis,** the red and white Burgundies, the wine of **Beaune,** Macon, **Meursault** and the **Beaujolais.** The former duchy of Burgundy is divided now into several *departments,* but extends roughly from the Chablis area southeast of Paris to Lyons in the south and east to the slopes of the Jura Mountains. The great vineyards of Burgundy, however, are centered in the *Cote d'Or* (the slope of gold), which include those of Beaune and **Nuits-St.-Georges.** The grapes, for the most part, face southeast on these gentle ridges in the "gold" of the sun. The area is ancient. The Romans brought with them the art of viticulture, though native grapes may already have been in cultivation. Charlemagne, an early father of the vine, planted vineyards on the *Cote d'Or* in the eighth century.

The great wines of Burgundy are essentially from two vine stocks, Pinot for the reds, and Chardonnay for the whites; though farther south—near Lyons, beyond the confines of historical Burgundy—the Gamay grape supplies the well-known Beaujolais. A white grape, Aligote, also produces a good dry white Burgundy. Unlike **Bordeaux wines,** which are grown on large estates or *chateaux* owned by syndicates, Burgundy wines come from vineyards which are often the property of several individuals. This can result in wine of great variance from year to year or even within the harvest from a single vineyard. Over the centuries, therefore, the French government has evolved a rather complicated legal system to ensure the quality of the nation's most famous product. These are the laws of *appellations d'origine.* Only the wines so codified by this system can legally bear the names of their region, district or specific vineyard. They are then labeled *Appellation Controlee.* Primarily, this system determines that blended and unblended wines be so designated and labeled. (A "blended wine" is mixed with wine from different years or different vineyards.)

The northern half of the *Cote d'Or* is world-famous for its production of red wines, with excellent white wines from the Cote de Beaune gradually supplanting them in the south. The spectrum of Burgundy wine concentrated in this area affords, then, a unique and delightful tour—from the darker, heavier reds in the north, gradually becoming lighter and smoother in the wines of **Pommard,** until they are totally replaced by the white Meursault and **Montrachet.**

Over the years Burgundy has supplied France with almost half of the wine consumed in that country, and has been first in the production of the *appellation controlee* wines sold and distributed outside of France, with nearby Switzerland and the United States among the major customers.

BURMEISTER CHEESE

This brand of cheese is similar to **brick cheese,** with a ripe, soft consistency. It is made in Wisconsin in the United States.

BURNET

Also GARDEN BURNET. A spring herb belonging to the rose family, burnet *(Poterium sanguisorba* or *Sanguisorba minor)* has a cucumberlike flavor. With small purple flowers and oval leaves, it is useful only in the spring and during the fall renewal when the leaves are tender. Like **borage** it goes well in drinks and salads, and both leaves and seed are used to flavor vinegar. It seldom makes an appearance in American and British cooking, but the French and Italians use it in butters and sauces. Burnet has an astringent quality, and 17-century herbalists maintained that its presence in a cup of claret refreshed the spirit and drove away melancholy.

BURRINI CHEESE

See **Buttiri.**

BUSH APPLE

A kind of plum, *Heinsia pulchella*, found in West Africa and Australia, the fruit has a pleasant flavor and may range in color from yellow to red.

BUSH TEA

A palatable beverage resembling China tea in taste, it is made by infusing the dried leaves of the South African shrub *Cyclopia genistoides.*

Bustard

BUSTARD

The great, or bearded, bustard *(Otis tarda)*, the largest land bird of Europe, is now all but extinct in England, France and other Western European countries. The largest specimens stand 3½ feet high and weigh up to 35 pounds. Its flesh is considered a great delicacy, and so it has been hunted assiduously for centuries.

The ancient Romans dubbed it *avis tarda* ("slow bird") because of its characteristic movements. Being large and heavy, it was slow to flight, needing a long takeoff run. Often hunting dogs could catch it before it became airborne. Consequently, it frequented open fields, where predators could be spotted a long way off. In Europe, urban encroachment on open spaces and improved weaponry gradually led to its extinction. The Roman name for the bird became *austarde* in Gallic, *outarde* in French and finally "bustard" in English. Another species, the little bustard *(Tetrax tetrax)*, is still considered a fine game bird. Its flesh is greatly esteemed, particularly the drumsticks.

The European bustard has many cousins in Asia, Africa and Australia. The largest species, *Choriotis kori*, is found in Senegal, where it is called *korossobounti.* Larger specimens of this bird stand five feet high. Close relatives are the *Choriotis arabs*, which inhabits the region just south of the Sahara, and the *pauuw* of South Africa. Writers compare the taste of the breast meat of the African bustard to the white meat of chicken, and the drumsticks to golden plover or hare. In France, a favorite way of preparing the little bustard is to roast it in butter and serve with a red wine sauce.

BUSTER

This term is used to describe a crab that is in a phase between hard and soft shell, i.e., the shell is loosened but not yet shed. It is considered a treat and is prepared by frying in batter. The word may also be used for a soft-shelled crab.

BUTCHER'S BROOM

See **Ruscus.**

BUTIFARRA

This fatty pork sausage is made in Spain and Latin America. Fat port is minced with white wine, spiced with cloves, nutmeg, salt and pepper, then shaped into links.

See also: **Chorizo, Salchichon, Sausage.**

BUTTEN KASE

See **Holstein Skim-Milk Cheese.**

BUTTER

Particles of fat are separated from whole milk or cream and solidified by churning. The product, butter, is oily, thick and usually yellow and may be salted or not. It is an ancient substance, used in all probability by all peoples who reached the pastoral stage. Nomads have prepared it from many different kinds of milk, including that of ewes, goats, mares, asses, buffaloes and camels. Nowadays, it is mostly made from cow's milk. The best butter is composed of at least 80 percent fat, and between 12 percent and 16 percent water. Of all natural fats, it is the best tasting and the most easily digested. In cooking, it is the best for enriching cakes, pastries and sauces. Indeed, it does quite well by itself as a sauce, e.g., over vegetables.

Butter used to be produced on small farms, and it was customary to start with aged milk, which had been allowed to stand for two or three days while the cream separated and it became slightly sour. This sourness enhanced the taste of butter, provided conditions were right. Since the advent of efficient refrigeration, large creameries have become the rule. There cream is separated from sweet milk in a centrifugal separator and then pasteurized. A special lactic acid starter is then added to the cream to recapture the slightly acid flavor. The butter is then churned and usually salted. If the butter's color is not judged yellow enough—a marketing essential—color is added. The artificial coloring is from carotene, annatto or marigolds.

As a rule, it takes nine quarts of milk to make one pound of butter. According to U.S. government standards, butter is rated on a scale of 100, which breaks down as follows: flavor, 45 points; body, 25 points; color, 15 points; salt, 10 points and packaging, 5 points. The grades are AA, A, B, and C, with the first scoring 93 or above, and the last equivalent to 89. The lowest grade is used only in baking and food processing. Butter which has a rank smell and a sour taste is said to be rancid, a condition caused by the formation of butyric acid. To avoid this condition, butter should be refrigerated at all times when not in use, preferably in a separate compartment of the refrigerator, which will prevent contamination by other food odors.

Butter was well known in antiquity, used often as a medicine for skin injuries, such as burns, and as a food. It is frequently referred to in the Bible, as for example in Psalms 7:21: "The words of his mouth were smoother than butter, but war was in his heart." When Isaiah prophesied the Messiah, he put it this way: "Behold, a virgin shall conceive, and bear a son, and shall call him Immanuel. Butter and honey shall he eat." Among ancient Greeks and Romans butter was a scarce commodity. Greek land did not lend itself to cow pasturage, and the milk obtained from sheep and goats was either drunk immediately or made into cheese, which was a lot less perishable. Roman cows, the *chianina* of Tuscany, were not milk cows, but made excellent beef. Butter became much more plentiful in the Middle Ages, and it is believed to be the Scandinavians who first used it extensively as food and introduced it to the rest of Europe. At first it was regarded with suspicion. The people of Paris, for example, were advised by a physician in 1648 that butter produced leprosy, a disease mistakenly thought to come from eating spoiled meat or fish. It was logical, since butter in those days was more often rancid than not.

Butter has figured in many memorable phrases in English, e.g., Jonathan Swift's, "She looks as if butter wouldn't melt in her mouth," and Sir Walter Scott's, "Fine words butter no parsnips." The butterfly got its name from an old belief that a witch assumed the form of a butterfly to steal milk and butter.

BUTTER BEAN

See **Lima Bean.**

BUTTER CHEESE

See **Bel Paese.**

BUTTERFISH

Also DOLLARFISH. This small food fish, *Stromateus triacanthus*, is found in great numbers off the Atlantic coast of the United States during the summer months. A member of the mackerel family, the butterfish more resembles the **pompano,** with its flat body, oval shape, blunt head and small mouth. It has a deep olive back with dark bars and generally attains a length of eight-11 inches, and a weight of one-half to one pound. Its flesh is highly regarded for its distinctive flavor and firmness. As a rule, the butterfish is quickly sauteed or broiled. It is also known as the gunnel, the dollarfish and the harvest fish.

A smaller fish, the *Peprilus paru*, goes by the same name, and is quite good to eat. Butterfish is also a name for the California pompano *(Palometa simillima)* found off the coast of central California during the summer.

BUTTERKASE

A full-cream, unsalted, soft cheese made in Austria, its taste is mild and slightly sour.

BUTTERMILK

Two commercial products are sold under this title. One is the natural fluid, that is, the liquid remaining after churning out butter from milk, and the other is manufactured from whole or skim milk fermented by adding "friendly" bacteria, then churned. Both are pleasantly sour tasting, containing all the proteins and casein of sweet milk. The souring and churning processes, however, make the casein more digestible. The "friendly" bacteria are *Streptococcus lactis* and *Leuconostoc citrovorum*. The buttermilk made from cultured whole or skim milk is often sprayed with tiny droplets of milk fat during processing so the end product will look like classic buttermilk.

BUTTERMILK CHEESE

An American farm-style cheese prepared from the fresh curd of buttermilk, it has a soft texture like **cottage cheese,** which it resembles, but is finer grained and has more fat. **Danish export cheese** is one example.

BUTTERNUT

The edible nut from the American tree, *Juglans cinerea*, is a member of the walnut family. The rich, sweet-flavored oil from this nut gives rise to the name. The butternut tree grows most abundantly in the northeastern United States but also as far south as Georgia and as far west as North Dakota. In some areas it is called the white walnut or long walnut.

Butternuts are used in candy, ice cream, cakes, cookies and also in pickles and catsup.

During the Civil War, Confederate Army uniforms were colored butternut, and the dye may have come from the husk of the butternut.

BUTTERSCOTCH

This chewy candy of Scotland is made of butter boiled with brown sugar, then beaten until creamy and allowed to set in a toffelike consistency. It is also used as a flavoring agent. A favorite ice cream topping in the United States is butterscotch sauce or syrup. It is essentially butterscotch with the addition of cream and lemon juice, cooked in a double boiler.

BUTTIRI

An Italian cheese containing a lump of butter in the center, it resembles ***caciocavallo*** and is made in Calabria. It may be made either of buffalo or cow's milk. *Buttiri* is sliced so that each segment has both cheese and butter in it. Another version, called *burrini*, is composed of cheese covered by a layer of butter.

See also: **Manteca.**

BUTTON MUSHROOM

See **Mushroom.**

BUTTON ONION

See **Onion.**

BYRRH

This French aperitif is based on red wine and has a slightly bitter taste, probably due to quinine, among other herbs. It is aromatic and fortified with brandy to bring its alcoholic content up to 19 percent. The practice of adding quinine to wine grew up during the colonial era when European soldiers were exposed to malaria. Army doctors inveigled the troops into taking their quinine by putting it in their wine. The taste caught on and quinine became a standard ingredient of aromatized wines.

C

CABBAGE

This most ancient of cultivated leafy plants was defined by Ambrose Bierce, in his *Devil's Dictionary*, as "a familiar kitchen-garden vegetable about as large and wise as a man's head."

Although two main types are distinguishable—those with smooth leaves and those with curly leaves—centuries of cultivation have brought innumerable varieties into existence. Common and Savoy cabbages, for example, have smooth, tightly-packed leaves, while **kale** has curly leaves. Among the specialized types are **brussels sprouts,** prized for their miniature cabbage heads; **cauliflower** and **broccoli,** for their edible flowers; and **kohlrabi,** for its stems. **Sea kale** is the only variety that still grows wild.

Cabbage ranks as the world's most popular vegetable, next to the potato, and is a source of abundant vitamin C. It was highly regarded by ancient Greeks and Romans, although the varieties they cultivated are not known precisely. Aristotle followed the Egyptian custom of eating cabbage before banquets to prevent inebriation. Cato considered it a remedy for many ailments, from sore throats to cataracts. Cabbage is not mentioned in the Bible, and the Israelites apparently did not know of it.

Cabbage heads may be flat, round or pointed. Those heads that are firmer and more compact have smoother, whiter and more tender internal leaves. When selecting cabbage, one should look for solid heads, somewhat heavy for their size, with closely trimmed stems and little or no discoloration of the leaves. The heads may be green, purple, red or white.

Cabbage is available all year, but tends to lose moisture rapidly and wilt at room temperature. It should be stored in a refrigerator in a covered container or plastic bag.

Cabbage typically costs less than most other vegetables and is a highly recommended addition to the diet. Raw, its high vitamin content remains intact; cooked, it is low in fat, fairly low in protein, a good diuretic agent and effective as roughage because of its high fiber content.

It gives off a strong odor during the first five minutes of cooking. A piece of bread placed in the cooking water minimizes the odor.

CABBAGE PALM

Also CABBAGE PALMETTO. The name includes the tender terminal bud of certain palm trees, especially the Caribee royal palm *(Roystonea oleracea)* and the cabbage palmetto *(Sabal palmetto).* On maturity the royal palm reaches a height of 100 feet with leaves ascending directly from the top, forming a crown. It is felled at three years or less, and the bud extracted from the crown. The latter is said to bear some resemblance to a cabbage and may be eaten as a green in salad, cooked and eaten as a vegetable or pickled. The bud is also called heart of palm, and is available canned. The pith is consumed as **sago,** and the tender shoots can be parboiled, then sauteed and eaten like asparagus.

While the *R. oleracea* is found generally in areas ringing the Caribbean, the cabbage palmetto grows from North Carolina to Florida, in Bermuda and in the Bahamas. It is valued for its timber and its leaves, which are used for thatching and hat making. The terminal bud is considered the equal of the royal palm's.

See also: **Coconut.**

CABECOU CHEESE

A goat's milk cheese from Quercy, France, its season is from April to November.

CABELLUDA

Edible fruit of a tropical tree, *Myrcia tormentosa*, found from Panama to Brazil, the cabelluda resembles a gooseberry, but is orange in color with a pleasant, subacid taste. It is used to make jellies.

CABERNET

This black grape is used in making some of the best red wines in the world particularly in Bordeaux and throughout Europe, in California, South Africa, and Australia. *Cabernet Sauvignon* is a smaller grape, but of like quality. *Cabernet Franc* is a popular grape grown in Bordeaux and along the Loire, in Anjou and Touraine. The Cabernet grape makes a full-

Cabernet Sauvignon grape

bodied and robust dry wine with a fruitiness and a bouquet that suggest the grape flower itself.

A major use of the Cabernet is in the making of the great rose wines of Anjou and Tours. Here the grapes are not crushed but allowed to ferment naturally. A pale, sweet liquid is the result, which in contact with the black grape skins becomes the distinctive light pink color of these famous wines. If the grapes are slightly crushed, a stronger color and richer bouquet is effected. "Ruby Cabernet" is made in California from a mixture of Cabernet and Carignane grapes, a University of California hybrid.

Cabernet Sauvignon wine may be aged up to 20 years, longer in cooler climates. In California, for example, this wine is often aged longer than it is in Bordeaux. The high tannic content and strong grape flavor are diminished through long storage. In Australia and South Africa another variety of the Cabernet is common, the *Cabernet Shiraz (Sirah)*, a tangy dry red wine of high caliber.

See also: **Bordeaux Wines.**

CABEZON

A fish of the *Cottidae* family characterized by spiny fins and head, the cabezon *(Scorpaenichthys marmoratus)* is the largest member of the family, weighing as much as 25 pounds. It is caught along the Pacific Coast of North America from Alaska to Baja California. The cabezon is frequently caught by anglers and is fished commercially in a modest way. The flesh of the cabezon is well regarded, but its roe is said to be poisonous.

CABRALES

In Spain, these cheeses made from goat's milk are farmhouse cheeses from the highlands of Santander and Asturias and are eaten locally. Some varieties have blue veining in the style of Roquefort.

CABREIRO CHEESE

A cheese made from sheep and goat's milk in the Castelo Branco district of Portugal, it is formed into plate-shaped loaves with rounded edges, weighing one to two pounds. If eaten young, it is very mild and creamy; if allowed to mature for three months, the flavor becomes very sharp.

CABRION CHEESE

A local goat's-milk cheese made in Burgundy at the time of the grape harvest, it is saturated in *eau de vie de marc* and aged in grape husks. It is also made from cow's milk.

CABRIOUS

See **Goat's Milk Cheese.**

CACAO

See **Chocolate and Cocoa.**

CACCIATORI SAUSAGE

A salami in the style of Milan, but less salty, *cacciatori* is small, weighs six to eight ounces and requires less aging than the larger Milan sausages.

CACHACA

Also PINGA. A Brazilian rum made from sugarcane juice that has been nautrally fermented. The juice is distilled in a pot still and sold unaged for local consumption. High in congenerics, cachaca is very strong and crude. Although it has many local adherents, few visitors like it.

CACHAT CHEESE

A highly flavored cheese of the Provence region of France, it is made from sheep or goat's milk cured with wine vinegar and then pressed. Cachat has a creamy texture and is very popular. It is served in an onion skin and is often accompanied by red wine.

CACHIATO

This blue-striped grunt is a member of the *Haemulon* genus of tropical food fish, which are plentiful off the coast of Florida and the West Indies. When pulled from the water, it emits a characteristic grunting noise.

See also: **Grunt.**

CACIOCAVALLO

A traditional Italian cheese, *caciocavallo* is molded by hand into the shape of a gourd. The cheese is molded while the curd is hot, expelling the whey and producing a compact, eyeless texture and a sealed surface. If unopened, the cheese keeps well and is suitable for warm climates.

It is quite similar to **provolone,** but it is not smoked and has less fat, even though whole cow's milk is its chief ingredient. In curing, pairs of cheeses are tied together with raffia and draped over poles, which, some say, gave rise to its name, a shortened version of *cacio a cavallo* ("cheese on horseback"). For table use, it is cured two to four months; for grating, six to 12 months. The cured cheese has a smooth, firm body with a whitish interior.

It originated in the south of Italy, but is also made in Sicily and northern Italy during summer months. Typically one cheese weighs from four to five pounds.

Caciocavallo's salty flavor make it a good accompaniment to dry, red wine. It is often baked in pasta dishes, such as lasagne.

CACIO FIORE

Also, CACIOTTA, CACIOTTO. An Italian ewe or goat's milk cheese, *cacio fiore* has a soft curd and a delicate, buttery flavor. The flower, *fiore*, in its name refers to the type of rennet used to make it, which contains wild artichoke flowers. Such rennet produces the soft, delicate curd. Cacio fiore is colored with saffron, and is ready to eat after only 10 days' curing. One cheese generally weighs from two to five pounds.

CACIOTTA, CACIOTTO

See **Cacio Fiore.**

CAERPHILLY

Caerphilly is a British cheese named after the Welsh village of the same name. It is a semisoft cheese made from cow's milk with a mild flavor, reminiscent of buttermilk, and a crumbly texture. Caerphilly requires only two or three weeks of curing, and must be eaten soon after that because it is perishable. It has a round, flat shape which is said to be a handy one for those Welsh miners who like to eat a slice while working.

CAESAR'S MUSHROOM

See **Orange Amanita.**

CAFFEINE

Caffeine is one of the group of chemical compounds termed methyl xanthines, which includes theophylline and theobromine, present in tea, plus adenine and guanine, components of DNA. We ingest caffeine in coffee, tea, colas and other carbonated drinks, chocolate bars, cold and headache pills.

Caffeine is a mild stimulant acting on the heart and central nervous system. It is a diuretic and acts to relax smooth muscles. For some persons, the ingestion of caffeine can cause tenseness and insomnia.

Investigations pointing to serious, even fatal, results from the overuse of caffeine by pregnant women and in laboratory experiments on rats have caused the U.S. Federal Drug Administration to move caffeine off its "Generally Recognized as Safe" (GRAS) list to an interim list. This means that further study of the results of the use of caffeine in a variety of applications is required. Concern has developed that caffeine might bring about genetic mutations, since caffeine tests with bacteria have caused mutations. No such effect has, however, been established for humans.

CAFFRE

A type of **sago,** i.e., edible pith of a South African tree of the *Cycad* family, it is used to make Kaffir bread.

CAIMAN

See **Crocodile.**

CAJUADA

Cajuada is a fermented beverage based on cashew

fruit that is made in West Africa. The luscious, pearlike fruit of the cashew tree is also the basis of a sort of wine, called *maranon* that is made in El Salvador.

CAKE

Any of various kinds of baked dessert, ceremonial, or holiday treats requiring flour, eggs, milk, sugar and a leavening agent, such as baking powder, in their preparation. Basically, there are two kinds of cakes: those that are shortened (or which contain fat, usually in the form of butter) and those that are unshortened.

Shortened cakes may be made by one of three methods. Sugar and fat are first creamed together, in one method, then are beaten with eggs (either the yolk or the white or both). A mixture of flour, salt and baking power, the dry ingredients, are sifted in at intervals. The resulting mix is then baked in a moderately hot oven (350°–400° F) (177°–204° C). In the "one-bowl" method, all ingredients are mixed in a bowl with an eggbeater or power mixer, and the raising agent added last. The "muffin" method calls for the combination of the combined liquid (sugar, milk, fat, eggs) with the combined dry ingredients before baking. Although an easy process, this makes for a coarse-grained product, which does not keep long. In all three methods, the cake is baked in flat, well greased, shiny metal, layer pans at least 1½ inches deep.

Sponge cakes and angel food cake are examples of unshortened or "foam-type" mixtures. These depend mostly upon incorporated air for leavening and require the vigorous whisking of eggs (in angel food cake only the white of the egg is used). The blended sugar, flour and salt is then gently folded in. In sponge cakes the unseparated egg is whisked with sugar and flavoring, and the sifted flour is folded into this thick, airy mixture.

Cake or pastry flours are far more desirable for mixing than are ordinary flours used in breadmaking. Cakes are often iced after baking with chocolate, the sugared juice and rind of fruits, such as lemon and orange, syrup, thick vanilla-flavored cream, prepared frostings and nuts. Cakes may be flavored with all sorts of ingredients, particularly with candied fruits, currants, almond paste and liquors like rum and brandy. The word "cake", in French *gateau,* is closely connected to the verb *gater* "to spoil"—which indicates the highly perishable nature of this food. In English, there may be an obscure association of "cake" with "cook," which, if true, points to the ancient lineage of this food.

A rule in baking cake is that less butter and eggs are needed if (as in earlier times) yeast is added. A preheated oven kept at a steady, moderately hot temperature is essential to the finished product. A good way still to tell if a cake is done is to test it with a knife. If the knife inserted into the mixture emerges sticky, the cake is not done. Cakes made with yeast tend to keep less than those made with baking powder. Today, ready-made cake mixes sold at supermarkets and grocery stores make the preparation of this food much simpler than before.

CALABASH GOURD

See **Gourd.**

CALABRESE

An Italian variety of broccoli *(Brassica oleracea,* var. *italica),* calabrese is also known as green sprouting broccoli. The flower heads are green, not purple green like purple sprouting broccoli. It is also called asparagus broccoli because shoots grow out of the sides of the stalks and may be cut and cooked like asparagus. After the terminal head is cut, the side shoots may grow small heads, which have a delicate flavor. Calabrese are usually grown for quick freezing or canning and mature in the summer. In the kitchen, calabrese are treated like **cauliflower,** i.e., boiled or steamed, but they may also be pureed or added to soups.

See also: **Broccoli.**

CALABUR

Fruit of a small tree, *Muntingia calabura*, native to the American tropics, but naturalized in Asia as well, it produces small, five-celled berries that may be white or yellow and have many seeds. Calaburs are used to make jam or pies.

CALADIUM

This is a genus of tuberous-rooted plants that are native to the American tropics. The roots have sometimes been used as potato substitutes.

CALAMARY

See **Squid.**

CALAMINT

A perennial herb of Europe and Asia, calamint *(Calamintha officinalis)* has blue, thymelike flowers. Its aroma and taste are much like peppermint's, but it is less amenable to commercial exploitation.

CALAMONDIN

A hybrid citrus fruit, *Citrofortunella mitis*, calamondin is the result of crossing the mandarin and the kumquat. The calamondin is one of the most ornamental of citrus trees, having bright green leaves and bright orange fruit. The latter reaches 1½ inches in diameter and looks like a tangerine, whose characteristic loose skin it retains. The taste, however, is far more acidic, but still well flavored. The juice is a good source of naturally concentrated vitamin C, and is unsurpassed as a base for an ade-type drink. It is also used to prepare artificial flavorings. Calamondin is grown in the Philippines and in the United States where it is the hardiest of the citrus hybrids.

CALAMUS

Also SWEET FLAG, MYRTLE FLAG, FLAG ROOT. This perennial, aromatic herb, *Acorus calamus*, of the Northern Hemisphere has a stout, pink, rootlike stem. Both the stems and leaves have a pleasant, sweet flavor. The stems are boiled with sugar to make a kind of candy, and are thought to have medicinal value as well. The leaves are eaten as a salad green or used to flavor puddings and cooked fruits.

CALANGALL

See **Galingale.**

CALCAGNO

A hard Sicilian cheese made from ewe's milk, calcagno is suitable only for grating or cooking.

CALF

A term used for a young mammal aged under 12 months, but especially the young beef, which is further subdivided into heifers (females) and bull calves (males). Calf flesh is usually called veal, although in the strict sense, veal refers only to milk-fed calf. Calves not so carefully fed and slaughtered under 12 months of age would be more properly called baby beef. When compared to veal, its flesh is darker, coarser and grainier and the fat yellower. See also: **Veal.**

Other parts of the calf are eaten as variety meats, such as, for example, the calf's crow, which is the membrane covering the intestines. It is prepared in a number of ways. For more information on calf's variety meats, or offal, see also: **Brains, Head, Heart, Kidney, Liver, Sweetbreads, Tongue, Variety Meats.**

CALIFORNIA POMPANO

See **Whiting.**

CALIFORNIA WINES

Wine from the European wine grape *Vitis vinifera* is cultivated in nine major wine-growing regions of California: five in the San Francisco Bay area, three in the San Joaquin Valley and one east of Los Angeles, in the district of Cucamonga. The vine was introduced into California in the 18th century by Spanish missionaries. The first commercial California vineyard was established in 1824 in Los Angeles. Other European immigrants and connoisseurs—notably Jean Louis Vignes, a Frenchman, and a Hungarian nobleman, Agoston Haraszthy (called "the father of California viticulture")—imported over 300 varieties of Old World vines into California in the mid-19th century. In 1880 the California State Board of Viticultural Commissioners was created to stabilize an expanding industry. California today provides almost 90 percent of all the wine grown in the United States, surpassing Germany, South Africa and Portugal in wine production.

The relatively cool climate of the San Francisco Bay area is well suited to European grape varieties. The Napa Valley, whose reliable sunlight is tempered by foggy ocean breezes, is widely known for its red and white table wines made from the Cabernet Sauvignon, from **Bordeaux;** the Pinot Noir and Chardonnay, from **Burgundy;** the Sauvignon Blanc, from **Sauternes;** and the Barbera, from Piedmont in northern Italy; as well as for its native red **Zinfandel.** The warmer San Joaquin Valley, in the districts of Lodi, Modesto and Fresno, is ideal for the cultivation of sweet grapes—such as the Palomino and Tinta varieties from Portugal and various types of **Muscat.** Light and sweet table wines are grown in Cucamonga.

California wines are labeled generically, after the basic or predominant grape used in their making, as well as after specific wineries. Among the best reds are **Gamay,** Grignolino, Pinot St. George, Ruby Cabernet—a University of California hybrid of Cabernet Sauvignon and **Carignane Wine—Barbera,** Petit Sirah or **Shiraz, Chianti,** Pinot Noir and Zinfandel. These are generally lighter and less fruity than their French and Italian counterparts, apt for informal meals or even as summertime drinks when moderately chilled. Zinfandel is a dry, hearty red, superb—as is the robust Barbera—with roast meats and pasta. Gamay , Grignolino and Zinfandel grapes are also used in the making of rose, although the **Grenache Wine,** from southern France, takes precedence here. California white table wines are perhaps more full-bodied and "obvious" in their taste than are German and French whites. The Napa Valley is noted for its production of Emerald Riesling, Gewurtztraminer,

Green Hungarian, Grey Riesling, Johannisberg or White Riesling, Chardonnay, Chenin Blanc, **Semillon,** Sauvignon, Folle Blanche and Sylvaner. Of these the Chardonnay is especially rich, and the Folle Blanche particularly dry and subtle. The Johannesberg Riesling and Gewurtztraminer tend to be rich and even—for a white wine—robust. Both of these wines improve with aging. California Sauterne (without the "s" at the end) may be either sweet or dry, as is the "Mountain White" (a white Burgundy) that is grown both in the Napa and the San Joaquin Valleys.

Charles Krug founded the first commercial winery in the Napa Valley in 1861 near St. Helena. After the end of the Prohibition era this estate was purchased by the Mondavi family, although wines from these vineyards retain the Krug label. Some of the best California white wine is grown here, particularly Chenin Blanc. Other great Napa names are Beringer (founded in 1876), Beaulieu (1900), Inglenook (1879), Louis Martini (1933)—famous for its dry red Zinfandel and Barbera and for its white Folle Blanche Johannesberg Riesling and Gewurtztraminer—Souverain (1953) and Mondavi (1966). Christian Brothers—noted for its **Sherry** and **Brandy**—has a long history in the area as well. In Sonoma, just south of the Valley and across the Bay from San Francisco, are the wineries of Sebastiani, Buena Vista and Korbel, which makes a superb dry **champagne.** East of San Francisco, near Livermore, is the winery of Wente Brothers, noted for its Dry Semillon, one of the best white California wines to drink with fish. Urban pressure has caused Wente Brothers— opened by Karl Wente in 1883—to open new vineyards in Monterey County, about 100 miles farther south.

Wineries in the San Joaquin Valley include—in Modesto—the firm of Ernest and Julio Gallo, which makes wine in great volume and Cresta Blanca—noted for its sherry made from palomino grapes. The Almaden and Paul Masson wineries are located near San Jose. Almaden is probably the world's largest wine-growing estate given to the production of classic table wines. Paul Masson produces wine on a slightly smaller scale. Both wineries claim one founder, Etienne Thee, in 1852.

Cucamonga, the southernmost wine-growing district in California, must fight against the eastward sprawl of Los Angeles. Nevertheless, it provides numerous light red table wines along with sparkling Champagnes, aperitifs and dessert wines. Its hot, dry climate is not favorable to full-bodied wines, so the vintage from this area is best consumed when it is young. Its special soil gives—to connoisseurs—a unique and tangy *gout de terroir* ("taste of the soil"), which distinguishes this wine from those of northern California.

California wines have steadily grown in reputation. An excellent program in wine technology is provided at the University of California at Davis west of Sacramento. Other American wines—from New York, Arkansas, Ohio and Missouri—are made from *Vitis labrusca,* a native grape variety. In North America, so far, only California wines descend from "the noble grape," the European *vinifera.*

See also: **Wines, United States.**

CALIPASH

See **Turtle.**

CALIPEE

See **Turtle.**

CALISTOGA WATER

This bottled mineral water is taken from a geyser at Calistoga in the Napa Valley of California. Some minerals are removed from the water before bottling, and carbonation is added. Calistoga water contains sodium, bicarbonates, chlorides, carbonates and sulphates, as well as traces of calcium, magnesium and potassium. Compared to 23 other bottled waters, it contains relatively high levels of arsenic (.055 ppm) and flouride (6.2 ppm). A sensory panel sponsored by the Consumers Union in 1980 judged its taste to be good, and made the following comments on its flavor: mildly sour, mildly salty, distinctly bitter and distinctly soapy.

See also: **Mineral Water.**

CALLALOO

A spinachlike vegetable popular in the West Indies, it is believed to have been brought there by slaves from West Africa. Some sources tentatively identify *callaloo* as leaves of the taro, or eddo, plant *(Colocasia esculenta),* better known for its starchy roots. The leaves are used to make soup and flavor stew.

See also: **Taro.**

CALLOP

Also GOLDEN PERCH. An Australian river fish, *Plectroplites ambiguus,* that is valued for both food and sport, the callop has a distinctive olive to dark green back and golden sides and belly. Large specimens weigh up to 50 poiunds and attain a length of 30 inches. A perchlike fish, it is deep-bodied, with a small head and steep forehead. The callop is found in the Clarence, Richmond and Murray-Darling river systems and has been introduced elsewhere.

CALORIE

A measure of energy, expressed as a unit of heat. Thus the amount of potential energy contained in a particular food is counted in calories. A Calorie (upper case) is the amount of heat required to raise a kilogram of water one degree centigrade. A calorie (lower case) is the amount of heat required to raise one gram of water one degree centigrade.

It should be noted that a calorie is not a measure of nutritional quality. It says nothing of vitamins, minerals, protein and the like. Instead, it speaks of fuel available to maintain vital metabolic processes and sustain other activities of the body, such as work, exercise, growth and maintenance of body temperature. Asked about the calorie requirements of intense thought, American chemist Francis G. Benedict wrote, "The extra calories needed for one hour of intense mental effort would be completely met by the eating of one oyster cracker or one half of a salted peanut."

The average human adult needs between 2,500 and 3000 calories a day to carry on normal activities. There is great variation among individual needs depending on age, sex, body size, level of activity, climate and such special functions as growth and development, pregnancy and lactation. A laborer might require as many as 5,000 calories a day, while a dieter would make do with 1,500.

Certain health problems are associated with calories. Obesity is one. Where there is balance between calorie intake and expenditure, a stable weight is maintained. If more calories are taken in than burnt, the excess is stored as fat, and obesity results.

Other problems have to do with the source of calories, namely, fat, refined sugar and alcohol. Nutritionists agree that calories from fats should not exceed 35 percent of the total, and that a preponderance of these should be from polyunsaturated fat. This is because higher consumption of saturated fat tends to raise the serum cholesterol level of the blood stream, a condition believed to promote heart disease and other circulatory ailments. (See also: **Fat.)**

Overall figures for the United States show that the average adult obtains from 20 to 25 percent of his calories from refined sugar, and from 10 to 12 percent from alcoholic beverages. These cause concern because at such high percentages, nutritional adequacy is difficult to maintain. Sugar and alcohol are virtually "empty calories," contributing nothing in the way of vitamins, minerals and protein.

For the calorie content of more than 700 foods, see the chart under: **Nutritive Value of Foods.**

CALLOU

An unusual Arabian wine made from the flowers of the coconut palm, *callou* matures rapidly—within 24 hours of its manufacture—and rapidly goes sour if it not drunk soon thereafter.

CALSO WATER

A mineral water from Menlo Park, Calif., Calso is not spring water, but tap water put through a process which involves mixing it with various minerals and carbonating it. The resulting water has a high sodium content (397 mg. per 8-ounce glass). A sensory test sponsored by Consumers Union in 1980 judged the taste of Calso to be poor, and made the following additional comments: mildly bitter, distinctly salty, distinctly soapy flavor, mild salty aftertaste, mild soapy aftertaste.

See also: **Mineral Water.**

CALUMBA

Also COLUMBO. An evergreen plant, *Jateorhiza calumba*, native to Mozambique, it is grown also in southern India, Sri Lanka and elsewhere. Calumba roots are used to make bitters for tonics and aperitifs. There is an American plant, *Frasera caroliniensis* known also as columbo and green gentian, whose roots are used similarly.

CALVADOS

A French apple brandy, calvados is somewhat like American applejack, but is bottled at a greater age and has a more complex aroma, redolent of wood, fruit and apple blossoms. (Ordinary French apple brandy is called *eau de vie de cidre.)* Calvados takes its name from the department of Calvados in Normandy, which is the center of French apple production. Juice from ripe cider apples is allowed to ferment for a month, or until no sugar remains, and is then distilled. Calvados is aged in oak casks for as much as 10 years before being bottled but never less than six. The finest version, *calvados du Pays d'Auge,* is double-distilled in a pot still and may be allowed to age as long as 40 years, by which time it attains the fineness of a cognac. Standard calvados has a strong, fiery taste with a pronounced apple flavor. The finer calvados from Auge is smooth and soft, with a remarkable aroma.

According to tradition, Calvados was first made more than 1,000 years ago by Vikings who settled in the Normandy region. Calvados is bottled at from 80 to 100 proof. It is customarily taken as an appetizer, although some follow the custom of the *trou normand,* i.e., sipping a small glass at various points during a meal. Opinions differ as to the function of this practice. For some, it clears the palate and aids digestion. For others, it creates a "hole" *(trou)* for more food, or, conversely, fills a hole left in the stomach by certain dishes.

See also: **Applejack.**

CAMAS

Also CAMASS, CUMMAS, QUAMASH. An American plant, *Camassia quamash*, this starchy root grows in the western and northwestern United States. It was used as food by many Indian tribes only in times of famine, but was esteemed by the Nez Perce tribe. The bulbs were prepared for eating in various ways. They were boiled, grilled, made into flour and baked in loaves, smoked or merely dried in the sun.

Members of the Lewis and Clark exploration party, having been charged by President Thomas Jefferson with seeking out and reporting on any new edible plants in the Northwest, tried eating camas bulbs. Their reports were not enthusiastic. The meal resulted in violent attacks of dysentery.

The camas has basal linear leaves with racemes of blue, purple or white flowers. Typically it grows on flat, grassy areas among hills or small prairies within forests.

In central Idaho, near Grangeville, there is a rich agricultural area called Camas Prairie.

CAMBRIDGE CHEESE

Also YORK CHEESE. A soft farmhouse cheese made in England, where, among soft cheeses, it is the most important after **cream cheese,** cambridge cheese is white and has a tangy flavor. It is made from cow's milk and is eaten fresh, after standing only 30 hours; it does not keep well.

CAMBRIDGE SAUCE

An English cold sauce similar to mayonnaise, cambridge sauce consists of mashed yolks of hard-boiled eggs, mashed anchovy filets, capers, cayenne pepper, chervil, tarragon, chives, mustard, oil and vinegar. It is served with cold meats, especially mutton and lamb.

See also: **Sauce.**

CAMEL

There are two common types of camel, the dromedary, with one hump, and the Bactrian, with two. As a source of food, camels are mainly appreciated in the Middle East and North Africa. Archaeological evidence suggests, however, that the first humans to eat camels were the Indians of North America. It is generally agreed that the one-hump camel, and possibly the two-hump camel as well, originated in North America. They are believed to have migrated to Asia before or during the Warm Ice Age, more than 10,000 years ago, when a land bridge existed between the two continents where the Bering Straits are today. Camels appeared in appreciable numbers in the Middle East in historic times. Texts in Sumerian, the oldest written language, mention camels as a novelty, calling them "mountain elephants." The ancient Persians found them useful, both as a means of transportation and as food. They particularly favored smoked camel hump. King Cyrus, in a campaign against Croesus of Lydia in 540 B.C., employed a camel-mounted cavalry, which was such a novelty that it startled and stampeded the horses of the Lydian cavalry. The ancient Hebrews used camels as beasts of burden, but tabooed the eating of their flesh. They called them *gamal*, whereas the modern Arabic word for camel is *djamal.* Camels came into general use in Egypt only in Roman times, and did not spread to the far reaches of the Sahara until the Christian era.

The camel has not found favor with modern Western commentators, either as a work beast or as food. Arthur Weigall, a British Egyptologist, wrote, "The fact that a camel has yellow teeth, a harelip, a hump, corns and suffers from halitosis places the poor creature beyond the range of ordinary sympathy." Its low intelligence was a sore point with Sir Francis Palgrave. He wrote "He is from first to last an undomesticated animal, rendered serviceable by stupidity alone, without much skill on his master's part, or any cooperation on his own." *(Encyclopaedia Britannica).* Another commentator found the flesh fibrous and indigestible, with a less than mediocre taste. Yet, as noted, the ancient Persians found the flesh of camels tasty, as did the Greeks and Romans, who considered it a dish fit for the Emperor. The emperor Elagabalus was especially fond of camel's heel. The renowned Roman gourmet Marcus Gavius Apicius served a dish of camels' heels and flamingo tongues at one of his feasts. The trick, perhaps, lies in selecting the right camel to eat. According to modern Arabs, such a camel should be young, and raised especially for the table. As an industry, raising camels for the table is a fairly recent phenomenon, brought on by their decline in importance as work beasts. Camels are bred in the Sudan and driven to market in Cairo, where nowadays the vast majority are sold for food. Young camel, roasted on a spit, is considered right for a festive occasion. The taste is, depending on age, much like that of beef or a flavorful veal, with a slight aftertaste similar to that of horse meat.

CAMEL'S THORN

The sugary exudation of a Middle Eastern shrub, *Alhagi camelorum*, it is eaten like candy.

CAMEMBERT

Probably the most famous French cheese, camembert is soft and surface-ripened like **brie,** but with a distinctive aroma and slightly bitter taste. One Madame Harel, who lived in the hamlet of Camembert, near Vimoutiers in the Department of Orne, is credited with creating the cheese as we know it today, but this involved perfecting a local product whose history goes back to the 12th century in Normandy. Legend has it that Napoleon was offered a plate of the then unnamed cheese and dubbed it camembert. His joy of discovery was such that he kissed the waitress. The departments of Orne and Calvados are centers of production, but it is also made elsewhere in France and in other countries, including the United States. French law requires printing the place of origin on the package.

In processing, whole cow's milk is inoculated with *penicillim candidum* mold, which, in the curing, forms a gray, feltlike layer on the rind. Depending on the degree or ripening, the interior is waxy, creamy or runny. It is sold at an early stage of maturation (three weeks to a month), and connoisseurs like to eat it *a point*, i.e., when it is soft enough to be runny, but has not yet spoiled.

Cheeses are marketed in various sizes and are often packed in round, flat boxes.

CAMEROON CARDAMOM

Seeds of an African plant, *Aframomum hanburyi*, are cultivated as a cardamom substitute.

CAMOMILE

Also CHAMOMILE. The flowers of this daisylike herb, *Arthemis nobilis*, are steeped in water to make a celebrated tea. Its aroma is reminiscent of that of fresh apples, but its taste is bitter. A member of the aster family, "camomile" in Spanish is *manzanilla;* it is used to flavor a Spanish sherry of that name.

See also: **Manzanilla.**

CAMOSUN

Camosun is an American cheese developed in 1932 at Washington State College Agricultural Extension to make use of surplus milk supplies. It is semisoft and resembles **Gouda** and **Monterey Cheese** in taste and texture, but is processed using simpler methods. Curing takes one to three months.

CAMPANULA

See **Rampion.**

CAMPARI

A popular Italian aperitif, actually a beverage bitter, Campari is most frequently served over ice, with a twist of lemon peel and some soda water. It is flavored with bitter-orange peel, gentian, quinine and other ingredients. Although it is most in demand in Italy, where bottled Campari and soda is sold everywhere, it is used elsewhere as the basis for several cocktails, including the Americano (with vermouth) and the Negroni (with gin and vermouth). It may be used along with a sweetener such as grenadine or **cassis** to make a long, refreshing drink, or mixed with an equal amount of **Amer Picon,** a sweetener and soda water. It contains 16 to 18 percent alcohol.

CAMPEACHY WOOD

See **Logwood.**

CANA

A Paraguayan rum of the light-bodied, Puerto Rican sort, it goes well with fruit juices in mixed drinks.

See also: **Rum.**

CANADA DRY CLUB SODA

Club soda is ordinary tap water, filtered and carbonated, with minerals added. The mineral content of Canada Dry Club Soda was high enough in 1980 for it to be considered a mineral water under California law (i.e., it contains more than 500 ppm of total dissolved solids). As such, its flavor was compared to that of 22 other bottled mineral waters by a Consumers Union sensory panel. The panel judged its flavor to be good, and better than that of 20 competitors, such as **Perrier, Calistoga,** et al. Comments on its flavor included: mildly bitter and mildly salty.

See also: **Mineral Water.**

CANADA GOLDENROD

A flowering perennial herb, *Solidago canadensis*, its seeds are edible and are considered a good food source in case of scarcity.

CANADA LETTUCE

This lettuce plant, *Lactuca canadensis*, native to North America, is used mainly as a pot herb or spinach substitute. When young and tender the leaves are added to salads.

CANADIAN CHEDDAR

See **Cheddar Cheese.**

CANADIAN COLBY

See **Colby.**

CANADIAN GROUSE

A game bird similar to the **blackcock,** the canadian grouse *(Canuchites canadensis)* dwells in the woods of southeastern Canada and northeastern United States. It has been assiduously hunted and is becoming increasingly rare nowadays. At table, it is considered inferior to the blackcock, but may be prepared in any way suitable for the latter.

CANAIGRE

Also WILD RHUBARB. A perennial herb, *Rumex hymenosepalus*, of the dock genus, its leaf stalks are boiled and made into pie like rhubarb. The leaves are eaten as greens, usually cooked like spinach. It is native to the American Southwest.

CANARD

See **Duck.**

CANARY GRASS

Canary grass *(Phalarus canariensis)*, originally cultivated in the Canary Islands, bears a seed that is rich in edible starch. The islanders munched these seeds as food and also fed them to their canary birds. First carried to Spain, the grass was later introduced to the south of France, where it continues to flourish.

See also: **Garden Cress.**

CANARY MADRONE

This bright orange, edible berry of a shrub, *Arbutus canariensis*, is native to the Canary Islands. It is used to make sweets.

CANARAY SEED

See **Canary Grass.**

CANDIL

See **Squirrelfish.**

CANDLEFISH

Also EULACHON. A small, saltwater fish, *Thaleichthys pacificus*, of the Pacific Northwest, it resembles the smelt. A member of the salmon family, the candlefish spawns in fresh water and is plentiful at the mouth of the Columbia River. The candlefish is one of the oiliest of fishes and seldom exceeds 12 inches in length. Nevertheless, it is extremely good to eat, the fat being delicately flavored and easy to digest. Eaten fresh, it is best sauteed in butter, it is also available smoked, kippered and canned. Fat is so abundant in this fish that native Americans used it in place of a candle, first drying it then passing a wick through the length of its body. Similar species in other parts of the world include the South African halfbeak.

CANDLENUT

Also CANDLEBERRY TREE, INDIAN WALNUT, KUKUI. Seeds of a Malaysian tree, *Aleurites moluccana*, yielding a valuable oil. The tree is large, reaching 60 feet in height, and appears frosty or whitish at a distance. It has been widely transplanted to the tropics and in the Philippines, China and the Pacific Islands.

The candlenut seeds are contained in hardshell nuts about two inches in diameter. They are so rich in oil that they make a good candle when threaded on a thin stick and lit. The oil is used for cooking, and commercially in varnish in the area of production.

CANDLE TREE

A species of small tree, *Parmentiera cereifera*, native to Mexico and Central America, its fruit—yellow and up to four feet long—resembles a candle. It may be eaten raw or cooked.

CANDY

Also termed "sugar confectionery," candy has been with us for a long time. Egyptian hieroglyphics from 3,000 years ago record their candymaking. The Roman confectioner was a skilled craftsman, using tools not much different from the hand tools used today. In those times, before the appearance of sugar, honey was the sweetener. Persians in the Middle Ages increased sugar cane farming and refining, and sugar began to replace honey as sea trading Venetians began bringing sugar from Arabia to Europe. This trade vastly increased supplies of sugar and brought its price down. By the 16th century the candymaking industry was producing candy at popular prices.

Candy manufacturing machinery started to develop late in the 18th century, and by the 20th century yearly world output was valued in billions of dollars.

The main and basic ingredient in candy is sugar, usually in the form of invert sugar, a mixture of glucose and fructose. Other ingredients are milk, usually in concentrated or dried form, fats, usually vegetable fat or butter, maple sugar, corn sugar, corn syrup, honey, molasses, soya proteins, egg albumen, chocolate, licorice, powdered starch, gum arabic, flavorings and colorings of many kinds, emulsifiers such as lecithin and glyceryl monostearate, fruits, nuts, gelatin and pectin.

There are two general categories of candy. One is hard candy, boiled at a high temperature, noncrystalline, (i.e., its sugar crystals melt into a plastic mass), chewy or hard. The other is soft candy, crystalline smooth, creamy and easily chewed.

Examples of noncrystalline candy are fruit drops, lollipops, jawbreakers, butterscotch balls, clear mints, caramels, toffees, brittle and nougat, which is used as a filling for many candy bars.

Examples of crystalline candy are fondant (the filling for most chocolate-covered and crystallized cremes), fudge, Turkish Delight (which is traditionally flavored with Attar of Roses), marshmallows, pastes, marzipan (itself an almond paste), gums, pastilles, preserved fruits, cotton candy and pastel coatings.

Though candy is still made by hand, both in homes and, to a limited extent, commercially, the overwhelming bulk is made by machines. They provide speed, precise controls on proportioning ingredients, timing and temperatures, a sanitary shield against human handling and sufficient productive capacity to supply the steadily growing market. Fondant, for example, is made by continuous flow machines that produce 2,000 pounds per hour. Another machine receives the fondant and, by means of a series of processes, prepares it for chocolate covering. Covering, or enrobing, is done by a third machine, which forms a continuous curtain of liquid chocolate through which the pieces of candy pass on a wire mesh conveyor on their way to cooling and machine packaging. This is a typical process by which many popular candy bars are turned out.

Homemade candy is still very popular. It can be made without any elaborate machinery, just a few kitchen utensils. Instructions for beginners are available from local public schools, libraries, cooking schools and book stores.

See also: **Caramel, Chocolate and Cocoa, Divinity, Fudge, Gum, Marshmallow, Marzipan, Nougat, Sugar**

CANELLA

Also WILD CINNAMON. The bark of this shrubby West Indian tree, *Canella winterana*, is highly aromatic and is used as a spice and as medicine. It is cultivated in south Florida.

CANESTRATO CHEESE

See **Incanestrato.**

CANISTEL

Also TI-ES. Fruit of a tropical tree, *Pouteria campechiana*, of the *sapodilla* family, native to Central America and the Caribbean islands, it is round to pear-shaped and grows up to four inches long. Canistel has green-to-brownish yellow skin and orange pulp, which is sweet, soft and mealy. It has a musky, but good, flavor and is eaten raw or used to flavor custards and sherbets. The tree is cultivated in southern Florida for its fruit. A spice is also extracted from the plant.

CANNED FOODS

This heading applies to food preserved in tin cans sterilized by heat and, in the United States, all foods hermetically sealed whether in tin or glass containers. In Great Britain the term "bottling" is used for food stored in glass jars. A French confectioner, Francois Appert, was the first to invent this method of food preservation. In 1809 he managed to preserve food in glass bottles, which were kept in boiling water for various lengths of time. His work was experimental, with no clear definition of how or why the process worked. Louis Pasteur, in 1860, explained Appert's method—the destruction of all microorganisms by the exclusion of air. Microorganisms are induced by **fermentation**—the action of oxygen upon sugar and various bacteria. Canning prevents these growths from forming—through sterilization by boiling and through the careful exclusion of oxygen.

An Englishman, Peter Durand, experimented further with Appert's method, but the invention of the modern tin can is generally ascribed to an American, Thomas Kensett, in 1823. Using glass, the industry had spread to the United States in 1819, when the bottling of fish and shellfish grew into a major industry. The Civil War gave a huge boost to the industry, with the tin can providing a convenient receptacle for all sorts of food. Today the United States is the most important producer of canned foods in the world.

The modern tin can is actually about 98 percent sheet steel with only a thin coating of tin. The sanitary or "open top" can came into regular use in the first decade of the 20th century. This design eliminated the use of solder in sealing the can, with a double seam on the top and the soldering required only on the sides.

Commercial canning makes use of several basic steps in its operation. First the food is cleaned—by air or water blasting and shaking. Then the various inedible portions of the food are removed—by husking, sorting, trimming, vining, slicing, peeling, etc. Some foods, such as beets, carrots, spinach and peas, are then blanched. The cans are then filled and the air exhausted by the release of carbon dioxide gas, as the food itself expands to drive out the oxygen. The can is next sealed, boiled and sterilized. The final step in the process is the cooling of the cans, with labeling and storage for marketing.

Commercial canneries should be very close to the source of the fresh food to be canned—particularly in the case of fish: sardines, shrimp, crab and squid. Probably the most vivid insight into a large-scale cannery operation is John Steinbeck's novel, *Cannery Row.* The first sentence of the book eulogizes the industry. "Cannery Row in Monterey in California is a poem, a stink, a grating noise, a quality of light, a tone, a habit, a nostalgia, a dream." With the disappearance of the sardine from Monterey waters in the 1940s, the eighteen canneries that existed in Steinbeck's time dwindled to one, which now packs squid, mostly for shipment to Greece.

In home canning the process is virtually the same as that followed commercially. The jars are filled and sealed, whether packed raw in brine (the cold-pack method), or after the food has been slightly cooked (the hot-pack method). The jars are then boiled in a water bath—not long for fruits and preserves, but up to five hours for meats. Or the food may be steamed first in a pressure cooker, then sealed quickly in jars. The procedure is tricky—and hot, especially in a steamy kitchen on a late summer day after the picking or harvest. There are many recipes for the home canning of food. A precaution is to boil thoroughly, although overcooking tends to produce food with a mushy texture.

Essential in both commercial and in home-canning is the elimination of oxygen. A slight bulge in a sealed can, however, hints at the activity of *Bacillus botulinus*, a bacteria that can live and flourish without free oxygen. A sour smell upon opening the can indicates the presence of this poisonous matter, so a good precaution is to boil all food slightly—especially home-canned goods—before serving. Foods that are highly acid, or mixed with brine or syrup, are least likely to be affected by botulism.

CANNELLONI

See **Pasta.**

CANNIBALISM

See **Human Flesh.**

CANNING

See **Preservation of Foods.**

CANNOCCHIE

See **Squill Fish.**

CANNONBALL FRUIT

This edible fruit of the cannonball tree *(Couroupita guianensis)* is native to the West Indies and other parts of tropical America. The fruit is reddish brown and round with a maximum diameter of eight inches. Though edible, it is not appetiszing due to an ill-smelling inner pulp.

CANNONAU WINE

One of the best known red wines of Sardinia, it is heavy, on the sweet side and rather too high in tannin to appeal to many visitors.

CANQUILLOTE

Also FROMAGERE, TEMPETE. *Canquillote* is a fermented cheese produced in eastern France. A curd is formed naturally by allowing milk to sour. The curd is heated, pressed, then broken up and left to ferment for a couple of days to develop flavor. After that, it is heated and mixed with water, salt, eggs and butter. The mixture is pressed into molds of different shapes.

CANTAL

Also FOURMES DE CANTAL. Cantal is a hard, yellow French cheese that has been made in the mountains of Auverge, Department of Cantal, since at least Roman times. Pliny the Elder mentioned it with approval. It is made from whole cow's milk and has a salty, piquant flavor, as well as a firm, close body that results from having been hard pressed into cylindrical molds *(fourmes).* Cheeses generally measure 14 inches in diameter, and weigh on the average 75 pounds. Cantal is produced in early summer and requires from three to six months' curing.

CANTALOUPE

See **Muskmelon.**

CANTHIUM

Edible fruit of a small African tree or shrub, *Canthium longiflorum*, it is highly regarded for its excellent quality.

CANTONESE SAUSAGE

A Chinese sausage made from pork and flavored with wine and fruit rind, it looks like a long frankfurter. Boiling is the usual method of preparation.

CAPACOLA

See **Capicolla.**

CAPE ANTEATER

See **Aardvark.**

CAPE BRANDY

This flavored brandy is popular in the Cape Province of the Republic of South Africa. South Africa is a prolific producer of wine and brandy, of which cape brandy is just one type. The grape distillate is improved with aromatic herbs and spices.

See also: **Brandy; Wines, South African.**

CAPE GOOSEBERRY

Also TIPARI, POHA. The cape gooseberry is an edible berry produced by a bushlike plant, *Physalis peruviana*, native to Mexico and North America. It is just one of several species of *Physalis* that bear small tomatolike fruits, varying in color from red to orange-yellow to green to purple. This variety grows well in the warmer parts of Europe, especially France, where it is also known as *alkekengi*, *coqueret* or *physalis*. The berry is contained in a straw-colored calyx, which resembles a Chinese lantern. It is eaten raw and has a slightly acid flavor. It also makes good jam or jelly.

See also: **Ground Cherry, Tomatillo.**

CAPE GRAPE

This purplish black berry comes from the South African woody vine, *Vitis capensis*. The pulp is reddish and is used to make jelly.

CAPELIN

Also CAPLIN, ICEFISH. A small fish of the smelt genus, *Mallotus villosus*, inhabiting the cold Arctic waters of North America and Siberia, it is found as far south as Alaska in the Pacific and Cape Cod in the Atlantic. It is a very tasty fish, rather resembling fine herring. The capelin is prepared like smelt or may be dried. It is often used for cod bait.

The capelin spawns on cold water beaches, such as those of Newfoundland, Iceland and Alaska. During spawning season, capelins are so plentiful that they can be scooped up off the beaches with a shovel.

CAPERCAILLIE

Also CAPERCAILZIE, WOOD GROUSE. This member of the grouse family is the second largest game bird of Europe. Its plumage is predominantly black, interspersed with green, white and red. The capercaillie *(Tetrao urogallus)* reaches the size of a small turkey and inhabits forested and mountainous regions of northern Europe. It is hunted in Norway, Sweden and Germany, the pine forests of the Jura, the Alps and the Carpathians and in Siberia. At one time it was extinct in the British Isles, but was reintroduced into Scotland, where it has become a favorite game bird.

The flavor of the capercaillie is largely determined by the season in which it is hunted. If it is killed in April or May, it is likely to taste of turpentine, having spent the cold season perching high in pine trees and feeding off the needles, cones and seeds. If bagged in the later summer or fall, however, its fine white meat has a delicate, pheasantlike taste. This is because it has been feeding on wild fruit, bilberries and aromatic vegetation.

Cooking strategies to mask or draw out the taste of turpentine include soaking the carcass in milk for several hours before cooking it and stuffing the bird with raw potatoes, which are discarded after cooking.

The bird should be drawn immediately after it is bagged. Some connoisseurs say the carcass should be hung for at least a week to promote tenderness and a gamey flavor.

CAPER

This is the unopened flower bud of the caper bush *(Capparis spinosa)*. A wild plant in Mediterranean regions, it is under cultivation in such temperate countries as Britain, France and the United States. In the wild, the caper bush is a prickly plant, but the cultivated varieties, as in France, are smooth. Its tuliplike flowers close at night, so they are usually harvested at daybreak before they can reopen.

The buds are pickled in vinegar, which has usually been flavored with **tarragon,** and then bottled. They are used to spice sauces and to garnish cold meats, fish and seafood. Capers have a pleasant, peppery flavor. Good capers are olive green and firm to the touch; the smaller the caper, the better its flavor. Nasturtium seeds, called false capers, are sometimes unscrupulously substituted for the real thing.

See also: **Nasturtium.**

CAPER SAUCE

Basically a white sauce, caper sauce is prepared according to several different recipes, depending on whether it is to be served with mutton, salmon or white fish. The version served with mutton consists of milk, mutton gravy and chopped capers, plus a little cream and tarragon vinegar. It is served hot.

See also: **Sauce.**

CAPICOLLA

Also CAPACOLA, CAPOCOLLO, CAPPO COLLO, COPPA. An Italian sausage made from boneless pork shoulder and spiced with sweet red peppers, capicolla is pressed, rather than chopped, put into casings, cooked and air-dried. It is a specialty of Parma, but is made in many parts of the world.

Coppa, a Corsican specialty, is very similar, except that chili peppers and cayenne are substituted for the sweet peppers, making the sausage a lot spicier.

See also: **Sausage.**

CAPLIN

See **Capelin.**

CAPO COLLO

See **Capicolla.**

CAPON

A rooster that has been gelded and fed intensively so that it is larger and plumper than the ordinary chicken, a capon averages six to eight pounds in weight, while a normal broiler-fryer would weigh from 1.5 to four pounds. The capon has an abundance of white flesh that is marbled with fat, unlike the regular fowl, whose fat is pocketed. The capon was an invention of the ancient Romans, who at one point banned the raising of hens in the city of Rome. Accounts differ as to why this was thought necessary. According to one story, raising hens for the table was so popular and widespread that chickens in the street became a public nuisance. In another version, the Roman Senate feared hens would become extinct due to their continuous consumption by wealthy gluttons. As a result, the Consul Caius Fanius promulgated a law banning hens, but mentioned nothing about cocks. They were omitted, it seems, because until then they had been of no culinary interest. Adhering to the letter of the law, Romans began raising cocks for the table.Noting, perhaps, the effects of castration on other mammals, they began snipping roosters at the age of three months. They were confined indoors, usually in a darkened room, and fattened on a porridge of flour and milk. The result was a bird that was at once meatier, but more tender and succulent than hens. At the age of seven to 10 months, the capon was considered ready for the table.

The capon has retained a certain popularity down through the years, particularly in Italy, where at Christmas it occupies the place of the turkey in the United States and the goose in other European countries. After World War II, breeders developed a new method of caponization, which dispensed with the gelding operation, a trauma that all too often proved fatal to the fledgling cock. A female hormone pill was grafted into the neck of the cock at the age of six or seven weeks. This prevented normal development of male characteristics. *Caponette* was the term coined for those birds that were gelded chemically. It was soon discovered, however, that often the pill did not dissolve completely, and traces of the hormone remained in the flesh. As a consequence, chemical caponization has been banned in many countries.

Capons are usually prepared simply— roasted on a spit or in an oven with a bland stuffing, if any at all. But they can be prepared in any way appropriate to a chicken or a turkey. The term "capon" has been applied to other foods, usually implying a degree of luxury. A Norfolk capon, for example, is a type of red herring. And the French use the term for a rare and delicious fish of the Mediterranean which has a large, boxlike head. It can also refer to a castrated rabbit.

See also: **Chicken.**

CAPPADOCIA

Cappadocia was a type of bread favored by the wealthy of ancient Rome. Of the 62 different kinds of bread baked in Rome, cappadocia was considered the finest. It was yeast-raised and contained finely sieved whole wheat flour, along with olive oil, honey, salt and milk. The result was a dome-shaped loaf with a soft, salty crumb.

See also: **Bread.**

CAPPO COLLO

See **Capicolla.**

CAPRINO

See **Goat's Milk Cheese.**

CAPSICUM

Various bushy, many-branched plants of the nightshade family, particularly *Capisicum frutescens* with its several types, bear hot chilies or peppers. Pepper plants are found throughout the world, though the genus, *Capsicum*, seems to be original to Central and South America. The name stems from the Latin *capsa*, meaning "box" or "chest" and describes the box-like enclosure of the seeds and internal tissues. The small-fruited plants are the most pungent, and are called "chilies." The larger fruit is commonly named "peppers." In the American Southwest, the green (or red) chiles are said to clean out the sinuses, drive away headaches, and induce clear thinking. Traditionally, hot peppers are a stimulant to the appetite.

The conical or elongated fruit of the capsicum is green when immature, red when ripe. It may be eaten as a vegetable, made into relishes, or ground into powders—as cayenne pepper, ordinary red pepper, paprika or as an ingredient in tabasco sauce. Its use, then, is as a **spice** as well as a vegetable. *Capsicum frutescens cerasiforme* is known as cherry pepper. The variety *conoides* is known as tabasco, *fasciculatum* as bell or sweet pepper, *longum* as chili or yellow pepper, sometimes called "banana pepper." Fruit of the capsicum may also be pickled, once the pods are slit and the seeds removed, in a mixture of brine, vinegar, mace and nutmeg.

CAPULIN

Fruit of a tropical American tree, *Prunus capollin*, it has red or yellow skin and a pleasant, sweet flavor.

CAPYBARA

An edible mammal of Central and South America, which is believed to be the largest living rodent, the capybara looks like a **guinea pig** but can weigh as much as 110 pounds, stand 1½ feet high and be up to four feet long. There are two species, *Hydrochoerus hydrochaeris*, which is found east of the Andes and as far south as the Parana River; and *H. isthmius*, the smaller of the two, which is found in Panama east of the canal. Capybaras band together in groups of 20 or so and live in woods with dense vegetation around a body of water. Capybaras are unagressive beasts, peaceful and quiet. When closely pursued, they head for water where they are very much at home. Their flesh, though edible, is said to be of poor quality. They are more often killed for destroying crops than as food. Indians fancy their teeth as ornaments.

CARACU

This herbaceous plant, *Xanthosoma caracu*, is native to tropical America. In the West Indies, its young leaves are cooked and eaten much like spinach or used in soups and stews. Its thick tuberous roots are eaten as a potato substitute.

CARAMBOLA

A fragrant tropical fruit, native to India and southeast Asia, but also cultivated in Hawaii and the West Indies, particularly in Jamaica and Haiti. The name derives from *karambal*, a word from the Marathi language of Bengal, which comes to English via Portuguese. The fruit is oval—perhaps five inches long by two inches thick—with smooth, waxy skin and five prominent ribs, which give slices the shape of a star. For this reason, it is sometimes confused with the **star apple,** an unrelated fruit. There are two kinds, sweet and sour. The sweet carambola *(Averrhoa carambole)* has a bland, sweet taste and yellow green color, while the sour, or mild, carambola *(Averrhoa bilimbi)* is darker and has a nicely tart taste. Both are eaten raw or used to make iced drinks.

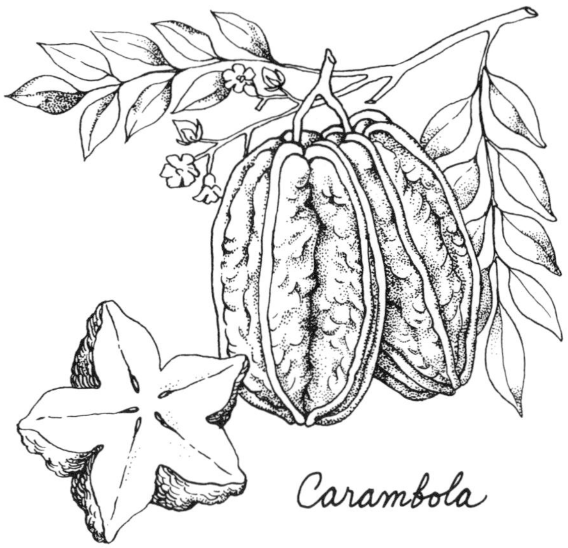

CARAMEL

Sugar is heated in a skillet until it liquifies and turns amber, then boiled with a little water until it becomes dark amber (but not burnt). Caramel is used as a coloring agent for gravies, syrups, jellies, stocks and the like. It may be strained and bottled, and it keeps indefinitely. Caramel is also a widely used commercial coloring agent in prepared foods, soft drinks etc.

"Caramelize" means to heat sugar as described, or to coat another food, such as ham, with sugar, which then caramelizes during roasting or other cooking. Other foods, such as malt and coffee, which contain sugar or starch, can caramelize if roasted.

A caramel is a piece of soft, chewy candy made of sugar syrup, corn syrup, cream and flavoring.

CARAMONTE

See **Norway Lobster.**

CARANDA

Also KARANDA, KARONDA. Here is a fruit of an Indian shrub or small tree, *Carissa carandas*, which resembles a gooseberry. The berries are red to black, about ¾ inch in diameter and are made into jellies or used in pies. There are related species found in Indonesia and Australia.

CARASSIN

See **Crucian.**

CARAWAY

This hardy biennial plant, *Carum carvi*, is valued for its tiny brown seeds, which in the United States are used to season rye bread. Germans and Austrians also use the seeds to improve the flavor of pastry and cheese.

In taste, the seeds fall somewhere between parsley and dill. They yield an oil much favored by Danes, Germans and Russians to flavor liquors such as **akvavit** and **kummel.**

It is grown commercially in many parts of Europe, but not in Britain, where it has lost popularity since Tudor times, when it was used medicinally as well as in the kitchen. Caraway roots resemble parsnips, and when young and tender, they make a fine vegetable.

CARBOHYDRATE

Carbohydrate is a class of foods whose importance in human nutrition is comparable to that of protein and fat. Although carbohydrates differ greatly in characteristics—composition, appearance, properties and nutritional value—they are all made up of carbon, hydrogen and oxygen. From a culinary point of view, the significant carbohydrates are starches and sugars. A third type, cellulose, is indigestible by humans but plays a role in nutrition as dietary fiber.

Carbohydrates are brought into existence by plants, which synthesize them out of carbon dioxide and oxygen in the presence of chlorophyll, using the energy provided by sunlight. The process is called photosynthesis. It would be hard to overestimate their importance structurally to plants and, as part of the food chain, to animals, since the latter depend, directly or indirectly, solely on carbohydrates.

Typical starch carbohydrates are provided by such things as potatoes, leguminous vegetables or cereal products. Sugar carbohydrates are obtained from sucrose (refined sugar), glucose and fructose. Sugar is the most concentrated carbohydrate, containing about 1,820 calories to the pound. Carbohydrates provide about two-thirds of the energy needs of the body. They are readily converted into fat by the human body, so dieters do well to limit their intake.

CARBONATED BEVERAGE

Also SODA, SODA POP. Potable water is charged with carbon dioxide gas under pressure, then used as a beverage either unsweetened or sweetened and flavored in a variety of ways. The term does not cover naturally carbonated water, such as might emerge from a spring; it is discussed under the topic, **Mineral Water.**

Unsweetened carbonated water is called club soda, seltzer water (after the village Nieder Selters near Wiesbaden in West Germany where it occurs naturally), or soda water. It may be drunk chilled and undiluted as a refreshing beverage, and is said to be always cooler at a given temperature than still water because the bubbles of escaping gas draw heat from the liquid. More often, club soda is mixed with whisky, rum or other alcoholic beverage to make a highball.

Sweetened carbonated drinks are a far more popular beverage, especially in the United States where they originated in the early 19th century. They constitute the most important class of soft drink (i.e. nonalcoholic). Others include similar noncarbonated drinks and milk-based drinks such as milk shakes. This kind of drink is commonly known as soda or soda pop and is descended from beverages made in the home, such as pennyroyal tea, sassafras tea, sweet cider, cranberry juice, etc.

Soda pop first appeared in Philadelphia in the 1830s, and by 1900 there were 2763 bottling plants throughout the United States doing business amounting to $25 million. Thirty billion bottles were produced for American consumption in 1960, and by the mid-1970s the number had swelled to more than 107 billion bottles, that is, about 485 bottles a year for each person in the United States. The American taste for soda pop has spread to all parts of the globe, aided by modern distribution and advertising techniques. The People's Republic of China is the most recent convert.

Fruit flavors—especially lemon-lime and orange—are widely popular as well as such flavorings as root beer and ginger. The leading flavor is cola. Cola beverages account for half of the top ten selling brands in the United States. The first among those is **Coca-Cola.** One reason for their popularity is that cola drinks usually contain caffeine, a mild stimulant, although not more than 0.02 percent by weight.

The leading ingredient of soda pop apart from water, is sugar, amounting in some cases to five teaspoonsful per six to eight ounce serving. Formulas can be quite complex—as a glance at a label shows—and, in addition to sweetening and flavoring include such things as natural and artificial color; acidifying agents; buffering agents; emulsifying, stablizing or viscosity producing agents; foaming agents and chemical preservatives.

CARDAMINE

Also LADY'S SMOCK. A perennial herb, *Cardamine pratensis*, of temperate Europe, Asia and North America, it has white or rose-colored flowers, and its leaves are eaten in salads, and though a little milder, they are often compared in taste to watercress.

CARDAMOM

An aromatic spice related to ginger, cardamom has a sweet, pungent, lemony flavor which in the West seems to appeal most to Scandinavians and, to a lesser extent, Germans and Russians. They especially favor it in breads, pastries and sausage. It is also popular in the Near and Far East. Arabs add ground cardamom seeds to their coffee. For Indians, it is a standard ingredient of curry powder. They also chew seeds of the finest quality with betel nut as a digestive.

Two plants of different genera, *Eletteria cardamomum* and *Amomum cardamomum*, produce seeds which commercially are called cardamom. The finest

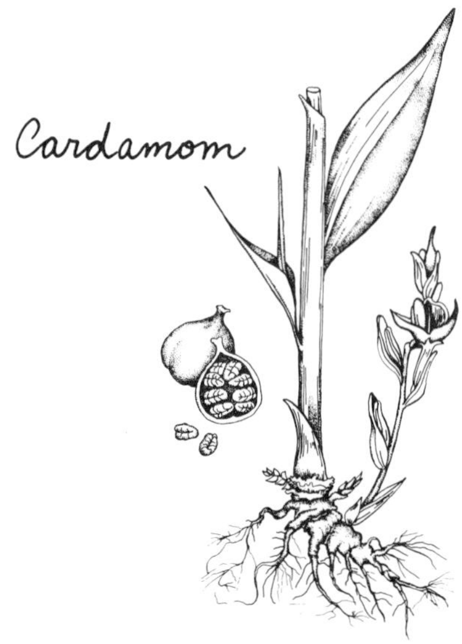

cardamom comes from the Eletteria plant, which is native to the Malabar Coast of India, but which also grows in Ceylon and Guatemala. It is a reedlike plant that propagates itself, like ginger, by means of large rhizomes. Only cardamom seeds, however, are valuable, and they are found in single pods, about the size of peas, widely spaced along the stalk. These pods are whitish-green and three-sided. The seeds are brown or black, and are so tiny that it takes four pods to yield one-quarter teaspoon of seeds. To prevent adulteration, the seeds are sold in the pods, but must be separated before using. Pods are treated differently depending on their destination. For the United States they are bleached. Oven-dried brown pods are more common in European and Asian markets. Sun-dried green pods are preferred in India. These last reputedly give the best flavor—clean, precise and pungent. Cardamom plants are not amenable to mass cultivation, but must be found in the wild state and carefully tended. For this reason, it is the second most costly spice, after saffron. Once removed from the pod, cardamom is easily adulterated with pepper, mustard seed or cheaper grades of cardamom.

The second variety, *Amomum cardamomum*, is native to Indochina. Like the first, it is tended in the wild. Pods are larger and more plentiful on these plants, clustering like grapes, but the seeds are not as sweet and pungent as the first kind. The prime areas in which this type of cardamom are found are parts of Vietnam and Cambodia; as a result, for many years supplies of this spice have been disrupted by war.

Cardamom was first brought to the West by soldiers of Alexander the Great returning from India. It was well-known in ancient Rome, but used chiefly in making perfume. When Roman trade routes collapsed, it disappeared from Europe, to reappear when Crusaders returned from the Holy Land. For the remainder of the medieval period, it was a favorite spice because of its sweet odor and strong flavor.

Cardamom seeds are known as "grains of paradise" in the East, where they are chewed with betel and, in sufficient quantity, are said to have a soporific effect. In cooking, they can be substituted for cinnamon. Cardamom is used to flavor certain liqueurs and some vermouths.

CARDIGA CHEESE

Here is a Portuguese sheep's milk cheese with a mild flavor. Its texture is oily and rather hard.

CARDINAL FISH

See **Mullet.**

CARDON DE CANDELABRO

The round, edible fruit of a treelike, Chilean cactus, *Trichlocereus chiloensis*, is made into brandy and syrup in Chile and Argentina.

CARDOON

This vegetable is a member of the thistle family and is a close relative of the globe artichoke, although it looks more like celery. Cardoon *(Cynara cardunculus)* is cultivated for its fleshy root and stems, some of which are six or seven feet long. There are also many wild varieties, but they are smaller and less tender. Tenderness in the cultivated varieties is ensured through blanching, which involves tying the leaves together after they have attained maximum growth and storing them for some time before marketing. The stems are white below and grayish-green above.

The artichoke enjoyed by the ancient Greeks and Romans was actually cardoon. It also figured prominently in medieval cooking. It is popular in Europe today, but less so in the United States, where the stems are often known as chard. They should not be confused with real chard, or spinach beet.

The main root, which is thick, fleshy and tender, is often boiled, then served cold in salad. It may also be sauteed in butter or served in Bechamel sauce. The stems may be treated like asparagus or celery, and the leaves, like spinach.

CARIBBEAN GRAPE

The sour fruit of a woody vine, *Vitis caribaea*, is found in North America and the West Indies and can be used to make jellies and jams.

CARIBOU

A wild cousin of the reindeer, the caribou *(Rangifer tarandus)* is native to North America, inhabiting Alaska, northern Canada and Greenland. It is not exclusively North American, however, because some species are found in Siberia and in Spitzbergen. The caribou has been called a relic from the last Ice Age, when it roamed as far south as southern China, Turkey, southern France, Spain and Central America. It was a prime source of food, clothing and tools for humans during the Stone Age, and when the glaciers receded some 10,000 years ago, many tribes who were dependent on them followed the caribou north. Their descendants are the Eskimos, particularly inland Eskimos, who live in the regions mentioned above.

The tundra caribou *(Rangifer articus)* is the most important species, and is very similar to the domesticated reindeer, which is herded by the Laplanders of northern Scandinavia. Caribou flesh is much gamier, however, than that of the reindeer. Other species are the woodland caribou *(Rangifer caribou)*, which is heading for extinction; the rare mountain caribou *(Rangifer novaterrae);* and the smaller *Rangifer platyrhyncus*. The word "caribou" comes from the Algonquin language and means "shoveler," "pawer" or "scratcher." It describes the caribou's activities in getting at reindeer moss through the snow.

The caribou is an antlered animal, and is considered excellent game. The meat is sometimes cooked exactly like beef, except that all the fat is trimmed off. It can also be cooked like venison, i.e. broiled, or roasted with strips of salt pork over the top. To attenuate the gamy taste, it is best to marinate it in a wine mixture for several days. Caribou meat is often accompanied by a tart relish made from berries, such as lingonberries. If caribou meat is seen in food stores, it is usually frozen.

See also: **Reindeer.**

CARIGNANE WINE

A varietal wine produced in California from the highly colorful Carignane grape, it is also a very sweet French dessert wine. The grape is used in the Rhone wine region to produce roses, in California for ports, and in Algeria, Morocco and Tunisia for red table wines.

CARLINE THISTLE

This is a genus of shrubs, *Carlina acanthifolia*, or *C. acaulis*, native to Europe, West Asia and the Canary Islands. A variety found the the Cevennes region of France is used as food. The young flower heads are eaten in salads, and the roots are prepared and eaten like fennel root and are used medicinally.

CARNATION

The petals of this popular ornamental flower, *Dianthus caryophyllus*, are sometimes used to flavor mustard, a syrup and a cordial.

CAROB

Also, BOKSER, ALGARROBA, ST. JOHN'S BREAD, LOCUST BEAN. Carob is the fleshy pod of an evergreen tree *Ceratonia siliqua* that is native to the Levant, but grows well throughout the Mediterranean area. The trees are handsome, long-lived, 25 to 35 feet high and prolific in pod production. The pods are reddish-brown, four to eight inches long and leathery on the outside but succulent and sweet on the inside. They contain up to 50 percent sugar, and have a substantial protein content as well.

Carob tastes somewhat like chocolate and is substituted for it by health-food enthusiasts and by

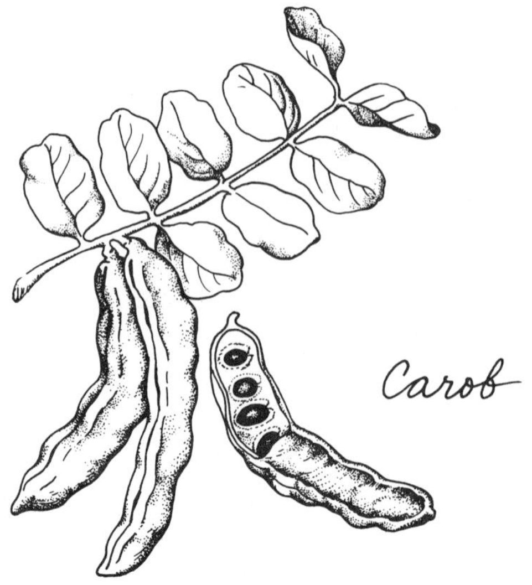

those who cannot eat chocolate. Except for a few very hard seeds, the whole pod may be eaten fresh, or dried, as a candy. Some authorities claim that the locusts St. John the Baptist ate in the wilderness (Matthew 3:5) were actually carob pods, as were the husks that the Prodigal Son hungered for as he fed them to the pigs (Luke 14:16).

The pods are ground up and fed to cattle, which is their chief commercial use. They served as forage for Wellington's cavalry during the Peninsula campaign and for Allenby's cavalry in Palestine.

Carob makes a good thickener for food, and drug companies use it to make a cough medicine. It flavors certain aromatic liqueurs made in Egypt and Sicily. Also, in the United States it is added to chewing tobacco and dog biscuits.

CAROLINA MOUNTAIN WATER

A bulk drinking water bottled in plastic containers in the United States, Carolina Mountain Water is relatively low in mineral content. A 1980 Consumers Union sensory panel rated the taste of this water as good, with the following qualifications: mildly bitter, mild bitter aftertaste, distinctly plastic flavor, heavy, thick mouthfeel.

See also: **Mineral Water.**

CAROTENE

Also CAROTIN. A reddish yellow pigment is found in fruit, egg yolks and many vegetables, such as carrots, peas and pumpkins. The human body converts this carotene to vitamin A, which is beneficial to eyesight and growth. Carotene is extracted from its natural sources and used to color foods, such as cheese and margarine.

CARP

Carp *(Cyprinus carpio)* is a member of the minnow family, and so widely distributed that it is probably the most important freshwater food fish in the world. Many claims have been made about the longevity of carp, particularly those in the royal pools at Fontainebleau, which are alleged to have lived hundreds of years. On this basis a character in Aldous Huxley's novel *After Many A Summer Dies the Swan* devised a diet consisting almost entirely of the bellies of ancient carp, which enabled him to live for centuries. More realistically, it would appear that the average life span of a carp is 13 to 15 years; one carp is known to have lived in captivity to the ripe old age of 47.

The common, or golden, carp has two fleshy barbels on each side of its upper jaw and a single dorsal fin; its golden-olive color above shades to golden-yellow and then to golden-white below. Each of its many scales has a dark spot at the base and dark edges, giving the fish a cross-hatched appearance. Carp have been selectively bred to eliminate scales. One result was the leather carp, which has no scales, but rather a thick, brownish skin which resembles leather. Another was the mirror carp, which has a single line of large, mirror-like scales running the length of its body. Both of these, especially the mirror carp, taste better than the common carp.

Carps grow rapidly, and one that reaches maturity can weigh from 15 to 25 pounds. Carps weighing 70 pounds have been landed in the United States. France claims the record; according to Alexandre Dumas, a 154-pound carp was caught there in 1711. But for average size, no European carp can approach the *mahseer*, or giant carp, which inhabit the large rivers of India. Specimens of 120 pounds are common; when they are taken with rod and reel they fight like tarpon.

The carp is native to eastern Asia, probably China, but was introduced at a very early date into Europe. Carps were mentioned by Aristotle in 350 B.C. They were a popular food fish during the Middle Ages, as evidenced by the carp pools that are a frequent adjunct of the monasteries dating from that era. Far from being ornamental, these carp pools represent serious efforts at fish farming. In England, carp were quite common by Shakespeare's time. He made reference to carp in *Hamlet* (1604) with, "Your bait of falsehood, takes this carp of truth," as did Ben Jonson in *Forest* with, "Fat, aged carps that runne into the net." They were introduced into the United States in 1876 by the U.S. Fish Commission, and are now distributed from coast to coast.

The carps that were transplanted to America were obtained from Germany, where the cultivation of carp has been pursued with considerable ardor. Germans developed the leather and mirror carp. More recently, they have come to be farmed in Taiwan on flooded pasture lands south of Taipei; the preferred type is called, appropriately, the grass carp. The French have never been great carp fanciers, but carp are bred in the Sologne and the Dombes for export to Germany and Israel. Carp plays an important role in

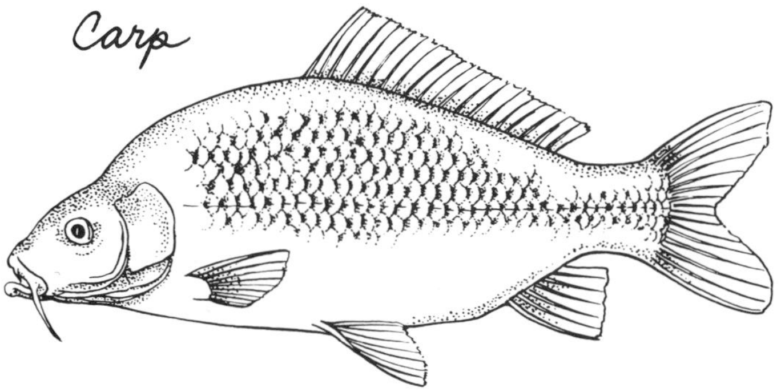

Jewish cuisine; it is often used, for example, in the preparation of gefilte fish, and especially for carp roe, a reasonable substitute for sturgeon caviar, which is forbidden to the Jews by dietary laws. A 26-pound female carp can produce during its lifetime, more than two million eggs. Carp roe can be cooked in butter or pureed, as in the Greek *taramosalata*.

Carp have never been a popular food fish in the United States perhaps because they prefer placid waters and rooting in muddy bottoms, and as a result their flesh often has a muddy taste. This taste can be eliminated by washing the flesh thoroughly in running water, then letting it soak in a weak vinegar solution for a few hours. Only small carp are fried; the larger ones are better stewed or baked. The Japanese are very fond of carp; to them the carp represents virility, strength and endurance, qualities they think a person can acquire by eating the flesh of the carp.

CARRAGEEN

Also CARRAGHEEN, from a town near Waterford, Eire. Carrageen is a purple, branching seaweed *Chondrus crispus*, found on northern European and American coasts. After harvesting, it is dried and bleached and sold commercially as Irish Moss. In cooking, it is used in making jellies and blancmange and may be eaten as a vegetable, like spinach. In pharmacy, it is used as a demulcent.

See also: **Dulse.**

CARRE

Also CARRE FRAIS, DOUBLE CREME CARRE, FROMAGE DOUBLE CREME. A French cream cheese of the neufchatel type, small and very rich, carre is made from a milk and cream mixture and eaten fresh. It is sold in two-inch squares, weighing about four ounces. *Demisel* cheese is similar, but saltier.

CARRE DE L'EST

A mold-ripened French cheese made in Alsace-Lorraine, *carre de l'est* emulates **camembert** in style, while resembling a mild **maroilles** in taste. Indeed, some U.S. camembert is made using the French method for *carre de l'est*. This involves cutting the curd to accelerate drainage of whey, which results in a softer curd than that of traditional camembert. Local variations include *fleur*, a fresh cheese coated with white mold, and *lave*, whose rind is washed in water.

CARRE FRAISE

See **Carre.**

CARROT

A common garden vegetable, the carrot *(daucus carota* var. *sativa)* is cultivated for its thick, fleshy root, which is usually conical, but sometimes round. Carrots can vary in color from red to yellow and even translucent white. The best, however, are orangish yellow. Darker carrots contain a greater amount of carotene, a substance which the human body converts to Vitamin A. Carotene has also been used to color butter and margerine. Carrots are eaten raw or cooked. Best for eating raw are the small, tender carrots of early summer. Larger, older carrots develop a hardy, woody core which is practically inedible raw. They are particularly good, however, when cooked with meat or in stews, because they retain their flavor and do not lose their shape.

A native of Afghanistan, the carrot was under cultivation in the Mediterranean area as early as 500 B.C. Although the ancients did not regard carrots highly as a food, they put them to other uses. The Greeks used them as a remedy for venereal disease, reasoning, apparently, that the vegetable's shape was a clue to the organ of the body that could be helped by it. The Arabs, applying similar logic but reaching a different conclusion, considered it an aphrodisiac. Pliny mentioned the carrot, citing its powers as a stomachic. It was cultivated in Europe during the Middle Ages, but it did not become popular until the 16th century, after improved varieties were developed. It has retained its popularity ever since.

Besides A, carrots are rich in vitamins B, C and E. The carrot contains about 10 percent to 15 percent sugar, more than any other vegetable except the beet. In early Celtic literature it was known as "honey underground." The Irish make a sweet pudding of it, and the Indians bake it into small, sweet cakes called *gajar halva*. Carrots are used to make the Jewish *tzimmes*, a Rosh Hashanah dish symbolizing gold coins and hence prosperity. Mineral salts abound in carrots, including those of iron, magnesium, calcium and phosphorus. Carrots are principally water (80 percent), however, and are low in calories, containing 42 per 3½ ounces (100 grams).

Carrots are used as hor d'oeuvres and in soups. As a side dish they often accompany meat, especially beef. With their mildly laxative effect, carrots complement beef, which can sometimes be constipating.

CARROWGARRY CHEESE

A creamy but firm-textured Irish cheese made at Roscommon, it is prepared from full-fat cow's milk.

CARSENZA

See **Crescenza.**

Carrots

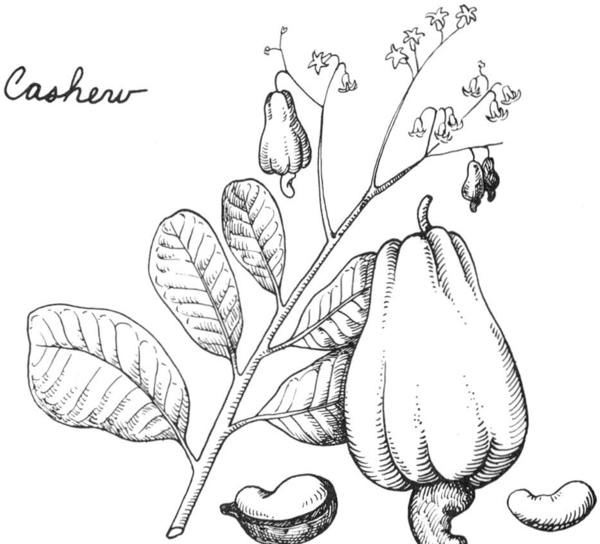

CASABA

See **Muskmelon.**

CASABANANA

Also CURUBA, MELOCOTON. The scented gourd-like fruit of a South American vine, *Sicana odorifera*, is club-shaped, about 10 to 15 inches long and three inches wide. It may be eaten when green as a vegetable or made into preserves. The name *casabanana* is sometimes mistakenly applied to *Benincasa hispida*, the **Chinese watermelon.**

CASCAVAL CHEESE

See **Katschkawalj.**

CASEIN

This phosphoprotein is abundant in milk and certain leguminous vegetables, such as soybeans. Eighty percent of milk protein is casein, and the latter is the principal raw material of cheesemaking. It is coagulated as solid matter from milk through the action of rennet or hydrocloric acid, which separates the milk into two constituents, curds and whey. The curds are mostly casein. If fermented, they become the nutritious substance known as cheese. They may, however, be thoroughly washed, dried by the application of heat, then pressed ground, bagged and stored. Casein in this form is a crumbly sort of powder. It is added to certain prepared foods, or it may be used industrially in paint, papermaking, or in such plastic items as bristles, buttons and billiard balls.

CASHEW

The cashew tree *(Anacardium occidentale)* produces a double fruit, the principal one being the cashew nut. The nut develops on the outside tip of the cashew apple, a colorful, juicy tropical fruit which is much appreciated locally. The apple's juice makes a passable wine called *cajuada* in Brazil and *maranon* in the Spanish-speaking tropics.

The tree originated in Brazil. Its name derives from the Arawak word *acaeju*, which means "to pucker the mouth," and describes the effect of some varieties of the fruit.

The nut itself develops inside a very hard shell, or rind, which exudes an acrid, irritating oil that is removed in the roasting process. It is kidney-shaped and has a delicate, sweet flavor which many consider far superior to that of the **peanut.** Its popularity is on the increase in the United States; cashews now constitute more than half the nuts imported into the country.

Cultivation of the cashew spread to other parts of tropical America, and the Portuguese took the tree to their Indian colony Goa. India is the main exporter of cashew nuts today; Mozambique, a former Portuguese colony, is also an important exporter. The nut's popularity, which came relatively recently, had to wait for the introduction of an adequate canning method.

Cashew nuts are generally eaten roasted, with salt, as a snack. They are not very suitable for baking because of their tendency to soften when heated.

CASIGIOLU

Also PANEDDA, PERA DE VACCA. *Casigiolu* is a Sardinian cow's milk cheese similar to ***caciocavallo.***

Sweet Cassava

CASSAREEP

This condiment or flavoring agent is prepared from the juice of the **cassava** plant. The cassava juice is boiled to make a thick syrup to which spices are added. It is used as the basis for many sauces in the West Indies and is an indispensable ingredient of the West Indian pepper pot.

CASSAVA

Also MANIOC. Cassava *(Manihot utilissima)* is a tuberous vegetable of American origin which was the principal source of flour for the pre-Columbian Indians of Brazil and the West Indies. It remains popular there today, and is also cultivated intensively in tropical Africa and Asia. Three products come from the cassava: cassava flour, **cassareep** and **tapioca.** Of the two main varieties of cassava, sweet and bitter, the latter is more important commercially because its roots grow to a larger size: roots weighing 30 pounds are not unusual. Although the term "manioc" is used as a synonym for cassava, it is usually applied to bitter cassava. Raw manioc contains prussic acid, enough in some seasons and climates for a lethal dose. But the acid is readily dissipated by cooking or sun drying the root or flour or by commercial processing.

Cassava has certain industrial uses, mainly as source of starch for such products as compressed yeast, sizing material and laundry starch. As a food, it has never appealed to Europeans and North Americans, except in the form of tapioca. But the flour, or meal, is an important food in several tropical countries. In Malaysia, it is a staple food, as important as bananas and coconuts. In Brazil cassava flour, called *farinha* is sprinkled liberally on the national dish, *feijoada,* which consists mainly of black beans, onions and sausage. Cassava tubers are composed of about 40 percent starch, 30 percent glucose, 10 percent tapioca and tiny amounts of protein, minerals, salts and lipids. The rest is water. Corn has at least twice as much protein as cassava, although the latter yields 10 times as much food per acre as either corn or wheat.

CASSETTE CHEESE

Also BOULETTE. A soft Belgian cheese, made from cow's milk, it is fermented at high temperatures and seasoned with salt and pepper before being shaped by hand into balls that are usually wrapped in walnut leaves. Cassette is a specialty of the Namur, Dinant and Huy districts.

CASSIA

Cassia buds and cassia bark—two flavoring agents—are produced by two different trees, both tropical, but belonging to separate botanical families. Cassia buds are tiny, unopened flowers of the *Cassia fistula,* a small tree named the golden shower, or pudding pipe tree. They have a weak cinnamon taste, and resemble small, spiky cloves. They are used whole in pickling or ground in spicing cakes and bread. The cassia family contains about 500 leguminous trees and shrubs that inhabit tropical or subtropical lands.

Many are used for medicinal purposes. *C. fistula*, for example, has pods containing a laxative pulp. Other varieties yield senna leaves. (See also: **Bedagosa.)**

Cassia bark, sometimes called the poor man's cinnamon, comes from the *Cinnamonum cassia* tree which is native to China. It was long considered an inferior grade, or even cinnamon substitute, when compared to Ceylon cinnamon *(C. zeylanicum)*. Cassia bark's taste is coarser, stronger and less volatile than Ceylon cinnamon. Its cultivation in this century in Indochina and Indonesia has led to its wide acceptance, especially in the United States. In cassia, the cinnamon taste extends also to the leaves, and it was in this form that cassia was introduced to the West in Classical Antiquity. Cassia leaves, called *malabathrum*, were mentioned as a spice in the Roman cookbook of Apicius, a first century gourmet. Cassia leaves are used today in India to flavor curries.

See also: **Cinnamon.**

CASSINA

Also CASSENE, YAUPON, YAPON. This tea made by native Americans comes from the dried leaves of either of two varieties of holly, *Ilex cassine* or *I. vomitoria*. These two species are native to the southeastern coast of the United States from North Carolina to Florida.

Holly is a shrubby evergreen tree with flat, leathery, glossy and dark green leaves that are evenly scalloped on the edges. The leaves and twigs contain both caffeine and tannin. When infused like ordinary tea, they make a mild, light-colored- stimulating drink that is bitter to the taste.

Native Americans, however, boiled the leaves for half an hour or more, producing a dark, bitter brew packing considerably more wallop. Each year they would travel from all over the southeast to the coast to collect a supply of leaves to last them for the year. They made this the occasion of the two- or three-day tea-drinking spree, which they thought of as a sort of cure. They valued the laxative and diuretic effects of the "black drink," as they called it, and consumed prodigious amounts of it at near boiling temperature.

The term "yaupon" comes from the Catawba word *yupon*, a diminutive of *yop*, a shrub.

CASSIRI

A sweet, alcoholic beverage is made in Guyana from a mash of sweet potatoes, sweet cassava and sometimes corn. When corn is used, the brewers chew it before adding it to the mash. This provides the necessary enzymes to convert cornstarch to sugar. Cassiri is mild and has a pleasant taste.

CASSIS

Cassis is the French word for black **currant,** and also the name of a liqueur based on black currant juice. There is more than one version. One, made in Burgundy, consists of black currrant juice, brandy and sugar. It contains 15 to 20 percent alcohol. A sweeter, heavier version, called *creme de cassis*, has the same percentage of alcohol. It can be taken alone as a digestive liqueur, or, typically, used to make a vermouth Cassis, which consists of a teaspoon of Cassis added to a third of a glass of dry vermouth, plus ice and soda water. The drink is deep purple in color.

The name Cassis is also given to French wines from a certain part of the *Cotes de Provence*, a region that runs along the Mediterranean coast from Nice to Marseilles. The Cassis area produces reds, roses and whites, the last generally acknowledged as the best. The area is a few miles southeast of Marseilles, and the wines are considered an ideal accompaniment to the local seafood.

CASTANOPSIS NUT

Also CHINQUAPIN. Edible fruits of several species of evergreen trees *(Castanopsis)*, native to Asia and North America, they include the chinquapin of Virginia and other southern regions of the United States, the Tonkin chestnut, the golden-leaved chestnut, the Sumatra *castanopsis*, the Philippine chestnut, the Chinese and Tibetan chinquapins and the Henry chinquapin.

They resemble small chestnuts and are enclosed three to a bunch in a spiny covering. But the actual seed more resembles an oak seed. The flavor is reminiscent of both chestnut and acorn. They are prepared by roasting, boiling or parching.

CASTELLO

Also CREMA DANICA. This popular soft Danish cheese has a sharp taste, rather like a cross between Camembert and **Brie.** It is good accompanied by fresh fruit or red wine.

CASTELLO BRANCO

See **Serra Da Estrela.**

CASTELMAGNO

Castelmagno is an Italian cheese of the blue-mold type, similar in taste and texture to **Gorgonzola.**

CASTELO BRANCO

This medium soft Portuguese cheese is found in nearly all parts of the country. It is made from sheep's milk or from a mixture of sheep and goat's milk.

CASTLE CHEESE

See **Schlosskase.**

CAT

Few modern peoples eat the domestic cat *(Felis catus)* with anything but reluctance. An exception to this are Italians of the Valle d'Aosta, where, in the villages of Pont St. Martin and Donnaz, they raise cats especially for the table. Apparently, though, cats are eaten only at Christmas, as a special treat. They reputedly taste like hare, only better, and for diners who like a little more flavor, some cats are hung for 48 hours to give them a gamey taste. There seems to be no cultural group that includes cats as a regular part of its diet.

This has not always been the case. When Marco Polo visited China, he noted that cats were on the menu for rich and poor alike, although the latter had to make do with alley cats. In the West, cat bones have been found in prehistoric caves. It is assumed that these bones are the remains of meals because, so far as can be documented, the ancient Egyptians were the first to domesticate the cat. Their stores of grain needed protection against the rodents, so they tamed the wild African cat *(Felis lybica)* to do the job. Cats were so successful at the task that a cat god appeared in the pantheon, and some were honored with mummification. Domestication occurred about 3000 B.C. and since then there has been a general taboo in the West against eating cats.

Exceptions are made in times of famine. The most notable and well-publicized of these occurred in 1870–71, during the Franco-Prussian War, when the Germans laid siege to Paris. By Christmas 1870 the siege had lasted 99 days, and stocks of normal food were exhausted. Parisians were obliged to resort to dogs, cats, rodents and zoo animals. On Christmas Day, the famous *Restaurant Voisin* carried on its menu, "Cats garnished with rats."

The similarity between cat and hare has been the subject of humorous verse. An example is this bit of doggerel by the Rev. Richard Harris Barham:

She help'd him to lean, and she help'd
him to fat,
And it look'd like hare—but it might
have been cat.

CATALO

See **Beefalo.**

CATAWBA

The Catawba is a red grape native to North America, and the wine produced from it. The Catawba vine was originally found in woods near the Catawba River in North Carolina in 1801. It was first thought to be a **Tokay,** on the strength of an assertion by a German priest. But it is in fact a hybrid of *Vitis labrusca* and *Vitis vinifera.* It produces a dark, rich, red wine, with a taste slightly akin to that of muscat. The cultivation of the Catawba helped to establish successful grape growing in the Atlantic states.

CATECHU

A red brown sap is obtained from various Asian trees including the *Acacia catechu* and the *Areca catechu* or betel nut palm. It is chewed for its astringent taste and stimulating effect. It is mixed with sugar and gum tragacanth to make tablets, which sweeten the breath and settle the stomach. The acacia sap also yields an important khaki dye, black cutch.

See also: **Betel Nut.**

CATERPILLAR

Several types of caterpillars—the worm-like larvae of butterflies—are considered edible. Nutritional analysis has shown them to consist of about 37 percent protein and 14 percent fat. Mexicans delight in eating toasted or fried maguey worms, which are the caterpillars of skipper butterflies. "Caterpillar pretzels" are eaten as an hor d'oeuvre accompanying mezcal, the brandy made from the maguey cactus. Most people have probably sampled the coffee-borer caterpillar, since minute portions of it are frequently present in ground coffee. The Laotians, however, are particularly fond of it, eating roasted caterpillars with rice and a dash of salt. The silkworm *(Bombyx mori)*, has long been considered a nutritious and flavorful dish by the Chinese and Vietnamese. It is eaten after it has pupated, i.e., formed a cocoon. In this stage it contains 23.1 percent protein and 14.2 percent fat. After unreeling the silk, the Chinese soften the caterpillars in water and cook them in omelets, or stir fry them with onions. The Vietnamese first boil the pupae, then fry them, or put them in soup with cabbage and *nuoc-mam.* Cooking silkworms are reputed to have a very pleasant smell.

CATFISH

A class of fish whose long feelers, called barbels, around its mouth are thought to resemble a cat's whiskers, the catfish is a freshwater fish, in the main, although certain European marine fish, such as the sea wolf and the dogfish are sometimes referred to as catfish. There are 25 families (2,000 species) of catfish worldwide, but only the North American varieties are of much gastronomic importance. Nevertheless, the largest catfish, the Wels, or sheatfish

(*Silurus glanis*), which can attain a length of 10 feet and a weight of 400 pounds, is European. Considered a delicacy, it is found mainly in the Danube, Elbe, Vistula and Oder rivers. The most commonly eaten American varieties can range in weight from two to 150 pounds. The American lake catfish (*Amiurus lacustris*), one of the larger kinds, inhabits Midwestern lakes, such as the Great Lakes. It has a broad head, long barbels and a rather stout body. The Mississippi, or blue, cat (*Ictalurus furcatus*) is found in the Mississippi and Gulf states, along with the mud cat, or goujon (*Leptops olivaris*). Both can attain weights well above 100 pounds. The mud cat has a flat head and short barbels, while the blue cat has a narrow head, narrow mouth and long barbels. The most popular smaller variety is the bullhead (*Amiurus nebulosus*), also called the horned pout or the Schuylkill cat (after a river in Pennsylvania). The bullhead has a much wider range; it is found in nearly every section of the United States. It adapts well to new environments, and in 1855 fingerlings of the bullhead were imported into France to be bred for the table on fish farms. They escaped captivity, however, in 1871 and bred so prolifically in French rivers as to threaten valued native fish. To make matters worse, the French did not develop a taste for catfish. The bullhead usually weighs a pound or two, and seldom exceed 12 inches in length.

Catfish are scaleless, and their flesh is finely grained, with few bones. The taste is sweet, tending towards muddiness, particularly in bullheads, which are bottom feeders. The larger fish are cut into thick steaks and grilled. Smaller fish are always skinned, then fried or deep-fat fried, perhaps after being rolled in cornmeal or batter.

Catfish are a specialty of the southern United States and, to a lesser extent, the Midwest. They are often raised in captivity for the table; channel catfish are the preferred type for this treatment. They can be bought live at fish farms or, in many instances, eaten on the spot at nearby restaurants. Fisherman handle catfish gingerly because the barbels are reputed to be poisonous, but in reality it is the spines on the fins that are dangerous.

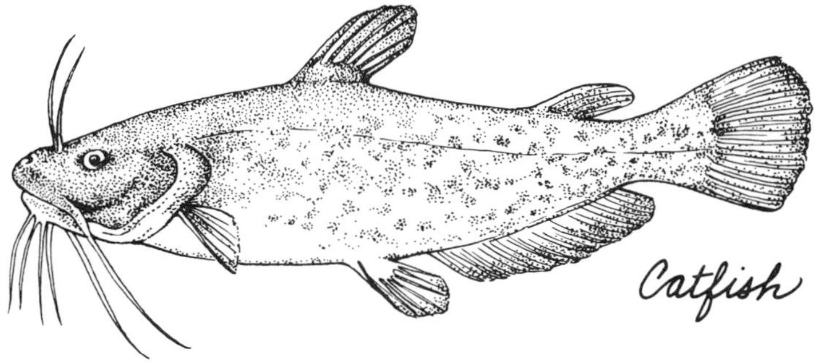

CATMINT

See **Catnip.**

CATNIP

Also CATMINT. This aromatic herb, *Nepeta cataria*, of the mint family grows in temperate areas worldwide. Its leaves and young shoots have a refreshingly minty and somewhat bitter taste. It may be added to salads as a seasoning. The dried leaves are sometimes used to make an herbal tea taken as a restorative. The odor of catnip is attractive to cats who love to play with catnip balls.

CAT'S EAR

A perennial herb, *Hypochoeris maculata*, of Europe and Siberia has young leaves that make an excellent salad. It is rarely eaten except in times of food shortage.

CATTAIL

Also BULRUSH. A wild marsh plant that is a versatile source of food in the wilderness, the cattail is a tall plant, easily identifiable with its long, flat reedlike leaves and cylindrical flower spikes that look like fuzzy, brown brushes. The cattail (*Typha latifolia*) has many other names including elephant grass, reed-mace, club rush and cattail flag. It grows in damp areas along the edges of freshwater lakes and streams and, at one time or another during the year, all its parts are edible.

In the spring, the tender young shoots can be eaten raw in salads or boiled as greens. They are called "cassock asparagus," for they are said to be a favorite with the Don Cossacks of Russia. In France, the leaves are used in salads. The green bloom spikes, before they develop pollen, can be eaten raw, or cooked and dipped in melted butter. They resemble sweet corn in that the core is inedible. May and June are the most appropriate months for this. After pollen develops, the bloom spike can be boiled as a porridge or used as a flour to make bread dough. It can be mixed half-and-half with wheat flour for pancakes or muffins. The rootstalk can also be ground and used as flour. It is full of stored starch and quite nutritious. Often it is simply peeled and either boiled or baked. Cattail sprouts, which spring from the root ends under the surface of the water, are broken off to serve as sweet vegetables or to be pickled. The bulrush of Biblical fame is not this plant, but a type of papyrus (*Cyperus papyrus*).

CAUL

A membrane enclosing the stomach and adjacent viscera of mammals, the caul is an extension of the peritoneum, the membraneous sack that holds the guts. Caul is also known as the omentum.

The caul is the best part of the peritoneum for cooking purposes because it is generously ribbed with fat, so that it looks like a net or thick veil. It is used to wrap ground meat, offal or forcemeats when cooking to protect them from direct heat. The caul's fat adds moisture.

The caul is also used as sausage casing. Pork caul is most often used, followed by that of sheep or calf. In French, the caul is the *crepine* or *toilette. Crepinettes* are small caul-encased sausages made from minced pork, lamb, veal or chicken.

CAULIFLOWER

Queen of the cabbage clan, this plant is cultivated for its edible flower. Mark Twain dubbed it "cabbage with a college education." Indeed, this vegetable has been much improved over the years by careful selection and cultivation.

The flower formed by the stalk and bud is a compact white mass, sometimes referred to as the "curd." Long leaves surrounding the bud are cut down to within an inch of the curd, which should be solid and creamy white in color. Spotting indicates that it might not be fresh, and a granular appearance that the flowerettes have begun to grow. Large ones are as good as small, and size bears no relation to age.

Cauliflower *(Brassica oleracea*, Botrytis group) is among the most important vegetables produced in the United States, where it is grown primarily in California and New York. It is available nearly the year around.

If eaten raw, it is usually pickled in vinegar. The customary method of cooking is boiling, after which it still retains some vitamin C, thiamine and carotene.

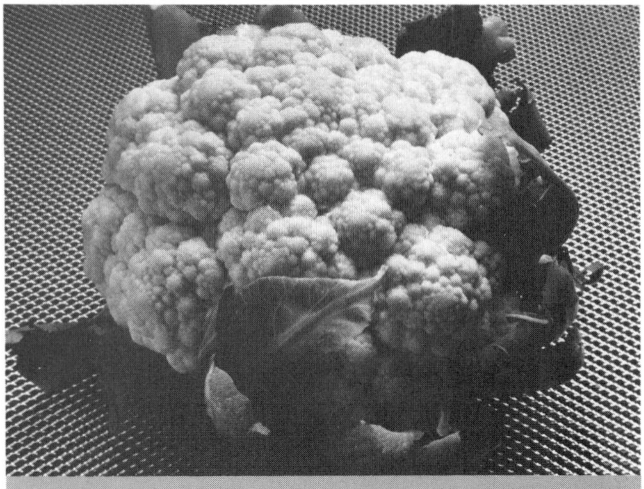

Cauliflower

CAVALLA

Also CREVALLE JACK, JACK. A genus of tropical fish of the pompano family, cavallas have the oblong, compressed body of the pompano, plus a high forehead. Perhaps the most abundant species is the crevalle jack *(Carangus hippos)*, which can weigh from three to 35 pounds and reach a length of three feet.

It is found on both coasts of tropical America, going as far north as Cape Cod in the Atlantic, and in the East Indies. The crevalle jack has a greenish brown back, golden sides and underparts and a black spot on the pectoral fins. It is a food fish of considerable importance. Along with several other fish, it is sometimes called the horse mackerel.

CAVE LOBSTER

See **Spiny Lobster.**

CAVIAR

Also CAVIARE. In the strictest sense, caviar is the roe, or eggs, of various species of **sturgeon,** a freshwater fish that can weigh up to 2,000 pounds. Iran produces the most caviar, then Russia. It is an unusual and expensive delicacy. The roe of other fish compete as caviar substitutes—lumpfish, tuna, mullet and salmon; the last is called "red caviar." But connoisseurs consider the competitors feeble by comparison with true caviar.

The species of sturgeon *(Acipenseridae)* that produce caviar are, in order of size, beluga, osetra, sevruga, sterliad and sterlet. The best fishing grounds are in the rivers around the Caspian Sea, the Black Sea and the Sea of Azov. The color of caviar is generally black, but one also finds various shades of yellow, gray, dark green and brown. The test of fine caviar is its good taste; it can be found in any of those colors. The size of individual eggs ranges from very small to the size of a pea.

Beluga caviar is the most plentiful. It is pearly gray, and the eggs are large. Many caviar fanciers prefer the sevruga, because it is the finest grained.

Caviar is processed as follows: It is removed from the fish and pressed through a sieve to remove membrane, fibers and fatty tissue. The finest eggs are mixed with salt—enough to make up four to five percent of the finished product—and put in cans or jars as fresh caviar. It is called *malossol* ("lightly salted"). A coarser product, which consists mostly of roe that is premature or damaged in the sieving process, is more heavily salted (10 percent), pressed in bulk and shipped for canning elsewhere. This is called *payusnaya*, and is a staple food in Russia and Eastern Europe.

Centuries ago sturgeon was plentiful in the rivers of England, France and Germany. Tastes then were the reverse of ours. Sturgeon flesh was thought fit for a king ("royal sturgeon"), while the roe was not considered anything special. An Italian proverb expressed the contemporary wisdom: "Who eats caviar eats flies, dung and salt."

Near the end of the 19th century, the United States had its day in the sun as the world's prime source of caviar. But overfishing and industrial sprawl turned the sturgeon to a rare species in North America. Lately the industry has been making a small comeback, with production centers on rivers in Oregon and Washington on the West Coast, and the Hudson River on the East Coast. Approximately 20,000 pounds of caviar similar to the Beluga and Sevruga types were expected to be produced in 1980.

Caviar will spoil if not kept below 40° F. It is usually served on ice. It may be eaten by itself or spread on toast, with a dash of lemon juice.

Red caviar (salmon roe) is larger and saltier than black. To offset the saltiness, it is often served with cream cheese, sour cream or eggs.

CAVY

See **Guinea Pig.**

CAYENNE

A dullish red powder made from the hottest of chili peppers *(Capsicum frutescens)* and used as a spice, cayenne takes its name from the town of Cayenne, French Guiana, although it is made in many places, including Japan, which produces the mildest form. Cayenne is made in two different ways. The small pods may be dried and ground to fine powder and marketed in that form. Alternatively, the powder may be mixed with dough and baked into hard biscuits, which are then reduced to powder. Nepaul pepper is a very hot Indian variety, yellowish red in color.

Cayenne is very pungent and hot and should be used sparingly; a pinch is sufficient to add zest to most dishes. It is commonly sprinkled on clam chowder and on oysters. The bite in barbecue sauce usually comes from cayenne. In small doses, it reputedly facilitates digestion, especially of vegetables. *Capsicums* are rich in vitamin C.

CEBRERO

This Spanish cheese has faint blue veining, but not enough to be classed as a blue cheese. It is formed in the shape of a mushroom and has a creamy, but moderately sharp, taste. The rind is pale yellow.

CEDRAT

See **Citron.**

CELERIAC

A variety of **celery,** *Apium graveolens* var. *rapaceum*, it has a large, brownish, edible root. In the United States, celeriac is better known as celery root, celery knob, or turnip root celery. It is not the root of ordinary celery, as some believe, and does not develop large stalks above the ground.

Celeriac is best served as a cooked vegetable, much in the manner of **cauliflower,** which its taste slightly resembles. Typically, it is first washed and pared, then cut into chunks or large slices, blanched and lightly boiled with pepper, salt and butter. It may also be steamed and sprinkled with grated parmesan or swiss cheese.

Celeriac is usually sold in bunches of three or four roots, which vary in size from small knobs of about two and one-half inches thick to larger ones from four to five inches across. A pound of celeriac should easily serve four persons. It may also be eaten raw or used with salads, soups and stews. Its large size also allows it to be stuffed with any ingredients used to stuff bell peppers or tomatoes.

Celeriac

CELERY

Celery is a garden vegetable, *Apium graveolens* var. *dulce*, cultivated for its crisp, rounded leaf stalks, which are eaten raw or cooked. The kind generally found in United States markets is the Pascal variety, which has greenish stalks that are practically stringless. Another variety is yellow or golden celery, whose stalks have been blanched. Pascal celery has the more pronounced flavor of the two. When celery is fresh, a rib broken off the head snaps cleanly. The celery heart (at the base, where the stalks join) is also delicious, and the leaves make a nice garnish for meat or poultry.

Americans and the British generally prefer to eat celery raw, serving it in many ways: Celery curls may be eaten as an appetizer; the stalks may be chopped fine for use in salads or sandwich fillings; or

A celery field in the Santa Clara Valley, California

Celery

whole stalks may be eaten, alone or stuffed with cheese or other fillings. Cooked celery is preferred on the Continent. The French favor braising, or frying, celery and serving it with Bechamel sauce. The French also consider it a basic aromatic flavoring, and use it to season soups, stocks, casseroles and creamed dishes. The Italians, whose ancestors, the ancient Romans, were the first Europeans to eat celery as a table vegetable, also prefer cooked celery, but for this purpose often buy *ache*, a wild variety, whose flavor is stronger than that of cultivated celery.

Ache is native to the Mediterranean areas, growing in seaside soils impregnated with brackish water. It was first gathered by the ancient Egyptians and used as a seasoning. According to Homer, who mentioned *ache* in the *Odyssey*, the ancient Greeks continued this practice. It remained for the Romans to cultivate the celery plant and discover its use as a table vegetable. They also believed that wearing a wreath of *ache* prevented hangovers. Horace wrote:

> *Fill the cups with Massic wine, which makes us forget all our ills; imbibe the flowers of these mighty springs, and make in haste crowns of ache and myrtle.*

With the collapse of the Roman Empire, *ache* disappeared from the European diet, to reappear again in Renaissance Italy; from there its cultivation spread to France and England. Large-scale commercial cultivation of celery in the United States was initiated by Dutch farmers near Kalamazoo, Mich. in 1874. California and New York are also large celery-producing states.

Celery is highly perishable. The fresh stalks should be washed, then wrapped in absorbent paper and stored in a dry, very cool place. Though not rich in calories, celery contains abundant mineral salts, vitamins and iron.

Perhaps the last word on celery belongs to the American writer Ogden Nash, who wrote:

> *Celery raw, develops the jaw,*
> *But celery stewed is more quietly chewed.*

CELERY ROOT

See **Celeriac.**

CELERY SALT

A prepared seasoning consisting of ground celery seed and salt crystals, it is added to soups, stews and salads and imparts a celery taste to the dish while salting it.

1 Apples

2 Sun-dried apricots

3 Artichokes

4 Bananas

5 Blackberries

6 An assortment of Brie cheeses

7 Broccoli

8 Brussels sprouts

9 Red cabbage

10 The Cabernet grape

11 Houses of cake

12 Ceriman

CELERY SEED

Celery seed is in fact the tiny fruit, resembling a seed, of a wild celery plant, also known as smallage. Either whole or ground, these seeds are a popular flavoring. Whole, they are used on rolls and crackers and in cheese, salads and sauces, as well as for pickling. Ground, they are used in soups, stews, chowders and vegetable juices. They are an ingredient of celery salt; in that form they find even more uses.

CELLULOSE

An indigestible form of carbohydrate abundant in plants, it makes up the fibrous or woody part of their cell walls. It is a polymer of glucose. Animals with more than one stomach, such as cows, are nourished by it. Humans, however, cannot digest cellulose. It does play a role in human diet, however, as roughage, providing bulk for intestinal functioning.

See also: **Carbohydrate.**

CENDRE DE LA BRIE

See **Brie.**

CEPE

See **Bolete.**

CEREALS

Cereals have been mankind's basic food since Neolithic times. Before that, nomads roamed the land searching for game. Then, in the Neolithic era, came the birth of agriculture, which basically involved the cultivation of wild grasses. This tied humans down to one place, bringing social stability and, eventually, the urban civilization that still characterizes human culture.

Cereals are members of the grass family cultivated for their edible seed. The main cereals are wheat, barley, corn (maize), rice, oats, rye, millet and sorghum. They played a crucial role in the formation of human culture because cereals are the one category of food that can sustain human life practically unaided. True, their vegetable proteins must be supplemented with food that contains complete protein, such as eggs, meat, milk, fish or soya. Also, cereals generally lack calcium and vitamin A. Yet millions of humans live on diets consisting primarily of cereal, such as rice, with tiny supplements to make up for missing nutrients. Cereals are the one indispensable food.

More than half the world's arable land is devoted to the cultivation of cereals, with wheat being the most important, making up 31 percent of total production. It is the most nourishing cereal, and it predominates in the relatively dry areas of the world. Second in importance is rice, which accounts for 15.5 percent of world cereal production, practically all of it going for human consumption. It is the mainstay in the relatively hot and humid areas of the world. Corn (maize), though constituting a larger portion (22.5 percent) of total production than rice, plays a lesser role in human nutrition because the majority goes to fatten animals. Less important grains are barley (10.25 percent), oats (7.5 percent) and rye (2.5 percent). Millet and sorghum (9.5 percent together) are important to human nutrition only in parts of Africa, Asia and the Soviet Union which are too dry for other grains. Otherwise, it is fed to animals. Because it is not a member of the grass family, **buckwheat** is excluded here.

There term "cereal" derives from the name of the ancient Roman goddess of the harvest, Ceres, and from a ritual in her honor called *Ceralia.* The overwhelming importance of cereal grains in ancient times can be deduced from the story of Joseph's rise to power in Egypt, as told in the Bible. Joseph, an Israelite and a talented interpreter of dreams, was languishing in jail, where a former member of the royal household had told him about a disturbing dream that the Pharoah had had. Sent for by the Pharoah, Joseph told him that this dream presaged seven years of bountiful harvests, to be followed by seven years of lean harvests. Joseph was put in charge of a program to store grain for the lean years, and everything transpired as he had predicted. Because he had averted famine, and possibly political instability, Joseph became the second most powerful man in Egypt, after Pharoah.

All cereals can be made into bread, and consequently played a key role in the ancient Roman formula for domestic peace. Each citizen was entitled, during Imperial times, to free grain from the public dole, as well as free public entertainment. This policy was summed up in the terse slogan, "Bread and circuses." For more information, see entries on specific grains.

See also: **Breakfast Food.**

CERIMAN

Also FALSE BREADFRUIT. This delicious fruit is a member of the Arum family. Native to tropical and subtropical America, including Florida, it is plentiful in Mexico and Guatemala. The ceriman plant *(Monstera deliciosa)* is a tree-climbing vine, with perforated leaves two to three feet long and dangling, cordlike roots. The fruit bears no resemblance to real breadfruit; conelike in shape, it looks more like a greenish-yellow banana—up to 14 inches long—whose skin is textured by a mosaic of squarish platelets like a pineapple's. Perhaps this appearance has influenced the description of its taste, which is said to resemble that of a cross between pineapple and banana. At any rate, the husky skin is easily removed and the pulp is sweet and luscious. Ceriman is always eaten raw.

CERO

Also PAINTED MACKEREL. A good food fish of the tropical western Atlantic, found from New England to Brazil and in the Gulf of Mexico, the cero *(Scomberomorus regalis)* is a Spanish mackerel that can weigh up to 35 pounds and attain a length of six feet. Average size of a landed fish is about 10 pounds. It has the typical spindle shape and large mouth of the genus. It is deep blue above with silvery sides and belly, sprinkled with yellow and bronze spots. It is a popular fish with anglers and is eaten fresh, smoked or canned.

See also: **Mackerel, Spanish Mackerel.**

CERTOSINA

An Italian cow's milk cheese from the Veneto region, it is white and has a creamy texture.

CERVELAS

See **Cervelat.**

CERVELAT

Also CERVELAS. Cervelat, a French sausage, is made from lean and fat pork and highly spiced with garlic. The small cervelat resembles a **frankfurter,** but is shorter, fatter and redder. The larger ones look like **bologna sausage,** but their taste is much spicier.

The name "cervelat" is related to the French word for brain, *cervelle.* The name is an old one, and there is reason to believe that, a couple of centuries ago, cervelat contained pig's brains. Brains are no longer an ingredient, yet the texture of the cervelat is still smooth and tender.

The modern cervelat contains approximately five parts of lean pork to one part of either lard or chopped bacon, plus chopped parsley, the green parts of scallions, thyme, basil, clove and nutmeg. The most important flavoring agent is garlic, which in France doesn't make much of an impression, because there cervelat is commonly eaten with a hot mustard that overwhelms any other taste. After the mixture of meat and flavorings is stuffed into casings, the sausages are air-dried and, usually, poached in beef bouillon.

A variation, made in Lyons, is *cervelas truffe*, which includes chopped truffles and, sometimes, pistachio nuts and is lightly smoked.

The cervelat is also known as the *saucisson de Paris*, yet failed to win over one of Paris' most famous gourmets, Alexandre Dumas *pere*, who made this acerbic comment in his *Le Grand Dictionnaire de Cuisine:*

> *Pork cervelat has all the bad qualities of pig meat, and the manner in which it is prepared makes it even more indigestible. Cervelat is also made with fish. This is less indigestible, but the high proportion of spices used makes it anything but healthful, especially if it is eaten frequently.*

Nevertheless, cervelat continues to be quite popular in Europe and the United States. A British version, called "saveloy," is made from the extremities of pigs, and is somewhat coarser than the French version. *Cervelatwurst*, a German sausage, is made from finely minced pork and beef filets. It is highly spiced and smoked, and soft enough to be spread.

See also: **Sausage.**

CEVENNES

See **Goat's Milk Cheese.**

CEYLON GOOSEBERRY

See **Ketembilla.**

CEYLON SPINACH

See **Basella.**

CEYLON TEA

The island of Sri Lanka produces various kinds of black tea, the best coming from the high districts of Uva, Nuwara and Eliji. These teas are known for their rich and unique flavors, but much tea is also grown at lower altitudes. Among the best, the leaves smell of flowers and the flavor is intense. The color is bright and the aroma pleasant. A special drying process is employed in some districts, involving two firings. In the first, a very high temperature is used, sealing in flavor and essential oils; in the second, a lower temperature is used to insure a longer period of freshness.

See also: **Tea.**

CHABICHOU

A French goat's milk cheese with a soft texture, it is a product of the Pitou district and is in season from May to November.

CHABICHOUS

See **Goat's Milk Cheese.**

CHABLIS

Chablis is an elegant dry white wine grown in the Chablis district in northern Burgundy, about 50 miles northwest of Dijon. In earlier times the wines of Auxerre (as the region was then called) were predominantly red, and for centuries supplied much of the vintage consumed by Parisians. Chablis, from the Chardonnay grape, is extremely dry and has an almost "flinty" taste—like **champagne.** It is clear, almost pale in color and is traditionally *the* wine to drink with oysters—though it of course complements other shellfish and seafood of all kinds. In the 20th century the production of Chablis has declined somewhat, and consequently the best of this vintage is now rather expensive. A good Chablis—dry, but more intensely flavored than the great French wine—is made in California.

See also: **Burgundy Wines.**

CHABOISSEAU

A Mediterranean food fish, its striking appearance has won it such nicknames as "devil fish," "scorpion fish," and "toad." It has a large, ugly head, and when held makes a curious grumbling noise, which earned it the nickname, "grumbler." It makes fine eating but should be avoided during the spawning season from November to May. It is often used in fish stews, such as bouillabaisse.

CHABOT

See **Chub.**

CHAD

See **Bream.**

CHALLAH

Also HALLAH, TWIST. The traditional Jewish Sabbath bread, Challah is a light, yeast-raised loaf, made with eggs and braided in a beehive shape. A pinch of saffron is often added to the dough, producing a light gold color. Often poppy or sesame seeds are sprinkled over the top of the loaf. According to one authority, the braided shape is reminiscent of shewbread, the 12 loaves of unleavened bread placed at the altar before Jehovah every Sabbath by the ancient Hebrew priests and eaten by them alone at the end of the week.

See also: **Bread.**

Challah

CHAMBERTIN

Chambertin is a name given to some of the most celebrated red wines of Burgundy, from vineyards near Dijon in the northern part of the Cote d'Or. The vineyard of Chambertin itself was planted in the seventh century next to the *clos* (or "vineyard") of Beze, and was named for the peasant, named *Bertin*, who owned the property *champs*, or field, of Bertin. Wine from this vineyard and from the Clos de Beze is still the most prized of all the red Burgundies, dark red, full-bodied and robust ("masculine") in its flavor.

See also: **Burgundy Wines.**

CHAMLAGU

The yellow flowers of this Chinese pea tree *Caragana chamlagu* are eaten locally. It is a bushy tree or shrub indigenous to the north of China and is able to withstand cold conditions.

CHAMOIS

Also ISARD, IZARD. The only western European antelope, the chamois *(Rupicapra rupicapra)* is a small goatlike creature inhabiting the higher regions of the Alps, Pyrenees, Appenines, Carpathians and Caucasus mountains. The Pyrenees variety, called the *izard*, is slightly smaller than the chamois and reddish in color. Because of its agility and fleetness of foot, the chamois is a favorite with hunters. But due to the chamois' increasing scarcity, hunting is greatly restricted. The flesh is considered venison, of a subtle type with a pronounced but not overwhelming gamey flavor. It is relatively tender. The two most likely places to find chamois meat (except for those hunting it themselves) are Andorra, where it is a great favorite, and in Italy near the Valle d'Aosta, where chamois are more numerous than elsewhere. The young chamois is spit roasted while older animals, tougher and dryer, are baked in a marinade of white wine and spices. A special delicacy is the liver, which is baked in wine with onions.

The chamois has been considered fair game since Neanderthal times, which perhaps accounts for its sparse numbers and its liking for inaccessible terrain. The ancient Greeks and Hebrews ate chamois. According to the Bible (Deuteronomy 14:4–5), "These are the beasts which ye shall eat, the ox, the sheep, and the goat. The hart and roebuck and the fallow deer and the wild goat and the pygarg (antelope) and the wild ox and the chamois." Apart from Europe and western Asia, New Zealand is the only place in the world that has wild chamois. They are descendants of a small herd that was presented as a gift of state by the Emperor Francis Joseph of Austria-Hungary before World War I.

The soft, porous leather known as chamois (pronounced "chammy") that is used to polish cars in the United States was originally made from the skin of the chamois. Now deer or antelope hide is used for better "chamois," while cheaper varieties are made from split sheep's skin.

Chamois

CHAMPAGNE

This is the noble sparkling wine from the Champagne district, east of Paris. Although good still wines have been cultivated in this region (along the Marne) from ancient times, the history of champagne really began in the 17th century when it was *the* fashionable drink. Dom Pierre Perignon, a Benedictine monk, is usually credited with being the father of champagne. Almost certainly it was he who devised the process of sealing the bottles with bits of cork. Vintners had earlier used a film of oil, wax, an oil-soaked cloth, or even a wooden peg for this purpose. Very possibly, Dom Perignon also discovered the *methode champenoise*, responsible for making the wine sparkle.

Most champagne is made from a blend of green and black grapes, although the finished wine is a clear, pale gold. Some champagne is made from green grapes (Chardonnay) only, and is called Blanc de Blancs. This is one of the most highly prized of all champagnes. A pink champagne results from allowing the skin (or *must)* from the black grapes to remain in contact with the pressed liquid for a short time, or by adding a small amount of red wine to the mixture. The chalky soil of the Champagne region adds importantly to the wine's particular brightness and flinty taste.

A sparkling wine requires a second fermentation. With champagne, this takes place in the individual bottles. After the first pressing of grapes carefully chosen and blended from all parts of the region—unlike the practice elsewhere in France, where the grapes come from single estates or vineyards—the wine is stored in casks until late winter or early spring. The first fermentation—called *bouillage*, or "boiling"—is completed by this time. A mixture of liquid sugar *(liqueur de tirage)* dissolved in older wine is then added to the vintage. This brings on a second fermentation in April or May, when the additional sugar produces a gas from carbonic acid. This makes the champagne bubble. The bottles are kept on their sides with the necks pointing down *(sur pointe)* for several years. At carefully selected times the bottles are tipped at angles, turned, wiggled, twisted, until at last a skilled technician (called the *degorgeur)* quickly removes the cork—where sediment has collected—and examines the beverage. The small amount of wine lost in this process is then replaced, more sugar is added if needed, and the wines are recorked, secured with a wire mesh, and labeled for sale. Often—to make this tricky job easier—the necks are prefrozen in a brine solution. The ice is blown out when the corks are removed, and almost no wine at all is lost.

This method of double fermenation is typical of all wine called champagne, whether it is produced in France, the United States, South America or the Soviet Union. The *methode champenoise* is characterized by the *remuage* (the deposit of sediment towards the cork), the uncorking or *degorgement* (removing the cork and, along with it, the sediment) and the *dosage* (the addition of more liqueur to the bottle). Another method used to produce sparkling wines, or *vins mousseux*, is known as the *cuve* (or vat) *close*. In this process the second fermentation takes place in huge vats rather than in the bottles. It is forbidden by French law to produce champagne in this way. In the United States, especially in California, sparkling wine called champagne is made in a manner similar to the *methode champenoise*, but the second fermentation occurs in large glass containers holding up to a gallon of wine.

Chief among the grapes used in the making of champagne are the Pinot Noir, the Pinot Meunier and the Chardonnay. The climate of Champagne is uncertain—not like the more stable weather of the Loire farther west—and the great champagnes do vary in excellence from year to year, although every effort is made by the vintners to maintain blends of high quality. Types of champagne are named according to the amount of sugar added in the second fermentation. Brut—prized especially by the English—is the driest champagne, with an absolute minimum of added sugar (0.5 to one percent). Extra Dry *(Extra Sec)* has from one to two percent of additional sugar. Dry or *Sec* has from three to six percent. *Demi-Sec* has seven to 10 percent. And Sweet *Douce* or *Doux* has from 10 to 15 percent. The carbonic acid helps preserve the wine for long periods of time, safeguarding it from bacteria.

Champagne inspires toasts, for occasions of great festivity, the following dialogue from Hemingway's *The Sun Also Rises* notwithstanding: "I say, that is wine,' Brett held up her glass. 'We ought to toast something. Here's to royalty.' 'This wine is too good for toast-drinking, my dear. You don't want to mix emotions up with a wine like that. You lose the taste.'" *Brut* and *Extra Sec* are superb aperitifs. *Sec* and *Demi-Sec* are appropriate with any meal, or for their own sake. The *Douce* is a luxurious wine with dessert.

See also: **Loire Wines.**

CHAMPEDEK

Fruit of this southeast Asian tree, *Artocarpus polyphema*, is similar to the **jackfruit** but smaller. When immature the fruit may be eaten as a vegetable in soups, or, when ripe, it may be eaten raw. The flavor is somewhat stronger than jackfruit's. The seeds are also edible.

CHAMPENOIS CHEESE

A cow's milk cheese made in France's Champagne region, it is in season from September to June.

CHAMPOLA

Also CHAMPOLO. Champola is a refreshing soft drink made in El Salvador and Nicaragua from the soursop *(Annona muricata)*, a fruit known locally as *guanabana*.

See also: **Soursop.**

CHAMPOLEON

Also QUEYRAS. A hard French cheese made from skim milk in the Haute-Alps region, champoleon is similar to ***canquillote.***

CHANNEL BASS

See **Bass.**

CHANTELLE

This is the trade name of a semisoft American cheese with a mild flavor, open texture and smooth, waxy body similar to that of **Port du Salut.** It is closer to **Bel Paese** in the making and curing, however. The surface is coated early in the processing to hinder the action of surface organisms; hence it never becomes as soft as Bel Paese. It is shipped after three weeks' curing. Cheeses are round, eight inches in diameter, flat and weigh about five pounds.

CHANTERELLE

Also GIROLLE. The name "chanterelle" applies to several vase- or trumpet-shaped, edible mushrooms that grow in temperate areas around the world, including Japan, India, Europe and the United States. The most representative of this group is the golden chanterelle, or *girolle (Cantharellus cibarius)*, whose receptable is shaped like a crumpled cup with a pleated outer surface. The mushroom is egg-yellow; its pleats function like gills to produce spores. Chanterelles are small, not more than one to three inches across and about the same in height. The texture of their flesh is thick and meaty, and has a fragrance, in European varieties at least, of apricots. It is found on the ground in open evergreen and deciduous woods, usually in summer and fall, but in California on into the winter.

The chanterelle ranks high with gourmets for its delicious flavor, and is widely eaten in Europe, where it is available in markets in both fresh and dried forms. It is virtually ignored in the United States, except by connoisseurs who pick their own. Dried chanterelles, however, are available in Italian grocery stores in America. The chanterelle is a versatile mushroom, excellent with scrambled eggs, in sauces or stewed with meat. It keeps well under refrigeration for a week, or, when frozen, for up to a year.

Other chanterelles are the white chanterelle *(C. subalbidus)*, which closely resembles the golden chanterelle, except that it is white and slightly larger; the gillless chanterelle *(Craterellus cantharellus)*, which is thinner and lacks pleats but otherwise resembles the golden chanterelle, and the horn of plenty *(Craterellus cornucopioides)*, which the French call the "trumpet of death." Despite the hyperbole, this last mushroom is not poisonous. On the contrary, it is so delicious that it earned the nickname "black truffle," although it is not a truffle. French cooks sometimes substitute it in pates for truffles. It is small, grayish-brown to black in color, and has the typical trumpet, or funnel, shape.

In picking golden chanterelles, the amateur must beware of the beautiful jack-o'-lantern fungus *(Omphalotus illudens)*, which is toxic, causing stomach

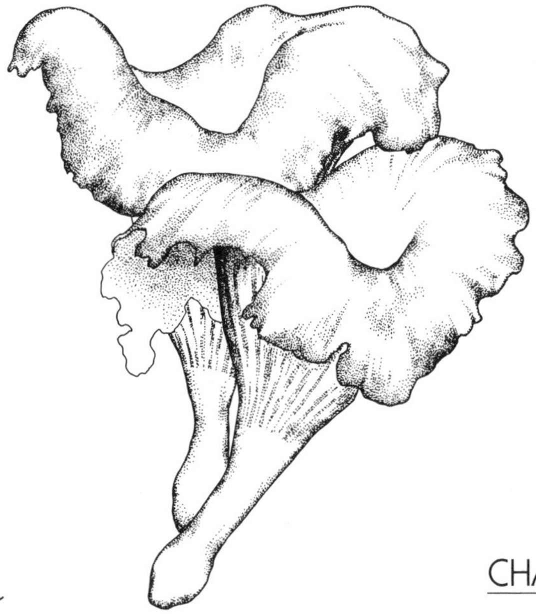
Chanterelle

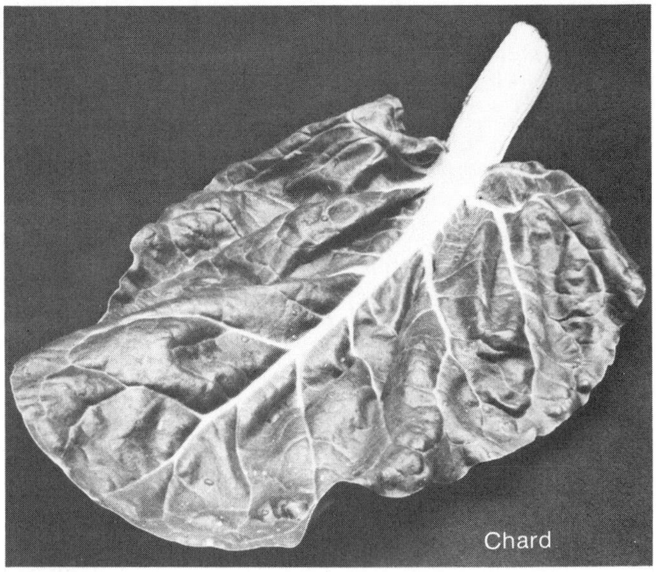
Chard

upsets and diarrhea. Although it resembles the golden chanterelle, there are several differences: the jack-o'-lantern fungus is pumpkin-colored (rather than golden), has sharp gills (rather than blunt pleats) and glows in the dark (the golden chanterelle does not).

CHANTILLY SAUCE

In general, "Chantilly" means "with fresh cream" or "whipped cream added." When applied to sauces, it can refer to a cold sauce, consisting of mayonnaise and whipped cream; a hot sauce, consisting of bechamel or veloute mixed with whipped cream; or, for a sweet course, whipped cream stiffened with a beaten egg and sweetened with vanilla sugar. Other versions involve adding whipped cream to Hollandaise or allemande sauces. The unsweetened versions are served with eggs, poultry, sweetbreads and brains.

See also: **Sauce.**

CHAOURCE

A soft, creamy cheese made in the Champagne district of France, chaource resembles **Camembert,** but is larger in size. Made from whole cow's milk, it is eaten fresh or slightly fermented. It is in season from October to June.

CHAPATI

See **Chupatty.**

CHAPON

The Mediterranean food fish, *Scorpaena scrofa*, has a pinkish red color and is often used in bouillabaisse.

CHAR

A troutlike fish and member of the salmon family, genus *Salvelinus*, the char prefers cold water. The word "char" comes from the Gaelic *ceara*, meaning blood-colored. Chars are characterized by reddish orange bellies, and black or black-spotted backs. Various types of char are known as trout, e.g. the Dolly Varden trout *(S. malma)* and the eastern brook trout *(S. fontinalis)*, while others are known as salmon-trout.

For eating, the most renowned char is the *omble chevalier* of Swiss, Italian and French lakes. The great depth of these lakes—Lake Geneva, 500 feet; Lake Constance, 817 feet—or their high altitude keeps the water temperature low, which produces larger fish, some reaching a weight of 35 pounds. The *omble chevalier* is a variety of Arctic char *(S. alpinus)*, an ocean fish, certain species of which became land-locked after the last Ice Age. There are many other varieties of European char, all much smaller. Those in Scandinavian lakes average five pounds, while those in British and Irish lakes average a pound or two.

The smaller char are distinguished from trout not only by their pinkish flesh, but by the fineness of their scales, which are sometimes almost imperceptible. In North American the eastern brook trout is considered both a fine game fish and a fine food fish. The same is not true of the Dolly Varden, which is found in the northern Pacific coastal region. It is not considered a game fish, and its flesh is only mediocre eating. Char is generally prepared like trout.

See also: **Salmon, Trout.**

CHARACIN

This small, freshwater fish, related to the carp and the catfish, is represented by many species in Africa, and South and Central America. Characin are valuable food fish in Africa, especially the *Alestes macrolepidotus*, which is found in Lake Albert and in the Nile, Niger, Chad, Volta and Congo Rivers. This characin reaches a length of 22 inches, and has a flattened head, pointed snout and a deep body with large scales. It is silver with a bluish gray back.

Related, but smaller fish, are the long-finned characin *(A. longipinnis)* of tropical West Africa and *A. nurse*, which reaches a length of 10 inches and is widely distributed in tropical Africa. It is distinguished by a brassy iridescent color. The pike characin *(Hepsetus odoe)* of Central Africa is a game fish highly regarded by anglers who fish for it with a small spoon. It reaches a length of 14 inches, and is found from Senegal and the Congo Basin to the Upper Zambezi and the Kafue River.

CHARD

Also SWISS CHARD. A variation of the common white beet *(Beta vulgaris cicla)*, it is grown for its spinachlike leaves and thick stalks. Chard does not have the thick, terminal root normal for beets. It is known by a number of different names, including leaf beet, leaf chard, sea kale beet, silver beet, white leaf beet, spinach beet and Swiss chard.

Despite the last name, it is not a Swiss specialty and is native to the Mediterranean area. It grew wild in several varieties over wide areas of the Mediterranean basin, Asia Minor, the Caucasus and the Near East. Chard was cultivated in prehistoric times, and, apparently, it was the only kind of beet the ancient Greeks knew. By the second century B.C. the Romans had both the white beet and the chard. A variety of the latter grown in Pompeii was particularly prized. The word chard derives from the Latin, *carduum*, which means artichoke or thistle, such as the **cardoon.** Chard may have been the ancestor of the common white beet.

The different parts of chard are frequently eaten separately. The flat or curly leaves may be pale to dark green, yellow or bright red. They may be prepared as greens, or in any way suitable for spinach. They taste like an earthy spinach. The stalks and midribs are steamed or boiled in salted water and served with melted butter.

Unlike spinach, chard withstands heat well and so is available from July to the first frost. It does not travel well, however, so is generally eaten close to its source.

The name "chard" is also given to the leaf stalks of artichokes and cardoons, which are blanched and used as a vegetable.

CHARENTAIS

This small French melon has deep yellow skin and a rich aromatic flavor. The flesh has a pink orange color and a luscious, soft texture. It is thought to be a smaller variety of cantaloupe *(Cucumis melo cantalupensis).*

See also: **Muskmelon.**

CHARENTE

See **Cognac.**

CHARLOCK

Also CALIFORNIA RAPE. An annual herb of the field mustard type, probably native to the Mediterranean region, charlock *(Brassica kaber)* has small yellow flowers and is considered a troublesome weed in many places, yet is sometimes cultivated as mustard, although its seeds are not pungent.

CHAROLLES CHEESE

A goat's milk cheese made in the Maconnais area of France, it is at its best from April to December.

CHARQUI

See **Beef, Bison.**

CHARTREUSE

Chartreuse is a spicy, aromatic plant liqueur manufactured in France by Carthusian monks, who were given the formula in 1607 by Henry IV. In its original form, Chartreuse was an elixir, containing 136 herbs and spices combined in an alcohol base. Chief among them were hyssop, angelica, balm, cinnamon bark, saffron and mace. The recipe was modified and improved by Brother Gerome Maubec in 1757, and is a closely guarded trade secret. The liqueur is made by adding honey, sugar and brandy to the elixir. It is marketed in two forms: the yellow, which is very sweet and 86 proof, and the green, which is drier and 110 proof. The elixir is still marketed, but is banned from sale in the United States by drug labeling laws which require a listing of ingredients.

As a result of anticlerical legislation, the monks were expelled from their priory, La Grande Chartreuse, near Grenoble, in 1903. They took refuge in Tarragona, Spain, and continued to make the liqueur. Meanwhile, the French government auctioned off the trademark and the distillery. Lacking the true recipe, a company began to manufacture an imitation Chartreuse. At Tarragona, the true liqueur was issued with two labels, the original French one, plus another testifying to its Spanish origin. This continued until 1927 when the French company went bankrupt. Local businessmen bought up the nearly worthless shares, and sent them to the Carthusian Fathers, who in the 1930s illegally reestablished operations in France. The expulsion order was officially lifted after World War II. Preexpulsion Chartreuse is rare and expensive. The bottles are nearly identical to those containing imitation Chartreuse, except for a printer's mark in the left corner of the label. The label of the genuine article reads *Lith. Alier*, while the label of the imitation version contains only the word *Lith.*

CHASCHOL

Also, CHASCHOSIS. This hard, skim-milk cheese is made in the canton of Grisons in eastern Switzerland. It is sold in wheels that range from 17 to 20 inches in diameter and weigh from 22 to 45 pounds.

CHASCHOSIS

See **Chaschol.**

CHASSEUR SAUCE

A French sauce, used with meat or game, it consists of a white wine base with minced mushrooms, chopped shallots, butter, chopped parsley and a meat glaze.

See also: **Sauce.**

CHASTE TREE

This aromatic shrub or small tree, *Vitex agnus-castus*, grows in the Mediterranean area. Its one-seeded fruit is eaten as an anaphrodisiac, hence the name.

CHATEAU D'YQUEM

A "superior growth" of strong, sweet white wine from **Sauternes** and **Barsac** south of Bordeaux in western France, Chateau d'Yquem is the best of the Sauternes, rivalling the white wines of Germany as "the greatest sweet wine in the world." Chateau d'Yquem is produced mainly from Semillon grapes when these have overripened on the vine. It is very strong—in some years up to 20 percent or more in alcohol content—a brilliant gold in color, very smooth and sweet (almost a liqueur rather than a wine), with a beautifully delicate bouquet. It should be experienced at the end of a meal or on special occasions. Its rich flavor eclipses that of any food.

See also: **Bordeaux Wines.**

CHATEAU HAUT-BRION

Both red and white wines are bottled at the Mission (or *chateau)* Haut-Brion in the **Graves** region near Bordeaux. The only "classified" growth (since 1855) is the red Chateau Haut-Brion, an outstanding dry wine. A good dry, white Chateau Haut-Brion has not been so classified—under the French *Appellation d'Origine* system. But many claim it to be the peer of the more touted red.

See also: **Bordeaux Wines.**

CHATEAUNEUF-DU-PAPE

This warm, heady French red wine comes from the vineyards of Chateauneuf-du-Pape between Orange and Avignon on the banks of the Rhone. A medieval ruin dominates the vineyards—the site of a former summer residence of the popes *(papes)* in Avignon. The wine itself is a mellow red, made from a blend of as many as thirteen grapes, chief among them the Syrah and Grenache. Chateauneuf has a special bouquet, evocative of oriental spices. There is great variance among the wines that bear this label, but generally they are rich in color, strong (at least 12 percent in alcohol content) and fruity. **Hermitage** may be a superior red Rhone wine, but the yield of Chateauneuf-du-Pape is more ample, and the wine can be drunk and appreciated much sooner.

See also: **Rhone Wines.**

CHATEAUROUX

See **Goat's Milk Cheese.**

CHAUD-FROID SAUCE

A classical French sauce, made in white and brown versions, it is used for various cold foods. White *chaud-froid* consists of veloute sauce and aspic much reduced, then mixed with cream and egg yolks, colored and seasoned to taste and served cold, usually with eggs, white meat or fish. Brown *chaud-froid* consists of half-glaze (from *espagnole* sauce) and aspic or gelatin flavored with truffles and madeira. It is used on cold meats.

In French cuisine, the *chaud-froid* preparation is fowl or game that is cooked as a hot dish, but served cold. The tradition dates from the mid-18th century. Yet there is evidence that the ancient Romans had their own *chaud-froid* dishes. For example, a jar containing fragments of jellied meat bearing the inscription *calidus-frigidus* was found in the ruins of Pompeii.

CHAYOTE

Also CHRISTOPHINE, CUSTARD MARROW, MIRLITON. A tropical vine of the gourd family, chayote *(Sechium edule)* is related to cucumber and squash. The vegetable is round or pear-shaped with color ranging from white to dark green. The outside may be smooth or corrugated and is sometimes covered with soft spines. It is usually three to eight inches long. Inside there is only one seed, which has the unusual property of germinating inside the fruit. Chayote has no odor and hardly any taste. Its composition is about one percent protein, three to four percent carbohydrates, a trace of lipids, and 90 to 92 percent water. Its young shoots, and tuberous roots are also edible.

A perennial climbing plant, chayote is native to Mexico and Central America. Its name comes from the Nahuatl word, *chayotl.* Cultivation of chayote spread to many tropical countries, and it is particularly popular in the West Indies. In 1850, it was transplanted to Algeria, and from there was imported into France, where it is called *brionne.* In the United States, it will grow as far north as South Carolina and southern California. Its popularity has been on the rise recently in the British Isles.

Chayote is prepared in many ways. It may be stewed, stuffed, fried or boiled. It may be sweetened for dessert. For example, when cooked in sugar and fresh lime juice, it resembles stewed apples. It is available year round in some Latin American markets, and keeps for two to four weeks in the refrigerator.

CHEBULE

See **Myrobalan.**

CHECKERBERRY

Also MOUNTAIN TEA, TEABERRY, WINTERBERRY. This scarlet fruit of an evergreen shrub, *Gaultheria procumbens*, is native to Canada and the northern United States. The berries have a spicy flavor reminiscent of sweet birch. They are boiled in water to make a kind of tea, or they can be cooked and used like cranberries in stuffings, sauces and pies.

Checkerberry contains oil of wintergreen and formerly was used as a commercial source of flavoring for candy, chewing gum and medicines. Nowadays, oil of wintergreen is extracted from the sweet birch tree *Betula lenta* or synthesized artificially. Checkerberry plants favor cool, damp woods and often grow in the shade or evergreen trees.

CHECKER TREE

Also WILD SERVICE TREE. Native to Europe, North Africa and Asia minor, the checker tree *(Sorbus torminalis)* produces a small, oblong fruit that is used to make wine, brandy and vinegar.

CHEDDAR CHEESE

One of the oldest English cheeses, whose reputation has grown steadily in English speaking countries, cheddar is the most popular cheese in America by far. It originated in the Somerset district of Cheddar in the 16th century. In subsequent years, it was customary for many farmers to pool their milk to make huge cheeses. The largest cheddar on record, which was presented to Queen Victoria, weighed more than 1200 pounds. A fine quality cheese, called farmhouse cheddar, is still made in country districts, particularly in Somerset, but it is factory cheddar that has come to dominate American cheese production.

Cheddar is usually made from sweet, whole cow's milk, (if from skim, it must be noted on the label), which has been pasteurized. The resulting paste is smooth and fairly hard, ranging in color from white to orange, the latter shade often enhanced by carrot or marigold juice. Curing requires three to six months minimum, but larger cheese may need a year or more. The flavor ranges from mild to sharp, becoming mellower as aging progresses.

Cheddar is marketed in a wide variety of shapes, sizes and weights. The most common style also takes the name cheddar. It is 14 inches in diameter, 12 inches thick and weighs from 70 to 78 pounds. Rectangular blocks or prints range from the barrel size at 600 pounds down to the popular one-pound block.

Cheddar was brought to the New World by English colonists, and the first factory was founded in 1851 by Jesse Williams near Rome, New York. Since then, cheddar-type cheeses have become so ubiquitous in the United States that they are often referred to simply as American cheese.

Cheddar also refers to a process in the manufacture of cheese, namely, the consolidation of the curds, where they are piled along the floor of the vat, becoming in the case of cheddar, one rubbery sheet of curd.

See also: **American Cheese, Cheese.**

Varieties of cheese

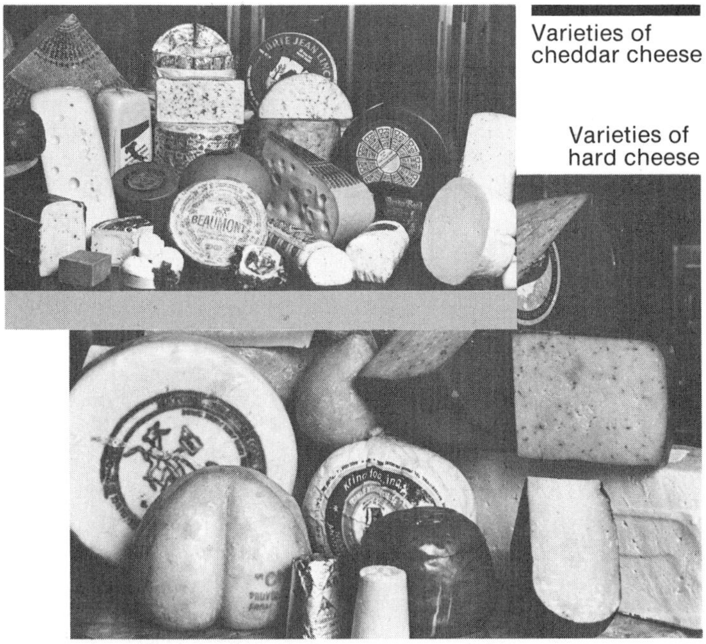

Varieties of cheddar cheese

Varieties of hard cheese

CHEESE

Cheese is a food made from the curd of milk, which is separated from the watery part, whey, and usually pressed in a hoop or mold. Most cheese is made from cow's milk, because it is most abundant, but cheese is produced in every culture where animals are milked, be they goats, sheep, camels, asses, mares, buffalo or reindeer.

In the simplist form of cheese, lactic acid bacteria cause the milk to sour, coagulating the curd. Apart from this, cheese is usually coagulated with rennet, a substance containing two enzymes, rennin and pepsin. It is obtained from the fourth stomach of unweaned calves, kids and lambs, or from such plants as thistles, figs and yellow bedstraw.

The union of milk and rennet, according to legend, occurred accidentally when an Arab merchant, setting out on a day's journey across the desert, stored his milk supply in a pouch made out of the stomach of a sheep. During the day, rennet from the stomach's lining caused the curds to separate from the whey. At the end of the day, he ate the curds and drank the whey, satisfying both hunger and thirst, and, so the story goes, discovering a new food.

The curds contain much of the food value of milk, including casein (main protein), a lot of the fat, some lactose (milk sugar), albumin salts and water. The whey, which is mainly water, contains most of the lactose, some albumin and a little fat. After draining, the curd may be heated or pressed to remove more whey, stirred or cut up to achieve a more uniform consistency, then packaged or molded. In a day or so, it is ready to be eaten fresh, or it may be stored for aging. Aging can last for years and enables a cheese, if uncut, to keep indefinitely. Thus, the perishable nourishment in milk is transformed into a highly palatable food which, treated correctly, can last a long, long time. It is a highly effective and economical way of using surplus milk.

The history of cheese can be documented as far back as 4,000 years—Sumerians recorded its existence on clay tablets, and Egyptians and Chaldeans made reference to it. Greeks recommended it for athletes in training and used baskets called *formos* for draining off the whey. From that word, we get the Italian *formaggio* and the French *fromage*. Romans had a sophisticated knowledge of cheese, and it was a staple in the diet of legionnaires. From their word *caseus* we get the English word, "cheese" (by way of Old English *"cese,"* or *"cyse"*), plus the German *kase*, the Dutch *kaas*, the Italian *cacio*, the Irish *cais*, the Welsh *caws*, the Portuguese *queijo* and the Spanish *queso*. From the fall of the Roman Empire to the Renaissance in Europe, monasteries dominated cheesemaking, carrying on and in some cases improving techniques inherited from the ancients.

Cheesemaking spread to all parts of the Western World and, especially in Europe, permeated the culture to such an extent that each district of each country has its own distinct cheese or variation on a well-known cheese. Many local cheeses resulted from happy accidents that occurred using tried and true methods, and others from peculiarities of climate or bacteria that changed a standard taste or texture. Today there are hundreds of different types of cheese, often only distinguishable by an expert. France alone lays claim to 500.

Sour-milk cheeses such as cottage, cream and Neufchatel owe their flavor mainly to lactic acid bacteria. Apart from these, cheese flavor is a result of complex interaction among bacteria, molds and yeasts and the constituents of milk, such as lactose and lactic acid. Combining these elements successfully has long been considered a high art, which is now shading into a science. For example, in the cheddar process, lactic acid bacteria are allowed to multiply greatly in the milk before renneting. Because of this, microorganisms that feed on it are encouraged to grow during maturation.

The same is not true of Swiss, Camembert and Limburger. Camembert has more whey left in the curd than cheddar, so more lactose is present for fermentation. This is an important factor in Camembert's flavor. Mold/bacteria activity may be confined to the surface, as in Camembert, or spores may be injected directly into the curd as in Roquefort, Stilton and Gorgonzola so that it permeates the entire body of the cheese. The art is in balancing the action of these microorganisms. The temperature of curing rooms does much to control the level of mold/bacteria action.

Many of these microorganisms are not necessary to produce basic cheese, but they are essential in providing the wide variations in flavor and texture demanded by the sophisticated tastes of cheese consumers.

According to the United States Department of

Agriculture, there are only 18 types of cheese, archtypes, if you will, whose characteristics are easily distinguishable, and whose methods of manufacture are clearly different. Examples of these types are brick, Camembert, cheddar, cottage, cream, Edam, Gouda, hand, Limburger, Neufchatel, Parmesan, provolone, ricotta (a whey cheese), Romano, Roquefort, sapsago, Swiss and Trappist. These are discussed fully under separate headings.

A more useful breakdown classifies them by degree of firmness and type of ripening agent, such as the following taken from the USDA's handbook on cheeses:

1. Very Hard (grating):
   a. Ripened by bacteria: asiago old, Parmesan, Romano, sapsago and spalen.
2. Hard
   a. Ripened by bacteria, without eyes: *caciocavallo*, cheddar and granular or stirred curd.
   b. Ripened by bacteria, with eyes: Gruyere and Swiss.
3. Semisoft:
   a. Ripened principally by bacteria: brick and muenster.
   b. Ripened by bacteria and surface microorganisms: Limburger, Port du Salut and Trappist.
   c. Ripened principally by blue mold in the interior: blue, Gorgonzola, Roquefort, Stilton and Wensleydale.
4. Soft:
   a. Ripened: Bel Paese, Brie, Camembert, cooked hand, fresh ricotta, and Neufchatel (as made in France).
   b. Unripened: bakers', cottage, cream, fresh ricotta, Neufchatel (as made in United States), *myost*, pot and *primost*.

CHERIMOYA

Also CHIRIMOYA. A tropical fruit of the *Annonceae* family, closely related to the sweetsop, soursop and custard apple, cherimoya is native to the highlands of southern Ecuador and northern Peru, but is cultivated in Australia, Spain, Argentina, Chile, Mexico and the Caribbean. To achieve its best qualities it requires both a tropical climate and an altitude of from 3,000 to 7,500 feet. The tree, *Annona cherimola*, is cultivated for its ornamental value as well as the fruit. It achieves a height of 15 to 25 feet, has velvety green leaves and flowers that are green outside and white inside.

The size and shape of the fruit vary greatly. It can weigh from three ounces to 15 pounds. Its shape can be oval, spherical, conical or heartshaped, with a surface that may be smooth, sculptured or knobby. The outside sometimes suggests a dusty artichoke, but the pulp is cream-colored, fragrant and sugary, but with enough acidity to prevent its being cloying.

The taste has been described as a cross between pineapple and banana. It is usually eaten raw and may be sliced and floated in white wine or champagne. One cooking method is to dip slices into batter and deep fry them.

Cherimoya

CHERRY

This small, pulpy fruit is colored bright red, reddish black or yellow and contains a single hard seed. The cherry tree is a member of the *Rosaceae* family, and some varieties are grown as ornamentals. The latter usually do not bear fruit, or if they do, it is inedible. Cherries grow in the temperate zones of Europe, Asia and the Americas, and although there are numerous varieties, they all fall into one of three categories: sweet, sour or a hybrid of the two.

The sweet cherry *(Prunus avium)* is believed to have originated in northeastern Asia, and spread throughout the temperate zones in prehistory. It is said to have had such a wide dispersal early on because it is a great favorite with birds, who carried the cherry stones far and wide. Hence the scientific designation *avium*. Joseph Addison wrote in the *Spectator*, "I value my garden more for being full of blackbirds than of cherries." It is not unusual in a very hot summer for wild cherries to ferment on the tree and become so alcoholic that the birds who partake of them get drunk and fall to the ground unconscious around the tree. The ancient Greeks first knew it as a wild fruit, but did not care much for it since it tended to be small, bitter and hard. The Etruscans cultivated it, and the cherry later became a favorite fruit of the Romans, who brought its cultivation to the rest of Europe and Britain.

Sweet cherries are the kind most often eaten fresh, and they are larger and plumper than the sour kind. There are two leading types: the *geans* or

Cherries

guigne, and the *Bigarreau* or *Napoleon*. The *geans* are soft, sweet and juicy, either black on the outside with dark flesh, or red with translucent flesh. Well known varieties are black tartarian, elton heart and frogmore. *Bigarreaus* have firmer flesh and are often identified by the color of their skins, e.g., white hearts or black hearts, which are mottled. Other well known varieties are Bing, and Queen Anne. In the United States 85 percent of sweet cherries are grown in the western states of California, Washington, Utah and Oregon, which have relatively mild winters and hot, dry summers. Irrigation is required, however.

The sour cherry *(Prunus cerasus)* is the kind preferred for cooking, canning and distilling. Not much is known of its history, except that it spread more slowly than the sweet type, perhaps because birds don't like it. Nowadays its production far exceeds that of the sweet cherry, at least in the United States where the ratio is two to one. The main varieties are amarelles, morellos and *damasca*. Although of the sour type, amarelles are not too acid to be eaten fresh. They are pale red and have a colorless juice. The morellos are either dark red or black, and always very bitter. For cooking pies or cobblers, for making jams or canning, these cherries are superior to the sweet varieties. *Damasca* is a small, dark, very bitter cherry grown in Dalmatia, Yugoslavia and used for making Maraschino liqueur. In the United States 90 percent of the crop of tart cherries is produced in Michigan, Wisconsin and New York.

Hybrids are known as dukes, and among the many varieties there are reds and blacks, with both light and dark flesh. Many dukes are suitable for cooking, for eating fresh or more especially for bottling as brandied cherries.

See also: **Maraschino.**

CHERRY BAY

See **Cherry Laurel.**

CHERRY BRANDY

This term is used to designate two different drinks. The first is a brandy distilled from grapes and steeped in cherries with sugar added. This is really a sweet, cherry-flavored liqueur, or cordial but is the only product permitted to be called cherry brandy in the United States since the law provides that only liquor distilled from grapes may be labeled "brandy." (See also: **Peter Heering.)**

The second is a liquor distilled from a mash consisting of cherries with stones intact. The color is clear and the taste dry, with overtones of bitter almond. It is marketed in the United States under trade names, such as **Kirsch** or Kirschwasser.

CHERRY ELAEAGNUS

Also GUMI. The scarlet fruit of the small shrub, *Elaeagnus multiflora*, is native to Japan and China. Growing on a slender stalk, the cherry elaeagnus is used to make jam or beverages.

CHERRY GUM

Product of a small tree, *Amygdalus leicocarpus*, it is consumed as a confection in Iran and Arabia. Cherry gum is also known as Persian gum or *kirsch-gummi.*

CHERRY HEERING

See **Peter Heering.**

CHERRY LAUREL

Also CHERRY BAY. This is an evergreen shrub, *Prunus laurocerasus*, whose leaves are sometimes used as a flavoring agent. When crushed they exude an aroma of bitter almonds and have been used in France to flavor sweet desserts. They must be used with discretion, however, because the essence contains hydrocyanic acid.

CHERRY MARNIER

A fruit liqueur, Cherry Marnier is used mainly as an after-dinner drink because it is considered an aid to digestion. It is similar to what Americans call a cordial, being sweet, 50 to 60 proof and consumed by sipping. The firm in Cognac, France, which produces *Grand Marnier*, also makes Cherry Marnier.

CHERRY PLUM

Also MIRABELLE. This sweet, red or yellow fruit of a shrubby tree, *Prunus cerasifera*, is native to western Asia. It grows easily in Europe and the British Isles. The cherry plum is round with a small point and customarily reaches one inch in diameter.

The fruit is rather tasteless fresh but improves with cooking. It is mostly used in jellies, preserves, pies and tarts. Cherry plum is also known as "cloth of gold" in Great Britain, and as the *mirabelle* in France.

The Alsace region is the center of French production. There the *mirabelle* is used principally to make a liquer of the same name, or a brandy which has a clear color, a pleasant aroma of plums, but a strong burning taste. The cherry plum is also called the *myrobalan* and may be related to the East Asian fruits of the same name. According to one authority, the *mirabelle* was first encountered in Borneo by members of Magellan's round-the-world expedition. This is not certain however.

See also: **Emblic, Myrobalan.**

CHERRYSTONE

See **Clam.**

CHERVIL

An annual herb, chervil *(Anthriscus cerefolium)* looks like parsley, but its taste, while similar, is subtler and has overtones of aniseed. Native to Russia and Asia, it is at home in Europe and the United States.

Because of its delicate but aromatic flavor, it is rarely used alone. In France, it forms the basis of many mixed herb seasonings and improves the flavor of salads, sauces and stuffings for poultry, fish and shellfish.

It is not important in British cooking, but is very popular in the American South. Chervil leaves are used to garnish or season soups, stews and omelets, but because of the delicate flavor they are not suitable for dishes that require long cooking.

In Europe, there is another variety, *Chaerophyllum bulbosum*, which has a turniplike root. It is prepared and eaten like carrots.

Chervil

CHESHIRE CHEESE

Also CHESTER CHEESE. Blue-painted Britons were making Cheshire cheese as early as 43 A.D. when the Roman legions invaded, so it ranks as the oldest English cheese, or at least the first mentioned in history. Its popularity rivals cheddar's, and like **cheddar cheese** it is made from whole cow's milk, and has a hard-pressed, firm curd. Unlike cheddar, the texture tends to be crumbly. This cheese was first made in the village of Chester, on the River Dee, in Cheshire county. On the continent of Europe, it is generally known as Chester cheese.

Cheshire may be early, medium or late ripening, the medium being the most common, and the late having the best flavor, maximizing between 12 and 18 months. Its curd color may be nearly white, blue or orange yellow, this last achieved with the aid of annatto food dye. The blue curd develops through the natural veining action of *penicillum glaucum* mold during aging. The fine, rich flavor of blue-veined Cheshire is perhaps the best of the three, yet the classic orange Cheshire is preferred by Londoners and is most commonly exported.

The mild, mellow flavor of Cheshire is held impossible to imitate, though many have tried, because the Cheshire county soil gives the grazing a saline content that adds a unique flavor to the milk. Typically, the cheese is cylindrical in shape, 14 inches in diameter and weighs from 50 to 70 pounds.

CHESHIRE-STILTON

This English cheese combines the manufacturing and curing methods of **Cheshire Cheese** with the mold that gives **Stilton** its characteristic blue green veins.

CHESIE

See **Plum.**

CHESTER CHEESE

See **Cheshire Cheese.**

CHESTNUT

A sweet, starchy nut, the chestnut is the fruit of several varieties of the tree genus *Castanea*, most notably the European chestnut *(Castanea sativa)*, which is widely cultivated in Southern Europe. Superior in size and taste was the American chestnut *(Castanea dentata)*, but American chestnut trees were wiped out by a blight in the first three decades of the 20th century. Chestnuts are grouped into two commercial varieties, the marron and the domestic chestnut.

Marrons are favored for preserving because they are sweeter and keep well. They are heart-shaped with reddish brown shells, and within the shells the meat is detached from the inner skin. Domestics are generally larger, less sweet, though pleasant tasting, and have dark brown shells with the meat firmly attached to the inner skin.

Pliny described no less than eight varieties of chestnut, claiming the tree originated in the town of Sardis, onetime home of King Croesus. There is no doubt that it is native to the Mediterranean area, and the ancient Romans delighted in them, but only in roasted form.

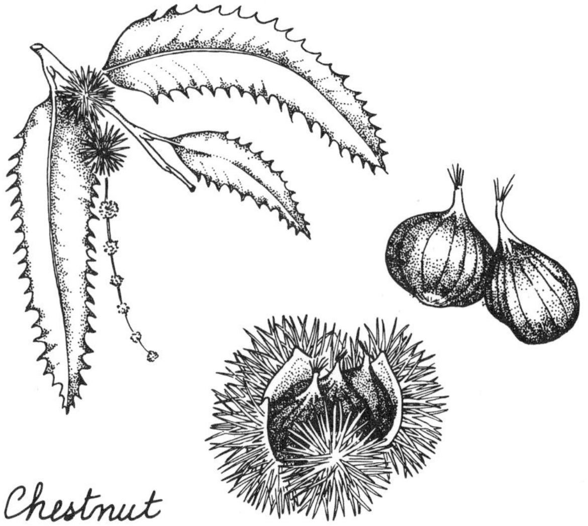

Chestnut

Italy and France are the main producers of chestnuts. In some parts of Italy, they are known as "mountain bread," and indeed with their high starch and sugar content (37 percent), they can be made into a passable flour.

Chestnut flowers grow in clusters called catkins, which characteristically cover almost the entire tree. The nuts are borne in groups of three inside a prickly bur, which splits open when ripe. The shells are thin, and the inner skin astringent to the taste.

Chestnuts may be roasted, boiled, steamed, grilled and mashed. They are preserved whole, in a vanilla syrup, or as a paste called *polenta* in Southern Europe. It is an excellent spread, or can be served in tarts, with whipped cream or ice cream. In the United States chestnuts used to be popular in poultry stuffings. *Marrons glace* are candied chestnuts.

Chincapin, or chinquapin, is a small, sweet chestnut, produced by the American Dwarf variety. It is native to Virginia and other southern states.

CHEVRE

See **Goat's Milk Cheese.**

CHEVRET

Here is a soft, goat's milk cheese made in Bresse, France and in the Maconnais, where it known as *chevreton*. It is at its best from April to November.

CHEVROTIN

See **Goat's Milk Cheese.**

CHEVROTINS

Also CHEVROTTON. This is a small, French goat's milk cheese. Among the best are the *chevrotins d'ambert* from the Savoie, and the *chevrotton de Macon*. They are in season from March to December and May to September respectively. A Bourbonnais' version is the *chevrotin de Moulins*.

CHEVROTTIN DE MACON

See **Maconnais.**

CHEVROTTON

See **Chevrotins.**

CHEWING GUM

Not quite a candy, chewing gum is a flavored and sweetened substance used for chewing. Since about 1890 the usual base for chewing gum has been chicle, a latex extracted from the *Achras sapota*, a tropical evergreen tree, which also produces the **sapodilla,** a delicious fruit. In recent years the demand for chewing gum has outstripped the supply of chicle, giving rise to the use of other natural substances such as jelutong and sorva, from the East Indies, and artificial gum bases.

Chewing gum is most popular in the United States, Latin America and Canada. American colonists picked up the habit from the Indians of New England, who chewed the resin of the black spruce tree. The first commercially produced chewing gum appeared in 1850 and was based on this resin. Later on, paraffin wax was used as a base, and in 1890 chewing gum manufacturers discovered chicle, which had been chewed as gum by the Mayan Indians for centuries. The combination of a better base and modern advertising techniques had by the early 1900s created the great American chewing-gum habit. The habit reached such proportions that pundits were moved to denounce it. Elbert Hubbard, an American editor and writer, wrote, "This will never be a civilized country until we expend more money for books than we do for chewing gum." The American humorist Will Rogers saw it a little differently. He said, "All Wrigley [the biggest chewing manufacturer] had was an idea. He was the first man to discover that American jaws must wag. So why not give them something to wag against?"

Some authorities theorize that the compulsion to chew gum bespeaks a dietary deficiency. Like twig chewing, could it be an attempt to balance the diet? One beneficial effect of chewing gum, however, is that it stimulates the flow of saliva and is thus an aid to digestion. Also, gum chewing, like chewing betel nuts, is reputed to calm nervous tension. Accordingly, gum chewing increased dramatically during both world wars.

A stick of chewing gum consists of about 60 percent sugar and 19 percent corn syrup, plus flavorings (most often peppermint and spearmint), which may contain a trace of vitamins. Each stick provides about nine calories. For more information on the chicle tree, see: **Sapodilla.**

CHHANA

This is Asian sour-milk cheese made from whole cow's milk.

CHIA

A relative of sage, the chia plant *(Salvia columbariae)* produces edible seeds believed to have a stimulating effect. Chia is native to Mexico and the American southwest, and chia seeds were widely consumed in Aztec Mexico. At the time of the Spanish conquest, Montezuma, the Aztec emperor, received as tribute 6,000 tons of chia seeds annually from subject tribes. This amount was exceeded only by corn (maize) at 10,000 tons, and beans at 7,800 tons. The name comes from the Mayan word *chiabaan*, meaning "strong," or "strengthening." The Aztecs, who made it into cakes, believed it to have fortifying qualities. Modern Mexicans use the seeds to make a hot drink or to press an edible oil from them.

CHIANTI

A dry red wine from Tuscany, in central Italy, it represents almost 75 percent of the wine produced in a specific area between Florence and Siena. By an official decree in 1967, Chianti should contain a certain percentage of at least three basic vines: Sangiovese, Cannaiolo Nero, and Malvasia (Malmsey) del Chianti. A small quantity of must made from grapes hung on hooks or trellises is added to the new wine in November. The fermentation of this added liquid gives a special tang to the finished product, as carbon dioxide is released and dissolved in the hermetically sealed wine.

The Tuscans say of Chianti that "it kisses and bites" *("bacia e morse").* Unlike many other Italian red wines, Chianti can be drunk soon after fermentation—in early spring after the harvest—although it does improve with age. Chianti Vecchio is a name applied to the wine after it has aged for at least two years in wooden casks.

Chianti is typically sold in *fiaschi*—straw-covered flasks or bottles of one and two liters—and complements beautifully dishes of pasta and light meats. A white version of this wine (Chianti Bianco) is also produced in the area, but has a slightly sweeter taste, similar to the Roman Frascati.

CHIAVARI

A hard, Italian cheese made from sweet or sour, whole cow's milk in the Chiavari region of Genoa province, it is considered a local version of ***cacio fiore.***

CHICHA

A fermented corn (maize) drink made in South America, particularly Peru, chicha has a yellow color, a sweet taste and is mildly alcoholic. This sort of drink was made by natives of both North and South America before the arrival of European explorers and colonists. The latter did not take to it with enthusiasm, perhaps because the corn had to be chewed before it was added to the mash. This supplied the enzymes necessary to convert the cornstarch to sugar. People hire themselves out as corn chewers in both Brazil and Peru.

CHICKEN

Uncooked chicken

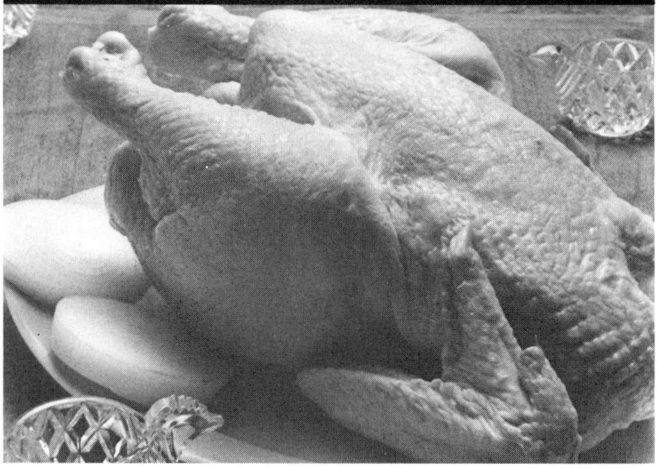

The domestic fowl *Gallus gallus* is commonly known as the chicken. The word "chicken" used to apply only to younger birds, but the meaning has spread to include birds of all ages—from squabs to stewers—provided they are killed for meat.

Authorities agree that the progenitor of the modern chicken was a wild jungle fowl from India which was tamed around 2000 B.C. The domestic chicken spread both east, to China and the Pacific Islands, and west, to Europe, where it first appeared in Central Europe around 1500 B.C. Egyptian funerary paintings suggest the chicken had become commonplace there by 1350 B.C. On Biblical evidence, Old Testament Hebrews did not know of the chicken, but it was present in Asia Minor: Assyrian seals from the 8th century B.C. bear a picture of a chicken. About this time the first historical mention of the chicken was made by citizens of Sybaris, a Greek colony on the bottom of the Italian peninsula. They enacted a law banning roosters in the city so they would not be awakened by crowing at dawn. Chickens became important economically to the Greeks mainly for the eggs they produced. This tradition was carried forward in Rome, where the breeding of hens became something of a science.

It wasn't until the second century B.C. that the eating of chickens became widespread in Rome. It has been theorized that, before then, chickens were too scrawny to be appetizing. They had to forage for themselves, and no attention was paid to fattening them up. The latter practice developed first on the Greek island of Cos and perhaps spread to Rome from there. At any rate, chicken-eating bloomed, and by the reign of Trajan (98–117 A.D.) the chicken was a staple in the kitchen, as attested in the works of Apicius, a celebrated Roman gourmand, who left behind many varied and ingenious recipes for chicken.

Chicken raising had been established in northern Europe, including Britain, long before Roman hegemony was established. Consequently, chicken eating, unlike many Roman culinary tastes, did not die out with the collapse of the Empire but continued to thrive. Romans had been particularly fond of the **capon,** a male bird castrated early in its life; capon retained great favor throughout the Middle Ages. But the chicken was not an aristocrat; it was a true bird of the people—so much so that France's first Bourbon king, Henry IV (1589–1610), used it as a symbol for prosperity when, on the occasion of his coronation, he said, "I wish that every peasant may have a chicken in his pot on Sundays." This proved to be an enduring image, since as recently as 1928 a variation of it was adopted by the United States Republican Party as a campaign slogan. The Republicans did not restrict the chicken/pot idea to Sundays and won the election.

In the 20th century, chicken raising has become a science, with a consequent rise in efficiency and productivity and lowering of cost. It is termed the broiler industry, and has become one of the largest agricultural businesses in the United States. In 1974 almost three billion broilers were produced in the

United States, mainly in the states of Arkansas, Georgia, Alabama and North Carolina. Within a controlled environment, chicks are fed a carefully balanced diet consisting of a mash that, typically, contains yellow corn, wheat or wheat by-products, oats, soybean meal and alfalfa meal, with animal, fish and milk by-products as protein supplements. Whereas in the 1940s it took 13 to 14 weeks to bring a chick to fryer size (three to four pounds), by 1974 the time span had been reduced to seven to eight weeks.

Worldwide, chicken is probably the most universally eaten meat, surpassing even beef. Marketers of chicken, on the other hand, claim to have detected a phenomenon they call "chicken fatigue." This is a way of saying people get tired of the taste of chicken faster than they do of, say, hamburger, a major competitor in the fast-food market. Be that as it may, chicken consumption continues to rise, perhaps because it is such a versatile food. It is good broiled, roasted, baked, steamed, fried, boiled, fricasseed, barbecued or made into chicken pie or chicken soup.

In the United States chickens are marketed according to government standards. The terminology is regulated by law, and runs according to age (which usually determines size). A broiler is a very young bird (four to six weeks old), which can weigh up to 2½ pounds. The French word for this bird is *poussin*, a term often used in the United Kingdom. They are usually cooked whole, by roasting on a spit or deepfrying. Broilers can be of either sex, but have little flavor or flesh. Fryers may weigh as much as 3½ pounds; their flesh is nearly as tender as that of broilers and somewhat tastier. Also known as a spring chicken, the fryer may be roasted whole, jointed (as in pies) or sauteed. In these very young chickens the bones are soft and pliable, with a gelatinous quality that makes good soup stock. A roaster may be of either sex; it is less than eight months old and weighs from 3½ to five pounds. Capons are marketed in this category, but their weight runs much higher—six to 10 pounds. Yet their flesh is tender, and their skin soft and pliable. A chicken of roasting size has a taste robust enough to be poached or boiled, although moist cooking methods are customary only with the last category, which is the hen, stewing chicken or boiling fowl. It is more than 10 months old, perhaps even elderly—i.e., more than 1½ years old. These are female birds, and are stewed, used in soups or minced.

Among breeders, chickens are divided into five races: Asiatic, Continental European, Mediterranean, English and American. The most popular examples of these races are the *brahma* (Asiatic); the *bresse* (Continental European) of France; the *leghorn* (Mediterranean) of Italy, a better producer of eggs than meat; the Jersey (English) and the Wyandottes, Rhode Islands and Plymouth Rocks (American).

See also: **Capon.**

CHICLE

See **Chewing Gum.**

CHICKLING

Here is a type of vetching or wild pea, *Lathyrus sativus*, with an edible seed. The green leaves may be eaten when very young and the dried seeds used like beans or lentils.

CHICK-PEA

Also GARBANZO. A small, round seed of very ancient cultivation, it is an important food in India, the Near East, Italy, France and most Spanish-speaking countries. The chick-pea is not a true pea, although it grows two to the pod, but is a member of the *Leguminosae* family. It owes its scientific name, *Cicer arietinum*, partly to its shape, which is flattened on two sides, and resembles a ram's head. The chick-pea is slightly larger than an ordinary pea, and can vary widely in color, including white, black and red. The white, garbanzo, variety is reputed to be the best.

Chick-peas have been found in the remains of Neolithic villages and were cultivated in the Hanging Gardens of Babylon. The "pulse" of the Biblical Hebrews is believed to be chick-peas. The ancient Greeks cultivated it under the name *erebinthos*, and the ancient Romans in Pompeii canned in amphorae a concoction of chick-peas and bacon for export. The chick-pea has garnered many alternative names in English, including Egyptian pea, chestnut bean, Bengal gram, Spanish pea, dwarf pea, chich and caravance. The standard French term is *pois chiche* from the Latin *cicer*. In English this became chich pea and evolved into chick-pea.

The chick-pea is extremely nourishing. Its yield of protein per acre cultivated is higher than any other leguminous grain except peanuts and lupine seeds. There are about 350 calories in 3½ ounces (100 grams) of dried chick-peas.

The dried chick-peas must be soaked before cooking. This is not necessary with canned varieties. Chick-peas are of minor importance as food in the United States. They are most frequently served cold in salads. In Mediterranean lands, however, a staple item is *hummous*, chick-peas mashed with sesame oil. Roasted, they are served as *meze*, an hors d'oeuvre in Greece. One of the most important foods of the Sahara is the classic North African *couscous*, which consists of a small amount of floured semolina and chick-peas shaped into a ball and eaten with the hand. In Spain, chick-peas form the basis of such national dishes as *olla podrida* and *cocida*, which are types of stew. Elsewhere in Europe, they are most often served in soups, stews and salads. The taste of chick-peas is very bland. They are most often marketed in dried or canned form.

Belgian endive, one of the several varieties of chicory

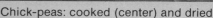

Chick-peas: cooked (center) and dried

CHICORY

Chicory *(Cichorium intybus)* is an herbaceous plant that grows wild in Europe, temperate North Africa and the United States. It somewhat resembles the dandelion, except that it has delicate blue flowers, which have earned the nickname, "blue sailors." The plant is native to countries bordering the Mediterranean, and over the centuries many cultivated varieties have been developed from it, including the witloof (white leaf), or Belgian endive, the Catalonia or asparagus chicory, red chicory and *grumolo.* These will be discussed more fully below. Wild chicory, as well as some of the cultivated varieties, have long parsniplike roots. The roots are white and fleshy, attaining a length of 10 to 14 inches. When roasted and ground, they look like coffee, and since the 18th century have been used as a coffee substitute. The French, particularly, prefer coffee flavored with chicory root, in a ratio of about one ounce of chicory to the pound. It has its adherents in the United States too, especially in New Orleans.

The naming of cultivated varieties of *Cichorium intybus* is confused by opposite usage in England and Germany, on the one hand, and France and the United States on the other. What the English call chicory, the Americans often call endive. To compound the confusion, United States usage is gaining ground in England.

A characteristic of chicory leaves in the wild is bitterness, so to reduce this the popular cultivated chicory, witloof (Belgian endive, *barbe-de-bouc),* is blanched. This is accomplished by uprooting nearly mature plants, pruning them severely, then replanting them for a two to three week period in darkness. The result is a long vegetable with tightly folded, nearly white leaves that are tender and crisp. It is eaten in salads, like lettuce, and may be substituted for lettuce. It may also be braised and served as a vegetable.

The Catalonia, or asparagus chicory, much resembles its namesake, and is popular in Italy as a potherb. Red chicory and grumolo are broad-leaved varieties that resemble, in shape if not in color, head or romaine lettuce. All varieties of chicory are rich in vitamin C.

See also: **Endive.**

CHILDREN'S TOMATO

This African plant, *Solanum anomalum,* produces a tomatolike fruit. It is eaten in sauces and soups or may be preserved by drying. The children's tomato is seldom cultivated.

CHIHLI

See **Wong Bok.**

CHILEAN FIG

Also SEA FIG. This fruit of a low growing shrub, *Carpobrotus chilensis,* is closely related to the ice plant. It is found from Oregon to Baja California, and in Chile. The many-lobed fruit is eaten in the areas of cultivation.

CHILEAN GUAVA

Also CHILEAN MYRTLE. The red to black fruit of an evergreen shrub, *Ugni molinae*, native to Bolivia and Chile, Chilean guava is a member of the **myrtle** family. The fruit is a round berry, containing several seeds and reaching a diameter of about one-quarter inch. Its flavor and aroma are described as delightful, and it is used mainly to make jam.

CHILEAN NUT

Also CHILEAN HAZEL. Edible seed of a Chilean tree, *Gevuina avellana*, it resembles a hazel nut, ranging in color from coral-red to black and is cherry-sized. The seed has a pleasant taste and is highly regarded where grown. The tree is occasionally grown in southern California.

CHILEAN WINEBERRY

Also MACQUI. This fruit of a small evergreen shrub, *Aristotelia chilenses*, is native to Chile and much appreciated there. The plant is grown in California as an ornamental. In Chile, the juice is sometimes used to adulterate wine.

CHILI

Also CHILLI. Some species of chili, *Capsicum frutescens*, are the hottest food in the world. They originated in Brazil and Peru and are featured in many Latin American cuisines, particularly Mexico's. They are popularly called peppers, although *capisicums* are not botanically related to the Eastern pepper plant *(Piper nigrum)*, which provides most of the world's black and white pepper and originated in India.

Christopher Columbus was the first to call *capsicums* pepper. The arawaks of the West Indies gave him spicy dishes to eat. Thinking he was in India, Columbus concluded the spice was pepper. Thus began a semantic overlap that remains today in English. It does not exist in Spanish, however, because pepper is *pimienta*, while *capsicums* are either *aji*, the Arawak word, or *chile*, from the Aztec *chilli*. Green or bell pepper and pimento, or red pepper, larger members of the *capsicum* genus, are generally much milder than chili. They are eaten as a vegetable rather than a spice, and will be discussed elsewhere.

The redder a chili is, the hotter it generally is. One of the active substances is capsicin, which is capable of producing a burning sensation on the bare skin. For this reason, cooks who handle chili are well advised to wear rubber gloves and keep their hands well away from their eyes.

Capsicums were transplanted to Japan, Europe, India and Africa, where chili is called *pili-pili*. Capsicums are the basis of such spices as **cayenne, paprika** and **tabasco.** Nowhere, though, is there a greater variety of chili than in Latin America. Following are some examples:

Ancho—a dark red, heart-shaped chili, three inches long by 2½ wide. Mild and full-flavored. Available dried.

Chipotle—A plump, brick-red chili, two inches long, tapered and twisted. It has a distinct flavor and is very hot. Available canned.

Guero—Also called California green pepper, it is plump and a pale yellow green in color, three to four inches long by 2½ wide. Available fresh in the fall; otherwise canned in California. Mild.

Hontaka—Very hot Japanese chili, exported to Latin America. It is thin, red and wrinkled, about two inches long. Available dried in jars and cellophane packets.

Jalapeno—A hot, rather stringy chili with smooth, grass-green skin, about two inches long. Widely available canned.

Malagueta—A small, slender, tapering green or red chili, very hot, used in Bahian (Brazil) cooking. Not available in the United States.

Mulato—Often used with the *ancho*, it is darker, larger and hotter. Available dried.

Pasilla—A dark mahogany, thin chili, hotter than the *ancho*, but not as flavorful. Sold dried.

In cooking the whole chili may be used, or the soft inner lining of the skin may be scraped off and added to the dish. *Capsicums* are often available in powdered form, which is usually very hot. Chili growers and canners have a pungency scale to judge chilis by, which ranges from one to 120. The *jalapeno* mentioned above, which seems hot to the North American palate, is rated at 15.

See also: **Pepper; Pepper, Green and Red.**

CHILLI

See **Chili.**

CHILOE STRAWBERRY

Also BEACH STRAWBERRY. This strawberry plant, *Fragraria chiloensis*, native to Chile, is one of the parents of the hybrid cultivated strawberry. The other is *F. virginiana*, the Virginia strawberry. The Chiloe strawberry is found from Alaska to California and in Pacific regions of South America. It is cultivated in Andean countries and sold in local markets there.

See also: **Strawberry.**

CHIMAJA

A condiment used to flavor ***mole* sauce** in Mexico, it is made from the root of the wild cherry *Prunus ilicifolia*. It is used fresh or in powder form after being chopped, dried and ground.

CHINAMAN LEATHERJACKET

Also YELLOW LEATHERJACKET. A member of the triggerfish family, *Balistidae*, found in Australian waters, it is highly regarded for its white, tender, well flavored flesh. Chinaman leatherjacket is brightly colored and reaches a maximum length of about 20 inches.

CHINAMAN'S HAT

See **Limpet.**

CHINA ORANGE

See **Chinois.**

CHINA ROOT

Rootstock of the woody vine, *Smilax china*, it is a relative of sarsaparilla, and like the latter is used as a flavoring ingredient in soft drinks. It is native to Japan and China and was formerly used medicinally as a purgative.

CHINCHARD

Chinchard is the French name for an Atlantic Ocean fish of the same family as the saurel and the **cavalla,** that is, the *Carangidae*. It resembles a horse mackerel and is eaten in both Africa and France, where it is highly regarded and usually filleted.

CHINESE ARALIA

A shrub or small tree, *Aralia chinensis*, it is native to China and similar to **udo.** Its young leaves make an excellent vegetable.

CHINESE ARTICHOKE

See **Crosne.**

CHINESE CABBAGE

See **Petsai.**

CHINESE CHIVES

Also GARLIC CHIVES. A strong-flavored member of the onion genus, *Allium tuberosum*, it is an important vegetable in parts of Asia. The plant has long, poorly developed bulbs on a stout rhizome, but the parts used in cooking are the young leaves and flower stalks whose flavor resembles that of garlic. They are used to season meat dishes.

CHINESE GOOSEBERRY

See **Kiwi Fruit.**

CHINESE LANTERN

See **Ground Cherry.**

CHINESE LAUREL

Also BIGNAY. This red, currantlike fruit of an evergreen tree, *Antidesma bunius*, is native to Indian and Malaysia. The berries are used to make jellies, preserves and syrup, as well as in a sauce that accompanies fish dishes.

CHINESE MEDLAR

See **Loquat.**

CHINESE MUSHROOM

See **Straw Mushroom.**

CHINESE MUSTARD

Also INDIAN MUSTARD. A mustard plant, *Brassica juncea*, cultivated in Europe, Asia and the United States for its green leaves, it is particularly well liked by the Chinese who cook and eat the leaves like spinach. Varieties include curley mustard *(B. juncea* var. *crispifolia)* and broadleaved *(B. juncea* var. *foliosa)*. A variety of field mustard *(B. rapiformis)* grown for its turniplike root is also called Chinese mustard. The conical roots are cooked and eaten like turnips. The hot condiment served in Chinese restaurants is prepared from powdered English mustard and water.

See also: **Mustard.**

CHINESE PERCH

A freshwater species of China where it is regarded as a moderately important commercial food fish, the Chinese perch *(Siniperca chuatsi)* attains a length of up to 39 inches and can weigh as much as 18 pounds. Colors are green brown with a pattern of light patches. It is found as far north as the Amur River, which forms a border with the USSR.

CHINESE RADISH

See **Radish.**

CHINESE UNONA

The aromatic, somewhat acid fruit of a tree, *Unona discolor*, indigenous to tropical Asia, it may be used as a pepper substitute or otherwise as a condiment.

CHINESE WATERMELON

Also ASH GOURD, WAX GOURD. Fruit of a long-running vine, *Benincasa hispida*, native to southeast Asia, it is oblong or cylindrical in shape, nine to 16 inches long, with waxy, hairy skin and firm white flesh. The seeds are cucumberlike. Chinese watermelon is eaten as a fresh vegetable, like pumpkin or squash, or used to make preserves, such as sweet pickles.

CHINESE WOLFBERRY

Also CHINESE MATRIMONY VINE, DUKE OF ARGYLL'S TEA TREE. This shrubby vine, *Lycium chinensis*, is native to temperate Asia but was transplanted to Europe, North America and the British Isles. Its scarlet or orange berries are edible, and the tender young leaves can be eaten like spinach.

CHINESE YAM

Also IGNAME, CINNAMON VINE. A yam, *Dioscorea batatas*, its tubers reach a length of three feet or more. Though usually grown in the United States as an ornamental vine, it is a popular food variety in temperate East Asia and in French possessions in the West Indies whence it is shipped to France under the name, *igname*.

CHINOIS

Also CHINA ORANGE. A small Chinese orange, *Citrus myrtifolia*, it is similar to the tangerine. Chinois is considered a delicacy in France, where both green and yellow varieties are crystallized or preserved in brandy.

CHINQUAPIN

See **Castanopsis Nut.**

CHIODINI

See **Honey Mushroom.**

CHIOTILLA

Fruit of a treelike cactus, *Escontria chiotilla*, of southern Mexico, chiotillas are round, purple and about two inches in diameter. They are sold in local markets.

CHIPOLATA

A Spanish sausage, resembling the **chorizo,** but much smaller and softer in texture, Chipolata's main ingredient is pork, and chives are used as a flavoring. *Chipolatas* are added to vegetable casseroles or used as a garnish on various roasts, chops and poultry.

See also: **Sausage.**

CHIPPED BEEF

See **Dried Beef.**

CHIRIMOTE

Fruit of an Ecuadorean shrub, *Disterigma margaricoccum*, sold in local markets there, chirimote is tender, crisp and juicy.

CHIRIMOYA

See **Cherimoya.**

CHITO MELON

Also MANGO MELON, VINE PEACH. A small melon, *Cucumis melo* var. *chito*, about the size of a lemon or orange, its skin is yellow or orange, and its flesh is white, firm and without fragrance. It rather suggests a cucumber. Chito melon is sometimes eaten as a cooked vegetable, but it is most frequently used for pickling and in chutneys. It is known also as orange melon, garden melon, melon apple and vegetable orange.

See also: **Muskmelon.**

CHITON

Also AMPHINEURAN. Here is a class of marine mollusks whose "shell" consists of a series of overlapping plates giving them something of the look of tiny armadillos or long sowbugs. They are found on both coasts of North America and are known as sea beef in the West Indies. A Pacific species, *Cryptochiton stelleri*, reaches a length of 13 inches and is known as seaboots, or gum boots. It is eaten by native Americans. Most species are smaller, such as the *Acanthopleura granulata* of Florida and the Gulf of Mexico, which averages three inches. The chiton may be prepared in any way suitable for whelk or limpet.

CHITTAGONG AND SYLHET TEAS

These are well-known varieties of black tea grown in what was once India, but is now Pakistan. These are heavier, darker and more pungent than the finest Indian teas, such as **Darjeeling tea,** which are cultivated a higher altitudes (7,000 feet or more).

See also: **Tea.**

CHITTERLING

The small intestines of swine, chitterlings or "chit'lins" are, in the United States, an item of Soul Food, i.e., dishes favored by generations of black Americans and southern whites. The usual method of cooking is to boil them for about four hours in seasoned water, then serve hot with vinegar or hot sauce. Alternatively, they may be fried, cooked in a pot with other ingredients or stuffed. Chitterlings have never been generally accepted in the northern and western United States.

In England, they are used to make a dumpling called Down Derry, in which they are cut up, fried and embedded in a potato mixture, then baked. They may also simply be dipped in egg and breadcrumbs and fried in bacon fat. The Russians prepare them like tripe, serving them with sour cream. Chitterlings are also used as sausage casings.

See also: **Sausage, Pig.**

CHIVE

Related to the onion, chive is a grasslike herb, *Allium shoenoprasum*, whose leaves have hollow stems with a delicate onion flavor. It is used to garnish as well as to season soups, stews and salads. The plant, which has attractive pink flowers, grows in clumps six to eight inches high and thrives well in pots or home gardens. Stems may be clipped freely, since they easily grow back.

Because its flavor is subtle, it will not withstand much cooking. Customarily, it is chopped finely and sprinkled on the dish just before serving.

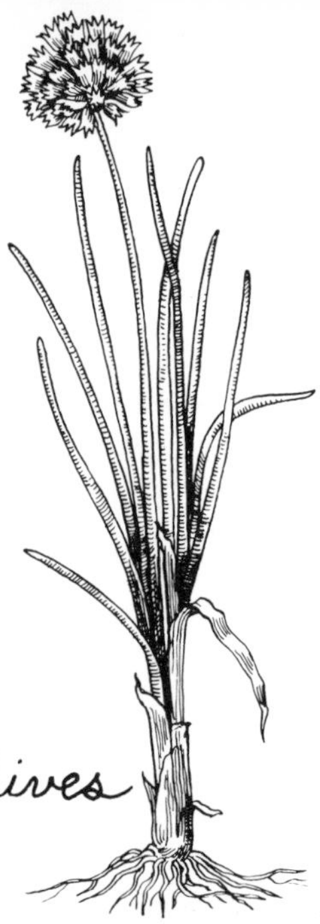

Chives

Chocolate and Cocoa

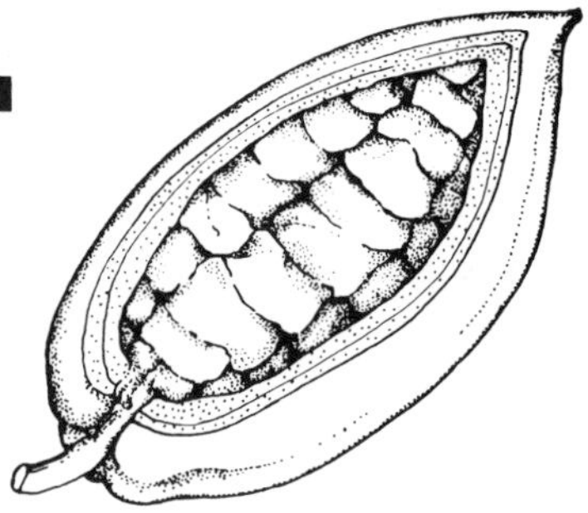

CHOCOLATE AND COCOA

Both of these are foods refined from cocoa beans, fruit of the cacao tree *(Theobroma cacao)*, which is indigenous to the American tropics. Highly nutritious substances, they are widely consumed as a beverage, a candy and as a confectionary coating on bakery products.

In pre-Columbian Mexico, the beans were the base for two drinks of the Aztec elite, *cacaoquahitl* and *chocolatl*. Bernal Diaz, a Spanish chronicler of the conquest of Mexico, recorded that Montezuma, the Aztec emperor, drank more than 50 cups a day of *cacaoquahitl*, a bitter brew made by boiling the dried and roasted beans in water. The Spaniards much preferred *chocolatl*, a thicker brew of chocolate sweetened with honey and flavored with vanilla and other spices. Both drinks were found to be refreshing and stimulating due to the presence in cacao of two alkaloids, theobromine and caffeine.

Chocolate, as a drink, was introduced into Spain shortly after 1519, where it remained a closely guarded secret for nearly 100 years. It gained acceptance in France in the 17th century, and in 1657 a Frenchman opened a hot chocolate shop in London. The idea spread across Europe in succeeding years and to the American colonies in the 18th century.

A process was developed in Holland in 1828 to obtain powdered chocolate by pressing much of the cocoa butter from the ground and roasted beans. Fry and Sons, an English firm, combined cocoa butter with chocolate liquor and sugar in 1847 to produce eating chocolate. Milk chocolate was developed in 1876 by Daniel Peter, a Swiss, by adding milk solids to chocolate liquor.

The cacao tree grows from 20 to 40 feet in height, and bears clusters of flowers that stem directly from the trunk and main branches. It has been said that they look like small beech trees with squashes hung from the trunk. The flowers produce oval pods, filled with a whitish, sweet, slimy material that encloses from 30 to 40 seeds. Twenty to 30 cocoa beans are in a pound.

The pods are gathered as they ripen, split in two by a machete, and allowed to dry out for 24 hours. Seeds in the pulp are stored in boxes and "sweated" (fermented) for several days. To a great extent, the sweating determines the quality of the commercial bean. Over-fermentation ruins them, and under-fermentation leaves them prone to deterioration and mildew and tasting like raw potato. During fermentation several changes take place: the juicy sweatings of the pulp are drained away, the germ of the seed is killed, bitterness is reduced, flavor develops and the beans take on a reddish tint. The beans are then dried in the sun, or in artificial heat.

In the first step of processing the beans are cleaned and roasted. The latter reduces acidity, moisture content and helps develop flavor. The beans are dehulled, cracked and winnowed, leaving them in the form of "nibs" or small pieces. To extract the benefit of the untreated cocoa bean, cocoa nibs can be steeped in boiling water and made into a wholesome beverage.

Cocoa nibs are screened by size, and then combined with those from other plantations to form blends that match varying criteria of taste. After blending, the nibs are put into heated grinders. This reduces them to an oily liquid called chocolate liquor.

The liquor is processed in two different ways according to whether the end product is to be cocoa or chocolate. For cocoa, the chocolate liquor is pressed hydraulically to remove a determined amount of cocoa butter. Cocoa sold in the United States contains from 11 to 22 percent cocoa butter, while that sold in Britain must contain a minimum of 20 percent. It is then pulverized and sifted. Sometimes the chocolate liquor is "dutched," that is, treated with an alkalai solution to reduce natural acidity, mellow the flavor and darken the color.

For chocolate, additional cocoa butter is added to the liquor, and it is "conched," a process, requiring from four to 72 hours, that aerates, emulsifies and develops further flavor in the chocolate mass. The process is completed by molding, where the chocolate is cast in small bar or blocks and then cooled.

Baking or plain chocolate, either natural or alkalized, is little more than pure chocolate liquor molded into cakes and chilled. Sweet chocolate contains between 15 and 35 percent chocolate liquor, plus sugar, added cocoa butter and such flavorings as vanilla beans, vanillin, salt, essential oils, and spices, such as cinammon or cloves.

Milk chocolate is sweet chocolate with milk or milk solids substituted for a portion of the chocolate liquor, the proportions being 12 to 15 percent chocolate liquor, and 15 to 20 percent milk solids. It is lighter in color, milder and sweeter than ordinary sweet chocolate. Bittersweet chocolate is similar to sweet chocolate, but contains less sugar and more chocolate liquor. Chocolate coatings are usually based on cocoa powder, with vegetable fats added rather than cocoa butter.

Cocoa and chocolate should be kept cool and dry. In high heat, fat bloom occurs. It is a condition in which cocoa butter infiltrates the surface, turning products grey or white. Excessive moisture can cause mustiness, mold or sugar bloom, where the sugar dissolves out then recrystallizes on the surface.

Most cocoa comes from the species *Theobroma cacao* the first term meaning literally, "food of the gods." It has a high nutritious content. The bean itself contains 49 percent oil, 18 percent protein, 10 percent starch and 7 percent other carbohydrates. Typically, milk chocolate contains 520 calories per 100 grams (3½ oz.), and is 8 percent protein, 57 percent carbohydrate and 32 percent fat. It is particularly rich in potassium, calcium and magnesium, and contains vitamins A, B_1, B_2 and B_3.

CHOKECHERRY

Red fruit of a small shrub or tree, *Prunus virginiana*, with an acid, astringent taste, chokecherries are sometimes used to make jams and preserves.

CHOLESTEROL

A substance necessary to human metabolism, cholesterol is a fatty alcohol found abundantly in animal fat, blood, nerve tissue and bile. Most of the cholesterol present in the human body is manufactured by the body itself. Yet high levels of cholesterol in the blood stream, called serum cholesterol, are associated with the fatty degeneration of the arteries that leads to heart disease and stroke. This is because cholesterol combines with other substances to form plaques, little platelets that stick to artery walls. These are mushy at first, but later harden and narrow the passageway for blood circulation. If the process continues unchecked, the artery may become completely blocked, a condition that can cause a heart attack or a stroke.

Serum cholesterol is measured by the number of milligrams per 100 cubic centimeters of blood. In the United States, 225 milligrams or less is considered low, 226–259 medium and 260 or more high.

A number of factors influence the serum cholesterol level, one of them being ingestion of saturated fat. A saturated fat is one that has hydrogen atoms attached at all available points on its carbon chain. It remains solid at room temperature. For reasons yet unexplained a high intake of saturated fats raises the serum cholesterol level, which in turn causes plaquing. Most saturated fats are animal fats. Butter is a good example.

The opposite of a saturated fat is one that is said to be polyunsaturated. It does not have hydrogen atoms at all available points on the carbon chain, and it is liquid at room temperature. Research shows that polyunsaturated fats do not increase the serum cholesterol levels. Most polyunsaturated fats are fish, vegetable or seed oils. A good example is soybean oil. Many margarines are made from polyunsaturated fats, soybean oil being the most common. Its being liquid at room temperature is an inconvenience that the manufacturer eliminates through hydrogenation, that is, by treating the liquid oil with hydrogen transforming it into a solid fat.

One dietary factor that seems to have an effect on the cholesterol level is pectin, a carbohydrate substance found in many ripe fruits. It is water soluable and yields a gel, which is the basis of most jellies. In one study, a dosage of 15 grams of pectin per day reduced the serum cholesterol level of nine subjects by 15 percent over a three week period. Perhaps this property of pectin is the basis of the old saw, "An apple a day keeps the doctor away."

CHORIZO

A small pork sausage that originated in Spain, it is popular with all Spanish-speaking peoples. The chorizo is highly spiced—sometimes very, very hot—and has a pronounced garlic flavor. Ingredients include pork fillet, pork fat and pig's liver, which are minced together with sweet red peppers, cayenne pepper, juniper berries, salt, white pepper and garlic. The mixture is stuffed into casings, smoked and dried. The best comes from the Estremadura area of Spain. Chorizo is often cooked with chickpeas.

See also: **Chipolata, Sausage.**

CHOWDER BEER

Here is a beverage obtained by boiling black spruce bark *(Picea mariana)* in water, then mixing the resulting liquor with molasses. Black spruce yields a sap that has antiscorbutic qualities.

CHRISTALINNA

This is a hard, rennet cheese made from cow's milk in the cantons of Grisons and Graubunden in Switzerland.

CHRISTE-MARINE

See **Samphire.**

CHRISTIAN IX CHEESE

A Danish cheese that contains such spices as cumin and caraway seeds, it is nearly identical to **Kuminost,** differing mainly in size and shape. While the latter is marketed in small loaves, Christian IX comes in flat cylinders that weigh around 35 pounds. It is coated with yellow paraffin or wax.

CHRISTOPHINE

See **Chayote.**

CHRIST'S THORN

Also CROWN OF THORNS. A spiny shrub or small tree, *Ziziphus spini-christi*, of the *jujube* genus indigenous to North Africa and Arabia, its fruit is eaten dried and in that condition tastes like shriveled apple.

CHRYSANTHEMUM

A genus of edible plants whose leaves and flowers are often used in Japanese and Chinese cooking, chrysanthemums can be herbs or shrubs, with many small flowers or a single, large-stalked flower. They bloom in late summer and fall in a variety of colors, mostly yellow, white or red. They have a characteristic odor and a taste most often compared to that of cauliflower, but more delicate. In the West, chrysanthemum petals are sometimes strewn on salads, more for decorative purposes than for their taste. Less often, finely chopped chrysanthemum leaves are served in vinaigrette sauce. The chrysanthemum, however, is the national flower of Japan; there it is served in a variety of ways. In Kyoto, chrysanthemum fritters are a specialty. Also, the leaves and petals are finely shredded, mixed with cream and served as a salad. In various forms, they are a common article of diet. Many species of chrysanthemum are used, but the deep yellow blossoms are best liked for salad purposes. The word "chrysanthemum" comes from the Greek words *khrusos* (gold) and *anthemon* (flower).

Chrysanthemum leaves

Chufa

CHUB

In Europe, this freshwater fish, *Leuciscus cephalus*, of the carp family is found in rivers and streams. The chub has acquired a variety of names, usually having to do with head, because is is bigheaded. Hence it is called *chevenne* and *testard* in France. There the chub commonly reaches a length of 10 to 15 inches (maximum two feet) and may weigh up to 12 pounds. English chub are smaller, 15 inches and 10 pounds being the maximums.

The taste of chub varies depending on its habitat. Like many members of the carp family, it may frequent muddy bottoms and have a muddy taste. Chub taken from fast-moving or clear waters are much better tasting. They are not fished commercially, however, and rarely appear in markets or restaurants, except perhaps as one ingredient in a mixed fry or chowder. The flesh is bony and not too firm. On the whole, it is considered mediocre as either food or game.

In the United States, the name "chub" is given to a number of fish in both fresh and salt water. It is applied to both the lake herring *(Argyrosomus artedi)* and whitefish (genus *Coregonus)* of Lakes Michigan and Superior. The whitefish is excellent broiled, planked or smoked. Its roe is considered a plausible caviar substitute. The river chub *(Hybopsis kentuckiensis)* and the silver chub *(Semotilus corporalis)*, found mainly in the South, are distantly related to the European variety. Among saltwater fish, the tautog, spot and Bermuda bream are also called chub.

CHUFA

Also EARTH ALMOND, GROUND ALMOND, RUSH NUT. Chufa is a small, scaly tuber, resembling a peanut, that grows from the roots of a reed or sedge *(Cyperus esculentus)*, which is native to Egypt. The tubers are dark brown outside, creamy white inside and sweet to the taste. They are eaten raw or cooked, fresh or dried. Drying seems to improve the flavor. In Africa, the dried tubers are ground into meal and used to make bread. Chufa grows extensively in Europe, Asia and America. It enjoyed a period of general popularity in Europe as a spice during the Middle Ages. It was called **galingale** in England and *souchet* in France.

Chufa has a slight gingery flavor, and its use declined when that spice became widely available in Europe. It is still a commercial crop in Spain, and is the basis of a popular drink called *horchata*, which is a kind of chufa **orgeat.** Chufa grows easily in the southeastern United States, and went through a spell of commercial cultivation there in the middle of the 19th century. Although the yield was bountiful, a market for the crops was never found.

The word "chufa" comes from the Spanish. It is an old word meaning "trifle" or "tidbit."

CHUFLE

A flowering herb, *Calathea macrosepala*, native to Costa Rica, its young flower clusters are cooked and eaten as a vegetable. Chufle is also found in Mexico and some South American countries. A closely related plant, violet *chufle*, is similarly used.

CHUKAR

An Iranian or Indian rock partridge which has been introduced into the western United States as a game bird with some success, chukar is reputed to have an excellent taste and may be prepared like any other small game bird.

CHUNO

See **Potato.**

CHUNO DE CONCEPCION

Chuno de Concepcion is a tuberous-rooted herb, *Alstroemeria ligtu*, of the Peruvian lily type, but native to Chile. Its roots yield a flour useful for baking or cooking as porridge and gruel.

CHUPATTY

Also CHAPATI. The traditional unleavened flat bread or pancake of northern India, the chupatty is made from a coarse wheat flour called *atta*, plus water and salt. They are mixed into a stiff dough, shaped by hand into a flat disk and then baked on an iron griddle over an open fire. Chupatties are the staple native bread of upper India, and go well with curry, rice and *dal*, a kind of lentil stew. The disks can serve as envelopes for food, or pieces are torn off to dip into sauces or to scoop up portions of food. The chupatty has a rather tough texture, and much resembles the Mexican **tortilla.**

According to John Masters in his *Nightrunners of Bengal*, the chupatty played a key role in the Sepoy Mutiny, which rocked the British Raj in 1857. Mutineers dispatched runners from village to village in Bengal, bearing a coded message which gave the date of the impending uprising. Runners would hand the village watchman two chupatties, one torn in five parts (to signify the fifth month) and another torn in ten parts (to signify the 10th day), i.e., May 10, 1857.

CHUPONES

These edible berries of a perennial plant, *Greigia sphacelata*, are native to Chile.

CHUREK

An Armenian flatbread or pancake. The *churek* is unleavened, and consists of flour, salt, sugar, butter and water. A soft dough is mixed, then rolled into the thinnest cakes possible, sprinkled with sesame seeds and baked until light brown.

See also: **Bread.**

CHURRO

See **Doughnut.**

CHUTNEY

This relish or condiment originated in India but is now manufactured in a number of countries. It contains pickled fruits and vegetables and has a sweet, often spicy, flavor. The most popular variety is mango chutney, which, in addition to mangos, contains raisins, tamarinds, limes, ginger, vinegar and sometimes chili. Other varieties contain shallots, apples, pimientos, mustard, brown sugar, tomatoes, bananas, celery and such spices as turmeric and cinnamon. Garlic is featured in some chutneys, particularly those of Sri Lanka.

Mango chutney is usually eaten with curry, and other chutneys accompany stews or cold meats and sausages. In making homemade mango chutney, green peaches are a plausible substitute for the mangos.

CIBOL

Also JAPANESE BUNCHING ONION, STONE LEEK, WELSH ONION. A bulbless onion, *Allium fistulosum*, it looks something like a scallion. The plant has hollow cylindrical leaves that may reach a height of 20 inches. They do thicken at the bottom forming a sort of bulblet, which is not much thicker than the stem. The leaves may be broken off without uprooting the plant and used singly as a seasoning like chives. In this sense, the plant is perennial. It may also be uprooted and used as a spring onion. The flavor is mild like that of a leek.

Cibol is native to Siberia, and has been the principal garden onion in Japan and China for centuries. It was introduced into Europe in the late Middle Ages, and into England in the 17th century. It has never attained much popularity in the West, and despite the name, Welsh Onion, it has never been much planted in Wales. "Welsh" is apparently a corruption of the German word for "foreign" which the onion acquired on introduction from the Far East. It is a home garden crop in the West.

CICALA DE MARE

See **Squill Fish.**

CICELY

See **Sweet Cicely.**

Cider Making:
1. Washing apples
2. Crushing apples
3. Apple-pressing machine
4. Bottling the freshly pressed cider
5. Pasteurizing the cider

1. 2. 3. 4. 5.

CIDER

The juice pressed from the pulp of apples, it may be used as a drink or made into vinegar. There are two basic drinks, sweet apple juice or sweet cider, and fermented apple juice, called hard cider, containing from two to eight percent alcohol.

Sweet apple juice as pressed will not remain sweet but will ferment from natural action of its components. To prevent fermentation, the sweet juice may be filtered and pasteurized before bottling or canning. This is a very popular drink in America.

Just leaving sweet, fresh, apple juice alone in a container will soon produce hard cider. Well filtered, it makes a palatable drink. Before the Revolutionary War, it was the American national drink. In northwest France today, in the apple-growing country, it is a more popular drink than wine. The French call it *cidre.*

In England and Spain, a secondary fermentation may be induced producing a sort of sparkling cider, sold commercially as champagne cider. It is a very lucrative export to Latin America, has a sweet, apple flavor and costs only half the price of real champagne.

Americans of old considered hard cider a mild drink: John Adams, second United States president, downed a pitcher of it each morning at breakfast and still thought himself a nondrinker. This indulgence may have affected his longevity. He died at 91 years of age.

Apple cider vinegar is refermented hard cider with a high acetic acid content. It is an indispensable flavor and condiment in the kitchen.

CIDER VINEGAR

See **Vinegar.**

CIMARRONA

See **Mountain Soursop.**

CINA

Also CABEZA DE VIEJO. Edible fruit of the whisker cactus *(Lophocereus schottii)*, a treelike plant native to Sonora and Baja California, it measures one inch in diameter and is in season in spring and summer.

CINCHO CHEESE

A Spanish cheese made from sheep's milk, it has a firm texture and is also known as *campos* for Tierra de Campos, its area of origin.

CINCHONA

Also PERUVIAN BARK. This bark of a South American tree, *Cinchona ledgeriana*, is used to flavor certain fortified aperitif wines and carbonated drinks, such as tonic water. Cinchona takes its name from the Countess Chinchon, wife of a 17th century viceroy of Peru. According to legend, she was dramatically cured of a fever by an infusion of bark from what, up to then, had been called the fever-bark tree. The botanist Carl Linnaeus was so impressed by the story that he named the tree *cinchona*, after the fortunate countess. Today the tree grows abundantly in Ecuador, Peru, Bolivia, Java and India.

Cinchona bark yields the alkaloid, quinine, which has an extremely bitter taste. It is a specific against the chills and fever of malaria. Together, these two factors account for its presence in aperitif wines, such as **vermouth.** Malaria was the scourge of the tropics in the 18th and 19th centuries when European countries sought to establish colonies there. Yet, European troops did not like the bitter taste of quinine, the only thing that could stave off the debilitating chills and fever of malaria. Then an enterprising army surgeon conceived the idea of mixing quinine with sweet wine, a combination that overcame the soldiers' reluctance. Thus the French and Italians acquired a taste for quinined wines that they have never lost.

CINNAMON

There are two main varieties of this warm, fragrant spice: Ceylon cinnamon and cassia cinnamon. Ceylon cinnamon *(Cinnamomum zeylanicum)*, considered by many authorities to be the true cinnamon, is judged to have a flavor that is richer, more aromatic and milder than the other variety. The cinnamon plant, a kind of laurel tree, grows wild in Ceylon, and in the wild state it achieves heights of 20 to 30 feet. Today its cultivation is one of Ceylon's chief industries, and by careful pruning, the height of the cultivated trees is kept to 10 feet or less. The spice consists of the inner bark of this tree. When the tree is about six years old, or otherwise regarded as ripe, branches that have a thickness of at least an inch are lopped off in four-foot lengths. The bark is separated from the wood but allowed to rest in place to ferment for three to six hours. Then the outer bark is scraped away to lay bare the yellow inner bark. Upon drying, the bark forms tight, concentric rolls called quills, which are the commercial cinnamon.

Cassia cinnamon *(Cinnamomum cassia)*, known also as Chinese cinnamon, was brought to the West originally from China. It is believed to be a species developed by the Chinese in ancient times from the original Ceylon type, one better adapted to the

climate and conditions of southern China. It is now grown in many parts of Southeast Asia, including Indochina and the islands of Indonesia and Malaysia. This is sometimes referred to as the "poor man's cinnamon," yet many people prefer its more pungent and longer-lasting flavor. It is less volatile than the Ceylon type and reputedly retains its flavor longer. There is a wider range of quality in the cassia type in that the lowest grades are cheaper than any Ceylon, while the highest grade is more expensive than its competitor. At the quill stage, the two types can be distinguished by the thickness of the bark. Cassia bark is thicker, rougher and paler than the Ceylonese cinnamon bark. In powdered form, which is extremely common, the two are difficult to distinguish.

The term "cinnamon" derives from the Hebraic/Arabic term *anomon*, meaning "fragrant," with the prefix *kin*, meaning "plant of China." Arabs first brought the spice to the West in the days of ancient Israel, Greece and Rome. They concealed its place of origin, however, and it was not well known until the 14th century that much of the cinnamon came from Ceylon. The Italians called it *cannella*, and the French, *cannelle*, meaning "little reed." During the Middle Ages, cinnamon became the rage among those who could afford spices, despite its high cost. With the discovery of the Spice Islands and their exploitation by the Dutch, cinnamon became one of the most widely used spices in Europe.

Today cinnamon in quill form is used in pickling and to spice coffee and puddings. The powdered form is sprinkled on puddings, hot cereals, rice and farina dishes and apple pie and is used to flavor baked goods.

CIPOLLINO

See **Tassel Hyacinth.**

CISCO

The name includes any of various whitefishes of the genus *Leucichthys*, important food fish found in the Great Lakes region, such as the menomenee whitefish, mooneye cisco and the lake herring.

Cisco may be the favorite food fish caught in inland American waters. Planked whitefish is a prime delicacy around the Great Lakes. The catch of cisco is probably largest in Lake Michigan with the smallest in Lake Ontario.

CISTANCHE

Cistanche is a perennial, parasitic plant, *Cistanche lutea*, of North Africa. It stems and shoots are eaten like asparagus.

CITEAUX CHEESE

A cow's milk cheese much like *Port du Salut*, it is made in France by the Trappist monks at Citeaux and is in season all year long.

CITHAR

An important commercial food fish of tropical Africa, the cithar *(Citharinus citharus)* is widely distributed in lakes and rivers including the Nile, Niger, Volta, Senegal and Gambia, plus Lake Albert. It is a deep-bodied fish of a silvery color, with red touches on its fins. It is extremely abundant and can reach a length of 30 inches.

CITRANGE

This hybrid fruit, developed in the United States, is a cross between the sweet orange and the trifoliate orange *(Poncirus trifolia)*. The latter is a thorny, ornamental tree, whose fruit is so bitter as to be inedible. It is, however, a hardy plant, and when not used in hedges, it has been employed as rootstock for budding the fruit orange.

The citrange *(Citroncirus webberi)* has a very strong flavor, but is tarter than the ordinary orange. It varies greatly in size and appearance, from small to large, and from red to green. In some the pulp is greenish and the peel fuzzy. The citrange is chiefly used in cooking and for making summer beverages and preserves.

CITRANGEQUAT

This citrus fruit is a second generation hybrid. One parent is the citrange, a cross between the orange *(Citrus sinensis)* and the trifoliate orange *(Poncirus trifolia)*. The other parent is the kumquat *(C. japonica)*.

CITRON

Also AIGRE DE CEDRE, CEDRAT. Citron is a citrus fruit, *Citrus medica*, which, though closely related to the lemon, is cultivated for its thick, spongy rind. The citron is a larger fruit than the lemon—large ones weigh as much as 20 pounds—and is shaped more like a quince. The skin is greenish yellow, with a warty, knobby surface. In many varieties, the fruit is too bitter to be eaten fresh; in others, the taste is less acid than the lemon and is thought palatable. Yet, the fruit is rarely consumed fresh because the skin and pulp are too valuable as commercial products. Most often the skin and pulp are candied, glaceed or crystallized. They are eaten alone as a confection or used in bakery products, such as fruit cake. Citron is used in marmalade, and in Corsica, one of the world's largest producers, it is used as a base for a liqueur, Cedratine. Oil of the skin is used in making perfume.

Citron is thought to have originated in Persia or Media (hence the scientific name *medica)*, but was cultivated in the West as early as 300 B.C. The Romans inherited its cultivation from the Etruscans, and the Moors introduced it into Spain, where they established large groves near Granada. The Spaniards brought it to the Caribbean, where it has become a specialty of Puerto Rico. The United States consumes about one-half the world's production of citron.

Candied citron may be purchased by the piece in the market for use in cooking and baking. It should be moist and sticky, not hard and crystallized. It is finely diced, or shaved before mixing into a cake.

CITRONELLA

An aromatic grass, *Cymbopogon nardus*, native to the Asian tropics, it is widely cultivated in other tropical areas, such as south Florida. It is the chief source of oil of citronella, which is distilled from its leaves and is perhaps best known as an insect repellant. The oil is pale yellow, inexpensive and has a lemony scent disliked by flying insects. Citronella is also used in cheap perfumes.

The leaves are sometimes used sparingly to season salads, in Africa to make tea or in the Far East to flavor soybean sauce. The flowers are used in France to flavor digestive liqueurs.

Another plant of the mint family, *Collinsonia canadensis,* native to North America, is also known as citronella. It has lemon-scented flowers.

CITRON MELON

A small, round melon of the watermelon genus, citron melon *(Citrullus lanatus* var. *citroides)* has the outer color and patterning of watermelon, but its inner flesh is hard and white. It is never eaten raw but is used to make pickles and preserves. The latter are usually prepared by boiling the rind for 20 minutes in a sugar and water solution strongly flavored with lemon and ginger. It is also known as preserving melon.

CITRUS

This genus of trees and shrubs produces several types of popular and useful fruits, namely the orange, tangerine (mandarin), citron, bergamot, grapefruit, lemon, lime and kumquat. They share a tart taste, which may be predominantly sweet or sour; a juicy pulp divided into easily separable cells and a leathery rind, which is easy to remove. The plants themselves are woody perennials with evergreen leaves. They vary in size from six to 20 feet, and grow best in the mild climates of southern Italy, Sicily, Spain, Greece, Brazil, Mexico and in the states of Florida and California of the United States.

The term "citrus" is from the Latin, and derived from a Greek word, *kedros*, meaning "cedar." When the fruit first appeared in Greece, it was wrongly supposed to be from a type of cedar tree. The Romans believed cedar apples, as they were called, to come from the Canary Islands, or Hesperides. When Roman writers referred to the "golden apples of the Hesperides," it is believed they meant the orange. It was not the sweet orange of today, however, but the bitter orange, or bigarade, which was the only one known in classical antiquity. Oranges were shipped to Rome from Egypt, which in turn got them from India. India got its orange trees from their original home, China.

In a commercial environment, few citrus trees are grown from seed. Trees grown from seed tend to be thorny and take up to 15 years to become fruitful. Most citrus trees are propagated by budding or grafting the top half, or scion, of one variety onto the bottom half, or rootstock, of another variety. For example, lemon scions are budded with rootstocks from a type of orange tree. This easy union among different species produces trees with few or no thorns that bear fruit within five years. It also facilitates hybridization, with such results as the citrange (sweet orange and trifoliate orange), the temple (sweet orange and tangerine), and the tangelo (tangerine and grapefruit). Freaks also result, which include chimeras (fruit fusing the tissues of two species), and a single tree that bears lemons, limes, oranges, tangerines, kumquats and grapefruit on its branches at the same time.

Citrus fruit is rich in vitamins, particularly vitamin C. See also under the specific fruits.

CITRUS AURANTIUM

See **Orange.**

CITRUS MEDICA

See **Citron.**

CLABBER

See **Milk.**

CLAIRETTE

This is a French wine grape used in the Rhone region to make one of the wines mixed in Chateauneuf-du-Pape, and in the Herault Department to make vermouth. By itself, the clairette grape produces a characterless white wine that becomes very dry as it ages. For this reason, it is usually improved in some way or used to mix with another wine to add a particular quality. Two French varietals are Clairette de Bellegard, which is almost dry white wine that may be served either as an aperitif or a table wine, and Clairette du Languedoc, a golden dry white wine, produced in Herault, that does not age well.

The grape is used to produce white wines of many countries, including Israel, Algeria, Morocco, Australia and South Africa. As in France, it is usually used as a mixing wine.

CLAM

Any marine mollusk with a two-part, hinged shell that buries itself in wet sand is a clam—provided it's not called something else. Clams exist in all parts of the world in incredible variety that defies neat definition. They range from a Japanese clam that is so tiny as to be practically tasteless to the giant clam of the Indian Ocean whose weight approaches 500 pounds. Many of these species are edible, but only a few are prominently so. The latter include the hard- and soft-shell clams of the Atlantic Ocean; the soft-shell and razor clams of the Pacific Ocean and, less importantly, the pismo clams and geoducks.

Clams may be angular, heart-shaped, wedge-shaped or conical. An important anatomical feature is the neck, or siphon. When buried in the sand, the clam extends its neck up into the water to take care of its digestive and respiratory needs. The neck has two parts, one to take in water and food and the other to expel waste, but they are usually bound together in a single tube. The ridges on clam's shells are an indication of their age. Clams normally live one to 10 years, but one pismo clam is known to have lived to the age of 26.

Refuse sites indicate that prehistoric man ate clams with gusto, and many ancient historic people followed suit; an exception was the Hebrews, whose kosher laws forbade them to eat any seafood without scales or fins. Although today clams are popular worldwide, they are not an American predilection, even though they are the most common American shellfish. To judge from statistics, Americans prefer shrimp and lobster by a long margin. Native Americans introduced colonists to the hard-shelled clam, or quahog *(Venus mercenaria).* "Quahog" is the colonists' approximation of the word *poquauhock*, which means "closed shell." The Native Americans ate the clams and used its shell for money, or wampum. Although dirty gray outside, the quahog has a creamy white interior with purple patches. These purple parts were highly esteemed and set at twice the value of the white wampum, made from conch shell. For eating purposes, hard-shelled clams are divided into three grades: littlenecks, which at one year old measure 1½ inches across, and are the smallest; cherrystones, which after two years measure three inches; and quahogs, or adult clams, which measure more than three inches. Quahogs bigger than 3½ inches are not eaten raw, but are ground up for chowder. The quahog was transplanted to French waters, where it is known as *le clam*. Other, similar, French clams are the *palourde*, the *clovisse* and the *praire*. In Italy the hard shell clam is called *vongole*, but is generally eaten when young and small.

Clams

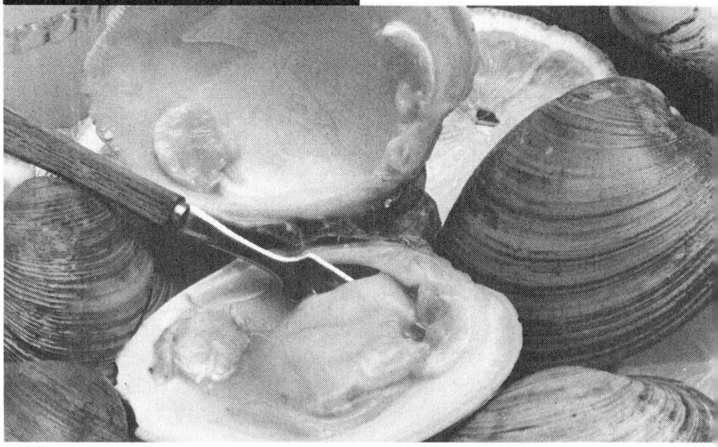

The soft-shell clam *(Myra arenaria)* is also called the long-necked, or steamer clam in the United States, where it is most popular. It is thinner than the quahog, chalky white and oval in shape. In the New England area, steamers are found in wet sand between high- and low-water marks, and are gathered at low tide. In the Mid-Atlantic states, they are found farther out to sea, and are gathered by dredges. Steamers are the most important clams commercially, and were successfully transplanted to the West Coast in the 1880s, where they are now plentiful from Monterey to Alaska. Soft-shell clams are called *clanque* in France; in Britain, though readily available, they are not nearly as popular as mussels.

The razor clam *(Solen siliqua)* is so called for its resemblance to an old-fashioned straight razor in a folded position. Pacific razor clams, when sold frozen or canned, are marketed as ocean clams. They are plentiful in Oregon, Washington, British Columbia and Alaska, but not in California, where the beaches slope too steeply to suit them. They are six to eight inches long, and are frequently prepared by being baked in their own shells.

The increasingly rare pismo clams *(Trivela stultorum)* were once so plentiful that farmers plowed them up at low tide and fed them to pigs. To be legally gathered they must now measure at least five inches across. They are now found in great numbers only in Baja California.

The geoduck *(Panope generosa)* is the largest intertidal bivalve and is found from Northern California to Alaska. It is best gathered at extraordinarily low spring tides.

Clams are an extremely healthful food when eaten raw, provided they are fresh, because they are rich in mineral salts, especially calcium, phosphorus, iron and potassium. Cooking destroys some of these and much of the vitamin content, yet even they they are unusually nutritious. The chief hazard in buying clams is the possibility of lack of freshness. Only those whose shells are tightly closed are unmistakably fresh. A gaping shell means that the abductor muscle is relaxed; thus the clam is dead or dying.

When eaten raw, clams are usually accompanied by lemon juice or vinegar sauce. They also may be broiled, fried, steamed, stewed or baked. Clam chowder is a favorite soup in the United States.

See also: **Nutritive Value of Foods.**

CLARET

This English name is used for dry red French wine in general, but in particular the "clear" red wine of Bordeaux. The English wine trade with Bordeaux dates from the 12th century when most of southwestern France belonged to the dukes of Aquitaine who were also the kings of England. The name has persisted through the centuries. Samuel Johnson pronounced the virtues of *claret* to be puerile: "Claret is the liquor for boys; Port for men; but he who aspires to be a hero must drink Brandy."

See also: **Bordeaux Wines.**

CLARY

A perennial plant of the sage genus, clary *(Salvia sclarea)* reaches three feet in height and has white, pink and mauve flowering stalks. It is a native of southern Europe. Clary was formerly used as a potherb and its leaves dried and used as a flavoring agent in French and English cooking.

The leaves and flowers are strongly scented, a fragrance reminiscent of grapefruit. When used as a flavoring, however, the taste combines something of mint, sage and muscatel sage. For this last quality, it is one of the herbs still used to flavor Italian vermouth. In England, it was used to flavor pastries and added to beer and ale in place of hops. Clary flowers are still occasionally used to make an herbal tea or are added to salads. The leaves can serve in wine cups in place of sweet woodruff.

CLAVARIA

See **Coral Fungus.**

CLEAVERS

Also BEDSTRAW, GOOSE GRASS. An herbaceous plant *Galium aparine*, its leaves and stems can supposedly curdle milk, much like rennet. Authorities differ on this point, however. It is certain that some species, those with delicate yellow and white flowers, are added to cheese (e.g., Chester cheese) as a coloring agent. Cleavers enjoyed some popularity in England and the United States as a garden vegetable during the 19th century, but since then it has gone out of usage, except among wild food enthusiasts. It resembles spinach somewhat when boiled.

Cleavers is a member of the same botanical order as coffee, *Rubiaceae*, and its seeds were occasionally used as a coffee substitute. In England, the leaves, buds, stems and all were used to make Lenten pottage, to which was often added mutton broth or oatmeal. It garnered some esteem as a medicinal herb. Cleavers tea was regarded as an effective diuretic and was thought to dissolve kidney stones and gravel.

Cleavers grows wild in the northern temperate regions of America, Europe and Asia. It earned the name "cleavers" from its practice of hooking onto neighboring plants by means of downward-pointing hooks that grow on its stems, leaves and fruit.

CLEMENTINE

A hybrid citrus fruit, *Citrus nobilis*, var. *deliciosa*, the clementine is a cross between the tangerine and the orange, specifically the wild North African variety. It is less flattened than the tangerine, is darker, smoother skinned and is closer to the orange in flavor. It is very juicy, and in the best variety, the *misserghia*, is practically seedless. Another variety, the *Monreal*, contains up to 20 seeds and is a prolific bearer of fruit, used in cooking and for its juice. All varieties are said to be descended from a single tree that was discovered in an Algerian garden in 1902 by the French missionary, Father Clement. It is grown only in North Africa, Spain, Italy and Israel. The clementine is in season during winter months.

CLERIMBERT

See **Alpin.**

CLIDEMIA

Also TRIANA. Clidemia is the fruit of a Mexican plant of which there are four species, *Clidemia chinantlana*, *C. dependens*, *C. deppeana* and *C. hirta.* Clidemias are eaten by native Mexicans.

CLIMBING ENTADA

Also ST. THOMAS BEAN. This climbing vine, *Entada gigas*, is found in many of the tropical areas of the world. The fruit is a very long legume, averaging three to six feet and as much as four inches across. The beans are roasted and eaten and the leaves cooked as a vegetable. The legumes also provide fiber and saponin.

CLONEVAN

A mild-flavored Irish cheese, *clonevan* is produced in County Wexford and somewhat resembles **Camembert** in looks if not in flavor. The shape is round and flat, the texture firm and the flavor creamy. It comes packed in a round straw box.

CLOS MARIOUT

This is a dry white Egyptian wine grown near Lake Mareotis. Traditionally, Clos Mariout was the wine offered by Cleopatra to Caesar when he visited Egypt. Some wine of this type is bottled and sold in Egypt today under the label Cleopatra. In its own name, Clos Mariout, is exported and highly regarded.

See also: **Wines, North African.**

CLOTTED CREAM

Also DEVONSHIRE CREAM, CORNISH CREAM. This English cream is made in the western counties of Devonshire and Cornwall. Raw milk is placed in shallow pans and the cream is allowed to rise for from 12 to 24 hours, depending on the season. The milk is then scalded until the cream begins to show a ring around the edge. When cool, the cream is skimmed in layers for use in desserts. This method produces a very smooth cream with a yellow crust on top.

CLOUDBERRY

A reddish yellow fruit resembling the raspberry that grows in arctic and subarctic regions, especially in Sweden, Norway and Finland. In the United States cloudberry *(Rubus charaemorus)* is plentiful in Alaska, where it is also called the dwarf mulberry, and as far south as Maine and New Hampshire, where it prefers mountainous regions or peat bogs. In general, it grows in regions where there is little nutritive competition. For example, in Great Britain it is found on mountains, desolate moors and exposed heaths. The plant itself is herbaceous and trailing. It has a stunted appearance and its drupes, which measure an inch across, seem too large for it. Except for the color, the cloudberry looks like a large blackberry. Its flavor is sweet, not tart, and its admirers claim to detect in it the taste of moss, mountain moor and burnt caramel. Cloudberries are rich in vitamin C.

It is a popular fruit in Quebec, where it is called yellow berry, and in the Maritime Provinces of Canada, where it is styled baked-apple berry. Its most ardent consumers are in the three Scandinavian countries named above. It is called *suomuuian* in Finland, *hjortron* in Sweden and *multe* in Norway. The job of gathering berries falls mainly to the Lapps, a nomadic people who herd reindeer across the desolate northern regions of the three countries. In summer months, whole families of Lapps pick cloudberries, managing to amass as much as 2,000 pounds per family for sale in markets. A cloudberry liqueur is also manufactured.

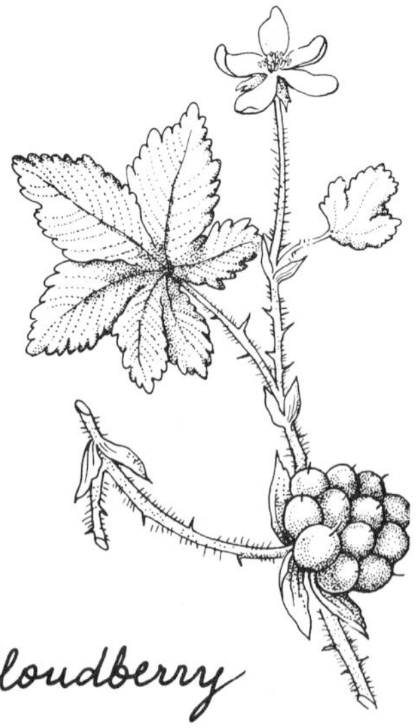

Cloudberry

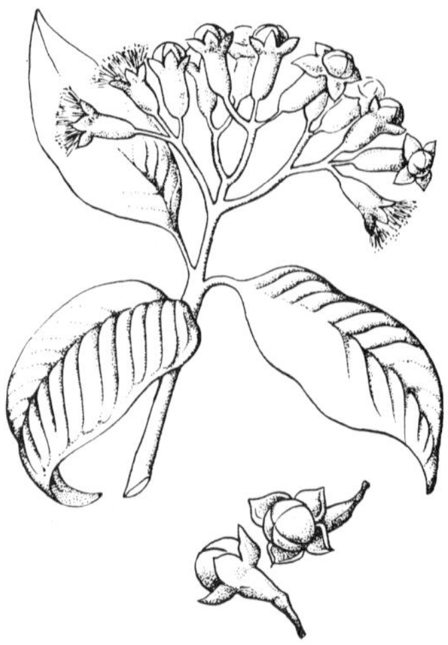

Cloves

CLOUD EAR

See **Black Tree Fungus.**

CLOVE

Cloves are the dried buds of a tropical evergreen tree, *Eugenia carophyllata.* They look like small, brown nails, hence the name, which derives from the French for nail, *clou.* Their aromatic and astringent qualities have made them a major spice, while their essential oil has important medical uses.

The Moluccas in the East Indies were the original home of the clove tree. The Chinese were using cloves in the third century before Christ, one emperor requiring courtiers to hold cloves in their mouths when addressing the court. Reportedly, this was to overcome the odor of garlic, of which the Chinese were prolific users.

The ancient Romans used cloves, particularly in love philtres, yet the spice was not introduced to the rest of Europe until the Middle Ages, where it became a tremendous success. The daily fare was dull, and food spoilage everpresent even in wealthy circles, so that people were desperate for spices to enliven taste and mask unpleasant odors. Against this background, exorbitant demand developed for cloves.

Even the smallest of maritime nations saw a chance to gain great wealth by controlling the spice trade to the Moluccas. After much strife with the Portuguese, the Dutch managed in 1605 to establish a monopoly of production on Amboina, one of the Moluccas. They then stamped out production in the rest of the Moluccas and tried to prevent it everywhere else. In spite of this, commercial ingenuity prevailed, and smugglers managed to bring trees to Zanzibar and the West Indies, which became, and continue to be, important producers.

Under the best of conditions, a clove tree can attain a height of 40 feet and bloom year round. At first the blooms are pale, then green, then bright red, which signals the picking stage. Drying them changes the color to dark brown and prevents decay. They are about 18 percent oil, which can be extracted by distillation.

In the home, cloves are used to flavor mincemeat, to stud ham and pork and to spice pies and puddings. Commercially, cloves are important flavoring in pies, candy and dentifrices. Oil of cloves is best known medicinally as a reliever of toothaches. Recently, the oil has become an important source of synthetic **vanillin.**

CLOVE BARK

This is the bark of a tropical American tree, *Dicypellum caryophyllatum*, from which an aromatic oil is extracted that may be used as flavoring in place of cloves.

CLOVER

With rare exceptions, humans do not eat clover, save at one remove in such things as meat, milk and honey. The exceptions usually occur in times of famine, but there are others. For example, some Icelanders boil white clover *(Trifolium repens)* as a green vegetable. Wild red clover *(T. pratense)*, a European variety, is used to make a tea and a cough syrup. A bitter variety, *T. campestra*, is occasionally used to flavor beer when hops are lacking. The Swiss put sweet clover in their cheese to flavor it (but sweet clover is not a true clover—it is melilot). There are 250 species of clover throughout the world. It is cultivated chiefly as fodder.

CLOVISSE

See **Clam.**

CLUSTER BEAN

Also GUAR BEAN. A bushy perennial plant, *Cyamopsis tetragonolobus*, common in India, is cultivated for the young pods, which grow in clusters and are eaten beans and all. If allowed to mature, the pods reach four to five inches in length and yield black, gray and white beans that are a source of industrial guar gum.

See also: **Gum.**

COALFISH

See **Pollack.**

COATI

Also COATIMUNDI. A mammal related to the raccoon and the panda, the coati *(Nasua nasua)* is found from the southwestern United States down through South America. It is an omnivorous animal, living in dens and traveling in bands of up to 40 individuals. A large specimen will weigh as much as 25 pounds. It has a long body (up to 27 inches) and a narrow head with a long, pointed muzzle. Its tail is prehensile and longer than the body and head combined.

Coatis are hunted for meat by natives who train dogs for that purpose. Though generally inoffensive and easily trained, the coati can inflict serious wounds if cornered.

COCA

Coca is a shrub, *Erythroxylum coca,* native to the east Andean region of South America, whose dried leaves, when processed, yield the crystalline alkaloid cocaine, a powerful stimulant drug. Used externally, cocaine is also an effective local anesthetic. Many Indians of the Peruvian and Bolivian *altiplano* chew coca leaves on a daily basis for their refreshing effect. Coca enables them to work long hours and resist the effects of hunger, fatigue, cold and high altitude. Francesco Carletti, an Italian traveler, made the following observation at the turn of the 17th century:

> *[The indians] keep [coca] constantly in their mouths, chewing it together with a small amount of ground lime [calcium oxide]. . . . They say that chewing this leaf gives them strength and vigor, and such is the superstition and faith that they have in it that they cannot work or go on trips without having it in their mouths. And, on the contrary, having it, they work happily and walk a day or two without refreshing themselves otherwise or eating anything.*

The Indians' habits have not changed to this day. The effect seems to be part soporific and part stimulating and has been compared to that of chewing **betel nut,** as is customary in Southeast Asia, and of chewing the kola nut, as is done in West Africa. The latter contains caffeine, which accounts for its stimulating effect like drinking strong coffee or tea.

It is said, however, that the proportion of cocaine in the leaves is higher than caffeine in coffee, tea or the kola nut. It is therefore more potent, and more likely to be habit-forming.

Coca leaves are grown in other parts of South America, in Ceylon, Java and Taiwan for the commercial production of cocaine, which has many medicinal uses. The leaves are also used to flavor cola beverages, but only after they have been decocainized.

COCA-COLA

Also COKE. This sweet carbonated beverage is the leading soft drink in the United States and probably in the world. It takes its name from the coca plant, which is the source of cocaine, and the kola nut, an African bean that contains the stimulants caffeine and kolanin. The amount of these ingredients in Coca-Cola is reputed to be so small as to be undetectable under chemical analysis. What Coca-Cola does contain is mostly sugar (five teaspoonfuls per small bottle) and water, plus caramel (for coloring), caffeine (less than either coffee or tea), phosphoric acid and such flavoring agents as cinnamon, nutmeg, vanilla, lavender, lime juice, citrus oils and vegetable glycerine. It also contains a secret ingredient, and the formula giving the proportion of the other ingredients is also a secret. The traditional 6½-ounce bottle of Coca-Cola contains between 81 and 86 calories.

The name "Coca-Cola" became the issue in a law suit brought under the Pure Food and Drug Act in 1906. The company was accused of misbranding because the drink, in actual fact, contained neither coca nor cola. It came to trial in 1909, and after nine years of courtroom battling, reached the Supreme Court, where Justice Charles Evans Hughes rendered a decision against the company. He said the company must put in at least trace elements of coca and cola if it wished to continue using the name. Otherwise, he said, a company could put out a product labeled "Chocolate-Vanilla" that contained neither chocolate nor vanilla.

The alternative name "Coke" is a registered trademark of the company, but only the first half of the Coca-Cola name is protected. Other soft drinks such as Pepsi and Diet Rite are free to use the "cola" part.

COBIA

Also SERGEANT FISH. A fish of the Atlantic Ocean that inhibits warm water and is generally found from Chesapeake Bay south to Florida, the cobia *(Rachycentron canadum)* is a long fish—reaching four to five feet—with a heavy body and a broad head. It frequents open water and is considered a fine food fish. The cobia is also known as coalfish because of its swarthy aspect, and it often reaches a weight of 25 pounds.

COBNUT

See **Hazelnut.**

COCCINEA

Also IVY GOURD. Fruit of a tropical vine, *Coccinea grandis*, native to Asia and Africa, it is oblong, smooth and scarlet, and may be eaten raw, candied or cooked. The shoots are also eaten as a vegetable.

COCHINEAL

This red food dye is obtained from the female *Coccus cacti*, a scale insect that lives on any of several species of the prickly pear cactus, such as *Opuntia ficus-indica* and *O. tuna*. There are gray, red and black varieties of the insect, but the gray is considered best. The dye is called carmine, and consists of the dried, crushed bodies of the insects, 70,000 of which are required to make up one pound.

The first European to encounter carmine was Bernal Diaz del Castillo, chronicler of the conquest of Mexico, who ran across it in the main market of Tenochtitlan. Cochineal was shipped to Europe in

1518 and there it was assumed to be of vegetable origin, resembling as it did a shriveled currant. Later, its insect origin was revealed under a microscope.

The insect is native to Central America and Peru, but is produced commercially mainly in Mexico, Guatemala and certain parts of North Africa. A cochineal farm consists of large plantings of cacti, which are kept trimmed low to facilitate harvesting. The female attaches itself to a cactus, and is collected after being fertilized but before complete development of the eggs. They are brushed off into baskets, and are dried in an oven heated to 150° F.

Carmine is used to color icings, creams, jellies, cakes and candies, as well as wines and liqueurs. It is tasteless and odorless.

See also: **Prickly Pear.**

COCHLEARIA

See **Scurvy Grass.**

COCKLE

A heart-shaped, seawater shellfish, cockle has traditionally meant only the small *Cardium edule*, which is found in sandy beaches and estuaries of Great Britain, France and Mediterranean countries. This is the one Molly Malone sang of in, "Cockles and mussels alive, alive O!" Today the name is applied more generally to hundreds of heart-shaped bivalves in many areas of the world. The European cockle is a relative of the oyster. It is small and nutritious, with pale, delicately flavored flesh. It is usually boiled, then served cold with a variety of condiments.

On tidal beaches the cockle is easier to gather than than the clam because it has no neck and cannot burrow deeply into the sand. On the other hand, it is capable of taking huge leaps to meet the incoming tide.

Cockles have been a popular food in northern Europe since prehistoric times. In the Middle Ages, the term "cocked hat" was coined because of the public's familiarity with cockles. Pilgrims to the shrine of St. James of Compostela wore on their hats a badge representing a scallop shell, which resembled a cockle shell, and was called in French *coquille St. Jaques.* It became known as a cockle hat and finally "cocked hat."

The original cockle is not found in the United States. On the East Coast, the best known is the giant Atlantic cockle *(Dinocardium robustum)*, which is found from Cape Hatteras to Mexico. It measures better than five by four inches, is strong-tasting and is usually served stuffed or in chowder. The smaller prickly cockle *(Trachycardium egmontianum)* of Florida and the Gulf states is prepared similarly.

On the Pacific coast, the most plentiful is the basket cockle *(Clinocardium muttallii)* found from Alaska to Baja California. It averages three inches in size, has good flavor but is usually somewhat tough. The giant Pacific spiny cockle *(Trachycardium quadragenarium)* is found from Santa Barbara to Baja. Less important are the Pacific egg cockle, which remains in deep water and has come to prominence recently with the increasing popularity of skin diving, and the rock cockle, which is small, sweet and tender. It is best when cooked and is not a true cockle but a relative of the quahog.

COCKSCOMB

Also COXCOMB. The fleshy, red crest from the head of a rooster, once a familiar garnish, has all but disappeared from the human diet. Modern methods of raising and distributing poultry do not lend themselves to the production of what has always been a marginal food. Yet, cockscombs are available canned in France, and they are something of a local specialty around Padua, Italy.

A century ago, according to Alexandre Dumas' *Grand Dictionnaire de la Cuisine*, they were so commonly used in rice casseroles or vol-au-vent as to be considered too ordinary to be served at important dinners. Three centuries earlier they were thought to be a royal dish, and formal court dinner nearly always began with a course garnished with cockscombs. They were nearly always served together with cock's "kidneys," i.e., testicles. Louis XV is supposed to have remarked on the aphrodisiac virtues of cockscombs thus accompanied.

Unless canned, cockscombs need rather elaborate preparation. They must be pricked with a needle, then the blood must be squeezed out with the fingers under flowing cold water. They are blanched to loosen the skin, which must be completely removed, then soaked until they are white. Boiling in salted water for half an hour completes the preliminaries. In *cretes de coq en attereaux*, the French marinate prepared cockscombs, spit them on small skewers, dip them into batter and fry them until golden. They are used to decorate entrees.

COCKSPUR GRASS

Also KHERI. This annual grain plant, *Echinochloa crus* var. *galli*, is valued in Japan and other temperate regions for its seeds. These can be milled into flour for porridge or dumplings. The United States variation, called barnyard millet, is considered a noxious weed.

COCKTAIL

A cocktail may be either alcoholic or nonalcoholic, and both kinds are intended as appetizers. The nonalcoholic cocktail is served as the first course of a meal and is a small tidbit designed to whet the appetite. It consists of a glass of fruit juice, such as tomato juice; a small dish of diced fruit, say melon or mixed fruit, or it may be a dish of chilled seafood in a sauce, such as a shrimp cocktail.

The alcoholic cocktail is a short drink taken just before lunch or dinner, usually no more than three or 3½ ounces. It is most often based on a strong liquor, such as whiskey, gin or rum, but sometimes wine is the base. The base is mixed with fruit juice, another liquor, such as vermouth, or a variety of flavoring agents, such as bitters, syrups or sprigs of mint, then shaken or stirred with ice. A good deal of attention is paid to the appearance of a cocktail, since its look as well as its taste must be appetizing.

The martini is probably the most popular and best known cocktail in the world. It is composed of gin and dry vermouth, in varying proportions according to taste, but usually nowadays 15 parts gin to one part vermouth, plus a garnish such as a stuffed olive, or a twist of lemon peel. Other well known cocktails are the champagne cocktail (sugar cube, bitters and dry champagne), the daiquiri (rum, lime juice and sugar), the manhattan (rye or blended whiskey, sweet vermouth, and aromatic bitters), the margarita (tequila, lemon or lime juice and triple sec) and the whisky sour (bourbon whiskey, lemon or lime juice and sugar).

There are several accounts of how the word "cocktail" came to be attached to this class of drinks, two of which seem to be given equal credence. One account says it derived from the French word *coquetel*, a term used around Bordeaux at the turn of the 19th century for a drink consisting of a sugar cube saturated with brandy then covered with dry champagne. The drink became popular in England as the brandy cocktail, and the name "cocktail" stuck to the new type of short drink.

Another account insists that the cocktail is an American drink which, up to the time of the American Revolution, was called the "bracer." During the war, American officers frequented a tavern near Yorktown, New York, owned by one Betsy Flanagan. Betsy, a renown mixer of bracers, always kept a glass filled with rooster tail feathers on the bar, and, one way or another, the cock's tails became associated with Betsy's concoctions.

COCOA

See **Chocolate and Cocoa.**

COCOA BUTTER

A vegetable butter extracted from cacao (cocoa) beans, it is yellowish in color and has the attractive and useful property of being solid at room temperature but melting at just below body temperature. The main gastronomic use of cocoa butter is in milk chocolate candy bars, and in chocolate coatings for other confections. At room temperature, the chocolate impregnated with 15 to 30 percent cocoa butter breaks with a satisfying snap, yet melts refreshingly if put into the mouth.

Cocoa butter makes up about 50 percent of the volume of cacao beans, but most of it is removed in processing the beans to make cocoa and other commercial chocolate preparations. When the latter are then used to make candy, the cocoa butter is restored to a proportion of 15 to 35 percent. More than that is cloying to the taste. Cocoa butter has a slight chocolate taste. Swiss "white chocolate" is sweetened cocoa butter.

A main commercial use of cocoa butter is in the pharmaceutical and cosmetic industries, again because of its fortuitous melting point, 92.1°–93.9° F (33.4°–34.4° C.).

See also: **Chocolate and Cocoa.**

COCO DE MER

Also DOUBLE COCONUT, SEA COCONUT. A huge variety of coconut, *Locoicea maldivia*, the coco de mer grows only on one or two islands of the Seychelles group, which are located in the Indian Ocean 1,000 miles east of Africa. It acquired the name "sea coconut" because empty husks were found floating in the sea long before the point of origin was known. This turned out to be the Vallee de Mer on Pralin Island. Unlike the ordinary coconut, *Cocos nucifera*, the coco de mer does not propagate by chance. Flowering stalks of *Cocos nucifera* float from place to place and can take root where conditions are propitious because each stalk has male and female flowers. This is not true of the coco de mer, which has separate male and female trees. The only other place where it is under cultivation, apparently, is Curieuse Island, also of the Seychelles group.

The coco de mer has some claim to be the largest and heaviest fruit in the world. Specimens weighing 50 pounds are not uncommon. It needs about 10 years to ripen, and it has two lobes, looking as if two large coconuts were fused together, hence the name double coconut. The two-lobed shape has occasioned the nickname in French of *coco-fesse* or buttocks coconut. The flesh is white and tastes like that of the ordinary coconut, although it is not quite as firm as the latter. It is popularly credited with unusual therapeutic properties, e.g., the ability to dissolve gallstones, cure paralysis and restore flagging virility.

Coco de Mer

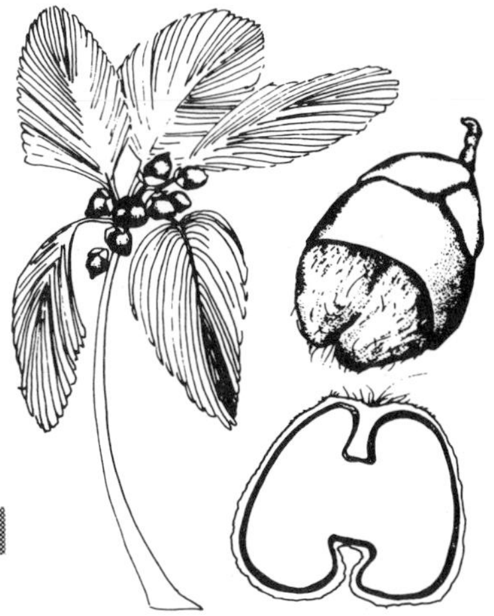

Coconut

COCONUT

Fruit of the palm *Cocos nucifera*, the coconut is one of the most useful plants in the world. Although it probably originated in the area of Malaysia and Indonesia, the tree yields important food and commercial crops throughout the world's tropics. "He who plants a coconut tree," the saying goes, "plants food and drink, vessels and clothing, a habitation for himself and a heritage for his children." Reaching heights of 75 to 100 feet, the tree has a slender, nearly round trunk that is crowned by a thatch of feather-shaped leaves nine to 18 feet long. Perhaps a dozen times a year flower stalks emerge from the crown and develop a cluster of from six to 12 nuts, which take up to six months to mature. Ideal climatic conditions for the tree are a temperature that stays above 68° F year-round and an average of 70 inches of rain annually. They grow best within a few steps of the sea, but have proven viable at altitudes of 2,000 feet or more. The production of nuts falls off rapidly, however, as the distance and altitude increase. In the wild, trees produce from 50 to 100 nuts a year. Cultivated trees produce at least 75, and usually many more. Coconut trees begin bearing at about the age of five years and can continue up to 75 years.

The coconut consists of several layers, which together are about the size of a man's head. The outer layer is a fibrous husk, green when immature and brown when ripe. Next comes a hard nut, six to eight inches across, and inside that a kernel of white, oily "meat," which contains a quantity of sweet liquid called coconut water in its hollow center.

Nearly all parts of the coconut tree have a practical use or commercial value. In certain places the native populations make a medicine from the root. The leaves may be woven into baskets, platters, mats and hats. They may be converted into fans or clothing or used to make the roofs of dwellings. In the Moluccas they are used as sieves for filtering **sago** flour.

Wood from coco palms is called porcupine wood because its surface pattern suggests porcupine quills. If cut down near the sea, it is naturally moisture-resistant and is good raw material for dwellings, bridges and dams. If not, it may be exported for cabinet-making. Fiber from the husk is called coir. It makes excellent rope that is resistant to rot in a marine environment. Coir is also used to make fishing lines, carpets, mats, baskets, brooms and brushes. The coconut shell may be used for bowls, cooking utensils and the like; failing all else, it may be burned for fuel. A particular delicacy is palmetto cabbage or palm heart, which is the terminal bud nestled in the crown of the tree. It is an unusual and expensive, salad vegetable with a crisp and crunchy texture and a taste somewhere between that of white asparagus and bamboo shoots. Removing it results in the death of the tree, so it is generally taken from trees that have been felled for lumber. Sap from the palm is made into wine or, when distilled, a fiery liquor. Another beverage, called toddy, or tuba, is obtained by milking the unopened flower stalks. It is very sweet and may be drunk fresh. Toddy is frequently fermented or distilled to make alcoholic drinks, or converted to vinegar.

The most commercially valuable part of the coconut is the white meat, or copra, as it is called after sun-drying. The local population has the first chance to sample it when the coconut is at the half-ripe, or green, stage. At this point the meat is no firmer than the pulp of a melon; it may be eaten out of the shell with a spoon and has fresh, fruity flavor. The liquid is more abundant and similar to fresh water. As the nut ripens and the husk turns brown, the meat becomes solid and the water thicker and less abundant. With the husk removed, the ripe nut weighs on the average 1½ pounds, of which 28 percent is meat. For commercial purposes it is scraped from the shell and dried, preferably in the sun. A portion of the copra is shredded for use in cooking and confections, but much is pressed for its oil, which constitutes about 60 percent of the whole.

Coconut oil, also called coconut butter, is a white fatty solid at room temperature. It is the world's leading vegetable oil and is used for cooking and to make margarine the world over, except in the United States. It also goes into soaps, detergents, shaving cream, shampoos, face creams, perfumes and candles. Coconut oil is also a major ingredient in glycerine, synthetic rubber, safety glass and hydraulic brake fluid.

Coconut milk is not the natural liquid of the nut. It is made by grating fresh, white coconut meat, mixing it with water and then straining the mixture through cotton cloth. It looks somewhat like cow's milk, and, in some cases, has been used as a substitute for it.

COCO PLUM

Also ICACO. This plumlike fruit of a shrubby tree, *Chrysobalanus icaco*, is native to the American tropics and West Africa. The coco plum is a pulpy, one-seeded fruit that reaches 1½ inches in length. It grows as far north as southern Florida. A popular fruit in Africa, the coco plum is mostly used for jams and preserves in the Western Hemisphere.

COCO YAM

Coco yam is a West African variety of taro or dasheen *(Colocasia esculenta* var. *antiquorum)*. It is a tropical plant with wet and dry varieties. The edible part is thickened root, or corm, which yields a fine grained, easily digestible starch. The wetland variety is most appropriate for making poi, a South Pacific specialty. The dry variety sprouts tubers that are eaten like potatoes.

See also: **Taro.**

COCOZELLE

A variety of summer squash *(Cucurbita pepo* var. *melopepo* cv. *cocozelle)* related to the **zucchini,** but generally larger, *cocozelle* is oblong and cylindrical, reaching perhaps 18 inches, with a diameter of five inches. The skin is dark with yellow or green stripes. The flesh is yellow. Like other summer squashes, cocozelle is best eaten young. It should be free of discolorations and soft spots and should be stored in the refrigerator. It has an excellent flavor and is available in Europe, Great Britain and North America, perhaps more plentifully in the last.

See also: **Squash.**

COCUY

Also COCUI. A brandy distilled in Venezuela from the maguey cactus, it is somewhat like Mexican mezcal and tequila but cruder.

See also: **Mezcal.**

COD

Also ATLANTIC COD. A food fish widely distributed in the North Atlantic Ocean, the cod *(Gadus morhua*, or *callarias)* has been commercially important since the 15th century. Due to its excellent quality and great abundance it became known as "beef of the sea" and "the poor man's friend." Cod is a member of a family that includes the haddock, pollock, hake and cusk and is distinguished from them by its color, which varies from reddish brown to grayish black, with many dark spots; a pale lateral line from tail to gill; and a single barbel on its chin. It averages six to 12 pounds in size. Fifty pounders are not unusual, and the record cod weighed more than 200 pounds. Its important food qualities are lean flesh, good flavor, comparatively few bones and adaptability to dry-salting.

Although present in the eastern Atlantic from the Baltic Sea to the Bay of Biscay and in the western Atlantic from Greenland to Cape Hatteras, the cod's greatest abundance is in the waters off Newfoundland. The "Newfoundland Banks " proved to be a great incentive for the colonization of North America, particularly New England. These banks were first discovered in the 14th century by Basque fishermen who were chasing increasingly scarce whales. It remained their secret until the Cabot brothers, Sebastian and John, explored the eastern coast of North America in 1497 and reported on the huge numbers of *baccalo*, as the Indians called them, teeming in the waters at the edge of the continental shelf.

Shortly thereafter the Basques were joined by the English, the Bretons, the Dutch, the Spanish and the Portuguese. A few years later the Portuguese learned to preserve cod in salt, an innovation that brought cod into all major cuisines and gave a tremendous boost to the industry. By 1640, Massachusetts colony was sending 300,000 dry codfish to market. Peter Faneuil, an early codfish tycoon, built Faneuil Hall in Boston, an edifice which came to be known as the "Cradle of Liberty." In 1784, respectful legislators were moved to hang a wooden carving of the Sacred Cod in the Massachusetts House of Representatives. Later on, the American poet and novelist, Wallace Irwin, penned these lines on the status of the cod:

Of all the fish that swim or swish
In ocean's deep autocracy,
There's none possess such haughtiness
As the codfish aristocracy.

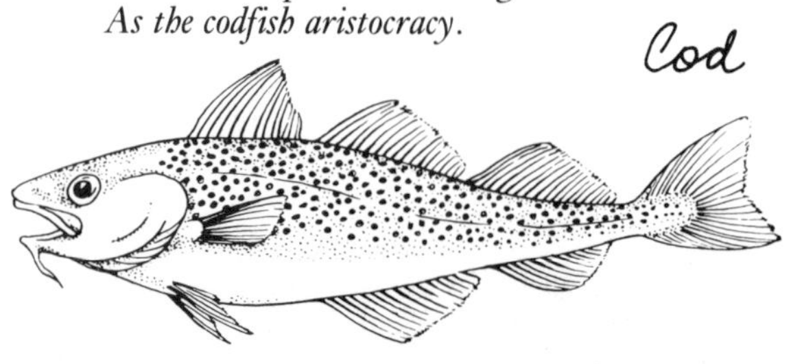

Meanwhile the cod appeared on Nova Scotia banknotes with the legend, "Success to the Fisheries," and on Newfoundland stamps, while the law courts there held that the word "fish" if used unmodified, must mean codfish.

The boom in codfish was based on salting, which was usually accomplished immediately after catching. The fish was thoroughly cleaned of blood, split from head to tail, washed repeatedly in salt water, had part of the backbone removed and was placed in a vat and covered with salt. When deemed to be cured, it was washed and dried in the sun. When it "bloomed" (assumed a whitish appearance), it was ready for market. An alternative method of preserving cod was developed in Norway and involved splitting the cod and drying it in the sun, but omitting salt. The result is called "stockfish," meaning dry as a stick.

Cod prefer deep waters in summer and shallow waters in the winter, and thus are a cold weather fish. The season is roughly October to March, with the best fishing from October to December. Cod are taken on hand lines, trawl lines and gill nets.

Fresh cod is prepared in a variety of ways, including frying, grilling, boiling, stuffing, baking and smoking. Salt cod is the basis of many dishes in France, Spain, Italy and Portugal where it is called respectively, *morue*, *bacalao*, *baccala*, and *bacalheu*. Cod liver oil is taken as a vitamin supplement.

Auguste Escoffier, in his authoritative book, *Le Guide Culinaire*, had this to say about cod, "If cod were less common, it would be held in as high esteem as salmon; for, when it is really fresh and of good quality, the delicacy and delicious flavor of its flesh ranks it among the finest of fish."

COD BURBOT

A freshwater fish, *Lota maculosa*, allied to the cod, cod burbot is found in the Great Lakes, northern New England and Canadian lakes. It has several common names: coneyfish, eelpout, freshwater cusk and ling. Cod burbot is a good food fish and should be prepared like cod.

See also: **Burbot, Cod, Cusk.**

COEUR A LA CREME

See **White Cheese.**

COFFEE

The name applies both to the roasted, ground beans or seeds of the coffee plant (genus *Coffea*), and to the aromatic drink made from the seeds. In the commercial sense, coffee is the most important caffeine beverage plant in the world. Its main species, *Coffea arabica*, is native to Ethiopia, but now grows prolifically in other coffee areas.

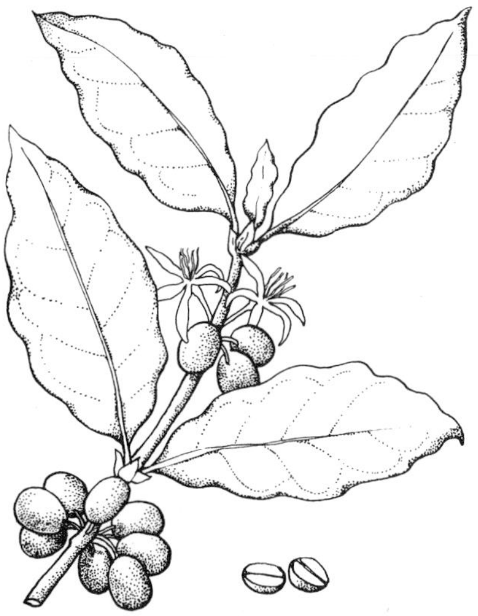

The coffee plant is a slender tree whose foliage forms a rough pyramid. In the wild, it grows to a height of 10 to 20 feet, but under cultivation, it is pruned back to about six feet, a practice that facilitates berry production and harvesting. A coffee plant begins bearing at from four to six years of age, reaches a maximum yield at from 10 to 15 years of age (as much as 12 pounds of berries annually, or four to five pounds of beans), and continues on the average to 40 years of age. Coffee leaves are evergreen and waxy bright; its blossoms, which bloom briefly before the berries appear, are white and smell of jasmine.

The beans grow in pairs inside berries, which are first green, then on maturing turn a deep red. Lesser but significant species are *C. liberica*, from the Liberian lowlands, a hearty tree whose beans have an inferior taste; *C. robusta*, a fast-growing type with a marked flavor of its own, whose *canophora* variety, native to Uganda, is best known; and *C. caturra*, a high-yielding dwarf species whose output accounts for one-third of Colombia's harvest.

The right climate is essential to the production of first-rate coffee, i.e., near 70° F temperatures yearround, at least two hours of sunlight a day and abundant rainfall distributed throughout the year. In addition, the coffee plant needs shade to protect it from direct sunlight and flourishes in rich, well-drained soil. These conditions are generally met in the tropics at a certain elevation. The so-called coffee belt girdles the globe between the latitudes of 25 degrees North and 30 degrees South. Coffee producers are grouped in Central and South America, the West Indies, Africa, the East Indies, Southeast Asia and India. Brazil is the leading producer.

After being harvested, the beans must be extracted from the berries. This is accomplished by first curing the berries, then stripping off the pulp, parchment and skin coverings of the beans. The age-old dry method of curing involves exposing the berries to the sun until they shrivel up, then milling off the skins. The wet method is more complex, but allows the grower more control over the process, a factor that affects the flavor of the final product. It involves removing the outer skin, fermenting the berry to loosen the other coverings, then milling them off. The end product of both processes is the green coffee bean. Green beans are shipped to an exporter who grades them according to a host of factors, such as growing altitude, method of curing, size, weight, etc. Each country has its own grading scheme and nomenclature. After being graded, the beans are loaded in hemp bags weighing 132 pounds and transported to the packer, who does the roasting and blending. Following is a list of coffees by country, with comments taken from Norman Kolpas' *Coffee Lovers' Companion:*

Angola: mostly *Robusta.* strong flavor but not much character.

Brazil: Used mostly for blending. Best is Bourbon Santos, smooth, sweet, medium-bodies, with a high acidity when aged.

Colombia: Full body, rich flavor and balanced acidity. Best is Medellin.

Costa Rica: Very aromatic, full bodied and rich, with good acidity.

Dominican Republic: Known as Santo Domingos. Good body, sweet and well flavored.

Ecuador: Sharp flavor, not much body. Usually blended.

El Salvador: Smooth, good body and acidity, but not much flavor. Good in blends.

Ethiopia: A rich flavor almost reminiscent of wine. Pungent and sharp. Best known is Harrar.

Guatemala: Flavorful, with a real tang, full body and good aroma. Best are Antigua and Coban.

Haiti: Mellow, sweet and mild, with medium body and acidity.

Hawaii: Known as Kona. Flavorful, medium body, slightly nutty.

India: best known is Mysore. Low acidity, good body and light flavor.

Indonesia: Home of Java, heavy-bodied and very rich. Often blended with Yememi Mocha. Also good are coffees of Sumatra and Celebes.

Jamaica: Famous for Blue Mountain, one of the most mellow, rich, aromatic and sweet coffees of the world.

Kenya: Full-bodied, sharp and slightly winey.

Mexico: Sharp, aromatic, medium-boiled. Best are Coatepec, Oaxaca and Pluma.

Nicaragua: Good body, bitey acidity.

Peru: Good body and acidity, slight sweetness. Best is Chanchamayo.

Puerto Rico: Full, rich body and sweet flavor.

Tanzania: Rich flavor, good body and sharp acidity.

Venezuela: Low acidity, good body and mild flavor.

Yemen: Home of Mocha, a rich, almost chocolate-flavored coffee. Often blended with Java. The name Mocha has also been given to mixtures of coffee and chocolate because of the original Mocha taste.

With the different strains, roasts and blends as well as ways of brewing, the taste of coffee varies widely from place to place. Mark Twain, in *Tramps Abroad*, remarked on this phenomenon: "The average American's simplest breakfast consists of coffee and beefsteak; well, in Europe, coffee is an unknown beverage. You can get what the European hotel keeper thinks is coffee, but it resembles the real thing as hypocrisy resembles holiness. . . ."

Coffee owes its stimulating effects mainly to caffeine, and to a less extent, theobromine. Caffeine stimulates the cerebral cortex, allaying drowsiness and fatigue, but it also has a diuretic effect and, in some people, may even cause diarrhea. Coffees vary in caffeine content, e.g., Brazilian coffee has more caffeine than Colombian or Central American, while Philippine has more than all three.

Depending on all the factors discussed above, a six-ounce cup of coffee can contain from 72 to 150 milligrams of caffeine. It was this stimulating effect of coffee that led to its discovery, according to legend. One day an Ethiopian goatherd named Kaldi noticed that his normally lethargic goats were dancing on their hind legs and bleating for joy. He also noticed that they'd been feeding on some bright red berries. He sampled the berries himself, and experienced an immediate boost in his spirits and energies. Impressed, he took some berries to the local monastery, where the head monk, on hearing Kaldi's story, condemned the berries as the devil's work. He flung them in the fire, whereupon a heavenly aroma came forth from the fireplace, filling the air. The head monk was inspired to rescue the berries from the fire and infuse them in hot water. So pleased was he with taste and effects of the fragrant beverage that he proclaimed it heaven-sent and henceforth gave it to the monks in the evenings to keep them from falling asleep during prayers.

Coffee plants were first cultivated in southern Arabia and the berries exported from the port of Mocha. Partly because alcoholic beverages are forbidden to Moslems, coffee became popular in the medieval Moslem world both for its stimulating effects and as a social drink. The first coffee house is said to have been the Kiva Han, which was built in Constantinople about 1475. Europeans began to sample coffee in the 16th century, first in Venice, then in Germany. The Dutch were the first to take it up seriously, then the Spanish and the Italians. The initial reaction from the Roman Catholic Church was to condemn it as "the wine of Islam." On tasting it, however, Pope Clement VIII had a better idea, and said, "This

Satan's drink is too delicious to let the heathen have it all to themselves. We shall baptize it and make a Christian beverage of it."

Coffee houses became the rage first in Venice, then Vienna, then Paris and eventually, in the 18th century, London, where they became the center of the city's social and political life. It has been said that in England the coffee house developed into the exclusive club, but elsewhere in Europe it became the ordinary cafe. Also, the great insurance institution, Lloyd's of London, had its humble beginnings in a coffee house kept in Lombard Street by one Edward Lloyd in the early part of the 18th century.

Despite strict security on the part of the Arabs, the Dutch managed to smuggle a coffee plant out of Mocha and plant it in Java, thus adding a second landmark name to the history of coffee. A Frenchman brought the first coffee plant to Martinique in the West Indies in 1720, and it is said all the coffee bushes that grow so fruitfully in Latin America (producing 90 percent of the world crop) are descended from this single plant.

The United States consumes about 70 percent of the world coffee crop, which comes to about 15 to 16 pounds of coffee a year for each American, or about three cups a day. This per capita consumption is low, however, when compared to Scandinavians. The Finns, according to the *Guiness Book of World Records*, are the world's greatest coffee drinkers with a per person consumption of 37.5 pounds a year. The Swedes give good competition but manage a mere 30 pounds a year. Coffee has made inroads into such traditional tea markets as Japan, where the coffee house has become a ubiquitous institution since World War II. For example, Jamaica's Blue Mountain coffee is unavailable in many parts of the world because the bulk of it is exported to Japan, where it fetches the highest prices.

COFFEE BREWING

For brewing at home, there are three basic grinds of coffee: *regular*, a granulated texture used mostly in percolators; *medium*, a little finer, used in various drip systems, and *fine*, a texture close to powder. To make good coffee, these preliminaries are important: use clean equipment; start with fresh water, and after boiling it, wait a minute or so, because the best brewing temperature is a few degrees below boiling, and use at least two tablespoons of coffee per cup. At two tablespoons per cup, a pound of coffee will yield 40 cups.

The simplest, but often least satisfactory, way of making coffee is *open pot* brewing: water is brought to a boil in a sauce pan, then regular grind coffee is added; the heat is turned off, the pot is covered and left to stand for five minutes. It is then uncovered and several spoonfuls of cold water are added to settle the grounds. The coffee is ready for careful pouring.

Drip coffee is a more sophisticated method that appeals to many connoisseurs. It brings the coffee into contact with the water for the shortest possible time, and extracts the maximum of flavor and aroma with a minimum of bitter taste. Drip pots may use a paper or cloth filter, or simply a perforated top. Coffee is placed in the top part of the pot, and the water poured over it, seeping down into the lower portion of the pot. The water is never poured through more than once.

The *vacuum* involves two bowls, usually glass but sometimes metal. Water is boiled in the lower, serving container. The upper bowl, which is open-topped, and whose bottom has a long tube with a filter in it, fits snugly into the lower bowl. The water rises through the tube and filter into the upper bowl, where it infuses for about a minute. When the coffee maker is removed from the heat, a vacuum forms in the lower bowl, which brings the brewed coffee filtering back down through the tube. The upper bowl is removed, and the coffee is ready to be served.

Percolation is the most automated method, and therefore involves the least fuss. It is preferred in the United States. Yet, experts deplore it because it relies on boiling the coffee, which, in their opinion, brings out the bitterness. A coffee percolator contains a basket for the coffee grounds fitted on top of a long stem. When the water boils, the water rises through the stem, and falls on the coffee grounds, seeping through them and the basket (which is perforated) back into the pot. It continues this cycle until the coffee reaches the desired strength.

Caffe expresso is an Italian invention involving the use of a machine that forces boiling water through very dark, Italian roast coffee at a pressure of 60 pounds per square inch. This extracts the coffee's full flavor as quickly as possible. A rich, tasty brew, *espresso* is served in demitasse cups.

Turkish or *Middle Eastern* coffee utilized pulverized coffee grounds and the *kanika*, or long-handled eastern coffee pot. Coffee, water and sugar are added to the pot, and the mixture is brought to a boil three times, then poured into tiny cups. When the grounds settle, there remains a thimbleful of strong, sweet coffee for careful sipping.

COFFEE, DECAFFEINATED

Caffeine is a stimulant that affects the central nervous system, allaying drowsiness and fatigue. It also has a diuretic effect and in some people may cause diarrhea. It is present in coffee, but the quantity varies according to the strain, the blend, the roast, etc. Consequently, a six-ounce cup of coffee may have from 72 to 150 milligrams of caffeine. Since some persons can not tolerate caffeine, yet wish to drink coffee, about five percent of coffee is sold decaffeinated.

The process of decaffeination involves first either steaming the green coffee beans or soaking them in hot water for about five hours to soften them and open their pores. They are then treated with chlorinated solvents, which extract about 97 percent of the caffeine. In a second steaming, the solvents evaporate, taking the caffeine with them. The beans are then dried and ready for roasting.

COFFEE, INSTANT

There are two basic methods of making instant coffee: spray drying and freeze drying. Spray drying, a technical development of the 1930s, involves use of a tall drying chamber. Extra strong coffee is brewed, then sprayed into the top of the drying chamber, which has a current of hot air passing through it. When the coffee reaches the bottom of the chamber, all the water has evaporated, leaving the familiar grains of instant coffee. This method, unfortunately, dissipates much of the coffee's flavor and aroma.

To get around these undesired effects, freeze drying was developed. Again, extra strong coffee is brewed. Instead of being sprayed into a heated chamber, which removes the flavorful but volatile coffee oils, the coffee is cooled to a slush of coffee and ice crystals. The mixture is then moved to a vacuum chamber where the ice is removed from the liquid and the concentrated liquid coffee is dried at temperatures below zero. Finally, the distinctive chips of freeze-dried coffee are left.

Instant coffee accounts for more than 25 percent of coffee drunk at home in the United States. It is much more popular elsewhere. For example, in the United Kingdom, instant coffee accounts for nearly 75 percent of all coffee sold. Like other convenience foods, instant coffee is gaining ground. It offers certain advantages: It is fast, easy and clean to make. It stays fresh longer and can be mixed by the cup to individual taste at a lower price than fresh coffee.

See also: **Coffee.**

COGNAC

This world-famous grape **brandy** comes from Cognac, a small town in the district of Charente, in the vicinity of Bordeaux in southwestern France. Only brandies produced in this regions—along the right bank of the Gironde, in the valley of the Charente, and near La Rochelle on the Atlantic—are entitled to bear the name "Cognac," although the word is often loosely applied to mean any brandy. Cognac is best made from white grapes, especially the Blanche, Colombac,Folle Jurancon, Monfils, Sauvignon and **Semillon.** The growths are classified, in descending order of smoothness, as *Grande Champagne*, *Petite Champagne*, *Borderies*, *Fine-bois*, *Bons-bois*, *Bois ordinaires*, and *Bois du terroir*. Another classification, *Bois communs dits a terroir*, pertains to the Cognac made near La Rochelle.

Cognac is produced by a method of distillation called *brouillis* or the *methode charentaise*. After the grapes have been pressed, the juice is allowed to ferment naturally without the addition of sugar or sulfur dioxide. In the winter months the wine is heated in large pot-stills enclosed in brick kilns and fired by wood or coal. Since alcohol has a lower boiling point than water—173° F (78.3° C)—the stills are heated to above 173° F (78.3° C) but below 212° F (100° C). The alcohol then vaporizes and separates from the original liquid. It is then gathered and recondensed into a liquid of much greater alcoholic strength. This, essentially, is the process by which any brandy is made. The first distillation, or *broullis*, is thus collected and returned to the still for a final distillation. The resulting brandy, or *bonne chauffe*, is colorless and has an alcohol content of about 35 percent. The liquid is then sweetened with sugar syrup (about one-half to one percent by volume) and is stored in barrels of white oak or of Limousin oak where with age it acquires its characteristic golden brown color.

The particular flavor of Cognac comes partly from an oily substance produced by yeast cells in the distilling process but also from the kinds of grapes used, the type of oak, the length of aging, and the blending with other brandies. Most Cognacs are from five to 10 years old, but may be aged safely for twenty-five years. Cognac has been proudly described locally as "liquid gold." Its special fiery smoothness—especially in *Grande* and *Petite Champagnes*—as well as its heady bouquet, make it easily the best grape brandy in the world. The chalky subsoil of the Charente region is very similar to that in the district of **Champagne** much farther north, thus the classification of the best Cognacs as "champagnes." *Borderies*, slightly less mellow but richer in body than the two *Champagnes*, refers to a series of little hills that border the Charente on both banks, and where the Cognac grapes are grown. Cognac is an ideal after-dinner drink with espresso but is also drunk typically in France as an "eye-opener," especially on cold winter mornings, or mixed with black breakfast coffee.

See also: **Bordeaux Wines, Brandy, Jurancon Wine.**

COGSWELLIA

Several species of this thick-rooted perennial herb, *Lomatium* spp., are valued for the flour that can be made from the roots when they are dried and milled. The plants are native to western North America. The flour is used in making bread, cakes or porridge.

COHUNE NUT

The fruit of a Central American palm tree *Orbignya cohune* yields an edible oil called cohune oil. The tree may reach 45 feet in height and a foot in diameter. The fruit averages three inches in diameter and two inches in length. It has a hard shell, and the meat consists of about 50 percent oil. The oil is similar to coconut oil and is used commercially in making margarine.

COING

Also COINGUARDE. *Coing* is the French word for quince, and also the name of a liqueur flavored with quince that is made in Alsace-Lorraine. *Coinguarde* is the name of another quince-based liqueur made in France.

COINTREAU

This colorless, orange-flavored liqueur is a very fine **Triple Sec.** It is bottled at 80 proof and is made in Angiers, France. The Cointreau family developed this popular drink and put their name on it as a trademark. All liqueurs are generally used as after dinner drinks and are believed to aid digestion.

See also: **Cherry Marnier, Curacao, Grand Marnier.**

COLA

Also KOLA NUT. Cola is a genus of African trees whose seeds or nuts contain the stimulants caffeine, theobromine and kolanine. There are many species of cola tree, and their fruits are known by a variety of names, including ombene, temperance nut, *bissy-bissy* nut, *guru* nut, *goro de gonsha* and *ecla*.

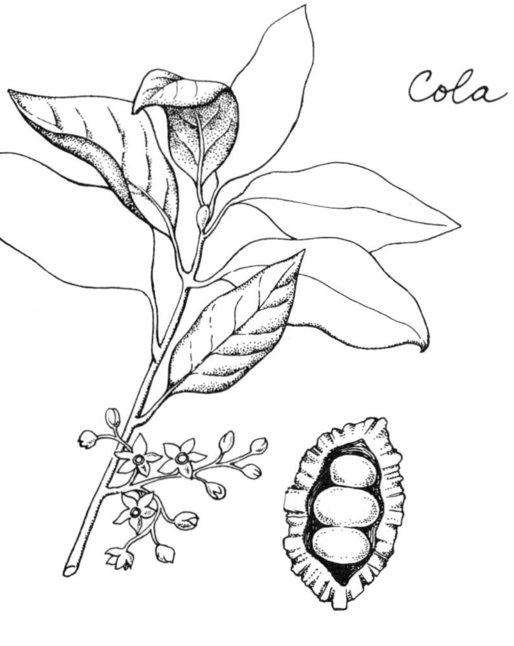

Cola trees have been transplanted to the Western Hemisphere, growing well in the West Indies and tropical South America. According to the species, cola trees can vary in height from 30 to 60 feet. The seed or nut grows in a pod, beanlike, and may be white, red or brown. The size of the nut has been compared by some to a hazelnut and by others to that of a horse chestnut. The nut has no odor, and its taste has been described as bitter and astringent. Yet it is gathered in huge quantities by the natives of West Africa both for export and for domestic consumption.

Although cola has no nutritive value, the nut is a popular thing to chew on because of its stimulating properties. A kola nut contains more caffeine than a coffee bean, plus theobromine and kolanine, which is reputed to be beneficial to muscle tone and stimulating to the appetite. It is also said to quench thirst, diminish fatigue, permit long marches through the jungle, banish sleepiness and stimulate sexual desire. This last quality is attributed to the oil of the nut. The most popular type of nut comes from the species *Cola nitida*, which bears both white and red fruit. The white is considered best and is consumed at home, while the red is exported.

According to an early Coca-Cola advertisement, the newspaperman Henry Morton Stanley might never have found Scottish missionary David Livingstone ("Dr. Livingstone, I presume."), had it not been for the kola nut, which energized his native bearers as they beat their way through Darkest Africa. Cola drinks, however, may or may not have cola in them. The Coca-Cola company was sued in 1909 for misbranding because the drink had neither coca nor cola in it. Supreme Court Justice Charles Evans decided in 1916 that the company must include a bit of each or lose its trademark. Consequently, the company did put them in the formula, but in such minute amounts that they do not show up in laboratory analysis. Considering the taste of cola—described as discouragingly astringent and bitter—one is just as happy without it.

The French, perhaps, are the only non-Africans to include the kola nut in their cuisine, chiefly in desserts where the bitter taste is offset by sweetening. *Gateau a la kola* is a tea biscuit. It is also combined with chocolate, whose taste it complements in creamy desserts. Powder from dried nuts is made into a tincture and used for medical purposes.

COLBY

Here is an American cow's milk cheese made by the cheddar process but with a softer, more open texture. Its higher moisture content makes it more perishable than cheddar.

COLD-PACK CHEESE

This American creation consists of a number of cheeses, usually of the cheddar type, ground together and mixed with an acidifying agent, water, salt and spices. It is packed in a variety of handy containers and meant to be used as a spread or sandwich filling. Other cheeses appropriate for mixing in a cold pack are Roquefort, Gorgonzola, Gruyere and Limburger, but not soft, unripened cheeses, or the hard, grating variety. There are various legal limitations on the contents, including a ceiling of 42 percent on moisture. Cold pack is kept under refrigeration and has a sharp cheese flavor.

A variation on this is cold-pack cheese food. The difference lies in the addition of another dairy product to the mixture, plus a sweetener. The dairy product may be milk, skim milk, cheese whey or albumin.

COLE

See **Rape.**

COLE SLAW

See **Cabbage.**

COLIN

See **Quail.**

COLLARD

Collard is a type of cabbage, *Brassica oleracea acephala*, whose broad, straight leaves do not form a compact head. It is like **kale** in this respect, except that kale leaves are narrow and frizzled. Experts have speculated that collard may be the original form of cabbage because when cabbage first came under cultivation by the ancient Romans it did not form a head. They taught it to do so.

The word collard is a contraction of the earlier name "colewort," which means a nonheading cabbage. Indeed, either word can be used for the young, tender leaves of any type of cabbage that has not yet formed a head. Collard leaves can be picked progressively, a handy quality that allows the main plant to keep growing and providing fresh leaves. Alternatively, the young plant can be stripped of leaves while they are still very tender.

Collard bears up under intense heat much better than common cabbage, and is very popular in the southern United States. It is frequently referred to there in the plural, as collards, or collard greens, or collie greens. It is a standard item of "soul food,"

Collard

i.e., certain dishes favored by generations of black Americans and southern whites. A favorite way of preparing it is collard greens and beans. "Pot likker" is the juice remaining after collard and pork have been cooked together in water. It is rich in vitamins and minerals. Collard may be prepared in any way suitable to cabbage. The leaves are low in calories and are nutritious, containing only 33 calories in 3½ ounces (100 grams), but plenty of calcium, iron, vitamin A, thiamin, riboflavin, niacin and vitamin C.

COLOCYNTH

Also BITTER APPLE, BITTER CUCUMBER, BITTER GOURD. This round yellow fruit, *Citrullus colocynthis*, about the size of an orange, is known for its bitter taste and cathartic properties. Its closest relative is the watermelon, so perhaps it might be classed as a melon or a gourd.

The colocynth is a decorative plant with a thick rind and a spongy pulp. It is native to the Mediterranean area but also grows in Africa, India, Ceylon, Iran, Arabia, Syria and the Cape Verde Islands. The fruit is no longer eaten in Europe today, but was a familiar item in the 15th, 16th and 17th centuries. In Shakespeare's *Othello*, Iago remarks, "The food that to him now is as lucious as locusts, shall be to him shortly as bitter as coloquintida." At that time, colocynth was used mainly as an emetic and imported into England from Cyprus. To be used for this purpose, the fruit is picked when it has attained full size but is not yet ripe. This maximizes its purgative qualities.

Natives of the Sahara Desert—the Tibesti and the Teda—gather colocynth for its seeds. To attenuate the bitter and purgative properties of the seeds, they are dried, walked on to crack the husks, winnowed, mixed with the ashes of camel dung, ground and stored away. The resulting flour is mixed with dried dates and eaten as traveling rations. Alternatively, the seeds are pressed for their heavy oil, which is used for various purposes.

COLONIA HARD CHEESE

See **Reggiano.**

COLUMBINE MEADOWRUE

Here is a perennial herb, *Thalictrum aquilegifolium*, of Europe and northern Asia. The roots may be boiled and roasted and eaten as vegetables.

COLOMBO

See **Calumba.**

COLWICK

See **Slipcote.**

COLZA

See **Rape.**

COMFIT

This candy or sweetmeat, originally consisted of a grain of spice, anise or caraway seed coated in successive layers of sugar. Later, it came to mean any fruit, root, nut or seed so coated, and still later candy such as bonbons. The term is old-fashioned, and the candy has a long history. Consider the cynical statement by Lysander, a Greek general (d. 395 B.C.): "Children are to be deceived with comfits, men with oaths." At one time, a box of comfits was an indispensable accessory to the person of fashion, carried at all times. Comfits served to allay hunger and sweeten the breath, but the practice went out of style at the end of the 16th century.

COMFREY

A rough, hairy, perennial plant, *Symphytum officinale*, whose leaves are used raw to garnish salads or cooked as a potherb, comfrey is similar to **lamb's lettuce** and **spinach** in its preparation and taste. Its French name, *Consoude*, comes from the Latin *consolida* ("solid") and indicates its earlier medicinal use as an astringent.

The plant, eaten raw or ground into powder, was thought to be especially beneficial for liver ailments. Comfrey is best served lightly steamed with salt and butter and is a good complement with chicken or pork.

COMMENDARIA

A dessert wine of Cyprus, Commendaria is believed to be the oldest named wine in the world. It was dubbed *commendaria* by the Knights Templar in 1191 and has been made continuously since. Commendaria is somewhat like cream sherry. It has a dark amber color and a sweet, rich flavor. The method of blending and aging is similar to the *solera* system used for **sherry.** Unlike other European vines, those on Cyprus were not attacked by the phylloxera (wine louse), and are thus growing on their original rootstock.

COMMERCIAL GLUCOSE

See **Corn Syrup.**

COMMISSION CHEESE

A Dutch cheese from the provinces of North Holland and Friesland made from slightly skimmed milk, it is similar to **Edam** in taste, texture and shape, but a cheese usually weighs eight pounds, twice the size of Edam.

COMTE

A hard, French cow's milk cheese made for generations in Franche-Comte country near the Swiss border, it is nearly identical to **Gruyere** a Swiss product. Indeed, over the years it has lost its original name, *vacherin*, and has become known as the French Gruyere. However, it is marketed in somewhat larger sizes than Gruyere, each cheese weighing from 100 to 120 pounds.

CONCH

Also LAMBI. This marine gastropod inhabiting the waters from Cape Hatteras to Texas is popular as food only in the Bahamas, south Florida and some Caribbean islands. Conch (pronounced "conk") is better known elsewhere for its large, spiral shell,

Conch

which is often shaggy on the outside, but a lustrous pink fading to pearl gray on the inside. Conch shells make crude, but effective, trumpets, and in the Old South were used to call plantation hands in from the fields.

Outside of its shell, the conch looks like a giant pink snail, complete with large horns that have yellow eyes at the tips. Two varieties are generally eaten, the king conch *(Strombas gigas)* and the queen conch *(Cassis madagascarensis)*. A Mediterranean **whelk** often referred to as *concha* or *conchiglia* or *scungilli* in Italian is much appreciated in Italy but is not the conch discussed here.

Conch tastes like clam, but is quite a bit sweeter. The flesh is liable to be tough, especially if cooked, and so is usually pounded vigorously with a mallet before being eaten. It is invariably cut into small pieces before being prepared in one of three typical ways. It may be eaten raw, marinated in lime juice in a salad or appetizer, deepfried in batter or made into chowder.

CONCORD

The name refers to a North American red wine, a grape, a grape juice and a jelly. The concord grape was discovered by Ephraim W. Bull of Concord, Massachusetts in 1845 from seeds saved from wild grapes handed him by some boys who had been grape-hunting in the woods. Since then, this variety has been cultivated more than any other grape of *Vitis labrusca* east of the Rocky Mountains. Its juice needs to heavily sweetened to make a wine that will keep any length of time, and it has a decidedly "foxy" taste. Concord makes a good fresh grape juice, however, and is the basis for a great many *labrusca* red wines.

CONDENSED MILK

Also EVAPORATED MILK. Both products are condensed milk achieved by evaporation of the water content by 40 to 50 percent. Sugar is added to condensed milk so that it is sweet with the consistency of thick cream. It also keeps better after the container is opened. No sugar is added to evaporated milk but it usually has a specified amount of milk fat and milk solids. It does not keep as long after opening.

CONDIMENT

Any substance, often aromatic, added to food at the table may be called condiment. "Seasoning" refers to substances added to the food beforehand in its preparation and cooking. Ordinary table salt is a condiment, thought to improve the taste of meat, vegetables, soups and stews by its sharpness and to stimulate digestion.

Acid condiments—vinegar and lemon juice—complement salads and fish. Bitter condiments—garlic, onion, mustard, horseradish—go well with both cold and hot meats, especially roast beef, as well as with salads. Bitter aromatic condiments—pepper, paprika, savory herbs—are used to accompany both meat and vegetables.

Salad oil, butter, honey and sugar are all widely used, natural condiments. Worcestershire sauce, curry powder, soy sauce and ketchup are so-called ready-made condiments manufactured and designed to enhance specific foods, such as steaks, rice, cooked vegetables and luncheon meats. The name derives from the Latin *condire*, which means "to pickle" or "make sharp" the appetite.

CONEY

Also NIGGER-FISH. The coney is a vividly colored, West Indian grouper *(Cephalopholis fulvus)* found from Bermuda to Brazil that reaches a length of about 12 inches. It has a yellow or deep red color marked with many small, usually blue, spots. It frequents reef areas near the shoreline and out to about 150 feet of depth. The coney is good to eat.

CONGER

This large, snakelike, saltwater fish is commonly called a sea eel, although some experts dispute whether it is a true eel. Unlike the common **eel** the conger inhabits saltwater exclusively and has no scales. Females of the European conger *(Conger conger)* often reach a length of eight feet. Males are much smaller. Conger flesh is much like that of the common eel, but more coarse and less oily. Congers are called *anguille de mer* in French, and *seeaal* in German, both terms meaning sea eel.

Congers are plentiful in European waters from April to November, when they disappear only to reappear the following March. Not much is known of their life cycle, but it is thought that they migrate to the Sargasso Sea to spawn along with hordes of the common eel, whose life cycle is well known. A large female is capable of laying eight million eggs.

Conger has been a well-known food fish in Europe since ancient times. It was sold in the fish markets of Periclean Athens, and the Romans had a famous recipe for conger flavored by oregano. It was highly regarded in the Middle Ages, and a 13th-century French proverb claimed that the best conger were brought into the port of La Rochelle.

It has always been appreciated more in France than elsewhere, but less so nowadays except as a cheap substitute for common eel. Apart from that, it is used almost exclusively in bouillabaisse, where its taste seems to bring out the flavor of the other ingredients.

The American conger *(Conger oceanicus)* is found from Cape Cod to North Carolina. It is a smaller fish, averaging four to six feet. The so-called California conger is really a **moray.**

CONGO PEA

Also DHAL, GRAY PEA. A yellow pulse, *Cajanus cajan*, closely related to the **pea,** it grows prolifically in tropical regions of the world. The Congo pea is a bush that grows as high as 10 feet, producing yellow flowers that are followed by flattened pods containing four or five yellow seeds. These are eaten either fresh or dried, but in any case the outerskins are removed to avoid a bitter taste. It is in this form that the name *dhal* fits most appropriately, since it means the pea divested of its skin.

The Congo pea has been under cultivation for so long that no wild species are known, though it is believed to have originated in the Far East. Congo peas constitute one-fifth of all pulses grown in India, where it is commonly called Bengal bean, yellow *dhal* or *dhall*. It is extremely important in Africa, where it is known by a variety of names depending on the country, but including pigeon pea, *pois cajan*, *pois d'Angole* and *alverja*. It is a staple food in Jamaica, where it is called the goongoo pea. It was brought there by African slaves.

In certain areas there are fringe benefits to growing the Congo pea. In the Far East, the bush attracts an insect, *Carteria lacca*, which pierces the bark causing the bush to secrete a gum from which lacquer is made. In Madagascar it attracts a caterpillar whose silklike cocoon is worth more than the peas which, incidentally, often survive the infestation.

CONSOMME

See **Soup.**

CONZATT'S ROSE APPLE

Edible fruit of a Mexican tree, *Eugenia conzattii*, of the myrtle family, it is eaten in the south of Mexico.

COOKED CHEESE

Also KOCHKASE. This cheese is obtained by heating and flavoring fermented skim-milk curds. The result has a buttery consistency, agreeable flavor and is eaten uncured. It is made in the United States and other countries and is known by several names including cup cheese, Pennsylvania pot cheese, *topfen* and *fresa*.

The curd is generally prepared like cottage cheese, put through a grinder and placed in a vat to ripen for three days to a week. The shorter the ripening period the milder the cheese. The ripe curd, plus flavoring materials such as cream, salt, caraway seeds, eggs, pimentos and olives, are heated to 180° F, and stirred continuously until the consistency is like honey. It is poured into pots or molds and when cool is ready to eat. It will keep for a few days under refrigeration.

COOKIE

A small, sweet cake, usually flat and unleavened. In England it would be called a sweet biscuit. Basic cookie ingredients include a flour, a fat (often butter), sugar, eggs and milk. These make a dough that may be soft or stiff depending on the type of cookie desired. Soft-dough types are usually dropped from a spoon onto a greased cookie sheet before baking; stiff doughs may be rolled out, then cut into fancy shapes with a cookie cutter or shaped into a long roll, refrigerated and then sliced and baked. Cookies may also be put through a forcing tube or a cookie press.

The term "cookie" comes from the Dutch word *koekje*, meaning "little cake." According to one authority, the word "cookie" enjoyed a period of popularity in the British Isles in the 19th century. It was well known enough to be mentioned several times in the novels of Anthony Trollope. Yet, today it has dropped out of British usage altogether.

See also: **Biscuit, Bread.**

COOKING, MENU AND CANNING TERMS

Following is a list of words commonly used in cooking, on menus or in the canning of foods. If a word you seek does not appear below, it may be explained in another article, and can be located by consulting the index:

a blanc. (French) Cooked gently so that it does not brown in methods such as braising, poaching and sauteeing; also, a preliminary cooking in salted water, lemon juice and flour to blanch a food or retain its whiteness.

a brun. (French) Cooked until brown, or browned before poaching or braising.

acid food. A food is deemed acid when it normally contains 0.36 percent or more natural acid, such as fruits, rhubarb and tomatoes. In canning, they may be safely processed in a boiling water bath canner at 212° F. (100° C.). Low-acid foods preserved in vinegar, such as sauerkraut, pickles or relish, may be similarly treated.

agneau. (French) Lamb.

ail. (French) Garlic.

a la. (French) In the style of; or, as done in, by, for or with. Examples: *a la creme* (with cream), *a la moutarde* (in mustard sauce).

a la bourguignonne. (French) In the style of Burgundy, which usually means braised in red Burgundy wine with mushrooms and small onions. The *a la* is often omitted on menus, and a dish becomes simply *bourguignon*, as in *boeuf bourguignon*. See also: **Bourgignonne Sauce.**

a la grecque. (French) Greek style, i.e., cooked in a marinade of olive oil and herbs.

a la king. In the United States, to prepare meat, fish or poultry in a creamy seasoned sauce.

a la mode. (French) Made in a certain style, often used with a place name as in *a la mode de Caen*, that is, in the style of Caen. Appearing on a menu without a place name, it may mean prepared in the style of that particular restaurant. In the United States, it means serving cake or pie with ice cream.

a l'ancienne. (French) In the old style; old fashioned.

amande. (French) Almond.

anchois. (French) Anchovy.

anguille. (French) Eel.

antioxident. In canning, a chemical agent that inhibits oxidation, such as ascorbic acid (vitamin C), and which controls discoloration of fruits.

antipasto. In Italy, the dish served before the main or pasta dish. It usually consists of hot or cold *hors d'oeuvres*, such as an assortment of cold meat, stuffed peppers, mushrooms, fish and vegetables.

aperitif. (French) A drink taken before a meal to stimulate the appetite. It is often a fortified wine, such as vermouth.

a point. (French) Medium rare, when applied to beef, especially steak.

appetizer. A small portion of food or drink served before a meal to stimulate the appetite. It may be juice, fruit, seafood, or perhaps a dry, fortified wine, such as sherry.

artichaut. (French) Artichoke.

ascorbic acid. Vitamin C found in some fruits and vegetables. In canning, it is commercially available in white, crystalline form to be used to control discoloration of fruits.

asperge. (French) Asparagus.

aspic. A jelly made from meat, fish or vegetable stock, usually with gelatin added, it is used to coat meat, poultry or fish or can be served as a relish or as a main dish when molded and filled with meat, fish, poultry or vegetables.

au. (French) With, in, or of.

aubergine. (French) Eggplant.

au bleu. (French) When applied to freshwater fish (especially trout), it means to cook immediately after killing and cleaning by plunging the fish in boiling court bouillon with vinegar added. This turns the fish's skin a metallic blue. When applied to meat, especially steak, it means cooked very rare.

au choix. (French) Of your choice.

au gratin. (French) Said of a dish topped with a sprinkling of butter, bread crumbs or cheese and baked or placed under a flame until brown. The word *gratin* refers to the brown coating thus formed.

au jus. (French) Served with its own natural, unthickened, pan juices. Said of meat, usually beef.

au naturel. (French) Cooked plain.

baba. (French) A sponge cake, with raisins, usually steeped in a mixture of syrup and either rum, brandy or kirsch.

bacteria. Microscopic organisms found in the soil, water and air, some of which are harmful. In canning, the latter present a problem if low acid food is to be preserved. To prevent production of harmful toxins, these bacteria must be neutralized by superheating to 240° F. (116° C). This is accomplished using a steam pressure canner.

bain-marie. (French) A large saucepan filled with water, which is a sort of bath for keeping smaller pans warm, in the manner of a steam table or for cooking certain dishes that must never boil. It sits on top of the stove, or may fit into the oven. It is like a double-boiler, but differs in that the water in the *bain-marie* surrounds the smaller pan as high as half-way up, providing heat from all sides, rather than just from the bottom.

bake. To cook by dry heat usually, but not necessarily in an oven.

banane. (French) Banana

band. See *metal band*, below.

bar. (French) Bass.

barbecue. Any meat broiled on a rack, or spit, over an open fire. Such meat is usually basted with a highly seasoned sauce, so by extension anything cooked in such a sauce is said to be barbecued; also, by extension, the meal at which such food is served.

bard. To wrap meat or poultry in fat, using thin sheets or strips. The fat is tied on, and provides automatic basting, which enhances the flavor and protects delicate parts of the meat or poultry.

baste. To spoon melted fat, butter or other liquid over food to keep it from drying out during cooking and to enhance the flavor.

batter. A thin mixture of flour, eggs and milk, liquid enough to be poured or dropped from a spoon onto a griddle. It is easily beaten or stirred. Batter too thick to be poured or spooned is called **dough.** If yeast is added, the mixture is called sponge batter.

bearnaise. (French) In the style of the Bearn region. See also: **Bearnaise Sauce.**

beat. To stir or mix rapidly with a circular up-and-down motion to introduce air into the mixture, which makes it lighter or fluffier.

beignet. (French) A fritter. Served as an hors d'oeuvre, first course or dessert, beignets may be simply puff paste or yeast dough deep-fried, or they may be stuffed with savory or sweet fillings.

beurre. (French) Butter.

beurre blanc. (French) A warm, creamy sauce for fish, made from butter, shallots, vinegar, lemon juice and seasonings.

beurre clarifie. (French) Clarified butter. Butter is heated until it liquifies. The milk solids separate and sink to the bottom of the container, and the clear liquid can be poured off. The latter does not burn easily at high temperatures.

beurre manie. (French) Kneaded butter. Butter is softened and mixed with flour to form a paste that is used to thicken sauces.

beurre noir. (French) A sauce consisting of butter, vinegar or lemon juice, and capers or parsley, which is heated until it turns brown. It is served over eggs, fish or vegetables.

binder. Anything added to a liquid mixture to thicken and hold it together. Common binders are egg yolks, flour, potatoes and rice.

bisque. (French) A thick, rich soup, usually made of fish or crustaceans but also of pureed vegetables, poultry or game. Alternatively, a frozen creamy dessert consisting of fruit, macaroons or nuts.

blanch. To plunge a food into boiling water (or to pour boiling water over it) to remove an unwanted skin, to set the color or flavor, to remove an unwanted odor, to partially precook or to remove excess salt as in the case of bacon. Also, to bleach the stalks of vegetables such as asparagus or endive by banking the earth over them or by growing them in darkness.

blanquette. (French) A stew of veal, lamb, chicken or sweetbreads in a cream sauce, garnished with small white onions and mushrooms.

blend. To mix food thoroughly by stirring with a spoon, beater or blender so that the resulting mixture is uniform in texture, color and flavor.

boil. To heat a liquid until bubbles break on the surface and it begins to vaporize. Also, to cook food in such a liquid, usually water.

boiling water bath canner. A kettle used for sterilizing acid foods and their containers. It is large enough to immerse completely and fully surround canning jars.

bone. To remove bones from meat or fowl.

bonne femme. (French) A simple, home-style method of preparing food. Also, a way of cooking meat or poultry, usually in a casserole, accompanied by button onions, mushrooms and bacon. *Soupe bonne femme* is based on white stock and contains chopped leeks and sliced potatoes with butter added to the last minute.

botulism. Food poisoning caused by a toxin produced by the bacillus *Clostridium botulinum,* which can thrive in the tightly sealed can or jar of any low-acid food if the container is not properly sterilized. These bacteria do not normally grow in acid foods, and cannot grow in the presence of air. They are destroyed when low-acid foods are correctly processed in a pressure canner. Botulism paralyzes the motor-nerve centers, and small amounts can be fatal. Symptoms include nausea, vomiting, muscular weakness and sometimes disturbance of vision.

bouillir. (French) To boil.

bouillon. (French) A broth meat stock, obtained by boiling meat, usually beef, together with vegetables and seasoning and straining the result. Also, any clear soup made by cooking meat, fowl, or fish in a liquid. See also *court bouillon,* below.

bouquet garni. (French) A small bundle of herbs tied together or wrapped in cheesecloth and used to season soups, stews or sauces. Herbs commonly included are thyme, bay leaf and parsley.

braise. A moist method of cooking foods, especially meats with a considerable amount of connective tissue. Meats are first seared until brown in a small amount of fat, then cooked in a tightly covered pan in a small amount of liquid, which may be juice, water, milk, cream, stock, vinegar or vegetable juices.

bread. To coat food with dry bread or cracker crumbs after first dipping it in milk or beaten eggs so that the crumbs will stick. Food thus coated is usually fried.

brochette. A small spit or skewer used to impale morsels of food for broiling or frying. *En brochette* means "cooked on a skewer."

broil. To cook by exposing to direct heat, usually under a very hot flame or over hot coals.

broth. A clear soup, consisting of the liquid in which other foods have been broiled, such as meat, fish, poultry or vegetables.

brouille. (French) Scrambled.

brown. To scorch the surface of a food (particularly meat) by quickly searing it in fat or under a hot flame in the oven. The purpose is to produce an appetizing color, or, in the case of meat, seal in the juices.

brush on. Use a small brush to apply liquid to the surface of food.

can. To preserve food by sealing it hermetically in containers. Also, a container of tin-coated steel in which to preserve food for future use.

canape. (French) A small open-faced sandwich consisting of bread, toast or fried bread, upon which is spread seasoned pastes, flavored butters or savory tidbits. In France, it accompanies winged game. In the United States, it is served as an appetizer with cocktails.

caneton. (French) Duckling.

cap. In canning, any of various closure devices for sealing mason jars. Included are metal screw bands used to hold vacuum lids in place during processing and zinc caps with porcelain liners and rubber sealing rings.

capres. (French) Capers.

carmelize. To melt white granulated sugar in a small amount of water, and cook until brown. The resulting syrup is used to color and flavor other foods or to line a dessert mold.

cerise. (French) Cherry.

cervelles. (French) Brains.

champignon. (French) Mushroom.

chantilly. (French) Lightly whipped cream, and, by extension, a term used to modify a dish prepared or served with whipped cream.

charcuterie. (French) Pork butchery, or a shop specializing in port and sausage.

chasseur, a la. (French) *Chasseur* means "hunter," but the phrase in cooking usually means a dish accompanied by a sauce of sauteed mushrooms, shallots and white wine.

chateaubriand. A cut of beef named after the French statesman and writer the Viscount Francois August Chateaubriand (1769–1848), whose chef invented it. It is a thick fillet, taken from the tenderloin, large enough for two or three persons, that is broiled and traditionally served with *bernaise* sauce.

chill. To cool, but not freeze, in a refrigerator or over cracked ice.

chop. To cut into fine pieces; also, a cut of meat from the rack or loin, as in pork or lamb chop.

chou. (French) Cabbage.

choucroute. (French) Sauerkraut.

chou-fleur. (French) Cauliflower.

citric acid. In canning, an acid derived from citrus fruits and used as an antioxident to control discoloration of fruits.

clarify. To purify a substance or make it clear. For clarified butter, see *beurre clarifie.* Stock is clarified by boiling it with eggwhite and crushed eggshell, then straining it through a sieve or cheesecloth.

coat. To cover food lightly but thoroughly with a layer of liquid, flour, breadcrumbs, crackercrumbs, mayonnaise, etc.

coat a spoon. A test to determine whether a sauce has reached the desired thickness. Dipped into a cream soup, the spoon emerges covered with a thin film; dipped into a sauce, it emerges with a thicker, but even, film.

cocotte. (French) A heavy casserole or cooking dish, often of iron or copper, which has a close-fitting cover. It may be large enough to hold a chicken or small enough for just an individual serving. Cocottes sometimes have glass covers, and are used in the oven as well as on top of the stove. They are used for braising meats and chicken, for boiling vegetables and for deep-fat frying. If cooked and served in a small cocotte, a dish is said to be *en cocotte.*

coddle. To cook in a liquid (usually water) that is just below the boiling point.

cold pack. In canning, to fill jars with raw, rather than hot, food before processing. Also called raw pack, it is used for foods that need delicate handling after cooking.

combine. To mix, or blend, two or more ingredients so that they cannot be separated.

compote. Fresh or dried fruits simmered together and served in a sugar syrup. It may be flavored with spices or spiked with liqueur.

concombre. (French) Cucumber.

condiment. A seasoning or relish for food added to enhance its flavor or stimulate the appetite. Typical condiments are salt, pepper, capers, horseradish, mustard, etc.

confit. (French) Preserved, especially as in *confit d'oie*, a goose meat that has been cooked and packed in its own fat. Also *fruits confits*, fruit that has been cooked and preserved in sugar or alcohol.

consomme. (French) A strongly flavored but clear stock or broth made from meat or poultry and concentrated by having half its original bulk boiled away. It is used as a basis for various soups and sauces or as a soup by itself.

cool. To let a food stand until it is no longer warm to the touch.

cool place. In canning, this means an area with a temperature of 50° F. (10° C.). This is ideal for storage of canned jars of food.

core. To remove the central capsule that contains the seeds of certain fruits and vegetables.

correct seasoning. As cooking proceeds, to taste the food at various stages and add seasoning if required.

cote. (French) Rib, or a cut of meat including part of the rib. Also, in wine parlance, the hill or slope covered with vineyards.

cotelette. (French) Chop or cutlet.

cotriade. (French) A fish soup, made in Brittany, which is somewhat like bouillabaise, but is made with butter instead of olive oil, and mackerel and sardines but no shellfish and no garlic.

coupe. (French) A shallow dessert dish; also, the dessert usually served in it, consisting of ice cream, with various toppings, chopped nuts and whipped cream.

courgette. (French) Zucchini.

court bouillon. (French) A liquid used for poaching fish or vegetables. It is highly seasoned and aromatic, containing the essence of root stock and vegetables that have been boiled in it plus some wine. It enhances the flavor of the food simmered in it. It may be strained and used as stock. Also called *short stock*.

cream. To soften and mix other foods with a solid fat, usually by rubbing them together with the back of a spoon, to achieve a creamy consistency. Butter and sugar, or butter and garlic may be creamed, for example. An electric mixer may also be used for this purpose.

crecy. (French) A town famous for its carrots, and hence any dish cooked or served with carrots, e.g., *potage Crecy*, a soup of pureed carrots.

creole. Describes a dish served with a sauce consisting of tomatoes, green pepper, onion, celery, okra and seasonings. A Louisiana speciality.

crepe. (French) A thin, light pancake made from a batter of egg and flour.

cresson. (French) Watercress.

croquette. Small balls or cylinders of food, composed of minced meat, vegetables, fish or rice that are rolled in a batter and deep-fried. They are usually served in a creamy sauce.

croute. (French) The word for crust, but also a case made of toasted French bread or brioche dough, to be stuffed with a filling, which may vary, and served as an hors d'oeuvre. Also, toasted or sauteed slices of French bread used as a garnish.

crouton. (French) Small cubes of French bread, buttered or plain, that are baked in a slow oven or sauteed until crisp, then used as a garnish for soups and salads.

crumb. The soft, inner part of bread, as opposed to the crust. Also, to coat or cover food with crumbs before frying or baking.

cube. To cut into medium-sized squares, one-quarter to one-half inch across.

custard. A dessert consisting of sugar, eggs, milk or cream and a flavoring. A custard may be of the baked type, which has a jellylike consistency, or of the boiled type, which is thinner.

cut in. A way of combining solid fat with dry ingredients in pastry-making without melting it. Two knives are used to break the fat into small pieces resting on a bed of dry ingredients. The mixture has a coarse, mealy consistency.

daube. A cooking method for meat, poultry or game in which a cut is braised in red wine stock with herbs and vegetables. It is much like a stew.

deep-fry. To cook food by immersing it completely in hot fat or oil.

deglaze (Fr: deglacer). To loosen and dissolve the fat and browned particles left in a pan after sauteeing or roasting foods by heating and stirring in wine, stock or other liquid. The resulting glaze is used as a base of a sauce or gravy.

degrease. (Fr: degraisser). To skim the grease off the the surface of a hot liquid. Or, to chill a liquid until the fat rises to the top and congeals, then removing it.

demi-tasse. (French). A very small coffee cup, and by extension, the drink of coffee contained therein, which is customarily strong and black.

devein. In cleaning shrimp, to remove the black or white dorsal vein, usually by making a shallow cut along the vein line and scraping out the vein.

dice. To cut food into smallish cubes, i.e., one-quarter to one-eighth inch, which is midway between cubing and mincing.

dilute. To thin or weaken a liquid by adding another to it.

disjoint. To cut or break into pieces at the joint, usually applied to poultry or a cut of meat.

dot. To distribute small pieces of butter or other substance over the surface of food.

dough. Basically a mixture of flour and liquid (water, eggs or milk) thick enough and firm enough to be kneaded or worked by hand. Dough generally contains other ingredients such as shortening, sugar, salt and yeast. Compare this to *batter*, above.

dredge. To sprinkle or coat a food with a dry substance such as flour, sugar, bread or cracker crumbs.

drippings. The juice and fat that exude from meat or fish during cooking.

dry pack. When freezing food, to pack without added liquid sugar.

duglere, a la. (French) A method of cooking and serving white fish named after chef and restauranteur Duglere who poached them in white wine and butter and served them with a sauce featuring peeled and chopped tomatoes.

dust. To sprinkle the surface of food a dry ingredient such as sugar, flour or crumbs.

duxelles. (French) A mixture of minced mushrooms, onions, shallots and parsley sauteed in butter or oil, with stock or wine added and then much reduced. It is used as a flavoring for stuffings and sauces.

echalote. (French) Shallot.

ecrivisse. (French) Crayfish.

enrich. To add cream, eggs or butter.

entrecote. (French) A boneless steak cut from between two ribs of beef, especially from the first cut on the loin end, ribs nine to 11.

entree. Traditionally in France, the third course, generally a hot dish in white or brown sauce. In the United States, the main course of a meal.

entremet. (French) A side dish. Originally, dishes served between meat courses, often of vegetables, to which guests helped themselves. Today usually sweet dishes, hot or cold desserts, such as a custard, an ice or a charlotte.

enzyme. A protein that changes other substances by catalytic action, such as starting the process of decomposition of food, which changes the flavor, texture and color. Canning and freezing both neutralize the action of enzymes.

epinard. (French) Spinach.

escalope. (French) A thin slice of meat or fish, usually flattened slightly, and without bones, gristle or skin. Also, a round veal steak cut in this fashion.

escargot. (French) An edible snail.

farce. (French) Stuffing or forcemeat.

farci. (French) Stuffed or filled.

fermiere, a la. Literally in the style of a farmer's wife, and refers to braised or pot-roasted meat with vegetables.

fillet. A boneless cut of lean meat or fish, generally taken from a choice part, such as the tenderloin (of beef).

fines herbes. (French) A mixture of finely chopped herbs used to flavor soups, stews, omelets and fish. Traditionally included are tarragon, chervil, chives and parsley. Thyme is occasionally added.

flake. A small, loose chip of food; also, to break up food into flakes using a fork, said especially of cooked seafood, tuna, crabmeat and the like.

flambe. (French) Flamed, said of foods—meat, crepes, cake, etc.—that are served drenched in an alcoholic liquid, then ignited. Brandy is most frequently used. A residue of flavor remains after the alcohol burns off.

flan. In French, a straight-sided open pastry shell, usually filled with a sweetened fruit mixture or pate. In Spain and Latin America, a caramel egg custard baked and served as dessert.

flat-sour. In canning, an organism in canned vegetables that gives food an unpleasant, sourish flavor. It is caused by bacteria and is heat resistant, yet can be avoided by correct and sanitary canning methods.

flour. The finely ground meal of any edible grain, such as wheat, rye, buckwheat, etc. Also, to coat a food evenly with a thin layer of flour or to coat a pan after first rubbing grease on the surface. See also: **Flour.**

foie. (French) Liver. See also: **Foie gras.**

fold. To blend a delicate mixture—such as stiffly beaten eggwhites—into a heavier mixture, such as a souffle sauce. The technique involves putting a portion of the light mixture on top of the heavy mixture, then with a spatula, cutting down through both to the bottom of the bowl, scraping along the bottom and up the side and depositing a dollop of the heavy mixture on top of the light, then cutting down again and so on until the lighter mixture is incorporated. Care must be taken not to deflate the lighter mixture.

fonds de cuisine. (French) Basic stocks or broths kept ready to form the basis of sauces or soups.

fondue. A Swiss dish in which Emmenthaler or Gruyere cheese is melted together with white wine, kirsch, garlic and seasonings in a chafing dish. Chunks of bread are dipped into the heated mixture and eaten off of long-handled forks. Also, an American dish that is a baked mixture of eggs, milk, cheese and either bread or cracker crumbs. A vegetable fondue is a dish in which vegetables have been cooked until they are soft and pulpy. In fondue *bourguignonne*, cubes of lean beef are dipped into very hot fat for a few moments, then dipped into a sauce and eaten. Long forks are used, and each diner helps him or her self.

forcemeat. A mixture of minced meat, fowl, eggs or vegetables that has a pastelike consistency and is used as a stuffing, filling or spread. Forcemeats are made in infinite variety and may even be served as separate dishes, as in the case of the quenelle, which is a kind of forcemeat that is poached and served by itself.

fraisage. (French) Kneading of dough.

fraise. (French) Strawberry.

framboise. (French) Raspberry.

frappe. (French) Iced; also the name given to a flavored ice or sherbet consisting of pureed fruit and chipped ice chilled to a mushy consistency. Also a liqueur poured over crushed ice and served as an after dinner drink. In the United States, a type of very thick milk shake.

freezer burn. Dehydration of food that has been improperly packed for freezing. It causes loss of flavor, texture and color.

fricassee. (French) A method of cooking chicken in which it is first browned in butter, then cooked in a seasoned liquid until tender; used especially for older birds.

fritter. A small batter cake fried in deep fat; also any food, such as fruit, fish, meat, poultry or vegetables, that is first dipped in batter and then deep-fried.

friture. (French) Fried in deep fat, but generally refers to a platter of very small fish.

frosting. Icing, i.e., a sweetened mixture used to coat or decorate cakes, cupcakes and cookies.

fruits confits. (French) Glaceed or candied fruits.

fruits de mer. (French) Seafood generally, but specifically a dish of crustaceans and shellfish served together, often raw, as an hors d'oeuvre.

fry. To cook in hot fat. See also *deep-fry*, above.

fume. (French) Smoked.

fumet. A concentrated broth, or even jelly that is extracted from fish, meat or vegetables by slow cooking. It is used to give flavor and body to sauces and stocks.

galette. (French) A round, flat cake, usually of flaky pastry, and sometimes flavored with cheese or sweetened and served with a dessert.

garni. (French) Garnished or used as a garnish.

garnish. Anything (usually another food) used to embellish, trim or decorate another food. Typical garnishes are sprigs of parsley, vegetables, sauteed mushrooms, watercress and olives.

gateau. (French) Cake.

gelee. (French) Jelly; *en gelee* is said of a food served with a gelatin coating.

glacage. (French) A glaze or frosting.

glace. (French) Glazed or iced. It may refer to a sweet frozen liquid or to any food that has been coated with a thin, sweet syrup and cooked at a high heat until the syrup forms a hard coating that cracks.

glace de viande. (French) Meat glaze.

glaze. A thin coating of syrup, jelly or aspic on the surface of food that usually gives it a glossy sheen. Also a concentrated form of meat or fish stock obtained by boiling it down to the consistency of syrup, which, on cooling, turns to jelly. Like stock, it is used to flavor gravies, sauces, etc.

goujon. (French) A gudgeon (a freshwater fish).

goulash. A spicy Hungarian beef or veal stew.

grate. To reduce a food to shreds or particles by rubbing it against the rough, indented surface of a utensil called a grater.

gratine. (French) Said of a dish with a brown top crust formed usually of bread crumbs or grated cheese cooked under a broiler.

grease. To rub fat or oil on the surface of a food or utensil to prevent sticking.

grenouille. (French) Frog. *Cuisses de grenouilles:* frogs legs.

grill. To cook food on a gridiron over hot coals or under a broiler. Also the gridiron itself and the food prepared by grilling.

grind. To crush or cut food into small pieces or to reduce it to powder using any of a number of devices such as a meat grinder, a food mill or mortar and pestle.

hacher. (French) To mince, or chop finely.

haricot. (French) Kidney bean in any of its various forms.

head space. In canning, the area left unfilled between the top of the food in a jar and the inside bottom of the lid. Too much head space may cause exposed food at the top of the jar to discolor or prevent a proper seal; too little can cause food to boil out of the top of the jar, possibly ruining the seal or in freezing may cause the jar to break when the food expands from the cold.

high-altitude cookery. Above 3,000 feet, cooks must take into account the effects of lower atmospheric pressure, especially in boiling and baking. This causes water to boil at a lower temperature, hence more quickly, yet the time needed to boil foods must be lengthened. Breads and cakes rise more readily. Slightly less flour and leavening are needed than would be standard at sea level, and ovens should be set at slightly higher temperatures.

homard. (French) Lobster.

hors d'oeuvres. (French) Small tasty bits of food served as an accompaniment to cocktails or small amounts of food eaten before a meal or as a first course. Typical hors d'oeuvres include cheese, olives, celery and bite-size bits of meat or fish.

hot pack. In canning, the filling of jars with precooked hot food before processing. It is the method of choice with firm food because it permits tighter packing and requires fewer jars.

huile. (French) Oil.

huitre. (French) Oyster.

icing. Frosting, i.e., a sweet coating for cakes, cupcakes or cookies usually made of sugar and butter plus flavoring.

incorporer. (French) To *fold* (see above).

infusion. The beverage resulting from the steeping of herbs, vanilla or tea in water or another liquid for the purpose of extracting the flavor.

jambon. (French) Ham.

jar. In canning, a glass container specially designed and heat-treated for use in home canning. Often called a mason jar.

jardiniere. (French) Garden style, said of a dish served with a garnish of freshly cooked vegetables.

juilienne. (French) To cut into small, matchlike strips; usually applied to meats, fruits or vegetables. Also a soup featuring vegetables cut *julienne* style.

knead. To mix and work (usually dough) into a plastic mass by pressing it, folding it and turning it repeatedly. This is done by hand or, in large bakeries, by machine.

laitue. (French) Lettuce.

langouste. (French) **Spiny lobster.**

lapin. (French) Rabbit.

lard. To insert strips of fat into lean meat. This can be done by threading it through the meat with a larding needle or by cutting a slit in the meat and forcing the fat through. The fat bastes the meat internally and improves the flavor.

lardon. (French) The thin strip of fat used to lard lean meat.

lard de poitrine fume. (French) Bacon.

leavening. The agent used to make dough rise and hence to make bread lighter. This is usually accomplished through the production of carbon dioxide gas in the dough with such agents as yeast, baking soda and baking powder.

legume. A class of vegetables that is formed in pods having a single row of seeds, such as peas, beans and lentils. In French, *legume* means vegetable.

lyonnaise, a la. (French) Prepared in the style of Lyon, i.e., with sauteed onions. See also: **Lyonnaise Sauce.**

macedoine. (French) A dish of mixed vegetables or fruits. They are evenly cut, may be raw or cooked and are served hot or cold.

macerate. To steep food (usually fruit) in a liquid so that it may absorb certain flavors. In the case of fruit the liquid is often a liquor, such as brandy. Compare *marinate*.

madrilene, a la. (French) Madrid-style, i.e., flavored with tomato juice or tomato pulp. Also a consomme flavored with tomatoes and served hot or chilled and often jellied.

maigre. (French) Thin or lean; but when applied to a soup or sauce, it means containing no meat fat. It also can mean meatless as in *un jour maigre*, a meatless day.

maison. (French) House; when tacked on to the name of a dish, such as *pate maison*, it means prepared in the special style of the house or restaurant.

maitre d'hotel. (French) Headwaiter. In the United States often shortened to *maitre d'*.

marengo. (French) Way or preparing chicken or veal, first sauteeing it in olive oil with garlic and tomatoes, then cooking it in white wine or brandy, water, parsley, olives, onions, seasonings and lemon juice. It is garnished with crayfish and fried eggs. So named by Napoleon's chef, who improvised it out of materials at hand after the battle of Marengo in 1800.

marinade. A liquid in which food (usually meat) is soaked for the purpose of tenderizing it or enhancing its flavor. Typically, a marinade is a brine solution or a mixture of oil and soy sauce or of wine or brandy all seasoned with herbs and assorted flavorings.

marinate. To place food (usually meat) in a marinade. Compare with *macerate*.

mariniere, a la. (French) Mariner's style; said of seafood, often shellfish, steamed in a broth of white wine and seasonings. Mussels so cooked may be used as a garnish for fish, which is said to be *a la mariniere*.

marmite. (French) A soup kettle or stock pot. It is a deep vessel of metal, enamel or earthenware. The term is also used for the individual china or earthenware bowls the soup is served in. See also *petite marmite*, below.

marron. (French) Chestnut.

marzipan. An icing or candy made of almond paste, eggwhites and sugar. It is often molded into fancy shapes, made into cake decorations or used as a center for dipped candies.

mash. To crush or beat food into a soft, uniform mass using a masher or other utensil. Also crushed malt or other cereals steeped in hot water and used for making beer and certain liquors.

mask. To cover a prepared dish completely with a sauce or aspic before serving it.

matelote. (French) A stew of freshwater fish prepared with wine.

melange. (French) A mixture of foods; also a preserve consisting of various pitted, uncooked fruits soaked in a mixture of sugar and brandy and aged in a stone crock.

melt. To change from a solid to a liquid form, usually by applying heat. Also in the United States, a term used to designate a dish covered in or garnished with melted cheese, such as a *tuna melt*.

meringue. Stiffly beaten eggwhites blended with sugar.

metal band. In canning, a threaded screw band used with a metal vacuum lid to form a two-piece metal cap.

meuniere. (French) "Miller's wife," a term used to describe food made or served with melted butter, lemon juice and parsley. Most often applied to fish, which is lightly floured before cooking.

microorganism. In canning, a living plant or animal of microscopic size, such as molds, yeasts and bacteria that can cause spoilage.

mijoter. (French) To simmer.

mille-feuille. (French) Literally "thousand-leaf," meaning a pastry consisting of many thin layers of puff pastry dough filled with custard, cream, fruit puree, etc.

mince. To chop into very fine cubes; smallest in the descending order of cube, dice and mince.

mincemeat. A spicy mixture used as a pie filling and consisting of the following minced ingredients: suet, apples, candied fruits, raisins, nuts and sometimes meat. It is spiced with cinnamon, clove and allspice and flavored with brandy, rum or other spirits.

mirepoix. (French) Diced vegetables, usually carrots, onions and celery, sometimes flavored with ham. They are cooked slowly in butter with bay leaf and thyme and used to flavor meats, stuffings, sauces and braises.

mold. To shape food into a particular form; also a dish or pan used to effect the shaping. Also microscopic fungi that appear as fuzz on decaying food. In canning, they are easily destroyed at processing temperatures between 140° and 190° F. (60° to 88° C.).

moule. (French) Mussel.

mousse. (French) Froth; any light dessert containing whipped cream or beaten egg whites, such as cream or custard. Also an aspic or pureed meat, fish, poultry or vegetables.

moutarde. (French) Mustard.

nap. To coat a food with sauce that is thick enough to stick but pliant enough to reveal the outlines of the food.

navarin. (French) Mutton or lamb stew made with onions, turnips, potatoes and sometimes with fresh spring vegetables.

navet. (French) Turnip.

nesselrode. A pudding made with preserved fruits and nuts, chestnut puree, maraschino flavoring and whipped cream. Named for the Russian diplomat Count K. R. Nesselrode (1780–1862), whose chef created it. Also a cream pie topped with shaved chocolate, filled with candied fruits and flavored with rum. Also a game soup garnished with tiny chestnut-stuffed cream puffs.

noisette. (french) Hazelnut. Also a small, round slice of meat with the bone and fat removed.

nouille. (French) Noodle.

oeuf. (French) Egg.

offal. Variety meats, i.e., internal organs.

oie. (French) Goose.

oignon. (French) Onion.

open kettle. In canning, an older method no longer considered safe. Food is cooked in an open pan and then quickly put into jars and sealed without further processing. This method can be used safely only when canning jellies.

overnight. Approximately 12 hours.

pain. (French) Bread.

pan-fry. To fry in a skillet in a small amount of hot fat. Also the fat that accumulates from the meat as it cooks.

papillote. (French) Parchment paper to wrap food while cooking so as to retain juices. The wrapped food is said to be *en papillote.* Also frilled or curled paper decorations used on food.

parboil. To boil food for a short time, leaving it partly uncooked. It is then completed by another method, such as baking.

pare. To cut off the outer covering and stem of a fruit or vegetable using a small knife or other utensil.

parfait. In France, a frozen whipped cream and egg mixture with flavored fruit and sometimes brandy served in a tall slender glass. In the United States, an ice cream dessert consisting of layers of various flavors in a parfait glass topped with syrup, nuts and whipped cream.

paramentire, a la. (French) Prepared or served with potatoes.

paste. A smooth blend of a dry ingredient and a liquid or any food that has been ground, pounded or reduced to a soft, creamy mass.

patate. (French) Sweet potato.

pate. (French) Any dough for bread, rolls or pastry.

pate. (French) A blend of ground meats, poultry or fish that is well seasoned and often baked in a crust. It is often baked in a dish lined with strips of fat, in which case it is called a *terrine,* after the dish. *Pate* is usually served cold as an hors d'oeuvre or luncheon dish. See also: **Foie Gras.**

pate a choux. (French) Puff pastry dough.

pate brisee. (French) Short pastry; pie dough.

pate en croute. (French) Pate baked in a pastry crust.

patty shell. A small puff-pastry shell used to hold a creamed mixture of chicken or fish.

peche. (French) Peach.

pectin. A colloidal substance found in ripe fruits such as apples, that is available commercially in powdered and liquid form. In canning it is used to make jellies jell.

peel. To remove the outer coating of a fruit or vegetable. For fruits and vegetables with thin skins, this can be facilitated by dropping them into boiling water for five or 10 seconds.

persil. (French) Parsley.

petit four. (French) Small, individual, fancy cakes or cookies that have been decoratively iced. Also fruits that have been dipped into sugar frosting.

petite marmite. A clear soup made of beef, chicken, marrowbones, vegetables and seasoning often served with toasted bread and grated cheese. The name derives from the bowls in which it is traditionally served. See also *marmite,* above.

pH. An abbreviation meaning the "potential of hydrogen," a measure determining the acidity or alkalinity of a solution. It is useful to know in canning because foods are classed as acid or low acid and processed differently.

pickling. Preserving or flavoring a food in a solution of brine or vinegar and spices.

pilaf. A Middle Eastern dish in which rice is first cooked briefly in fat, then braised in a seasoned liquid.

pit. To remove pits or stones from fruits or vegetables.

poach. To simmer food immersed in a liquid. An exception is to poach foods in butter, which means to saute them.

pocher. (French) To poach.

poire. (French) Pear.

poireau. (French) Leek.

pois. (French) Pea.

poisson. (French) Fish.

poivre. (French) Pepper.

potage. (French) Soup, sometimes thick, sometimes clear. The word is used interchangeably with *soupe.*

pot-au-feu. (French) A thick soup or stew prepared with meat, usually beef, and vegetables. Sometimes the meat is eaten separately with a condiment, such as pickles.

potee. (French) Usually a hearty soup of pork and cabbages but also any dish cooked in an earthenware pot, including soups, stews and bean dishes.

poulet. (French) A young spring chicken, such as a broiler or fryer, in contrast to a *poule* or stewing chicken.

praline. A flat candy made in New Orleans of pecan nuts and caramel sugar. In France, a mixture of carmelized sugar and almonds that is crushed or ground. The powder is used to flavor sweet sauces or to decorate desserts.

preheat. To bring an oven or broiler up to the desired temperature before using. Fifteen minutes is considered the standard time necessary.

preserves. Fruit cooked whole in sugar syrup, served as a condiment or used in desserts. Also fruit made into a jam or jelly and then canned.

press. A kitchen utensil for extracting the juice of such foods as garlic or lemons. Also to force food through a fine strainer or sieve.

pressure-canner. In canning, a heavy kettle used to process low-acid foods. It has a lid that makes a steam-tight fit, a pressure gauge and a petcock. The steam under pressure reaches a temperature of 240°

F. (116° C.), which destroys harmful bacteria that thrive in low acid foods.

printanier. (French) A dish that is cooked or garnished with tender, young spring vegetables, such as asparagus tips, carrots, peas, turnips, green beans and onions.

processing. In canning, the stage of sterilizing jars and the food they contain in a pressure or boiling bath canner.

provencale. (French) Cooked in the style of Provence, i.e., with garlic and usually with olive oil and tomatoes.

puree. Any food reduced to a thick, smooth liquid by first being cooked, then forced through a sieve or food mill.

pruneau. (French) Prune; dried plum.

quenelle. (French) An oval ball of finely minced meat, fish or poultry that is well seasoned and poached in stock. It is usually served hot as a first course in a thick sauce. A *quenelle* is often mixed with puff-pastry dough before cooking.

queue de boeuf. (French) Oxtail.

quiche. (French) An open-face pastry or pie shell filled with a savory custard and cooked until brown. Best known variety is *quiche lorraine*, containing a mixture of eggs, bacon and cream.

rafraichir. (French) To cool or chill, especially to plunge vegetables from boiling water into cold water to halt the cooking process. Also an ice served between the fish and meat courses.

ragout. (French) A highly seasoned stew made of meat or fish accompanied by assorted vegetables. Also a thick sauce, especially a meat sauce.

ramekin. A shallow baking dish in the shape of a long oval or a size to hold an individual portion. Also a prepared dish, usually of cheese, made in such a vessel.

raw pack. Same as *cold pack* (see above).

reduce. Also *reduire* (French). Concentrating and intensifying the flavor of a liquid by evaporation through boiling it rapidly.

refresh. Same as *rafraichir* (see above).

releve. (French) The remove, i.e., the course in formal dinners that follows the soup or fish course and precedes the main course.

remove. See *releve*, above.

render. To melt solid fat by slowly heating it.

ribbon. As used in the phrase, "to beat an egg yolk and sugar mixture to form a ribbon," it describes a desirable stage in the blending when the mixture, dropped from an uplifted beater, will form a slowly dissolving ribbonlike line on the surface. Eggyolks may become granular if beaten beyond this stage.

rice. Small particles resembling rice obtained by forcing food through a sievelike utensil called a ricer.

rillettes. (French) A variety of pate in which shreds of fat and lean pork are simmered with seasonings, then ground or pounded and packed into jars and usually served as an hors d'oeuvre.

rissole. A puff-pastry or turnover shell stuffed with a savory or sweet filling and deep-fried like a fritter.

riz. (French) Rice.

roast. To cook (usually meat) uncovered in an oven or over an open fire, charcoals or ashes.

rognon. (French) Kidney.

roti. (French) A roast; roasted.

rouille. (French) A hot red pepper sauce served with *bouillabaisse.*

roulade. (French) Thin slices of meat, especially beef or veal, rolled around stuffings, such as bacon with onion, and cooked in a seasoned liquid or sauteed.

roux. (French) A thickener for sauces consisting of a cooked mixture of butter and flour.

rubber. In canning, a flat rubber ring used as a gasket between a zinc cap or glass lid and the lip of the jar. They should be placed on the jar wet and not greatly stretched. Used rings should be discarded, not reused.

salpicon. (French) A filling made up of diced ingredients held together by a sauce. It may consist of a single ingredient—meat, fish, a vegetable—or a mixture of several. It may be stuffed into a rissole or used as a garnish or croquette. Fruit salpicon may be served as a dessert.

salt. To season a food with salt or rub it with salt.

saucisse. (French) Small sausage.

saumon. (French) Salmon.

saute. Also *sauter* (French). To cook a food rapidly in an open pan in a small amount of hot fat. It may be done to brown a food as a preliminary to further cooking, or it may be the only cooking as with chicken or thin strips of beef.

scald. To heat a liquid, such as milk, to just below the boiling point; also to *blanch* (see above).

score. To make shallow cuts in the surface of a food for decorative purposes, or in order to prevent curling, turning or crumbling, or to permit seasonings to penetrate. Hams are often scored in diamond patterns.

sear. To brown and seal the surface of a food by quickly subjecting it to high heat. This may be done on top of the stove or in the oven.

season. To enhance the taste of a food by adding salt, herbs, spices or other ingredients. Also treating a cast iron cooking utensil with oil and heat before regular use.

separate. Egg yolks are separated from whites by cracking the shell in half and then carefully pouring the yolk back and forth from one half to the other while letting the white run into a bowl.

set. To coagulate liquid foods either by subjecting them to heat, as with custard, or to cold, as with gelatin.

shred. To cut, shave or break food into slivers.

shuck. To remove the husk of an ear of corn or

the shell of a clam, oyster or mussel.

sift. To pass a food (usually a powder or grain) through a sieve or metal screen to remove impurities and to make it lighter or fluffier.

simmer. To cook foods or liquids at or just below the boiling point.

singe. To remove pinfeathers, down or bristles from an animal carcass by exposing it to direct flame.

skewer. Originally a wooden pin, today the skewer is usually a short, sharp metal pin used to hold meat in place during cooking. On longer varieties, small pieces of food are threaded for grilling.

skim. To remove floating matter—fat, scum, etc.—from the surface of a liquid with a perforated spoon called a "skimmer" or with a ladle.

smother. To cook food in a tightly covered dish, using very little liquid or to cook food under a mass of other food, such as *smothered in onions.*

soft ball stage. In candymaking, the temperature at which a drop of boiling syrup dropped into cold water forms a soft ball. This occurs at 234°–245° F. (112°–118° C) on a candy thermometer.

sorbet. (French) A sherbet or water ice.

soubise, a la. (French) Dishes garnished with an onion puree. The name derives from Charles, prince of Soubise, an 18th century gastronome who was fond of onions.

souffle. A baked dish made light and fluffy by combining stiffly beaten egg whites with a flavored sauce that may be sweet or savory. When heated, the egg whites cause the mixture to puff up.

soupe. (French) Soup. Usually interchangeable with *potage,* yet sometimes implying a thicker consistency.

souper. (French) Supper.

spit. A long, pointed metal rod on which food is threaded for roasting or grilling. It may be positioned horizontally or vertically and operated by hand or electric power.

steam. To cook food by exposing it to the vapor from a boiling liquid. This is usually accomplished either by cooking in a closed pot with just enough liquid to generate steam or by using a steamer, a sort of colander with folding leaves that can fit into many different-sized pots and supports the food over the boiling liquid.

steep. To place a dry substance, such as tea, in a boiling liquid and allow it to stand for a while to extract the flavor. Also to marinate or soak a food in an aromatic liquid.

stew. To cook a food or foods in a seasoned liquid for a long time at low temperatures; a way of cooking certain cuts of meat until tender. Also a thick combination of foods, usually meat or fish and vegetables that have been cooked in this fashion.

stock. A liquid or jellied base for sauces, soups and gravies made by boiling meat, poultry or fish trimmings and vegetables together in a seasoned liquid. Then it is strained and often reduced before use.

superheating. In canning, to heat water above the boiling point under pressure without vaporizing it. It a pressure canner water reaches 240° F. (110° C.), which is sufficient to kill harmful bacteria in low-acid food.

syrup. A sweet, sticky, thick liquid made by boiling sugar with water or by reducing the juice of certain fruits, sugar cane or maple sap, etc. In canning, a mixture of water, sugar and juice is used to add liquid to canned or frozen products.

tart. A small, open pastry shell or pie crust that is filled with a sweetened mixture (fruit-flavored, custard or jam) and baked. In France, a *tarte* may also contain a nonsweet food, such as meat or cheese, as in *quiche.* The word also is used to describe a sharp, sour taste.

tartare, a la. Breaded fried foods accompanied by a highly seasoned **sauce.** Also applied to lean steak served raw and accompanied by a raw egg and condiments.

terrine. (French) An earthenware baking dish used for cooking and serving pate. The word is used to refer to both the dish and its contents.

thicken. To make or become thick. It is usually said of liquids to which thickening agents (flour, cornstarch, egg yolks, etc.) have been added or which have been reduced by evaporation.

timbale. (French) A metal or ceramic pastry mold; a pastry crust cooked in the mold, and by extension, any food prepared in a pastry crust of that sort. Also a custardlike mixture of finely chopped meats, fish or vegetables, or cheese baked in molds or ramekins and then served unmolded.

toss. To flip food over by tossing the pan, familiarly used with pancakes but also useful when cooking vegetables in a covered casserole. The latter may be grasped with both hands and gently tossed to shift the cooking levels of the contents.

tournedos. (French) Medallions of beef, i.e., very small, thin slices of fillet cut from the tenderloin. Tournedos are usually an inch thick and 2½ inches in diameter.

tranche. (French) Slice.

truite. (French) Trout.

truss. To secure the wings and legs of a fowl to insure that it retains its shape during cooking. Wings or legs may be bound with string or fastened with pins, skewers and the like.

tutti-frutti. (Italian) Mixed fruits; also a mixed fruit preserve used as a topping for ice cream or pudding; also, ice cream made with chopped fresh, dried or candied fruit.

unmold. To remove food from a mold. Techniques include running a thin knifeblade around the inner edges of the mold, or dipping the bottom in hot water, then covering the top of the mold with a chilled plate and inverting it. The bottom should be gently tapped to loosen the contents.

vacuum seal. In canning, the absence of normal

atmospheric air pressure in airtight jars. The jar and its contents are heated, causing the air and food inside to expand, forcing some air out and decreasing the atmospheric pressure. The jar is capped, and as it cools the contents shrink, forming a partial vacuum. Normal pressure on the outside holds the lid down, which along with rubber gaskets, keeps the cap sealed, preventing the air from reentering.

vacherin. (French) A type of Swiss and French **cheese.** Also a meringue case made originally in the shape of the cheese but now used as a container for whipped cream desserts, fruits or ice cream.

venting. Permitting the air to escape from a pressure canner; also forcing air out of a jar by applying heat. Also known as *exhausting*.

viande. (French) Meat.

volaille. (French) Poultry.

vol-au-vent. (French). Puff pastry formed into a patty shell, baked, then filled with a creamed mixture of meat, poultry or fish. It is covered with a pastry lid.

wet pack. In canning, to pack fruit in a sugar syrup; in freezing, to pack in plain sugar.

whip. To beat a food, such as eggs, cream or butter, quickly and steadily to introduce air into it, increase its bulk and lighten its consistency. This is done with a fork, whisk, rotary beater or electric mixer.

COON

Here is an American cheddar-type cheese whose flavor is extremely sharp and tangy owing to a special patented curing process. Only cheese of high quality can be used because the curing involves unusually high temperatures and humidity, which encourage mold growth. Coon has a very dark rind and crumbly body.

COONTIE

Also SEMINOLE BREADROOT, ZAMIA. This is the starchy pith of a small, palmlike tree, *Zamia* spp., native to Florida, the West Indies and Mexico. The flour or meal made from the pith resembles **arrowroot** and **sago,** and the plant is sometimes called Florida arrowroot or sago cycad. Of the more than 40 species of Zamia, only three yield a useful starch. They are *Z. floridana*, *Z. integrifolia* and *Z. pumila*. The stems of these plants remain wholly underground or at the most extend six inches above the surface of the ground. Their leaves have the feathery appearance of ferns.

Zamia bread, a specialty of the Taino Indians of the Caribbean Islands, was one of the first local staples offered to Christopher Columbus and his men on their arrival in the New World, but the Spaniards were put off by its appearance and the method of preparation. The Indians first grated the stem of the plant, then shaped the gratings into little balls, which they left out in the sun for two or three days. During this time, the balls turned black and became wormy, telltale signs that the zamia starch was safe to eat. They then pressed the balls flat and baked them on a griddle. Eating the starch before it turned black and wormy could result in death for the eater, the Indians said. Subsequent analysis has shown that zamia pith contains curarine, a constituent of curare arrow poisoning. It is dissipated by heat or can be removed by thorough washing.

COOT

The coot is a common aquatic bird of North America, Europe and Africa. Though considered game in a marginal sense, it is rarely eaten because of the general unpalatability of its flesh. It tends to be dark, dry and bland. This is true if the bird is skinned shortly after being killed. Otherwise, oil from the skin permeates the flesh giving it a strong, unpleasant taste. In former times when fasting was taken more seriously, coot was more widely eaten by Roman Catholics because it figured on a list of birds that could be eaten on fast days.

The European coot *(Fulica atra)* is a small bird, rarely exceeding two pounds in weight, that inhabits marshes and lakes and occasionally brackish river mouths and bays. It is eaten in northern Italy more than anywhere else, especially in the Polesine region south of Venice and the marshy coastal areas of Tuscany. Coot is prepared there with heavy sauces and strong tasting accompaniments designed to compensate for the blandness of the flesh. The North American coot *(Fulica americana)* resembles the **moor cock** and is often called mud hen or swamp hen. It is almost never eaten in the United States.

The playful antics of coots in their watery habitat has given rise to such phrases as "crazy as a coot," and "old coot," i.e., a silly, harmless person, perhaps not too bright.

COPPA

See **Capicolla.**

COPRA

See **Coconut.**

COQUILLES ST. JACQUES

See **Scallop.**

COQUITO

Also CHILEAN WINE PALM. This chilean palm tree, *Jubaea chilensis*, is valued chiefly for its sap, which is made into a type of honey or a palm wine. The tree has also adapted well in California. It reaches a height of 30 feet or more, the trunk attaining a width of three feet. In Chile, the wild tree was felled and the sap extracted from the trunk. The sap would be boiled and then consumed much like **maple syrup.** Wild stands of coquito have been pretty much depleted in Chile, however.

The fruit of the tree is also eaten. It resembles the coconut but in miniature, generally being no more than 1½ inches long. Nevertheless, the coquito nut has meat and oil similar to the true coconut. It is sometimes called monkey's coconut. The fiber is suitable for making cordage.

CORAL

A soft greenish substance found in the ovaries of the hen lobster, it is the stuff from which lobster roe is made. Coral turns bright red on cooking and is the basis, especially in France, of lobster sauces, pastes and butters. It is rich and tasty and takes its name "coral" from its appearance after being cooked.

See also: **Lobster.**

CORAL FISH

The name applies to any of several small fish that live around coral reefs, including *Abudefduf saxitilis*, also known as the sergeant major, and *A. sordidus*, a larger fish found in the Indian and Pacific Oceans. The sergeant major is either blue or yellow with dark stripes and is worldwide in its distribution. It reaches a length of about nine inches and has a deep, flattened body. Although its flesh is deemed insipid, it is an important food fish in many areas. Its cousin, *A. sordidus*, is likewise deep-bodied, reaches a length of 10 inches and is found from East Africa to the Hawaiian Islands. Gray brown, it has light longitudinal stripes. This species too is important as food, though there seems to be no commercial exploitation.

CORAL FUNGUS

Also CLAVARIA. A class of edible fungi that grow in small clumps like bushes or miniature coral, coral fungus has small clublike branches, which vary in color according to species, e.g., ashy coral fungus *(Clavaria cinerea)*, rose pink coral fungus *(Clavaria subbotrytis)*, purple tipped coral fungus *(Clavaria botrytis)* and pale yellow clavaria *(Clavaria flava)*. Various species are native to North America, the British Isles and Europe. They vary in height from two to six inches and occur in woodlands during a warm, wet spell. The inner flesh is white but generally is said to be tough, insipid tasting and sometimes indigestible. The pale yellow clavaria is considered the best of the lot. It may be prepared like other mushrooms. The French first sautee it in butter or oil, then add it to a variety of dishes.

See also: **Mushroom.**

CORAL VINE

Also MOUNTAIN ROSE. A climbing vine, *Antigonon leptopus*, native to Mexico and Central America, coral vine bears bright pink flowers. Its tubers are edible and have a nutty taste. It grows wild in tropical climates, or it may be cultivated as a summer plant in temperate latitudes.

CORB

Also BROWN MEAGRE. A Mediterranean croaker, the corb *(Sciaena umbra)* is a good eating fish but is not often caught due to its living habits. The corb frequents rocky bottoms in coastal waters, hovering at the mouths of caves or crevices. It feeds at night. It reaches a length of more than 27 inches and is a beautiful golden bronze color above, shading lighter below. The name "corb" is related to the French word for crow, *corbeau*.

See also: **Croaker.**

CORBINA

Also CORVINA. This Spanish name is common to several salt-water fish. Two species caught along the coast of Southern California, *Ericcion parvipinnis* and *Ericcion reticulatus*, are excellent food fishes. They are frequently pulled in by surf fishers. Corbina are related to the weakfish and the croaker of Atlantic coastal waters.

See also: **Croaker, Weakfish.**

CORDIAL MEDOC

Cordial Medoc is a mixture of liqueurs—creme de cacao and orange curacao—and fine brandy. It is bottled at 80 proof in Bordeaux, France.

COREOPSIS

This herbaceous annual plant, *Coreopsis cardaminifolia*, is native to the southern and southwestern United States. The flowers are deep purple at the center with yellow rays. The whole plant may be boiled to produce a pleasant drink.

CORIANDER

Both the leaves and the seeds of this aromatic herb, *Coriandrum sativum*, are valued as seasoning. It is an annual plant, native to the eastern Mediterranean and has feathery leaves and tiny yellow seeds.

It was popular with the ancient Romans, who introduced it to the rest of Europe. Its name derives from the ancient Greek word for bedbug because its seeds, if bruised in the unripe state, give off a nauseating smell.

Coriander is much esteemed as a general seasoning in Chinese, Indian and Mexican cuisines. Its finely ground seeds are a major ingredient of curry powders. In Europe and the United States, the leaves are used to flavor soups, while the seeds are used to flavor cakes, cookies, pastries, sausages and liqueurs. In earlier times its sugar-coated seeds were a popular candy in Scotland.

CORMORANT

This is a voracious sea-bird better known for its abilities as a fisher and a producer of guano than for its gastronomic value. Yet in earlier times the great cormorant *(Phalacrocorax carbo)* was a frequent item at table. This was perhaps due to its everyday presence in the homes of the great where its native abilities as a swimmer and diver were used to provide fish for the household.

The neck of the cormorant was fitted with a ring, which allowed it to breathe but prevented it from swallowing fish it caught. In the royal households of Renaissance England the master of cormorants had his official place alongside the master of hounds. This use of cormorants persists today in the Far East. A bird thus used often ended its career by itself becoming a meal for the master.

Because the flesh of the older bird is dark and strong smelling, however, the squab cormorant is considered much more palatable. It reputedly tastes like hare, and enjoys a certain esteem in the Hebrides, Orkney and Shetland Islands. In France, the bird is still eaten in Brittany, but the standard recipe seems designed to hide the taste of the bird rather than to enhance it.

It is in Peru that the cormorant makes its greatest contribution to the modern world. The Peruvian cormorant or white-breasted guanay *(Phalacrocorax bougainvillei)* nest by the millions on Guanapo Island and leave behind guano, a valuable fertilizer and source of nitrates.

The word "cormorant" derives from the Latin name for the bird, *corvus marinus*, meaning sea crow or sea raven.

CORN

Also INDIAN CORN, MAIZE, SWEET CORN. Corn in the culinary sense means the cereal grain *Zea mays*, which is native to the Americas. That is what will be discussed here, although in England the term means wheat, and in a larger sense, any grain or all grains. Corn, a grass of the family *Gramineae*, is believed to be descended from *teosinte*, a plant that grows wild in the Mexican highlands.

The cultivation of corn began in southern Mexico before recorded history and spread to the south as well as the north, reaching what is now the United States more than 2,000 years ago. It formed an important part of the diet of the Pueblo, Hopi, Zuni and later the Navaho. Corn was well entrenched among the Indians of the East Coast by the beginning of the 17th century when European colonists began to arrive. It played an important role in the survival of many of the colonies because the strains of wheat that the Europeans brought with them would not grow in the American soil. On the very day the

Pilgrims debarked from the Mayflower at Plymouth in 1621, Captain Miles Standish, leading a foraging party, came across an Indian cache of corn and beans that lasted the whole group through the winter. Later, they learned to plant corn Indian style, i.e., to scratch a hole in the ground with a stick, put in some corn kernels, together with a fish or two, then make a tiny hill of soil over the spot.

Corn remained the primary grain of the colonies for 200 years. After that, adaptable strains of wheat and rye began outproducing corn. The Indians taught the colonists how to make corn chowder, several corn breads, such as corn pone and hoe cakes, and a cornmeal mush, samp. Elsewhere, the Indians used corn to make beer, such as the modern day *chicha*, a corn beer brewed in Peru.

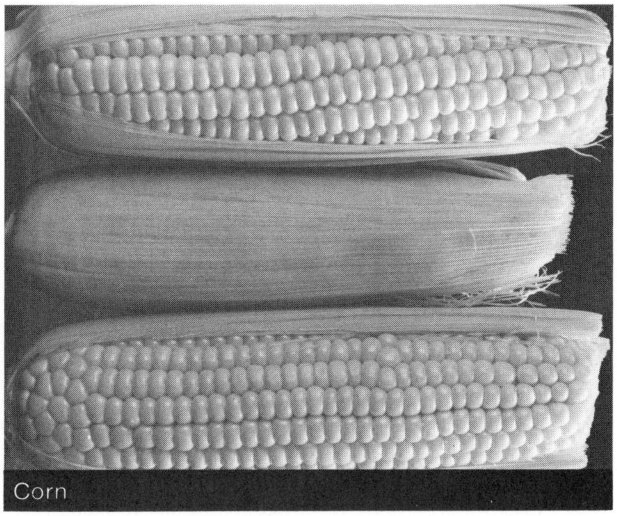

Corn

Corn is cultivated all over the world, and today is probably the largest and most luxuriant of all grain grasses. Dent corn *(Z. mays*, var. *indentata)*, a common variety in the United States, easily reaches heights of nine or 10 feet. The fruit of corn, the kernels, grow in rows on large ears, which measure up to 15 inches. Rows number from eight to 24 depending on the variety of corn. A kernel consists of three parts: a starchy core called the endosperm; the embryo or germ, which is made up of as much as 50 percent oil; and the hull or bran, which encloses the other two parts. The structure and texture of the kernel vary according to the type of corn.

In the United States, dent or field corn is the most prevalent. Dent has a small indentation on the top of the kernel at a spot where the endosperm is exposed. It is caused by shrinkage of the endosperm. Rarely eaten fresh, dent instead is used as livestock feed and in such industries as food processing, distilling and starch. It provides different kinds of fodder, including ripe grain, chopped, shredded stalk and ensilage, which is the green plant ears and all. It is chopped fine and fermented in silos before being fed to cattle.

Flint corn *(Z. mays* var. *indurata)* has a shorter growing season and is more adaptable to northern climates. Though otherwise similar to dent, the flint kernel completely encloses the endosperm, and thus retains its natural curvature at the top. Varieties of flint are more important in human nutrition than are dent.

Sweet or green corn *(Z. mays* var. *saccarata)* is the kind used for corn on the cob and canned corn. The ear is picked just short of ripeness while the kernels are plump and well filled but still soft and milky. A small genetic difference between sweet and field corn prevents the former from converting most of its sugar to starch as does the latter. It is important to eat or can sweet corn as soon as possible after harvesting, because the process of converting the sugar to starch begins on picking. The husk should be bright and fresh-looking. Dry, yellowed or straw-colored husks are indications of age or damage.

Within the above varieties are yellow and white strains. Yellow corn is good source of vitamin A, while white corn is not. Both are rich in vitamins B (thiamine) and C and riboflavin and in small amounts of minerals, such as phosphorous and iron. **Corn oil,** a polyunsaturated fat, is extracted from the germ. Other products, such as **cornmeal, cornstarch, corn sugar,** and **corn syrup** will be discussed under separate headings. The disease pellegra was formerly associated with eating corn because many poor people who fed principally on corn suffered from it. It is not caused by corn, however, but by a deficiency of niacin, a vitamin of the B complex, which corn lacks. A corn diet must be supplemented to make up for that deficiency.

CORN BREAD

A specialty of the southern United States, corn bread is traditionally made from cornmeal (maize) rather than flour, although modern recipes usually call for the addition of wheat or rye flour. Typically, stone-ground cornmeal is combined with baking powder, sugar, salt, an egg and milk to form a batter that is baked in a shallow pan. It is served hot and has a bright yellow color. Other varieties, such as creole corn bread are much lighter in color, using only the finest white cornmeal.

Early corn breads, such as corn pone, jonnycake, ashcake and hoe cake, were made using techniques the colonists learned from the Indians. They were unleavened and consisted of cornmeal, water and sometimes salt. They were shaped by hand into broad, flat cakes. Baked in an oven, the cakes were called corn pone; baked in the ashes of the hearth, they were called ashcakes. The same mixture baked on the broad blade of a hoe over an open hearth fire would be called hoe cake. Corn dodgers utilized the same dough cut into thin rectangles and baked in a skillet or greased baking sheet.

On the move, early Americans preferred the jonnycake or journeycake, which was a dried cornmeal pancake. The modern formula calls for flour, cornmeal, salt, baking soda, sugar, butter, milk and eggs. In earlier days, it was nearly identical to the ashcake.

See also: **Bread, Cornmeal.**

CORN COCKLE

An annual plant, *Agrostemma githago*, with magenta purple flowers, it is native to the eastern Mediterranean. It has been naturalized in most temperate regions as a noxious weed found in grain fields. The young leaves, however, may be cooked and eaten like spinach—flavored with bacon and steeped in vinegar. It is seldom eaten except in emergency situations. The seeds should be avoided because they are poisonous.

CORNCRAKE

Also LAND RAIL. Corncrake *(Crex pratensis)* is a small, migratory game bird with a short bill. It is particularly popular in France. It is common throughout southern Europe—frequenting meadows in southern France, Spain, Italy and Greece—where it spends the winter, and in the British Isles, where it spends the spring and summer. The corncrake is becoming increasingly rare in the British Isles and has been declared a protected species. In France the bird is called *roi de cailles* because it arrives and departs at the same time as quail and was thought to be their guide in migratory flight. It has a fine flavor and is at its best in October and November. It may be prepared like snipe or **quail.**

CORNED BEEF

This is a form of brisket, plate or rump beef cuts cured by the corning process. Corning consists of salting, pickling, adding sugar, nitrate, nitrite and spices and aging for about a month at 36° F (2° C).

Preparing canned corned beef is a matter of following instructions on the label; but if a solid, three-pound hunk is to be handled, more care is required: wash in running water to remove surface brine, place in a suitable deep kettle, fill kettle with boiling water and simmer three hours. By that time a fork should easily penetrate to the center.

CORNELIAN CHERRY

Also CORNEL. This is the bright red fruit of a tree, *Cronus mas,* which is a member of the dogwood family and native to south-central Europe and western Asia. The tree itself is shrubby, reaching 20 feet in height at the most, and in summer is covered by yellow-green flowers. Its wood is very hard, and has been used to make golf-club heads.

The cornelian cherry has a tart but pleasant flavor. It may be eaten fresh, but more often is is pickled like an olive, which it approximates in size. In France, the cornelian cherry is often preserved in honey or sugar. It may be used in the preparation of alcoholic drinks. The cornelian cherry is popular in Russia where it is used to make sauces and a dessert called *kisel.*

According to Homer, Circe fed Ulysses' companions cornelian cherries after she turned them into swine.

CORNFLOUR

Flour made from corn (maize) is cornmeal ground and sifted until it is as fine as flour made from wheat. It is generally not sold at retail, but is used by commercial bakers for dusting, in the manufacture of pancake mixtures or in sausagemaking. English "corn flour" is **cornstarch.**

CORNHUSKER

An American cow's milk cheese, similar to **cheddar** and **colby,** it was developed by the Nebraska Agricultural Experiment Station in 1940. Cornhusker takes less time to make but is moister than average, which gives it softer body, while increasing perishability.

CORNISH CREAM

See **Clotted Cream.**

CORNISH JACK

A valuable African food fish, *Mormyrops deliciosus,* of the lower and middle Zambezi, the Congo Basin and rivers of West Africa, the cornish jack can reach a length of five feet and weigh up to 40 pounds. It has a dark gray to bronze back and a silver belly. The cornish jack is considered the tastiest of the *Mormyridae.*

See also: **Elephant-Snout Fish.**

CORNMEAL

Grains of corn—both yellow and white—are ground to varying degrees of fineness to make cornmeal. The white type, ground very finely and sifted, is called cornflour, a term that in England refers to **cornstarch.** Two types of cornmeal are distinguished by process, stone-ground (water-ground) and granulated. The latter is the newer process, which involves grinding the corn on steel rollers after it has been kiln-dried. Most cornmeal is made in this fashion. The rollers break and remove the husk and the germ almost entirely, which gives the meal a dry and granular feel. It contains only small amounts of fat and not more than 15 percent moisture. The stone-ground process avoids heating the grain and employs the whole kernel. Many people think its flavor is richer because the germ and oil are left in. It is excellent for simple forms of cornbread but does not keep well, nor does it blend as easily with wheat flour. Consequently, it is harder to find and may be available only through mail order. **Hominy** and **hominy grits** are corn grains broken into particles of uniform size, which are larger than the granules of cornmeal.

Cornmeal is used to make bread, cakes and pastries. In Europe, coarse cornmeal is used to make cornmeal mush, which has several national variations including Rumania's *mamaliga*, Italy's *polenta* and France's *armotte*. Mealie porridge, also a cornmeal mush, is a staple food in Africa.

Early settlers of North America learned to make cornmeal from the native Americans and used it to make a mush called samp, a word taken from the Narragansett word *nasaump*. Their early attempts to make bread from cornmeal failed, because the latter, unlike wheat flour, has very little gluten. The native Americans taught them to make simple corn breads, such as corn pone (from the native American *appone)* and ash cake. These are broad, flat cakes placed on platters of wood and either baked in an oven (corn pone) or in the ashes of a hearth fire (ash cake). Later on, the colonists learned to mix the cornmeal with wheat flour and to produce fluffy cornbread, muffins and Boston brown bread, which contains 50 percent or more wheat flour.

In Mexico, the Indians bypassed the process of making cornmeal. Instead, they boiled the kernels and mashed them into a paste. This they used as a dough to make *tortillas*, thin, flat unleavened bread.

CORN OIL

This edible oil is extracted from the germ of the corn (maize) kernel. The germ is a byproduct of milling the grain for cornmeal. The germs are dried, ground and formed into cakes, which are then pressed to extract the oil. After refining, corn oil has a golden yellow color and a slight taste and aroma of freshly ground corn. Corn oil is polyunsaturated and is therefore desirable for low-cholesterol diets. It is excellent for frying and pastry-making. Increasingly, it is used to make margarine but has not found much favor as a salad oil.

CORN SALAD

See **Lamb's Lettuce.**

CORN SMUT

See **Cuitlacoche.**

CORNSTARCH

A highly refined and pulverized starch made from corn (maize), it is used chiefly to thicken liquids. (In England this product is called corn flour.) Another desirable property is that of lightening the texture of cakes and pastries when mixed at a ratio of one to four with flour. In refining, the raw starch is broken up, washed, siphoned, repeatedly strained to remove particles of fiber, pulverized and finally dried to reduce the moisture content about 10 percent.

As a thickener cornstarch is first mixed with a little cold liquid, then added to the soup, pudding, etc and the whole thing brought to a boil. It must be stirred constantly to avoid lumps forming. The resulting paste is more translucent than one ordinary flour can produce. It works equally well in sauces and pie fillings and is one of the easiest starches to digest. Cornstarch is used in many Chinese dishes. In addition to the thickening effect, it gives them a slightly glazed aspect as well.

CORN SUGAR

This dextrose is produced from cornstarch in the same manner as **corn syrup,** i.e., hydrolysis. More acid is used in the process, however, plus extensive evaporation. Its principal uses are industrial, e.g., in the manufacture of beer, vinegar and caramel. There are various grades of starch sugar, such as brewer's sugar, which contains no less than 70 percent dextrose; climax, with 80 percent and anhydrous, which looks like yellow cornmeal and must have at least 95 percent dextrose. The early Mexican and Peruvians made a kind of corn sugar, which is not related to this. They pressed the juice from stalks of sweet corn, then evaporated it.

CORN SYRUP

A product obtained by heating cornstarch with certain acids. The resulting liquid is two-thirds sugars (dextrose and maltose) and one-third gum (dextrin). It varies in color from clear to amber. Light corn syrup has been clarified and decolorized, and has no taste other than sweet. It is used as a general sweetener in the manufacture of jams, in baking and in candy making. It is especially valuable in the candy industry because corn syrup does not crystallize when cooked, nor does it disintegrate or get grainy. It maintains a softness and elasticity indispensable in chewy candies. Also, since it has no flavor itself, it does not interfere with flavors added to it. Dark corn syrup usually has additives for coloring and flavor, such as caramel, maple syrup or refiners syrup (a residue of beet and cane refining). It is used a a table syrup.

Corn syrup is a commercial glucose, and the process used to produce it works well with other starches, such as potato starch. The process was invented during the Napoleonic wars when the English naval blockade cut the French off from imported cane sugar. Like the beet **sugar** industry, it flourished until the blockade ended, then languished when cane sugar became available. The industry came to life again in the last quarter of the 19th century when an improved process lowered the cost of producing sugar from starch.

CORN WHISKY

A whisky prepared from a mash consisting of 80 percent or more corn (maize). Corn is also the principal grain in the mash for bourbon whisky, the difference being that the mash for bourbon need be only 51 percent corn. Straight corn whisky must satisfy other legal requirements apart from the mash; it must be aged at least two years in new white oak barrels or used charred oak barrels. The whisky aged in the barrel must have been distilled at no more than 160 proof, and at the time of bottling it may be diluted by nothing but distilled water to a proof no lower than 80.

See also: **Whisky.**

COS LETTUCE

See **Lettuce.**

COSTMARY

See **Alecost.**

COTHERSTONE

An English farmhouse cheese made in the valley of Tees, Yorkshire, it is similar to **Stilton** but not so well known. It has the familiar blue veins and is prepared from double cream cow's milk.

COTRONESE

A peppery Italian cheese that originated in Calabria, Italy, it is made from ewe and goat's milk and has a plastic curd, much like **moliterno**.

COTTAGE CHEESE

Also POT CHEESE, DUTCH CHEESE, SCHMIERKASE. This soft, uncured cheese made from skim milk is probably the oldest form of soft cheese and is greatly favored by weight watchers because of its high protein and low fat content. There are two main styles: A large-grained, low acid variety called sweet-curd, flake type or popcorn cheese. It is obtained by renneting the milk, then cutting the curd into large cubes and washing them thoroughly to reduce the acid; and a small-grained version called country or farm style.

Curds are white, and have a clotted appearance. Although the whey is drained, the curds are not pressed and so retain quite a bit of moisture. Cottage cheese is highly perishable and is usually eaten within two or three days. Sometimes cream is added, and if this raises the butter fat content to 4 percent, the mixture is called creamed cottage cheese. Flavorings such as peppers, olives or pimentos are often added. Cottage cheese is primarily a table cheese and is often added to salads. It is a good source of protein and calcium.

COTTONSEED

Oil and meal are the two most important foods derived from cottonseed. The meal is used principally as fertilizer and fodder, but cottonseed oil occupies a significant place in international commerce as an economical alternative to olive and peanut oil for use in shortenings, margarine and as salad or cooking oil. By weight, the cotton plant produces twice as much seed as fiber. The seed resembles a small coffee bean in size and form. One hundred pounds of seed yields about 16 pounds of oil, which is polyunsaturated and high in protein and vitamin E. It is also used in food packing, e.g., as a medium for canned sardines. The United States produces about one-third of the world's supply of oil, followed by India, China, Mexico, Egypt and Brazil.

The cotton plant, whose name derives from the Arabic *qutun*, is native to Asia, but was cultivated in America long before recorded history. The plant fiber was used to make cloth for thousands of years before the food value of the seed was appreciated. The latter had to wait for machinery sophisticated enough to separate the seed from the fiber, express the oil from the seeds and refine the oil. The oil industry began in 1855, and had its first major growth period between 1875 and 1930 when the percentage of seeds refined rose from 5 percent to 80 percent of the crop. Today it is a major growth industry in the new states of Africa.

As a cooking oil, cottonseed oil is appreciated mainly in the countries of origin. Japan, a nonproducer, is an exception to this rule. Cottonseed oil is highly esteemed there for cooking tempura, i.e., shrimp, vegetables and other tidbits dipped in a thick batter and then deep-fried.

COUCH GRASS

Also QUICK GRASS. A species of grass, *Triticum repens*, closely related to barley, it is generally considered a pest by farmers because of its rapid and persistant growth. The medieval English, however, collected its rhizomes and used them to make a tea that was valued for its diuretic qualities. The French still value it for that purpose today to such an extent that the rhizomes are imported in quantity from Italy. Its name in French, *chiendent*, means dogtooth, and derives from the observation that a sick dog seeks out the plant instinctively and chews the rhizomes. It is a European plant that has been naturalized in North America.

COULOMMIERS

Here is a soft, mold-ripened French cheese, very similar to a small **Brie,** made in the vicinity of Coulommiers (Seine-et-Marne). What generally distinguishes Coulommiers from Brie and Camembert is its short ripening period. It is made from whole cow's milk and is sold when only a few days old, before it acquires the reddish brown crust typical of Brie. Although some persons prefer to hold it for a week or two, it is usually eaten fresh. Cheeses are small and round, measuring five inches across by two thick and weighing about one pound. Coulommiers is considered a good cheese but inferior to Brie. Modified versions of Coulommiers are made in the United States and Canada.

COUMA

The guava-sized fruit of a tree, *Couma guianensis*, native to Guyana is round, sweet and pleasant tasting.

COUMARIN

See **Tonka Bean.**

COURGETTE

See **Zucchini.**

COUSCOUS

This cereal dish originated with the Berbers of North Africa and is especially popular in the Maghreb, the area made up of Algeria, Tunisia and Morocco. The basic ingredient is semolina or other cracked grain. It is dusted with flour, then steamed over a stock, stew or sometimes water. The steaming is done in a special utensil called the *couscousier*, which has two parts: a round pot on the bottom for the stock, and a sievelike upper part that holds the semolina.

Couscous is usually served heaped on a platter with a little butter or olive oil worked into it. The meat or poultry used for the stock is arranged around it, along with vegetables, chick peas, etc. It is generally accompanied by a fiery hot sauce, which is passed separately. Couscous may be eaten alone as a kind of porridge or as a dessert. In the latter case it is steamed over water, sweetened and mixed with raisins and nuts.

Couscous has been adopted in many variations by the rest of the Moslem world. It achieved a modicum of popularity in France, and since World War II this popularity has been extended to parts of the United States.

COW

Along with its major use as a dairy animal, the cow—especially sterile adults and heifers—has been a delicacy in 19th-century England and in France, where braised cow's udder is still prepared and eaten. The udder is first soaked in cold water, then blanched, cooled and flattened. It is then studded with bacon fat (or *lardons)* and after braising in a tight-lidded pan with very little water or stock it is served plain or with seasoning. Calf's udder is best prepared as a roast like the rump of veal. It may be garnished with jelly or with any herb or vegetable commonly added to cold meats and poultry.

COWBERRY

Also FOXBERRY, MOUNTAIN CRANBERRY. This small red fruit of an evergreen shrub, *Vaccinium vitis-idaea*, grows wild in the Northern Hemisphere. The fruit is sour tasting and after being gathered wild is used in jams, jellies and sweet sauces. It tastes like cranberry. A variety of the cowberry called the **lingonberry** is quite popular in Scandinavia.

COWCOD

Also **Rock Cod.**

COWFISH

A type of boxfish *(Ostraciontidae)*, it has a hornlike projection jutting out over each eye giving rise to the name cowfish. Like other boxfish, its body is encased in a bony shell that may be rectangular or triangular.

The cowfish *(Lactophrys quadricornis)* is a sluggish swimmer with a tail that acts more as a rudder than a propeller. It prefers warm waters and is common in the coastal waters of North Carolina and the Bahamas. It is considered fine eating, its flaky meat resembling that of a young lobster. The cowfish is usually cooked in its own shell.

COW PARSNIP

Also HOGWEED, MEADOW PARSNIP. This weedy plant, *Heracleum sphondylium*, is commonly found in the temperate areas of Europe, Asia and North America. The leaves may be cooked and eaten as a green vegetable and taste somewhat like asparagus. In Central Europe, the shoots are cooked and eaten like asparagus, and in Lithuania and Poland a home-brew beer is made from the stems and seeds.

See also: **Dandelion.**

COWPEA

Also BLACK-EYED PEA, PEA BEAN. Despite the name, this legume *(Vigna sinensis)* is botanically more a bean than a pea. Native to India and Iran, it is widely cultivated in warm and temperate regions, most notably Africa, China and South America. The cowpea is known under a variety of names, e.g., *cubia beledi* in Arab countries, *dan tua* in the Far East, *niebe* in Africa and *pois chique* in the Antilles.

It is a highly nutritious food, similar to the kidney bean in food value. In dried form, it contains 23 to 24 percent protein, one percent fat and 56 to 57 percent carbohydrate. It is also eaten fresh, as a green bean and shelled. Africa is the greatest consumer of cowpeas. For example, in Nigeria it is the second most important legume after the peanut. It is known as the kaffir bean in South Africa, and in the Congo both the tuberous roots and tender young pods are eaten.

In the United States it is chiefly used for forage and soil enrichment. Yet, it is a staple ingredient of "soul food," i.e., the cooking of the blacks of the American South. Cowpeas were brought from Africa by slaves, appearing first in Jamaica in 1674. A typical soul food dish, Hoppin' John, contains cowpeas, chopped ham and rice in ham broth. A spot at one end of the seed accounts for the sobriquet, "black-eyed."

COW PILOT

The Caribbean fish *Pomacentrus saxitilis* is considered to be of fair eating quality. It has bright black and green bands around its body. The cow pilot is taken in the coastal waters of southern Florida and the West Indies.

COWSLIP

Cowslip is a European wildflower, *Primula veris*, of the primrose genus. In England its sweetly scented flowers are added to salads or used to make wine, vinegar or mead. The flower may also be crystallized in sugar and eaten as candy. The dried leaves are infused in boiling water to make a kind of tea. In the United States the term "cowslip" is used for the marsh marigold.

See also: **Marigold.**

COWTREE

The name applies to any of several species of South American trees, e.g., *Brosimum utile* or *B. galactodendron* whose milky sap may be drunk mixed with water as a milk substitute. One obtains the sap by making slits in the tree trunk.

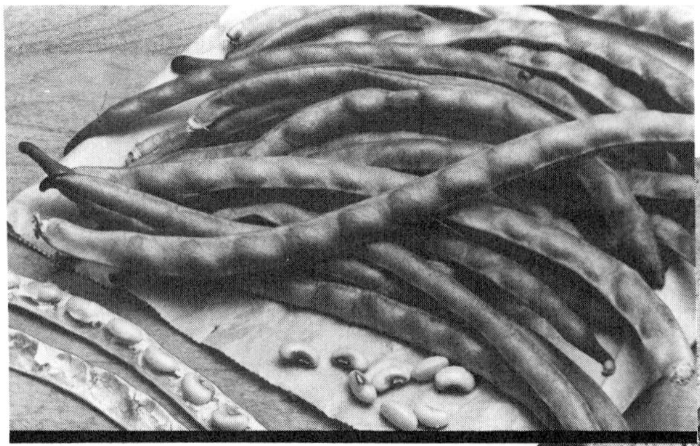

Cowpeas

Blue crab

COW WHEAT

Plants of the genus *Melampyrum* whose seeds are similar to wheat grains may be ground and used like ordinary wheat grains.

COXCOMB

See **Cockscomb.**

COYAL

Fruit of the coyoli palm, *Acrocomia mexicana*, is found from Mexico to Honduras and is used to make a palm wine.

CRAB

This is a short-tailed crustacean with a hard shell, eyes mounted on stalks and five pairs of legs, the front pair armed with claws. There are more than 4,000 species of crab worldwide, all of the order *Decapoda*, and most of them edible. On the subject of crabs, John Hay, American diplomat and journalist, wrote: "There are three species of creatures who when they seem coming are going, and when they seem going are coming: diplomats, women and crabs."

Shallow-water and beach crabs do move sideways with a body that is very wide relative to the length of their legs, but deep-water crabs with longer legs walk forward. With so many species, the variation in size, shape and habitat is tremendous. At the small end, there are tiny pea crabs that live in the shells of other mollusks; at the large end are such giants as the Japanese giant crab *(Macrocheira kaempferi)*, of which one specimen measured 12½ feet across, and the Tasmanian giant crab *(Pseudocarcinus gigas)*, which weighs as much as 30 pounds. They are lumped into rough categories by shape of shell: quadrangular, triangular or round. As for habitat, these include deep-water, shallow-water, fresh-water, brackish-water, beach and land. However, land crabs return to the water to spawn.

Crabs are the second most popular crustacean in the United States after shrimp. On the East Coast, the most frequently eaten is the blue crab, which is very plentiful in Chesapeake Bay. It constitutes about three-quarters of the fresh crab meat sold, much of it from the soft-shell crab. The soft-shell crab is a blue crab that has molted, i.e., shed its hard shell preparatory to growing a larger one. The peak season for this process is July and August, and the whole thing takes six to eight hours, including the new shell hardening a bit so that the crab can be shipped. Farther south is the preserve of the stone crab, whose territory includes the shores of Florida and the Gulf Coast as far as Texas.

The favorite West Coast crab is the Dungeness, which is found all the way from Alaska to Baja California in Mexico. It takes its name from a place in Washington State. Specimens taken in northern parts are considered better, particularly those from San Francisco and Crescent City in California. Second in popularity are the large king crabs, taken in deep water off the coast of Alaska. Other species also esteemed for the table are the swimming crab, the deepwater red, or sea, crab and the rock crab.

In Europe, the best edible varieties are the common crab, the giant crab and the spider crab. The long-legged thornback, a variety of spider crab, has particularly good flesh. The red zodiac crab is a British delicacy. In the Far East, the Japanese enjoy both the king crab and the Dungeness, while the Chinese have a succulent freshwater crab.

Land crabs (family *Gecarcinidae)*, though born in the sea, develop body cavities like lungs for breathing, unlike other crabs, which breathe through gills. They are found in tropical areas and while disdained in Florida are highly appreciated as food in Puerto Rico and other Caribbean islands and on the west coast of Africa. Called *jeuyes* in Puerto Rico or *courlourou* in Martinque, they are caught and penned up for three days—to be both fattened and purged—before being cooked and served as stuffed land crab. A common land crab in the Pacific Islands and Asia is the coconut, or robber, crab, which climbs palm trees to pick coconut. The flesh of this crab strikes most Westerners as oily, but it finds great favor with the locals.

The large Samoan crab *(Scylla serrata)* and Hawaiian Kona crab *(Ranina serrata)* are considered by some to be better than the Dungeness and are exported to the United States mainland.

Crabmeat from blue, Dungeness, king or rock crabs is usually available in cans. Otherwise, crabs are available in a variety of forms: live, cooked in the shell, cooked and frozen and fresh cooked meat. Soft-shell crabs travel well, and are shipped live for hundreds of miles, packed in seaweed and ice. Live hard-shells are eaten close to the point of origin because of their perishability. Softshell crabs are often sauteed, while the hard shell variety is invariably boiled or steamed. A dressed crab is one that has had all the meat removed from its body and claws, mixed with cream, seasonings and often breadcrumbs, then put back into the shell and served cold.

CRABAPPLE

This small apple, usually bright yellow or red, which is too sour to eat fresh, makes excellent jams, jellies, preserves and cider. Siberia is thought to be the original home of the crabapple, and the Siberian crabapple *(Malus baccata)* to be the parent of all other varieties that are grown all over the world for their beauty as well as their fruit. Many of the best fruit-bearing trees are hybrids of the Siberian crabapple and the ordinary apple *(Pyrus malus).*

The fruit averages about one inch in diameter but in hybrid varieties may be considerably larger. The crabapple tree, known also as the crab tree, is renowned for the hardness of its wood, and in earlier times it was a favorite material for cudgels. The tree is ornamental, and many of its species, especially those from Asia, are grown in the West for the beauty of their blossoms, which bloom so thickly that the tree is a mass of flowers. Crabapples make delicate and delicious jelly. They are liberally endowed with pectin and are often added to other fruit jellies to improve consistency.

The United States has several indigenous varieties of crabapple, including the eastern *(M. coronaria)*, which inhabits the Northeast and goes as far west as Wisconsin; the prairie *(M. ionensis)*, and the Oregon *(M. fusca)*, whose habitat extends from California to Alaska. American varieties tend to be larger and tastier than those found in Europe, where the term "crabapple" may be applied rather more loosely to any small, sour apple, even wild varieties of the ordinary apple.

CRACKER

This thin, dry bread wafer may be plain, salted or slightly sweet. The basic cracker dough consists of flour, a little salt, a little fat, water and maybe milk. It may be unleavened or leavened with soda. This is what is known in England as a dry biscuit. The dough is pricked on top and baked dry and crisp. The finished product may be an even light brown, as in the case of soda crackers, or white with tiny brown bubbles on the surface. Adding fat to the recipe produces a more crumbly cracker.

Modern crackers are a close relative of a twice-baked bread known as a ship's biscuit, hard tack or pilot's biscuit. It was popular in the days before the improvement of food storage as a bread for travelers. It was twice-baked to make it as dry as possible. This improved its keeping qualities, and made it more compact for storage. (See also: **Knackebrod).**

Other varieties of cracker include the Graham cracker, a dark brown cracker prepared with whole wheat flour; the oyster cracker, which is tiny and served atop oyster stews and bisques, and the cream cracker, a plain, flat variety, one of the first to be marketed in air-tight containers and exported worldwide from Ireland.

To retain their crispness, crackers must be kept in their moisture-proof container. Softened crackers may be heated in a slow oven to regain their crispness.

See also: **Bread, Flour.**

CRACKLING

This is pork skin cooked until it is brown and crisp. In England and the United States, this is usually the skin of a pork roast, which is cut into thin strips for easy eating. In Cuba, the skin is cut into squares or diamonds and deep-fried. It is called *chicharon.* In Mexico the latter refers to much larger pieces of pork skin that have been cooked until all the fat is rendered out. They have a crisp bubbly texture. In France, three-inch squares are baked with fat attached until all the fat is rendered, and the skin is crisp and golden brown. The squares are called *grattons.* In English, the plural form "cracklings" usually refers to the latter method of preparation.

CRAKEBERRY

See **Crowberry.**

CRANBERRY

This small, acid, ruby-red fruit grows wild in the bogs and marshes of northern Europe and is cultivated in the United States. The native American variety *(Vaccinium macrocarpon)* is the largest cranberry of all (up to one-half inch across) and the only one that is cultivated.

Early American colonists learned from the Indians how to make a sweet sauce from the berries, which grew wild in the Northeast, particularly in the Cape Cod area of Massachusetts. The cranberry was too tart to be eaten raw by the colonists (although the Indians did it); but boiled in sugar syrup, it produced a jelly or sauce with a tart, slightly bitter, yet pleasant smoky taste. This sauce or jelly has become the traditional accompaniment to roast turkey at the Thanksgiving and Christmas holidays. Also, more recently, cranberry juice has been made into a refreshing drink, often containing an admixture of a sweeter juice like apple and has been marketed nationally in the United States.

Opinions differ on the derivation of the name "cranberry." One explanation is that at an early stage of development, the cranberry flower resembles the head of a crane, hence craneberry. Another is that the word comes from the French, *canneberge*, or shore reed, the name given it by French colonists in Canada. Cultivation of cranberries is a risky business. Whole crops are destroyed by the cranberry worm. Moreover, although cranberries grow only in cold climates, the shrub may be killed by an early frost. For planting ground, cultivators select a peat swamp or salt marsh that has some source of fresh water for winter flooding. The peat is covered by five inches of sand, and the vines are planted in this layer, taking root in the peat. After the harvest, which takes place in September or October, the bogs are often flooded as a means of insulating the roots from temperatures lower than freezing, which they cannot survive.

In Europe, the closest relative to the American cranberry is the Finnish *karpolo*, which grows in marshes and is picked wild. It is smaller, somewhat sweeter and is used by the Finns to make preserves and some liqueurs. The French *airelle (Vaccinium oxycoccos)* is similar to the Finnish variety yet grows on dry ground.

Two-thirds of American production of cranberries, which totals three million bushels a year, comes from Massachusetts and the rest from Wisconsin and New Jersey. Fresh cranberries should be firm to the point of hardness. To make the sauce, they should be boiled in sugar syrup until they pop, but no longer because further cooking makes them bitter.

CRANBERRY TREE

A deciduous tree, *Viburnum opulus*, of temperate Europe, North America and Asia bears scarlet fruit that makes good jellies. It can be used in place of cranberries. The bark is used medicinally. This plant is also known as the cranberry bush, the European cranberry, the guelder rose and the whitten tree.

CRANE

An ungainly bird that once enjoyed a secure place in the diets of Europe and China, the crane is seldom eaten nowadays except in tropical Africa, where the natives occasionally dine on crown crane *(Balearica pavonina)*. Even in its heyday, only the young bird was considered palatable. The ancient Egyptians were fond enough of the bird to domesticate it and fatten it for the table. The same was true of ancient Romans, who kept them in aviaries and stuffed them like Strasbourg geese. Crane was forbidden to ancient Hebrews, as was the heron, a close look-alike. Europeans of the Middle Ages ate it with gusto. It was prepared in a number of ways, often highly spiced with ginger and mustard or boiled in caramel sauce.

The crane's appearance has contributed a number of vivid images to modern languages. It is a wading bird, with long, sticklike legs, an equally long, thin neck and a hesitating gait. Its name was borrowed to describe a derrick with a long boom. The same process occurred in both French and Spanish, where the words *grue* and *grua* mean both the bird and the machine. In a crowd you can crane your neck to get a better view of something. Apparently the French have noted some similarity between the movements of the hunting crane and the streetwalking prostitute, because they nicknamed the latter *grue*. In Washington Irving's *The Legend of Sleepy Hollow*, the protagonist was a tall, gangly character named Ichabod Crane who was pursued by the headless horseman.

CRANIOLARIA

A plant, *Craniolaria annua*, of the West Indies, its fleshy roots are preserved in sugar and considered a delicacy.

CRAPPIE

This fresh-water food fish, *Pomoxis annularis*, of the sunfish family is native to North America and found in the Great Lakes region south to the Mississippi Valley. About eight inches long, the white crappie (pronounced "croppy") resembles the **perch** in appearance and taste, but has a single, large, spiny dorsal fin. It frequents warm, muddy lakes and sluggish streams and is particularly fond of brush and stumps.

Crappies are bony but are very sweet tasting when lightly fried. The black crappie *(Pomoxis nigromaculatus)* is slightly larger, more like a **bass** in appearance, mottled with dark spots. It is very bony but is also good to eat when fried, though at times it has a muddy taste. Local names include calico bass, strawberry bass and grass bass.

CRAWFISH

See **Crayfish.**

CRAYFISH

Also CRAWFISH. A freshwater crustacean much resembling the lobster, but smaller, it is found in rivers and lakes and eaten, sometimes reluctantly, in many parts of the world. There are two main types, the *Astacus*, found in Europe, Asia and the West Coast of the United States, and the *Cambarus*, which inhabits the eastern and southern United States.

The large crayfish *(Astacus fluviatilis)* runs six to eight inches in length, has large claws and is red in color. The smaller *Astacus pallipes* runs three to four inches in length. During the Middle Ages, crayfish were the only crustacean widely eaten because they, unlike saltwater crustaceans, were found inland where most of the eating was done. The others were eaten only near the seashore due to the spoilage problem. These varieties have been successfully farmed in France where in the 19th century the popularity of crayfish reached the level of a national craze. The American crayfish *(Cambarus affinis)* averages three to four inches in length and is most popular in Louisiana and neighboring areas of Texas, where they are fished more intensively than anywhere else in the world. The season in the United States is September to April.

Crayfish never stop growing, shedding and replacing shells as they get larger, and may reach an age of 30 years. Their flesh is delicately flavored and should be prepared simply, but they may be prepared in any way that lobster is. The French serve it in a bisque, a cold mousse and *au gratin*, while the Swedish enjoy it between swallows of *aquavit*. During the season in Louisiana, fried crayfish are sold in the streets in paper cones.

The **spiny lobster** is erroneously called crayfish in Australia and South Africa.

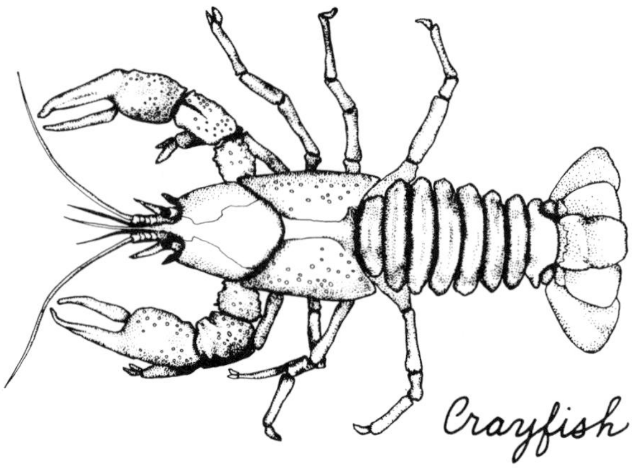
Crayfish

CREAM

Cream is the yellow-tinged part of whole milk that is rich in butterfat and gradually rises to the top. Formerly cream was skimmed from the top of milk left to settle in shallow pans. Fluid skimmed after 12 hours was called cream, while fluid skimmed after 24 hours of settling was called double cream.

Now the cream that most of us buy is not skimmed, but separated in a machine by centrifugal force. Butterfat content of the three official types is: light (for coffee), 18 percent; for medium cream, 30+ percent; and whipping cream, 36 percent.

CREAM CHEESE

This soft, uncured, white cheese is like **cottage cheese** but is much richer because it is made from cream or a mixture of cream and milk. Probably the mildest of all cheese, cream cheese is spread on bread, used as a sandwich filling, put in salads or serves as the principal ingredient of cheesecakes. It is like an unripened *Neufchatel* with a higher fat content. For a discussion of French cream cheeses, see **Carre** and **Fromage a la Creme.**

Processing starts with cream or a homogenized and pasteurized mixture of milk and cream. A lactic acid starter and rennet are added, and when the curd is formed it is heated to facilitate draining of the whey. When drained, the cheese is salted and often flavored with pimento, olives, pineapple or relish. It is usually packed in metal foil for market. Cream cheese must be eaten fresh and is highly perishable.

See also: **Slipcote.**

CREAM NUT

See **Brazil Nut.**

CREAM OF TARTAR

This is a white acid crystal also known as potassium acid tartrate. The principal acid in the crystals acts on sodium bicarbonate to release carbon dioxide gas, hence its use for several generations as a raising agent in breads where yeast is not used. It is an ingredient in certain baking powders for this same reason.

Traditionally cream of tartar has been derived from the tartar contained in wine lees. These are removed from the bottom of a wine barrel, dried and powdered. When the powder is boiled in water and cooled the crystals form on top of the liquid. These are skimmed, redissolved, decolorized and reprecipitated. The term "cream" comes from the way the potassium acid tartarate crystallizes at the top of the liquid. Cream of tartar is also used in some prepared fruit drinks and to stabilize egg whites beaten for an angel food cake.

CREMA DANICA

See **Castello.**

CREME DE CACAO

Here is a popular sweet liqueur with flavor derived from cacao and vanilla beans. It is bottled at 54 to 60 proof, has a strong chocolate taste and is produced either white or brown. The word *Chouao* often appears on the label and refers to a region in Venezuela where the finest cacao beans were once produced. It is served alone or as a cocktail ingredient.

CREME DES BARBADES

See **Barbados Cream.**

CREOLE CHEESE

An American mixture peculiar to Louisiana, it combines fresh, rich cottage cheese with equal portions of rich cream. It is made especially for the New Orleans market.

CREPE

See **Pancake.**

CRESCENT

See **Croissant.**

CRESCENZA

Also CARSENZA. A soft, Italian cow's milk cheese is made in Lombardy from September to April. It is yellow, of the **Bel Paese** type, with a creamy, sweet fast-ripening curd. Crescenza cheeses are ready to eat after only 15 days' curing and weigh between one-half and 3½ pounds.

CRESS

See **Garden Cress.**

CRETAN DITTANY

A pink-flowered dwarf shrub *(Origanum dictamnus)* of the marjoram genus, it is native to the mountains of Greece and Crete. Cretan dittany is aromatic; in former times it was used to flavor treacle and continues to be used as a herbal flavoring for certain liqueurs.

CREUSE

A French farmhouse cheese from the Department of Creuse, it is made from skim milk and is marketed in two forms: aged for a year or two, or fresh. If fresh, it comes in tightly closed, straw-lined containers and has a soft, yellow curd with a pronounced flavor. The cured version is very dry and firm.

CRICKET

This leaping insect, closely related to the locust, is eaten by a number of peoples. There are about 1,400 species worldwide. Crickets have long antennae, and the males produce a characteristic chirping noise by rubbing parts of the forewings together. In the West, this is considered a cheerful sound, and the cricket has often symbolized good luck, quiet and peace. In "Il Penseroso," Milton expressed it thus:

Far from all resort of mirth,
Save the cricket on the hearth.

Elsewhere, crickets are relished as a food, and one of high nutritional value, since they consist of about 50 percent protein. They are usually prepared for cooking as follows: the wings and small legs are removed along with the terminal portion of the hind legs. The head is pulled off, bringing with it any attached viscera.

Crickets are eaten grilled and roasted in Africa and Madegascar, and also ground into flour. Mexicans of Oaxaca state make a venerable dish from a variety called *chapulin*, which they gather in the cornfields. Two United States species, the Morman cricket *(Anabrus simplex)* and the field cricket *(Acheta assimilis)* were eaten by native Americans. Perhaps the best known cricket dish is the Vietnamese *con-de-com*, fried mole crickets. They are mixed with shelled peanuts, fried in lard and served as a condiment.

CROAKER

Also DRUMFISH, MAIGRE. The name applies to several species of food fish of Europe and America that make croaking or grunting noises. Most are members of the *Sciaenidae* family and include the *maigre*, or hardy croaker *(Sciaena aquila)* of the Atlantic seaboards of England and France, the *ombrine (Sciaena cirrosa)* of the Mediterranean and the Atlantic croaker *(Micropogon undulatus)* of the United States Atlantic seaboard south of Cape Cod and of the Gulf coast. Croakers produce their peculiar noises from air bladders, which they squeeze in a rapid rhythm. The sound has been described as croaking, grunting and even drumming. They are a carnivorous fish, inhabiting sandy shores in warm, temperate climates, extending in some cases to the tropics. They make excellent eating and sometimes are sold under the names of better known fish, such as sea bass or sea trout.

The largest of the type is the *maigre* or hardy croaker, which reaches lengths of six and seven feet. It is easy to serve and eat because its flesh, which is mostly white, is free of small bones. The *ombrine* was a favorite fish with the ancient Romans, and is known by a different name in each country (and sometimes district) bordering on the Mediterranean. It can attain a length of 40 inches and a weight of 35 pounds. It is a highly prized food fish. Smaller Mediterranean croakers are the corb *(Sciaena umbra)* and the Canary croaker *(Umbrina canariensis).*

On the American side of the Atlantic, the

Atlantic croaker is a relatively small (12 inches) but important food fish. It is yellow above with dusky and dark brown bars and spots. This fish is a favorite around Baltimore, where it is called the hardhead. The channel bass, or red drum *(Sciaenops ocellatus)*, a close relative of the croaker, inhabits the Atlantic coasts of both North and South America. A Pacific Coast variety is the spotted croaker *(Roncador strearnsii)*, which is regarded as a game fish as well as food fish. The Australian mulloway, or jewfish *(Sciaena antarctica)* is practically identical to the *maigre*.

CROCODILE

Also ALLIGATOR, CAIMAN. This large, lizard-like amphibious reptile is an important source of protein in some parts of Africa and South America. Crocodile is a generic term that includes alligators, caimans and gavials. They range in size from four feet for the South American caimans to 20 feet for the estuarine, or marine, crocodile. There are 24 species worldwide. The tail is considered the best portion of the animal tasting like lobster according to most authorities. At Victoria Falls, Zimbabwe, hotel dining rooms regularly offer such delicacies as crocodile thermidor and crocktail cocktail. Other experts claim many parts of the crocodile are edible and highly prize the feet.

The South American caiman *(Paleosuchus palpebrosus)* is a staple food of some Brazilian Indians. Burmese of the Irrawaddy River delta are great hunters of the marine crocodile *(Crocodylus porosus)* and use a duck as bait to lure it within killing range. Natives of tropical Africa are the greatest crocodile eaters, particularly the pygmies. Alligator tripe is popular in Ethiopia.

Ancient Romans highly prized the tail of the *Crocodilius niloticus* of Egypt, claiming to find in it aphrodisiacal properties. An ancient belief that crocodiles shed tears as they devoured their prey gave birth to the English phrase, "crocodile tears," which means a hypocritical show of grief.

CROISSANT

Also CRESCENT. The croissant is a crescent-shaped roll, especially popular in France for breakfast accompanied by a cup of *cafe au lait*. It is made from puff pastry or a specially leavened bread dough consisting of flour, salt, sugar, yeast, water, milk, either lard or butter and perhaps an egg. In any case, the croissant is very light and is best served with butter and maybe a little jam.

There are two schools of thought on the origin of the crescent roll, both having to do with the Turks, whose flag bears the emblem of the crescent moon. One story traces its birth to Budapest in 1686, when the city was under siege by the Turkish army. Turkish sappers were tunneling under the city walls. Night bakers heard the racket caused by the excavating Turks and raised the hue and cry. The Turkish plan was foiled, and in recognition of their heroic role the city's bakers created the crescent-shaped roll, which became a favorite in Budapest and later in France.

A second, perhaps more believable story, places the emergence of the crescent roll in Vienna in 1683 when that city was threatened by a Turkish invasion. The Viennese bakers created the *kipfel* (their word for crescent) to curry favor with the Turks, whom they soon expected to be masters of the city. Some reverse the story, i.e., the roll was created to symbolize Vienna's finest hour in escaping Turkish domination. Nevertheless, the roll found favor with the aristocracy. A century later when Marie Antoinette, an Austrian princess, married Louis XVI of France, she brought with her the *kipfel* recipe. It was naturalized by French bakers and became France's favorite breakfast roll.

See also: **Bread.**

Croissants

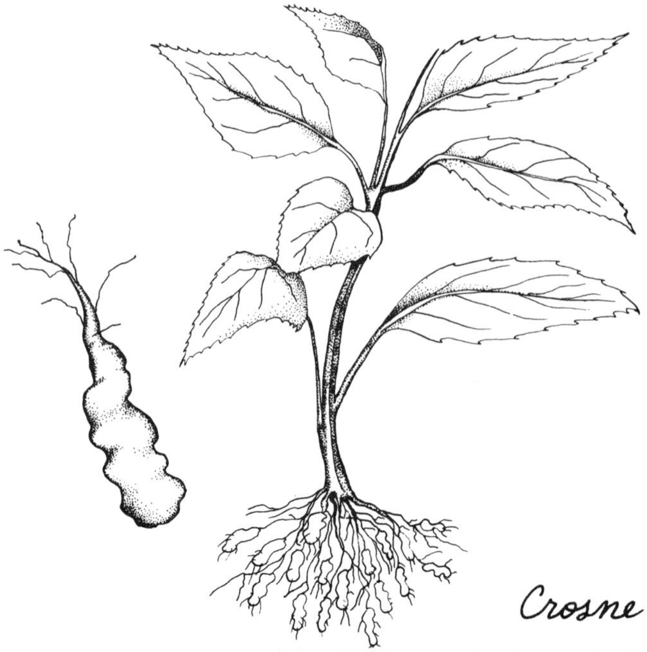

Crosne

CROSNE

Also CHINESE ARTICHOKE, CHOROGI, JAPANESE ARTICHOKE, STACHYS. Sometimes called knotroot, the *crosne* is a perennial plant cultivated for its tubers or underground rhizomes, which have been compared in flavor to the Jeruselem artichoke. The flavor is more delicate, however, and practically nonexistent if the tubers are overcooked. *Crosne (Stachys sieboldi)* is related to the mint family but does not resemble mint in either appearance or taste. It has a curious shape, i.e., like a short string of fat beads, which accounts for the name knotroot.

The *crosne* originated in either China or Japan and appeared in Europe three decades after Commodore Perry's visit to Japan. The vegetable received some acceptance in France and began to be farmed commercially in 1887. It takes its name from the village of Crosnes, not far from Paris, but the center of production seems to have been Sully-sur-Loire. The skin of the *crosne* has a white color when freshly unearthed, but turns brown as it dries out.

Crosnes are soaked to enhance flavor and sometimes peeled before cooking. They are high in carbohydrates, especially sugar, and easily digestible. They have become rare in recent years, even in France, but if a menu item is announced *a la Japonaise*, it is garnished with *crosnes.* They are little known in the United States, but occasionally may be served marinated in French dressing and served with quartered tomatoes and water cress.

CROW

This is a general name for various large, glossy black birds of the genus *Corvus*, family *Corvidae*, and allied genera. They are also called rooks, hooded crow, carrion crow, piping crow and fish crow. In England, rooks are considered a game bird and are shot for sport. In America, their large numbers and hearty appetites cause farmers to shoot them to protect their crops. Sometimes a scarecrow is used instead of a gun.

Crows are not choice eating, but the young birds are more tender and palatable. Cooking them in a bouillon is one recommended method. Crows are one of the few birds to be named in the title of a poem: Edgar Allen Poe's "The Raven," which is *Corvus corax*, a type of crow.

CROWBERRY

Also CRAKEBERRY. This black fruit of a small shrub, *Empetrum nigrum*, grows wild in temperate North America, Europe and Asia. The crowberry has a slightly acid taste and is popular with young people in northern Scotland and northern Russia. In Iceland, the berries are made into a beverage by mixing them with sour milk.

CROWFOOT PLANTAIN

Also BUCKSHORN PLANTAIN. Crowfoot plantain is an herbaceous plant, *Plantago coronopus*, native to Europe, Asia and North Africa. It has been naturalized in Australia and New Zealand as well. Its leaves may be consumed in salads.

CROW GARLIC

Also FIELD GARLIC. This wild species of garlic, *Allium vineale*, is native to Europe but naturalized in the United States. It possesses the requisite aroma and pungency to be substituted for regular garlic, and it is occasionally used as a flavoring ingredient. This plant is also known as stag's garlic.

CROWN OF JAPAN

See **Crosne.**

CRUCIAN

Also CARASSIN. A carplike fish inhabiting lakes and ponds of Central Europe and Asia, the crucian *(Carassium carassius)* has a short, thick body and a deep yellow color. It is smaller than many other members of the carp family and, unlike the carp, does not have barbels on its chin. It is also known as the German carp or Prussian carp, and—by breeding and selection—varieties of this species have become the domestic goldfish. It may be prepared like carp but is usually made into a soup.

CRUCITO

Also TINTERO. Fruit of a woody plant, *Basanacantha armata*, found wild in Central America, crucito is eaten locally in the area of cultivation.

CRULLER

See **Doughnut.**

CRUMPET

An English batter cake, the crumpet is served at breakfast or teatime. As a rule it is bakery-made and consists of unsweetened dough made from flour, eggs, milk, salt, butter and baking powder or yeast. The mixture is poured onto a griddle or baking sheet fitted with small crumpet rings and baked on one side only. When the crumpet is done, its uncooked top is left pierced with many tiny holes.

When served at home, the crumpet is usually toasted, often on the grate of a fireplace. At breakfast, crumpets are toasted, liberally spread with butter or served with jam. Alternatively, they may be toasted and served with a poached egg or bacon on top. The typical crumpet is only one-half inch thick and has a soft, woolly texture. It has been called a blanket soaked in butter.

CRUSTACEANS

The name applies to shellfish closely related to insects, of the phylum *Arthropoda.* Many of them, such as lobsters, prawns, crayfish, crabs and shrimp, are valuable human foods. Crustaceans differ from other shellfish or mollusks by having a hard exterior skeleton (often a shell), segmented bodies and jointed, paired legs. Their flesh is white, firm and close-grained, somewhat sweet and without a fishy taste. The meat of lobsters and shrimp, particularly, contains a high degree of protein.

Two types of lobster are found in American waters, the homard or clawed lobster from Maine and Nova Scotia and the spiny or rock lobster, which prefers warmer temperatures. Both are best served boiled—which produces the bright red color of the shell. Crayfish (or crawfish) are smaller, fresh-water cousins of the lobster. They are sold in large quantities in France, in the Pacific Northwest and in New Orleans. By far the majority of crustaceans consumed in the United States are shrimp, especially the large varieties from the Gulf of Mexico. Also popular are crabs from Alaska and the Pacific Coast. Crustaceans include over 25,000 separate species and range in size from minute water fleas and barnacles to giant land crabs with leg spans of nine to 10 feet. A major caveat in their preparation as food is never to overcook.

CUBEB

Cubeb is the dried berry of a vinelike shrub of the pepper family, *Piper cubeba,* whose spicy flavor combines elements of both black pepper and allspice. It is native to Java, Sumatra and Borneo but is also grown in Sri Lanka, Africa and the West Indies. Nothing is known about the use of cubeb in antiquity, but Arab traders brought it to Europe during the Middle Ages, and it was widely used as a spice there through the Renaissance. Cubeb has a pleasant aroma and a pungent taste, which is acrid and slightly bitter. It contains an essential oil (about 15 percent by weight), which is light green in color. From this is made a solid substance called cubeb camphor.

In the West, cubeb has fallen into disuse as a seasoning agent but is still credited with medicinal properties. It is thought to be a remedy for catarrh and asthma, and during the 19th century the dried berries were rolled into cigarettes and smoked to relieve those conditions. It is a diuretic and rubifacient and was formerly used in treating diseases of the urinary tract. Cubeb has long had a reputation as an aphrodisiac, especially among Arabs and East Indians.

The name "cubeb" comes from the Arabic word, *kubbabab.* They brought it also to Africa, where it is still frequently used as a spice. Should you run across it in a recipe and wish to approximate its taste, try mixing in equal portions of black pepper and allspice.

CUCHIA

An Indian eel, *Monopterus cuchia,* it is an important food fish in the states of Bengal, Orissa, the Punjab and Assam. It is also found in Burma. *Cuchia* reaches a length of 28 inches and is dull green with yellowish spots. The *cuchia* inhabits rivers, swamps, ditches and lagoons.

CUCKOO

This is a songbird about the size of a small pigeon that is found in most temperate and tropical regions. There are many genera, but the most common species are the European cuckoo *(Cuculus canorus)* and the American yellow-billed cuckoo *(Coccyzus americanus).* Like many other songbirds, the cuckoo is considered a delicacy in parts of France and in other Mediterranean countries. It may be roasted or grilled whole and served on a crouton or boned and then stuffed.

The cuckoo is well known for its habit of placing its eggs in the nests of other birds. By extension, a man whose wife commits adultery is said to have been cuckolded. About the cuckoo, Shakespeare wrote in *Love's Labour's Lost:*

> *The cuckoo then, on every tree*
> *Mocks married men; for thus sings he, Cuckoo!*
> *Cuckoo! Cuckoo! O word of fear,*
> *Unpleasing to the married ear.*

CUCUMBER

The cucumber *(Cucumis sativa)* is an annual herbaceous plant, closely related to the watermelon, that requires lots of hot weather to thrive. It does well in temperate climates provided the summers are hot. The fruit is a large, long berry with tough, dark green skin and rounded ends.

This refreshing vegetable, noted for its cooling qualities, is one of the oldest cultivated plants. Recent carbon datings point to its cultivation as early as 9750 B.C. and to its origin in Thailand, rather than in India as earlier supposed. Reports of cucumbers are as old as history. They were grown throughout Mesopotamia and were represented in the hanging gardens of Babylon. The Hebrews were fond of them as were the ancient Romans. The Emperors Augustus and Tiberius found them so refreshing that they obliged the imperial gardeners to grow them year around, which necessitated their devising a method of hothouse cultivation. Other monarchs, including Charlemagne and Louis XIV, were passionately fond of them. Their cultivation spread to England in the 14th century and to Germany in the 16th century. The Spaniards eventually took them to the New World, where they were adopted by the Pueblo.

In spite of their age, they have not received much veneration in print. For example, Dr. Samuel Johnson had this to say, "A cucumber should be well sliced and dressed with pepper and vinegar, and then thrown out as good for nothing." He exaggerated, of course, yet he came close to the truth for, nutritionally speaking, the cucumber's value is next to nil. It is mostly water with tiny amounts of protein, carbohydrate and minerals. It is rich in vitamins A and C, provided you don't peel it. The small amounts of sulfur in cucumber are reputedly good for the complexion, hair and fingernails, so that quite a few beauty products are based on cucumber.

Very young cucumbers are most often used for pickling, although the mature fruit is also suitable. Fresh cucumbers are usually eaten slightly unripe and raw, although in some Slavic countries they are cooked with meat dishes.

CUCUMBER TREE

Also BILIMBI. This tree of tropical Asia, *Averrhoa bilimbi*, has green yellow fruit somewhat resembling a cucumber. It averages two to four inches in length and is five-angled. The pulp is acid-tasting and is generally not eaten raw but used for drinks, marmalade, jellies and syrups. It is also candied and pickled. The cucumber tree's fruit is closely related to the **carambola,** a more palatable fruit. This species is believed to have its origin in Malaysia, but it has been naturalized in other tropical areas, such as South America.

In the United States the *Magnolia acuminata* is also called cucumber tree because of its purplish red fruit that resembles the cucumber in shape. This tree reaches 100 feet in height and grows well in the Southeast.

Cucumbers

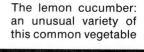

The lemon cucumber: an unusual variety of this common vegetable

CUDRANIA

Fruit of a genus of spiny trees found in Asia from China to Australia, the *Cudrania tricuspidata* bears round, orange red, multiple fruits that may be eaten fresh or preserved. Two other edible species are *C. javanensis* and *C. triloba*. In China *cudrania* leaves are fed to silkworms.

CUITLACOCHE

Also HUITLACOCHE. Cuitlacoche consists of galls or tumors obtained from an ear of corn afflicted with corn smut. They are considered a great delicacy in Mexico and are used to flavor typical dishes, such as *quesadillas*. Corn smut is a plant disease caused by the fungus *Ustilago maydis*, which is regarded as a serious pest in the United States. Microscopic spores invade grains of corn while on the stalk, and eventually swell up into large, gray galls or tumors. When ripe, these tumors burst and are seen to be full of black dust, which are the fungus spores. In Mexico, they are picked unripe and cooked, producing a black fluid that reportedly has a delicious mushroom flavor. The name derives from the Aztec words *cuitlatl* ("waste") and *cochi* ("black"). The tumors are considered poisonous when ripe.

CULRAGE

A pepper plant, *Polygonum hydropiper*, of the knot weed genus native to the United States, it grows in damp or boggy places.

CULTUS COD

See **Lingcod.**

CUMIN

An herb of ancient vintage, cumin *(Cuminum cyminum)* bears a fruit remarkable at once for its powerful aromatic flavor and tiny size. Thus in Spanish something of no importance is likened to a *comino*, or cumin seed. It is mentioned in the Bible and probably reached its heyday of domestic use in Europe during the Middle Ages, when it was important in German cooking and baking.

Despite its obscurity in United States and European kitchens, it is quite popular in Latin America, the Balkans and in oriental cooking. Commercially, cumin is a staple flavoring agent in curry powder, chili powder, chutney, sausages, and in cheeses, meats and pickling solutions. It is a versatile culinary herb and can be used to enhance the flavor of soups, stews, rice dishes and bread.

CUMQUAT

See **Kumquat.**

CUNNER

Also BLUE PERCH, BURGALL. This small food fish is found on both sides of the Atlantic. The European cunner is *Crenilabrus melops*. It has real gastronomic merit and may be prepared like smelt. The American species, *Tautolabrus adspersus*, is caught from Labrador to New Jersey. It is very good to eat.

Both species are members of the wrasse family. The American variety is known by sundry other names, such as American blue perch, the chogset, the nipper and the sea perch.

CUNNINGHAM PLUM

This orange red fruit of a small Australian tree, *Diploglottis cunninghamii*, has a pleasant, subacidic flavor and is mostly used for preserves.

CURACAO

A fruit liqueur made in France and Amsterdam, Curacao is orange colored and orange flavored, 50 to 60 proof, and spiced. Its main flavor is imparted by the dried, bitter peel of the Curacao orange from Curacao Island in the Netherlands Antilles.

Grand Marnier, Cointreau and **Triple Sec** are based on Curacao. Such liqueurs are used as after dinner drinks and are believed to aid digestion.

CURASSOW

Named for the Caribbean island of Curacao, it is a turkeylike bird native to Central and South America. The name covers several species belonging to the *Crax* and *Pauxi* genera. One of the better known is the crested curassow *(Crax alector)*, which is found in Guyana, Mexico and Brazil. Many others are found from Mexico to Paraguay, but only east of the Andes. It is considered the finest game bird of South America, and in many places it has been domesticated.

The curassow is short-legged, heavy and has a short bill. The bird has abundant white flesh, much like the turkey, and its diet of berries and insects insures a palatable flavor.

CURATELLA PLUM

This is the fruit of a tropical African tree *Parinarium curatellafolium*. It is well liked in the area of cultivation.

CURCUMA

Also EAST INDIAN ARROWROOT, ZEDOARY. This is a genus of tropical Asian herbs valuable for their tuberous rhizomes. The best known is *C. domestica* or **turmeric,** widely used as a spice and a yellow coloring agent in food, especially in mustard and curry powder. Two other species, East Indian arrowroot *(C. angustifolia)* and zedoary *(C. pallida)*, are cultivated in India, Ceylon and south China. Their rhizomes are used to produce an easily digestible starch, which, though not utilized industrially, is of local importance as a food thickener and as pablum for invalids and infants.

CURCUMA OIL

See **Turmeric.**

CURING

See **Preservation of Food.**

CURLEW

This shore bird is related to the woodcock, sandpiper and plover. There are many species native to Europe and North America, the commonest being the Eurasian curlew *(Numenius arquata)*. Formerly, it was widely regarded as a game bird, and its flesh is considered excellent eating, provided its diet consists of berries, grubs and insects, rather than sealife such as mollusks.

Nowadays the number of curlews is much reduced, and the only place it is commercially available is in the Polesina region of Italy, south of Venice. There, unfortunately, the curlew has a fishy taste due to its diet of small crustaceans, mollusks and seaweed. The name of the bird is onomatopeic, deriving from one of its calls, a loud, clear "curl-e-e-e-u-u-u."

The eskimo curlew was once one of the most plentiful game birds in the United States and considered second only to the passenger pigeon as a table delicacy. They were generally killed at the beginning of their migratory journey south when they were at their fattest. They earned the nickname "dough-birds" because their skin was so taut with fat that it would explode on being shot. Another, more effective method of hunting, was called "fire-lighting." A bonfire would be built on the beach near their nesting grounds. Attracted to the light, they would be killed by the thousands. Once considered inexhaustibly numerous, the eskimo curlew, along with the passenger pigeon, became extinct by the end of the 19th century.

Curlew

CURLY CHICORY

See **Endive.**

CURRANT

Currants are berries of the *Ribes* genus of the *saxifrage* family, of which there are many species. The two most common edible types are the red currant and the black currant, which resembles the **gooseberry.** They share the name "currant" with a seedless raisin that has been grown in Greece since ancient times and exported principally from the town of Corinth. "Currant" is a corruption of "Corinth." (For more about raisin currants, see **Raisin.)**

The red currant *(R. rubrum)* is a shrub native to northern Europe and Asia. Its semitransparent berries range in color from red through yellow to white. Its taste is pleasantly sour, and while part of the crop is eaten fresh, most is used commercially to prepare jelly, preserves, syrup and currant wine. A famous red currant jam comes from Bar-le-Duc, France and is a frequent accompaniment to roast mutton, lamb, hare and venison.

The black currant *(R. nigrum)* is somewhat bitter and is less often eaten fresh than the red, except perhaps in England. It is reputed to have some therapeutic value against sore throat, and black currant lozenges are available for that purpose. It is cultivated heavily in France near Dijon, where it is used to prepare the famous liqueur Cassis.

Cultivation of currants has been discouraged for many years in the United States because it serves as an intermediate host for the fungus *Cronartium ribacola*, which causes white pine rust. At one time this pest destroyed 650 million board feet of white pine yearly. Currants, especially the black variety, are rich in vitamin C.

CURRY

This word is used in cookery for two different, but related, items. First, it is a condiment in powder form, originally from India, made up of curry leaves, garlic, pepper, ginger, yellow turmeric and other spices. Second, it is the fish, meat, eggs or vegetables that make up the dish to be curried. In India, curry powder is not usually bought as a blend. Indian cooks blend their own, so the strength and flavor of curry as a dish is subject to almost infinite variations.

In America, curry powders are bought already blended. While nothing can be subtracted, additions may be made. Curry powder is increasing in popularity, not just for curries but to flavor chicken, lamb, veal, rice and other dishes.

CURRY LEAF

The strong-smelling leaf of a small tree, *Murraya koenigii*, native to southern India and Ceylon, curry leaf has a pungent flavor and is a standard ingredient in curries in the area where the tree is found.

CURUBA

A species of passion fruit *Passiflora mollissima* native to the American tropics from Venezuela to Bolivia and naturalized in Mexico, *curuba* is yellow and oblong and somewhat resembles a banana. It is also known as banana passion fruit. A related species, the *curuba de tasco*, is cultivated in Ecuador and Colombia where the fruit is eaten raw or used to make drinks, ice creams and sherbets.

See also: **Passion Fruit.**

CUSCUS

A tree-dwelling mammal of New Guinea, the Celebes and adjacent islands and tropical eastern Australia, the *cuscus (Phalanger maculatus)* is related to the koala and somewhat resembles the American opossum. It has a heavy, powerful body and a large specimen might reach a length of 30 inches. The *cuscus* is highly prized as food by natives of New Guinea.

CUSK

A large ocean fish found on both sides of the North Atlantic, the cusk *(Bromius brosme)* is similar to the cod but larger, and its flesh is coarser. It is sold fresh or salted. The cusk may be broiled, baked or steamed or prepared in any way suitable for cod. The **cod burbot** is also known as the freshwater cusk.

CUSTARD

This is a mixture of eggs, milk and flavoring agents sweetened according to taste and cooked either soft or hard. Soft custard is cooked in a double boiler until the mixture coats a metal spoon. It may be used as a sauce, e.g., poured over strawberries, or mixed with fruit and spongecake, a dessert the English call "trifle." Hard custard is baked in an oven and has a gelatinous consistency. It is variously flavored and is used mostly as a pudding dessert as in caramel custard, which is flavored with vanilla and baked with a caramel topping. Other favorite flavorings are apricot, chocolate, coconut, coffee and macaroon. Unsweetened custard may be used in a savory main dish, such as quiche Lorraine.

CUSTARD APPLE

See **Bullock's Heart.**

CUSTARD MARROW

See **Chayote.**

CUSTARD SQUASH

See **Chayote.**

CUTTLEBONE

See **Cuttlefish.**

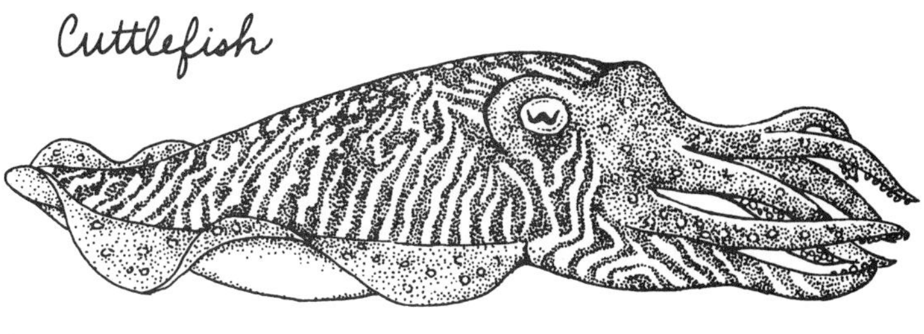

CUTTLEFISH

Also CUTTLE. This small marine animal, which is not really a fish but a mollusk, much resembles the squid and more distantly, the octopus. Growing to a length of six to 10 inches, it has a broad head, two distinctive eyes and 10 suckered tentacles. Behind the head is an oval-shaped body supported by an internal shell that is calcified. Cuttlefish are a popular food in Spain, Italy, Greece, Japan as well as in India, Malaysia, China and the Pacific Islands. They are plentiful in the British Isles and the United States, but are generally spurned as food, except by immigrants from southern Europe and Japan or their descendants. There is no culinary enthusiasm for them in France or Germany, either. This was not always so. In 13th-century France, a variety caught in Normandy figured in a list of preferred fish.

The tradition in southern Europe is much longer and stronger. The ancient Romans considered it an aphrodisiac. According to legend, Diogenes, an ancient Greek, died while trying to eat a raw inkfish. Diogenes' distress is understandable because the flesh of inkfish, including cuttlefish, is very tough and must be thoroughly pounded with a mallet and then cooked before being palatable. Cuttlefish was not specified in the legend, but like the octopus, cuttlefish propel themselves away from the scene of trouble by squirting water liberally laced with ink through a narrow tube.

The European cuttlefish *(Sepia officinalis)* is the most common in the Mediterranean. Its color varies, but it usually has brown stripes. The smaller *Sepia rondeleti* is also eaten. The Japanese are fond of the pygmy cuttlefish *(Idiosepius paradoxus)*, which rarely exceeds three-quarters of an inch. The cuttlefish is frequently prepared in its own ink.

Cuttlefish ink is used to make sepia pigment for water colors. Its shell, called cuttlebone, is marketed in pet stores as a beak sharpener for canaries.

CYMBIDIUM

A member of the orchid family, this variety of cymbidium *(Cymbidium virescens)* is found in Japan and China. The flowers are white or greenish white with purple blotches. In Japan, they are eaten after salting or preserving in plum vinegar, or they may be infused in hot water and the result drunk as a hot beverage.

CYMLING

Also PATTYPAN. This variety of summer squash *(Cucurbita pepo* var. *melopepo)* has the shape of a flattened disk with ribbed sides and scalloped edges. Large specimens reach nine inches in diameter and 3½ inches in height. It is white and thin-skinned. The cymling is often baked or boiled, mashed with butter and usually cooked without being peeled.

CYNAR

Cynar is an Italian wine aperitif, whose name and principal flavor are derived from the artichoke. The ancient Romans, who called the artichoke *cynara*, believed it to have properties that keep the liver young. It remained for a modern Italian, Angelo dalle Molle, to combine this beneficial ingredient with wine to produce a drink that now rivals **vermouth** in popularity in his native country.

CYNOMORIUM

This is a North African shrub, *Cynmorium coccineum*, whose roots are ground in to a powder and used as a condiment.

CYPRUS WINES

See **Wines, Cyprian.**

D

DAB

This small flatfish is the tastiest member of the flounder family, edging out the **plaice** and the summer and winter flounders. The dab is a small saltwater fish found in both the Atlantic and Pacific Oceans. It has adapted to living on the bottom of the sea, has eyes placed on its upper (right) side and is light brown with small dark spots. Its blind (down) side is white. The European dab *(Limanda limanda)* reaches a length of between eight and 12 inches and is more oval in shape than the **sole.** Each side has a thick layer of meat that is free from bones, white, rather soft and easily digested. The flavor is distinctively sweet, not oily. It may be cooked like plaice or sole.

American dabs are similar but not identical to the European. On the Pacific Coast the Alaska dab is considered best, while the rusty dab *(L. ferruginea)* and sand dab *(Hippoglossoides platessoides)* are the pick of Eastern dabs. The latter is the largest of the three.

See also: **Flounder.**

DACE

A European freshwater fish, *Leuciscus leuciscus*, held in low esteem as a food, the dace is a small fish whose name derives from the Old French word *dars*, for "dart," after its diminutive size and dartlike movement. The flesh is tough, coarse and rather tasteless and is most popular in France. It is used mainly for soups and *matelots*, but it may be fried, broiled or baked whole.

The American dace is more highly regarded as food. The name refers to several species of carplike fish, the best known are the dace *(Rhinichthys astronasis)* and the horned dace *(Semotilus atromaculatus)*. They may be prepared like **smelt.**

DADAK

A tree of the breadfruit genus, *Artocarpus dadak*, is found in Sumatra and Java. Its fruit, however, are small, no larger than hens' eggs. The pulp is acidulous and used mostly for making jellies.

DAHLIA

A plant of the *Compositae* family characterized by bright, showy flowers and tuberous roots, the dahlia is native to Mexico and Central America. It is widely cultivated as an ornamental. The roots, however, are edible and are similar in taste to the **Jerusalem artichoke.** The petals are sometimes used to decorate salads, but they have no taste.

DAHOMEY OLIVEPLANT

A shrub, *Solanum olivare* of West Africa and the Congo region, its fruit is eaten locally.

DAHURIAN LADYBELL

Dahurian ladybell is a perennial herb, *Adenophora triphylla*, of Japan, Taiwan and China. Its tuberous roots may be cooked and eaten as a vegetable.

DAIKON

See **Radish.**

DAING

This dried, salted fish is native to the waters of the Philippine Islands. The first Westerners to taste it were the crew members of Fernando Magellan's fleet in 1521 on its round-the-world voyage of 1519–1522.

DAISY

The daisy is a common plant and field flower, *Bellis perrenis.* Daisy blossoms consist of a yellow disk surrounded by white or pink rays. The leaves and buds may be eaten in salads. In former times in England, the flower heads were candied. A related species is the *Chrysanthemum frutescens* or marguerite.

DAKOTA POTATO

See **Ground Nut.**

D'AMBERT

See **Forez.**

DAMBOSE

This is a kind of sugar obtained from dambonite, which is itself a white crystalline substance derived from the latex of the *n'dambo* tree native to the Gabon River area of West Africa. The percentage of dambonite is small in the latex, which otherwise is used to make India rubber.

DAMEN CHEESE

Also GLOIRE DES MONTAGNES. A cheese fit for the ladies, according to its name, it is soft, uncured, with a mild flavor and made from cow's milk in Hungary and Austria.

DAMIANO

Also LICOR DAMIANO. This is liqueur made in Baja California and flavored with leaves and flowers of the plant *Turnera aphrodisiaca.* It is sometimes used in the Margarita cocktail in place of triple sec or is taken as an aperitif. This liqueur is reputed to have aphrodisiac properties.

DAMSON

See **Plum.**

DANDELION

Also COW PARSNIP. The familiar wild plant, *Taraxacum officinale,*—some would say weed—has a single yellow flower, deeply notched leaves and a perennial, milky root. The dandelion is considered by many to be a delectable spring green. The leaves, which have a slightly bitter taste, are served raw in mixed salads or cooked in any manner suitable for spinach. The word "dandelion" is probably an anglicized form of the French name, *dents de lion,* or lion's teeth, a reference to the notched leaves. The French also commonly call it *pissenlit* ("pee in bed") because of the unpleasant milky substance the oozes from the stem when it is plucked.

Dandelions are also cultivated. The French heap earth up around the plant to blanch the leaves, which tends to soften the texture and reduce the bitterness in the flavor. Other parts of the plant are edible too, including the flower buds, which when fried in butter taste like mushrooms; the petals of opened flower, which may be sprinkled on salads; the crowns of the leaves in very early spring, and the long taproot, which has been compared favorably with parsnips and salsify. The root tends to be too bitter during the summer, and should be gathered only in spring or after the first frost of autumn. In certain parts of Europe, the ground, roasted root is used to adulterate coffee or even substituted for it altogether. It tastes much like coffee but lacks caffeine.

The dandelion is similar to **chicory** in food value and caloric content (13 per 3½ ounces [100 grams]). It is rich in vitamins A and C and contains smaller amounts of vitamins B and E, plus calcium, potassium, iron, magnesium and phosphorus. Protein and carbohydrate are each about 1 percent. Medicinally it is known for its diuretic properties. Dandelion juice is reputed to be beneficial for the complexion, banishing splotches, freckles and even warts.

Petals of the flower are made into dandelion wine and the leaves into tea. In French, the expression "to eat dandelions by the roots" is the equivalent of the English phrase, "to push up daisies."

DANISH EXPORT CHEESE

Made from a mixture of buttermilk and skim milk, Danish export is small, flat and round about the size of a **Gouda,** It takes about five weeks to ripen.

DANUBE BLEAK

Also SHEMAIA. A shoaling fish of the carp family, *Chalcalburnus chalcoides,* it is found in the Danube and other rivers flowing into the Black Sea, Sea of Azov, the Caspian and the Aral Sea. It is a migratory fish that is netted during the spawning migration when it is at its fattest. The Danube bleak reaches a maximum length of about 12 inches. The fish is generally cured before eating and is considered a table delicacy. The range of this fish also includes parts of Iran and the basins of the Tigris and Euphrates Rivers.

DANZIGER GOLDWASSER

A liqueur containing flecks of gold leaf in suspension that swirl about colorfully when the liquid is shaken or poured, Goldwasser was originally made in the old port city of Danzig (now Gdansk), but has been copied elsewhere. The best is made in Germany.

Goldwasser is bottled at 80 proof. It is clear in color (apart from the gold) and is flavored predominantly with orange peel, with anise and other spicy herbs. The taste is sweet.

Goldwasser dates from the days when gold was thought to be a cure-all. Its presence in liqueur is natural since liqueurs were originally concocted for medicinal purposes. The gold leaf is tasteless and today is considered a harmless novelty.

DARALAG

See **Bgug-Panir.**

DARJEELING TEA

This black tea is grown in the foothills of the Himalayas at altitudes of 7,000 feet or more. Named for the district in which it grows, Darjeeling is considered by many to be the finest Indian tea. It is slow-brewing, has a rich, red color and a rich, rather fruity taste reminiscent of muscatel. It is full-bodied and leaves a pleasant aftertaste. Because of its distinction, it is used in many blended teas, particularly in the American market.

See also: **Tea.**

DARLING PLUM

Also RED IRONWOOD. This fruit of a shrubby tree, *Eugenia confusa*, native to the Bahamas and southern Florida, is very small, pleasant tasting and purple to black.

DART

Also LADYFISH, MOONFISH, SWALLOW-TAIL. A food fish of the Indian and Pacific Oceans, the dart *(Trachinotus russelli)* is a member of the *Carangidae* family, which includes the jacks, scads and pompanos. Like the pompano, it is deep-bodied but flattened from side to side. It attains a length of about two feet and is considered a good sportfish by anglers. Its flesh is rated moderately good eating. The dart has a dark blue back, silver sides and white belly. It is closely related to the ***permit*** and the ***palometa.***

DARUM

Also MAHUA SPIRITS. A distilled liquor is made from the flowers of the *mahwa* or Indian butter tree *(Bassia latifolia)* in India. The tree grows especially well in Bengal but is also found in appreciable quantities in Africa and the Malay Peninsula. In addition to making up the mash for darum, the creamy white flower petals are eaten fresh and dried. The former is reputed to be highly intoxicating and has an offensive odor. Despite the odor, it is quite popular because it is so very cheap.

DASHEEN

See **Taro.**

DATE

The sweet, fleshy fruit of the date palm, *Phoenix dactylifera*, which is perhaps the oldest cultivated plant, the date is shaped somewhat like a long olive, and varies in color when mature from tan to a darker brownish yellow. The color depends on the type of date and the degree of curing.

Authorities differ on where the date palm originated, some saying Africa, others the northern shore of the Persian Gulf.

The date palm grows wild in the Middle East, but early on humans found it necessary to improve yields through cultivation. Date palms are either male or female, and in the wild pollen is distributed by the wind, since no insect has been induced to perform this service. The Arabs learned to do this by hand, which enabled them to reduce the ratio of bearing trees (females) to nonbearing trees (males) from 50–50 to 50–1. Archeological data shows that this began in the Stone Age, somewhere between 50,000 and 10,000 B.C. There are records of date cultivation in Mesopotamia beginning in 3,000 B.C. and indications that it began in India and North Africa as early as 2,000 B.C. In Mesopotamia, date palms grew along the banks of irrigation canals and were so productive that dates were cheaper than grain. Dates became the staple food of the poor, and grain-based beer was replaced by date wine as the popular drink.

Xenophon, the Greek general and historian who participated in a military expedition to Persia in the 4th century B.C. sampled Middle Eastern dates and recorded these observations, "Their color was just like amber, and the Babylonian villagers dried them and kept them as sweets."

Dates were well known in Europe during medieval times and later but were very expensive. The price did not come within the reach of the average

Date palms

person until after 1830 when the French conquered Algeria. Cultivation in California did not begin until around 1902.

Dates grow most prolifically in Iraq, which is the world's largest exporter. They are raised commercially in a belt of hotlands extending from northern India, through southwestern Asia and North Africa to the Canary Islands. The trees grow readily outside this belt, but the fruit does not ripen because the crucial climatic variables are lacking. From April through September, dates need a constant temperature above 70° F (21.1° C), preferably much higher, with no hint of atmospheric humidity. In addition, they need water at the roots, which means either irrigation or an oasis situation. In Europe these conditions are present only in southeastern Spain, near Alicante, and the United States only in the low deserts of California and Arizona. The vast majority of U.S. dates are grown in the Coachella Valley, near Indio, California, where the summer temperatures hover between 100° and 120° F (37.8° and 49° C) at 20 feet below sea level.

Dates are grouped into two commercial categories: sweet and semi-sweet moist dates, and dry dates. The choicest in the first category are large and soft but not sticky. This is the kind packed for export and also the sort selected for transplantation in California and Arizona. An example is the Deglet Noor date of the Algerian Sahara. The semi-sweet soft date is most often eaten fresh near its place of origin. The dry date is the indispensable staple food of many Arab countries. Grown mostly in North Africa, they have good keeping qualities. Pressed whole into blocks, or ground into flour, they can be kept for a year or more under the right conditions. Regardless of category, each date contains a single hard seed that is deeply grooved on one side.

The date is a wholesome food and one of the most complete. It is 65 to 70 percent carbohydrate by weight, mostly sucrose and dextrose. In addition, the date contains abundant mineral salts, vitamins A, B, C and D, and fiber for roughage. Calorie content is about 300 per 3½ ounces (100 grams), roughly equivalent to that of a small steak. Date protein is not complete, but when supplemented by complete protein, such as that contained in milk, the date is considered a sustaining diet.

The juice of dates is extracted in various ways to make date honey, which may be used as a packing medium for fancy fruit or fermented and drunk as palm wine. The latter may also be made from the fermented sap of the palm tree, in which case it is called "toddy."

The tree itself has been put to a multitude of uses. Huts are built from the stems and leaves, the fiber in the latter is made into baskets, ropes, hats and mats. The wood of the tree is used for fuel. It is at the very top of the tree, where new leaf shoots are born, that the sap for toddy is tapped. This part also houses the terminal bud, which is called "heart" or "cabbage." Removing this causes the death of the tree, so that it is not usually harvested until a tree is past its bearing prime, i.e., after it is past 80 or 100 years of age.

DATE PLUM

Also LOTUS PERSIMMON. A date-sized fruit of the persimmon genus, *Diospyros lotus*, found in west Asia, China and Japan, the date plum is yellow turning black when ripe. It is eaten fresh, dried or overripe. The tree is often used for grafting stock for the *kaki*.

See also: **Persimmon.**

DATE SHELL

Also DATTE DE MER. This edible mollusk, a bivalve of the *Lithdomus* genus, whose shell is shaped like a date, is similar to the mussel.

DATTE DE MER

See **Date Shell.**

DAUCUS

An annual herb of the Mediterranean region, *Daucus muricata*, has spiny fruit whose seeds are used in the preparation of some liqueurs. This plant is closely related to the carrot *(Daucus carota* var. *sativum).*

DAUPHINE WINES

See **Wines, French.**

DAURADE

See **Bream.**

DEEP ROCK WATER

A bulk drinking water sold in recyclable glass containers and distributed in Southern California. It has a high mineral content when compared to nine other bulk waters (600 ppm of total dissolved solids). A 1980 Consumers Union sensory panel rated the taste of this water as excellent (inferior only to New York City tap water) with no sensory defects. Bulk waters are sold as alternatives to tap water.

See also: **Mineral Water.**

DEEP-SEA TREVALLE

A medium-sized, ocean fish of the cooler waters of the Southern Hemisphere, *Hyperoglyphe antarctica* is caught off Tristan da Cunha, South Africa, southern Australia and New Zealand. The deep-sea trevalle reaches a maximum length of about 4½ feet. It is a member of the blackfish family *Centrolophidae* with a large mouth and steel-blue coloring above shading lighter below. Its taste is described as delicious, and the species is considered an untapped food source. A closely related species, *H. japonicus*, is just now beginning to be intensively fished. It is found in the North Pacific.

See also: **Blackfish.**

DEER

Also VENISON. The name includes any one of a number of four-legged ruminants that belong to the family *Cervidae*, such as the red deer of Europe, the white-tailed deer of North America, reindeer, elk and moose. Their flesh is called venison. Humans have hunted deer since prehistoric times.

For centuries a favorite pasttime of the European aristocracy was hunting deer on horseback. Many of the customs and rites of the hunt date back to the ancient Gauls of pre-Roman France. The chase was introduced into England after the Norman conquest. Stag hunting on horseback behind a pack of hounds reached its peak in the Middle Ages and ceased to change much in form or content after the age of Elizabeth I.

Early settlers of North America remarked on the abundance of the white-tailed deer, of which there are about 20 species. Native Americans had been hunting them for centuries without threatening their existence, yet less than 100 years after the arrival of the Pilgrims, the colonies had to place restrictions on deer hunting to ensure the survival of the species.

Although venison has lost its role as a staple item in the modern diet, deer is still the most readily available form of game in many parts of the world. Stone-age cultures, such as the Tasaday of the Philippines, who trap the midget deer, still rely on it as the major source of meat. It is also the principal fare in Arctic regions such as Lapland, where herding reindeer is the main occupation.

Deers are antlered and have a coat of fur that ranges in color from reddish brown to gray above and white on the belly. They are noted for their grace and speed. As a rule, deers are at least five years old before being taken for food, as young deer meat tends to be rather tasteless. A male deer is called a buck and is best as food from May to September. The female is called a doe, and is at its peak from September to December. Venison is usually hung for a short period of time before being cooked to improve flavor and tenderness.

In temperate Europe the principal deer are the roe deer, the fallow deer and the red deer, and are preferred as venison in that order. As hunting prey, the red deer has the richest history and ritual. Its terminology is more elaborate, the male being called a stag or hart, and the female a doe or hind.

About one million deer are killed each year by hunters in the United States, a kill rate that maintains the total deer population at about six million. Very little of this venison, however, finds its way into meat markets.

See also: **Moose, Reindeer.**

DEERBERRY

Also SQUAW HUCKLEBERRY. Two species of *Vaccinium* are called deerberry: *V. caesium*, a two- to three-foot shrub bearing dark blue berries, and *V. stamineum*, a shrub reaching 10 feet in height and bearing green, blue or purple berries. Both are found in the eastern United States from Massachusetts to Florida. Like blueberries, these are rather tart when fresh and are often made into jams or pies.

DEER PARK SPARKLING WATER

A mineral spring water carbonated and bottled in the United States, Deer Park is low in mineral content. A 1980 Consumers Union sensory panel rated the taste of this water as fair with the following qualifying comments: mildly bitter, mildly sour, mild bitter aftertaste, mild chemical flavor.

See also: **Mineral Water.**

DEER PARK WATER

A still spring water bottled in plastic containers for bulk drinking in the United States, it has a relatively low mineral content. A 1980 Consumers Union sensory panel rated the taste of this water as good with the following qualifications: distinctly plastic flavor and heavy, thick mouthfeel.

See also: **Mineral Water.**

DELAWARE WINE

This is a North American red grape wine. The Delaware grape is a hybrid of *Vitis labrusca* and *Vitis vinifera*. It originated in the garden of Paul H. Provost, a Swiss vineyardist of Frenchtown, New Jersey, where it was found after Provost moved away, about 1850. It was then brought to public notice by A. Thompson of Delaware, Ohio in 1855. The grape makes a dark red, full-bodied wine. Like most *labrusca* wines, much sweetening needs to be added to make it palatable, although it serves well as an aperitif or "late afternoon wine."

DELFT

A Dutch cheese made from partly skimmed cow's milk with spices added, it is similar to **Leyden.**

DEMARARA RUM

See **Rum.**

DEMI-GLACE

See **Half-Glaze Sauce.**

DEMISEL

See **CARRE.**

DENDE OIL

See **Palm Oil.**

DENTEX

Also DENTICE. A saltwater fish of the *Sparidae* family, related to the sea bream and the gilthead, it is found in the Mediterranean Sea, most often off the coast of Italy where it is known as *dentice*. Its exterior is gray, but its flesh is firm and white. The dentex is highly regarded as food, expecially in Italy where it is usually roasted or baked.

DEPPEI

A variety of wood sorrel, *Oxalis deppei*, native to Mexico, its pleasantly acidulous leaves are eaten as boiled greens. Its tender, juicy but largely tasteless roots are also edible. It attains a length of four inches and is usually added to stews. *Deppei* is also known as good luck leaf, good luck plant and lucky clover because it looks like four-leaf clover.

DERBEYSHIRE CHEESE

See **Derby.**

DERBY

Also DERBEYSHIRE CHEESE. An English cow's-milk cheese with a hard-pressed, sweet curd, it is flakier and moister than cheddar, yet firmer than **Chesire.** It ripens rapidly in one to four months. The flavor markedly improves with age but peaks at six months. Holiday variations included a flavoring of sage leaves as well as spinach, which produce a pleasant green tinge.

DESERT LEMON

Fruit of a shrub or small tree, *Atalantia glauca*, found in the Australian states of New South Wales and Queensland, it is usually eaten in jellies or as preserves.

DESERT PEPPERWEED

A shrub, *Lepidium fremontii*, of the U.S. Southwest whose seeds are used as food and as a seasoning, it grows wild and is related to garden cress.

DESSERT

A sweet served at the end of a meal, usually dinner or supper has been customary in the United States for 100 years or more. Until recently, the last course of a French dinner was fresh fruit and cheese, perhaps following the sweet course. More often nowadays, the sweet is included at the end. In England, the last course used to be fresh fruit and nuts accompanied by a sweet wine, such as port. There again the custom is changing towards a sweet at the end.

Gastronomic theory holds that the dessert should harmonize with the rest of the meal. That is, it should repeat nothing that has gone before, e.g. a fruit dessert would not be appropriate in a meal that included a fruit salad. It should also balance the meal. A heavy meal should be followed by a light dessert, such a fruit or gelatin. A light meal, on the other hand, can support a heavy dessert, such as a pudding, a custard or a pie. A starchy dessert would go well after a meal without a starch course like spaghetti.

Typical desserts are fresh or canned fruit, ice cream, sherbet, gelatin, puddings, custards, pies, frosted cakes and rich pastries.

DEVIL FISH

See **Angler.**

DEVONSHIRE CREAM

See **Clotted Cream.**

DEVONSHIRE CREAM CHEESE

A specialty of the west of England, this is **clotted cream** carried a step further. Cream is allowed to rise on fresh milk, which is then scalded without stirring. After cooling, the cream is skimmed and set in small molds. The cheeses are marketed when they are firm enough to retain their shapes.

DEW BEAN

See **Moth Bean.**

DEWBERRY

A variety of bramble, closely related to the **blackberry,** dewberry is known also as the trailing blackberry. Species in the United States include *Rubus flagellaris, R. macropetalus, R. mirus, R. ursinus* and *R. vitifolius.* Dewberry canes characteristically trail on the ground, while blackberry canes are erect and self-supporting. The dewberry ripens earlier than the blackberry and is not as thickly clustered. The yield is generally lower too, although the individual berry may be larger than the blackberry and has a distinctive flavor of its own. The English dewberry *(R. caesius)* produces smaller fruit than American varieties. The important producing states for dewberries are Oregon, Texas, California, Washington, Michigan, Arkansas, Oklahoma, Alabama and North Carolina.

Dewberries may be prepared like blackberries. They make a superb pie, or "cobbler," cherished in the southern United States and—if highly sweetened —a fermented wine. "Considered together," says Euell Gibbons, "these berries are easily the most valuable wild fruit crop in America."

See also: **Blackberry, Loganberry.**

DHAL

See **Congo Pea.**

DIABLE SAUCE

This French sauce is served with meats and consists of a mixture of white wine and wine vinegar greatly reduced, then mixed with half-glaze, boiled and seasoned with cayenne pepper and *fines herbes.*

See also: **Sauce.**

DIAMONDFISH

Also FINGERFISH, KITEFISH. A small, diamond-shaped fish, *Monodactylus argenteus*, the diamondfish is found in coastal waters from the Red Sea to Australia. It is good to eat and a popular aquarium fish. The diamondfish is able to live in salt or fresh water. It reaches a length of eight inches, but is twice as high as it is long. A close relative is *M. sebae* of the coast of West Africa.

DIBS

A thick and luscious syrup made in some Arabic countries, most notably Syria, it consists of wine that has been much reduced plus the juice of dates and figs.

DIKA NUT

Fruit of a West African tree, *Irvingia barteri*, it is eaten locally and used to make an oily, chocolatelike substance called *dika bread*, which is prized as food.

DIK-DIK

This tiny African antelope is popular game for the pygmies of the Ituri Forest. They net them in large numbers and even sell them by the roadside. The dik-dik (genus *Madoqua)* stands 1½ feet high when full grown and weighs up to 12 pounds. There are six species found from Somalia and Ethiopia down to Angola and Namibia. In some areas it is protected by law, and in others it is avoided for superstitious reasons. For example, the Bakete tribe of the Congo believe a person's teeth will fall out if he or she kills or eats a dik-dik.

DILL

This potherb, *Anethum graveolens,* is best known for its pungently flavored seeds, which are used in pickling cucumbers. It is a vividly green annual plant, resembling **fennel** and growing from two to three feet high.

Native to Asia, but common throughout Europe and the United States, dill has been important plant since ancient times, medicinally as well as in the kitchen. Its name derives from the Norse *dilla,* meaning "to lull," and it was given to infants as a soporific.

The leaves are lacy, delicate and highly aromatic. Finely chopped, they are used to season stews, potatoes, fish, vegetable salads and broiled meats. With a taste akin to caraway, the seeds are a favored seasoning in Scandanavian and Russian cooking. Dill is considered a general seasoning in Asia and is reputed to stimulate the appetite.

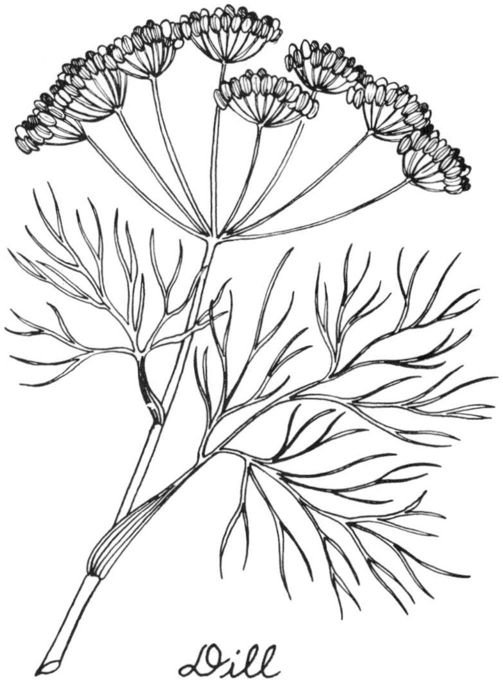

Dill

DILLENIA

Fruit of a genus of evergreen trees, *Dillenia spp.* of tropical south Asia, which may be lofty forest trees or shrubs, it is usually round, segmented, with a gelatinous pulp. The color varies according to species from black to yellow or red. There are four edible species in the Philippines alone. They are seldom eaten raw but used to make sauces or jellies or to season curries.

DIPLOMAT SAUCE

A French sauce used with fish, it is an elaboration of **Normande sauce.** It includes lobster butter, brandy and mushroom essence and is garnished with chopped truffles and diced lobster meat.

See also: **Sauce.**

DISHCLOTH GOURD

See **Loofah.**

DISTILLATION

In distillation, a liquid is converted to a gas through heating, then caught in a condenser and reconverted to a liquid through cooling. The final liquid, called the distillate, is a purer form of the original, i.e., an essence. This may be done to capture the essence of a solid, such as rose petals, which have been macerated in water. Or it may be used to purify the original liquid, as in distilling water. Distilled water is purified of mineral salts and air. It has a flat taste and does not make palatable drinking water, yet it is ideal for diluting a liquid, such as high-proof whisky, without altering its taste.

Distillation has had its greatest gastronomic impact in the area of separating a more volatile liquid from less volatile ones, i.e., the distillation of alcoholic spirits. Ethyl alcohol vaporizes at 173° F (78.3° C), and water at 212°F (100°C). Thus, heating a fermented liquid to a temperature between 173° and 212° F results in a distillate of high alcohol content.

This process was discovered long before the Christian era by many peoples, including the Chinese who distilled spirits made from rice wine, and the East Indians who were distilling *arak* from sugarcane juice before 800 B.C. The Greeks and Romans of Classical Antiquity knew about distillation. Aristotle, in his treatise on *Meteorology*, mentioned that "seawater can be made potable by distillation; wine and other liquids can be submitted to the same process." There was no discussion of distillation in the West, except by Arab scholars, until the 12th century A.D. when alchemists began to apply the process in their researches.

Of course, distillation was practiced before this time—nobody is quite certain when it started—by Celts of Scotland and Ireland to make the potent spirit *uisgetbeatha* ("water of life"), which developed into modern whisky. The alchemists' method applied to wines and ales produced *aqua vitae*, also meaning "water of life," which is still with us, in name at least, in *eau de vie* and *akvavit*. The Germans called the distillate *gebrannter Wein*, meaning burnt or distilled wine. The Dutch termed it *Brandewijn* which became brandywine in English and finally "brandy."

We are indebted to the Arabic language for the terms *alcohol* and *alembic*, the latter being the basic distilling apparatus and the word for still in most European languages. Distilling methods have been greatly refined over the centuries but have not changed much in basic apparatus. The pot stills used by Cognac manufacturers today would be easily recognizable to their 16th-century ancestors. The essential parts consist of a copper pot (the still) with a broad, rounded bottom and a long, tapered neck, and a worm condenser, which is a spiral copper tube connected to the still by a copper pipe and fitted with a jacket containing cold water to speed the condensation of the vapors. The pot still produces distillate in batches and has been replaced in certain branches of the distilling industry by the patent or continuous still, which was invented in 1826.

See also: **Brandy, Cognac.**

DIVINITY

The traditional divinity candy is prepared by combining sugar, water and white corn syrup, which is then cooked to a soft ball stage. The resulting syrup is poured while hot slowly into the whites of stiffly beaten eggs and stirred constantly until peaks form. Flavoring, nuts and candied fruits may then be added. This produces a white, creamy candy with a light texture. There are many variations, depending upon the candymaker's skill and imagination.

See also: **Candy.**

DOCK

See **Sorrel.**

DOCMAC

This large African catfish, *Bagrus docmac*, is of commercial importance in several areas of the continent. Large specimens may weigh as much as 50 pounds and be 3½ feet long. The *docmac* is found in Nigeria, Ghana, the Nile Basin and the Great Lakes of Africa.

DOG

Among modern cultures, it seems the Chinese are the only people who eat dog as a regular part of the diet. Dogs are raised specially for the table and are eaten while still pups no more than six months old. Dog flesh is sold in Chinese markets under the name, "fragrant meat," or "hornless goat." It reputedly tastes somewhat like mutton. One breed favored for this purpose is the chow.

Dog eating is an ancient custom in China, dating back at least to the fourth century B.C. when the philospher Mencius extolled dog flesh as a panacea for ailments ranging from malaria to jaundice. Many hoary recipes survive, such as this one from the Han dynasty (202 B.C.–220 A.D.), which calls for dog's liver to be wrapped in a thin casing of its own fat and roasted to achieve a crackling finish. The practice was outlawed by the Manchus, who conquered China in the 17th century. Later, dog eating became a symbol of rebellion against the Manchus, particularly among the followers of Sun-Yat-Sen who plotted to overthrow the dynasty in the early 20th century.

Many ancient peoples fancied dog flesh, including the Phoenicians, Greeks, Romans, Aztecs and, more recently, the Tahitians encountered by Captain Cook on his first voyage of discovery in the South Seas. The Aztecs were particularly fond of a special hairless breed, a larger version of the modern Chihuahua. The dog favored by Tahitians was herbivorous and quickly became extinct, bred out of existence by the larger carnivorous dogs introduced by the Europeans. Cook and his men were taken aback when offered roast dog by their Tahitian hosts but quickly acquired a liking for it, Cook noting, "There were few but allowed that South Sea dog was next to English lamb."

Scholars have speculated that the current Western taboo against eating dog has to do with the dog's greater value as a hunter and herder—practical considerations that led to its domestication in the first place. A notable exception to this taboo was made during the siege of Paris in the Franco-Prussian War (1870–71) when dogs as well as cats were butchered and sold openly in Parisian meat markets.

The Chinese custom of eating dogflesh came into conflict with the Western taboo against it in Hong Kong, which became a British colony in the 19th century and where the practice is outlawed, although the ban is widely ignored. The dog-loving British impose a prison sentence and a stiff fine on anyone convicted of butchering a dog or consuming its flesh. The Chinese, on the other hand, regard the ban as yet another example of European arrogance toward and intolerance of Asian civilization. To circumvent the law, a small group of friends cooperate in raising a dog for eating. When it is six months old, they butcher it in secret and have a feast. This also protects them against unscrupulous butchers who have been known to capture stray dogs, butcher them, then allow the flesh to age unrefrigerated, so that it supposedly bears a greater resemblance to mutton and can thus fool the meat inspector.

DOGFISH

Also GRAYFISH, SPUR DOG. Most commonly this name refers to a small shark, *Squalus acanthias*, with a sharp spine in front of each dorsal fin. It lives in the North Atlantic and Pacific Oceans, with related species in the Mediterranean and South Atlantic. The term is applied in a derogatory manner to several other fish, including the bowfin, New World burbot, the mud puppy and the blackfish, discussed under separate headings.

Dogfish gained their name apparently because they are a schooling fish and hunt in packs of 1,000 or more, ranging from the surf out to about 100 fathoms. In the United States they were a constant source of irritation to fishermen until World War I when they became commercially valuable for their livers because cod liver oil was scarce. Dogfish liver makes up one-sixth of the fish's body mass, and its oil is even richer in essential vitamins than cod liver oil. Americans learned to eat the flesh then and again in World War II, when the scarcity again occurred.

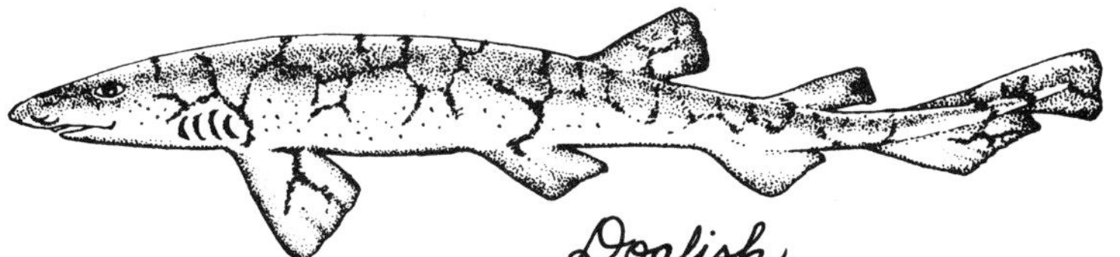

Dogfish

Of all dogfish species, the one found in U.S. North Atlantic waters is the best eating, which is no great compliment. In fish markets, the labeling is often euphemistic: "grayfish" in the United States, "flake" in England and *saumonette* in France. The word means "little salmon" and was inspired by the salmonlike red tinge of the flesh of skinned dog fish. Second best is the flesh of smooth hound *(Mustelus mustelus)*, which is common in the Mediterranean and nearby Atlantic.

Dogfish are brown or slate-colored on back and sides, shading to gray or white underneath, with white spots along the sides of smaller specimens. They average two to three feet in length, four being a maximum, and weigh seven pounds on the average, with a 20-pound maximum.

They may be cooked like cod or any large fish. One recommended way is cut one into strips, dip these in batter and fry them like English fish and chips.

Dogfish skin is used to polish wood and metal.

DOG NETTLE

Also SMALL NETTLE. The stem and leaf tops of this annual herb *(Urtica urens)* may be boiled and eaten as spinach or used in soups. It is seldom resorted to, however, except in emergencies.

DOGTOOTH VIOLET

Also DOG'S TOOTH LILY. A perennial herb of Europe and temperate Asia, its dried bulbs or corms are ground for a flour that makes excellent cakes or noodles. The leaves of the dogtooth violet *(Erythronium dens-canis)* are mottled red brown and white, and the flowers vary in color from pink to purple.

DOILY

It is a Chinese-American term for a thin wheat pancake used in Chinese cooking. The doily is used to wrap hor d'oeuvres and dumplings. Food may be rolled in a doily, then picked up and eaten with the fingers.

DOLICHOS BEAN

This genus of tropical legumes is native to Africa and Southeast Asia. The most prominent species of the genus, as far as human foods goes, is the hyacinth or **lablab bean.** Other members of the genus include the Sarawak bean *(Dolichos hosei)* and the Australian pea *(D. lignosus)*. Characteristically, the *dolichos* pod resembles a string bean.

DOLLARFISH

See **BUTTERFISH.**

DOLPHIN

The dolphin is a highly intelligent aquatic mammal of the *Cetacea* order, which also includes whales and porpoises. There are marine and freshwater varieties. Only the latter, it seems, is eaten with any regularity. Freshwater dolphins of the family *Platanistidae* are found in the rivers Ganges (India), Yangtze (China) and the Amazon and La Plata of South America. Both the flesh and the blubber of these creatures are sometimes eaten. The largest of them rarely exceeds 10 feet in length and 500 pounds in weight.

Marine varieties, such as the common dolphin *(Delphinus delphis)* and the bottled-nosed dolphin *(Tursiops truncatus)*, are fished commercially in some areas for their oil, which is put to industrial use.

DOLPHINFISH

This popular gamefish, *Coryphaena hippurus*, is found in warm marine waters throughout the world and is prized by gourmets for its delicate fillets and steaks. The dolphinfish, also called "dorado" because of its brilliant gold sides and dark yellow tail, should not be confused with the mammalian dolphin *(Delphinus delphis)*, which swims around ocean-going ships, has a beak and is actually a species of whale.

The adult male dolphinfish is characterized by a blunt vertical head like a battering ram and may attain a length of four to five feet, although the average catch (in the Gulf Stream, where the fish travel in large schools) is usually smaller than this. In the Pacific Ocean the dolphinfish is more widely known as the *mahi-mahi*, and is often served in restaurants under this Hawaiian name. It is a voracious eater, will take any bait, strikes in an explosive manner and fights spectacularly. The dolphinfish is particularly fond of flying fish. A good indication that the game is near is to see a school of these smaller creatures skimming frantically over the water. At death the dolphinfish undergoes a rapid change in color from bright green to brilliant blue and gold before fading to a uniform yellow or silver.

The pompano dolphin *(Coryphaena equiselis)* is related but lacks the blunt vertical head of the male dolphinfish. It is also smaller and has a rounder, less streamlined body.

Dolphin Fish

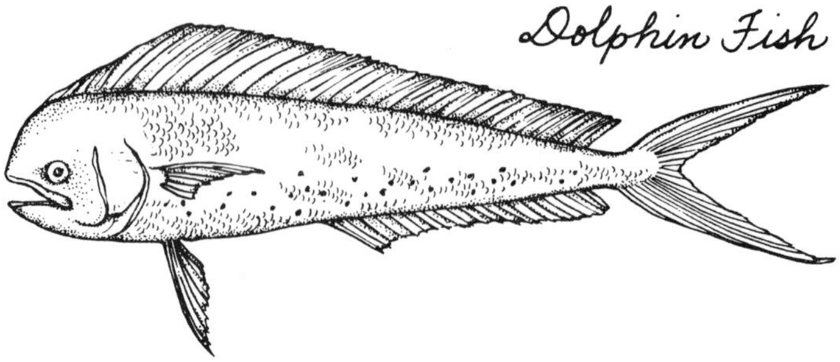

DOMIATI

This buffalo or cow's milk cheese is popular in Moslem countries, particularly Egypt. When fresh it is salty and mild, but in the cured form it is "pickled," and has a cleanly acid taste. It is distinguished from other cheese by the addition of salt at a early stage of processing before the rennet. Then, during the curing, *domiati* is pickled in salt whey or salt milk brine for four to eight months. It may also be canned in brine for shipping. If kept for a year or more, the cheese develops a dark surface and strong flavor.

DOM PERIGNON

See **Champagne.**

DONKEY

Also ASS. A four-legged animal of the horse genus, the donkey *(Equus asinus)* is generally much smaller and has longer ears and a shorter mane than its larger relative. It is a slow but sure-footed animal, and is thus useful for transport in steep, rocky places. Donkey flesh is said to be far tastier than that of horse, but benefits from the general taboo against eating horse flesh prevalent in English-speaking countries. Only in Africa is the donkey eaten with regularity as fresh meat. Certain types of Sicilian salami are said to be made from the meat of the small Sicilian donkey. The meat of donkey foal (under two years of age) is said to be excellent for making pate, indeed superior to veal.

Mention was made of donkey flesh by the ancient Romans, who were particularly fond of donkey foal. In China, wild asses were hunted to provide food for the army in war time. In time of siege or blockade, when the populace was forced to resort to such things as rat, cat, dog and donkey, donkey won high praise. This was true of the siege of Paris in 1870 when Labouchere, a liberal politician, declared, "I should never wish to taste a better dinner than roast of donkey." When the English blockaded Malta, the Maltese were introduced to donkey's meat and—so the story goes—came to prefer it to beef and veal. To some it is reminiscent of mutton and may be prepared like mutton, horsemeat or beef.

DONZELLE

Also GIRELLE, OPHIDIUM. A small eellike fish of the Mediterranean, a member of the *Ophidiidae* family, it is used in France as an ingredient of **bouillabaisse.**

DORAB

Also WOLF HERRING. Here is an ocean fish related to the herring but much, much larger, reaching lengths of 12 feet or more. The *dorab (Chirocentrus dorab)* is caught by Arab fishermen in the Red Sea but is also widely distributed from East Africa to Australia. It is edible but is not highly valued as food because of the many small bones in its flesh. It is also a dangerous fish to catch because of its sharp teeth, well-developed fangs and vigorous leaps.

DORADE

See **Bream.**

DORADO

A freshwater fish, *Salminus maxillosus*, found in South American rivers, especially the Parana and Uruguay Rivers, it is the continent's most renowned game fish. There are several species, all called *dorado*, and large specimens can weigh up to 50 pounds. The *dorado* has a troutlike appearance and beautiful coloration, including an overall golden hue, dark on the back and bright on the sides, and bright red fins. It is good to eat. This fish should not be confused with the **dolphinfish,** which is also called the *dorado*.

DORSET CHEESE

Also, BLUE DOREST, BLUE VINNY. A hard English cheese with blue veins was developed in Dorset County more than 200 years ago. It is a farmhouse cheese, and not so plentiful as the better known **Stilton.** Unlike Stilton, the blue mold in Dorset does not produce an overall marbling effect, instead, bright blue veins run in streaks through the cheese. Otherwise, the curd is white with a dry crumbly texture and a sharp, frequently acid flavor. It is made from partly skimmed cow's milk, pressed and bandaged during curing so that is develops a natural thick rind. The finished cheese is circular and flat and weighs 14 to 16 pounds. Double Dorset is a richer, creamier version.

DORY

See **John Dory.**

DOTTED SAXIFRAGE

This perennial herb, *Saxifraga nelsoniana*, is found in Europe, northern Asia and North America. Its succulent leaves may be eaten raw in salads or dressed with oil.

DOTTER

This German skim milk cheese made in the Nuremberg area is unusual. Egg yolks are added to the milk before renneting.

DOTTEREL

Also GUIGNARD. A European shore bird, *Eudromias morinellus*, of the plover family, it is small, plump and good to eat, but protected by law in such places as Great Britain. Its name derives from the Middle English word for dunce or foolish person. The dotterel is so tame that it can often be taken by hand. It is migratory and visits England in the summer. In France, it is considered at its best from October to December. It may be prepared like **plover.**

DOUBLE COCONUT

See **Coco de Mer.**

DOUBLE CREME CARRE

See **Carre.**

DOUGH

A thick, pliable mass is mixed from such dry ingredients as flour or meal, salt and leavening and is moistened with water, eggs or milk. After kneading, this mixture is baked into bread, pastry, etc. Dough may vary in firmness depending on what it is intended to make. Softer doughs are made into bread, firmer ones into pastry. It is always too stiff to stir or pour. A similar mixture liquid enough to be poured is called batter and is used to make pancakes or waffles.

DOUGHNUT

Also CHURRO, CRULLER. The doughnut is a small cake, usually leavened with yeast or baking powder, fried in deep fat and then served hot or cold. It is a popular treat in Europe and the United States. The traditional form is round with a hole in the center, but it may be round with some jelly at the center instead of a hole or oblong and twisted, in which case it is called a cruller. A recent refinement is the doughnut hole, which is a ball of dough the size of a golf ball, cooked like a doughnut. The Spanish *churro* is ribbonlike and crunchy and tied in a loose knot.

In cooking, the temperature of the fat is a crucial factor, and must be kept between 350° and 370° F (176.7° and 187.8° C). At lower temperatures, the doughnut absorbs too much fat. Doughnuts may be served plain, but more often they are sprinkled with sugar, glazed or covered with flavored icings, spices or nuts.

Fried cakes are a truly ancient food. Achaeologists have found the fossilized remains of what appear to be doughnuts in the kitchen middens of prehistoric Native American settlements. Modern doughnuts were supposedly introduced into colonial America by the Dutch at New Amsterdam who called them *olykoeks* ("oily cakes"). The doughnut with a hole is said to be a recent invention, developed by a sea captain who loved doughnuts but found them indigestible. After some experimentation, he found doughnuts with the hole sat better on his stomach and attributed this to a more thorough cooking at the center.

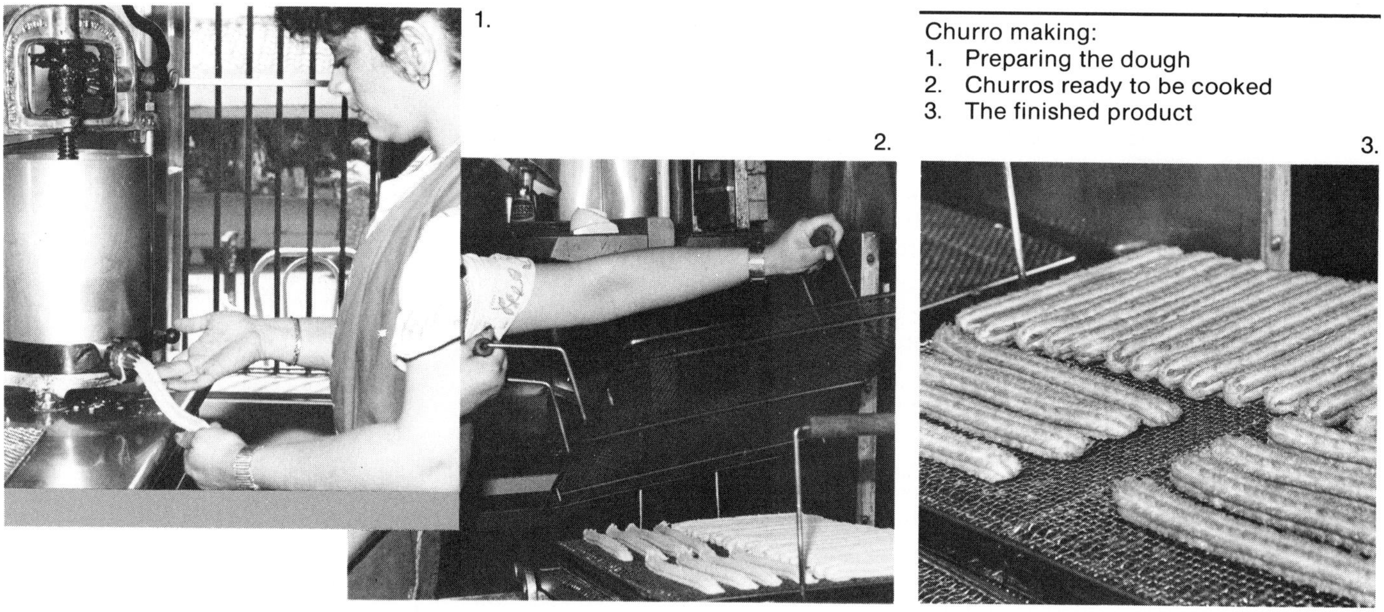

1. 2. 3.

Churro making:
1. Preparing the dough
2. Churros ready to be cooked
3. The finished product

It is not known whether the sea captain was an optimist or a pessimist, but his discovery opened the way for the following observation by American writer Mclandburgh Wilson:

Twixt optimist and pessimist
The difference is droll:
The optimist sees the doughnut,
The pessimist, the hole.

DOUGLAS KNOTWEED

A perennial herb, *Polygonum douglasii*, of western North America, its seeds can be ground into flour appropriate for making bread or porridge.

DOUM PALM

Also DOOM PALM, GINGERBREAD TREE. A small, sometimes forked palm tree, *Hyphaene thebaica* is native to the Nile region of North Africa. The fruit attains a length of 3½ inches and has a mealy outer husk or pulp the taste of which resembles gingerbread.

DOUNDATE

The reddish fruit of a straggling shrub or small tree, *Nauclea latifolia* is native to tropical Africa. The fruit grows to 3½ inches across and has a sweet juicy pulp and an applelike flavor.

DOVE

See **Pigeon.**

DOWITCHER

A shore bird of the Americas that ranges from Alaska to Peru and Brazil, the dowitcher is known also as the redbreasted or graybacked snipe and is related to the American snipe. It has a chunky body that reaches a length of 12 inches. Its bill is fully half as long as its body. The dowitcher *(Macrorhamphus griseus)* may be prepared like **snipe.**

DOWNY ROSE MYRTLE

Also HILL GOOSEBERRY, HILL GUAVA. This fruit of a shrub, *Rhodomyrtus tormentosa*, is found in India and east to China to the Philippines. It is a round, juicy berry with a sweet aromatic taste, which is eaten fresh or used to make jam and pies.

DRAGON'S EYES

See **Longan.**

DRAMBUIE

A clear, pale brown Scottish liqueur reputed to be the oldest made there, it is a mixture of old highland malt Scotch whiskey, heather honey and a variety of herbs and spices. The taste is half-dry, and the name derives from the Gaelic phrase, *an dram buidheach*, "the drink that satisfies." It is 80 proof.

According to tradition, the MacKinnon family obtained the original recipe from Prince Charles Edward Stuart, "Bonny Prince Charlie." It was his favorite liqueur, and he had brought the formula with him to Scotland from France in 1745. When he and his highland allies were defeated in the Battle of Culloden, the MacKinnons protected him and helped him escape to France. He gave the MacKinnons the secret recipe for Drambuie in gratitude. It is generally served as an after-dinner cordial but is the basis of at least one cocktail, the Rusty Nail.

DRIED BEEF

Also CHIPPED BEEF. This meat is usually selected from the flank, then pickled in a brine solution, smoked for a few days, then dried for two weeks. It is sliced thinly by machine, then sold in plastic bags, jars or cans. In small, wafer-thin slices it is called chipped beef. Its color is dark red and its flavor nutty and salty. Chipped beef in a cream sauce served over toast or biscuits is an old standby that has outworn its popularity. It is fine in an emergency, however.

DRIMYS

Also WINTER'S BARK. An evergreen tree, *Drimys winteri*, native to South America, its bark is ground into powder and used as a condiment in Brazil and Mexico. An Australian species called pepper tree *(D. tormentosa)* bears fruit that may be dried and used as a pepper substitute.

DROMEDARY

See **Camel.**

DRUMFISH

See **Croaker.**

DRY CHEESE

Also SPERRKASE, TROCKENKASE. This German skim milk cheese is made in small dairies for home consumption in the eastern Bavarian Alps and Tyrol. Often flavored with caraway seeds, it is allowed to dry before serving until it is very hard.

DUBLIN PAY PRAWN

See **Norway Lobster.**

DUBONNET

This is the famous trade name for an aromatic French **aperitif** made from semi-dry white or red fortified wine flavored with herbs and quinine. Quinine, long an ingredient favored by European colonists in the tropics, is considered medicinal as well as thirst-quenching.

The alcohol content of Dubonnet is 15 to 20 percent. It can be drunk straight but is often mixed with soda and garnished with lemon or lime to make a thirst-quenching wine cooler. The white, or "blonde" Dubonnet (really a greenish gold color) is best for this prupose.

White Dubonnet can also be used to make a Martini, when it is added to gin in place of **vermouth.** Red Dubonnet is sweeter, more syrupy and is usually drunk straight or with a slice of lemon. The Dubonnet Company in Paris now also makes and bottles its product in Fresno, California.

DUCK

A swimming bird with a flat bill, short neck and legs and webbed feet, its flesh is darker in color and stronger in flavor than that of a chicken or turkey. There are at least 60 or 70 species of duck. Most domesticated ducks, however, are descended from a single wild species, the mallard or common wild duck of North America *(Anas boscas)*.

Ducks were domesticated rather late in history. This was probably due to their abundance in the wild and the ease of capturing them. The ancient Chinese, Japanese and Romans kept them in a semi-wild state, perhaps knowing that the wild bird tastes better than the domesticated one. At any rate, ducks were domesticated by the 15th century in Europe and probably earlier in China.

Returning crusaders gave considerable impetus to the eating of wild duck in the Middle Ages when they brought back citrus fruit from the Holy Land. Placing an orange or some lemon juice in the body cavity of a duck will dispel the fishy taste encountered in ducks that feed mainly on fish. The trick was known to the ancient Romans, but was lost when the empire collapsed in the West. *Canard a l'orange* remains a popular dish today.

Wild ducks are very lean, much more than tame ducks, and their flesh, even without fishy overtones, has a more pronounced flavor than that of the domesticated type. It is gamy without being hung, and the dark color of the meat is due to the rich blood supply needed to sustain the exertion of flying. It should be cooked quickly after death, and perhaps larded to prevent drying out.

Following are common breeds of domestic duck:

The Aylesbury duck: A favorite in England, this white duck is a little heavier than the Pekin. It is generally roasted and served with applesauce after being stuffed with a mixture of breadcrumbs, chopped onion and a little fresh sage.

The Muscovy duck: a native of Brazil, the Moscovy duck, known also as the Barbary duck, acquired its name from being a musk duck *(Cairina moschata)*, "Muscovy" being a corruption of that, rather than from any relationship to Russia. Glands in this bird's rump exude secretions that can give its flesh a strong taste that sometimes renders it inedible. The French use them to cross with Nantais ducks. The resulting hybrid produces good ***foie gras*** and is a better table bird. Like all true hybrids, it is sterile. Lesser known ducks are the Cayuga, the Indian Runner and the Khaki Campbell, all kept for both meat and eggs.

The Nantais duck: Smaller than the Rouen, the Nantais is regarded by some as the best French duck. It weighs about four pounds when fully grown at four months. The Nantais is crossed each year with wild drakes to improve the flavor.

The Pekin, or Long Island duck: This most popular of ducks in the United States is white and is descended from Chinese ducks imported in 1872. It can attain a weight of 10 pounds, but is best at eight-12 months old when it weighs between four to seven pounds. Its flesh is juicy and lighter in color than a wild duck's. The Chinese use it to make Pekin Duck, a specialty that involves pumping air between the bird's body and skin so that after cooking in a kilnlike oven the duck emerges with an aromatic and crackly skin.

The Rouen duck: This is considered to be the tastiest French duck. Taste is attributed in great part to the way it meets its death, i.e., by smothering. Blood is retained in the body and gives the flesh a dark red hue and gamey taste. The Rouen is used for the spectacular pressed duck, made famous by the *Tour d'Argent* restaurant in Paris.

Wild ducks are generally conceded to have better flavor, and this is attributed mainly to what they feed on: grain and acquatic plants. Birds—such as the Merganser—that feed on fish are best avoided if one objects to a fishy taste. Wild rice and wild celery also improve the taste of duck flesh.

The Black duck: Called the black mallard in the United States, this bird has a dark brown head and dull brown body. Ranging from Canada to North Carolina, it is a highly regarded table bird.

The Canvasback duck: This duck feeds on wild celery and is reputed to be the tastiest of North American ducks. It takes its name from the color of its black plumage, i.e., ashy white, marked with zigzag black lines. Average market size is 2½ to 4 pounds. American author Jack London liked to gorge himself on canvasback. A few days before his death in 1916, according to biographer Richard O'Connor, London's usual meal consisted of "two large wild ducks cooked for eight minutes." Despite doctor's orders, "he refused to stop eating underdone mallards or canvasbacks at every meal; it was duck season and he meant to have his fill of them."

The Mallard duck: This ancestor of domestic ducks is omnivorous and found throughout the world. In the male the back is brown and gray and the head and neck a glossy green. The female is brown and buff. It averages 2½ to 3 pounds and has a delicate flavor. Its abundance make it an important wild duck.

The Pintail duck: Popular for sport as well as food in Britain, the pintail is beautiful, with a long slender neck and pointed tail.

The Teal: Both green-winged and blue-winged teal are common. The former is the smallest of wild ducks and is often called the puddle duck. These and other varities of teal are found in freshwater streams, ponds and lakes throughout Europe, Asia and the Americas.

The Widgeon: A freshwater pond bird averaging two to three pounds in weight. It has a back of brown and black, green sides and white or buff top. Its distinctive flavor make it a sought-after table bird.

The Wood duck: This elaborately plumed bird once faced extinction from overhunting but now is extensively protected. It is good to look at and good to eat. The North American Carolina wood duck and the Asian Mandarin ducks are representative of this species.

Other common wild ducks are the Redhead, the Ruddy, the Gray duck and the Blackhead or Scaup. Wild ducks should be plucked dry, singed, then wiped inside and out but never washed. The breast should be larded to prevent its drying out, and the carcass should be oiled. Wild duck is generally roasted rare, then served hot.

Although duck is the general term for both sexes, the female is a duck and a male a drake. Duck flesh is rich in minerals and vitamins, expecially iron, thiamin and riboflavin.

DUEL CHEESE

A soft, cured cheese made in Austria and Germany from renneted cow's milk and marketed in two-inch squares.

DUGONG

See **Manatee.**

DUHART

See **Java Plum.**

DUKU

See **Langsat.**

DULSE

Also DELISK and IRISH MOSS. This may be any of several species of coarse, purple seaweed. Dulse is usually *Phodymenia palmata*, but *Dilsea edulis* is also used. Dulse is used for food in coastal regions of Scotland, Ireland, Iceland, Canada and New England. When dried, it can be chewed like candy. It also finds use as thickener in jellies and aspics. In addition, dulse is a prime source of iodine and iron. Bleached and dried, it forms the commercial Irish Moss.

See also: **Carrageen.**

DUNLOP

This rich, moist, Scottish cheese was developed in Dunlop, Ayreshire. Once considered the national cheese, it has since been superseded by **cheddar,** which it much resembles. Dunlop is white, firm and close textured, but due to its high moisture content, it does not keep or travel well.

DURIAN

An unusual tropical fruit, durian *(Durio zebethinus)* combines a delicious flavor with an unpleasant odor, much like certain kinds of aged cheese. The fruit is native to Malaysia but is also found in Sumatra, Java, the Celebes, the Moluccas, Thailand, India and the Philippines.

The durian tree is tall and stately, rather like an elm. The fruit is oval, about the size of a large melon or soccerball and when ripe is a dull yellow. Durians generally weigh five to eight pounds. The skin of the durian is covered with hard, stubby spikes, but opens to reveal a yellow pulp with chestnut-sized seeds embedded in it. Both the seeds and pulp are edible, the seeds being roasted much like chestnuts. It is the pulp, however, that attracts durian fanciers. Its taste has been described in various ways, e.g., cream and vegetables, almond custard and robust, overripe Roquefort. Obviously, the flavor is complex, and differences may be explained by the fact that there are a dozen species of durian.

They all share the problem of foul odor, however, which definitely discourages the uninitiated. It has been compared to rotting vegetables, sewage, putrid flesh or simply described as fetid. Refrigeration minimizes it. It is so penetrating, however, that in air-conditioned spaces, it is picked up and carried throughout the system. For this reason, certain Asian airlines will not let passengers carry it on board.

Durian is customarily eaten raw, but it may also be used in cakes, jams and even sherbet.

DURRA

See **Sorghum**

DURUM WHEAT

See **Wheat, Pasta.**

DUTCH CHEESE

See **Cottage Cheese.**

DWARF ALMOND

Also DWARF RUSSIAN ALMOND. This succulent fruit of small tree, *Prunus tenella*, is native to eastern Europe and Siberia.

DZEREN

Also DZERON. A swift antelope, *Procapra gutturosa*, inhabiting the arid deserts of Central Asia, Tibet, China and southern Siberia, it is often used for food in Mongolia. The *dzeren* is also known as the Chinese antelope.

DZIGGETAI

See **Hemione.**

E

EARL GRAY TEA

This hearty and aromatic blend of Indian and Ceylon black teas was created for one Earl Gray, an early English investor in tea ships. The blend is not unique anymore and varies with the manufacturer. Some are scented with bergamot and others with lavender.

See also: **Tea.**

EARLY BLUE VIOLET

Also WILD OKRA. The purple flowers of this perennial herb, *Viola palmata*, are used for thickening soups. The entire plant is very mucilaginous. It is found in eastern North America.

EARTH ALMOND

See **Chufa.**

EARTH CHESTNUT

Also GROUNDNUT PEAVINE, TUBEROUS VETCHLING. The edible tubers of a climbing or trailing vine, *Lathyrus tuberosus*, native to Europe and west Asia, they are boiled and eaten as vegetables. This vine has been transplanted to North America and is related to other legumes, such as the everlasting pea and the sweet pea. Earth chestnuts are seldom seen for sale except in the local markets of Syria and the Balkan states.

EARTH NUT

Tuberous roots of a perennial plant, *Carum bulbocastanum*, native to Europe and temperate Asia, consist of a nutlike series of bulbs, which are black on the outside and white on the inside. These are a useful emergency food and are occasionally seen in markets. After boiling, they taste like chestnuts. The plant is closely related to **caraway** and its seeds may be substituted for caraway seeds as a flavoring agent. In England the name "earth nut" is also given to a type of small truffle, *Bunium flexuosum*, about the size of a hazelnut. It has no commercial value. This truffle is also known as the pig nut or fairy potato.

EARTHWORM

Round, segmented worms that burrow in the soil, earthworms are 72 percent protein and less than 1 percent fat. They are abundant in North America, yet it is safe to say that the overwhelming majority of Americans seek their protein elsewhere. Exceptions are the enthusiasts who enter the annual earthworm recipe contest sponsored by Gaddie's North American Bait Farms of Ontario, California, which raises earthworms commercially The contest has drawn as many as 500 recipes, which include such delicacies as dried earthworms (tasting like shredded wheat) suitable for sprinkling on top of salads or baking into oatmeal cookies.

In frontier days the woodcock, a bird that dined chiefly on earthworms, was a frequent prey of hunters who considered the undigested contents of the stomach—a meaty spaghetti of earthworms—to be an extra treat to be consumed with the rest of the innards. The Chinese make an earthworm broth—a time-honored dish—by slitting the worm, washing them to remove all particles of earth, then simmering the worms in water until the broth is reduced by half.

EAST AFRICAN CARDAMOM

East African cardamom is a perennial plant, *Aframomum mala*, of tropical Africa, whose seeds provide a condiment like cardamom.

EASTERN SHAD

See **Shad.**

EAU DE FRAMBOISE

This brandy distilled in France from a fermented mash of raspberries is often referred to as white alcohol because it is colorless. Framboise is distilled at a fairly low proof—100 or less—so as to retain a maximum of raspberry aroma, which is its chief attraction. It is bottled unaged, again to retain the aroma. This brandy is expensive due to the huge amount of fruit required to produce it. It is served chilled. Framboise is also used to make a liqueur.

EAU DE VIE

A French phrase meaning "water of life," applied generally to brandy and other distilled spirits, especially European products. Swedes call their spirit **aquavit,** Danes say *akvavit*, ancient Romans ordered *aqua vitae*, ancient Celts tippled *usque baugh*, Americans followed the Celts with **whiskey,** while Germans favor **schnapps.**

These are all potent liquors, 80 proof and up, distilled from grain, potatoes or grapes. The brandies are usually after-dinner drinks and considered by some to aid digestion. Aquavit and whiskey are usually before-dinner drinks considered by some to stimulate the appetite. They are rich in calories but have limited food value.

EAU DE VIE DE MARC

See **Marc.**

ECHINOCACTUS

Also EAGLE'S CLAW, MULE CRIPPLER CACTUS. A small cactus, *Echinocactus horizonthalonius*, of the *visnaga* genus native to western Texas, southern New Mexico and northern Mexico, its pulp is used to make sweets.

EDAM

Also MANBOLLEN, KATZENKOPF, TETE DE MAURE. This Dutch cheese has been made in the town of Edam near Amsterdam since at least the 13th century but widely imitated in Denmark and the United States. Edam is produced from partly skimmed cow's milk and has a sweet curd with semisoft to hard texture. It has a mild, sometimes salty flavor and a crumbly body that is free of eyes. The curd is orange yellow. The Dutch dye the rind bright red for export. Edam is usually dipped in red paraffin in the United States. Owing to its spherical shape, it is known in many places as red ball cheese. Sizes of the cheese range from one to 14 pounds, and it is also sold in loaves.

EDDO

See **Taro.**

EDIBLE CANNA

See **Tous-les-Mois.**

EDIBLE TULIP

A type of tulip *(Tulipa edulis)* native to Japan and China, its leaves are used as a salad green.

EEL

Eels are long, snakelike, freshwater fish that spawn in salt water. The American eel *(Anguilla rostrata)* and the European eel *(Anguilla anguilla)* are closely related. Their flesh is oily and gelatinous but firm and delicious if prepared correctly. The eel has a pointed snout and a large mouth and may live anywhere from five to 20 years, attaining a length of three to five feet.

All European and American eels apparently begin life in the Sargasso Sea, south of Bermuda and 1,000 miles east of Florida. After spawning, the adults die. The eel larvae are carried by the Gulf Stream to the East Coast of North America and to Europe, where they enter the mouths of rivers in hordes. Males remain in the tidewater areas, but females ascend the rivers and remain there until they are fully grown and ready to spawn. At that time, they cease feeding, go back down the river, join the males and head for the spawning area. The journey is one year for American eels and two and one-half to three years for European eels. Not having eaten the whole way, they are ready to collapse on arriving and die after spawning. Eel fishing is best in the spring when the females are heading for the sea.

Eels were considered a delicacy in ancient Rome, and they were a particular favorite with the Emperor Heliogabalus (218–222 A.D.), who fattened conger eels in tubs, feeding them the flesh of Christian martyrs. From this practice, perhaps, comes the legend that eels have a predilection for human flesh. There is no evidence to back this up, nor is there any support for the belief that they are poisonous. Repugnance due to their reptilian appearance probably accounts for the evil stories about them and also for a certain reluctance on the part of many people to eat them for the first time.

England, the Low Countries, Denmark, Sweden, northern Germany and Italy are big eel-eating areas. Jellied eel—a small piece of eel in pale green aspic—has been a favorite snack in East London for centuries. It is seasoned with chili vinegar. Hamburg eel soup has as big a cult following as Marseilles bouillabaisse. Comacchio is the eel capital of Italy. Tokyo is another center of eel eating. A typical dish is marinated eel, broiled over charcoal, spiced with ginger sauce and skewered on bamboo slivers.

Elvers are small eels, usually at the larval stage, rarely measuring more than three inches and thin as matchsticks. Two famous elver dishes are the Belgian *anguilles en vert* (eels with potherbs) and the Basque *angulas a la bilbaina* (baby eels fried in oil).

Eels are eaten in the northeastern United States but not on the Pacific Coast, where there are none.

See also: **Conger.**

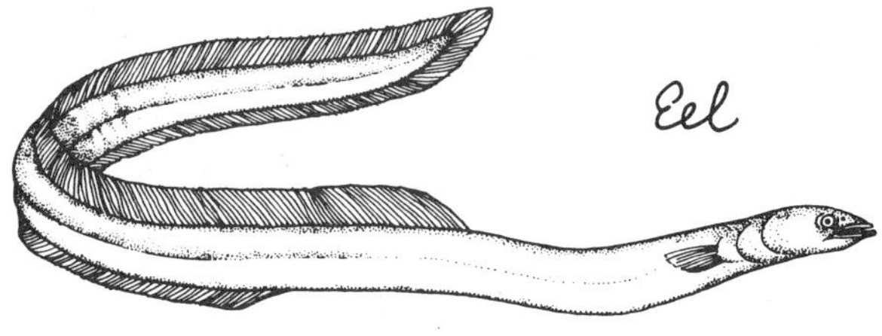

EGG

A germ of offspring—encased in a shell or tough membrane—is produced by birds and some reptiles. (Fish also produce eggs, but they are discussed under **Roe).** The egg is a rounded or oval body containing a thick transparent liquid called the white or albumen, which surrounds a blob of colored matter called the yolk. The white consists mainly of protein and the yolk of protein, fat, vitamins and minerals. A hen's egg contains about six grams of high-grade animal protein, all the essential vitamins except C and most of the minerals essential to human nutrition. Eggs, moreover, are easy to digest, especially if eaten raw, soft-boiled, hard-boiled or poached. Other methods of cooking usually involve fat, and the eggs will be as digestible as the fat is.

The hen's egg is the kind most commonly used as food, justifiably so, since it comes very close to being a complete food. A distant second in popularity is the duck egg, which enjoys a following in China, England, Holland and Belgium. It has a stronger taste and an oilier consistency than hen's egg. Geese and turkey eggs are palatable but rarely appear in markets. Plover eggs are much appreciated by gourmets, especially in Holland; they were eaten by Native Americans of the colonial era and much resemble hens' eggs in taste and composition. The Japanese relish quail eggs and eat them raw as a topping on *sushi;* the English like both quail and gull eggs. Rarer still are partridge eggs, guinea hen eggs (available mainly in France), peacock eggs (popular with the ancient Roman aristocracy) and penguin eggs (consumed by Eskimos or other inhabitants of polar regions). Pigeon eggs are considered a delicacy in China; and in Africa the ostrich egg, tipping the scales at three pounds, is produced commercially in some areas.

Of reptile eggs, the only one eaten with any frequency is that of the turtle, and then only in the vicinity of their nesting areas. Best are those of the sea **turtle.**

It is believed that the chicken was first domesticated in India around 2000 B.C. and that the Indians were the first to eat eggs from tame hens. The Chinese, however, are credited with first incubating eggs about 1400 B.C. In the West, the ancient Egyptians made no mention of chickens, neither does the Old Testament. Domesticated chickens seem to have reached ancient Greece through Central Europe and were common by the fifth century B.C. Hens' eggs were a staple food relied on by ordinary folk; but the rich in both Greece and Rome fancied such rare delicacies as peacock eggs. Hens' eggs kept their importance throughout the Middle Ages and Renaissance and were among the foods to be landed by Columbus in the New World when he made his first landfall in the West Indies in 1493. There were no domestic chickens in the Western Hemisphere until that time but apparently no dearth of eggs because Leif Ericsson, who landed in North America in 1000 A.D. had already reported, "There were so many birds that it was scarcely possible to step between their eggs."

Two varieties of hens' eggs are common in markets, brown-shelled and white-shelled. Opinions differ on which type is tastier and healthier, although there seems to be no firm evidence to support either side. Fertilized eggs are also alleged to be better than the unfertilized variety. In some cultures this preference is based on religious belief, e.g., some Hindu castes eat only unfertilized eggs, and since they contain a spot of blood, fertile eggs are not kosher. But many health-food enthusiasts believe the fertilized egg to be nutritionally superior and more flavorful and are willing to back it up by paying a sizeable premium (10 to 20 percent) in the supermarket.

Two factors clearly do affect the taste and nutritional quality of the hen's egg: chicken feed and freshness. Such grains as wheat, corn and oats are best, plus whatever insects the animal can forage. In commercial operations, fish meal and bone meal are added to the egg-layers' diet, and too much of either can give an unpleasant taste to the egg. (Marigold petals are sometimes added to insure a bright yellow yolk). Under cold storage conditions eggs may be kept wholesome for nine months to a year, but when it comes to taste the rule is the fresher the better. A freshly lain egg one hour old delights the palate, and a day old egg is far tastier than one two weeks old, but after that the law of diminishing returns sets in. A traditional way of judging the relative freshness of an egg (one that has not gone bad) is to place it in a glass of lightly salted water. A newly laid egg will sink to the bottom, while an older one will float. This is due to the amount of air inside the shell, which increases as the egg ages.

Egg consumption in the United States has remained relatively constant over the past 20 years, fluctuating between 27 and 30 eggs per person per

Eggs

Eggplants

year. Statistics suggest that the U.S. figure is closely followed by those of Canada, Belgium, England and France.

Eggs are a versatile food. According to the 18th-century French gastronome Grimod de la Reyniere, "They know in France 685 different ways of dressing eggs, without counting those which our savants invent every day." Apart from being eaten raw or cooked separately in ways we have mentioned in passing, they are used either whole or the white and yolk separately in making cakes, puddings, souffles and sauces. About 10 percent of the annual egg production is processed into egg products, which may be liquid, frozen or dried.

Hen's eggs in the market are packed and sold according to size, which ranges from jumbo, or extra large, to the very small. If you need to separate the yolk from the white, it is easier to do if the egg is cold.

EGG CHEESE

A Finnish cheese, originating in Nyland, combines fresh eggs with whole cow's milk at a ratio of about two eggs per quart. Usually the eggs and a starter are first mixed, then added to the milk.

EGGNOG

A festive beverage made and drunk usually at Christmas, eggnog has the consistency of thick cream and is, in fact, a sort of liquid custard consisting of beaten eggs, milk or cream and sugar. It is often flavored with vanilla and a dash of nutmeg. Eggnog is served chilled and may be drunk by itself, or fortified with whisky, rum, other spirits or perhaps wine. The Germans make a sort of beer eggnog which they call *biersuppe*. In former times it was customary to make eggnog a month before Christmas and let it age. Nowadays it can be purchased readymade in the market.

EGGPLANT

Also AUBERGINE. A member of the potato family, eggplant *(Solanum melongena)* is a large, heavy vegetable that is usually pear-shaped and dark purple. Both the shape and color can vary widely, however. There are round and cucumber-shaped eggplants, and the color ranges from purple through red and striped to white. The white variety is well liked in Britain and Europe. Its resemblance to the egg accounts for its English name.

Eggplant has worldwide acceptance, but it is best known in oriental, Middle Eastern and Balkan cooking. It is believed to have originated in India, although no wild plant has ever been found. Unknown to ancient Greeks and Romans, eggplant was introduced into Spain by the Arabs in the 12th century. Records show it in England and Italy in the 16th century but as a decorative plant whose fruit was suspected of causing madness and thus called "mad apple." By this time the Spaniards greatly favored it, believing it to be an aphrodisiac, and gradually it came to be accepted in Northern Europe.

Eggplant is not a very nutritious food, having only 1 percent protein, 3 percent carbohydrate and no fat. On the other hand, it is filling and very low in calories—if not fried. The basic ingredient of such well-known dishes as *ratatouille* and *caponata*, eggplant can be served as a cold appetizer, stuffed as a main course or used as a vegetable accompaniment to almost any meat. It is never eaten raw.

The flavor of eggplant has an underlying bitterness, which can be attenuated by cutting the plant in half, salting it and letting it soak in water for an hour before cooking.

In the market, eggplants should be firm to the touch, with a clear, satiny color that covers the surface evenly. They should not be bought by size or weight, because larger ones have more seeds. The young, tender plants have a better flavor.

EGG TREE

A tree, *Garcinia xanthochymus*, of the western Himalayas and northern India, its dark yellow fruit reaches the size of a small orange and has a pointed projection at one end. This tree is related to the mangosteen. The yellow, juicy pulp has a pleasantly acidic flavor.

EGLANTINE

Also SWEETBRIER. This shrubby variety of rose, *Rosa eglanteria* is grown chiefly in the West as an ornamental and is interesting for its fragrant foliage. It is native to western Asia, however, and there and in India its flowers are used to make a confection called *gulangabin*, which consists of rose petals and honey. The name is also applied to the dog rose *(R. canina)*, and some sources speak of making preserves from the hips of the eglantine. This most probably refers to the dog rose and is considered under **rose hips.**

EGUSI MELON

Varieties of gourd, *Cucumeropsis edulis* and *C. manii*, cultivated in West and Equatorial Africa are valued solely for their oily seeds, which are cooked and eaten.

EGYPTIAN LOTUS

See **Lotus.**

EGYPTIAN ONION

See **Tree Onion.**

ELAND

A large antelope inhabiting the plains of Central and southern Africa, the common eland *(Taurotragus oryx)* can weigh as much as a ton and stand nearly six feet at the shoulder. It has long spiral horns and a characteristic oxlike massiveness about its forequarters. Elands are popular game because they yield large quantities of tender meat, and their hides make excellent leather.

ELATERIUM

Young specimens of this gourdlike fruit of a Central American plant, *Elaterium ciliatum*, are cooked and eaten as vegetables.

ELBINGER

See **Werder.**

Elderberry

ELDERBERRY

The name includes the fruit of several species of the elder, especially the dark purple berries of the American or sweet elder *(Sambucus canadensis)*, a roadside shrub found throughout North America. The berries are generally cooked or made into jelly or used for elderberry wine. In Europe, elderberries were thought to have medicinal qualities, were used to make wine, or served as a common adulterant of **port.** The berries of the American elder grow in large torch-like clusters that weigh down the stems. They are far richer in vitamin C than are citrus fruits, but have a rank, woody taste when eaten raw.

Elderberries make the best jelly when mixed with juice pressed from the fruit of the scarlet **sumac** *(Rhus glabra)*, a shrub that usually abounds in the same vicinity. The resultant jelly is "a clear transclucent red," according to Euell Gibbons, without any "cloying sweetness," with "a delightful, clean tartness that invited you to eat more, and then more."

In the Old World the elder (the name is akin to the alder, and perhaps elm) has had a magical association. Medieval belief insisted that Judas Iscariot hanged himself on an elder. A crown of elder became "a token of shame and disgrace." In Germany one was to doff one's hat to an elder in the notion that this tree was the wood of the cross of Christ's crucifixion.

ELDERFLOWER

The white blossoms of the American elder *(Sambucus canadensis)* are used to flavor jams, jellies and wines.

EL-DHAMBALA BEAN

A climbing plant, *Dolichos bracteata*, related to the lablab bean, has pods that grow to about three inches in length. The pods are narrow and well filled. *El-dhambala* beans are an important food source in tropical areas of Africa and Asia. This plant produces purple or mauve flowers.

See also: **Lablab Bean.**

ELECAMPANE

Also ELECAMPE, SCABWORT. A relative of the daisy, elecampane *(Inula helenium)* is a wild perennial plant with large clusters of yellow flowers. Its roots were once used to make candy. It is native to Europe and parts of Asia; the roots are spicy but bitter to the taste. They contain, however, a starch called inulin, which can be converted to **fructose** and gives the plant a commercial value.

The ancient Greeks and Romans held it in high esteem, mainly for its medicinal properties, but also as a food, provided it was taken with something sweet, such as grape sugar. As a medicine, it was deemed good for respiratory problems, such as shortness of breath and coughing. It was preserved by steeping in sweetened wine. After the fall of the Roman Empire, it seems to have disappeared from the European diet, only to reappear in the 19th century as a candy favored by English schoolboys. They liked its bittersweet flavor and believed it would strengthen their wind and improve their endurance in athletics. The root was also occasionally eaten as a boiled vegetable.

ELECAMPE

See **Elecampane.**

ELECTRIC CATFISH

An edible catfish, *Malapterurus electricus*, of tropical Africa is capable of delivering an electrical shock powerful enough to render a human unconscious. It can reach a length of four feet, and a large specimen will weigh more than 30 pounds. Its flesh is described as firm, white and well flavored. The range of this fish includes the Nile River system, rivers of West Africa, the Chad, Lake Rudolph and the Zambezi system.

ELECTRIC EEL

An edible, freshwater eel, *Electrophorus electricus* of South America, is capable of delivering a powerful electric shock. It can attain a length of eight feet and is found in the Guyanas and in the basins of the Orinoco and Amazon Rivers. This eel is only occasionally used for food, but it is frequently kept in public aquariums for its novelty value. Its electrical potential has been measured at 500 volts, enough to severely shock a human. This ability has been used in the experimental treatment of rheumatism.

ELEPHANT

A four-footed mammal, the elephant is the world's largest land animal and exists in two species, the African elephant *(Elephas africanus)* and the Indian elephant *(Elephas indicus)*. The former is the larger of the two and seems to be the only kind eaten with any regularity. According to most sources, elephant flesh is tough and tasteless, the trunk and feet being the best parts. The African pygmies specialize in hunting elephants, and they prefer the foot. "Biltong" is a South African word for elephant meat that has been turned into dried strips. When the herds are being thinned at Kruger National Park, biltong is available in butcher shops throughout the country. South Africans regard it as a delicacy and describe it as "tasty, but a little coarse."

The first recorded European to eat elephant meat was probably the Italian Alvise de Cadamosto, who partook of some on the Gambia River in Africa in 1456 and left us these notes;

> *I had a portion cut off, which, roasted and broiled, I ate on board ship . . . to be able to say that I had eaten the flesh of an animal which had never been previously eaten by any of my countrymen. The flesh, actually, is not very good, seeming tough and insipid to me.*

The Germans laid siege to Paris in 1871 during the Franco-Prussian War, cutting off the food supply. Citizens of Paris were reduced to eating the animals in the zoo, two of which were the elephants, Castor and Pollux. Cuts of elephant trunk sold for 40 francs a pound and were reportedly eaten with bearnaise sauce.

ELEPHANT APPLE

Also WOOD APPLE. This edible fruit of a small, spiny tree, *Feronia limonia*, is native to India and Ceylon. The fruit is about the size of an orange and has a glutinous, aromatic pulp that can be eaten raw or used in jellies and sherbet. It is thought stimulating and good for the stomach. The rind is a dull red and the pulp pinkish. Although of different genera, citrus species can be grated onto this tree.

ELEPHANT GRASS

A type of cattail, *Typha elephantina*, it is indigenous to southern Europe, southern Asia and Africa. At one time or another during the year, all parts of a cattail are edible, including shoots, leaves, green bloom spikes, rootstalks, etc.

See also: **Cattail.**

ELEPHANT'S FOOT

Also HOTTENTOT-BREAD. This vine of the yam family, *Dioscorea elephantipes*, native to South Africa, has a tuberous root that resembles an elephant's foot. It protrudes half above ground and may be up to three feet in diameter. It has a starchy consistency and was once cooked and eaten by Hottentots as a famine food.

ELEPHANT-SNOUT FISH

Probably the most widely found fish of the African *Mormyridae* family, *Mormyrus kannume* is characterized by a long, trunk-shaped snout. It is good to eat, if rather oily, and it is fished commercially in many areas of the Nile River and the great African lakes, including Victoria, Albert, Edward and George. A closely related species, *M. proboscyrostris*, is found in the Upper Congo River.

The elephant-snout fish attains a maximum length of about 32 inches and is colored dull bronze above, shading lighter below. This fish was held sacred by the ancient Egyptians and appears frequently in their art. *M. kannume* is able to generate an electrical field that it uses as a kind of radar.

ELEPHANT YAM

Also TELINGO POTATO. Edible corm of a perennial herb, *Amorphophallus campanulatus*, found in tropical southeast Asia and southern India, it is a food of some importance there.

ELETARIA

Also JAVA CARDAMOM. This perennial herb, *Elettaria speciosa*, has stout rhizomes whose seeds are used to make candy. It is native to Java and is related to **cardamom.**

ELISAVETPOLEN.

See **Eriwani.**

ELK, AMERICAN

See **Wapiti.**

ELK, EUROPEAN.

See **Moose.**

ELLIPTICAL SUNPLANT

A shrub, *Solanum ellipticum*, of South Australia, its fruit is eaten locally.

ELM TREE PLEUROTUS

This edible mushroom, *Pleurotus ulmarius*, of the British Isles and North America, grows on stumps and dead branches of elm trees and occasionally other hardwoods. It is a relative of the oyster mushroom and appears in the late summer, fall and early winter. It reaches four inches in height, and the cap may reach six inches in diameter. The color of the cap ranges from white to cream, buff or pale fawn with white gills and stem.

The elm tree pleurotus has a pleasant aroma and is delicious eating when young. It is tougher and has little flavor when older, but may be used to extend a number of dishes. This mushroom was a favorite of the Dakota tribe of the American Midwest. Squaws sought it out in boxelder trees, especially in decayed spots caused by their tapping the trees for sugar sap.

See also: **Mushroom.**

ELOPS

See **Ladyfish.**

ELVERS

See **Eel.**

EMBLIC

Tart but edible fruit of a deciduous tree, *Phyllanthus emblica* of tropical Asia, emblic is at its best in preserves and jellies. It is also called myrobolan or myrobalan along with a number of other fruits.

See also: **Myrobalan, Cherry Plum.**

EMILIANO

This Italian hard cheese of the *grana* or Parmesan type is very similar to **Reggiano.** The exterior is dark and oily, but the curd is light yellow with a mild to sharp flavor and granular texture. The cheeses are cylindrical in shape, 12 to 16 inches in diameter and weigh 44 to 66 pounds. They are aged from one to two years. The latter type is most suitable for grating.

EMMENTAL

See **Swiss Cheese.**

EMMENTHAL

See **Swiss Cheese.**

EMPEROR

The *Lethrinidae* family of fish frequents coral reefs in the Indian and western Pacific Oceans. The sweetlip emperor *(Lethrinus chrysostomus)* is abundant along the northern coast of Australia and on the Great Barrier Reef. It weighs as much as 20 pounds and may be up to 3 feet long. It is much admired both as food and as a sport fish.

This and other emperors are characterized by long snouts, deep cheeks, and by otherwise resembling a **grunt.** Another valuable food fish is the long-nosed emperor *(L. miniatus)*, also known as the scavenger and Mata Hari. The range of this fish is much broader, extending from the Red Sea and East Africa to the east coast of Australia. Similarly distributed is the spangled emperor *(L. nebulosus)*. This is the most abundant and heavily fished of the three species. It is somewhat smaller, attaining a maximum length of only 30 inches.

EMU APPLE

See **Bulloo.**

ENDIVE

These are curly-leaved, green vegetables of the species *Cichorium endivia*, which are commonly called salad chicory, or curly chicory in the United States. A closely related species is escarole *(chicoree scarol)*. The plant is thought to be native to India, having been introduced into Europe as far back as the time of the ancient Greeks. Endives are used chiefly as salad greens, and their leaves have the slight bitterness characteristic of true chicory. To attenuate the bitterness they are frequently blanched. (For an explanation of this process, see **Chicory.)**

There are two broad categories of *Cichorium endivia:* the *crispa* with curly, deeply indented leaves, of which endive is an example; and the *latifolia* with whole leaves, curly at the edges, of which escarole is an example. In France, endive is known as *chicoree frisee*. Escaroles grown in the summer have tougher leaves than the fall and winter varieties and are therefore served more appropriately as a cooked vegetable. Braising is a common method of cooking both endives and escaroles.

ENGADINE

A mild, rennet cheese made in the Swiss canton of Grisons, it is produced from whole cow's milk and has a medium-firm texture.

ENGLISH BREAKFAST TEA

Trade name for a Chinese black tea, reputedly **Keemun** or a blend of similar teas that make a full-bodied, rich, mellow and fragrant brew. The name is used in Canada and the United States, but not in England.

See also: **Tea.**

ENGLISH CRESS

See **Garden Cress.**

ENGLISH DAIRY CHEESE

Despite the name, this was an American cheese, similar to **cheddar,** but cooked much longer and consequently having a much harder curd.

Escarole, a close relative of endive

Enoki mushrooms

ENOKI MUSHROOM

Also ENOKIDAKE, SNOW PUFF MUSHROOM. Featured in Japanese cuisine, the enoki mushroom is small and white, and has a long, smooth stem. It looks something like a bean sprout, but is an exotic form of the velvet foot mushrom *(Flammulina velutipes)*, a mushroom that grows wild in the United States. Commercially cultivated enoki mushrooms are available fresh during the fall and early winter months in Oriental grocery stores. They are rich in trace minerals, and have a delicate, perfumed aroma. The canned variety are available year round, but they lack the delicate taste of the fresh mushrooms.

ENSETE

This genus of tropical plants, *Ensete* spp., is closely allied to the banana and found in both Africa and Asia. In some places the flower stalks are eaten, first being fermented, then made into a bread. An Ethiopian species, *E. Ventricosum*, also known as Abyssinian bread, produces edible flower heads and seeds.

ENTRE-DEUX-MERS

This white wine comes from western France between the Garonne and the Dordogne rivers (the two *mers* or "seas"), east of **Bordeaux.** Only white wine from this region can be labeled "Entre-deux-Mers." The red wines grown here are sold simply as Bordeaux. Entre-deux-Mers is the largest wine-growing district in Bordeaux—not as important as the **Medoc** and **Sauternes,** but noteworthy for its dry but fruity wine from the Semillon and Sauvignon grapes.

EPAZOTE

See **Mexican Tea.**

EPINOCHE

See **Stickleback.**

EPOISSE

A soft, mold-inoculated French cheese from the Cote d'Or department is made from renneted, whole or partly skimmed cow's milk. *Epoisse* is an important cheese in the Burgundy area. It is sometimes eaten fresh in the summer months and sometimes seasoned with pepper, cloves or fennel seeds and soaked in white wine.

ERIOGLOSSUM

This edible fruit of a shrubby tree, *Erioglossum edule*, native from tropical Asia to northern Australia, is red turning to black, has a single seed, is round in shape and reaches a diameter of about three-quarter inch.

ERIWANI

Also KARAB, TALI, KURINI, ELISAVETPOLEN, KASACH. This Russian cheese is made from fresh ewe's milk chiefly in the Caucasus. The curd is pressed and salted in brine.

ERMITAGE WINE

See **Hermitage.**

ERVY

A soft French cheese resembling Camembert in taste and texture, it is named for the village of Ervy in the Champagne district. In season from November to May, the cheese typically measures seven inches in diameter and weighs four pounds.

ERYNGIUM

The *Eryngium* is a large genus of perennial herbs, one species of which, the *Eryngium foetidum*, is used as a condiment. The valuable parts are the roots, which have an unpleasant odor but when added to soups or meat dishes impart a pleasant taste. This species is native to tropical America.

ERYTHRIN

Also TIGERFISH, JEJU. The *Erythrinidae* are a group of predatory fish found in tropical South American waters. The live in freshwater and are considered excellent food fish. A marked characteristic is their ability to use atmospheric oxygen, which the *erythrin* gulps above the surface and stores in a bladder. Its preferred habitat is stagnant pools.

The most abundant and commercially valuable species is the tigerfish *(Hoplias malabarucus)*, which attains a length of two feet. It is found from Venezuela and the Guianas south to Argentina. Others are the jeju *(Hoplerythrinus unitaeniatus)* and the pikelike *Erythrinus erythrinus*.

ESCARGOT

See **Snail.**

ESCAROLE

See **Endive.**

ESPAGNOLE SAUCE

Also BROWN SAUCE. A concentrated dark sauce is made from beef and a small amount of vegetables and thickened with flour or starch. It is one of the basic French sauces, along with bechamel and *veloute*. Like the latter two, it is used as a basic ingredient of many other sauces, called "compound sauces" *(sauce composee)*. For example, add madeira, stock, gravy and butter and you have madeira sauce; with duck gravy and orange peel added, you have *bigarade* sauce, and so on.

Espagnole sauce, though rich, is simple in concept. A roux is made of chopped vegetables (tomatoes, onions, carrots), herbs (thyme, bay leaf), butter and cornstarch by heating and mixing. Beef stock is gradually added to the roux, allowed to boil for an hour or more, then strained and skimmed. The result is a clear, lightly thickened, amber liquid. It will keep in a cool place for three to four days.

See also: **Sauce.**

ESSENTIAL OIL

Also VOLATILE OIL. The term applies to a liquid expressed, extracted or distilled from a flower, fruit or plant that possesses the distinctive odor or flavor of the original. It is frequently oily, highly volatile and subject to evaporation at ordinary temperature. Examples are oil of coffee, tea, lemon, anise, cinnamon, clove etc. Frequently they are not soluble in water but are mixed with such vehicles as alcohol, ether, fatty oils or mineral oils. Essential oils are used by manufacturers of flavoring extracts, and perhaps even more by perfumers.

EST! EST!! EST!!!

A straw-colored Italian wine from the ancient town of Montefiascone on Lake Bolsena in the province of Latium north of Rome, it is dry with a fruity, fresh bouquet. A legend attaches to the origin of its name. A German bishop, Johannes Fuger, was traveling to Rome for the coronation of the Emperor Henry V in 1110. Being a lover of good wine, he sent his valet ahead to search out accomodations, instructing him to chalk the word *est* (meaning "it is.") on the wall of any inn with good wine. At Montefiascone, the valet was so impressed by the quality of wine that he expressed his enthusiasm by writing *Est! Est!! Est!!!* on the wall of the local inn.

The story goes that the wine proved so beguiling to the bishop that he never left Montefiascone, preferring to end his days within reach of his favorite tipple. His tomb, which lies just within the entrance to the basilica of Saint Flaviano, bears this inscription: *Est, Est, Est et propter nimium est, Johannes de Fuger, dominus meus, mortuus est.* ("It is, it is, it is, and through too much "it is," my master, Johannes de Fuger, dead is.") The bishop bequeathed all his money to the town on condition that every year the town fathers pour a barrel of wine over his grave, a practice long discontinued.

ESTUARY CATFISH

An abundant Australian species, *Cnidoglanis macrocephalus*, the estuary catfish is said to make very good eating despite its hideous appearance. It lives in salt or brackish waters, favoring the muddy bottoms of estuaries or sandy bays of inshore waters. Its head is broad and flat and its body long and slender. Its large mouth is surrounded by eight barbels, and its spiny pectoral and dorsal fins can inflict painful wounds. It is black brown above with a white belly.

ETHIOPIAN APPLE

The fruit of an herbaceous plant of the nightshade family, *Solanum aethiopicum*, it is found and eaten in the warm regions of Asia and Africa.

EULACHON

See **Candlefish.**

EVAPORATED MILK

See **Condensed Milk.**

EVENING PRIMROSE

Also GERMAN RAMPION. The roots of the evening-flowering plant *Oenothera biennis* may be eaten as vegetables. The young shoots are also tasty and are used in salads. This species is found both in Europe and eastern North America.

EVIAN WATER

A still mineral water bottled in France, it is a natural spring water, relatively low in mineral content (330 ppm total dissolved solids). A sensory panel sponsored by the Consumers Union in 1980 judged its taste to be good and made the following comments on its flavor: heavy, thick mouthfeel, mild soapy flavor.

See also: **Mineral Water.**

FAIRY RING

Also SCOTCH BONNET. A small edible mushroom of North America, the British Isles and Europe, it is so named because it is customarily found in groups forming a loose circle. It fruits in autumn in meadows, lawns, golf courses and the like, often creating unsightly and unwelcome bare patches in the turf. On maturing, it measures up to four inches in length, and the cap can reach 2½ inches across. The cap is white to tan.

The fairy ring *(Marasmius oreades)* is best for eating when young and tender. It has a pleasant mushroom taste and fragrant aroma and holds its flavor well when dried. It is good broiled and served with steak. Its small size also makes it particularly suitable for soups, sauces and stews.

See also: **Mushroom.**

FAIRY SPUDS

Also SPRING BEAUTY. These are the small tuberous roots of a perennial herb, *Calytonia virginica*, whose small pink flowers are known as spring beauties. Fairy spuds are eaten as a cooked vegetable and have a flavor resembling potatoes or chestnuts.

FALERNIAN WINE

The great red wine of ancient Rome, praised by Horace and Martial, is today a thick, dry, heavy vintage made in the province of Caserta, northeast of Naples. Catullus, too, sang its praises:

Come, my boy, bring me the best
of good old Falernian . . . and no more water;
water is the death of wine.
Serve the stuff to solemn fools
who enjoy their sorrow,
respectable, no doubt—
but wine!
Here's wine!
The very blood of Bacchus!

Falernian wine—from the Aglianico, or Ellanico, grape—has a high tannin content, which gives it a rather bitter taste. It is also very strong (13 to 16 percent alcohol). It often retains some nonfermented sugar, which mitigates the bitterness. A dry white Falerno is also grown in the region of Lazio, farther north.

FALSE BREADFRUIT

See **Ceriman.**

FALSE SPIKENARD

Also WILD SPIKENARD, SOLOMON'S PLUMES. A perennial herb of North America, *Smilacina racemosa* has white flower spikes and edible berries that may be red or spotted purple. The fruit is consumed where grown.

FARINA

This is the Italian word for flour. All variations of the word derive from the Latin word *far*, which is spelt, a staple grain of the ancient Phoenicians and other early Mediterranean peoples. In English, the term is used for a flour or meal obtained from any number of products, including cereal grains, potatoes, nuts, beans, etc. Specifically, in the United States, farina is a white granular cereal made from the white inner portion of the wheat kernel, or endosperm. It is generally prepared as a hot breakfast cereal served with milk.

In a different context, farina is another name for semolina, or wheat middlings. These are hard particles of wheat left in the milling machine after the finer flour has sifted out. Semolina from very hard, or durum, wheat is used to make macaroni. Farina consists mainly of starch, and from this comes the adjective, farinaceous, which is used to describe food made up mainly of meal, flour or starch.

In Portuguese, *farinha* refers to a fine flour made from the bitter manioc or **cassava.** It is a popular product in Brazil and used, among other ways, to sprinkle on top of the national dish, *feijoada*, which consists of rice, black beans, sausage, pork chops, onions, bananas and chilled orange slices.

FARM CHEESE

Also FARMER CHEESE. This firm, pressed cheese is made on farms in the United States. Methods vary considerably from place to place, but usually the curd is formed from whole or partly skimmed cow's milk by renneting or natural souring. The curd is drained, then pressed overnight. To be eaten fresh, it is immediately wrapped in parchment. If it is to be cured, it is dried and dipped in paraffin and stored in a moist cellar. The paste should slice without crumbling. The flavor should be clean and mild.

The term is also applied to a French farmhouse cheese that is very close to both **white cheese** and **cottage cheese.** French names include *mou*, *maigre* and *ferme*. The curd is formed by souring from whole or skim milk. The cheese is then drained and kneaded to expel more whey. Salt and sometimes cream are mixed in. Then it is molded into various shapes and sizes.

FARMER CHEESE

See **Farm Cheese.**

FASEOLE

A type of kidney bean, *Phaseolus vulgaris*, grown in the south of France, it is comparable in shape and use to the white haricot or navy bean, except that it is smaller and green. It has a very good flavor.

FAT

Chemically speaking, fat consists of glycerine combined with three acids: stearic, palmitic and oleic. It may be saturated or unsaturated, and current theory holds that the distinction is important for health. Saturated fat contains a relatively low proportion of oleic acid and is solid at room temperature. Butter is one example. Unsaturated fat contains a relatively high proportion of oleic acid and is liquid at room temperature. Vegetable oil is an example. It has been recommended that persons seeking to keep a low cholesterol blood level or who suffer from arteriosclerosis restrict their intake of saturated fats and substitute the unsaturated. There is no conclusive evidence that this is beneficial, however. See also: **Cholesterol.**

Fat is a major source of energy and is found in the connective and nervous tissue of all animals and in parts of many plants, especially fruit, seeds and nuts. It is one of the three main constituents found in all body cells, the other two being protein and carbohydrate. Of the three, it is by far the greatest producer of energy, i.e., nine calories per gram, as opposed to four per gram in the other two. Normally, body weight consists of about 20 percent fat, although this may vary in colder climates where fat serves as an excellent insulator to prevent loss of body heat.

Fat enters the diet either by being contained in the food we eat or through the use of fats in cooking. In animal tissue, fat is a white substance interlarding or encompassing a carcass. It turns to oil when heated and hardens into a thick grease when cold. Vegetable fats are more commonly called "oils" because they are liquid at room temperature. To a certain extent, all natural fats are mixtures of saturated and unsaturated. Among the animal kingdom, highest saturation is found in beef and mutton fat, then pork, then veal and poultry, and finally fish oils, such as herring and salmon. Butter, a highly saturated fat, is a case apart because it is a concentrate formed by human intervention.

The type of fat you ingest can be controlled to a great extent by what fat, if any, you use in cooking. There are some relatively fatless methods of cooking, such as boiling, which is also the least flavorful. Others usually requiring no added fat are spit roasting and grilling. Added fat, however, greatly enhances taste in such methods as frying and roasting.

Vegetable and nut oils, with the exception of coconut, are generally unsaturated. They include the following in order of increasing saturation: safflower seed, sunflower seed, corn, sesame seed, peanut and olive.

The normal amount of fat for an adult in a temperate climate to eat is 75 grams per day. Staying power is a characteristic of a fatty meal. That is, fatty food leaves the stomach more slowly, slowing down digestion, so that the eater does not feel hungry so quickly. On the other hand, too much fat can cause stomach upset.

See also: **Margarine.**

FAT SLEEPER

A food fish of the goby family, the fat sleeper *(Dormitator maculatus)* is found in the western Atlantic from North Carolina to Brazil, including the Gulf of Mexico. It lives close to shore, preferring brackish waters and sometimes freshwater river mouths. The fat sleeper reaches a length of 18 inches and has a short, thick body with dark brown skin and red fins.

FAUFAL

See **Couscous.**

FAVA BEAN

See **Broad Bean.**

FEABERRY

See **Gooseberry**

FEATHERBACK

This freshwater fish, *Notopterus chitala*, is found from India to Sumatra but is most highly valued as food in Thailand. Its name derives from its small, featherlike dorsal fin. Featherback reaches a length of about three feet and lives in rivers, swamps and canals. The fish is cultured in Thailand and sometimes carried live hundreds of miles to market.

FECULA

Also FECULE. A powdered starch used to thicken soups and sauces, it is obtained by washing down the starchy pulp of vegetables such as potatoes, cassava, yams, arrowroot and other legumes.

FEDELINI

See **Pasta.**

FEIJOA

Also PINEAPPLE GUAVA. The guavalike fruit of an evergreen tree, *Feijoa sellowiana*, of southern Brazil, Paraguay, Uruguay and northern Argentina, the feijoa is green tinged with red and two to three inches long. It has a pleasant flavor much like guava, although it varies greatly from tree to tree and cultivar to cultivar. It is eaten raw but more often made into a jam, jelly or stew.

FENDENT WINE

See **Wines, Swiss.**

FENDLER'S CYMOPTERUS

A perennial herb of the western United States, especially Colorado, Utah and New Mexico, *Cymopterus fendleri* has aromatic roots. When dried, these are used to flavor meat dishes.

FENNEL

There are three plants generally known as fennel: ordinary fennel, sweet fennel and Italian fennel. They are native to Italy but have been naturalized throughout Europe and in the United States, mainly in California. Fennel was an important culinary herb for the ancient Romans and all three varieties have maintained that popularity in modern Italy.

Fennel

Ordinary fennel *(Foeniculum vulgare)* grows wild, but it is the cultivated plant that is valued for its foliage and seeds, whose flavor much resembles **anise.** The stalks often reach five or six feet, supporting delicate, feathery leaves and yellow blossoms. The stalks and leaves are a traditional seasoning for fish dishes, while the seeds are used in cookies, pastries and sweet pickles. An essential oil is extracted and used to flavor liqueurs. The ancient Romans considered a fennel infusion to be therapeutic to eye diseases, particularly cataracts.

Sweet, or Florence, fennel is a smaller plant with a bulbous root and heavier stalks that give it a celerylike appearance. Anethole, its essential oil, gives this plant a fragrance of anise that is both appetizing and refreshing. It is eaten both raw and cooked as a vegetable and is quite low in calories, yet has little nutritive value. The Greeks considered it an aid in losing weight, and they called it *marathon* after their verb to grow thin. It is called *finocchio* in Italy, where it is used to season a sausage with a similar name.

Italian fennel *(Foeniculum vulgare piperitum)*, also called *carosella* or *cartucci*, is relished for its fresh stalks, which are prepared like asparagus.

FENNEL FLOWER

Also ROMAN CORIANDER. An aromatic herb, *Nigella sativa*, of the Mediterranean region, whose seeds are used for seasoning, it has blue, yellow or white flowers.

FENNEL WATER

Here is a cordial or liqueur made in France and flavored with fennel. It tastes like anise.

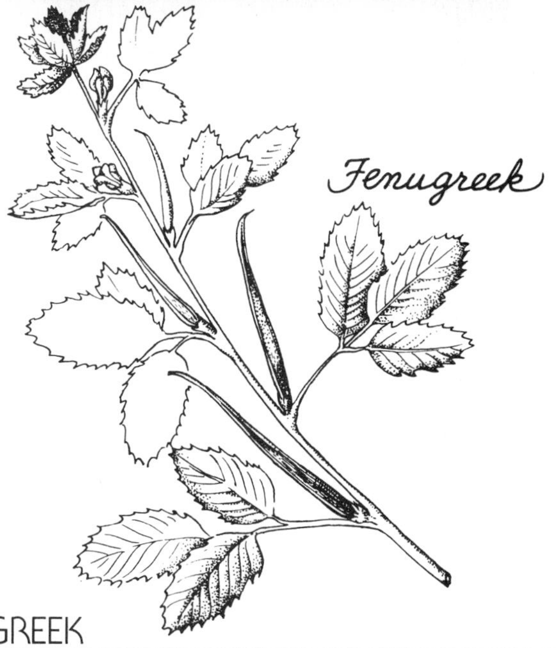

FENUGREEK

Seeds of the herbaceous fenugreek plant *(Trigonella foenumgraecum)* are an important ingredient of curry powder. The seeds are very tiny—2,500 to the ounce—and are actually a pulse like the pea. Fenugreek seeds must be dried, ground and heated before the characteristic flavor and aroma emerge. They are very hard and must be ground with stone or in a poppy-seed grinder. The leaves and seed pods are also eaten as vegetables in India and some parts of Africa. The seeds, especially, are an important vegetable in Ethiopia.

In the West, fenugreek has been cultivated as far back as early Roman times. It has never received much notice as a food or spice, however. As a medicine, it was a standard item in Roman and medieval herbals, and early Egyptians used fenugreek seeds as we do quinine today. A flour ground from the seeds makes a good poultice for boils and abcesses. Taken internally, it relieves inflammation of the digestive tract. In veterinary medicine, the flour is used as conditioning powder for horses and cattle. The rather odd name comes from the Latin, and means "Greek hay." Fenugreek is still used as fodder in some parts of North Africa, and in California small amounts are grown and used as green manure.

In curry powder, fenugreek seeds impart a pleasantly bitter taste and aroma. They are reddish brown or yellow. Oddly enough, in small amounts the seeds have a maplelike flavor and have been put to commercial use in the United States to flavor candy. The seeds are high in calories—335 per 100 grams—and in India are taken by persons who want to gain weight. They are also rich in calcium, and for this reason are taken by lactating mothers.

FERA

A European lakefish much favored by gourmets, the *fera (Coregonus ferus)* is considered second only to the *omble chevalier* in the delicate flavor of its flesh and is equalled only by the *bouting* or *lavaret (C. lavaretus)*, a close relative. Both the *fera* and the *bouting* are found in Lake Geneva and in several other lakes of Switzerland, Bavaria, Austria and France. The best *fera* are taken from Lake Geneva in May from the shallow waters near the sandbank or *travers*, and are called *fera de travers*.

The *fera* is a member of the whitefish genus of the salmon family and is thus akin to the cisco *(C. artedii)* of American lakes. It reaches a maximum length of about two feet and varies in color from white to blue to black, depending on age and the depth at which it is feeding. It may be prepared in any way suitable for trout but is best cooked simply, such as *a la meuniere*, or broiled.

FERMENTATION

This is a biological process whereby a chemical change is produced in foods by the action of various "ferments," such as yeast or certain bacteria. Popularly, fermentation is best associated with the making of wine and beer. This is known as vinous fermentation, where the action of yeast on sugar and malt produces a liquid: alcohol, and a gas: carbon dioxide. If the process is allowed to continue unchecked, acetous fermentation results, when acetic bacteria oxidize the alcohol and produce vinegar. The French *vin aigre* means, literally, "sour wine." The souring of milk is caused by lactic fermentation, when some of the milk sugar is converted into lactic acid by the action of lactic bacterià.

Louis Pasteur was the first to prove conclusively the correspondence between fermentation and oxidation. He linked fermentation to putrefaction, or the spoiling of organic matter by microorganisms in the absence of—or with very little—air. Thus, putrefactive fermentation is involved in the rotting of meat. Generally in fermentation, a sugar substance yields a product with a pleasant odor and taste, while proteins give rise to a foul-smelling change.

Fermentation can provide foods unfit to eat as well as foods that are among the finest in the world. It is a highly valuable process in food production vital to the production of wine, beer, cheese, soured milk, pickles, sauerkraut, olives, breads and sausages.

FERMENTED FISH SAUCE

See **Nuoc-mam.**

FERMENTED MILK

This includes milk that has fermented through natural action or whose fermentation has been enhanced by such agents as rennet, bacteria and yeasts. The purposes of fermentation are several: to improve the milk's transportability, to preserve it for a longer time, to make it easier to digest, to make it available to persons who cannot tolerate fresh milk, to make it a mild stimulant and to alter its flavor and textures.

Sources of milk for fermentation are or have been cows, horses, goats and buffaloes. Fermented milk bears various names. Some examples include **acidophilus milk, buttermilk,** *dahdi* (India), *mazyn* (Armenia), *huslanka* (Carpathians), *lab en zebodi* (Egypt), *busa* (Turkestan), *cieddu* (Italy), *kuban*, **kefir, kumiss** (USSR) and *taetta* (Scandinavia), as well as cheese and yogurts.

See also: **Cheese, Yogurt.**

FERNET BRANCA

Fernet Branca is a dark brown bitters, particularly popular in Italy where it comes from, and relatively so in America where it is made by a branch of the parent company, Fratelli Branca Co. The infusion and distillation of a variety of aromatic plants, seeds, barks, roots, herbs and fruits blended into an alcohol base are sometimes a shock for those who taste it for the first time.

In Italy, it is used in cocktails for flavoring. Italians also drink it straight, esteeming the quinine-like taste as a tonic and an aid to digestion.

English distillers have developed an orange bitters as a comparable drink. They infuse the dried peel of the bitter Seville orange. This is the same orange that has proved so successful in orange marmalade.

FERRARELLE WATER

A naturally sparkling mineral water bottled in Italy, Ferrarelle water has a relatively high mineral content (1400 ppm total dissolved solids). A 1980 Consumers Union sensory panel rated the taste of this water as fair, with the following qualifying comments: mildly bitter, mild soapy flavor, mildly salty.

See also: **Mineral Water.**

FETA

Feta is a soft, white Greek cheese with both farmhouse and factory varieties that was originally made by shepherds in the mountains north of Athens. Feta is a "pickled" cheese with a salty, astringent taste. Made from fresh ewe's or goat's milk for local consumption, it is salted and packed into kegs, and is ready to eat in four or five days. For the export variety, pasteurized milk is used, and the curd is either kept in kegs for a month after salting or packed in tin containers. Cow's milk is used in the feta made in the United States.

FETERITA

See **Sorghum.**

FETTUCINE

See **Pasta.**

FETTICUS

See **Lamb's Lettuce.**

FEVERFEW

The leaves and flowers of this perennial herb, *Chrysanthemum parthenium*, are used to make a soothing tea. At one time, the plant was thought to have extraordinary curative powers, especially in reducing fevers, hence the name. Feverfew is a member of the chyrsanthemum family and has yellow disc flowers and white petals. The leaves are also used to flavor soups and stews.

FIBER, DIETARY

Also ROUGHAGE. Plant fiber, or "roughage," as it used to be called, is thought to play a beneficial role in the human diet. In the common definition, fibers are thin, threadlike structures that combine with others to form vegetable tissue. More to the point, fiber is a complex of substances that appear not to be absorbed or digested by humans. Thus fiber passes through the intestine unchanged but absorbs and holds water, adds bulk to the diet and acts as a laxative.

Most of the fiber is found in the wall of the plant cell, and cellulose is its largest component. Other components are pectin, hemicellulose and lignin. Plant gums, such as guar gum and mucilages, can also be classified as fibers.

Early interest in dietary fiber focused on wheat bran, the husk or outer covering of the wheat grain, which is high in cellulose. Bran has been taken as a laxative since the 14th century, so it was not a completely new idea when, in the 1820s, it became what was probably America's first food fad. In that decade the Reverend Sylvester W. Graham of West Suffield, Connecticut, began to popularize a diet based on bread made from coarse, unbolted or unsifted flour. He denounced white bread, which for centuries had been a symbol of the good life. White bread was made from flour that had the bran removed in the milling process and thus had no laxative effect. Dr. Graham was obsessed with bowel regularity, and he banned white bread from his diet. The doctor's name is still with us today in Graham flour (coarse, whole wheat flour) and the Graham cracker. His ideas influenced a whole generation of reformers and led to the founding of the modern breakfast food industry.

More recent interest has focused on fiber and how its components affect the incidence of heart disease, diabetes and colon cancer. For example, the effects of cellulose, pectin and guar gum on the level of serum cholesterol have been studied. The results suggest that while cellulose appears to have no effect, both pectin and guar gum—at a level of 15 g and 36 g per day respectively—lowered the cholesterol level of heart patients over a three-week period. Data regarding diabetes and colon cancer are not so clear, yet there are apparent correlations between incidence of colon cancer and low-fiber diets.

Two disadvantages of a high-fiber diet appear to be increased flatulence and the possibility that the fiber may reduce the absorption of essential nutrients as they move through the digestive system. So, a dietary rule of thumb is that a little fiber is good, but a lot is not necessarily better.

FICIFOLIA

Also MALABAR GOURD. Ficifolia is the fruit of a long-running perennial vine, *Cucurbita ficifolia*, that is native to tropical America but often cultivated in eastern Asia. It is a member of the squash family, and may be nearly spherical or oblong and can reach 12 inches in length. It is green with white stripes. *Ficifolia* is cooked and eaten as a vegetable or used to make preserves.

FIDDLER CRAB

This small, edible crab of the genus *Gelasimus* is particularly plentiful in Florida between Tampa and Key West. The fiddler crab is a burrowing variety, with one claw much larger than the other. Its taste is good, but the yield of meat per crab is very low.

FIELDFARE

See **Litorne.**

FIELD GARLIC

Also CROW GARLIC, STAG'S GARLIC. A weedy species of garlic, *Allium vineale*, native to Europe has been naturalized in the United States. The bulbs have the aroma and pungency suitable to being substituted for ordinary **garlic.**

FIELD MUSHROOM

Also MEADOW MUSHROOM. Probably the best known of all wild mushrooms, the field mushroom *(Agaricus campestris)* is also called the common mushroom and appears on lawns, pastures, fields and golf courses, but never in woods. It is closely related to the cultivated mushroom *(A. bisporus)* found in markets and to Rodman's mushroom *(A. bitorquis)*, which also appears in the open but is larger and prefers hard-packed soil.

The field mushroom is short, stocky and white with pink or brown gills. It appears at the end of summer, when nights are cooler and there is occasional rain. The field mushroom grows in scattered groups or may form circles or "fairy rings." The stem is very short, so that the mushroom often appears to be all cap and no bottom. The cap may reach a diameter of up to four inches. It is possible to confuse this mushroom with the deadly white amanitas, or destroying angels to which it bears a passing resemblance. In contrast to the field mushroom, however, the white amanitas are tall stately mushrooms with white gills. (See also: **Orange Amanita.)**

Field mushrooms have been grown commercially on a small scale since the Middle Ages. This is the *champignon de Paris* and is believed to be the fungus that was first called *mouscheron* by the French, from which we derive our English word.

The taste of this mushroom is delicious and can be eaten raw or cooked. In fact, it is one of the few wild mushrooms that can be eaten raw in salads without concern. It has a stronger flavor than the commercial *A. bisporus* yet may be substituted for it in any recipe. It is good in steak sauce or mushroom soup.

See also: **Mushroom.**

FIELD PEA

This pulse, *Pisum arvense*, is closely related to the common or garden **pea** but is more often used as livestock fodder or green manure than as human food. Though not as appetizing as the garden pea, the field pea is as nutritious and is similar in appearance. Both are annual leafy plants that grow up to five feet long, but the field pea has purple instead of white flowers and gray or dun-colored instead of green seeds. At maturity the seed has a smooth covering, whereas in the garden pea this covering is wrinkled. For human consumption, the field pea is dried, then split. It is used to make pea meal.

The field pea is a hardy plant and grows wild in certain parts of Europe. For this reason, it was long thought to be the wild ancestor of the garden pea. But current botanical opinion holds that it is merely another variety of garden pea that escaped from cultivation in earlier times and reverted to the wild.

There are many different varieties of field pea, some better suited for drying than others, including small bluish green types, speckled varieties of the black-eyed Susan type, and bigger, dimpled kinds. The better known are the Bavarian winter pea, the black-podded pea, the capuchin pea, the Smyrna pea, the Konigsberger pea, the East Prussian pea, the paluschke pea and the sand pea.

See also: **Cowpea.**

FIELD POPPY OIL

Oil is expressed from the seeds of this common European wild flower *Papaver rhoeas*. It is also known as the corn poppy and the Flanders poppy. In France the oil is used in the kitchen in the same way as olive oil. The flowers may be cinnabar-red, deep purple, scarlet or white and are used both medicinally and to color wine.

FIELD SALAD

See **Lamb's Lettuce.**

FIG

Fig

This is the sweet fruit of the fig tree *(Ficus carica)*, which is a member of the mulberry family. There are several hundred varieties. For this reason the fruit varies greatly in size, shape and color. The plant may be a vine, a shrub or a tree. The fruit may grow underground or high in the air, dangling from a tree limb, which is the usual case for figs of commercial importance. The fruit may be black, brown, red, purple, violet, green, yellow green or white. It customarily ripens in early or late summer, and can be relatively large or small. One thing is invariable. If the fruit is allowed to ripen, it is sweet. Fig trees do best in hot climates, although some varieties have borne fruit as far north as the British Isles and northern France.

The fig tree originated, in this geological era at least, in southwestern Turkey, near Smyrna (Izmir), which was once part of the ancient kingdom of Lydia. Throughout the Mediterranean area, it rivaled the date in popularity because, although not as useful, it could grow in areas that were not suitable for the date. Figs, especially dried, were a major sweetner in early historic times. It has been theorized that forerunners of the Etruscans migrated to the Italian peninsula from Lydia, bringing with them the cultivation of the fig tree. At any rate, legend has a fig tree sheltering Romulus and Remus, the founders of Rome, as they were being suckled by the wolf. Greek soil is particularly hospitable to fig trees, and Attic figs became one of ancient Greece's most celebrated products. Throughout the ancient world demand was so high for Attic figs that laws were enacted to restrict their export.

Figs were introduced to all of temperate Europe by the Romans. Later the Spaniards introduced figs into America, where they flourished, especially in California. There is some evidence that native fig trees grew in America before the last Ice Age, but none survived. The mission fig tree, introduced by the Spaniards, and the Smyrna fig tree, imported from Turkey, are the backbone of the California fig industry.

The Smyrna variety produces the finest figs in the world, and is the only one of the four major commercial species that requires "caprification," or pollination, to produce mature fruit. Pollination is accomplished as follows: Male fig trees, caprifigs, produce flowers, not fruit. The fig wasp *(Blastophaga grossorum)* lays its eggs in the caprifig blossom. When the larvae mature, the female wasp bursts out of the blossom laden with pollen. Just before this occurs, caprifig blossoms, containing perhaps 1,000 larvae are cut off the male tree and hung on the branches of the female tree, whose blossoms are contained inside the fruit. The wasp enters the fruit unsuccessfully attempting to lay its eggs, but managing to fertilize the fruit. Without this pollination, Smyrna figs drop off the tree at an immature stage.

The mission fig, the white pedro fig and the common fig bear fruit without pollination, but cannot propagate without it. For this reason, commercial trees are usually grown from cuttings. Fig trees are longlived. Some trees at California missions are more than 100 years old and measure more than 18 feet across at the trunk.

Figs do not travel well, so fresh figs are eaten only near where they grow. Figs are eaten by most people in preserved form, which is the more nutritious. Fresh figs are 80 percent water and 12 percent sugar; but as dried fruit they contain five times as much sugar, and one-fourth the water. They are rich in iron, and contain vitamins A, B, C and D.

Apart from fruit bearing, fig trees have proved useful in other ways. In making cheese, shepherds in ancient Greece stirred the milk with branches from a fig tree, which hastened the curdling process. Modern Mallorcans still employ this practice. At various times and places, fig trees provided much needed shade. The most celebrated example is the *bo*, or *bodhi* tree *(Ficus religiosa)*, which sheltered Gotama Buddha during his quest for enlightenment.

Our word "sycophant" derives from a situation in ancient Athens where fig trees were planted in a sacred grove dedicated to Ceres. To prevent poaching from this grove, authorities employed fig-informers, *sykophantes* from *sykon*, "fig," and *phaintain*, "to make known." These men abused their office by falsely accusing persons to extract bribes.

In some places, figs are roasted and ground and then used to flavor coffee, much in the way that the French use chicory. They are also used as a base for alcoholic drinks, especially in Moslem countries.

FILE

File (pronounced *fee-lay)* is a powder made from the tender, young leaves of the Sassafras tree *(Sassafras albidum)*, which is native to the eastern United States from Maine to Florida. File is used as a condiment and binder in Creole cookery, especially in gumbo. Creole cooks learned to use file from the Choctaws, who still produce and sell it. They pluck the leaves, dry them and then gently rub them between the fingers to reduce them to powder.

File is never cooked but added to a dish as a condiment just before it is served. The powder is mucilagenous, and it thickens and binds the dishes it is added to.

See also: **Okra.**

FILEFISH

This group of marine fish (family *Balistidae)* is so named because of their rough, finely toothed scales that required them to be skinned before being cooked. Filefish are tasty but small, rarely exceeding 10 inches in length. An African species, *Stephanolepsis auratus*, is found in shallow water around the southeastern coast and marketed locally. *S. cirrhifer* is fished commercially in the east China Sea and is popular in Japan and Korea. The lîver of this fish is rated a delicacy.

Filefish are very deep-bodied and are characterized by a flap of skin that hangs down below the belly and is stiffened somewhat by a thick spine.

FILLED CHEESE

To make this cheese, milk is used from which the butterfat has been removed and then replaced by a different fat of either animal or vegetable origin. The new fat is either stirred in quickly with the rennet or homogenized in. The milk is then processed in the normal manner. The motive is economic, i.e., the resulting product is either cheaper or keeps better. The process is defined and limited by law.

FINANCIERE SAUCE

This is a French sauce consisting of basic **espagnole sauce** enriched with madeira and chicken stock, much reduced and flavored with chopped mushrooms, chicken livers and truffle trimmings. It is strained and served hot on sweetbreads and calf's head.

See also: **Sauce.**

FINDLER POTATO

The tubers of this wild plant, *Solanum fendleri*, of the southwestern United States, Mexico and Central America, are edible and considered a palatable potato substitute.

FINE

(Pronounced *feen)* This French word for brandy usually appears in the phrase, *fine de la maison*, that is, "house brandy." Practically every French restaurant will have its house brandy, and usually it is not cognac but another type of lesser quality served in a carafe, not a bottle.

See also: **Brandy, Cognac.**

FINE CHAMPAGNE

A French brandy made from grapes growing in the Cognac regions of Grande and Petite Champagne, it is a blend of liquors from the two regions with at least 50 percent coming from Grande Champagne. As a rule, it is a very good cognac.

See also: **Brandy, Cognac.**

FINNAN HADDIE

See **Haddock.**

FINTE

This European saltwater fish, *Alosa finta*, is closely related to the shad and swims upriver to spawn. It has a somewhat longer body than the ordinary shad but is considered equally good eating. The French rate it a delicacy and prepare it like **shad.**

FIOR D'ALPE

Also FLORA DI ALPI, FLOR ALPINA. Fior d'Alpe is a sweet, yellowish liqueur flavored with a mixture of Alpine herbs, such as juniper, mint, thyme, arnica, wild marjoram and hyssop. It was originally concocted for its medicinal properties and probably originated in Italy. Smooth and refreshing, it is sold in tall thin bottles, each containing an herb sprig, upon which form tiny sugar crystals. It is 92 proof.

FIORE SARDO

When immature and soft this Sardinian cheese, made from ewe's milk, serves as table cheese. When fully ripe and hard, it is grated and used as a condiment in pastas and soups.

See also: **Sardo.**

FIRECREST

A small European songbird, *Regulus ignicapillus*, also known as the fire-crested wren, it has a bright red crest and generally resembles a wren. Like the **lark,** it is considered a delicacy in France and may appear in *brochettes* of small birds.

FISH

Throughout history, the fish has been an important sustainer of human life, second only to cereals in that respect. It ranks first as a source of complete protein, edging out meat because of the latter's relative scarcity and consequent higher price. "Fish" here means a cold-blooded animal that lives in water, has a backbone and permanent gills for breathing and uses fins to propel itself. This definition excludes fishlike mammals, such as porpoises and whales, shellfish, cuttlefish, crustaceans and creatures such as starfish and jellyfish. Recent worldwide catch of fish was estimated at about 35 million tons annually.

The fish is the largest family in the animal kingdom with about 20,000 species, most of which are edible. This is more than mammals, birds, reptiles and amphibians put together. Fish can be divided into two major groups, freshwater and saltwater. Certain exceptional species can exist in both, such as the salmon, the eel and the gray mullet. Salmon grow to maturity in saltwater but are born, breed and usually die in freshwater. Eels are born in the sea, live to maturity in freshwater, then return to the sea to breed and die. Gray mullet seem to be able to adapt to either environment if necessary. Most fish, however, can survive in only one type of water and perish if any major change occurs. A case in point was the rise in the general level of the oceans at the end of the last Ice Age. This caused saltwater to pour into the Black Sea, which up until then had been a freshwater sea, killing so many fish that the rotting of their bodies poisoned the entire sea. The environment is still poisonous below 250 fathoms.

There are other limitations on fish according to water temperature. A fish from northern or southern cooler temperature waters cannot survive in or even cross equatorial waters. Some fish, with varying success, have been transplanted by humans within the two cool zones. Tropical fish are also limited to their environment, which is somewhat larger than the temperate areas. An exception to the above rule is the tuna, which can live in cool or warm waters, finding the desired temperature by adjusting the depth at which it swims. There are more species of fish in tropical seas, but individual species, such as herring and cod, are more numerous in colder waters.

Ocean fish generally prefer shallow water—100 fathoms or less—but commercial fishing is still viable down to 250 fathoms. Although the area of continental shelves constitutes no more than 10 percent of the ocean surface, it produces most of the food fish.

There are certain rules of thumb to distinguish fish best suited for eating. Saltwater fish are generally tastier than freshwater fish. Fish from fast-moving water are preferred to fish from sluggish water since the latter might have a muddy taste. Fish from clean water taste better than those from polluted water. Finally, when buying fresh fish in a market, select those whose flesh is firm, i.e., finger pressure does not leave a mark on the skin.

In preparation, the important rule is not to overcook. Fish is naturally tender and overcooking makes it tough. For more information, see under names of specific fish.

FISH MAW

The air or sound bladder of a fish, the maw is taken from certain varieties of fish and used in Chinese cookery to flavor several dishes. It is first air dried, then cut into thin strips.

FISSURELLE

Gastropod mollusks of the genus *Fissurella* abound in the Mediterranean Sea. They resemble limpets and barnacles and exist in more than 100 varieties. The keyhole limpet is an example of the *fissurelle*, and so is the St. Peter's ear, which is plentiful off Grecian shores. *Fissurelles* are prepared like octopus.

FISTULANE

See **Beefsteak Fungus.**

FIUGGI WATER

A natural, still mineral water bottled in Italy, Fiuggi has a relatively low mineral content. A 1980 Consumers Union sensory panel rated it as good-tasting with the following comments: heavy, thick mouthfeel, stale, old flavor; mild soapy flavor and very mild metallic flavor.

See also: **Mineral Water.**

FIVE FRAGRANCE POWDER

This mixture of spices, favored by the Chinese, contains cloves, cinnamon, aniseed, star anise and pepper.

FLAGEOLET

Also CHEVRIER. A small kidney bean, *Phaseolus vulgaris*, was developed in France by a man named Chevrier. It is a specialty of the Arpajon district. The flageolet remains very small and green on reaching maturity and is shelled before being eaten. It is delicious and much used in France in stews and casseroles.

FLAGROOT

See **Calamus.**

FLAMINGO

A bent-beaked, long-legged, tropical wading bird (genus *Phaenicopterus)* with pink or red plumage, the flamingo achieved some popularity among ancient Romans as an exotic food. The Emperor Vitellius (reigned 69 A.D.) is said to have gluttonized on a mixture of peacock brains and flamingo tongues. Nobody since has paid much attention to it, save the Sardinians, who eat it occasionally but do not rate it highly as a delicacy.

FLATHEAD

This is a food fish (family *Platycephalidae)* of the Indian, Pacific and tropical eastern Atlantic Oceans. The largest species is the dusky flathead *(P. fuscus)*, which is found in Australian waters. It is taken in shallow, often muddy waters and reaches a length of four feet. Large specimens weigh as much as 32 pounds. The dusky flathead has firm, white, well flavored flesh and is considered a commercial species of some importance.

A close relative is the river gurnard *(P. indicus)* found throughout coastal waters of the Indian Ocean. Though somewhat smaller than the dusky flathead, it is found in similar habitats, and its flesh is considered very good eating. It is also known as the sand gurnard. Both of these fish are distinguished by a flattened forebody and head with widely spaced eyes.

FLAT HERRING

This herringlike fish, *Hilsa kelee*, of the Indo-Pacific area, ranges from China to East Africa. Its body is highly compressed and flattened and reaches a maximum length of about 12 inches. It has a greenish back, brilliant silver sides and belly and dark blotches along the sides. It is an abundant schooling fish that supports several fishing industries in the area. The flat herring is eaten fresh, salted or smoked.

FLAVORING EXTRACT

This is the oily, usually volatile, essence of a nut, fruit, spice, etc. bottled in an alcohol solution (30% or more) and used to flavor food or drink. Common extracts are those of almond, anise, cinnamon, clove, lemon, orange and vanilla. Commercial products often use an artificial flavoring rather than the active principle of the named flavoring agent. For more information, see **Vanilla Extract.**

FLORA DI ALPI

See **Fior D'Alpe.**

FLOR ALPINA

See **Fior D'Alpe.**

FLOTOST

This Norwegian cheese is made from boiled whey, much like **Myost,** but contains more fat, amounting to at least 20 percent of the solids.

FLOUNDER

Flounder is a flat, bottom dwelling fish that lives in salt or fresh waters in most temperate zones. There are hundreds of varieties of which the species *Plueronectes* and allied genera may be the largest saltwater group. Other important saltwater species are the English *(Flesus flesus);* the American winter flounder *(Pseudopleuronectes americanus);* the fluke or summer flounder *(Paralichthys dentatus)*, and the southern flounder *(P. lethostigmus)*, also called **plaice.**

The flounder resembles many other flat fish, such as young halibut, brill, lemon sole, dabs, sole, turbot, bream and sunfish. These last two are freshwater varieties found in creeks of the United States and are called golden shiner. They are also caught in the river Seine in France.

Flounders are white on the underside and have both eyes on the topside. Their color varies from green brown to a black yellow with red markings. Some species, however, have developed protective coloration that belies this description.

Flounders are very good food, firm in flesh and delicate in flavor. A whole fish may be baked or broiled. If filleted, it may be poached or grilled and dressed with melted butter and lemon juice. The Norwegians like them smoked.

See also: **Bream, Dab, Halibut, Sole, Sunfish, Turbot.**

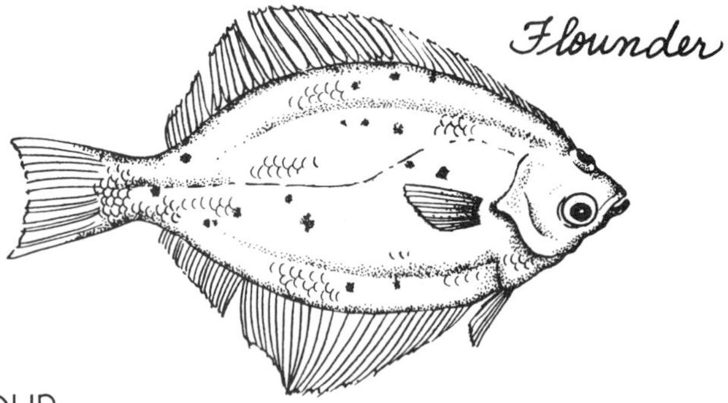

FLOUR

Flour is a fine powder obtained by grinding the meal of wheat or other grains. It is the basic raw material of bread, cake and pastry and is used as a thickening agent in puddings, sauces, soups and stews. Apart from wheat the principal grains ground for flour are rye, buckwheat, oats, barley and corn (maize). Certain beans and other farinaceous products are also ground for flour, including cassava, chestnuts, potatoes, soya and rice. For use in bread or other baked goods, they must be combined with wheat flour, because the latter is richest in gluten, a protein substance needed to contain the leavening agent and give structure to the raised loaf or cake. Even rye, which contains nearly as much gluten as wheat, needs an admixture of wheat flour to produce a light loaf.

Wheat flour is classified by the type of source grain (i.e., hard or soft) and by the degree of milling. Hard wheats produce strong flours with high gluten content, which are most suitable for bread. Soft wheats produce weak flour with low gluten and high starch content, most suitable for pastry and cake. The two are often mixed together and marketed as all-purpose flour. The latter may even be "prepared" or "self-raising," i.e., it contains baking powder.

As for milling, the coarsest is called whole wheat, whole meal or Graham flour (Grant flour in England). It is thought to be the most nutritious, since it contains the whole of the grain—germ, endosperm and bran. This type of flour is often stoneground, always unsifted and is brown. It has several drawbacks: the presence of wheatgerm limits its shelf life, and the presence of bran may cause intestinal irritation. Other grades of wheat flour are ground on steel rollers and may contain germ and bran in varying proportions down to none at all, as is the case with fine white flour. The latter is a pale yellow on leaving the mill but whitens with age or with the addition of bleaching chemicals, which diminish still further the vitamin content. White flours are always bolted (sifted) at the mill, leaving a residue of bran and middlings, which are hard grains. Middlings of the hardest wheat, called durum, are marketed as semolina, the raw material for Italian **pasta.**

White flour that has been cleaned of germ and bran and perhaps bleached is usually then "enriched" with vitamin B1, nicotinic acid, iron, riboflavin, calcium and phosphorus. These are the very elements removed in the milling. Other additives often include enzymes to increase fermentation; potassium bromate or chlorine dioxide, which produce oxygen to strengthen the gluten, and other compounds to retard mold growth.

Rye flour, wheat's only rival in gluten content, is generally darker and in its coarsest form, rye meal, is very popular in Germany, Russia, Central Europe, Scandinavia and the Baltic States. When a recipe calls for flour, you may be sure it means wheat flour unless otherwise specified.

See also: **Bread, Rye, Wheat.**

FLOWER CHEESE

This soft but cured English cheese takes its name from the addition of flower petals, usually from roses or marigolds, to the curd. Whole cow's milk is used.

FLY

According to Ogden Nash:

God in His wisdom
Made the fly
And then forgot
To tell us why.

Several tribes of California, however, while still living in their aboriginal state, found several species of fly useful as food. The Modocs of the Pitt River relished the female of the snipe fly (species *Antherix*), which congregated in great masses during egg-laying time. They collected them by the bushel, mashed them, formed them into loaves and baked them. The result was a reddish brown loaf the consistency of **head cheese.** It was sliced and eaten cold. The Modoc word for this fly was *koo-cha-bee*, a name they also gave to the brine fly *(Ephydra glacilis)*, which was also eaten by the Paiutes as well as the Mono and Koso tribes.

Though tiny, countless millions of these flies swarmed over the alkaline and saline lakes of eastern California (Mono Lake, Owens Lake, East Lake, Borax Pond) during the summer. Their larvae and pupae were driven by wind onto the lake shores and the tribes came from afar to gather the heaped larvae by the basketful. The larvae were handled two ways: either dried and pounded into a flour or peeled of their cuticle. In this case the "kernel," like a grain of rice, could be eaten immediately or saved to be eaten later as a snack, like popcorn.

In more recent times, Chinese in the Canton area reared the larvae of the green bottle fly *(Chrysomyia megalocephala)* commercially for use as a medicine and a food. Similar to American screwworms, the maggots were washed and sun-dried before being sold. They were eaten without further preparation. Breadfruit maggots are said to be preferred by some Pacific Islanders to the **breadfruit** itself.

FLYING FISH

A family of fish, *Exocoetidae*, with enlarged pectoral, and sometimes pelvic, fins that enable them to leap clear of the water and skitter along the surface for extended distances. Typical of them is the *Exocoetus volitans*, a two-winged species widespread in tropical and semitropical seas of all oceans. It reaches a length of 12 inches and is blue above, silver on the sides and white below.

It is popular as food in Barbados and is said to have a pleasant, nutty taste, but eating is a laborious chore due to myriad small bones. A favorite way of preparing it is in flying fish pie topped with a crust of mashed potatoes.

FOGAS

Also FOGOSCH. A type of pike-perch found in the Hungarian lakes of Tisza and Balaton, the *fogas (Lucioperca sandra)* can reach a weight of 20 pounds and is a highly regarded food fish. The flesh is translucent when raw and white when cooked. It is said to be deliciously tender and nearly devoid of bones. The same fish is found in the Danube but having had to struggle against a strong current is not nearly as tender.

A *fogas* weighing two pounds or less is called a *fogasullo*. A closely-related fish is the *fogosch* of Lake Platen in Austria, which reaches the same size and weight and possesses the same good gastronomic qualities. These fish are usually prepared simply—fried, broiled, baked—because their delicious flavor does not require enhancement and, being delicate, is easily overwhelmed by a rich sauce.

FOGGIANO

This Italian's ewe's milk cheese is made in Apulia and is similar to **Cotronese** and **Moliterno.**

FOIE GRAS

The liver of a goose that has been artificially fattened, usually by forcible feeding, *foie gras* is a great delicacy and very expensive.

An ancient Roman is credited with inventing *foie gras*. He was Consul Quintus Caecilius Metullus Pius Scipio, the father-in-law of Pompey, a Roman general and statesman (106–48 B.C.). He used figs as feed. Marcus Gavius Apicius elaborated the technique 50 to 75 years later, using dried figs and honeyed wine and expanding the list of animals to include ducks and pigs. The Latin term for *foie gras* was *iecur ficatum* ("fig-fattened"), and from the second half of it derives the French word for liver, *foie*. Until the end of the 18th century, *foie gras* could mean any kind of fattened liver (from pigs, hens or capons), not just goose liver. Then Jean-Pierre Clause, a chef working in Strasbourg, invented a dish incorporating goose liver, chopped veal and bacon cooked in a crust. It caught the attention of King Louis XVI, and soon Clause went into business for himself to capitalize on its popularity. Since then *foie gras* has meant goose liver and, with a little stretching, duck liver.

It is a French specialty, and the best goose livers are produced in the area surrounding the cities of Strasbourg and Toulouse. Fine *foie gras* is also imported into France from Austria, Bulgaria, Czechoslovakia, Hungary, Israel, Luxembourg and Poland. Much of the imported liver is processed in France—preserved in cans or earthenware containers—and exported under a French label, which fetches a higher price than would otherwise be attainable. Similar *foie gras* is made from ducks, but the livers tend to be smaller and may disintegrate in cooking. Duck *foie gras* is considered an inferior product and is not as widely used.

The Toulouse goose, a large species, is usually selected for fattening, an inhumane ordeal for the bird. Two methods are used. When the goose reaches six months of age, food is crammed down its throat for a period of three to five weeks. Three times a day the goose is held between the knees of the feeder, a funnel outfitted with a crank is forced down its throat, and mash poured in the funnel. The mash is then cranked into the bird's stomach. Alternatively, an electric needle may be inserted into the goose's brain, destroying a portion of the hypothalamus that tells the bird it has had enough to eat. After that, the bird eats constantly. The second method is more economical, but does not produce as large a liver as the first. A goose thus fattened may reach a weight of 25 pounds and have a liver of 2¼ pounds. Livers vary in weight between 1¼ and 4 pounds, the smaller ones being tastier.

Experts describe the color of the finest *foie gras* as somewhere between a rosy white and beige. The fresh product is extremely perishable and must be eaten within two or three days of the goose's demise. Preserved *foie gras* has been thoroughly cooked before being canned or potted and will keep for up to three years before going off. The best foie gras is labeled *foie gras naturel entier*, and consists of a single liver with nothing cut away from it.

Pate de foie gras, a smooth paste, consists of about 75 percent *foie gras* combined with pork fat, onions and mushrooms and formed into a loaf. Sliced truffles are often added to this mixture. The flavor of *foie gras* is discreetly rich with a touch of acidity. It is often served on toast or French bread as an hors d'oeuvre. Otherwise, there is no consensus about when in a meal the *foie gras* should be served. It may be served at the beginning with white wine, at the end with a heavy red wine or in the middle with a salad. *Foie gras* frequently comes larded with anything from strips of beef tongue to a thick border of yellow goose fat.

France consumes about 800 tons of *foie gras* annually, and it exports about 2,200 tons for a total of 3,000 tons. Of this total, it produces about 700 tons and imports the rest from the countries named above.

See also: **Goose.**

FONTINA

A firm, but creamy, Italian cheese of note from the Aosta Valley near the Swiss border, it is made from ewe's milk, and its delicate, nutty flavor seems to combine the best of Swiss and Gruyere with a spicy quality all its own. Fontina requires at least two months' curing, and if eaten at this stage makes a good table cheese. When fully cured, it is grated for use as a condiment.

The cheeses come in round, flat wheels oiled on the outside, which range in weight from 25 to 75 pounds. The curd has small holes. There are numerous imitators, such as *fontal*, *fontinella* and *fantina*, which are sometimes marketed in the United States as fontina. *Fonduta*, the Piedmontese version of fondue, calls for fontina cheese.

FOOD ADDITIVES

Chemical substances are often added to food in its production, processing, storage and packaging to preserve color, flavor, texture or nutritive value, or to prevent microbial spoiling and oxidation. Insecticides and other chemical agents used to safeguard animals and plants from diseases may also be found in food, but they are not considered additives.

The largest group of food additives are those used for flavoring. Commonly, these are natural spices, essential oils and extracts and synthetic chemicals—aldehydes, esters, alcohols—which give food such flavors as strawberry, cherry, pineapple, walnut and wintergreen. Monosodium glutamate, called *aji-no-moto* in Japan, is a widely used flavoring in meat and in meat broths. Soft drinks, confectioneries, including ice cream, baked goods and gelatin desserts all use many flavoring agents.

Iodine, added to salt, has a high nutritional value and prevents the disease known as goiter. Vitamin D added to fluid milk stems the growth of rickets. Most flour and bread sold in the United States are "enriched" with iron, thiamine, riboflavin and niacin. Sodium fluoride and silicon fluoride are well-known nutritional additives in water. Thiamine in polished rice combats beri beri. Salt is a common nutritional additive, controlling the growth of microbes in most foods, as does sugar when added to jams and jellies.

Sodium benzoate and other benzoates are important chemical preservatives. Sulfur dioxide and sulfites are added to wine, vegetables and meat to counterract oxidation. If added to chopped meat when it has begun to decompose, for example, sodium sulfite produces a bright red color that makes the food look deceptively fresh.

Other types of food additives include emulsifiers to maintain consistency in salad dressings, baked goods and cake mixes, clarifiers, firming agents, coloring agents, aerating agents, humectants (which readily absorb moisture and are useful in the dried-fruit industry), sequestrants to separate mineral trace elements, anti-caking agents, foaming agents, buffering agents, leavening agents, bleaching agents, thickeners and artificial sweeteners.

Thickening agents, such as glycerol, sorbitol, gelatin and pectin, impart body to processed cheeses, salad dressings, ice cream and frozen desserts and also prevent the loss of flavor in cake mixes, gelatin desserts and puddings. Yeast and sodium bicarbonate (the source of carbon dioxide in baking powder) are well-known leavening agents. Coloring agents—whether "natural," such as turmeric, caramel, carmine and carotene or "synthetic"—are commonly added to soft drinks, confectionery, cheese, butter, margarine and meat products. Cyclamates, the artificial sweetener, were banned in the United States in 1970 because of their possibly harmful side-effects.

As food processing becomes a more exact science, and as the need for wider distribution and longer storage of food continues, so does the necessity for careful regulation of the industry in all its phases. In the Food Additives Amendment of 1958, all additives then in use but not considered safe by qualified experts became subject to approval by the U.S. Food and Drug Administration. In most countries now, all additives—with the exception of the possible residue of pesticides and fungicides, but including antibiotics—are clearly labeled on the food package or container.

FOREZ

Also D'AMBERT. This French cheese at its best is comparable to **Roquefort,** but its processing is so crude that it is often spoiled by unwanted mold and bacteria.

FORKBEARD

Forkbeard is a small, delicate Mediterranean fish of the cod family *(Gadidae)*. Its English name derives from two ventral fins near the head that give the appearance of a forked beard. It is good to eat and is usually fried. The Spanish are fond of this fish and call it *bistola de roca*. There is also a freshwater species, somewhat like the **burbot.** Its liver is a highly esteemed food.

FORMAGELLE

A small, soft Italian cheese made from ewe's or goat's milk in the northern mountains, formagelle is made in the spring and autumn and eaten fresh. It is similar to what is called **cacio fiore** or caciotta in the South.

FORMAGELLE BERNARDE

See **Bernarde.**

FORMAGERE

See **Fromage Fort.**

FORMAGGINI

The term means "small cheeses" and refers to several kinds of Italian dessert cheeses, all small, that are sweetened and flavored or spiced in various ways. Two prominent examples are:

Formaggini di Lecco, from Lecco in Lombardy, is made from cow's milk, sometimes with an admixture of goat's milk. It may be eaten fresh, when it is sweet or at any stage of maturation, although it is very piquant when fully cured. Spices and other additives include pepper, sugar, cinnamon and occasionally oil and vinegar.

Formaggini de Montpellier contains white wine, thistle blossoms and other flavorings.

FORMAGGIO DI CAPRA

See **Goat's Milk Cheese.**

FORMAGGIO DI PASTA FILATA

Also DRAWN-CURD CHEESE. This generic term applies to a group of Italian plastic curd cheeses, so called because during processing the curd is heated and drawn into ropes for kneading and shaping. This eliminates holes, pockets of air and whey. Cheeses so treated have better keeping qualities, even in warm climates. Some are eaten early as table cheese, others are allowed to ripen until firm and sharp for grating. Examples are provolone, *caciocavallo*, *moliterno*, mozzarella, *provatura* and *scamorze*. Non-Italian cheeses treated similarly are *katschkawalj*, *kaskaval*, *oschtjepek*, *parenica* and *panedda*.

FORMAGGIO SALAME

See **Salame Cheese.**

FORMOSA JAMBOSA

The edible fruit of a tropical Asian tree, *Eugenia formosa*, Formosa jambosa is cultivated in Vietnam. The fruit is small and round and has a bland taste.

FORTUNE COOKIE

This specialty of Chinese restaurants in the United States is presented at the end of the meal, along with the check. It consists of a round wafer that has been baked on a grill, removed while still pliable, then folded around a strip of paper. The paper carries a telegraphic message, such as "Bear good fortune modestly." Fortune cookies are made from a batter consisting of rice flour, eggs, powdered sugar and flavorings.

Fortune cookies

FOURDERAINE

This home-made liqueur is made from sloes *(Prunus spinosa)* that are steeped in alcohol. It is a specialty of the north of France but not as popular as it used to be. The sloes are picked after the first frost to increase their sweetness.

FOURME D'AMBERT

See **Ambert.**

FOUR-WINGED SALTBUSH

Also CENIZO, CHAMISO. A gray shrub, *Atriplex canescens*, found in the western United States and Mexico and as far east as South Dakota and Texas. It grows well on saline soils and has edible seeds, which were eaten by Native American tribes.

FOWL

See **Poultry.**

FRANCHE–COMTE

See **Wines, French.**

FRANCOLIN

This partridgelike bird, *Francolinus* spp., is found in southeastern Europe and Asia Minor. When the bird's natural food supply has been adequate, its white flesh is considered delicious. Marco Polo remarked on it in the account of his travels. It may be prepared like partridge.

FRANKFURTER

Also HOT DOG, WIENER. This is America's favorite sausage, usually prepared as a hot dog, i.e., boiled or grilled, placed in a similarly shaped bun and eaten with ketchup, mustard, onions and other garnishes. The frankfurter originated in Europe centuries ago, although specialists disagree on where. Some trace its lineage to the linked sausages of Frankfurt, Germany, others to the Austrian wiener.

It gained popularity in the United States more than a century ago under the nickname "dachshund's sausage." It was dubbed "hot dog" by cartoonist T. A. "Tad" Dorgan in 1906, who depicted a dachshund inside an elongated bun as a character in his comic strip. The hot dog was greatly popularized by Nathan's of Coney Island (Brooklyn, New York) whose excellent Coney Island Red Hot achieved a nationwide reputation. Americans now consume more than 8½ billion hots dogs a year.

The original frankfurter sausage contained both beef and pork, the proportions being three parts pork to one beef. These proportions are now usually reversed, but by law the frankfurter may contain the ground meat of sheep or goats and even up to 15 percent chicken. It may contain no more than 30 percent fat, and 2.5 percent carbohydrate filler, which usually consists of cereals, dry milk solids, corn syrup or vegetable starch. The typical frankfurter is five to six inches long and three-quarter inch in diameter, contains 4½ to six grams of protein, and consists of about 58 percent water by weight (48 percent natural liquid, 10 percent added).

Frankfurters have a firm, easily chewable consistency and are sold ready cooked and lightly smoked. They are usually reheated by gently boiling or grilling and are often added to casseroles, bean dishes and soups. Frying toughens them. The Germans prefer them hot with sauerkraut or cold with potato salad.

See also: **Sausage.**

FREEZE DRYING

This is a method of preserving food wherein the food is frozen in a vacuum and the water removed by sublimation. The water goes directly from the solid phase, i.e., ice, to the gaseous phase, i.e., water vapor. The advantages of this process are that the food retains its original size, shape and cellular structure. The last feature makes for quick rehydration.

Freeze drying has been used for forty years in laboratories for preservation of unstable biological materials. One of its most successful commercial applications has been instant coffee. Freeze drying seems to deliver a better flavor than the alternative, spray drying, because the latter is accomplished at high temperatures that destroy taste values. A more recent application has been to camping food and survival rations where freeze drying provides both superior flavor and light weight.

See also: **Preservation of Food.**

FREEZING

See **Preservation of Food.**

FREMONT'S GOOSEFOOT

A weedy herb, *Chenopodium fremontii*, is found in western North America. Its seeds are ground into flour and mixed with corn meal to make porridge or bread. It is most plentiful in the state of Oregon.

FRENCH BREAD

The French make a wide variety of breads, but the kind thought of as uniquely French is the long, narrow loaf with diagonal slashes across the top. The best known loaf of this type is the *baguette*, which is shaped like a long thin wand approximately two feet in length. It weighs about nine ounces.

This is the ordinary bread of French cities, and is made from flour, salt, sugar, yeast and water. The shape of the *baguette* maximizes the crust area, and during the baking the loaf is brushed several times with water or an egg-yolk glaze to insure adequate crustiness.

Compared to other breads, there is proportionately less crumb, but, as the French point out, the crust is easier to digest. Customarily, the bread is cut into convenient pieces for the table—and always on the diagonal to provide a greater area for the spreading of butter. Other loaves of this type include the *ficelle* (thinner) and the *flute* (shorter, broader).

See also: **Bread.**

FRESA CHEESE

A Sardinian cooked cheese with a soft texture and a mild, sweet flavor, Fresa is made from cow's milk, sometimes with the addition of goat's milk. It is eaten fresh in the spring and autumn.

See also: **Cooked Cheese.**

FRESCO

See **Milano Cheese.**

FRESHWATER CATFISH

An Australian species, *Tandanus tandanus*, found in the rivers of southern and eastern Australia, it reaches a length of two feet. Its flesh, though quite good to eat, is not often marketed due to its unattractive appearance.

FRESHWATER DRUM

See **Gasperou.**

FRIBOURG

This hard cheese, of the **Swiss** variety, originated in Switzerland but is also produced in the Po Valley of Italy. It most closely resembles **Spalen.**

FRIJOL

See **Kidney Bean.**

FRISIAN CLOVE CHEESE

A Dutch cheese, much resembling **Leyden**, Frisian clove cheese is made from partly skimmed cow's milk, spiced with cloves and occasionally cumin. It is round and flat in shape and weighs from 20 to 40 pounds.

FROG

Properly speaking, only the legs of this common amphibian are eaten. Frog's legs are generally considered to be a gourmet's dish; their taste is often compared to that of chicken. They are most closely associated with French cooking. Charles Lamb, the English author, recorded his first encounter with them in a letter to his sister, Mary:

> *Since I saw you I have been in France, and have eaten frogs. The nicest little rabbity things you ever tasted. Do look about for them. Make Mrs. Clare pick off the hind quarters, boil them plain, with parsley and butter. The fore quarters are not so good. She may let them hop off by themselves.*

There are more than 20 species in Europe, but the most generally eaten are the green frog *(Rana esculenta)* and the mute frog. In the United States, three species are edible and run twice the size of the European: the green frog, the American bullfrog *(R. catesbeiana)* and the leopard frog *(R. pipiens)*. Florida is the principal source of American eating frogs.

FROMAGE A LA CREME

A French **cream cheese** is made either by double-creaming the milk before renneting or working fresh cream into the drained curd. It is soft and rich and, although eaten fresh, will keep for several days under refrigeration. When set into heart-shaped molds, it is called *coeur a la creme.*

FROMAGE A LA PIE

See **White Cheese.**

FROMAGE BLANC

See **White Cheese.**

FROMAGE BLEU

See **Blue Cheese.**

FROMAGE DE BOITE

See **Box Cheese.**

FROMAGE DE BOURGOGNE

See **Burgundy Cheese.**

FROMAGE DE CHEVRE

See **St. Marcellin.**

FROMAGE DE FOIN

See **Hay Cheese.**

FROMAGE DE TROYES

See **Barberey.**

FROMAGE DOUBLE CREME

See **Carre.**

FROMAGE FORT

Also FORMAGERE. The term means "strong cheese," and refers to a French variety of **pot cheese** or **cooked cheese** from the Morvan and Lyon districts. Skim milk curd is melted, pressed and grated. After ripening for a week or so, it is mixed with milk, butter, salt, pepper, chopped herbs and wine or leek juice to form a paste. It is then sealed in stone pots and fermented for another two or three weeks. A strongly flavored cheese is produced.

See also: **Canquillote.**

FROMAGE MOU

See **Maquee.**

FROMAGE PERSILLE

See **Blue Cheese.**

FROMAGE RAFFINE DE L'ISLE D'ORLEANS

See **Island of Orleans Cheese.**

FROMAGERE

See **Canquillote.**

FRONSAC

This robust, ruby-colored wine comes from the Cotes de Fronsac on the Dordogne in western France near **Bordeaux.** Fronsac is a region associated with the amorous Duc de Richelieu, who introduced the wine of Bordeaux to the French court in the 18th century.

FRONTIGNAN WINE

See **Wines, Swiss.**

FROST FISH

See **Tomcod.**

FROST GRAPE

Also WINTER GRAPE, CHICKEN GRAPE. The fruit of a high-climbing, woody vine, *Vitis vulpina*, the frost grape is native to the eastern half of the United States. The frost grape is black and glossy and very acidic until the first frost when it becomes sweet. It is generally gathered wild but is occasionally cultivated.

FRUCTA DE MACACO

Here is an edible fruit of a shrub or tree, *Rolliniopsis discreta*, native to Brazil.

FRUCTOSE

Also FRUIT SUGAR, LEVULOSE. A very sweet sugar is found naturally in honey, fruit juices and the nectar of plant glands. It can be obtained through hydrolysis from **sucrose,** which breaks down into fructose and glucose (grape sugar). However, in industrial production it is usually obtained from inulin, a polysaccharide contained in the roots of dahlia, chicory and other plants of the *Compositae* genus, which yields only fructose. Fructose is more readily soluble in water than glucose and more easily tolerated by diabetics.

FRUHSTUCK CHEESE

This small, Limburger-type cheese is made from whole or partly skimmed cow's milk. It has been variously characterized as being delicate and eaten for breakfast, luncheon, dessert or as an appetizer. It is made in both Germany and the United States. During curing, yeast and mold grow on the surface and are followed by red cheese bacteria, which form a surface smear. At an early stage of ripening it is usually wrapped in tinfoil or parchment paper and is brought to full maturity at 42° to 45° F (5.6° to 7.2° C). It may be eaten at any point in this process.

FRUIT

There is no easy definition of fruit that does not violate some conventional idea of what is a fruit and what is a vegetable. In the broad sense, a fruit is any plant product, such as grain, flax or vegetables, as in the expression "fruits of the earth." This, however, is too broad a definition for a food book. A more narrow definition, which comes closer to the popular conception of fruit, is the edible, seed-bearing product of trees, shrubs, bushes, vines, etc. However, this would include such items as cucumbers, zucchini, eggplant and tomatoes, which are usually considered vegetables.

To get the definition still more narrow, further qualifications must be added, such as "succulent," "fleshy" and, especially, "sweet." "Sweet" coincides with most persons' idea of fruit. Yet olives, avocados and lemons are, after all, fleshy and succulent.

Our definition so far, however, still excludes such a highly regarded "fruit" as the strawberry, which is not a seed container. The actual fruit is the tiny achene on the outside skin of the strawberry. The strawberry belongs to a class of products called false or freak fruits. The latter, however, should be included in any popular definition of fruit.

One definition, taking all these exceptions into account, might be: Any succulent, fleshy or sweet plant product that contains seeds or is partially formed from other flower parts such as receptacles, sepals, petals or bracts.

The following are major categories of fruits:

Berries: A huge category containing thousands of members, containing the *Rubus* genus (example: blackberry), the *Ribes* genus (examples: currants and gooseberries) and a branch of the *Ericaceae* family (examples: cranberries, blueberries).

Citrus fruits; Fruits with a thick rind or outer casing enclosing a juicy pulp, such as oranges, lemons and kumquats.

Drupes: These are fleshy fruits containing one large seed, such as apricots, cherries, peaches and plums.

False, or freak fruits: Fruits that are not, strictly speaking, seed containers but are formed from other parts of the flower. Examples: strawberries, pineapples.

Nuts: Botanically speaking, these are fruits, but are excluded from the popular definition. (See **Nut.**)

Pomes: A class of fleshy fruits containing a core and seeds, such as the apple, the pear and the quince.

Fresh, raw fruits are full of vitamins, and some, like the date and the banana, can sustain life for a long time. Citrus fruits are particularly rich in vitamin C, while others contain calcium, iron and vitamins A and B. Apart from being wholesome, they are eaten for taste and to vary the diet.

FRUIT BUTTER

Fruit butter is a spread like jelly, jam and marmalade but differs by not being so sweet and by having a smooth, butterlike consistency. Fruit butter contains five parts fruit pulp to two parts sugar. Jelly, by contrast, contains 45 parts fruit juice to 55 parts sugar, a ratio that pertains also to jam, preserves and marmalades.

In the home, fruit pulp is sieved and cooked with sugar and perhaps spices until it reaches the desired consistency. This is done over very slow heat to insure that the pulp does not scorch and that the spice oils are properly absorbed. Constant stirring is necessary.

A variety of fruits

Tart apples make the best known fruit butter, but other popular fruits are fresh or dried apricots, grapes, peaches, plums and quinces.

FRUIT JUICE

The fruit squeezed from raw fruit, as a commercial product fruit juice is usually marketed as a frozen concentrate. This is especially true of citrus juice, but also of apple and grape juice. Many of the juices canned or bottled at ready-to-drink strength are reconstituted from concentrate.

Frozen concentrates are a post-World War II development, that hinged on the discovery of the overconcentrate/juice cut-back method of dehydration. It was applied first to the **orange juice** industry, which resulted in a drastic reduction in the consumption of fresh citrus fruit, oranges in particular, but saved the orange-growing industry from an already declining market.

One difference between fresh-squeezed juice and juice made from concentrate is the presence in the latter of some peel oil, or a flavor enhancer from peel oil called d-lemonene, which, for some people, makes the juice a little harder to digest.

FRUIT WINE

Apart from grapes, fruits frequently used to make wine include apples, pears, cherries, berries, plums, pineapples, citrus fruit and dried figs, dates and raisins. Two popular fruit wines are cider and perry, made from apples and pears respectively.

The word "cider" comes from the Hebrew word *shekar*, meaning strong drink. It is fermented from the freshly pressed juice of apples not suitable for eating. The alcoholic content varies from two to eight percent. In the United States, it is known as "hard" cider to distinguish it from "sweet," i.e., nonalcoholic cider. Both, however, are sweet to the taste. Hard cider was the favorite table drink of 19th century Americans, especially in rural areas where apple trees were abundant and the water supply often polluted. Hard cider fell from favor during Prohibition and owing to changed circumstances never regained its popularity when Prohibition ended. Cider is a popular beverage in northwestern France, where apples are a major crop, and the famous apple brandy *Calvados* is produced, as well as in Spain and England. In Spain, cider is often given a second fermentation in the bottle, making an effervescent drink referred to as champagne cider.

Perry shares many of cider's characteristics: its sweetness, its alcoholic content and the pronounced flavor of the original fruit.

Berry wines are made from blackberries, raspberries, strawberries, elderberries, loganberries, boysenberries and currants. Each is sweet and fruity but with the characteristic flavor of the original fruit. They may be made from fresh juice, fresh frozen fruit or the concentrated fruit juice, which is usually supplemented with dried fruit. Because of the distinctly acidic flavor of the berries, all berry wines have water and sugar added. The finished product is usually fortified and ranges from 12.5 to 20 percent alcohol. Berry wines are aged very little because the color and taste deteriorate with age. Czechoslovakia, Israel, Holland, Japan, Poland and Yugoslavia are major producers of berry wines.

Cherry wine is made from sour cherries, particularly the Langeskov cherry of Denmark, which is a major exporter of cherry wine. The flavor is often improved with the crushed pits, which adds a subtle touch to a beverage that is otherwise richly fruity and very sweet. The wine is bottled unaged at an alcoholic strength of up to 19 percent. It is customarily served chilled and often used in desserts.

Japan, with its humid climate, is famous for its plum wines that may have either the natural plum flavor, or almond overtones from the inclusion of the stones in the fermentation. They are sweet and fortified. Both plum and apricot wines are produced in California. China exports an unusual *litchi* wine.

Pineapple wine is a specialty of Puerto Rico. The Spanish red pineapple is used, and the wine is fortified with pineapple brandy. The taste is unusually tart for a fruit wine, and the color is golden.

A variety of citrus wines are produced in Florida. They are fortified, having up to 20 percent alcohol, and have a sherrylike flavor. Dried figs, dates and raisins are used to make wine by shredding the pulp and steeping it in hot water that becomes the fermenting must.

Fruit wines are usually served chilled, often with ice and soda water. They make a good dessert topping, and come in handy as glazes for ham or game birds.

FUDGE

A soft, rich, American candy is made with milk, butter and sugar. Chocolate or cocoa, walnuts and vanilla flavoring are almost always added to produce the traditional fudge. When the syrup is cooked to the right consistency, it is beaten to give it a creamy consistency, at which time the melted chocolate, vanilla and nuts are added. There is a method that adds marshmallow to the cooking process, in which case the beating is eliminated.

See also: **Candy.**

FUGU

Also GLOBEFISH. A fish of the genus *Tetrodon* is popular as a food in Japan and widely believed to be a virility builder. The *fugu*, however, can be deadly poison unless cleaned by a specially trained chef. The liver and ovaries of the fish contain a virulent toxin that can spread throughout its body unless they are removed as the first step of cleaning. What's more, to the unpracticed eye, the fish's liver greatly resembles its testes, the desirable part for virility seekers.

Feasting on *fugu* is certainly expensive and can be dangerous if the diner doesn't patronize the restaurants licensed to serve it. The season is from October 1 to March 31, and each year approximately 200 *fugu* fanciers pay the ultimate price of their avocation. Many are fishermen who arrogantly assume they know how to clean a *fugu*. Perhaps they have the heady feeling of a man playing Russian Roulette. An old Japanese proverb states: "One who dines on *fugu* should first have his last will and testament in order."

There is no danger in the licensed restaurant since the chef must pass an oral, written and practical examination. *Fugu* is served in soups and stews or sliced thin and dressed with sauces. *Fugu* sashimi is reputed to be the most expensive dish served in Japanese restaurants. Such a meal may be topped off with a cup of hot sake containing the *fugu's* testes.

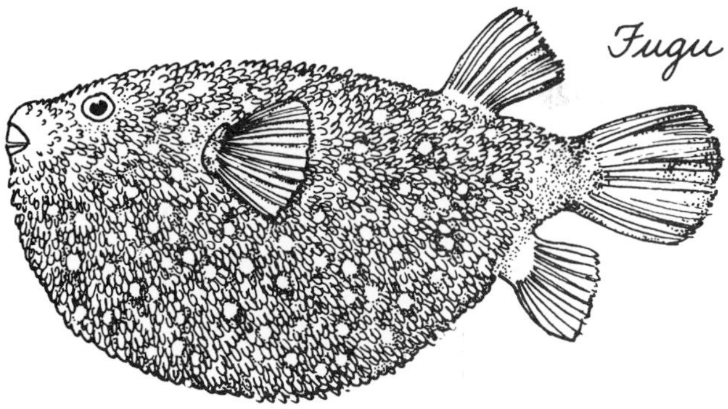

Fugu

FUKI

Also JAPANESE COLTSFOOT, JAPANESE PETASITES. The flower buds of the perennial herb, *Petasites japonicus*, are eaten as a vegetable or dried and used as a condiment. The plant is native to China, Korea and Japan, but it is grown extensively in Japan.

FUNGHI

See **Honey Mushroom.**

FUNGUS

This is a group of more than 2,000 plants characterized by a lack of green color, leaves or flowers. Typically, fungi thrive in damp shady places on dead organic matter or as parasites on plants or animals. They run the gamut from mushrooms to microscopic molds, rusts and smuts. The best known edible fungi include mushrooms, truffles and such things as beefsteak fungus, puffballs and tree ears. An unusual edible fungus is corn smut, which is described under **Cuitlacoche.** For more information consult the index or check under the specific name.

G

GADWALL

Also GRAY WIDGEON, SAND WIDGEON. A wild duck, *Anas strepera*, of Europe, North America and north Asia, the gadwall is a migratory bird, like the **mallard** in size. Being a vegetarian, the gadwall has a little better flavor than other shoal-water ducks that feed on fish. It is considered one of the better table birds and may be prepared like mallard.

See also: **Duck.**

GAILLAC

These are wines—especially white and semisparkling—grown near the town of Gaillac, about 30 miles northeast of Toulouse in southern France. A rough, sweet Gaillac is drunk soon after its harvest. The name better describes a light, dry white wine from the Mauzac grape. Gaillac Mousseux and Gaillac Perle are sparkling wines. The Perle is a natural and creamy sparkling wine obtained from no other product than its grape. It is delicate and rather low in alcohol content, unlike most other sweet and sparkling wines. The red wines of Gaillac are not very highly regarded but are agreeable in color and in body.

GAISKASLI

This soft, pleasant-tasting goat's milk cheese is made in Switzerland and Germany. It is molded into three-inch cylinders and takes three weeks to ripen. See also: **Goat's Milk Cheese.**

GALAM BUTTER

See **Shea Butter.**

GALAMUS

This sweet dessert wine of the Midi in France is not as well known as the famous Muscat de Frontignan and **Banyuls,** which come from the same region. It has a tawny color and a prematurely old or rancid flavor. Galamus is made in the vicinity of Roussillon.

GALANGAL

See **Galingale.**

GALANGALE

See **Galingale.**

GALANTINE

Galantine is the meat—generally white—of veal, chicken, turkey or duck that has been cooked, boned, seasoned and then pressed and molded into a roll. It is served cold, usually glazed or covered in its own jelly. It is often decorated with truffles and pine nuts. Galantine is a popular dish in Poland and enjoyed a vogue in Edwardian England.

GALETTE

Various kinds of French cake are called galettes, including a thin, round one made of flaky pastry eaten traditionally on Twelfth Night in the Paris region, a puff pastry or breakfast roll made of yeast dough and a potato cake that is round and savory.

GALILEE CICHLID

A perchlike food fish, *Sarotherodon galilaeus*, found in fresh water from Lake Galilee south through Egypt to East and Central Africa, it reaches a length of about 15 inches. A closely related species is the Mozambique chichlid *(S. mossambicus)*, which is similarly sized and whose range includes eastern and southern Africa. A larger African cichlid is the Nile mouth brooder *(S. niloticus)*, which can weigh up to 14 pounds and consequently is considered a more valuable food fish. It is found in freshwater all over central and northern Africa and as far north as Syria and Israel.

GALINGALE

Also CALANGALL, GALANGAL, GALANGALE. This name is given to two botanically unrelated spices that were quite popular until the late Middle Ages but are rarely used nowadays. Both types consist of tubers or rootstock.

One type, which seems to have been preferred especially in England, originated in China and is related to the ginger plant, which it resembles in taste. The English word derives from the Chinese name, *Kao-liang-kiang*, which first passed through Arabic as *khalanjan*. Its use was first noted in Europe in the eighth century and grew to be widespread by the end of the 15th century. In those days of heavy spicing, it was used alongside ginger, mace, cloves and cinnamon.

A second type of galingale was the root of the reed *Cyperus longus*, which originated in Africa and is related to **chufa.** This version was known to the ancient Romans, who imported it from Egypt. Its arrival in England may have antedated the gingerlike galingale. Its flavor was similar to the latter but not as pungent. It was, however, capable of being grown both in England and in France, where it was called *souchet* or *amandes de terre*. When cooked the tuber had a pinkish color and somewhat resembled a hamburg parsley root.

Although the Chinese import grew to be favored over the reed, neither competed well with ginger and were abandoned as the latter became increasingly available. Ginger also has better cooking qualities, dissolving into a prepared dish, while galingale does not. The latter was lowered into a pot in a muslin wrapping, then removed when cooking was finished.

GALL

This is bile, a bitter liquid secreted from the liver and stored in the gall bladder, which is attached to it. If the gall bladder is broken in poultry or game, the bitter flavor can ruin the taste of meat.

GALLINULE

The name includes any bird of the genus *Gallinula* but is a term often used to refer to the moor hen (see **Moor Cock).** Well-known species of gallinule include the European purple gallinule *(Porphyrio porphyrio)*, a much larger bird than the moor hen and found mainly in southern Spain, Sardinia and Sicilia. It has also been introduced into New Zealand. Another is the American purple gallinule *(Porphyria martinica)*, which is closer to the moor hen in size and is found from the southern United States to Central America and the West Indies. A second American species is the red-billed mud hen *(Gallinula galeata)* of Florida. Gallinule is prepared like moor cock.

GAMAY

A small village in southern **Burgundy** has given its name to one of the most prolific vines, Petit Gamay, in that wine-growing area. The Gamay vines have an exceptionally high yield, higher than those of the Pinot, and are used in the making of **Beaujolais,** particularly in the vineyards of Moulin-a-Vent and Les Thorins.

The grape is red with a white juice, well suited to the warmth of the Beaujolais region. The Gamay grape is also grown successfully in central France near Tours and in California, where it usually results in a fruity rose.

GAMBRA

See **Partridge.**

GAME

Wild animals, including mammals, birds and fish, hunted for sport, and for food: this is the traditional meaning of the word. It remains true today, except that some "game" animals, such as pheasant, are raised in captivity for the table, blurring the definition somewhat. Usually a game animal raised domestically ceases to taste like game. According to the best authority, the taste of game animals, particularly deer and fowl, depends on the fodder, which in the wild differs radically from the domestic. Moreover, in the wild, animals are intensely active and thus tend to be lean to such an extent that many must be larded to prevent excessive drying out in the cooking. These conditions, according to one authority, "create a warm fragrance unfound in any other kind of flesh."

Oddly, most lovers of game—in Europe if not in the United States—would not themselves be able to appreciate this subtle difference due to the practice of hanging game before cooking it. That is, game is hung until it is "high," i.e., beginning to putrify. This gives it a strong, acrid, "gamy" flavor, unlike its natural one. It also makes it harder to digest. A taste for hung game developed in Europe in the Middle Ages when there was no handy way of preserving it. Since those who had access to game were the landed aristocracy, the style-setters of the era, the practice took hold, solidified into doctrine and is with us still, long after improved technology made it unnecessary. This tradition has always been stronger in Europe than in America, but now there are signs of change, especially in France. Many Parisian restaurants specializing in game are serving notice to their customers that game will be served fresh, i.e., within 24 to 48 hours of killing.

In various epochs, game has constituted an important element in the human diet and strongly influenced social behavior. Stone Age populations in Europe and America that depended on game were nomads who moved on after exhausting the local game population, or who regularly followed the migrations of herds of animals, such as buffalo. On the other hand, those who depended chiefly on crops led a sedentary life, a style that led to the growth of large cities.

Within particular cultures, according to the latest theory, a primitive division of labor developed between the sexes, with men pursuing the hunt and women tending the crops. As agriculture became the predominant source of food, hunting became a perquisite of the aristocracy. In medieval times, hunting game was the main pastime of the landed gentry and nobility when they weren't making war as an occupation. For them, game was the major source of meat for the table. This was not true for humbler folk of that era, because game legally belonged to the landowner and poaching (illegal taking of game) tended to be severely punished.

When North America was first settled, game was a major sustenance for native Americans, and then for the colonists. The latter made such inroads on the game population with their superior technology (muskets and blunderbusses) that by the end of the 17th century restrictive laws had to be enacted to save some species from extinction. Some species that seemed inexhaustible at the time, like the passenger pigeon and the eskimo curlew, are now extinct. The buffalo, likewise, has been reduced to negligible numbers. Increasingly the hunting of game is subject worldwide to a maze of restrictive legislation that limits the season as well as the number of animals that can be taken and protects threatened species.

The most common game animals are deer, rabbit, hare, bear, boar, duck, geese, pheasant, partridge, grouse, quail, snipe, woodcock, pigeon, squirrel and raccoon. The chief challenges in cooking are to counteract the tendency towards dryness in the flesh of some game and to overcome strong tastes that might be caused by a particular type of fodder, e.g., fish. To minimize the latter, marinating in wine sauce for a day is recommended.

See also: **Quail, Deer, Pheasant,** etc.

GAMMELOST

This very popular Norwegian skim-milk cheese is semisoft and mold-ripened. The word *gammel* means "old" and refers to the use of sour (i.e. old) milk rather than rennet, to obtain a curd. Gammelost has a grainy texture and a sharp, aromatic flavor, resulting in part from the action of the *mucor*, *rhizopus* and *penicillium* molds that are injected into the curd. The interior is shot through with blue green veins, and the rind is brownish, tending to darken with age.

Cheeses are round and flat, six inches in diameter and generally weigh six to nine pounds. Curing takes one month, but often after partial curing, cheeses are put into chests lined with straw that has been treated with juniper extract. Some cheese fanciers object to the resulting flavor.

GAMOTE

A tuberous-rooted plant, *Cymopterus montanus*, has young roots that make a good substitute for parsnips. Gamote is native to western North America and is especially plentiful in Kansas. Another variety is globular gamote *(C. globosus)*.

GANSEBRUST

This type of sausage consists of smoked breast of goose wrapped in a casing of goose skin.

See also: **Sausage.**

GAPER

A bivalve mollusk, *Mya truncata*, gaper is found buried in the sand at low water all around the British and French coasts and the Atlantic Coast of the United States. It favors the mouths of rivers and estuaries. The gaper has a large shell that gapes at either end. It is boiled and eaten like a cockle.

Gaper is known by a host of alternative names including the horse clam in the United States, the *brelin* in Brittany, the spoon shell in Devonshire and the cockle brillion around Belfast in Northern Ireland.

GAPERON

A French cheese made of cow's milk in Limagne, it is at its best from September to July.

13 Chayote

14 A wide variety of cheeses

15 Some medium-soft cheeses

17 Bottled apple cider

18 The Dungeness crab

19 Crabapples

20 Cranberries

21 Cuitlacoche

22 Figs

23 French bread

24 Garlic

GAR

This fish lives in salt or fresh water and has a long, slim body with long, narrow jaws. Saltwater gars are *Teleosts*, bony fish of the group *Percesoses*, family *Belonidae*, and are also called billfish, garpikes, needle fish or sea eels. In Australia and New Zealand gars are mostly from an allied family, the half beaks. *Teleosts* and half beaks are all good eating. Freshwater gars, found in North America, are *Ganoids*, large fish of the group *Holostei*, with hard, shiny scales and tough, rank flesh. They are of two species, commonly termed long-nosed gar *(Lepisosteus osseus)* and short-nosed gar *(Cylindrosteus Platystomus)*, and are found in the central and eastern United States. Alligator gars are the really superb fishes. Some have been caught that measured up to seven feet long. They inhabit the lower Mississippi River and its tributaries in Louisiana. Gars are fierce predators, living on other fish.

Saltwater gars may be prepared for the table like any bony fish: baked or fried like eels, which they resemble, or in fish stews. Freshwater gars lend themselves mostly to the stewpot, where long boiling and additional ingredients tend to mitigate their rank flavor and tough fiber.

See also: **Bowfin, Paddle Fish, Sturgeon.**

GARAM MASALA

Garam masala is the Indian term for curry powder, the principal ingredients of which are allspice, anise, bay leaf, capsicum, cardamom, cinnamon, chili, coriander, cumin, fenugreek, ginger, mace, mustard seed, black and white pepper, saffron and turmeric.

GARAPINA

In Mexico and the Caribbean, this drink is made of fermented pineapple juice, flavored with tamarind and oranges and sweetened with sugar.

GARBANZO

See **Chick-Pea.**

GARDEN BALM

See **Balm.**

GARDEN CRESS

Also ENGLISH CRESS. This piquant herb *(Lapidium sativa)* of the mustard family is well known as a garnish as well as a seasoning. Rich in vitamin A, its curly leaves are a frequent ingredient of hors d'oeuvres, salads and sandwiches. It is native to Iran, but common in Ethiopia, Egypt, Moslem countries and Europe. When grown commercially, it is generally sown together with mustard.

See also: **Barbarea, Cardamine, Nasturtium, Water-cress.**

GARDEN MINT

See **Spearmint.**

GARDEN WARBLER

Also BECCAFICO. This small European songbird, *Sylvia hortensis*, is fancied as a table delicacy in both France and Italy. Garden warbler won high praise from the French gastronome Jean Brillat-Savarin (d. 1826), who wrote:

> *[it] gets at least as plump as robins and ortolans and nature has given its flesh a slight bitterness and a unique flavor so exquisite that they engage, gratify and stimulate all the degustatory powers. If the garden warbler were the size of a pheasant it would certainly be worth the price of an acre of land.*

GARLIC

This bulbous member of the lily family far surpasses its cousins, onions and shallots, in the pungency of its flavor and odor. Accordingly, garlic *(Allium sativum)* has as many detractors as adherents, yet if it is used with a light hand, it enhances the flavor of many cooked dishes as well as cold salads.

A native of Central Asia, garlic has stirred controversy in Europe since the dawn of history. Ancient Greeks, on the whole, disliked it, forbidding recent garlic eaters entry to the temple of Cybele. On the other hand, they recommended it as a strengthener to warriors before battle and to athletes before a contest. Ancient Romans divided on the subject, nobles avoiding it, but recommending it as healthy food for plebians, who took to it with relish—at least in the South. It is used with abandon in the southern regimes of Calabria and Sicily, while the rest of Italy claims **basil** as a favorite seasoning.

Use of garlic has gained a lot of ground in the United States and northern Europe over the past 50 years, yet its social acceptability is still questionable. It is a staple seasoning in Chinese cooking, and Koreans greatly favor it as a pickler of vegetables, especially in **kim chi.**

Garlic has several varieties, and the bulbs, or heads, may be covered with white, pink or mauve skin. The head is divided into 10 or 12 sections, called "cloves," not to be confused with the spice, **clove.**

Cloves of garlic may be used fresh or in powdered form. If fresh, they are taken raw and cut into slivers before being added to hearty stews or pot roasts. Sometimes garlic slivers are inserted into the flesh of a leg of lamb before roasting. With salads, the bowl is rubbed with a cut clove of garlic before the salad is mixed.

To minimize the smell of garlic after eating, chewing a sprig or two of **parsley** is recommended.

GARUM

Also LIQUAMEN. A liquid condiment or seasoning, made from fermented fish, which the ancient Romans used in place of salt, garum was usually a clear, golden liquid that added a salty, slightly fishy, slightly cheesy flavor to any dish. The common use of anchovies and anchovy paste in French and other Mediterranean cooking is a direct sequel to the Roman use of *garum.* It has been called Roman soy sauce. The closest thing to it in modern terms is the Vietnamese **nuoc-mam,** a fermented fish sauce, which is labeled "fish soy" in Chinese grocery stores. The liquid from salted anchovies comes closest in the West.

The Romans made *garum* in factories, using small fish such as anchovies, sprats, small mackerels and scombers, plus the entrails of larger fish, such as tuna. These were put together in a large trough and thoroughly salted. Sometimes shrimps, sea urchins, spiny lobsters or oysters were added. After 24 hours, the concoction was put into an earthenware vessel and set in a sunny spot to ferment for two or three months. The resulting liquid was drained off and put into small pots, such as mustard is today.

One of these pots was found in the ruins of Pompeii, bearing the legend, "Best strained liquamen. From the factory of Umbricus Agathopus." The coarse lees, or sediment, left at the bottom of the vessel was called *halec.* It was a paste, somewhat resembling anchovy paste, which, according to Pliny, was used not only in cooking, but as a mange cure for sheep. Later, in the serving, *garum* might be flavored individually by the addition of vinegar, oil or pepper. The most popular variety was that flavored by pepper, called *garum nigrum.*

According to one authority, the use of garum survived into the 19th century in Turkey. *Pissalat,* a garumlike material, is made in Provence from larval anchovies or sardines. It is mixed with onion puree and ripe olives, spread on bread dough and then baked. *Bagoong* is a Filipino variation on *nuoc-mam,* in which the fish entrails are removed so that the fermentation results from the fish enzymes rather than from the intestinal bacteria.

The Eskimos create a paste along the lines of *halec* by storing fins, heads, tails and guts of fish in underground pits for a few months. The resulting paste tastes like strong cheese with virtually no flavor of fish.

GASPEROU

Also FRESHWATER DRUM. A large North American fish, *Aplodinotus grunniens,* it is found from Canada to the Gulf of Mexico, especially in the Mississippi River system. The gasperou is a night feeder, moving into shallow water and consuming bottom-living mollusks, crustaceans and insect larvae. It is popular among anglers because of its large size, ranging up to 50 pounds and averaging 15. Its flesh, however, is rated as only mediocre. Consequently, it has only local importance as a food fish.

The name "drum" is accounted for by its ability to make audible sounds that have been variously described as croaking, grunting or drumming. In addition, its earbones (otoliths) have an L-shaped groove that gives them curio value. They are kept as "lucky stones." Earbones have been unearthed at prehistoric American sites, and these suggest that the primeval version of this fish was much larger, weighing up to 200 pounds.

GAUDI

The edible berry of a Hawaiian shrub, *Clermontia gaudichaudii,* the gaudi is sweet and yellow.

GAUR

Also GAYAL. A large wild ox of India, Burma and Malaysia, the gaur is a magnificent animal and highly regarded as food where available. The *gayal (Bos frontalis)* is a closely related but smaller species native to Burma. The *gayal* has been domesticated in certain areas, and some authorities claim the *gayal* is a cross between the gaur and domestic cattle.

GAUTRIAS

This cylindrical French cheese of the Mayenne department resembles **Port du Salut** and generally weighs five pounds.

GAVOT

A French cheese, it is made from cow's, ewe's or goat's milk in the department of Hautes-Alpes.

GAYAL

See **Gaur.**

GAYETTE

A small French sausage made of pork liver, bacon and seasonings, it is wrapped in pork caul and baked. The *gayette* is a specialty of Provence. It is flat and is served cold as an hors d'oeuvre.

GAZELLE

These small, wild antelope, genus *Gazella* and allied genera, are noted for their lustrous eyes and great speed. They inhabit a wide area of the world. Some of the better known species are the springbok *(Antidorcas euchore)* of southern Africa, the common gazelle *(G. dorcas)* of northern Africa, the goitered gazelle *(G. subgutturosa)* of Persia and the Indian gazelle *(G. bennetti)*. They make a palatable food.

Gazelle is prepared like venison after being marinated to mitigate the gamey taste.

GEANS

See **Cherry.**

GEECHEE LIME

See **Ogeechee Lime.**

GEHEIMRATH

A mass-produced Dutch cheese with a deep yellow curd, it closely resembles, but is not as good as, the small **Gouda.**

GEHIRNWURST

See **Pork Brain Sausage.**

GELATIN

Gelatin is obtained from the boiling of animal bones, hides and other tissues. If dissolved in a hot liquid, it forms a jellylike mass when the liquid cools. A similar substance obtained from fish is called **isinglass.** If from vegetable matter, it is called **agar.** In the 19th century gelatin was made at home through the laborious process of boiling calves' feet, straining the liquid, allowing it to set, skimming off the fat the next day, sweetening and flavoring it and then letting it set again in molds. Today it is universally available in standard forms and quantities. Six sheets, or one-half ounce (sold in small envelopes), is the correct amount to dissolve in a pint of water. Incidentally, with the old method, the gelatin was not obtained from the hooves themselves, but from the connective tissue still clinging to them.

As a food, gelatin is used mainly in gelatin desserts; in meat products such as canned hams, meat loaves, luncheon meats and head-cheeses; in candy, such as marshmallows, wafers and fondants; in ice cream, sherbets and water ices; in canned soups, such as jellied consomme; and in bakery items, such as icings, frostings, cake fillings and chiffon pie fillings. It is also used to make the flavor of chewing gum last longer by coating some of the flavoring particles.

As early as the 1840s, powdered gelatin was available commercially and was even sweetened and flavored. But it was not until the 1890s in the United States—when the arts of merchandising, packaging and advertising were better developed—that gelatin desserts began their popularity. Charles B. Knox, a salesman of Johnston, New York, got the idea of packaging the powder in easy-to-use form after watching his wife make jelly from calves' feet. He had salesman go door to door teaching housewives to use gelatin sheets to make aspics, molds and desserts. It wasn't long before Jell-O came into being. Widespread home refrigeration broadened the market and between 1936 and 1976, the use of gelatin as food increased sixfold in the United States.

Gelatin is nearly all protein. In the dry form, it is 85.6 percent protein with only 56 calories. Unfortunately, from a nutritional point of view, the protein in gelatin is not complete, i.e., it is low in amino acids. It makes a fine complement to other proteins, however. For example, it supplies amino acids lacking in wheat, barley and oats and would make a good addition to diets high in those cereals.

Gelatin has industrial uses, such as in making medicine capsules, pill coatings and suppositories; emulsions for photography; hectograph duplicating equipment and in clarifying wine and beer.

GELOSE

See **Agar–Agar.**

GENEVA

See **Gin.**

GENEVER

See **Gin.**

GENEVOISE SAUCE

This French sauce used with fish consists of **espagnole sauce** and is based on fish stock plus butter, parsley, mushrooms, lemon juice, shallots and dry white wine. It is much reduced and served hot, especially on trout and salmon.

See also: **Sauce.**

GENIPAP

Also MARMALADE BOX. The greenish or russet brown fruit of a large tree, *Genipa americana,* found in Mexico, the West Indies and in South America as far south as Brazil and Peru, *genipap* is about the size of a small orange and grows in clusters. It may be eaten raw but is said not to be particularly palatable that way. The flavor is subacidic.

More frequently, genipap is made into preserves of the marmalade type, hence the tree name "marmalade box." These preserves are popular in Puerto Rico and Brazil. The tree yields an indelible blue dye once used by Indian tribes as body paint. *Genipapado* is a cooling drink made from the fruit.

This fruit is not to be confused with the Spanish lime or **ginep.**

GENTIAN

A large genus of flowering herbs, *Gentiana* spp., is widely distributed in temperate, arctic and in mountainous tropical areas. Gentian flowers may be white, yellow, blue, purple, red or spotted, depending on the species. The flowers are sometimes used in the Alps and Pyrenees to flavor aperitifs and cordials. The roots of the yellow gentian *(Gentiana lutea)* yield a bitter juice that is one of the standard flavoring agents in certain **vermouths.** It is the principal flavoring agent of the liqueur, *gentiane,* which is produced in Switzerland and France.

GEODUCK

See **Clams.**

GEONOMA

A small palm tree, *Geonoma interrupta,* whose young flower clusters are cooked and eaten in Mexico, geonoma is also found in the Lesser Antilles, Trinidad and in South America as far south as Peru.

GERARDMER

See **Gerome.**

GERMANFISH

An excellent food fish, *Formio niger* is found from East Africa across the Indian and Pacific Oceans to Hawaii, but nowhere in sufficient numbers to warrant a commercial fishery. It is a silver gray fish, much like the jacks and crevalles in body shape. It can attain a length of two feet. The Germanfish is important as a food fish throughout its range.

GERMON

See **Tuna Fish.**

GEROLSTEINER SPRUDEL WATER

A carbonated mineral water bottled in West Germany, Gerolsteiner Sprudel Natural Mineral Water is relatively high in mineral content (1750 ppm of total dissolved solids) and in sodium content (33 mg. per 8-ounce glass). A 1980 Consumers Union sensory panel rated the taste of this water as good, with the following qualifying comments: mildly bitter, mildly sour, mildly astringent, mild soapy flavor, mildly salty.

See also: **Mineral Water.**

GEROME

Also GERARDMER. A soft French cheese that has been made for a century or more in the valleys of the Vosges mountains, particularly around the village of Gerardmer, and in Switzerland, Gerome tastes much like **Munster.** These cheeses are sometimes flavored with aniseed, fennel or cumin, in which case they are called *Gerome anise.* Whole cow's milk is used, often supplemented by goat's milk. Curing takes six weeks to four months, depending on size, which ranges from eight ounces to five pounds. The interior is yellow and the rind a brick red. It is available all year round, but is best in winter.

GERVAIS

Gervais is a very rich, delicate, French cream cheese of the Neufchatel type. Soft and perishable, it is available all year round, but is especially good in summer. Although a particular cheese named after its maker, Gervais has come to be a generic term for French cheese of the soft, cream type. It can also be a cow's milk cheese from Normandy sold in small packages that resembles a *demisel.*

See also: **Carre.**

GETMESOST

Also GETOST. A goat's-milk cheese made in Sweden and Norway from whey, it has a soft texture and slightly sweet taste.

GEX

A hard French cow's milk cheese that has delicate blue veins streaking an otherwise pure white curd, it originated more than a century ago in the town of Gex, department of Ain, which remains the principal center of production. Some *Gex* is also made in the southeast in the departments of Isere and Jura, where it is known as *bleu du Haut-Jura*.

Gex is one of a group of cheeses matured with the aid of a blue mold, in this case the *penicillium glaucum*. Others include **sassenage, septmoncel** and **roquefort.** In some, like Roquefort, the mold is injected early on in processing, but with *Gex* the mold grows naturally during curing, which takes three to four months. The rind is yellow or red on the cured cheese, and the latter weighs around 14 pounds. *Gex* has been compared favorably with **Stilton,** the best-known English blue cheese. Its season is November to May.

See also: **Blue Cheese.**

GHEE

Ghee, or clarified buffalo butter, an essential cooking medium in the Indian subcontinent, is the liquid remaining after the butter has been boiled and strained. Unlike fresh butter, it can be kept for months even in a hot climate. As a dairy product, ghee has religious significance among high-caste Hindus, since anything cooked in it is automatically purified.

GHERKIN

This is any small pickle usually made from the immature fruit of certain pickling cucumbers that are especially prickly. The original gherkin was the **anguria** or West Indian gherkin, a variety of cucumber native to West Africa and the West Indies that is very prickly and reaches a maximum length of two inches. Both the word *anguria* and "gherkin" are probably derived from the old Dutch word *agurkje*. Gherkins are most often flavored with dill and used as a garnish.

GIANT BUR REED

A perennial aquatic herb, *Sparganium eurycarpum*, of northern North America, the giant bur reed has tubers that make good vegetables. It has stiff, flat leaves and reaches a height of 4½ feet.

GIANT HYSSOP

Also ANISE HYSSOP. Giant hyssop is a tall perennial herb, *Agastache foeniculum*, of the central and western United States. Its leaves are used to make an herbal tea. The dried leaves are used for seasoning as well.

GIANT PERCH

Also PALMER. A valuable food fish, the giant perch *(Lates calcarifer)* is found in both fresh and saltwater along the coasts of the Indian Ocean and as far east as China and the Philippines. The saltwater varieties are said to be more flavorful than the freshwater, but both kinds grow very large, exceeding six feet in length and topping 90 pounds in weight. Those brought to market range from three to 30 pounds; their flesh is described as firm and white. It is a slender-bodied fish with a flattened head, large mouth and prominently spined dorsal fin. It is greenish gray above and white below and has brilliant red eyes.

A close relative is the Nile perch *(L. niloticus)*, another giant that can weigh as much as 180 pounds and is best known as a sport fish. It is a good fighter and has been stocked in many African lakes and reservoirs. Heaviest of all the Lake Albert perch *(L. albertianus)*, which is found only in Lake Albert and the Albert and Murchison Niles. It too is a sought-after sportfish but is more often taken with nets. A good-sized specimen weighs around 360 pounds. It is an important food fish.

GIANT TOAD

Also SILVER TOADFISH. A pufferfish *(Lagocephalus scleratus)* found in the Indian and Pacific Oceans from East Africa to Australia and Japan, this species prefers the open ocean and is a long, slender fish unless annoyed. Then it inflates its body like a balloon, which brings erect a whole series of densely packed spines on the surface of its skin.

The flesh of this fish is virulently poisonous, unless prepared by an expert. Such experts flourish in Japan. (See **Fugu)** The famous navigator, Captain Cook, reportedly sampled the flesh of this species and narrowly escaped death from poisoning.

GIANT WILD RYE

This robust, perennial grass, *Elymus condensata*, is found in California and elsewhere in western North America. The seeds are suitable for milling into flour used to make bread.

GIBEL

Also GOLDFISH, PRUSSIAN CARP. A species of carp, *Carassius aurantus gibelio*, found throughout

Europe and in many other parts of the world, it may be used as a food fish, but is more often kept in aquaria for ornamental purposes. The gibel is distinguished from other carp by its lack of barbels around the mouth and by its strongly serrated dorsal and anal fins. Young gibels are golden red in color and do not reach a pure gold color until the age of 18 months. Gibel can tolerate low oxygen water and in the wild are often found in marshy pools, backwaters of rivers and lakes or other mildly polluted water.

See also: **Carp.**

GIBLETS

The term refers to the interior organs of fowl and includes the heart, liver and gizzard, plus odds and ends like the neck, feet and cock's comb. They are cooked separately and used as ingredients in gravy, stuffing, or sometimes made into a stew. Giblets may also be used to flavor stocks and soups. The livers of geese and ducks are excluded from the term "giblet," since they are considered special delicacies on their own.

GILTHEAD

Several fish of the sea-bream family *(Sparidae)* are called by this name. They inhabit the Mediterranean Sea and warmer Atlantic coastal waters of Europe. They have gold markings on the head and stripes on the belly. Though not generally considered as good as the sea bream *(Pagellus centrodontus)*, several species make excellent eating. The Spanish are particularly fond of the red gildhead, which they call *besugo de laredo* and prefer fried, poached or cooked in a casserole with tomatoes and sweet peppers.

See also: **Bream.**

GIN

The juniper berry gives this liquor its distinctive taste, which is never strong in the English and American types of dry gin. For this reason, it is a favorite base for cocktails, unlike the Dutch type called *genever*, which has a pronounced flavor and is usually drunk straight.

"I never drink anything stronger than gin before breakfast," quipped the American humorist W. C. Fields, yet gin of the dry type is distilled at higher proof than other spirits and is, therefore, the purest. The mash consists of corn, malt, rye and other grains. The product of the first distillation, is cut with water, then distilled again with the flavoring agents called botanicals. This method imparts a delicate flavor.

The name derives from the French word for juniper, *genievre*, but the drink was invented in the 17th century by a Dutch professor of medicine, Dr. Franciscus Sylvius, who sought a cure for certain tropical diseases. Barley malt is used exclusively in the mash for *genever*, or Hollands gin. Moreover, the botanicals are added directly to the mash, which accounts for the stronger taste. It is distilled at lower proof, 90 to 94, with heavier body. Old Tom, or Plymouth gin, is sweetened. **Sloe gin** is not, strictly speaking, a gin, but a liqueur.

Gin is usually bottled unaged at between 80 and 100 proof. It is usually colorless unless mixed with fruit syrups to produce flavored gin.

GINEP

Also MAMONCILLO, SPANISH LIME. The green, plum-sized fruit of the *Melicoccus bijugatus* tree, ginep is found in the Caribbean Islands and in south Florida. The rind is leathery but thin and contains a sweet-tart translucent pulp surrounding an egg-shaped seed, which is also edible. The whole is about one inch in diameter. The ginep is popular as a fresh fruit, especially in Cuba and Puerto Rico. The seed is roasted before eating.

GINGELLY OIL

This oil is pressed from the gingili or sesame seed.

See also: **Sesame.**

GINGER

This venerable spice comes from the rootstalk of a reedy, herbaceous plant, *Zingiber officinale*, which probably originated in India but is also native to other countries in tropical Asia. It was the first oriental spice to be transplanted in the New World, and today Jamaican ginger is the most valuable of all.

The rootstalk looks like a potato that grew upon itself, broadening out into the shape of a knobby "hand," a term used to refer to ginger root. The taste is piquant and peppery but can vary widely depending on where the plant was grown, and whether the cook uses whole root or powdered ginger.

Whole ginger root is often used in Indian and Chinese cooking, while powdered ginger is generally preferred in the West. After being harvested, the rootstalk is washed and dried in the sun. It is then ground with the skin on (black ginger) or peeled (white ginger). Generally, the lighter the color, the more "bite" to the flavor. The portion nearest the stem has a more delicate flavor and is frequently preserved in heavy syrup or crystallized sugar.

Different forms of ginger root: crystallized (front right); the root itself (center); and powdered (rear left)

Ginkgo nuts

Powdered ginger is used in ginger snaps and gingerbread and as a flavoring base for carbonated beverages. Red pickled ginger is a staple in Japanese cuisine. Ginger is a standard ingredient in curries and chutney.

GINGER ALE

Ginger ale is a nonalcoholic carbonated beverage impregnated with **ginger** *(Zingiber officinale).* It is sold commercially as a soft drink. Two types of ginger ale are marketed. "Pale dry" is less sweet and more highly carbonated than the "golden" or aromatic ginger ale. Caramel coloring supplies the rich, warm hue of both types. A unique ingredient in ginger ale is **capsicum,** which gives the beverage its special pungency.

Ginger ale differs from ginger beer in being transparent rather than cloudy and by the presence of the capsicum extracts. Also, **fermentation,** common in the production of ginger beer, has been replaced by the artificial infusion of carbon dioxide gas. Ginger ale is a pleasant, refreshing drink, particularly when a sprig of mint is added to the glass. It is less sugary in flavor that other commercial soft drinks and mixes well with some whiskies.

GINGERBREAD PLUM

This edible fruit of an African tree, *Parinarium macrophylla,* is found in the warm regions of that continent and is highly regarded there as a fresh fruit.

GINGERBREAD TREE

See **Doum Palm.**

GINGER WINE

A fermented beverage flavored with ginger and served as a liqueur or mixed with other alcoholic drinks, it usually consists of ginger essence, water, tartaric acid, cream of tartar, sugar and yeast.

Stone's Green Ginger Wine is currant wine flavored with ginger. It has an alcohol content of 13 percent and is drunk as an aperitif or often mixed in equal proportions with whisky as a cocktail. A ginger liqueur is also made and bottled at 70 proof.

GINJAS

A type of sour cherry, *Prunus cerasus* var. *austera* cultivated in Madeira, it is used to make jam, or a type of liqueur. The latter is made as follows: *ginjas* are steeped in alcohol or brandy for several weeks, then water and sugar are added. After further steeping, the liquid is filtered and bottled with three to four *ginjas* in each bottle. The liqueur is called *ginginha.* The *ginja* is similar to the morello.

See also: **Cherry.**

GINKGO

Also GINGKO, GINKO. The maidenhair tree *(Ginkgo biloga)* of northern China and Japan bears yellow fruit that contains an edible seed used in Japanese cookery. The tree is a handsome ornamental that grows to a great height (140 to 160 feet) and whose fan-shaped leaves stream out on longer, slender branches like banners. It is considered a living fossil, since it belongs to an order of plants that were typical of the Permian period several hundred million years ago. It seems to be susceptible to no pests or diseases, which perhaps explains its survival. It is frequently planted near Buddhist temples or on other sacred ground. The maidenhair tree has been transplanted to Europe and the United States for its ornamental qualities combined with its ability to resist both great cold and prolonged drought.

The seed, called ginkgo nut, is cooked in a variety of dishes, but when eaten alone, it is usually roasted. It is sweet and mildly resinous. The seed is thought to aid digestion and goes well in soups and with poultry.

GINSENG

This root plant, *Panax quinquefolia*, or *scheninseng*, is native to both Asia and North America and is highly prized, especially in China, as a cure-all and aphrodisiac. The name derives from the Chinese *jen-chan* meaning "man-root," and the more the root resembles a man the greater are said to be its powers. It is expensive, and depending on the quality, it can fetch anywhere from $60 to $600 an ounce. In the West, it is occasionally used as an ingredient in bitters, but its chief value has been as an item of trade with China beginning back in the 1770s and continuing to the present.

Although ginseng has been under cultivation in the United States since 1870, the wild variety is considered more potent and fetches twice the price of the cultivated. The Chinese occasionally use it as a seasoning, e.g., in squab and ginseng soup, to which it adds a faint licorice flavor. But customarily, the root is powdered and made into a tea, which is reputed to be refreshing and stimulating. It has been reported that Soviet cosmonauts are issued pieces of ginseng to take along on missions into space as a preventive against possible ailments.

GIODDU

This is a fermented milk product like yogurt made in Sardinia.

See also: **Fermented Milk, Yogurt.**

GIRAFFE

The tallest of existing animals and a native of Africa, the giraffe *(Giraffa camelopardis)* can reach a height of 18 feet, much of it taken up by a very long neck. It chews a cud and lives largely on a diet of leaves and twigs from the giraffe acacia tree. The giraffe usually has a light fawn color marked with darker spots. Its head has two bony excrescences that look like horns.

It is hunted by several primitive African tribes who usually kill it with poisoned darts. Though edible, the meat is not considered to be of high quality, but the bone marrow is regarded as a great delicacy.

GIRELLA

A member of the wrasse family, the girella *(Labrus vulgaris)* is a small, brightly colored fish of the Mediterranean. In French cuisine, the girella is used mainly in **bouillabaisse.** It may also be fried. Three varieties are the common girella (violet with an orange stripe), the red girella (bright scarlet) and the Turkish girella (green with turquoise blue stripes). The girella seldom exceeds 12 inches in length.

GIROLLE

See **Chanterelle.**

GISLEV

This is a hard Danish cow's milk cheese.

GIZZARD

A bird's second stomach, the gizzard is a muscular pouch with a tough lining that the bird uses to grind food mixed with gastric juices in the first stomach.

Before preparing it, one should slit open the side and remove any bird food remaining in it. The gizzard is added to the **giblets** when making a gravy for poultry, or it may be prepared on its own by braising or roasting. The gizzard is considered a delicacy by many people in Europe.

GJETOST

This firm Norwegian cheese is made from a boiled whey mixture that comes from cow's milk (90 percent) and goat's milk (10 percent). The prefix *gje* indicates a goat's-milk product, but if the whey comes entirely from goat's milk, the cheese is labeled *ekte* (genuine) or *geitmyost*. The curd is golden brown and sweet due to a high lactose content. The cured cheese generally weighs around nine pounds and is eaten all year round.

See also: **Mysost.**

GLARNERKASE

See **Sapsago.**

GLASSWORT

Also MARSH SAMPHIRE. A European marsh plant of the goosefoot family, glasswort *(Salcornia herbacea)* has bright green, jointed branches but no leaves. The shoots are steeped in malt vinegar and then pickled. They are sold as marsh samphire and have a bitter, salty taste.

GLIADIN

See **Gluten.**

GLOBE ARTICHOKE

See **Artichoke.**

GLOIRE DES MONTAGNES

See **Damen Cheese.**

GLOUCESTER CHEESE

A cheddar-type cheese similar to **Derby,** Gloucester comes in two sizes, which have distinct characteristics. Single Gloucester, which weighs about 15 pounds, is round and flat with a clear yellow curd. The texture is smooth and waxy and the flavor mild. Double Gloucester has the same general shape but is thicker and weighs around 24 pounds. The curd is dyed brownish red with annatto, and though firmer than the single, it is crumbly. Its flavor is also mild, but richer. Some authorities consider it the best red cheese in England. It is good for toasting and other uses.

GLUCOSE

Also DEXTROSE, GRAPE SUGAR. Glucose is a monosaccharide, or simple sugar, and the most abundant sugar to be found in a natural state. It is formed by the action of sunlight in all higher plants and is sometimes stored in a readily available form, as in cane and beets. There are concentrations of it in sweet fruits, especially grapes and figs, and in honey. In other plants, it combines with other substances to form starch, as in potatoes, and corn (maize).

It can be separated from these starches by treating them with acids. The resulting glucose is used as a syrup, which is about half glucose and named after the plant contributing the starch, e.g., corn syrup. This type of glucose does not crystallize readily and is thus very useful in the manufacture of jams, syrups and candies. Glucose is not as sweet as sucrose and **fructose.**

GLUMSE

This German cottage cheese is made in western Prussia. Skim milk is curdled by souring, the whey is drained off, and either milk or cream are added before eating.

See also: **Cottage Cheese.**

GLUTEN

Protein matter in wheat or rye flour that forms a spongy mass when mixed with water, gluten enables raised bread to retain its shape.

Gluten is composed mainly of two proteins, gliadin, which has elastic properties, and glutenin, which gives strength. Gluten can be isolated by repeatedly washing bread dough until all the starch is removed. It is a grayish, sticky substance. Gluten bread has a higher proportion of gluten and lower proportion of starch than other breads.

GLUTEN BREAD

This is any bread low in starch and high in gluten content. **Gluten** is a sticky, protein substance in cereal flour that gives a leavened loaf its elastic, tough consistency. Wheat flour is particularly rich in gluten, which makes it so appropriate for breadmaking. In making gluten bread, the dough is kneaded under a stream of water until most of the starch is washed away. It makes a light elastic loaf suitable for diabetic diets or for those who otherwise wish to limit their starch intake.

See also: **Bread.**

GLYCERINE

Also GLYCEROL. This colorless, odorless, syrupy liquid slightly sweet to the taste, is formed from the decomposition of animal and vegetable fat. It is often a by-product of soap manufacture. Glycerine is also present in all wines and beers in minute quantities as a result of fermentation. It is used in food manufacturing as an additive to candies and cake icings where it helps retain moisture.

GNEMON

A woody plant or shrub with edible fruit in the form of catkins, *gnemon (Gnetum gnemon)* is found in tropical Asia. The catkins are roasted and eaten in the Philippines. There is a related species in India.

GNU

Also WILDEBEEST. An African antelope with the head and horns of an ox and the mane and tail of a horse, it has an ungainly and somewhat ferocious appearance that is only partly misleading. It is peaceful if unprovoked, but has been known to charge and kill handlers in captivity. Two species inhabit the African plains from Tanganyika and Kenya southward. The white-tailed gnu *(Connochaetes gnou)*, or black wildebeest, is considered an excellent game animal, and perhaps for this reason is practically extinct in the wild. The brindled gnu *(C. taurinus)*, also known as the white-bearded gnu or blue wildebeest, is still plentiful in Central Africa. Its flesh, however, is coarse, dry and tough.

GOAT

The goat is a four-legged ruminant with hollow horns that is found all over the world. In certain areas of southern Europe, the meat of the unweened **kid** is highly esteemed as food. The flesh of the adult male is not eaten under any conditions other than famine because it is tough and has a disagreeable odor. The flesh of the doe, although tough, does not smell bad. It is eaten with some regularity in the Philippines, Indonesia and Jamaica, either in a stew or a highly spiced curry because its toughness requires lengthy cooking. An unusual English specialty is goat ham, which is rubbed with saltpeter, pickled in brine, smoked for three weeks, then cooked as one would a cured pork ham.

The domestic goat *(Capra hircus hircus)* is kept in many countries for the milk it gives, which may be drunk fresh or made into cheese. It has been dubbed "the poor man's cow." Americans are prejudiced against goat meat, and only in Texas are goats raised in any quantity. In the United States goat's milk is often drunk by persons allergic to cow's milk Some varieties of goat—notably the Cashmere and the Angora—are valuable for the wool they produce.

See also: **Kid** and **Goat's Milk Cheese.**

GOATFISH

This name is applied to several species of fish of the red mullet family *(Mullidae)*, which are found in the Indian, Pacific and Atlantic Oceans. Goatfish prefer inshore, shallow waters. They share certain characteristics, such as a reddish color above, a long body and a pair of long barbels on the chin, to which they owe the name "goatfish."

The golden banded goatfish *(Pseudupeneus auriflamma)* is native to the Indian Ocean and the Red Sea but has also entered the eastern Mediterranean where it competes with the red **mullet** as a valuable food fish. The largest of the goatfishes is *P. barberinus*, which is also known as red mullet, but should not be confused with *Mullus surmuletus*, a famous species native to the Mediterranean. *P. barberinus* is found in the tropical Indo-Pacific from Africa to Australia. It reaches a length of 20 inches and is highly regarded as food. A companion species is *P. fraterculus*, also known as the surmullet. It inhabits roughly the same territory and reaches a maximum length of about 18 inches.

GOATNUT

Also JOJOBA. The goatnut is the edible seed of a perennial, evergreen, woody shrub, *Simmondsia chinensis*, native to semiarid regions of California, Arizona and Baja California. The seeds have been used as food, dried or roasted, or as a source of cooking oil. It has been found that goatnut meal, although it consists of about 30 percent protein, contains a substance called *simmondsin* that acts as an appetite suppressant when fed to animals. This limits its use as feed.

The oil, called jojoba oil, is not a true oil but a liquid wax. It is quite similar to sperm whale oil and can be substituted for it in most uses. Commercial exploitation of this product has begun in such markets as cosmetics, waxes, pharmaceuticals and lubricants. Because of its ease of cultivation and drought- and fire-resistant character, goatnut has attracted some interest as a landscape and soil-conservation plant.

GOAT'S BEARD

Also JACK-GO-TO-BED-AT-NOON. This biennial, tap-rooted herb, *Tragopogon pratensis*, is closely related to **salsify.** It is native to Europe but naturalized in North America. Its blanched shoots are eaten like asparagus, and its roots, which are coarser than salsify's, are nevertheless sometimes prepared in the same way. The plant is rarely cultivated but grows freely in meadows. It is considered a weed in North America.

GOAT'S MILK CHEESE

This is cheese made in the usual way except that goat's milk is used instead of cow's milk. Mixtures of the two are common, some of which also contain ewe's milk. Goat's milk has a stronger flavor than cow's milk and is somewhat richer in protein and fat.

Goat's milk cheese is not always identified as such, but the following names are well known. France: *Cabriou*, *Cevennes*, *Chabichou*, *Chateauroux*, *Chevret*, *Chevrotin*, *Gratairon*, *La Mothe*, *Loches*, *Pamproux*, *Poitiers*, *Rigottes*, *Rougerets*, *Rougernis*, *Sainte-Maure*, *and Vendome;* Italy: *formaggio de capra*, or one bearing the adjective, *caprino;* German areas: *ziegenkase*, or *gaiskasli* (see also under **Gaiskasli** for a specific cheese).

See also: **Cheese.**

Varieties of goat's milk cheese

GOBO

See **Burdock.**

GOBY

This large family of small fish, *Gobiidae*, includes both fresh and saltwater species. Typically gobies have a long body, a large head and a big mouth.

The black goby *(Gobius niger)* is the largest European saltwater species and the most important as food. It reaches a length of about seven inches and, despite its name, is not conspicuously black but dusky gray or brown. It is especially plentiful in the Mediterranean, but its habitat extends from the Black Sea to the North Sea. The black goby has a thick-set appearance and the characteristic suction cup formed by its pelvic fins. This fish is greatly appreciated in France for its delicate flavor. It is often caught in areas of low salinity and is known as *goujon de mer*. Frying is the favorite method of preparation.

The freshwater goby *(Chaenogobius isaza)* of Japan rarely exceeds three inches in length. It is found in Lake Biwa and is a valued food fish, despite its small size. The freshwater goby is netted in large numbers and eaten either fresh or pickled in a sweet sauce.

GOLDEN APPLE

See **Bengal Quince.**

GOLDEN NEEDLES

The dried buds of the tiger lily *(Lilium lancifolium)* are gold-colored and are used to season meat or poultry dishes in Chinese cooking.

GOLDEN PLOVER

This small shore bird of Europe and North America, has been appreciated as a game bird since Classical Antiquity. The European varieties are the *Pluvialis apricaria* and the *Pluvialis apricaria altifons*, which has a black head. The American golden plover *(P. dominica)* breeds in North America but migrates to Ireland. They are prepared for cooking like **plover.**

GOLDEN SPOON

See **Nance.**

GOLDEN SYRUP

See **Treacle.**

GOLDEYE

A valued food fish of North America, the goldeye *(Hiodon alosoides)* is found in the Mississippi basin and in the rivers of the Great Plains as far north as the Mackenzie Great Slave Lake. It reaches a length of about 20 inches and resembles the herring.

The name derives from the golden iris of its eyes; its back is blue black against an overall silver. The goldeye has a reputation as a gamefish and may be eaten freshly caught. Its gastronomic fame, however, comes from the way it is prepared in Winnepeg, Canada. Oak-smoked goldeye is a local delicacy and reckoned to be the most flavorful of all Canadian fish.

A close relative, the mooneye *(H. tergisus)*, is smaller but also good to eat and is considered a passable game fish. It is found in the United States from the Great Lakes south to Alabama.

GOLDFISH

See **Gibel.**

GOLDLINE

Also SAUPE, BAMBOOFISH. A saltwater fish of the sea bream family, the goldline *(Sarpa salpa)* is found throughout the Mediterranean and in the Atlantic from the Bay of Biscay to South Africa and beyond into the Indian Ocean. It reaches a length of 18 inches and always swims in tightly packed shoals. The goldline has a fairly deep body, full scales on body and head, and a large mouth. It is a food fish of some importance within its range.

GOOBER

See **Peanut.**

Good King Henry

GOOD KING HENRY

Also WILD SPINACH, HUAUZONCLE. A member of the goosefoot genus, this herbaceous plant, *Chenopodium bonus henricus*, grows wild in England but is cultivated in the Americas, particularly Mexico. It is related to spinach and is rich in iron. The fresh tops resemble asparagus.

It can be prepared like spinach or eaten in salads. It is sometimes used as a flavoring ingredient and is believed to have medicinal properties. Legends tie it to King Henry VIII of England, whose sore legs were treated by application of this plant.

GOONCH

This big catfish, *Bagarius bagarius*, is found in the larger rivers of certain countries of Asia, including India, Burma, Thailand, Vietnam and Indonesia. Large specimens weigh as much as 250 pounds and measure up to 6½ feet long. The *goonch* has a wide, flat body, which is a deep olive green marked with dark blotches and spots. It is considered a valuable food fish.

GOOSE

The goose is a ducklike aquatic bird of the genus *Anser* with a long neck and webbed feet. Several species, both wild and domesticated, are appreciated for their rich, dark meat. While wild geese tend to be lean, poultry geese carry considerable fat, much more than chickens, turkeys or ducks. The goose was domesticated in the Neolithic era, and during much of the time since has been an important poultry bird, particularly for the poor. Like the goat and the pig, the goose is an expert forager and thus tends to be an economical animal to raise. Even so, it takes less grain to put a pound of flesh on a goose than on a chicken or a turkey. Geese are less bother to raise than ducks, because, although they are aquatic birds, they require far less water.

The popularity of geese in the West is not what it was in former times. The ancient Romans particularly treasured the geese of Gaul, which they imported through the Bay of Naples and fattened in the nearby town of Morino. Then, according to Pliny, the geese were walked 125 miles to market in Rome. It was a favorite on feast days with rich and poor alike in the Middle Ages and Renaissance, particularly so in England where it took second place only to the chicken. According to tradition, Queen Elizabeth I was eating roast goose on the day the English defeated the Spanish Armada, September 29. She decreed that that day (Saint Michael's day) be celebrated annually with a feast of roast goose, much as Thanksgiving is celebrated with roast turkey in the United States.

The Northern Hemisphere is the best breeding ground for the goose, whose natural habitat extends from Lapland to Spain and from Canada eastward to China. The wild graylag goose *(Anser anser)* is believed to be the progenitor of all species of geese in the West, both domesticated and wild. In the East, the Chinese goose *(Cygnopsis cygnoid)* is thought to be the original species. The latter is the largest species of wild goose in existence, dwarfing the Canada goose, which is the largest species of the Western Hemisphere, weighing as much as 14 pounds, and having a wingspan of six feet.

The male goose is called a gander, but in the culinary sense, both sexes are called goose. Under the right conditions, a goose can live to a great age. To avoid toughness, however, one should eat it young. For a wild goose this means under a year old, under two for the domestic variety. The best age is seven or eight months, the corresponding weight being six to eight pounds. A bird under six months of age is referred to as a gosling, or green goose.

Although the goose has maintained its following in Germany, and to a lesser extent in England, there seems to be no large-scale commercial exploitation of the kind we associate with chickens and turkeys. Rather they are raised on small farms. There is no mass-marketing of geese in the United States due perhaps to the bird's large size and high fat content. Because of the latter, 1½ pounds must be allowed for each serving of the domesticated bird because there is comparatively little meat. To counteract the fattiness of goose, a stuffing of potatoes flavored with onions and herbs is used when roasting it. The potatoes absorb a lot of the fat.

The most popular domesticated geese are the Embden, the Toulouse and the Chinese. The Embden is white, has an orange bill, and averages about 15 pounds in market weight, although the mature bird can weigh as much as 20. The Toulouse, named for the city in France where it is raised in large numbers, is gray and larger than the Embden. The adult gander reaches a weight of 26 pounds. It reaches market weight toward the end of the year and has thus been the traditional Christmas goose. The Chinese, with both brown and white varieties, is a smaller bird.

Well-known types of wild geese are the Canada (the largest in the West), the snow goose, blue goose and the brant, or black goose. They have a distinctive gamy flavor that varies according to breed and diet. Inevitably, those that feed on fish have a fishy taste.

Geese have a reputation for being foolish, as in our phrase "silly goose." But, in fact, they are warier than ducks when it comes to being hunted. An exception to this is the Hawaiian *nene.* Although it is said to have evolved from the Canada goose, it has lost its aquatic habits and most of the webbing on its feet and is as easy to hunt as a duck. The geese of Strasbourg are famous for their fat livers, which are developed by unusual forced feeding methods. They are used to make the expensive delicacy *foie gras.*

See also: **Foie Gras.**

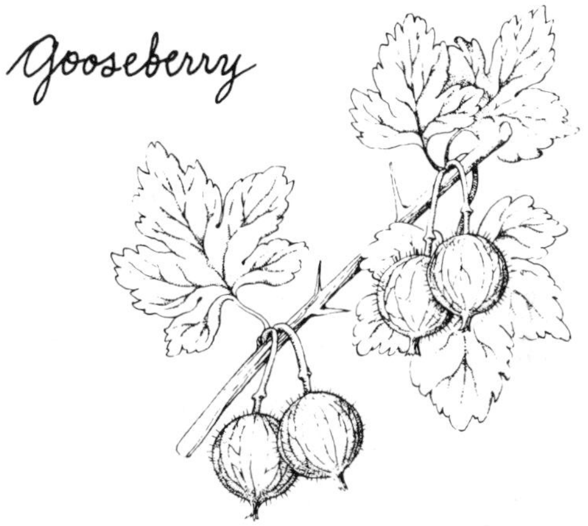

GOOSEBERRY

A fruit seldom seen fresh in U.S. markets, the gooseberry is native to both Europe and North America, although the latter varieties are much inferior. The main European species is *Ribes grossularia.* The fruit is round, tart and may be red, yellow, green or white depending on the variety. The size varies accordingly, as does the skin texture, which may be smooth or hairy. It is a close relative of the currant and does well in cool climates, such as England's where there is little direct sunlight.

Gooseberry is of little importance gastronomically and has virtually no following anywhere but Great Britain, where it is much appreciated and where its cultivation has reached perfection. The English varieties bear the largest fruit (up to one ounce each) and have the least thorns. Gooseberry pie is a traditional dessert there at Whitsuntide. The berries make excellent jams and preserves. The fruit can also be fermented to make a wine of considerable alcoholic content. In France, a sauce made from green gooseberries is a traditional accompaniment to mackerel. Perhaps this accounts for the French term for gooseberry, *groseille a maquereau,* mackerel currant.

The most important American species is *Ribes hirtellum.* It is seldom cultivated and grows wild in the Northeast, on the shores of the Great Lakes, the Northwest or Alaska. The season for gathering them lasts for only two to three weeks in July. Attempts to grow the English varieties in the United States have failed because of their susceptibility to gooseberry mildew. Gooseberry cultivation has been discouraged also because, like the currant, the gooseberry plant transmits blister rust, a blight that kills the American white pine, a tree of considerable commercial importance. For the Chinese gooseberry, see **Actinidia.**

See also: **Cape Gooseberry.**

GOOSEBERRY FIG

This edible fruit of a succulent shrub, *Carpobrotus acinaciformis*, is found in the Cape Province of South Africa and in the Mediterranean region. The fruit has 10 to 15 cells and is about the size of a gooseberry. The taste is reported to be insipid.

GOOSEFOOT

A few members of this large family of plants, mostly weedy herbs, are grown as potherbs or for their seeds. One grows wild in the United States and is known by the name "pigweed." Some of the more respectable members of the family are food plants. They include lamb's quarters *(Chenopodium album)*; anserine *(C. amaranticolor)*; wormseed, or Mexican tea *(C. ambrosioides)*, valued for its essential oil; Good King Henry *(C. bonus-henricus)*; strawberry slite *(C. capitatum)*, and quinoa *(C. quinoa)*, whose seeds are an important cereal food in the Andean highlands. The name "goosefoot" derives from the shape of the leaves. See under the common name of each species for more information.

GOOSE GRASS

See **Cleavers.**

GORAKA

This edible and pleasant-tasting fruit of *Garcinia cambogia*, a tree native to Indochina, is closely related to the mangosteen, one of the best tropical fruits. The sap of this tree yields commercial gamboge, a resin used in artists' pigment and as a cathartic.

GORGONZOLA

Also STRACCHINO DE GORGONZOLA. This is the foremost blue-veined Italian cheese. It takes its name from the village of Gorgonzola, near Milan, although little is produced there now. Its origin dates back to the ninth century A.D. and came about accidentally. The owner of a wineshop, who accepted cheese from farmers as payment for his wares, stored them in the cellar where they ripened. Blue mold formed naturally on their surface. They became famous, and an industry was born that still flourishes in the Lombardy and Piedmont districts.

Gorgonzola travels well and has attained an international reputation for strong flavor and unusually creamy texture. It is made in other countries as well, including the United States, mainly in Wisconsin and Michigan. It goes particularly well with fresh fruit and crusty white bread.

The peculiar blue green mottling of Gorgonzola curd is achieved by sprinkling mold powder *(Penicillium glaucum)* on it during an early stage of processing. During the second stage of curing, many holes are punched into the cheese to facilitate growth of the mold. Curing takes from three to 12 months, and a cured cheese, which is cylindrical in shape, weighs from 14 to 17 pounds. In earlier days, the surface bore a protective red coating but now is usually wrapped in tinfoil.

Gorgonzola curd is yellowish, but a white Gorgonzola, called *pannerone*, is also marketed. Though highly appreciated in Italy, it is little known elsewhere.

GOUDA

Perhaps the Dutch cheese best known overseas, Gouda has a sweet, yellow curd, ranging from semisoft to hard. It is similar to **Edam** in this respect and in its production; but Gouda contains more fat, is flatter and has a wider range of sizes, some weighing as much as 50 pounds. Curing requires anywhere from two to six months, and while the younger Goudas may be roughly comparable to Edam in quality, connoisseurs consider the aged Gouda a truly great cheese.

Gouda is made from whole or partly skimmed cow's milk. In the processing the curd is heated to give it firmer body and better keeping qualities. Although cheese average between 10 and 15 pounds, there is a baby Gouda weighing one pound. It is coated with red wax and wrapped in cellophane.

Gouda is often served at breakfast with coffee and fresh white, black or pumpernickel bread. It is excellent with cocoa. Kosher Gouda is also available.

GOURAMI

This freshwater fish, *Osphroneum goramy*, is widely cultured in parts of Asia, especially India, Sri Lanka, Southeast Asia, the Philippines and China. The fish is able to survive in a variety of habitats, including streams, rivers, ponds and swamps with open water. This adaptability is due in great measure to its possession of accessory breathing organs that enable it to breathe atmospheric oxygen. This, together with the general high quality of its flesh, greatly enhances its marketability, since it can be brought to market alive.

The *gourami* reaches a length of up to two feet, and, although it has a rather flat body, large specimens weigh several pounds, carrying much of the weight in the front part of the body near the head. Adult fish have an overall dark, brownish red color.

GOURD

This general term covers the fruits of a wide variety of annual plants, usually with hard or durable shells, that are closely allied to cucumbers, pumpkins and melons. Gourds are grown as ornamentals as well as for food. In North America, the term "gourd" is usually applied to fruits grown as ornaments or curiosities rather than as food.

Some of the more common gourds are the yellow flowered gourd *(Cucurbita pepo* var. *ovifera)*, the white flowered gourd *(Lagenaria siceraria)*, the snake or serpent gourd *(L. siceraria*, or *Trichosanthes anguina)*, the white or wax gourd *(Benincasa hispida)*, the dishcloth gourd or louffa *(L. aegypticiaca)*, the anguria *(C. anguria)*, the hedgehog gourd *(C. dipsaceus)*, the bitter gourd *(Momordica charantia)*, the bottle gourd *(Lagenaria vulgaris)* and the Egusi melon *(Cucumeropsis edulis*, or *C. manii)*. For more information, check the index or look under the specific common name.

GOURNAY

A soft French cheese, resembling American-style **cream cheese,** it takes its name from the village of Gournay in Normandy. It is made from whole milk, and is similar to **Neufchatel** in its very rich, creamy white texture. Gournay is in season from November to June and is marketed in round, flat tinfoil packages weighing four ounces, or in two-inch squares.

Another version, *Gournay Fleuri*, is ripened with the aid of a surface mold *(Penicillium candidum)* and achieves a flavor reminiscent of Camembert.

GOUTWEED

Also BISHOP'S ELDER. This coarse European herb, *Aegopodium podagraria*, naturalized in North America, attains a height of two feet and has broad leaflets. Goutweed leaves can be boiled and eaten as a spinach substitute or added raw to salads.

GOYA

An Argentine cheese made from whole or partly skimmed milk, it has a granular texture and resembles medium-curd **Asiago.**

GRAHAM BREAD

Graham bread is made from whole-wheat, or Graham, flour. This flour contains all of the wheat grain, including the germ, endosperm and much of the husk, which is mostly bran. The name derives from a Dr. Sylvester Graham, an American Presbyterian minister and food crusader, who in the 1840s advocated temperance and a vegetarian diet based on bread made from coarse, unsifted wholewheat flour. His original loaf was made without yeast or other leavening agents and was thus heavier than yeast bread, yet it was sweet and fairly palatable.

The crucial thing to Dr. Graham was that the bran was retained in the flour and could work its laxative effects on the consumer. Although nothing was known about vitamins in those days, Dr. Graham began the debate on the nutritional merits of whole-wheat bread versus white bread that continues to this day. (See: **Bread).** The term "Graham flour" is still in use in the United States, France and Finland, while in England the term "Grant flour" is used. The bran in Graham flour may irritate some persons' intestines.

GRAHAM FLOUR

An unsifted, whole-wheat flour, Graham flour contains the bran, or outer covering, of the wheat berry. It is named for the Rev. Sylvester Graham, an American health-food enthusiast who originated a vegetarian diet based on a coarse bread made from this flour, called **Graham bread.** Dr. Graham came to prominence in the 1840s. Dr. Graham's doctrines influenced Dr. Harvey Kellogg who, together with his brother, Will K., invented a dry cereal called Granose, thereby launching the American breakfast food industry.

GRAIN

See **Cereal.**

GRAINS OF SELIM

Also GUINEA PEPPER, NEGRO PEPPER. Fruits of the tree *Xylopia aethopica* are used as a pepper substitute. They are sold in local markets in Senegal and other countries of West Africa.

GRANA

This is a group of Italian cheeses that combine a granular texture with other characteristics, such as sharp flavor, hardness, small eyes and good keeping and traveling qualities. They have been made for centuries in the Po Valley and fall into two main types: grana Lombardo, made in Lombardy north of the Po, which includes Lodigiano; and Grana Reggiano, made in Emilia province south of the Po, which includes Emiliano and Parmigiano. They are known for their grating qualities, and most are exported under the name of Parmesan.

See also: **Emiliano, Lodigiano, Lombardo, Parmesan, Parmigiano, Reggiano.**

GRANA BAGOZZO

See **Bagozzo.**

GRANADILLA

See **Passion Fruit.**

GRAND COMB

Also GREAT SCANDIX. A perennial, herbaceous plant, *Scandix grandiflor*, grand comb is common in Greece and Asia Minor. The young leaves are used in salads, or boiled or fried and eaten as greens.

GRAND MARNIER

Grand Marnier is a French liqueur based on **Cognac** and flavored with orange peels. Grand Marnier makes a tasty addition to roast duck. The heated liqueur, mixed with orange juice and fatty broth from the cooking, provides an excellent sauce.

GRAND VENEUR SAUCE

This French sauce is used with venison and other furred game. It consists of **poivrade sauce** plus venison juice, red currant jelly and cream. It is heavy and brown and should be served hot.

See also: **Sauce.**

GRAPE

A type of berry that grows in bunches on a woody vine, grapes are small, usually round, smooth-skinned and juicy. The number of varieties is enormous—8,000 or more—and the colors vary accordingly. Most often encountered are the red, purple and green. Grapes are eaten raw as table fruit or dried as raisins. The juice may be pressed out and drunk as fresh fruit juice or fermented and made into wine.

The grape is probably the most widely cultivated fruit in the world, and 90 percent of the plants are varieties of one species, *Vitis vinifera.* This is an Old-World vine believed to have originated in the neighborhood of the Caspian Sea.

Grapes were eaten in the Middle East and Europe in prehistoric times and perhaps cultivated too. Painting in Egyptian tombs indicate grapes were under cultivation there as early as 4,000 B.C. Grape culture was extensive in Greece by 1500 B.C. Special varieties were cultivated for table grapes, and the fruit was especially popular with ancient Romans who imported them from Greece, Sicily and Spain by the first century A.D. Grape culture was established in France long before the Romans got there, but the latter did introduce them into England and perhaps Germany along the Rhine River. During these centuries, an important by-product of grapes was grape sugar, an important sweetener, second only to honey. It retained this importance until after the Crusades when cane sugar began to be imported from the Near East. In the Middle Ages, the juice of unripe grapes, called "verjuice," was a staple cooking ingredient used to add tartness to such things as sauces much as lemon juice is used today.

Table grapes, left to right: Champagne; Thompson seedless; and Black Rebier

In North America certain native species have retained interest, because *V. vinifera* does not thrive east of the Rocky Mountains. These include *V. lambrusca* and *V. aestivalis*, the "fox grapes" of the central and northern regions, and *V. rotundifolia*, the Muscadine grapes of the southeastern and Gulf regions.

All of these species produce table grapes as well as wine grapes, but special varieties have been developed for each purpose, i.e., as a rule, table grapes do not make good wine, and vice versa. Grape varieties developed especially for wine making are fully discussed elsewhere, under **Wine** and **Wine Grapes,** and they will be largely excluded from the following discussion.

The *V. vinifera,* which predominates in the western United States and elsewhere in the world, is above all a wine grape, yet it produces a number of excellent table grapes. In many cases, they have a higher sugar and pulp content than the indigenous U.S. species mentioned above. They travel well, and the skins adhere tightly to the flesh. Favorite U.S. varieties are the Thompson Seedless, which is long, almost seedless and greenish white; the Emperor, which is light red, also long and has seeds; the black Cornichon; the bright red Flame Tokay; the light green Malaga and the Zinfandels and Alicantes. Muscats, also popular, are ideal for raisins.

The best known western European varieties are the July or Saint Anne (yellowish, oval, ripening at the end of July); the Golden Chasselas (amber or rose yellow, medium sized and medium sweet, ripening in July); the Baresana (amber, not too sweet, ripening in August); the Bicane (oval, sweet, ripening in August); the Muscatel, which includes the white Frontignan and the black Muscatele, and the Gros Vert (roundish, hard yellow skin, slightly acidic taste). Some varieties are used to make raisins, which are called sultanas (originally a seedless variety from Turkey) or currents (having originated in Corinth). Raisin grapes are also used to make a wine called *passito*. (See also: **Wine and Liquor Terms).**

Among native American grapes, the Concord (a black *lambrusca)* is the best known. Consumed as a fresh fruit, it is even more popular as a source of fresh juice and grape jelly. Other *lambruscas* are the Catawba (medium-sized, round, purplish red, excellent flavor), the Niagara (green, fair quality), the Worden (similar to the Concord). The Delaware is a hybrid of *vinifera* and *lambrusca* and is small, red and costlier than the others yet possesses a very delicate, sweet flavor. Unlike the *vinifera*, the skin of the *lambrusca* separates easily from the pulp which has earned it the nickname "slip-skin." The **Muscadine,** also known as scuppernong, are valued chiefly for their juice and for making jellies, syrups and pastes. The fresh grapes have a musky taste ("foxiness") that is not pleasing to everyone.

Young, tender grapes leaves still form a part of the cuisines of Greece, Rumania and the nations of Asia Minor and North Africa. They are used raw in salads or stuffed with rice or meat and baked. Grape seeds are edible, and in some places the oil is pressed from them and used in cooking. See also the names of particular grapes, **Wine,** and **Wine Grapes.**

GRAPEFRUIT

Also POMELO. As citrus fruits go, the grapefruit *(Citrus paradisi)* is of very recent origin, having been formally recognized as a species only in 1840. It is the second-largest citrus fruit, exceeded only by the pummelo, or shaddock, of which it is believed to be a mutation.

The grapefruit is round and ranges in diameter from four to six inches. It is marketed in two general types: white and pink. The skin and pulp of the white varieties are actually pale yellow, while the pinks vary from reddish yellow to reddish brown. The taste of both types ranges from sour to sweet, always, however, with the bitter overtone that makes the grapefruit so distinctive. The United States grows about 75 percent of the world crop, mainly in Florida, Arizona, California and Texas. About half of the total crop is processed for juice or canned segments, while the other half is sold fresh. The number of seeds usually determines which fruit are marketed fresh, since the seedless variety (i.e., fewer than five seeds per fruit) is preferred for table use.

The grapefruit was first described by John Lunan in his *Hortus Jamaicensis* of 1814 as a variety of pummelo *(C. grandis)*, a citrus fruit native to Indonesia that was brought to Barbados by the English Captain Shaddock in 1696. Although it was mistakenly called "shaddock" for a number of years in England, the grapefruit was soon seen to be a completely different species, perhaps a mutation. How it got to Jamaica is unknown. Lunan likened its taste to that of the grape, hence the origin of the name "grapefruit." An alternative derivation of the name is attributed to the grapelike clustering of fruit that occurs on a grapefruit tree, which may be laden with 40 to 50 fruits on a single stem.

The first commercial plantings of grapefruit took place in Florida in 1885. They were marketed in New York but were slow to catch on because they were of the seedy variety. With the introduction of the Marsh seedless variety, the grapefruit rapidly gained in popularity; production mounted to one million boxes annually by 1910. A seedless pink variety, the Thompson, was discovered in 1924. It shares its predominance today with the Red Blush, a red-fleshed, seedless variety discovered in 1929. The grapefruit was introduced into Europe from America but did not gain widespread acceptance until after World War II. Besides the United States, other leading producers are Israel, the West Indies, Argentina and South Africa.

Grapefruit is a versatile food. It is eaten fresh as a first course at breakfast, in salads and in fruit cups. A grapefruit half may be sprinkled with brown sugar and broiled as a first course at other meals. Peeled segments of grapefruit are canned in syrup. The pleasant bitterness of grapefruit lends itself to making marmalade.

See also: **Citrus, Shaddock.**

Grapefruit and grapefruit juice

GRAPE HYACINTH

See **Tassel Hyacinth.**

GRAPE SUGAR

See **Glucose.**

GRAPPA

The Italian equivalent of the French *marc*, this brandylike liquor is distilled from the spent stalks, seeds and skins of grapes after the wine has been pressed from them. It has a touch of sweetness but is often strong and crude. It is bottled unaged and has a devoted following. Care should be taken that it comes from a reputable distiller.

See also: **Marc.**

GRASS SNAKE

See **Snake.**

GRASSHOPPER

See **Locust.**

GRATAIRON

See **Goat's Milk Cheese.**

GRAVELET

See **Chub.**

GRAVENCHE

A large European lake fish of the salmon family, it is similar to the ***fera*** *(Coregonus ferus)*, but smaller, and may be compared to the lake cisco of the U.S. Great Lakes. The *gravenche* is found mainly in Swiss lakes, such as Lake Geneva, and in Bavaria. It is prepared like trout.

GRAVES

This famous wine-growing region of western France on the west banks of the Garonne near **Bordeaux** offers both red and white wine of superior quality. For centuries the Graves red wine was known by the English as "claret" so called for its clear, rich color and flavor. The Graves vineyards extend for about 35 miles between the Garonne and the Atlantic in loose gravelly soil deposited over the years by the Garonne and the Gironde. The area takes its name from a type of clay—called *graves*—common to the region, which may have the same root as the English word, "gravel."

The northern part of Graves produces red wines for the most part, including the aristocratic **Chateau Haut-Brion.** Excellent white wines, both sweet and dry, are commonly grown in southern Graves—just above the vineyards of **Sauternes** and **Barsac.** The entire district produces about three times as much white wine as red. A dry white Graves with a faint acid touch is ideal with seafood. The historic claret, or dry red wine of Graves—with its subtle bite and clear, almost stained-glass color—is still said to be "food for the body and the soul."

GRAY CHEESE

This firm, pleasant tasting cheese is made in the Tyrol from sour skim milk. The name derives from the grayish color of the curd, whose proper ripening is ensured by the addition during processing of granules of ripened cheese or bread with the desired mold growing on it.

GRAYFISH

See **Dogfish.**

GRAYLAG GOOSE

Also GREYLAG. The common wild goose *(Anser anser)* of Europe is believed to be the ancestor of all domestic geese of the West. Its opposite number of the Orient is the Chinese goose *(Cygenopsis cygnoid)* called the Guinea goose when domesticated.

See also: **Goose.**

GRAYLING

Also OMBRE, UMBER. A genus *(Thymallidae)* of the salmon family found in clear, cold rivers, streams and lakes of the Northern Hemisphere. The European grayling *(Thymallus thymallus)* attains a length of 18 inches and a weight of up to five pounds, although two pounds is the average. It is troutlike in shape but has a distinctively high, many-rayed dorsal fin. It has a gray back and silver sides with horizontal violet stripes. The European grayling is found from eastern England to European Russia. It is a fine-tasting fish whose flesh, when fresh, has a slight flavor of thyme, hence its Latin name. It is usually cooked simply e.g., sauteed in butter, but it may be prepared in any way suitable for trout.

The most common American grayling is the arctic grayling *(T. articus)*, whose habitat extends

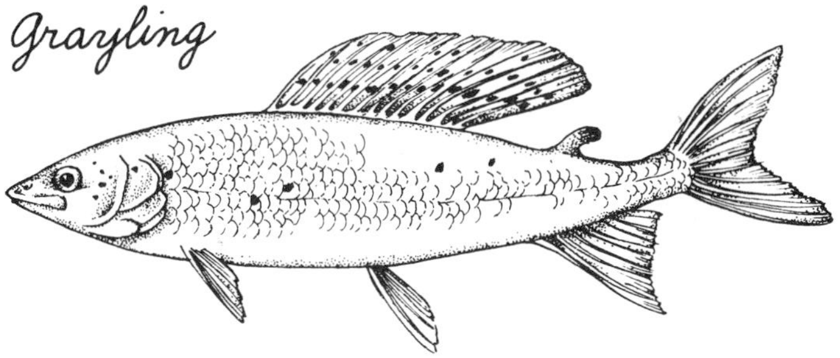

from central Russia across Alaska to Lake Superior in northern Michigan. Due to pollution and other factors, it has become increasingly rare in the lower 48 states, but is still plentiful in Alaska. People of the arctic region depend on it as food for both themselves and their dogs. Elsewhere it is sport for anglers. The arctic grayling is larger than its European cousin, attaining a length of two feet. Other North American species are the Montana grayling *(T. montanus)* and the Michigan grayling *(T. tricolor)*.

GRAY PEA

See **Congo Pea.**

GRAY SNAPPER

Also MANGROVE SNAPPER. A cousin of the **red snapper,** the gray snapper *(Lutjanus griseus)* is a saltwater fish found on both sides of the tropical Atlantic and in the Gulf of Mexico. It is a good sport fish and a commercially valuable food fish. Its coloring varies but tends to be green gray with a reddish head and orange fins. It weighs up to 20 pounds but averages two to five pounds and may be up to three feet long. The gray snapper has the typical long snout of the snapper genus but a rather slender body. It frequents inshore water, rocky areas, reefs and even brackish or freshwater areas, such as mangrove-covered creeks. It may be prepared like red snapper.

GRAY WIDGEON

See **Gadwall.**

GREAT BEAR WATER

A natural spring water bottled in plastic containers for bulk drinking, it has a relatively low mineral content. A 1980 Consumers Union sensory panel rated the taste of this water as very good, with the following qualifying comments: mild plastic flavor, mildly bitter.

See also: **Mineral Water.**

GREAT SCANDIX

See **Grand Comb.**

GREAT SNIPE

See **Snipe.**

GREAT SOLOMON'S SEAL

A large perennial herb, *Polygonatum communtatum*, of the lily family whose rhizomes are a source of starch and flour, it is found in eastern North America from New Hampshire to the Mexican border and in temperate Asia and Japan. It has yellowish green or greenish white flowers.

GREEN BEAN

See **Kidney Bean.**

GREEN CHEESE

See **Sage Cheese.**

GREENGAGE

See **Plum.**

GREEN GRAM

See **Mung Bean.**

GREEN LAVER

See **Laver.**

GREENLING

This small family *(Hexagrammidae)* of marine fishes found on both sides of the north Pacific includes the **lingcod,** the kelp greenling and the ainame. The kelp greenling *(Hexagrammos decagrammus)*, which is found from Southern California to Alaska, seldom exceeds 21 inches in length but is an important food fish in the northern extreme of its range. Elsewhere it is considered good sport for anglers.

The *ainame (H. otakii)* is the most common greenling on the Asian side of the Pacific and though a smaller fish (16 inches or less) is of commercial importance in Japan. It is eaten raw or prepared in a variety of other ways.

Greenlings have a brownish red to dark purple coloring. The male kelp greenling is distinguished by large blue spots on its head, each surrounded by a rust brown ring.

GREEN ONION

See **Scallion.**

GREEN SAPOTE

A delicate tropical fruit, green sapote *(Pouteria viride)* is closely related to the **mammee sapota** and is grown and eaten in Central America. Its pulp is pale brown and very sweet and juicy. It may be consumed fresh or preserved.

GREEN SAUCE

Also SAUCE VERTE. This French sauce based on **mayonnaise** is served with hard-boiled eggs, poultry and fish. Mayonnaise is blended with either the juice of pounded parsley, chervil and tarragon leaves or with a puree of spinach.

See also: **Sauce.**

GRENACHE WINE

This is "cooked" wine made from the Grenache species of wine grape. The name comes from the Italian *granaccio,* meaning large grain. The grape is grown mainly in the south of France and makes a sweet, highly intoxicating wine that is usually red. Among the best of the Grenache wines is the Grenache Noir, a rich red wine from **Banyuls** in the eastern Pyrenees. A good Grenache Rose is also produced in California.

GRENADINE SYRUP

See **Pomegranate.**

GREYERZERKASE

See **Gruyere.**

GRIBICHE SAUCE

A French sauce for cold fish and shellfish, Gribiche consists of oil and vinegar mixed with pounded hard-boiled egg yolks, chopped gherkins and capers seasoned with parsley, chervil and tarragon. It is garnished with strips of hard-boiled eggwhite.

See also: **Sauce.**

GRIFFITH'S CAMBOGE

A tropical fruit related to the **mangosteen,** Griffith's cambodge *(Garcinia griffithii)* is found in Assam and Malaysia. The fruit is large and yellow and has an astringent taste. To be palatable raw, it must be sweetened with sugar. It is sometimes cut up and used to make soup, but it makes excellent jelly and compote. This tree is seldom cultivated.

GRITS

Also GROATS. Either term refers to grain that has been hulled and coarsely ground. "Grits" is an American term and is probably a corruption of "groats." By itself, it refers to hominy grits, i.e., grains of hulled corn ground as a coarse meal and eaten as a breakfast cereal or as a potato substitute. The English term "groats," usually refers to oats that have been hulled and coarsely ground. Groats are used for thickening soups and making gruel.

Either term can be applied to wheat, barley or other grains so treated provided that it is modified by the name of the grain, as in "wheat groats," "barley groats," etc.

See also: **Hominy.**

GROG

A nickname for rum and an alcoholic drink consisting of rum, lemon juice, sugar and hot water, the term derives of the British naval practice of issuing ordinary seamen a daily rum ration. In 1740 Admiral E. Vernon, disliking its intoxicating effects, began watering the daily rum ration. Admiral Vernon was known by the nickname "Old Grog" because he habitually wore an old grogram cloak during foul weather. His nickname was transferred to the drink. Later, lemon juice was added to the mixture as an antiscorbutic agent. Any seaman showing the effects of the drink was said to be "groggy." "Grog" is also used as a general term for any alcoholic drink.

GROSSE CERISE DE MARTINIQUE

Similar to the **Barbados cherry** and the **West Indian cherry,** this species *(Malpighia urens)* is a shrub that produces reddish fruits and is found in tropical America and the West Indies. The cherry-like fruit has a juicy pulp, a refreshing taste and a high vitamin C content.

GROUND ALMOND

See **Chufa.**

GROUND CHERRY

Also ALKEKENGI, STRAWBERRY TOMATO, WINTER CHERRY, CHINESE LANTERN, HUSK TOMATO. A berry from the *Physalis* group of plants, specifically *P. alkekengi* or *P. pubescens*, the ground cherry grows prolifically in North and South America and in central and southern Europe. The fruit is the size of a large cherry and resembles a green tomato, although its color can vary from red to orange yellow to purple. It is contained in a straw-colored calyx, or husk, that looks like a chinese lantern. This species is sweeter than other types and tastes somewhere between a tomato and a strawberry. The ground cherry is cultivated commercially in Europe, Mexico and the United States. It is a frequent ingredient in chili sauce but is equally good raw or in preserves.

GROUND NUT

Also DAKOTA POTATO, INDIAN POTATO, WILD BEAN. An American twining herb whose tubers were once a valued source of food for certain tribes in what is now the eastern United States, ground nut *(Apios tuberosa)* should not be mistaken for the peanut *(Arachis hypogea)*, which is sometimes called ground nut in Great Britain.

It is grown in Europe and America today for its ornamental value, i.e., its small, fragrant, dark purple flowers, but in colonial times it excited some interest as a starchy vegetable and was transplanted in Europe as a food plant. It was found to be inferior to the potato, however, and was soon eclipsed by the latter.

The tubers were one to two inches long, attached by stringlike roots. Native Americans ground them to make a meal, which they used to make cakes. Sag Harbor, on the eastern tip of Long Island, takes its name from a place just to the south called Sagaponack, which means "place of the groundnuts" in the Shinnecock language.

GROUPER

A large family of fish *(Serranidae)*, closely resembling and related to the sea bass, groupers are found in warm inshore waters throughout the world but notably off the coast of Florida and the West Indies.

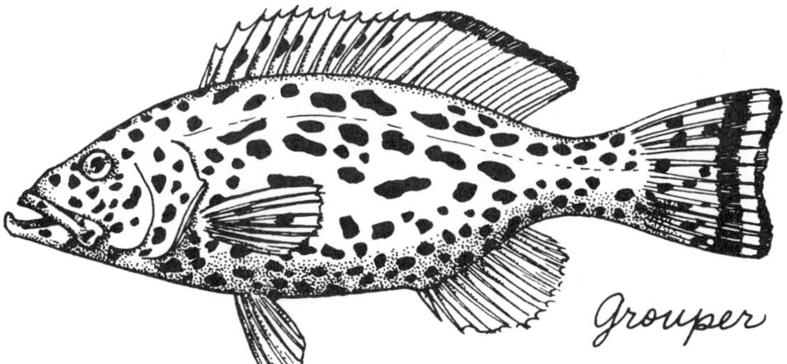

The grouper has a stout and rather compressed body. The Nassau grouper *(Epinephelus striatus)* is perhaps the best known food fish. In the market it usually weighs from five to 15 pounds. The jewfish *(Epinephelus itajara)* is the largest of the groupers and has been known to reach a weight of 700 pounds. It is common in the Florida Keys. Both are excellent eating at any size.

Others in the family include the gag, scamp, rock hind, black grouper, red grouper, misty grouper, snowy grouper and yellowfish. The skin of all varieties is tough but strongly flavored. The firm white flesh of the grouper should be cut into finger-shaped wedges for deep frying or for use in chowder.

GROUSE

A class of game birds with plump, henlike bodies and feathered legs, grouse generally prefer to live on the ground, and many molt with every changing season to match the foliage. Grouse inhabit parts of North America, Europe and Asia and generally prefer cool weather. They tend to be excellent eating, and this has helped bring a few species near extinction.

In English-speaking areas the most celebrated species is the red or Scotch grouse *(Lagopus scotius)*. It has reddish brown plumage speckled with white. A choice, younger bird may be expected to measure 13 to 15 inches in length. In Great Britain grouse season runs from August 12 to early December, timed to take the birds after a summer of foraging on berries, seeds and tender heather shoots, which gives them a clean, often delicately spicy flavor.

Though known in France, the bird is of less gastronomic interest because it more likely to subsist on pine cones, seeds and needles, which can give it a slight turpentine taste. This can be alleviated by soaking the carcass in milk for several hours before cooking. Other common grouse of Europe are the wood grouse *(Tetrao urogallus)* and the hazel grouse *(Tetrates bonasia)*.

The red grouse is a member of the *ptarmigan* genus which is represented in North America by the fine-tasting willow ptarmigan *(L. lagopus)*, a lover of cold weather common in Alaska, and by the white-tailed ptarmigan *(L. leucurus)* of the western United States. At one time, the latter was hunted mercilessly for its fine feathers, which found a ready market in the hat industry.

The ruffed grouse *(Bonasa umbellus)* is the tastiest American species. It is also called "pheasant" in some parts of the country, and "partridge" in the South. Again, its excellent flavor is attributed to its diet of fruits, herbs and seeds. The ruffed grouse is a larger bird than the red grouse and owes its name to "ruffs" of feathers on each side of its head. The bird is generally chestnut colored on top with a buff breast and whitish underparts.

Next to the wild turkey, the sage grouse *(Centrocercus urophaesianus)* is America's largest game fowl. It may weigh as much as eight pounds and subsists largely on the leaves and shoots of the sage brush. This imparts a strong flavor. In earlier times two favorite grouse were the now extinct heath hen *(Typmanuchus cupido cupido)* of the eastern states and the prairie chicken or prairie hen *(T. cupido americanus)* of the West, so named because it looks like a hen. It has practically disappeared, except in some areas of Texas. Other American species include the Canadian spruce grouse, Franklin's grouse, the Sierra grouse and the blue grouse.

Due to the sedentary nature of the grouse, its flesh is generally white with only a hint of gaminess. Only young birds—up to a year old—are suitable for roasting. Care should be taken to avoid overcooking, which renders them tough and dry. Older birds are better braised, baked in pies or potted.

In American slang, "to grouse" means to complain or to grumble, whereas in Australia a "grouse" is anything extraordinary or wonderful.

See also: **Game, Capercaille.**

GROYER

See **Gruyere.**

GRUMICHAMA

This cherry-sized fruit of an ornamental tree is found in tropical and subtropical regions of southern Brazil and Peru. The *grumichama (Eugenia braziliensis)* is dark red turning black and has a pleasant flavor when eaten raw or when used to make jellies or pies. It is known also as the Brazil cherry and is similar to the *E. uniflora*, which usually goes by the name Brazil cherry.

See also: **Surinam Cherry.**

GRUMOLO

See **Chicory.**

GRUNERKASE

See **Sapsago.**

GRUNERKRAUTERKASE

See **Sapsago.**

GRUNION

These small silvery fish, *Leuresthes tenuis*, are found along the coast of southern California and Baja California. Grunions are most easily caught by hand when they leave the water to spawn. At night, shortly after high tide, thousands of grunions may be found on moist sandy beaches. This lasts for two or three hours for three or four nights after each full or new moon, when tides are highest. They are best when broiled or deep fried and taste like **smelt.**

GRUNT

Several species of tropical fish of the *Haemulon* and *Orthopristis* genera are considered good eating. These include the white, yellow and blue-striped grunts, all members of the snapper family. The grunt is also known as the grumbler and pigfish owing to the peculiar grunting noises it emits when pulled from the water. Those generally caught weigh one-half to two pounds. Large specimens can weigh as much as 20 pounds and be three feet long.

Grunt are found in the South Atlantic and are particularly plentiful around the West Indies and off the coast of Florida. Their taste has been compared to that of the butterfish, and they are prepared in a variety of ways when freshly caught.

GRUYERE

Also GREYERZERKASE, GROYER, VACHELIN. This noted cheese originated in a village of the same name in the canton of Fribourg in Switzerland. Gruyere resembles **Swiss** or Emmenthaler cheese but has a sharper, slightly acidulous taste and smaller eyes, and is produced in smaller sizes. The texture is firm, but creamier than that of Swiss and is excellent for eating by itself or for cooking.

Gruyere is made from whole cow's milk. A typical cheese is round with a diameter of 20 inches, a thickness of five inches and a weight somewhere between 55 and 110 pounds. It is cured for a minimum of three months and may be eaten then or when very ripe. It keeps well if uncut. The rind is a golden brown. For local consumption more salt is used, and the cheese is wrapped in cloth soaked in brine or white wine to better maintain the pungent flavor.

Gruyere is produced in other cantons of Switzerland and in eastern France, often under the name of **Comte.** It is widely imitated abroad, but the American process Gruyere is not at all like the original.

GUAGUANCHE

A small variety of barracuda, the *guaguanche (Sphyraena guachancho)* is found in the western Atlantic from New England to Brazil, including the Caribbean and the Gulf of Mexico. It reaches a maximum length of about two feet. It is olive green above, and silver along the sides with a faint golden stripe. It shares the predatory habits of other **barracuda** and is regarded as a fine sport fish. The flesh of the *guaguanche* is more highly regarded than that of the Atlantic barracuda; it has a finer taste and is not known to pass along the *ciguatera*, or fish poisoning, as does its larger cousin.

GUANACO

A wild form of **llama,** the guanaco *(Lama guanacoe)* is found in southwestern areas of South America at elevations ranging from sea level to 15,000 feet. The guanaco vaguely resembles a camel (without a hump), and has a long wooly coat of hair. It can be up to six feet long and weigh up to 200 pounds. Its flesh is edible but judged to be of only fair quality. The guanaco prefers open country, such as high pampas and plateaus, since it depends on its foot speed to escape capture.

GUARANA

These are caffeine-bearing seeds of a Brazilian climbing shrub, *Paullinia sorbilis* or *P. cupana.* After processing, the seeds are used to make a stimulating hot drink on the order of coffee or tea. They are also the basis of a popular soft drink of the same name.

Seeds that have been dried, ground into a meal moistened and shaped, are sold in five to six inch, sausagelike rolls that weigh 12 to 16 ounces. They are dried to a very hard consistency, and resemble chocolate. To prepare a drink, a roll is grated into hot water. The taste is bitter unless sweetened. Guarana is also known as Brazilian cocoa.

GUAR BEAN

See **Cluster Bean.**

Guava: fruit; juice; and jelly

GUAVA

There are more than 150 varieties of guava, a small, usually oval fruit native to tropical America. The common guava *(Psidium guajava)* is thin-skinned, may vary from yellow to red and averages two inches in diameter.

Other varieties of guava include the strawberry guava *(Psidium cattleianum)* a smaller, hardier fruit with purple skin and a taste like strawberry; the Brazilian guava *(P. guineense)* and the pineapple guava, which is not a true guava but a ***feijoa.***

Guavas are grown in tropical areas throughout the world. Mexico and the Caribbean Island are major producers. In the United States, only southern Florida grows them commercially.

Guava pulp is aromatic, sweet and sometimes slightly acidic. The fresh fruit gives off a musky odor that some people find unpleasant. In some varieties, masses of seeds are embedded in the pulp which makes eating the fresh fruit raspy to the throat. On the whole, guava is considered mediocre fresh but superior when cooked. It is eaten stewed or preserved in jams, jellies or in paste form. Guava paste, or "cheese," is made by boiling the pulp until it is reduced to the consistency of gelatin. It is firm enough to be sliced with a knife, and is often eaten with fresh cream cheese. Guava paste has a tendency to crystallize and therefore should be eaten as fresh as possible.

Guavas as rich in minerals and vitamin C. The juice is sold in cans, and is called guava nectar.

GUCHHIA

See **Threadfin.**

GUDGEON

A small, freshwater fish very common on the bottom of lakes, rivers and streams from the British Isles across Europe to Asia, the gudgeon *(Gobio gobio)*, seldom exceeds eight inches in length and has a green brown back, yellow sides with dark blotches and a light belly. It has a long, fully scaled body and a barbel at the corner of each mouth.

Gudgeon has an excellent flavor and in some parts of Europe it is eaten with gusto. In others, however, it is deemed only good bait for larger fish. A favorite method of preparation is to dip it in flour or batter and fry it in deep oil.

The gudgeon takes bait readily and when hooked does not put up much of a fight. For this reason, it became a slang term for one who is easily cheated or ensnared, or for something that can be gained without ability or merit.

GUIGNARD

See **Dotterel.**

GUINARD

See **Dotterel.**

GUINEA CORN

See **Sorghum.**

GUINEA FOWL

Also GUINEA HEN. This pheasantlike bird, originally from West Africa, has been reared domestically for centuries but never completely domesticated. Of several varieties, the most common is the pearl guinea fowl *(Numida meleagris)*. Despite its bare, vulturelike head, this is a handsome bird with lustrous pearl-gray plumage that is evenly dotted with white.

The ancient Greeks, who were the first Europeans to import and rear guinea fowl, explained the spots with the following legend. The sisters of Meleager, son of the king of Calydon, wept so uncontrollably when their brother died that they were changed into guinea hens. The spots were their tears. The guinea fowls emit a screeching that has been likened to the sound of a rusty windmill. The bird's taxonomic name alludes to this legend.

The Greeks, nevertheless, much appreciated the bird's flavor, which remained slightly gamey despite domestic rearing. The Romans imported guinea fowl from North Africa for the tables of aristocrats. When the Roman Empire collapsed in the West, the guinea fowl, like so many delicacies savored by the Romans, lapsed into obscurity.

They were reintroduced into Europe in the 16th century by the Portuguese, who brought them from West Africa. Since then, the guinea fowl has been a luxury item, appearing today only in high-priced restaurants. The reason for this is that the guinea fowl is not amenable to the assembly-line methods that make contemporary poultry farming profitable. Only in France are they produced on a large commercial scale. If cooped up, they will not lay eggs. If allowed to roam freely, they will perch on the highest limb of a tree and descend only at feeding time.

As a result, guinea fowl production in the United States peaked in 1939 and has been going downhill ever since. Those raised today are aimed at the specialty meat market, or high-priced restaurants or for use as watchfowl, protecting flocks of poultry from predators with their shrill, grating cry. Guinea fowl have no trouble dominating other barnyard fowl, including much larger turkeys.

Guinea fowl are eaten young, usually from four to eight months. They reach this size in late summer or early autumn and range from three-quarters to 2½ pounds. They may be roasted, braised, served in a casserole or prepared in any way suitable to pheasant.

GUINEA PEPPER

See **Cayenne, Grains of Selim.**

GUINEA PIG

Also CAVY. This rodent is native to the Andean region of South America and is still regularly eaten there, usually prepared like chicken or rabbit. The guinea pig *(Cavia procellus)* is a domesticated relative of the wild cavy *(Cavia cutleri)*, a source of meat for Peruvians from time immemorial. If available, the wild, olive-colored cavy is still eaten in western South America, but it is the domestic guinea pig that provides perhaps 50 percent of all the animal protein eaten in modern Peru.

The Arawaks, the first Americans encountered by Columbus in 1492, kept guinea pigs. When Pizarro's men arrived in Peru, they found the Incas raising them, and took to them with relish themselves. The Spaniards sent guinea pigs back to Europe where they enjoyed a brief fad as food in both England and Spain. The Arawaks called the animal *cuy*, but the Spaniards dubbed it "guinea pig" although it was not a pig and had nothing to do with Guinea.

The guinea pig is a compact, short-eared, almost tailless animal, about seven inches long, and weighs up to two pounds when mature. It is usually black, white and orange. The wild cavy reproduces only once a year, but the guinea pig can produce up to six litters a year. A guinea pig requires minimal housing and can be raised entirely on vegetable and fruit scraps. A mature animal provides more than enough meat for one adult.

Only in South America is the guinea pig regularly taken as food. In North America and Europe, they are kept as pets or raised as laboratory animals.

GUINEA PLUM

Guinea plum is the fruit of a West African tree, *Parinarium excelsum*, with long leaves and large terminal bunches of flowers. It is closely related to the guiana, curatella, gingerbread and mobola plums.

GUINEA SUNPLANT

This West African shrub, *Solanum macrocarpon*, of the nightshade family, produces a fruit eaten in the area of cultivation.

GUIOLE

See **Laguiole.**

GULL

The name applies to various sea birds of the genus *Larus*, which have webbed feet and feathers of white, black and gray. Common gulls include the great and less black-backed gulls and the herring gull. On account of its diet, the gull is too fishy-tasting to be palatable. This can be remedied if the gull is trapped and fed on milk or buttermilk for two to three weeks. Gull's eggs, on the other hand, have good flavor and are delicious hard-boiled, made into omelettes or otherwise used like hen's eggs.

GUM

This sticky substance, derived from trees or plants, dries to an uncrystallized mass but when put into water thickens or stabilizes the solution. Gum is found in a wide variety of foods, sometimes occurring naturally, but often added. The term "gum" is loosely applied to many substances, but for industrial purposes it is limited to plant polysaccharides and their derivatives. This would exclude chicle, the major raw material for **chewing gum,** and resinous saps from balsam and other evergreen trees, but would include water-soluble cellulose and mucilages.

Following are the major gums, classified by source: *Seaweeds:* Agar, from red algae *(Gelidium* sp.); algin, from brown algae *(Macrocystis pyrifera);* carrageenin, from red algae *(Chondrus crispus, Gargartina stellata);* fucoidan, from brown algae *(Fucus* sp., *Laminaria* sp.), and laminaran, from brown algae *(Laminaria* sp.).

Plant exudates: Gum arabic, from acacia trees; ghatti, from *Anogeissus latifolia;* karaya, from *Sterculia urens* and gum tragacanth, from *Astragalus* spp.

Plant extracts: Pectin, from the cell walls of all plants but commercially from citrus waste; larch arabinogalactan, from the Western larch, and ti, from the tubers of *Cordyline terminalis.*

Plant seeds: Corn-hull gum, from the seed coating of corn (maize); guar, from the seeds of a leguminous plant, *Camposia teragonolobus*, or *Cyamopsis tetragonoloba;* carob, from the endosperm of the carob tree *(Ceratonia siliqua);* quince seed, of *Cydonia vulgaris;* psyllium seed, of the plant species *Plantago;* flax seed, from *Linum usitatissimum;* tamarind, from the *Tamarindus indica* and wheat gum.

Miscellaneous: These include cellulose derivatives from plant cell walls, wood pulp and cotton; starch (amylose and amylopectin) from cereal grains and tubers; dextran, produced by bacterial action on sucrose, and chitin which is derived from the exterior covering of crustacea and insects.

Ranked by order of importance to industry, they are gum arabic, gum tragacanth, guar, cellulose, carrageenin, carob, agar and then other vegetable gums.

The many uses of these gums include emulsifying beer and pie fillings, retarding the settling of particles in diet foods and chocolate milk, keeping the air in whipping cream, retarding crystal growth in ice cream and candy, giving added body to soft drinks, cheese spreads, gravies, icings, salad dressings and syrups, and gelling such things as marshmallows, jellied candies and fruit jellies.

For more information on specific gums, look elsewhere in the alphabet under the name or consult the index.

GUM ARABIC

Also GUM ACACIA. A gum that is important to the manufacture of marshmallows, syrups, jellied candies and such things as licorice and jujubes, it is secreted by various species of acacia trees or shrubs, usually *Acacia arabica* and *Acacia vera.* Acacia is a small, pretty tree that grows in dry, desert country. It is often thorny, and the flower of some varieties are used to make fritters in France.

Medicinally, gum arabic is useful in cough syrups. Other commercial applications are in ink and adhesives.

See also: **Gum.**

GUMBO

See **Okra.**

GUMI

See **Cherry Elaeagnus.**

GUMMY SHARK

A common shark in coastal waters south of Australia and New Zealand. Gummy shark *(Mustelus antarctica)* is related to the **dogfish** of the Atlantic coast of North America. It reaches a length of five feet.

It supports an important commercial fishery for its firm, white flesh, marketed as "flake" in Australia. Its liver was formerly an important commercial source of vitamins A and D, but the market for shark liver oil collapsed after World War II.

GUM TRAGACANTH

See **Tragacanth.**

GUNDI

A tiny North African rodent, *Ctenodactylus gundi* is trapped for food by the inhabitants of the mountainous areas of Libya, Tunisia, Algeria and Morocco. The *gundi* has silky fur and reaches a maximum length of about six inches.

GUNPOWDER TEA

This pungent, rather bitter Chinese green tea can be made from any of the regional varieties of China green teas. Only the smallest and youngest leaves are selected, and these are rolled into pellets whose shape and gray green color recalls gunpowder. Most comes from Taiwan and Anhwei Province in China. The brewed tea has a yellow green color and is best drunk plain.

See also: **Tea.**

GURNARD

Also SEA ROBIN. This family *(Triglidae)* of small sea fishes is widely distributed through the world. It is characterized by a bony head and large pectoral fins with fingerlike feelers. The largest species found in European waters is the yellow gurnard *(Trigla lucerna)*, also known as the gurnet. It is found from the North Sea to the Mediterranean and Black Seas and south to South Africa. It is brilliantly colored and reaches a length of up to two feet and a weight of 11 pounds. The yellow gurnard is fished both commercially and for sport.

A more common and smaller species is the gray gurnard *(Eutrigla gurnardus)*, which is distributed over the same area. It is a bottom-dweller with gray color relieved by a pink tinge and white spots on its back. The gray gurnard reaches a length of 16 inches. It is often used in Bouillabaisse, or may be prepared like mullet, although its flesh does not compare in flavor or delicacy.

A common Indo-Pacific species is the red gurnard *(Chelidonichthys kumu)* which is especially abundant in Australian waters. It is bright red above and white below with a green inner surface on its pectoral fins. It is considered excellent eating and is fished commercially. This species reaches a length of two feet.

GURNET

See **Gurnard.**

GUSSING

An Austrian cheese quite similar to **brick cheese,** Gussing is made from skim milk rather than whole. Individual cheeses weigh from four to eight pounds.

GUYANA PLUM

The *Parinarium campestre*, a tropical tree of the rose family, produces this good-flavored fruit.

GUYANA UNONA

The aromatic fruit of the tropical tree, *Unona concolor*, is used as a condiment. This species of unona, a member of the *Anonaceae* family, is native to Guyana.

GWYNIAD

See **Houting.**

GYNANDROPSIS

Also SPIDER WISP. This woody tropical to subtropical plant, *Cleome gynandra*, is considered a weed in many places, but its seeds are valued in parts of Africa and India for their oil. The oil has some of the properties of mustard oil or garlic and is used to flavor sauces or stews. In Senegal, the ashes of this plant are used as a salt substitute. Medicinally, the seeds are considered antihelminthic.

GYOKURO TEA

Gyokuro is a Japanese green tea of high quality, indeed the best exported. The name means "pearl dew" and the taste is mild and slightly sweet.

See also: **Tea.**

H

HACKBERRY

Also SUGARBERRY. Hackberry is the orange red fruit of a very tall nettle tree, *Celtis occidentalis*, found in eastern North America from Quebec to Alabama. The fruit turns dark purple when ripe and grows to about three-quarter inch in length. It is tart until touched by frost, when it becomes sweet and aromatic. A closely allied species, the western hackberry *(Celtis reticulata)*, bears edible fruit and is found in the southwestern United States and northern Mexico.

HADDOCK

A member of the same family, but smaller than, the Atlantic cod, haddock *(Melanogrammus aeglefinus)* is an important food fish of the North Atlantic. When eaten fresh its flesh is fine, white, flaky and somewhat firmer than the cod's. It has a delicate flavor.

Though much resembling the cod, the haddock has dark lines running along both sides from tail to gill, a purplish gray back and a dark spot above each pectoral fin. In legend, these are said to be bruises inflicted by Saint Peter when he removed a shekel for temple wax from the mouth of a haddock.

Haddock is present on both sides of the Atlantic from the Bay of Biscay to Iceland and from there down to New Jersey. A cold water fish, it is generally taken in deeper water than the cod. It is in season from September to February.

Haddocks average one to two feet in length and from one to five pounds in weight. The largest on record weighed 37 pounds and ran 44 inches. They are eaten fresh or smoked. Smoked haddock from the Scottish fishing village of Findon (pronounced "Finnan") near Aberdeen has achieved a wide reputation for excellence. In making finnan haddie, as it is called, the haddock is split open, part of the backbone removed, the head cut off, the whole lightly salted, then smoked rather far from the fire. It emerges golden. Another Scottish smoked haddock, called Abroath smokies, are held much closer to the fire and emerge black and sooty.

See also: **Cod.**

Haddock

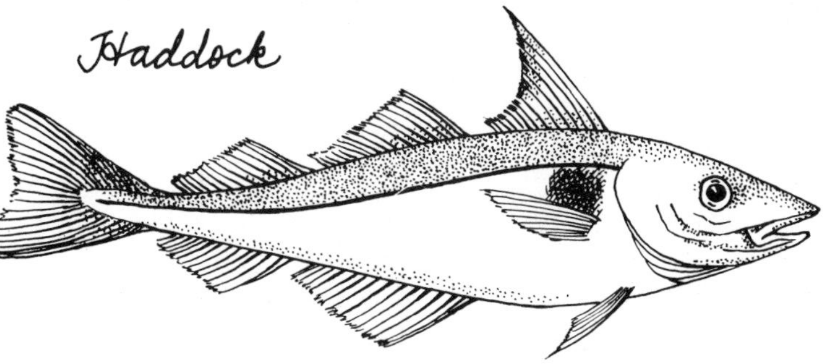

HAGFISH

Hagfish is an eellike fish (family *Myxinidae)* regularly eaten in Japan but regarded with disgust nearly everywhere else. The hagfish lives in the mud, is nearly blind and survives by attacking fish that are caught in nets or on lines. It uses its sharp teeth and slimy body to bore into a helpless fish through its gill openings, then consumes it from within. The hagfish of Japanese waters is *Eptatretus burgeri*, which reaches a length of about two feet. Very similar species are found in the eastern Pacific and the Atlantic, and are regarded as pests by fishermen both for their depredations and their extreme sliminess.

HAGGIS

A Scottish national dish that has been described as "a sort of Paleolithic sausage," haggis consists of minced innards (heart, liver, lung, etc., usually of a sheep) ground together with oatmeal and beef suet and seasoned by nutmeg, pepper, cayenne pepper and salt. This mixture is stuffed into a cleaned sheep's stomach and boiled for three to four hours in salted water. It is allowed to cool, then reheated before serving, usually with mashed turnips and boiled potatoes.

The haggis is served with much ritual—to the skirling of bagpipes—on Burns' Night, which is January 25, the anniversary of his birth. Scotland's most famous poet, Robert Burns wrote a paean entitled, *To a Haggis*, which runs like this:

Fair fa' you honest, sonsie face,
Great chieftain of the pudding race!
Aboon them a' ye tak your place,
Painch, tripe, or thairm:
Weel are ye worthy o' a grace—
As lang's my arm.

How haggis achieved its exalted status is obscure. It has been speculated that it was prepared by Scottish wives for warrior husbands as battlefield rations. The ancient Romans almost certainly brought haggis to Britain, although of course they did not subjugate Scotland. The Romans themselves were probably indebted to the Greeks for their knowledge of haggis. In 400 B.C. the Greek satirical dramatist Aristophanes wrote a comic description of "a stuffed sheep's stomach" that exploded at the dinner table upon being carelessly broached. The Roman epicure Caelius Apicius of the first century A.D. left us a recipe for haggis in his cookbook *De re coquinaria* that differs little from the contemporary Scottish one. Haggis was also popular in England until the 18th century. *Afronchemoyle* is a Norman-French form of haggis. A simpler version of haggis is prepared in a saucepan and called pot haggis.

See also: **Sausage.**

HAIRY THORN APPLE

Also DOWNY THORN APPLE, HORN-OF-PLENTY, METEL. This is the thorny but edible fruit of an annual herb, *Datura metel*, native to southwest China. This plant is widely cultivated in both hemispheres as an ornamental and as a source of the drug scopolamine. Hairy thorn apple is closely related to the rank smelling jimson weed *(D. stramonium)*, whose roots were consumed by Carlos Casteneda (with hallucinogenic effect) as part of his apprenticeship to the Yaqui shaman, Don Juan Matus. His experiences are recounted in *The Teachings of Don Juan: A Yaqui Way of Knowledge*.

HAKE

A fish of the cod family *(Gadidae)*, hake is found in the cold and arctic seas of the Northern Hemisphere. The European hake *(merluccius merluccius)* is long, slender, sharp-toothed and voracious. Its shape suggested a hook ("hake") to early mariners. The hake is called *merlan* (whiting) in Provence, *colin* (cod) in Paris, and is also served as *saumon blanc* on some French menus.

The New England or silver hake *(Merluccius bilinearis)* is caught off the Grand Banks but may range as far south as Cape Hatteras. Hake is an important food fish. Its meat is white, soft, flaky and tender. In the United States, hake is usually sold in packaged or frozen form, along with cod, haddock and other white fish, as "deep sea fillets." It tastes like cod and also contains liver oil, used in medicine.

HALCYON

Also KOOKABURRA, LAUGHING JACKASS. The Australian kingfisher *(Dacelo gigas)* is a bird with brilliant blue plumage and a harsh, cackling cry suggesting harsh laughter. It has naturalized in China and Indochina and is of some culinary interest because one authority has claimed that its nest is used by the Chinese in bird's nest soup. Other authorities agree, however, that the nest of the salangane swallow or swift is used.

See also: **Bird's Nest.**

HALF-GLAZE SAUCE

Also DEMI-GLACE. This French sauce, based on **espagnole sauce,** is mixed with meat stock and then reduced by boiling to one-half to one-tenth its original volume. Its consistency should be such that it half-glazes or coats the food it is used on. Madeira or sherry is often added as flavoring.

See also: **Sauce.**

HALIBUT

A huge flatfish, the common halibut inhabits the coldest waters of the North Atlantic and Pacific Oceans. Like its smaller cousins the **sole** and the **flounder,** the halibut generally lies flat on the bottom. Accordingly, it has a up-side (the right) where both eyes are placed, and a down-side, which is white. As a rule, the right side is dark brown, but the halibut is able to change this color depending on the character of the sea bed so as to blend into the setting.

The North Atlantic halibut *(Hippoglossus hippoglossus)* is one of the largest of edible fishes, running to lengths of 10 to 12 feet, and weighing up to 700 pounds. The highest weights are for the female; the male seldom exceeds 500 pounds. Catches of 50 to 100 pounds are common. The flesh of the halibut is firm and white but is coarse from the larger fish. The flesh of the "chicken halibut"—from three to 10 pounds—is finer and therefore considered best. Due to over-fishing, the Atlantic halibut is plentiful nowadays only in arctic waters, but in former times it was common as far south as 40° north.

Three-quarters of the world halibut catch is now taken out of the North Pacific where the Pacific halibut *(H. stenolepsis)* is second in commercial importance only to the salmon. Called the barndoor halibut, it matches its Atlantic cousin in size and appearance and is found from central California north to Alaska and the Bering Sea in depths from 60 to 3,000 feet. The California halibut *(Paralichthys californicus)* is a much smaller fish and not a true halibut, being "lefteyed." A record fish of this species was caught in 1980; it tipped the scales at 78 pounds, 8 ounces.

Halibut are in season all year, although in the Atlantic the "chicken" halibut is best from March to October, and the large ones from August to April. Eaten fresh, halibut is usually cut into steaks or fillets and broiled, but it is also popular smoked. Halibut liver oil may be taken as a dietary supplement for deficiencies of vitamins A and D.

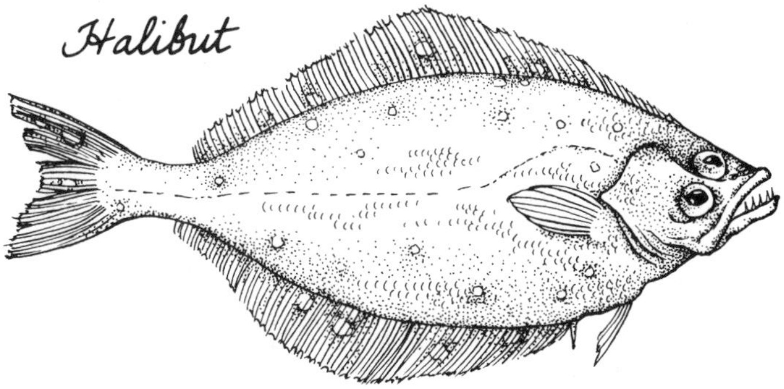

HALLAH

See **Challah.**

HAM

The upper part of a pig's hind leg, ham is sold smoked and/or salted but usually both. Sometimes part of the shoulder—cured and smoked—is sold as ham. This used to be called a "picnic" or California ham but is fatter and less flavorsome than the hindquarters.

Processing a ham involves the following operations: trimming, chilling and immersing in brine (a mixture of salt, sugar and a trace of saltpeter), washing, drying and smoking. Hickory wood or mahogany sawdust are the favorite fuels in the United States for smoking, which takes at least three days. In other countries beechwood is preferred. Germany uses juniper bush.

English and American hams are first soaked in water then simmered for several hours before a final baking. Other hams, usually those from France, Germany and Italy, can be served without additional cooking. Tenderized hams are those that have been partially or entirely cooked before marketing. Thus they need only roasting or warming to be ready to eat. Consult the label for cooking instructions.

Some of the best known hams are the following:

United States: Virginia hams have the best reputation, especially those from the town of Smithfield, which boasts that its hams come from pigs fattened on peanuts as a supplement to the basic diet of corn (maize). Smithfields are dry-salted, spiced with black pepper and matured for at least a year after being smoked. Kentucky hams are also dry-salted: they are hung for two years after being smoked over corncobs, hickory bark and sometimes sassafras wood.

England: York, Suffolk and Bradenham hams are all excellent. The last is marked by black skin. Lightly smoked, they are characterized by a mild, sweet flavor and pink flesh.

European Continent: Most celebrated of these are the *jambon de Bayonne* (France), *prosciutto di Parma* (Italy), *jamon de Asturias* (Spain), Danish ham and Prague ham. As a rule, these hams may be eaten without being cooked. They are often thinly sliced and served as hor d'oeuvres. Many consider the Prague ham to be the finest. It is salted and left in brine for many months before being smoked over a beechwood fire. It is matured in cellars for months before marketing.

See also: **Pig, Pork.**

HAMLET

Also NASSAU GROUPER. This saltwater food fish, *Ephinephelus striatus*, of the grouper family, is found in the Caribbean Sea and Gulf of Mexico. The average market size is ten pounds, but this fish can reach a length of three feet and weight of 50 pounds. Its overall color is olive-gray with brown vertical bars and white spots. It is considered very good eating.

See also: **Grouper.**

HAMMERHEAD SHARK

A family of sharks *(Sphyrnidae)* is characterized by a flattened head that has the appearance of a mallet. They are found worldwide in tropical and temperate waters. Two well-known species are the great hammerhead *(Sphyrna mokarran)*, which reaches a length of 20 feet, and the smooth hammerhead *(S. zygaena)*, which seldom exceeds 14 feet. Both these sharks are considered dangerous to man, and they seem to be eaten with regularity only in Japan where their fine-grained flesh is highly regarded.

The smooth hammerhead was fished commercially in Mexico and Florida for the oil content of its large liver, which used to be a valuable source of vitamin A. This fishery suffered a serious setback in the 1940s when vitamin A was synthesized in the laboratory.

See also: **Shark.**

HAND CHEESE

Also HANDKASE, QUESO DE MANO. It is so called because it used to be molded by hand, although this practice has been discontinued in most parts. Hand cheese is a small, surface-ripened cheese made from sour milk or butter milk that is very popular among German-speakers. Although often flavored with caraway seeds, the fully ripened cheese has a very sharp taste and aroma that take some getting used to.

Hand cheese is made in several countries, including the United States where people of German descent operate factories in Pennsylvania, New York, Wisconsin and Illinois. The curd is prepared like **cottage cheese,** then molded by hand. Bacteria cause surface smear during ripening, but it is carefully controlled. Curing takes six to eight weeks, and finished cheeses are round, with a diameter of two to three inches.

The Latin American version, called *queso de mano*, has some goat's milk added to what is basically a cow's milk curd. These cheeses are somewhat larger, averaging six to seven inches in diameter.

HANDKASE

See **Hand Cheese.**

HARD SAUCE

Also BRANDY BUTTER. A sweet sauce used on puddings and fruit desserts in the United States and Britain, it consists of confectioner's sugar and butter mixed and beaten into the consistency of a creamy paste, then flavored with lemon juice, brandy or rum. It is served cold.

See also: **Brandy Sauce, Sauce.**

HARDTACK

See **Knackebrod.**

HARE

This term applies to all small, wild rodents of the *Leporidae* genus, excepting rabbits. Known as jackrabbits west of the Mississippi, they are larger than wild rabbits, having longer ears, hind legs and feet and wider muzzles.

European varieties are larger than the American, the best coming from France, then Germany. The Belgian hare is actually a rabbit.

Hare are highly esteemed as a game food when young, preferably six months old or less. At that age, the hare-lip is barely noticeable. After the hare is a year old, the meat, particularly of the males (bucks) becomes coarse, dry and stringy.

The flesh of the hare is dark and has a gamey taste. It should be cooked through, not eaten red. Younger hares are jugged or roasted. Older hares are marinated, and allowed to age for a day or so, then made into brawn, terrines or soup. If the flesh is "high." it should not be eaten.

HARICOT BEAN

See **Kidney Bean.**

HARMAND'S GRAPE

This fruit of a high-climbing, woody vine, *Tetrastigma harmandii*, of Southeast Asia, is found from Malaysia to the Philippines. It is a kind of berry with a grapelike taste and is used to make jellies.

HARONGA

A Madagascan shrub *(Haronga madesgascariensis)* bears this edible fruit.

HARRACHER

See **Romadur.**

HARTSHORN

In medieval times, the antlers of a stag were reduced to powder. The powder was used to make gelatin or, because of its ammonia content, to make a leavening agent in quickbreads. It was a precursor of modern baking powders. Modern hartshorn is salt of hartshorn, or ammonium carbonate, a rarely used baking powder. The term "hartshorn" may also be used to refer to the **buckshorn plantain.**

HARTWEG'S BERRY

A reddish fruit of a South American shrub, *Cyphomandra hartwegi*, Hartweg's berry is related to the **tree tomato.** It is sold in local markets in Colombia, Argentina and Chile. It is consumed as a vegetable and cooked before eating.

HARZKASE

A German **hand cheese,** *harzkase* is made from sour milk and often flavored with caraway seeds. Cheeses are small and round with a diameter of two inches. They typically weigh four ounces. They are made in the Harz Mountains.

HATAHATA

A food fish of some consequence in Japanese waters, the *hatahata (Arctoscopus japonicus)* is a sandfish that reaches a length of no more than 11 inches. It is found on coastal mud or sand from Kamchatka to Japan and on the east coast of Korea. The *hatahata* is the indispensable item in the Japanese New Year dinner. If not eaten fresh, it is pickled in salt and yeast. The roe is conisdered a delicacy and is called *buriko*.

HATHAWARIYA

Also SICKLE THORN. The stems and fleshy roots of this woody vine, *Asparagus falcatus*, are eaten like asparagus. It is found in eastern India, Sri Lanka and tropical and southeastern Africa. The roots may also be candied and eaten as a confection.

HAUSA GROUNDNUT

A West African legume, *Kerstingiella geocarpa*, similar to the bambara groundnut, it is more suitable for the drier areas.

See also: **Bambara Groundnut.**

HAUSA MILLET

An annual cereal grain, *Digitaria exilis*, of the crabgrass genus, it is sometimes cultivated in Africa for its seeds. The seeds are used for flour and meal.

HAUSA POTATO

The tubers of this tropical African plant, *Coleus rotundifolius*, of the flame nettle genus, are often cultivated and eaten as a substitute for the common potato.

HAUSKASE

This German cheese of the **Limburger** type is disk-shapted with a diameter of about 10 inches.

HAUT-BRION

See **Chateau Haut-Brion.**

HAVARTI

A Danish cheese, *havarti* is acidic tasting when fresh but sharp and aromatic when aged. The cheese has an unusual flavor. It originated in New Zealand more than 100 years ago and was adopted by the Danes who also called it Danish Tilsit. The cheese has large and small holes. Normally round in shape, it may also be pressed into leaf shapes. It is packed in foil and weighs between eight and 11 pounds.

HAW

Also HAWTHORN, MAD APPLE. Edible fruit from a wide variety of shrubs and trees from such genera as *Crataegus*, *Viburnum* and *Bumelia*, haws range in size from one-half to one inch in diameter and may be round, oval or pear-shaped. They are generally sweet and juicy. Though sometimes eaten fresh as a dessert fruit, more often they are used to make jellies.

Some of the better species include the summer haw *(C. flava)*, a pear-shaped, yellow-fruited variety found in the southern United States from Virginia to Florida; the Hupeh haw *(C. hupehensis)*, a dark red variety up to one inch long, which is often cultivated in west China; the Mexican hawthorn, used for preserves and jellies; the American hawthorn *(C. mollis)*, a red variety of the Midwest and South used for making jellies; the May hawthorn or English hawthorn *(C. laevigata)*, a deep red variety that thrives in cooler regions of Europe, North Africa and

Hazelnuts

west Asia and is sometimes ground into flour and added to bread, and the Chinese haw *(C. pentagyma)* a species cultivated in north China and Siberia, frequently stewed, candied, preserved or made into jelly.

The hawthorn is common enough in England to have occasioned these lines by Shakespeare from *Henry VI:*

Gives not the hawthorn-bush a sweeter shade
To shepherds looking on their silly sheep
Than doth a rich embroider'd canopy
To kings that fear their subjects' treachery?

HAWAIIAN LAUREL

A native Hawaiian tree, *Antidesma platyphyllum*, has pink fruit used to make jellies and syrups. A local wine is also made from the Hawaiian laurel.

HAWFINCH

Also GROSBEAK. This is the common grosbeak *(Cocothraustes vulgaris)* of Europe, a bird of the finch family with a thick, conical beak. This small bird is considered a delicacy in France where it is usually roasted.

HAY CHEESE

Also FROMAGE DE FOIN. A French skimmed-milk cheese, produced in the department of Seine-Inferieure, it is so called because it is ripened on freshly cut hay. This results in a special aroma, which is somewhat like that of **livarot.** Most is consumed locally.

HAZELNUT

Also COBNUT, FILBERT. With its many varieties, the fruit of the shrublike hazel tree *(Corylus avellana)* assumes different shapes, and the terminology varies accordingly. Roughly speaking, there are two groups: oblong nuts and round nuts. Hazelnuts are oblong; cobnuts are round. Filberts are cultivated hazelnuts, but by shape may fall into either group. The name "filbert" comes from the day upon which the nuts ripen, St. Philbert's day, August 22.

Hazelnut trees grow well in temperate, moist climates. The fruit has a hard, woody shell, encased in a green outer husk. The kernel is a single seed, which is 65 percent oil by weight. Major producers of filberts are Spain, Italy and Turkey.

Cultivation of this nut is very old, especially in Italy, where it still flourishes in Sicily and around Naples. Three varieties are common in England: the white, the red and the frizzled. The first two take their names from the color of the skin on the kernel; the last has a frizzled husk, cut at both ends. There are many other varieties including Californian, Chinese, Siberian and Japanese, plus hybrids.

Until 1940, the United States imported most filberts from Italy and Spain but since then has intensely cultivated a native hazelnut, improving the size and flavor greatly over the original.

Hazelnuts are good fresh, when easily peeled. According to the recipe, they may be ground, sliced or chopped. They are used in chocolate candy bars and certain kinds of nougat. Although seldom seen in the kitchen, hazelnut oil is used in cosmetics and perfumes.

HEAD

The heads of cattle, sheep and other animals contain a reasonable amount of good, edible meat. Nevertheless, head is not a popular food in the United States, except as part of an ethnic cuisine, such as Mexican or Basque. This is due partly to aesthetic considerations, as in the Texas barbecue, where calf's head is traditional, but where nowadays it is usually not displayed at table.

Heads are eaten in other forms, however, for example in headcheeses and brawns. Apart from the muscle meat, brain and sensory organs, the head contains lots of bone, cartilages and ligaments, which yield gelatin-rich stock when boiled. Moreover, the meat, being carcass meat, is readily removed only after cooking. After boiling, the meat and the stock are pressed into molds, or wrapped tightly in cloth. When cooled, it has a jelly-like consistency that is easy to slice and a mosaic appearance that is attractive on the plate. The English and northern Europeans make headcheese from both calf's and pig's head.

In 19th-century New England, the meat from simmered calf's head was served in a beef gravy with brain fritters. In contemporary Hungary, the sliced meat from calf's head is dipped into batter, fried and served with baked potatoes and tartar sauce.

Apart from headcheese, hog's head is prepared in a number of ways. Where wild swine are available, the classic boar's head makes an imposing dish. The head is carefully skinned, all the meat is diced and cooked together with the tongue, then mixed with a dressing and stuffed back into the skin, which is shaped to resemble the original head. An alternative is the French boar's head with pistachio. The Irish are fond of pig's face and cabbage, while in the southern United States hog's head is made into a hearty stew, which includes the head plus boned pork, stew beef, a hen and lots of onions, tomatoes and potatoes.

Americans have little enthusiasm for lamb and mutton, and none at all for lamb or sheep's head, except for enclaves of pastoral peoples such as the Basques in Nevada and Colorado. In Sweden, lamb's head is grilled or roasted, then eaten with the fingers, dipping meat, tongue and eyes in mustard sauce. The Norwegian *smala-hovud* features boiled lamb's head as does the North African *bouzellouf*. Boiling enables one to recover all the meat that is difficult to remove otherwise.

Poultry heads, usually discarded in the United States, are often added to stews or soups in Europe. For preparation they are scalded, plucked and cleaned. The beak is also removed. The French *alicuit* (fowl stew) includes them along with feet, innards and muscle meat. They are also a standard ingredient of the Hungarian goose giblets fricassee and the German fowl giblets soup.

Fish heads are raw material for fish stocks and fumets. Fish head soup is an item of American soul food, and cod's head and shoulders a traditional English seafood melange the includes cockles, mussels and oysters.

See also: **Variety Meats.**

HEADCHEESE

This is not cheese at all but a kind of sausage consisting of meat from calf or pig's head seasoned and molded in its own natural jelly. In England it is called brawn.

Headcheese is prepared as follows: The eyes and brains are removed from the heads and the hair singed off. The heads are boiled in seasoned water for four hours, then the meat is cut from them in coarse pieces, which are placed in a mold. The stock from boiling is simmered, bouillon and gelatin are added, then this mixture is poured over the meat in the mold. It takes 24 hours to set. Tongue and innards are often added to the head meat and even chunks of chicken or roast beef.

In Scotland, this is called jellied head. But both the Dutch and French have terms analogous to headcheese, i.e., *hoofdkaas* and *fromage de tete de porc*. It is served cold, in slices, as from a cheese.

See also: **Head, Sausage.**

HEALTH FOOD

The term applies to foods raised "organically" (vegetables and fruit not sprayed with pesticides; meat from animals that have not been inoculated with growth-stimulating hormones or drugs and fed "naturally" on plants that have not been sprayed). Health food has long been associated with faddists, or with religious movements, but now appears in most of the larger supermarkets and in special health-food stores in the United States. An early exponent of health food was Sylvester Graham (father of the Graham cracker) whose followers insisted that "candy led directly to the grave." Graham expounded temperance, vegetarianism, whole grains and strict personal cleanliness. Certainly it seems to be true that the United States and western Europe consume far more than a healthy intake of animal protein and fat. Obesity, with its relation to heart disease, is a major problem.

Health-food theorists include "lacto-vegetarians", whose diet adds eggs to dairy products; and "nondairy frutarians." Other groups urge raw foods only, or maintain yoga and macrobiotic regimes. In the macrobiotic diet, emphasis is placed on the proper balance of the *yin* and the *yang*. (*Yin* foods are those that contain acidity and expansion, while *yang* foods contain alkalinity and contraction.) Some vegetarians, also, insist that the eating of any meat is harmful because the consumer takes into his or her nervous system the muscular tension of the animal at the moment of its death.

Health food, such as oatmeal, was used in the 19th century as a steady diet for invalids and for those with digestive problems. Vegetarianism is practically identified with health-food cookery, although organically prepared meat is considered acceptable in some diets. Health-food staples are wheat germ, alfalfa sprouts, soy beans, soy flour, soy sauce, honey instead of sugar, brown rice instead of white or polished rice, yogurt, whole grain wheat and oats, nuts and sunflower seeds. Chief villains in a health food diet are sugar and solid vegetable shortenings.

The cost of most health foods in the United States is generally higher than foods more normally known and available. Also, a continuing challenge to the purely vegetarian health food consumer is to find a balanced diet that includes a sufficient amount of protein, generally supplied by nuts and vegetables. Another challenge is to make the food—especially vegtables and grains—palatable and not monotonous. Scores of health-food cookbooks exist today in the United States, all purporting in their several ways to meet this challenge.

Modern advances in the food-processing industry, with the apparent necessity to preserve food for longer periods of time and, hence, the inclusion of **food additives** has brought with it a counter industry—health foods that contain no synthetic additives or the residue of pesticides, fungicides, antibiotics, hormones or drugs. In addition, the amount of food wasted in the large-scale preparation of meat argues for a more efficient economy and the changing of personal diet to include the highly nutritious and lower priced animal organs generally discarded or ground into pet food: liver, kidneys, brains and sweetbreads.

American contact with the Far East, especially since World War II, has led to the study of diets connected with Buddhism, but more so with the Japanese generally, who subsist on little or no red meat, making do instead with soy beans, seaweed, sea salt, organic vegetables, fish and rice. Nostalgia plays its part, too, in the current popularity of health food—if one can remember or fantasize the fresh taste of garden vegetables and fruits and the smell of freshly baked bread served "in Grandma's day."

HEART

Also PLUCK. One of the **variety meats,** heart of beef, lamb, pig and other ruminants makes an economical and high protein dish and is a good source of vitamin B. Beef hearts are the largest and toughest and must be braised or simmered until tender. Calves' and lambs' hearts are smaller and more tender. They are usually stuffed with breadcrumbs and herbs, then braised with vegetables and stock. Sheeps' and pigs' hearts are a frequent ingredient of sausages. Hearts range in size from one-quarter pound for a lamb heart to about three pounds for beef heart. Heart is almost all muscle meat, but unlike other muscle cuts, it does not improve in taste by aging. Heart should be bought as fresh as possible like all viscera meat. Basic preparation for heart is to trim all veins, arteries fat and valves, then wash thoroughly.

Beef heart is classic barbecue fare. In Peruvian *anticuchos*, for example, beef hearts are cubed, marinated overnight, then grilled on skewers. The Italians slice beef heart very thinly, marinate the slices for several hours in olive oil, salt and pepper, then grill them over charcoal. The Hungarians make a rich soup of calf's heart, lung and rice, thickened with sour cream. The Chinese stir-fry a julienne of beef heart with mushrooms. Mock goose is an English holiday dish consisting of stuffed, simmered beef heart, roasted with strips of bacon.

Lamb and sheep's hearts are usually sold together with the lungs (also considered pluck). They have about the same amount of protein as a leg of lamb, but a lot less fat. The Italians prepare a dish of lamb organs with artichokes, including the heart, lungs and livers.

Pork heart is rich in thiamine and higher in protein than ham. The Chinese stir-fry pig's heart with scallions, and in France a casserole of pork heart is prepared with orange sauce. A rich Filipino stew called *binagis,* or pork organ pepperpot, includes pig's heart and kidney, plus pork meat and liver together with onions, garlic and sweet and hot peppers.

Goat heart may be substitued for sheep's in most recipes. The Moroccan *tagine bel kharouf* is a stew of kid meat and organs that combines chopped liver, heart, kidneys, lung and pancreas and is eaten as an accompaniment to *couscous.*

HEDGEHOG

This small, rodentlike, nocturnal mammal, *Erinaceus europaeus,* common to northern Europe and Asia, is characterized by a long snout, protective spines and a short tail. In North America the **porcupine** is also called a hedgehog but differs in size and appearance. It also has barbed instead of straight quills.

The hedgehog bears no resemblance to a pig. The name actually comes from "hedge haunter" due to the animal's habit of digging its burrow under a hedge or dense bush. It rolls itself into a tight ball at the slightest cause for alarm.

Hedgehog meat is edible, especially when the gamey taste is eliminated by overnight soaking in cold brine. Although esteemed a delicacy by the Romans, very few hedgehogs are consumed in Europe today.

HEDGEHOG MUSHROOM

See **Horse Mushroom.**

HEDGE LIME

Also DOG LIME. This perennial herb, *Sisymbrium canescens*, grows wild in North America. Its seeds are used to make a refreshing drink by mixing them with lime juice, claret and syrup.

HELMET CRAB

See **King Crab.**

HELVELLES

Also MONK'S MOREL. A European fungus with several edible varieties, including the *Helvella crispa*, the *H. lacunosa* and the *Cyathipodia macropus*, somewhat resembles the morel but has a crinkly appearance.

Helvelles should not be eaten raw but should be simmered for five minutes in water (and the water thrown away) before final cooking. They may be prepared in any way suitable for **morel.** This fungus is known to cause indigestion in some persons.

See also: **Mushroom.**

HEMIBARBUS

Hemibarbus is a genus of deep-bodied food fish of the Amur and other rivers of north China. The most important member of the genus for food is *H. maculatus*. It reaches a length of 16 inches and is halfway between a barbel and a goby. It has barbels at the corner of its mouth, a high dorsal fin and a pointed snout. The fish is taken in seine nets and the fishery is considered moderately important.

HEMIONE

Also DZIGGETAI. This wild donkey, *Equus hemionus* of central Asia, has edible flesh that may be prepared like domestic **donkey.**

HEN OF THE WOODS

See **Polypore.**

HERB

The herb is defined as a plant that does not develop a woody stem above the ground and dies away after flowering. There are thousands of plants in that category, but we are concerned here only with the few that are commonly used to season and flavor food. One or more parts of the plant may serve, including the leaves, stems, seeds and root.

This kind of use goes back before the dawn of history. For example, poppy and caraway seeds were found at Swiss prehistoric lake sites in circumstances suggesting they were used as condiments. In historical times, herbs received extremely wide use in the ancient civilizations of the Middle East, India and China, and during classical antiquity. Indeed, the trend in herb use is one of narrowing the list down to a precious few. In this connection, Waverly Root wrote:

> *Of the 2,500 recognized species of edible herbs, Assyria used at least 250; Mesopotamia as many; Egypt listed 877 recipes in the Ebers Papyrus of the 16th century B.C.; the ancient Hindu Sambita herbal more than 500; and in China the Pen Tsao of about 2,000 B.C. named 365, a number which may entitle us to wonder whether they were not held to this limit in order to provide one herb for each day of the year. Hippocrates used 400 herbs and Coelius Apicius, in his* De Obsoniis et Condimentis, sive Arte Coquinaria, *called for a variety of seasoners which would stagger a modern restaurant pantryman.*

Some of the lists he cites may be more comparable to the U.S. Pharmacopeia than a cookbook. Still, by the middle of the 19th century the number in use in French kitchens was minuscule by comparison. Alexandre Dumas in his gastronomic encyclopedia set the number at 28.

Modern encyclopedists are able to agree on only 25 as being truly common. They are: angelica, anise, balm, basil, bay, borage, burnet, caraway, chervil, chives, coriander, dill, fennel, hyssop, marjoram (sweet marjoram), mint, oregano, parsley, rosemary, saffron, sage, savory, sesame, tansy and tarragon.

Receiving an occasional mention are: camomile, celery seed, cress, cumin, dittany, horehound, lemon thyme, lemon verbena, lovage, mandrake, mustard seed, poppy seed, purslane, rue and sorrel.

Garlic and shallot are mentioned in some lists. They are popular flavoring agents, but most writers seem to think of them in a different category than the herbs mentioned above, more like vegetables in their own right.

Herbs are classified in various ways. For cooking purposes, there are strong herbs (known as potherbs) and mild herbs. Potherbs are: basil, bay, dill, marjoram, mint, oregano, resemary, sage, tarragon and thyme. Used indiscreetly, any one can overpower the taste of the food it is supposed to enhance. Milder herbs are chervil, chives, parsley and savory. For homegrowing, certain herbs are easy to dry and store for later use. They retain their flavor well, indeed their potency is increased by half when dried. They are sage, basil, chervil, dill, fennel, lovage, marjoram, parsley and thyme.

Practically all of the common herbs have been put to one medical use or another over the ages, have been used in a love potion or have been held to be magical in some sense. See also in this volume under the name of the individual herb, such as **Angelica, Anise,** etc.

See also: **Spice.**

HERB BENNET

See **Bennet.**

HERB IVY

See **Buckshorn Plantain.**

HERKIMER

This once-popular American cheddar-type cheese named after its place of origin, Herkimer County, New York, is made from cow's milk and has the following characteristics: sharp flavor, white curd, dry crumbly texture.

HERMITAGE

These are wines, especially red, from the vicinity of L'Hermitage, a town in the valley of the Rhone in southern France. The red Hermitage is distinguished by a rich, almost purple color, and an exquisite bouquet. It is made from the Syrah (or Sirah) grape. The origin of the name perhaps stems from the tenth century, when Henri Gaspart de Sterimberg, a knight under Louis VIII, grown weary of war, petitioned a corner of land, a "hermitage," where he could retire.

Hermitage was an especially popular wine in the 19th century and a favorite of the czar's court in Russia. Hermitage is known for a berry taste, which lingers in the mouth. It should be aged for several years before being drunk. When young it is rough, like **Chianti.** A white Hermitage from a mixture of grapes is also grown in small quantities.

See also: **Rhone Wine.**

HERMIT CRAB

A small crustacean of the genus *Paguridae* of the crab family, the hermit crab has no natural shell of its own except for a hardened band around its middle. It occupies the shells of univalve mollusks either by finding an abandoned one or by killing and eating its rightful owner. As it grows, it moves into ever larger shells. The hermit crab may be cooked like shrimp or cleaned and broiled or baked in its borrowed shell.

HERRGARDSOST

A popular Swedish cheese, *herrgardsost* is mostly factory made, although its name, *herrgard*, means "manor house" and implies that it is farmhouse or homemade. In the half-cream version it has a medium-firm, pliable curd and a mild, sweet, nutty flavor much like that of **Gouda.**

Curing takes three to four months, and finished cheeses, which are dipped in paraffin or cheese wax, weigh from 26 to 33 pounds. The full-cream version, which is aged four to six months, is more like a hard **Swiss** cheese. It is called *herrgard-elite* and weighs as much as 40 pounds.

HERRING

As a food fish, the herring *(Clupea harengus)* is rivaled only by the **cod.** It is a small fish, averaging 12 inches in length and 1½ pounds in weight; but it has always appeared in legendary abundance in the North Atlantic, surfacing in schools whose length and breadth stretched for miles.

Archeological evidence points to its appearance in the northern European diet in early Neolithic times. By the 6th century A.D., the Danes had achieved a modicum of prosperity through fishing for it commercially. Apart from its abundance, herring owed its popularity, like cod, to an easy method of preservation, a decisive commercial advantage in the days before refrigeration. Cod was preserved by sun drying and salting; herring was preserved by smoking. Herring fishing boomed in the Middle Ages, and by the 12th century its ready availability caused it to lose all prestige among the elite. Although herring was delicious and nutritious, its cheapness earned it a reputation as food for the poor, and the well-to-do shunned it except as a donation to charitable institutions. Herring became a staple in all northern European countries and has remained so to this day. Considering its history, it is not surprising that herring is more often preferred in cured form than fresh.

The Atlantic herring *(Clupea harengus harengus)* is the most prolific and popular member of herring family, which has 27 species. It has a greenish blue back and silver belly and side and is found throughout the North Atlantic from North Carolina, north past Greenland to Novaya Zemlya and back down to Gibralter. Other important species are the wall-eyed herring *(Pomolobus pseudoharengus)* and Pacific herring *(Clupea pallasii)* in the United States, the **alewife** in Britain and the silver sild and thread herring of the Atlantic.

Herring were long thought to be a migratory fish, but recent studies have shown that what was thought to be one school migrating south actually were many schools rising to the surface in response to a cooling trend in the ocean water as the seasons changed. All herrings in a particular school are of the same age and size. Rather than swim abreast, they mass together in staggered formation with uniform spacing, each fish's head ranged opposite the midpoint in the body of his neighbor. This limits their freedom to maneuver and facilitates netting them in huge scoops or gill nets because they cannot scatter in all directions.

In the days before coining was standardized, the uniform size of herring made them attractive as an informal unit of calculation. In the Middle Ages, most cities issued their own coins. The resulting variety was so bewildering that merchants from different jurisdictions found it easier to calculate the value of a sale in so many herring, which was then immediately translatable into local currency. In this sort of transaction, no fish changed hands.

Herring has a fairly high fat content (6 percent), and if eaten fresh is best when grilled, stuffed or baked. There are many varieties of cured herring including: kippers, where fish is split, salted dried and smoked; bloaters, which are fat specimens, lightly smoked and salted; Bismarck herring, where the entire fish is pickled in a solution containing spices, red pepper and onion; soused herring, i.e., pickled; and rollmops, which are rolled pickled fillets.

"Red herring" has entered the language as a figure of speech. It is an English specialty in which the whole fish is salted and smoked. It acquired a figurative meaning because, if dragged across a fox's trail, it destroyed the scent, throwing the hounds off the chase.

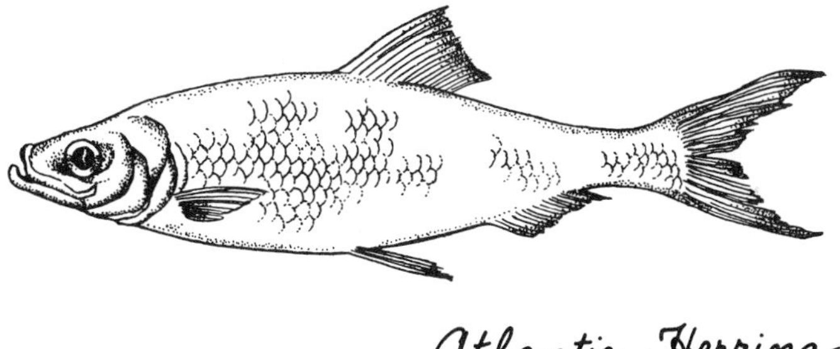

Atlantic Herring

HERVE

A soft, fermented Belgian cheese of the **Limburger** type, it is made from cow's milk in full-cream, half-cream and partly skimmed versions, with herbs often added for flavoring. The cheese is pressed into squares six inches to the sides and three inches thick, then ripened in beer-soaked cloth.

HICKORY NUT

Here is the fruit of several varieties of large North American trees *(Carya* spp.) of the walnut family. Hickories are very tall, handsome shade trees, attaining heights of up to 150 feet. The best known hickory-type nut is the **pecan,** which will be treated separately. After the pecan, in order of quality comes the shagbark *(C. ovata)* and the shell bark *(C. laciniosa)*, also known as the king nut. Another variety, the pignut hickory *(C. cordiformis)*, sometimes yields edible nuts.

The seed of the hickory nut is enclosed in a green husk, which is relatively light ("paper-shelled") in the pecan, heavier in the shagbark, and thickest in the shell bark. The names of the last two varieties refers to characteristic peeling of the bark in mature trees. The shell bark's strips are narrower than the shagbark's.

The shagbark nut has an oblong, slightly angled shape and white meat. It is found from Quebec south to Florida and Texas. The shellbark nut is nearly round with yellow or reddish meat. It is found from New York to Pennsylvania and south to Oklahoma.

Hickory nuts are rich in oil, and native Americans extracted from them a milky fluid that they used to make a gruel and to moisten corn (maize) cakes. Today hickory nuts are used in making candy and other confections.

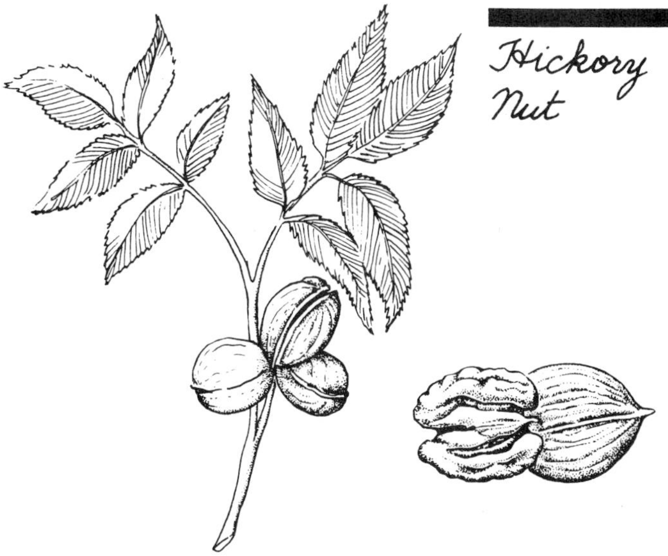

Hickory Nut

HILSA

Also FLAT HERRING. Two food fish are known by this name. One is a freshwater fish, *Clupea ilisha*, of the Ganges River, which is highly esteemed as food and is sometimes referred to as the Indian salmon. A second is the flat herring *(Hilsa kelee)*, which ranges from China to the east African coast. Typically, it is 12 inches long with a compressed, flattened body. Its back and sides are green, and its belly is silver. The flat herring is fished commercially and is eaten salted or smoked.

HIMALAYAN ASH

Also GRIFFITH'S FRAXINUS. This species of ash tree *(Fraxinus griffithii)* is found in China, Malaysia and the Philippines. If smoked, its leaves produce the same scent and taste as opium but neither its narcotic nor other unpleasant effects. It is said to be helpful in the treatment of addiction.

HINCKLEY & SCHMITT WATER

This still, natural spring water bottled in the United States is relatively low in mineral content. A 1980 Consumers Union sensory panel rated the taste of this water as good, with the following comments: heavy, thick mouthfeel; mild soapy flavor and soapy mouthfeel.

See also: **Mineral Water.**

HIND

Also ROCK HIND. This term is used for a female red deer that is three or more years old. The hind was once considered the finest venison.

Among fish, the rock hind *(Epinephelus adscensionis)* is a small member of the grouper family, reaching a maximum length of about two feet. It is found in the Atlantic Ocean from the Canary Islands to South Africa and in the west from Massachusetts to Brazil. The rock hind is grayish green with dark spotting over its head and body. It is a significant food fish. Closely allied to it is the speckled hind, a grouper found off the west coast of Florida. It reaches a maximum weight of 30 pounds.

HING

See **Asafetida.**

HINNY

See **Mule.**

HIPPOCRAS

Also IPOCRAS, YPOCRAS. A sweetened and aromatized wine that was popular in Europe from the Middle Ages on into the 18th century, it is reckoned now to have been a way of salvaging wine that was souring. Hippocras was the **vermouth** of its epoch.

A quantity of wine was boiled with spices such as cinnamon, ginger, cloves plus herbs and raisins. When the liquid was reduced by two thirds, sugar, and perhaps more wine, was added. This was allowed to cool, then it was strained through a flannel bag called Hippocrates' sleeve, hence the name "hippocras." Often it was sweetened with honey as well.

Hippocras was drunk cold or, if possible, iced, usually before meals or on special occasions. It achieved renown as an aphrodisiac, and in Holland newlyweds were presented bottles of hippocras to be drunk on their wedding night.

HIPPOPOTAMUS

The hippopotamus is an African mammal whose name means "river horse" in Greek, which is a good first impression. It is an amphibious member of the hog family that lives in or near the rivers of Africa.

The hippopotamus *(H. amphibius)* has nocturnal habits, submerging itself during the day and feeding at night on plant life. It is a huge ungainly beast with a thick square head, a large muzzle, a wide, heavy body and short legs. It can be dangerous if roused, upsetting boats and wreaking havoc on their passengers.

Hippopotamus flesh is considered a succulent dish by East Africans, so much so, according to one authority, that a thousand years ago it changed its eating habits from diurnal to nocturnal so as better to avoid hunters. Pliny the Elder (d. 79 A.D.) recommended eating the snout and foot of the hippo to boost sexual potency.

HOANG ME

See **Shiitake.**

HOCCO

See **Curassow.**

HOCHSTRASSER

See **Romadur.**

HOCK

The name is an English contraction for a German white wine grown at Hochheim, on the Rhine, though the word was carelessly used in the 19th century to denote all German **Rhine wine.** Hock was thought to have a tonic quality ("A good hock keeps the doctor away"), and Lord Byron recommended it as a cure for hangover:

(but I write this reeling,
Having got drunk exceedingly today,
So that I seem to stand upon the ceiling)
I say—the future is a serious matter—
And so—for God's sake— hock and soda water!

Hochheim today is a smooth and superior white wine, low in alcohol content, from the Rheingau in the "elbow" of the Rhine near Koblenz.

HOECAKE

See **Ash Cake, Cornbread.**

HOG

See **Pork.**

HOG APPLE PLUM

See **Spondias.**

HOGFISH

Also RASCASSE. The term "hogfish" is the popular name of more than one species. Most prominent, perhaps, is the Mediterranean *Scorpaena scrofa*, known as *rascasse* in French, which is an indispensable ingredient of **bouillabaisse.** It is a small (maximum length, 20 inches), ugly fish, which the French also call *diable de mer* (sea devil) and *crapaud* (toad) because of its poisonous spines.

Another species is the *Lachnolaimus maximus* or hogsnapper of the western Atlantic and Gulf of Mexico. It is an excellent food fish that weighs up to 25 pounds. *L. maximus* is a member of the wrasse family and is easily recognized by the first three spines of its dorsal fin, which are very long and thick. It has been fished into scarcity in the West Indies.

Other hogfish are the *Bodianus pulchellus*, the spotfin hogfish; and *B. rufus*, the Spanish hogfish, both dwelling in the western Atlantic but of negligible food interest.

HOG PLUM

In American usage, the hog plum refers to the yellow or red fruit of a small tree or shrub, *Prunus americana*, found in the eastern United States from New England south to Florida and west to New Mexico. Its fruit is also known as the wild plum, the August plum, the goose plum and the sloe. Equally, it could apply to the *P. reverchonii*, a similar looking fruit of a small shrub native to Oklahoma and Texas. Sometimes the Allegheny plum or sloe *(P. alleghaniensis)* is called hog plum, as are the wild lime *(Ximenia* spp.) of Florida and the West Indies and the chickasaw or sand plum *(P. angustifolia)* of Kansas and the Southwest. In international parlance, hog plum most often refers to tropical fruit of the *Spondias* genus, most notably the **yellow mombin** and **red mombin.**

HOGWEED

See **Cow Parsnip, Dandelion.**

HOHENBERG

See **Box Cheese.**

HOHENHEIMER

See **Box Cheese.**

HOLLANDAISE SAUCE

This French sauce consists chiefly of butter and egg yolks mixed to a thick consistency and seasoned with peppercorns and lemon juice. It is one of the basic sauces and may be used by itself on fish, eggs and vegetables or serve as an excellent base for other sauces.

See also: **Sauce.**

HOLLY

Holly exists in many species and varieties, two of the most common being English or European holly *(Ilex aquifolium)*, an evergreen tree of Europe, North Africa and western Asia; and American holly *(I. opaca)*, also an evergreen tree but native to the United States.

Hollies are characterized by bright green, leathery leaves with scalloped edges and tiny, bright red berries. In many places, holly serves as an ornamental plant, used especially in Christmas decorations. In

Corsica, however, the berries are roasted and ground, then used to make a coffeelike beverage. *Houx*, a distilled spirit made in Alsace, is prepared from a mash of holly berries. The most notable drink made from the holly plant is **mate,** a tealike drink very popular in the southern cone of South America.

The shoots of knee holly or butcher's broom *(Ruscus aculeatus)* are eaten like asparagus.

HOLLYHOCK

The roots of the flowering plant *Alcea rosea* can be used to make a nourishing starch. It is native to the Mediterranean region, and, according to one source, the ancient Egyptians ate its pickled leaves. The hollyhock is also known as rose mallow, and the color of its flowers varies from white to pink or purple.

HOLSTEIN DAIRY CHEESE

See **Leather Cheese.**

HOLSTEINER MAGERKASE

See **Holstein Skim-Milk Cheese.**

HOLSTEINER MARSCH

See **Wilstermarsch.**

HOLSTEIN GESUNDHEITSKASE

See **Holstein Health Cheese.**

HOLSTEIN HEALTH CHEESE

Also HOLSTEIN GESUNDHEITSKASE. This German **cooked cheese** is made from sour skim milk. After the curd is mixed and pressed, cream and salt are added. Then the mixture is heated and poured into half-pound molds.

HOLSTEIN SKIM-MILK CHEESE

Also HOLSTEINER MAGERKASE, BUTTENKASE. A German skim-milk cheese, originating in the Schleswig-Holstein area, it is colored with saffron and often flavored with caraway seeds. Fresh buttermilk is often added before renneting. The curd is hard-pressed and requires five or six months for full curing. Cheeses weigh 10 to 14 pounds.

HOLY THISTLE

Also ST. MARY'S THISTLE. This is a thistlelike herb, *Silybum marianum*, native to the Mediterranean region, whose young leaves are suitable for salads. It is sometimes cultivated there for its ornamental value, yet it has naturalized in California and elsewhere in the United States as a weed.

HOMINY

Hulled and degermed corn (maize) broken up or ground into various degrees of coarseness. The finest ground hominy (which is still coarser than **cornmeal)** is called hominy grits. This is a popular food in the American South, where it may be eaten as a breakfast cereal with milk and butter or may be boiled, made into a mush and fried. Very coarse, or nearly whole-kerneled, hominy is called samp, or pearl hominy. It is eaten as a dinner vegetable or as a rice or potato substitute.

Pearl hominy is closest to the old-fashioned lye hominy, which early American colonists learned to make from the native Americans. The word "hominy" derives from a native American language. Its origin—depending on which expert you believe—comes from *auhuminea*, meaning "parched corn," or *tackhummin*, an Algonquin word meaning "hulled corn." The native Americans hulled the corn by soaking it in water to which they added a bag of wood ashes. Under this treatment, the kernels swelled and acquired a distinctive taste. Colonists adopted the practice and later dispensed with the ashes, using instead a lye solution.

See also: **Grits.**

HONEY

Honey is a syrupy food produced by bees from plant nectar and stored in wax cells called honeycombs. Nectar is a kind of sweet sap secreted by flowers in special glands. It consists of from 50 percent to 90 percent water, 10 percent to 50 percent sugar (mainly sucrose), and 1 percent to 4 percent minerals, coloring materials and aromatic substances that later determine the special flavoring of the honey.

Bees collect nectar and store it in honey sacs. They later disgorge it into the cells of the honeycomb. In the process, the bees add two enzymes to the nectar, and through evaporation reduce its moisture content to about 18 percent. One enzyme inverts the sucrose, creating levulose and dextrose. The second, glucose oxidase, retards bacterial growth during the evaporation. It is inactive at the normal moisture level of honey, but should the honey be diluted, as it is when it is fed to bee larvae, the enzyme becomes active again and protects the honey from attack by microbes. Because of this antiseptic property, honey made an effective wound dressing in the days before the discovery of modern salves and creams. Also, its thick, sticky consistency prevented outside bacteria from passing through to the wound. When the bees finish processing it, honey consists of about 45 percent levulose, 34 percent dextrose, 2 percent sucrose, 18 percent water, plus minerals, B-complex vitamins, amino acids and of course, the enzymes (which may later be destroyed by pasteurization).

From the most remote times until the advent of cane sugar, honey was the chief sweetner for humans. It loomed large in the minds of ancient Hebrews as a symbol of richness and ease. When Moses led them out of captivity in Egypt, the promised land was described as, "a land rich and broad, where milk and honey flow" (Exodus 3:8). The honeybee was a royal symbol in ancient Egypt, and the Greeks and Romans considered honey a food fit for the gods. Norsemen diluted honey, allowing it to ferment, and made the alcoholic beverage mead, which remained popular in Europe through the Middle Ages. Napolean chose the likeness of the honeybee to adorn his personal crest.

The honeybee was introduced into North America around 1640, quickly adapted to the new environment, and by 1812 had spread as far west as Texas. America had native bees, but they produced no honey. Apiculture was a crude affair, and honey production low, until the middle of the 19th century, when L. L. Langstroth, an American, discovered the phenomenon of bee space and developed the movable frame hive. In the next 22 years, such developments as the frame of foundation, the centrifugal honey extracting machine, and the bellows-and-nozzle smoker laid the basis for modern beekeeping.

On the average, a bee colony contains from 50,000 to 70,000 bees, which produce a harvest of from 60 to 100 pounds of honey per year (5 to 8.3 gallons). A little more than a third of the honey produced by the bees' is retained in the hive to sustain its population. To produce one pound of honey, bees must gather about four pounds of nectar, which requires the bees to tap about two million flowers. The honey is gathered by worker bees, whose lifespan is three to six weeks, long enough to collect about a teaspoon of nectar.

The taste, color and viscosity of honey depends in large part on the source of the nectar. Color ranges from water white (sage honey) through amber (clover and orange) to black red (avocado) and dark green (winter-blooming eucalyptus). The palest honeys are often the mildest. Sage, for example, is quite bland, but extremely thick, having a very low moisture content (14 percent). Alfalfa honey is amber and has a pronounced flavor with mint overtones. Buckwheat honey has a strong flavor and the color of molasses.

In Europe, the honeys of France, Greece and Scotland are highly regarded. French honey of Narbonne, gathered from rosemary blossoms, crystal white and granular, is similar to American clover honey. It is reputed to be the world's oldest honey, having been mentioned by Julius Caesar in his dispatches home from Gaul. Scotch heather honey, dark and strong tasting, normally has a jellylike consistency and is a major ingredient of the liqueur Drambuie. Honey from wild thyme, gathered at Mount Hymmettus in Greece, is world famous. It has a resinous flavor.

Honey is marketed in three forms, comb honey, chunk honey and extracted honey. Comb honey is more or less straight from the hives, while chunk is bottled with small chunks of comb. The flavor and freshness of honey is at its best in these forms, and the chewiness imparted by the wax is relished too. Most honey sold in stores is extracted honey, i.e., liquid honey extracted from the comb by centrifuge. Much of the extracted honey has been heated, which tends to destroy some of its health-enhancing properties. Honey should be kept in a warm, dry place because it tends to absorb and retain moisture. Honey does not spoil, but if it absorbs too much moisture, it becomes thin and may ferment. Its tendency to retain moisture is considered an asset in the baking industry and in the tobacco industry, both of which use it too keep their goods fresh and moist. All pure honey crystallizes, or granulates, a condition preferred by some consumers. To return honey to a liquid state, place the jar of honey in a pan of water and heat it to a moderate temperature.

See also: **Bee Grub.**

HONEY AGARIC

See **Honey Mushroom.**

HONEY BALL MELON

This delicious, green-fleshed melon of the inodorus group *(Cucumis melo inodorus)* is closely related to the winter, honeydew and casaba melons. It is round, lightly netted or smooth and may have a white, green, gray or yellow skin.

See also: **Muskmelon.**

HONEYBERRY

See **Ginep.**

HONEYDEW

See **Nanna.**

HONEYDEW MELON

See **Muskmelon.**

HONEY FUNGUS

See **Honey Mushroom.**

HONEY MUSHROOM

Also CHIODINI, FUNGHI, HONEY AGARIC, HONEY FUNGUS. A fleshy, edible mushroom that grows prolifically in the woodlands of Europe, the British Isles and North America, honey mushroom *(Armillariella mellea)* resembles the king **bolete** but is apricot-yellow in color. It is usually found on stumps or at the base of living trees, on which it is a destructive parasite. It is harvested by the bushel and often pickled for later enjoyment. On the other hand, it is frequently shunned by amateur mushroomers because of the difficulty in distinguishing it from the poisonous *Galerina* mushrooms, which also grow on wood and have a similar appearance.

The honey mushroom is held in particularly high esteem in Italy, and is sold canned in Italo-American neighborhoods. They prefer this mushroom at the button stage. When raw, it is slightly bitter, but when cooked, it rivals the bolete and the morel for flavor.

The honey mushroom fruits in summer, autumn and early winter. The height of the plant averages six inches, and the cap reaches six inches in diameter.

See also: **Mushroom.**

HONEYWARE

See **Badderlocks.**

HONEY WINE

See **Mead.**

HOP CHEESE

Also HOPFEN. This small German cheese is cured with hops, hence the name. It shares this distinction with **Nieheimer,** and although both are prepared from sour milk, they are not identical. For curing, the fresh curd is spiced with caraway seeds, mixed with ripened curd and molded into small cheeses that when dry, are packed in casks between layers of hops.

HOPFEN

See **Hop Cheese.**

HOPS

The conelike clusters of flowers of the female hop plant *(Humulus lupulus)* are used to flavor beer and help preserve it. In some places, the tender, spring shoots of the hop—they resemble asparagus tips—are eaten raw in salads or boiled like asparagus.

Hop is a common plant in the temperate areas of the world, growing wild in Europe, England and the United States. It has perennial roots that grow new tops each year in the form of climbing vines that can reach a length of 25 feet. Male and female plants are separate, fertilization being effected by airborne pollen. On blooming, the clusters of female flowers are dotted with yellow, resinous glands, which contain the active ingredients *lupulin* and *humulone.* These resins impart the pleasantly bitter taste to beers and ales, act as an antiseptic by retarding wild bacteria growth and help the brew retain a head of foam. Some other effects may not be so desirable. According to F. Bianchini in *The Complete Book of Fruits and Vegetables:*

> *The hop has an estrogenic action, feminizing and anaphrodisiac, so that, besides serving as a sedative, it is believed by some to be the cause of the disorders (obesity, sterility, hepatic degeneration) afflicting hard beer-drinkers.*

It is not clear when hops came into general use as a beer ingredient. According to the old rhyme,

> *Hops, Reformation, Bays and Beer*
> *Came into England all in one year.*

The year in question was 1518, but hops were definitely present in England as early as as the 8th century in *humularia,* hop gardens. Most authorities place the introduction of hops into beer in the 14th century, which might make the rhyme right for the first *commercial* crop in England.

The eating of hop shoots is practically unknown today in England and the United States, yet not too unusual on the European continent. They are available in markets in Belgium, where creamed hop shoots is a popular side dish. They are also enjoyed with poached eggs and omelettes. In Germany, near Lake Constance, hop shoots are served with melted butter or whipped cream and a squeeze of lemon juice. Two centuries ago in England, a hop sauce was made by boiling the buds and mixing the result with melted butter. It was poured over fish, chicken and boiled mutton. In former times, hops were believed to be helpful in inducing sleep. Pillows stuffed with hop leaves were recommended to insomniacs.

HORCHATA

This popular Spanish soft drink is made sometimes from **chufas,** and sometimes from a kind of almond syrup called **orgeat** in France. *Chufas* are the small tubers of a type of reed, *Cyperus esculentus.* They have a slight gingery flavor and were once widely used as a spice in Europe. *Chufas* are still a commercial crop in Spain. The term *orgeat* refers both to the beverage and to the syrup, which used to be made of barley but now consists of almond essence, sugar and sometimes orange-flower water.

HOREHOUND

An aromatic but bitter herb of the mint family, horehound *(Marribium vulgare)* has been used for centuries as a flavoring and as a medicine. Its modern uses have been pretty much reduced to two: as the essential ingredient in cough drops or sore-throat lozenges, and as a flavoring in a candy of the same name. Yet, some cooks find its leaves a welcome occasional substitute for bay leaf in flavoring soups, stews and sauces.

HORSE

The meat of this familiar quadriped, *Equus caballus,* is nutritious and tasty yet not much used as human food, except in France and Belgium. Traditionally in France, horsemeat has been sold through special butcher shops, which display a golden horse's head over the door.

The meat is brighter red in color than beef but is similar in texture and protein content. The taste differs in that there is a definite sweetness not present in beef. It may be that horsemeat is healthier than beef or pork, because the horse is not subject to tuberculosis like beef, nor tapeworm like hogs.

The French partiality for horsemeat had its origin in the Napoleonic wars, although before then it had been eaten in times of famine. After the battle of Eylau in 1807, the surgeon general of the Army, Baron Larray, together with the battle casualties, was cut off from supplies and stranded on the Isle of Lobau. There were plenty of freshly killed horses on the battlefield, so for lack of anything better, he fed the sick and wounded roast horse seasoned with gunpowder. The troops ate it with gusto and seemed to thrive on it. As a result of this experience, Baron Larray became an enthusiast, and after the wars, campaigned for its acceptance as a regular part of the diet. He was joined in this campaign by the eminent agronomist Antoine-Auguste Parmentier, who had already popularized the potato. It gained wide acceptance and became an item of daily consumption.

The popularity of horsemeat in France peaked in the early 1960s when per capita consumption came to about five pounds a year. By 1972, that figure had declined to 3¾ pounds. Part of the decline was due to the wide publicity given an outbreak of food poisoning, which was traced to chopped horsemeat. Contrary to law, a butcher had been adding old, tainted scraps of meat to the fresh meat he was grinding for customers. This resulted in the salmonella contamination, which causes a virulent gastroenteritis. One person died and others were hospitalized. Although other foods are susceptible to salmonella contamination—particularly poultry—horsemeat bore the brunt of the bad publicity.

A hippophagic society was formed in London in the 17th century to popularize the eating of horsemeat. Also, during both world wars, horsemeat was made available in special shops on a ration-free basis. Neither effort made much headway in getting the British public to accept horsemeat. For Jews horsemeat is not kosher. In the United States, it has achieved acceptance only as pet food. There is an ancient Christian taboo on horsemeat, which, according to one account, had its origin in a pagan "horse feast" celebrated in October by ancient Danes and Saxons. The early Church was unable to work this feast into its calendar, as it had other pagan festivals at Christmas and Easter, so the festival was banned, and the taboo stuck on horseflesh.

Horsemeat is eaten in steaks, roasts or mixed with other meat in sausages. The French are fond of eating ground horsemeat raw, seasoned with onions or garlic or very lightly cooked.

See also: **Donkey, Mule.**

HORSE BEAN

Also JACK BEAN, SWORD BEAN. These terms are used indiscriminately for two species of tropical legume, *Canavalia ensiformis* and *C. gladiata.* However, *C. ensiformis,* the jack bean, does not have a climbing habit, while *C. gladiata,* the sword bean, does. Both produce pods up to 14 inches long, which are broad and swordlike. They contain up to a dozen large seeds that are white in the case of the jack bean, and usually dark red, pink or brown in the case of the sword bean.

These plants are grown mainly as green manure or fodder crops, yet both the young pods and the mature seeds can be cooked and eaten. Caution is advised regarding *C. ensiformis*, since the fresh, immature seeds of some varieties are poisonous. Its cultivation is limited to tropical America, while *C. gladiata* is grown in Asia.

Horse bean is also an alternative name for the Windsor or **broad bean.**

HORSE CHESTNUT

See **Buckeye.**

HORSE MACKEREL

The name is used for several different species of fish including the **cavalla** *(Carangus hippos)*, the **tuna fish** and the saurel or scad *(Trachurus trachurus)*. This last is a small fish of the eastern Atlantic, Mediterranean and Black Sea. It has a blue gray top, silvery sides and white belly. The saurel is used for food in the Mediterranean and off the South African coast where, under the name *maasbanker*, it is caught in large numbers and eaten fresh, canned or smoked. It seldom exceeds 16 inches in length and is, therefore, not much of a game fish.

T. symmetricus, a close relative, is sometimes called horse mackerel, but it is best considered under **Jack Mackerel.**

HORSE MUSHROOM

This close relative of the **field mushroom** is similar in appearance but larger. The two often grow together, and the horse mushroom *(Agaricus arvensis)* can be distinguished by its double ring or collar on the stem. Larger specimens can measure eight inches in length and eight inches across the cap. This mushroom is associated with pastures, especially if horses have grazed there. The cap is white, turning yellowish with age, and the stem white. The flesh is white too but stains brownish yellow when cut.

The horse mushroom is sometimes confused with the poisonous (to some) yellow-staining mushroom *(A. Xanthoderma)*, but may be distinguished from the latter by its faint smell of aniseed. It has a strong but pleasant taste and is considered almost as desirable as the field mushroom. Its flesh is coarser, however.

See also: **Mushroom.**

HORSE PARSLEY

See **Alexanders.**

HORSERADISH

Horseradish *(Armoracia rusticana)* is a member of the mustard family cultivated for its peppery root, which may attain a length of 18 inches and a diameter of 1½ inches. It is a native of eastern Europe and the Orient, but it is also popular in the Alpine regions, Britain and the United States.

It may be eaten raw, grated or slivered as an accompaniment to roast beef or steak. It is excellent with seafood when mixed into a savory sauce. It is often mixed half-and-half with mustard to add a spicy tang.

HORSERADISH TREE

The leaves and roots of this tropical African and Asian tree *(Moringa pterygosperma)* are pungent; their taste is compared to that of horseradish. They are chopped up and mixed with water or milk to make a sauce for meat thought to aid digestion. The seed pods, which reach a length of 18 inches, can be eaten as a green vegetables. They are sometimes called "drumsticks." The horseradish tree has been naturalized and widely cultivated in other tropical areas.

HORSESHOE CRAB

See **King Crab.**

HOSPICE DE BEAUNE WINE

This great dry red (and some white) wine comes from the vineyards of Hospice de Beaune in Burgundy, in the Cote de Beaune in eastern France. Vineyards in this area cover 130 acres and include the growths of Corton-Charlemagne and **Meursault** for white wines and those of **Aloxe-Corton,** Beaune, **Pommard** and **Volnay** for the famous reds.

See also: **Beaune; Burgundy Wines; Wines, French.**

HOT DOG

See **Frankfurter.**

HOTTENTOT FIG

This edible fruit of a perennial succulent shrub, *Carpobrotus edulis*, is native to the Cape Province of South Africa. The fruit has 10 to 15 cells.

HOUTING

Also GWYNIAD. A European whitefish, *Coregonus lavaretus,* found from the British Isles across Europe and Russia to Siberia, it has a herringlike appearance and is closely related to the ***fera*** and the American lake **cisco.** It is essentially a freshwater fish, preferring large lakes, but there are saltwater and migratory varieties. The houting is known by various local names, such as the *gwyniad* in Wales, the *powan* in Scotland, and the skelly or schelly in the English Lake District. The houting is an excellent food fish and is usually fried, broiled or baked. It is widely bred and stocked in eastern Europe and the USSR.

See also: **Whitefish.**

HOWLER MONKEY

The howler monkey *(Alouatta belzebub)* is the largest New World monkey. Its flesh is eaten, but it is not considered as good as **spider monkey.** The howler monkey is found in forested tropical areas from Veracruz, Mexico southward to Guayaquil, Ecuador and east of the Andes through Bolivia, Brazil and Paraguay. It can be up to three feet long and weigh 20 pounds. The name derives from its ability to howl so loudly that it can be heard two to three miles away.

HUAUZONCLE

See **Good King Henry.**

HUCHEN

See **Huck.**

HUCK

Also HUCHEN. This large fish of the salmon family, *Hucho hucho,* is found only in the Danube River and some of its tributaries as well as in lakes within the system. Pollution has reduced it to a rarity nowadays, but it is considered very good eating and an angler's delight. The huck possesses good fighting qualities in addition to its generous size, which ranges up to five feet in length and 114 pounds in weight. Thirty-five pounds is deemed a good weight these days. It is prepared like **salmon.**

HUCKLEBERRY

The name applies to any of a number of native American blue or black berries that belong to the *Gaylussacia* genus and are gathered wild. The huckleberry much resembles the blueberry and, popularly, many people use the name "huckleberry" for wild varieties (be they huckleberry or blueberry) and "blueberry" for cultivated varieties. There are a number of differences, though. Blueberries belong to the *Vaccinium* genus and they are generally larger and sweeter than huckleberries. Blueberries are cultivated, while huckleberries are not; and a huckleberry has ten large, gritty seeds, while the blueberry has many tiny ones.

The huckleberry is used for making tarts, pies, preserves and syrups and, in the summer, is available in markets in the Northeast, South and Northwest. Of huckleberries and blueberries available in markets, Henry David Thoreau, American naturalist, philosopher and writer, had this to say:

> *The fruits do not yield their true flavor to the purchaser of them, nor to him who raises them for the market. There is but one way to obtain it, yet few take that way. If you would know the flavor of huckleberries, ask the cowboy or the partridge. It is vulgar error to suppose that you have tasted huckleberries who never plucked them. A huckleberry never reaches Boston; they have not been known there since they grew on her three hills. The ambrosial and essential part of the fruit is lost with the bloom which is rubbed off in the market cart, and they become mere provender. As long as eternal justice reigns, not one innocent huckleberry can be transported thither from the country's hills.*

See also: **Blueberry.**

HUITLACOCHE

See **Cuitlocoche.**

HUMAN FLESH

Also CANNIBALISM. There are two sorts of cannibalism. The first, survival cannibalism, is resorted to in the face of extreme deprivation. Examples of this sort are found in all cultures, and they are regarded with extreme repugnance, even by the perpetrators. Americans are familiar with the plight of the Donner party, a group of 10 men and five women snow-bound in the Sierra Nevada en route to California in the winter of 1846/47. They were trapped in what is still called the Donner Pass for nearly a month, and during that time the seven who eventually survived dined off the flesh of four white men of the party, who died in a snowstorm, and of two Indians who were shot for the purpose.

The second sort of cannibalism might be called customary cannibalism, i.e., a cultural or ethnic group eats human flesh as a settled practice, either for ritual purposes, or because the members like it. These people willingly violate what must be regarded as a universal taboo. While the first have merely gone through a harrowing experience and survived as best they could, the second stand out as true savages.

The literature of history, anthropology and archeology is replete with examples of customary cannibalism.

Classic examples from archaeology include most species of early humans such as *Australopithicus*, *Homo erectus*, Neanderthal man, Java man, Peking man and Cro-Magnon man. Conclusions of cannibalism are based on the broken condition of bones and their presence in caves used for living quarters or in underground ovens. The Western Hemisphere also yielded similar evidence. James Trager, author of *The Food Book*, writes:

> *Fossil bones believed to be the oldest remains of man ever found in the Western Hemisphere were unearthed by a bulldozer in the State of Washington in the spring of 1968. The bones, those of a young pre-Indian nomad, date back between 11,500 and 13,000 years. They indicate the man's enemies or fellow tribesmen split his bones to eat the marrow, just as they did with animal bones.*

From history, the Caribs must be considered a classic example, if only because our word "cannibal" is derived from their name, which was corrupted from *Caribal* to *canibal.* Their shocking practices were reported to Europe by none other than Christopher Columbus who encountered them on Hispaniola during his first voyage to the New World in 1492. It should be noted that he was not an eye-witness to cannibalism, but merely repeated what he had been told by their close neighbors (and enemies) the Arawaks.

When the Spaniards invaded mainland Mexico, their chief adversaries, the Aztecs, were accused of cannibalism. The Aztec practice of ritual human sacrifice is well supported by evidence, but the charge of cannibalism is not. None of the chroniclers of the Conquest witnessed cannibalism; rather, they relied on reports from other (non-Aztec) tribes, or merely leaped to the conclusion that human sacrifice went hand in hand with cannibalism.

In the 17th century, reports of cannibalism focused on the Upper Congo where war prisoners were fattened for the table, and woman children were bought and sold for food. During the 18th century, interest switched to the South Pacific where Fiji chiefs were alleged to dine on human flesh, and where on the island of New Britain human flesh was said to be sold from butcher stalls. Nineteenth-century colonization again focused attention on Africa where the Azande of Central, and the Mende of West Africa were said to practice ritual cannibalism. In the 20th century, reports of cannibalism have been pretty much confined to New Guinea, the last frontier, as it were.

W. Arens, a professor of anthropology at the State University of New York at Stony Brook, recently (1979) conducted a review of the literature on cannibalism and was disturbed by one fact: as regards customary cannibalism, *there are no eyewitness reports.* This statement applies to the whole corpus of historical and anthropological literature. Somewhat shaken, Professor Arens advertised in professional journals for contemporary eyewitness accounts. He received none; instead, he received a query from a German graduate student who, having decided to do his dissertation on cannibalism in the Amazon, couldn't produce a single first-hand account of the act itself.

In his carefully written and completely absorbing study, *The Man-Eating Myth*, Professor Arens presents his conclusions. He teeters on the brink of stating that customary cannibalism does not exist, and has never existed, but stops short, reflecting that it is nearly impossible to prove a negative. Instead, he writes:

> *Although the theoretical possibility of customary cannibalism cannot be dismissed, the available evidence does not permit the facile assumption that the act was or has ever been a prevalent cultural feature. It is more reasonable to conclude that the idea of the cannibalistic nature of others is a myth in the sense of, first, having an independent existence bearing no relationship to historical reality, and, second, containing and transmitting significant cultural messages for those who maintain it.*

What then of modern anthropology which, according

to Professor Arens, unquestioningly accepts the existence of customary cannibalism?

> *The misguided notions about the savage mode of life have fallen, one by one, against the onslaught of [social anthropology's] techniques, but the cannibal remains inviolate, never to be seen or forgotten. In a sense, social anthropologists of all persuasions have had to avoid applying their own lessons to the study of their own discipline for the purpose of maintaining a crude cultural opposition between "we" and "they." As a consequence, the general tone of modern anthropological commentary on cannibalism emerges as little more than 19th century reinterpretations in contemporary scientific jargon.*

HUMBLE PIE

See **Umbles.**

HUMPBACK WHITEFISH

Also GREAT LAKES HERRING, LAKE WHITEFISH. This is the common whitefish *(Coregonus clupeaformis)* of North America. It is an important and popular food fish and is found from the Bering Straits to Labrador and south to the Great Lakes. The humpback whitefish has a conical head, an elongated, heavy and flat-sided body, and a thick, projecting upper lip. It looks a lot like a herring and reaches a maximum weight of about 42 pounds, although the average fish weighs from two to five pounds. Its coloring is bluish olive on the back with silvery sides.

The flesh of the humpback whitefish is sweet and white and may be prepared like bass, flounder or pike. It is delicious smoked and is used as an hors d'oeuvre on canapes or as sandwich filling. Its roe is dyed black and used as a caviar substitute.

See also: **Whitefish, Fera.**

HUNDRED-YEAR-OLD EGG

See **Preserved Egg.**

HUSK TOMATO

See **Ground Cherry.**

HUTIA

Also JUTIA. *Hutia* is a ratlike rodent *(Capromys* species) found on certain islands of the Caribbean Sea. Three species inhabit Cuba where they are well regarded as food. Cubans hunt them with the help of dogs who chase them up trees and hold them at bay until the hunter arrives. A large adult *hutia* reaches a length of about 12 inches and weighs up to 15 pounds. The *hutia* is covered with coarse fur that ranges in color from gray to reddish brown to black. It subsists on a diet of fruit, leaves, bark lizards and small animals. The predominant species is *C. pilordes.*

A larger species, *Geocapromys brownii*, is found on Jamaica and the Bahamas. At one time it was an important food species, and people hunted it with dogs. Today it is rare and is protected legally.

HVID GJETOST

A Norwegian goat's-milk cheese resembling **Gjetost** but stronger and meant for local consumption, it is pressed into rectangles measuring nine by six by four inches.

HYDROMEL

This mixture of honey and water was used as a beverage by ancient Greeks and Romans. If allowed to ferment, the mixture becomes **mead,** a honey wine.

HYSON TEA

A Chinese green tea named for an East Indian merchant who first imported it, Hyson is made from the hard, twisted older leaves. It has a blue color, yet the brew is fragrant, light and mellow. The Chinese term for it, *hsi-ch'un*, means "blooming spring."

See also: **Tea.**

HYSSOP

An herb of the mint family, hyssop *(Hyssopus officinalis)* is often mentioned in the Bible, but experts say that that was a different plant altogether. This is highly aromatic and has a hot, bitter taste. Plants average two feet in height with blue, white or pink flowers. It is native to southern Europe and Asia but has been naturalized in the United States and the British Isles.

It was revered by earlier generations for its religious and medicinal as well as its culinary values. Hyssop tea, for example, was thought to be good for the complexion. Also, hyssop was dubbed the "holy herb" and used in purification rites.

In recent times its popularity has waned. It is a standard ingredient in some French liqueurs and a seasoning in some sausages. Hyssop can add zest to soups, stews and salads but must be used sparingly.

HYSTRIX

An edible citrus fruit, *Citrus hystrix*, of the Philippine Islands, it resembles the lemon.

I

IBURUA MILLET

Here is an African plant, *Digitaria iburua*, of the crabgrass genus whose seeds are sometimes used as a cereal grain.

ICACO

See **Coco Plum.**

ICE

See **Ice Cream, Preservation of Food.**

ICE CREAM

Also SHERBET, WATER ICE. Ice cream is a frozen confection usually, but not necessarily, based on a dairy product. In the broad sense, the term extends from French ice cream, which has a rich milk, egg and cream base, through French custard, ice milk, "frozen dairy confection" and "dietary frozen dairy dessert," to such things as sherbets, water ices and mellorine, an imitation ice cream based on other animal fats or vegetable oil.

The Chinese invented ice cream in the form of the fruit-flavored water ice sometime before the 14th century A.D. when Marco Polo, the enterprising Venetian, paid a visit to China. According to tradition, he brought the recipe back to Italy, which took to the new delicacy with gusto. At this time, or perhaps earlier, the Chinese also taught the Indians and the Arabs to make water ices, which they called *sherbets*. Catherine de Medici, who became queen of France in the 16th century, brought with her a chef who delighted the French court with his iced confections. But it wasn't until the mid-17th century that water ices became an item of popular consumption in Paris. A Sicilian named Procopio opened the Cafe Procope in 1660 at the Rue des Fosses-Saint-Germain-des-Pres where he sold water ices and ice creams in various flavors. The novelty was quickly accepted, and within 16 years he had more than 250 competitors among the *limonadiers* of Paris. By the end of the next century the *bombe glacee* (ice cream molded in spherical shape) had become the indispensable dessert at formal French banquets. The industry grew and prospered under Napoleons I, II and III. Ice cream bases became richer and more refined and were molded into elaborate shapes. In the meantime, Italian ice cream developed apace, Signori Pratti and Tortoni achieving a worldwide reputation for the delicacy of their ices.

American luminaries of the Revolutionary period appreciated ice cream. Thomas Jefferson brought back a recipe from France that made use of the pot freezer in which the ingredients were first beaten by hand, then shaken up and down in a pan of ice and salt until frozen. In 1784 George Washington made an entry in his account book about "a cream machine for making ice," and both Mrs. Alexander Hamilton and Dolly Madison helped popularize ice cream in high political circles. In 1846 America made its first contribution to ice cream technology when Nancy Johnson invented the portable, hand-cranked freezer. An Italian immigrant, Giovanni Bosio, began to sell Italian ices to the public, and in 1851 Jacob Fussel set up the first wholesale ice-cream business in Baltimore. Later American creations included the ice cream soda (Philadelphia, 1874) and the ice cream cone (St. Louis fair of 1904).

In the 20th century, ice-cream making has developed into a highly automated, highly competitive industry. A typical product may contain any or all of the following ingredients: milk fat, nonfat milk solids or other milk-derived substances, sugars, corn syrup, water, flavoring, egg products, stabilizers and emulsifiers, plus a generous amount of air. Just which of these goes into a product, and in what proportion, are regulated by the U.S. government in its Federal Frozen Dessert Standards of Identity. Minimum standards require that a gallon of ice cream weigh at least 4.5 pounds, contain not less than 10 percent milk fat and 2.7 percent protein and have at least 1.6 pounds of food solids per gallon. In practice the average trade brand by weight is 12 percent fat, 11 percent milk solids (nonfat), 15 percent sugar and 0.3 percent vegetable gum stabilizer.

Annual production of ice cream in the United States amounts to about 15 quarts a year per person, or, adding in all the other related products, 23 quarts a year per person. Following are some frequently encountered terms related to ice cream:

Baked alaska: Sponge cake is filled in the center with ice cream, covered on the top and sides with a layer of meringue and then browned in a hot oven. Insulated by the meringue, the ice cream does not melt, and the whole is served hot from the oven. The French term is *omelette a la norvegienne.*

Cassata: A molded ice cream from Naples that is filled with layers of diced fruit and nuts or macaroons.

Coupe glacee: The French version of the ice cream sundae (see below). Served in a stemmed glass or silver cup, it consists of liqueur-soaked fruit, one or two scoops of ice cream, plus a topping of creme chantilly or candied fruit.

Dietary frozen dairy dessert: A low-calorie product made in the United States with certain minimum standards specified by law, including less than 2 percent milk fat, at least 7 percent milk solids by weight, at least 1.1 pounds of food solids per gallon and a minimum weight of 4.5 pounds per gallon.

French ice cream: A rich, solid type of ice cream that has a higher fat content and deeper color than the average trade variety. It is made from a sweet custard base with egg yolks and cream.

French custard: A product similar to French ice cream but usually sold as a soft-serve item. By law it must contain at least 1.4 percent egg yolk solids for plain flavor and 1.12 percent for bulky flavors.

Frozen dairy confection: The generic term for ice cream bars on sticks, ice cream sandwiches, popsicles, etc., which are made in individual servings.

Gelato (plural: *gelati):* The Italian word for ice cream.

Glace: French for ice cream.

Granita: Italian for water ice (see below).

Ice milk: A product quite similar to ice cream that satisfies all the legal requirements of ice cream mentioned above with these exceptions: it must contain between 2 and 7 percent milk fat, at least 2.7 percent protein and not less than 1.3 pounds of food solids per gallon.

Melba: A dessert named after Nellie Melba, a famous Australian opera singer. It consists of vanilla ice cream served with a ripe peach that has been poached in vanilla syrup and the whole topped with raspberry puree.

Mellorine: An imitation ice cream which, though made like ice cream, is not limited to milk fats and solids, but may incorporate fats from other animals or from vegetables. It must, however, have at least 6 percent fat, and 2.7 percent protein.

Neapolitan: Three-flavored ice cream—usually vanilla, chocolate and strawberry—arranged in layers and sold in brick form.

Parfait: A soft ice-cream dessert served in a tall glass. It may be flavored with fruit or a liqueur or topped with a syrup.

Philadelphia ice cream: A soft, smooth ice cream made of thin cream, or milk and cream and no eggs.

Popsicle: A frozen dairy confection (see above) of the water ice variety, sold in many flavors.

Sherbet: Closer to a water ice than ice cream, it contains a small amount of milk products. Sherbet is usually made in fruit flavors and in the United States must weigh at least six pounds per gallon and contain 0.35 percent edible citric or natural fruit acid.

Soda: A beverage consisting of a scoop or two of ice cream, a flavoring agent and carbonated water. Its invention is attributed to Elias Durand, who owned a drugstore in Philadelphia in 1825, the year carbonated water came on the market.

Soft-frozen dairy products: This category includes the French custard mentioned above, but three-fourths of the total sold is accounted for by ice milk. It is drawn from a mixing/freezing machine at a temperature of 18 to 20 degrees F. (−7.8° to −6.7°C) and sold directly to the customer.

Sorbet: French for water ice (see below) or sherbet (see above).

Spumoni: An Italian ice cream or sherbet that, like Neopolitan, incorporates more than one flavor and is filled with chopped nuts and candied fruit.

Sundae: A dish of ice cream topped with fruit, syrup or a sauce and usually garnished with chopped nut and whipped cream. An American invention, the sundae has given rise to numerous and fantastic variations.

Water ice: The original ice cream, it is made of fruit juice, sugar and water. Sometimes egg white is added as a thickener, binder and stabilizer. It is not to be confused with sherbet, which contains milk products. It is believed to have been made by the Chinese as early as the eighth century A.D.

ICE FISH

This term is most often used for the **capelin,** but it also applies to the *Chamsocephalus esox*, which inhabits the waters off Patagonia, the Falkland Islands and the Straits of Magellan. It reaches a length of about 14 inches and is considered a good food fish. Its overall coloring is light brown with flecks of black and iridescent purple on its back. The ice fish is called pike where it is caught. It is the only member of its family *Channichthyidae* occurring outside the antarctic area.

ICELAND MOSS

A type of lichen, *Cetraria islandica*, found in Norway, Iceland and Arctic regions, it can be ground into a flour and used to make bread, mixed with wheat flour or consumed by itself. It is filling but not particularly nutritious and can be readily made into a soothing infusion for medicinal use. It readily yields a gelatin as well.

ICE MILK

See **Ice Cream.**

ICE PLANT

A succulent plant, *Mesenbryanthemum crystallinum*, native to southwestern Africa and the Cape Province of South Africa, it has been naturalized in the Mediterranean area, the Canary Islands and California. It is often cultivated as ground cover or soil binder. The leaves may be eaten like spinach or in salads.

IDE

Also ORFE. This freshwater fish, *Leuciscus idus*, of eastern Europe and Russian Asia, is closely related to the **chub** and the **dace.** In addition to being a valuable commercial fish, the *ide* is quite ornamental and is stocked in garden ponds and park lakes. It has a overall golden color. The *ide* attains a maximum length of about two feet and lives mainly in rivers and large lakes. Its flesh is said to be very tasty. Extensive commercial fishing of the *ide* is carried on in eastern Europe and the USSR.

IGARA GLADIOLUS

The short, fleshy underground stems of this African species of gladiolus *(Gladiolus quartinianus)* are used to make a cooling beverage. The plant is characterized by its blood-red to pale yellow flowers.

IGNAME

See **Chinese Yam.**

IGUANA

A large lizard with a number of species in North, Central and South America, it was one of the first native foods encountered by Christopher Columbus in Cuba. In the West Indies and South America it sometimes reaches a length of five feet. The iguana dwells in trees, dunes and rocky coastlines. Eaters at both ends of the economic spectrum appreciate iguana meat, i.e., common folk and gourmets. As for the great mass of people in the middle who have never eaten lizard, one writer suggests that the iguana would seem more palatable if one thought of it as a turtle without a shell. According to best authority, however, iguana meat more resembles chicken than turtle.

In preparation, the animal is skinned and eviscerated, then roasted or barbecued over charcoal. The meat is white, tender and appetizing. In French Guiana, iguana is prepared *a la Provence*, although there are no iguanas in Provence. In some places, iguana eggs are considered a delicacy; they are dried, pickled or fried.

In Mexico and the American Southwest, the pygmy iguana *(Dipsosaurus dorsalis dorsalis)* is the preferred food species. It rarely exceeds a foot in length and is commonly eaten in Mexico. There are species of iguana in the Fiji Islands and Madagascar that most resemble the larger Central and South American varieties.

ILAMA

Also ANONA BLANCA. A small tree, *Annona diversifolia* of Mexico and Central America whose fruit resembles the cherimoya, ilama is of the same genus as cherimoya and grows in lowland tropics. The fruit has very tender, pale green or pink skin, which may be smooth or knobby. It is usually round or slightly oblong and six inches long. The fruit is often cultivated and has a fine flavor.

ILHA

The name means "island," referring to the Azores, where this cheese is made for export to Portugal. It is a firm cow's-milk cheese like ripe cheddar, shaped in wheels that are four inches thick and 10 to 12 inches across.

IL PESTO

One of the most distinguished of Italian sauces and a specialty of Genoa, it consists of basil, garlic, grated Parmesan or *pecorino sardo* cheese, pine nuts and olive oil. This mixture is beaten to the consistence of creamed butter and served with pasta, minestrone or baked potatoes.

IMPERIAL TEA

This Chinese green tea has leaves that, like **gunpowder tea,** are rolled into pellets. Its leaves are older and therefore larger than the latter's. It is a fine quality tea, brewing a cup somewhat less pungent than gunpowder.

See also: **Tea.**

IMPEYAN

Here is a type of pheasant, *Lophophorus impeyanus*, found in the cooler regions of India. The male is distinguished by its crested head and spangled, iridescent plumage. It is said to have excellent flavor.

INCANESTRATO

This is a Sicilian cheese whose curd is pressed into wicker molds. These leave a basketlike imprint on the surface, earning it the name *incanestrato*, which means "basketed." It has a plastic curd (see **Formaggio di Pasta Filata)** and is usually made from a mixture of ewe's milk and cow's milk. If from ewe's milk alone, it bears the adjective ***pecorino.*** *Pepato* is a variety spiced with pepper, which is just one of many spices that may be added. *Incanestrato* is also made in the United States, usually by the **Romano** process. A Messina version, containing olive oil, is called *majocchino.*

INCA WHEAT

Also QUIHUICHA, LOVE-LIES-BLEEDING, TASSELFLOWER. A tropical annual herb, *Amaranthus caudatus,* whose leaves and seeds are edible, it is much cultivated in India as a food plant and was highly esteemed as such by the Incas of pre-Columbian Ecuador, Peru and Bolivia.

The leaves are eaten in salads or boiled as a potherb. The seeds are ground into flour and used for breadmaking. Inca wheat is still grown extensively in South America and prefers elevated tropical areas but can be grown as a summer crop in temperate regions.

INCONNU

Also NELMA. This is a large whitefish, *Stenodus leucichthys*, found in the USSR and the arctic regions of North America. The Russian species *(S. Leucichthys leucichthys)* inhabits the Caspian Sea and associated rivers, particularly the Volga and Ural. It mounts these rivers to spawn and is usually netted during migration. The *inconnu* is an extremely important food fish in that region due to its abundance and large size. A large fish may attain a length of up to five feet and weigh as much as 88 pounds.

The North American species *(S. l. nelma)* frequents the muddy rivers and lakes of the Arctic Circle. Nonmigratory varieties are found in lakes a little farther south but not below northern Canada. Like other whitefish, its flesh is very good eating. The fish's name means "unknown" in French and is attributed to the fact that, since the fish did not occur in warmer regions, it was unknown to early French explorers.

INDIAN ALMOND

See **Myrobalan.**

INDIAN ARTICHOKE

See **Ipomea.**

INDIAN BREADROOT

See **Breadroot.**

INDIAN BUTTER TREE

See **Mahwa.**

INDIAN CORN

See **Corn.**

INDIAN CRESS

See **Nasturtium.**

INDIAN CUCUMBER

The thick, white rootstock of this perennial herb of North America is edible. Indian cucumber *(Medeola virginica)* is found from Nova Scotia to Minnesota and south to Florida, Alabama and Louisiana. The texture of its rhizome is crisp and its taste reminiscent of cucumber.

INDIAN FIG

See **Prickly Pear.**

INDIAN KALE

Also PRIMROSE MALANGA, SPOON FLOWER. A type of **yautia** native to Colombia, Indian kale *(Xanthosoma lindenii)* has edible tubers and large arrow-shaped leaves that can be chopped up and boiled like spinach.

INDIAN MUSTARD

Also LEAF MUSTARD, MUSTARD GREENS. The type of mustard most commonly cultivated for its green leaves, Indian mustard *(Brassica juncea)* is indigenous to both Europe and Asia and has been introduced to North America where it grows spontaneously as a weed. After being cooked, the leaves are eaten like spinach.

INDIAN POTATO

See **Ground Nut.**

INDIAN SORREL

See **Roselle.**

INDIAN SPINACH

See **Basella.**

INDIAN SUGAR TREE

This tree of northern India, *Madhuca latifolia*, has flowers that are a good source of sugar. The nectar-rich blossoms are used to sweeten food and as a base for fermented liquors.

INDIAN SUNPLANT

A plant native to Southeast Asia whose fruits are eaten in India and Southeast Asia, Indian sunplant *(Solanum indicum)* is a member of the nightshade family.

INDIAN TROUT

A prime sportfish of the Indian hills, the Indian trout *(Barilius bola)* resembles a European trout but belongs to the carp family. It reaches a length of 12 inches, has a slender body, small scales, a pointed head, an olive green back and silvery sides with a pink tinge. *B. bola* is found in northeastern India in clear streams from the Punjab to Assam and Burma. It is a gallant fighter and is usually taken with a fly or spoon. It may be cooked like trout.

INDIAN TURNIP

See **Breadroot.**

INDIA WHEAT

Also TARTARY BUCKWHEAT. This variety of buckwheat *(Fagopyrum tataricum)* is indigenous to India and northern Asia. The seeds are ground for flour.

See also: **Buckwheat.**

INGAS

A genus of shrubby trees *(Inga* spp.) of tropical America, *Ingas* have pods that contain a sweet edible pulp surrounding inedible seeds. Edible species include the *huamuchil (I. dulcis)*, *cujin (I. reusoni)*, food *inga* or *guavobejuco (I. edulis)*, *guavo de Castilla (I. spectabilis)*, *guavo peludo (I. macuna)*, *guavo real (I. radians)*, *nacaspilo (I. spuria)*, *paterno (I. paterno)* and *toparejo (I. ruiziana)*.

INK CAP

Also INKY COPRINUS. This genus of edible mushrooms has the unusual characteristic of melting into black ink shortly after reaching maturity. The common ink cap *(Coprinus atramentarius)* is a chunky gray mushroom that grows in clumps in grass, around decaying trees and almost anywhere on dung heaps. It appears in spring and fall during cool, wet weather.

The flesh of the inky cap is tender and palatable but should be eaten as soon as possible before deterioration sets in. There is nothing sinister about this process, as it is the plant's method of releasing spores, and the mushroom is harmless, if unpalatable, in the inky state. Care should be taken, however, not to ingest alcoholic drinks after eating the common inky cap. A substance found in it, coprine, reacts with the alcohol to cause an Antabuse effect, i.e., nausea and vomiting, which may last up to two hours.

Another valuable species is the glistening coprinus *(C. micaceus)*, a small, brown mushroom that grows around stumps on buried wood in the spring and into the fall. It does not cause a reaction with alcohol. Neither species requires much cooking, and both are good prepared *au gratin.* They are common in North America and the British Isles.

See also: **Shaggy Mane** and **Mushroom.**

INKY COPRINUS

See **Ink Cap.**

IPOMEA

The name includes a large group of herbs and shrubs of the morning glory family *(Convolvulaceae)* that tend to climb and entwine. Both ivyleaf *(Ipomoea hederacea)* and the tall morning glory *(Ipomoea purpurea)* abound in the United States, where they are a serious pest in fields of soybean and corn, tying the plants together before harvest. By far the most important food crop in this family is the **sweet potato** *(Ipomoea batatas)*, a tropical vine with an edible root. The dark brown or black seeds of the morning glory are said to be mildly hallucinogenic.

IRISH BREAKFAST TEA

This medium-strong blend of black Indian and Ceylon teas seeks to balance pungent, malty types with full-flavored varieties.

See also: **Tea.**

IRISH MIST

Irish mist is the trade name for a liqueur based on a blend of Irish whiskeys sweetened with honey—from heather, clover and foxglove—and with the addition of several aromatic herbs. Irish Mist sold in the United States usually contains from 35 to 40 percent alcohol, is dark brown to gold and lacks the "smoky" taste of liqueurs based on Scotch whiskey, such as Drambuie.

IRISH MOSS

See **Carrageen.**

IRISH SODA BREAD

This is a white bread leavened with soda rather than yeast. The dough is moistened with buttermilk or sour milk, which reacts with the soda in the leavening process. Soda bread may be baked on a griddle or in an oven. The loaf is usually round, eight inches across and has a cross cut into the top to the depth of three-quarter inch. Soda bread is usually eaten warm. It is popular in Ireland.

See also: **Bread.**

ISARD

See **Chamois.**

ISIGNY

Isigny is an American cheese that looks like **Camembert,** but tastes rather like a mild **Limburger.** Named for a town in France, the small cheeses (five inches in diameter, one to two inches thick) are made in the Camembert way, except that the growth of the surface mold is checked by frequent washing.

ISINGLASS

A kind of gelatin obtained from fish, it is finer than other commercial **gelatin,** which comes from animal sources, and has been pretty much replaced for household use by cheaper products. It is made from the air bladders of certain fish, such as sturgeon and cod. When dry, it is a tough whitish substance.

Isinglass is still used in a winemaking process called fining, which clarifies the wine before bottling. Isinglass is mixed with a small quantity of wine, then introduced into the vat. It coagulates all foreign matter floating in the wine, and it slowly sinks to the bottom, bringing with it all the impurities. This is usually done twice, the process taking a week or two each time.

ISLAND OF ORLEANS CHEESE

Also FROMAGE RAFFINE DE L'ISLE D'ORLEANS. A soft Canadian cheese with a characteristic flavor much like piquant French cheeses of a similar consistency, it is made from whole cow's milk on an island in the St. Lawrence River below Quebec. It is cured in part by surface molds and yeasts and reaches its peak in about three weeks, after which it deteriorates rapidly.

ITALIAN MARROW

See **Zucchini.**

ITALIAN PASTE

See **Pasta.**

ITALIAN SWEET SAUSAGE

Also SALSICCIA DOLCE. This fresh pork sausage contains both lean and fat meat and is seasoned with coarse black pepper and herbs. The meat is not as finely ground as in American pork sausage, and the taste is much spicier from the pepper and, perhaps, from the coriander and fennel seeds.

Salsiccia dolce are short (three to four inches) and fat. They are usually grilled or broiled and served with stewed sweet peppers or bell peppers.

See also: **Sausage.**

IVY GOURD

See **Coccinea.**

IZARD

See **Chamois.**

IZARRA

A liqueur produced by the Basque people of the French Pyrenees, it has a brandy base and is flavored with herbs of the region, especially angelica. Two grades are produced: green, which is 100 proof; and yellow, which is 86 proof and sweeter.

J

JABOTICABA

This edible fruit of the Brazilian tree, *Myrciaria cauliflora*, grows best in the cool, moist southern part of the country. It is small, round and dark purple. *Jaboticaba* is highly regarded and much cultivated in Brazil but little-known elsewhere except in Hawaii. There are three other related species, including the *M. jaboticaba* or *jaboticaba do matto.*

JACK BEAN

See **Horse Bean.**

JACK CHEESE

See **Monterey Cheese.**

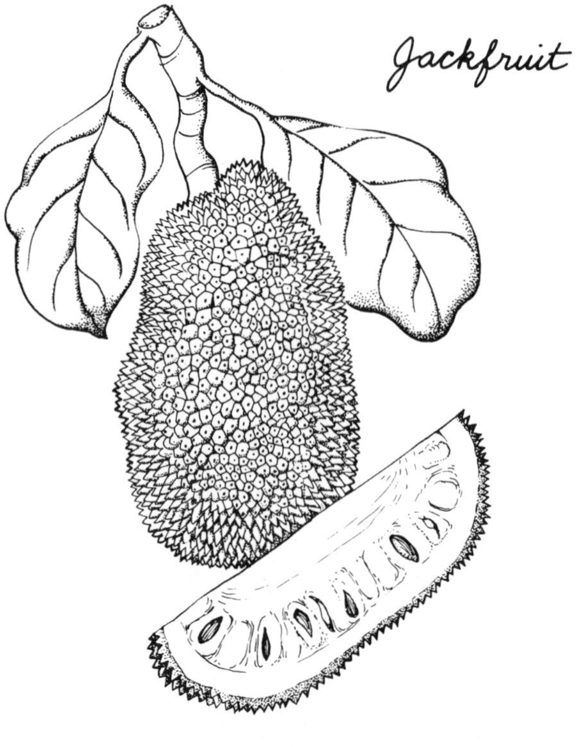

JACKFRUIT

Jackfruit grows on a large tree, *Artocarpus integrifolia*, of tropical Asia and the South Pacific islands. A member of the same genus as **breadfruit,** jackfruit is even larger than the latter, often attaining a weight of 40 to 50 pounds. The fruit is covered by a granulated, greenish skin and has an irregularly oblong or round shape. The coarse-textured pulp is yellow and contains a number of chestnut-sized seeds, which are also edible.

The pulp is sweet, but seems somewhat insipid to the Western palate. Locally, however, it is a staple and versatile food, eaten raw, boiled or fried, used in curries or pickled. Jackfruit is a particular favorite of elephants. *Chempedak* is a smaller species of jackfruit found in Malaya.

JACK MACKEREL

A Pacific Ocean fish, *Trachurus symmetricus* of the *Carangidae* family, jack mackerel closely resembles the mackerel, but it is quite a bit larger, reaching a length of 30 inches and a weight of five pounds. The jack mackerel is found from Baja California to British Columbia and is commercially exploited on a small scale. It is a surface feeder and a popular sport fish.

JACOPEVER

This South African redfish (family *Scorpaenidae)* reaches a length of about 16 inches. It is found in the South Atlantic as far west as Tristan da Cunha and is considered to be a moderately valuable commercial species. The *jacopever (Sebastichthys capensis)* may be prepared like red snapper.

JAGGERY

See **Palm Sugar.**

JAM AND JELLY

Basically, these are confections or spreads made from fruit and sugar. The distinction between the two is that jelly is made from the juice of the fruit, while jam utilizes the fruit itself. Preserves are a subcategory of jam in which the original shape of the fruit is retained, i.e., whole or cut fruit is preserved in a clear sugar syrup. What causes these products to "gel" is **pectin,** a natural constituent of many fruits. The proper amount of pectin (1 percent) boiled with the right concentration of acid (pH 3.1) and sugar (65 percent) produces the best jelly. Too much pectin produces a rigid gel, and too much sugar a sticky gel. If fruits low in pectin and acid are used—such as peaches, figs and pears—those constituents must be added, either by combining a fruit such as crabapple, which is high in them, or by adding commercially available pectin and acid.

U.S. law requires that jams and jellies consist of 45 parts of fruit juice (or solids) for every 55 parts sugar by weight. Fruit butter, on the other hand, contains five parts fruit ingredient for every two parts sugar. See also: **Marmalade.**

Fruits with good natural gelling properties include crabapples, sour apples, sour berries, citrus fruits, grapes, sour cherries and cranberries. Fruits low in pectin include strawberries and apricots, while sweet cherries, quinces and melons are low in acid.

See also: **Gelatin.**

JAMAICA PEPPER

See **Allspice.**

JAMAICA SORREL

See **Roselle.**

JAMBO

See **Rose Apple.**

JAMBOLANA

See **Java Plum.**

JAMBOLIFERA

The leaves of this small tree, *Acronychia laurifolia*, are used as a condiment in tropical Asia.

JAMES' POTATO

The tubers of this North American vine, *Solanum jamesii*, can be cooked and eaten like potatoes. It is found in the United States Southwest and adjacent areas of Mexico.

JAPANESE APRICOT

Japanese apricot is the sour or bitter fruit of an ornamental tree, *Prunus mume*, native to China and Japan. *P. mume* is a popular garden tree. Many varieties are used for bonsai. The fruit is round, about one inch in diameter, yellow green and has a single stone. Japanese apricot is most often pickled or used to make a sweet liqueur, but it may be preserved in sugar as candy, or salted, or boiled.

JAPANESE ARTICHOKE

See **Crosne.**

JAPANESE ELEAGNUS

A deciduous tree, *Eleagnus umbellata*, of the Himalayas, China and Japan, it reaches a height of 18 feet. Its fruit is silvery, turning scarlet when ripe. It is eaten after being scalded.

JAPANESE GOURD

This small fruit of the plant *Trichosanthes japonica* is closely related to the **snake gourd.** It grows up to three inches long and is oval in shape. The plant is native to Japan, where the young fruits are salted or kept in soy sauce for eating.

JAPANESE HORSERADISH

See **Wasabi.**

JAPANESE MEDLAR

See **Loquat.**

JAPANESE MUSTARD

Also CURLED MUSTARD. Here is a variety of mustard *(Brassica juncea* var. *crispifolia)* much cultivated in Japan. The soft, thin leaves are cooked to produce a green spring vegetable.

JAPANESE QUINCE

See **Japonica.**

JAPANESE RAISIN TREE

This deciduous tree, *Hovenia dulcis*, of Japan, China and the Himalayan region, has small, reddish fruit that is much esteemed in some parts of China and Japan. It is fleshy, club-shaped, about one-quarter inch across and dry, but the flavor is sweet and subacidic.

JAPANESE SLOUGHGRASS

A perennial grass, *Beckmannia erucaeformis*, of temperate Asian and North America, produces seeds that are eaten in Japan.

JAPANESE STAUNTON VINE

The purple fruit of this woody climbing vine *(Stautonia hexaphylla)* is cultivated in Japan and China. The fruit is a berry, reaching perhaps two inches in length, with a pulpy texture and a sweet, honeylike taste. It is highly regarded in Japan.

JAPAN PEPPER

See **Zanthoxylum.**

JAPONICA

Also JAPANESE QUINCE. The fruit of the ornamental shrub, *Chaenomeles japonica*, was introduced into Europe around 1815 and is now widely grown on the continent. Only certain varieties produce fruit. Japonica is yellowish green, large and fragrant but also hard and exceedingly bitter when fresh. It is round or oval, resembling the true quince in that respect, and it has some of the latter's mucilaginous and demulcent properties. Consequently, it makes excellent jellies and preserves but is inedible fresh. It is sometimes combined with apples and pears to enhance their flavor in cooked dishes.

JARILLA

Edible fruit of a small Mexican shrub *(Jarilla caudata)*, it is candied or used to make preserves.

JASMINE

A genus of shrubs *(Jasminum* spp) of the olive family, many species of which have showy, white, yellow or pink flowers, jasmines are heavily scented, and the blossoms are used in oriental cookery. A variety of tea is also mixed with jasmine petals before curing. The result is a delicately aromatic, red tea.

JAVA ALMOND

The edible seed of an East Indian tree, *Canarium commune*, also grows in the Pacific region. It is highly regarded locally and is often eaten with rice or in pastries. The taste is described as pleasant.

JAVA APPLE

See **Mankil.**

JAVA JAMBOSA

Also WILD ROSE APPLE. This dark red purple berry of a shrubby tree, *Syzygium pycnanthum*, is found in the Malay Peninsula, Sumatra and Java. Java *jambosa* is round, about one-half inch across and has an outer covering or "calyx." It is eaten raw and considered to be of fair quality.

JAVA PLUM

Also DUHAT, JAMBOLANA. The olive-sized fruit of a tropical evergreen, *Syzygium cumini*, native to India and Ceylon, Java plum is cultivated throughout Southeast Asia as far as the Philippines. There are several varieties, ranging in sweetness and astringency, all having maroon to dark purple skin. Some have dark flesh, and some have white flesh. The latter are sweeter.

The sweet types are eaten fresh, but more often the java plum is used to make preserves or, as in the Philippines, to make wine. The java plum is related to a wide variety of fruits of the *Eugenia* and *Syzygium* genera that are generally called rose apples and include, for example, the jamrose, the jambo, the pitanga and the Surinam cherry. All, according to legend, are descended from the mythical Hindu *jambu*, or *gambu*, a tree that bore the golden fruit of immortality.

JAY

The common European jay *(Garrulus glandarius)* is considered a table delicacy in France when young. It is skinned, not plucked, and may be prepared like a game bird, except that it does not require hanging. Older birds are sometimes eaten but should be boiled before cooking or soaked in a marinade. The American jay, or bluejay *(Cyanocitta cristata)* is different bird, but both are of the family *Corvidae*. The European jay is an overall brown.

JELLY BEAN

This small, bean-shaped candy has a chewy gelatinous center and a glazed exterior. It comes in many different colors and flavors.

JENNY STONECROP

The leaves of this succulent perennial, *Sedum reflexum*, are eaten in soups and salads. It is indigenous to Europe.

JERBOA

Also KANGAROO RAT. A squirrel-sized rodent with long hind legs reminiscent of a kangaroo's, it is found in Europe and Africa under the name *jerboa*, and in the American Southwest under the name "kangaroo rat." The jerboa is widely eaten in Africa, but only rarely in the United States. It may be prepared like squirrel or rabbit.

JERUSALEM ARTICHOKE

This edible tuber of the sunflower genus, *Helianthus tuberosus*, was found initially in the New World but is now widely spread throughout North America, Europe and Asia. The most common variety resembles a potato. It has a thick brown, edible skin and is knobby, chewy and white.

The Jerusalem artichoke contains inulin, a carbohydrate, which is beneficial to diabetics and others who require a low-starch diet. The root has a sweet taste and is more watery than the potato. It is normally eaten raw, though it can be prepared like a potato—boiled, roasted, fried or mashed with butter. A common practice in the southern part of the United States is to peel and slice the artichoke to garnish salads.

The name comes in part from an Anglicization of the Spanish word for sunflower, or *girasol*. The "artichoke" label was perhaps applied by the French explorer Champlain, who called the root *artichaut du Canada*. He may also have introduced the plant into France in the 17th century. In France, however, the artichoke was given the new name *topinambour*—a nonsense word—under which it was marketed primarily as famine food. The spread of the plant was hindered for a time by the belief that its roots caused leprosy—perhaps because they resembled deformed fingers.

The Jerusalem artichoke grows prolifically (it is one of those plants that always threatens to take over the garden). From six to 10 feet tall, it differs from the common wild sunflower in having a thinner, reedlike stalk and in its preference for thick, gregarious clusters. The flowers, too, are smaller, less brightly yellow and lack the seed-bearing brown disk in the center. The roots should be dug after the first frost—and can stay in the ground, providing a natural storage all winter.

George Gurdjieff mentions that in the Middle East the Jerusalem artichoke, in addition to supplying an abundant food, makes a perfect fence to shade gardens. "In many parts of Turkestan it is the custom to fence off one garden from another and from the road, by planting hedges of Jerusalem Artichokes, which grow very high and thick and serve the purpose of wooden or wire fences." This practice can be observed, as well, in many parts of the southern and southwestern United States where the wild sunflower plant abounds.

JERUSALEM OAK PAZOTE

See **Mexican Tea.**

JEWFISH

Also BLACK SEA BASS. This name is applied to a number of fish, most notable among them being the huge grouper, *Epinephelus itajara*, found on both the Atlantic and Pacific Coasts of the United States. It prefers warmer, southern waters and may reach a length of eight feet and a weight of 700 pounds. It has a broad, flat head and a dark brown color marked by five irregular broken bands running across the sides. It is considered excellent eating and a fine sport fish. Another jewfish of the same genus is the *garrupa (E. lanceolatus)*, which is found in the Indian and Pacific Oceans. Largest specimens reach 12 feet and 600 pounds. The *garrupa* is a sought-after sport fish but has been known to attack humans.

In Southern California, the jewfish is the giant sea bass *(Stereolepsis gigas)* or black sea bass. Its range extends south to the coast of Mexico, and it lives in inshore waters. Catalina Island is a favorite fishing ground for *S. gigas*, which can weigh up to 600 pounds. It has a deep, heavy body—yellow when young but dark brown when older—and short-based dorsal fins. It is good to eat and a fine game fish and is, consequently, becoming increasingly scarce.

Other jewfish include the longtooth, or snapper salmon *(Otolithes ruber)*, of the eastern Pacific and Indian Oceans. It is an important food fish throughout its range. The mulloway *(Johnius antarctica)* inhabits Australian waters and weighs up to 130 pounds. It is good eating when young, but larger specimens have coarse flesh with an insipid taste. The *Promicrops itaira*, an Atlantic tarpon much prized as game, is too bony to make good eating.

JEW'S EAR

See **Black Tree Fungus.**

John Dory

Jerusalem artichokes

Jicama

JEW'S MALLOW

See **Jute.**

JICAMA

Also YAM BEAN. Jicama is a leguminous plant with a large tuberous root, two species of which are fairly well known. The smaller one, called the yam bean *(Pachyrhizus erosus)*, which is common to the tropics of both hemispheres, has a root that reaches six to eight inches in length. It is eaten raw and boiled. The larger one, called *jicama (Pachyrhizus tuburosus)* grows in the temperate and tropical regions of America and is a major crop in Mexico. Its root reaches eight to 12 inches in length and up to one inch in thickness. It is almost invariably eaten raw and is a good thirst quencher, being both juicy and nutritious. *Jicama* is often cut into thin slices and sprinkled with sugar or added to a salad.

Jicama is a word that derives from the Aztec word, *Xicamatl.* It is a bean vine whose blossoms and pods are pinched off to promote growth of the root. Two types are recognized in Mexico: the *agua*, which has a watery juice, and the *leche*, which has milky juice. The roots take five months to mature. Authorities urge moderation in eating *jicama*, as it can prove indigestible. An extract of the seeds, which are considered poisonous to eat, is used to treat skin ailments.

JOBO

See **Yellow Mombin.**

JOB'S TEARS

An annual grass plant, *Coix lacrymajobi*, has large, shining, pear-shaped seeds that are milled into flour, especially in Southeast Asia. The plant reaches a height of three feet and has broad leaves. It thrives under the same conditions as corn (maize). The seeds are also used as beads for necklaces and rosaries.

JOCHBERG

Here is a fair quality cheese made in the Tyrol from a mixture of cow's and goat's milk. Individual cheeses are 20 inches in diameter, four inches thick and weigh about 45 pounds.

JOHANNISBERG WINE

See **Wines, German; Wines, Swiss.**

JOHN BROWN

Also BLUE HOTTENTOT, BRONZE BREAM. A sea bream of South African waters, the John Brown *(Pachymetopon grande)* is highly regarded as food and is popular with anglers as well. It seldom exceeds two feet in length and possesses a deep body approaching oval in outline with deep bronze coloring and a head of iridescent blue. The fish is mainly a plant feeder and is, therefore, difficult to hook, but once on the line it is reputed to be a game fighter.

JOHN DORY

A European food fish renowned for both its firm, delicately flavored flesh and its ugly appearance, the John Dory *(Zeus faber)* is a flat fish, seeming substantial when viewed from the side but quite thin viewed head-on. A good size for this fish is 12 pounds, but two-thirds of that is taken up by head and viscera. It is precisely this huge head that strikes many buyers as repulsive, and for this reason it is often removed before the fish is displayed. Not a very agile fish, the John Dory possesses a jaw that can be thrust forth suddenly to snap up its prey. In repose, this outsize jaw gives it a hangdog look.

The name "John Dory" is said to be taken from the French *jaune doree* (bright yellow) which refers to its overall color. It is a popular food fish in the Mediterranean area in general and the south of France in particular, where it is known as the *Saint Pierre.* This name comes from the legend that St. Peter caught a John Dory, grasping it behind the gills. It uttered such loud groans, however, that he took pity on it and threw it back, leaving a fingerprint behind each gill. The fish's markings include a yellow-ringed black spot on each side of its body, the fingerprints of legend.

The John Dory may be cooked whole by braising, poaching or broiling; it is most often filleted and cooked like other flat fish. Its flesh has been compared to lobster meat in firmness and flavor. One variety, *Zenopsis ocellata*, is found along the Atlantic Coast of the United States.

JOJOBA

See **Goatnut.**

JOLLYTAIL

Also INANGA. A small, schooling fish, *Galaxias maculatus* of Australian waters, the jollytail is caught and eaten as **whitebait** when it is at an immature stage. Its range also includes New Zealand and Tasmania.

JOLTHEAD PORGY

This excellent food fish, *Calamus bajonado*, inhabits the western Atlantic from New England to Brazil, including the Gulf of Mexico and West Indies. There are several edible members of the *Calamus* genus, but the jolthead porgy is the largest, reaching a length of two feet and a weight of 10 pounds. *C. bajonado* has a large, brown head, brassy cheeks, a blue line beneath the eyes and an orange patch at the corner of the mouth. It is silver with bluish highlights in the scales.

JORA

In South America this sprouted corn is frequently used to make **chicha,** a type of corn (maize) beer, which is called *chicha de jora*.

JOSEPHINE CHEESE

A Silesian cheese made of whole cow's milk with a soft paste, it is cured in small cylindrical packages.

JOYAPA

See **Popenoei.**

JUAN FERNANDEZ LANGOSTA

A type of **spiny lobster** caught in the coastal waters of the Juan Fernandez Islands, which lie some 500 miles to the west of Chile, this crustacean is reputed to have a particularly fine taste and texture.

JUDAS TREE

This small tree, *Cercis siliquastrum*, of southern Europe and western Asia, has purplish rose flowers that are eaten in salads or used to make fritters. The flowers are strongly scented. In bud form they may be pickled in vinegar and used like capers. Judas is said to have hanged himself on this type of tree.

JUJUBE

Also CHINESE DATE. This sweet, olive-sized fruit of the shrubby tree, *Ziziphus jujuba*, is native to China, India and Syria. Jujubes are green in the development stage and rust-colored when ripe. After picking, they are left to dry for some time so that the pulp becomes sweeter and spongy.

Jujube

Jujube are often boiled in honey or syrup, or candied. They taste somewhat like a dried date, and like a date, the raw fruit contains a single, pointed stone. Jujubes are a feature of Chinese cuisine, but they are also under cultivation in California and the south of France.

Candy jujubes, which used to contain juice of the fruit, now consists of gum arabic, plus some flavoring.

JULEP

Variously this might be a cool, sweet drink flavored with aromatic herbs; a sweet syrup used as a vehicle for medicine; or a cold, alcoholic drink containing sugar, whiskey or brandy, shaved ice and an herb flavoring. In the United States, the best-known julep is the mint julep, which is served in a collins glass and features bourbon whiskey and a sprig of mint. There are many other "julep cups" known in England. Milton referred to them when he wrote in *Comus:*

> *This cordial julep here*
> *that flames and dances in its crystal bounds.*

The word "julep" comes from the Persian *gulab* and the Arabic *julab*, both meaning rosewater, a powerfully aromatic liquid distilled from rose petals and used in perfumery.

JUMPY BEAN

Also WHITE POPINAC. The tropical shrub, *Leucaena glauca*, is native to America but widely naturalized in the tropics. Its flowerheads, which measure an inch across, are eaten in Java as a side dish with rice. Elsewhere the shrub is grown as forage or as shade for banana trees. The seeds are used to make necklaces.

JUNEBERRY

Also SHADBUSH, SERVICEBERRY, SUGAR-PLUM. This is the edible fruit of the genus *Amelanchier*, which consists of about 25 species of shrubs and small trees native to temperate North America. Depending on the species, the Juneberry can range from the size of a pea to more than three quarters of an inch across. The color varies from red to purplish black. The fruit has a heavy bloom like the blueberry.

As the name implies, the Juneberry ripens in late June, and it is sweet, juicy, but rather insipid. On the other hand, it is extremely hardy and drought-resistant, and for these reasons it played a significant role in the diet of native Americans, particularly in the Northwest. Pioneers, particularly the Mormons, had to depend on the Juneberry for survival on more than one occasion.

Cultivars of the species *A. Alnifolia* are grown commercially in a few areas and are much more productive than the wild varieties. Nowadays, Juneberries are used for pies and preserves. The flavor is usually improved by the addition of lemon juice.

JUNIPER BERRY

The aromatic dark blue fruit of the common juniper shrub or tree *(Juniperus communis)* of the cypress family are too acrid for eating raw. In the American Southwest, however, they are frequently gathered to make a strong savory tea. Juniper berries and seeds are also used to flavor wine and the distilled liquor, **gin.**

See also: **Gin, Juniper Wine.**

JUNIPER WINE

An alcoholic drink, believed to be medicinal, *Vin de Genievre* is brewed in Europe with berries from the common juniper tree or shrub *(Juniperus communis).* The fruit is also used to flavor **gin,** an English contraction of the word *genievre* or "Juniper." The name also applies to a wine formerly made in France, using wormwood (absinthe) and juniper seeds.

See also: **Juniper Berry.**

JUNKET

Here is a pudding consisting of curds and cream or of milk that has been curdled by rennet. The mixture is sweetened and variously flavored. Junket tablets are made out of rennin, the principal ingredient of rennet, which is obtained from the stomachs of calves and used to coagulate milk.

JUPITER'S BEARD

See **Artichoke.**

JURA BLEU

See **Septmoncel.**

JURANCON WINE

The white wine from Jurancon in the ancient province of Bearn, near Pau in southern France, is well known. It is unusually full-bodied and strong in alcohol content with a slight flavor of **Madeira.** Red Jurancon wines are typically blends of several grapes—none of which, oddly, come from local vines. White Jurancon grapes—Mansenc, Cruchen, and Courbu—are used to make an exceptional dessert wine and for **cognac.**

The French wine industry was given a royal boost, it is often said, when the king of Navarre gave his newborn grandchild—later to become Henry IV of France—a few drops of Jurancon wine before the infant had tasted his mother's milk.

JUTE

Also JEW'S TALLOW, TOSSA JUTE. This species of jute *(Corchorus olitorius)* is a secondary source of fiber, but its leaves make good spinach. It is an erect, annual plant, reaching more than 12 feet in height. It grows in low-lying areas of warm districts. This plant is often eaten in West Africa.

K

KABANOS

This long sausage, popular in both Poland and the Ukraine, consists mainly of pork with some beef added. It is seasoned with mace and garlic.

See also: **Sausage.**

KAFIR BREAD

See **Breadfruit.**

KAFFIR PLUM

The dark red fruit of a small tree native to South Africa, the kaffir plum *(Harpephyllum caffrum)* is about an inch in diameter and has a juicy, acidic pulp that is best when made into jelly.

KAFFIR POTATO

Tubers of an African herbaceous plant, *Plectranthus esculentus*, found commonly in Zimbabwe, Natal and adjacent regions, they are often cooked and eaten like ordinary potatoes. The taste is said to be pleasant. The kaffir potato is known as *umbondive* where it grows.

KAJMAK

Also KAYMAK. The name is Turkish for cream, and this Balkan specialty is close to both **clotted cream** and **cream cheese.** It is so popular in Yugoslavia that its nickname is Serbian butter. The Bulgarians consider it a national dish. Quality varies widely because methods are primitive. Essentially, fresh milk is boiled and then allowed to stand for 12 hours. The cream is skimmed off and either sold fresh or allowed to ripen in molds. When unripe, *kajmak* has a mild, pleasant flavor, but when fully ripe it approaches Roquefort in its sharpness and has a consistency like butter. It is often served with bread as an hors d'oeuvre.

KAKI

See **Persimmon.**

KALE

Also BORECOLE. Kale is a winter cabbage whose leaves do not form a head but grow freely. Its many varieties may be wavy, curly or toothed. Colors range from bluish green and reddish brown to purple.

It is a coarse vegetable, which bears cold weather well. Indeed, frost seems to mellow the flavor. Rich in vitamin A, kale is cooked like cabbage or served raw in a green salad.

Kale

KALPI

Also WEBB'S ORANGE. This species of orange, *Citrus webberi*, is used much like an ordinary lemon.

KAMANI

See **Myrobalan.**

KANGAROO

A plant-eating marsupial mammal of Australia, it was formerly an important food source for the aborigines. The kangaroo *(Macropus giganteus)* has short forelegs and stands nearly upright on its long, strong hind legs and thick tail. It moves by leaps and bounds.

The flesh of the kangaroo's tail is reckoned a gourmet dish, although most Australian's have never tried it. It is exported in cans and usually made into a soup. Many people inadvertantly tried kangaroo meat in southern California. In 1981 it was discovered that what was thought to be ground beef imported from Australia was in fact part horse meat and part kangaroo meat. Much of the shipment had already been sold through fast food outlets as hamburgers. Imports were temporarily halted while Australian authorities set up stringent controls. In Australia, kangaroos are now a major source of dog food.

KANGAROO APPLE

This yellow, oval fruit of an Australian shrub, *Solanum aviculare*, is eaten raw, boiled or baked.

KANGAROO RAT

See **Jerboa.**

KANTEN

See **Agar-Agar.**

KAOLIANG

The name refers either to a kind of grain-bearing **sorghum** grown in eastern Asia or to a strong, alcoholic liquor made from this grain in China. It is often referred to as a wine, but it is bottled at 100 proof.

KAPOK

A tropical tree, *Ceiba petandra*, also known as the silk-cotton tree, is the source of the commercial fiber, kapok. In West Africa, however, it is cultivated for its seeds, which are ground into an edible meal.

KARAB

See **Eriwani.**

KARATAS

This tropical plant, *Karatas plumieri*, of the West Indies and South America, bears pleasant-tasting, edible fruit. Its young flower clusters are also eaten as a vegetable. The *karatas* is related to the pineapple.

KAREISH

An Egyptian sour-milk cheese that is cured in brine, giving it a pickled quality, it is much like **domaiti,** except that in the making salt is added to the curd rather than to the milk.

KARKALIA

Edible fruit of a succulent shrub, *Carpobrotus aequilaterus*, found in Australia, Tasmania and western South America, it is red, has eight–10 cells and usually reaches a length of two inches. The karkalia is eaten raw. It is known also as pig's face.

KARONDA

See **Caranda.**

KARUT

This skim-milk cheese made in Afghanistan and northwestern India is very dry and hard.

KASACH

See **Eriwani, Ossetin.**

KASHA

Kasha is Russian for a coarse meal of cracked buckwheat, barley or millet that is eaten as a hot cereal, either boiled or otherwise cooked. It is a staple food occupying a place similar to that of rice in China or pasta in Italy. Kasha is used in a versatile manner: to accompany cooked meats, game or poultry, as a stuffing for fish, meat and poultry; as a garnish for soups or mixed with other vegetables.

KASHKAVAL

See **Kaskaval.**

KASKAVAL

Also KASHKAVAL. A plastic-curd, ewe's milk cheese, made in Rumania and Bulgaria, kaskaval is similar to the Italian **formaggio di pasta filata** and to **katschkawalj.** The curd is heated and stretched until it is elastic, a procedure that smooths and firms the texture and improves keeping and traveling qualities. Curing takes two or three months, and cheeses weigh four to seven pounds. This cheese may be used like **Parmesan** in cooking. *Peneteleu* is a drier version of this cheese.

KASSERI

Kasseri is a firm Greek cheese made from ewe's milk, goat's milk or a mixture of the two. The paste is white and the flavor mild. It is like **kefalotyri** but a little softer, so that when fresh it is a good table cheese, but when fully ripe it may be grated.

KAT

See **Khat.**

KATSCHKAWALJ

The name is a transliteration of **caciocavallo** and describes a plastic-curd, ewe's milk cheese made in Serbia, Macedonia, Rumania and Bulgaria that closely approximates the Italian model. The curd is heated and worked like bread dough until elastic. It is hand-molded into six pound spheres and placed in forms. The Turkish cheese *zomma* is quite similar.

KATURAY

Edible flower of a tree native to the South Pacific and parts of Asia, it is probably from either *Sesbania grandiflora*, the scarlet wisteria tree, or *S. sesban*, a closely related species. *Katuray* flowers are used as food, especially in the Philippines.

KATZENKOPF

See **Edam.**

KAURIE

Edible fruit of a robust, herbaceous plant, *Astelia nervosa*, found in New Zealand, the kaurie is a berry with black, lustrous seeds. It is eaten locally. The plant is perennial and reaches a height of 10 feet. It should not be confused with the Kauri Pine, a tree that produces Kauri gum.

KAVA

Also AVA, ARVA, KAWA KAVA, YAVA, YANGONA. Kava is a fermented drink made from the roots of a pepper plant, *Macropiper latifolium*, called *yangona* in Fiji but also any of the alternative names in various islands of the South Pacific. It is drunk in Polynesia, Melanesia and in New Zealand by the Maoris.

The roots of the plant are dried in the sun, then mixed with water or saliva and allowed to ferment. It is said to be nonalcoholic, yet intoxicating if drunk in sufficient quantity. One authority says it produces a pleasant, slightly numbing effect in the mouth and makes the drinker weak in the legs but not in the head. Herb Payson, writing of a cruise to Fiji in *Sail* magazine, recounted this experience with it:

> *The men sat around drinking kava, which they call grog, while the women did the work. Grog is what Fijians make out of the yangona roots. They chop the roots into a coarse powder, put the powder into a muslin bag much like a large teabag, and then knead the bag in water in a large wooden, ceremonial bowl. The result is a mixture which looks like diluted milk of magnesia, tastes like a mud puddle, and has an even less salubrious effect than 3.2 beer. After hours of continuous drinking, the dedicated could achieve a state of drowsiness along with thoroughly flushed kidneys. I tried, having discovered that the taste was not quite so repulsive as I remembered, but only achieved the flushed kidneys.*

KAYA

Also JAPANESE TORREYA. An evergreen tree, *Torreya nucifera*, provides edible nuts that are rich in oil. They are highly regarded in Japan and used in candies.

KAYMAK

See **Kajmak.**

KEEMUN TEA

Keemun is a high quality, black Chinese tea, probably the best made available through export from China and Taiwan, although the quality varies from year to year. It is full-bodied and comparable in strength to Indian teas. It has a spicy, smoky taste and is dark amber in color. Keemun is often taken with sugar and milk and is excellent served with food.

See also: **Tea.**

KEFALOTYRI

A hard goat's or ewe's milk cheese made in Greece and Syria for grating purposes, it has a yellow curd and a sharp, salty flavor. This cheese has different names depending on where it is made, but this version takes its name from its shape, which is like a hat or head *(kefalo)*. It is 10 inches thick. It is used like **Parmesan** in cooking. An American version is made in the Ozarks region of Arkansas.

KEFIR

This fermented milk beverage originated in the Caucasus Mountains region of southeastern Europe. The original kefir was made from camel's milk, and more recently from goat's milk and cow's milk. It was the Russian version of **kumiss.**

Kefir is similar to yogurt, except that it is fluid rather than custardlike, and, if the traditional procedure is used, it contains about 1 percent alcohol. *Streptococcus* and *Lactobacillus* bacteria convert the milk sugar to lactic acid, giving the drink a slightly tart taste, and lactose-fermenting yeast produce the alcohol. The yeast collect in globules the size of wheat grains and float on the surface.

See also: **Fermented Milk, Kumiss, Yogurt.**

KEI APPLE

Also UMKOKOLO. Smooth, yellow fruit of a South African tree, *Dovyalis caffra*, it is apple-shaped and about 1 to 1½ inches in diameter. It has a juicy, acidic pulp. The fruit is pickled or made into jams, jellies, compotes or marmalade.

KELADI

This is a Southeast Asian plant whose yamlike tubers are eaten like potatoes and whose leaves may be eaten as a green vegetable. Frying is the best method of preparing the tubers, since they have a soapy taste when boiled. They are best avoided when raw because they may irritate the mouth. *Keladi* is popular in Malaysia.

KELP

Kelp is a general term for several species of brown seaweed that find many industrial uses in the United States and form a significant portion of the Japanese diet. The major member of the kelp group of seaweeds is the giant Pacific kelp *(Macrocystis pyrifera)* which grows in strands of up to 100 feet long. About 170,000 tons of this are harvested yearly in the United States, mostly off the coast of California.

As a food, it is sought after for the jellylike alginates it contains, which provide body for salad dressings, ice cream and other prepared desserts. Increasingly, it is used as a substitute for the red seaweeds that have a longer history of exploitation in the West, such as **carrageen** and **agar-agar,** which have similar properties. Most of the U.S. kelp harvest, however, goes into paint and rubber compounds, the processing of paper and textiles, pharmaceutical and cosmetic products or beer, where it helps reduce the size of the head when pouring.

Seaweed makes up about 10 percent of the Japanese diet, and among the six principal varieties, kelp is considered the best. After processing, it is called *kombu* and is sold as a powder for use as a seasoner, or in sheets. The latter are combined with fish in many dishes, put into soup or stripped and woven into tiny, edible baskets that are deep-fried and filled with meat or vegetables. Boxes of assorted *kombu* are often brought by Japanese guests as house gifts.

Kelp is gathered on the west coast of Ireland, where it is boiled to make a green gruel used to accompany mutton. It is also gathered in France but goes into food processing or is used as fertilizer. Kelp contains little protein or digestible carbohydrate, but is rich in potassium and iodine. As a source of the latter, it enjoyed a vogue as a health food in the 1960s, such that marine biologists and ecologists began to fear for the destruction of kelp beds, so necessary to marine creatures as food and shelter. Such fears proved groundless, however, and the chief food use of kelp in the United States continues to be as a source of algae gelatins.

Kelp tablets are a food supplement commonly sold in health-food stores. The U.S. Food and Drug Administration warns that kelp tablets may contain high levels of arsenic, "as do many other products from the sea." It reports that elevated levels of arsenic were found in the urinary tract of persons who consumed kelp tablets, and that industrial workers exposed to high levels of arsenic experienced a greater occurrence of cancer.

KENTJUR

Also KENCHOER. A Southeast Asian plant whose pungent-tasting root has a flavor similar to that of ginger, it is used as a spice in Malaysia and Java.

KERGUELEN CABBAGE

This antarctic plant, *Pringlea antiscorbutica*, is noted for its vitamin C content. The leaves are used in salads.

KETCHUP

Also CATCHUP, CATSUP, TOMATO SAUCE. Ketchup is a sauce or condiment usually made of tomatoes that have been boiled, pureed and strained, then mixed with vinegar and seasoned with onions, sweet peppers, sugar and sometimes soya. Ketchup is believed to be of Chinese origin and started out with salted, spiced mushrooms as the chief ingredient.

The word "ketchup" is said to come from the Malay or Thai word *kachiap*, which derived from the Chinese *koe-chiap* or *ke-tsiap*, meaning the brine of pickled fish. In former times, ketchup might be made from a variety of main ingredients—cranberries, green walnuts, anchovies, shellfish—but nowadays such ketchups are rare. Ketchup almost invariably means tomato sauce.

Ketchup is a very popular sauce and comes in various grades depending on how high the concentration of tomato solids. Fancy grade, for example, consists of more than 32 percent tomato solids, while standard grade will have as little as 25 percent. Sugar has become an increasingly important ingredient, and some ketchups contain as much as 25 to 30 percent sugar.

Ketchup is used to add flavor to such things as hot sandwiches (hamburgers, hot dogs), cold meats, sausages, cheese dishes and fried fish. It is best used sparingly as it can easily overwhelm the taste of the food it accompanies.

KETEMBILLA

Also KITEMBILLA, CEYLON GOOSEBERRY. This is the sweet, juicy fruit of a small tree or shrub, *Dovyalis hebecarpa*, native to subtropical Asia but widely transplanted elsewhere. The *ketembilla* has a velvety texture somewhat resembling a gooseberry, is round in shape, maroon purple in color, and three-quarters to one inch in diameter. It is mostly used in jams, jellies and in sauces for meat or fish.

KETJAP

An Indonesian hot sauce, *Ketjap* is an indispensable flavoring ingredient in Indonesian cuisine. Its name derives in all probability from the Chinese *ke-tsiap*, as does the English "ketchup."

KHAT

Also ARABIAN TEA. Khat is an evergreen shrub, *Catha edulis*, native to Ethiopia and Somalia, whose leaves and tender shoots are chewed by Moslems as a favorite daily stimulant. The dark green leaves and twigs are also dried and used to make a tea. This is an ancient drink, perhaps antedating the use of tea by the Chinese, but it is not nearly as popular as it used to be.

The leaves are mixed with honey to produce a palatable wine. This drink was once forbidden by the Prophet Mohammed. Later the ban was lifted on the grounds that its use promoted only hilarity and good humor.

KIBBEH

The national dish of Lebanon, *kibbeh* consists basically of ground lamb and crushed wheat or *burgall*, rolled in sausagelike patties similar to Greek **soudzoukakia** or meatballs. Traditionally, *kibbeh* is prepared by pounding the lamb and wheat for an hour in a large stone mortar. The mixture is then kneaded and seasoned with mint and with ground **pine nuts.** It is lightly cooked with olive oil or can be eaten raw—as in *kibbeh nieheh*, a kind of steak tartare.

KID

Kid is the flesh of a young goat, preferably unweaned and less than three months old. The English and Americans are prejudiced against goat meat, yet in Mexico roast kid is an everyday dish. It is enjoyed in France and in Mediterranean countries, such as Italy, Greece and Lebanon, especially at festive occasions. For example, suckling kid is a specialty at Easter.

In earlier times, kid was often preferred to lamb. *Le Menagier de Paris*, a 14th-century domestic manual, lists a menu for a wedding banquet, saying, "a quarter of a kid is better than a lamb." Indeed, in the Middle Ages, kid was so much more popular than lamb that the latter was often disguised as kid in the markets by the addition of a kid's tail. The rarest delicacy was *capretto incaporchiato*, or "trapped kid"; the tiny offspring was strapped under its mother's belly in a wicker basket so that it could reach the udder but not the grass. This assured that its flesh would be milky white. In the 18th century, kid was common fare in England and the United States, so there is no accounting for the current prejudice. Authorities speculate that it stems from the bad odor associated with goats, although strictly speaking, this only applies to the adult male goat.

KIDNEY

This is an internal organ of all mammals, but only those of lamb, veal, pork, beef and mutton are of any gastronomic importance. So called cock's kidneys *(rognons de coq)* are actually testicles. Kidney, like liver, is classed as a variety meat (offal), but it is far less popular than liver. It is a nutritious food, high in protein, minerals and vitamins A and B.

Lamb and calve's kidneys are the most esteemed because they are the tenderest and have a delicate flavor. They are usually grilled or sauteed, but only briefly so as not to make them tough. Pork liver has a stronger taste and coarser texture and is most frequently used in pates. Beef liver, toughest and strongest tasting of all, is thoroughly cooked, usually by braising, or included in a steak and kidney pie.

The kidney is an excretory organ, and it is said that the kidney of an aged animal will taste of urine. Leopold Bloom, in James Joyce's novel *Ulysses*, counted this a plus. "Most of all he liked grilled mutton kidneys which gave to his palate a fine tang of faintly scented urine."

The taste for kidney has declined greatly in the United States since the beginning of this century. It is an exotic food encountered, perhaps, in a mixed grill or in a fancy French restaurant. At an Algerian barbeque *(mechoui)*, on the other hand, the kidneys are considered the choicest part of the roasted animal. Throughout Africa, kidneys are singled out as a treat, perhaps because many people believe, as did the early Europeans, that they give courage and strength to those who eat them. Eskimos eat seal kidney.

In the market, kidneys may be sold with a layer of fat surrounding it. Usually this is trimmed before cooking along with the outer membrane, fat white veins and the core. This image of kidney is evoked by Thomas Hood in this portrait of a 19th-century English butcher:

Whoe'er has gone thro' London Street,
Has seen a Butcher gazing at his meat,
And how he keeps
Gloating upon a sheep's
Or bullock's personals, as if his own;
How he admires his halves
And quarters—and his calves
As if in truth upon his own legs grown;—
His *fat!* His *suet!*
His *kidneys peeping elegantly thro' it!*

KIDNEY BEAN

Also HARICOT BEAN, NAVY BEAN. Beans are the seeds of leguminous plants, and the kidney bean *(Phaseolus vulgaris)* is the basic variety of New World bean, which was brought back to Europe by the early explorers of North America. Eventually, it replaced in popularity the fava or **broad bean,** which had been the only bean in the European diet since ancient times. There are many well-known varieties of this bean, such as the *adzuki*, the lima, the mung, the pinto, the scarlet runner and the tepary. These will be discussed under separate headings. Green, or string beans, are simply the unripe pods of different types of kidney bean.

Shelled, dried kidney beans are highly nutritious, containing approximately 24 percent protein, 48 percent carbohydrates, three percent fat and four percent ash. They also contain ample fiber. They are known as "the poor man's meat." Caloric content is about 300 per 3.5 ounces (100 grams).

Haricot is an approximation of the Aztec word, *ayacotl*. The Aztecs had developed many different species of the bean, adapted to the various climates of Mexico. The two mainstays of their diet were beans and corn (maize). They complemented each other both dietetically and agriculturally. Nutritionally, beans provided the protein that corn lacks. They were also planted together in the same fields. Corn provided stalks for the beans to climb on, while beans enriched the soil with nitrogen. Without this enrichment, corn would soon have exhausted the soil.

The Italians were the first Europeans to cultivate the kidney bean in the 16th century, calling it the *fagiolo*. It caught on in France in the 18th century with the first plantings near Soissons, which is still famous for its beans. It spread from France to England, where it gradually replaced the broad bean in the worker's favorite dish, beans and bacon.

Both fresh and dried kidney beans are used for cooking, the dried ones needing two to three hours soaking in water before use. They are prepared in a variety of ways, such as in soups, stews or baked dishes. Baked beans are a specialty of New England, where according to tradition, native Americans taught the Pilgrim Fathers the technique of baking beans in an earthen pit lined with hot stones.

Green beans have a different nutritional content than the mature bean, containing only two percent protein and three percent carbohydrates, and amounting to only 18 calories per 3.5 ounces (100 grams). Their principal use is as a boiled vegetable or as an ingredient of salads.

KIELBASA

See **Polish Sausage.**

Kidney beans, clockwise from top: black, kidney, fresh green, adzuki and (center) pinto

KIMCHI

Also KIM CHEE. *Kimchi* means pickled vegetables. The dish is a Korean staple and probably the best known Korean food outside Korea. There are hundreds of varieties, some highly spiced with peppers, some mild, some highly fermented, others not. *Kimchi* usually includes cabbages, radishes, cucumbers, onions, chili peppers and, especially, garlic. Often it contains pickled shellfish as well. It is a good source of vitamin C.

Kimchi is fermented in earthenware jars that are filled with salted water and often buried in the earth for protection against cold weather. In Korea *kimchi* is on the table at all meals.

KING BARRACUTA

A large fish of Australian and New Zealand waters, the king barracuta *(Rexea solandri)* resembles a tuna, is stout-bodied and can be as much as 4½ feet long. It is deep blue above and silver below. Its flesh is described as having a fine texture and flavor. Although an important commercial fish in the 19th century, catches after 1880 dwindled to practically nothing. Nowadays it is occasionally taken on lines or by trawlers in open ocean.

KING CRAB

Also ALASKA KING CRAB. This giant variety of crab, *Paralithodes camschatica*, is found in the extremely cold waters of the North Pacific Ocean and the Bering Sea. It has a spiderlike appearance and a leg span that reaches six feet in the largest specimens. Four to five feet is closer to average. A good sized crab weighs from 15 to 25 pounds.

Still, it is not the largest edible crab in the world. That honor goes to the Japanese giant crab or the Tasmanian giant crab, both of which are edible. The king crab, however, wins the prize for the tenderness, succulence and beautiful flavor of its flesh, which is white with pinkish borders. Most of the meat is extracted from the crab's long, tubular legs, which yield chunks up to nine inches long. Some meat is also extracted from the crab's body, but in bits and shreds.

These good qualities of the king crab have made it attractive to canners; and industries have sprung up in Alaska, Russia, Japan, Canada and Chile, which has its own southern version of the king crab. Canned king crab has proven a popular luxury item worldwide.

The name "king crab" is also applied to the European spider crab *(Maia squinado)*, which is deemed a delicacy; and to the Atlantic horseshoe crab *(Limulus polyphemus)*, which is inedible except for its eggs.

See also: **Crab.**

KINGFISH

This name is given to a number of good food fish. The largest, also called the "king mackerel" *(Scomberomoru cavalla)*, is found in the western Atlantic from North Carolina to Rio de Janeiro and in the Caribbean. It can reach a length of more than five feet and weigh as much as 80 pounds. It is characterized by plain coloring: deep blue above and silvery below. The king mackerel is taken as food throughout its range but has occasionally proven toxic.

Two species of the Pacific and Indian Oceans are called kingfish, the great *trevally (Caranx sexfaciatus)* and the golden *trevally (C. speciosus)*. The great trevally is found from East Africa to the Hawaiian Islands and is caught for food throughout this range. Large specimens measure up to four feet long and weigh as much as 40 pounds. Its colors range from golden yellow with dark cross bars in young fish to blue above and silver sides in adults. It is a fine sport fish. The golden trevally is somewhat smaller and is found from East Africa to Australia.

The northern kingfish *(Menticirrhus saxatilis)* is found in the western Atlantic from Cape Cod to Florida. It is a favorite fish for beach anglers and makes excellent eating. The northern kingfish is distinguished by a single barbel on its chin. It is bluish gray above and silver below and has dusky bars on back and sides. It reaches a length of 17 inches.

KINGFISHER

See also: **Halycon.**

KINGKLIP

Also LING. An eellike fish, *Genypterus capensis,* found in the coastal waters off South Africa, it is the center of an important commercial fishery from Walvis Bay to Algoa Bay. Large specimens attain a length of five feet. Characteristically, the kingklip has a flat head and a large mouth. It is dull brown above and mottled on the sides. The flesh of this fish is very highly regarded in South Africa, and its liver is considered a great delicacy, on a par with chicken liver.

A close relative is the ling *(G. blacodes)*, a cusk-eel found in New Zealand and Australian waters. Its flesh, especially its liver, is also highly prized, but the fish is not abundant enough to warrant commercial fishing. It reaches a maximum length of about three feet. It should not be confused with the Atlantic ling *(Molva molva)*.

KING ORANGE

Also NAARTJE. The small, sweet orange of South Africa, king orange *(Citrus nobilis)* closely resembles the tangerine, of which it is a variety or mutant. It is a delicious citrus fruit, probably the country's best, and is eaten as a dessert, in fruit salads, crystallized in sugar or in jellies and preserves.

KIPPERS

See **Herring.**

KIRGISCHERKASE

See **Krutt.**

KIRSCH

Also KIRSCHWASSER. Kirsch is a potent cherry brandy made from the small, wild, black cherries of the Rhine Valley. Ripe fruit is mashed and allowed to ferment in wooden tubs with stones intact for six weeks. The mixture is then twice distilled and allowed to mature in earthenware containers.

Kirsch is light, dry and colorless. It has a definite aroma of cherries and, due to the oil in the stones, overtones of bitter almonds. It is bottled at from 80 to 100 proof. Kirsch is produced in Germany, Switzerland and France, although which country produces the best is a matter of some dispute. It may be drunk neat or is frequently used to flavor fruit or crepe dishes.

KIRSCHWASSER

See **Kirsch.**

KISHKA

Kishka is a shiny, black Russian sausage whose ingredients are pig's blood, fat trimmings, groats, salt, pepper and chopped onions. The flavor is strong and salty.

See also: **Sausage.**

KITE

Also KITEFISH. In British usage, this is a flatfish of the **turbot** family. It is also the diamondfish *(Monodactylus agrenteus)* found from East Africa to Australia. A common fish throughout the area, frequenting river mouths and often living in freshwater, it is good to eat, but rather small, reaching a length of only nine inches.

KIWI FRUIT

Also ACTINIDIA, CHINESE GOOSEBERRY. Kiwi is a fruit about the size of a large plum, a fuzzy brown on the outside and a bright green on the inside. Its flavor is pleasantly sour, and many find it delicious raw. It may be eaten with the skin on, in which case it is thought advisable to rub off the fuzz.

Kiwi fruit *(Actinidia sinensis)* is thought to be of Chinese origin, and since its seeds (which are eaten) look like a gooseberry's, it was first called Chinese gooseberry. The main source of the fruit, however, is New Zealand (hence the name *kiwi* after the native bird), and some authorities think it may have originated there. A close relative, the *kokuwa (Actinidia callosa)* is native to Japan and Manchuria. It too is edible, and its flavor has been described as very delicate.

There are about 40 species of *Actinidiaceae* in East Asia, many of which were imported to Europe in the 19th century as ornamentals. The kiwi is of recent introduction, however. California is the only other source of substantial production. The tree is small, reaching 18 to 25 feet in height, with velvety round leaves and white or brown flowers. The fruit matures at the beginning of winter.

As for food value, the kiwi contains protein, salts of iron, calcium and phosphorus, and considerably more vitamin C than the lemon. When eaten as a dessert—raw or cooked—sugar or a liqueur is often added.

Kiwi is the basis of a favorite New Zealand dessert, which is something of a national dish—the Pavlova. It is creamy and presumably as light on the stomach as the Russian ballerina was on her feet.

KJARSGAARD

Kjarsgaard is a hard Danish cheese made from skimmed cow's milk.

KLEVOVACA

Klevovaca is a ginlike liquor produced in Yugoslavia by redistilling plum brandy with juniper berries.

KLOSTER

Also KLOSTERKASE. A soft, ripened cow's milk cheese made in both Germany and France, it is similar to **Romadour** and is produced in quarter-round cubes.

KNACKEBROD

Also HARDTACK. This hard, dry, biscuitlike bread of Swedish origin is made from rye flour and rye meal combined with sugar, salt and milk. It is a variety of hardtack, which was the sailors' name for ship's biscuit, staple fare aboard ship in the days before refrigeration. In U.S. parlance, they were called hard crackers or pilot's crackers. In the heyday of exploration, ship's biscuit was notorious for being so hard that it was practically impossible to bite into them unless they were either honeycombed internally by weevils or softened in water.

Knackebrod dough is rolled out very thin, shaped into rounds, then the center of each round is cut out. Both shapes are baked.

See also: **Bread.**

Kiwi fruit

KNACKWURST

See **Knockwurst.**

KNAOST

See **Pultost.**

KNOBBARD

Also KNOB. An edible shellfish found along the English coast, it is mentioned in Shakespeare's *Henry V*. The knobbard is small, similar to the **whelk,** and of only fair quality. It is probably related to the knobbed whelk, reputed to be the largest shellfish on the Atlantic Coast of North America north of Cape Hatteras.

KNOBLAUCH SAUSAGE

Knoblauch is German for garlic, and this sausage is quite similar to the **frankfurter,** i.e., basically minced beef and pork, but has more fat and garlic in it and is encased in shorter, thicker links.

See also: **Sausage.**

KNOCKWURST

Also KNACKWURST. This is a short, thick German sausage made with fat and lean pork, lean beef and seasoned with garlic, cumin seeds and salt. Knockwursts are tied in pairs for drying and smoking. They resemble certain types of **cervelat sausage.** They may be served cold or poached.

See also: **Sausage.**

KNOTTED WRACK

Also YELLOW TANG. A type of brown seaweed with branching fronds and conspicuous bladders, it is common off sheltered beaches of the British Isles and other Atlantic countries. Knotted wrack *(Ascophyllum nodosum)* is not very palatable in its natural state but is a fecund source of alginates used to thicken soups, ice cream, confectionaries, jellies and puddings.

KNOUTBERRY

See **Cloudberry.**

KOB

See **Waterbuck.**

KOCHKASE

See **Cooked Cheese.**

KOHLRABI

A variety of **cabbage,** much like a **turnip,** it is cultivated for its thickened stem, or root, that grows just above ground. The root has a delicate taste, much like that of a sweet and tender turnip.

For best flavor, the size of the root should not exceed three inches in diameter. Much of the kohlrabi's flavor resides in the skin, and it should not be peeled before cooking. It is often diced and cooked like cauliflower or sauteed in oil and garlic. When young and tender, its sprouting leaves can be cooked like spinach.

Kohlrabi

KOLA NUT

See **Cola.**

KOMBU

See **Kelp.**

KOMIJNE KAAS

See **Leyden.**

KOMMENOST

See **Kuminost.**

KONIGSWURSTE

Also PARTRIDGE SAUSAGE. This is called "king's sausage" due to the expensive ingredients, namely, partridges and truffles. The partridges are poached and boned, then supplemented by a couple of small chickens or cornish hens. The meat is finely ground, then mixed with minced truffles and chopped mushrooms and seasoned with salt, a little Rhine wine, coarsely ground pepper and mace. The mixture is stiffened by the addition of two eggs, then stuffed into pork intestines, which are twisted into links five to six inches long. The links may be braised or poached and served hot, or allowed to cool, then sliced to be served as hors d'oeuvres. It should not be fried, as the flavor of the game is lost.

See also: **Sausage.**

KONJAC

This edible tuber of a perennial herb, *Amorphophallus rivieri* var. *konjac* of the Asian tropics, may be as much as 10 inches in diameter. It is cultivated from Indonesia to Japan. It has a yamlike consistency.

KOPANISTI

A Greek cheese similar to **feta** but ripened with blue-green mold, it has a sharp, peppery flavor, and the texture is firmer and somewhat finer than feta's. *Kopanisti* is cured in earthenware containers, a process that takes one to two months.

KOPPEN

Also BAUDEN. A Czechoslovakian sour-milk cheese made by goatherders in the Sudetes Mountains between Silesia and Bohemia, *Koppen* has a firm texture and a sharp, pungent flavor. Individual cheeses weigh one or two pounds and may be either cup-shaped or cylindrical.

KOSHER

The term means clean or fit to eat according to Jewish dietary laws contained in a code called *halakhah*, which is based on passages in the Old Testament books of Leviticus and Deuteronomy. Religious Jews are guided by these laws in what they eat, when, and how they eat it. The laws spell out classes of forbidden food, e.g., birds of prey, reptiles, any animal except those that chew the cud and have cloven hooves. In the last example, an animal must both chew the cud and have cloven hooves to qualify. Therefore, both pork and horsemeat are nonkosher, as are camels and hares, which chew the cud but do not part the hoof. Other nonkosher items are animal blood and seafood that does not have fins and scales, which excludes eels, sharks, oysters, clams, lobsters, shrimp and mussels.

The laws also prescribe the way in which an animal is to be slaughtered. It must be done by a religious slaughterer, the *shochet*, who accomplishes his task with one clean slash of the throat. This facilitates bleeding, which removes a nonkosher food, animal blood. To remove as much blood as possible, the butcher may soak, drain, rinse and rerinse the meat. Incidentally, only the forequarters of an animal are kosher, so among beef cuts, kosher butchers sell meat from only the following: chuck, brisket, plate and rib.

An example of kosher laws relating to eating is the prohibition against mixing meat and dairy products. A Jew who "keeps kosher" would never use cream or butter at the same meal in which meat is served. Households where this is strictly observed must have two sets of dishes, one for meat dishes and one for dairy dishes, and each set is washed separately.

It has been suggested that a practical advantage of eating kosher is that kosher meat, for example, is more closely inspected, thus protecting the health of the consumer. One disadvantage is that it is more expensive. Indeed, the emphasis in dietary laws is on the "unclean" nature of tabooed food, such as pork. The whole raison d'etre of kosher is thought by many people to derive from ancient wisdom on health matters, which dates from an unrefrigerated age. Animals with questionable eating habits, such as pigs, and scavengers, such as birds of prey and crustaceans, are ruled out. These rules would seem to support a health-enhancing rationale for the foundation of dietary laws. On the other hand, skeptics point out that the chicken is kosher, and its eating habits can be as filthy as a pig's.

Several other theories of dietary taboos have been advanced, one of the most convincing of which is the "enemy food" theory. James Trager, in his fascinating and well-written treatise entitled *The Food Book*, remarks:

> *To us the most reasonable explanation is that the pork taboo was a vestige of the cultural conflict between range and grange. Swine were the domestic animals of farmers; early Jews were herdsmen. (Cain in the Book of Genesis, son of Adam and Eve, was a "tiller of the ground," but his brother Abel was a "keeper of sheep"; the "mark of Cain" after he slew his brother was to keep him from being killed in vengeance, which sounds like an effort by the Scripture writers to make range-grange adversaries cool it.) Just as the Chinese may have avoided milk products because they were the foods of their herdsmen enemy, Jews and Mohammedans and others avoided the meat of their farmer antagonists.*

KOSHER CHEESE

This is made in accordance with Jewish dietary laws and without the use of animal rennet. Curd is usually formed by natural souring or sometimes by a lactic starter. Various kinds include soft cheeses like cream and cottage, a Gouda and a cheese like Limburger eaten fresh.

KRAKORSO

The seeds of this cardamon-type plant, *Amomum thyrsoideum*, are used as a condiment or to spice such dishes as curry. It is found in Southeast Asia, especially Indochina.

KRAKOWSKA

A pork sausage of Ukrainian origin flavored with garlic, pepper, salt, mace and caraway seeds, it is heavily smoked and usually served cold as an hors d'oeuvre with thin-sliced rye bread.

See also: **Sausage.**

KRAUTERKASE

See **Sapsago.**

KREMSTALER

See **Romadur.**

KROBONKO

Also OYSTER NUT. These oily seeds of a perennial African vine, *Telfairea occidentale*, are eaten cooked in tropical regions. A related species with edible seeds is the Zanzibar oil vine *(T. pedata)*.

KRUPNIKOPF

A caraway-flavored liqueur, popular in Latvia and Lithuania, it is sweetened mainly with honey.

KRUTT

Also KIRGISCHERKASE. This crude, sour-milk cheese is made by nomads of the middle Asian steppes. The skim milk of cows, goats, sheep or camels is used, and the finished cheeses are sun-dried.

KUBACHER

A soft German cheese from upper Bavaria, it is made from cow's milk and is eaten ripe. Cheeses are marketed in two-pound cylinders.

KUDU

Kudu is a wild antelope of Africa, second in size only to the **eland.** There are two species, the lesser kudu *(Tragelaphus imberbis)* of eastern Africa and Somalia, and the great kudu *(T. strepsiceros)* of Africa south of the Zambezi Rivers, west to Angola and north to Ethiopia. Of the latter, a large male might stand as high as 4½ feet at the shoulder and weigh as much as 600 pounds. Kudus have been hunted for meat, hides and sport since prehistoric times. Their flesh, however, is said to be dryer and coarser than that of the deer.

KUDZU VINE

Kudzu is a woody, hairy vine, *Pueraria lobata*, native to China and Japan. Its root, leaves, pods and seeds are all edible. The kudzu has a long taproot that can be cooked and eaten as a vegetable. The plant is widely grown in the southeastern United States as fodder and to renovate exhausted land.

KUKUI

See **Candlenut.**

KUMINOST

Also KOMMENOST. A Scandinavian cow's-milk cheese, *Kuminost* is spiced with cumin and caraway seeds. Otherwise it resembles **Colby** and **grana.** Cheeses are formed in loaves weighing from five to seven pounds.

KUMISS

Also KOUMISS, KUMYS. A fermented milk drink of the ancient Mongols, *kumiss* is still made in the Russian regions of Uzbek, Bashkir and Krighiz. The original *kumiss* was made from mare's milk; a similar beverage made from camel's milk was called *kefir*, and from yak's milk, *airan*. *Kumiss* was fermented in two stages, first with a lactic acid bacteria, which produced a sour yogurtlike substance, and second with yeast, which gave it an alcoholic content of .1 to .2 percent and a slight effervescence. The first stage took 24 hours and the second an additional 12.

Kumiss has a long tradition in Central Asia. Herodotus, the Greek historian, reported the Scythians consuming it around 650 B.C. Marco Polo described the making of it in the 14th century. He wrote that Genghis Khan liked *kumiss* and kept a stable of 10,000 white horses to insure a ready supply.

Traditionally, a portion of the previous batch was added to start the *kumiss* fermenting. Modern versions, which at one time were available in the United States, are made from cow's milk and utilize commercial cultures. American *kumiss* was a creamy liquid with the consistency of buttermilk. It used to be sold in drugstores and was not alcoholic.

See also: **Kefir.**

KUMMEL

A clear liqueur flavored with caraway and cumin seeds, it varies in sweetness depending on where it is made. As a base, a highly distilled liquor is used, generally made from grain or potatoes. For decades, German kummel has been the standard of excellence, particularly Gilka Berliner Kummel. However, according to the Dutch, Bolskummel was the original, first distilled in 1575. It made such an impression on the Russian czar that he popularized it among the aristocracy. Today Russia is the principal producer and consumer of kummel. With crystallized sugar it is sold as Kummel Crystallize. It is bottled at from 70 to 86 proof.

KUMQUAT

This plum-sized citrus fruit has an orange gold rind and a bittersweet flavor. Some varieties of kumquat *(Citrus japonica)* are round like tiny oranges, while others are oblong. The fruit is native to China and was widely cultivated in Japan, Indochina and Java before reaching the West. Now it is extensively grown in the Mediterranean basin, Florida and California. The rind is sweet and aromatic, and frequently the fruit is eaten whole, rind and all.

Kumquats are enjoyed as a fresh fruit, as a dessert or in salads. They are also candied, used in preserves or marmalade, cooked in syrup to be served with ice cream, or pickled in wine vinegar, like cucumbers or melon. In France they are cooked as a garnish for roast duck. Kumquats are available in markets during the winter, and the fresh fruit should have firm, unblemished skin. The best specimens are heavy for their size.

Kumquat trees are ornamental plants that normally reach 10 to 15 feet in height. In China and Japan they are often set in pots and dwarfed to only two to three feet in height. The tiny trees bear normal fruit.

Kumquats

KUMYS

See **Kumiss.**

KUNDOL

Small, round, many-seeded fruit of a tropical tree native to the Philippines, the *kundol (Artocarpus odoratissimus)* is closely related to the **jackfruit.**

KURINI

See **Eriwani.**

KVASS

Also KVAS, KWASS, QUASS. A beer of ancient origin made in Russia, it is brewed in the home, is effervescent, mildly alcoholic and has a slightly sour taste. A simple version can be made by fermenting black rye bread, sugar and water. More elaborate versions may also contain white flour, raisins, lemon juice, sprouted barley and mint leaves or juniper berries. Kvass is also used as the basis for some Russian soups.

L

LABAN

This cultured-milk drink is like yogurt and is popular in the Middle East.

See also: **Fermented Milk, Yogurt.**

LABLAB BEAN

Also HYACINTH BEAN. A bean obtained from a variety of hyacinth plant, *Dolichos lablab* is widely cultivated in North Africa, the Middle East and Southeast Asia. It comes in two types—white or black—and is popularly known as the Egyptian bean and the "kidney bean of Asia." The mature seeds are rich in protein but hard-skinned. The young pods can be prepared and eaten like string beans. They are low in calories and rich in vitamin C.

Outside of Asia the plant is chiefly valued as an ornamental to decorate garden walls and arbors. The bean has been accepted somewhat in the southern United States where conditions are right for heavy yields. It is also known as the bonavist.

See also: **Bean.**

LABNEH

This Syrian sour-milk cheese is produced in very large quantities.

LABRADOR HERRING

See **Herring.**

LABRADOR TEA

Two species of evergreen shrubs, *Ledum groenlandicum* and *L. palustre*, have leaves that are infused to make a tea. These shrubs are native to damp, cold places of North America and Eurasia. The leaves yield an aromatic oil that is reputed to be mildly narcotic in its effect. Ledums were frequently served in place of ordinary tea in the American colonies during the years immediately before the Revolution due to the proscription on the importation of tea.

LABRUS

This is a genus of colorful fish of the wrasse family. Two common European species are the ballan wrasse *(L. bergylta)* and the cuckoo wrasse *(L. mixtus)*. The ballan is the largest of the European *labridae*, reaching a length of 20 inches. It is found in the Mediterranean and in the eastern Atlantic from the Canary Islands to Scotland and Norway. It is moderately popular among anglers, although its flesh is considered mediocre, being coarse and rather sweet.

The cuckoo roams the same territory, but is smaller. It is recognizable by its coloring, which combines red and blue in irregular patterns. It is often caught in lobster pots, scavenging for food. These species are often used in bouillabaisse and other fish stews.

See also: **Wrasse.**

LACCARIA

These are small edible mushrooms of North America and the British Isles. The most common are the waxy laccaria *(Laccaria laccata)* and the amethyst laccaria *(Laccaria amethystina)*. The latter is a deep violet and occurs in damp woodlands in the summer and autumn. The former is a pale red to lilac rose and appears in open, moist woodlands in late summer to early winter. They are both about the same size, i.e., height up to four inches, cap up to two inches across.

See also: **Mushroom.**

LACHSSCHINKEN SAUSAGE

This German sausage is made from the fillet of pork, which is pressed rather than minced or ground. Cured pork loins are faced and stuffed into large beef casings, tied off at about 16 inches, then dried and lightly smoked.

See also: **Sausage.**

LACRIMA CRISTI

This dry white wine from the Bay of Naples is known for its golden yellow color, subtle bouquet, velvety flavor and moderate alcoholic content. The wine is cultivated on the Italian mainland, on the slopes of Mount Vesuvius. It is made from the Falanghina, Greco di Torre and Fiana vines. Its Italian name means "the tears of Christ"—symbolic of the tears shed by Jesus Christ on Capri after Lucifer plundered the island from Paradise and let it fall into the sea.

It is an excellent addition to fish and shellfish—for which the Bay of Naples is famous. There is also a red Lacrima Cristi, which is produced in smaller quantities but which is not nearly so well known. A Spanish Lacrima Cristi—thick, sweet, old gold in color—is produced near Malaga.

LACTIC ACID

A clear, syrupy acid with a sour taste, it is produced during fermentation by the action of bacteria on lactose, or milk sugar, and by certain other processes. Lactic acid is the chief curdling agent in sour milk, cheese, yogurt and the like. Lactic-acid producing bacteria, such as *streptoccocus lactis* and *lactobacillus bulgaricus*, are usually introduced by inoculation.

Lactic acid has preservative properties and is present in pickling solutions, the making of sauerkraut and in wines and beers. In some places, sour milk is used to preserve meat and as a tenderizing marinade. Lactic acid is partly responsible for the inimitable taste of San Francisco sourdough bread.

A by-product of energy production, lactic acid helps preserve the flesh of game after the kill. During the chase, the pursued animal breaks down stored glycogen to produce energy and in the process deposits lactic acid in its muscle tissue.

The same thing occurs when a person overindulges in alcohol. The presence of excess lactic acid in muscle tissue is a major cause of the fatigue associated with a hangover. It is eliminated by the metabolic system at a steady rate that cannot be hurried. This explains why the hangover responds only to rest and time.

LACTOBACILLUS BULGARICUS

See **Yogurt.**

LACTOSE

A white, crystalline sugar naturally present in milk, it can be crystallized by concentrating and evaporating the whey.

LADIES FINGERS

See **Okra.**

LADOIX-SERRIGNY

Dry wines, notably red, come from this district near **Beaune** on the *Cote d'Or* in **Burgundy.** Both red and white wines from this district are usually labeled as Cote-de-Beaune-Villages. The best of the Ladoix-Serrigny red wine approaches the quality of the **Aloxe-Corton,** which is grown in the same vicinity.

LAD'S LOVE

Also SOUTHERNWOOD. An aromatic herb, *Artemisia abrotanum*, native to southern Europe but found also in the United States, it has a taste similar to that of **tarragon** and may be added raw to salads or cooked like spinach. A pleasant-tasting herb tea is made by infusing the leaves in boiling water.

LADYFISH

Also ELOPS, GIANT HERRING, TENPOUNDER. The *Elopidae* are a family of tropical seafish that superficially resemble the herring. The most prominent species is the ladyfish or tenpounder, *Elops saurus*, a gamefish of some importance off the coast of South Africa, Australia and the United States. Adults reach a length of up to four feet, but their flesh tends to be of only fair quality and rather bony. It is prized by anglers, however, because of the way it leaps and fights to escape. The ladyfish is found close inshore, sometimes in the surf, and in estuaries. It is silver blue above and brilliant silver on the sides.

LADY APPLE

See **Azarole.**

LADY'S SMOCK

See **Cardamine.**

LAFITE, CHATEAU

See **Bordeaux Wines.**

LAFITE ROTHSCHILD

See **Bordeaux Wines.**

LAGER

See **Beer.**

LAGOPUS

Also LAGOPEDE. The Pyrenean partridge (genus *Lagopus*), which is a member of the **grouse** family, it is fancied by gourmets in spite of the slightly bitter taste of its flesh attributed to its feeding on myrtle berries, rowan berries and birch shoots. White in winter except for black splotches on the tail, it turns tawny in summer with thin black streaks in its plumage. It is prepared like grouse.

LAGUIOLE

Also GUIOLE. This hard French cow's-milk cheese is rather like ***Cantal*** but generally considered better. It is named for the village of Laguiole, in Aveyron. Curing takes one month, and the cheese is available all year round.

LAGUNE, CHATEAU LA

See **Bordeaux Wines.**

LAITERON

Also MILKWEED. A plant of the *Asclepias* genus, which is sometimes eaten in France, it has a milky sap and its flavor combines that of lettuce and chicory. Young leaves are added to salads; mature leaves, which become leathery, may be cooked and eaten like spinach. Its roots are reminiscent of salsify and in winter are prepared in the same way.

LAKE HERRING

See **Cisco.**

LAKE TROUT

A large troutlike fish that inhabits the northern rivers and the deep, cold lakes of Europe and North America, lake trout are actually chars, i.e., members of the *Salvelinus* genus, rather than the *Salmo* genus. The best known European char is the *omble chevalier*, which is discussed under **Char.** The North American lake trout *S. namaycush* is widely distributed from Alaska to Labrador and as far south as the Great Lakes and the upper reaches of the Mississippi River system. It has also been stocked in certain deep, cold lakes, such as Lake Tahoe.

S. namaycush has been known to reach a length of four feet, but such fish are increasingly rare. It is a slow grower, and its fighting qualities make it a popular fish for anglers. Five pounds is considered a good size nowadays. The lake trout has a dark green to gray back and a white to yellowish belly, with light spots all over the head, back and sides. It has the characteristic pinkish flesh of the char and is excellently flavored. The lake trout is an important commercial fish in the far northern reaches of North America.

Lake Trout

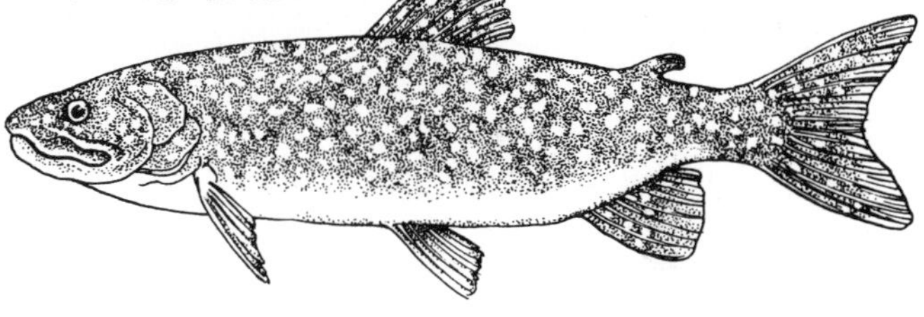

LAKKA

Also SUOMUURAIN. This is a cloudberry liqueur made in Finland. Cloudberries are a specialty of the arctic region and have a delicate, bittersweet flavor.

LAKOOCHA

Also MONKEY JACK. The edible fruit of a large deciduous tree, *Artocarpus lakoocha*, found in tropical Asia from India to Burma and Malaysia, lakoocha is related to breadfruit and jackfruit, but unlike those two it is relatively small, measuring about three inches across. It is round and has a pleasant subacidic flavor.

LALANDE WINE

This is a chiefly red wine from Lalande, a flat, sandy basin southwest of **Bordeaux,** near the Atlantic

Ocean in France. Lalande produces the great **Pomerol,** among the best of Bordeaux dry red wines, and the many labels from the commune of Neac, including those of Chateau Lacroix, Chateau Moulin-a-Vent and Chateau Nicole.

LAMB

Lamb is a sheep less than 12 months old. Its flesh, in some parts of the world—most notably the Middle East and Spain—is considered the best of all meats. There are three categories of lamb. The first is baby, or hothouse lamb, which is milk-fed and seldom more than six weeks old. It is very flavorful, but rare and extremely expensive. The second is spring lamb, which is also milk-fed but ranges up to four months in age. This is the one normally seen in U.S. markets, stamped "Genuine Spring Lamb" by the U.S.D.A. The meat is nearly white, tender with a delicate flavor and carries little fat. The third type is older than four months, but less than a year, and has been weaned and fed on grass. Its flesh tends to be more flavorful than the spring lamb's and in some instances is preferred over the latter, especially if it grazed in certain areas, such as the salt meadow in the estuary of the Gironde River at Pauillac, France, or in Holland's Frisian Islands. At 12 months the lamb becomes a yearling sheep, whose flesh is considered mutton, a meat not much liked in the United States because of its strong taste.

For that matter Americans are not great consumers of lamb, eating four pounds per capita a year, as compared to more than 100 pounds of beef. The French consumption is at least 50 percent higher than the American, and the British consumption is ten times as high, if you include mutton. Lamb, however, is completely dominant as the meat of choice in southeastern Europe, North Africa, the Middle East and Moslem India. Archeological evidence in Iraq shows that the preference for lamb was already established there by 9000 B.C.

Lamb flesh spoils faster than beef and should be eaten as soon as possible after purchase. The choice cuts of lamb are the legs, saddle or loin. These are the tenderest yet least economical cuts since the ratio of bone to meat is proportionately higher than in the neck, breast and shoulder, which are less tender but just as nutritious.

Because of its delicate flavor, lamb is usually cooked as simply as possible. The *gigot*, or roast leg of lamb, is held in high esteem in France. It is seasoned with garlic and accompanied by white beans. Roast leg of lamb in Great Britain and the United States is usually accompanied by mint jelly. Spitroasted, suckling lamb enjoys popularity throughout Italy, while Finland specializes in sauna-cured lamb, which though shriveled and dry-looking on the outside, remains juicy and tender inside. Lamb variety meats are particularly appreciated, including brains, heart, kidneys, liver, sweetbreads and tongue. See accompanying chart for the principle cuts of lamb.

In England, even lamb's tail is used to make a traditional dish. It is called lamb's tail pudding. The tails are docked between March and June and after being skinned, washed and stewed, are mixed with batter and potatoes and baked in the form of a pasty. Lamb's fries are testicles, which are parboiled, halved and skinned before cooking.

LAMBI

See **Conch.**

LAMB MINT

See **Spearmint.**

LAMBRUSCA

This very bright, dry red wine, tempered by sweetness and with a thick but short-lived froth is produced in the region of Emilia Romagna in northern Italy. A mixture of dryness and sweetness is characteristic of this wine, which well suits the highly flavored and rather greasy cuisine of the area (based largely on pork), which includes the culinary centers of Parma, Bologna, Modena and Reggio Emilia. This wine, like the **Barbera,** is named for its vine. There are many kinds of Lambruschi in this region, but all have the slight sweetness and the sparkling froth.

LAMB'S LETTUCE

Also CORN SALAD. A prolific plant or weed, lamb's lettuce *(Valerianella locusta)* is best prepared like spinach—raw in salads or lightly boiled or steamed—and much resembles spinach in taste. Only the young tender plants should be collected, when less than a foot high.

The "lettuce" label probably comes from the white, milky coloring of the underside of the leaves. The word "lettuce" is from the Latin *lactucus*, or "milky."

LAMB'S QUARTERS

Also WHITE GOOSEFOOT. An annual weedy herb, *Chenopodium album* found in Europe, Asia and North America, it is sometimes cultivated as an edible green for its stems and thick, tooth-shaped leaves, which are often mealy white beneath. Boiled, the leaves and young tops make a good spinach substitute. This plant is suited to cold, temperate climates and can reach a height of 10 feet. Its seeds may be milled for flour and used to make cakes, bread and porridge. They taste like buckwheat.

LA MOTHE

See **Goat's Milk Cheese.**

LAMPERN

This small river lamprey, *Lampetra fluviatilis*, is found in rivers and coastal waters of northwest Europe and the British Isles. A valuable food fish at one time, the lampern has suffered from pollution and obstruction of many rivers in its range.

See also: **Lamprey.**

LAMPREY

The lamprey is an eellike fish that appears to have gone out of fashion as a food, except in France. In earlier times it was considered good fare in England, Germany and Italy. Of the 25 species worldwide, the sea lamprey *(Petromyson marinus)* is the largest, attaining a maximum length of three feet. It is present on both sides of the Atlantic, from which it ascends rivers and streams to spawn, sometimes permanently adapting to the fresh-water environment, as it has in the Great Lakes of the United States.

Despite the resemblance, the lamprey is no relation to the eel. It is a parasite on other fish using an oval sucking disk instead of a mouth. After attaching to the host, it gnaws through the skin with its rasplike tongue and sucks out blood and other vital juices, leaving only when satiated or when the host dies. The sucking disk is also useful when it migrates upstream to spawn. With it, the lamprey attaches itself to a rock, wriggles to the top of it, then attaches to the next and so on. This habit earned it its scientific name, which means "stone sucker."

It was a popular food with the ancient Romans. According to Horace, knights and patricians doted on lamprey. During the Middle Ages, lampreys were caught in the Rhine River and made into a stew. They fetched high prices in Italy and France, while in England lamprey became the traditional Easter dish for English kings. In the present day, the city of Gloucester traditionally makes a Christmas gift of lamprey to Queen Elizabeth II.

In the United States lamprey were eaten before 1850 but since then have disappeared from the fish markets. The lamprey in the Great Lakes are reputedly inedible, although there seems to be no proof of that. Two lampreys that are also common in the United States are the freshwater silver lamprey *(Ichthyomyzon unicuspis)* and the Pacific lamprey *(Lampetra tridentata)*, which ascends West Coast rivers from the sea. They are both smaller than the sea lamprey.

Lamprey are somewhat inconvenient to prepare in that they must be bought live and killed by the cook. Although they have no bones, they are very slimy and must be skinned. The most renowned contemporary lamprey dish is *lamproie a la Bordelaise*, i.e., lamprey in the style of Bordeaux. This is a kind of stew whose other principal ingredients are leeks and red wine. Lamprey flesh has been described as fat and delicate.

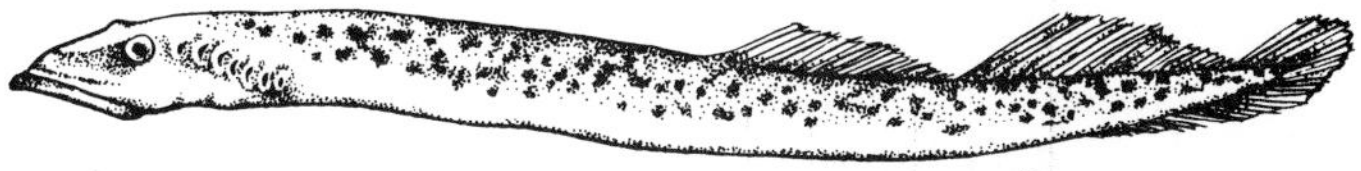

Lamprey

LAMPSANA

See **Lapsana.**

LANCASHIRE CHEESE

A popular English cheese that is very good for cooking, Lancashire has a white curd that is softer, more moist and more strongly-flavored than **cheddar** and **Cheshire.** Curing takes at least one month, but even at three months this cheese can be spread on bread like butter. Lancashire does not travel well, and most is consumed locally. Cheeses may weigh anywhere from 10 to 50 pounds.

LANDJAEGER

A small, thin, red brown sausage of the **cervelat** type, landjaeger is heavily smoked and hard to the touch. It is of German/Swiss origin.

See also: **Sausage.**

LAND RAIL

See **Corncrake.**

LANGOUSTE

See **Spiny Lobster.**

LANGOUSTINE

See **Norway Lobster.**

LANGRES

A soft, crusty French cheese from the Champagne region whose origin dates back 1,000 years or more, it is yellow and smooth-textured, with a strong aroma and flavor. Much of it is eaten fresh from September to April, otherwise it is aged from two to three months. Most is consumed locally as it does not travel well.

LANGSAT

Also DUKU. Edible fruit of a Malaysian tree, *Lansium domesticum*, also found in Indonesia, it is a pale, yellow berry that grows in dense clusters. The pulp is whitish, aromatic and succulent. Langsat is eaten as a dessert fruit.

LANGWAS

Also GREATER GALANGAL. An herb of the ginger family, *Alpinia galangal* is native to tropical Asia. The plant is often cultivated in Java. There the flower may be eaten raw with vegetables or along with pickles.

LANTANA

Also SHRUB VERBENA, WILD SAGE. A genus of tropical and subtropical shrubs found in North and South America and in Africa, the purple fruit of the *Lantana salviifolia* is eaten in West Africa.

LAOS

This pungent root of the ginger lily *(Alpina galanga)* is used as a seasoning in Southeast Asia.

LAPHROAIG

A brand of unblended Highland malt whiskey, unlike 99 percent of Scotch whisky it contains no grain whiskey. It is fuller-bodied than the blended whiskies and is considered to be of finer quality.

LAPLAND

A very hard cheese made by Laplanders from reindeer's milk, it resembles **Swiss** cheese. The finished product is shaped like a dumbbell.

LAPSANA

Also LAMPSANA. A genus of European plants, including the *Lapsana communis*, which is a sort of wild endive, it is best eaten raw in salads. It becomes tough and bitter when cooked.

LAPWING

See **Plover.**

LAPSANG-SOUCHONG TEA

This hearty, black Chinese tea has a rich, smoky taste and aroma with sweet overtones. It is a strong, slow-brewing tea produced chiefly in Hunan and Fukien provinces and Taiwan. It is often used in blends with Assam or Ceylon teas.

See also: **Tea.**

LARD

Lard is hog fat that has been rendered, clarified and deodorized. Fine lard is white and semisolid in texture. For use in such things as margarine, it is hydrogenated to firm up the texture. Up until around 1950 in the United States lard was the most commonly used fat in margarine, cooking and baking. Then, animal fats began to be replaced with hydrogenated vegetable and seed oils. Still, many consider lard to be the best shortening for cakes and pastries and the best fat for deep frying. It does not sputter when heated and has a high smoking temperature. *Leaf lard* is considered to be the finest quality lard. It comes from the leaf fat around a hog's kidneys.

LARGE CANE

Also SOUTHERN CANE, CANEBRAKE. This type of bamboo, *Arundinaria gigantea*, is found in the eastern and southern parts of North America. Its seeds may be used as a substitute for wheat.

LARK

Lark is a small songbird common in Europe, North America, Asia and Africa. The European skylark *(Alauda arvensis)* is considered excellent eating and fair game in France and Italy. It is a small, brown bird weighing no more than an ounce when dressed. The flavor is described as delicate. Larks are made into a pate in France, the city of Pithivier being famous for it. They may also be roasted on skewers, casseroled or boned and cooked in butter.

Larks used to be popular fare in England, particularly if baked into lark pie. This is no longer true. Lark has completely disappeared from the English diet, and the same goes for the United States where it is generally illegal to hunt them. Before the middle of the 19th century, however, small birds were a normal part of the American diet.

LASAGNE

See **Linguine.**

LASCASES, CHATEAU LEOVILLE

This is one of the finest dry red wines produced in the commune of St. Julien, in the **Medoc** area of Bordeaux in southwestern France. Chateau Leoville-Lascases is almost annually classified as a great growth. The label designates a robust, "masculine" wine, rich in tannin and ideal for roast meats and game.

See also: **Bordeaux Wine, Medoc, Leoville Wine.**

LASSI

Also LHASSI. This popular drink in east Asia is made from sour milk or yogurt, sugar, salt and water or soda water. It is whipped together to make a long, cool drink.

LA TACHE

A famous vineyard in the Vosne-Romanee commune of France's Burgundy region, it is a *grand cru* producer whose red wines are described as having beautiful color, a deep bouquet and flavor, body, elegance and breed.

See also: **Burgundy Wines, French.**

LATEX

This is the milky sap of a number of different plants, an edible variety of which comes from the cowtree *(Brosimum utile* or *B. galactodendron)* of South America. The sap is mixed with water and drunk as a milk substitute. The latex of the papaya tree contains the enzyme papain, which is much like the digestive enzyme pepsin and is used as a meat tenderizer.

LA TOMME

See **Tomme.**

LATOUR, CHATEAU

See **Bordeaux Wines.**

LAUREL

See **Bay Leaf.**

LAVARET

See **Fera, Houting.**

LAVENDER

Aromatic shrubs *(Lavandula* spp.) of the mint family have leaves and purple flower spikes that may be used as a flavoring agent. Two of the most common lavenders are the English lavender *(L. angustifolia)* and Spanish lavender *(L. stoechas)*. They originated in the Mediterranean region, northeastern Africa and India.

Their flavor is bitter, so they are used sparingly in jellies, marinades, punches and stews. Lavenders are widely grown as ornamentals. Oil of lavender is distilled from the flowers and used in perfumery.

LAVER

This is an edible seaweed found on both coasts of the United States, in Europe and the Far East. Purple or red laver *(Porphyra laciniata)* is eaten in Scotland and Ireland under the name *slouk* or *sloke*. It may be boiled and served as a hot vegetable or pickled and served with cold meats. Red laver is rich in iodine and is harvested from June to March.

Green laver *(Ulva lactuca)*, also known as sea lettuce, has bright green, crinkly leaves. It is also served as a cooked vegetable. In the British Isles, laver is also used to flavor oatmeal, flat cakes and bread. In the Far East, laver is the preferred food of the swift or salangane, whose saliva is the precious ingredient of the birds' nests used to make soup in Chinese cuisine.

See also: **Bird's Nest.**

LAVILLE HAUT-BRION

Here is a dry white wine from the region of **Graves** in the Bordeaux area of southwestern France. The label "Chateau Laville Haut-Brion" heralds a "classified growth" produced in the commune of Talence and marks a dry white Graves superb with shellfish and seafood.

See also: **Bordeaux Wines, Graves.**

LEAF CHEESE

See **Tschil.**

LEAF MUSTARD

See **Indian Mustard.**

LEAST CISCO

One of the smaller whitefish with both migratory and nonmigratory varieties, least cisco *(Coregonus sardinella)* is an important food fish in Siberia, arctic Russia and adjacent areas of North America. It commonly reaches a length of about 16 inches and has a protruding lower jaw. Migratory populations live in the mouths of estuaries, then ascend the rivers in great shoals during the summer. They are commonly caught in gill nets and seines.

See also: **Cisco, Whitefish.**

LEATHER CHEESE

Also LEDER, HOLSTEIN DAIRY CHEESE. This is a variation of **Holstein skim-milk cheese** where all the fat is removed from the milk before butter milk is added. It is made in the Schleswig-Holstein area from cow's milk. The cheeses have small eyes and are cured for four months. Their weight ranges from 15 to 25 pounds.

LEBANON

A type of bologna sausage made in Lebanon, Pennsylvania, it is precooked and consists entirely of beef that is heavily smoked. The taste is rather sharp.

See also: **Sausage.**

LECITHIN

A fatty substance found in egg yolks, nerve tissue, milk, brains and most abundantly in soybeans, lecithin is a natural emulsifier, that is, it disperses oils in other liquids and holds them in suspension. Lecithin from egg yolks is the emulsifier in mayonnaise. Commercial lecithin comes mainly from soybeans and in the crude state is dark colored. It is bleached by hydrogen peroxide to a light straw color. It contains a lot of phosphorus and is used as emulsifier in chocolate coatings, margarine, shortening and greaseless frying compounds.

LEDER

See **Leather Cheese.**

LEECHEE

See **Litchi.**

LEEK

A close, but more delicately flavored, relative of the onion, the leek *(Allium ampeloprasum*, var. *porrum)* is a member of the lily family and is cultivated chiefly for its blanched stems and terminal bulblet. It is a hardy plant that survives cold winters yet also does well in subtropical climates, such as that of the Mediterranean area.

The cultivated leek is herbaceous and biennial, achieving a height of about three feet in the second year. In cultivation, the edible lower portions, i.e., stem and bulb, are banked with earth so that they become blanched. The trimmed green tops are also eaten. The raw leek has a strong odor, but this disappears in the cooking, leaving a mild onion flavor. It is used chiefly to flavor soups, stews and stock, but in European countries it is often treated like asparagus, i.e., boiled and served hot with butter or cold with vinaigrette sauce.

The leek is a plant of very ancient cultivation, and due to its adaptability to various climates was admired by such diverse cultures as the ancient Egyptian, Roman and Celt, including the Irish, Welsh and Scots. In his *Satires*, Juvenal wrote, "Egypt is a country where onions are adored and leeks are gods." The Romans believed leeks to be beneficial for the vocal cords. The Emperor Nero therefore drank leek soup every day to deepen and clarify his voice for speechmaking. The leek is a patriotic symbol of the Welsh nation, a reminder of a Welsh victory over the Saxons in 640 A.D. in which Welshmen identified themselves by fastening leeks to their caps. On the continent, they were a mainstay during the Middle Ages. In more recent times, the leek's popularity has waxed and waned, especially in France. It is presently on the rise. Although frequently available in supermarkets, the leek has never enjoyed much popularity in the United States. Cock-a-leeky soup, whose principal ingredients are chicken and leeks, is a Scottish specialty.

LEGUME

This large group of plants whose fruits consist of seed-bearing pods includes peas, beans and lentils. By extension, the word "legume" is applied to the seed too. In French *legume* and Spanish *legumbre* the meaning has been broadened to encompass all vegetables. Technically, legumes belong to the botanical family *Leguminosae*, which contains about 12,000 species of spiny herbs, shrubs, trees, vines or lianas. Common legumes eaten by humans are peas, beans, soybeans, lentils, peanuts, chickpeas and cowpeas. Common forage legumes are alfalfa, clover, kudze, the lespedezas and the vetches. See separate articles on many individual legumes.

Legumes combine a number of beneficial qualities. As food, they are high in protein and carbohydrates. Taken together with grains, such as wheat or corn (maize), they can provide all the amino acids essential to complete protein. In the dry state, legumes are made up of from 18 to 25 percent protein, and soybeans even more. As an agricultural crop, they can restore depleted soil through bacteria living symbiotically in their roots. Legumes absorb nitrogen from the air, and the bacteria fix it in the soil.

LEICESTER CHEESE

This hard, mildly sharp, English cheese has much in common with other popular English cheeses, such as cheddar, Derby and Cheshire. The curd is pale orange (from annatto), moist and fast ripening, but with a flaky texture. The cheeses are round, weigh an average of 40 pounds and may be marketed after only two months curing, although six to eight months improves the flavor. Some consider this the finest mild English cheese of its type.

LEMON

A citrus fruit whose cultivation goes back at least 2,500 years, the lemon *(Citrus limon)* has an acidic flavor and yellow skin, which contains an essential, aromatic oil. The lemon tree, a small evergreen, is believed to have originated in the Indus Valley of northern India and does best in subtropical climates, such as those of Sicily and Southern California. For best results, its cultivation requires even temperatures, because the tree does not respond well to harsh sunlight, frost or heavy rains, although plenty of water is needed. In Southern California, where lemons are never grown more than 40 miles from the sea, both irrigation and heating are needed in the orchards. Under these conditions, the trees bear both fragrant flowers (white, tinged with red or purple) and fruit all year round. Commercially, the tree is never grown from seed, but propagated by budding or grafting onto the rootstock of a type of orange tree. Following this method, the tree is ready to bear in five years. Grown from seed, it might take 15 years to reach bearing size, and then it produces inferior fruit.

Lemons are oval shaped and range in size from small, smooth and thin-skinned to large, rough and thick-skinned. There are three categories of lemon: the common or acid type, which appears in markets; the rough lemon, whose rootstock is used for budding orange trees; and the sweet lemon, which lacks the tartness of common lemon and whose flavor is insipid rather than sweet. The fruit is usually picked unripe as soon as it reaches a specified size considered marketable. It is then kept from one to four months while it "cures," i.e., turns yellow. Once ripe, the fruit will deteriorate rapidly unless it remains unbruised and is kept at a temperature of around 40° F (4.4° C). Under those conditions, it will keep for eight-12 weeks.

Leek

Lemons

The lemon has countless uses in the kitchen. Lemon juice is used mainly as a souring agent. As such, it is interchangeable with vinegar for anything but pickling. It goes into salad dressings, lemonade, sherbet, ice cream and is a general seasoner of seafood. Aromatic oil of lemon is contained in small cysts in its skin. Sometimes called "zest" of lemon, it is obtained by grating the skin or rubbing it with cubes of sugar. The oil is useful medicinally too, as it has antibacterial properties. Lemon juice contains high amounts of vitamin C, about 60 milligrams per 3½ ounces (100 grams).

From India, cultivation of the lemon spread west to Persia and Palestine, and possibly to Greece and Italy, although throughout Classical Antiquity lemons remained a rare and expensive luxury. Lemons disappeared entirely from Europe with the collapse of the Roman Empire in the West, but were reintroduced by the Moors during the Eighth and Ninth centuries into Spain and Sicily. There was not much demand for lemons in the rest of Europe until the 13th century after the Crusaders returned from Palestine where they found an abundant supply. Still, they were priced for the well-to-do, and it was not until the 15th century that lemon juice began to replace **verjuice** as the principle souring ingredient in cooked dishes. According to tradition, Christopher Columbus brought lemon seeds to the New World, and the first large plantings occurred in Florida in the 16th century. Florida proved too damp for successful lemon-growing, and in the 19th century California became the pre-eminent lemon state. Today California produces 80 percent of the U.S. lemon crop.

LEMON BERRY

Also LEMONADE BERRY. The bright, red berry of a variety of sumac, *Rhus integrifolia*, native to southern and Baja California, it has been used as a flavoring in foods and for making cooling drinks.

See also: **Sumac.**

LEMON CURD

This is a thick custard made of lemon juice and rinds, eggs, sugar and butter. The mixture is cooked, bottled in jars and eaten like jam.

LEMON EXTRACT

See **Flavoring Extract.**

LEMON FISH

See **Amber Fish.**

LEMONGRASS

Also FEVER GRASS. This perennial, tropical grass, *Cymbopogon citratus*, reaches a height of six feet or more. It is widely cultivated in the Asian tropics for the essential oil distilled from its leaves. Lemongrass oil is highly aromatic; it is used in perfumery and medicine and is used freely in Vietnamese cooking as a flavoring agent.

LEMON MINT

Also LEMON BEE BALM. This perennial plant is eaten as a condiment with meat dishes. *Monarda citriodora* is native to the southern United States from South Carolina to New Mexico and to adjacent areas of Mexico.

LEMON OIL

A pale, yellow liquid found in the tiny, balloon-shaped sacs contained in the outer rind of the **lemon,** it is used to add flavor or fragrance to such products as carbonated soft drinks, laundry detergents, candies, ice creams and baked goods. An element of lemon and other peel oils, d-limonene, is used as a flavor enhancer in frozen juice concentrates.

LEMON SOLE

This common European flatfish, *Microstomus kitt*, is not a member of the sole family, but belongs to the *Pleuronectidae*, which includes the plaice, halibut, dab and flounder. Its name in English seems to derive from the French *limande-sole*.

The lemon sole is most plentiful in the cold waters of the North Atlantic around Iceland, northern Norway and the Faeroes but is found as far south as the Bay of Biscay. It is fished most intensively by the Danes. *M. kitt* resembles the sole with its oval shape, small head and brown coloring, but by concensus of authorities its flesh is definitely inferior in taste and texture, being rather insipid and stringy unless absolutely fresh, when its taste is very delicate. Lemon sole is broiled and served with a good sauce or prepared like sole or dab.

The California Dover sole *(Microstomus pacificus)* is the lemon sole's American counterpart. Like the lemon sole, it rarely exceeds 28 inches in length. The dover sole is heavily fished from Baja California to the Bering Sea, and its fillets are marketed both fresh and frozen. Its flesh is also definitely inferior to the English or true Dover sole *(Solea solea)*. Thus its name on a menu is a potential source of confusion to the consumer.

LEMON THYME

Also WILD THYME. A species of thyme *Thymus serphyllum* that grows wild all over Europe and has a delightful fragrance and rich flavor of lemon, it is a prostrate, mat-forming plant with a woody base, erect stems and purple, headlike flower clusters. It is good pasturage for sheep.

The ancient Greeks and Romans used it to flavor wine, and early herbalists considered it a specific against nightmares. It makes a good accompaniment for fish dishes, as well as for chicken and veal, and is excellent for flavoring soups.

LEMON VERBENA

This lemon-scented herb *Lippia citriodora* is cultivated chiefly for its fragrance but does have its culinary uses. Chopped finely, its leaves are added to salads, stuffings and fruit drinks. It is extremely aromatic and must be used sparingly. It makes a good herb tea. Commercially, its oil is extracted for use in perfumes.

LEMUR

Natives of Madagascar are fond of the flesh of two local varieties of lemur, the sportive lemur *(Lepilemur ruficaudatus)* and the weasel lemur *(L. mustelinus)*. These lemurs are small (up to 13 inches long), tree-dwelling, nocturnal mammals. They are captured during daylight hours when they are sluggish. The natives knock them out of the trees with sticks.

LE-NATURE'S WATER

A carbonated mineral water bottled in the United States, Le-Nature's Crystal Clear Mineral Water is relatively low in mineral content (365 ppm of total dissolved solids). A 1980 Consumers Union sensory panel rated the taste of this water as good, with the following qualifying comments: mildly bitter, mildly sour, mildly salty.

See also: **Mineral Water.**

LENGUADO

Also PEACOCK FLOUNDER. This colorful species of flounder, *Bothus lunatus*, is found in the western Atlantic and Caribbean from Bermuda to Brazil. It is left-eyed and reaches a length of 18 inches. The lenguado is a highly regarded food fish throughout its range and is generally taken in shallow water.

LENTIL

This leguminous plant has been cultivated by humans since the Bronze Age for its flat, dishlike seeds, which are highly nutritious. The seeds are 25 percent protein, more than any other legume, and rich in vitamin B, iron and phosphorus.

A staple in the diets of the ancient Greeks, lentils were also the object of snobbery. "Now he doesn't have to eat lentils anymore," was a proverbial way of alluding to a person's rise to riches. They are also thought to be the mess of pottage for which the biblical Esau sold his birthright.

Lentils may be green, yellow, orange or black. The two main types are the Egyptian, which are orange, small, and sold split in two; and the French, which are larger, tastier and gray green in color.

They are most popular in India, where they form the basis of the dish, *dahl*. In the West, they are usually made into soup or added to a salad.

LENTISK

See **Mastic.**

LEOGNAN WINE

A superior wine, both red and white, produced in the commune of Leognan in the **Graves** region of **Bordeaux,** Leognan is characterized by its smoothness and by a distinctive and delicate aroma. Among the famous reds are those of Chateau Hault-Bailly and **Chateau-Haut-Brion.** Chateau Carbonnieux and Chateau Olivier make both red and white wine in this district, while the best white Leognan may be that of Domaine de Chevalier.

LEON LEMON

Also TURK'S HEAD. Edible fruit of a large, ribbed cactus, the Leon lemon *(Ferocactus hamatacanthus)* is greenish and is used as a substitute for lemon in cooking. The Turk's head, as it is also known, is found mainly in south Texas, New Mexico and northern Mexico.

LEOVILLE WINE

This is a dry red **Bordeaux** classed among the best "second growths" in the region of **Medoc,** world famous for its great red wines. Among the most highly prized are the wines of Chateau Leoville-Lascases, Chateau Leoville-Poyfere and Chateau Leoville-Barton.

See also: **Lascases, Chateau Leoville.**

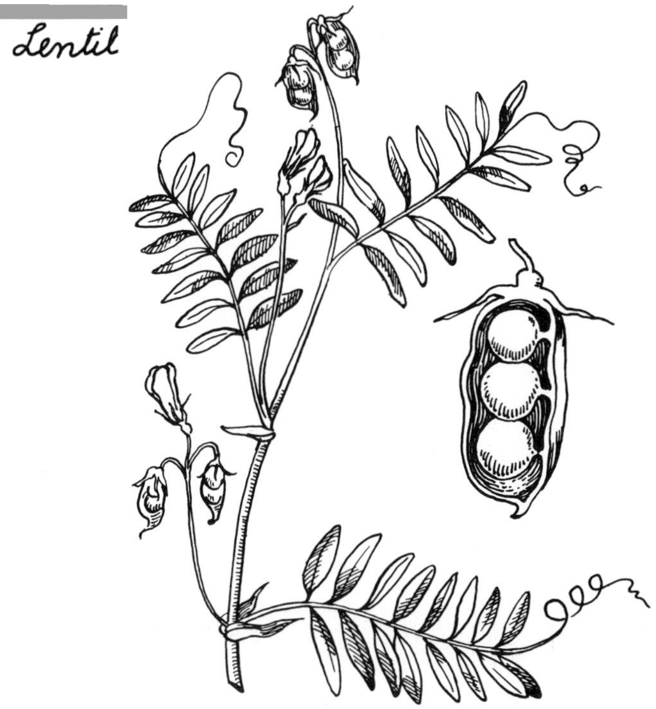

Lettuce: butterhead (left) and romaine (right)

LEPIOTA

See **Parasol Mushroom.**

LEREN

An edible tuber produced by several species of plants of the *Calathea* genus, most notably *C. allouia*, the *leren* is native to the Caribbean region but has been transplanted to other tropical areas, such as India, Sri Lanka, Malaysia, Indonesia and the Philippine Islands. The tubers are relatively unknown outside their immediate areas of cultivation. They look somewhat like potatoes, measuring from two to 3½ inches in length and up to two inches in diameter.

They are boiled for 15 to 20 minutes before eating, and the resulting starchy vegetable can be eaten with dinner or by itself. Its white flesh has a crisp, crunchy texture and a taste that resembles sweet corn. It is considered a superior hor d'oeuvre.

LESCIN

A Russian ewe's milk cheese, it is made in the Caucasus region.

LESSER CELANDINE

Also PILEWORT. A wild plant found in Europe, western Asia and North America, lesser celandine *(Ranunculus ficaria)* has stalks and heart-shaped leaves that can be cooked and eaten as vegetables.

LETTUCE

The well-known garden vegetable *Lactuca sativa* has crisp, succulent leaves without peer in popularity as a salad ingredient. The name "lettuce" derives from the Latin word *lactuca* for milk, because, when cut, lettuce exudes a milky juice. The Assyrians, Greeks and Egyptians considered lettuce an aphrodisiac, chiefly, it seems, because they grew asparagus lettuce, with its phalluslike central stalk. In contrast, the Romans thought it an anaphrodisiac and called it "eunuch's salad." Of course, they were dealing with head lettuce, a form they developed that lacks the requisite form to suggest potency.

The ancient Romans ate lettuce in salad with dressing, as we do, and when it came into vogue under the Emperor Augustus (27 B.C.–14 A.D.) it was eaten at the end of the meal. Later under Domitian (81–96 A.D.), it was switched to the beginning of the meal. Debates still take place on the question of when the salad should be eaten. Nevertheless, the Roman change is attributed to their discovery that lettuce arouses the appetite.

There are three main types of lettuce plant: cabbage or head; cos or romaine, and leafy lettuce. A fourth, rare type is asparagus lettuce *(L. sativa* var. *angustana)*, which has a fast-growing central stalk.

Head lettuce (L. sativa var. *capitata)* is further divided into two groups: Boston or butter head lettuce, which has a round spreading head, fairly small with soft, dark green leaves whose texture is almost oily, and hard-headed types such as iceberg, which is firm and crisp with whitish green leaves. Iceberg is the most common variety found in U.S. markets. It is easiest to pack and ship but is inferior from the point of view of taste and nutrition.

Cos or romaine lettuce (L. sativa var. *longifolia)* has long, coarse, green leaves which loosely form a cylindrically shaped head. Of all lettuces, this is the most heat resistant. Despite its name "romaine," it did not originate in ancient Rome, although it was known there, but on Cos, a Greek island in the Aegean Sea.

Leafy or cutting lettuce (L. sativa var. *crispa)* does not form a head, or at best a very loose one. It is handy in the home garden because, unlike other varieties, it does not run to seed but instead produces a succession of leaves for cutting during the summer months.

Lettuce leaves are usually green or greenish white but may also be brown or mottled red and brown. Lettuce is extremely rich in vitamins and mineral salts. It contains vitamins A, B, C and E, plus calcium, iron and magnesium. Because of its magnesium content, it is considered a calmative and a mild sedative. The milky juice of wild lettuce is classed by some authorities as an hypnotic or narcotic similar to opium. It was formerly used in treating nervous disorders, insomnia, rheumatism, colic and the like. Similarly, bolted lettuce is reputed to have a soporific effect. This is lettuce that has been subjected to intense heat early in life and has consequently gone to seed prematurely, creating an unnatural chemistry.

LEVERET

See **Hare.**

LEVOVANGAN

A small but important food fish found from the Red Sea to Hawaii, levovangan *(Monotaxis grandoculis)* reaches a length of 30 inches and has a broad deep head and large eyes. Otherwise it resembles members of the sea bream family *Sparidae.* It is silver gray above, shading lighter on the sides with red or yellow fins. The levovangan is found at the edges of reefs in fairly deep water and is abundant enough to be a valuable subsistence fish throughout its range.

LEVULOSE

See **Fructose.**

LEYDEN

Also KOMIJNE KAAS. A Dutch cow's-milk cheese, both farmhouse and factory made, it is spiced with cumin, caraway seeds and sometimes cloves. It is a hard cheese, and in some variations the curd is shot with green veins. Leyden has a hard crust, which is generally light-colored but at times tinted blue. The shape is round and flat like **Gouda,** and the weight ranges between eight and 20 pounds. The outside is marked with crossed keys, borrowed from the University of Leyden's emblem.

LICHEE

See **Litchi.**

LICHEN

These mosslike plants grow under difficult climactic conditions—severe cold, aridity, high altitude—on such surfaces as rock, dead trees and barren soil. They have neither stems nor leaves and consist of a complex association of algae and fungi. The best-known edible lichen is **iceland moss.** Other lichen serve as reindeer fodder and a source for fabric dye.

LICORICE

Also LIQUORICE. A slow-growing herb, *Glycyrrhiza glabra*, has roots that produce a sweet juice used in candymaking, medicines and as a flavoring agent. The licorice plant is native to southern Europe and western Asia. It prefers sandy, moist soils and is so plentiful in some areas of Italy and Sicily as to be considered a pesky weed. The licorice plant reaches a height of about three feet and has small bluish or violet flowers, a long taproot and stolons (rootlike runners that fan out beneath the soil). The taproot and stolons are harvested to produce the extract when the plant is at least three years old.

The roots are allowed to dry out for six months or so, then are steeped and pressed. The juice is evaporated until it is thick and black. With a little starch and sugar added, it can be pressed into glossy, black sticks and eaten as candy. The extract is valued in medicine as a emollient and expectorant and has been found useful in cough preparations. In areas where the plant is plentiful, the roots are infused to make a sweet drink.

Licorice is a corruption of the Greek term *glycerrhiza* meaning "sweet root." The taste is sweet, yet bitter, and reminiscent of the taste of anise. Among licorices, Spain's is known for its sweetness and that of Turkey for its bitter quality. In England, licorice extract is used to flavor stout and porter. At

Pontefract in Yorkshire, licorice grows prolifically and is used to produce the licorice candy known as Pontefract cakes.

Recent studies have shown that too much licorice can cause high blood pressure in some people.

LIEBFRAUENMILCH

This is a light German white wine from Rheinhesse. *Liebfrauenmilch* or *Liebfraumilch* is a name applied to all the sweet wine of this region that possess the qualities of a good Rhine wine: lightness, freshness, bouquet and moderate alcoholic content. The name means "Virgin's milk" in German but really derives from the word *minch*, a dialect word for "monk," after vineyards cultivated in the Middle Ages by monks near the Church of Our Lady of Worms.

LIEDERKRANZ

This is an American variation, some say improvement, on the Belgian **Limburger** cheese. The art of making it was discovered by Emil Frey of Monroe, New York in 1892. It was named after a singing society to which Frey's employer belonged. The name *Liederkranz*, meaning "wreath of song," is trademarked.

It is a soft cow's-milk cheese in most respects like Limburger, but the flavor and aroma are milder. Red slime bacteria are the principal ripening agents, working from the surface inward. Liederkranz is rather perishable. Cubes weighing five or six ounces are wrapped and shipped to market after 12 to 15 days' curing.

LIGHTS

Also LUNGS. This culinary term means mammalian lungs, especially those of calves, beef, lamb and pork. Lights are used in stews in various parts of Europe, such as Hungary's calf's lung and heart in paprika sauce and in **haggis.** In the United States, however, the Wholesale Meat Act was amended in 1971 to declare lungs unfit for human consumption, a position considered unenlightened by some food experts in view of lungs' high protein and low fat content.

See also: **Variety Meats.**

LILLET

A French aperitif wine sold in both red and white versions, like **vermouth,** it contains quinine and other flavoring herbs. It is best served chilled.

LILY BULB

The bulbs of certain lilies are nutritious and may be ground to make a flour for baking or cooking as porridge and gruel. Edible lily bulbs include those of the gold-banded lily *(Lilium auratum)*, the tiger lily *(L. lancifolium)*, the martagon lily *(L. martagon)*, the Carolina lily *(L. michauxii)* and the Turk's cap *(L. superbum)*.

Henry David Thoreau (d. 1862), American essayist, poet and naturalist, reported making a soup from lily buds, which he thought "palatable enough, but it reminded me of the Irishman's limestone broth."

Limas, a variety of sweet lemon

LIMA

Also MILLSWEET. This variety of sweet lemon, *Citrus limonia*, originated in Palestine, but in the Western Hemisphere it is grown mainly in Mexico, Arizona and California. The tree reaches a height of 16 feet and is quite thorny. The lima is very low in acid and appeals to lovers of citrus fruit who cannot tolerate acid. When ripe, the lima is yellow, and in rare cases orange, and reaches a diameter of 1½ inches. It is eaten raw or used to make juice.

LIMA BEAN

Also BUTTER BEAN. A New World plant, *Phaseolus lunatus* has broad, flat, usually light green beans widely cultivated in tropical and subtropical areas of the world. The lima bean was domesticated by the Indians of Peru and its cultivation had spread to North America before the arrival of colonists. The Algonquins of the Northeast used it as one of the main ingredients of their staple dish, succotash.

Depending on the variety, the lima bean plant can be a large climbing vine or a small bush. The varieties break down into two basic types, the Sieva or Carolina bean, which is small, and the Cape or Madagascar bean, known as the true lima bean, which is larger. Both are floury in texture, high in food value (like all the *Phaseolus* genus) and popular, especially in the United States, Great Britain and Brazil. Most of the U.S. crop is produced in California, while Great Britain imports lima beans from Mauritius and Madagascar, where they have been cultivated since the 18th century. The larger varieties are often referred to as butter bean in the American South and in England. Lima beans also function as a rotation crop with sugar cane in tropical areas.

The lima bean is sold both fresh and dried. Size doesn't indicate tenderness (since they are different varieties), although the flavor may vary. To retain the flavor, they should be steamed. Older beans may be blanched in boiling water before steaming. Canned or frozen lima beans are also available.

See also: **Bean, Kidney Bean.**

LIMAO DO MATTO

Lemonlike fruit of a small South American tree, *Rheedia edulis*, it is sometimes cultivated in Brazil and is used to make jam.

LIMBURGER

This semisoft Belgian cheese is celebrated for its remarkably strong flavor and aroma, characteristics caused mainly by the ripening action of *Bacterium linens*. During the curing process, bacteria form a red slime on the surface, giving the cheese a red yellow color. It is made from whole, skim or partly skimmed milk, and the curd has small, irregular holes. Cheeses vary in size from three-inch cubes, weighing one pound, to six-inch squares, weighing 2½ pounds.

Although named for the town of Limbourg, province of Liege, where it was first produced, more Limburger is now made elsewhere. Germany, Austria and the United States are the leading producers. Other cheeses identical or very similar to Limburger are *Allgauer Limburger*, *Backsteiner*, *Herve*, *Marienhofer*, *schloss*, *stanger* and *Void*.

See also: **Liederkranz.**

LIME

Also ADAM'S APPLE. A small, aromatic citrus fruit with refreshingly sour juice, the lime *(Citrus aurantifolia)* is usually green and about half the size of the average lemon, the fruit it most resembles. Probably native to India, limes are grown in most subtropical regions, but the West Indies and Mexico supply most of the limes in international trade. There are many varieties of limes, but two of the better known are the Dominican and the Persian, or seedless, which is the larger. Most are nearly round and measure one to 1½ inches in diameter. On the average, limes contain one third more citric acid than lemons and are an excellent source of vitamin C. In the market, limes are occasionally seen spotted with purplish brown marks called "scald." Despite the poor appearance, the flesh is often not affected. Limes are grown an a small scale in California and on a larger scale in Florida, whose climate is more appropriate. Two well-known Florida varieties are the Tahiti and the Key.

Lime is used to make thirst-quenching beverages and to flavor ice creams and desserts. It is frequently an ingredient in chutney and marmalades. In Mexico, limes are used as a general seasoner, especially in seafood, soups and on other fresh fruit. Mexicans use a wedge of lime to clear their palate after drinking tequila neat.

LIMEQUAT

This hybrid citrus fruit crosses the lime *(Citrus aurantifolia)* and the kumquat. Two different species are produced depending on which species of kumquat is used, the marumi kumquat *(Fortunella japonica)* or the nagami kumquat *(F. margarita)*.

The *X Citrofortunella floridana* crosses the lime and the marumi to produce an excellent acidic limequat with a diameter of from one to 1½ inches. The *X Citrofortunella swinglei* crosses the lime and the nagami kumquat to produce an oval, yellowish fruit with a mustard-yellow pulp. Limequats tend to be hardier than their contributing parents.

LIME TREE

See **Basswood.**

LIMOUX, BLANQUETTE DE

See **Blanquette de Limoux.**

Limpet

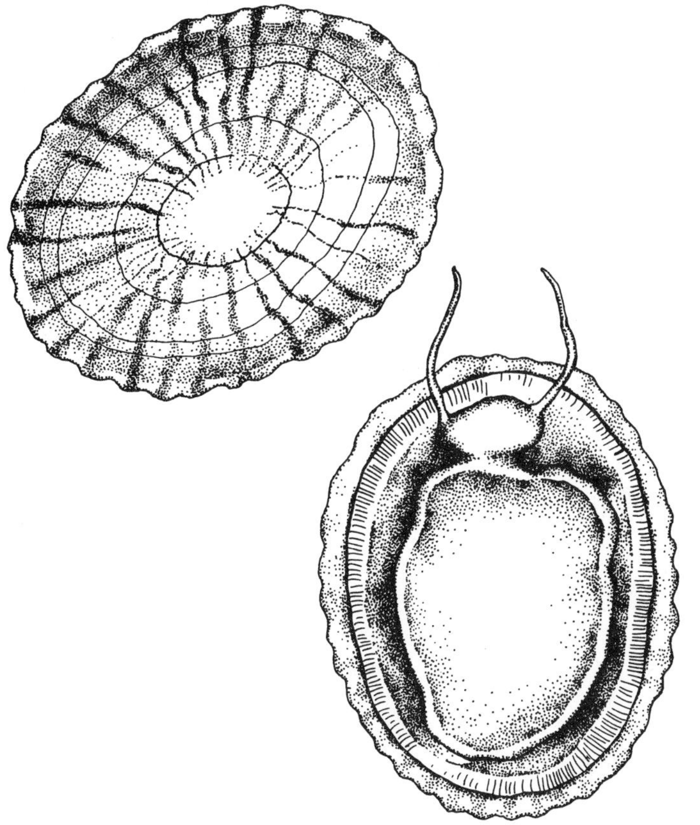

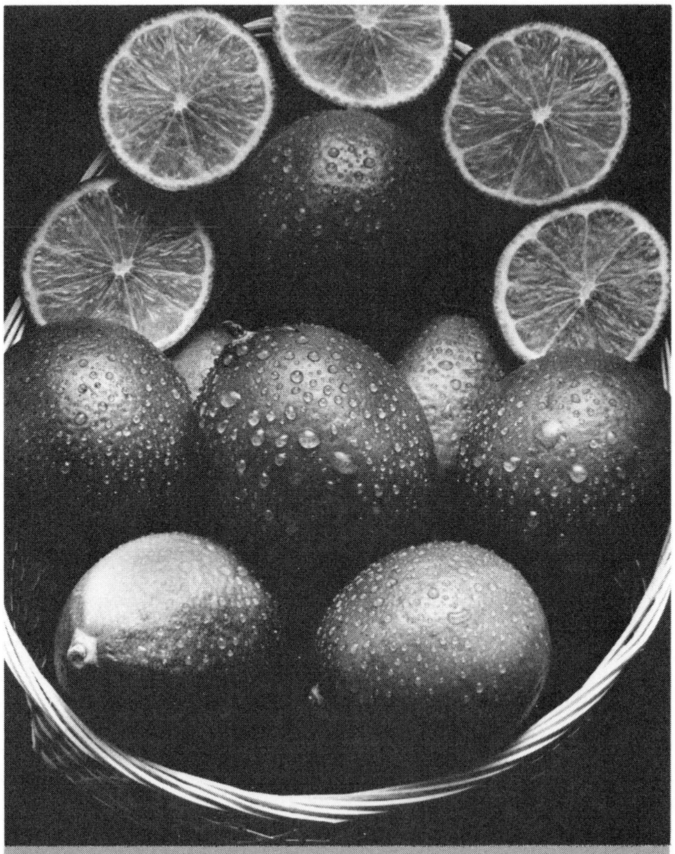

Limes

LIMPET

Also CHINAMAN'S HAT. A marine shellfish of unprepossessing appearance usually found clinging to intertidal rocks, the limpet has a single, open shell and clings to the rock by means of a muscular foot, as does the **abalone.** It can be pried off using a knife or a screwdriver. Limpets have real gastronomic merit and can be prepared using any recipe appropriate for clams or oysters.

Common limpets on the Atlantic Coast of North America are those belonging to the *Acmea* and *Crepidula* genera. They are quite small, but the Pacific coast *Lottia gigantea* can be up to four inches across, and the giant keyhole (volcano) limpet reaches a diameter of seven inches. In Hawaii, limpets are often eaten raw flavored with **limu** seaweed. Their shells are made into puka-shell jewelry.

In the British Isles, the most common limpet is the *Patella vulgata,* which has a fine taste but little popularity. Limpet pie is a traditional dish.

LIMU

An edible seaweed served in Hawaii and on other Pacific Islands, it is fleshy and sharp-tasting. It is often mixed with peppers and nuts and served as a relish.

LINCOLN CHEESE

This English cream cheese is soft and perishable and is about two inches thick. It was originally produced in Lincolnshire.

LINDEN

See **Basswood.**

LINDENLEAF SAGE

This sage variety, *Salvia tiliifolia,* is indigenous to an area stretching from Mexico to Ecuador. The seeds are used to make a drink that is sometimes mixed with barley water.

LING

A large ocean fish, *Molva molva,* of the cod family *(Gadidae),* the ling dwells in the eastern Atlantic from Norway to the Bay of Biscay. It is a long, slim fish, attaining weights of around 45 pounds and lengths of six feet or more. It is greenish brown above and white below.

It is a good fish to eat and is often marketed smoked or salted. The ling is an important commercial fish in Norway, Scotland, Ireland and Iceland. Occasional specimens are taken off the eastern coast of Canada.

In the United States the name "ling" is sometimes applied to the **burbot** and in Australia and New Zealand to a species of cusk-eel, *Genypterus blacodes.*

Lingonberry

LINGCOD

Also CULTUS COD. An important commercial and sports fish of the Pacific Coast of North America, the lingcod *(Ophiodon elongatus)* is found from Alaska to Baja California in shallow rocky areas and in deep water. It has a long, slender body reaching a length of five feet and a weight that seldom exceeds 100 pounds. It is greenish brown marked with dark blotches and golden spots on its sides.

Lingcod are taken by trawlers and sold fresh in fish markets. Although the flesh sometimes has a green tinge, it is considered very good to eat. The lingcod is not a true cod but a member of the greenling family *(Hexagrammidae).*

LINGONBERRY

Also LINGBERRY, MOUNTAIN CRANBERRY. This is a small, dark red, sour-tasting fruit of a variety of the cowberry *(Vaccinium citis-idaea* var. *minor).* The plant is not much cultivated but grows wild in the colder regions of North America from Alaska to Massachusetts and in northern Europe and Asia.

The berry is particularly popular in Scandanavia where it is used in desserts, made into a sweet sauce for Swedish pancakes, etc. In Russia and Scotland it is used extensively in purees, compotes and fruit soups. In North America, it used to be thought of as famine food for trappers, but it occasionally appears in the market and is prepared like the **cranberry.**

See also: **Cowberry.**

Linguine

LINGUINE

Also LASAGNE. This is a type of Italian pasta consisting of flat, ribbonlike noodles ranging from one-eighth inch to four inches wide. The flour, or semolina, used in this pasta dough comes from hard durum wheat. The vast majority is factory made and is *pasta secca*, that is, flour and water. Lasagne, which is the broadest of all, is sometimes made at home, in which case the flour is mixed with eggs to form *pasta all'uovo*.

The nomenclature of this pasta depends on the size. *Lingue de passero* ("sparrow tongues") are the smallest, then in ascending order come *bavettine*, *linguine*, *bavette*, *tortiglioni* and *fusili* (like *bavette*, but twisted), *tagliolini*, *trenette*, *lasagnette*, then *lasagne secche* (the broadest).

This is generally considered *pasta asciutta*, that is, to be cooked apart (not in soup) and served with a sauce. The largest types, such as lasagne, are often baked in a deep dish with layers of pasta alternating with a filling of meat, sausage, cheese, tomatoes or eggs.

See also: **Pasta.**

LINNET

Songbirds of Europe, Asia and Africa belonging to the family *Fringillidae*, linnets are eaten in France and Italy, especially the *Linota cannabina*, which is known as the red, gray or brown linnet depending on the sex and season of the year. It is prepared like **lark.**

LIPOTI

This edible fruit of a medium-sized tree, *Eugenia curranii*, found in the Philippines, is round and white, turning to dark red or black, and has a pleasant, acidic flavor. It ranges from three fourths to 1½ inches in diameter. The *lipoti* is highly regarded in the Philippines as a base for wine-making. It is also eaten raw and made into excellent jelly.

LIPTAU

See **Liptauer.**

LIPTAUER

Also LIPTOI, LIPTAU. Here is a sour-milk cheese made from cow's, sheep's or goat's milk and combined half and half with butter, spices and some paprika to give it a pink color. It is popular in Hungary, Austria, Germany and Holland. Flavorings include chopped anchovies, caraway seeds, capers and chives. It has a fine, granular texture and a sharp taste like **Brinza,** which in some places is also called **Liptauer.**

LIPTOI

See **Liptauer.**

LIQUAMEN

See **Garum.**

LIQUEUR

Also CORDIAL. The term includes any sweetened, flavored alcoholic beverage usually drunk after a meal as a digestive, but sometimes served as an ingredient in a cocktail. A liqueur and a cordial are the same thing, with "cordial" being more of an American term. Homemade liqueurs are sometimes called "ratafias."

A liqueur consists of a distilled spirit (usually brandy) but also whisky, rum, gin, potato spirits, etc.) plus flavoring materials (fruits, flowers, herbs, seeds, barks, roots, peels, berries, juices and other natural flavoring substances) and sweetener, which must make up 2.5 percent of the volume by weight, but often runs as high as 35 percent. If the sweetener amounts to no more than 10 percent, the liqueur is considered *dry*, and it may be so stated on the label.

According to tradition, liqueurs originated in the Middle Ages and were developed in monasteries. They began as elixirs, that is, medicines incorporating curative herbs that still remain in the pharmacopoeia, such as caraway seed, coriander, angelica root, oil of orange, oil of lemon and various herbs. The general population was quick to appreciate their revivifying and digestive properties, and thus a secular industry was born. The oldest liqueur still made by a religious order is Chartreuse, which is based on a secret formula originated in 1605 and improved by the monks in 1737.

There are two principal types of liqueurs: fruit liqueurs, which generally have the natural color of the fruit; and plant liqueurs, which are colorless. Each has its typical method of manufacture. Fruit liqueurs are made by cold methods, such as infusion or maceration, where the aroma, flavor and color is obtained by steeping crushed fruit (and sometimes fruit stones) in alcohol. The resulting liquid is filtered, sweetened and bottled. Another cold method is percolation, which involves separate receptacles for the fruit mass (above) and the spirits (below). The spirits are pumped up over the fruit mass and allowed to percolate through it to the receptacle below. The process is repeated, like coffee percolating, until all the essence is extracted from the fruit.

Liqueurs from plants, seeds, roots and herbs are usually made by a hot extraction method that involves first steeping the flavoring agent in alcoholic spirits and then distilling the resulting liquid. Certain delicate flavoring agents, such as flowers, may be distilled in water, and the essence thus obtained added to the alcoholic spirits. Hot methods yield a colorless liqueur that is sweetened to taste and often dyed any color thought to be desirable from a marketing point of view.

Typical fruit liqueurs are made from apricots, blackberries, cherries, peaches and plums (sloe gin). Well-known plant liqueurs are Benedictine, Chartreuse, anisette and kummel. Liqueurs are bottled at from 40 to 110 proof. For more information, look under the names of specific liqueurs.

LIQUEUR WINE

The name is given to any sweet and intoxicating wine that is aromatic, infused with herbs and drunk as a dessert wine or as an **aperitif.** Liqueur wine, or *vin de liqueur*, is also used in cooking and in the making of certain candies. Among the most widely known wines of this nature are **Malaga, Madeira, malmsey,** the Portuguese Moscatel de Setubal, **port, sherry, Lacrima Cristi,** and the French **lunel.**

LIQUOR

Also SPIRITS. The term "liquor" is used for any alcoholic drink but applies especially to distilled spirits, such as brandy, whisky, rum and the like. These last differ in taste and character depending on the raw material used for the mash (wheat, rye, corn, molasses, etc.), the proof at which they are distilled, the containers used for aging and the length of the aging period. For more information, look under the specific name of various liquors and under **Wine and Liquor Terms.**

In a broader sense, it can mean any liquid, broth or juice, such as meat liquor or pot liquor.

LIQUORICE

See **Licorice.**

LIQUORICE ROOT

The long, sweet roots of the perennial plant, *Hedgsarum mackenzii*, make good spring vegetables. They resemble sticks of licorice in appearance and are indigenous to North America from central Canada to Alaska.

LIRAC

This wine comes from the valley of the **Rhone** north of Avignon in southern France. This region produces red, white and rose wines—all characterized by a fragrant bouquet. Lirac rose is similar to the great **Tavel** grown slightly farther south. The reds and roses are made primarily from the Grenache, Cinsault and Mourvedre grapes, while the Clairette grape predominate in the making of the whites. All of the local grapes are mixed in the same vat at harvest, a major reason for the strong bouquet of this amiable vintage.

LISTRAC WINE

The name includes red and white wine from the vineyards of Listrac in the **Haut-Medoc** region of **Bordeaux.** The vineyards are situated on one of the highest hills in the area, and the yield of red wine is particularly full-bodied and "winy." A good white wine, similar to that of **Graves** is also produced.

LITCHI

Also LICHEE, LYCHEE. This is the fruit of the soapberry tree, *Litchi chinensis*, native to China but now cultivated in many parts of the world. The litchi grows in clusters on a small tree that has been cultivated in southern China for about 2,000 years. Nowadays it is also grown in India, South Africa, Hawaii, Burma, Madagascar, the West Indies, Brazil, Honduras, Japan, Australia and the southern United States.

The litchi is popularly referred to as a nut, but it looks more like a strawberry, especially when fresh, and has a sweetly acidic flavor like a citrus fruit. On maturity, it generally reaches a diameter of one to 1½ inches, and has an outer skin that is hard, brittle and bright red. Inside, a single, hard seed is completely covered by a fleshy, white pulp that, when eaten fresh, has a sweet, acidic, slightly musty flavor. The litchi is usually canned for export in dried form. Dried in the shell, the pulp turn black and shrinks raisinlike around the seed. In this form, it has a taste that has been compared to that of a very sweet Muscat grape.

The litchi is eaten fresh in the areas where it grows but is nearly as good canned as fresh. Fresh litchis may be shelled, pitted and served in a salad. They make excellent preserves.

LITES

See **Lights.**

LITORNE

Also FIELDFARE. This species of European songbird, *Turdus pillaris*, of the thrush family is considered a delicious tidbit in France. It reaches a length of about 10 inches, has an ash-colored head, chestnut back and wings and a black tail. It is prepared like **thrush.**

LITTLENECK

See **Clams.**

LIVAROT

This soft French cheese is made from goat's or cow's milk and mold-ripened. Its flavor is reminiscent of **Camembert.** It is made in the Normandy region, chiefly around the village of Livarot. Skim milk is used, and some of the output is sold fresh as white cheese. The more familiar, aged variety, is inoculated with mold, formed into small cheeses of six-inch diameter, wrapped in *laiche (Typha latifolia)* leaves and cured from three to five months. A crusty surface and pungent flavor develops. Before marketing, the cheese is dyed reddish brown with annatto. It is best eaten from January to March.

LIVER

An internal organ of mammals, birds and fish, the liver is the largest and most nutritious of the variety meats (offals). In order of palatability come veal or calves' liver, the tenderest of all, and best when the animal is slaughtered young; lamb's liver, which runs a close second and is more economical; sheep's liver, which is tougher and stronger-tasting; pig's liver, which is often used to stuff sausages; and beef (ox) liver, which due to its toughness is most often ground for pates or terrines.

Poultry liver has its special constituencies and uses. Very finely chopped chicken liver is a Jewish delicacy. Goose liver, when artificially fattened, produces the delicacy, **foie gras.** Turkey liver is usually part of the stuffing when the bird is roasted.

Cognoscenti highly prize some of the rarer livers such as those of game, particularly deer; fish, especially skate and turbot, and lobster, which is green, and is also known as tomalley. Valuable oils are extracted from cod and shark livers.

Probably the greatest recorded connoisseur of human liver was the American mountain man Jeremiah Johnson, who boasted of having eaten the livers of 247 Crow. He was following the custom of certain native American tribes who believed the human liver to be the repository of manly virtues, such as courage.

Perhaps due to its vital role in digestion, the liver is a storehouse of valuable food elements. It has a high content of calcium, iron, vitamins A, D, E, K and vitamins B_1, B_2, B_6 and B_{12}, not to mention protein. In the market, liver should be a bright, yellowish red. It is generally tender, except for the outside membrane and the tubes running through it, which should be removed before cooking. To maintain the tenderness, liver should be cooking very lightly, or else it becomes leathery. It is most frequently sauted in butter, less often broiled or braised. When cooked, poultry liver becomes soft and crumbly.

The importance of liver has been summed up humorously in the following pun: "Is life worth living? It all depends on the liver."

LIVER FISTULA

See **Beefsteak Fungus.**

LIVER PUDDING

See **Liverwurst.**

LIVERWURST

Also BRAUNSCHWEIGER. This highly seasoned sausage, consisting largely of pork liver, originated in Germany. The livers are minced together with pork trimmings and various flavorings and seasonings, such as onions, pistachio nuts, cardamom, salt and pepper. The mixture is stuffed into straight casings and smoked for three hours, usually over hickory wood, although sometimes it is sold fresh.

Braunschweiger, which is made like liverwurst, takes its name from Brunswick Province in Germany. It has more liver than regular liverwurst, and thus spreads easily on bread, crackers or toast. It too may be sold smoked or fresh and is usually a little spicier than the normal liver sausage.

Both make good cold cuts and luncheon meat and may be used to stuff fowl, potatoes, green peppers and squash. Liverwurst makes an acceptable substitute for pate de foie gras when mashed with mayonnaise to achieve spreadable texture.

See also: **Sausage.**

LIZARD

The term covers a large group of reptiles with long, slender bodies, tails, scaly skin and four legs. In a loose sense, the term includes the salamander, one species of which, the **axolotl,** was greatly relished by the Aztecs. The kind of lizard most commonly eaten in the Western Hemisphere is the **iguana.** The best one of these for eating is reputed to be the pygmy iguana *(Dipsosaurus dorsalis dorsalis)* of the southwestern United States and Mexico. The taste of its flesh is often compared to that of chicken. The iguana also lives in Madagascar, but the African lizard most commonly eaten is the monitor, a name referring to any of several species of huge, flesh-eating lizards. It acquired its name through the notion that this lizard monitored the movements of crocodiles and warned of their presence.

LIZARDFISH

Also SPOTTED-TAILED GRINNER. Of the many lizardfishes (family *Synodontidae*), an Indo-Pacific species, *Saurida undosquamis*, is one of the largest and one of the few used as food. It reaches a length of 20 inches and has the typical reptilian look of its family, with broad bony head, pointed snout and heavy shiny scales on its body. It is found in deep water from East Africa across to Australia. This is a well regarded, but not important, food fish. It is usually prepared in fritters.

LLAMA

The llama *(Llama peruava)* is a four-footed, South American animal that is related to the camel but lacks its hump. The Indians of the Andean region use the llama as a beast of burden and as a source of milk and wool. Its flesh is edible and may be prepared like beef. Llamas are rarely slaughtered for the table, however, for they are much too valuable in their other capacities. When they do reach the table it is because of age and incapacity, and then they are too tough to be palatable.

LOACH

A genus, *Cobitidae*, of small freshwater fish found in Europe and Asia, numbering perhaps 200 species, they are distinguished by long, flattened bodies and barbels about the mouth. One of the most common is the stone loach *(Noemacheilus barbatulus)*, which inhabits clear streams and rivers from Ireland across Europe and Russia to Korea. It does not usually exceed five inches in length, it has a delicate flavor, and it may be cooked like smelt or used in soup or stew.

Throughout the same range is found the spined loach *(Cobitis taenia)*, which has spines projecting above its eyes that protect it from predators. It prefers clear lakes and slow-flowing rivers with muddy bottoms. It is eaten fried, in stews or *a la meuniere*.

LOAF CHEESE

The term defines the cheese by the shape in which it is packaged, i.e., a rectangular block. For years it was synonymous with **process cheese,** which was practically the only cheese packaged in loaves. But more recently, many natural cheeses are packaged thus, including brick, cheddar, cream and Swiss.

LOBSTER

This large, saltwater crustacean is renowned for its delicious flavor as well as its high price. There are two main species, which are similar in most respects, except for average size. They are the European lobster *(Homarus gammarus)* found from Norway to the Mediterranean, and the American lobster *(Homarus americanus)*, found from Labrador to Cape Hatteras. The American variety is larger. The best specimens come from the colder reaches of the Atlantic, such as the waters off Nova Scotia, Maine and Brittany. Other crustacea are called lobster, such as the spiny lobster *(Balinurus vulgaris)* and the Norway lobster *(Nephrops norvegicus)*, or Dublin Bay prawn, but they differ significantly from the varieties under discussion and are dealt with under separate headings.

Lobsters are covered by a hard shell that is a mottled blue black when taken from the sea and turns bright red after cooking. Its two claws are of unequal size, one a heavy crusher good for smashing other shellfish, the other a more maneuverable pincer. Many consider the flesh of the claws to be the best part of the lobster. Lobsters grow continuously in their lifetime, taking seven to eight years to go from the larval stage to the U.S. legal minimum size, one pound. During that time, it sheds its shell and grows a larger one 20 times. During the shedding stage, it is most vulnerable to attack from predators, except for one, man.

The flesh is lean and watery during shedding and undesirable for eating. If unmolested, American lobsters can reach a length of five to six feet, and weigh more than 40 pounds. Such specimens were not unusual before the mid-19th century when lobster-eating came into vogue in the United States. Lobsters caught nowadays average a pound and a half, and are better eating than the giant ones.

In Europe, lobsters have been fished since the Stone Age and consequently were in scarce supply long before this occurred in America. Thus, they have long stood as symbols of luxury, along with champagne and caviar. Thomas Hood, writing in 1825, penned these lines *To Minerva:*

My temples throb, my pulses boil,
I'm sick of Song, and Ode, and Ballad—
So, Thyrsis, take the Midnight Oil,
And pour it on a lobster salad.

Yet in colonial America lobster was so plentiful as to be spurned as poor people's food. The lobster boom did not take off in the United States until after the Civil War, when improved transportation enabled a wider distribution of the catch. The latter peaked in 1885 at 133 million pounds, then dropped to 33 million by 1918. Strict conservation laws in Maine have allowed the industry to rebound to half of what it was at the peak, but the prognosis for lobster is continued scarcity—and high prices—unless a breakthrough occurs.

There are four commercial sizes: chicken, medium, large and jumbo, ranging from about one pound to four pounds. Lobsters must be eaten fresh and therefore should be purchased live. When turned on its back, it should be able to wriggle its legs and flap its tail. If it doesn't do this, select another because there is no guarantee that a lobster is fresh even if it is kept in a tank of water. A lobster begins to die when taken from the sea, and storage in a tank merely slows the process.

Other parts of the lobster are edible besides the firm flesh of the tail, legs and claws. The greenish liver, called tomalley, is considered a delicacy. In the female, the bright red coral, or ovaries, is tasty and rich. The coral may be mixed with butter and put through a seive to make lobster butter. A female lobster with roe clinging to her underside is considered the finest eating lobster in France, where it is called *paquette*. In the United States that condition is called "in berry." It is illegal to catch females in berry.

Lobsters are most often steamed or boiled. A favorite method is to pop a live lobster into a pot of boiling salt water, preferably seawater. Experts say that this method produces a toughness in the flesh that can be avoided by starting with the lobster in cold water, which is then brought to a boil. Apparently, this way is also more humane because the lobster suffers less. Other cooking methods are broiling, which again can cause some toughness, and baking.

LOCHES

See **Goat's Milk Cheese.**

LOCUST

Also GRASSHOPPER. The locust is a large winged insect, which is essentially a grasshopper in its migratory phase. It is one of the most widely eaten insects, especially in Africa and Asia, where it can reach a length of up to four inches. Only the smaller varieties, less suitable for eating, are found in Western Europe and North America.

The locust, when dried, may yield as much as 75 percent protein, and 20 percent fat. Small wonder, then, that it is eaten in a wide diversity of forms, including boiled, roasted, grilled, salted, dried and reduced to paste. Before cooking, the locust must be prepared as follows: The wings and small legs are removed, plus the terminal portion of the hind legs. The head is also pulled off, bringing with it any attached viscera. Among locust eaters, Ethiopians are known for failing to prepare them in the foregoing manner, and consequently they sometimes suffer severe intestinal obstructions.

Among the ancients, fried locusts were a delicacy of Mesopotamia. Greeks roasted them. Moses declared

four varieties kosher (Leviticus 11:21–22). Modern peoples eat them in the following ways: roasted (Navahoes), dried locusts and milk (Arabic North Africa), locust dumplings (Arabic North Africa), fried grasshoppers (China, Thailand, Japan, Arab countries), locust stew (pioneer America), boiled locust with rice (Vietnam), boiled locust with couscous (Arabic North Africa), locust soup (Arabic and Jewish North Africa).

LODIGIANO

This is a hard Italian cheese of the **grana** type made near Lodi, south of Milan. The surface of the cheese is dark and oily, and the curd yellow, with a sharp, fragrant, somewhat bitter flavor. These cheeses are larger (65 to 110 pounds) and slower ripening than other *granas*, with three to four years the customary aging time. They are used for grating, like **Parmesan.**

LOGANBERRY

This dark purplish red berry, *Rubus loganobaccus*, has a tartly flavored pulp that is more suitable for preserving than eating fresh. The loganberry was discovered a century ago in the California garden of Judge J. H. Logan. It is thought by some to be a hybrid of the American blackberry and the red raspberry. The shape does resemble the blackberry's, and the color that of the red raspberry until full maturity, when it darkens. Moreover, the flavor is quite like that of the red raspberry, except it is more acidic. Others find no merit in these comparisons and maintain that the loganberry is a variety of the American dewberry, or trailing blackberry, another member of the *Rubus* genus.

Fresh loganberries rarely appear on the market, as the entire crop is bought up for canning. As it is, none but the ripest would be palatable fresh because of the tartness. Loganberries are used in jams, jellies, pies and ices.

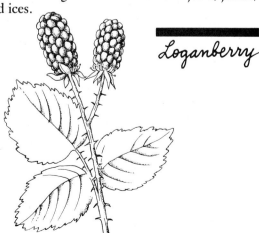

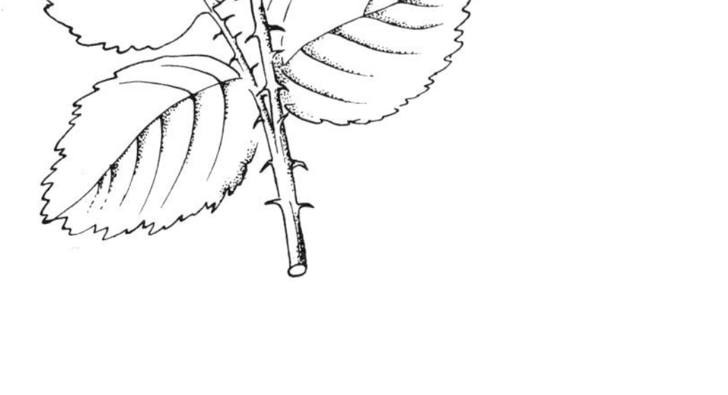

LOGWOOD

Also CAMPEACHY WOOD. Red or violet dye extracted from the bark of this tropical American tree, *Haematoxylum campechianum*, is used to improve the color of some liqueurs and wines. The dye is called hematoxylin.

LOIN

Loin is the lower part of the back extending from the ribs to the hips. In a slaughtered animal, then, it is the upper portion of the hindquarters with the flank removed. The loin includes the vertebrae.

In lamb, beef and pork, the loin is usually split down the middle and, if not, is known as a saddle of lamb, a baron of beef or a double loin of pork. In pork, the loin extends from the ham to the shoulder and includes the ribs. Various cuts are made from the loin, such as loin chops, tenderloin, sirloin and short loin.

LOIRE WINES

These are wines from both banks of the longest French river, which flows some six hundred miles west in to the Atlantic at Saint Nazaire. The Loire, an unusually gentle stream, flows through the beautiful "chateaux country" west of Orleans, through Touraine and Anjou. It is watered by several still more placid tributaries: the Cher, the Indre and the Vienne. The wine of this region is said to be as gentle and refreshing as the rivers. The most important grape associated with this region, the Pineau de la Loire, known more commonly in the United States as Chenin Blanc, is certainly worthy of this description, and is responsible for the great white wines of Touraine and of the sparkling white wine of Saumur.

The Loire is noted for all three colors of wine, red, white, and rose (Anjou makes some of the best rose in France) and for its *petillant*, or semisparkling wine. Near Nevers, before the river makes an arc northwest to Orleans, is produced probably the most famous white wine of the Loire, the **Pouilly-Fume.** This very dry wine is similar—in flavor as well as in name—to the **Pouilly-Fuisse** of **Burgundy,** but is made from grapes blended with dominant Sauvignon. West of Nevers, along the right bank of the Cher, is the vineyard of **Quincy,** which proveds a dry white wine similar to **Chablis,** excellent with oysters. Between Blois and Tours another well-known white wine of the Loire is made, the **Vouvray.** This has a distinctive, aromatic quality and a dry but fruity taste. Frequently, depending on the particular vintage, Vouvray wines are sparkling.

Very delicate red wines are grown in Touraine, near Chinon—a wine beloved by Rabelais (" 'I know where Chinon is,' said Pantagruel, 'and I know the painted cellar. I've drunk many a glass of fresh wine there, and I don't doubt that Chinon is an ancient city. . . .' ") Chinon wines are light in color and body and also in alcoholic content, and have a soft violet bouquet. They are made from a grape grown almost solely in the Loire area, the Cabernet Franc.

Farther down the river, towards Angers, the Saumur vineyards yield an exceptional white wine similar to the **Sauternes.** The same process is used in the production of these wines as is used with Sauternes, that of allowing the grapes to overripen on the vines *(pourriture noble*, or "noble rot") to increase their sugar content. These are often sparkling, unlike the Sauternes, and are made from not more than 40 percent of black grapes, which are normally used to produce red wines only. Saumur, like Anjou, its neighbor, also is known for its high-quality rose wines. In Saumur these are made from the Cabernet grape only, while in Anjou the Groslot grape is commonly used. The Saumur rose differs from that of Anjou in being much paler—a light glassy pink—in color.

East of Nantes, where the river widens on its way to the Atlantic, the driest of all the wines of the Loire is made, the Muscadet, a white wine of a golden color, picked and bottled early to retain a small amount of carbonic gas, its trademark.

In all, the wine of the Loire is among the most amiable and most subtle in France, much like the countryside itself. It is ironic, perhaps, that Rabelais, the French writer whose very name brings images of rough-and-tumble earthiness to the mind, should so have loved this gentle country and its wine.

LOLLIPOP

Also SUCKER. This is a piece of hard candy, usually clear toffee, attached to, or impaled on, a small stick. It comes in various flavors.

LOMBARDO

A hard Italian cheese of the ***grana*** type, similar to **Lodigiano**, but smaller and faster ripening. It has a sharp, aromatic flavor and is usually grated for use as a condiment, like **Parmesan.** The cheeses are round and flat, weighing between 40 and 60 pounds.

LONGAN

Also LUNGAN, DRAGON'S EYES. Fruit of a subtropical evergreen tree native to India but much cultivated in Malaysia and southern China, Longan *(Euphoria longan)* has been transplanted elsewhere, more notably in protected areas of Florida and California. The longan averages about an inch across and has a yellow brown skin. It grows in yellow clusters looking like grapes. Its taste resembles the litchi's, though it is generally considered inferior to the latter when eaten fresh. It is dried for export or made into preserves and is popular in Chinese communities.

LONGANIZA

A Spanish pork sausage, similar to **chorizo,** but spicier, it contains lean pork, garlic, oregano (wild marjoram), pepper and *achiote*, which are annatto seeds and add color as well as flavor.

See also: **Sausage.**

LONGHORN

See **American Cheddar.**

LONG RICE

These are translucent, cellophanelike Chinese noodles made from either rice flour or mung beans.

LOOFAH

Also DISHCLOTH GOURD. The fruit of this tropical vine, *Luffa aegyptiaca*, is cylindrical and up to two feet long at maturity. It may be eaten like squash when young and tender but is usually cultivated for its reticulate, fibrous interior, which, when dried, is a kind of vegetable sponge. This is the loofah of commerce. It is used as a dishcloth, or, more commonly, as a washcloth to scour the body while bathing.

LOOFAH, ANGLED

See **Sing-Kwa.**

LOOKDOWN

A good food fish found on both sides of the tropical Atlantic and in the Gulf of Mexico, the lookdown *(Selene vomer)* reaches a length of about 12 inches, and its trapezoidal body and silvery color make it quite distinctive. It is caught both by anglers and trawlers in fairly shallow coastal waters.

See also: **Opah.**

LOQUAT

Also BIWA, CHINESE MEDLAR, JAPANESE MEDLAR. An orange-colored fruit somewhat like a small apricot, the loquat *(Eriobotrya japonica)* originated in China, was developed in Japan and is now cultivated in Europe and the United States. It grows on a small evergreen tree that was first cultivated in the West for its ornamental qualities, and whose wood is prized by violin-makers. It was introduced into Europe in the 19th century, and, though not the tastiest of fruits, it excited interest because of its early ripening, i.e., March. In those days, it was considered highly exceptional to have fresh fruit that early in the year.

The flavor of loquat has been described as acidic, and when fully ripe, sweet and cherrylike. The fruit varies in color from yellow to deep orange and contains a number of seeds. If eaten raw, loquat is usually combined with other fruit in a salad, or fruit cup. It may be peeled and served cooked with cream. It makes excellent jams and jellies, especially if the less ripe, more tart fruit is used. A loquat liqueur is made whose taste has overtones of bitter almonds.

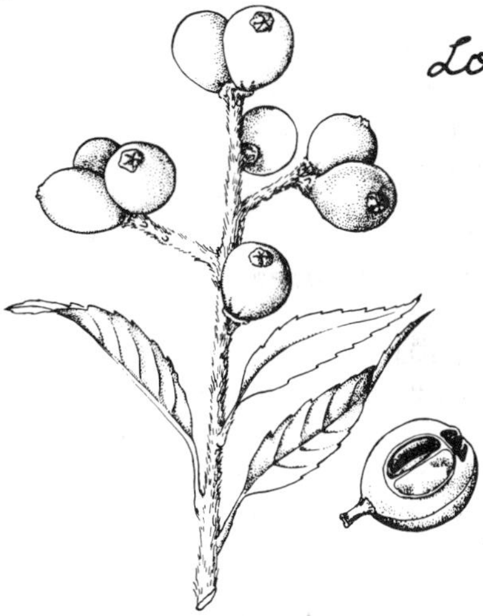

Loquat

LORDS AND LADIES

See **Arum Maculatum.**

LORRAINE CHEESE

Here is a small, hard, highly-priced cheese that is seasoned with pepper, salt and pistachio nuts. Prepared from sour milk, *Lorraine* is eaten comparatively fresh and considered a delicacy. It is made in the Lorraine region, near the French-German border. It is marketed in two-ounce sizes.

LOTE

See **Burbot.**

LOTUS

The name includes any of several species of the water lily family, *Nymphaeaceae*, whose rhizomes and seeds are edible. Prominent among these is the sacred lotus *(Nelumbium nuciferum)* indigenous across southern Asia to Australia. The flowers of this plant are sacred to Buddhists. The rhizomes have an unprepossessing appearance, like a decayed root, yet they have a good, crisp texture and a taste something like artichoke. They should be gathered young. Thinly sliced, they can be served raw in salads. Usually, however, they are roasted, steamed or pickled. As a sweet, they may be stuffed with rice or preserved in sugar. The seeds are somewhat like small hazelnuts. The embryo has a bitter taste and is removed, then the seeds may be eaten raw (the taste is fresh and delicate), boiled, or roasted. They are sometimes soaked in water, then cooked in sugar to make a stuffing for duck.

Lotus: fresh (front) and dried (rear)

The Egyptian white lotus *(Nymphaea lotus)* is the lotus of ancient Egyptian art, along with its close relative, *N. caerulea*. It belongs to the same family as the sacred lotus, but its leaves float on the surface of the water while the sacred lotus stands well above the surface on long stalks. In ancient times, the rhizomes of white lotus were roasted, ground into flour, and used to make bread for the humbler classes. Herodotus, a Greek historian of the fifth century B.C., tasted this bread and pronounced it very good. This may have been more a reflection on the poor quality of Greek bread. The Egyptians had discovered the art of leavening bread with yeast, thus their bread was the envy of the ancient world. The rhizomes are still used today to make meal in Egypt as well in other parts of Africa. White lotus seeds are roasted, then usually ground into meal. Another edible species is the blue lotus *(N. stellata)* of India, considered there to be a famine food.

In Greek legend, the lotus was a fruit that induced a state of dreamy languor in the eater, so that he became indolent and forgetful. The Greek hero, Odysseus, encountered the lotus eaters, or *lotophagi*, during his wanderings. They lived in an area that is now Libya. Experts agree that the lotus of legend was not a water lily. They speculate that it may have been the date plum *(Diospyros lotus)*, a fruit the Greeks used to make both a bread and a wine for the poor, who used it to forget their troubles. Others speculated that it was bird's foot **trefoil,** a seed-bearing plant for which magical properties were claimed.

LOUDENNE, CHATEAU

This dry red wine comes from the **Medoc** region of **Bordeaux** in southwestern France. The Chateau Loudenne vineyards are located in the commune of St.-Yzans. Their yield has been classified under the French system of *appellations controlees* as an "exceptional great bourgeois growth" among the many great "masculine" red wines of the district.

See also: **Wine, French.**

LOUKANIKA

This Greek sausage is made from minced pork and beef seasoned with garlic, cinnamon, allspice, orange peel, cracked whole peppercorns, wine and lemon juice. It may be served hot as an hors d'oeuvre or fried with eggs and tomatoes.

See also: **Sausage.**

LOUP DE MER

See **Bass.**

LOUPIAC

This semi-sweet white wine comes from the vineyards of Loupiac, south of **Bordeaux** on the right bank of the Garonne in western France. The only grapes of this tiny district are the Semillon, Sauvignon and Muscatelle. These are harvested when they are over-ripe, in the manner of **Sauternes.** Loupiac wine is a clear, pale gold and, like the Sauternes, possesses a delectable fragrance and warmth.

LOVAGE

An aromatic herb used since Classical Antiquity as a flavoring agent and a salad vegetable, lovage *(Levisticum officinale)* resembles **angelica,** and is a member of the parsley family. Like angelica, its shoots are used in candymaking. Its seeds are somewhat like celery seeds and can be used similarly. Both roots and seeds are flavoring agents in some liqueurs. The fresh leaves are added to salads, but always with discretion because the taste is strong. Lovage is native to southern Europe, and is a popular ingredient in Balkan cooking.

Scotch lovage *(Legusticum scoticum)* has heavy stalks that look like celery. They are eaten raw in salads or cooked by braising. The taste has been described as pleasantly musky, a lemon-scented celery.

LOW WINES

See **Whisky.**

LOX

See **Salmon.**

LUCMO

A tropical fruit of the sapote type, the lucmo *(Lucuma obovata)* is native to South America. It is round to oval and has a yellow pulp, which is mealy. It should be kept in straw for a few days before being eaten.

LUCUMA

See **Star Apple.**

LUDERICK

Also BLACKFISH, BLACK BREAM. An Australian food fish of the rudderfish family *Kyphosidae*, the luderick *(Girella tricuspidata)* is also a popular sport fish along the coasts of Queensland, New South Wales, South Australia and West Australia. It is also found in Tasmanian and New Zealand waters. The luderick is a deep-boiled, blunt-nosed fish that reaches a length of 28 inches. It has a brown back, marked by 10 to 12 dark bands, and a grayish belly. It is most plentiful around New South Wales, where it is marketed fresh, usually as black bream. This fish is closely related to the **opaleye.**

LUGANA

These Italian wines are produced in the southern part of Lombardy near the shores of Lake Garda, including a fairly good dry red wine with a distinctive tartness, and a pleasant, light white wine made from the Trebbiano grape.

See also: **Wines, Italian.**

LULO

See **Naranjillo.**

LUMPFISH

Also LUMPSUCKER. The roe of this large, clumsily shaped sea fish is often sold as caviar. The lumpfish *(Cyclopterus lumpus)*, so called because of its lumplike dorsal fin, is found on both sides of the North Atlantic but prefers the colder waters around Scandinavia. The fish has thick, green skin with knobby protuberences. Its pelvic fins come together to form a sucker, hence its other name, lumpsucker.

The lumpfish deposits huge quantities of pink roe in large holes in the rocky ocean beds off Scandinavia where much of it is harvested by fishermen. The eggs are dyed black, salted and pressed before being sold as Danish or German caviar. Though not as fine as the real thing, it makes a good, inexpensive substitute.

See also: **Caviar.**

LUNAR-TAILED ROCK COD

This is a large bottom fish of the Indo-Pacific region, plentiful from the Red Sea and East Africa to northern Australia and the Marshall Islands. It frequents coral reefs and lagoons. Its flesh is considered very good eating. The lunar-tailed rock cod *(Variola louti)* reaches a length of up to three feet and makes a fine game fish.

LUNEBERG

An Austrian cheese with characteristics midway between **Swiss** and **Limburger,** it is made from cow's milk in the mountain valleys of Vorarlberg. The curd is colored with saffron.

LUNEL WINE

This is an aromatic **Muscat** dessert wine from the commune of Herault near Lunel in Languedoc in southeastern France. Muscat de Lunel is very sweet, with from 15 to 20 percent alcohol content, and is similar to the white, muskier wine made from the Frontingnan grape in Switzerland.

LUNG

See **Lights.**

LUNGFISH

Also MUDFISH. A family of large, freshwater fish of Africa *(Protopteridae)* remarkable for their possession of lungs in addition to gills, lungfish are relicts of an earlier geologic era, when they were very abundant and are are thus considered "living fossils." They are, nevertheless, widely eaten in Africa.

The common lungfish *(Protopterus aethiopicus)* reaches a length of 6½ feet and is found through East and Central Africa in rivers and lakes. The lungfish prefers shallow water and must rise to the surface every half hour or so to breathe, giving fishers opportunity to net it or spear it. During dry seasons or droughts it estivates, i.e., burrows deep into damp mud and lies dormant, using lungs alone to breathe. It can last as long as four years in this condition, unless dug up by a hungry fisherman.

A closely related, but smaller, species is *P. annectens* found in Senegal, Nigeria, Lake Chad and in the Zambezi system. It is the kind most often exported to Europe as lungfish. Also known as the mudfish, it rarely exceeds 3½ feet in length.

LUPINE

This flat, yellow bean is the fruit of a leguminous plant *(Lupinus* spp.), native to the Mediterranean basin and cultivated since ancient times. The beans must be soaked in water for three hours before cooking to free them from a bitter taste.

The lupine has the good food value of other legumes yet is of negligible importance as human food today. In Italy, it is occasionally eaten roasted as a snack, as one would salted peanuts or pumpkin seeds. In Roman times, the lupine was considered food fit for the poor and during public festivals was cooked in large batches and distributed free. Since then three species—the blue, yellow and white, named for the color of their blossoms—have been grown as rotation crops and green manure. The nitrogen nodules in their roots improve the soil. Certain sweet varieties, developed in the 20th century, are used as animal fodder.

LYCHEE

See **Litchi.**

LYNNHAVEN

See **Oyster.**

LYONNAISE SAUCE

Here is a French onion sauce consisting of chopped onions fried in butter, flavored with white wine and wine vinegar, mixed with **half-glaze** and strained. It is usually served with ragouts, left-over and braised meats.

See also: **Sauce.**

LYONS SAUSAGE

Also SAUCISSON DE LYONS. A large, dry French sausage of the type called **saucisson,** it is made entirely of pork, mostly lean from the ham, but with a small portion of dry salted fat pork, which is diced. The lean is finely chopped, mixed with the fat and seasoned with garlic, salt, pepper and white peppercorns. After the ingredients are well mixed, they are stuffed into wide hog casings, which are tied off at a maximum of 18 inches. The sausage is dried for two days, pressed and retied, then wrapped in string to preserve a straight shape during the next three to four months of drying. Occasionally, some lean beef or pork rind is added to the above mixture to hasten the drying.

Lyons sausage is customarily served sliced cold as an hors d'oeuvre, but it may be boiled or broiled and served on an English muffin with a topping of cheese.

See also: **Sausage.**

LYSIMACHIA

This is a genus of annual or perennial herbs, *Lysimachia* spp., of the primrose family native to China, Japan and North Vietnam. The dried leaves of two species are used as a condiment.

M

MAATJES

See **Herring.**

MABOLO

Also BITTER FRUIT. A persimmon-type fruit, *Diospyros discolor* of Malaysia and the Philippines, it is round and about four inches in diameter. It has brown, velvety skin and dry flesh with a dark cream color.

MACADAMIA NUT

Also, QUEENSLAND NUT. Nutritionally rich and very costly, the macadamia nut is native to Australia and takes its name from Dr. John MacAdam, a scientist and early promoter of its cultivation in Australia. The nut, with its steely shell, is covered by a muddy, brown husk—the whole about the size of a golf ball. The husk is easily removed, but the shell is formidably strong, requiring a hammer and pliers to open. The nut meat is white, crisp and slightly sweet in flavor. It is also rich in oil. It most closely resembles the hazel nut, though many claim it is superior in flavor and aroma. Luther Burbank proclaimed it the perfect nut. The macadamia tree *(Macadamia ternifolia)*, which resembles the holly tree, is valued as an ornamental shrub.

From Australia, it has been introduced into the southern United States, the West Indies, South Africa and the Mediterranean area, but only in Hawaii has it achieved major commercial importance. Although the tree was brought there in the 1880s for use an an ornamental shrub, it was not until 40 years later that it came to be studied as a potential cash crop. Two scientists at the Hawaiian Agricultural College first developed a way of separating the kernels from the shells by shrinking them in drying bins. They then invented a commercial cracker. These two developments made macadamia farming commercially feasible.

Hawaiian macadamia nuts are shelled, roasted, salted and packed in glass jars. They are usually served as cocktail hor d'oeuvres but may be grated and sprinkled on desserts or other dishes. Macadamia nuts also make an excellent nut butter. They are high in calories, one dozen containing about 196. In 1980 a ten-ounce package of shelled, salted macadamia nuts cost $7.00, which is rather higher than such competitors as pistachio or pine nuts.

MACARANDIBA

A Brazilian fruit of the sapote type, the macarandiba *(Lucuma procera)*, is highly regarded raw, as a dessert fruit or for making preserves.

MACARONI

Also MACCHERONI. This is a type of Italian pasta consisting of long, hollow tubes made from a mixture of hard durum wheat flour and water. The numerous types of macaroni vary quite a bit. *Bucatini* and *fischietti* are the smallest. *Fischietti* means small whistle, which refers to the sound produced when they are eaten with gusto. The tubes get wider as follows: *perciatelli*, *maccheroncini*, *maccheroni*, *mezza zite*, *zita* and *zitone*. The short tubular pasta have different names. *Penne* and *maltagliati* are short tubes with a smooth exterior, while *denti d'elefante* and *mezzi rigatoni* have ribbed exteriors. *Mille righi* and *mille righi grandi* have elbow bends and ribbed exteriors. *Rigatoni* is the largest short tubular pasta.

Invention of the name *macaroni* is credited to a 13th-century king or cardinal, who, when first presented with a dish of this pasta, exclaimed, "Ma caroni!" This has been translated as, "How very dear!" or "The little dears!" It is possible to obtain macaroni in various colors, including green and red, which are tinted with spinach juice and beet juice.

Macaroni is cooked as follows: water is brought to a boil, salt added, then the pasta added a little at a time so the water doesn't come off the boil. Long shapes may be broken up into shorter ones, as pasta doubles its length in the cooking. It is timed following the *al dente* rule, i.e., remove it when the pasta is still biteable, not mushy but has just lost any recognizable taste of flour. When this point is reached, after some testing, pour the macaroni into a large colander.

See also: **Pasta.**

1.

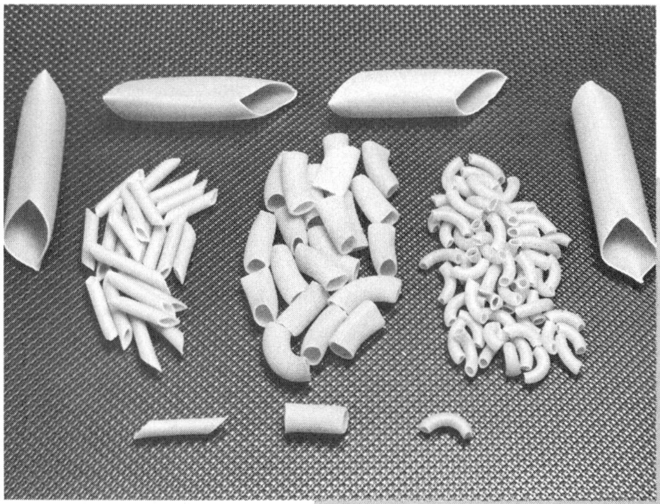

2.

1. Macaroni: manicotti (top), mostaccioli (left), rigatoni (center) and elbow (right)
2. Macadamia nuts

MACAROON

A small cookie (biscuit), which is crisp on the outside and chewy on the inside, the macaroon is usually made from sugar, egg whites and either almond paste or shredded coconut. The almond macaroon is believed to be the original, first produced in Italy under the name *amaretti*, but popularized in France during the 16th and 17th centuries. The coconut macaroon is better known in the United States.

MACCHERONI

See **Macaroni.**

MACE

A mild and fragrant spice, mace, *(Myristrica fragrans)*, is the second covering of nutmeg, that is, a scarlet, lacy fiber coming between the outer husk and the hard inner shell containing the kernel of nutmeg. On being harvested, it is peeled off the shell, dried and usually ground finely, becoming a rich orange brown. It is also sold in "blade" form. The nutmeg tree is native to the Banda Islands of the Molucca group in the East Indies. The West Indies are another important source of mace and nutmeg.

With a flavor reminiscent of nutmeg and cinnamon, it is used to flavor mashed potatoes, cauliflower, cheese, meat and fish dishes and puddings. As a commercial flavoring, it is added to a wide variety of sweets, pickling solutions, tomato ketchup, Worcestershire sauce and frankfurters.

MACKEREL

Beautiful and strong tasting, the mackerel is a schooling fish whose season lasts from April to October in northern latitudes. It is plentiful in the Pacific Ocean, on both sides of the Atlantic Ocean, and in the Mediterranean, Black and Red Seas. Of the pelagic fish, it is second only to herring in commercial importance.

The Atlantic mackerel *(Scomber scombrus)*, whose striped back ranges in color from iridescent steel-blue to greenish blue, averages 18 inches in length, and 12 to 18 pounds in weight. It is very fatty and gamy tasting, but it can be very good if cooked fresh without fat. It may also be poached, baked, or broiled and served with clarified butter. Mackerel is best in spring before spawning. Much of the mackerel catch is consumed salted, smoked, pickled or canned.

Ancient Egyptians liked it and sometimes pickled it. Romans, who distributed salted mackerel all over the empire, also used it to make their universal seasoner, *garum*, a liquid prepared from the decomposed remains of fish and fish entrails.

In the United States south of Chesapeake Bay, the king mackerel *(Scombrus cavalla)* predominates, running as far south as Brazil. It is a much larger fish, weighing up to 100 pounds. On the Pacific Coast, the chub, or Pacific mackerel *(Scombrus japonicus)* is most common. This species is also found in the Mediterranean.

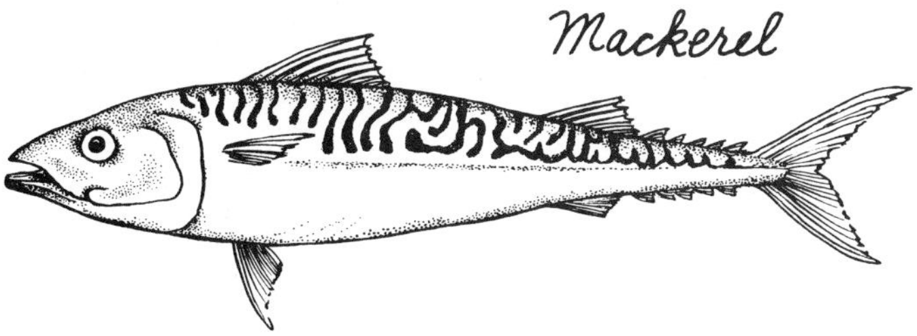

MACONNAIS

Also CHEVROTTIN DE MACON. This French goat's-milk cheese, marketed in two-inch squares, is in season from May to September.

See also: **Goat's Milk Cheese.**

MACON WINE

See **Burgundy Wine.**

MACOUCOU

Tropical fruit of an evergreen tree found in Guyana and related to the **star apple,** the macoucou, *(Chrysophyllum macoucou)*, is yellow orange in color and attains the size of a pear.

MACQUELINE

This soft, mild flavored French cheese is mold ripened like **Camembert** and **Brie** but does not compare to them in quality. It is made from whole or partly skimmed milk, with production centering in Senlis in the Oise department. The cheeses are round and flat, weighing four ounces. They are cured for about 20 days.

MACQUI

See **Chilean Wineberry.**

MACROBIOTICS

A theory of diet whose basic objective is to prolong human life, it has a philosophical basis in the Yin-Yang conception of forces in the universe. Common foods are classified as being either predominantly Yin or Yang and are then eaten in a prescribed proportion. Macrobiotic diets emphasize cereals, vegetables and fish; meat and other animal protein is usually avoided. One of the more popular macrobiotic diets was originated by Georges Osawa.

MADDERWORT

This is a perennial herb, *Rubia tinctorum*, native to the Mediterranean region, whose roots were used as a source of the dye, alizarin. The dye is now made artificially, but the roots can be used to make a kind of beer. The roots are chopped coarsely and left to ferment for five to six days in a mixture of water, sugar and yeast. The resulting brew is strained and bottled.

MADEIRA

Here is a Portuguese wine from the Madeira Islands in the Atlantic Ocean. In Portuguese the name means "wood." Sailors of Henry the Navigator landed in Madeira in 1419 and found dense, aromatic forests. Lured by their reports, colonists came and brought the vine with them.

Madeira wine is made from a mixture of black and white grapes, which are made separately into wines called *tinta* and *verdelho*, from the names of the grapes. Four great Madeiras—Malvasia (malmsey), Sercial, Verdelho and Boal—are made from varieties of grapes bearing these names. Malmsey, pressed from long, conical, yellow grapes, was introduced to the island from Crete. It is a sweet, exotic, gold-colored wine. The Sercial, from Rhineland plants, makes a dry, amber, very strong wine and is usually aged from eight to ten years. The Verdelho is semidry, and the Boal semisweet.

The harvesting of Madeira is similar to that of **port** in the Douro Valley of Portugal. The volcanic soil is broken by hand tool. The vines overhang island paths on trees and trellises and cover tiled roofs. The grapes are picked by hand and are carried on the backs of workers called *borracheiros* to the large vats for pressing. The pressed wine is left open to the sun, however, where it caramelizes.

Like port, there are two types of Madeira: vintage and *solera* ("blended"). In the *solera* method, the wine is kept in the same barrels, but as the original liquid evaporates, new wine is added, the barrels filled continuously to the brim. This process is repeated until a desired result is attained. Unlike port, Madeira travels easily. An attempt is even made to agitate the wine to reproduce the commotion caused by early sea voyages when Madeira was shipped to Great Britain and to the British colonies in America.

As with port, the British have long been connoisseurs and faithful customers of this wine. The British consul at Funchal (the principal city on Madeira), a Mr. Bolton, was able to arrange special privileges for the importation of Madeira in the 17th and 18th centuries in exchange for wheat and dairy products from Ireland, wood and rice from America and fish from Newfoundland. But the British love of Madeira goes back to the 15th century. Falstaff sold his soul for "a cup of Madeira and a cold capon's leg" *(Henry IV* Part I); and the duke of Clarence, after all, was drowned in a butt of Malmsey ("like a cat," exclaimed Huck Finn).

MADEIRA SAUCE

This French sauce used with steak or roast meat consists of **espagnole sauce** and butter much reduced and added to a mixture of stock, juice (from the meat being served) and Madeira wine. It is flavored with mushrooms, and occasionally sliced truffles are added. It is served hot.

See also: **Sauce.**

MADEIRA VINE

Also MIGNONETTE VINE. A rapidly growing, twining plant whose leaves are cooked and eaten like spinach, Madeira vine *(Anredera cordifolia)* is a native of tropical America and grows from Mexico south to Chile along the western side of South America. The Madeira vine is widely cultivated in the tropics.

MADRAS BEAN

Also HORSE GRAM. The seeds of this annual plant, *Dolichos biflora*, are considered an excellent food. They have both high protein and high carbohydrate content. The plant is semierect, reaching two to three feet in height and has narrow, curved pods about three inches long. It is common in India and Sri Lanka, and is grown extensively in drier areas. The Madras bean is closely related to the **lablab bean** but is more oily and fibrous than the latter. It is also used as horse fodder, hence the name "horse gram."

MADRUNO

Edible fruit of a small tropical American tree, *Rheedia madruno*, it is yellow with a rough, leathery rind and a juicy berrylike pulp. The madruno is sold in local markets in Ecuador. The taste is slightly aromatic. It can be eaten raw or used to make jams and preserves.

MAGALIS

Scarlet fruit of a small South African tree related to the **star apple,** the magalis, *(Chrysophyllum magalis)*, is round, about one inch in diameter and has a pleasant flavor.

MAGERE SCHWEIZERKASE

See **Radener.**

MAGHREB HOPS

The leaves of this North African herb, *Origanum glandulosum*, are used as a condiment. It is a member of the marjoram genus.

MAGPIE

This is the name given to several small birds of the crow genus *(Corvus)*. The magpie is eaten with some regularity in France, especially in country districts. Its flesh is dark and strong-tasting. The flesh of small birds tends to be dry and must be larded or barded before cooking. In France, magpies are used to make stock or cooked in a casserole.

The ancient Egyptians were fond of eating small birds. Herodotus, the Greek historian, mentioned in his *Histories* that Egyptians pickled magpies in brine for a few days, then ate them raw.

MAGUEY

This is the Mexican name for agave, or century plant, of which more than 400 species exist in North America. It has a short, fleshy base fringed by broad, spiky leaves in roseate arrangement, which can be up to seven feet long. On reaching maturity (10 to 12 years), the base sends up a flowering stalk as high as 25 feet.

In preconquest Mexico, the plant was an economic mainstay, providing building materials (fencing and roofing from the leaves), clothing and sandals (from the fiber), needles and thread (from the thorns and fiber), food (from the base, tender inner spikes, stalk, buds and blossoms), soap (from the roots), fuel (when dead) and a multitude of medicinal remedies.

The base tastes somewhat like artichoke, or when candied, like sugar cane. Tender upper portions of the stalk are roasted, and the buds, taken just before flowering, are roasted or baked and eaten as a sweet preserve. The sweet juice of the maguey can be harvested by scooping out the base just before maturity and allowing it to collect inside. Called *agua miel* (honey water), it is a yellowish liquid, which, when taken fresh, is considered a general tonic.

The chief modern use of the maguey *(Agave americana)* is in the preparation of two popular Mexican alcoholic drinks, **pulque** and **mezcal,** of which tequila is the best known variety.

MAGUEY WORM

See **Caterpillar.**

MAHALEB

A small, ornamental cherry tree, *Prunus mahaleb*, whose blackish fruits are used to make a fermented liquor like **kirsch,** it is native to Europe and western Asia.

MAHLEB

See **Mahaleb.**

MAHSEER

This is an Indian fish of the barbel group, some species of which are much larger than their European cousins. (See **Barbel).** Best known is the *tor mahseer (Barbus tor)*, which reaches a length of four feet. It is India's most famous angling fish, and it is found in the rivers of the foothills of the Himalayas from Bihar to Assam. The *tor mahseer* is a member of the carp family and locally is an important food fish.

Putitor mahseer (B. putitora) is the largest of the group, having a long torpedo-shaped body, a broad, deeply forked tail and a high dorsal fin. It is a famous sportfish of India, and large specimens are nine or more feet in length. The *putitor mahseer* has a tendency to develop large, thick lips, and it has the characteristic four barbels at its mouth. This fish is found in rivers all along the Himalayas from Kashmir to China. The *bokar (B. hexagonolepsis)* is one of the smaller *mahseers*, weighing at most 21 pounds. Nonetheless, it is sought out by anglers. It is found in rivers of the eastern Himalayas and is also known as the *katli*. *Mahseers* may be prepared in any way suitable for carp.

See also: **Barbel** and **Carp.**

MAHUA SPIRITS

See **Darum.**

MAHWA

Also INDIAN BUTTER TREE. A tree of tropical India, Africa and Malaysia, the mahwa *(Bassia latifolia)* has edible flowers, and its seeds yield a butterlike oil. Mahwa flowers have creamy white petals, which are eaten fresh or dried. They also serve as a mash to make the potent spirit, ***darum.*** Typically a mahwa tree produces 200 pounds of flowers a year, and Indian production of these flowers amounts to about 25,000 pounds a year. A closely related species, the *mee* tree *(Bassia longifolia)*, also produces edible flowers.

MAIA

Maia is fermented milk used as a yogurt starter in southeastern Europe.

See also: **Fermented Milk.**

MAIDENHAIR FERN

This type of fern, *Adiantum pedatum*, is characterized by fine, hairlike composite leaves. The leaves are edible at the fiddlehead stage. The leaves are also dried and used for decorating cakes.

See also: **Bracken.**

MAIGANG

This dark-red, edible fruit of a large Philippine tree, *Eugenia polycephaloides*, reaches a diameter of three-quarter inches and has a tart flavor. It is made into a delicious jelly.

MAIGRE

See **Croaker.**

MAILE

Also MAILE PENER. A Russian ewe's milk cheese, made in the Crimea, it has a pleasant taste and a crumbly, open texture. Maile is cured in brine and keeps very well.

MAINAUER

A surface-ripened cream cheese named for an island in Lake Constance that touches the borders of Germany, Austria and Switzerland, it is similar to **Munster** and **Radolfzeller cream cheese** which is also made in the same area. These cheeses are round, with a red surface and a medium-soft yellow paste. Each weighs about three pounds.

MAINZER HAND CHEESE

Also MAINZER HANDKASE. A superior **hand cheese**, Mainzer is made in both Germany and Austria. It has the sharp, acidic flavor and a pungent aroma typical of the type. Partly skimmed cow's milk is soured. The curd is kneaded by hand and pressed into very small cakes that average two ounces. Curing takes six to eight weeks. Mainzer hand cheese is sometimes called pimp cheese.

MAINZER HANDKASE

See **Mainzer Hand Cheese.**

MAITRANK

Also MAIWEIN. A German wine cup consisting of young, white Rhine wine flavored with woodruff shoots *(Asperula* spp.) and a little brandy, it is a popular spring drink and in English is sometimes called May wine punch.

MAIZE

See **Corn.**

MAJOCCHINO

See **Incanestrato.**

MALABAR NIGHTSHADE

See **Basella.**

MALAGA WINE

See **Wines, Spanish.**

MALAGUETA PEPPER

See **Cardamom.**

MALAKOFF

This soft, creamy white French cheese of the **Neufchatel** type is eaten fresh or ripened. It is made in the Normandy region in very small units, averaging two inches in diameter by a half-inch thick. Malakoff is in season from November to June.

See also: **Gournay.**

MALAY APPLE

See **Rose Apple.**

MALAYSIAN SUNPLANT

This plant of the nightshade family, *Solanum ferox*, is found in India and Southeast Asia, where its fruits are consumed.

MALLARD

Properly, the term refers to the male, or drake, of the common wild duck *(Anas platyrhyncos)*. In the Northern Hemisphere, particularly in the United States, "mallard" is often used to identify the common wild duck of both sexes. The male is distinguished by its dark green head, white neck band and rusty breast. The female is a mottled brown. Mallards thrive in ponds and marshes and are surface feeders rather than divers. They are the ancestors of the domestic species of ducks. As Mrs. Isabella Beeton wrote in her *Book of Household Management* (London, 1861):

> *It is to be regretted that domestication has seriously deteriorated the moral character of the duck. In a wild state, he is a faithful husband, desiring but one wife, and devoting himself to her; but no sooner is he domesticated than he becomes polygamous, and makes nothing of owning ten or a dozen wives at a time.*

Mallard meat is dark. The most widely used preparation is that of roasting, especially with orange wedges and orange flavoring.

MALLOW

These are plants of the genus *Malva*, most particularly the high mallow, *M. sylvestris*, a European wildflower whose rose purple flowers are used to make an herb tea and whose leaves can be eaten in salads or cooked as a vegetable, like spinach. The flowers are also used medicinally to sooth chest complaints. The plant has been naturalized in the United States where it is cultivated as an ornamental.

MALMSEY WINE

This strong, usually sweet wine is now made in **Madeira,** Cyprus, Sardinia and the Canary Islands, but it originally spread throughout the Mediterranean from the Greek port of Monemvasia (Malvoisie) in the Bay of Epidaurus. The wine is similar to that of Frontignac (or Frontignan), sweet and somewhat musky in flavor.

It is frequently drunk as an **aperitif** or as a dessert wine and is also used in cooking and to flavor certain sauces. Tradition has it that the Duke of Clarence was drowned in a butt of malmsey (Shakespeare's *Richard III).* Its popularity was perhaps highest in the 16th century, when "Malmsey" meant any strong, syrupy dessert wine from Greece, Italy or elsewhere in the Mediterranean.

MALT

Malt is germinated grain—usually barley—that is kiln-dried and used principally in brewing, baking and the preparation of malt-extract. Germination is induced by first steeping the grain in cisterns for 48 to 72 hours. After that, it is spread out on growing floors and allowed to sprout; then it is dried and screened. In the process, most of the starch in the grain has been converted to maltose (malt sugar). In addition—and this is the key to its great commercial value—a considerable amount of diastase has been developed. Diastase is an enzyme that promotes conversion of starches into sugar.

Diastase performs this important function in the preparation of many alcoholic beverages, and this explains why the latter can be made from basic ingredients that contain no natural sugar, such as cereals and potatoes, but do contain a lot of starch. The diastase converts the starch to sugar, which is then consumed by the yeast to produce alcohol.

Malt itself is not a popular food product. An infusion of malt, however, is evaporated at low temperatures to produce extract of malt either as a syrup or a powder. Extract of malt is highly nutritive, containing a large proportion of sugar and fair amounts of vitamin B. It may be taken as a tonic or used to moisten the cereal of very young babies. Apart from its nutritive value, the diastase in it will promote the easy digestion of the starches. Malt is also used in malted milk powders, soups and medicines.

Malt is a major ingredient of **beer** and ale. This prompted the poet A.E. Houseman to write the following lines in *The Shropshire Lad:*

And malt does more than Milton can
to justify God's ways to man.
Ale, man, ale's the stuff to drink
For fellows whom it hurts to think;
Look into the pewter pot
To see the world as the world's not.

MALT BREAD

A bread that is sweet, soft and dark from the addition of malt extract, molasses and raisins, it is leavened with yeast and has a moist quality due to the dextrin formed.

See also: **Bread.**

MALTED MILK

Dried extracts of malted wheat and barley mixed with powdered milk, it is a nourishing product used as an additive in broths and especially sweet fountain drinks concocted with fresh milk, ice cream, flavoring syrups and preserved fruits of various kinds.

MALT LIQUOR

This term is used to describe fermented beverages made from malted barley, such as beer, ale, porter and stout. More particularly, malt liquor is a beverage made in the United States like beer, but it contains more alcohol than beer. The percentage of alcohol varies according to the regulations of each state, e.g., 3.2 to 7 percent in Ohio, and 4 to 8 percent in Oregon. Malt liquor is usually light, pale and mild tasting.

MALTOSE

Also MALT SUGAR. This is a white, crystalline sugar obtained by the action of diastase of malt (an enzyme) on starch, usually cornstarch in the United States. It is a disacharide, a sugar containing sucrose, maltose and lactose. This starch-digesting property of diastase has been of great importance for thousands of years in converting starch to sugar in the process of alcoholic fermentation.

See also: **Fermentation.**

MALUNGAY

See **Horseradish Tree.**

MAMMEE

Also MAMEY, MAMEY APPLE. This succulent fruit is plentiful in the West Indies and the tropical parts of Central and South America. Perhaps because of its size (three to six inches in diameter) and shape (roundish), the mammee has been called an apple. It is not a pome, however. Its rind is thick, leathery and brown, and the bright yellow pulp contains one or more large seeds. The mammee grows on a very large and beautiful tree *(Mammea americana)* whose flowers, in the West Indies, are used in distilling a liquor called *Eau de Creole.*

The taste of the mammee is closer to apricot than any other temperate fruit. The fruit may be eaten raw, out of hand, with wine or sugar, cooked or in preserves. It is also used as a flavoring for ice cream.

Mammee

MAMMEE SAPOTA

This fruit of the marmalade tree *(Pouteria zapota)* of the American tropics is one of the **sapodilla** group. The *mammee sapota* is oval, measures five to six inches in length and has coarse, reddish brown skin and pulp that may vary in color from yellow to orange crimson. It generally contains two or three shiny black seeds.

It has a bland taste. For the latter reason, it is often combined with a more acidic fruit when cooked or made into preserves.

MAMONCILLO

See **Ginep.**

MANATEE

Also DUGONG, SEA COW. The manatee is an American aquatic mammal that inhabits tropical rivers or brackish coastal sea waters. It is a member of the *Sirenia* family, which contains two other genera, the dugong of the Indian Ocean, and the extinct Stellar's sea cow of the Bering Strait. All three are herbivorous, subsisting on underwater plants. It has a large body, weighing as much as 600 pounds, shaped somewhat like a seal's. The manatee has prominent shoulders, a barrel-shaped trunk that tapers toward a crescent-shaped tail, and flippers.

The dugong has the peculiar habit of rising halfway out of the water when suckling its young, holding the infant in its flippers. This posture, and its face, which is said to be a homely caricature of a human face, are believed to have given rise to our mermaid legends.

The Stellar sea cow was hunted out of existence in the 18th century by Russian seal hunters for its hide, fat and especially meat, which, if anything like the manatee's and dugong's, was very tasty. The taste of the latter has been likened to pork or a good veal cutlet. A kind of bacon is made from it in the West Indies. The oil of the dugong is prized in Asia as a medicine for dysentery, constipation, headaches, earaches and diseases of the skin. Dugongs weep on being taken from the water, and their tears are caught and sold to be used in love potions.

Both the dugong and the manatee are threatened species. The North American species, *Trichechus manatus*, seems to be surviving best in Florida rivers where it is protected from hunters by law. There are thought to be 1,000 to 1,200 extant. The South American manatee, *T. inunguis*, inhabits the estuaries of the Amazon River where it is diligently hunted for meat and hide. There manatee steaks are broiled or stewed, and the fat, which is sweet, is rendered down and used to make pastry.

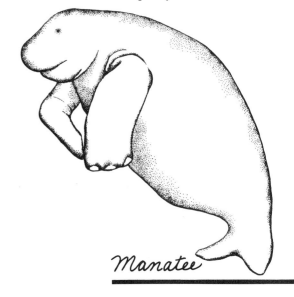

MANBOLLEN

See **Edam.**

MANCHEGO

This cow's milk cheese, produced in Spain, is also popular in Latin American countries, particularly in Mexico. *Manchego* tastes pleasant and mild when young, but it ages into an exceptionally fine cheese, with a nutty flavor and crumbly texture. These cheeses are ripened in molds lined with esparto grass, which leaves an imprint on the rind. They are usually cylindrical, five inches high, with a diameter ranging from two to five inches. Interior color varies from white to golden yellow and some cheeses have small, irregular holes.

MANDARIN

See **Tangerine.**

MANDUBA

This South American catfish, *Ageneiosus brevifilis,* is renowned for its fine flavor. The manduba is found in rivers and backwaters from Guyana through the Amazon basin to Peru, Uruguay and Argentina. It reaches a length of 21 inches, and large specimens weigh from four to five pounds. The manduba is a dull grayish brown above and has silvery sides and belly. It feeds on crustaceans and small fish.

MANGABEIRA

Edible fruit of a small Brazilian tree, *Haucornia speciosa*, it is reddish yellow in color, oval and about the size of a plum. In Brazil mangabeira is used to make marmalade.

MANGEL-WURZEL

See **Mangold.**

MANGO

This uniquely flavored fruit is so widely eaten that it is called the "apple of the tropics." It grows on a huge tropical evergreen tree, *Mangifera indica,* which is believed to have originated in India, but which is cultivated extensively in such areas as Malaysia, the East Indies, the Philippines, southern Florida, Mexico and Hawaii. The tree often reaches heights of 115 feet and is valued for its ornamental qualities and ability to provide shade. A mango vaguely resembles a peach, although it is usually kidney-shaped and can weigh as much as eight pounds. The skin is thin but leathery and may be red or yellow in color. The pulp is fragrant and juicy, with a flavor that varies depending on the variety, of which there are more than 30. The taste seems to combine elements of the pear, apricot, pineapple and banana. The fruit has a large central pit, which, in inferior specimens, is hard to remove due to an abundance of fibrous matter in the pulp. Inferior fruit also has a strong undertaste of turpentine, which may explain why some visitors to the tropics do not like mangoes on first trying them. This is not a problem with good quality, fully ripened mangoes.

Mangoes are a staple food throughout the tropics, but especially in India. Indians frequently pick them green, and eat them as a vegetable with salt and pepper. They are also picked when green to be used as an ingredient in chutney. When ripe, they are eaten as a sweet dessert or used in preserves and jams.

MANGOLD

Also MANGEL, MANGEL-WURZEL. A large, coarse field beet, *Beta vulgaris* var. *crassa,* used more often as fodder than as human food, it is genetically related to the garden beet and the leaf beet (Swiss chard) and is the variety from which the sugar beet was developed. It is also used to make mangel-wurzel beer.

MANGO MELON

Also ORANGE MELON, GARDEN LEMON, MELON APPLE, VEGETABLE ORANGE, VINE PEACH. A small melon, *Cucumis melo* var. *chito,* whose firm, white flesh is used to make preserves and pickles, it is also cooked and eaten as a vegetable. About the size and shape of a lemon or orange, the mango melon has yellow or orange skin and is not edible raw.

MANGO PLUM

There are several varieties of this fruit of tropical Asia, especially in Burma, Malaysia and Indochina, including the *Bouea macrophylla* and the *Bouea burmanica.* The fruit usually resembles a yellow plum and has a slight mango taste. It may be eaten raw, cooked or pickled.

MANGOSTAN

This annual herb, *Amaranthus mangostanus*, is grown in Japan during the summer months. Its leaves are boiled like spinach and may be eaten salted as a side dish. This is not to be confused with the mangosteen, which is a tropical fruit.

MANGOSTEEN

Also MANGOSTAN. One of the most delicious tropical fruits, the mangosteen is also one of the rarest, due to the difficulty of cultivating and transporting it. It is the fruit of a small tree, *Garcinia mangostana*, which is native to Malaysia, Indonesia and the Molucca Islands. On maturity, the mangosteen reaches the size of a tangerine and has a purplish red rind that suggests the pomegranate. This thick, leathery rind contains a pinkish white pulp divided into segments like an orange. The pulp is soft and melting, suggesting that of a ripe plum, and has a sweet, slightly acidic flavor.

The mangosteen has been transplanted successfully to the Western Hemisphere, most notably in the West Indies, the Panama Canal Zone and Honduras. Plantings have been on a commercial scale only in Honduras where the annual output amounts to between 40 and 60 tons. If planted as a seed, the tree requires 15 years before bearing; if budded, eight to 10 years. The fruit is best if picked when fully ripe.

The flavor of the mangosteen is said to combine the best properties of the pineapple, apricot, orange and grape. Some authorities say it is best when chilled. It is sometimes pureed and used as a topping for ice cream or sherbet. In the East Indies, the pulp may be cooked with rice *(lempog)* or with syrup *(dodol)*.

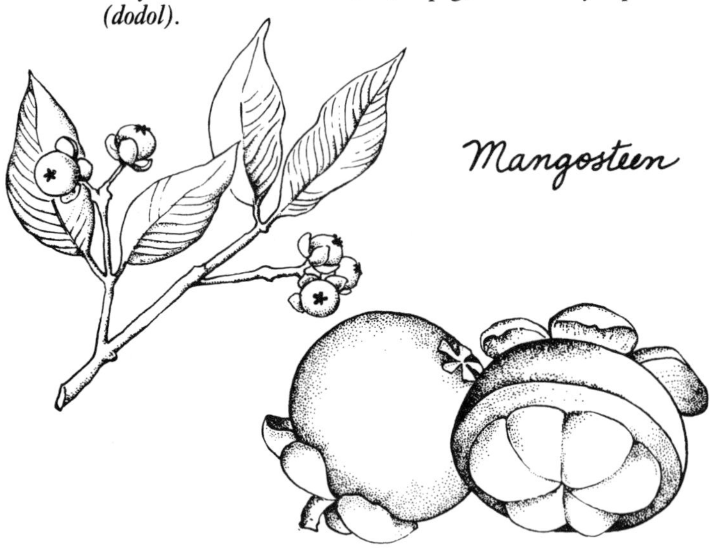

MANGROVE

This is the edible fruit of a tropical tree, *Rhizophora mangle*, of the same name. The mangrove tree grows along seashores in muddy areas and tidal estuaries. It is remarkable for its aerial roots that form stilts. The mangrove fruit reaches a length of about an inch and a half, is oval and has a single seed. It is sweet and pleasing to the taste and is healthy to eat before it germinates and puts out roots. The bark of the mangrove is an important source of tannin.

MANIOC

See **Cassava.**

MANKIL

Also JAVA APPLE, SAMARANG ROSE APPLE, WAX APPLE. This edible fruit of a handsome ornamental tree, *Syzygium samarangense*, found in Malaysia, Indonesia and the Philippines, may be white or red and is pear-shaped with a fleshy, acidic pulp. It reaches a length of one to 2½ inches. The Java variety is highly regarded, but in other areas its flavor tends to be insipid.

MANNA

Also HONEYDEW. According to Don and Patricia Bothwell, authors of *Food in Antiquity*, Biblical manna was the secretion of an aphid or scale insect living on the tamarisk shrubs in the Sinai. It is still collected there today by Bedouins. The oak wax scale *(Cerococcus quercus)*, a similar insect that infests oak trees in Arizona and southern California, produces a bright, yellow wax which native American tribes in California collected. It was called "Indian honey" or "honeydew," and the native Americans used it like chewing gum.

Aphids and scale insects are plant lice which, in certain seasons, excrete this sweet liquid "honeydew" almost continuously. It is normally harvested by ants. However, according to the Bible [Exodus 16:13], the manna, or bread from heaven, fell during the night and was visible on the ground after the dew had evaporated. It is more evident at that time of day because the ants have not yet gotten to it. Manna is granular and sweet, and, according to one source, a modern gatherer of manna can collect up to four pounds in a morning. The word "manna" derives from the Arabic word *man*, meaning aphid or honeydew, and *man-es-simma*, meaning manna from the skies. It occurs elsewhere in the Arabic world, including Iran and Iraq, where manna-bearing branches are gathered and beaten until the manna drops off. It is sold to confectioners who make it into candy and other sweets.

Other possible sources of Biblical manna have been advanced. These include saps or resins from the flowering ash *(Fraxinus ornus)*, the tamarisk *(Tamarix gallica)* and the camel's thorn *(Alhagi maurorum)*, all without benefit of insects; the fruit of an Iranian type of pea plant, *Astragalus florulentus;* an edible lichen living on the trees named above and, finally, the one perhaps closest to the original concept, a shower of food from the heavens, caused not by Jehovah, but by a near collision of Venus and Earth. This last was put forward by Immanuel Velikovsky in his *Worlds in Collision*.

A type of manna is also found in Australia on the leaves of Eucalyptus trees, secreted by the larvae of psyllid insects. The white conical structures are collected by aborigines, who prize it for its sweet taste.

MANN'S CHERIMOYA

A small African tree, *Annona manii*, closely related to other *Annonaceae*, suoch as cherimoya, sweetsop, and soursop, produces large fruits that are eaten locally. They have a fine flavor.

See also: **Cherimoya.**

MANTECA

Also MANTECHE. This is an Italian specialty that consists of a flask-shaped hollow cheese filled with butter, usually whey-butter. The bag has walls one half-inch thick and is formed of cheese with a plastic curd like ***caciocavallo.*** It contains from one-quarter to one-half pound of butter, which maintains its freshness for a long time. Whey butter is a byproduct of making *caciocavallo* and provolone.

Manteca looks like a small caciocavallo cheese. The outer surface is usually a smoky yellow brown, and the interior straw colored. The precise methods of manufacture remain a closely guarded secret. It is known also as *butirro*, *burriello*, *burrino* and even *burro* (butter).

MANTECHE

See **Manteca.**

MANTIS SHRIMP

See **Squill Fish.**

MANUR

Also MANURI. A Serbian cheese made from either cow or ewe's milk with buttermilk added, it is kneaded by hand and salted.

MANY CAPPED POLYPORE

See **Polypore.**

MANZANILLA

A dry white Spanish wine, very similar to dry **sherry** from Jerez de la Frontera in the province of Cadiz. Manzanilla differs from sherry in its much shorter and simpler aging process. The alcohol content is maintained at 15.5 percent, until it is stabilized and bottled as Manzanilla Fina, which is smooth and rather bitter. Some Manzanilla is allowed, however, to increase in strength, and is bottled at from 17 to 20 percent, when the *flor*, or yeast, dies. This is called Manzanilla Pasada—and has an odor something like the golden sherries—but is much drier. Manzanilla is also the Spanish work for camomile and some authors have suggested that this wine was once flavored with camomile.

MANZANITA

Edible berries of an evergreen shrub *Arctostaphylos manzanita* native to Northern California, manzanita are white turning to red and are used mainly for jellies and cider.

MAO-T'AI

See **Pai Chiu.**

MAPLE SUGAR

This is a sugar obtained by boiling down **maple syrup** until sufficient evaporation is produced to cause the residue to granulate. The yield is about three pounds of sugar from 1¼ quarts of syrup. The syrup is obtained from the sap of the sugar apple tree *(Acer Saccharum)*. Although today maple sugar is an expensive delicacy, in former times it was a staple sweetner in the northeastern United States.

MAPLE SYRUP

This sweet liquid is obtained by boiling the sap of the sugar maple *(Acer Sacharinum)* or black maple tree. This is no ordinary sap but one produced by the tree during the cool spring seasons typical of the northeastern United States and nearby regions of Canada. For reasons that remain obscure, the tree exudes the sugar sap only if there is a succession of days in which the temperature drops below freezing at night, but rises well above it during daylight hours. These conditions are fulfilled sometime between mid-February and mid-April and can last anywhere from five days to six weeks.

The sap is extracted as follows: a hole is bored into the bark of the tree about three feet from the ground; a spout is driven into this hole to a depth of two to three inches, and a bucket is hung from the spout. For a good tree, the flow ranges from 120 to 400 drops a minute, which amounts to an average of

12 gallons of sap per season. This boils down to about 1¼ quarts of syrup, which can then be reduced by evaporation to about three pounds of sugar. A tree trunk must be 10 to 12 inches in diameter to be of tappable size. This takes a tree 35 to 50 years to attain.

American colonists learned about "tree sweetner" from the native Americans for whom it was the sole means of sweetening and seasoning. For about the next two hundred years, it was the cheapest, and for many who lived inland, the only readily accessible sweetner. Honey was available in some places as was molasses near the seacoast, although the latter suffered the stigma of having been produced by slave labor. In the 18th century, Americans consumed four times the amount of maple sugar that they do today, despite an enormous rise in population. Because of the peculiar combination of conditions needed to produce sugar sap—the right trees and the right climate—true maple syrup and maple sugar are luxury items today. To be profitable nowadays, a stand of maple must contain at least 500 trees. Most of the sweetner is marketed today in roadside stands or by mail order. Maple syrup and sugar have never been produced elsewhere, although attempts have been made to transplant the trees to the Old World.

Maple syrup can be made two ways: by boiling down the sap or by adding water to maple sugar. It is poured over hot biscuits, griddle cakes or French toast.

MAQUEE

Also FROMAGE MOU. This name is applied to three Belgian cheese. The first is a soft, brick shaped cheese made from cow's skim milk. The second is made from the whey created in making the first type. The third is a homemade cottage cheese.

MAQUI

See **Chilean Wineberry.**

MARANG

A tropical fruit of the Philippines, the marang *(Artocarpus odoratissimus)* is related to the **jack fruit,** but is much smaller. It is round or oblong, juicy, well flavored, sweet and aromatic. It is borne by a large, evergreen tree.

MARANON

See **Cajuada.**

MARASCHINO

This strong, clear-colored liqueur derives its special flavor from the marasca or damasca cherries of Dalmatia, Yugoslavia. It is made by pounding the fruits and crushing the stones. Honey is added, and the mixture is left to ferment before being distilled. Sugar is usually added to make a sweet drink, but occasionally maraschino is bottled as a dry liquor. It is 60 to 78 proof.

MARC

Also EAU DE VIE DE MARC. In French, the word refers to the residue of skins, seeds and stems left in the wine press after the grape juice has been squeezed out. By extension, it means a potent liquor distilled from a mash composed of this residue. A sort of brandy, marc (pronounced "mar" with the "c" silent) has a strawlike, woody taste and rustic character that appeals to some enthusiasts. It can be very crude, though, and requires years of aging to make it palatable. It is usually identified by origin, such as *marc de Bourgogne* (Burgundy), or *marc de Champagne.* It can also be made from the residue of pressing apple cider, in which case it is known as *eau de vie de cidre.*

See also: **Grappa.**

MARCHES

This hard, Italian sheep's-milk cheese is named for the province of the Marches but is made chiefly in Tuscany an adjoining provinces.

MARE'S-TAIL

A water plant, *Hippuris vulgaris,* found in many areas of the world, including Europe, Asia, North America and Patagonia, it has slender, erect stems, tiny flowers and long, hairlike leaves. The young shoots are edible and are prepared like asparagus. In certain regions of France the shoots have been eaten since Roman times. They may also be pickled.

MARGARINE

Also OLEOMARGARINE. This fatty substance used as a spread and in cooking started out as a butter substitute. Present-day margarine consists of about 80 percent fat—mostly commonly soybean oil—emulsified in a liquid, usually water, milk or solutions of dairy or vegetable protein. It may contain a number of additives, such as salt, vitamins A and

D, sweeteners, antioxidants, preservatives, edible colors, flavors, acids and alkalies.

Although margarine is now considered a food in its own right, the connection to butter has remained important. This is because overwhelming public acceptance of margarine is dependent on how closely it approximates butter in looks and taste.

Margarine was invented in 1869 by an enterprising French chemist, Hyppolyte Mege-Mouries, to win a cash prize offered by the French government for "a cheap butter for the Army, Navy and needy classes of the population." This first effort consisted of suet, chopped cow's udder and a little warm milk, all mixed under pressure and churned into solid fat. The product was pearly white, and Mege-Mouries dubbed it *margarine* after the Greek word *margarites*, which means pearly. It was marketed under the name *butterine*.

Butter producers have waged a bitter fight against margarine ever since it first appeared in markets in 1873. They have been particularly concerned with its being fraudulently passed off as butter to the public. This led to restrictive legislation in the United States, especially in dairy states, prohibiting the sale of yellow margarine (one had to color it oneself using an enclosed capsule of yellow coloring matter), or imposing a special tax on colored margarine. This restruction has dropped away over the years as the price of butter rose to a level well above that of the costliest margarine.

In the battle for public acceptance, a number of different bases were used in margarine, including whale oil, palm oil, peanut oil and coconut. Money was invested in research on utilizing other vegetable oils and on how to "cream" them, mature them, add vitamin concentrates, keep them soft, etc. More recently soybean oil has begun to dominate, followed by corn oil, then in much smaller amounts cottonseed oil, palm oil, safflower oil, beef fat and lard.

Margarine use has been rising steadily in the United States since the 1920s as a middle-class alternative to butter, rather than as a butter substitute for poor people. In the past two decades research into circulatory ailments has tended to favor the use of unsaturated fats (most margarines), as against saturated fats (butter). Saturated fat, i.e., one that is solid at room temperature, tends to increase the amount of cholesterol in the bloodstream, which promotes fatty deposits in the arteries leading to arteriosclerosis.

Over a seven year period in the 1970s, per capita consumption of margarine in the United States averaged 12 pounds a year, more than twice as much butter at 4.8 pounds. The British and French much prefer butter to margarine. If figures from the 1960s are still accurate, the French have a per capita consumption of four pounds of margarine and 20 pounds of butter a year.

MARGATE

The largest of the western Atlantic grunts, and an important food fish, the margate *(Haemulon album)* is found from Bermuda and Florida to Brazil. It is a relatively deep-bodied, slender fish with a high dorsal fin. It attains a length of 25 inches, and its skin has a grayish overall cast but is otherwise variably colored. The margate favors shallow areas of open seas.

A close relative is the black margae *(Anisotremus surinamensis)*, a fish similar in appearance but smaller. Grunts are so named for the audible noises they make both in and out of the water by grinding their teeth and amplifying the sound with their swim bladders.

See also: **Grunt.**

MARIENHOFER

A soft, fermented Austrian cheese made from partly skimmed cow's milk in Carinthia, it is highly aromatic, like **Limburger** and is marketed in four-inch, tinfoil-wrapped squares.

MARIGOLD

Three different marigold plants have culinary uses, the pot marigold *(Calendula officinalis)* the marsh marigold *(caltha palustris)* and the sweet marigol *(Tagetes lucida)*.

Pot marigold is the common garden flower of Europe and North America with yellow to deep orange flowers. It is grown chiefly as an ornamental, but the flower heads and petals are useful both fresh and dried as flavoring and coloring agents. Pot marigold has been nicknamed "the poor man's saffron" on account of the yellow coloring it can add to soups, stews and custards as well as to margarine and even cheese. It is especially popular in Holland for such things as conger eel soup and meat soup. In England, the petals are used in marigold pie, a crusty egg custard. Marigold flowers must be used sparingly, however, because they have a pungent flavor, and formerly were infused to make an herbal beverage called calendula tea, which was taken as a stimulant.

Marsh marigold grows in swampy areas of North American and Eurasia. The leaves and stems may be cooked and eaten as a green vegetable. It is best known, however, for its flower buds, which are pickled and eaten as caper substitutes. This plant is also known as cowslip.

The sweet marigold is native to Mexico and Guatemala. The leaves resemble **tarragon** in flavor and are used in much the same way.

MARINKA

This carplike fish, *Schizothorax argentatus*, of the southern USSR, inhabits fresh waters of the Lake Balkhash basin in Kazakhstan. It reaches a length of 20 inches and is fished commercially in the lake. The marinka is usually eaten dried. Its unshed eggs are discarded as poisonous.

MARJORAM

This herb is a member of the mint family, but only two of its many varieties are important as seasonings: sweet marjoram and pot marjoram (oregano).

Sweet marjoram, *Marjorana hortensis*, is a perennial in its native Mediterranean region, but an annual in colder climates. Its leaves have a fragrance and taste that are at once pleasantly sharp and aromatically bitter, with a hint of camphor. It has been put to many uses over the centuries. It was long thought to have the power of keeping milk fresh, hence the sobriquet "sweet." Marjoram tea was prescribed for chest infections. Currently, its essential oil is used commercially in soaps and perfumes. Its leaves, both fresh and dried, are a highly popular seasoning. Sweet marjoram can be added to practically anything, but is considered perfect for chicken and turkey stuffings, sometimes substituting for sage, which has a stronger flavor. It enhances taste when cooked with mushrooms and is an excellent garnish or salad green.

Pot marjoram, *Origanum vulgare*, also called wild marjoram, is a hardy perrenial plant, common throughout Asia, the British Isles, North America and Europe, particularly Italy, where it is called *oregano*. The flavor is much stronger than sweet marjoram's, but only plants grown in southern regions have the necessary fragrance for seasoning. It is an indispensable adjunct of Italian and Mexican cooking and is popular throughout Latin America.

Marjoram

MARKHOR

This wild goat, *Capra falconeri* of the Himalayas, is eaten by the people of northern India. Its flesh is described as stringy, but edible. The markhor attains a maximum length of about 4½ feet and weighs up to 260 pounds. It is crowned by a remarkable set of horns that curve backward nearly matching the length of its body.

MARKISH HAND

This soft, piquant German cheese is pressed more heavily than most **hand cheeses,** but otherwise is made in the usual way. It is marketed in small, oblong pieces and is judged to be of fair quality.

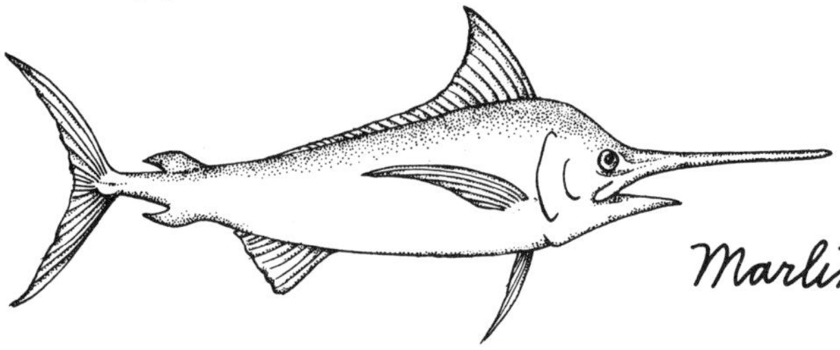
Marlin

MARLIN

Any of several species of this large to very large game fish are highly prized as food. Top weight goes to the black or white marlin *(Makaira indica)*. It can be as much as 12 feet long and weigh 2,000 pounds. *M. indica* ranges the Indian and Pacific Oceans and is especially plentiful off Australia, New Zealand, Peru New Guinea and Hawaii. It is one of the world's great game fishes and an important commercial food fish throughout its range. Characterized by a long, pointed snout forming a bill, it is heavy-bodied with a deep chest and flattened sides. In the water *M. indica* is a deep slaty blue above and silver below, but after death it is covered by a whitish haze, hence the two contradictory names.

A companion species is the blue marlin, *M. nigricans*, which is found worldwide in tropical and warm temperate seas. It runs longer than *M. indica* (up to 15 feet) but only achieves half its maximum weight. It is an avidly sought sport fish, and commercial catches in the Pacific alone run more than one million pounds a year. The blue marlin is a dark steely blue on its back and white on its belly. The much smaller white marlin and striped marlin belong to the *Tetrapturus* genus. The former is a familiar game fish of the United States Atlantic Coast, reaching a top length of 8 feet. The striped marlin *(T. audax)* inhabits the Indopacific area and is reputed to be the best tasting of all marlin and hence correspondingly popular in commercial fisheries. It has the usual blue back and white sides but is distinguished by up to 15 white or pale blue vertical stripes.

See also: **Sailfish.**

MARMALADE

As generally understood, marmalade is a preserve, or jam, made from bitter oranges. In the making, the rind of the fruit is boiled with the juice, sugar and corn syrup. The result has a vaguely bittersweet flavor. Marmalades may be made from other citrus fruits, such as lemons and grapefruits. Marmalade has a stiff consistency and contains solid matter. It is a popular preserve in Great Britain where it is eaten at breakfast with toast and butter. Perhaps the best known is Dundee marmalade from Scotland.

In former times, the word "marmalade" was also applied to sweet jams made from apples, peaches, etc., which were flavored with the rind of a tart citrus fruit. To confuse matters a bit, the similar word, *marmelade*, is used in France for many types of thick jam, but not for orange jam. In Spanish, the term *mermelada* is used for any type of jam.

The English word "marmalade" derives from the Portuguese *marmelada*, a jam originally made from quince, which is called *marmelo*.

MARMOT

Also WOODCHUCK, GROUND HOG. This is a small rodent, *Marmota marmota* plentiful in parts of North America, western Europe and Asia. Several species are hunted for flesh and fur in North America and Asia. The species *M. monax* is said to have been a staple item of diet for several North American tribes. A large marmot can attain a length of up to 25 inches and weigh up to 16 pounds. It has a thick coat of fur ranging in color from bright brownish yellow through reddish brown to dark brown. Marmots live in the ground in burrows and feed during the day on herbaceous vegetation. The marmot may be prepared in any recipe suitable for rabbit or squirrel. It should be noted that rodents from the western United States can host ticks that transmit Rocky Mountain spotted fever (a form of typhus) and tularemia. Animals that behave oddly or lethargically should be avoided.

The African ground hog *(Thryonomys semipalmatus)* or cane rat is considered an important source of protein for many people. This rodent is found in reedbeds, marshes, swamps, the borders of lakes and streams and occasionally among bushes and rocks in higher ground. There are six different species that are widely distributed from the southern edge of the Sahara south to the Cape province. Since it often does considerable damage to cane fields, it is the object of organized hunts. The Zulus are said to be particularly fond of this rodent's flesh. By way of preparation, they first pluck out its bristly fur like feathers from a chicken.

MAROILLES

See **Marolles.**

MAROLLES

Also MAROILLES. A soft, fermented French cheese, *Marolles* originated in a medieval village of the same name, but is now made in numerous villages in the departments of Aisne and Nord. Its long and illustrious history was brought to public attention in 1960 when a celebration was held in Marolles to mark its 1000th anniversary.

Marolles is made from whole, skim or partly skimmed cow's milk. It has a brownish red rind, yellow paste and a sharp smell, which has caused the French to nickname it *vieux puant*, old stinker. There are minor variations in size and shape, depending on the village of origin, but it is usually square, with a side rarely measuring more than six inches or less than two. One unusual variation is shaped like a half-moon and is seasoned with herbs. Cheese are aged from three to five months and are eaten from October to July.

MARRON

See **Chestnut.**

MARROW

See **Bone Marrow, Squash.**

MARSALA

A sweet white dessert wine from western Sicily, it has a high sugar content (5 to 10 percent) and very little acidity. In its preparation a mixture of cooked concentrated must (wine lees) is added to the fermented liquid. Marsala varies in sweetness and strength according to the proportions of this mixture. Its alcoholic content is very high (17 to 20 percent), and it is usually aged for at least two years in wooden casks.

The debut of Marsala outside Sicily occurred in 1773, when a British entrepreneur, John Woodcock, imported the wine into England. He then settled in Sicily to cultivate and produce the wine on a larger, more advanced scale. Marsala is frequently used in a sauce, with veal. Traditionally, it is often served chilled—with antipasto—before a festive meal.

MARSH HEN

See **Grouse.**

MARSHMALLOW

This confection was originally made from the roots of the marsh mallow *(Althea officinalis)*, a European plant naturalized in the coastal marches of the United States. The marshmallow today is made from sugar, starch, corn syrup and either gelatin or stiffly beaten egg whites. It is a spongy, white candy, resembling a gum drop in shape, which may be eaten all by itself or used in icings and desserts. A traditional custom in the United States is to toast marshmallows over an open fire at the end of a long twig or fork.

MARSH SAMPHIRE

This small, fleshy herb, *Salcornia herbacea*, of the coastal zones of Europe, has succulent stems and leaves that are cooked and eaten like spinach. This annual plant is sometimes collected and sold as produce in the markets of France, Belgium and Holland.

MARSH WOODWORT

The tubers of this perennial herb, *Stachys palustris*, may be cooked and eaten as vegetables. It is found in freshwater marshes of Europe and North America. Marsh woodwort is related to *chorogi*, a plant much cultivated in Japan for its slender, white edible tubers.

See also: **Crosne.**

MARTAGON

See **Lily Bulb.**

MARTINIQUE CHERRY

Edible fruit of a small tree, Martinique cherry *(Flacourtia inermis)* is probably native to the West Indies. The fruit is a cherry-sized berry, brilliantly red and slightly acidic, although some varieties are sweeter than others. It is customarily used to make jellies, and if eaten fresh is generally sweetened with sugar.

MARTIN'S GRAPE

The edible fruit of a woody vine, *Ampelocissus martini*, native to the Philippines, these grapes grow in large bunches. Their color is dark maroon red to black, and their taste is tart. They are used to make jellies.

MARTYNIA

Also UNICORN PLANT. A low, spreading plant whose curved seed pods are pickled like cucumbers, martynia *(Proboscidea louisianica)* is found from Delaware to Indiana and south to New Mexico. The martynia plant has a hairy, sticky texture. Its pods, which end in a sort of curved beak, attain a length of six inches. Pickled pods are eaten by themselves or used in mixed pickles.

MARUMIA

This is a woody vine, *Marumia mucosa* of Java, whose berries are made into a pleasant drink.

MARVOLA NUT

Plum-sized fruit of a South African tree, *Sclerocarya caffra*, it is one-seeded, reputed to have good flavor and used often to make jellies.

MARZIPAN

Also ALMOND PASTE, MARCHPANE. This is a sweet paste made of ground almonds, sugar and egg whites. When made right it is as pliable as putty and is often used to make tiny candies in the shapes of fruit such as bananas, oranges, etc. Marzipan also makes delicious cookies (biscuits), cakes and icings.

The origin of marzipan is ancient, and obscure. Some authorities trace it back to ancient Rome, others attribute to it an Arabic origin. It was popular among the Elizabethan English who called it first "St. Mark's pain" (after the French *pain* for bread), then "marchpane," and finally "marzipan." The French use it to make small cookies which they call *massepains.*

MASCARPONE

Also MASCHERPONE. A soft, Italian cream cheese with a mild, acidic, buttery flavor that is eaten fresh, it is made in Lombardy during winter and marketed in four-ounce cylinders wrapped in muslin.

Mascarpone has a consistency somewhat like cottage cheese and is the basis for a classic cheese cake. It is also served with chocolate cake, fresh fruit or bread. Like a whipped cream, it can be beaten into a liqueur or brandy, and sprinkled with sugar.

MASCHERPONE

See **Mascarpone.**

MASKED TRICHOLMA

See **Blewit.**

MASKINOGE

See **Muskellunge.**

MASTIC

Resinous sap from the bark of the lentisucus *(Pistacia lentisucus)*, a small evergreen shrub from the Greek island of Chios, mastic (the word comes from an early Greek word for "mouth," and is related to the English "masticate") is a natural chewing-gum or breath-sweetener in Greece and Turkey and was used in ancient times to make the alcohol beverage **mastika.** The well-known wine, **retsina** may owe its popularity to this early (and acquired) taste for mastic. The gum is very soft—and thus easily chewable—transparent and has a faint yellow or glassy-green tinge. Mastic today is a prime ingredient in the making of varnish.

MASTIKA

Mastika is a distilled liquor made in Greece of grape spirit flavored with gum **mastic.** It originated on the island of Chios. The taste of Mastika is similar to that of Ouzo and other anise-flavored liqueurs. It is manufactured much in the manner of **gin,** and may be drunk as an aperitif or as a liqueur. Mastika is not well known outside Greece, and few non-Greeks acquire a taste for it.

MATAI

See **Water Chestnut.**

MATASANO

Also GUATAMALAN SAPOTE. A tropical fruit closely related to the **white sapote,** the matasano *(Casimiroa tetrameria)* reaches the size of a small orange, is greenish yellow and has a soft, melting pulp and a bittersweet flavor.

MATCHA

This powdered green tea is used in the Japanese tea ceremony. It is made from the young leaves of mature tea plants and produces a thick, bitter and frothy brew.

See also: **Tea.**

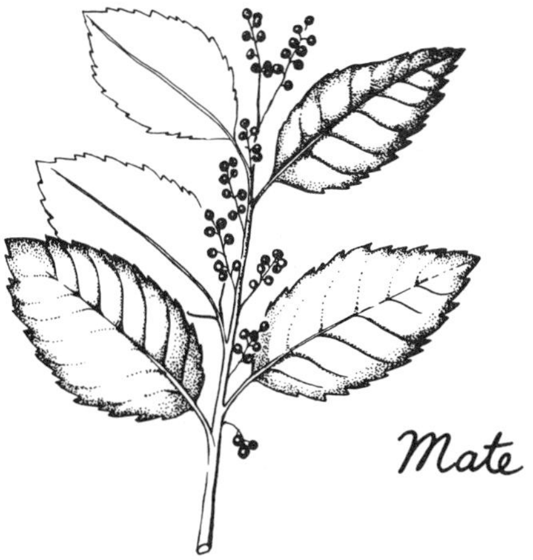

MATE

Also PARAGUAY TEA, YERBA MATE. A beverage made by infusing the buds and leaves of a type of holly, *Ilex paraguayensis,* it is a popular drink in several countries of South America, including Brazil, Argentina, Paraguay, Uruguay and Chile. In certain areas, mate occupies a place in the diet similar to that of tea in Great Britain and coffee in the United States. Indeed, the stimulating principle of mate is the same, i.e., caffeine, although according to Gaylord Hauser:

> Mate *is often extolled because it is thought to be less harmful than Chinese tea. This is true in most cases, but there are varieties of* mate *which contain just as much caffeine as Chinese tea.*
>
> *Dr. Moreau de Tours of the Pasteur Institute states that the alkaloid in* mate *contains the different properties of caffeine without presenting any of the inconveniences.*

The buds, leaves and young shoots of *Ilex paraguayensis* are dried, or fumigated, then pulverized before packaging. The powdered leaves have a yellowish green color. In the traditional method of brewing, the powder is placed in a hollowed-out gourd (or a silver vessel of the same shape), boiling water is poured on it, and it is allowed to steep for about 10 minutes. The resulting "tea" is sipped through a metal straw (called *bombilla)*, which has a small basket-work bulb, or filter at the lower end to strain out particles of mate. The original powder is good for two or three infusions. The drinking vessel is called *culha* in Brazil and *mate* in Spanish-speaking areas from the Indian word *mati* for calabash. The word *mate* is now generally used for the beverage and the plant as well, although properly speaking it should be *yerba* (herb) *mate.* The taste resembles that of green tea, but is slightly more bitter. The traditional brewing method is still in use among Argentine *gauchos* (cowboys) and other country folk, but in the cities, *mate* is brewed like Chinese tea, hot with water or milk, with sugar or iced. It may also be flavored with lemon juice, rum or kirsch. Because of its high alkali content, *mate* is thought to be beneficial in the treatment of gout.

MATELOTE SAUCE

This French fish sauce consists of red wine and fish stock, much reduced and thickened with fish half-glaze and seasoned with mushrooms. Butter and cayenne are added just before serving.

See also: **Sauce.**

MATEUS

This is the trade name for an internationally-known rose and dry white wine from Portugal. Mateus is exported throughout the world—particularly to the United States, Canada and Australia—in distinctive flask-shaped dark green bottles. Foreign demand for Mateus is so high that it absorbs the entire harvest from Tras-os-Montes ("across the mountains")in north-eastern Portugal. Mateus Rose is especially prized. Its taste, slightly sparkling, is said to rival that of the great French **Tavel.**

MATISIA

Edible fruit of a South American tree, *Matisia cordata*, of the sapote type, it has brownish green, leathery skin and a sweet, pleasant-tasting, orange yellow pulp.

MATSUTAKE

Also PINE MUSHROOM. A large edible mushroom of Japan, which is regarded gastronomically as the equal of the **king bolete,** the matsutake *(Tricholoma matsutake)* grows wild on the ground under red pine trees. It has a brownish color, a ring on its stem and a cap (often cracked) that can measure up to 10 inches across. It is considered a great delicacy in Japan and has been described as "superb, with an aroma and flavor quite unlike any other mushroom."

The October fruiting of the matsutake is a noteworthy event in Japan where hordes of city people head for the pine forests to search for the mushroom and have picnics. A second variety, the *Armillaria matsutake*, is also collected. Much of the wild crop is canned for export. The Japanese use the matsutake in sukiyaki, or marinated in soy sauce and sake, then grilled, or steam with fish, chicken and ginkgo nuts.

The matsutake is related to the native North American mushroom the wood-blewit *(Tricholoma nudum)*, which is inferior in taste, but may be substituted in the event *matsutake* is not available. Japanese immigrants to the United States, however, prefer the "white matsutake" *(Armillaria ponderosa)* or pine mushroom, which is abundant in the pine forests of the Pacific Northwest and especially in the Douglas fir forests of the Puget Sound area. It is a large, white mushroom (height up to six inches; cap up to eight inches across) and weighs up to four pounds.

The Japanese cultivate the matsutake commercially as a side industry to reforestation by transplanting mastutake mycelia in pine tree plantations.

See also: **Mushroom.**

MATUGUNGO

See **Wild Medlar.**

MATZO

Also MATZOTH. Jewish unleavened bread that has much the appearance of an unsalted soda cracker, it is made from flour and water and contains no yeast or baking powder.

Matzo has an ancient history. According to tradition, it originated during the exodus of the Jews from Egypt, a story recounted in the Old Testament. Fleeing in a great hurry, they carried flour already mixed with water, some of which was baked by the torrid desert sun, surprising them with its palatability. The Exodus is commemorated each year at the Jewish feast of the Passover, at which religious Jews partake of matzo, calling it the "bread of affliction."

The baking of matzo is highly automated. It comes out of the oven a flat cracker, one-eighth of an inch thick, usually square or round in shape. The top surface has a regular pattern of brown baking marks. Matzos may be ground into matzo meal and used to make matzo balls or dumplings, which are served in soups and stews. Matzo dough is also mixed with egg and used to make blintzes or egg pancakes. Many people find that matzos make fine hors d'oeuvre crackers.

MAVRODAPHNE

Mavrodaphne is a sweet red Greek dessert wine from near Patras in the Peloponnesus. *Mavro* means "black" or "dark," and the wine is a very dark red, intoxicating and syrupy. Perhaps the best description of its flavor is this one by Henry Miller in *The Colossus of Maroussi:*

> *It slips down like molten glass, firing the veins with a heavy red fluid which expands the heart and the mind. One is heavy and light at the same time; one feels as nimble as the antelope and yet powerless to move. The tongue comes unloosed from its mooring, the palate thickens pleasurably, the hands describe thick, loose gestures such as one would love to obtain with a fat, soft pencil. One would like to depict everything in sanguine or Pompeiian red with plashes*

Matzo

of charcoal and lamp black. Objects become enlarged and blurred, the colors more true and vivid, as they do the myopic person when he removes his glasses. But above all it makes the heart glow.

See also: **Wine, Greek.**

MAY APPLE

This North American woodland plant of the barberry family has a single, edible, egg-shaped fruit the size of a large cherry. The May apple *(Podophyllum peltatum)* is commonly known as American mandrake, because of its resemblance to the poisonous European mandrake *(Mandragora officinarum).* This misnomer on the part of the early settlers no doubt contributes still to a fear of the may apple.

The fruit, which ripens in late August or early September, has a flavor similar to that of strawberries or guavas. It is waxy, yellowish, about two inches long and contains several seeds. Many of these "berries" make an excellent marmalade. In May the plant yields a fragrant white flower, and shoots up quickly to about fifteen inches in thick wide-leaved clusters that often hide the ground.

May apple is sometimes called "wild lemon," although the fruit has no such bitter taste and is also known as raccoon berry and hog apple. Ozark folklore has it that the May apple always grow in areas that furnish the more precious and rare **ginseng.** The rootstalk is poisonous and embodies the powerful drug *podophyllin.*

MAY CORDIAL

A German liqueur used to flavor other drinks, it is made by infusing hawthorn blossoms in brandy sweetened with a little sugar. After three months, it is strained and bottled.

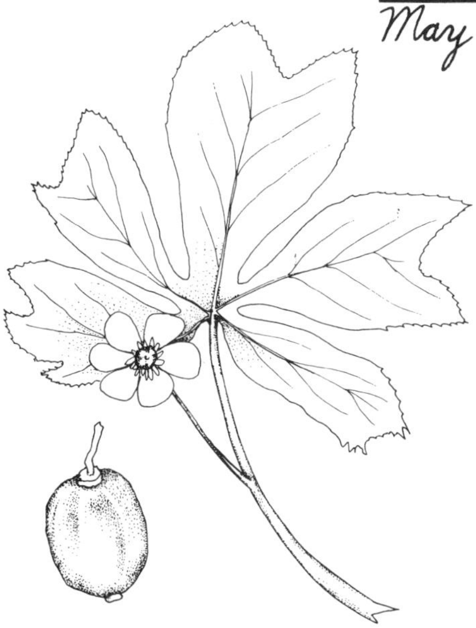

MAYONNAISE

This cold sauce is one of the basic French sauces. It may be used by itself or served as the base for innumerable compound sauces. Mayonnaise is a stable emulsion of eggs, oil, spices and vinegar or lemon juice. It is used the world over as a salad dressing and a sauce for a variety of dishes. Mayonnaise is produced commercially in vast quantities. The commercial variety must be refrigerated after it is opened, and the homemade should always be kept at a low temperature because it spoils easily. Mayonnaise should not be frozen, however, as it separates into its constituent parts when thawed. The same separation occurs if it is overheated.

The derivation of the name "mayonnaise" is the subject of some dispute. Some authorities claim the original spelling was *mahonnaise,* after the Irish General MacMahon, whose chef is said to have invented it. The great French cook and culinary writer Antonin Careme held that the true spelling should be *magnonaise,* from the French verb *manier,* meaning "to stir," and referring to the prodigious amount of stirring (now blending) needed to achieve the correct smooth, creamy consistency. Another source claims that the original spelling was *moyeunaise* from the old French word *moyeu* for egg yolk, the heart of the emulsion. The debate goes on, with no conclusive proof for any theory.

MEAD

Also HONEY WINE. An alcoholic beverage, usually consisting of fermented honey, water and spices, it is an ancient drink dating back to biblical times and was once popular in northern Europe, especially Anglo-Saxon England. Today it is made in California, England and Poland.

In its heyday, there were many types of mead. Two favorites were sack mead, flavored with **hops,** and cowslip mead, seasoned with cowslip blossoms. Nowadays, a mild-flavored honey is used for fermenting, which is then sweetened and fortified with alcohol or brandy to bring it up to 18 to 20 percent. Kosher mead is produced in New York State.

MEADOW LEEK

See **Wild Onion.**

MEADOW MUSHROOM

See **Field Mushroom.**

MEADOW PARSNIP

See **Dandelion.**

MEADOWSWEET

Also QUEEN-OF-THE-MEADOW. This is a wild herb, *Filipendula ulmaria* of the Northern Hemisphere. In England, its cream-colored flowers are used to make an herbal tea good against colds. The leaves may be chopped finely and added (sparingly) to soups. The leaves are also used to flavor certain liqueurs and wines, such as vermouth.

MEAGRE

See **Croaker.**

MEAT

This term refers to the flesh of animals, especially mammals, used as food. It frequently refers to fish and fowl as well. The definition also stretches to include the flesh of nuts, such as walnuts.

Meat is particularly rich in protein, the substance needed to rebuild body tissue, and 95 percent of it is digestible. If fatty, meat digests slowly, affording the eater a longlasting feeling of satiety. It has been said that meat gives the body a feeling of well-being that no other food can provide. It is usually the main course of a meal.

Its high esteem is attested in this 17th-century before-meal prayer:

Some have meat but cannot eat;
Some could eat but have no meat;
We have meat and can all eat;
Blest, therefore, be God for our meat.

The principal meats are beef, lamb, mutton (sheep), pork and veal. These will be discussed at length under separate headings, so a few words here will suffice.

Beef, which comes from steers fattened in feed lots, is America's favorite meat, although in Shakespeare's time it was thought to cause stupidity and melancholy. In *Twelfth Night*, Shakespeare wrote, "I am a great eater of beef, and I believe that does harm to my wit."

The Japanese, on the other hand, eat about one-tenth as much meat as Americans. Yet, with their growing affluence, meat has gained some acceptance. It has meant, however, overcoming a distaste for the smell of people who eat meat.

Although Westerners do not notice it, meat eaters give off a definite odor of butyric acid, which is contained in animal fat. It is noticeable, though, to those who eat little meat, such as the Japanese. In the 19th century, they dubbed Westerners, "butter-stinkers," due to this characteristic smell of heavy meat-eaters.

Veal, the flesh of a calf less than 14 weeks old, was preferred in ancient Rome and has maintained its popularity in modern Italy. Italians, per capita, eat about 16 pounds of veal annually, which is four times the American consumption.

Of the world's livestock, sheep are the most numerous, so lamb and mutton are at the top of the list in many countries. The English, for example, eat five times as much as Americans, who find the taste of mutton too strong.

Pork, a favorite in early America, used to rival beef in annual production, but has remained constant in the past 60 years, while beef eating has doubled. This has been blamed on the steady drop in farm population, the theory being that farmers like pork better than city dwellers do. Though not as popular, hogs may be the most efficient meat source, because, as the saying goes, meat packers use "everything but the oink."

MEAT EXTRACT

See **Beef Extract.**

MEAT PASTE

See **Potted or Deviled Meat.**

MECKLENBURG SKIM

This hard, saffron-colored cheese is made of skim milk in the northern German province of Mecklenburg.

MEDLAR

Fruit of a tree, *Mesopilus germanica*, native to the Mediterranean area, it grows as far north as England, but in those climes it never becomes fully ripe on the tree. Medlar is brown, about the size of a small apple and has an open top ringed by five lobes. The taste is astringent and tart in the unripe state. In warm climates, such as southern Italy, it ripens on the tree and can be eaten directly after picking. In colder climates it never really ripens on the tree, although if left through the first frost, it becomes somewhat palatable. Usually, the fruit is harvested sometime in November and left on the shelf for two or three weeks, until bletting (i.e., rotting) sets in. Then the acidity is much reduced and the flavor is described as unique and agreeably winelike.

It is eaten alone in warm climates, but elsewhere appears in compotes, preserves and jellies. The medlar was known in antiquity and was cultivated by the Assyrians and Greeks. It is related to the pear family, and a common wild variety is protected by thorns. Medlars grow freely in the United States, where the tree was introduced by the Jesuits.

MEDOC

Here is wine from the rich tidewater plain of the Medoc, which forms a peninsula between the Gironde and the Atlantic north of **Bordeaux** in western France. Several "great growths" *(grands* or *premier crus)* of red wines have been classified in this region, including the Chateau Lafite-Rothschild, Chateau Margaux, Chateau Latour, and Chateau Mouton-Rothschild. The Medoc, with its fine, gravelly soil, is divided into two major wine-growing districts: Medoc proper and, towards Bordeaux, Haut Medoc, which includes the subdistricts of Margaux, Moulis and Pauillac.

The Margaux wine is full-bodied but at the same time light and elegant. Thirty miles north of Bordeaux are the famous vineyards of Pauillac, where the chateaux of Latour, Lafite-Rothschild and Mouton-Rothschild are located. These latter two estates have been the property of the barons de Rothschild since 1853. All of the Medoc wines are distinguished by a rich smoothness and an exquisite bouquet. They are bottled—with few exceptions—at the chateaux that bear their names. This is stated on the label as *"mis en bouteille au chateau,"* which guarantees the historic perfection of these prime French red wines.

MEGRIM

Also LANTERN FLOUNDER, SAILFLUKE. A flatfish *(Lepidorhumbus whiffiagnois)* of the western Mediterranean and the Atlantic coasts of Europe, it reaches a length of two feet and lives on the soft muddy bottoms of fairly deep water. The megrim is fished commercially. Its flesh is considered good but not equal to turbot or sole. This fish was first described as the whiff, hence its curious scientific name. It got to be known as sailfluke because early writers claimed it put up its tail vertically to sail before the wind.

MEIWA KUMQUAT

A round, sweet variety of kumquat, *Fortunella crassifolia* is found in China and Japan. It is sometimes cultivated, is sweet and is often eaten raw.

MEKONG CATFISH

One of the largest of the giant Asian catfish, the Mekong catfish *(Pangasianodon gigas)* is valuable as food. It is found only in the Mekong river system, but this includes many of the larger rivers of Thailand, Laos, Cambodia, Vietnam and some parts of China. This fish has a wide reputation and is celebrated in the literature of the area. It can reach a length of eight feet, but due to overfishing such specimens are becoming increasingly rare.

See also: **Pungas Catfish.**

MELBA TOAST

These thin slices of toast are cooked in a slow oven until very, very dry and golden brown. Melba toast may be bought packaged in the market. It is named for Dame Nellie Melba (d. 1931), an Australian soprano, to whom it was first served.

MELILOT

Also SWEET CLOVER. A fragrant herb, *Melilotus officinalis* of Europe and Asia, that has been naturalized in North America, it reaches a height of four feet or more and has minutely toothed leaflets and yellow flowers. The leaves and flowers are dried and used to flavor stews and marinades. In France, melilot is added to the stuffing of freshly killed rabbits. In Switzerland, it is used to flavor Gruyere and sapsago cheeses. In Iceland, the roots are cooked and eaten like carrots.

MELISSA

See **Balm.**

MELON

See **Muskmelon, Watermelon.**

MELON FRUIT

See **Papaya.**

MELON PEAR

See **Pepino.**

MELON THISTLE

This is a cactus plant, *Melocactus*, of Mexico, Guatemala, the West Indies and Colombia, which is also called a Turk's cap cactus. These names derive from its resemblance to a large cantaloupe surmounted by a crown of spines filled with wooly, fibrous matter. The body, or "melon" is deeply ridged, rounded and one to two feet in height. It produces round or oval, small, red fruit, which are tart. The body of the cactus is juicy and is used by cattle for forage during periods of drought.

MELON ZAPOTE

See **Papaya.**

MELUN

Also BRIE DE MELUN. This if a French cheese of the **brie** type noted for its strong odor. Individual cheeses are smaller and thicker than the standard Brie de Meaux and have a yellow curd. Its taste is saltier and more piquant than Brie's. It is sometimes called *Brie d'amateur*.

MENHADEN

Also POGY, MOSSBUNKER. A small but at times extremely plentiful fish along the Atlantic coast of North America, the menhaden *(Brevoortia tyrannus)* is dark blue above with silver sides and reaches a maximum length of 18 inches. It is edible but, being extremely oily, it is not too palatable. Nevertheless, the menhaden is important commercially for production of fishmeal, oil and fertilizers. It is vital to the food chain, since swordfish, tuna, shark and cod all prey on it. The menhaden is related to herrings and sardines.

MENPACHI

This Pacific Ocean food fish is highly regarded in Hawaii. The menpachi *(Myripristis amaenus)* has a luminous red color and reaches a length of about 14 inches. The range of this fish extends from Hawaii to Indonesia. It lives close inshore and is characterized by large, black-pupiled eyes.

MERCUREY

This is wine from the vineyards of Mercurey near the Cote d'Ore in **Burgundy** south of **Beaune.** This district is also known as the Cote Chalonnaise, for its principal town, Chalon-sur-Saone. The name *Mercurey*, reminiscent of the ancient Roman presence in Burgundy, is most frequently linked with red wine, known for its frank "drinkable" quality and strong perfume. But two superior white wines are also grown in this region, in the vineyards of Rully and Givry. Rully white wine is perfumed, strong and often semisparkling (a "sparkling Burgundy"). A similar wine is produced in Givry, as is a somewhat thinner red wine with the Mercurey label.

MERGA

A sauce served on the North African dish, ***couscous,*** it is made from the stock of the meat served with the *couscous* and, if seasoned with red pepper, can be very hot.

MERGANSER

This wild duck is characterized by a crested head and a long, slender toothed beak with a hook at the tip. The merganser *(Mergus merganser)* is an excellent diver and lives on fish. Its flesh is edible but usually has a fishy taste.

MERINGUE

Egg whites are beaten until stiff and then blended with sugar and a little salt. Meringue is used as a topping for desserts, in which case it is delicate and fluffy. Thicker meringue, with more sugar blended in, is used as a shell in which to serve ice cream or other desserts. The thickest meringue is used to cover ice cream in such dishes as baked Alaska.

According to tradition, meringue was invented in 1720 by a Swiss pastry cook named Gasparini, who practiced his trade in a small town called Mehrinyghen.

MESITRA

A soft Russian cheese made in the Crimea of whole ewe's milk, it is eaten unsalted and fresh.

MESONA

The leaves of this perennial herb, *Mesona palustris*, are used to make a cooling drink. The plant is a native of Java and is well liked.

MESPIL

See **Medlar.**

MESQUITE

Also ALGARROBA, SCREW BEAN. A plant of the Western Hemisphere, mesquite *(Prosopis* spp.) has seeds whose pods resemble **carob** and are an important range food for cattle. In former times, the seeds of certain varieties of mesquite were eaten by Native Americans and early white settlers in the Midwest and Southwest of the United States. These varieties included the honey mesquite *(P. glandulosa)* var. *glandulosa)* whose pods range in length from four to nine inches and are white or yellow. The pods were eaten fresh or dried and used to make a molasses-like syrup. People also ate the screw bean or tornillo *(P. pubescens)* whose pods are tightly coiled and hairy.

METAXAS

Trade name for a dark, strong, semisweet grape brandy (pronounced "Met-ock-SAH") from southern Greece. Mextaxas, or Metaxa, is bottled in Pireaus, south of Athens but is widely exported, chiefly to the United States. Its brownish red color is partially the result of caramel flavoring. Served typically in tall slender bottles, Metaxas can be drunk straight or with ice. Perhaps the smoothest of these brandies is the "five-star" *(pende astiria)*, with an alcohol content of up to 42 percent. A stronger "seven-star" Metaxas is also very popular.

METCALF BEAN

Both the fruit and foliage of this drought-resistant plant, *Phaseolus retusus*, are edible. It is indigenous to New Mexico and Arizona and is sometimes cultivated there.

METEL

See **Hairy Thorn Apple.**

METT SAUSAGE

Also METTWURST. A German sausage composed of chopped pork, pig's liver and spices, it is stuffed into beef casings and smoked. The texture of this sausage is soft and spreadable. Mett sausage is a popular filler for sandwiches and can be served as a canape, spread on rye bread.

See also: **Sausage.**

MEURSAULT

This is a superior white Burgundy wine grown near the village of Meursault south of **Beaune.** White Meursault is produced from the Chardonnay grape and is characterized by being both dry and mellow, even "fruity." The wine maintains a clear gold-green color for up to five years, but if aged longer, it usually turns dark and becomes *maderise*, or "like **Madeira".** Many connoisseurs, however, prefer this development and the consequent "nutty" taste.

MEXICAN APPLE

This highly regarded, yellow green fruit of a Mexican shrub, *Solanum piliferum* of the nightshade family, is about the size of a hen's egg and scented like an apple.

See also: **White Sapote.**

MEXICAN TEA

Also EPAZOTE. This Mexican herb, *Chenopodium ambrosioides* of the goosefoot genus, is used as a condiment in certain typical dishes especially beans, where it reportedly minimizes the stomach gas often produced by beans. It is also used to make a medicinal tea.

MEZCAL

Mezcal is Mexican brandy distilled from the heart of the **maguey** plant, is also known as the agave or century plant. Mezcal has a sharp, herbaceous flavor, which goes well with salt and lime juice. It is usually bottled at from 80 to 86 proof.

Of the more than 400 species of maguey, only a few are suitable for the preparation of mezcal, the best being the *agave tequileana.* Contrary to popular belief, mezcal is not distilled from **pulque.** Instead, the plant is trimmed of leaves, then processed to produce a mash which, when twice distilled, becomes mezcal. Other mezcal regions center on Oaxaca in the south and on San Luis Potosi in the center of Mexico.

Tequila is the best known variety of mezcal. It takes its name from a town near Guadalajara in the state of Jalisco. By law only mezcal from this region may be called "tequila." The joys and sorrows of drinking mezcal are harrowingly recounted by Malcolm Lowry in his novel, *Under the Volcano.*

MICHINO

Edible fruit of a South American evergreen tree, *Chrysophyllum michino*, found in Colombia and Peru, the michino is related to the **star apple** and has yellow skin and white pulp.

MIGNOT

A soft French cheese made for a century or more in the Calvados, *Mignot* department may be eaten either fresh or ripened. The former is called *Mignot blanc.* It has a mild flavor and is made from April to September. The latter is *Mignot passe.* It is a fermented cheese resembling **Pont l'Eveque** or **Livarot,** ripened by a naturally occuring mold. It is available the rest of the year.

MILANO CHEESE

Also FRESCO, QUADRO, STRACCHINO DE MILANO, STRACCHINO QUARTIROLO. This soft, Italian table cheese of the **Bel Paese** type has a creamy, sweet, yellow curd. It is fast-ripening and most resembles ***Crescenza.*** Milano is ready to eat after 20 days' curing and does not last longer than 60 days. The cheeses are square, wrapped in muslin and weigh between three and six pounds.

MILK

This white or yellowish liquid is obtained from the udders and breasts of female mammals. Meant primarily for the suckling of offspring, it has great nutritive value, containing protein, sugar (lactose), fats, mineral salts, plus vitamins A, C and certain B vitamins. In the United States and western Europe, milk, especially cow's milk, plays an important role in the nutrition of growing children and some adults. Elsewhere, it is not so important because many people lose the ability to digest milk. This occurs if there is any interruption in milk consumption after a person is weaned from mother's milk. A baby's intestines secrete plenty of lactase, an enzyme whose presence is necessary to digest lactose. After weaning, however, the infant stops secreting lactase unless milk, usually cow's milk, is supplied continuously. In many parts of Asia and Africa this is not possible, or, as among native Americans, not thought desirable. Hence, the ability to digest milk is lost, and the process seems to be irreversible in many. If a nondigester drinks milk, it causes bloating, and intestinal cramps or diarrhea. Many of these persons can and do consume milk in indirect form, such as butter, cheese, casein and yogurt.

Milk has often been called the perfect or complete food, but this seems to be true for humans only of mother's milk. Indeed, provided the mother is healthy and the flow is adequate, mother's milk is tailored individually to a baby's needs since the baby and the mother were once a single organism. For the first three or four days after giving birth, the mother secretes not milk but colustrum. Colustrum contains a lot of protein but little sugar and fat, since these are difficult to digest. Then the colustrum gives way to a sort of natural skim milk, which eventually reaches full-fat status between the fifth and tenth day. In the 1960s and 1970s mother's milk was found to be polluted with DDT, a pesticide, some samples to the extent of quadrupling the legal limit (0.05 parts per million) imposed on marketable cow's milk. It is expected that this situation has improved since the banning of DDT.

Cow's milk is the most important nonhuman milk in human nutrition. It consists of 84 percent to 90 percent water and 10 percent to 16 percent solids, of which 2 percent to 7 percent is fat, 2.5 percent to 4.5 percent is casein (a protein) 2 percent to 6 percent is sugar, and the rest albumin (another protein) and mineral salts including a large amount of calcium. In addition to the vitamins mentioned above, vitamin D is often irradiated into milk at the processing plant. One cup of whole milk contains about 160 calories. For skim milk, the figure is 90.

Dairy cows, usually special breeds in the United States, are efficient producers of nutritious food, i.e., they produce milk at one-fourth the cost of producing beef. Holsteins are the most numerous and the most productive. They routinely produce more than 8,000 pounds of milk per year. However, it has the lowest butterfat content of any dairy breed (3.45 percent). Jerseys, on the other hand, have the highest butterfat content (5.14 percent), but average only 5,500 pounds of milk a year. The grand champion producer was a Holstein, Carnation Ormsby Madcap Fayne, who gave 41,943 pounds of milk (19,508 quarts) in one year.

Milk is marketed in several ways.

Raw milk: is essentially unchanged from that delivered by the cow, simply cooled and packaged. It is also called certified milk, i.e., certified by a medical commission as coming from healthy cows and hygenic premises.

Pasteurized milk: (named after bacteriologist Louis Pasteur who in 1860 discovered the process) is heated to 145°–150° F (62.8°–65.6° C) and held there for sufficient time to kill pathogenic bacteria, then quickly cooled. In addition to disease bacteria, heating also kills the natural lactic acid bacteria so that pasteurized milk does not sour, but it does go bad. In any case, it remains fresh longer than raw milk.

Homogenized milk: has been forced through fine openings at great pressure to break up the fat globules and casein. As a result, cream does not separate and rise to the top (as it does in nonhomogenized milk), and the milk itself is smoother and more easily digestible. Most milk marketed in the U.S.A. has been both pasteurized and homogenized.

Skim milk: has had its cream removed, which gives it a thinner, bluer appearance. A variation of this is *low-fat milk*, which has had its fat content reduced to a fixed percentage, e.g., 2 percent.

Fermented milk: includes such things as kefir, acidophilus, kumiss and yogurt, which will be discussed fully under separate headings. Suffice it to say that the lactose in these preparations has converted to lactic acid or alcohol by the action of bacteria or yeast.

Buttermilk: is the liquid that remains after **butter** has been made. Often, nowadays, it is made from nonfat milk by the addition of a bacterial culture.

Condensed milk: is produced by reducing the water content in milk through evaporation until the milk has the consistency of honey. Sugar is added.

Evaporated milk: goes through a similar process, but the result is thinner than condensed milk, because not as much water is removed and no sugar is added. It can be reconstituted to the approximate level of fresh, pasteurized milk by adding water.

Filled milk: is a commercial product that has had vegetable oil substitute for its butterfat. It feels and tastes much like milk and is more economical.

Imitation milk: is made from such ingredients as corn-syrup solids, vegetable fat, sugar, salt, artificial thickeners, colors and flavors, sodium caseinate and water. It is generally a lot less nourishing than real milk.

Goat's milk and sheep's milk are consumed fresh to a far lesser extent than cow's milk. Goat's milk has a higher percentage of fat and protein than cow's milk and a stronger flavor. because the fat globules are smaller, it is easier to digest. Sheep's milk also has a higher percentage of fat than cow's milk and more sugar.

All three types of milk are widely used in the manufacture of **cheese.** The cheese-making process is begun by souring the milk. This is accomplished naturally, through the action of lactic acid bacteria (milk's natural bacteria) or artificially by the introduction of a coagulant, such as rennet or yellow bedstraw. The milk separates into curds and whey. Curds are the semisolid part of the milk, and whey is the watery liquid. Curds form the basis of most cheeses, but some also are made from whey. Curds may provide a dish for immediate consumption, such as **cottage cheese** or junket, in which the curds are sweetened and flavored.

Of the countries that keep statistics, the Finns have the highest per capita consumption of milk and cream, 250 quarts a year (as of 1969). Milk and cream consumption have been declining in the United States. The per capita figure was 157 quarts a year in the late 1950s. This declined to 133 in the late 1960s, and by the mid-1970s was down to 120. The change was attributed to anxiety about cholesterol (from milk fat) and weight.

David Ogilvy, in his *Confessions of an Advertising Man*, remarked that many fine advertising slogans had been conceived that would never appear as such. Consider the following, which extols a brand of evaporated milk:

> *Carnation milk is the best in the land.*
> *Here I sit with a can in my hand.*
> *No tits to pull, no hay to pitch,*
> *Just punch a hole in the son of a bitch!*

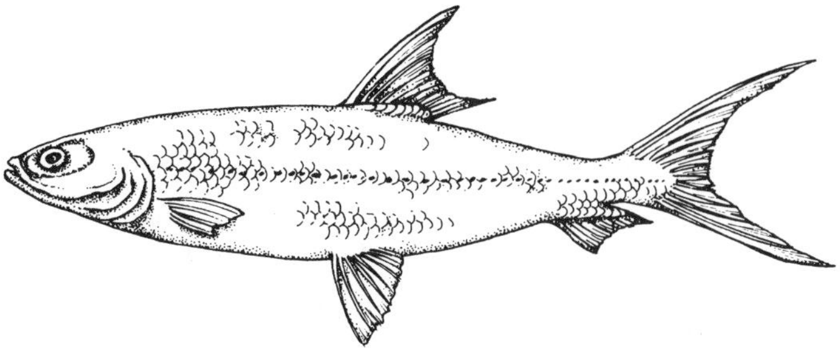

Milkfish

MILKFISH

Also SALMON HERRING, BANDANG, BANGOS. This ocean fish, *Chanos chanos*, which is extensively farmed in Southeast Asia, is enormously valuable as a food fish. In its natural habitat, the milkfish reaches a length of six feet. It prefers open ocean, except at spawning time when it comes inshore. Commercial fisheries by and large ignore it, but anglers seek it out as a hard-fighting and difficult quarry.

Its economic importance begins when it spawns in estuaries, lagoons and even rivers. In the Philippines and other Southeast Asian countries milkfish fry are collected from water neighboring the spawning grounds, put into brackish rearing ponds and later transferred to lakes where they mature to market size. The milkfish is a planteater, surviving first on algae and later on larger plants. Although the milkfish's pinkish flesh has many bones, it is deemed to be of very high quality.

The adult milkfish is characterized by a brilliant silver color, a high dorsal fin and a deeply forked tail. It is an active and fast swimmer. Its range includes the Red Sea, the coastal waters of East Africa and the western Pacific.

MILK POWDER

See **Milk.**

MILK SUGAR

See **Lactose.**

MILKWEED

This is a perennial wild herb *(Asclepias* spp.) plentiful in North America and Africa. The name derives from its milky sap. The plant is edible but bitter-tasting unless boiled thoroughly before eating. The young shoots are sometimes added to salads.

MILLER'S THUMB

Also BULLHEAD. A flat-headed, European fresh-water fish, it inhabits small streams, large rivers and lakes and attains a length of about four inches. The miller's thumb *(Cottus gobio)* is sometimes eaten; frying is the preferred method of preparation. It is found from the Caspian Sea area as far west as England and Wales, and from the Baltic south to the Alps and Pyrenees.

MILLET

This cereal grain, encompassing many species and varieties, is of little importance as food in the West but is highly regarded as such in Africa and Asia. Millets are grasses that produce very small seeds, sometimes in great abundance, as in the case of Italian millet *(Setaria italica)*, which under the right conditions can outproduce wheat. Usually, however, millet is grown under adverse conditions, because one of its most attractive qualities is its hardiness, i.e., its ability to withstand drought, extreme heat and infertile soils. Another desirable quality is that it keeps well, escpecially if unthreshed.

Finger millet *(Eleusine coracana)*, a tropical variety so called because the grain bearing spikes radiate from the ear like fingers from a hand, has been kept for as long as five years unthreshed before being eaten. The variety most often seen in Western countries is common millet *(Panicum miliceum)*, which is used for pasturage, green silage or hay. In Britain, it is a popular bird seed. Other major varieties are Japanese millet *(Echinochloa frumentacea)* and pearl millet *(Pennisetum glaucum)*, both staples in India and Africa. Teff *(Eragrostis abyssinica)*, which is called love grass in English, is an essential Ethiopian crop used to make a flatbread that is very similar to the Mexican tortilla.

In prehistoric and early historical times millet was the leading grain crop in the West, but its less attractive qualities led to its virtual abandonment as barley and wheat came under cultivation. The small seeds are hard to handle and contain no gluten, hence they are not suitable for making leavened bread unless mixed with wheat or rye.

As a rule, millet is made into a coarse porridge or gruel, such as the *puls* of the ancient Etruscans, which was adopted by the Romans and called *pulmentum*. It was the staple food of the poor. Later, barley replaced millet as the principal ingredient. Gruel, porridge and flatbreads are still the standard uses of millet in Asia and Africa.

MILLSWEET

See **Lima.**

MILT

Also LAITE, LAITANCE. Milt is soft roe, i.e., the sperm of the male fish and the reproductive glands containing it. Some of the best milt comes from carp, catfish, herring, mackerel and sturgeon. Basic preparation includes washing, stripping away the membrane that contains blood vessels and poaching in a mixture of lemon juice, water, butter and salt. It may be served immediately or elaborated in such dishes as fritters, tartlets, and crepes. Sturgeon milt is canned in Russia in tomato sauce or with vegetables.

MIMOSA

See **Acacia.**

MINDANAO PLUM

Edible fruit of a Philippine shrub, *Flaucourtia euphlebia*, it is round, dark purple, about three-quarter inch across and has a subacidic flavor. It is used to make jellies.

MINERAL WATER

Chemically all waters but distilled water are mineral waters, since they all contain dissolved minerals. Even rainwater contains many impurities. In the commercial sense, however, the term "mineral water" is used to describe most bottled waters but excludes such types as bulk water, club soda and seltzer. Perrier water is a prominent mineral water.

Such waters have a long history of popularity in European countries, stemming from a centuries-old custom of "taking the waters," i.e., visiting a resort or spa featuring natural spring waters for a health cure. This custom was popular with the ancient Greeks and Romans and remains so today in Europe where the names Spa (Belgium), Baden-Baden (Austria) and Wiesbaden (Germany) conjure up images of rest, dieting and bathing amidst luxurious surroundings. Part of the cure was drinking the local spring water, which had the value of being nonalcoholic and otherwise innocuous. Some were also claimed to be of medicinal value. From this came the supposition that drinking them at home might be equally valuable, and so the tradition grew.

In 19th and early 20th-century America, luxurious spas, such as Calistoga, California; Saratoga, New York; Poland Springs, Maine; and Hot Springs, Arkansas, were popular resorts for the rich and famous. The fashion passed, however, and bottled mineral waters were relegated to the shelves of gourmet shops where they sold for fancy prices. All this changed in the 1970s when bottled mineral waters experienced a boom in the United States as a "healthful" alternative to alcoholic beverages or diet soda. The beverage industry has undergone an overall trend toward lightness—wine instead of cocktails, light beer—and mineral water represented the ultimate in lightness, i.e., very little taste and no calories at all.

Some definitions are necessary to distinguish among various types of bottled water.

Still water means without gas bubbles, such as ordinary tap water, a mineral water such as Evian, and bulk water, which is sold in large containers for use as drinking water.

Sparkling water has bubbles made by dissolved carbon dioxide gas, which may occur naturally in subsurface water or be added later. Water that contains enough gas to be bubbly underground is called "naturally sparkling" on the label. Usually the gas escapes when it reaches the surface, and must be reinjected before bottling. This is the case with Perrier and Saratoga. Other waters, that are naturally still, such as Poland Spring Sparkling, have been injected with "natural" carbon dioxide, which is supposed to produce longer-lived bubbles than manufactured carbon dioxide.

Spring water emerges from the earth's surface under its own pressure. This must be true of water labeled as such under truth-in-labeling legislation. "Natural spring water" implies no processing before bottling, while mere "spring water" may or may not be processed.

Mineral water, as we noted above, is a broad term, but the state of California, in a piece of pioneering legislation, has defined mineral water as that containing 500 parts per million or more of total dissolved solids (TDS). Water with fewer PPM cannot be labeled "mineral water." This caused some consternation in the industry because some mineral waters have fewer PPM of TDS than a lot of ordinary tap water. For example, Poland Spring, which had been calling itself mineral water for several decades, had to be relabeled for sale in California because it had only 125 PPM. "Natural mineral water" means that minerals have been neither added nor removed.

Club soda is tap water that has been filtered, and has had carbonation and minerals added.

Seltzer is filtered tap water with carbonation added.

Soft water has low mineral content and may occur naturally or be softened artificially by the exchange of sodium ions for some of the calcium or magnesium ions in the water.

Hard water has high mineral content and is reputed to be good-tasting.

According to *Consumer Reports*, a publication of the Consumers Union, Americans drink bottled water for a number of reasons, including health, the desire to appear sophisticated and dissatisfaction with the taste of tap water. In mid-1980, Consumers Union analyzed 38 widely available waters for mineral content, including New York City tap water, then submitted them to a panel of sensory consultants to be ranked by taste. It should be noted that Craig Claiborne, food editor of the *New York Times*, had organized a taste test of mineral water in 1979, which pitted Perrier, the leading prestige brand, against several others. The winner was Canada Dry Club Soda. There were three categories of water in the CU judging; bulk still waters, other still waters and sparkling waters. Ratings ran the gamut from excellent to poor. Following is a list of the waters and their ratings as published in the September, 1980 issue of *Consumer Reports*. (Since then, of course, the waters may have been reformulated.):

BULK STILL WATERS

New York City tap water (U.S.A.), excellent;
Deep Rock Artesian Fresh Drinking (U.S.A.), excellent;
Arrowhead Mountain Spring (U.S.A.), very good;
Great Bear Natural Spring (U.S.A.), very good;
Mountain Spring (U.S.A.), very good;
Carolina Mountain (U.S.A.), good;
Deer Park 100% Spring (U.S.A.), good;
Sparkletts Crystal-Fresh Drinking (U.S.A.), fair;
Bonniebrook Spring (U.S.A.), fair;
Borden Polar Spring (U.S.A.), poor

OTHER STILL WATERS

Mountain Valley (U.S.A.), excellent
Poland Spring Pure Natural Mineral (U.S.A.), very good;
Hinckley & Schmitt Natural Spring (U.S.A.), good;
Evian Natural Spring (France), good;
Fiuggi Natural Mineral (Italy), good;

SPARKLING WATERS

Peters Val Naturally Sparkling Mineral (West Germany), good;
Canada Dry Club Soda (U.S.A.), good;
Le-Nature's Crystal Clear Mineral (U.S.A.), good;
Gerolsteiner Sprudel Natural Mineral (West Germany), good;
Apollinaris Natural Mineral (West Germany), good;
Saratoga Naturally Sparkling Mineral (U.S.A.), good;
Montclair Sparkling Natural Mineral (Canada), good;
a Sante Napa Valley Mineral Sparkling (U.S.A.) good;
Calistoga Sparkling Mineral (U.S.A.), good;
Canada Dry Seltzer Pure Sparkling (U.S.A.), good;
Poland Spring Sparkling Pure Natural Mineral (U.S.A.), good;
Perrier Naturally Sparkling Mineral (France), good;
Vittelloise Natural Spring (France), fair;
Ferrarelle Naturally Sparkling Mineral (Italy), fair;
Schweppes Sparkling Mineral (U.S.A.), fair;
Bartlett Mineral Spring Sparkling (U.S.A.), fair;
Sheffield's 0_2 Sparkling Spring (U.S.A.), fair;
Deer Park Sparkling 100% Spring (U.S.A.), fair;
Safeway Bel-Air Sparkling Mineral (U.S.A.), fair;
Vichy Celestins Naturally Alkaline Mineral (France), fair;
San Pellegrino Natural Sparkling Mineral (Italy), fair;
Black Forest Naturally Sparkling Genuine Mineral (West Germany), fair;
Calso Mineral (U.S.A.), poor.

It is worth noting that the waters were tasted by the sensory consultants in unmarked containers, and at a strictly controlled temperatures (40–45° F, 4.4–7.2° C). Absence of bad taste was the main attribute of good-tasting water, plus clarity, freedom from sediment and color, a clean taste and a refreshing quality with some hint of sweetness, bitterness or sourness. None of the sparkling waters were rated excellent because, according to the consultants, bubbles of carbon dioxide seemed to exaggerate slight off-flavors and to impart a taste of their own, chiefly bitterness. For more information on some particular waters, see under the specific name.

MINNOW

Small freshwater fish usually with a bronze or olive back and shining silver or gold sides, the minnow belong to the *Cyprinidae* family, which also includes the goldfish *(Carassius auratus)* and the much larger **carp.** Most are an important source of food and hence bait for gamefish and are raised for this purpose in the United States where "minnow farms" are a million-dollar industry.

Especially important to anglers are the many varieties of chub, shiners and dace. The common shiner is said to be the best of all bait for bass and the redbelly dace for brook trout. Minnows are good eating when they are large enough (most varieties rarely exceed eight inches). The word itself means small, from the Anglo-Saxon *myne*.

MINT

This general term includes a large genus of aromatic herbs, *Mentha*, which includes apple mint, bergamint or orange mint, dittany, horehound, hyssop, marjoram, peppermint, rosemary, spearmint and thyme. See separate articles on each of these varieties.

Mints are characterized by a fragrant aroma and a pleasant taste, which has overtones of menthol. It was a favorite seasoning in ancient Greece and Rome and in the Middle Ages, when strong flavors were needed to mask rancidity. Mint oils are important commercially in medicines, confections, liqueurs and in toothpaste. Black peppermint *(Mentha piperita vulgaris)* is the preferred source of commercial oil, but is not used in the kitchen because of its coarseness. Spearmint is the common seasoning herb. Mint sauce or jelly often accompanies lamb or mutton. Mint teas were once popular.

Pennyroyal *(Mentha pulegium)* has declined in favor both as a seasoning and as an insecticide, a use that earned it the name *pulegium*, from the Latin for flea.

MINT SAUCE

A sauce usually served with lamb and consisting of fresh mint leaves, chopped fine, mixed with wine vinegar and sugar and allowed to stand for a few hours before serving. Horsemint *(Menta longifolia)* is often used for this purpose.

See also: **Sauce.**

MINTZITRA

This soft, ewe's milk cheese is made in the Macedonia region on the Greek-Yugoslavian frontier.

MIRABELLE

See **Cherry Plum.**

MIRIN

This is a sweet, sherrylike, rice wine made in Japan.

MIRLITON

See **Chayote.**

MIRROR DORY

A close relative of the John Dory, the mirror dory *(Zenopsis nebulosus)* is found in the Indian and Pacific Oceans. It is good to eat but is fished commercially only off New Zealand and Japan. The mirror dory reaches a length of about 18 inches and has bright silver coloring with one dark blotch on each side. It has a deep body, flattened from side to side, and a large extensible mouth. It is prepared like **John Dory.**

MISKET KARLOVA

This semidry Bulgarian wine made from the Muscat grape has a golden color and an excellent aroma. "Karlova" refers to the region where the wine is produced.

MISO

See **Soybean.**

MISSEL THRUSH

Also MISTLETHRUSH. A European songbird, the missel thrush *(Turdus viscivorus)* is so called because it feeds chiefly on mistletoe berries. Its plumage is brown, but of a darker hue than that of the common **thrush.** Small song birds, such as the thrush, are prized morsels in France, Italy and Corsica, and they are prepared in a variety of ways, including roasting over charcoal, baking (after being boned and stuffed), and being made into pate.

MISSION HAUT-BRION WINE

This French red wine comes from an ancient vineyard in the Pessac commune slightly west of the city of **Bordeaux.** A red **Graves,** the best of this wine bears the label Chateau la Mission Haut-Brion and is grown only a few steps away from the more renowned **Haut-Brion** vineyards.

MISTOL

Mistol is a shrub or small tree of the jujube genus, *Ziziphus mistol* found in the Argentine and Andean regions. Its edible berries are sweet and juicy. In Bolivia, they are used to prepare *chicha*, a fermented beverage of low alcoholic content.

MITZITHRA

This soft, oily cheese is made from the whey by-product of **feta** cheese by Greek shepherds in the vicinity of Athens. The whey is mixed with some fresh ewe's milk to begin the processing.

MOBOLA PLUM

Mobola plum is the wild fruit of the South African tree *Parinarium mobola.* Its strawberry taste makes it one of the best fruits of the *Parinarium* genus.

MOCHA

A fine type of coffee with a rich, almost chocolate flavor, it came originally from the town of Mocha in Yemen. Early coffee growing was controlled by Arabs, and up until about 1720 the English and the Dutch had to go to Mocha for their coffee supplies. Continuing in the Arab tradition, coffee made from mocha beans (which are produced elsewhere now) is served in tiny cups.

"Mocha" is also a descriptive term for sweets or flavoring agents that combine the tastes of coffee and chocolate.

See also: **Coffee.**

MOCKERNUT

See **Bullnut.**

MOCK TURTLE

This is a mixture of veal, calf's head meat and seasonings used to make a soup that is supposed to resemble green turtle soup. It has a gelatinous quality and a strong flavor. Mock turtle soup is available canned in both the original and clear varieties.

MOLASSES

A thick syrup produced as a by-product of sugar refining, it ranges in color from bright amber to dark brown. The lighter the color of molasses, the finer the grade. It used to be a common sweetener in the United States, but now is used more as a flavoring agent.

In sugar production, cane juice is put through three successive boiling and crystalization procedures. Molasses left after the first round is the finest and is dedicated to kitchen use. That left after the third round is very dark and very low in sugar content. It is called mother liquor, or blackstrap, and is used principally as cattle feed. Molasses from beet sugar has an unpleasant taste and smell. In many areas, molasses is the chief raw material for the distillation of rum.

See also: **Rum.**

MOLE SAUCE

This Mexican sauce comes in many variations, some dating from Aztec times most probably. The word *mole* derives from the Nahuatl word *molli,* meaning "sauce flavored with chili." Mole sauces are used in Mexican dishes of turkey, chicken and meats, and particularly with tacos. Two popular versions are green *mole* and *mole poblano* (Puebla mole) which is dark brown. The green mole consists of a puree of chili peppers, tomatoes, onions, coriander and garlic, flavored with ground pumpkin seeds, walnuts and almonds, seasoned with salt and pepper, then mixed with chicken stock and cooked for five minutes. It is frequently served with chicken, in which case the chicken, when nearly done, is cooked for 10 minutes in the mole sauce.

Mole poblano is certainly the most famous version of mole, and is the essence of Mexico's holiday meal, *Mole Poblano de Guajolote* (turkey in Peubla mole). This sauce includes chili peppers, onions, tomatoes, raisings, tortilla, and garlic, all pureed then mixed with ground almonds, sesame and anise seeds, which are then added to chicken stock and seasoned with cinnamon, cloves, coriander, salt and pepper. After simmering for five minutes, the sauce receives its most unusual ingredient, bitter chocolate. Although it cannot be tasted, neither can it be omitted because it adds a necessary something without which the mole loses its character. If served with turkey, the bird is simmered for 30 minutes in the sauce before being served. *Mole poblano* is also used with chicken and pork.

The tedious business of pureeing and grinding the ingredients can now be circumvented by purchasing a dry packaged mix in the supermarket or a prepared paste version by the pound in Mexican traditional markets. To be good, mole need not be so hot as to be unacceptable to nonMexicans. The degree of heat can be controlled by the amount of chili used.

See also: **Sauce.**

MOLINA

A fruit of the sapote type, the molina *(Lucuma bifera)* is roundish, the size of an apple and must be eaten very ripe. The taste is excellent, but molinas are sold only in local markets. The tree is native to Peru and Chile.

MOLITERNO

This Italian cheese has a plastic curd and is made from ewe's and cow's milk in Calabria, Lucania and Basilicata. If from ewe's milk only, it is called *pecorino moliterno*. Production methods are similar to those used in making ***caciocavallo.***

See also: **Formaggio de Pasta Filata, Pecorino.**

MOLLUSK

This is a type of small animal found on land and in the sea and usually possessing a shell of one or more parts. Mollusks are invertabrates, i.e., animals without backbones. Their bodies are soft and unsegmented. The land mollusk eaten with the greatest regularity is the snail. Popular marine mollusks are oysters, clams and scallops. Less popular but still widely eaten are cockles, mussels, abalones, periwinkles, limpets, whelks, squid, cuttlefish and octopuses. For more information, see under the name of a specific mollusk.

MOLUCCA BERRY

Here is a type of raspberry, *Rubus moluccanus,* found in India, Malaysia and Indochina. The fruits are well-flavored and eaten raw.

MONBAZILLAC

Here is a strong, sweet, white French wine from the Dordogne basin east of **Bordeaux.** The harvest in this area occurs when the grapes have overripened on the vine. This is the "noble rot" *(pourriture noble)* condition encouraged by many growers of sweet wines, particularly those in **Sauternes** and along the German Rhine. Monbazillac wine quickly turns a clear gold but gains a deeper, richer color with age. In excellent years, Monbazillac rivals the wine of **Loupiac** and other great sweet Bordeaux wines.

See also: **Rhine Wines.**

MONCENISIO

This small Italian cheese is ripened by blue mold like **Gorgonzola.**

MONDSEE

See **Box Cheese.**

MONDSEER SCHACHTELKASE

Also MONDSEER SCHLOSSKASE. This is an Austrian cow's-milk cheese of the Munster type, that is, surface-ripened by red smear bacteria. The taste and aroma are acidic and sharp but milder than Limburger's. The full-cream variety is called *Schlosskase. Schachtelkase* is half or three-quarters cream.

These cheeses are round and six inches in diameter or loaf-shaped. They average about two pounds in weight. They are cured three to six weeks, wrapped separately and packed in wood containers called *schachteln.* This cheese is produced in the Mondsee district. Most of it is consumed locally.

MONDSEER SCHLOSSKASE

See **Mondseer Schactelkase.**

MONKEY BREAD

See **Baobab.**

MONKEY JACK

See **Lakoocha.**

MONKEY NUT

See **Paradise Nut.**

MONKS HEAD

See **Bellelay.**

MONOSODIUM GLUTAMATE

Also ACCENT, AJINOMOTO, MSG. This food additive, sold in the form of a white powder, enhances the flavors of certain foods, most notably soups, meat, vegetables, fowls and fish. MSG has no taste itself, and its exact mode of operation is not known. It is thought to increase the sensitivity of the taste buds or to stimulate the formation of saliva.

MSG was first isolated in 1908 in Japan from an extract of the seaweed kombu *(Laminaria japonica),* which had been used by the Japanese for centuries to bring out the flavor in various foods. MSG is a salt of glutamic acid, a common amino acid, which is most easily extracted from gluten, a vegetable protein. Today the large commercial producers utilize two processes, one employing wheat gluten, and another based on beet molasses.

MSG is immensely popular in Asia, where the per capita consumption is four times the U.S. average. It is a common commercial food additive in the United States, especially in canned soups.

In 1968 an allergic reaction to MSG was identified and called "Chinese Restaurant Syndrome" because a few cases were traced to the heavy-handed use of MSG in the kitchens of some Chinese restaurants. The symptoms are headache, dizziness, facial pressure, chest pain, burning sensations in the back of the neck and numbness. At first it was though that only large doses could produce the symptoms, but further investigations showed that smaller doses could cause them too in susceptible persons. In the resulting furor, babyfood manufacturers decided to stop using MSG in their products, and the New York City Department of Health was moved to warn Chinese restaurants to lower the amount of MSG added to such things as wonton soup and egg rolls.

MONOSTORER

A popular Rumanian cheese made of ewe's milk in the Transylvania district, it is hard pressed and salted in brine.

MONRUE

See **Cod.**

MONSTERA

See **Ceriman.**

MONTANA GRASS

Also INDIAN RICEGRASS. This is a perennial grass, *Oryzopsis hymenoids*, of western North America, whose seeds are edible as grain.

MONTASIO

This Italian hard cheese, similar to **fontina** and ***bitto,*** is made in the Friuli area near the Austrian border. It is made from cow's and goat's milk and sometimes sheep's milk. This cheese can be eaten fresh as table cheese, in which case the curd is white and mild tasting. If allowed to mature 12 months or more, the curd turns yellow and granular and acquires a sharp taste and characteristic aroma. Such cheeses are usually made from partly skimmed milk, and are grated for use in cooking and as a condiment. The rind is dark and oily.

MONTAVONER

Here is an Austrian sour-milk cheese to which seasoning herbs are added during processing.

MONT CENIS

A hard, French blue-veined cheese in the style of ***Gex*** and ***Septmoncel*** that is made in the Mont Cenis area, *Mont Cenis* is made from a skimmed and whole milk mixture taken from cows, ewes and goats. It is mold-inoculated and matured in cellars for three to four months. Cheeses are large and round, averaging 25 pounds in weight, with a curd that is white shading to yellow. Parsley is often added as seasoning.

MONTCLAIR WATER

This is a Canadian sparkling mineral water that a 1980 Consumers Union sensory panel rated as good-tasting, with the following comments: mildly bitter, mildly sour, mildly astringent, mild chemical flavor, mildly salty. It has a relatively low mineral content (200 ppm total dissolved solids).

See also: **Mineral Water.**

MONT D'OR

This soft French cheese like ***Pont l'Eveque*** originated in the Lyon area more than 300 years ago. In former times, it was made exclusively from goat's milk and achieved a reputation for high quality. This reputation has declined in recent years as manufacture spread to other areas and cow's milk was substituted. It is often sold fresh, but much is cured with the aid of surface mold. Curing takes one week in summer and three weeks in winter. It is best between December and April. The name *Mont d'Ore* is also given to a large Munster-type cheese made in Franche Comte.

MONTEREY CHEESE

Also JACK CHEESE. A fine cheddar-type cheese first produced in Monterey County, California, it is made from pasteurized cow's milk in whole, skim and partly skimmed versions. Monterey is made much like **Colby,** with one variation, called high-moisture Jack, using a slightly different process.

Monterey made from whole milk is semisoft and mild when young but becomes sharper when aged, a process that takes from three to six weeks. Monterey made from partly skimmed, or skim milk, is intended for grating and is called dry Monterey or dry Jack. It is generally aged at least six months and has a much sharper flavor. Cheeses generally weigh between nine and 12 pounds. The grating variety may be coated with a peppery oil. There is a Mexican imitation of Monterey with a firmer texture and a biting taste.

MONTHERY

This soft French cheese is of the **Brie** type, surface-ripened and made of cow's milk in the Seine-et-Oise department. Milk may be whole or partly skimmed. The cheeses, which are round and flat, comes in five and three pound sizes. Curing, with the aid of blue mold, takes about one month.

MONTIA

A member of the miner's lettuce genus, montia *(Montia fontana)* is native to southern and central Europe. It is a small, soft perennial herb which is eaten in salads, especially in parts of France.

MONTRACHET

This is a wine-growing district in **Burgundy** south of **Beaune.** The vineyards span two villages, or communes: those of Puligny and Chassagne, both of which have added Montrachet to their names (e.g. Puligny-Montrachet).

Many experts claim that the Montrachet vineyards give the greatest white wine in the world. In any event, the best white wine from this district is frequently compared with the great white wine of **Bordeaux,** the **Chateau d'Yquem.** It is called "the divine wine" (a pun in French, *le vin divin* or, loosely, "wine of wines"). The French would pronounce the name as "Mon-rah-shay," omitting the "t."

Several well-known white wines are produced in this district, including the Chevalier Montrachet and the Batard (or "bastard") Montrachet, named, it is said, for the offspring of an early feudal lord who was too old to go on a crusade and who was, instead, "tempted by the devil" and a bevy of local maidens. The wine resembles **Meursault** in having both a dry and mellow, or "fruity," taste, but unlike the Chateau d'Yquem it leaves the palate dry and refreshed.

MOONFISH

An edible fish, moonfish *(Mene maculata)* is found in coastal waters from East Africa throughout the Indian and Pacific Oceans to the Hawaiian Islands. Although it rarely exceeds eight inches in length, it is a very deep-bodied fish, nearly plate-shaped in profile. It is an important food fish along the Indian coasts. It is silver-gray overall with a green back interspersed with green gray patches on the upper sides. It frequents reefs and sometimes enters estuaries.

See also: **Opah.**

MOONFLOWER

A white, trumpet-shaped flower of the tropical morning glory plant, *Ipomea alba*, this fragrant, night-blooming flower is eaten as a vegetable. It is probably native to the American tropics but is found in both hemispheres.

MOONSHINE

Also POTEEN. In the United States, moonshine is illegally made whisky. Distilling is done in secret, usually at night, i.e., by the light of the moon. The term "moonshine" is most closely associated with the hills of Kentucky and Tennessee where "moonshiners" for decades have carried on a running battle with "revenooers," that is, federal revenue officers who were attempting to shut down illegal stills. The term "moonshine" is often used to cover smuggled whisky as well. The Irish equivalent of moonshine is *poteen*.

MOOR COCK

The male of the moorfowl, or red grouse *(Lagopus scoticus)*, has long been a favorite game bird in the British Isles. The red grouse is plump, rarely weighing much over a pound and is similar to the **quail** in shape and behavior. The moor cock's plumage is a rich chestnut with black stripes. The red grouse is a species of ptarmigan and is not found in North America, where the ruffed grouse *(Bonasa umbellus)* is a popular distant cousin. Its flavor when roasted and liberally basted with butter and meat drippings is considered exquisite, a touch of the heathery moors where it is most commonly found.

MOOSE

Also EUROPEAN ELK. The largest members of the deer family belong to this class of ruminant. The species native to the northern United States and Canada is called the moose *(Alces americanus).* The closely related species of northern Europe is called the elk *(Alces alces).* The American elk is more like the red deer and is discussed under **Wapiti.**

Apart from its large size, the moose has several distinguishing characteristics: huge, flattened antlers; short, stout neck; a long face with tiny eyes and a square upper lip so deeply furrowed as to appear cleft; a black beard at its throat; forequarters that are higher than its hindquarters, and an overall deep gray color. The short neck and tall front legs sometimes make grazing awkward. It must kneel down to reach short grass; consequently it prefers to browse on the young shoots and leaves of trees.

The moose is the traditional prey of Canadian and Alaskan Eskimos who use its meat, hide and antlers. The nose and tongue are considered great delicacies, especially when smoked. Otherwise the meat is light, digestible and not markedly gamy, unless hung for more than 48 hours. It may be cooked in the manner of any venison or beef, but should be larded to avoid its drying out in the cooking. Moose steaks are customarily placed in a marinade for 24 hours or less, then slowly broiled.

See also: **Wapiti.**

MOOSEBERRY

These red berries of a deciduous shrub, *Viburnum pauciflorum*, of northern North America and northeast Asia are eaten fresh or preserved, particularly in Alaska.

MORA

The name refers to varieties of raspberry growing in Latin America, including the *mora comun (Rubus adenotrichos)* of Mexico and Ecuador, and the *mora de Castilla (R. glaucus).* The *mora comun* has a good flavor and is eaten fresh or cooked. The *mora de Castilla* produces fruit of excellent quality with a pronounced raspberry flavor. The berries commonly measure from three-quarter to 1½ inches long. They are eaten fresh, used to make *jaropa de mora* syrup or to make raspberry preserves. The *mora de Castilla* is found in Ecuador and adjacent regions.

MORAY

This large (three to ten feet) species of eel found in tropical seas throughout the world is very pugnacious and dangerous to man when provoked. It belongs to the family *Muraenidae*. The moray differs from other eels by having round small gills and no pectoral or pelvic fins.

They are a frequent menace to skin divers. Their large mouths studded with sharp teeth are designed to grip and hold their prey, notably abalone and octopus. The sailors of the raft Kon-Tiki were chased from a lagoon by morays in Polynesia, where the giant eel is generally feared and shunned by natives.

Its rather oily flesh was considered delectable by the Romans. The Mediterranean moray, *Muraena helena*, is still hunted and consumed today. Species of moray are also common around coral reefs in Florida, Polynesia and off the coast of Southern California.

MORCILLA BLANCA

Morcilla is Spanish for blood sausage and is generally seen in two types, *morcilla asturiana* and *morcilla negra*. For more information, see **Blood Sausage.** *Morcilla blanca* is an exception, however, because it is made up of minced chicken, hard-boiled eggs, fat bacon, black pepper, parsley and seasonings.

See also: **Sausage.**

MOREL

Also SPONGE MUSHROOM. This is an edible fungus or mushroom whose cap has the honeycomb appearance of a sponge. It is found in wood clearings and orchards during the spring. Most often seen is the common morel *(Morechella esculenta)*, which has a yellow brown to brown spongy head and is generally two to five inches high. Larger is the thick-footed morel *(Morchella crassipes)*, which often achieves a height of one foot and nearly matches the common morel in color. The black morel *(Morchella angusticeps)* has a slender, more pointed cap and, though often found on the border of woodland or in evergreen forests, especially favors recently burnt-over areas. The smallest is the white morel *(Morchella deliciosa)*, which rarely exceeds three inches in height. Morels are found throughout North America and Europe.

The morel is one of the easiest wild mushrooms to gather. It is not easily confused with poisonous mushrooms and usually appear in abundance. The morel fruit is completely hollow inside its cap and stem. It should not be eaten raw, as it may cause stomach upsets; nor should it be taken with alcoholic beverages. The combination also seems to cause upset stomachs.

The morel is said to be one of the most delicious of all mushrooms. It may be sauteed and eaten by itself or added to eggs, stuffed or creamed to accompany beef or fish.

See also: **Mushroom.**

25 Goat's milk cheeses

26 Hominy

27 Honeycombs (rear, middle front), honey (far right) and pollen (front center)

28 Iceberg lettuce

29 Maine lobster

30 Maguey

31 Mangoes

32 Mammee sapota

33 A variety of mole sauces

34 Morel

35 A variety of mushrooms

36 Pakchoi

37 The large Mexican papaya

38 The papaya plant with fruit still attached

39 Peanuts: shelled and unshelled

40 Dried chili peppers

MORELLA

Edible fruit of a small tree, *(Myrica rubra)* native to Japan, southern China, Korea and the Philippines, the *morella* has a deep red purple color, a succulent pulp and reaches a diameter of about one inch. It is eaten fresh or used to make a drink.

MORETON BAY CHESTNUT

Also BLACK BEAN. These edible seeds of an Australian tree, *Castanospermum australe*, are found in the Australian states of Queensland and New South Wales. The seeds are contained in a woody spongy pod up to nine inches long and two inches wide. The seeds are round and can be ground into flour for gruel or baking.

MORINGA

See **Horseradish Tree.**

MORNAY SAUCE

This elaboration of the classic French **bechamel sauce** was named after De Mornay, a friend of King Henry IV of France, responsible for its creation. If used with eggs and vegetables, it consists of bechamel sauce combined with sweet cream and flavored with Gruyere and Parmesan cheese. If it is to be used with chicken, chicken stock is substituted for the cream. For fish, fish stock is substituted for the cream.

See also: **Sauce.**

MOROCCAN ASH

Moroccan ash is a species, *Fraxinus oxyphylla*, found in North Africa. Its fruits are used as a condiment and aphrodisiac in the Maghreb region.

MORTADELLA

This large Italian sausage, originating in Bologna, mixes lean pork and beef chopped fine with cubes of pork fat. It is flavored with coriander and white wine. This mixture is stuffed into casings four to six inches wide and then smoked, preferably over beech or oak shavings. It is also cooked by a steam process or baked. Cheaper versions can contain such ingredients as tripe, pig's head, donkey meat, potato or soya flour. In some, the flavor is excellent, and in others it is rather insipid. Pistachio nuts are used to flavor some *Mortadella*.

See also: **Sausage.**

MORTINO

Also MORTINIA. A variety of blueberry, *Vaccinium mortinia*, indigenous to Ecuador and Peru, it is purple, about one-quarter inch across and has a heavy bloom. It is highly regarded in the area of its cultivation.

MORWONG

Also BLACK PERCH. The name refers to three species of Australian sea fish. The morwong or black perch *(Nemadactylus morwong)* is actually green and is found in southeastern coastal waters and reaches a length of about two feet. It is fished commercially, and the quality of its flesh is rated good.

A companion species is the blue morwong *(N. valenciennesi)*, which reaches a length of 30 inches. It is distinguished by a bright blue color and a broader range, extending to the west, south and east coasts of Australia. Its flesh is rated on a par with *N. morwong*, and it is a common commercial species. The dusky morwong *(Psilocranium nigricans)* is a smaller fish (up to 16 inches). It is edible but of not commercial value.

MOSTELLE

Also MUSTELE. A Mediterranean fish, *Gaidropsarus mediterraneus*, of the cod family, somewhat resembling the **whiting,** it has a slender body, white flesh and attains a length of about 28 inches. The *mostelle* is often found in the estuary of the Rhone River, but nowhere is it plentiful. Its liver is considered a delicacy. *Mostelle* is its name in the south of France, where the fish is used in bouillabaisse. Alternative names for it are *mostele*, *motelle*, *moutelo* and *mutelle*.

MOTH BEAN

Also DEW BEAN. A legume native to southern Asia and often grown in India, the moth bean *(Vigna acontifolia)* is an annual plant. Its pods are cylindrical, one to two inches long and may be eaten when fresh. Otherwise the beans are dried for later consumption.

MOUFLON

Also BIGHORN, DALL, MOUNTAIN SHEEP. These wild sheep inhabit mountainous regions in various parts of the world. They do not have the woolly coat of the domestic species, but a growth of coarse, heavy hair ranging in color from creamy white through gray and brown. Males have heavy spiral horns. A large adult attains a maximum length of about six feet, stands up to 19 inches high at the shoulder and can weigh as much as 440 pounds.

Mouflon flesh is considered comparable in eating quality to that of the **chamois.** Marination for several hours before cooking is recommended. It may be prepared in any way suitable for venison or mutton. The mouflon is believed to be the ancestor of the domestic sheep *(Ovis aries).*

The mouflon *(O. musimon)* is the wild sheep of Sardinia and Corsida; the bighorn sheep *(O. canadensis)* is found in western Canada, north to Saskatchewan and British Columbia, east to the Black Hills of North Dakota, and south to Nebraska, Colorado and New Mexico; the Dall sheep *(O. dalli)* occurs in northwestern Canada and in Alaska; the argali *(O. ammon)* inhabits the mountains of central and eastern Russia, east to Shansi in western China, and south to Ladak and Nepal; the Asian mouflon or urial *(O. orientalis)* is found in the mountains of southern and western Russia, Iran, Afganistan, Cyprus, Kashmir, Pakistan and Baluchistan; and the Laristan sheep *(O. Laristanica)* ranges in southern Iran.

MOULIN A VENT WINE

See **Beaujoleais.**

MOUNTAIN COCK

See **Capercaillie**

MOUNTAIN HERRING

See **Rocky Mountain Whitefish.**

MOUNTAIN LETTUCE

Also DEER TONGUE. This is a perennial herb, *Saxifraga erosa*, of the eastern United States, whose leaves are used in salads. It grows wild in the mountains of southern Pennsylvania.

MOUNTAIN MINT

The name applies to any of several species of perennial herb *(Pycanthemum* spp.) of North America. When crushed, the leaves have a mintlike odor. They may be used as a mint substitute. Mountain mint is also an alternative name for **basil.**

MOUNTAIN PAPAYA

A type of papaya grown in the highland tropics of South America, mountain papaya *(Carica pubescens)* has very aromatic fruit that is eaten cooked. It is often candied or made into jam or preserves. The fruit is smaller than *C. papaya*, its one advantage being that it may be grown at higher altitudes.

MOUNTAIN PHELLOTROPE

The roots of this perennial plant, *Phellotropus montanus*, may be dried or baked, then ground into meal that is used to make porridge. This plant is indigenous to Texas and New Mexico.

MOUNTAIN ROSE

See **Coral Vine.**

MOUNTAIN RYE

This wild cereal grass, *Secale montanum*, is thought to be the ancestor of common **rye** *(S. cereale)*, an important food and fodder crop of northeastern Europe.

Mountain rye is indigenous to southern Europe, North Africa, the Middle East and southwestern Asia. It has several varieties, some annual, some perennial, but it is still well known as a grain crop in certain areas.

MOUNTAIN SOURSOP

Also CIMARRONA. A small West Indian tree, *Annona montana*, bearing fruit that is smaller than the **soursop,** it has a yellowish pulp and a pleasant, refreshing flavor.

MOUNTAIN SPRING WATER

A spring water bottled in plastic containers for bulk drinking in the state of Pennsylvania, it has a relatively low mineral content. A 1980 Consumers Union sensory panel rated the taste of this water as very good, with the following comments: mild plastic flavor, mildly sour, mild plastic aroma.

See also: **Mineral Water.**

MOUNTAIN VALLEY WATER

This is a still mineral water bottled in the United States. A 1980 Consumers Union sensory panel rated the taste of this water as excellent with no sensory defects.

See also: **Mineral Water.**

MOUSE DEER

Also CHEVROTAIN. A small mammal, of the family *Tragulidae* found in Asia and Africa, the mouse deer is more closely related to camels and pigs than deer. A large adult might weigh as much as 11 pounds.

It has a small head, pointed snout and a body that reaches a maximum length of about three feet. It looks like an **agouti.**

The water chevrotain *(Hyemoschus aquaticus)* is found in Africa from Gambia and Sierra Leone in the west to the Ituri Forest at the eastern border of the Congo Basin, and southward to the Cameroons. It frequents dense forest along watercourses. The flesh of this animal is well liked by natives who hunt it using dogs, snares and long nets. The Asian mouse deer *(Tragulus javanicus)* is found from India throughout Southeast Asia to the East Indies. It is a favorite food.

MOUSSELINE SAUCE

Also SAUCE MOUSSEUSE. This light French sauce builds on the classic **hollandaise sauce** by incorporating stiffly whipped cream. It is seasoned to taste. Mousseline sauce is heated very carefully and served over fish, asparagus, broccoli and cauliflower.

See also: **Sauce.**

MOUTARDE SAUCE

This sauce, based on either **hollandaise** or **bechamel** sauce, is flavored by French or English mustard or a combination of the two.

See also: **Sauce.**

MOZARINELLI

This is a soft Italian cheese made from either cow or buffalo milk.

MOZZARELLA

A soft, rubbery cheese that originated in the south of Italy, but is made extensively elsewhere, especially in the United States, mozzarella is not ripened and is usually, but not always, cooked in some form before eating. Although originally it was made from buffalo milk, it is now made from cow's milk. Its curd is white, and unsalted. Individual cheese are ball-shaped and weigh from eight ounces to one pound.

Variations include *mozzarella affumicata*, which is smoked; *treccia*, which is braided, and *uova de buffalo*, small and egg-shaped. Methods of manufacture are similar to those of ***caciocavallo*** and ***scamorze.*** **Ricotta** is often made from the whey.

Mozzarella is a classic cheese for pizza and for cassaroles such as lasagne.

MRSAV

See **Sir Posny.**

MSG

See **Monosodium Glutamate.**

MUD BASS

See **Sunfish.**

MUDFISH

See Bowfin, Lungfish.

MUG

See **Mung Bean.**

MUGWORT

The dried leaves of this perennial European herb, *Artemesia vulgaris*, were much used formerly as a flavoring agent to season goose and pork as well as stews, stuffings, sweets and ale. They are aromatic and slightly bitter tasting.

Another variety, Chinese mugwort *(A. verlotorum)*, is more aromatic still. Mugwort is closely related to **wormwood** and sagebrush.

MULBERRY

This is the sweet fruit of several varieties of the mulberry tree, chiefly the black mulberry *(Morus nigra)*, the white mulberry *(M. alba)* and the red mulberry *(M. rubra)*. The tastiest of the three is the black mulberry. If very ripe it has a distinctive flavor all its own and may be used in any way suitable to blackberries or loganberries. It is of Asian origin but has been grown in Europe since the days of Classical Antiquity. These berries are invariably sweet, but other taste components—acid content, for example—vary considerably from tree to tree, unless they are carefully tended in a greenhouse.

The red mulberry is an American species, whose original territory extended along the East Coast from New England to Florida and west to Texas. It has been introduced into all parts of the country.

The red mulberry is less tasty than the black, but if eaten perfectly ripe it makes an acceptable dessert fruit and is delicious cooked in pies and tarts. It is also used to make jelly, a liqueur and mulberry gin.

The white mulberry, a native of China, is the blandest of all, though very sweet. Because of the insipid taste it has no following in the West, but is a staple food in Afghanistan, where, after being dried and ground into flour, it is used to make bread. The white mulberry is cultivated chiefly because its leaves are the preferred food for silkworms. This has caused mulberry trees to be planted in Italy, Georgia (U.S.A.) and London, to little avail in the last two places. A tree planted in the garden of Buckingham Palac dates back to 1609 when James I planted 400 acres in St. James's Park aiming to found a silkworm industry. Unfortunately, it was the wrong kind of mulberry and the project failed.

Mulberries grow in the temperate zones of the Northern Hemisphere, or at fairly high altitude in the tropics, and do best in warmer areas, such as the southern United States. They have a limited popularity in Europe, but there is virtually no demand for them in the United States. In addition, they are rarely carried in supermarkets because of difficulties in handling, i.e., they are perishable and easily bruised, thus difficult to ship and keep.

The Latin poet Ovid related how white mulberries were turned to red by the blood of the ill-fated lovers, Pyramus and Thisbe. Another Latin writer, Horace, thought them salubrious, or so it would seem from these lines in his *Satires:* "A man will pass his summers in health, who will finish his luncheon with black mulberries."

MULE

Also HINNY. A mule is the offspring of a male donkey, or jackass, and a mare. A hinny is the offspring of a stallion and a female donkey. The latter is much less common. Mules attain about the same size as horses; they have long ears, small hoofs, and are highly esteemed for their endurance and surefootedness. In areas where horsemeat is well regarded, mule meat is highly prized, considered, perhaps, the best equine meat of all. The meat of mule foals is used to make pate. Mule meat may be prepared in any way suitable for horsemeat.

See also: **Horsemeat.**

MULLET

Two families of fish are called mullet, the gray mullet *(Mugilidae)* and the red mullet, or goatfish *(Mullidae).* They are not related. Both are good to eat, with the red mullet having the edge.

Gray mullet are a schooling, migratory fish, very plentiful in the Atlantic and Pacific Oceans, with some 100 species worldwide. Of the family, the striped mullet *(Mugil cephalus)* is the most important food fish in U.S., British and European Atlantic waters. It is torpedo-shaped, blue gray or green above and silver below. It grows to as much as three feet and 15 pounds, but 10 pounds is considered a good size.

The smaller white mullet *(Mugil curema)* is common in U.S. waters. Mediterranean varieties include the thinlipped mullet *(Mugil capito)*, the thick lipped mullet *(Mugil chelo)*, the golden mullet *(Mugil auratus)* and the jumping mullet *(Mugil saliens).* A marked characteristic of the gray mullet is that it rapidly adapts to fresh water and then can easily switch back to saltwater. It loves to feed on aquatic plants in shallow brackish water. For this reason, although its flesh is very white and delicate, it should be washed thoroughly before cooking to avoid a muddy taste.

In European waters the best red mullet *(Mullus surmuletus)* or *(M. barbatus)* are caught in the Mediterranean. A very similar fish *(Mullus auratus)* is found on the Atlantic coast of the United States from Cape Cod to Pensacola, Florida. Much smaller than the gray mullet, the red mullet is an elongated fish with bright colors, usually red, but sometimes yellow splotches or stripes and two barbels on its chin. Twelve ounces is considered a good sized fish, but weight can range as low as two ounces.

Red mullet has been known as a fine eating fish since ancient times and, indeed, was the object of an extraordinary craze on the part of the Romans during the first and second centuries A.D. According to Juvenal, the waters near Rome were fished out, and mullet had to be brought from Corsica, Taormina or

Marseilles. Yet, such was the demand that a knight, Crispinus, paid 60 gold pieces for one fish. When the Emperor Tiberius was presented with a 4½-pound red mullet (a size unheard of in modern times), he sent it to the market to be auctioned off. After spirited bidding between Apicius (a famous epicure) and P. Octavius, the latter carried it off for 5,000 sesterces. Such extravagance among Roman epicures continued on into the reign of Caligula.

According to tradition, the red mullet, like the woodcock, secretes no bile and may therefore be cooked with very little cleaning. At any rate, the liver is considered a delicacy and is often cooked with the fish. The flesh is firm and white. Baking or grilling are the preferred cooking methods, often with a sprig of fennel.

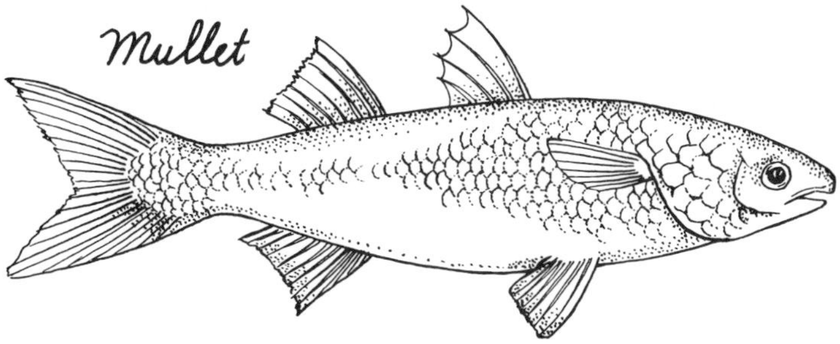

MULLEY

A giant Asian catfish found in the freshwaters of India, Sri Lanka, Burma, Indochina, Thailand, Java and Sumatra, the mulley *(Wallagonia attu)* can reach a length of 6½ feet, but such a large specimen, due to its slender build, would weigh only about 120 pounds. It is considered a good game fish, but opinions differ on its value as food. In some places it is eaten readily, while in others it is avoided on the grounds that it has unclean eating habits. The mulley has light green coloring above and sides of a golden cream.

MULLIGATAWNY

This is an Anglo-Indian soup based on chicken or lamb and seasoned with curry powder. The original Indian dish consisted of a rich cream soup flavored with curry powder and other spices and garnished with small pieces of chicken. It was served with a side dish of rice or cold bananas and tomatoes, peeled and sliced. The name derives from the Tamil words *milagu* (pepper) *tannir* (water).

The Western version is made with a boiling chicken or breast of lamb, soup stock or broth, chopped, sauteed onions, curry powder, spices and herbs, lentils, coconut cream or milk of almonds, cream or milk. Rice and slices of lime or lemon are added as garnishes.

MULSE

See **Hydromel.**

MUNDU

Edible fruit of a small tree, *Garcinia dulcis* native to the Molucca Islands, the mundu is yellow, smooth-skinned, about the size of an apple and has a subacidic flavor. It has a number of seeds, which are surrounded by a palatable aril. The mundu is eaten raw or cooked and makes a good jam.

MUNG BEAN

Also GREEN GRAM. This is a green bean about half the size of a pea, widely cultivated in India and China, which provides most of the bean sprouts used in Chinese and Indian cookery. Mung beans *(Phaseolus aureus)* have a good flavor and are high in protein and vitamin content. In dried form, they can be boiled like peas, used in stews or ground into a floury meal. The beans sprout readily if kept in a warm, damp place, and in that form they are eaten raw in salads, incorporated into a variety of Chinese dishes or cured in India.

See also: **Bean, Bean Sprouts.**

MUNSTER

This semisoft, surface-ripened cheese originated in the Munster Valley of the Alsace region and is popular on both sides of the German-French border. It is similar to the French ***gerome*** cheese. In Europe, Munster is made from whole cow's milk, often flavored with aniseed or caraway and cumin seeds. It is frequently colored with annatto, and that, combined with red-smear bacteria used in ripening, give it a brick red tint. Curing takes as much as three months, and the result is a fully flavored cheese. Sizes range from two to ten pounds, and cheeses are individually wrapped and packed in boxes.

Munster made in the United States is considerably milder, resembling **brick cheese** with somewhat less ripening. Pasteurized milk is used. These cheeses are yellow and generally marketed in oblong loaves.

MURIN

See **Mirin.**

MURRAY COD

The king of Australian freshwater fishes, the Murray cod *(Maccullochella macquariensis)* can weigh as much as 200 pounds and reach a length of six feet. It is good to eat—although the larger fish are said to be tough and oily—and is a prized sportfish as well. The Murray cod is found in the Murray-Darling river system, in the headwaters of the Richmond and Clarence Rivers of New South Wales, and in the Dawson and Mary rivers of Queensland. The fish has a dark green coloring with bluish mottling on the back and sides. It is a member of the *Serranidae* family, which also includes the giant sea bass.

MUSCADET

This dry white wine comes from the **Loire** in western France, from Sevre et Maine near the city of Nantes. The best Muscadet is produced *sur lie*, which means that the wine is kept in longer contact with the pulp of the grape in order to realize a natural fruitiness. This is, however, the driest white wine of the Loire. Its taste is much like that of good **champagne,** though without the carbonation. It is ideal with seafood. It should be served chilled and kept that way throughout the meal.

MUSCADINE

The name refers to two species of North American grapes, *vitis rotundifolia* and *vitis munsoniana.* A wild fruit, known variously as bullace, muscadine and fox, it grows on vines that commonly reach the tops of the tallest trees. The plant is sometimes trained for ornamental use in the southern United States, as poet Karl Kopp describes here:

> *his house no different from most—*
> *rough weathered slabs of oak tin-roofed*
> *but tied more closely to the earth*
> *(like a tent) by morning-glories roses*
> *honeysuckle and wild muscadine*

The Muscadine grape is used in the making of **Scuppernong wine.** The abundance of Muscadine may well have prompted the Vikings to call the entire New World "Vinland."

MUSCARI

See **Tassel Hyacinth.**

MUSCAT

The name includes any of several varieties of white or black musky sweet grapes from Spain, Greece, the general Mediterranean area and California. The Muscat grape is used frequently in the making of raisins, but also is an important ingredient in the production of a strong, usually sweet **aperitif** or dessert wine. Of the better known wines made from this grape are the Muscat d'Alsace, the Muscat d'Alexandrie grown in Algeria and Tunisia, the Muscat de Lunel from southern France and the Greek Muscats from Patras, Rhodes, Limnos and Samos.

See also: **Alsace, Muscat d'; Lund Wine.**

MUSCATEL WINE

This strong sweet wine is made from the **Muscat** grape. In Europe, Muscatel can be either red or white or even sparkling. In the United States, the name applies to a very cheap fortified yellow to amber wine called simply Muscatel. A good white dessert wine of this name is produced in Israel. Perhaps the finest Muscatel wine is the Moscatel de Setubal, a very sweet liqueur wine, which should never be drunk before it is five or six years old.

MUSCATEL SAGE

See **Clary.**

MUSCOVY DUCK

Also MUSK DUCK. This domestic duck is descended from a species found wild from Mexico to southern Brazil. The Muscovy duck *(Cairina moschata)* is rather combative and ill-tempered but does not quack. It is characterized by a large crest and red wattles. The Muscovy duck is one of the 12 major breeds in the United States. It was imported to Europe in the 16th century and has been domesticated throughout the world.

Young birds are considered excellent eating. Older birds have a musky smell and tend to be tough. Muscovy duck is prepared like wild duck.

MUSHROOM

This is an edible fungus. The term brings to mind a small plant, consisting of a single stem topped by an umbrella-shaped cap. There are, however, about 38,000 kinds of mushroom in the world, so the variety in size and shape is considerable. Three-quarters of these, according to the experts, are edible in the minimal sense, while no more than 2,000 would be thought palatable. The remaining one-quarter are toxic to a greater or lesser extent, causing discomfort to the eater ranging from indigestion to mortal agony. Only 1 or 2 percent are deadly. Poisonous mushrooms used to be called *toadstools.* Unfortunately, there is no foolproof way for the

1.

2.

1. The commom mushroom
2. Tree mushroom

layman to distinguish between a mushroom and a toadstool, the familiar old wives' tales notwithstanding. Even the skillful are wary when collecting wild mushrooms, gathering only the familiar, not wanting to put their expertise to the ultimate test, for, as one source put it, "It's the 'experts' who die of poisoning."

The fleshy parts of the mushroom, i.e., the stem and the cap, are not the fungus, but the fruit of the fungus. The fungus remains underground and consists of a mass of thin, threadlike roots, or stems, called mycelium, or "spawn." Commercially grown mushrooms are often started from spawn, rather than from seeds, which are called spores. Spawn is used because it brings quicker results. In natural propagation, mushroom spores are dispersed from gills on the underside of the cap. Mushrooms are found wild in all temperate parts of the world, either in open spaces or woodlands. In the latter case, they are often in a symbiotic relationship with certain species of trees (elm, oak, beech), a fact that has hindered their commercial cultivation. Mushrooms range in size from that of a small button to more than a foot in diameter at the widest part of the cap.

In Asia and Africa nearly everybody eats a variety of mushrooms. In the West, acceptance of mushrooms varies widely from region to region and country to country. A strip of northern Europe, from Russia, through the Baltic states, and on through Scandinavia is an enthusiastic area of mushroom-eating. The Finns stand out in particular enjoying about 50 varieties. Another, southern, concentration of mushroom fanciers includes northern Spain (Catalonia), southern France (Provence) and Italy. Still, in France, where 80 species are considered edible, only about 20 are available in markets, the dominant species being the common mushroom *(Agaricus campestris)*, called there the *champignon de Paris*. The English are a lot less enthusiastic than the French, but it is in the United States where adventuresomeness toward mushrooms approaches nil. Virtually the only mushroom available in American markets is the common mushroom, in two or three varieties. Although at least 50 American mushrooms are classified as edible, the other 49 are generally accessible only to those who are willing to go out and pick them.

Mushrooms have been eaten by humans since long before the dawn of history, and contemporary evidence points to their importance in the diet of aborigines. Charles Darwin, for example, made this observation in his *Voyage of the Beagle* about the Patagonian mushroom:

> *In Tierra del Fuego, the fungus in its tough and native state is collected in large quantities by the women and children and is eaten uncooked. With the exception of a few berries, chiefly of a dwarf arbutus, the natives eat no vegetable food besides this fungus.*

Of such importance were they to the diet of Australian aborigines that there mushrooms were nicknamed, "Blackfellows' bread." The Maoris of New Zealand eat several varieties, and the same is true of the natives of the Solomon Islands and New Guinea.

In some ancient cultures (and modern ones as well) certain mushrooms were revered for their mind-altering effects. Scholars have speculated that hallucinogenic mushrooms were the legendary "ambrosia" of the Greek gods, and that the *soma* of the Hindu *Rig Veda* (thought to be a liquor of the gods) was the fly agaric mushroom *(Amanita muscaria)*. The ancient Aztecs had classified more than 20 varieties of hallucinogenic mushrooms as *Teonanactl*, i.e., "food of the gods." Modern day cultists in Mexico consume the mushroom *Psilocybe mexicana* as a means of achieving enlightenment or consulting a spirit entity. The effects of ingesting *Psilocbe mexicana* are hinted at in this bit of dialogue between the Indian sorcerer Don Juan Matus and his apprentice, anthropologist Carlo Castenada, taken from his *The Teachings of Don Juan: a Yaqui Way of Knowledge*. Casteneda had just smoked a powdered form of the mushroom ("little smoke"):

> *"Mescalito is a protector because he talks to you and can guide your acts,"[Don Juan] said. . . . The smoke on the other hand is an ally. It transforms you and gives you power without ever showing its presence. . . . You never see it. But it is there giving you power to accomplish unimaginable things, such as when it takes your body away."*
>
> *"I really felt I had lost my body, Don Juan."*
>
> *"You did."*
>
> *"You mean, I really didn't have a body?"*
>
> *"What do* you *think yourself?"*
>
> *"Well, I don't know. All I can tell you is what I felt."*
>
> *"That is all there is in reality—what you felt."*

Despite long human experience with mushrooms, their value as a food is questionable. In modern cuisines, they are treasured for their contribution to the flavor and texture of dishes rather than for their nutritive content. They have virtually no fats, sugars or assimilable carbohydrates. Whatever carbohydrates they have is mostly cellulose, which, though nonnutritive, makes good roughage. Mushrooms do have, however, more protein than practically any other vegetable. In fact, mushrooms come closer to meat than any other vegetable in taste and texture, so that it has been called the "beefsteak of the poor." This is somewhat overoptimistic, since only five grams of protein per 100 grams of mushroom are assimilable by themselves. The rest, lacking in essential amino acids, must be accompanied by complete proteins, such as are found in meat.

Mushrooms have been cultivated as food since the 17th century. Although about 20 kinds are under cultivation in France, the most popular is the common field or meadow mushroom *(Agaricus campestris)*. In the United States it is virtually the only one available fresh, if you include the cultivated subvarieties, *A. bisporus* and *A. hortensis*. Sold in markets, they come in three grades, the smallest known as button mushrooms; the medium-sized as cups and the largest (and most strongly flavored) as open or flat mushrooms. The largest may reach a height of four inches, and the cap (which varies in color from white to cream to brown) a diameter of five inches. They thrive in a compost consisting mainly of horse manure, straw and sterilized soil. Essential environmental elements are controlled temperature and moisture.

The mushroom industry got rolling in the United States during the early 20th century and centered near Downington, Pennsylvania, southwest of Philadelphia, an area enjoying the natural advantage of extensive limestone caves. Air conditioning enabled other areas to compete, and in the 1970s the industry boomed, involving such widely scattered areas as Southern California, Florida, Tennessee, Texas, Connecticut and Utah. Per capita consumption spurted during the 1970s from one-half pound annually of cultivated mushrooms to 2.2 pounds, and growth continues.

For most cooking purposes, mushrooms are regarded as vegetables, although they lack chlorophyll and therefore lack the characteristic green coloring. The peculiar and delicate mushroom flavor is present in both the fresh and dried forms, but not in canned mushrooms. The former should be cooked just briefly, to avoid toughening them and to preserve the flavor. They may also be eaten raw, dressed with lemon juice, olive oil, cream or yogurt. By way of preliminaries, mushrooms should be cleaned and trimmed, though experts favor only a minimum of washing.

Following is a list of familiar mushrooms and fungi, which, though not possessing all the characteristics of mushrooms, are commonly regarded as such. They will be discussed under separate headings: Beefsteak Fungus, Black Tree Fungus, Blewit, Bolete, Chanterelle, Coral Fungus, Elm Tree Pleurotus, Fairy Ring, Field Mushroom, Horse Mushroom, Ink Caps, Laccaria, Matsutake, Morel, Orange Amanita, Oyster Mushroom, Polypore, Puffball, Red Staining Mushroom, Saffron Milk Cap, Shaggy Mane, Shitake, Straw Mushroom, Truffle.

MUSIGNY

This wine comes from an important vineyard in the Cote de Nuits section of the Burgundy wine region, which is located a few miles south of Dijon. Les Musigny, as it is called, produces red wines of *grand cru* rank, noted for their finesse, suppleness and elegance. A small amount of Musigny Blanc is also produced.

MUSK DEER

Also KASTURA. This small Asian deer is valued as food when young and as a source of musk when mature. The musk deer *(Moschus moschiferus)* lives at altitudes of from 8,500 to 12,000 feet, and is found from China, Manchuria, Korea and the Sakhalin Islands to the Amur region and through Siberia to western Mongolia. It stands two feet tall at the shoulder, reaches a maximum length of about three feet and weighs up to 25 pounds.

The adult male secretes a brownish, waxy substance, called musk, into a pouchlike gland. Musk is used extensively in the manufacture of soap and perfume, as a flavoring (in minute doses) in some liqueurs, and as a flavoring in Turkish pastries called musk cakes. A high price is placed on musk, and since a single deer yields hardly more than an ounce of musk, this species has been hunted to near extinction. The flesh of the young deer is prepared like kid.

MUSKELLUNGE

Also MASKINONGE. A prized North American game fish, the muskellunge *(Esox masquinongy)* is the largest member of the pike family. There are three varieties, the northern, the chatauqua and the Great Lakes, all of which inhabit northern rivers, lakes or streams. It has the long, thin body and duckbill jaws characteristic of the pike, with greenish, spotted back shading to yellow sides. Individual fish average 15 to 30 pounds in weight, while a 50 to 60 pound fish is not unusual. A record catch from the Great Lakes came in at eight feet and 110 pounds. It is considered very good eating and may be broiled, baked or fried.

MUSK LIME

This is a very small species of orange, *Citrus microcarpa*, with a musky fragrance.

MUSKMELON

Also CANTALOUPE, CASABA, HONEYDEW, WINTER MELON. Melons are members of the cucumber family, and there are two distinct types, muskmelons *(Cucumis melo)*, which will be discussed below, and **watermelons,** which will be discussed under a separate heading.

The origin of the muskmelon is not certain, some authorities claiming the Indian subcontinent, others Africa. The Egyptians cultivated them, and so did the ancient Romans, although the size was much smaller than that achieved today. Cultivation seems to have lapsed until the Renaissance when a delicious and larger variety of the old melon was developed in Italy, near the papal villa at Cantalupo. This melon, *Cucumis melo cantalupensis*, is probably the most popular musk melon. It is not the melon called "cantaloupe" in the United States, which is actually the netted melon *(Cucumis melo reticulatus)*, also called nutmeg melon.

This American cantaloupe is small, usually two to four pounds, round or oval, with a coarse, corklike netting on the surface and a light green tinge behind it. Its flesh is very sweet and orange, with the seeds contained in a cavity in the center.

The European cantaloupe, on the other hand, is more football-shaped, with coarse, deeply grooved green skin, sometimes warty, and covered with markings resembling scribbling. The flesh is dark, orange and very sweet and juicy. To be fully enjoyed, these melons should be vine ripened.

Canteloupes are often eaten at breakfast in the United States, but in Europe are usually served as a dessert. This melon is frequently halved fresh and eaten with a little salt. The taste blends well with other fruit and sweet liqueurs, and it is sometimes marinated in port wine. These melons are perishable and should be kept chilled.

Casaba and honeydews are known as winter melons, as opposed to cantaloupes, which are summer melons. The casaba is a large American variety, round in shape, with a ribbed, tough skin. The flesh is creamy white and sweet, yet not aromatic like the cantaloupe's. Golden and pineapple are the most

Muskmelons

Mussels

common types, and a good specimen may be eight inches in diameter and weigh eight pounds. The honeydew melon is similar in size but has smooth creamy-white to grayish skin and green flesh. The latter is sweet and fragrant, more appropriate for desserts. Both sweet and sour pickles are made from these melons.

Ripeness can be detected in muskmelons—provided part of the stem is present—by the presence of a thin crack where the stem meets the crown of the melon. When this crack extends all the way around the stem, the melon has been fully ripened on the vine.

MUSK OX

Here is a large, shaggy animal, somewhat sheeplike in appearance, that inhabits parts of Alaska, northern Canada and Greenland. The musk ox *(Ovibos moschatus)* is valuable as a source of wool as well as meat, which is said to be excellent. It has substantial, curved horns that meet across its brow, humped shoulders, and an ungainly look that belies its agility. A large adult attains a length of up to 7½ feet and a weight of up to 900 pounds. The name derives from the strong scent given off by bulls in mating season. Musk oxen are hunted chiefly by Eskimos.

MUSKRAT

Also MARSH RABBIT, MUSQUASH. This is a North American aquatic rodent valued chiefly for its pelt, but well regarded as food in certain parts of Canada, Maryland and Louisiana. The muskrat *(Ondatra zibethicus)* inhabits fresh and salt water marshes, lake, ponds, rivers and streams. It behaves somewhat like a beaver, and in some areas is regarded as a pest because it burrows through dams, irrigation banks and channels.

An adult muskrat is generally between nine and 13 inches long and weighs up to four pounds. It looks generally like a rat, but has a luxurious brown fur pelt that makes it a very lucrative quarry for fur trappers. Despite a heavy toll (400,000 a year trapped in the state of New Jersey alone), the animal is nowhere near extinction due to its prolific breeding habits.

Despite a dark color and gamy flavor, muskrat flesh has been described as being "like beef, better than rabbit," when properly prepared. After the animal is skinned, musk glands must be removed from the groin area. Older animals may be soaked in cold, salted water overnight before being cooked. In Canada, muskrat is stuffed and baked. In Louisiana, it is made into a spicy stew called Cajun muskrat. It often appears on a menu as "marsh rabbit."

MUSSEL

This "hairy," marine shellfish is often found clinging to rocks or some other support in shallow water. The blue mussel *(Mytilus edulis)* is found on both sides of the Atlantic Ocean and is a popular seafood in Europe, yet is little appreciated in the United States. The blue mussel is farmed extensively on France's Atlantic coast, using a method supposedly invented by the Irishman Patrick Walton in 1235. It involves setting out stakes as supports for mussels in shallow water. However, there is evidence that the ancient Gauls cultivated mussels before the arrival of the Romans.

Mussels raised in cultivated beds are smaller than ocean mussels, yet the flesh is more tender and pale—tending to yellow rather than orange. Although twice as expensive as the wild variety, 45,000 tons of cultivated mussels are produced annually in France, and this supplies only one-half the demand. Mussels are almost always cooked, being either steamed, fried or stewed. Yet the Dutch and Belgians, who are also mussel devotees, often purchase them from street stands and eat them raw along with french-fried potatoes.

Although not native to the United States, the blue mussel is plentiful along the East Coast, having been brought there most probably clinging to the hull of a ship. Its lack of popularity is something of a mystery, since most early settlers came from mussel-eating areas. Much of the early colonists' selection of local food, however, was guided by native American practice, and many tribes tabooed shellfish. Mussels can also be poisonous if their environment is tainted, yet this has rarely been true for the blue mussel and does not explain the tepid response to it.

The West Coast mussel *(Mytilus californianicus)* is a different case. It is dangerous to eat from May to October due to the presence in the water of the plankton, ganyaulax. A poison from this plankton, saxitoxin, builds up in the mussel's liver to levels dangerous to humans. Native Americans living on the California coast thrived on this mussel because they learned to avoid it when the plankton was present, and they passed the knowledge on to European settlers.

The Mediterranean has distinct and larger species of mussels, e.g., the Provencal mussel *(Mytilus galloprovincialis)* whose flesh tone is closer to red than orange, and the bearded mussel *(Modiolus barbatus)*. They are frequently eaten raw with a dash of vinegar and green onions. Mussels are called *cozze* by Italians, who especially favor a small variety called the "sea date." It bores its way into stone and is found studding undersea rock formations.

Freshwater mussels *(Unionadae)* are rarer, although one was plentiful enough around Muscatine Iowa in the 1890s to provide shell for a pearl-button industry.

MUSSELCRACKER

Also BLACK BISKOP, STEENBRAS. A large ocean fish related to the sea breams, and found off the coast of South Africa, musselcracker *(Cymatoceps nasutus)* is a favorite angler's fish. It reaches a length of 50 inches and fights doggedly. Large specimens weigh as much as 100 pounds, but the flesh of smaller fish is more highly regarded, being less coarse. The head muscles of this fish are considered a special delicacy. It is taken close inshore, in rocky areas.

MUSTARD

"Mustard bites the tongue," wrote Ralph Waldo Emerson, describing the quality that has made this condiment second only to salt and pepper in popularity. From prehistoric times it was the custom to chew tiny mustard seeds with meat. The ancient Romans created a mustard sauce, which they made by crushing the seeds and mixing them with verjuice, the unripe juice of grapes or other fruit.

The modern product dates from the 18th century. An Englishwoman is credited with creating the first popular mix. Mrs. Clements of Durham powdered the seeds in a mill, mixed them with secret ingredients, and in 1729 sold the powder going from town to town on horseback. With the addition of water, it became something like the mustard of today. Her fortune was made when King George I became a loyal patron.

There are two types of seeds, black or brown, from the black mustard *(Brassica nigra)* and pale brown or yellow seeds from the white mustard *(Sinapis alba)*. These plants are native to southern Europe and the Mediterranean area but have been naturalized in many more temperate regions. The cultivated varieties customarily grow to a height of two to three feet. Their leaves and stems, when young and tender, are eaten in salads. A third, wild variety does particularly well in California, attaining heights of more than 14 feet. It is seen growing between rows of wine grapes in the northern part of the state, where vintners claim its presence indicates that the soil is right for grapes.

Mustard is marketed today as a powder or a paste, and in varying degrees of pungency. The finest mustards use black seeds, but many combine the two, or use just the light seeds. The paste type, called prepared mustard, can have a smooth or "whole grain" texture. Manufacturers variously add verjuice, vinegar, wine and vinegar, sugar, champagne and spices. The usual spices include either **turmeric** or **saffron** to ensure a bright, yellow hue. **Horseradish** is sometimes added to strengthen the taste.

The English still buy mustard in powdered form and mix it with water or milk just before using. Although very hot, it must be used when fresh because it loses its potency overnight. Quite similar is Chinese mustard, which is also sold in powdered form but is milder in taste. American salad mustard—the kind you see in ballparks—comes from light seeds and is mild.

France produces several types of fine mustard, which are widely exported. The most prominent is Dijon type, named for the capital of the Burgundy region. This must be made from dark seeds unless labeled *blanc*. The seeds are mixed with wine vinegar, and the taste is of medium strength. The Bordeaux type is mixed with unfermented wine, and the Florida type with champagne.

Many German mustards have a "whole grain" consistency, and are classified as Dusseldorf types.

MUSTARD GREENS

See **Indian Mustard.**

MUSTARD SPINACH

Also TENDERGREEN. An herb of the mustard family whose leaves are cooked and eaten like spinach, mustard spinach *(Brassica rapa* var. *perviridis)* is closely related to the **turnip.** It is also known as tendergreen. The plant reaches a height of six feet. Although it is grown in North American only for its edible leaves, Asians also cultivate it for its thick, tuberous crown, which they pickle.

MUTTON

Also SHEEP. This is the flesh of an adult sheep, preferably between one year and 18 months old, but often as much as four years old. In order of palatability, the meat of the ewe (adult female) ranks first, followed by that of the wether (castrated male), and finally by the ram, whose flesh is coarsest in texture and strongest in flavor.

Probably due to its reputation for pronounced flavor, mutton has never had much of a following in the United States. According to some authorities, the American aversion to mutton may stem more from the poor quality of the sheep—animals past their prime, or of a breed famed more for wool yield than eating qualities—than the natural inferiority of mutton to its competitors, beef and pork. Certainly, mutton enjoys greater popularity in Europe, especially in England.

Mutton Cuts

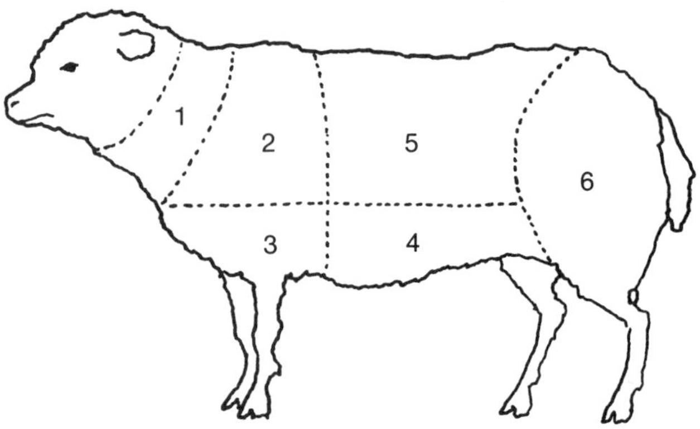

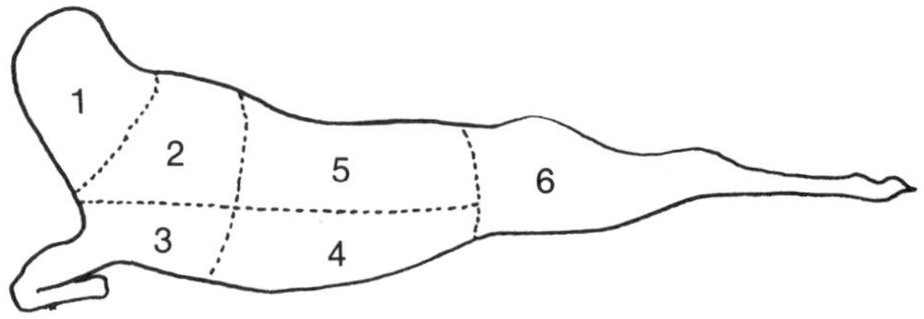

1. Neck
2. Chuck
3. Shoulder
4. Flank
5. Loin
6. Leg

The English word "mutton" comes from the French *mouton*, and indeed it was the Norman French, who conquered England in the 11th century, who established the English tradition of fancying mutton. In contrast to mutton, the word "sheep" comes from old English and antedate the Norman invasion. It is said that one can tell how a slaughtered animal was divided in those days by looking at how the cuts are named today, e.g., *mutton* chops for the Norman overlords, but *sheep's* tongue for humbler folk.

In England, a distinction is made between mountain sheep and lowland types. Welsh is considered the best of the mountain breeds, which are usually leaner than their lowland counterparts. Southdown is regarded as the finest flatland breed. The two types present different problems in cooking, i.e., fat must be added to the mountain breed to prevent its drying out, while care must be taken with the flatland type to prevent its being greasy. Flavor is often dependent on what sort of fodder the animals had. Welsh sheep are often grazed on wild thyme, which gives them a unique taste. Salt meadows, i.e., land reclaimed from the sea, are prized grazing areas for lowland sheep, providing a sort of built-in seasoning. French sheep raised near Mont St. Michel, or in the estuary of the Gironde at Pauillac, are noted for this quality.

Mutton is held in the highest esteem by the Arabs of the Middle East and North Africa. There the premier breed for eating is the famed fat-tailed sheep, whose tail often accounts for as much as one-sixth of its body weight. Their praises were being sung in the West as far back as the Greek historian Herodotus (5th century B.C.). Marco Polo, who ran across them in Afghanistan, reported, "There . . . are sheep as big as asses, with tails so thick and plump that they weigh a good 30 pounds. Fine, fat beasts they are, and good eating."

Increasingly, in both the United States and England, mutton masquerades on menus as lamb, a more popular and costly meat. Checking the color of the meat, though, should clear up any doubts. Fine lamb is pinkish or white, while good mutton has a bright red color, with a close grain and a firm texture. The most popular cuts of mutton are chops from the tenderloin and a roast from the hind leg. Mutton has a tendency to spoil more rapidly than other meats and more readily absorbs odors from other foods, and so should be protected from exposure to them. For further information on cuts of mutton, see the accompanying chart.

MUTTON SNAPPER

Here is a good food fish of the western Atlantic from New England to Brazil, including the Caribbean and the Gulf of Mexico. The mutton snapper *(Lutjanus analis)* has variable coloration, usually greenish above with pink flanks and red ventral fins. It prefers shallow bays, tidal creeks and open water with sandy bottoms. It reaches a length of 30 inches and a weight of up to 28 pounds. It is prepared like **red snapper.**

MYROBALAN

Also CHEBULE, MYROBOLAN. The name includes the fruit of several species of the *Terminalia* genus of Asian trees: *T. bellirica; T. Catappa*, which is also known as the tropical almond, Indian almond and the kamani; *T. Chebula*, known also as the chebule; and *T. karnbachi*, or New Guinea myrobalan. They are found from India, through Malaysia and the Philippines to New Guinea.

T. bellirica's fruit is smooth, dark red and pleasant-tasting, measuring about 1¼ inches across. It is most useful in preserves. The New Guinea variety has an almondlike flavor. The other varieties are used in the unripe state as a source of dyes and tannins.

The term myrobalan is also used for the **emblic** and the **cherry plum.**

MYRSINITES

Also ALPINE WINTERGREEN. The scarlet fruit of the shrub, *Gaultheria humifusa*, is found in western North America from British Columbia to California and east to Colorado. The fruit ripens in summer and is used to make preserves.

MYRTLE

Also GREEK MYRTLE, SWEDISH MYRTLE. This evergreen shrub, which reaches 15 feet in height, is native to the Mediterranean region and southwestern Europe. It has been naturalized in the United States particularly in Florida and California. Myrtle *(Myrtus communis)* is valued for its glossy leaves, which are highly aromatic and are used like bay leaves, and for its blue black berries, which are used fresh as a flavoring agent and dried as a pepper substitute. The plant was cultivated by ancient Egyptians and then by Greeks and Romans who used the berries to flavor *myrtalum* a sort of stew, and *mytridanum*, a spiced wine. Today, myrtle is especially popular in Sardinian cookery.

The myrtle family, *Myrtaceae*, contains more than 3,000 species of trees and shrubs, many of whose fruits are important economically (but of different genera than the classic myrtle). These include the guava *(Psidium)*, the rose apple *(Syzygium jambos)*, jaboticaba *(Myrciaria cauliflora)*, Surinam cherry *(Eugenia uniflora)*, and the spices, allspice *(Pimenta dioica)*, clove *(Syzygium aromaticum)* and oil of bay *(Pimenta racemosa)*. For more information, look under the specific name.

See also: **Sweet Gale** and **Chilean Guava.**

MYSOST

Also MYTOST. This is a Scandinavian cheese made from cow's-milk whey that is left over from the manufacture of other cheese. The composition of the whey varies depending on what cheese was made, but it consists chiefly of lactose (milk sugar) and small amounts of fat, protein and minerals. It is condensed by boiling until it has the consistency of a heavy cream. At this point, brown sugar may be added, as well as spices, mainly cloves or cumin seed. The reduced whey is called *prim*, with the result that mysost is often called *primost*. If cream is added before condensing, the result is called *flotost*.

The *prim* is poured into molds, and finished cheeses are round and flat, weighing 18 pounds. *Mysost* dries quickly, and little ripening takes place, so it must be carefully packed to ensure keeping qualities. *Mysost* has a light brown color, a buttery consistency and a mild sweet flavor. A considerable quantity is made in the United States.

See also: **Gjetost.**

N

NAARTJE

See **King Orange.**

NAGELES

Also NAGELKAZEN. This Dutch cheese made from cow's skim milk is spiced with cloves and cumin seed. It is eaten fresh.

NAIBOA

See **Yucca.**

NAMPLA

See **Nuoc-Mam Sauce**

NANCE

Also GOLDEN SPOON. Edible fruit of a small tree or shrub, *Byrsonima crassifolia*, native to the American tropics, the *nance* is single-seeded and yellow and reaches a diameter of about one-half inch. In El Salvador, it is eaten fresh or used to make a sweet wine called *nance*, which in turn is used to make a cocktail called *nancito*. The *nance* is found in the West Indies and from Mexico south to northern South America.

NANNYBERRY

See **Sheepberry.**

NANNYGAI

See **Redfish.**

NANTUA SAUCE

This is a fish sauce based on the classic French white sauce, either of the bechamel or veloute type. To the white sauce are added mixed diced vegetables, cream, crayfish butter, fish stock, a dash of wine or cognac and tomato puree. It is seasoned with salt, pepper and a pinch of cayenne and garnished with crayfish tails.

See also: **Sauce.**

NAPOLEON BRANDY

This is a labeling designation used on certain French cognacs. As defined by French law, Napoleon must have been kept in the cask for a minimum of 5½ years. It does not refer to brandy casked during the time of Napoleon I, or to brandies from 80 to 104 years old; these, according to best authority, are romantic nonsense.

NARA CHERRY

Edible fruit of a shrub or small tree, *Acanthosyris falcata*, found in southern South America, it is about the size of a cherry and red in color.

NARANJILLO

Also LULO. Bright orange, edible fruit of a small shrub found in the northern Andean region, the naranjillo *(Solanum quitoense)* is tomato-shaped, 1½ to two inches in diameter, and has a thick, leathery rind covered with small hairs. The pulp is juicy and refreshing and is used mainly for drinks and sherbets. This plant is cultivated in Ecuador, Peru, Colombia and Costa Rica. It thrives at altitudes between 3,000 and 5,800 feet.

NARASPLANT

This is a thorny shrub, *Acanthosicyos horrida*, of Africa, whose orange-sized fruit is relished by Hottentots. The taste is pleasantly acidic, and the fruit is eaten fresh or preserved.

NARDOO

This is an aquatic or marshy fern, *Marsilea drummondii*, found in Australia, whose spores and spore cases are dried and ground into flour by the aborigines, who use it to make bread.

NARWHAL

See **Whale.**

NASE

A freshwater fish of the carp family found in rivers of the Rhine and Danube basins, nase *(Chondrostoma nasus)* reaches a length of 20 inches and has an olive-green or gray back with silvery sides and belly. It is fished extensively along the Danube. Smoked nase is considered a particular delicacy.

NASEBERRY

See **Medlar, Sapodilla.**

NASTURTIUM

Also INDIAN CRESS. A new world plant, which was cultivated by the Incas, the nasturtium *Tropaelum minus*, is highly decorative as well as useful in the kitchen. Its pervasive fragrance earned it the name "*nasturtium*," or nose twister, from *nasus* (nose) and *torquere* (to twist).

The nasturtium develops brilliant yellow, orange and red flowers, which are edible and were once highly popular in salads. Nowadays it is the leaves and stems that are put to that use. Its unripe, green seeds have a peppery taste and, when pickled, are sometimes substituted for **capers.**

A tuber-rooted nasturtium *(Tropaeolum tuburosus)* is cultivated in Peru and Bolivia. Looking not unlike potatoes, they are usually dried for some days in the open air, then boiled. They may also be prepared like parsnips, although the taste is not similar.

Nasturtium

NATAL PLUM

Also AMATUNGULU. This scarlet fruit of a dense South African shrub, *Carissa grandiflora*, grows prolifically in Natal and other warm regions. The natal plum is an oval berry about 2 inches long used in making pies, jellies and preserves. It is often sold in markets.

Natal plum

NATIVE CURRANT

Edible berry of a woody plant native to Tasmania and southeastern Australia, the native currant *(Leptomeria acida)* has a subacidic flavor and is used to make jellies and preserves.

NAVY BEAN

See **Kidney Bean.**

NEBBIOLO

This Italian wine grape is used to produce the rich, full red wines of Piedmont and Lombardy, which include the Nebbiolo Piedmontese, a moderately sweet wine, and the well-known dry wines, Barolo and Barbaresco. Nebiolo vines have been put to good use elsewhere, including the Ticino region of Switzerland, California and Uruguay.

See also: **Wines, Italian.**

NECTAR

In Greek mythology, this drink of the gods was distilled from refined dew and was supposed to confer immortality. In the modern sense, the term is applied to any sweet, delicious beverage, such as apricot nectar, guava nectar, etc. Nectar is also the name of the sweet fluid secreted by plants and gathered by bees who use it to make honey.

NECTARINE

This is a variety of peach whose flesh is firmer and skin smoother than ordinary types. Its rich flavor inspired these words by the English poet, John Keats.

> *Talking of pleasure, this moment I was writing with one hand and with the other holding to my Mouth a Nectarine—good God how fine. It went down soft, pulpy, slushy, oozy—all its delicious embodiment melted down my throat like a large Beautiful strawberry. I shall certainly breed.*

It is a late summer fruit, coming chiefly from California and Oregon in the United States. It is cultivated in Britain under glass, and also in France where it is known as the *brugnon*.

NEEDLEFISH

See **Gar.**

NEOPOLITAN MEDLAR

See **Azarole**

NEOZA

Also CHILGHOZA PINE, NEPAL NUT PINE. This is a pine tree, *Pinus gerardiana*, native to Afghanistan and the Himalayan region of India, whose cones contain edible nuts. The tree attains a height of 80 feet, has bluish green leaves and cones up to nine inches long. Each cone contains many seeds.

See also: **Pine Nut.**

Nectarines

NEPAL ELEAGNUS

Also OLEASTER, WILD OLIVE. This shrub or small tree, *Eleagnus latifolia*, found and eaten in tropical Asia from India to China, has red, drupelike fruit that grows up to 1½ inches long.

NEROLI OIL

An essential oil distilled from orange blossoms, it is a volatile substance used in the manufacture of soaps and perfumes and as a flavoring agent in syrups, confections and pastry. Neroli oil is extracted from the white flowers of the Seville or sour orange *(Citrus aurantium)*. The distillation process also produces a condensation called orange flower water, which is put to the same uses as the oil.

NESSEL

A soft, cured English cheese made from whole cow's milk, it is marketed in round, thin cheeses.

NEST

See **Bird's Nest.**

NETTLE

See **Bigstring, Dog Nettle.**

NETTLE TREE

See **Hackberry.**

NEUFCHATEL

A soft cheese originally made in the Normandy region of France but widely copied elsewhere, it is made from cow's milk, either whole or skim, or a mixture of milk and cream. The following cheeses are considered mere variations of Neufchatel: *bondon*, *Malakoff*, *petit*, *carre*, *petit Suisse*.

Neufchatel may be eaten fresh or at more than one stage of ripening. The fresh cheeses are round and flat and weigh eight ounces. Curing is accomplished by white surface mold that appears during the first week, then a red mold that remains for another two weeks. Neufchatel is matured in small cheeses, two and a half inches in diameter and two to three inches thick. If eaten during the white-mold stage, it is called *Neufchatel fleur*. At the end of three or four weeks, it is firmer and pungently flavored and called *Neufchatel affine*. These cheeses are wrapped individually in parchment or metal foil. Their best season is from October to May.

American Neufchatel is made from pasteurized milk generally mixed with cream, as for cream cheese. It has less fat and more moisture than the European product.

NEVADA JOINT EPHEDRA

This desert plant, *Ephedra nevadensis*, found from Nevada to California, has seeds that are roasted and ground into flour used to make bread. These seeds are said to be beneficial for urogenital complaints. The best known species in the *Ephedra* genus is *E. distachya*, whose alkaloid ephedrine is used medicinally in conditions of low blood pressure, shock, hemorrhage, hay fever and asthma. It causes constriction of the swollen or inflamed blood vessels. *E. distachya* is found in southern Europe and northern Asia.

NEWBURG SAUCE

This sauce was created by a chef of New York's (once) famous Delmonico Restaurant for shellfish that has been boiled, broiled or baked. It consists of butter and sherry simmered together, then mixed with cream and seasoned with salt and paprika. The mixture is stirred into beaten egg yolks and cooked until smooth. It is served hot, usually with lobster, but it is also suitable for shrimp and other seafoods, even if reheated.

See also: **Sauce.**

NEW JERSEY TEA

Also WILD SNOWBALL, MOUNTAINSWEET. This is an evergreen shrub, *Ceanothus americanus*, found on the eastern seaboard of the United States from Maine to South Carolina and west to Texas. Its finely toothed leaves are dried and infused to make an herbal tea. It bears white flowers. It is also cultivated as an ornamental.

NEW ZEALAND DAMSON

Purple gray fruit of a New Zealand tree, *Elaeocarpus dentatus*, it is oval and measures about one-half inch in length. It resembles the common damson (see **Bullace)** and is highly regarded.

NEW ZEALAND ICE PLANT

See **New Zealand Spinach.**

NEW ZEALAND SPINACH

Also NEW ZEALAND ICE PLANT. A vegetable native to Australia and New Zealand, it resembles ordinary spinach in appearance and flavor but thrives in hot weather that spinach cannot stand. The plant was first brought to England by Captain James Cook and planted in London in 1772. It is now cultivated in the United States and in France, where it is very popular. The French word for it is *tetragone.*

New Zealand spinach *(Tetragonia expansa)* has other advantages over spinach: it bears repeated cutting of its leaves during the summer, and it has a more open growth so that it is less likely to be sandy. New Zealand spinach must be cooked to be palatable. Cooking reduces it to a pulpy mass, which has a more creamy consistency than spinach. Nutritionally, it is similar to spinach but has far less iron. It belongs to the ice plant family and shares with other members the presence of minute dots on its leaves that reflect the sun as if the plant had a coating of ice.

NGAI CAMPHOR

The camphor-scented leaves of this Asian shrub, *Blumea balsamifera*, are used to flavor food. It is found from Nepal to Indonesia and the Philippines.

NIAM-NIAM

The leaves of this tropical plant, *Sparganophorus vaill*, are used as a condiment in soups. It is found in countries bordering on the Gulf of Guinea (West Africa) and in the West Indies.

NIBE

A Pacific croaker whose tasty flesh is eaten raw in Japan *(Nibea mitsukurii)* and prepared in a number of other ways, nibe reaches a length of two feet and is common in the Sea of Japan, the Pacific coast of Japan and in the Yellow Sea. The *nibe* is a long fish with a prominent dorsal fin. It is light gray above, paling below, with dark brown bands.

See also: **Croaker.**

NIDWALDNER SPALENKASE

See **Sbrinz.**

NIEDERUNGSKASE

See **Werder.**

NIEHEIMER

This German sour-milk cheese, originating in the Prussian city of Neiheim, is flavored with caraway seeds. It is similar to **hop cheese,** but not identical. The curd is dried in small cakes, then broken up and mixed with salt, caraway seeds and either milk or beer. It is then fashioned into small cheeses weighing four ounces. When these are dry, they are packed into casks with hops for ripening.

NIGER SEED

Also GUIZOTIA SEED, RAMTIL. These small black seeds of an annual herb, *Guizotia abyssinica*, native to Ethiopia, are pressed to extract an edible oil. The oil is sweet and bland, and in India is used for cooking. In Africa the seeds are mixed with honey or sugar and made into cakes. The plant has been natururalized in California where the oil is used in birdseed mixtures.

NIGHT-BLOOMING CEREUS

See **Strawberry Pear.**

NIGHTSHADE

Also BLACK NIGHTSHADE, POISONBERRY, BREDES. This is an annual herb, *Solanum nigrum*, whose leaves are cooked and eaten like spinach and whose berries are made into pies and preserves. A native of Europe, this plant has been widely naturalized in other parts of the world, for example, in the West Indies. It has been reported as a poisonous plant, but this is erroneous.

It is perhaps confused with deadly nightshade, or belladonna *(Atropa belladonna)*, a Eurasian plant that yields the important drug belladonna and the alkaloids atropine and hyoscyamine. Deadly nightshade is poisonous if eaten. Both plants are members of the *Solanaceae* family.

NINGU

An African freshwater fish most plentiful around Lake Victoria where it is the basis of a smoked-fish industry, the *ningu (Labeo victorianus)* has a slender body and a high dorsal fin that give it a sharklike appearance. It rarely exceeds 16 inches in length. The ningu has an olive-green back and a creamy color on sides and belly.

NIPA

This fermented liquor is made from the sap of the nipa palm tree *(Nypa fruticans).* This tree has no erect trunk. It is native to estuaries and brackish swamps of India and eastern Asia from the Malay Archipelago to the Solomon and Ryukyu Islands. It has been naturalized in southern Florida, where it is considered an ornamental.

NIPPLEWORT

This bitter herb, *Lapsana communis*, is related to the dandelion and the sow thistle. Its leaves are sometimes added to salads or cooked and eaten as a green vegetable. Usually, nipplewort is mixed with cultivated vegetables, such as spinach and lettuce, which are less bitter. It is a wild plant, and its curious name survives from an age when it was used as an external application to the breasts of women.

NITTANUT

High-protein seeds of an African tree, *Parkia biglobosa*, found in tropical areas, are contained in a flat pod, eight to 12 inches long and an inch wide. These seeds are eaten where the tree is native. The tree is also known as African locust.

N'KUPE

This African freshwater fish, *Distichodus mossambicus*, somewhat resembles the **characin.** It inhabits rivers and lakes of southern tropical Africa and is especially plentiful in the Zambezi and Sabi Rivers and in Lake Kariba. It is an important food fish throughout its range.

The n'kupe reaches a length of about 28 inches and has an olive-green back with a series of eight dark bars across the back and upper sides. The body is deep and compressed and has a prominent snout and a long dorsal fin. The n'kupe is usually taken with nets but also has fighting qualities attractive to anglers.

NOEKKELOST

Also NOGELOST, NOEKKLEOST. This spiced cheese, originally Norwegian, is flavored with cumin seeds, cloves and caraway seeds. It is hard and similar in taste and quality to Edam or Gouda. Those from Norway are made from partly skimmed milk and are cylindrical and weigh from 18 to 32 pounds.

U.S. Noekkelost are made from whole or partly skimmed milk, and formed into loaves weighing from five to seven pounds. The cheeses are usually coated with paraffin or cheese wax and are available year round.

NOEKKLEOST

See **Noekkelost.**

NOGELOST

See **Noekkelost.**

NONDA

This is the fleshy edible fruit of an Australian tree, *Parinarium nonda.* It is single-seeded.

NOODLE

This is a thin strip of dough that may be cut into a wide variety of lengths, widths and shapes. The dough usually consists of flour, eggs and water, but, as in the case of some types of Italian *pasta*, the egg may be dispensed with. The word "noodle" derives from the German *nudel.* Noodles are sold fresh and dried. They are usually boiled in water or some other liquid but may be baked or fried. They may be served by themselves or used to garnish meat, egg or cheese dishes.

Noodles are an ancient food, springing up independently in ancient Rome and ancient China, and remaining a strong tradition in both places down through the centuries. The Italian tradition spread throughout the Western world, and the Chinese tradition spread throughout Asia, including Japan, Southeast Asia, and westward through Burma, India and the Middle East. While the western tradition is restricted to wheat flour, the Chinese relies also on rice, soy and mung beans, potatoes and seaweed.

Italian ***pasta*** is a popular type of western noodle. Because of its complexity, a separate article has been devoted to it. German-style noodles differ from Italian *pasta* in that ordinary wheat flour is used in place of semolina flour. Moreover, those of commercial manufacture must contain 5 percent egg solids. They are flat in shape, varying in width from one-sixteenth of an inch up to one-half inch. Noodle dough is also used in stuffed dishes, such as ravioli and the Chinese equivalent, *shiu mai.*

Some of the more common Asian noodles are:

Bean thread noodles: Made from the mung bean, these are thin, translucent noodles. They are added to Chinese hot-pot dishes and Japanese *mizutaki* and generally simmered in soups or soaked in hot dishes. The Japanese term is *shirataki.*

Japanese noodles, left to right: rice sticks, somen, soba, udon and saifun bean threads

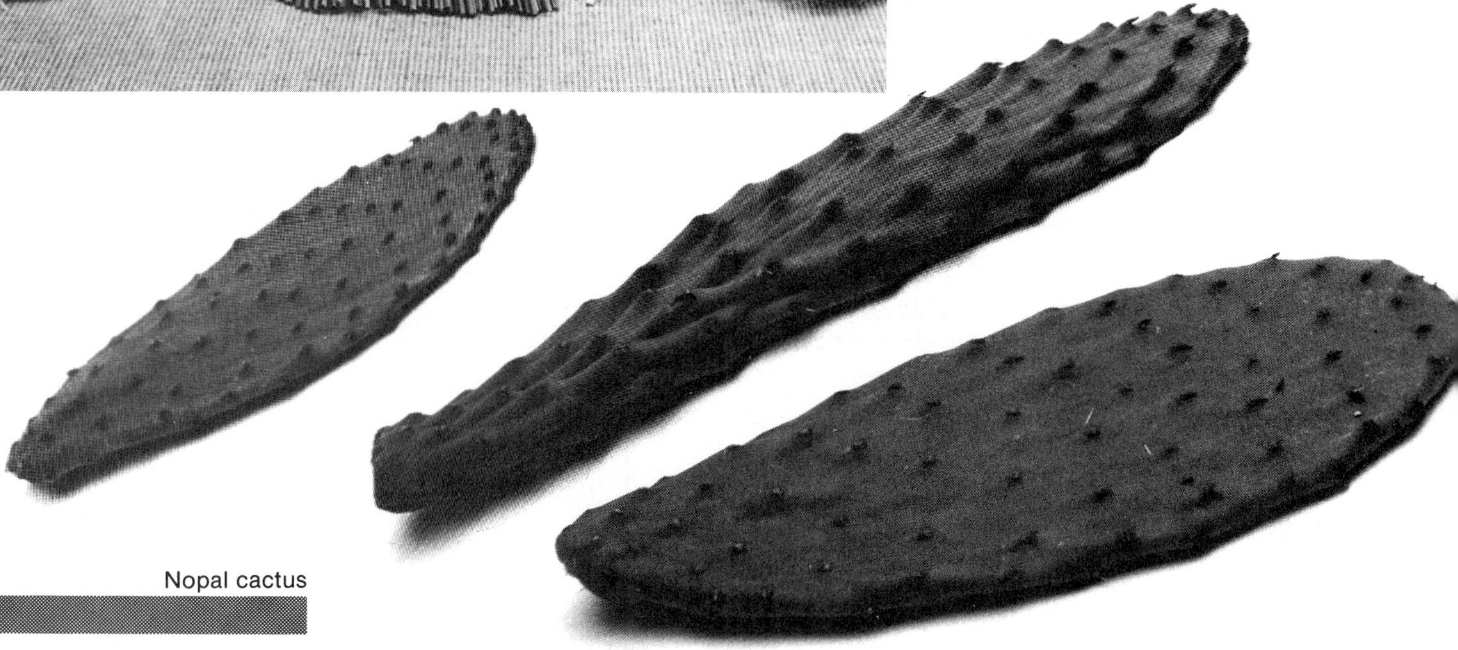

Nopal cactus

Cellophane or vermicelli noodles: A very fine translucent noodle that is employed much like the bean thread noodle. It is usually made from seaweed and is favored for cold dishes.

Phaluda: An Indian noodle made from cornstarch paste. Often served cold with ice cream and syrup, or fruit.

Potato starch noodles: Similar in appearance and use to the bean thread noodle.

Rice sticks: A long thin noodle which greatly increases in bulk when tossed in hot oil, becoming light and crisp. It may be stir-fried, soaked, simmered or deep fried.

Rice chips: The same dough as rice sticks, but formed into small chips. Both forms are popular in China and Southeast Asia. They are prepared like rice sticks but most often deep-fried.

Shrimp noodles: Made of shrimp paste and wheat flour. A Southeast Asian specialty that may be purchased (among other places) in Philippine grocery stores.

Soba: Japan's most popular noodle and a ubiquitous fast food, served with a variety of garnishes from eel to ice cubes and minced ham. It is made from buckwheat flour and has a slightly greenish color.

Somen: Used in soups and cold noodle dishes, this is a Japanese wheat vermicelli.

Udon: The thickest of Japanese wheat noodles, used in both cold and hot dishes.

Wheat, or egg-and-wheat noodles: Like linguine, Chinese egg noodles come in both narrow and wide lengths. They are sold both fresh and dried. The wheat noodles are usually flat.

NOOMAIE

Also BALEMO, CLOWN FIG. Edible fruit of a shrub found in the south Pacific Islands and Australia, particularly in the states of Victoria and Queensland, the noomaie *(Ficus aspera)* reaches no more than an inch in diameter and is green with pink stripes, turning black on maturity. It is consumed locally.

NOPAL CACTUS

Several species of bushy or treelike cacti are called *nopal* in Mexico. They are of the *Opuntia* genus and are common hedge plants in some parts of the country. The oval, fleshy joints of the plant are edible, and the smaller and thinner the better. By way of preparation, the thorns are scraped off (but leaving most of the green outer layer of skin), and the joints are cut into small pieces and cooked in salted water until tender. After draining, they exude a slimy substance (like okra), which is washed away under cold running water. Mexicans put them into scrambled eggs or use them in a salad. They are canned in both plain and pickled versions. For information on the fruit of the *nopal* cactus, see **Prickly Pear.**

NORI

This is a sheet of edible dried seaweed, usually purple laver *(Porphyra laciniata).* The Japanese use it as a wrapper for certain kinds of *sushi*, their classic fish and rice dish, and as a seasoning and decoration in other foods.

See also: **Laver.**

NORMANDE SAUCE

This classic French fish sauce has been elaborated from basic *veloute* sauce. There are variations, but in a standard form the *veloute* is increased by fish stock, then reduced by half and mixed with egg yolks and cream. While the sauce is still on the fire, fresh butter is beaten into it. After the sauce is strained, fresh cream is added. It is served hot over cooked fish.

See also: **Sauce.**

NORTHERN REDHORSE

Also SHORTHEAD REDHORSE. This large fish of the **sucker** family is found in central and eastern Canada and in adjacent areas of the United States. Northern redhorse *(Moxostoma macrolepidotum)* attains a maximum length of about two feet and is a fairly important food fish throughout its range. This species has prominent lips and a long body. It is olive-green on the back and yellow on the belly. It inhabits rivers, streams and lakes.

NORWAY LOBSTER

Also DUBLIN BAY PRAWN, LANGOUSTINE, SALTWATER CRAYFISH, SCAMPI. A clawed, saltwater crustacean found in the northern and eastern Atlantic Ocean and in the Mediterranean Sea, Norway lobster *(Nephrops norvegicus)* resembles its larger relative the *Hormarus gammarus*, but it seldom exceeds 10 inches in length, has a pale pink color and a slender body and claws. Those taken in the Irish Sea, called Dublin Bay prawns, average three inches in length; the Italian *scampi*, found in deep Adriatic waters, generally measure about six inches. A large crustacean of the Gulf of Gaeta, called *mazzancolle*, is believed to be of the same species.

These crustaceans are marketed fresh or frozen. In Great Britain, fresh Dublin Bay prawns are steamed, shelled and then dipped in a mixture of butter, salt and lemon juice. Frozen ones, having a little stronger taste, are used in prawn cocktails. They may also be served fried, curried or in a cream sauce. The flavor is shrimplike.

In Venice, *scampi* are boiled or fried in deep oil and served with a garlic sauce. In an recipe calling for Norway lobster, large shrimp may be substituted. Indeed this is frequently the case in restaurants that list *scampi* on the menu. If you are particular, it is wise to ask to see the *scampi* before ordering.

See also: **Crayfish, Lobster, Shrimp.**

NOSTRALE

This is the name for two kinds of cheese made from cow's milk in northwestern Italy, but more generally it is an Italian term meaning "homemade" and is used in rural areas to refer to things produced locally for local consumption, such as cheese, wine or salami. One of the *nostrale* cheeses is hard *(formaggio duro)* and is produced in the spring. The other is soft *(formaggio tenero)* and is produced in the summer.

NOUGAT

This chewy candy is made of nuts, usually almonds, and either honey or caramelized sugar. The name derives from the Latin word for nut, *nux*, (usually walnut). It appears to be of ancient origin and was originally made from walnuts. Today almonds are most common, but walnuts may be used, as well as pistachios and hazelnuts. Nougat was introduced into modern Europe by the Arabs through Spain. It remains today most popular in Spain and France.

There are two principal types. White nougat is made from stiffly beaten egg whites, honey sugar, orange flower water and nuts. Candied cherries are often added. This makes a fairly hard but chewy candy. Caramel nougat consists of chopped, browned almonds mixed with confectioner's sugar that has been melted into a caramel consistency. It is soft enough to be molded into various shapes.

NOYAU

A sweet French liqueur based on the pits of certain fruits, such as peaches, apricots and cherries, it is made by steeping the pits in brandy or white alcohol, then sweetening the resulting liquor. The predominant flavor is that of almonds, but this is enhanced with other flavoring agents, such as orange peel.

NUITS-ST.-GEORGES

One of the most celebrated wine-growing areas of **Burgundy** is in east-central France near the village or wine-growing commune of Nuits-St.-Georges. The Cote (or "slope") de Nuits makes up the northern half of the Cote d'Or ("slopes of gold"), so named for the sun that warms these hills laden with vineyards. This area, north of **Beaune,** is famed for its dry red wines, among them the **Chambertin, Vougeout** and **Vosne.**

Wines from Nuits-St.-Georges itself are generally full-bodied and a rich, dark red (the red Burgundy that the world knows and appreciates). They are excellent with steak or roast beef and with other roast meats and game. "Burgundy is for those with strong heads and constitutions," reported the epicure, Louis Vaudable. The robust red wine from Nuits-St.-Georges lives up to this description. In the Nuits a sparkling red Burgundy is also made by the method used in the production of **champagne.**

NUOC-MAM SAUCE

Also FERMENTED FISH SAUCE. This fermented fish sauce is popular in Southeast Asia and is known by various names, such as *nam pla* in Thailand, *tuk trey* in Kampuchea and *bagoong* in the Philippines. *Nuoc mam*, a salty, clear, brown liquid, is essential to Vietnamese cooking and is based on the principle of controlled spoilage. That is, certain kinds of fresh, ungutted fish are placed in a vat and covered with salt. After three days, much liquid is drawn off, but enough is left to cover the fish with a layer about two inches thick. The vat is covered with a wicker disk and left in the sun for a few months. Then the liquid is drained off and is ready to be used as a seasoning, while the residue at the bottom is used as fertilizer.

Nuoc-mam is used much like **soy sauce.** In the Philippine version, the fish are gutted so that the fermentation results from enzymes in the fish itself, rather than in its intestinal tract. From this is obtained a paste with a cheeselike odor, which is used as a sauce. Tens of millions of gallons of fermented fish sauce are consumed in Southeast Asia. It is sold in Chinese grocery stores under the label "fish soy."

The closest Western equivalent to *nuoc-mam* was ***garum,*** the favorite seasoning of the ancient Romans.

See also: **Sauce.**

NUT

What is popularly called a "nut" in English is usually something else, such as a seed, a legume, a rhizome or a tuber. Technically, the nut is defined as a fruit with a hard or leathery shell that contains a single, edible kernel, which is enclosed in a soft inner skin. Often the concept of indehiscence is added, which means the shell does not open spontaneously at maturity to expose the kernel. Examples are the acorn, the pecan and the hazelnut. This definition excludes a host of things that most people would call nuts, e.g., the peanut, which is a legume; the Brazil nut, which is a seed, and the almond, which is the seed of a fruit resembling a peach.

Yet the popular idea of nut combines a number of qualities that are highly useful for classifying edibles on the pragmatic level. Popular usage would include any edible fruit or seed, usually hard and oily, contained in a hard or brittle shell. This gets around precise botanical criteria and handily identifies a group of delicious and highly nutritious foods.

Nuts are a touchstone for persons concerned

that their diets be natural and healthy. They are available to eat with a minimum of processing and contain generous proportions of protein, carbohydrates and oil. Indeed, some nuts are as much as 70 percent fat, which is usually polyunsaturated. Examples of these are lychees, chestnuts, chufa nuts and water chestnuts. Those high in carbohydrates are pecans, hickory nuts, Brazil nuts, butternuts, coconuts and pistachios. Consumption of nuts is on the increase worldwide and this fact is probably a testimonial to their food value, as well as modern distribution methods. Nuts contain some minerals, especially magnesium, but only vitamin B is usually present. For more information, see also the names of specific nuts.

NUTGALL TREE

This is a small tree, *Rhus chinensis*, native to temperate eastern Asia, which bears an edible fruit called nutgall. The fruit is small, red and hairy and of mediocre quality.

NUTMEG

This familiar spice consists of the inner kernel of the fruit of the nutmeg tree *(Myristica fragrans)*, which also yields **mace.** It is native to the Banda Islands of the East Indies, but has transplanted well, particularly to Grenada in the West Indies.

The fruit has four layers. First is a fleshy outer covering that splits into two when ripe. Then comes a lacy, red aril enveloping a hard nut, which encloses the nutmeg proper. The kernel commonly measures three-quarters inch by 1¼ inches. The spice is highly aromatic but slightly bitter to the taste.

Although the fruit is eaten whole in the East Indies, preserved in heavy syrup, it is reduced to its constituent spices for export. The outer flesh is removed and discarded. The aril is stripped off, dried, ground and sold as the popular spice, mace. The nut is dried over low heat until the kernel is heard to rattle around inside. The shell is then removed and discarded. The larger kernels are sold as whole nutmeg, while the smaller are ground.

The ground form is most familiar to us nowadays, and it finds its greatest use in confections, baked products, apple sauce and all sorts of desserts. Nutmeg goes well with all forms of cabbage, and can add the right finishing touch to such festive drinks as milk punch, egg nogs and flips. Nutmeg must be used with discretion, since large quantities can be poisonous.

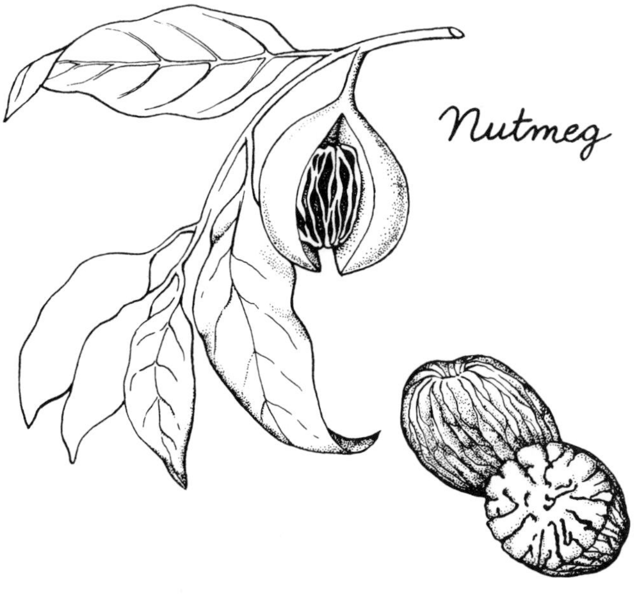

NUTMEG FLOWER

See **Black Cumin.**

NUTMEG PIGEON

A white pigeon (genus *Myristicivora)* of India, Burma and Sri Lanka, it feeds on nutmeg. It is considered game of good quality, especially when young.

NUT PALM

Also AUSTRALIAN NUT PALM. An Australian palm tree, *Cycas media*, that produces edible nuts. it is related to the sago palm.

NUTRIA

Also COYPU. This is a beaverlike rodent, *Myocastor coypu*, of central and southern South America. Its flesh is palatable, but the creature is best known for its velvety, plushlike underfur, which is used to make fur garments. The nutria domesticates easily and thrives in captivity. Nutrias have been farmed for their fur in Europe and parts of the United States. Escapees from these farms have adapted to the wild.

A nutria reaches a maximum length of about 25 inches and a weight of about 20 pounds.

NUTRITIVE VALUE OF FOODS

The following table lists the nutritional value of 730 common foods. It is adapted from the U. S. Department of Agriculture's *Home and Garden Bulletin, Number 72*, dated September 1978.

Nutritive Values of the Edible Part of Foods

(A dot • denotes lack of reliable data for a constituent believed to be present in measurable amount; the letter T indicates that a trace of the constituent in question is present.)

Foods, approximate measures, units and weight (edible part unless footnotes indicate otherwise)			Water	Food Energy	Protein	FAT: Fat (Total)	FAT: Saturated (Total)
		Grams	Percent	Calories	Grams	Grams	Grams
Almonds, shelled:							
Chopped (about 130 almonds)	1 cup	130	5	775	24	70	5.6
Slivered, not pressed down (about 115 almonds)	1 cup	115	5	690	21	62	5.0
Apple juice, bottled or canned	1 cup	248	88	120	T	T	•
Applesauce, canned:							
Sweetened	1 cup	255	76	230	1	T	•
Unsweetened	1 cup	244	89	100	T	T	•
Apples, raw, unpeeled, without cores:							
2¾-in. diam. (about 3 per lb. with cores)	1 apple	138	84	80	T	1	•
3¼ in. diam. (about 2 per lb. with cores)	1 apple	212	84	125	T	1	•
Apricot nectar, canned	1 cup	251	85	145	1	T	•
Apricots:							
Raw, without pits (about 12 per lb. with pits)	3 apricots	107	85	55	1	T	•
Canned in heavy syrup (halves and syrup)	1 cup	258	77	220	2	T	•
Dried							
Uncooked (28 large or 37 medium halves per cup)	1 cup	130	25	340	7	1	•
Cooked, unsweetened, fruit and liquid	1 cup	250	76	215	4	1	•
Asparagus, green:							
Cooked, drained:							
Cuts and tips, 1½ to 2-in. lengths:							
From raw	1 cup	145	94	30	3	T	•
From frozen	1 cup	180	93	40	6	T	•
Spears, ½-in. diam. at base:							
From raw	4 spears	60	94	10	1	T	•
From frozen	4 spears	60	92	15	2	T	•
Canned, spears, ½-in. diam. at base	4 spears	80	93	15	2	T	•
Avocados, raw, whole, without skins and seeds:							
California, mid- and late-winter (with skin and seed, 3⅛-in. diam., wt., 10 oz.	1 avocado	216	74	370	5	37	5.5
Florida, late summer and fall (with skin and seed, 3⅝-in diam.; wt., 1 lb	1 avocado	304	78	390	4	33	6.7
Bacon, (20 slices per lb. raw), broiled or fried, crisp	2 slices	15	8	85	4	8	2.5
Bagel, 3-in. diam.:							
Egg	1 bagel	55	32	165	6	2	.5
Water	1 bagel	55	29	165	6	1	.2

Unsaturated Oleic	Linoleic	Carbo-hydrate	Calcium	Phosphorus	Iron	Potassium	Vitamin A Value	Thiamin	Ribo-flavin	Niacin	Ascorbic Acid
Grams	Grams	Grams	Milli-grams	Milli-grams	Milli-grams	Milli-grams	Internat'l. units	Milli-grams	Milli-grams	Milli-grams	Milli-grams
47.7	12.8	25	304	655	6.1	1,005	0	.31	1.20	4.6	T
42.2	11.3	22	269	580	5.4	889	0	.28	1.06	4.0	T
•	•	30	15	22	1.5	250	•	.02	.05	.2	2
•	•	61	10	13	1.3	166	100	.05	.03	.1	3
•	•	26	10	12	1.2	190	100	.05	.02	.1	2
•	•	20	10	14	.4	152	120	.04	.03	.1	6
•	•	31	15	21	.6	233	190	.06	.04	.2	8
•	•	37	23	30	.5	379	2,380	.03	.03	.5	36
•	•	14	18	25	.5	301	2,890	.03	.04	.6	11
•	•	57	28	39	.8	604	4,490	.05	.05	1.0	10
•	•	86	87	140	7.2	1,273	14,170	.01	.21	4.3	16
•	•	54	55	88	4.5	795	7,500	.01	.13	2.5	8
•	•	5	30	73	0.9	265	1,310	0.23	0.26	2.0	38
•	•	6	40	115	2.2	396	1,530	.25	.23	1.8	41
•	•	2	13	30	.4	110	540	.10	.11	.8	16
•	•	2	13	40	.7	143	470	.10	.08	.7	16
•	•	3	15	42	1.5	133	640	.05	.08	.6	12
22.0	3.7	13	22	91	1.3	1,303	630	.24	.43	3.5	30
15.7	5.3	27	30	128	1.8	1,836	880	.33	.61	4.9	43
3.7	.7	T	2	34	.5	35	0	.08	.05	.8	•
.9	.8	28	9	43	1.2	41	30	.14	.10	1.2	0
.4	.6	30	8	41	1.2	42	0	.15	.11	1.4	0

Foods, approximate measures, units and weight (edible part unless footnotes indicate otherwise)			Water	Food Energy	Protein	Fat (Total)	Saturated (Total)
			Nutrients in Indicated Quantity			FAT	
Baking powders for home use:		Grams	Percent	Calories	Grams	Grams	Grams
Sodium aluminum sulfate:							
With monocalcium phosphate monohydrate	1 tsp.	3	2	5	T	T	0
With monocalcium phosphate monohydrate, calcium sulfate	1 tsp.	3	1	5	T	T	0
Straight phosphate	1 tsp.	4	2	5	T	T	0
Low sodium	1 tsp.	4	2	5	T	T	0
Banana flakes	1 tbsp.	6	3	20	T	T	•
Banana without peel (about 2½ per lb. with peel)	1 banana	119	76	100	1	T	•
Barbecue sauce	1 cup	250	81	230	4	17	2.2
Barley, pearled, light, uncooked	1 cup	200	11	700	16	2	.3
Beans:							
Lima, immature seeds, frozen, cooked, drained:							
Thick-seeded types (Fordhooks)	1 cup	170	74	170	10	T	•
Thin-seeded types (baby limas)	1 cup	180	69	210	13	T	•
Snap:							
Green:							
Cooked, drained:							
From raw (cuts and French style)	1 cup	125	92	30	2	T	•
From frozen:							
Cuts	1 cup	135	92	35	2	T	•
French style	1 cup	130	92	35	2	T	•
Canned, drained solids (cuts)	1 cup	135	92	30	2	T	•
Yellow or wax:							
Cooked, drained:							
From raw (cuts and French style)	1 cup	125	93	30	2	T	•
From frozen (cuts)	1 cup	135	92	35	2	T	•
Canned, drained solids (cuts)	1 cup	135	92	30	2	T	•
Beans, dry:							
Common varieties as Great Northern, navy and others:							
Cooked, drained:							
Great Northern	1 cup	180	69	210	14	1	•
Pea (navy)	1 cup	190	69	225	15	1	•
Canned, solids and liquid:							
White, with:							
Frankfurters (sliced)	1 cup	255	71	365	19	18	•
Pork and tomato sauce	1 cup	255	71	310	16	7	2.4
Pork and sweet sauce	1 cup	255	66	385	16	12	4.3
Red Kidney	1 cup	255	76	230	15	1	•
Lima, cooked, drained	1 cup	190	64	260	16	1	•
Bean sprouts (mung):							
Raw	1 cup	105	89	35	4	T	•
Cooked, drained	1 cup	125	91	35	4	T	•
Beef, cooked:							
Cuts braised, simmered or pot roasted:							
Lean and fat (piece, 2½ by 2½ by ¾ in.)	3 oz.	85	53	245	23	16	6.8
Lean only from above item	2½ oz.	72	62	140	22	5	2.1
Ground Beef, broiled:							
Lean with 10% fat	3 oz. or patty 3 by ⅝ in.	85	60	185	23	10	4.0
Lean with 21% fat	3 oz. or patty 3 by ⅝ in.	82	54	235	20	17	7.0

Unsaturated Oleic	Linoleic	Carbo-hydrate	Calcium	Phosphorus	Iron	Potassium	Vitamin A Value	Thiamin	Ribo-flavin	Niacin	Ascorbic Acid
Grams	Grams	Grams	Milli-grams	Milli-grams	Milli-grams	Milli-grams	Internat'l. units	Milli-grams	Milli-grams	Milli-grams	Milli-grams
0	0	1	58	87	•	5	0	0	0	0	0
0	0	1	183	45	•	•	0	0	0	0	0
0	0	1	239	359	•	6	0	0	0	0	0
0	0	2	207	314	•	471	0	0	0	0	0
•	•	5	2	6	.2	92	50	.01	.01	.2	T
•	•	26	10	31	.8	440	230	.06	.07	.8	12
4.3	10.0	20	53	50	2.0	435	900	.03	.03	.8	13
.2	.8	158	32	378	4.0	320	0	.24	.10	6.2	0
•	•	32	34	153	2.9	724	390	.12	.09	1.7	29
•	•	40	63	227	4.7	709	400	.16	.09	2.2	22
•	•	7	63	46	.8	189	680	.09	.11	.6	15
•	•	8	54	43	.9	205	780	.09	.12	.5	7
•	•	8	49	39	1.2	177	690	.08	.10	.4	9
•	•	7	61	34	2.0	128	630	.04	.07	.4	5
•	•	6	63	46	.8	189	290	.09	.11	.6	16
•	•	8	47	42	.9	221	140	.09	.11	.5	8
•	•	7	61	34	2.0	128	140	.04	.07	.4	7
•	•	38	90	266	4.9	749	0	.25	.13	1.3	0
•	•	40	95	281	5.1	790	0	.27	.13	1.3	0
•	•	32	94	303	4.8	668	330	.18	.15	3.3	T
2.8	.6	48	138	235	4.6	536	330	.20	.08	1.5	5
5.0	1.1	54	161	291	5.9	•	•	.15	.10	1.3	•
•	•	42	74	278	4.6	673	10	.13	.10	1.3	•
•	•	49	55	293	5.9	1,163	•	.25	.11	1.3	•
•	•	7	20	67	1.4	234	20	.14	.14	.8	20
•	•	7	21	60	1.1	195	30	.11	.13	.9	8
6.5	.4	0	10	114	2.9	184	30	.04	.18	3.6	•
1.8	.2	0	10	108	2.7	176	10	.04	.17	3.3	•
3.9	.3	0	10	196	3.0	261	20	.08	.20	5.1	•
6.7	.4	0	9	159	2.6	221	30	.07	.17	4.4	•

Foods, approximate measures, units and weight (edible part unless footnotes indicate otherwise)			Nutrients in Indicated Quantity			FAT	
			Water	Food Energy	Protein	Fat (Total)	Saturated (Total)
		Grams	Percent	Calories	Grams	Grams	Grams
Roast, oven cooked, no liquid added:							
Relatively fat, such as rib:							
Lean and fat (2 pieces, 4⅛ by 2¼ by ¼ in.	3 oz.	85	40	375	17	33	14.0
Lean only from above item	1¾ oz.	51	57	125	14	7	3.0
Beef, cooked-continued:							
Roast, oven cooked, no liquid added:							
Relatively lean, such as heel of round:							
Lean and fat (2 pieces, 4⅛ by 2¼ by ¼ in.)	3 oz.	85	62	165	25	7	2.8
Lean only from above item	2¾ oz.	78	65	125	24	3	1.2
Steak:							
Relatively fat, sirloin, broiled:							
Lean and fat (piece, 2½ by ¾ in.)	3 oz.	85	44	330	20	27	11.3
Lean only from above item	2 oz.	56	59	115	18	4	1.8
Relatively lean, round, braised:							
Lean and fat (piece, 4⅛ by 2¼ by ½ in.)	3 oz.	85	55	220	24	13	5.5
Lean only from above item	2½ oz.	68	61	130	21	4	1.7
Beef and vegetable stew	1 cup	245	82	220	16	11	4.9
Beef, canned:							
Corned beef	3 oz.	85	59	185	22	10	4.9
Corned beef hash	1 cup	220	67	400	19	25	11.9
Beef, dried, chipped	2½ oz. jar	71	48	145	24	4	2.1
Beef potpie (home recipe), baked (piece, ⅓ of 9-in. diam. pie)	1 piece	210	55	515	21	30	7.9
Beer	12 fl. oz.	360	92	150	1	0	0
Beet greens, leaves and stems, cooked, drained	1 cup	145	94	25	2	T	•
Beets:							
Cooked, drained, peeled:							
Whole beets, 2-in. diam.	2 beets	100	91	30	1	T	•
Diced or sliced	1 cup	170	91	55	2	T	•
Canned, drained solids:							
Whole beets, small	1 cup	160	89	60	2	T	•
Diced or sliced	1 cup	170	89	65	2	T	•
Biscuits, baking powder, 2-in. diam. (enriched flour, vegetable shortening):							
From home recipe	1 biscuit	28	27	105	2	5	1.2
From mix	1 biscuit	28	29	90	2	3	.6
Blackeyed peas, dry, cooked (with residual cooking liquid)	1 cup	250	80	190	13	1	•
Blackeyed peas, immature seeds, cooked and drained:							
From raw	1 cup	165	72	180	13	1	•
From frozen	1 cup	170	66	220	15	1	•
Blackberries, raw	1 cup	144	85	85	2	1	•
Blueberries, raw	1 cup	145	83	90	1	1	•
Bluefish, baked with butter or margarine	3 oz.	85	68	135	22	4	•
Bologna, slice (8 per 8-oz. pkg.)	1 slice	28	56	85	3	8	3.0
Braunschweiger, slice (6 per 6-oz. pkg.)	1 slice	28	53	90	4	8	2.6
Brazil nuts, shelled (6-8 large kernels)	1 oz.	28	5	185	4	19	4.8
Breadcrumbs (enriched):							
Dry, grated	1 cup	100	7	390	13	5	1.0
Soft, cubes	1 cup	30	36	80	3	1	.2
Soft, crumbs	1 cup	45	36	120	4	1	.3

Unsaturated Oleic	Linoleic	Carbo-hydrate	Calcium	Phosphorus	Iron	Potassium	Vitamin A Value	Thiamin	Ribo-flavin	Niacin	Ascorbic Acid
Grams	Grams	Grams	Milli-grams	Milli-grams	Milli-grams	Milli-grams	Internat'l. units	Milli-grams	Milli-grams	Milli-grams	Milli-grams
13.6	.8	0	8	158	2.2	189	70	.05	.13	3.1	•
2.5	.3	0	6	131	1.8	161	10	.04	.11	2.6	•
2.7	.2	0	11	208	3.2	279	10	.06	.19	4.5	•
1.0	0.1	0	10	199	3.0	268	T	.06	.18	4.3	•
11.1	.6	0	9	162	2.5	220	50	.05	.15	4.0	•
1.6	.2	0	7	146	2.2	202	10	.05	.14	3.6	•
5.2	.4	0	10	213	3.0	272	20	.07	.19	4.8	•
1.5	.2	0	9	182	2.5	238	10	.05	.16	4.1	•
4.5	.2	15	29	184	2.9	613	2,400	.15	.17	4.7	17
4.5	.2	0	17	90	3.7	•	•	.01	.20	2.9	•
10.9	.5	24	29	147	4.4	440	•	.02	.20	4.6	•
2.0	.1	0	14	287	3.6	142	•	.05	.23	2.7	0
12.8	6.7	39	29	149	3.8	334	1,720	.30	.30	5.5	6
0	0	14	18	108	T	90	•	.01	.11	2.2	•
•	•	5	144	36	2.8	481	7,400	.10	.22	.4	22
•	•	7	14	23	.5	208	20	.03	.04	.3	6
•	•	12	24	39	.9	354	30	.05	.07	.5	10
•	•	14	30	29	1.1	267	30	.02	.05	.2	5
•	•	15	32	31	1.2	284	30	.02	.05	.2	5
2.0	1.2	13	34	49	.4	33	T	.08	.08	.7	T
1.1	.7	15	19	65	.6	32	T	.09	.08	.8	T
•	•	35	43	238	3.3	573	30	.40	.10	1.0	•
•	•	30	40	241	3.5	625	580	.50	.18	2.3	28
•	•	40	43	286	4.8	573	290	.68	.19	2.4	15
•	•	19	46	27	1.3	245	290	.04	.06	.6	30
•	•	22	22	19	1.5	117	150	.04	.09	.7	20
•	•	0	25	244	.6	•	40	.09	.08	1.6	•
3.4	.5	T	2	36	.5	65	•	.05	.06	.7	•
3.4	.8	1	3	69	1.7	•	1,850	.05	.41	2.3	•
6.2	7.1	3	53	196	1.0	203	T	.27	.03	.5	•
1.6	1.4	73	122	141	3.6	152	T	.35	.35	4.8	T
.3	.3	15	25	29	.8	32	T	.12	.07	1.0	T
.5	.5	23	38	44	1.1	47	T	.18	.11	1.5	T

Foods, approximate measures, units and weight (edible part unless footnotes indicate otherwise)			Water	Food Energy	Protein	FAT: Fat (Total)	FAT: Saturated (Total)
		Grams	Percent	Calories	Grams	Grams	Grams
Breads:							
Boston brown bread, canned, slice, 3¼ by ½ in.	1 slice	45	45	95	2	1	.1
Breads-continued							
Cracked-wheat bread (¾ enriched wheat flour, ¼ cracked wheat):							
Loaf, 1 lb.	1 loaf	454	35	1,195	39	10	2.2
Slice (18 per loaf)	1 slice	25	35	65	2	1	.1
French or Vienna bread, enriched:							
Loaf, 1 lb.	1 loaf	454	31	1,315	41	14	3.2
Slice:							
French (5 by 2½ by 1 in.)	1 slice	35	31	100	3	1	.2
Vienna (4¾ by 4 by ½ in.)	1 slice	25	31	75	2	1	.2
Italian bread, enriched:							
Loaf 1 lb.	1 loaf	454	32	1,250	41	4	.6
Slice, 4½ by 3¼ by ¾ in.	1 slice	30	32	85	3	T	T
Raisin bread, enriched:							
Loaf, 1 lb.	1 loaf	454	35	1,190	30	13	3.0
Slice (18 per loaf)	1 slice	25	35	65	2	1	.2
Rye Bread:							
American, light (⅔ enriched wheat flour, ⅓ rye flour):							
Loaf, 1 lb.	1 loaf	454	36	1,100	41	5	.7
Slice (4¾ by 3¾ by 7/16 in.)	1 slice	25	36	60	2	T	T
Pumpernickel (⅔ rye flour, ⅓ enriched wheat flour):							
Loaf, 1 lb.	1 loaf	454	34	1,115	41	5	.7
Slice (5 by 4 by ⅜ in.)	1 slice	32	34	80	3	T	.1
White Bread, enriched:							
Soft-crumb type:							
Loaf, 1 lb.	1 loaf	454	36	1,225	39	15	3.4
Slice (18 per loaf)	1 slice	25	36	70	2	1	.2
Slice, toasted	1 slice	22	25	70	2	1	.2
Slice (22 per loaf)	1 slice	20	36	55	2	1	.2
Slice, toasted	1 slice	17	25	55	2	1	.2
Loaf, 1½ lb.	1 loaf	680	36	1,835	59	22	5.2
Slice (24 per loaf)	1 slice	28	36	75	2	1	.2
Slice, toasted	1 slice	24	25	75	2	1	.2
Slice (28 per loaf)	1 slice	24	36	65	2	1	.2
Slice, toasted	1 slice	21	25	65	2	1	.2
Cubes	1 cup	30	36	80	3	1	.2
Crumbs	1 cup	45	36	120	4	1	.3
Firm-crumb type:							
Loaf, 1 lb.	1 loaf	454	35	1,245	41	17	3.9
Slice (20 per loaf)	1 slice	23	35	65	2	1	.2
Slice, toasted	1 slice	20	24	65	2	1	.2
Loaf, 2 lb.	1 loaf	907	35	2,495	82	34	7.7
Slice (34 per loaf)	1 slice	27	35	75	2	1	.2
Slice, toasted	1 slice	23	24	75	2	1	.2
Whole-wheat bread:							
Soft-crumb type:							
Loaf, 1 lb.	1 loaf	454	36	1,095	41	12	2.2
Slice (16 per loaf)	1 slice	28	36	65	3	1	.1
Slice, toasted	1 slice	24	24	65	3	1	.1
Firm-crumb type:							
Loaf, 1 lb.	1 loaf	454	36	1,100	48	14	2.5
Slice (18 per loaf)	1 slice	25	36	60	3	1	.1
Slice, toasted	1 slice	21	24	60	3	1	.1

Unsaturated Oleic	*Unsaturated* Linoleic	Carbo-hydrate	Calcium	Phosphorus	Iron	Potassium	Vitamin A Value	Thiamin	Ribo-flavin	Niacin	Ascorbic Acid
Grams	Grams	Grams	Milli-grams	Milli-grams	Milli-grams	Milli-grams	Internat'l. units	Milli-grams	Milli-grams	Milli-grams	Milli-grams
.2	.2	21	41	72	.9	131	0	.06	.04	.7	0
3.0	3.9	236	399	581	9.5	608	T	1.52	1.13	14.4	T
.2	.2	13	22	32	.5	34	T	.08	.06	.8	T
4.7	4.6	251	195	386	10.0	408	T	1.80	1.10	15.0	T
.4	.4	19	15	30	.8	32	T	.14	.08	1.2	T
.3	.3	14	11	21	.6	23	T	.10	.06	.8	T
.3	1.5	256	77	349	10.0	336	0	1.80	1.10	15.0	0
T	.1	17	5	23	.7	22	0	.12	.07	1.0	0
4.7	3.9	243	322	395	10.0	1,057	T	1.70	1.07	10.7	T
.3	.2	13	18	22	.6	58	T	.09	.06	.6	T
.5	2.2	236	340	667	9.1	658	0	1.35	.98	12.9	0
T	.1	13	19	37	.5	36	0	.07	.05	.7	0
.5	2.4	241	381	1,039	11.8	2,059	0	1.30	.93	8.5	0
T	.2	17	27	73	.8	145	0	.09	.07	.6	0
5.3	4.6	229	381	440	11.3	476	T	1.80	1.10	15.0	T
.3	.3	13	21	24	.6	26	T	.10	.06	.8	T
.3	.3	13	21	24	.6	26	T	.08	.06	.8	T
.2	.2	10	17	19	.5	21	T	.08	.05	.7	T
.2	.2	10	17	19	.5	21	T	.06	.05	.7	T
7.9	6.9	343	571	660	17.0	714	T	2.70	1.65	22.5	T
.3	.3	14	24	27	.7	29	T	.11	.07	.9	T
.3	.3	14	24	27	.7	29	T	.09	.07	.9	T
.3	.2	12	20	23	.6	25	T	.10	.06	.8	T
.3	.2	12	20	23	.6	25	T	.08	.06	.8	T
.3	.3	15	25	29	.8	32	T	.12	.07	1.0	T
.5	.5	23	38	44	1.1	47	T	.18	.11	1.5	T
5.9	5.2	228	435	463	11.3	549	T	1.80	1.10	15.0	T
.3	.3	12	22	23	.6	28	T	.09	.06	.8	T
.3	.3	12	22	23	.6	28	T	.07	.06	.8	T
11.8	10.4	455	871	925	22.7	1,097	T	3.60	2.20	30.0	T
.3	.3	14	26	28	.7	33	T	.11	.06	.9	T
.3	.3	14	26	28	.7	33	T	.09	.06	.9	T
2.9	4.2	224	381	1,152	13.6	1,161	T	1.37	.45	12.7	T
.2	.2	14	24	71	.8	72	T	.09	.03	.8	T
.2	.2	14	24	71	.8	72	T	.07	.03	.8	T
3.3	4.9	216	449	1,034	13.6	1,238	T	1.17	.54	12.7	T
.2	.3	12	25	57	.8	68	T	.06	.03	.7	T
.2	.3	12	25	57	.8	68	T	.05	.04	.7	T

Foods, approximate measures, units and weight (edible part unless footnotes indicate otherwise)			Water	Food Energy	Protein	FAT: Fat (Total)	FAT: Saturate (Total)
		Grams	Percent	Calories	Grams	Grams	Grams
Breakfast cereals:							
Hot type, cooked:							
Corn (hominy) grits, degermed:							
Enriched	1 cup	245	87	125	3	T	T
Unenriched	1 cup	245	87	125	3	T	T
Farina, quick-cooking, enriched	1 cup	245	89	105	3	T	T
Oatmeal or rolled oats	1 cup	240	87	130	5	2	.4
Wheat, rolled	1 cup	240	80	180	5	1	•
Wheat, whole-meal	1 cup	245	88	110	4	1	•
Ready-to-eat:							
Bran flakes (40% bran), added sugar, salt, iron, vitamins	1 cup	35	3	105	4	1	•
Bran flakes with raisins, added sugar, salt, iron, vitamins	1 cup	50	7	145	4	1	•
Corn flakes:							
Plain, added sugar, salt, iron, vitamins	1 cup	25	4	95	2	T	•
Sugar-coated, added salt, iron, vitamins	1 cup	40	2	155	2	T	•
Corn, puffed, plain, added sugar, salt, iron, vitamins	1 cup	20	4	80	2	1	•
Corn, shredded, added sugar, salt, iron, thiamin, niacin	1 cup	25	3	95	2	T	•
Oats, puffed, added sugar, salt, minerals, vitamins	1 cup	25	3	100	3	1	•
Rice, puffed:							
Plain, added iron, thiamin, niacin	1 cup	15	4	60	1	T	•
Presweetened, added salt, iron, vitamins	1 cup	28	3	115	1	0	•
Wheat flakes, added sugar, salt, iron, vitamins	1 cup	30	4	105	3	T	•
Wheat, puffed:							
Plain, added iron, thiamin, niacin	1 cup	15	3	55	2	T	•
Presweetened, added salt, iron, vitamins	1 cup	38	3	140	3	T	•
Wheat, shredded, plain	1 oblong biscuit or ½ cup spoon-size biscuits	25	7	90	2	1	•
Wheat germ without salt and sugar, toasted	1 tbsp.	6	4	25	2	1	•
Broccoli, cooked, drained:							
From raw:							
Stalk, medium size	1 stalk	180	91	45	6	1	•
Stalks cut into ½ in. pieces	1 cup	155	91	40	5	T	•
From frozen:							
Stalk, 4½ to 5 in. long	1 stalk	30	91	10	1	T	•
Chopped	1 cup	185	92	50	5	1	•
Brown and serve (10-11 per 8-oz. pkg.), browned	1 link	17	40	70	3	6	2.3
Brussels sprouts, cooked, drained:							
From raw, 7-8 sprouts (1¼ to 1½ in. diam.)	1 cup	155	88	55	7	1	•
From frozen	1 cup	155	89	50	5	T	•
Buckwheat flour, light, sifted	1 cup	98	12	340	6	1	0.2
Bulgur, canned, seasoned	1 cup	135	56	245	8	4	•

Unsaturated Oleic	*Unsaturated* Linoleic	Carbo-hydrate	Calcium	Phosphorus	Iron	Potassium	Vitamin A Value	Thiamin	Ribo-flavin	Niacin	Ascorbic Acid
Grams	Grams	Grams	Milli-grams	Milli-grams	Milli-grams	Milli-grams	Internat'l. units	Milli-grams	Milli-grams	Milli-grams	Milli-grams
T	.1	27	2	25	.7	27	T	.10	.07	1.0	0
T	.1	27	2	25	.7	27	T	.05	.02	.5	0
T	.1	22	147	113	(*)	25	0	.12	.07	1.0	0
.8	.9	23	22	137	1.4	146	0	.19	.05	.2	0
•	•	41	19	182	1.7	202	0	.17	.07	2.2	0
•	•	23	17	127	1.2	118	0	.15	.05	1.5	0
•	•	28	19	125	15.6	137	1,650	.41	.49	4.1	12
•	•	40	28	146	16.9	154	2,350	.58	.71	5.8	18
•	•	21	(**)	9	.6	30	1,180	.29	.35	2.9	9
•	•	37	1	10	1.0	27	1,880	.46	.56	4.6	14
•	•	16	4	18	2.3	•	940	.23	.28	2.3	7
•	•	22	1	10	.6	•	0	.11	.05	.5	0
•	•	19	44	102	2.9	•	1,180	.29	.35	2.9	9
•	•	13	3	14	.3	15	0	.07	.01	.7	0
•	•	26	3	14	1.1	43	1,250	.38	.43	5.0	15
•	•	24	12	83	(**)	81	1,410	.35	.42	3.5	11
•	•	12	4	48	.6	51	0	.08	.03	1.2	0
•	•	33	7	52	1.6	63	1,680	.50	.57	6.7	20
•	•	20	11	97	.9	87	0	.06	.03	1.1	0
•	•	3	3	70	.5	57	10	.11	.05	.3	1
•	•	8	158	112	1.4	481	4,500	.16	.36	1.4	162
•	•	7	136	96	1.2	414	3,880	.14	.31	1.2	140
•	•	1	12	17	.2	66	570	.02	.03	.2	22
•	•	9	100	104	1.3	392	4,180	.11	.22	.9	105
2.8	.7	T	•	•	•	•	•	•	•	•	•
•	•	10	50	112	1.7	423	810	0.12	.22	1.2	135
•	•	10	33	95	1.2	457	880	.12	.16	.9	126
0.4	0.4	78	11	86	1.0	314	0	.08	.04	.4	0
•	•	44	27	263	1.9	151	0	.08	.05	4.1	0

(*)Value may range from less than 1 mg. to about 8 mg. depending on the brand. Consult the label.
(**)Value varies with the brand. Consult the label.

							FAT	
				Nutrients in Indicated Quantity				
Foods, approximate measures, units and weight (edible part unless footnotes indicate otherwise)			Water	Food Energy	Protein		Fat (Total)	Saturated (Total)
		Grams	Percent	Calories	Grams		Grams	Grams
Butter:								
Regular (1 brick or 4 sticks per lb.):								
Stick (½ cup)	1 stick	113	16	815	1		92	57.3
Tablespoon (about ⅛ stick)	1 tbsp.	14	16	100	T		12	7.2
Pat (1 in square, ⅓ in. high; 90 per lb.).	1 pat	5	16	35	T		4	2.5
Whipped (6 sticks or two 8-oz. containers per lb.):								
Stick (½ cup)	1 stick	76	16	540	1		61	38.2
Tablespoon (about ⅛ stick)	1 tbsp.	9	16	65	T		8	4.7
Pat (1¼ in. square, ⅓ in. high; 120 per lb.).	1 pat	4	16	25	T		3	1.9
Cabbage:								
Common varieties:								
Raw:								
Coarsely shredded or sliced	1 cup	70	92	15	1		T	•
Finely shredded or chopped	1 cup	90	92	20	1		T	•
Cooked, drained	1 cup	145	94	30	2		T	•
Red, raw, coarsely shredded or sliced	1 cup	70	90	20	1		T	•
Savory, raw, coarsely shredded or slice	1 cup	70	92	15	2		T	•
Cabbage, celery (also called pe-tsai or wongbok), raw, 1-in. pieces	1 cup	75	95	10	1		T	•
Cabbage, white mustard (also called bokchoy or pakchoy), cooked, drained	1 cup	170	95	25	2		T	•
Cake icings:								
Boiled, white:								
Plain	1 cup	94	18	295	1		0	0
With coconut	1 cup	166	15	605	3		13	11.0
Uncooked:								
Chocolate made with milk and butter	1 cup	275	14	1,035	9		38	23.4
Creamy fudge from mix and water	1 cup	245	15	830	7		16	5.1
White	1 cup	319	11	1,200	2		21	12.7
Cakes made from cake mixes with enriched flour:								
Angelfood:								
Whole cake (9¾ in. diam. tube cake)	1 cake	635	34	1,645	36		1	•
Piece, 1/12 of cake	1 piece	53	34	135	3		T	•
Coffeecake:								
Whole cake (7¾ by 5⅝ by 1¼ in.).	1 cake	430	30	1,385	27		41	11.7
Piece, ⅙ of cake	1 piece	72	30	230	5		7	2.0
Cupcakes, made with egg, milk, 2½ in. diam.:								
Without icing	1 cupcake	25	26	90	1		3	.8
With chocolate icing	1 cupcake	36	22	130	2		5	2.0
Devil's food with chocolate icing:								
Whole, 2 layer cake (8 or 9 in. diam.)	1 cake	1,107	24	3,755	49		136	50.0
Piece, 1/16 of cake	1 piece	69	24	235	3		8	3.1
Cupcake, 2½ in. diam	1 cupcake	35	24	120	2		4	1.6
Gingerbread:								
Whole cake (8 in. square)	1 cake	570	37	1,575	18		39	9.7
Piece, 1/9 of cake	1 peice	63	37	175	2		4	1.1
White, 2 layer with chocolate icing:								
Whole cake (8 or 9 in. diam.)	1 cake	1,140	21	4,000	44		122	48.2
Piece, 1/16 of cake	1 piece	71	21	250	3		8	3.0
Yellow, 2 layer with chocolate icing:								
Whole cake (8 or 9 in. diam.)	1 cake	1,108	26	3,735	45		125	47.8
Piece, 1/16 of cake	1 piece	69	26	235	3		8	3.0

Unsaturated Oleic	Linoleic	Carbo-hydrate	Calcium	Phosphorus	Iron	Potassium	Vitamin A Value	Thiamin	Ribo-flavin	Niacin	Ascorbic Acid
Grams	Grams	Grams	Milli-grams	Milli-grams	Milli-grams	Milli-grams	Internat'l. units	Milli-grams	Milli-grams	Milli-grams	Milli-grams
23.1	2.1	T	27	26	.2	29	3,470	.01	.04	T	0
2.9	.3	T	3	3	T	4	430	T	T	T	0
1.0	.1	T	1	1	T	1	150	T	T	T	0
15.4	1.4	T	18	17	.1	20	2,310	T	.03	T	0
1.9	.2	T	2	2	T	2	290	T	T	T	0
.8	.1	T	1	1	T	1	120	0	T	T	0
•	•	4	34	20	.3	163	90	.04	.04	.02	33
•	•	5	44	26	.4	210	120	.05	.05	.3	42
•	•	6	64	29	.4	236	190	.06	.06	.4	48
•	•	5	29	25	.6	188	30	.06	.04	.3	43
•	•	3	47	38	.6	188	140	.04	.06	.2	39
•	•	2	32	30	.5	190	110	.04	.03	.5	19
•	•	4	252	56	1.0	364	5,270	.07	.14	1.2	26
0	0	75	2	2	T	17	0	T	.03	T	0
.9	T	124	10	50	.8	277	0	.02	.07	.3	0
11.7	1.0	185	165	305	3.3	536	580	.06	.28	.6	1
6.7	3.1	183	96	218	2.7	238	T	.05	.20	.7	T
5.1	.5	260	48	38	T	57	860	T	.06	T	T
•	•	377	603	756	2.5	381	0	.37	.95	3.6	0
•	•	32	50	63	.2	32	0	.03	.08	.3	0
16.3	8.8	225	262	748	6.9	469	690	.82	.91	7.7	1
2.7	1.5	38	44	125	1.2	78	120	.14	.15	1.3	T
1.2	.7	14	40	59	.3	21	40	.05	.05	.4	T
1.6	.6	21	47	71	.4	42	60	.05	.05	.4	T
44.9	17.0	645	653	1,162	16.6	1,439	1,660	1.06	1.65	10.1	1
2.8	1.1	40	41	72	1.0	90	100	.07	.10	.6	T
1.4	.5	20	21	37	.5	46	50	.03	.05	.3	T
16.6	10.0	291	513	570	8.6	1,562	T	.84	1.00	7.4	T
1.8	1.1	32	57	63	.9	173	T	.09	.11	.8	T
46.4	20.0	716	1,129	2,041	11.4	1,322	680	1.50	1.77	12.5	2
2.9	1.2	45	70	127	.7	82	40	.09	.11	.8	T
47.8	20.3	638	1,008	2,017	12.2	1,208	1,550	1.24	1.67	10.6	2
3.0	1.3	40	63	126	.8	75	100	.08	.10	.7	T

Foods, approximate measures, units and weight (edible part unless footnotes indicate otherwise)			Water	Food Energy	Protein	FAT: Fat (Total)	FAT: Saturated (Total)
		Grams	Percent	Calories	Grams	Grams	Grams
Cakes made from home recipes using enriched flour:							
Boston cream pie with custard filling:							
Whole cake (8 in. diam.)	1 cake	825	35	2,490	41	78	23.0
Piece 1/12 of cake	1 piece	69	35	210	3	6	1.9
Fruitcake, dark:							
Loaf, 1-lb. (7½ by 2 by 1½)	1 loaf	454	18	1,720	22	69	14.4
Slice, 1/30 of loaf	1 slice	15	18	55	1	2	.5
Plain, sheet cake:							
Without icing:							
Whole cake (9 in. square)	1 cake	777	25	2,830	35	108	29.5
Piece, 1/9 of cake	1 piece	86	25	315	4	12	3.3
With uncooked white icing:							
Whole cake (9 in. square)	1 cake	1,096	21	4,020	37	129	42.2
Piece, 1/9 of cake	1 piece	121	21	445	4	14	4.7
Pound:							
Loaf, 8½ by 3½ by 3/14 in.	1 loaf	565	16	2,725	31	170	42.9
Slice, 1/17 of loaf	1 slice	33	16	160	2	10	2.5
Spongecake:							
Whole cake (9¾ in. diam. tube cake)	1 cake	790	32	2,345	60	45	13.1
Piece, 1/12 of cake	1 piece	66	32	195	5	4	1.1
Candy:							
Caramels, plain or chocolate	1 oz.	28	8	115	1	3	1.6
Chocolate:							
Milk, plain	1 oz.	28	1	145	2	9	5.5
Semisweet, small pieces (60 per oz.)	1 cup or 60–oz. pkg.	170	1	860	7	61	36.2
Chocolate-coated peanuts	1 oz.	28	1	160	5	12	4.0
Fondant, uncoated (mints, candy, corn, other)	1 oz.	28	8	105	T	1	.1
Fudge, chocolate, plain	1 oz.	28	8	115	1	3	1 .3
Gum drops	1 oz.	28	12	100	T	T	•
Hard	1 oz.	28	1	110	0	T	•
Marshmallows	1 oz.	28	17	90	1	T	•
Cantaloup, orange-fleshed (with rind and seed cavity, 5 in. diam., 2⅓ lb.)	½ melon with rind	477	91	80	2	T	•
Carbonated water	12 fl. oz.	366	92	115	0	0	0
Carrots:							
Raw, without crowns and tips, scraped:							
Whole, 7½ by 1⅛ in. or strips, 2½ to 3 in. long	1 carrot or 18 strips	72	88	30	1	T	•
Grated	1 cup	110	88	45	1	T	•
Cooked (crosswise cuts), drained	1 cup	155	91	50	1	T	•
Canned:							
Sliced, drained solids	1 cup	155	91	45	1	T	•
Strained or junior (baby food)	1 oz. (1¾ to 2 tbsp.)	28	92	10	T	T	•
Cashew nuts, roasted in oil	1 cup	140	5	785	24	64	12.9
Cauliflower:							
Raw, chopped	1 cup	115	91	31	3	T	•
Cooked, drained:							
From raw (flower buds)	1 cup	125	93	30	3	T	•
From frozen (flowerets)	1 cup	180	94	30	3	T	•
Celery, Pascal type, raw:							
Stalk, large outer, 8 by 1½ in. at root end	1 stalk	40	94	5	T	T	•
Pieces, diced	1 cup	120	94	20	1	T	•
Cheese:							
Natural:							
Blue	1 oz.	28	42	100	6	8	5.3

Nutrients in Indicated Quantity

Unsaturated											
Oleic	Linoleic	Carbo-hydrate	Calcium	Phosphorus	Iron	Potassium	Vitamin A Value	Thiamin	Ribo-flavin	Niacin	Ascorbic Acid
Grams	Grams	Grams	Milli-grams	Milli-grams	Milli-grams	Milli-grams	Internat'l. units	Milli-grams	Milli-grams	Milli-grams	Milli-grams
30.1	15.2	412	553	833	8.2	734	1,730	1.04	1.27	9.6	2
2.5	1.3	34	46	70	.7	61	140	.09	.11	.8	T
33.5	14.8	271	327	513	11.8	2,250	540	.72	.73	4.9	2
1.1	.5	9	11	17	.4	74	20	.02	.02	.2	T
44.4	23.9	434	497	793	8.5	614	1,320	1.21	1.40	10.2	2
4.9	2.6	48	55	88	.9	68	150	.13	.15	1.1	T
49.5	24.4	694	548	822	8.2	669	2,190	1.22	1.47	10.2	2
5.5	2.7	77	61	91	.8	74	240	.14	.16	1.1	T
73.1	39.6	273	107	418	7.9	345	1,410	.90	.99	7.3	0
4.3	2.3	16	6	24	.5	20	80	.05	.06	.4	0
15.8	5.7	427	237	885	13.4	687	3,560	1.10	1.64	7.4	T
1.3	.5	36	20	74	1.1	57	300	.09	.14	.6	T
1.1	.1	22	42	35	.4	54	T	.01	.05	.1	T
3.0	.3	16	65	65	.3	109	80	.02	.10	.1	T
19.8	1.7	97	51	255	4.4	553	30	.02	.14	.9	0
4.7	2.1	11	33	84	.4	143	T	.10	.05	2.1	T
.3	.1	25	4	2	.3	1	0	T	T	T	0
1.4	.6	21	22	24	.3	42	T	.01	.03	.1	T
•	•	25	2	T	.1	1	0	0	T	T	0
•	•	28	6	2	.5	1	0	0	0	0	0
•	•	23	5	2	.5	2	0	0	T	T	0
•	•	20	38	44	1.1	682	9,240	.11	.08	1.6	90
0	0	29	•	•	•	•	0	0	0	0	0
•	•	7	27	26	.5	246	7,930	.04	.04	.4	6
•	•	11	41	40	.8	375	12,100	.07	.06	.7	9
•	•	11	51	48	.9	344	16,280	.08	.08	.8	9
•	•	10	47	34	1.1	186	23,250	.03	.05	.6	3
•	•	2	7	6	.1	51	3,690	.01	.01	.1	1
36.8	10.2	41	53	522	5.3	650	140	.60	.35	2.5	•
•	•	6	29	64	1.3	339	70	.13	.12	.8	90
•	•	5	26	53	.9	258	80	.11	.10	.8	69
•	•	6	31	68	.9	373	50	.07	.09	.7	74
•	•	2	16	11	.1	136	110	.01	.01	.1	4
•	•	5	47	34	.4	409	320	.04	.04	.4	11
1.9	.2	1	150	110	.1	73	200	.01	.11	.3	0

Foods, approximate measures, units and weight (edible part unless footnotes indicate otherwise)			Water	Food Energy	Protein	FAT: Fat (Total)	FAT: Saturated (Total)
		Grams	Percent	Calories	Grams	Grams	Grams
Camembert (3 wedges per 4 oz. container)	1 wedge	38	52	115	8	9	5.8
Cheddar:							
Cut pieces	1 oz.	28	37	115	7	9	6.1
	1 cu. in.	17	37	70	4	6	3.7
Shredded	1 cup	113	37	455	28	37	24.2
Cottage (curd not pressed down):							
Creamed (cottage cheese, 4% fat):							
Large curd	1 cup	225	79	235	28	10	6.4
Small curd	1 cup	210	79	220	26	9	6.0
Low fat (2%)	1 cup	226	79	205	31	4	2.8
Low fat (1%)	1 cup	226	82	165	28	2	1.5
Uncreamed (cottage cheese dry curd, less than ½% fat)	1 cup	145	80	125	25	1	.4
Cream	1 oz.	28	54	100	2	10	6.2
Mozzarella, made with:							
Whole milk	1 oz.	28	48	90	6	7	4.4
Part skim milk	1 oz.	28	49	80	8	5	3.1
Parmesan, grated:							
Cup, not pressed down	1 cup	100	18	455	42	30	19.1
Tablespoon	1 tbsp.	5	18	25	2	2	1.0
Ounce	1 oz.	28	18	130	12	9	5.4
Provolone	1 oz.	28	41	100	7	8	4.8
Ricotta, made with:							
Whole milk	1 cup	246	72	428	28	32	20.4
Part skim milk	1 cup	246	74	340	28	19	12.1
Romano	1 oz.	28	31	110	9	8	•
Swiss	1 oz.	28	37	105	8	8	5.0
Pasteurized process cheese:							
American	1 oz.	28	39	105	6	9	5.6
Swiss	1 oz.	28	42	95	7	7	4.5
Pasteurized process cheese food, American	1 oz.	28	43	95	6	7	4.4
Pasteurized process cheese spread, American	1 oz.	28	48	82	5	6	3.8
Cherries:							
Sour (tart), red, pitted, canned, water pack	1 cup	244	88	105	2	T	•
Sweet, raw, without pits and stems	10 cherries	68	80	45	1	T	•
Chicken a la king, cooked (home recipe)	1 cup	245	68	470	27	34	12.7
Chicken, canned, boneless	3 oz.	85	65	170	18	10	3.2
Chicken chow mein:							
Canned	1 cup	250	89	95	7	T	•
From home recipe	1 cup	250	78	255	31	10	2.4
Chicken, cooked:							
Breast, fried, bones removed, ½ breast (3⅓ oz. with bones)	2¾ oz.	79	58	160	26	5	1.4
Drumstick, fried, bones removed (2 oz. with bones)	13 oz.	38	55	90	12	4	1.1
Half broiler, broiled, bones removed (10½ oz. with bones)	6¼ oz.	176	71	240	42	7	2.2
Chicken potpie (home recipe), baked, piece (⅓ or 9 in. diam. pie)	1 piece	232	57	545	23	31	11.3
Chili con carne with beans, canned	1 cup	255	72	340	19	16	7.5
Chocolate:							
Bitter or baking	1 oz.	28	2	145	3	15	8.9
Semisweet, see Candy, chocolate.							

Unsaturated Oleic	*Unsaturated* Linoleic	Carbo-hydrate	Calcium	Phosphorus	Iron	Potassium	Vitamin A Value	Thiamin	Ribo-flavin	Niacin	Ascorbic Acid
Grams	Grams	Grams	Milli-grams	Milli-grams	Milli-grams	Milli-grams	Internat'l. units	Milli-grams	Milli-grams	Milli-grams	Milli-grams
2.2	.2	T	147	132	.1	71	350	.01	.19	.2	0
2.1	.2	T	204	145	.2	28	300	.01	.11	T	0
1.3	.1	T	124	88	.1	17	180	T	.06	T	0
8.5	.7	1	815	579	.8	111	1,200	.03	.42	.1	0
2.4	.2	6	135	297	.3	190	370	.05	.37	.3	T
2.2	.2	6	126	277	.3	177	340	.04	.34	.3	T
1.0	.1	8	155	340	.4	217	160	.05	.42	.3	T
.5	.1	6	138	302	.3	193	80	.05	.37	.3	T
.1	T	3	46	151	.3	47	40	.04	.21	.2	0
2.4	.2	1	23	30	.3	34	400	T	.06	T	0
1.7	.2	1	163	117	.1	21	260	T	.08	T	0
1.2	.1	1	207	149	.1	27	180	.01	.10	T	0
7.7	.3	4	1,376	807	1.0	107	700	.05	.39	.3	0
.4	T	T	69	40	T	5	40	T	.02	T	0
2.2	.1	1	390	229	.3	30	200	.01	.11	.1	0
1.7	.1	1	214	141	.1	39	230	.01	.09	T	0
7.1	.7	7	509	389	.9	257	1,210	.03	.48	.3	0
4.7	.5	13	669	449	1.1	308	1,060	.05	.46	.2	0
•	•	1	302	215	•	•	160	•	.11	T	0
1.7	.2	1	272	171	T	31	240	.01	.10	T	0
2.1	.2	T	174	211	.1	46	340	.01	.10	T	0
1.7	.1	1	219	216	.2	61	230	T	.08	T	0
1.7	.1	2	163	130	.2	79	260	.01	.13	T	0
1.5	.1	2	159	202	.1	69	220	.01	.12	T	0
•	•	26	37	32	.7	317	1,660	.07	.05	.5	12
•	•	12	15	13	.3	129	70	.03	.04	.3	7
14.3	3.3	12	127	358	2.5	404	1,130	.10	.42	5.4	12
3.8	2.0	0	18	210	1.3	117	200	.03	.11	3.7	3
•	•	18	45	85	1.3	418	150	.05	.10	1.0	13
3.4	3.1	10	58	293	2.5	473	280	.08	.23	4.3	10
1.8	1.1	1	9	218	1.3	•	70	.04	.17	11.6	•
1.3	.9	T	6	89	.9	•	50	.03	.15	2.7	•
2.5	1.3	0	16	355	3.0	483	160	.09	.34	15.5	•
10.9	5.6	42	70	232	3.0	343	3,090	.34	.31	5.5	5
6.8	.3	31	82	321	4.3	594	150	.08	.18	3.3	•
4.9	.4	8	22	109	1.9	235	20	.01	.07	.4	0

Foods, approximate measures, units and weight (edible part unless footnotes indicate otherwise)			Water	Food Energy	Protein	Fat (Total)	Saturated (Total)
		Grams	Percent	Calories	Grams	Grams	Grams
Chocolate-flavored beverage powders (about 4 heaping tsp per oz.):							
With nonfat dry milk	1 oz.	28	2	100	5	1	.5
Without milk	1 oz.	28	1	100	1	1	.4
Chocolate milk (commercial):							
Regular	1 cup	250	82	210	8	8	5.3
Lowfat (2%)	1 cup	250	84	180	8	5	3.1
Lowfat (1%)	1 cup	250	85	160	8	3	1.5
Chop Suey with beef and pork (home recipe)	1 cup	250	75	300	26	17	8.5
Clams:							
Raw, meat only	3 oz.	85	82	65	11	1	•
Canned, solids and liquid	3 oz.	85	86	45	7	1	0.2
Coconut meat, fresh:							
Piece, about 2 by 2 by ½ in.	1 piece	45	51	155	2	16	14.0
Shredded or grated, not pressed down	1 cup	80	51	275	3	28	24.8
Cola drink	12 fl. oz.	369	90	145	0	0	0
Collards, cooked, drained:							
From raw (leaves without stems)	1 cup	190	90	65	7	1	•
From frozen (chopped)	1 cup	170	90	30	5	1	•
Cookies made with enriched flour:							
Brownies with nuts:							
Home-prepared, 1¾ by 1¾ by ⅞ in.:							
From home recipe	1 brownie	20	10	95	1	6	1.5
From commercial recipe	1 brownie	20	11	85	1	4	.9
Frozen, with chocolate icing, 1½ by 1¾ by ⅞ in.	1 brownie	25	13	105	1	5	2.0
Chocolate Chip:							
Commercial, 2¼ in. diam., ⅜ in. thick.	4 cookies	42	3	200	2	9	2.8
From home recipe, 2⅓ in. diam.	4 cookies	40	3	205	2	12	3.5
Fig Bars, square 91⅝ by 1⅝ by ⅜ in.) or rectangular (1½ by 1¾ by ½ in.)	4 cookies	56	14	200	2	3	.8
Gingersnaps, 2 in. diam. ¼ in. thick.	4 cookies	28	3	90	2	2	.7
Macaroons, 2¾ in. diam., ¼ in. thick.	2 cookies	38	4	180	2	9	•
Oatmeal with raisins, 2⅝ in. diam., ¼ in. thick.	4 cookies	52	3	235	3	8	2.0
Plain, prepared from commercial chilled dough, 2½ in. diam., ¼ in. thick.	4 cookies	48	5	240	2	12	3.0
Sandwich type (chocolate or vanilla), 1¾ in. diam., ⅜ in. thick.	4 cookies	40	2	200	2	9	2.2
Vanilla Wafers, 1¾ in. diam., ¼ in. thick.	10 cookies	40	3	185	2	6	•
Corn, sweet:							
Cooked, drained:							
From raw, ear 5 by 1¾ in.	1 ear	140	74	70	2	1	•
From frozen:							
Ear, 5 in. long	1 ear	299	73	120	4	1	•
Kernels	1 cup	165	77	130	5	1	•
Canned:							
Cream style	1 cup	256	76	210	5	2	•
Whole kernel:							
Vacuum pack	1 cup	210	76	175	5	1	•
Wet pack, drained solids	1 cup	165	76	140	4	1	•
Cornmeal:							
Whole-ground, unbolted, dry form	1 cup	122	12	435	11	5	.5
Bolted (nearly whole-grain), dry form	1 cup	122	12	440	11	4	.5
Degermed, enriched:							
Dry form	1 cup	138	12	500	11	2	.2
Cooked	1 cup	240	88	120	3	T	T

Unsaturated Oleic	Linoleic	Carbo-hydrate	Calcium	Phosphorus	Iron	Potassium	Vitamin A Value	Thiamin	Ribo-flavin	Niacin	Ascorbic Acid
Grams	Grams	Grams	Milli-grams	Milli-grams	Milli-grams	Milli-grams	Internat'l. units	Milli-grams	Milli-grams	Milli-grams	Milli-grams
.3	T	20	167	155	.5	227	10	.04	.21	.2	1
.2	T	25	9	48	.6	142	•	.01	.03	.1	0
2.2	.2	26	280	251	.6	417	300	.09	.41	.3	2
1.3	.1	26	284	254	.6	422	500	.10	.42	.3	2
.7	.1	26	287	257	.6	426	500	.10	.40	.2	2
6.2	.7	13	60	248	4.8	425	600	.28	.38	5.0	33
•	•	2	59	138	5.2	154	90	.08	.15	1.1	8
T	T	2	47	116	3.5	119	•	.01	.09	.9	•
.9	.3	4	6	43	.8	115	0	.02	.01	.2	1
0	0	37	•	•	•	•	0	0	0	0	0
•	•	10	357	99	1.5	498	14,820	.21	.38	2.3	144
•	•	10	299	87	1.7	401	11,560	.10	.24	1.0	56
3.0	1.2	10	8	30	.4	38	40	.04	.03	.2	T
1.4	1.3	13	9	27	.4	34	20	.03	.02	.2	T
2.2	.7	15	10	31	.4	44	50	.03	.03	.2	T
2.9	2.2	29	16	48	1.0	56	50	.10	.17	.9	T
4.5	2.9	24	14	40	.8	47	40	.06	.06	.5	T
1.2	.7	42	44	34	1.0	111	60	.04	.14	.9	T
1.0	.6	22	20	13	.7	129	20	.08	.06	.7	0
•	•	25	10	32	.3	176	0	.02	.06	.2	0
3.3	2.0	38	11	53	1.4	192	30	.15	.10	1.0	T
5.2	2.9	31	17	35	.6	23	30	.10	.08	.9	0
3.9	2.2	28	10	96	.7	15	0	.06	.10	.7	0
•	•	30	16	25	.6	29	50	.10	.09	.8	0
•	•	16	2	69	.5	151	310	.09	.08	1.1	7
•	•	27	4	121	1.0	291	440	.18	.10	2.1	9
•	•	31	5	120	1.3	304	580	.15	.10	2.5	8
•	•	51	8	143	1.5	248	840	.08	.13	2.6	13
•	•	43	6	153	1.1	204	740	.06	.13	2.3	11
•	•	33	8	81	.8	160	580	.05	.08	1.5	7
1.0	2.5	90	24	312	2.9	346	620	.46	.13	2.4	0
.9	2.1	91	21	272	2.2	303	590	.37	.10	2.3	0
.4	.9	108	8	137	4.0	166	610	.61	.36	4.8	0
.1	.2	26	2	34	1.0	38	140	.14	.10	1.2	0

Foods, approximate measures, units and weight (edible part unless footnotes indicate otherwise)			Water	Food Energy	Protein	FAT: Fat (Total)	FAT: Saturated (Total)
		Grams	Percent	Calories	Grams	Grams	Grams
Degermed, unenriched:							
Dry form	1 cup	138	12	500	11	2	.2
Cooked	1 cup	240	88	120	3	T	T
Crabmeat (white or king), canned, not pressed down	1 cup	135	77	135	24	3	.6
Crackers:							
Graham, plain, 2½ in. square	2 crackers	14	6	55	1	1	.3
Rye wafers, whole-grain, 1⅞ by 3½ in.	2 wafers	13	6	45	2	T	•
Saltines, made with enriched flour	4 crackers or 1 packet	11	4	50	1	1	.3
Cranberry juice cocktail, bottled, sweetened	1 cup	253	83	165	T	T	•
Cranberry sauce, sweetened, canned, strained	1 cup	277	62	405	T	1	•
Cream products, imitation (made with vegetable fat):							
Sweet:							
Creamers:							
Liquid (frozen)	1 cup	245	77	335	2	24	22.8
	1 tbsp.	15	77	20	T	1	1.4
Powdered	1 cup	94	2	515	5	33	30.6
	1 tsp.	2	2	10	T	1	.7
Whipped topping:							
Frozen	1 cup	75	50	240	1	19	16.3
	1 tbsp.	4	50	15	T	1	.9
Powdered, made with whole milk	1 cup	80	67	150	3	10	8.5
	1 tbsp.	4	67	10	T	T	.4
Pressurized	1 cup	70	60	185	1	16	13.2
	1 tbsp.	4	60	10	T	1	.8
Sour dressing (imitation sour cream) made with nonfat dry milk	1 cup	235	75	415	8	39	31.2
	1 tbsp.	12	75	20	T	2	1.6
Cream, sour	1 cup	230	71	495	7	48	30.0
	1 tbsp.	12	71	25	T	3	1.6
Cream, sweet:							
Half-and-Half (cream and milk)	1 cup	242	81	315	7	28	17.3
	1 tbsp.	15	81	20	T	2	1.1
Light, coffee, or table	1 cup	240	74	470	6	46	28.8
	1 tbsp.	15	74	30	T	3	1.8
Whipping, unwhipped (volume about double when whipped):							
Light	1 cup	239	64	700	5	74	46.2
	1 tbsp.	15	64	45	T	5	2.9
Heavy	1 cup	238	58	820	5	88	54.8
	1 tbsp.	15	58	80	T	6	3.5
Whipped topping, (pressurized)	1 cup	60	61	155	2	13	8.3
	1 tbsp.	3	61	10	T	1	.4
Cucumber slices, ⅛ in. thick (large, 2⅛ in. diam.; small, 1¾ in. diam.):							
With peel	6 large or 8 small slices	28	95	5	T	T	•
Without peel	6½ large, or 9 small pieces	28	96	5	T	T	•
Custard, baked	1 cup	265	77	305	14	15	6.8
Dandelion greens, cooked, drained	1 cup	105	90	35	2	1	•
Danish pastry (enriched flour), plain without fruit or nuts:							
Packaged ring, 12 oz.	1 ring	340	22	1,435	25	80	24.3
Round piece, about 4¼ in. diam. by 1 in.	1 pastry	65	22	275	5	15	4.7
Ounce	1 oz.	28	22	120	2	7	2.0
Dates:							
Whole, without pits	10 dates	80	23	220	2	T	•
Chopped	1 cup	178	23	490	4	1	•

Unsaturated											
Oleic	Linoleic	Carbohydrate	Calcium	Phosphorus	Iron	Potassium	Vitamin A Value	Thiamin	Riboflavin	Niacin	Ascorbic Acid
Grams	Grams	Grams	Milligrams	Milligrams	Milligrams	Milligrams	Internat'l. units	Milligrams	Milligrams	Milligrams	Milligrams
.4	.9	108	8	137	1.5	166	610	.19	.07	1.4	0
.1	.2	26	2	34	.5	38	140	.05	.02	.2	0
.4	.1	12	61	246	1.1	149	•	.11	.11	2.6	•
.5	.3	10	6	21	.5	55	0	.02	.08	.5	0
•	•	10	7	50	.5	78	0	.04	.03	.2	0
.5	.4	8	2	10	.5	13	0	.05	.05	.4	0
•	•	42	13	8	.8	25	T	.03	.03	.1	81
•	•	104	17	11	.6	83	60	.03	.03	.1	6
.3	T	28	23	157	.1	467	220	0	0	0	0
T	0	2	1	10	T	29	10	0	0	0	0
.9	T	52	21	397	.1	763	190	0	.16	0	0
T	0	1	T	8	T	16	T	0	T	0	0
1.0	.2	17	5	6	.1	14	650	0	0	0	0
.1	T	1	T	T	T	1	30	0	0	0	0
.6	.1	13	72	69	T	121	290	.02	.09	T	1
T	T	1	4	3	T	6	10	T	T	T	T
1.4	.2	11	4	13	T	13	330	0	0	0	0
.1	T	1	T	1	T	1	20	0	0	0	0
4.4	1.1	11	266	205	.1	380	20	.09	.38	.2	2
.2	.1	1	14	10	T	19	T	.01	.02	T	T
12.1	1.1	10	268	195	.1	331	1,820	.08	.34	.2	2
.6	.1	1	14	10	T	17	90	T	.07	T	T
7.0	.6	10	254	230	.2	314	260	.08	.36	.2	2
.4	T	1	16	14	T	19	20	.01	.02	T	T
11.7	1.0	9	231	192	.1	292	1,730	.08	.36	.1	2
.7	.1	1	14	12	T	18	110	T	.02	T	T
18.3	1.5	7	166	146	.1	231	2,690	.06	.30	.1	1
1.1	.1	T	10	9	T	15	170	T	.02	T	T
22.2	2.0	7	154	149	.1	179	3,500	.05	.26	.1	1
1.4	.1	T	10	9	T	11	220	T	.02	T	T
3.4	.3	7	61	54	T	88	550	.02	.04	T	0
.2	T	T	3	3	T	4	30	T	T	T	0
•	•	1	7	8	.3	45	70	.01	.01	.1	3
•	•	1	5	5	.1	45	T	.01	.01	.1	3
5.4	.7	29	297	310	1.1	387	930	.11	.50	.3	1
•	•	7	147	44	1.9	244	12,290	.14	.17	•	19
31.7	16.5	155	170	371	6.1	381	1,050	.97	1.01	8.6	T
6.1	3.2	30	33	71	1.2	73	200	.18	.19	1.7	T
2.7	1.4	13	14	31	.5	32	90	.08	.08	.7	T
•	•	58	47	50	2.4	518	40	.07	.08	1.8	0
•	•	130	105	112	5.3	1,153	90	.6	.18	3.9	0

Foods, approximate measures, units and weight (edible part unless footnotes indicate otherwise)			Nutrients in Indicated Quantity: Water	Food Energy	Protein	FAT: Fat (Total)	Saturated (Total)
		Grams	Percent	Calories	Grams	Grams	Grams
Deviled ham, canned	1 tbsp.	13	51	45	2	4	1.5
Doughnuts, made with enriched flour:							
Cake type, plain, 2½ in. diam., 1 in. high.	1 doughnut	25	24	100	1	5	1.2
Yeast-leavened, glazed, 3¾ in. diam., 1¼ in. high	1 doughnut	50	26	205	3	11	3.3
Eggnog (commercial)	1 cup	254	74	340	10	19	11.3
Eggs, large (24 oz. per dozen):							
Raw:							
Whole, without shell	1 egg	50	75	80	6	6	1.7
White	1 white	33	88	15	3	T	0
Yolk	1 yolk	17	49	65	3	6	1.7
Cooked:							
Fried in butter	1 egg	46	72	85	5	6	2.4
Hard-cooked, shell removed	1 egg	50	75	80	6	6	1.7
Poached	1 egg	50	74	80	6	6	1.7
Scrambled (milk added) in butter. Also omelet	1 egg	64	76	95	6	7	2.8
Endive, curly (including escarole), raw, small pieces	1 cup	50	93	10	1	T	•
Fats, cooking (vegetable shortenings)	1 cup	200	0	1,770	0	200	48.8
	1 tbsp.	13	0	110	0	13	3.2
Filberts (hazelnuts), chopped (about 80 kernels)	1 cup	115	6	730	14	72	5.1
Fish sticks, breaded, cooked, frozen (stick, 4 by 1 by ½ in.)	1 fish stick or 1 oz.	28	66	50	5	3	•
Frankfurter (8 per 1 lb. pkg.), cooked (reheated)	1 frankfurter	56	57	170	7	15	5.6
Fruit cocktail, canned, in heavy syrup	1 cup	255	80	195	1	T	•
Fruit-flavored sodas and Tom Collins mixer	12 fl. oz.	372	88	170	0	0	0
Gelatin dessert prepared with gelatin dessert powder and water	1 cup	240	84	140	4	0	0
Gelatin, dry	7-g. envelope	7	13	25	6	T	0
Ginger ale	12 fl. oz.	366	92	115	0	0	0
Grape drink, canned	1 cup	250	86	135	T	T	•
Grapefruit juice:							
Raw, pink, red, or white	1 cup	246	90	95	1	T	•
Canned, white:							
Unsweetened	1 cup	247	89	100	1	T	•
Sweetened	1 cup	250	86	135	1	T	•
Frozen, concentrate, unsweetened:							
Undiluted, 6 fl. oz. can	1 can	207	62	300	4	1	•
Diluted with 3 parts water by volume.	1 cup	247	89	100	1	T	•
Dehydrated crystals, prepared with water (1 lb yields about 1 gal.)	1 cup	247	90	100	1	T	•
Grapefruit:							
Raw, medium, 3¾ in. diam. (about 1 lb. 1 oz.).:							
Pink or red	½ grapefruit with peel	241	89	50	1	T	•
White	½ grapefruit with peel	241	89	45	1	T	•
Canned, sections with syrup	1 cup	254	81	180	2	T	•
Grape juice:							
Canned or bottled	1 cup	253	83	165	1	T	•

Unsaturated Oleic	*Unsaturated* Linoleic	Carbo-hydrate	Calcium	Phosphorus	Iron	Potassium	Vitamin A Value	Thiamin	Ribo-flavin	Niacin	Ascorbic Acid
Grams	Grams	Grams	Milli-grams	Milli-grams	Milli-grams	Milli-grams	Internat'l. units	Milli-grams	Milli-grams	Milli-grams	Milli-grams
1.8	.4	0	1	12	.3	•	0	.02	.01	.2	•
2.0	1.1	13	10	48	.4	23	20	.05	.05	.4	T
5.8	3.3	22	16	33	.6	34	25	.10	.10	.8	0
5.0	.6	34	330	278	.5	420	890	.09	.48	.3	4
2.0	.6	1	28	90	1.0	65	260	.04	.15	T	0
0	0	T	4	4	T	45	0	T	.09	T	0
2.1	.6	T	26	86	.9	15	310	.04	.07	T	0
2.2	.6	1	26	80	.9	58	290	.03	.13	T	0
2.0	.6	1	28	90	1.0	65	260	.04	.14	T	0
2.0	.6	1	28	90	1.0	65	260	.04	.13	T	0
2.3	.6	1	47	97	.9	85	310	.04	.16	T	0
•	•	2	41	27	.9	147	1,650	.04	.07	.3	5
88.2	48.4	0	0	0	0	0	•	0	0	0	0
5.7	3.1	0	0	0	0	0	•	0	0	0	0
55.2	7.3	19	240	388	3.9	8.0	•	.53	•	1.0	T
•	•	2	3	47	.1	•	0	.01	.02	.5	•
6.5	1.2	1	3	57	.8	•	•	.08	.11	1.4	•
•	•	50	23	31	1.0	411	360	.05	.03	1.0	5
0	0	45	•	•	•	•	0	0	0	0	0
0	0	34	•	•	•	•	•	•	•	•	•
0	0	0	•	•	•	•	•	•	•	•	•
0	0	29	•	•	•	0	0	0	0	0	0
•	•	35	8	10	.3	88	•	.03	.03	.3	(*)
•	•	23	22	37	.5	399	(**)	.10	.05	.5	93
•	•	24	20	35	1.0	400	20	.07	.05	.5	84
•	•	32	20	35	1.0	405	30	.08	.05	.5	78
•	•	72	70	124	.8	1,250	60	.29	.12	1.4	286
•	•	24	25	42	.2	420	20	.10	.04	.5	95
•	•	24	22	40	.2	412	20	.10	.05	.5	91
•	•	13	20	20	.5	166	540	.05	.02	.2	44
•	•	12	19	19	.5	159	10	.05	.02	.2	44
•	•	45	33	36	.8	343	30	.08	.05	.5	76
•	•	42	28	30	.8	293	•	.10	.05	.5	T

(*)For products with added thiamin and riboflavin but without added ascorbic acid, values in milligrams would be 0.60 for thiamin, 0.80 for riboflavin, and trace for ascorbic acid.
For products with ascorbic acid added, value varies with the bran, Consult the label.
(**)For white-fleshed varieties, value is about 20 International Units (I.U.) per cup; for red-fleshed varieties, 1,080 I.U.

						FAT	
Foods, approximate measures, units and weight (edible part unless footnotes indicate otherwise)			Water	Food Energy	Protein	Fat (Total)	Saturated (Total)
		Grams	Percent	Calories	Grams	Grams	Grams
Frozen concentrate, sweetened:							
Undiluted, 6 fl. oz. can	1 can	216	53	395	1	T	•
Diluted with 3 parts water by volume.	1 cup	250	86	135	1	T	•
Grapes, European type (adherent skin) raw:							
Thompson Seedless	10 grapes	50	81	35	T	T	•
Tokay and Emperor seeded types	10 grapes	60	81	40	T	T	•
Haddock, breaded, fried	3 oz.	85	66	140	17	5	1.4
Heart, beef, lean, braised	3 oz.	85	61	160	27	5	1.5
Honey, strained or extracted	1 tbsp.	21	17	65	T	0	0
Honeydew (with rind and seed cavity, 6½ in. diam., 5¼ lb.)	1/10 melon with rind	226	91	50	1	T	•
Ice Cream:							
Regular (about 11% fat):							
Hardened	½ gal.	1,064	61	2,155	38	115	71.3
	1 cup	133	61	270	5	14	8.9
	3 fl. oz. container	50	61	100	2	5	3.4
Soft serve (frozen custard)	1 cup	173	60	375	7	23	13.5
Rich (about 16% fat), hardened	½ gal.	1,188	59	2,805	33	190	118.3
	1 cup	148	59	350	4	24	14.7
Ice Milk:							
Hardened (about 4.3% fat)	½ gal.	1,048	69	1,470	41	45	28.1
	1 cup	131	69	185	5	6	3.5
Soft serve (about 2.6% fat)	1 cup	175	70	225	8	5	2.9
Jams and preserves	1 tbsp.	20	29	55	T	T	•
	1 packet	14	29	40	T	T	•
Jellies	1 tbsp.	18	29	50	T	T	•
	1 packet	14	29	40	T	T	•
Kale, cooked, drained:							
From raw (leaves without stems and midribs)	1 cup	110	88	45	5	1	•
From frozen (leaf style)	1 cup	130	91	40	4	1	•
Lamb, cooked:							
Chop, rib (cut 3 per lb. with bone), broiled:							
Lean and fat	3.1 oz.	89	43	360	18	32	14.8
Lean only from above item	2 oz.	57	60	120	16	6	2.5
Leg, roasted:							
Lean and fat (2 pieces, 4⅛ by 2¼ by ¼ in.)	3 oz.	85	54	235	22	16	7.3
Lean only from above item	2½ oz.	71	62	130	20	5	2.1
Shoulder, roasted:							
Lean and fat (3 pieces, 2½ by 2½ by ¼ in.)	3 oz.	85	50	285	18	23	10.8
Lean only from above item	2⅓ oz.	64	61	130	17	6	3.6
Lard	1 cup	205	0	1,850	0	205	81.0
	1 tbsp.	13	0	115	0	13	5.1
Lemonade concentrate, frozen:							
Undiluted, 6 fl. oz. can	1 can	219	49	425	T	T	•
Diluted with 4⅓ parts water by volume	1 cup	248	89	105	T	T	•
Lemon juice:							
Raw	1 cup	244	91	60	1	T	•
Canned, or bottled, unsweetened	1 cup	244	92	55	1	T	•
Frozen, single strength, unsweetened, 6 fl. oz. can	1 can	183	92	40	1	T	•
Lemon, raw, size 165, without peel and seeds (about 4 per lb. with peels and seeds)	1 lemon	74	90	20	1	T	•
Lentils, whole, cooked	1 cup	200	72	210	16	T	•

Unsaturated Oleic	Linoleic	Carbo-hydrate	Calcium	Phosphorus	Iron	Potassium	Vitamin A Value	Thiamin	Ribo-flavin	Niacin	Ascorbic Acid
Grams	Grams	Grams	Milli-grams	Milli-grams	Milli-grams	Milli-grams	Internat'l. units	Milli-grams	Milli-grams	Milli-grams	Milli-grams
•	•	100	22	32	.9	255	40	.13	.22	1.5	32
•	•	33	8	10	.3	85	10	.05	.08	.5	10
•	•	9	6	10	.2	87	50	.03	.02	.2	2
•	•	10	7	11	.2	99	60	.03	.02	.2	2
2.2	1.2	5	34	210	1.0	296	•	.03	.06	2.7	2
1.1	.6	1	5	154	5.0	197	20	.21	1.04	6.5	1
0	0	17	1	1	.1	11	0	T	.01	.1	T
•	•	11	21	24	.6	374	60	.06	.04	.9	34
28.8	2.6	254	1,406	1,075	1.0	2,052	4,340	.42	2.63	1.1	6
3.6	.3	32	176	134	.1	257	540	.05	.33	.1	1
1.4	.1	12	66	51	T	96	200	.02	.12	.1	T
5.9	.6	38	236	199	.4	338	790	.08	.45	.2	1
47.8	4.3	256	1,213	927	.8	1,771	7,200	.36	2.27	.9	5
6.0	.5	32	151	115	.1	221	900	.04	.28	.1	1
11.3	1.0	232	1,409	1,035	1.5	2,117	1,710	.61	2.78	.9	6
1.4	.1	29	176	129	.1	265	210	.08	.35	.1	1
1.2	.1	38	274	202	.3	412	180	.12	.54	.2	1
•	•	14	4	2	.2	18	T	T	.01	T	T
•	•	10	3	1	.1	12	T	T	T	T	T
•	•	13	4	1	.3	14	T	T	.01	T	1
•	•	10	3	1	.2	11	T	T	T	T	1
•	•	7	206	64	1.8	243	9,130	.11	.20	1.8	102
•	•	7	157	62	1.3	251	10,660	.08	.20	.9	49
12.1	1.2	0	8	139	1.0	200	•	.11	.19	4.1	•
2.1	.2	0	6	121	1.1	174	•	.09	.15	3.4	•
6.0	.6	0	9	177	1.4	241	•	.13	.23	4.7	•
1.8	.2	0	9	169	1.4	227	•	.12	.21	4.4	•
8.8	.9	0	9	146	1.0	206	•	.11	.20	4.0	•
2.3	.2	0	8	140	1.0	193	•	.10	.18	3.7	•
83.8	20.5	0	0	0	0	0	0	0	0	0	0
5.3	1.3	0	0	0	0	0	0	0	0	0	0
•	•	112	9	13	.4	153	40	.05	.06	.7	66
•	•	28	2	3	.1	40	10	.01	.02	.2	17
•	•	20	17	24	.5	344	50	.07	.02	.2	112
•	•	19	17	24	.5	344	50	.07	.02	.2	102
•	•	13	13	16	.5	258	40	.05	.02	.2	81
•	•	6	19	12	.4	102	10	.03	.01	.1	39
•	•	39	50	238	4.2	498	40	.14	.12	1.2	0

Foods, approximate measures, units and weight (edible part unless footnotes indicate otherwise)			Water	Food Energy	Protein	FAT: Fat (Total)	FAT: Saturated (Total)
		Grams	Percent	Calories	Grams	Grams	Grams
Lettuce, raw:							
Butterhead, as Boston types:							
Head, 5 in. diam.	1 head	220	95	25	2	T	•
Leaves	1 outer or 2 inner or 3 heart leaves	14	95	T	T	T	•
Crisphead, as Iceberg:							
Head, 6 in. diam.	1 head	567	96	70	5	1	•
Wedge, ¼ of head	1 wedge	135	96	20	1	T	•
Pieces, chopped or shredded	1 cup	55	96	5	T	T	•
Looseleaf (bunching varieties including romain or cos), chopped or shredded peices	1 cup	55	94	10	1	T	•
Limeade concentrate, frozen:							
Undiluted, 6 fl. oz. can	1 can	218	50	410	T	T	•
Diluted with 4⅓ parts water by volume	1 cup	247	89	100	T	T	•
Lime juice:							
Raw	1 cup	246	90	65	1	T	•
Canned, unsweetened	1 cup	246	90	65	1	T	•
Liquor, gin, rum, vodka, whisky:							
80 proof	1½ f. oz. jigger	42	67	95	•	•	0
86 proof	1½ fl. oz. jigger	42	64	105	•	•	0
90 proof	1½ fl. oz. jigger	42	62	110	•	•	0
Liver, beef, fried (slice, 6½ by 2⅜ by ⅜ in)	3 oz.	85	56	195	22	9	2.5
Macaroni, enriched, cooked (cut lengths, elbows, shells):							
Firm stage (hot)	1 cup	130	64	190	7	1	•
Tender stage:							
Cold macaroni	1 cup	105	73	115	4	T	•
Hot macaroni	1 cup	140	73	155	5	1	•
Macaroni (enriched) and Cheese:							
Canned	1 cup	240	80	230	9	10	4.2
From home recipe (served hot)	1 cup	200	58	430	17	22	8.9
Malted Milk, hom-prepared with 1 cup of whole milk and 2 to 3 heaping tsp. of malted milk powder (about ¾ oz.):							
Chocolate	1 cup of milk plus ¾ oz. of powder	265	81	235	9	9	5.5
Natural	1 cup of milk plus ¾ oz. of powder	265	81	235	11	10	6.0
Margarine:							
Regular (1 brick or 4 sticks per lb.):							
Stick (½ cup)	1 stick	113	16	815	1	92	16.7
Tablespoon (about ⅛ stick)	1 tbsp.	14	16	100	T	12	2.1
Pat (1 in. square, ⅓ in. high; 90 per lb.).	1 pat	5	16	35	T	4	.7
Soft, 2 8-oz. containers per lb.	1 container	227	16	1,635	1	184	32.5
Whipped (6 sticks per lb):							
Stick (½ cup)	1 stick	76	16	545	T	61	11.2
Tablespoon (about ⅛ stick)	1 tbsp.	9	16	70	T	8	1.4
Meat, potted (beef, chicken, turkey), canned	1 tbsp.	13	61	30	2	2	•
Milk:							
Fluid:							
Whole (3.3% fat)	1 cup	244	88	150	8	8	5.1
Lowfat (2%):							
No milk solids added	1 cup	244	89	120	8	5	2.9
Milk solids added:							
Label claims less than 10 g. of protein per cup	1 cup	245	89	125	9	5	2.9

Unsaturated											
Oleic	Linoleic	Carbo-hydrate	Calcium	Phosphorus	Iron	Potassium	Vitamin A Value	Thiamin	Ribo-flavin	Niacin	Ascorbic Acid
Grams	Grams	Grams	Milli-grams	Milli-grams	Milli-grams	Milli-grams	Internat'l. units	Milli-grams	Milli-grams	Milli-grams	Milli-grams
•	•	4	57	42	3.3	430	1,580	.10	.10	.5	13
•	•	T	5	4	.3	40	150	.01	.01	T	1
•	•	16	108	118	2.7	943	1,780	.32	.32	1.6	32
•	•	4	27	30	.7	236	450	.08	.08	.4	8
•	•	2	11	12	.3	96	180	.03	.03	.2	3
•	•	2	37	14	.8	145	1,050	.03	.04	.2	10
•	•	108	11	13	.2	129	T	.02	.02	.2	26
•	•	27	3	3	T	32	T	T	T	T	6
•	•	22	22	27	.5	256	20	.05	.02	.2	79
•	•	22	22	27	.5	256	20	.05	.02	.2	52
0	0	T	•	•	•	1	•	•	•	•	•
0	0	T	•	•	•	1	•	•	•	•	•
0	0	T	•	•	•	1	•	•	•	•	•
3.5	.9	5	9	405	7.5	323	45,390	.22	3.56	14.0	23
•	•	39	14	85	1.4	103	0	.23	.13	1.8	0
•	•	24	8	53	.9	64	0	.15	.08	1.2	0
•	•	32	11	70	1.3	85	0	.20	.11	1.5	0
3.1	1.4	26	199	182	1.0	139	260	.12	.24	1.0	T
8.8	2.9	40	362	322	1.8	240	860	.20	.40	1.8	T
•	•	29	304	265	.5	500	330	.14	.43	.7	2
•	•	27	347	307	.3	529	380	.20	.54	1.3	2
42.9	24.9	T	27	26	.2	29	3,750	.01	.04	T	0
5.3	3.1	T	3	3	T	4	470	T	T	T	0
1.9	1.1	T	1	1	T	1	170	T	T	T	0
71.5	65.4	T	53	52	.4	59	7,500	.01	.08	.1	0
28.7	16.7	T	18	17	.1	20	2,500	T	.03	T	0
3.6	2.1	T	2	2	T	2	310	T	T	T	0
•	•	0	•	•	•	•	•	T	.03	.2	•
2.1	.2	11	291	228	.1	370	310	.09	.40	.2	2
1.2	.1	12	297	232	.1	377	500	.10	.40	.2	2
1.2	.1	12	313	245	.1	397	500	.10	.42	.2	2

Foods, approximate measures, units and weight (edible part unless footnotes indicate otherwise)			Water	Food Energy	Protein	FAT: Fat (Total)	FAT: Saturated (Total)
		Grams	Percent	Calories	Grams	Grams	Grams
Label claims 10 g. or more of protein per cup (Protein fortified)	1 cup	246	88	135	10	5	3.0
Lowfat (1%):							
No milk solids added	1 cup	244	90	100	8	3	1.6
Milk solids added:							
Label claim less than 10 g. of protein per cup	1 cup	245	90	105	9	2	1.5
Label claims 10 g. or more of protein per cup (protein fortified)	1 cup	246	89	120	10	3	1.8
Milk:							
Nonfat (skim):							
No milk solids added	1 cup	245	91	85	8	T	.3
Milk solids added:							
Label claim less than 10 g. of protein per cup	1 cup	245	90	90	9	1	.4
Label claim 10 g. or more of protein per cup (protein fortified)	1 cup	246	89	100	10	1	.4
Buttermilk	1 cup	245	90	100	8	2	1.3
Canned:							
Evaporated, unsweetened:							
Whole milk	1 cup	252	74	340	17	19	11.6
Skim milk	1 cup	255	79	200	19	1	.3
Sweetened, condensed	1 cup	306	27	980	24	27	16.8
Dried:							
Buttermilk	1 cup	120	3	465	41	7	4.3
Nonfat, instant:							
Envelope, net wt., 3¼ oz.	1 envelope	91	4	325	32	1	.4
Cup	1 cup	68	4	245	24	T	.3
Muffins made with enriched flour:							
From home receipe:							
Blueberry, 2⅜ in. diam., 1½ in. high	1 muffin	40	39	110	3	4	1.1
Bran	1 muffin	40	35	105	3	4	1.2
Corn (enriched degermed cornmeal and flour), 2⅜ in. diam., 1½ in. high	1 muffin	40	33	125	3	4	1.2
Plain, 3 in. diam., 1½ in. high	1 muffin	40	38	120	3	4	1.0
From mix, egg, milk:							
Corn, 2⅜ in. diam, 1 ½ in. high	1 muffin	40	30	130	3	4	1.2
Mushrooms, raw sliced or chopped	1 cup	70	90	20	2	T	•
Mustard, prepared yellow	1 tsp. or individual serving pouch or cup	5	80	5	T	T	•
Mustard greens, without stems and midribs, cooked, drained	1 cup	140	93	30	3	1	•
Noodles, chowmein, canned	1 cup	45	1	220	6	11	•
Noodles (egg), enriched, cooked	1 cup	160	71	200	7	2	•
Ocean perch, breaded, fried	1 fillet	85	59	195	16	11	2.7
Oils, salad or cooking:							
Corn	1 cup	218	0	1,925	0	218	27.7
	1 tbsp.	14	0	120	0	14	1.7
Olive	1 cup	216	0	1,910	0	216	30.7
	1 tbsp.	14	0	120	0	14	1.9
Peanut	1 cup	216	0	1,910	0	216	37.4
	1 tbsp.	14	0	120	0	14	2.3
Safflower	1 cup	218	0	1,925	0	218	20.5
	1 tbsp.	14	0	120	0	14	1.3

Nutrients in Indicated Quantity

Unsaturated Oleic	*Unsaturated* Linoleic	Carbo-hydrate	Calcium	Phosphorus	Iron	Potassium	Vitamin A Value	Thiamin	Ribo-flavin	Niacin	Ascorbic Acid
Grams	Grams	Grams	Milli-grams	Milli-grams	Milli-grams	Milli-grams	Internat'l. units	Milli-grams	Milli-grams	Milli-grams	Milli-grams
1.2	.1	14	352	276	.1	447	500	.11	.48	.2	3
.7	.1	12	300	235	.1	381	500	.10	.41	.2	2
.6	.1	12	313	245	.1	397	500	.10	.42	.2	2
.7	.1	14	349	273	.1	444	500	.11	.47	.2	3
.1	T	12	302	247	.1	406	500	.09	.37	.2	2
.1	T	12	316	255	.1	418	500	.10	.43	.2	2
.1	T	14	352	275	.1	446	500	.11	.48	.2	3
.5	T	12	285	219	.1	371	80	.08	.38	.1	2
5.3	.4	25	657	510	.5	764	610	.12	.80	.5	5
.1	T	29	738	497	.7	845	1,000	.11	.79	.4	3
6.7	.7	166	868	775	.6	1;136	1,000	.28	1.27	.6	8
1.7	.2	59	1,421	1,119	.4	1,910	260	.47	1.90	1.1	7
.1	T	47	1,120	896	.3	1,552	2,160	.38	1.59	.8	5
.1	T	35	837	670	.2	1,160	1,160	.28	1.19	.6	4
1.4	.7	17	34	53	.6	46	90	.09	.10	.7	T
1.4	.8	17	57	162	1.5	172	90	.07	.10	1.7	T
1.6	.9	19	42	68	.7	54	120	.10	.10	.7	T
1.7	1.0	17	42	60	.6	50	40	.09	.12	.9	T
1.7	.9	20	96	152	.6	44	100	.08	.09	.7	T
•	•	3	4	81	.6	290	T	.07	.32	2.9	2
•	•	T	4	4	.1	7	•	•	•	•	•
•	•	6	193	45	2.5	308	8,120	.11	.20	.8	67
•	•	26	•	•	•	•	•	•	•	•	•
•	•	37	16	94	1.4	70	110	.22	.13	1.9	0
4.4	2.3	6	28	192	1.1	242	•	.10	.10	1.6	•
53.6	125.1	0	0	0	0	0	•	0	0	0	0
3.3	7.8	0	0	0	0	0	•	0	0	0	0
154.4	17.7	0	0	0	0	0	•	0	0	0	0
9.7	1.1	0	0	0	0	0	•	0	0	0	0
98.5	67.0	0	0	0	0	0	•	0	0	0	0
6.2	4.2	0	0	0	0	0	•	0	0	0	0
25.9	159.8	0	0	0	0	0	•	0	0	0	0
1.6	10.0	0	0	0	0	0	•	0	0	0	0

Foods, approximate measures, units and weight (edible part unless footnotes indicate otherwise)			Water	Food Energy	Protein	FAT: Fat (Total)	FAT: Saturated (Total)
		Grams	Percent	Calories	Grams	Grams	Grams
Soybean oil, hydrogenated	1 cup	218	0	1,925	0	218	31.8
(partially hardened)	1 tbsp.	14	0	120	0	14	2.0
Soybean-cottonseed oil blend,	1 cup	218	0	1,925	0	218	38.2
hydrogenated	1 tbsp	14	0	120	0	14	2.4
Okra pods, 3 by ⅝ in. cooked	10 pods	106	91	30	2	T	•
Olives, pickled, canned:							
Green	4 medium or 3 extra large or 2 giant	16	78	15	T	2	.2
Ripe, Mission	3 small or 2 large	10	73	15	T	2	.2
Onions:							
Mature:							
Raw:							
Chopped	1 cup	170	89	65	3	T	•
Sliced	1 cup	115	89	45	2	T	•
Cooked (whole or sliced), drained	1 cup	210	92	60	3	T	•
Young green, bulb (⅜ in. diam) and white portion of top	6 onions	30	88	15	T	T	•
Orange and grapefruit juice:							
Frozen concentrate:							
Undiluted, 6 fl. oz. can	1 can	210	59	330	4	1	•
Diluted with 3 parts water by volume	1 cup	248	88	110	1	T	•
Orange juice:							
Raw, all varieties	1 cup	248	88	110	2	T	•
Canned, unsweetened	1 cup	249	87	120	2	T	•
Frozen concentrate:							
Undiluted, 6 fl. oz. can	1 can	213	55	360	5	T	•
Diluted with 3 parts water by volume	1 cup	249	87	120	2	T	•
Dehydrated crystals, prepared with water (1 lb. yields about 1 gal.)	1 cup	248	88	115	1	T	•
Oranges, all commercial varieties, raw:							
Whole, 2⅝ in. diam., without peel and seeds (about 2½ per lb. with peel and seeds)	1 orange	131	86	65	1	T	•
Sections without membranes	1 cup	180	86	90	2	T	•
Oysters, raw, meat only (13-19 medium Selects)	1 cup	240	85	160	20	4	1.3
Pancakes, (4 in. diam.):							
Buckwheat, made from mix (with buckwheat and enriched flours) egg and milk added	1 cake	27	58	55	2	2	.8
Plain:							
Made from home recipe using enriched flour	1 cake	27	50	60	2	2	.5
Made from mix with enriched flour, egg and milk added	1 cake	27	51	60	2	2	.7
Papayas, raw, ½ in. cubes	1 cup	140	89	55	1	T	•
Parsley, raw, chopped	1 tbsp.	4	85	T	T	T	•
Parsnips, cooked (diced or 2 in. lengths)	1 cup	155	82	100	2	1	•
Peaches:							
Raw:							
Whole, 2½ in. diam., peeled, pitted (about 4 per lb. with peels and pits).	1 peach	100	89	40	1	T	•
Sliced	1 cup	170	89	65	1	T	•
Canned, yellow-fleshed, solids and liquid (halves or slices):							
Syrup pack	1 cup	256	79	200	1	T	•
Water pack	1 cup	244	91	75	1	T	•

Unsaturated											
Oleic	Linoleic	Carbo-hydrate	Calcium	Phosphorus	Iron	Potassium	Vitamin A Value	Thiamin	Ribo-flavin	Niacin	Ascorbic Acid
Grams	Grams	Grams	Milli-grams	Milli-grams	Milli-grams	Milli-grams	Internat'l. units	Milli-grams	Milli-grams	Milli-grams	Milli-grams
93.1	75.6	0	0	0	0	0	•	0	0	0	0
5.8	4.7	0	0	0	0	0	•	0	0	0	0
63.0	99.6	0	0	0	0	0	•	0	0	0	0
3.9	6.2	0	0	0	0	0	•	0	0	0	0
•	•	6	98	43	.5	184	520	.14	.19	1.0	21
1.2	.1	T	8	2	.2	7	40	•	•	•	•
1.2	.1	T	9	1	.1	2	10	T	T	•	•
•	•	15	46	61	.9	267	T	.05	.07	.3	17
•	•	10	31	41	.6	181	T	.03	.05	.2	12
•	•	14	50	61	.8	231	T	.06	.06	.4	15
•	•	3	12	12	.2	69	T	.02	.01	.1	8
•	•	78	61	99	.8	1,308	800	.48	.06	2.3	302
•	•	26	20	32	.2	439	270	.15	.02	.7	102
•	•	26	27	42	.5	496	500	.22	.07	1.0	124
•	•	28	25	45	1.0	496	500	.17	.05	.7	100
•	•	87	75	126	.9	1,500	1,620	.68	.11	2.8	360
•	•	29	25	42	.2	503	540	.23	.03	.9	120
•	•	27	25	40	.5	518	500	.20	.07	1.0	109
•	•	16	54	26	.5	263	260	.13	.05	.5	66
•	•	22	74	36	.7	360	360	.18	.07	.7	90
.2	.1	8	226	343	13.2	290	740	.34	.43	6.0	•
.9	.4	6	59	91	.4	66	60	.04	.05	.2	T
.8	.5	9	27	38	.4	33	30	.06	.07	.5	T
.7	.3	9	58	70	.3	42	70	.04	.06	.2	T
•	•	14	28	22	.4	328	2,450	.06	.06	.4	78
•	•	T	7	2	.2	25	300	T	.01	T	6
•	•	23	70	96	.9	587	50	.11	.12	.2	16
•	•	10	9	19	.5	202	1,330	.02	.05	1.0	7
•	•	16	15	32	.9	343	2,260	.03	.09	1.7	12
•	•	51	10	31	.8	333	1,100	.03	.05	1.5	8
•	•	20	10	32	.7	334	1,100	.02	.07	1.5	7

Foods, approximate measures, units and weight (edible part unless footnotes indicate otherwise)			Water	Food Energy	Protein	FAT: Fat (Total)	FAT: Saturated (Total)
		Grams	Percent	Calories	Grams	Grams	Grams
Dried:							
Uncooked	1 cup	160	25	420	5	1	•
Cooked, unsweetened, halves and juice.	1 cup	250	77	205	3	1	•
Frozen, sliced, sweetened:							
10 oz. container	1 container	284	77	250	1	T	•
Cup	1 cup	250	77	220	1	T	•
Peanuts, roasted in oil, salted (whole, halves, chopped)	1 cup	144	2	840	37	72	13.7
Peanut butter	1 tbsp.	16	2	95	4	8	1.5
Pears:							
Raw, with skin, cored:							
Bartlett, 2½ in. diam. (about 2½ per lb. with cores and stems)	1 pear	164	83	100	1	1	•
Bosc, 2½ in. diam. (about 3 per lb. with cores and stems)	1 pear	141	83	85	1	1	•
D'Anjou, 3 in. diam. (about 2 per lb. with cores and stems)	1 pear	200	83	120	1	1	•
Canned, solids and liquid, syrup pack, heavy (halves or slices)	1 cup	255	80	195	1	1	•
Peas, green:							
Canned:							
Whole, drained solids	1 cup	170	77	150	8	1	•
Strained (baby food)	1 oz. (1¾ to 2 tbsp.)	28	86	15	1	T	•
Frozen, cooked, drained	1 cup	160	82	110	8	T	•
Peas, split, dry, cooked	1 cup	200	70	230	16	1	•
Pecans, chopped or pieces (about 120 large halves)	1 cup	118	3	810	11	84	7.2
Peppers, hot, red, without seeds, dried (Ground chili powder, added seasonings)	1 tsp.	2	9	5	T	T	•
Peppers, sweet (about 5 per lb. whole), stems and seeds removed:							
Raw	1 pod	74	93	15	1	T	•
Cooked, boiled, drained	1 pod	73	95	15	1	T	•
Pickles, cucumber:							
Dill, medium, whole, 3¾ in. long, 1¼ in. diam.	1 pickle	65	93	5	T	T	•
Fresh-pack, slices 1½ in. diam., ¼ in. thick	2 slices	15	79	10	T	T	•
Sweet, gherkin, small, whole, about 2½ in. long, ¾ in. diam.	1 pickle	15	61	20	T	T	•
Relish, finely chopped, sweet	1 tbsp.	15	63	20	T	T	•
Pies, piecrust made with enriched flour, vegetable shortening, (9 in. diam.):							
Apple:							
Whole	1 pie	945	48	2,420	21	105	27.0
Sector, ⅐ of pie	1 sector	135	48	345	3	15	3.9
Banana Cream:							
Whole	1 pie	910	54	2,010	41	85	26.7
Sector, ⅐ of pie	1 sector	130	54	285	6	12	3.8
Blueberry:							
Whole	1 pie	945	51	2,285	23	102	24.8
Sector, ⅐ of pie	1 sector	135	51	325	3	15	3.5
Cherry:							
Whole	1 pie	945	47	2,465	25	107	28.2
Sector, ⅐ of pie	1 sector	135	47	350	4	15	4.0

Unsaturated Oleic	*Unsaturated* Linoleic	Carbo-hydrate	Calcium	Phosphorus	Iron	Potassium	Vitamin A Value	Thiamin	Ribo-flavin	Niacin	Ascorbic Acid
Grams	Grams	Grams	Milli-grams	Milli-grams	Milli-grams	Milli-grams	Internat'l. units	Milli-grams	Milli-grams	Milli-grams	Milli-grams
•	•	109	77	187	9.6	1,520	6,240	.02	.30	8.5	29
•	•	54	38	93	4.8	743	3,050	.01	.15	3.8	5
•	•	64	11	37	1.4	352	1,850	.03	.11	2.0	116
•	•	57	10	33	1.3	310	1,630	.03	.10	1.8	103
33.0	20.7	27	107	577	3.0	971	•	.46	.19	24.8	0
3.7	2.3	3	9	61	.3	100	•	.02	.02	2.4	0
•	•	25	13	18	.5	213	30	.03	.07	.2	7
•	•	22	11	16	.4	83	30	.03	.06	.1	6
•	•	31	16	22	.6	260	40	.04	.08	.2	8
•	•	50	13	18	.5	214	10	.03	.05	.3	3
•	•	29	44	129	3.2	163	1,170	.15	.10	1.4	14
•	•	3	3	18	.3	28	140	.02	.03	.3	3
•	•	19	30	138	3.0	216	960	.43	.14	2.7	21
•	•	42	22	178	3.4	592	80	.30	.18	1.8	•
50.5	20.0	17	86	341	2.8	712	150	1.01	.15	1.1	2
•	•	1	5	4	.3	20	1,300	T	.02	.2	T
•	•	4	7	16	.5	157	310	.06	.06	.4	94
•	•	3	7	12	.4	109	310	.05	.05	.4	70
•	•	1	17	14	.7	130	70	T	.01	T	4
•	•	3	5	4	.3	•	20	T	T	T	1
•	•	5	2	2	.2	•	10	T	T	T	1
•	•	5	3	2	.1	•	•	•	•	•	•
44.5	25.2	360	76	208	6.6	756	280	1.06	.79	9.3	9
6.4	3.6	51	11	30	.9	108	40	.15	.11	1.3	2
33.2	16.2	279	601	746	7.3	1,847	2,280	.77	1.51	7.0	9
4.7	2.3	40	86	107	1.0	264	330	.11	.22	1.0	1
43.7	25.1	330	104	217	9.5	614	280	1.03	.80	10.0	28
6.2	3.6	47	15	31	1.4	88	40	.15	.11	1.4	4
45.0	25.3	363	132	236	6.6	992	4,160	1.09	.84	9.8	T
6.4	3.6	52	19	34	.9	142	590	.16	.12	1.4	T

Foods, approximate measures, units and weight (edible part unless footnotes indicate otherwise)			Water	Food Energy	Protein	Fat (Total)	Saturated (Total)
		Grams	Percent	Calories	Grams	Grams	Grams
Pies-Continued							
Custard:							
Whole	1 pie	910	58	1,985	56	101	33.9
Sector, 1/7 of pie	1 sector	130	58	285	8	14	4.8
Lemon meringue:							
Whole	1 pie	840	47	2,140	31	86	26.1
Sector, 1/7 of pie	1 sector	120	47	305	4	12	3.7
Mince:							
Whole	1 pie	945	43	2,560	24	109	28.0
Sector, 1/7 of pie	1 sector	135	43	365	3	16	4.0
Peach:							
Whole	1 pie	945	48	2,410	24	101	24.8
Sector, 1/7 of pie	1 sector	135	48	345	3	14	3.5
Pecan:							
Whole	1 pie	825	20	3,450	42	189	27.8
Sector, 1/7 of pie	1 sector	118	20	495	6	27	4.0
Pumpkin:							
Whole	1 pie	910	59	1,920	36	102	37.4
Sector, 1/7 of pie	1 sector	130	59	275	5	15	5.4
Piecrust (home recipe) made with enriched flour and vegetable shortening, baked	1 pie shell, 9 in. diam.	180	15	900	11	60	14.8
Piecrust mix with enriched flour and vegetable shortening, 10 oz. pkg. prepared and baked	Piecrust for 2-crust pie, 9 in. diam.	320	19	1,485	20	93	22.7
Pineapple:							
Raw, diced	1 cup	155	85	80	1	T	•
Canned, heavy syrup pack, solids and liquid:							
Crushed, chunks, tidbits	1 cup	255	80	190	1	T	•
Slices and liquid:							
Large	1 slice; 2¼ tbsp. liquid	105	80	80	T	T	•
Medium	1 slice; 1¼ tbsp. liquid	58	80	45	T	T	•
Pineapple juice, unsweetened, canned	1 cup	250	86	140	1	T	•
Pizza (cheese) baked, 4¾ in. sector; 1/8 of 12 in. diam. pie	1 sector	60	45	145	6	4	1.7
Plums:							
Raw, without pits:							
Japanese and hybrid (2⅛ in. diam., about 6½ per lb. with pits)	1 plum	66	87	30	T	T	•
Prune-type (1½ in. diam., about 15 per lb. with pits)	1 plum	28	79	20	T	T	•
Canned, heavy syrup pack (Italian prune) with pits and liquid:							
Cup	1 cup	272	77	215	1	T	•
Portion	3 plums; 2¾ tbsp. liquid	140	77	110	1	T	•
Popcorn, popped:							
Plain, large kernel	1 cup	6	4	25	1	T	T
With oil (coconut) and salt added, large kernel	1 cup	9	3	40	1	2	1.5
Sugar coated	1 cup	35	4	135	1	1	.5
Popsicle, 3 fl. oz. size	1 popsicle	95	80	70	0	0	0

Unsaturated Oleic	Linoleic	Carbo-hydrate	Calcium	Phosphorus	Iron	Potassium	Vitamin A Value	Thiamin	Ribo-flavin	Niacin	Ascorbic Acid
Grams	Grams	Grams	Milli-grams	Milli-grams	Milli-grams	Milli-grams	Internat'l. units	Milli-grams	Milli-grams	Milli-grams	Milli-grams
38.5	17.5	213	874	1,028	8.2	1,247	2,090	.79	1.92	5.6	0
5.5	2.5	30	125	147	1.2	178	300	.11	.27	.8	0
33.8	16.4	317	118	412	6.7	420	1,430	.61	.84	5.2	25
4.8	2.3	45	17	59	1.0	60	200	.09	.12	.7	4
45.9	25.2	389	265	359	13.3	1,682	20	.96	.86	9.8	9
6.6	3.6	56	38	51	1.9	240	T	.14	.12	1.4	1
43.7	25.1	361	95	274	8.5	1,408	6,900	1.04	.97	14.0	28
6.2	3.6	52	14	39	1.2	201	990	.15	.14	2.0	4
101.0	44.2	423	388	850	25.6	1,015	1,320	1.80	.95	6.9	T
14.4	6.3	61	55	122	3.7	145	190	.26	.14	1.0	T
37.5	16.6	223	464	628	7.3	1,456	22,480	.78	1.27	7.0	T
5.4	2.4	32	66	90	1.0	208	3,210	.11	.18	1.0	T
26.1	14.9	79	25	90	3.1	89	0	.47	.40	5.0	0
39.7	23.4	141	131	272	6.1	179	0	1.07	.79	9.9	0
•	•	21	26	12	.8	226	110	.14	.05	.3	26
•	•	49	28	13	.8	245	130	.20	.05	.5	18
•	•	20	12	5	.3	101	50	.08	.02	.2	7
•	•	11	6	3	.2	56	30	.05	.01	.1	4
•	•	34	38	23	.8	373	130	.13	.05	.5	80
1.5	.6	22	86	89	1.1	67	230	.16	.18	1.6	4
•	•	8	8	12	.3	112	160	.02	.02	.3	4
•	•	6	3	5	.1	48	80	.01	.01	.1	1
•	•	56	23	26	2.3	367	3,130	.05	.05	1.0	5
•	•	29	12	13	1.2	189	1,610	.03	.03	.5	3
.1	.2	5	1	17	.2	•	•	•	.01	.1	0
.2	.2	5	1	19	.2	•	•	•	.01	.2	0
.2	.4	30	2	47	.5	•	•	•	.02	.4	0
0	0	18	0	•	T	•	0	0	0	0	0

Foods, approximate measures, units and weight (edible part unless footnotes indicate otherwise)			Water	Food Energy	Protein	FAT: Fat (Total)	FAT: Saturated (Total)
		Grams	Percent	Calories	Grams	Grams	Grams
Pork, cured, cooked:							
Ham, light cure, lean and fat, roasted (2 pieces, 4⅛ by 2¼ by ¼ in.)	3 oz.	85	54	245	18	19	6.8
Luncheon meat:							
Boiled ham, slice (8 per 8 oz. pkg.)	1 oz.	28	59	65	5	5	1.7
Canned, spiced or unspiced:							
Slice, approx. 3 by 2 by ½ in.	1 slice	60	55	175	9	15	5.4
Chop, loin (cut 3 per lb. with bone), broiled:							
Lean and fat	2¾ oz.	78	42	305	19	25	8.9
Lean only from above item	2 oz.	56	53	150	17	9	3.1
Roast, oven cooked, no liquid added:							
Lean and fat (piece, 2½ by 2½ by ¾ in.)	3 oz.	85	46	310	21	24	8.7
Lean only from above item	2½ oz.	68	55	175	20	10	3.5
Shoulder cut, simmered:							
Lean and fat (3 pieces, 2½ by 2½ by ¼ in.)	3 oz.	85	46	320	20	26	9.3
Lean only from above item	2¼ oz.	63	60	135	18	6	2.2
Pork link (16 per 1 lb. pkg.), cooked	1 link	13	35	60	2	6	2.1
Potato chips, 1¾ by 2½ in oval cross section	10 chips	20	2	115	1	8	2.1
Potatoes, cooked:							
Baked, peeled after baking (about 2 per lb. raw)	1 potato	156	75	145	4	T	•
Boiled (about 3 per lb. raw):							
Peeled after boiling	1 potato	137	80	105	3	T	•
Peeled before boiling	1 potato	135	83	90	3	T	•
French-fried, strip, 2 to 3½ in long:							
Prepared from raw	10 strips	50	45	135	2	7	1.7
Frozen, oven heated	10 strips	50	53	110	2	4	1.1
Hashed brown, prepared from frozen	1 cup	155	56	345	3	18	4.6
Mashed, prepared from—							
Raw:							
Milk added	1 cup	210	83	135	4	2	.7
Milk and butter added	1 cup	210	80	195	4	9	5.6
Dehydrated flakes (without milk) water, milk, butter and salt added	1 cup	210	79	195	4	7	3.6
Potato salad, made with cooked salad dressing	1 cup	250	76	250	7	7	2.0
Pretzels, made with enriched flour:							
Dutch, twisted, 2¾ by 2⅝ in.	1 pretzel	16	5	60	2	1	•
Thin, twisted, 3¼ by 2¼ by ¼ in.	10 pretzels	60	5	235	6	3	•
Stick, 2¼ in. long	10 pretzels	3	5	10	T	T	•
Prune juice, canned or bottled	1 cup	256	80	195	1	T	•
Prunes, dried: "softenized," with pits:							
Uncooked	4 extra large or 5 large prunes	49	28	110	1	T	•
Cooked, unsweetened, all sizes, fruit and liquid	1 cup	250	66	255	2	1	•
Puddings:							
From home recipe:							
Starch base:							
Chocolate	1 cup	260	66	385	8	12	7.6
Vanilla (blancmange)	1 cup	255	76	285	9	10	6.2
Tapioca cream	1 cup	165	72	220	8	8	4.1
From mix (chocolate) and milk:							
Regular (cooked)	1 cup	260	70	320	9	8	4.3
Instant	1 cup	260	69	325	8	7	3.6

Unsaturated Oleic	Linoleic	Carbo- hydrate	Calcium	Phosphorus	Iron	Potassium	Vitamin A Value	Thiamin	Ribo- flavin	Niacin	Ascorbic Acid
Grams	Grams	Grams	Milli- grams	Milli- grams	Milli- grams	Milli- grams	Internat'l. units	Milli- grams	Milli- grams	Milli- grams	Milli- grams
7.9	1.7	0	8	146	2.2	199	0	.40	.15	3.1	•
2.0	.4	0	3	47	.8	•	0	.12	.04	.7	•
6.7	1.0	1	5	65	1.3	133	0	.19	.13	1.8	•
10.4	2.2	0	9	209	2.7	216	0	.75	.22	4.5	•
3.6	.8	0	7	181	2.2	192	0	.63	.18	3.8	•
10.2	2.2	0	9	218	2.7	233	0	.78	.22	4.8	•
4.1	.8	0	9	211	2.6	224	0	.73	.21	4.4	•
10.9	2.3	0	9	118	2.6	158	0	.46	.21	4.1	•
2.6	.6	0	8	111	2.3	146	0	.42	.19	3.7	•
2.4	.5	T	1	21	.3	35	0	.10	.04	.5	•
1.4	4.0	10	8	28	.4	226	T	.04	.01	1.0	3
•	•	33	14	101	1.1	782	T	.15	.07	2.7	31
•	•	23	10	72	.8	556	T	.12	.05	2.0	22
•	•	20	8	57	.7	385	T	.12	.05	1.6	22
1.2	3.3	18	8	56	.7	427	T	.07	.04	1.6	11
.8	2.1	17	5	43	.9	326	T	.07	.01	1.3	11
3.2	9.0	45	28	78	1.9	439	T	.11	.03	1.6	12
.4	T	27	50	103	.8	548	40	.17	.11	2.1	21
2.3	.2	26	50	101	.8	525	360	.17	.11	2.1	19
2.1	.2	30	65	99	.6	601	270	.08	.18	1.9	11
2.7	1.3	41	80	160	1.5	798	350	.20	.18	2.8	28
•	•	12	4	21	.2	21	0	.05	.04	.7	0
•	•	46	13	79	.9	78	0	.20	.15	2.5	0
•	•	2	1	4	T	4	0	.01	.01	.1	0
•	•	49	36	51	1.8	602	•	.03	.03	1.0	5
•	•	29	22	34	1.7	298	690	.04	.07	.7	1
•	•	67	51	79	3.8	695	1,590	.07	.15	1.5	2
3.3	.3	67	250	255	1.3	445	390	.05	.36	.3	1
2.5	.2	41	298	232	T	352	410	.08	.41	.3	2
2.5	.5	28	173	180	.7	223	480	.07	.30	.2	2
2.6	.2	59	265	247	.8	354	340	.05	.39	.3	2
2.2	.3	63	374	237	1.3	335	340	.08	.39	.3	2

Foods, approximate measures, units and weight (edible part unless footnotes indicate otherwise)			Water	Food Energy	Protein	Fat (Total)	Saturated (Total)
		Grams	Percent	Calories	Grams	Grams	Grams
Pumpkin and squash kernels, dry, hulled	1 cup	140	4	775	41	65	11.8
Pumpkin, canned	1 cup	245	90	80	2	1	•
Radishes, raw (prepackaged) stem ends, rootlets cut off	4 radishes	18	95	5	T	T	•
Raisins, seedless:							
Cup, not pressed down	1 cup	145	18	420	4	T	•
Packet, ½ oz. (1½ tbsp.)	1 packet	14	18	40	T	T	•
Raspberries, red:							
Raw, capped, whole	1 cup	123	84	70	1	1	•
Frozen, sweetened, 10 oz. container	1 container	284	74	280	2	1	•
Rhubarb, cooked, added sugar:							
From raw	1 cup	270	63	380	1	T	•
From frozen, sweetened	1 cup	270	63	385	1	1	•
Rice, white, enriched:							
Instant, ready-to-serve, hot	1 cup	165	73	180	4	T	T
Long grain:							
Raw	1 cup	185	12	670	12	1	.2
Cooked, served hot	1 cup	205	73	225	4	T	.1
Parboiled:							
Raw	1 cup	185	10	685	14	1	.2
Cooked, served hot	1 cup	175	73	185	4	T	.1
Rolls, enriched:							
Commercial:							
Brown-and-serve (12 per 12 oz. pkg), browned	1 roll	26	27	85	2	2	.4
Cloverleaf or pan, 2½ in. diam., 2 in. high	1 roll	28	31	85	2	2	.4
Frankfurter and hamburger (8 per 11½ oz. pkg)	1 roll	40	31	120	3	2	.5
Hard, 3¾ in. diam., 2 in. high	1 roll	50	25	155	5	2	.4
Hoagie or submarine, 11½ by 3 by 2½ in.	1 roll	135	31	390	12	4	.9
From home recipe:							
Cloverleaf, 2½ in. diam., 2 in. high	1 roll	35	26	120	3	3	.8
Root beer	12 fl. oz.	370	90	150	0	0	0
Salad dressings:							
Commercial:							
Blue cheese:							
Regular	1 tbsp.	15	32	75	1	8	1.6
Low calorie (5 Cal. per tsp.)	1 tbsp.	16	84	10	T	1	.5
French:							
Regular	1 tbsp.	16	39	65	T	6	1.1
Low calorie (5 Cal. per tsp.)	1 tbsp.	16	77	15	T	1	.1
Italian:							
Regular	1 tbsp.	15	28	85	T	9	1.6
Low calorie (2 Cal. per tsp.)	1 tbsp.	15	90	10	T	1	.1
Mayonnaise	1 tbsp.	14	15	100	T	11	2.0
Mayonnaise type:							
Regular	1 tbsp.	15	41	65	T	6	1.1
Low calorie (8 Cal. per tsp.)	1 tbsp.	16	81	20	T	2	.4
Tartar sauce, regular	1 tbsp.	14	34	75	T	8	1.5
Thousand Island:							
Regular	1 tbsp.	16	32	80	T	8	1.4
Low calorie (10 Cal. per tsp.)	1 tbsp.	15	68	25	T	2	.4

Unsaturated											
Oleic	Linoleic	Carbo-hydrate	Calcium	Phosphorus	Iron	Potassium	Vitamin A Value	Thiamin	Ribo-flavin	Niacin	Ascorbic Acid
Grams	Grams	Grams	Milli-grams	Milli-grams	Milli-grams	Milli-grams	Internat'l. units	Milli-grams	Milli-grams	Milli-grams	Milli-grams
23.5	27.5	21	71	1,062	15.7	1,386	100	.34	.27	3.4	•
•	•	19	61	64	1.0	588	15,680	.07	.12	1.5	12
•	•	1	5	6	.2	58	T	.01	.01	.1	5
•	•	112	90	146	5.1	1,106	30	.16	.12	.7	1
•	•	11	9	14	.5	107	T	.02	.01	.1	T
•	•	17	27	27	1.1	207	160	.04	.11	1.1	31
•	•	70	37	48	1.7	284	200	.06	.17	1.7	60
•	•	97	211	41	1.6	548	220	.05	.14	.8	16
•	•	98	211	32	1.9	475	190	.05	.11	.5	16
T	T	40	5	31	1.3	•	0	.21	(*)	1.7	0
.2	.2	149	44	174	5.4	170	0	.81	.06	6.5	0
.1	.1	50	21	57	1.8	57	0	.23	.02	2.1	0
.1	.2	150	111	370	5.4	278	0	.81	.07	6.5	0
.1	.1	41	33	100	1.4	75	0	.19	.02	2.1	0
.7	.5	14	20	23	.5	25	T	.10	.06	.9	T
.6	.4	15	21	24	.5	27	T	.11	.07	.9	T
.8	.6	21	30	34	.8	38	T	.16	.10	1.3	T
.6	.5	30	24	46	1.2	49	T	.20	.12	1.7	T
1.4	1.4	75	58	115	3.0	122	T	.54	.32	4.5	T
1.1	.7	20	16	36	.7	41	30	.12	.12	1.2	T
0	0	39	•	•	•	0	0	0	0	0	0
1.7	3.8	1	12	11	T	6	30	T	.02	T	T
.3	T	1	10	8	T	5	30	T	.01	T	T
1.3	3.2	3	2	2	.1	13	•	•	•	•	•
.1	.4	2	2	2	.1	13	•	•	•	•	•
1.9	4.7	1	2	1	T	2	T	T	T	T	•
.1	.4	T	T	1	T	2	T	T	T	T	•
2.4	5.6	T	3	4	.1	5	40	T	.01	T	•
1.4	3.2	2	2	4	T	1	30	T	T	T	•
.4	1.0	2	3	4	T	1	40	T	T	T	•
1.8	4.1	1	3	4	.1	11	30	T	T	T	T
1.7	4.0	2	2	3	.1	18	50	T	T	T	T
.4	1.0	2	2	3	.1	17	50	T	T	T	T

(*) Product may or may not be enriched with riboflavin. Consult the label.

Foods, approximate measures, units and weight (edible part unless footnotes indicate otherwise)			Water	Food Energy	Protein	FAT: Fat (Total)	FAT: Saturated (Total)
		Grams	Percent	Calories	Grams	Grams	Grams
From home recipe:							
Cooked type	1 tbsp.	16	68	25	1	2	.5
Salami:							
Dry type, slice (12 per 4 oz. pkg)	1 slice	10	30	45	2	4	1.6
Cooked type, slice (8 per 8 oz. pkg)	1 slice	28	51	90	5	7	3.1
Salmon, pink, canned, solids and liquid	3 oz.	85	71	120	17	5	.9
Sardines, Atlantic, canned in oil, drained solids	3 oz.	85	62	175	20	9	3.0
Sauerkraut, canned, solids and liquid	1 cup	235	93	40	2	T	•
Scallops, frozen, breaded, fried, reheated	6 scallops	90	60	175	16	8	•
Shad, baked with butter or margarine, bacon	3 oz.	85	64	170	20	10	•
Shakes, thick:							
Chocolate, container, net wt., 10½ oz.	1 container	300	72	355	9	8	5.0
Vanilla, container, net wt., 11 oz.	1 container	313	74	350	12	9	5.9
Shrimp:							
Canned meat	3 oz.	85	70	100	21	1	.1
French fried	3 oz.	85	57	190	17	9	2.3
Soups:							
Canned, condensed:							
Prepared with equal volume of milk:							
Cream of chicken	1 cup	245	85	180	7	10	4.2
Cream of mushroom	1 cup	245	83	215	7	14	5.4
Tomato	1 cup	250	84	175	7	7	3.4
Prepared with equal volume of water:							
Bean with pork	1 cup	250	84	170	8	6	1.2
Beef broth, bouillon, consomme	1 cup	240	96	30	5	0	0
Beef noodle	1 cup	240	93	65	4	3	.6
Clam chowder, Manhattan type, (with tomatoes, without milk)	1 cup	245	92	80	2	3	.5
Cream of chicken	1 cup	240	92	95	3	6	1.6
Cream of mushroom	1 cup	240	90	135	2	10	2.6
Minestrone	1 cup	245	90	105	5	3	.7
Split pea	1 cup	245	85	145	9	3	1.1
Tomato	1 cup	245	91	90	2	3	.5
Vegetable beef	1 cup	245	92	80	5	2	•
Vegetarian	1 cup	245	92	80	2	2	•
Dehydrated:							
Bouillon cube, ½ in.	1 cube	4	4	5	1	T	•
Mixes:							
Unprepared:							
Onion	1½ oz. pkg.	43	3	150	6	5	1.1
Prepared with water:							
Chicken noodle	1 cup	240	95	55	2	1	•
Onion	1 cup	240	96	35	1	1	•
Tomato vegetable with noodles	1 cup	240	93	65	1	1	•
Spaghetti, enriched, cooked:							
Firm stage, "al dente," served hot	1 cup	130	64	190	7	1	•
Tender stage, served hot	1 cup	140	73	155	5	1	•
Spaghetti (enriched) in tomato sauce with cheese:							
From home recipe	1 cup	250	77	260	9	9	2.0
Canned	1 cup	250	80	190	6	2	.5
Spaghetti (enriched) with meat balls and tomato sauce:							
From home recipe	1 cup	248	70	330	19	12	3.3
Canned	1 cup	250	78	260	12	10	2.2

Unsaturated Oleic	*Unsaturated* Linoleic	Carbo-hydrate	Calcium	Phosphorus	Iron	Potassium	Vitamin A Value	Thiamin	Ribo-flavin	Niacin	Ascorbic Acid
Grams	Grams	Grams	Milli-grams	Milli-grams	Milli-grams	Milli-grams	Internat'l. units	Milli-grams	Milli-grams	Milli-grams	Milli-grams
.6	.3	2	14	15	.1	19	80	.01	.03	T	T
1.6	.1	T	1	28	.4	•	•	.04	.03	.5	•
3.0	.2	T	3	57	.7	•	•	.07	.07	1.2	•
.8	.1	0	167	243	.7	307	60	.03	.16	6.8	•
2.5	.5	0	372	424	2.5	502	190	.02	.17	4.6	•
•	•	9	85	42	1.2	329	120	.07	.09	.5	33
•	•	9	•	•	•	•	•	•	•	•	•
•	•	0	20	266	.5	320	30	.11	.22	7.3	•
2.0	.2	63	396	378	.9	672	260	.14	.67	.4	0
2.4	.2	56	457	361	.3	572	360	.09	.61	.5	0
.1	T	1	98	224	2.6	104	50	.01	.03	1.5	•
3.7	2.0	9	61	162	1.7	195	•	.03	.07	2.3	•
3.6	1.3	15	172	152	.5	260	610	.05	.27	.7	2
2.9	4.6	16	191	169	.5	279	250	.05	.34	.7	1
1.7	1.0	23	168	155	.8	418	1,200	.10	.25	1.3	15
1.8	2.4	22	63	128	2.3	395	650	.13	.08	1.0	3
0	0	3	T	31	.5	130	T	T	.02	1.2	•
.7	.8	7	7	48	1.0	77	50	.05	.07	1.0	T
.4	1.3	12	34	47	1.0	184	880	.02	.02	1.0	•
2.3	1.1	8	24	34	.5	79	410	.02	.05	.5	T
1.7	4.5	10	41	50	.5	98	70	.02	.12	.7	T
.9	1.3	14	37	59	1.0	314	2,350	.07	.05	1.0	•
1.2	.4	21	29	149	1.5	270	440	.25	.15	1.5	1
.5	1.0	16	15	34	.7	230	1,000	.05	.05	1.2	12
•	•	10	12	49	.7	162	2,700	.05	.05	1.0	•
•	•	13	20	39	1.0	172	2,940	.05	.05	1.0	•
•	•	T	•	•	•	4	•	•	•	•	•
2.3	1.0	23	42	49	.6	238	30	.05	.03	.3	6
•	•	8	7	19	.2	19	50	.07	.05	.5	T
•	•	6	10	12	.2	58	T	T	T	T	2
•	•	12	7	19	.2	29	480	.05	.02	.5	5
•	•	39	14	85	1.4	103	0	.23	.13	1.8	0
•	•	32	11	70	1.3	85	0	.20	.11	1.5	0
5.4	.7	37	80	135	2.3	408	1,080	.25	.18	2.3	13
.3	.4	39	40	88	2.8	303	930	.35	.28	4.5	10
6.3	.9	39	124	236	3.7	665	1,590	.25	.30	4.0	22
3.3	3.9	29	53	113	3.3	245	1,000	.15	.18	2.3	5

Foods, approximate measures, units and weight (edible part unless footnotes indicate otherwise)			Water	Food Energy	Protein	FAT: Fat (Total)	FAT: Saturated (Total)
		Grams	Percent	Calories	Grams	Grams	Grams
Spinach:							
Raw, chopped	1 cup	55	91	15	2	T	•
Cooked, drained:							
From raw	1 cup	180	92	40	5	1	•
From frozen:							
Chopped	1 cup	205	92	45	6	1	•
Leaf	1 cup	190	92	45	6	1	•
Canned, drained solids	1 cup	205	91	50	6	1	•
Squash, cooked:							
Summer (all varieties, diced, drained	1 cup	210	96	30	2	T	•
Winter (all varieties), baked, mashed	1 cup	205	81	130	4	1	•
Strawberries:							
Raw, whole berries, capped	1 cup	149	90	55	1	1	•
Frozen, sweetened:							
Sliced, 10 oz. container	1 container	284	71	310	1	1	•
Whole, 1 lb. container (about 1¾ cups).	1 container	454	76	415	2	1	•
Sunflower seeds, dry, hulled	1 cup	145	5	810	35	69	8.2
Sugars:							
Brown, pressed down	1 cup	220	2	820	0	0	0
White:							
Granulated	1 cup	200	1	770	0	0	0
	1 tbsp.	12	1	45	0	0	0
	1 packet	6	1	23	0	0	0
Powdered, sifted, spooned into cup	1 cup	100	1	385	0	0	0
Sweet potatoes:							
Cooked (raw, 5 by 2 in.; about 2½ per lb.):							
Baked in skin, peeled	1 potato	114	64	160	2	1	•
Boiled in skin, peeled	1 potato	151	71	170	3	1	•
Candied, 2½ by 2 in. piece	1 potato	105	60	175	1	3	2.0
Canned:							
Solid pack (mashed)	1 cup	255	72	275	5	1	•
Vacuum pack, piece 2¾ by 1 in.	1 piece	40	72	45	1	T	•
Syrups:							
Chocolate-flavored syrup or topping:							
Thin type	1 fl. oz. or 2 tbsp.	38	32	90	1	1	.5
Fudge type	1 fl. oz. or 2 tbsp.	38	25	125	2	5	3.1
Molasses, cane:							
Light (first extraction	1 tbsp.	20	24	50	•	•	•
Blackstrap (third extraction)	1 tbsp.	20	24	45	•	•	•
Sorghum	1 tbsp.	21	23	55	•	•	•
Table blends, chiefly corn, light and dark.	1 tbsp.	21	24	60	0	0	0
Tangerine, raw, 2⅜ in. diam., size 176, without peel (about 4 per lb. with peels and seeds)	1 tangerine	86	87	40	1	T	•
Tangerine juice, canned, sweetened	1 cup	249	87	125	1	T	•
Toaster pastries	1 pastry	50	12	200	3	6	•
Tomato catsup	1 cup	273	69	290	5	1	•
	1 tbsp.	15	69	15	T	T	•
Tomatoes:							
Raw, 2⅗ in. diam. (3 per 12 oz. pkg)	1 tomato	135	94	25	1	T	•
Canned, solids and liquid	1 cup	241	94	50	2	T	•
Tomato juice, canned:							
Cup	1 cup	243	94	45	2	T	•
Glass (6 fl. oz.)	1 glass	182	94	35	2	T	•
Tuna, canned in oil, drained solids	3 oz.	85	61	170	24	7	1.7

Unsaturated Oleic	Linoleic	Carbo-hydrate	Calcium	Phosphorus	Iron	Potassium	Vitamin A Value	Thiamin	Ribo-flavin	Niacin	Ascorbic Acid
Grams	Grams	Grams	Milli-grams	Milli-grams	Milli-grams	Milli-grams	Internat'l. units	Milli-grams	Milli-grams	Milli-grams	Milli-grams
•	•	2	51	28	1.7	259	4,460	.06	.11	.3	28
•	•	6	167	68	4.0	583	14,580	.13	.25	.9	50
•	•	8	232	90	4.3	683	16,200	.14	.31	.8	39
•	•	7	200	84	4.8	688	15,390	.15	.27	1.0	53
•	•	7	242	53	5.3	513	16,400	.04	.25	.6	29
•	•	7	53	53	.8	296	820	.11	.17	1.7	21
•	•	32	57	98	1.6	945	8,610	.10	.27	1.4	27
•	•	13	31	31	1.5	244	90	.04	.10	.9	88
•	•	79	40	48	2.0	318	90	.06	.17	1.4	151
•	•	107	59	73	2.7	472	140	.09	.27	2.3	249
13.7	43.2	29	174	1,214	10.3	1,334	70	2.84	.33	7.8	•
0	0	212	187	42	7.5	757	0	.02	.07	.4	0
0	0	199	0	0	.2	6	0	0	0	0	0
0	0	12	0	0	T	T	0	0	0	0	0
0	0	6	0	0	T	T	0	0	0	0	0
0	0	100	0	0	.1	3	0	0	0	0	0
•	•	37	46	66	1.0	342	9,230	.10	.08	.8	25
•	•	40	48	71	1.1	367	11,940	.14	.09	.9	26
.8	.1	36	39	45	.9	200	6,620	.06	.04	.4	11
•	•	63	64	105	2.0	510	19,890	.13	.10	1.5	36
•	•	10	10	16	.3	80	3,120	.02	.02	.2	6
.3	T	24	6	35	.6	106	T	.01	.03	.2	0
1.6	.1	20	48	60	.5	107	60	.02	.08	.2	T
•	•	13	33	9	.9	183	•	.01	.01	T	•
•	•	11	137	17	3.2	585	•	.02	.04	.4	•
•	•	14	35	5	2.6	•	•	•	.02	T	•
0	0	15	9	3	.8	1	0	0	0	0	0
•	•	10	34	15	.3	108	360	.05	.02	.1	27
•	•	30	44	35	.5	440	1,040	.15	.05	.2	54
•	•	36	54	67	1.9	74	500	.16	.17	2.1	(*)
•	•	69	60	137	2.2	991	3,820	.25	.19	4.4	41
•	•	4	3	8	.1	54	210	.01	.01	.2	2
•	•	6	16	33	.6	300	1,110	.07	.05	.9	28
•	•	10	14	46	1.2	523	2,170	.12	.07	1.7	41
•	•	10	17	44	2.2	552	1,940	.12	.07	1.9	39
•	•	8	13	33	1.6	413	1,460	.09	.05	1.5	29
1.7	.7	0	7	199	1.6	•	70	.04	.10	10.1	•

(*)Value varies with the brand. Consult the label.

Foods, approximate measures, units and weight (edible part unless footnotes indicate otherwise)			Water	Food Energy	Protein	FAT: Fat (Total)	FAT: Saturated (Total)
		Grams	Percent	Calories	Grams	Grams	Grams
Tuna salad	1 cup	205	70	350	30	22	4.3
Turkey, roasted, flesh without skin:							
Dark meat, piece, 2½ by 1⅝ by ¼ in.	4 pieces	85	61	175	26	7	2.1
Light meat, piece, 4 by 2 by ¼ in.	2 pieces	85	62	150	28	3	.9
Light and dark meat:							
Chopped or diced	1 cup	140	61	265	44	9	2.5
Pieces (1 slice white meat, 4 by 2 by ¼ in. with 2 slices dark meat, 2½ by 1⅝ by ¼ in.)	3 pieces	85	61	160	27	5	1.5
Turnip greens, cooked, drained:							
From raw (leaves and stems)	1 cup	145	94	30	3	T	•
From frozen (chopped)	1 cup	165	93	40	4	T	•
Turnips, cooked, diced	1 cup	155	94	35	1	T	•
Veal, medium fat, cooked, bone removed:							
Cutlet (4⅛ by 2¼ by ½ in.), braised or broiled	3 oz.	85	60	185	23	9	4.0
Rib (2 pieces, 4⅛ by 2¼ by ¼ in.), roasted.	3 oz.	85	55	230	23	14	6.1
Vegetables, mixed, frozen, cooked	1 cup	182	83	115	6	1	•
Vienna sausage (7 per 4 oz. can)	1 sausage	16	63	40	2	3	1.2
Vinegar, cider	1 tbsp.	15	94	T	T	0	0
Waffles, made with enriched flour, 7 in diam.:							
From home recipe	1 waffle	75	41	210	7	7	2.3
From mix, egg and milk added	1 waffle	75	42	205	7	8	2.8
Walnuts:							
Black:							
Chopped or broken kernels	1 cup	125	3	785	26	74	6.3
Ground (finely)	1 cup	80	3	500	16	47	4.0
Watermelon, raw, 4 by 8 in wedge with rind and seeds (1/16 of 32⅔ lb. melon, 10 by 16 in.)	1 wedge with rind and seeds	926	93	110	2	1	•
Wheat flours:							
All-purpose or family flour, enriched:							
Sifted, spooned	1 cup	115	12	420	12	1	.2
Unsifted, spooned	1 cup	125	12	455	13	1	.2
Cake or pastry flour, enriched, sifted, spooned	1 cup	96	12	350	7	1	.1
Self-rising, enriched, unsifted, spooned	1 cup	125	12	440	12	1	.2
Whole wheat, from hard wheats, stirred	1 cup	120	12	400	16	2	.4
White sauce, medium, with enriched flour	1 cup	250	73	405	10	31	19.3
Wines:							
Dessert	3½ fl. oz. glass	103	77	140	T	0	0
Table	3½ fl. oz. glass	102	86	85	T	0	0
Yeast:							
Baker's, dry, active	1 pkg.	7	5	20	3	T	•
Brewer's, dry	1 tbsp.	8	5	25	3	T	•
Yogurt:							
With added milk solids:							
Made with lowfat milk:							
Fruit flavored	1 container, net wt. 8 oz.	227	75	230	10	3	1.8
Plain	1 container, net wt. 8 oz.	227	85	145	12	4	2.3
Made with nonfat milk	1 container, net wt. 8 oz.	227	85	125	13	T	.3
Without added milk solids:							
Made with whole milk	1 container, net wt. 8 oz.	227	88	140	8	7	4.8

Unsaturated Oleic	*Unsaturated* Linoleic	Carbo- hydrate	Calcium	Phosphorus	Iron	Potassium	Vitamin A Value	Thiamin	Ribo- flavin	Niacin	Ascorbic Acid
Grams	Grams	Grams	Milli- grams	Milli- grams	Milli- grams	Milli- grams	Internat'l. units	Milli- grams	Milli- grams	Milli- grams	Milli- grams
6.3	6.7	7	41	291	2.7	•	590	.08	.23	10.3	2
1.5	1.5	0	•	•	2.0	338	•	.03	.20	3.6	•
.6	.7	0	•	•	1.0	349	•	.04	.12	9.4	•
1.7	1.8	0	11	351	2.5	514	•	.07	.25	10.8	•
1.0	1.1	0	7	213	1.5	312	•	.04	.15	6.5	•
•	•	5	252	49	1.5	•	8,270	.15	.33	.7	68
•	•	6	195	64	2.6	246	11,390	.08	.15	.7	31
•	•	8	54	37	.6	291	T	.06	.08	.5	34
3.4	.4	0	9	196	2.7	258	•	.06	.21	4.6	•
5.1	.6	0	10	211	2.9	259	•	.11	.26	6.6	•
•	•	24	46	115	2.4	348	9,010	.22	.13	2.0	15
1.4	.2	T	1	24	.3	•	•	.01	.02	.4	•
0	0	1	1	1	.1	15	•	•	•	•	•
2.8	1.4	28	85	130	1.3	109	250	.17	.23	1.4	T
2.9	1.2	27	179	257	1.0	146	170	.14	.22	.9	T
13.3	45.7	19	T	713	7.5	575	380	.28	.14	.9	•
8.5	29.2	12	T	456	4.8	368	240	.18	.09	.6	•
•	•	27	30	43	2.1	426	2,510	.13	.13	.9	30
.1	.5	88	18	100	3.3	109	0	.74	.46	6.1	0
.1	.5	95	20	109	3.6	119	0	.80	.50	6.6	0
.1	.3	76	16	70	2.8	91	0	.61	.38	5.1	0
.1	.5	93	331	583	3.6	•	0	.80	.50	6.6	0
.2	1.0	85	49	446	4.0	444	0	.66	.14	5.2	0
7.8	.8	22	288	233	.5	348	1,150	.12	.43	.7	2
0	0	8	8	•	•	77	•	.01	.02	.2	•
0	0	4	9	10	.4	94	•	T	.01	.1	•
•	•	3	3	90	1.1	140	T	.16	.38	2.6	T
•	•	3	17	140	1.4	152	T	1.25	.34	3.0	T
.6	.1	42	343	269	.2	439	120	.08	.40	.2	1
.8	.1	16	415	326	.2	531	150	.10	.49	.3	2
.1	T	17	452	355	.2	579	20	.11	.53	.3	2
1.7	.1	11	274	215	.1	351	280	.07	.32	.2	1

O

OAK MANNA

Also GAZ. A white substance produced by the European turkey oak tree *(Quercus cerris)*, oak manna is used to make a sweet called *gazenjubeen*.

OATMEAL

This is meal made from ground or rolled oats after the grain has been cleaned and the husks removed. In the United States over 90 percent of the oat crop is used for fodder, with the remainder—mostly of the "rolled oats" kind (the husked, sterilized grains are crushed into flakes by heated steel rolls)—going for breakfast cereals and for use in baking. Oats thrive in cool, high altitudes, where they invade and supplant wheat. In Scotland a popular dish is "brose," raw oatmeal mixed quickly with boiling water or broth. If the mixture is thickened and is boiled longer, it becomes "porridge." Oatmeal is best served hot, with milk and sugar. It absorbs salt readily. Norwegian *flat brod* is made of ground oats mixed with potatoes or pea-meal and baked on a hot griddle.

See also: **Oats.**

OATS

A cereal grain, *Avena sativa*, with more protein and fat than most others, it is a hardy plant that flourishes in climates that are too cold, wet, or warm for other grains.

Dr. Samuel Johnson, in his famous *Dictionary* of 1755, defined it as, "A grain which in England is generally given to horses, but in Scotland supports the people."

One of the earliest grains cultivated in Europe, oats played a key role in the three-crop rotation system, a breakthrough in medieval agriculture, and proved to be an excellent food for horses. It hastened their replacement of the ox in plowing. The Scots used it in oatcakes, an early unleavened bread, and in porridge.

In the United States, it is used principally as fodder but makes its appearance in the human diet as **oatmeal,** or rolled oats, a breakfast food.

OBA

See **Dika Nut.**

OCA

Also OCCA, OKA, ULLUCO. The edible tuber of a trailing South American perennial herb, *Oxalis tuberosa*, oca is much cultivated in Colombia, Peru and Bolivia. The tubers are round or kidney-shaped, 2½ to 3½ inches across, with reddish skin and a white pulp. They are too acidic to eat fresh. The natives age them in the sun for two weeks or more. This treatment renders them sweet and palatable, and they may be cooked and eaten like potatoes. If left to age longer, they shrivel and achieve the consistency of a dried fig and may be eaten raw.

The oca was transplanted in England in 1829, and grows well there, particularly in Wales. The plant produces a crop within four months of planting. Hence it grows well in northern summers.

The oca grows wild in French forests, and the tubers have found a place in classical cuisine. They are boiled in salted water, and may be served fried or in gravy. They make an excellent soup called *puree peruvienne*. The stems of the oca are cooked and eaten like rhubarb.

Another South American plant, the *ulluco (Ullucus tuberosus)* produces similar tubers. The leaves of both of these plants make first-class cooked greens.

OCHOCOA

The seeds of this West African tree, *Ochocoa gaboni*, are used as a condiment.

OCTOPUS

This eight-armed sea creature, much like the **cuttlefish** or **squid,** is most esteemed as food in Japan and the Mediterranean area. The octopus is a cephalopod, with a definite head, large eyes and a hard "beak" at the center of its suckered tentacles. It can change its

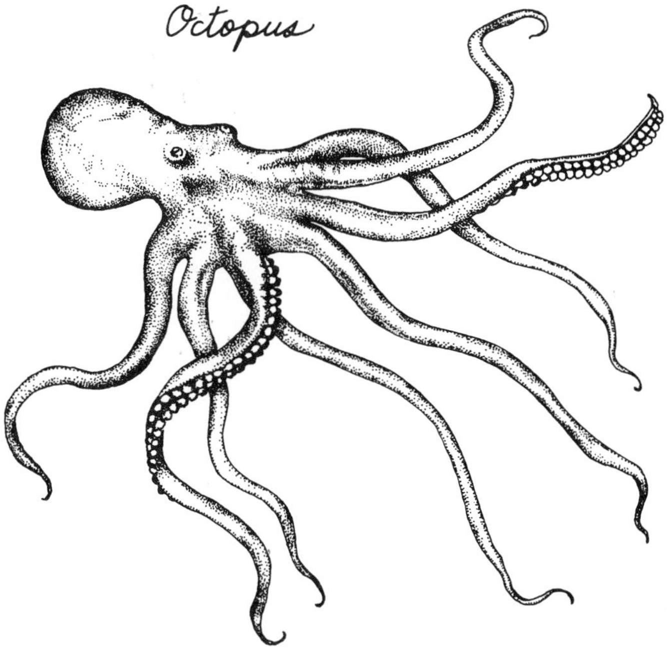

color at will to blend in with its surroundings, and when endangered squirts out a cloud of dark brown fluid to cover its escape.

The Atlantic octopus *(Octopus vulgaris)* is the preferred food species in France and Italy. It rarely exceeds three feet in length. The octopus is cleaned and prepared for cooking by turning the head inside out and detaching the ink sacs and internal organs. The flesh is then beaten until tender. Alternatively, fishermen of the Mediterranean beat it against a rock while it is still alive to achieve the same tenderizing effect. It is cut into pieces and usually deep-fried, although fancier cooking methods include Provence style (sauteed in oil and onions, then simmered in water, white wine, and seasoned with garlic and *bouquet garni)*, marinated Toulon style and flambeed *a la nicoise*.

In the Pacific, another small octopus *(O. hongkongensis)* is the one most often eaten. Hawaiians eat it raw, after cutting it into bite-sized pieces and mixing it with limu seaweed, grated onion and crushed red pepper. The Japanese boil or fry it.

The ancient Romans were fond of octopus and believed it to have an aphrodisiac effect.

ODARA PEAR

An African fruit related to the **star apple,** the odara pear *(Chrysophyllum africanum)* is a tropical species with a pleasantly acidic taste and a skin the color of apricot. It is popular in Nigeria.

OFFAL

See **Variety Meats.**

OGEECHEE LIME

This is the small, tart fruit of a North American gum tree, *Nyssa ogeche*, which is a member of the tupelo genus. The ogeechee is red and somewhat resembles an olive. It grows profusely along the banks of the Ogeechee River in southeastern Georgia. A chutney-like relish is made from the ogeechee and produced commercially in Savannah, Georgia. The formula for this relish originated in colonial times.

OIL

Edible oil is a liquid form of fat and, for cooking purposes, is generally derived from vegetables and nuts. Soluble in alcohol but not water, kitchen oil is used chiefly as a medium for frying, as an ingredient in pastry and cakes or as an ingredient in sauces and salad dressings. Some of the best known edible oils are almond, coconut, corn, cottonseed, olive, palm, peanut, poppyseed, rapeseed, safflower, sesame seed, soybean, sunflower and walnut. For a discussion of saturated vs. unsaturated fats in oil, see **Fat.**

An essential, or volatile, oil is the natural juice of a plant possessing its characteristic odor. It is extracted by distillation and used as a flavoring agent. Examples are clove oil, coffee oil, neroli oil (orange blossom), etc.

OILFISH

Also ESCOLAR. A large, deepwater fish, *Ruvettus pretiosus*, found in tropical and temperate seas worldwide, it resembles the mackerel and reaches a length of six feet or more. Its long, cylindrical body is an overall violet or purplish brown. The oilfish may be prepared and cooked like **mackerel,** but many people are put off by the excessive oiliness of its flesh. The oil, moreover, is said to have such a purgative effect that the fish has been nicknamed "castor-oil fish." The oilfish can weigh as much as 100 pounds.

OJEN

An anise-flavored, distilled spirit made in Spain, it has a rather dry flavor and is drunk as an aperitif and refresher, usually mixed with water. This mixture produces a drink with a cloudy, opalescent color. *Ojen* is similar to the French **pastis,** the Italian *anesone*, the Greek **ouzo** and the Turkish **raki.**

OKA CHEESE

This semisoft to soft Canadian cheese is produced by Trappist monks at Oka, Quebec. It is similar to **Port du Salut.**

OKARI

These edible nuts of the ornamental tree *Terminalia okari*, found in Papua and New Britain, are fairly large (three inches long by three-fourths inch in diameter), and fine-flavored. The okari is related to the **myrobalan.**

OKGUE

Also CREEPING FIG. Yellow, pear-shaped fruit of a creeping vine found in Japan, Taiwan and China, the okgue *(Ficus pumila)* reaches a length of two inches and is used to make jellies.

OKOLEHAO

A Hawaiian whiskey, known also as Oke, is distilled from the fermented mash of ti root, a variety of the taro plant. Ti roots are rich in fructose and were first used to produce a liquor in 1790 by William Stevenson, an Australian. He fermented the mash in the bottom of a canoe and improvised a still using a ship's cooking pot with a calabash for a lid and a gun barrel for a coil.

Two varieties are produced: Crystal clear and Golden Oke. Okolehao is not aged but filtered through charcoal after distillation. It has an unusual smoky flavor and aroma and is bottled at 80 proof. It is drunk straight, or mixed in highballs.

OKRA

Okra

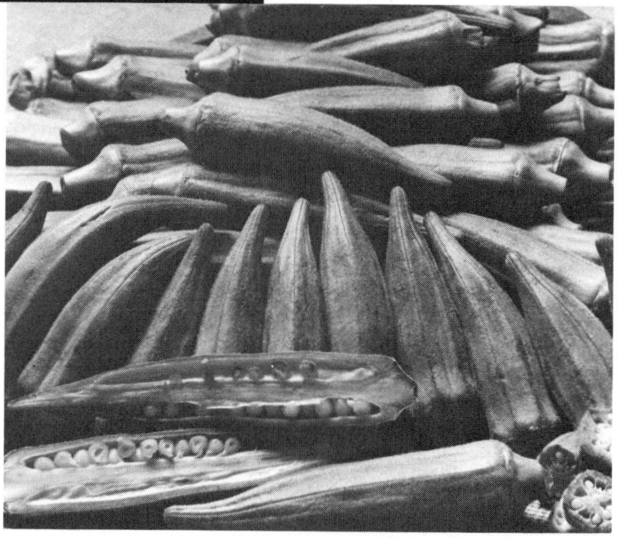

The okra plant *(Hibiscus esculentus)* is cultivated mainly for its sticky, furry pods, which find their chief use in the United States as a thickener in soups and gumbo. The home of okra is believed to be Africa, where in Angola it was called *ngumbo*. It was brought to the Western Hemisphere by slaves, who used it in a stew adapted from one made by native Americans in the southeastern United States. Okra gradually lost the name "gumbo," which was switched to the stew. The original thickener for the stew, which okra replaced, was file powder (dried sassafras leaves). It has been retained in some recipes, although they too are called "gumbo."

Okra is a large herbaceous plant, growing from two to eight feet high. The pods are ridged along their length, which runs two to nine inches. The pods are harvested unripe to avoid their becoming fibrous and indigestible. They are generally cut across the width into slices, whose ridges give them the look of small gear-wheels with seeds embedded in the center. Their taste is slightly tart, but pleasant. Apart from the Southeast, okra has received little acceptance in the United States, and is not often seen as a fresh vegetable. It is available frozen or canned, however. In the Western Hemisphere, it is most widely accepted in the West Indies, where it is the basis of callaloo, a thick stew or soup.

Okra was never popular in Europe, except in Spain and the Balkans, where historically Arab influence has been felt. It is relished in Greece, Egypt and other Middle Eastern countries, where it is called *bamyah* or *bamieh*. Not only the pods, but the leaves and young shoots are widely eaten throughout tropical Africa. In India, the pods are eaten fresh and in curries. They are pickled in the Middle East.

OLD HEIDELBERG

A soft surface-ripened American cheese made of cow's milk in Illinois, it is similar to **Liederkranz.**

OLDWIFE

A deep-bodied and brightly colored fish of southern Australian waters, the oldwife *(Enoplosus armatus)* has a pointed head and snout and is silver overall with eight dark brown bands ringing its body. It is considered very good to eat. The oldwife is taken by anglers in moderately shallow water. It is not commercially exploited. The oldwife's range includes the coasts of South Australia, Tasmania, New South Wales, with a few strays found off Queensland.

OLEOMARGARINE

See **Margarine.**

OLEASTER

See **Nepal Eleagnus.**

OLIVE

This fruit is generally eaten pickled as an appetizer or garnish but also yields a valuable cooking oil. The olive tree *(Olea europaea)* is native to the Mediterranean area, but is now cultivated in many subtropical regions of the world. Its berries are bitter and inedible on the tree and are made palatable only by pickling.

Two forms are popular commercially: green or unripe, and black or ripe. In the ripening process, olives reach full size while still green, then if left on the tree, gradually turn yellow and finally purplish brown. If pickled full grown, but still green, the resulting pickled olive will have a pleasingly tart flavor. It may be pickled whole, but often is pitted, then stuffed with pimento, anchovy, etc. The ripe olive contains from 10 to 30 percent oil, most developed in the final stages of maturation. This makes the ripe olive far more nutritious than the green and gives it a far mellower taste after pickling.

Large size and firm texture are desirable qualities in pickling olives, which are often twice the size of those grown for oil content. One inch in diameter by one and a half long would be about the maximum size. Pickling involves soaking the olives first in a soda or lye solution to remove the bitterness, then immersing them in brine or a salt and vinegar solution, perhaps with spices, such as fennel, thyme, coriander or laurel leaves.

Although cultivation of the olive tree is believed to have begun much earlier, the first historical mention of the olive occurred in Egypt in the 17th century B.C. It exerted tremendous influence on Mediterranean civilization, equalled perhaps only by the grape. In Mediterranean cuisine the olive occupied a far more central place than current practice would suggest. In many dishes, it was the principal element. Olive oil was ubiquitous, serving not only as the main cooking oil, but as fuel for lamps and as a liquid to rub on the body. The Greeks of Homer's time rubbed olive oil on their bodies to protect them from the cold. The later Romans followed a similar practice, but also used it as a vehicle for perfume and as a cleanser. It is said that in antiquity, a single large tree could supply a peasant family with all the fruit it wanted to eat, plus all the oil it needed for cooking, lighting and anointing.

Olive oil was an essential item of export for ancient Crete of the Minoan period (3,000–1,500 B.C.), and shared that role with wine in the economy of ancient Greece. Indeed, the Athenian decision to abandon wheat production in favor of olive oil profoundly affected the rural ecology. Substitution of olive trees, which have a deep tap root, for fibrous-rooted plants left the way open for radical soil erosion, a situation lamented in the fourth century B.C. by Plato, who gloomily commented that bare white limestone now stood in place of former green meadows.

The olive is a long-lived tree, and extremely hardy, thriving in poor soil and arid conditions that would stunt most other plants. Legends of its immortality abound. It is alleged, for example, that on the Mount of Olives in Jerusalem Christ was betrayed amidst trees that are still standing today. Likewise, it is claimed that certain trees in Italy date from the Roman Empire, and that a particular tree in the Vatican garden was already bearing fruit at the time of Charlemagne's arrival in Rome, an event that occurred about 1200 years ago. Longevity is verified in the case of the olive trees brought to California and planted at the missions by Jesuits more than three centuries ago, although this falls far short of legend.

Like all long-lived beings, olive trees are slow to mature, requiring 10 years to bear first fruit and 30 years to achieve mature production. Intensive cultivation and irrigation in California have succeeded in reducing these periods to four to eight years for first fruit and 15 to 20 for full maturity. Yet, these results have failed to have much impact on the major producing countries, Italy and Spain, where the saying goes, "Pamper an olive tree and spoil the fruit." Ninety to 95 percent of the world production of olives still comes from Mediterranean countries. The finest green olives come from the south of Spain, while the preeminent Italian varieties are the *cerignola*, an enormous green from Puglie; the rather bitter *oliva spagnola*, and the black Roman, which are small, wrinkled and have a smoky taste.

The olive growers of California and Arizona tend to concentrate on size, which brings a higher price in the marketplace. This is often achieved by severe pruning, which reduces the size of the crop but increases the size of the individual olive. The best-known varieties found in U.S. markets are:

Ascalano: A transplant from Italy, it produces the largest California olive. It has tender flesh, a small pit and light color.

Olives, clockwise from top right: black, green with almonds, green with pimento, Greek, and (center) Spanish green

Manzanillo: A Spanish olive of unusual quality, but rather too small for American tastes.

Manzanillo I: A deep-colored olive of Spanish origin, and unusually bitter before pickling.

Mission: It accounts for more than half of the olives cultivated in California. It is excellent for both pickling and as a producer of olive oil. It has firm, slightly tart flesh.

Sevillano: A Spanish olive particularly suited for pickling in both green and black varieties. It has a large pit and is deeply colored. The large queen olives are of this type.

The olive tree and olive oil have long had great symbolic meaning in Western culture. The Greeks believed the olive to be of divine origin, a gift of Athena, the goddess of wisdom. They maintained a sacred grove of olive trees and used the oil to anoint champion athletes. Since then it has often been used in sacred ritual. For example, the kings of both England and France were anointed with olive oil at coronation. It has been used as fuel for the lamps in both Jewish tabernacles and Christian reliquaries. The olive branch has been a traditional symbol of peace from the time of ancient Greece and Rome right down to the present. An olive branch is carried in the right claw of the eagle on the Great Seal of the United States.

See also: **Olive Oil.**

OLIVE OIL

This is oil extracted from the fruit of the olive tree, *Olea europaea.* Historically, the most important of all vegetable oils, and, by general agreement, the best tasting. In the Mediterranean area, it played an essential role in the cultures and economies of antiquity. Besides being the main cooking oil, it provided fuel for lamps. Also, Greeks of Homer's time rubbed olive oil on their skins to retain body heat. This custom was refined somewhat by the ancient Romans, who added perfume to the oil. In the absence of soap, it was used as a cleanser too.

The oil is removed from the olives as follows: They are crushed to the consistency of paste after being cleaned. The paste is folded into a type of reed cloth and pressed. The finest, or "virgin" oil comes from this first pressing. After refining, it has a straw-yellow color, and is redolent of the fruit. Second, and even third, pressings yield oil of inferior quality. The color of the second grade oil, after refining, tends to be greenish yellow. After these pressings, most of the oil still remains in the paste, and is extracted through processes involving heat and solvents. This lowest quality oil is whitish in color and spoils easily when exposed to the air. Another way of grading olive oil is by oleic acid content, the best having up to 4 percent and the lowest 1 percent.

On the average, 100 pounds of fine olives produces 13 to 15 pounds of edible oil. Olives pressed for oil may be of less than half the size of olives selected for pickling, where large size is highly prized.

French olive oil is reputed to be the most subtle and delicate in flavor, less fruity than the olive oil manufactured in Italy. Olive oil is also produced on a large scale in Spain, Greece, Lebanon and California. The fruit should be picked by hand as it first begins to soften, or else "combed" from the trees by wooden-teeth rakes. Thomas Jefferson was disappointed that he could not make olives grow in the eastern United States, not realizing that the Spanish had already introduced the tree successfully into Mexico and California. "Virgin" olive oil is a delectable and nutritious adornment in fresh green salads.

Olive oil is also an important agent in the packing of sardines, anchovies and tuna, as well as an aromatic ingredient in various soaps. "With us," says Mrs. Isabella Beeton, author of the *Book of Household Management* (London, 1861), "it is principally used in mixing a salad, and when thus employed, it tends to prevent fermentation, and is an antidote against flatulency."

Olive oil is sensitive to light, which fades it, and to heat, which hastens rancidity. It separates at low temperatures, and solidifies at 32° F (0° C). It easily picks up foreign odors, and for that reason should be kept in a tightly closed container.

See also: **Olive, Fat.**

OLIVET

This soft French cheese made from the milk of either cows or sheep is produced mainly in the town of Olivet in the Loiret. If *Olivet* is intended to be eaten fresh, as it is in the summer, it is made from whole milk, often with cream added. The result is a white or cream cheese. If it is intended to be eaten as a blue cheese, whole or partly skimmed milk is used, and the curd is salted and ripened for two to four weeks. Blue mold forms, and the flavor is like **Camembert.** A third variety is allowed to ripen for an additional two to four weeks. This variety is called *Olivet cendre* because during the second ripening period it is covered with ashes. The last two types are in season from October to June. Individual cheeses are round and flat, approximately six inches in diameter by 1¼ inches thick.

OLLA PODRIDA

This thick Spanish soup or stew is regarded by some as the national dish of Spain and is also known as *cocido* or *puchero.* Its character may vary depending on the ingredients. A wide range of meats and vegetables are used, but two indispensable items are chick peas and *chorizo* (sausage).

OLMUTZER QUARGEL

This sour-milk **hand cheese** made in Austria and Bohemia is spiced with caraway seeds. Individual cheeses are prepared from skim milk in very small sizes. Their flavor is sharp and rather salty. They are cured for eight to 10 weeks.

OLOMBE

Olombe is a small shrub, *Solanum pierreanum*, of the nightshade family found in Gabon and neighboring areas. Its applelike fruit is eaten locally.

ONAGA

An important food fish, the onaga *(Etelis carbunculus)* is widely distributed in the Indian and Pacific Oceans. It has an overall pink color, silver belly and red back, fins and mouth. It reaches a length of three feet and is a member of the snapper family. It is fished off East Africa, Mauritius, the Seychelles, Japan, the Philippines and Hawaii.

Onaga is its Hawaiian name. There it is considered a fine food fish. The onaga is caught near the shore rather than in deep water.

ONAGER

The wild ass of Asia, the onager *(Equus hemionne onager)* is found from Mongolia and Tibet to Syria and in the northern and eastern parts of Africa. It favors desert plains and can go for long periods without water. This is the wild ass of the Bible. Its flesh was considered a delicacy by the ancient Persians and ancient Romans.

The onager may reach a length of seven feet, stand 4½ feet at the shoulder and weigh up to 570 pounds. It is eaten today in parts of Africa.

See also: **Donkey.**

ONION

This common garden vegetable usually consists of an edible bulb with a pungent flavor and aroma. The onion *(Allium cepa)* and other members of the *Allium* genus, such as **garlic, shallots, leeks** and scallions, are members of the lily family. There are innumerable varieties of onions, many of them adapted to such narrow local conditions that they do not thrive elsewhere. They are classified in various ways: as growing single or multiple bulbs; as growing from seeds or from sets (small bulbs), and as growing above ground or below (partially or completely) ground. Bulbless onions are treated under **Scallions.**

Onions

Cultivation of the onion is older than history. It is believed to have originated in central Asia and to have been distributed in prehistoric times through both the Eastern and Western Hemispheres. It was held sacred by the ancient Egyptians. The onion was brought to Greece by Alexander the Great, yet the ancient Romans believed it to be native to Gaul. It was a staple food of the peasantry during the Middle Ages in Europe. When European explorers came to the New World, they found many native varieties, both in Mexico and what is now the United States. A French explorer, Pere Jacques Marquette, who traversed the southern shore of Lake Michigan in 1624, staved off starvation by eating a wild onion, which the native Americans called *chicago.*

The vast majority of mature onions are of the single bulb varieties and range in color from silvery white, through yellow to red. They are grown in all parts of the world and are probably the most widely used vegetable and flavoring agent. Mature onions are sold after a period of drying out, and if they are not perfectly dry in the market, it is probably an indication that they have begun to decay. They are quite variable in shape, running the gamut from perfectly spherical, through oval and pear-shaped, to rectangular. The flavor, though pungent as a rule, can approach bland sweetness in some varieties. The weather is an important factor in taste: the warmer the climate, the milder the onion. Following is a list of the most common types of onions:

Button onion: Also called pearl onion, it is much smaller than the ones discussed above, picked while still immature for use in cooking or pickling. As a rule, it is white or yellow-skinned.

Common or seed onion: The kind most commonly grown in the United States, and exceedingly variable in size, shape and pungency depending on the variety. Although the United States has more than 70 native species of onion, this is not one of them. Rather it is descended from varieties brought from Europe by settlers.

Egyptian or tree onion: Despite the name, it is native to the United States. Garliclike, it grows multiple bulbs among its roots. It also sends up a central stalk, at the summit of which develop still more tiny bulbs. Both sets can be used in cooking. See also **Rocambole.**

Potato Onion: An underground variety, so called because of its resemblance to the potato. It is propagated from sets and is believed to have originated in Egypt.

Spanish, or Bermuda, onions: Name given to many varieties of large, mild, single-bulb onions, which have the shape of a flattened sphere and usually a glossy brown skin. In the United States the name may be applied to any imported onion, although in recent decades importation of Bermuda onions had declined and their place in the market taken by onions grown in the southern states.

Much of the onion's pungency is due to its volatile oil, which contains much sulphur. It can be weakened somewhat by keeping the onion under water for a few minutes. Likewise, peeling the onion under water can prevent crying. Any form of cooking reduces the harshest of onions to relative mildness. It is extremely versatile both as a cooked vegetable—boiled or baked—or as a flavoring ingredient in sauces, soups, stews and in other meat dishes. The onion is about 91 percent water, and contains 28 calories per 3½ ounces (100 grams).

ONITES MARJORAM

A variety of marjoram, *Origanum onites,* whose leaves are used as a condiment, it is native to southern Europe and Asia Minor and is not widely cultivated.

ONKOB

This sour but edible fruit of a small, spiny tree, *Oncoba spinosa,* is found in Arabia and tropical Africa. The pulp tastes like pomegranate.

ONOPORDUM

Also WILD ARTICHOKE. This is a genus of coarse, thistlelike herbs, one of which is the wild artichoke plant. The latter is a tall plant, with wooly looking leaves and large heads of purple or white flowers. The leaf receptacles are eaten like artichokes, and the stalks like cardoons. The plant is native to Europe, North Africa and western Asia. The name of this genus tells what happens when these plants are eaten by wild asses: derived from the Greek, it says *onos* (an ass) and *porde* (flatulence).

ONOTO

See **Annatto.**

OOLONG BLACK DRAGON

Oolong is the compromise tea between black and green. It looks and tastes half-black and half-green and comes from several regions of China. Best known are those from Amoy, Foochow, Canton and Taiwan. The last one, for example, has a large leaf but makes a light infusion, redolent of ripe peaches. Others are also famous for a subtle, fruity taste and light color.

See also: **Tea.**

OPAH

Also MOONFISH, JERUSALEM HADDOCK. A large, deepwater fish whose salmon-pink flesh is highly prized as food, opah *(Lampris guttatus)* is found in all oceans except the Antarctic but is most plentiful in warm temperate and tropical seas. Despite its size (up to five feet long and 600 pounds), it is not commercially fished because of its mid-ocean, deep-water habitat.

The opah's markings are distinctive and beautiful: steel-blue back, rich green flanks, rose abdomen and crimson fins, all dotted with silver. Its flesh is excellent but a little dry. Due to its wide distribution, the opah is known by many names including lookdown, kingfish (Britain), sunfish, *gudhlax* (Icelandic for "God's salmon"), and *glansfisk* (Danish for "shining fish").

OPALEYE

This good-tasting, light-flavored fish is found off the California coast from San Francisco to Cape San Lucas. Opaleye *(Girella nigricans)* is green with silver sides and opalescent blue green eyes. The opaleye reaches a weight of four pounds and a length of up to 25 inches. The opaleye is a game fighter. Anglers take this fish off piers, in the surf or on rocky shores especially among kelp beds. It is also fished commercially. It is recognized by its deep body, high spiny dorsal fin and small, rounded head.

OPHIDIUM

See **Donzelle.**

OPOSSUM

Also POSSUM. This small, tree-dwelling, nocturnal marsupial mammal is native to the eastern and southeastern parts of the United States. Opossums can reach a weight of 12 pounds. They are omnivorous and eat insects, birds' eggs, meat, ferns and fruit, especially wild berries, which in the South, give their flesh an agreeable flavor. Opossum is also nutritious, containing twice the protein of beefsteak but only one-third the fat. Its taste has been compared to rabbit, or when roasted whole, to suckling pig.

The kind most frequently eaten is the common opossum *(Didelphis virginiana)*. It is skinned as quickly as possible after killing and the glands removed from the inside of the front legs and back. If not removed, they will impart a fetid taste to the meat. Excess fat is trimmed off, and the carcass may be aged or not depending on personal preference. The carcass is usually presoaked or parboiled before being cooked. The animal as a whole may be roasted, stuffed and baked or barbecued. It may be cut into pieces and prepared as one would a rabbit or fryer chicken. Fried opossum stew is a favorite in the rural South. The famous calalou of the Gulf states consists of opossum plus pork and the meat of small fowl, stewed with assorted seafood, okra, onions and eggplant. This is simmered to the consistency of a thick stew and served with rice.

OPUNTIA

See **Prickly Pear.**

ORACH

Also ORACHE, MOUNTAIN SPINACH, FRENCH SPINACH, SEA PURSLANE. Orach is a leafy plant, *Atriplex hortensis*, native to Asia but naturalized in Europe and North America. Its arrow-shaped leaves are cooked and eaten like spinach in England and especially in France, where three varieties are cultivated. The white variety has yellowish or light green leaves; the red variety has coppery to dark red leaves and stems; and the green has dark green leaves. Most popular is the white.

Oranges

ORANGE

This globose reddish yellow fruit of the *Citrus* genus has a juicy pulp that is divided into eight or ten oblong segments. Its leathery rind is easily separable from the pulp. Economically, the orange is one of the four to five most important fruits in the world. There are numerous varieties, which fall into two general classes, sour and sweet. The sour type is useful chiefly in cooking and in industry, while the sweet are mostly eaten fresh or squeezed for their juice. The orange tree is subtropical in nature and needs an equable temperature with some cool spells to improve the flavor of its fruit, but nothing below 28° F (−2.2° C).

Since they do not continue to ripen after being picked, all oranges are tree-ripened. The orange color of the fruit is not a sign of ripeness, but is a reaction to moderately cold weather. Oranges grown in the tropics remain green and are less flavorful than those exposed to cool weather.

The orange is native to southern China where references to it appear as early as 2,500 B.C. The first orange variety to appear in the West was the Bigarade, or bitter orange *(Citrus aurantium).* It was described around the first century B.C. by Roman writers, who referred to it as the "golden apple of the Hesperides." Hesperides was their name for the Canary Islands. The flavor of the Bigarade is quite tart and today is regarded as practically inedible when fresh, although this was not the general opinion until the sweet orange arrived in Europe some 500 years ago. The ancients did eat it as a fresh fruit, but not with the same gusto as we do the sweet orange today.

The Bigarade is believed to be the parent of all other varieties of orange. It is the hardiest of all orange plants. Commercial orange trees are not usually grown from seed, but are propagated by budding or grafting. Because of its hardiness, the bitter orange served for centuries as rootstock for sweet orange trees. This is no longer the case. It has been replaced by the rough lemon, which is more disease resistant. The tartness of the bitter orange makes it superior to the sweet as a seasoner in cooking and in marmalades and candied fruit. Its flowers and leaves are highly esteemed in the cosmetic industry for essences and perfumes. Essential oil is extracted from its rind for liqueurs, such as Curacao. Spain is its largest producer.

It is not clear when the sweet orange *(C. sinensis)* was introduced into the West—possibly as early as the 8th century A.D. by the Moors in Spain, or as late as the 16th century by the Portuguese from India—but it too originated in China. It quickly replaced the Bigarade as a fresh fruit and today is the most widely grown orange in the world. The sweet orange is a larger tree than the bitter, attaining heights of up to 35 feet. Those grafted on to root stock begin to bear in five years and continue to do so abundantly for 50 to 80 years. In Southern California, where orange trees seem to yield best, the average tree can be expected to bear 1,500 oranges a year. The dominant variety of sweet orange is the Valencia, which paradoxically is not much grown in Valencia, since Spain concentrates on the bitter orange, known also as the Seville orange. The Valencia is very sweet, juicy and almost seedless. Its popularity extends to most orange-growing centers, including Florida, California, Europe, Latin America, South Africa and Australia.

Other famous varieties of the sweet orange include: *Jaffa* of Israel, which is renowned for the same qualities as the Valencia. *Navel orange:* a recent mutant that appeared first in Brazil, has done much to enhance the reputation of California oranges. It is completely seedless. It keeps and travels well and is delicious to eat but is not as juicy as the Valencia. Well-known Florida varieties are the Parson Brown and the Indian River. *Pineapple orange* is so named because of its pineapplelike aroma. It is a favorite of juicemakers but is not popular as a fresh fruit because of its many seeds. *Blood orange* is a variety of the sweet orange grown chiefly in the Mediterranean area. It is very sweet, and its pulp is dark red or purple. Sicily is the principal producer. *Bergamot (C. bergamia)* is a hybrid of the sour orange cultivated for the essence extracted from its rind. (See also **Bergamot.)**

Another group of oranges are those of the tangerine (Mandarin) variety, which generally take the form of a flattened sphere, have looser skin than the Valencia type and are deliciously sweet. (For more information see also: **Chinois, Tangerine,** and **King Orange.)**

Due to the citrus genus' penchant for hybridization, there are many hybrids of the orange. See also: **Citrange, Citrangequat, Clementine, Orangequat, Ortanique, Shaddock, Tangelo, Tangor, Ugli.**

ORANGE AGOSERIS

Also MOUNTAIN DANDELION. A variety of mountain dandelion, *Agoseris aurantiaca*, the orange agoseris is found in western North America from British Columbia south to California and New Mexico. Its flowers are the color of burnt orange and turn purple with age. The leaves, which may reach a length of 10 inches, are edible and were well known to native Americans as greenfood.

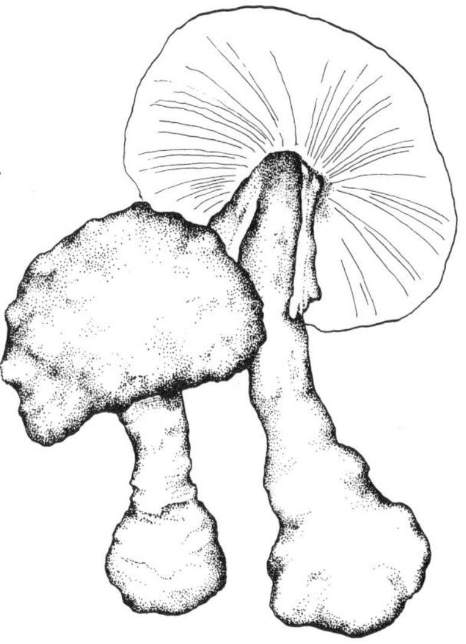

Orange Amanita

ORANGE AMANITA

Also CAESAR'S MUSHROOM. This is a delicious edible mushroom from a genus, the *Amanitaceae*, which numbers among its members the deadliest of poison mushrooms. The orange amanita *(Amanita caesarea)* gained the name "Caesar's mushroom" because it was the favorite mushroom of imperial Rome. The ancient Roman elite treasured their mushrooms like no other food, styling it "food of the gods." At a banquet, mushrooms were the only food personally cooked by the host, who used special pots called *boletaria*.

This mushroom has an orange yellow cap and a stem rising from a white, cuplike base. On reaching maturity, the stalk measures four to six inches, and the cap, which is flat, is three to six inches in diameter. Today it is considered, along with the **truffle** and the **bolete,** to be among the best mushrooms available. It is widely distributed in Europe, Asia, Africa and the United States. It generally appears in late summer or early fall near the roots of broadleaved trees. Because of its symbiotic relationship with the tree, it cannot be artificially cultivated.

Poisonous amanitas bear a family resemblance to the orange amanita, namely, white gills, a skirtlike ring on the stem, and a volva (the cuplike covering of the base). Amanitas account for perhaps 90 percent of mushroom deaths in the United States and Europe, and the deadliest of all is the death cap *(Amanita phalloides)*. It has an olive green cap, but does resemble the **field mushroom** in shape. The death cap is chiefly a European mushroom, but now appears to be widely distributed in the United States, since several deaths have been attributed to it.

The destroying angels are a related species that look a lot like the death cap except that they are entirely white. There are six of them, the *Amanitas verna*, *virosa*, *bisporigera*, *tenuifolia*, *suballiacea* and *ocreata*. They are often mistaken for the field mushroom or, in California, for the edible *Amanita calyptroderma*, a large mushroom with an orange brown cap. Another is the fly agaric *(Amanita muscaria)*, a red mushroom with white spots, which resembles the fairy ring mushroom. Its name comes from the ancient practice of adding fly agaric to milk to kill flies.

Apart from the fly agaric, whose toxin is muscaria, a nerve stimulant, the fatal substances in the amanitas attack the liver and kidneys. They are called *amatoxins* and are ten times deadlier than cyanide. Their effect is described as follows in *Mushrooms: Wild and Edible* by Vincent Marteka:

> *When a deadly amanita is eaten, the symptoms do not appear immediately. In fact, if a person quickly develops symptoms such as a stomach upset, it's most likely that the mushroom is not deadly. . . . The symptoms usually begin ten hours after the mushroom has been eaten, although they may occur as early as six or as late as 24 hours. The symptoms include severe abdominal pain, diarrhea, and vomiting. The symptoms usually last a day. Then, the person passes through a stage in which he seems to be improving. The victim, if in a hospital, may even be released from the hospital. However, the next stage is the critical stage, since the toxins have been steadily attacking the cells of the liver and kidneys. . . . By the final stage, about the fourth day after the amanitas have been eaten, the liver and kidneys may fail and death will occur.*

There is no antidote for amanita poisoning, but treatment with thioctic acid and penicillin have met with some success. In England, complete filtering of the blood through charcoal has saved the lives of several poisoning victims.

See also: **Mushroom.**

ORANGE FLAMETHROWER

The roots of this perennial herb, *Talinum aurantiacum*, of the American Southwest are cooked and eaten as a vegetable. A related species, potherb flamethrower *(T. triangulare)* has succulent leaves that are eaten as greens. It tastes like purslane and is also known as Surinam purslane. It is a native of tropical America.

ORANGE FLOWER WATER

See **Neroli Oil.**

ORANGE JUICE

The most popular of all fruit juices, especially in frozen, concentrated form, orange juice contains approximately 45 milligrams of vitamin C per liter, and none is permitted to be added during processing. Frozen concentrate is created using the "cutback" method, i.e., overconcentrating the juice, then cutting it back to the desired strength with fresh juice before freezing it. This technique was developed in the 1940s and revived the sagging market for oranges. Also included in the cutback are flavoring elements from peel oil, most notably d-limonene. Juice oranges are a specialty of Florida.

Since the development of frozen concentrate, the consumption in the United States of fresh oranges and single-strength juice has dropped by two-thirds, so that the number of oranges produced in Florida greatly exceeds that of California, which produces eating oranges. This was a reversal of the pre-1950 trend. More recent developments are synthetic orange drinks, and orange juice substitutes, i.e., a breakfast drink reconstituted with water from powder or crystals.

ORANGE MILD LACTARIUS

See **Saffron Milk Cap.**

ORANGEQUAT

A hybrid citrus fruit, crossing the orange with the kumquat, the orangequat is supposed to combine the orange's best qualities with the kumquat's hardiness and resistance to citrus cancer.

ORANGE ROCKFISH

A Pacific Ocean food fish, *Rosicola pinniger*, caught off the coast of California, it attains a length of two feet and resembles the **red snapper.** Its flesh is of high quality.

ORCHIS

This is a genus of orchids, particularly those of the species *O. morio* and *O. latifolia*, whose tubers are used to make **salep.** The tubers are dried and ground to powder, which, when mixed with hot liquid, becomes thick and gelatinous.

See also: **Salep.**

OREGANO

See **Marjoram.**

OREGON GRAPE

The black berry of an evergreen, thornless shrub found in northwest North America, the Oregon grape *(Mahonia aquifolium)* is used to make a substitute lemonade.

ORGEAT

This French syrup consists of an almond emulsion either mixed in barley syrup or with orange-flower water and sugar. It is used to make a soft drink or to flavor some cocktails. The term "orgeat" also refers to the beverage made from it. In Spain, this drink is called *horchata*.

ORIENTAL PICKLING MELON

The fruit of this trailing vine *(Cucumis melo* var. *conomon)* tends to be shaped like a cucumber. Mature specimens are used to make pickles, while the very young fruit is used in soups. The flesh of the latter is white or green and crisp. This species is native to China and Japan and is little grown in the United States.

ORMER

Also ORMIER, EAR SHELL. A species of shell fish related to the abalone, the ormer *(Haliotis tuberculata)* is abundant along some parts of the English coast, and particularly on the rocks of the Channel Islands. It is prepared like scallops or it is sometimes pickled.

ORONGE

See **Orange Amanita.**

ORSERA

See **Urseren.**

ORTANIQUE

A hybrid citrus fruit, crossing the sweet orange with the satsuma variety of tangerine, it is of Jamaican origin and is sometimes known as the Jamaican mandarin orange. The ortanique *(Glycosmis pentaphylla)* is loose-skinned, sweet and juicy with the characteristically flattened shape of the tangerine. It resembles another Jamaican hybrid called the **ugli** but is more regular in shape. It is seedless.

ORTOLAN

Also GARDEN BUNTING. This small European songbird, *Emberiza hortulana*, is prized as a table delicacy, especially in France. A corresponding U.S. bird would be the bobolink *(Dolichonyx oryzivorous)*, which is eaten in Louisiana and elsewhere. In France, the ortolan is a specialty of the Landes district where established custom was to net them and fatten them for market on oats and millet. A favorite way of cooking them is to roast them in their own fat. The bird is then eaten bones, tail and all. Ortolans were once plentiful in Italy, Spain and England but got so popular with gastronomes that their numbers have been drastically reduced by overhunting.

ORVAL

See **Clary.**

ORYX

Oryx is a genus of large antelopes found in Africa and Arabia and known for the excellence of their flesh. There are four species, three species of which have long, pointed horns projecting straight backward from behind the eyes. An exception is the Libyan and Saharan oryx *(Oryx tao)*, which has scimitar-shaped horns. A large adult can stand as high as seven feet at the shoulder and weigh as much as 460 pounds.

Other species are the Beisa oryx *(O. beisa)* of eastern Africa and the gemsbok *(O. gazella)* of the Kalahari in southern Africa. The Arabian and Iraqi oryx *(O. leucoryx)* is believed to be nearly extinct due to overhunting. Native people hunt the oryx mainly for the meat but also use the horn tips as spear points and the tough hide as shield coverings.

OSCHTJEPEK

Also OSCHTJEPKA. This Czechoslovakian cheese, much like **caciocavallo** is made from sheep's milk.

OSCHTJEPKA

See **Oschtjepek.**

OSOBERRY

Also INDIAN PLUM. Osoberry is the edible fruit of a deciduous shrub, *Oemleria cerasiformis*, native to the Pacific Coast of North America. The osoberry bush has fragrant, white flowers and reaches a height of 15 feet. It is found wild from British Columbia to California and is often cultivated as an ornamental. The fruit is a blue-black drupe that attains a length of one-half inch.

OSSETIN

Also, TUSCHKINSK, KASACH. This Russian cheese is made from sheep or cow's milk in the Caucasus. The sheep's milk variety is considered better. These cheeses are cured in brine for two months to a year. The younger cheeses are softer and milder.

OSTRICH

A large, flightless bird of Africa and Arabia, the ostrich *(Struthio camelus)* reaches a height of up to eight feet and inhabits areas of sandy plains. The flesh of the ostrich is edible but not highly thought of. It is described as tough and tasteless.

It had a good reputation among the gastronomes of ancient Rome, however, who set a high price on it. A special sauce was devised for ostrich meat by the famous epicure, Apicius. Today, it seems, ostrich is eaten with regularity only by some native people of South Africa, who dry the flesh before preparing it. The South American cousin of the ostrich is the rhea, which is similar in appearance but smaller. Regarding ostrich eggs, see **Egg.**

OSWEGO TEA

See **Bee Balm.**

OTAHEITE APPLE

See **Ambarella.**

OTAHEITE GOOSEBERRY

Also GOOSEBERRY TREE. This green, angled fruit of a small tree, *Phyllanthus acidus*, is native to Southeast Asia but has been naturalized in southern Florida and the West Indies. The size ranges from three-fourths to one inch in diameter. These fruits are used to make preserves and pickles.

OTOPHORA

Edible fruits of the East Indian trees *Otophora alata* and *O. spectabilis*, they are orange brown or dark purple and are of purely local interest.

OUZO

A colorless Greek alcoholic beverage, ouzo is very strong and is flavored with **anise.** It is drunk both as an **aperitif** and with food. Ouzo is normally a grape

liqueur, clear in the bottle, but when mixed with water, as is customary, it turns cloudy. George Gurdjieff points to the possible evolution of ouzo from the resin of the mastic tree *(Pistacia lentiscus)*, now used in varnish or as an astringent, and to the ritual and result of its use:

> *That evening we went to a small Greek restaurant for a little diversion after the period of difficulty and strain we had just been through. We were leisurely drinking the famous douziko [ouzo] and helping ourselves to this and that, as is the local custom, from the numerous small saucers piled with all kinds of hors d'oeuvres, from dried mackerel to salted chick peas. . . . After three rounds of the miraculous douziko —that worthy offspring of the beneficent mastikhe of the ancient Greeks—we began to talk more and more noisily and freely.*

The alcohol content of ouzo is about 50 percent.

See also: **Absinthe, Anisette, Arrack, Pastis, Raki.**

OVAR

Ovar is a Hungarian cheese with a medium-soft texture, a reddish yellow color and a flavor described as piquant but mild. Ovar is made from cow's milk. A typical cheese weighs 10 pounds.

OVCJI SIR

This Yugoslavian cheese is made from sheep's milk in the Slovenian Alps. It is cured three months and weighs from six to eight pounds.

OX

See **Beef, Variety Meats.**

OXEYE DAISY

The leaves of this common wild flower of Europe and Asia can be boiled as a vegetable or eaten fresh in a salad. This is seldom done, however, except in cases of famine. The oxeye daisy *(Chrysanthemum leucanthemum)* is an erect, perennial herb up to three feet high, whose flowers have yellow disks and white rays. It has been naturalized in North America as a weed.

OXTAIL

This is the tail of any beef animal, including the cow, the steer and the bull. The meat found on the tail is sparse but flavorful, and usually cheap. It has been used for centuries to make soups, stews and ragouts. Oxtail makes a gelatin-rich soup stock, and the traditional European oxtail soup is made from it. The tail is skinned, disjointed and braised, then simmered in water for several hours with vegetables, seasonings and perhaps red wine. Oxtail is also braised and served as a meat dish.

OYSTER

According to Jonathan Swift, "He was a bold man who first ate an oyster." That man's identity is lost in antiquity, however, since commercial cultivation goes back at least 2,000 years, and archaeological evidence suggests that early humans much appreciated its delicate flavor.

The oyster (family *Ostreidae)* is a marine bivalve mollusk. The best oysters come from commercial beds, which are located in brackish or salt water, in coves, bays and mouths of rivers, all shallow water areas. Oyster farming consists in providing a surface for a recently spawned oyster larva, called spat, to lodge upon along the shore near the low water mark. In a year or so, when the spat has attained sufficient size—one-half inch to one inch in diameter—it is carefully moved to deeper water, or other appropriate fattening grounds. At the end of three years, oysters are harvested if they have grown to legal size (three inches in diameter) and taken to a shucking house, where they are prepared for market.

Three commercial types are cultivated in the United States. The Eastern, or American, oyster *(Ostrea virginica)* abounds on the shorelines of the Northeastern and Mid-Atlantic States. It goes by various names including Blue Point, Cape Cod and Lynnhaven. The tiny Olympia is native to the Pacific Coast, while the larger Pacific, or King, oyster was introduced to the West Coast from Japan. It is cultivated from Eureka, California, north to the Puget Sound. The Pacific Coast varieties gained much in commercial importance during the 1960s when traditional beds in Chesapeake Bay, Delaware Bay and Long Island Sound suffered a combination of ecological disasters that cut the harvest of American oysters by two-thirds.

The finest-flavored oysters are reputedly the smaller English and French varieties, such as the English Colchester and Whitstable, or the French *marennes* and *belots.* The *marennes* have a characteristic green tinge from the algae upon which they live. It adds a slight coppery taste that is much esteemed. They are usually eaten raw in their own juices on the half shell. The larger types, such as the American and Portuguese, are often cooked in a variety of ways.

The oyster's nutrition content is high. It is rich in vitamins and organic salts, particularly iodine. Care

Pacific oysters

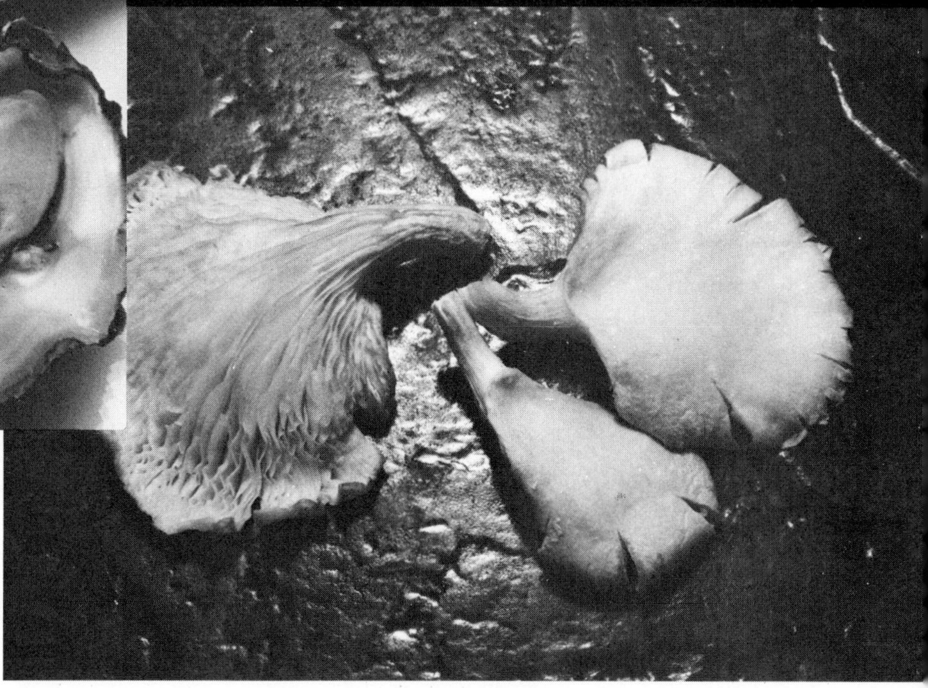

Oyster mushrooms

must be taken that oysters come from unpolluted waters and that their freshness has been maintained. Eating a spoiled oyster can cause serious illness.

Oysters are considered by many to be the perfect appetizer to a meal. They are delicious, yet more than a dozen can be eaten without exceeding the food value of an egg.

Although oysters will spoil in two days at room temperature, they keep well in the shell if maintained at 42° F (5.6° C). Oyster meat, if prepared correctly, will keep for three weeks at 32° F (0° C).

OYSTER CATCHER

Also SEA MAGPIE. This small, black and white wading bird is found in both Europe and North America. The European species is *Haematopus ostralegus*. The delicate flesh of younger birds is well liked in France where it is prepared like **plover.**

OYSTER MUSHROOM

This shell-shaped, edible mushroom, *Pleurotus ostreatus*, grows wild in temperate zones on dead or dying hardwood trees. It is also becoming one of the most widely cultivated mushrooms (after the *Agaricus bisporus* and shiitake), with industries in Taiwan, Japan, Europe, Australia, Canada and the United States. Most of the commercial crop is canned, but fresh mushrooms are often available in local markets in France and on the West Coast of the United States.

The oyster mushroom appears during the fall and winter in large colonies on rotten trunks or boles of beech, ash and the like. The plant is soft and pliant, with white, gray or tan caps (one to six inches across), whose underside features large white gills that look like knife blades. These fungi come in fan-shaped clusters, resembling clamshells from the top. One tree might yield as much as 40 to 50 pounds of oyster mushrooms. The taste and slippery texture of the plant when cooked suggests oysters, and the aroma is fishy, but pleasantly so.

The oyster mushroom is very good to eat when young, but even then it is a little tough, a quality considered desirable, since it is nearly always stewed or served in a soup or casserole. It is widely used this way in oriental dishes, but may also be dipped in egg batter, rolled in bread crumbs and fried. Prepared in this way, it is enough like fried oyster to fool some experts.

See also: **Elm Tree Pleurotus, Mushroom.**

OYSTER PLANT

See **Salsify.**

P

PACA

A South American rodent whose flesh is highly prized as food, the paca *(Cuniculus paca)* resembles the **guinea pig** but is much larger. A large adult can exceed 30 inches in length and weigh up to 22 pounds. Pacas are generally found in the high plateaus of the Andes of Venezuela, Colombia and Ecuador. They are inoffensive, nocturnal creatures; yet in some areas they are regarded as pests because they feed on the yam, cassava, vegetable and sugar cane crops. Paca flesh fetches a high price in native markets and is prepared like guinea pig.

PACARANA

Also BRANICK RAT. This South American rodent resembles the **paca** and is found in the valleys and lower slopes of the Andes Mountains in Colombia, Ecuador, Peru, Brazil and Bolivia. It looks like a huge guinea pig. A large adult might weigh as much as 33 pounds and reach a length of 31 inches. Its flesh is edible and, because of its large size, it is diligently hunted by native people. Consequently it has become rare and may be on the verge of extinction. The *pacarana (Dinomys branickii)* is cooked like **guinea pig.** It has been tamed on occasion but, unlike the guinea pig, it does not thrive in domestication.

PACIFIC OCEAN PERCH

A member of the **redfish** family, the Pacific Ocean perch *(Sebastes alutus)* is a valuable commercial species of the Pacific coast of North America. It reaches a length of about 18 inches, and is typically perchlike in shape with an exceptionally long lower jaw. It has deep red coloration relieved by dark back saddles. It is prepared like **red snapper.**

PADDLEFISH

Also CHINESE PADDLEFISH. This family of fish left over from prehistoric eras includes only two living species, the paddlefish *(Polyodon spathula)* and the Chinese paddlefish *(Psephurus gladius).* The first is found only in the Mississippi River and lives entirely on plankton. It has a paddle-shaped snout that it uses as a plankton net, which takes up one-third its length (ranging up to 6½ feet). The paddlefish resembles the sturgeon and used to be heavily fished both for its flesh and its caviar. Dams, pollution and fishing have greatly reduced its numbers.

The Chinese paddlefish reaches a length of 23 feet, much of which is taken up with a bony, swordlike snout. Eschewing plankton, it lives on smaller fish. It is greatly prized as food. *P. gladius* lives only in the Yangtze River in China.

PADI-STRAW MUSHROOM

See **Straw Mushroom.**

PAGLIA

This Swiss blue cheese made in Ticino is much like the Italian **Gorgonzola.** Cheeses are round and flat; their diameter measures eight inches. The paste is soft and yellow, with blue streaks, and has a pleasing, aromatic flavor.

PAGO

This is a Yugoslavian sheep's milk cheese from the island of Pag in the Adriatic Sea. Individual cheeses weigh from one-half to eight pounds.

PAGRUS

A sea bream *(Pagrus auriga)* that is locally important as a food fish in the Mediterranean and in the eastern Atlantic from Portugal to Angola, it reaches a length of about two and one-half feet. The pagrus has a rather flattened face, a humped profile and and a gold coloring marked by four or five dark vertical stripes.

PAHO

Mango-type fruit of a large Philippine tree, *Mangifera altissima*, the paho is green to yellow in color, two to 3½ inches long and smooth-skinned. It is used for pickling.

PAI CHIU

Also MAO-T'AI. This Chinese distilled liquor is made from grains. The most famous *pai chiu* is *Mao-T'ai*, which has a fiery taste and is distilled from fine millet and wheat. It takes its name from a town in Kweichow Province in southwest China. It is bottled at 53 proof or higher. Other well known *pai chiu* are *Fen Chiu*, *Ta Chu*, *Si Fen* and *Wu Liang Yu*.

PAILLE, VIN DE

See **Straw Wines.**

PAIN DE DIKA

See **Dika Nut.**

PAKCHOI

Also BOKCHOY. A Chinese variety of cabbage, *pakchoi (Brassica chinensis)* has dark green leaves and broad white stalks. It somewhat resembles chard, but the leaves do not form a head. The leaf itself, with its white midribs, is reminiscent of a spinach leaf. *Pakchoi* is used in Chinese cooking and can be served raw as a salad green or cooked. It retains its crisp texture better than most leafy vegetables when cooked. The term *pakchoi* means "white vegetable," so called because of the ribs and stems. Another variety of *pakchoi (B. napiformis)* is grown for its tuberous roots, which resemble white, tapered turnips.

See also: **Petsai.**

PALM

The large family, *Palmae*, of tropical or subtropical trees is best known for providing such foods as **sago, dates** and **coconuts.** This barely scratches the surface, however, because the palm numbers more than 1,200 varieties, which range from the 200-foot-high wax palm of the Andes, to the low scrub palmetto of the southeastern United States.

Palms yield a host of edible and useful products in addition to the familiar ones above. The edible list includes fruit, seeds and nuts, the terminal bud ("cabbage"), heart, leaves, stems, flower buds, flowers, pith, sap, ashes (as a seasoner), fresh juice, fermented juice (wine or toddy), distilled juice (arrack), sugar, flour, syrup, honey, salt, vinegar and oil. Useful items include wax, hemp, lubricating oil and vegetable ivory.

For information, look under specific palms and products, such as **Palm Wine, Palm Sugar,** etc.

PALMETTO

See **Cabbage Palm.**

PALM NUT

See **Palm Oil.**

PALM OIL

Also DENDE OIL, PALM KERNEL OIL. Two palm trees are important commercially in producing oil from palm fruit. They are the African oil palm *(Elaesis guineensis)* and the American oil palm *(E. oleifera)*. The trees will hybridize in cultivation, and their fruit is quite similar. This fruit is reddish brown and attains the size of a hazelnut or walnut.

Two sorts of oil are produced. The first, called palm or dende oil, is extracted from the fibrous flesh of the fruit. It is orange red and liquid at room temperature. Palm oil is an important cooking oil in West Africa and in Brazil. It is very popular in Brazilian cuisine. It has a pleasant taste but easily becomes rancid. When boiled, it produces a yellow fat resembling butter. Palm oil is also used to make soap and candles.

The second type is called palm kernel oil. It is extracted from the seeds of the fruit either by compression or by chemical means. This oil is solid at room temperature and is used commercially to make soap and margarine. In Africa, it is also used for cooking.

PALM SUGAR

Palm sugar is obtained from the sap of various palm trees, chiefly the *gomuti*, or sugar palm *(Arenga saccharifers)*, the palmyra *(Borassus flabellifer)*, the jaggery *(Phoenix sylvestris)*, the *coquito (Jubaea spectabilis)* and the **coconut.**

Of the first three, the sap of the *gomuti* is the richest, containing 15 percent to 20 percent sugar. Trees are tapped by making a triangular incision below the crown and draining off from three pints to three quarts of sap a day for up to seven weeks. Alternatively, in some palms the flower stalks can be milked, much in the way that toddy is obtained from the coconut palm. The sap is reduced to syrup, or sugar, by boiling, as is maple sap. Also, the syrup may be spread out to dry in the sun, forming thin sheets of sugar.

The *coquito* palm is native to Chile and under favorable conditions may grow as high as 60 feet. Its fruit is known as "monkey coconut" which, except for its tiny size—an inch or less in diameter—is like the true coconut. The *coquito* is cultivated for its sap, which is known as palm honey *(miel de palma)*. To obtain the sap, the tree must be cut down. After the leaves have been removed, the crown of the tree is tapped for the honey, which flows over a period of several months, and may amount to as much as 90 gallons. It boils down to the consistency of molasses.

PALM WINE

Also TODDY. Palm wine is an alcoholic drink made by fermenting the sap of any of several kinds of palm trees, including the coconut palm *(Cocos nucifera)*, the date palm *(Phoenix dactylifera)*, the jaggery *(Caryota urens)* and the palmyra palm *(Borassus flabellifer)*. In Asia the sap, called toddy, is drunk fresh or fermented. It is sweet in its natural state, containing up to 16 percent sugar. Toddy may also be distilled to produce a spiritous liquor.

PALOMETA

An edible fish of the western Atlantic, the palometa *(Trachinotus goodei)* resembles the **pompano,** to which it is closely allied. It is a deep-bodied, graceful fish with a silver back and sides and yellowish belly. The palometa reaches a length of about 20 inches and frequents sandy areas or reefs. It is found from Bermuda and New England to Argentina, including the Caribbean and the Gulf of Mexico.

PALO VERDE

The palo verde is a small bushy tree, *Cercidium floridum*, of the American Southwest and Baja California. Its seeds are used to make a beverage.

PAMPROUX

See **Goat's Milk Cheese.**

PANCAKE

The oldest form of bread is thought to have been a sort of unleavened pancake, but the pancake is still with us today as a more-or-less distinct entity. **Bread** has taken a separate line of evolution.

The ordinary pancake is a thin flat cake made from batter and fried on a griddle or a pan. The batter usually consists of eggs, flour, milk or milk and water, and some oil or melted butter. In former times English pancakes were moistened with ale, which had a leavening effect on cooking. Sometimes yeast or baking powder is added to American batter to lighten the cakes. The batter is beaten and allowed to stand until it has the consistency of thick cream. The size of a pancake may vary according to individual preference, the smallest generally being the size of a "silver dollar," and the largest big enough to cover the plate or require rolling to fit on a plate. The formula for batter is often varied to admit such ingredients as buttermilk or sugar. Pancakes may be spread with a sweet or savory mixture and rolled; if eaten plain, they are traditionally accompanied by butter and syrup or powdered sugar.

Given its ancient lineage, the pancake has assumed different forms in different countries. Following is a list of the better known variations:

Blini: A small pancake of Russia and Poland made of both wheat and buckwheat flour, plus yeast, butter, milk and eggs. Blini are often spread with caviar or slices of smoked salmon, stacked one on top the other and served with sour cream.

Blintz: The traditional pancake of Jewish cuisine with an eastern European origin, it is fried very thin and stuffed with cheese, cream cheese or fruits such as blueberries or apples. It is served with sour cream.

Cannelloni: An Italian hors d'oeuvre or entree, which may be made with noodle dough or pancake batter, the pancake is spread with a finely chopped, well-seasoned chicken, vegetable or meat mixture, or with cheese, then rolled, covered with a sauce and baked.

Crepe: A French pancake, very thin and light, made of a flour and egg batter, crepes are often spread with jam, fruit, whipped cream, or rolled in a sweet sauce and served as a dessert. The best known of these, *Crepes Suzette*, is doused with liqueur and set afire. Crepes may be filled with meat, poultry or cheese and served as an entree.

Eierkuckas: A rich pancake of Alsace Lorraine. The batter is mixed with cream and red currant jelly.

Flensjes: A very thin Dutch pancake made of egg batter and served as dessert with sugar, ginger, jam or marmalade.

Flaeskpannkaka: In Sweden, a pork or bacon pancake. The batter is cooked until nearly set, then the meat is laid on top and the cooking completed.

Palacsinta: This Hungarian pancake may be served for dessert or a main course depending on the filling. It may be spread with minced ham and mushrooms, plus grated cheese and sour cream, or topped with preserves and sour cream.

Pannekoeke: The basic Dutch pancake, it may be small, filled with custard and served as dessert; or made large, have bacon cooked in and served with molasses, constituting a meal in itself.

Pfannkuchen: The crepelike German pancake,

often served with a mixture of currants, candied peel, grated lemon peel and sour cream.

Platter or *Pannkaka:* Swedish pancake traditionally served with syrup, jam or spiced cranberries.

Po-ping: In Chinese cuisine, the thin Mandarin pancake used in such dishes as Peking duck and *moo shu* pork.

PANCREAS

See **Sweetbreads.**

PANDANUS

See **Screwpine.**

PANEDDA

See **Casigiolu.**

PANIR

See **Surati.**

PANNERONE

See **Gorgonzola.**

PAO D'EMBIRA

Also PIMENTA DE MACACO. The small fruits of a tropical American tree, *Xylopia carminativa*, taste and smell like pepper. They are used as a condiment. Similar fruits are produced by other members of the *Xylopia* genus and are known by such names as *malagueto, frusteca* and silky *embira.* An African variety is called African pepper.

PAPAIN

This enzyme, extracted from the tropical fruit papaya *(Carica papaya)*, acts much like pepsin in its ability to digest proteins. Commercial papain is obtained from the green fruit and forms the active principle in many meat tenderizing preparations.

PAPAW

This is the fruit of a small tree, *Asimina triloba*, of the **custard apple** family and is unrelated to the papaya, which is also called "papaw." The tree grows wild in the middle and southern United States. The fruit is banana-shaped, but thicker than the banana, and reaches from two to six inches in length and may weigh one pound or more. The pulp is yellow, mildly sweet, but distinctly aromatic—to such a degree that many people are put off by the odor. It is usually eaten raw but may be cooked.

Papaya

PAPAYA

Not really a tree, the papaya plant *(Carica papaya)* is a tropical evergreen with a slender stalk reaching as high as 25 feet. Its melonlike fruit grows in a cluster near the top. With its spray of fernlike leaves sprouting directly from the crown, it gives the overall appearance of a palm tree. The fruit varies in color from dark green through yellow to deep orange. The size can range from something that looks like summer squash and weighs 20 pounds, down to something the size of an oversized pear. It is hollow and contains a multitude of smooth, black seeds in a central cavity, which is surrounded by thick, pulpy flesh much like that of a soft melon. The mature flesh is pale yellow to pink; the taste is sweet, sometimes cloyingly so, occasionally redeemed by a slight acidity, and usually accompanied by a pronounced musky flavor, which is not pleasing to all. The papaya is best eaten as a dessert fruit. In the tropics, it is customarily seasoned with a few drops of lime or lemon juice. The seeds reportedly contain an enzyme like pepsin and are chewed by some people as an aid to digestion.

The rind of the unripe papaya is eaten as a vegetable. It is boiled or baked and tastes somewhat like sweet squash. The juice of the green fruit, as well as the latex of the leaves, is rich in an enzyme called papain, which breaks down the protein in animal tissue. For this reason, it is a remarkably effective meat tenderizer and is one of the main ingredients of commercial varieties.

The papaya is native to the West Indies and was a staple of the first people met there by Christopher Columbus, who wrote that the original Carib word *ababai* meant "the fruit of the angels." "Papaya" is an approximation of that word, as are "pawpaw" and "papaw," alternative names for the fruit in English. Another, unrelated, subtropical fruit is also called **papaw.** Cultivation of the papaya spread rapidly through other tropical areas of the world, and significant production today is recorded in the East Indies, India, the Philippines, Africa and Pacific islands such as Fiji and Hawaii. Nowhere does it grow more prolifically, though, than in its native ground of the Caribbean and Central America. Florida is the only U.S. state with viable commercial plantations.

PAPEDA

See **Hystrix.**

PAPRIKA

This bright red, mild chili powder was originally made in Hungary but is also produced extensively in Spain and California. In cooking, it is valued for both flavor and color. Paprika is made from the sweet bonnet pepper *(Capsicum tetragonum)*, whose taste varies somewhat according to where it is grown. Thus the Hungarian variety of paprika has some claim to distinction and has been a marked characteristic of Hungarian cuisine for the past 100 years. The finest grades of Hungarian paprika are mild, being made from the pods only. Lesser grades are hotter, being made from seeds and stems in addition to the pods. Spanish paprika is also available in mild and hot varieties and has a somewhat smoky flavor.

Industrially, paprika is used to color and season processed meats and some cheeses, such as *Liptauer.* In the kitchen, it is added to sauces, sour and fresh cream, butter, potatoes, rice and meat dishes. It is indispensable in goulash. *Capsicums* are rich in vitamins A and C.

PARA CRESS

The peppery leaves of this spreading herb, *Spilanthes acmella*, are used in salads to add a pungent flavor. It is widely distributed in the New and Old World tropics.

PARADISE NUT

Also SAPUCAYA, MONKEY POT NUT. This is an edible and finely flavored seed of the *zabucayo (Lecythis zabucayo)*, a tall forest tree native to French Guiana but found throughout the Amazon River Basin. It is similar to the **Brazil nut** but better tasting and easier to shell. It grows on the tree inside a large, urn-shaped pod, which has a diameter of six to 12 inches and holds many nuts. Harvesting these nuts is difficult because the pod falls from the tree (from a height of 70 feet or more)

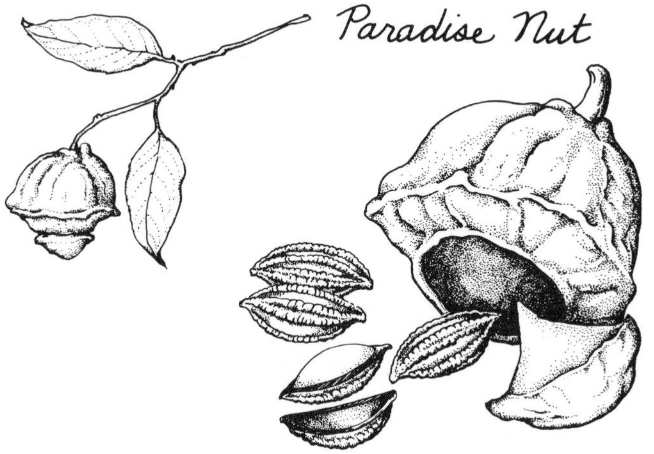

without warning when ripe, bursting upon impact. This sound attracts monkeys who feast on the nuts, hence the name "monkey pot nut."

PARASOL MUSHROOM

This large mushroom of elegant appearance and delicate flavor is found in a variety of habitats in North America, the British Isles and Europe. The parasol mushroom *(Lepiota procera)* may stand as high as 15 to 16 inches and have a cap measuring eight inches across. It appears in late summer or autumn in woods, pastures, meadows and especially in sandy soil. When young, the cap is nearly spherical and reddish brown, expanding to parasol shape on maturity, cracking and separating a bit so that the pigmentation breaks up into scales. The stem is bulbous below and tapers up, with a ring. Only the cap is eaten. The stem, being fibrous, is discarded. When young the flesh is thin, white and soft; when old, dry and leathery.

The parasol mushroom is prepared in a number of ways: it may be served as a separate vegetable with cream sauce, fried and served with bacon and eggs or stuffed, especially with sage and onions. It may be broiled on a quick fire or breaded and fried like a cutlet. Because of its distinctive appearance, it is not easily confused with toxic mushrooms. A close relative, the shaggy parasol *(L. rachodes)*, a smaller species, is also eaten.

See also: **Mushroom.**

PARCHA

Also SWEET GRANADILLA. A type of passion fruit native to the American tropics, *parcha (Passiflora ligularis)* grows on a climbing vine. It is oval in shape, 2½ to three inches long, with a white pulp and skin ranging from yellow to purple. *Parcha* is found in tropical areas from Mexico to western Bolivia. The fruit is considered superior to yellow granadilla. For more information on the yellow granadilla, see **Passion Fruit.**

PARENICA

Also PARENITZA. This sheep's milk cheese, much like **caciocavallo,** is made in Hungary and Slovakia.

PARENITZA

See **Parenica.**

PARFAIT-AMOUR

A liqueur flavored with grated citron peel, coriander, cinnamon and vanilla, it has a violet color and is made in France.

PARGO CRIOLLO

See **Porgy.**

PARKIA

This genus of trees is native to tropical Africa and Malaysia. Its edible seeds are used for flavoring and as condiments. The African species are the **nittanut** and the African locust bean *(P. filicoidea).* The seeds are contained in pods that can reach from 18 to 20 inches long and are also used in cooking. Two Malaysian varieties, *P. Javanica* and *P. Speciosa,* have pods with a slight garlic taste.

PARMESAN

Probably the best-known Italian cheese abroad, Parmesan is actually the name for a group of hard cheeses, commonly called **grana** in Italy, that includes Parmigiano, Reggiano, *Lodigiano*, *Lombardo*, *Emiliano*, *Veneto* or *Venezza*, and *Bagozzo* or *Bresciano*. The texture is grainy; the consistency ranges from very firm to extremely hard; it grates easily. Its high reputation comes from its use in cooking and as a condiment, where it seems to bring out the essence of other foods.

Parmesan is made in huge lots from cow's milk, which is skimmed more or less depending on place of manufacture. It is put through a complex process of heating and draining until a firm curd is achieved. During the first curing, which lasts a year, it is given a black coating that is airtight. Curing may continue for as long as four years, and an aged Parmesan cheese will last indefinitely.

The paste of the mature Parmesan is pale yellow, may have small holes, and has a very sharp flavor. Grated Parmesan is sprinkled on soups, salads and macaroni. Many consider it the best cheese for cooking because it does not become sticky or elastic when heated.

In Italy, it is made between April and November. Much Parmesan is made in the United States, mainly in the states of Wisconsin and Michigan, and is aged at least 14 months. See also the names of specific cheeses mentioned above.

PARMIGIANO

A hard Italian cheese of the **Parmesan** type that is used chiefly for grating, it is a variety of cheese called **grana** in Italy, because of its grainy texture. Parmigiano is made in Parma, Reggio Emilia, Modena, Mantua and Bologna from April to November. Cheeses are round and thick, weighing from 48 to 80 pounds, with a dark, oily surface and a pale yellow interior. Most are cured from one to two years and last extremely well.

See also: **Reggiano.**

PARROTFISH

Also SCARUS. So called because of their brilliant colors, parrotfish (family *Scaridae)* number many species worldwide in tropical and warm-temperate oceans. Most varieties are good to eat, and one, the Mediterranean parrotfish, or *scarus*, was highly prized as food by the ancient Greeks and Romans. This fish may be cooked in a court bouillon or fried.

Two of the largest parrotfish are the *Bulbometaphon muricatus* of the western Pacific and Indian Oceans, which has a grotesque bulbous forehead and reaches a length of four feet and a weight of 150 pounds; and the *Oplegnathus conwayi* of the southern Indian Ocean, which measures up to three feet. It has a parrotlike beak and a golden yellow body marked by dark vertical stripes. Its flesh is good but it is taken by anglers rather than commercial fishermen. It is also known as knifejaw.

Parrotfish inhabit coral reefs and feed on algae and coral that they scrape off the reefs with their strong jaws.

PARSLEY

This member of the carrot family was well known to the ancients, and the curly leaved variety *(Petroselinum crispum)* is the most popular garnish in the United States and Britain for fish, meat and poultry dishes. Parsley is extremely nutritious, rich in vitamins A and C, but all too often it is set aside by unadventurous eaters who regard it as mere decoration.

Among the ancient Greeks, parsley was associated with death. A mythological hero, Archemorus, the forerunner of death, was eaten by serpents while an infant as he lay on a parsley leaf. It was christened the herb of oblivion, and a hopelessly ill person was said "to be in need of parsley."

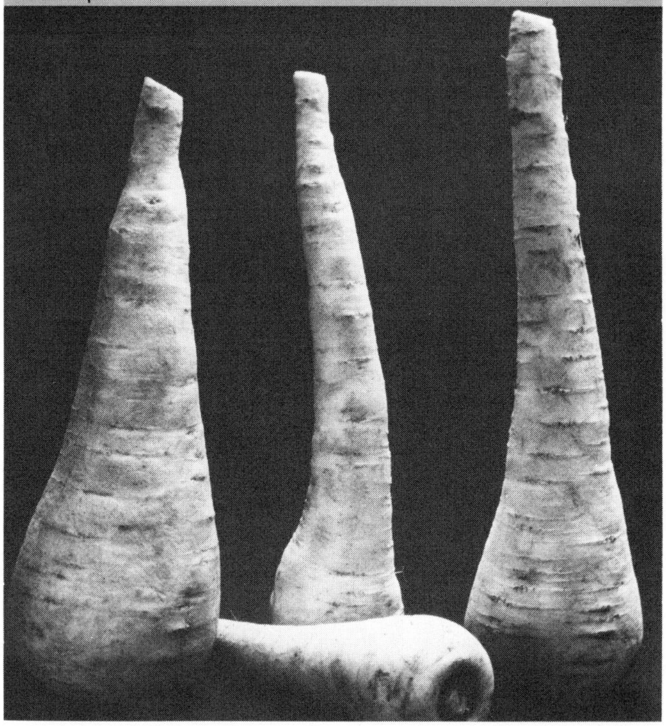

In medieval times, it was thought to belong to the devil, and consequently could be sown successfully only on Good Friday. The saying was coined, "Only the wicked can grow parsley."

It is a biennial plant with bright green leaves which comes in three main varieties: domestic, extra curly dwarf, and Italian. The curly variety is preferred as a garnish, and may be chopped and sprinkled over cooked dishes just before serving. The Italian variety, which has a stronger flavor, is preferred in cooking and may be added to soups and stews. It has flat leaves.

Turnip-rooted, or Hamburg parsley, is cultivated for its fleshy root. It is white, and typically may be six inches long and two inches wide. It is prepared like carrots and has a taste similar to parsnips and celeriac.

PARSNIP

A root vegetable with an assertive flavor, the parsnip *(Pastinaca sativa)* enjoyed great popularity in Europe up until the 18th century, when it began to lose ground in competition with the potato. Sir Walter Scott was referring to a dish that was past its heyday when he made this acerbic comment, "Fine words butter no parsnips."

The parsnip root comes in two forms: one is funnel-shaped, like a white carrot, and can be up to 20 inches long and seven inches across; the other is round and turnip-shaped. Like the potato, much of the parsnip's food value is in its starch. As a rule, parsnips are left in the ground until after the first frost, which converts much of the starch to sugar. It is prepared as one would a potato or Jerusalem artichoke, i.e., steamed, boiled, added to soups or stews or made into fritters.

The ancient Romans enjoyed parsnips, considering the best ones to be from Germany. Although today parsnip tops are regarded as a good green vegetable, the Romans thought them indigestible. Parsnips reached their peak of popularity in the Middle Ages, when they were considered the perfect accompaniment to salt cod and smoked herring, staple protein foods of the common folk. When explorers brought back the potato from the New World, it gradually took parsnip's place. The potato's blandness proved to have broader appeal than parsnip's pungent taste.

To some, cooked parsnips taste vaguely like lobster, and a salad based in it is called the "poor man's lobster salad."

PARTRIDGE

This term is used loosely to designate several species of small game birds, often wrongly, as in the United States, which has no true partridges. The two most common species are the gray *(Perdix cinerea)* and red-legged *(Alectoris rufa)* partridges, which are native to Europe and Asia. What is called "partridge" in the United States is either a quail or the ruffed grouse. The gray partridge is believed to have originated in England and averages 12 inches in length. It is a ground-nesting bird, which favors open country, moors or cultivated land. The red-legged partridge, often called "Frenchman" in England, is less common than the gray but similar in size. It is more inclined to perch in trees and more often frequents woods.

A third variety of partridge, the Greek or rock partridge *(Alectoris graeca)* is common to the Alpine regions of France, Italy and Switzerland and is also found in such distant parts as China.

Partridges are easily domesticated, but this causes loss of the wild game flavor. In cooking, a distinction is made between pullets, i.e., birds killed within a year of hatching, and adults. The pullet, called *perdreau* in French, is more tender and has a delicate flavor. Thus it is never cooked longer than 15 minutes, nor served with a highly seasoned sauce. It is never hung for more than three days, if at all. Often, fat is added in the cooking to prevent dryness. The adult bird, called *perdrix* in French, is, on the other hand, hung for as much as a week, cooked in a casserole and served with a sauce assertive enough to compete with the gamey flavor.

Recipes for preparing partridge that come down to us from ancient Rome are far less circumspect in treatment of what is, after all, not a strongly-flavored meat. Lucullus, a Roman general renowned for the luxury of his banquets, had his partridge boiled in court bouillon, then served in a sauce of verjuice (souring agent), mint and a mixture of strong seasoners. Under those conditions, only the gamiest of tastes would have escaped obliteration.

Partridge season begins in September and runs through December. The early season birds are reputed to be the best, while those of December are said to be flabby and stringy.

PARTRIDGE SAUSAGE

See **Konigswurste.**

PASSE-TOUT-GRAINS

This category of red Burgundy wine is chateau-bottled but combines a nonselective mixture of two Burgundy grapes, the Pinot Noir and Gamay. It is the least good of the quality reds.

Passion fruits

PASSION FRUIT

Also GRANADILLA. Here is a delicious tropical fruit of the passionflower vine, some varieties of which are also renowned for their beautiful flower. Some species of passionflower do well in subtropical and even temperate areas, but the latter do not bear fruit. Purple passion fruit *(Passiflora edulis)* is acknowledged to be the best eating. It is native to Brazil and grows only in the tropics.

The ripe fruit is about the size of a hen's egg. Its tough skin, purple red in color, wrinkles on ripening, which discourages some from eating it at the best moment. Those who persevere, however, discover a sweet, orange pulp, very juicy, with an unusual but excellent flavor. Many black seeds are embedded in the pulp and must be eaten along with the fruit. Purple passion fruit is grown extensively in South America, Hawaii, Australia and Malaysia and sparsely in the southern United States. It does not travel well, so most is consumed locally, either raw as a dessert or as juice. The juice is extracted by a method that eliminates the seeds, and it is bottled pure or used as the base for a soft drink. Passion fruit sherbet is also becoming available.

Maypop *(Passiflora incarnata)* is a passionflower native to the United States. Another is granadilla *(Passiflora quadrangularis)*, with greenish yellow fruit 10 inches long. Giant granadilla *(Passiflora caerulea)* is the most important commercial species, yet the ripe fruit is held to be inferior to the purple passion fruit. Giant granadilla is often picked when it is unripe and boiled as a vegetable. It grows easily in Southern California and Florida but is too fragile to ship. The yellow granadilla *(Passiflora laurifolia)* is popular in the West Indies. It goes by a number of names, including Jamaica honey-suckle, sweet calabash, water lemon, curuba and vine apple.

Passionflower gained its name because its bloom was thought to be symbolic of the Passion of Christ. The flower as a whole was said to represent the wound in Christ's side, filaments in its corona the crown of thorns, stiles of the pistils the nails, stamens the hammers used to drive them in, and so on.

PASSIONFRUIT GIN

Also GIN MARACUJA. A specialty of the Portuguese island of Madeira made from the *maracuja* or **passion fruit,** it is a sweet liqueur.

PASSOVER WINE

This strong, sweet, usually red wine with a grape or fruit base (wine made from grain is expressly forbidden) is blessed by a rabbi and drunk ceremonially during the Jewish holiday of Pesach, or Passover. Four cups of wine are tasted—by all members of the family or gathering—during the banquet, or "seder," on the first night of the holiday. The first cup is symbolic of sanctification, or *kiddush.* The second cup, after being blessed, is tasted during the reading of the Haggadah, or the relation of the history of the Exodus. Bitter herbs, called *maror* in Hebrew, are then crushed and added to the third cup of wine (the bitter with the sweet) to celebrate thanksgiving. The fourth cup attests to God's special providence. A fifth cup, "the cup of Elijah," is often added as a toast to the messianic vision but remains untasted by the celebrants.

PASTA

Also ALIMENTARY PASTE. Pasta is the generic term for a bewildering variety of Italian dough products, made from hard durum wheat flour and bearing such names as *macaroni, spaghetti, ravioli, canneloni, tagliatelli,* etc.

Pasta is a traditional Italian food, and various origins are attributed to it. The noodlelike kind may have been brought by the Ostrogoths, a Teutonic tribe that invaded Italy in about 405 A.D. On the other hand, some claim Marco Polo brought back pasta from China in the 13th century. Yet it is known that during the time of Imperial Rome, pasta of the *tagliatelle* type (flat, ribbonlike) was a common food, going by the name *laganum.*

Pasta can be sorted out by ingredients and by use. There are two main categories by ingredient: *pasta secca,* which consists of flour and water and is machine-made, and *pasta all'uovo,* which consists of flour and egg and is usually handmade. By use there are *pasta in brodo* and *pasta asciutta.*

Pasta in brodo serve as garnishes in clear broths or soups, fulfilling the same function as rice or croutons. They come in a variety of shapes, functional and fancy, some of which may also be served *asciutta.* Some of the more familiar shapes are *ascini di pepe* (small squares), *conchiglie* (sea shells), *crescioni* (crescents), *farfalle* (butterflies), *fiocchetti* (small bows), *lumache* (snail shells), *maruzze* (larger shells), *stellete* (stars) and *vermicelli* (fine noodles).

Pasta ascuitta means dry pasta, i.e., that which is not cooked and served in soup. It is a complex category, comprising both *secca* and *all'uovo,* which are cooked apart and served with sauce, or stuffed, then cooked and served with a sauce, or partially cooked in salted water, then baked with other ingredients.

Served with sauce: This is very often *pasta secca* of which the most important forms are cylindrical (archetype: **spaghetti**), tubular (archetype: **macaroni**), flat and ribbonlike (archetype: **linguine**). These are all long shapes. Short, smooth cylinders are *bombolotti.* Short tubular shapes have both smooth exteriors

Varieties of pasta, left to right: spaghetti, spinach fettuccine, fettuccine made with flour and eggs and linguine

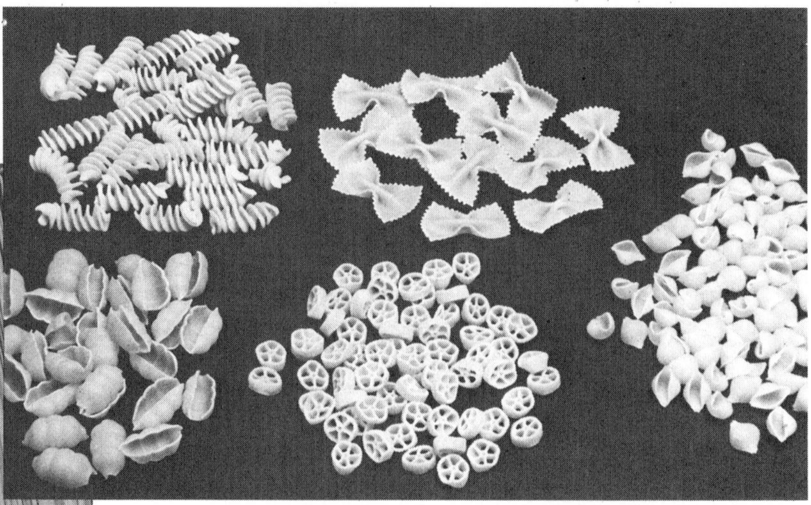

More pasta, clockwise from top left: rotelli, fiochetti, picciole rigate, ruoti, and gnocchi

(penne, maltagliati), and ribbed exteriors *(denti d'elefante, mezzi rigatoni)*. Short, ribbed tubes with an elbow bend are *mille righi* or *mille righi grandi*. The largest of the short, ribbed, tubular pasta is *rigatoni*.

The *pasta all'uovo*, being generally homemade, are limited to fairly simple flat, ribbonlike forms. From small to large the principal types are *tagliarini*, *tagliatelle*, *fettuccine*, *maccheroni alla chitarra*, *pappardelle* and *lasagne*.

Stuffed: Envelopes of pasta (usually *all'uovo*), filled with a savory meat stuffing (archetype: **ravioli**). The principle types are *agnolotti* (oblong shaped, vegetable or meat stuffing), *cannelloni* (large squares, rolled thinly, stuffed with cheese or meat), *cappelletti* (shape of tiny tricorn hat, filled with minced veal, ham, and pork with vegetables), *ravioli* (like *agnolotti*, but stuffed with ricotta and spinach), *rotoli* (giant *cannelloni)* and **tortellini** (half-moon shaped, variety of stuffings).

Baked: The larger varieties of *pasta secca (macaroni, rigatoni)* and *pasta all'uovo (lasagne)* are used in these dishes, which consist of alternate layers of pasta and different sorts of stuffings.

Modern Italians eat pasta with a wide variety of sauces, including bechamel, tomato, Bolognese and brown, and with such cheeses as Parmesan, mozzarella, ricotta, provolone, fontina and *mascarpone*.

PASTIS

A French **aperitif** flavored with **licorice** and similar to **ouzo, anisette,** and **raki,** pastis is distilled from grapes and is colorless until mixed with water. It then acquires a gray or smoky hue. It resembles Pernod in taste and in alcohol content (almost 50 percent).

PASTRAMI

A spicy, smoked meat of Rumanian Jewish origin, pastrami is usually a cut of beef taken from the shoulder, breast or top round. After the bones are removed and the fat trimmed, the meat is cured in spices and garlic for ten days, then smoked for an additional eight days. The result is a spicy, tasty meat used most often in sandwiches both hot and cold. In the United States turkey pastrami is sometimes encountered.

PASTRY

A general term for baked pies, "sweet rolls," cream puffs, tarts, etc., made of light puffy dough, the word also describes any of several doughs used in making pie crusts and tarts (small doughy shells that contain a filling). Pastry doughs are made of flour, fat (butter, margarine or lard) and a very little water. Salt, sugar or egg yolks may also be added to some doughs. Ready-made pie crust and pie filling mixes are today commonly available, but the making of pastry has long been an art requiring careful kneading with the hands, preferably on a slab of marble, with cold butter and ice water. To make plain pastry dough, the cook first sifts the flour and salt, then adds butter or other shortening, blending and pressing with the fingers, until this is distributed evenly through the flour. The mixture may then be kept rolled up in the refrigerator to chill for 20 to 30 minutes. Finally, the pastry is rolled out (with a gently floured rolling pin or by hand) to bake. In pies, either a one-crust or two-crust method is used. A top crust should be trimmed with a sharp knife. Holes are pricked in the crust to allow steam to escape in the baking.

Flakiness in pastry is caused by leaving the fat in pieces and by using a maximum amount of cold water. (Less water makes a pastry that is more mealy than flaky.) In puff pastry, the proportion of fat to flour is much higher than in plain pastry. Most of the fat is added to the dough during the rolling process, to form alternate layers of fat and dough. Hot-water crust is made by boiling the fat and water together and whipping this mixture quickly into the flour. Strong flours should be used for flaky, puff-type and hot-water pastries. In all preparations, the pastry should be handled as little as possible.

Types of pastry are almost infinitely various. Danish pastry consists typically of a yeast dough, enriched by folding in butter (as with flaky pastry), and molded into different shapes to hold fillings such as almond paste, vanilla *creme* or prunes. Danish pastry is marketed in the United States in a wide range of fillings—raspberry, strawberry, blueberry, lemon, pineapple, cheese.

Apfel strudel is a specialty of Austria. Here, plain pastry dough is pressed to paper thinness on a floured cloth, coated with fried bread crumbs, sliced apples, currants, sugar and cinnamon, then rolled up and baked before cutting into slices. Pears and peaches may also be used, with sour milk or cream, eggs, sugar and raisins. In France, puff pastry is widely used for fruit or cream tarts.

Eclairs are made with a rich dough beaten with eggs, which is then piped into a bag and cooked in a hot oven. The shells are then filled with icing or sweet sauce.

A favorite breakfast dish in Spain is **churros,** made from *chou* pastry, one of eight prominent doughs used in Europe for cakes. These are fritters cooked in hot fat, where they expand in long curls. *Churros* sprinkled with sugar are a tasty meal with black coffee or *cafe con leche*.

Pastries are also served in Great Britain in the form of meat pies. In this case, the pastry must undergo a comparatively long time of cooking. Thus, flaky and hot-water pastries are the kinds most often used. Flaky pastry is ideal for deep-dish pies, such as steak and kidney, veal, ham and chicken pies, where the filling is left uncovered. The usual way is to cook the pastry first, and then—with the pastry covered by wet, greaseproof paper—add and cook the meat filling. If cooked meat is used (as in chicken pie) the meal should be ready by the time the pastry is cooked. Pork and game are examples of meat pies cooked with the hot-water method. This is common for pastries that do not require a dish for support, the ingredients being sealed in the crust, which is readily filled and molded by hand.

See also: **Doughnut, Pastry.**

PASTY

In Great Britain, this is a meat pie or other savory baked in a shell of paste dough. It looks like a turnover. Pasties are traditional in Cornwall, with meat, turnips and potatoes the usual filling, but there are many alternatives including such sweets as berries.

PATAGRAS

One of the best Cuban cheeses, *Patagras* is made from whole or slightly skimmed, pasteurized cow's milk. It is similar in taste, texture and shape to **Gouda,** weighing from seven to nine pounds. Cheeses are coated with red wax and wrapped in cellophane.

PATE

Also TERRINE. *Pate* is a French word which, used strictly, means a meat, fish or fruit pie served hot or cold. The word *pate* is derived from the word for paste or dough, and originally a *pate* was always served encased in a shell of dough. As generally used nowadays in English, "pate" has come to mean the filling, with or without the dough, and a particular kind of filling at that. Pates are combinations of ground meat, usually pork, veal or liver. They are mixed to a smooth paste with small pieces of other meats, such as ham, bacon or fowl, plus pork fat, wine or brandy and sometimes truffles, then seasoned with herbs and baked. If the pate is baked in a pastry shell, it is called *pate en croute* and may be served either hot or cold. Otherwise, it is baked and then served in a small dish called a *terrine.* It is served cold and would be referred to in French as a *terrine*, but in English is simply called *pate*.

Pate is most often served as an hors d'oeuvre, and the best known is the legendary *pate de fois gras*, which is made basically of goose livers. See also **Fois Gras.** Other well known *pates* are *pate de canard*, basically duck liver interlarded with small pieces of duck meat; *pate dore*, a pork liver pate usually baked in an oven; *pate a la flamande*, a Belgian specialty including pork liver, bacon, garlic, pork fat and spices; *pate de foie d'oie*, made from at least 50 percent goose livers, the balance made up of pork liver or other meat; *pate de faisan*, pheasant pate; *pate maison*, a blending of ground meats, etc., specially prepared for the establishment on whose menu it appears; *pate de Paques*, an Easter pie consisting of sliced pork, chicken or rabbit, hard-boiled eggs, ground beef, all baked in a crescent-shaped pastry shell; *pate de Pithiviers*, larks, boned and stuffed with *foie gras*, then baked into a pie and served cold; *pate de tete*, ground meat from a pig's head blended into a paste; and *pate vendeen*, a specialty of the Pitou region consisting of wild rabbit and chopped pork.

PATELLA

See **Limpet.**

PATIENCE DOCK

See **Sorrel.**

PATTYPAN

See **Cymling.**

PATZCUARO WHITEFISH

A delicious whitefish (genus *Coregonus)* found in Lake Patzcuaro in the state of Michoacan in Mexico, it is related to the **cisco** of the United States, and the **fera** of Europe.

PEA

This is the seed of a leguminous, climbing plant, *Pisum sativum*, which is grown in many parts of the world, excepting tropical and subtropical regions. Nearly all edible peas are varieties of one species, the garden pea *(Pisum sativum* var. *hortense)*, which apparently originated in northern India, but which has been cultivated in Europe since very early times. The garden pea is unable to withstand long periods of intense heat or direct sunlight. Yet peas have been found in the tombs of ancient Egyptian kings. These turned out to be seeds of the oasis pea *(Pisum elatius)*, which continues to be cultivated in Egypt and other parts of North Africa.

Peas have been found at prehistoric sites in Europe, but it is not known whether they were

Pea pods

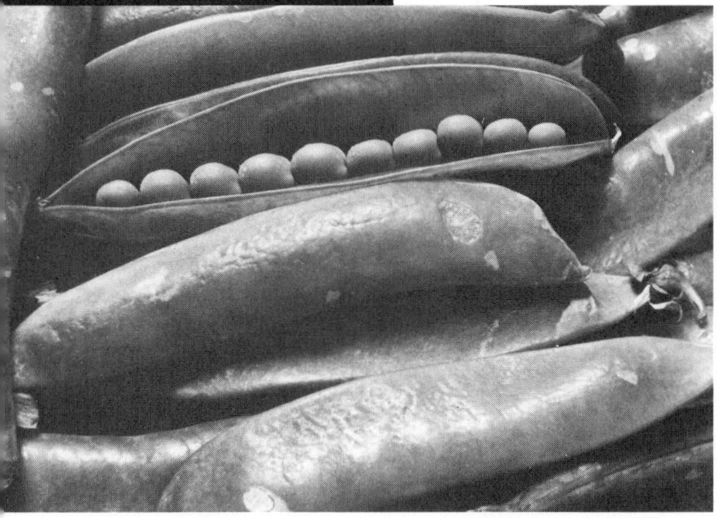

gathered wild or cultivated. Ancient Greeks did cultivate peas and ate them in dried form. They were a common food in ancient Rome with some 37 varieties available in Trajan's market.

Dried peas retained their popularity throughout the Middle Ages, because in that form, peas keep very well and could be stored as a reserve in case of famine. Green peas were a luxury reserved for royalty and the wealthy. The history of that era is replete with stories of royal gluttony inspired by green peas. King John of England is supposed to have died from overeating green peas. Another English king, William III (1689–1702), gained a reputation as a boor by, among other things, hogging the green peas whenever they appeared at the royal table, leaving none for anyone else. According to tradition, peas were brought to the New World by Christopher Columbus who planted them on Isabella Island in 1493. They soon caught on in the English colonies, and by 1614, according to Capt. John Smith, native Americans were growing them.

Peas are eaten fresh or dried. The rule for fresh peas is the younger and smaller they are, the better they taste. Also, to be appreciated fully, they must be eaten within hours of being picked, because they lose flavor rapidly, especially after shelling. The sugar in the pea soon turns to starch. Otherwise, canned or frozen peas may be preferable, having been preserved in a fresher state than that of most fresh peas found in the market. The finest peas are the *petits pois* of France, which are not merely small, unripe peas, but those from special refined varieties developed in Italy at the time of the Renaissance. They manufacture their sugar early. Canned *petits pois* is France's most popular preserved vegetable. Not far behind the *petits pois* are the small, wrinkled peas of England, which contain more sugar and less starch than the smooth, round peas that are preferred in the United States.

Most fresh peas are eaten shelled, even when very young, because the pod incorporates a parchment-like lining that is inedible. An exception is the sugar pea, which is also a variety of *P. sativum.* The young tender pods of this variety are eaten before the seeds begin to develop. At this stage, they are perfectly flat. If allowed to ripen, the pods become inedible as in the other varieties. The sugar pea is not much appreciated in the United States except among the Pennsylvania Dutch, whose predilection for it has caused it to be named the Mennonite pea. In Europe it is nearly equal in popularity to the garden pea, and is called by its French name, *mangetout*, meaning "eat everything." It is also a Chinese specialty, going under the name snow pea.

"Split pea" is a synonym for dried pea, because the drying process includes removing the outer skin and splitting the seed. Dried peas are often ground into powder for various culinary purposes, among them the making of split-pea soup. The difference between the food value of green and dried peas is considerable. The green contain approximately 7 percent protein, 12 percent carbohydrate, and yield about 80 calories per 3½ ounces (100 grams). In contrast, dried peas are 20 to 21 percent protein, 53 to 55 percent carbohydrate, 3 to 4 percent fat and contain 334 calories per 3½ ounces.

PEA BEAN

See **Cowpea.**

PEACH

The round, juicy fruit of the peach tree *(Prunus persica)*, the peach is a luscious fruit, and, as the scientific name suggests, one whose origin was first attributed to Persia. Now most authorities agree it is a native of China. The tree is a small one, with lance-shaped leaves and pink flowers. It thrives in temperate zones and is not particularly long-lived. Some commercial growers replant every eight to ten years. When perfectly ripe the flesh of the peach is strongly flavored and aromatic. It contains a single stone, which is rough and deeply furrowed. The skin is usually fuzzy. There are countless varieties, but these are broken down into rough classifications, such as white or yellow-fleshed, freestone or clingstone, and by time of ripening (very early, early, medium and late).

Clingstone peaches have firm flesh that adheres closely to the stone. They are early ripeners and are popular for canning because they hold their shape better. Well known varieties are Tuscan, Phillips Cling, Sullivan Cling, Walton, Peak, Sims and Libbee. In the freestone, the flesh is readily separated from

Peaches

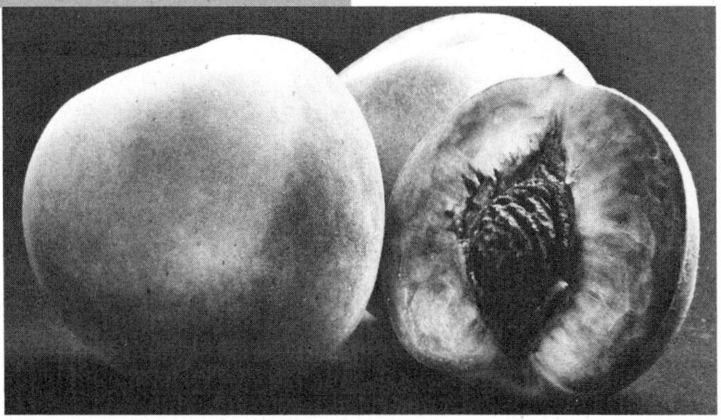

the stone. They are popular for general home use. The best known variety is the Elberta, but others include the J.B. Hale, the Golden Jubilee, the Mikado and the Eclipse. Italy and the United States are major peach producers, and within the latter, California and Georgia are preeminent.

Peaches, particularly the yellow-fleshed varieties, are rich in vitamins A and C. The sugar content is normally 9 percent. Peaches sold in markets are picked unripe and mature en route. Avoid peaches that have skin punctures, brown spots or shriveled skins. The fruit is usually eaten raw, sometimes with cream and sugar. Peaches may be baked and stuffed with almonds, butter and macaroons or stewed and used in pies, flans and jams. They are associated with ice cream, as in the famous Peach Melba dessert named after the Australian soprano, Nellie Melba (1861–1931). It consists of poached peaches in syrup on a bed of vanilla ice cream, with a puree of fresh raspberries and a sprinkling of almonds. Canned peaches are a staple in the home. Peach juice and bourbon whisky are the main ingredients of **Southern Comfort** liqueur.

American author James Fenimore Cooper commented on the difference between French and American peaches in this passage from *The Traveling Bachelor:*

> *A French peach is juicy, and, when you first bring it in contact with your palate, sweet, but it leaves behind it a cold, watery, and almost sour taste. It is for this reason so often eaten with sugar. An American is exceedingly apt to laugh if he sees ripe fruit of any sort eaten with anything sweet. The peaches here leave behind a warm, rich and delicious taste, that I can only liken in its effects to that which you call the bouquet of a glass of Romanee.*

PEACH BRANDY

In the United States, this is a liqueur consisting of a brandy base (distilled from grape) with peach flavoring and sweetening added. By law, this type of beverage must have at least 2½ percent sugar by weight and be at least 70 proof.

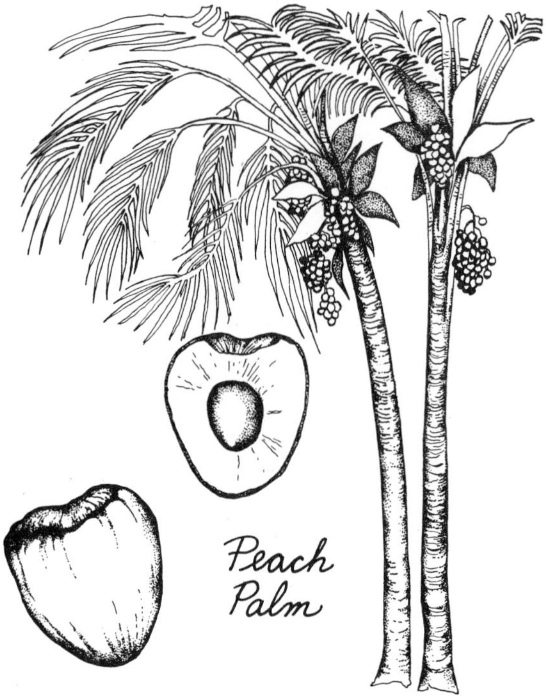

PEACH PALM

Also PEJIBAYE. Plum-sized, often seedless fruit of the South American peach palm tree *(Bactris gasipaes)*, the *pejibaye* can range in color from yellow through orange, red and purple, depending on the variety. It grows in bunches and is thin-skinned. Its pulp is mealy, high both in starch and fat content. The fruit is not eaten raw but usually boiled or roasted. When roasted, it is somewhat like a chestnut. The *pejibaye* makes a good poultry stuffing, or it may be used to prepare a pleasant-tasting drink.

The peach palm is a tall tree, reaching 60 feet or more in height, with long, densely spiny leaves. It has been cultivated since pre-Columbian times and is an important source of food in certain tropical areas. There are commercial plantings in Central America. The adult tree is prolific, bearing four to five bunches a year. The Brazilian spiny palm *(B. major)* is a closely allied species whose fruit is smaller but similar in characteristics.

The tough, fibrous wood of the tree, called *chonta*, is used by primitive tribes to make bows, spears and blowgun darts.

PEAFOWL

Also PEACOCK, PEAHEN. These are birds of the pheasant family, *Pavo cristatus*, renowned for the beauty of their plumage. The peacock especially was held in exalted esteem in medieval Europe. Charlemagne reportedly served several thousand peacocks at one of his banquets. The practice was to skin the bird while keeping the feathers intact. After the carcass had been stuffed and roasted, the skin and feathers would be replaced so that the visual splendor of the bird could be enjoyed by the dinner guests. Opinions differ on the quality of peacock flesh, some saying it is agreeable and delicate, others saying it is tasteless and dry, or at best mediocre. It is most often compared to turkey flesh; indeed, after the turkey began to be imported from the Americas, the peafowl ceased to be of much interest except as ornaments. There seems to be a limited market for young peahens, which are prepared like pheasants.

Peafowl are of southern Asian origin, and were brought to the West in Classical Antiquity. It is said that rich Athenians preferred peafowl eggs to any other. Probably the most lavish squandering of peafowl occurred in 69 A.D. during the reign of the Roman emperor Vitellius, who gorged himself on peacock brains. As many as 500 were killed at a time to provide him with the following exotic mixture: pike liver, pheasant brains, peacock brains, flamingo tongues and lamprey roe.

PEAMOUTH

A small, edible freshwater fish, *Mylocheilus caurinus,* found in rivers of the Pacific slope of Canada and the United States, it is a member of the carp family and is considered a fair gamefish by fly fishermen.

PEANUT

Also EARTHNUT, GOOBER, GROUNDNUT, MONKEY NUT. A member of the bean family, rather than a nut, the peanut plant grows in hot climates throughout the world. It is a vinelike plant, *Arachis hypogaea*, whose flowerstalks wither and bow to the ground after fertilization, burying the young pods, so that they come to maturity underground.

The pods are oblong, cylindrical and have a thin shell. The fruit has considerable food value, being rich in fat, protein, vitamin B, phosphorus and iron.

It was first thought that they were brought to the United States from Africa, and the term "goober" comes from the African word *nguba*. Later evidence showed that they originated in South America, probably Brazil, and that they traveled to North America before the European discovery.

Peanuts are a staple food in Africa and Asia, with India and China the leading growers. They are prized for their oil, which has industrial uses and is excellent for cooking, being particularly popular in France.

The United States produces more than a billion pounds of peanuts annually, chiefly for oil and to use as cattle feed, but much is marketed in the form of peanut butter. Peanuts also appear roasted and salted like nuts, as a hors d'oeuvre or snack. In that form, the saying goes, it is a courageous person who can eat just one.

Making peanut butter

PEANUT BUTTER

This is made from shelled, blanched and dry-roasted peanuts that have been ground to the consistency of a smooth paste. There are two types: smooth and chunk style, which contains pieces of whole nuts. Peanut butter is a nutritious food containing approximately 50 percent fat, 29 percent protein, 17 percent carbohydrate and 2 percent moisture. Commercial peanut butters may contain additives to improve smoothness, spreadability, and flavor, e.g., 1.5 percent salt, 0.125 percent hydrogenated vegetable oil, 2 percent dextrose, and 2 to 4 percent corn syrup or honey. It is used chiefly as a sandwich spread but also appears in prepared dishes and confections.

PEANUT OIL

The oil extracted from peanuts either by hydraulic pressing or by solvent action, it has a mild, pleasant flavor and is nearly colorless. It makes a good cooking oil and is favored for that purpose in oriental cooking.

See also: **Oil.**

PEAR

This is a soft, juicy fruit of the temperate zones, which is usually round at the base and tapering toward the stem. Among temperate fruits, it is second only to the apple in worldwide production. Originating perhaps in China or western Asia, the pear has been cultivated since at least 2,000 B.C. Since then about 5,000 varieties have been developed, elaborated from 15 or 20 species, all of which are descended from two wild species, the European

Varieties of pear, left to right: Nellis, Anjou and Bosc

common pear *(Pyrus communis)* and the Chinese pear *(Pyrus sinensis)*.

The tree *Pyrus communis* is a robust plant, having grayish, rough bark and white flowers. Aside from the so-called pear shape, the fruit may be elongated, oval or round. Although the dessert variety of pears is sweet, melting and juicy, there are harder varieties that are used mainly for cooking, canning and preserving. The pear's flavor is unique and delicate and is sometimes compared to wine. For example, the Bartlett's taste has been described as a "rich muscatel."

A peculiarity of the texture of some pears is grittiness. It is a characteristic of oriental species, many of which have been crossed with European species to improve the latter's resistance to disease. For this reason, some oriental varieties are called sand pears. The grit or stone cells multiply as the fruit approaches ripeness, and partly for this reason pears are usually picked unripe. They can be brought to full ripeness in storage, a quality that also enables the grower to time their arrival at the market and avoid a glut.

American pears are either European species or hybrids of those and oriental varieties. The dominant pear in the United States is the Bartlett. It is an English pear, known there as the Williams *Bon Chretien*, which was introduced into the United States by Enoch Bartlett of Dorchester, Massachusetts. It accounts for about ¾ of U.S. pear production. The Bartlett is yellow when ripe, highly aromatic, and has a white pulp, free of granulation. The crop is grown almost entirely in Oregon and Washington and is in season from July to November. It is popular with commercial buyers as well as individual consumers. Other well-known American pears are the Seckel, a hybrid of the oriental type, i.e., harder flesh and a gritty consistency; the big juicy Comice (see below); the Anjou; the Bosc, a winter pear, and the Kieffer, another hybrid.

France's most famous pear is the Comice, originally *Doyenne du Comice*, a phrase whose meaning is obscure, but can be translated as "best of the show." It is a large, fat pear, a pale yellowish green, and so soft when ripe that it can be eaten with a spoon. Another variety is the Durondeau, a very old variety of a type called *beurre* (butter), a commentary on its creamy texture.

Apart from the *Bon Chretien* and the Comice, which they are fond of, the English have a favorite pear called the Conference. It garnered first prize at the International Pear Conference held in London in 1885, and so was dubbed "Conference." It is a long, thin, yellow green to brownish pear, juicy and refreshing.

Pears are customarily eaten fresh, used in fruit cups, baked, cooked in syrup, cooked in wine and served with ice cream. Italians accompany fresh pears with **Gorgonzola** cheese.

PEARL BARLEY

This is the term for polished barley whose inner and outer husks have been removed. In cooking, the grains tend to swell and make a fine thickener for soups and stews, such as Scotch broth and mutton stew. The flavor is nutty and pleasant.

PEARL MOSS

See **Carrageen.**

PEARL PERCH

Also **EPAULETTE FISH.** Perhaps the finest food fish of Australian waters, the pearl perch *(Glaucosoma scapulare)* is found only in the coastal waters of Queensland and New South Wales. It has a deep body, a large head and mouth and a jet black spot at the end of its gill cover which, when rubbed, reveals a pearl-white bone. Otherwise, the body is greenish brown and silver below. The pearl perch reaches a length of two feet and is taken from the vicinity of sunken reefs. It is not available in large quantities.

PEA TREE

Also **SIBERIAN PEA TREE.** The young pods of this spiny shrub or small tree, *Caragana arborescens,* are eaten as a green vegetable. This plant is native to Siberia and Manchuria.

PECAN

Closely related to **hickory nuts,** pecans originated in North America, growing wild in the Mississippi Valley and in river bottoms in Texas and Oklahoma. Growing in clusters of four, pecans are enveloped in a hard, woody husk, which, like the walnut, splits open when ripe. The nuts are reddish, smooth and oblong with sharp-pointed tips. The taste has been likened to a good walnut, although in the wild varieties it tends to be tart due to the presence of tannin in the thin covering skin.

They were a staple food of native Americans. Cabeza de Vaca, the Spanish explorer, reported in 1528 that the tribes along the Gulf Coast gathered together in river bottoms during the fall to eat pecans. The native Americans extracted a milky fluid from pecans and hickory nuts, which they used for gruel in making corn cakes. The name "pecan" derives from their word, *pegan*, meaning bone shell. This is descriptive only of wild strains, because commercial pecans are "paper shelled."

Pecans

The pecan tree *(Carya illinoinsis)* is a member of the walnut family and reaches heights of 100 feet or more. It is intensively cultivated in Texas, Georgia, Oklahoma and Florida. Texas named it its state tree.

Pecan pie is a favorite dessert of the South, the chief ingredients being pecans, molasses and maple syrup. It is a popular flavoring for cakes, ice cream and puddings.

PECCARY

See **Wild Pig.**

PECORINO

This is a general term in Italy for cheese made from sheep's milk. The best known, and probably the oldest, is *pecorino Romano,* which was mentioned by Pliny. It is a hard pungent cheese that is eaten at the table when young, but when ripe is grated. **Romano** has goat's and cow's-milk varieties, as do many of the other *pecorinos* that will be discussed below. An identical cheese called **sardo** *(Sardo Romano* or *pecorino Sardo)* is made in Sardinia.

Some other *pecorinos* include *dolce,* which is hardpressed and dyed reddish yellow with annatto; *Toscano,* which is similar to Romano, but smaller; *Urbina* and *Grosseto,* which are mild, soft cheeses, and *Ancona, Cotrone, iglesias, leonessa, publia* and *Viterbo.*

See also: **Cotronese, Incanestrato, Moliterno** and **Pepato.**

PECORINO SARDO

See **Sardo.**

PECTEN

A genus of marine bivalves *(Pectinidae)* characterized by grooved, rounded shells. Gastronomically, the most important of these is the **scallop.**

PECTIN

This is a carbohydrate found naturally in certain fruits and vegetables, such as apples, cranberries, currants, gooseberries, quinces, lentils and peas. Pectin forms a gel when combined with the right proportions of acid and sugar, and it is the basis of the jellylike consistency in most jams and jellies. It is available as a commercial preparation, and when jelly is to be made from a fruit low in pectin, such as the raspberry, pectin must be added. This can also be accomplished by adding lemon juice, which is high in pectin.

Pectin is a valuable dietary fiber and has been shown to have a beneficial effect on the level of serum cholesterol in the bloodstream.

See also: **Fiber, Dietary.**

PEEPUL

Also BO TREE. A type of fig tree, *Ficus religiosa*, native to India and Southeast Asia, it is sacred to Hindus and Buddhists, but the small, dark purple fruits are eaten as famine food.

PEJIBAYE

See **Peach Palm.**

PELICAN

The name includes any bird of the genus *Pelecanus*, such as the brown pelican. The pelican is a large, ungainly waterfowl equipped with a fleshy pouch below its bill, which it uses to scoop up and hold fish, and webbed feet. Its flesh is edible but described as coarse, tough and oily.

PEMMICAN

A long-lasting food invented by native Americans, it takes its name from the Cree word *pimiy*, meaning "fat." Pemmican consisted of strips of dried meat, usually from bison, deer or bear, which were pounded to shreds and mixed with rendered fat (usually bear) and berries. The mixture was then stuffed into washed animal intestines, and the ends sewn up, making in effect a type of sausage. Lacking sausage casings, pemmican would be sewed into pieces of rawhide, or even canvas, and the whole dipped into tallow as protection against moisture. If kept quite dry, pemmican could keep indefinitely.

In their fascinating and well researched treatise, *Eating in America: A History*, Waverly Root and Richard de Rochemont wrote of pemmican:

> *Modern dieticians would be hard put to devise a better unspoilable and easily transportable food for men likely to be called upon to exert great physical effort. The iron ration of the Indians, it consisted of lean dried meat (proteins) pounded together with berries (vitamins) in melted fat (energy), sometimes with the addition of bone marrow. . . . It seems clear that they realized that the berries were not mere seasoning, but a necessary element in pemmican. . . . The Cree Indians used wild cherries, the Plains Indians used buffalo berries and the New England Indians used cranberries. Pemmican played an important role in the first crossing of the American continent: it was the basic food which in 1793 enabled Alexander Mackenzie, a fur trader, to travel from the Atlantic coast to the Pacific.*

A modified form of pemmican was later used in arctic exploration—dried beef and raisins. The latter was sometimes put up in cans, which would seem to add little to its keeping qualities, but a lot to its weight. Robert Falconer Scott, who led an ill-fated British expedition to reach the South Pole in 1910–1911, took along canned pemmican. It was found to be in edible condition 45 years later when a cache of his supplies was discovered by another expedition.

PENETELEU

See **Kaskaval.**

PENICILLIUM

Penicillium is a genus of fungi that grows as green mold on bread, cheese or fruit. Certain strains are used to produce the characteristic blue veining in cheeses such as Roquefort. These include *P. glaucum* and *P. roqueforti*.

PENNYROYAL

This plant of the mint family, *Mentha pulegium*, is native to Europe and western Asia. The leaves have a pungent minty aroma, and are sometimes used in cooking as a substitute for spearmint, or in wine cups and juleps. Its essential oil, oil of pennyroyal, was once produced in great quantities for use in medicines, but its popularity has declined. Due to its aroma, pennyroyal has traditionally been thought effective in repelling fleas, hence its species name *pulegium* from the Latin *pulex* for flea.

PEPATO

This Romano-type cheese, made from sheep's milk in Sicily and southern Italy, is heavily spiced with peppers and cured in layers between peppers. Some *pepato* is made in Michigan.

See also: **Incanestrato.**

PEPINO

Also MELON-PEAR. Pepino is the aromatic fruit of a spiny shrub, *Solanum muricatum*, native to the Andean regions of South America. The plant also grows well in temperate regions of North America and in the tropics at certain elevations. The fruit is

Pepino

egg-shaped, four to six inches long and is yellow with violet streaks or splotches. The pulp is solid and seedless and has an acidic but pleasant flavor. It is eaten as a table fruit and was formerly thought to have medicinal value in cases of rheumatism, bronchitis and various skin disorders.

The *pepino* is a member of the *Solanaceae* family, which contains such important foods as the white potato, the eggplant and the tomato, but also the bittersweet or deadly nightshade, a poisonous plant in all its parts. Some writers advise that it is unwise to eat too much of the *pepino* because it is slightly poisonous.

PEPINO DE COMER

This is the gherkin-sized fruit of an herbaceous vine, *Cyclanthera pedata*, indigenous to tropical America. In Peru and Bolivia it is eaten as a vegetable and also used to make pickles.

PEPPER

The basic and traditional spice—black or white pepper—belongs to the family *Piperaceae*, which was first domesticated on the Malabar coast of India. There are other, botanically unrelated, species popularly called pepper, such as cayenne, paprika, chili, green or bell peppers and pimentos, or red peppers. They are *Capsicums* of the family *Solanaceae*, which originated in Brazil and Peru, and were misnamed "pepper" by Christopher Columbus. On arriving in the West Indies, he thought he had reached India, home of pepper. When he encountered a native dish hotly

spiced with chili, he jumped to the wrong conclusion. The name stuck, however. *Capsicums* will be discussed under separate headings. See **Cayenne; Chili; Paprika; Pepper, Green** and **Red.**

Pepper was the first oriental spice brought to the West, and was a mainstay of the foreign trade of ancient Rome. It has been conjectured that the orgiastic feasting of wealthy Romans during the Imperial age was a way of conspicuously displaying wealth, since the dishes tended to be heavily spiced with pepper, and pepper was worth more than its weight in gold. In the 15th century, the exorbitant price of pepper spurred voyages of discovery, such as those of Vasco da Gama, whose first landfall after rounding the Cape of Good Hope in 1497 was the Malabar coast of India. Columbus too was seeking a trading route to the Indies when he discovered America. Spices, including pepper, later became commercial cornerstones of the British and Dutch colonial empires.

Of the more than 2,000 described species of pepper, the most prolific and commercially important is *Piper nigrum*. This is the source of most peppercorns—both black and white—that are used to spice food. It is a jungle plant that thrives best within 10° to 15° of the equator. Optimum conditions include high temperatures, a long rainy season and partial shade. *Piper nigrum* is a clinging vine that attaches itself to a convenient tree or other support, climbing sometimes as high as 25 feet. It bears small clusters of berries, measuring from one-fifth to one-fourth of an inch across at maturity. They are green at first, but ripen to a reddish yellow. Indonesia is the leading producer of pepper, but it is also important in Malaysia, Thailand, Ceylon and India.

The riper the pepper berries the more pungent their taste. They may be picked green, and sold while they are still fresh. This form has come into vogue over the past 20 years in the West, and is a good way to savor the full aroma of pepper without overwhelming pungency. Green peppers are tender and may be mashed into a paste for cooking or sprinkled whole over a variety of dishes.

Berries for black pepper are picked at a later, though still unripe, stage and sun dried. The drying turns the outer skin black. This black skin is the spiciest part of the pepper grain. Berries for white pepper are picked when ripe and also dried in the sun, but first they are soaked in water to loosen the skin, which is then rubbed off, leaving nothing to turn black. The extra processing and the weight loss when the skin is removed make white pepper more expensive. It is a matter for conjecture which of the two is spicier because, although black retains its skin (the spicier part), white is allowed to ripen longer to balance its loss of skin.

Americans greatly prefer black pepper, and to a lesser extent so do the British, while continental Europeans buy relatively more white pepper. The latter preference is attributed by some to black pepper's unaesthetic appearance in white sauces. In any case, peppercorns should be bought whole and ground as needed. Due to the volatility of its oils, ground pepper quickly loses its taste. Purchasing it in ground form also increases the risk of its being adulterated with such things as mustard husks, pea flour and juniper berries.

Second in importance to *Piper nigrum* is the long pepper *(Piper longum)*, which requires similar conditions for cultivation. The long pepper berries do not have the strength or aroma of the *Piper nigrum* and are put to such industrial uses as pickling. If ground and mixed with *Piper nigrum*, it is classified as an adulterant.

PEPPER DULSE

A red seaweed, *Laurencia pinnatifida*, found along the western coast of Scotland, it has a pungent, aromatic flavor and is dried for use as a spice in Scotland. It is not related to true **dulse.**

PEPPER, GREEN AND RED

Green, or bell peppers, and pimento, or red peppers, are larger, mild relatives of the hot chili pepper. In the kitchen, they are used as a vegetable rather than a spice. Both red and green are produced by the same plant *(Capsicum frutescens*, var. *grossum)*, the red being a ripe version of the green. Botanically, they are hard to distinguish from their spicy cousins, but there is no mistaking them in the market. Hot peppers are small, thin-skinned and have a kind of cap the stem sits on. Bell peppers are large and boxy, and the stem is recessed into the top.

Green peppers are picked before they are ripe and are very mild to the taste. They may be cooked as a vegetable, stuffed or used in relishes or salads or pickled. If allowed to ripen, they turn red and are hotter to the taste. Generally, reds are canned as pimento. Despite the name "pepper," they are not related to the tropical vine *(Piper nigrum)* that produces the traditional spice, black and white pepper.

Bell peppers grow well in subtropical areas such as the southwestern United States. They are very rich in vitamin C, and also contain vitamins A, B and E.

PEPPERMINT

The most commercially useful member of the mint family, peppermint *(Mentha piperita)* is cultivated for its essential oil, which is a popular flavoring for candy, chewing gum, toothpaste, liqueurs and medicines, where it usually disguises an unpleasant taste.

Peppermint's taste is pleasantly pungent and mentholated. It is a perennial herb with square stems and dark red leaves in the black mint variety, or green leaves in the white mint variety. The white is superior in flavor, but the black is preferred commercially for its higher oil yield.

Peppermint tea is still a popular tisane; a sprig of peppermint often garnishes the mint julep, a cocktail, but the choice of mint used is a subject of controversy.

See also: **Mint.**

PEPPERMINT SCHNAPPS

Also PEPPERMINT CORDIAL. Peppermint schnapps is a mint liqueur, bottled at from 40 to 60 proof, that is lighter bodied and less sweet than creme de menthe. Peppermint cordial is a liqueur obtained by combining oil of peppermint, 100 proof alcoholic spirits, sugar and water.

PEPPERONI

This is a firm Italian sausage that takes its name from the Italian word for chili pepper, *peperoni.* Like salami, it mixes pork and beef, with perhaps a higher proportion of pork, but it is much hotter and more highly spiced than salami. It is air-dried for a very long time. Pepperoni is a very popular topping for pizza in the United States; otherwise, it is eaten cold, sliced as an hors d'oeuvre or used to add spice to a casserole.

See also: **Sausage.**

PEPPER SAUCE

See **Tabasco.**

PERA DE VACCA

See **Casigliolu.**

PERA DO CAMPO

This is the pear-shaped fruit of a Brazilian shrub, *Eugenia klotzschiana*, cultivated in the central part of the country. The fruit is yellow, with a juicy, very aromatic pulp. It is used to make jellies.

PERCEBAS

Percebas is the Portuguese word for goose barnacle *(Lepas anatifera).* For more on this, see **Barnacle.**

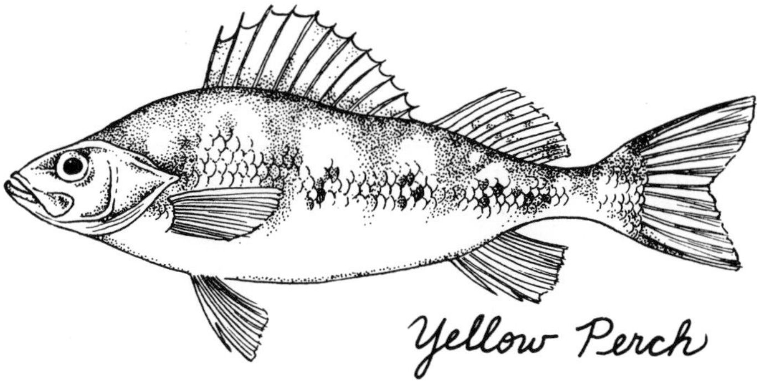

PERCH

This tasty, freshwater fish has many species found throughout the world. The largest member of the perch family is the Nile perch *(Perca nilotica)* of Africa, which can reach a length of six feet. The most common varieties are the yellow perch *(Perca flavescens)* in the United States, and the European river perch *(Perca fluviatilis).* These fish are nearly identical, both being small with greenish brown backs and yellow sides. They average 10 to 12 inches in length and one pound in weight with a maximum of about 4½ pounds.

Perch has been fished since the Stone Age in Europe. Izaak Walton in his 17th-century *The Compleat Angler* gave it high praise as a game fish. It is also esteemed by American anglers, yet it does not attract much commercial fishing, so is not often seen in fish markets. Simple recipes are best for perch; it may be prepared like a trout.

See also: **Walleye, Zander.**

PERCH-TROUT

See **Trout-Perch.**

PERCHE GOUJONNIERE

See **Pope.**

PERENNIAL LETTUCE

This is a southern European variety, *Lactuca perennis*, whose young or blanched leaves make good salad. In colder climates, it can be grown outside as a summer plant.

PERIGUEUX SAUCE

A famous sauce named after Perigueux, the chief city of the French district of Perigord, an area known for its truffles, it consists of **half-glaze** mixed with truffle extract, Madeira wine and diced truffles. Perigueux sauce is used with small cuts of meat, fowl, game, timbales and vol-au-vents.

See also: **Sauce.**

PERILLA

Perilla is an annual herb, *Perilla arguta*, of Southeast Asia, whose leaves, flower clusters and plant embryos are used to make a condiment. They have a minty flavor. It is cultivated in China, Korea, Japan and India. The species *P. frutescens*, a perennial, is cultivated for its oil seeds.

PERIWINKLE

Also WINKLE. These are edible sea snails of the genus *Littorina.* The periwinkle shell is cone-shaped and usually brown or yellow. The mollusk living inside is highly nutritious, having a protein content of 18 percent.

The species *L. littorea* is found on both sides of the Atlantic and was immensely popular in 19th-century England. Winkles, as they were called, were sold from little stalls in London's East End and at seaside resorts as well. They were customarily simmered in their shells, plucked out with a pin and seasoned with vinegar. Periwinkles are plentiful along French coasts as well and are even farmed in some areas.

They may be poached, pickled, roasted or, as in France, served as a garnish to fillets of bass. An edible species found on the Pacific Coast of North America is *L. scutulata.* In Hawaii, the periwinkle is called *opihi* and is often eaten raw with a seaweed garnish.

PERLON

Also SEVEN-GILLED SHARK. This edible shark, *Heptranchias perlo perlo*, is common in the Mediterranean Sea and in the Atlantic off Spain, Portugal and Cuba. Also found in the Pacific, it is recognized by its narrow, tapering head and snout and seven wide gill slits. The perlon is usually found in deep waters and is not considered dangerous to humans, although it can be as much as seven feet long.

PERMIT

A sport and food fish of the tropical Atlantic, the permit is a member of the *Carangidae* family, which includes jacks, scads and pompanos. A large specimen can be as much as four feet long and weigh up to 50 pounds.

The permit *(Trachinotus falcatus)* is a deep-bodied fish with an overall blue color, which is lighter on the belly, and a yellow patch in front of the anal fin. Like its relative, the pompano, the permit is considered excellent food. It is found from Massachusetts to Brazil and in the Gulf of Mexico. It frequents reefs and sandy flats.

PERRIER WATER

This is a sparkling, alkaline mineral water from La Source in Vergeze, France. In a 1980 rating by the Consumers Union, the taste of Perrier was judged good with the following additional comments: mildly bitter, mildly astringent, mild soapy flavor, mildly salty and lingering aftertaste.

See also: **Mineral Water.**

PERRY

A fermented drink made from the juice of pears, it is similar to hard cider, containing from 2 to 8 percent alcohol. Perry retains the flavor of the original fruit, which, as in the making of apple cider, are not the ones considered best for eating. Perry is not a well-known drink except perhaps in England and in the Normandy region of France, where most of the country's pears and apples are grown.

PERSIAN HERACLEUM

The seeds of this perennial plant, *Heracleum persicum*, are used as a condiment in Iran. It is a member of the cowslip genus.

PERSIAN MELON

A variety of muskmelon *(Cucumis melo* var. *reticulatus)*, and the largest of the reticulatus group, it is highly aromatic, sweet, with pink to orange flesh and a netted skin. Some cooling brings out the flavor, but it should not be served ice cold.

See also: **Muskmelon.**

PERSIMMON

Also KAKI. This autumnal fruit is celebrated for both its extreme sourness when green and its cloying sweetness when ripe. There are two main species, the American persimmon *(Diospyros virginiana)* and the Japanese persimmon, or kaki *(Diospyros kaki)*. The latter is larger than the American variety and of more predictable quality.

The American persimmon tree grows wild in southeastern United States and was encountered early on by explorers and colonists. It did not achieve much of a following, perhaps because of its small size—maximum diameter three inches—late ripening and the unpredictable quality of the wild fruit. Native Americans instructed the newcomers to eat them only after the first frost, i.e., October. Sampling one before then is a sour experience due to the presence of tannin compounds. In October, however, the fruit turns from green to bright orange and signals its ripeness by wrinkling slightly. At that point, the persimmon contains more glucose than most other tree fruit, and for this reason it was a great favorite with native Americans. Hernando de Soto, an early Spanish explorer, noted in 1540 that tribes in the Mississippi Valley made bread from a type of "prune," which was really the persimmon. They customarily dried them and then reduced them to a floury paste.

The Japanese persimmon tree, which is really a native of China, was introduced into the United States by Commodore Matthew Perry on his return from Japan in 1855. There are two types, one that is hard and astringent until ripe and one that is less astringent. They vary in color from yellow to deep red. It is the Japanese variety whose cultivation spread to France, Spain and Italy, where it is known as the *kaki*. When ripe, it is soft, pulpy and very sweet. Its size is like that of a large tomato or apple.

Persimmons are eaten raw or made into preserves.

PERUVIAN BARK

See **Cinchona.**

PERUVIAN POTATO

See **Ysano.**

PESTO

See **Il Pesto.**

PETER HEERING

Also CHERRY HEERING. A Danish cherry liqueur, reputed to be one of the finest in the world and

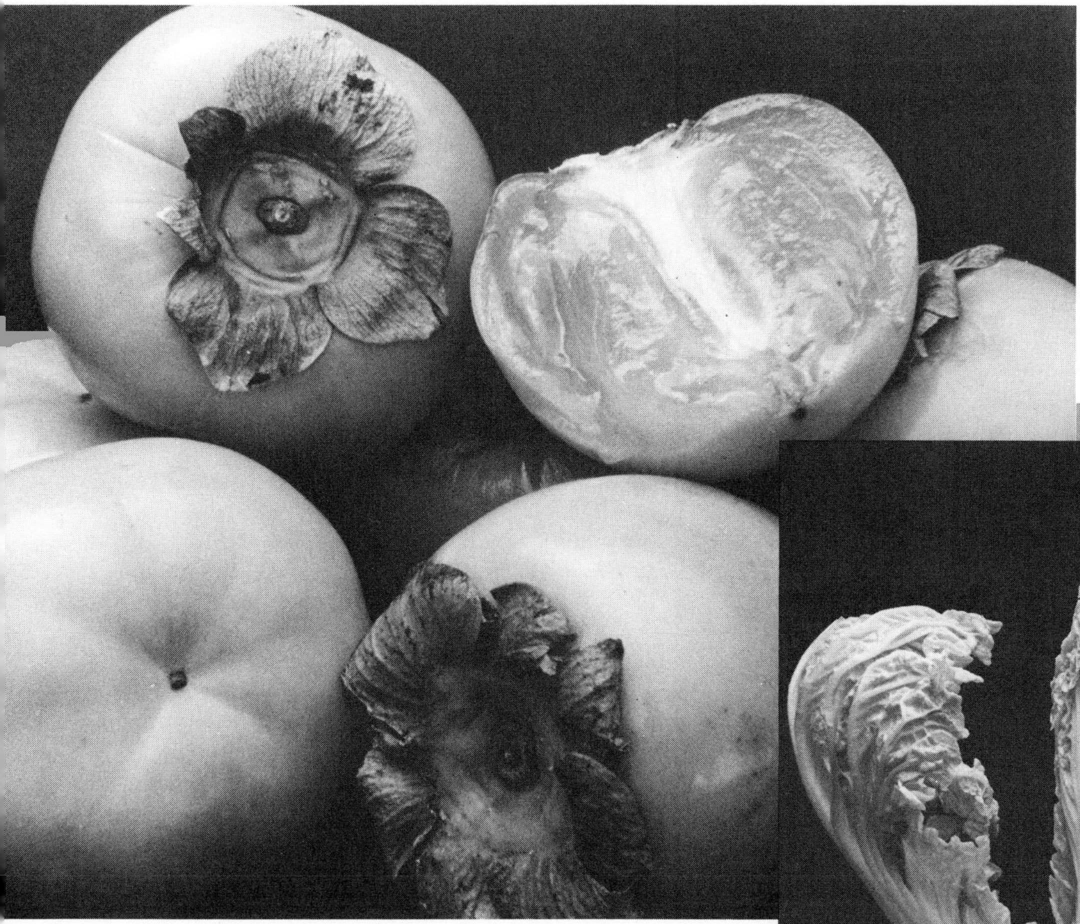
Persimmons

Petsai

formerly known as Cherry Heering, it has been produced in Copenhagen for more than 150 years. During that time, little has changed about it except the name and the shape of the bottle. It is sweet, and the flavor and aroma of cherries are remarkably full-bodied. It is 49 proof.

PETER VAL WATER

This is a naturally sparkling mineral water bottled in the Black Forest of West Germany. A sensory panel sponsored by the Consumers Union in 1980 judged its taste to be good, and better than that of 21 competitors. The panel made the following comments on its flavors: mildly bitter, mildly astringent, mild soapy flavor and mildly salty.

See also: **Mineral Water.**

PETIT SUISSE

A small, rich cream cheese that is made in France and eaten fresh, it is like **carre,** but contains no fat and is unsalted. Individual cheeses are round and flat, coming in two sizes: *gros* (two inches across by two inches thick) and *demi* (1¼ by 1-2/3 inches). They are eaten plain or with a little sour cream and sugar.

PETSAI

Also CHINESE CABBAGE. A garden vegetable of Asian origin, the *petsai (Brassica pekinensis)* has long, narrow, blanched leaves that form a cylindrical head 10 to 20 inches long. It is related to both cabbage and mustard but more resembles romaine lettuce or a cross between lettuce and celery. The leaves are thick, crisp and white to pale green in color. As a salad vegetable, the leaves are equal to the best lettuce.

Petsai is frequently used in Chinese cooking, either stir-fried or briefly boiled. Otherwise it is interchangeable with ordinary cabbage and has the advantage of giving off little odor when cooking. The blanched heart of *petsai* is often sold separately and makes an excellent salad, especially when chopped together with apple. *Petsai* is known in Japan as *hakusai*.

Seeds of *petsai* are available in the West, and the plant is easily grown in the garden, giving a larger yield than lettuce for the same investment of time and expense.

See also: **Pakchoi.**

PEZ ESPADA

See **Scabbard Fish.**

PEZ NEGRO

A small but economically important catfish found in the fast-running rivers of Colombia, *Pez Negro (Astroblepus grixalvii)* reaches a length of 12 inches and has dark coloring, a depressed head and well developed barbels. It is beginning to show signs of depletion due to overfishing, especially in the Central and Eastern Cordillera where it is particularly valued as a food fish.

PFISTER

Here is a type of **Swiss cheese** made from cow's skim milk and named after Pfister Huber, its originator. These cheeses are smaller than other Swiss, weighing no more than 50 pounds, and are cured for six weeks.

PHEASANT

A game bird that is as good to look at as it is to eat, the pheasant *(Phasianus colchicus)* is believed to be native to China, but it is plentiful worldwide. Unlike other birds considered to be good hunting, the pheasant is under no threat of extinction. Perhaps because it combines so many noble qualities—good looks, good hunting behavior, delicious taste—care is taken to stock it and prevent overhunting. Pheasant is also one of the few game birds whose flavor does not suffer much by domestication, so that raising pheasants for the table is a considerable industry.

In Europe, the common or English pheasant is most numerous, followed by the silver and golden pheasants. The male has the more beautiful plumage, characterized by a long tail and hairlike, maroon, silver or gold feathers on the lower back and red wattles around the eyes. The most common species in the United States are the Chinese ringneck and the English ringneck, the latter being a cross between the Chinese ringneck and the common European pheasant. They are marked by a white ring around the neck and hairlike feathers that are green in the Chinese and either mottled or maroon and green in the English.

The pheasant was introduced into Europe at an early date. Its name derives from the river Phasis (now called Rioni), which flows into the Black Sea from the Georgian Soviet Socialist Republic. According to Greek legend, Jason and the Argonauts, after capturing the Golden Fleece, sailed down the Phasis on their way home. While traveling through Colchis (as the area was then called) they discovered the pheasant and were so taken with the bird that they brought live specimens back to Greece. The birds naturalized there and later on became a favorite with the ancient Romans, who introduced them into the rest of the continent. The beauty of the bird inspired the Romans to culinary fantasy. A common way of preparing the bird was to skin it, taking care that the feathers remained intact, then after cooking, stuff it back into its skin so that it arrived at the table in all its natural glory.

During the Middle Ages, the pheasant was considered a noble bird by nature, a food fit only for the nobility. The latter was true of most game, a perquisite of the noble who owned the land. Yet with the pheasant, veneration reached such a level that it figured in chivalric rituals.

The pheasant arrived in America at a fairly late date. George Washington imported pheasants from Europe in 1789 to stock his Mt. Vernon estate. By the 1830s it was common enough to figure in cookbooks of the period. It did not become a regular game bird until after 1880 when large shipments of pheasant were brought from China and released in Oregon. It is now found wild in almost every state.

Though not as showy as the cock pheasant, the hen is usually a plumper bird and probably will be more tender unless the male selected is very young. It has been the custom for centuries to hang pheasant before cooking. During the hanging period, which lasts from four to 12 days depending on the season, the bird partially decomposes and acquires a gamey flavor. Although traditional gastronomic authority supports this practice, it is now passing out of fashion, especially in France. Current practice is to serve game within 48 hours of killing or thawing. Fresh birds are generally better between November and January. Young birds are usually roasted, while older birds may be braised, potted, baked in casseroles or used in salami.

PHELLOPTERUS

This perennial herb, *Phellopterus littoralis*, of northeast Asia, is often used as a condiment. It tastes like angelica or tarragon. Phellopterus is cultivated in Japan, China and Sakhalin.

PHILIPPINE ELEAGNUS

This is an evergreen shrub, *Eleagnus philippinensis*, whose pink to pale red fruit is tartly flavored and usually made into a very fine jelly. The fruit grows to about one inch in diameter.

PHOGALLI

Phogalli are edible flowers of the Indian plant *Calligonum polygonoides*. In northern India, the flowers are dried and ground into flour, which is made into bread, or they may be cooked in butter or ghee.

PHYTOLACCA

See **Pokeweed.**

PICAREL

Also BLOTCHED PICAREL. A beautifully colored fish of the Mediterranean Sea and adjacent Atlantic waters, *picarel*, *(Maena maena)*, is usually blue above and silver below with yellow pectoral fins. It reaches a length of about 10 inches. It is particularly abundant in the western Mediterranean and is important locally as a food fish. Salted picarel is a specialty of the island of Havar off the Dalmatian coast near Dubrovnik.

PICCALILLI

This relish of Anglo-Indian origin consists of chopped pickles, cauliflowers, green tomatoes, cucumbers, cabbage, button onions and more, all immersed in a mustard-vinegar sauce and seasoned with turmeric. Piccalilli is eaten with cold meats and cheeses.

PICHURIM

Also PICHRIM BEAN. The aromatic seed of a Brazilian tree, *Nectrandra puchury*, it is pepperlike and is used as a spice, condiment and medicine.

PICKEREL

In England, this term refers to immature northern pike, whereas in the United States, it applies to separate species of the pike family, namely, the chain pickerel *(Esox niger)*, found from the Great Lakes to Texas; the redfin pickerel *(Esox americanus americanus)*, found in southeastern states, and the grass pickerel *(Esox a. vermiculatus)*, found from Canada to Alabama. These are smaller members of the pike family and rarely exceed nine pounds in weight. They may be prepared in any way suitable for pike.

The term "pickerel" is also loosely applied to the pike-perch, or walleye.

See also: **Walleye.**

PICKLE

Also PICKLING. The term refers to any vegetable or fruit that has been immersed in a spiced vinegar or brine solution for varying lengths of time with the object of both preserving and flavoring it. There are many kinds of pickles. One of the best known is the dill pickle, a cucumber that has been steeped in a brine solution—perhaps briefly fermented—then canned or bottled in a vinegar solution that contains various herbs and spices, dill for sure, but perhaps also cloves, peppercorns, stick cinnamon, mace, red peppers, mustard seeds, allspice, bay leaf and root ginger. Also pickled, either by themselves or mixed, are cauliflowers, onions, gherkins, chilis, green tomatoes and green walnuts. Some relishes, such as **piccalilli,** contain pickles and other vegetables preserved in a mustard-vinegar-turmeric solution.

Fish and meat are also pickled, sometimes as a preliminary to another process such as smoking, as in ham, sometimes as an end in itself, as in the case of corned beef. Most often pickled are pork shoulders, hams and briskets of beef. The pickling solution in the case of meats contains, in addition to brine, sugar and spices, sodium nitrite and saltpeter (sodium nitrate), which gives meat a characteristic pink color as well as helping to preserve it. In England, pickled salmon is well known. Chinese hundred-year eggs are pickled, but only for about four weeks.

PICKLED CHEESE

The term refers to cheeses that are heavily salted during processing or cured in brine to improve their keeping qualities. Most are made in countries with warm climates bordering the Mediterranean Sea. The curd is usually soft and white, and the taste sharp and salty. Included in the group are *Domiati* and *Kareish* (Egypt); *feta* (Greece) and *Teleme* (Bulgaria, Greece, and Turkey). The last is also made in Rumania and called *Brandza de Braila*.

See also: **Domiati, Kareish, Teleme.**

PIDDOCK

This mollusk (genus *Phola)* found in European waters bores its way into soft rock, wood or clay. The species *P. dactylus* is eaten in England and France and may be boiled, pickled, or cooked in butter or prepared in any way suitable for **whelks** and **clams.**

PIE

Pie is a dish baked in a pastry crust. The filling may consist of meat, fish, fruit or vegetables, and it may be baked with an undercrust, an overcrust or both. These descriptions refer to pies baked in dishes, or pie tins, but a pie may also be baked in a pastry envelope, as in the case of a **pasty.** It is believed that pies originated in 14th or 15th-century England, and that in the early days they combined both sweet and savory ingredients. Taste has evolved into a separation of the sweet and the savory. In Great Britain a pie without a top crust is referred to as a "tart" or "flan," although an exception is made for such dishes as shepherd's and cottage pie, which are topped with a thick layer of mashed potatoes.

Savory pies have retained their popularity in England down through the ages. These include raised pies, made with hot-water crust and usually filled with pork, veal or ham; beefsteak and kidney pie, containing chunks of meat in a succulent gravy; game pies filled with venison, hare, pheasant or partridge; and mutton pies. The most common sweet pies are apple, rhubarb, blackberry with apple and gooseberry.

Americans are much more lax in their usage, including such items as lemon meringue pie (no crust on top, just meringue); unbaked pies consisting of a pie shell filled with chocolate cream or perhaps ice cream, and even Boston cream pie, consisting of layers of sponge cake with cream in between. One such off-beat pie is shoo-fly pie, a Pennsylvania Dutch creation. According to Waverly Root and Richard de Rochemont in their charming book, *Eating in America: A History:*

> *Shoo-fly pie [is] actually not so much a pie as a molasses cake, though it is baked in a pie-crust shell. Its name is usually explained as coming from the fact that flies are attracted by its sweet stickiness and must continually be shooed away, but there is another more recondite theory. Crumbs are sprinkled on the top of shoo-fly pie, which it is alleged make it look to some observers like the head of a cauliflower; hence "shoo-fly" is supposed to be a corruption of the French word for cauliflower,* chou-fleur. *How a French word could have insinuated itself into this setting is not explained.*

PIG

The name refers to a swine or hog, i.e., a domesticated animal with a long, broad snout and a thick, fat body covered with coarse bristles. The flesh of the pig is the world's most widely eaten meat, despite being tabooed by numerous cultures and religions. Pig as fresh meat is called "pork," a term that can be used to include cured meat too. Specifically, cured pork is ham and bacon.

Nearly all parts of the pig are edible or otherwise useful in some fashion. There is virtually no waste. It is a highly economical beast. This is why the pig, which was first domesticated by the Chinese more than 5,000 years ago, has maintained its worldwide popularity. Minor parts of the pig are used in the following ways: the skin is roasted to make crackling, a dry crisp honeycomb of bubbles; the blood makes black pudding, a type of sausage; intestines, or chitterlings, are used as sausage casings; brains may be poached or fried; variety meats, such as heart, liver, lights, sweetbreads and kidneys, are prepared like those of other animals; boiled pig's head is traditional Christmas fare in England or is used in brawns and head cheeses; cheeks can be baked, roasted or cured like bacon; and pig's feet, ears and tail can be boiled, fried, grilled and fricasseed. Pig fat boils down to a firm, white grease called lard, which is an excellent fat for frying and is good for making cakes and pastries.

As for the parts not eaten, the skin makes excellent leather; pharmaceutical essences are extracted from its glands; pepsin is obtained from its stomach; the inedible part of its fat is used as a lubricant, and its bristles serve as upholstery and insulation.

Ever since its first domestication in China, the pig has excelled in turning the seemingly useless byproducts of human existence into edible meat. It can thrive on such stuff as cotton leaves, corn stalks, rice husks, water hyacinths and peanut shells. For much of human history in the West, pig was the only meat available to the poor. Peasant and city-dweller alike found keeping pigs to be an economical proposition, since the animals could be left to fend for themselves. In the countryside, pigs foraged for acorns, beechmast and chestnuts, while in the city they roamed the streets living on garbage. They contributed in this way to hygiene as well as nutrition by keeping the streets clean. This was true of the citystates of Greece, ancient Rome, medieval London and Paris and even of New York City well into the 19th century. Charles Dickens made the following observations in his *American Notes* about pigs in New York City in that era:

> *They are the city scavengers, these pigs. Ugly brutes they are, having for the most part, scanty brown backs like the lids of old horsehair trunks, spotted with unwholesome black blotches. They have long,*

gaunt legs, too, and such peaked snouts, that if one of them could be persuaded to sit for his profile, nobody would recognize it for a pig's likeness . . . . Perfect self-possession and self-reliance, and immovable composure are their foremost attributes.

Hand in hand with widespread domestication of pigs came prohibitions against eating their flesh. The ancient Egyptians regarded the pig as an unclean animal, identifying it with Set, the god of evil. This may be the origin of the Jewish taboo against pork, i.e., the ancient Hebrews adopted the Egyptian practice during their captivity. It is also theorized that the taboo had its basis in hygiene, rather than religion, in that pork spoiled easily in the Middle Eastern climate. The mutton that replaced it, however, spoils just as easily as pork.

A more plausible theory is that pork was enemy food. The ancient Hebrews were nomads, herding sheeps and goats. Pigs are contrary animals, difficult to herd, and are thus a feature of sedentary life. When the Hebrews arrived in Palestine, they found the coastal plains occupied by Philistines, a sedentary people who kept pigs and ate shellfish (another food tabooed by Jews). The religious sanction may have been imposed to keep Jews from taking up pig-keeping, which meant defecting to the enemy lifestyle.

Islam, the religion of nomadic Arabs, also prohibits eating pork, probably for the same reason. And the Mongols, nomadic conquerors of China, disdained the eating of pork because it meant "going Chinese." Pork is also taboo to Laplanders, nomads of Northern Europe and to the American Navajo, a nomadic tribe that converted to agriculture in fairly recent times.

China is the leading pork-eating nation of the world, with an estimated pig population of 280 million. The Soviet Union has 75 million and the United States 60 million. These numbers pertain to 1978, but the U.S. figure fluctuates significantly depending on the price of pork. As for consumption, Austrians hold the top spot in Europe with a per-capita rate of 84 pounds a year, as compared to 74 for the West Germans, 61 for the French and 25 for the British. Americans eat about 70 pounds of pork, much less than they do of beef, which averages about 110 pounds.

Of all domesticated animals, pigs produce the most offspring, with the exception of the rabbit. In medieval Europe, the European pig and the Chinese pig were crossed to produce the lard pig, which was not broken down into different breeds until the 19th century. As the demand for animal fats in such things as margarine and shortening declined in the middle of this century, meat pigs replaced lard pigs in popularity. The emphasis now is on hogs with broad backs, flat sides, good hams and not too much fat. They are traditionally fed corn (maize) in the United States, which is supplemented by alfalfa, barley, skim milk and protein additives. They tend to be high in lean cuts and low in fat cuts. Typically a hog is slaughtered at the age of five to six months and weighs 220 pounds. Ham and loin make up about 44 percent of the carcass.

See also: **Bacon, Ham, Pork.**

PIGEON

The name refers to any bird of the *Columbidae* genus, of which there are many species, most characterized by small size, plumpness and short legs. Little distinction is made between doves and pigeons, and their distribution is world-wide. Chief among European varieties are the wood pigeon *(Columba palumbus)*, the stock dove *(C. oenas)*, and the rock dove or rock pigeon *(C. livia)*. These pigeons are very good to eat, especially the wood pigeon.

A special delicacy is the squab, or young pigeon, which is never more than four weeks old nor more than 14 ounces in weight. At that point, it has developed to where it is just about to leave the nest, and it may be recognized by its small, pinkish legs and downy feathers under the wings. These birds are tender and plump but, because of their small size, do not carry much meat. Squab is usually split and fried, but it may also be roasted. Mature pigeons are often baked in pigeon pie or another type of moist cooking, such as a casserole or stew. Pigeons are often raised domestically for the table and, in killing them, it is important that they be kept without food for 24 hours just prior, so that the meat has a pale color. The liver has no gall and may be left in the bird during cooking. Pigeon eggs are much relished in China.

Pigeons are found wild in most parts of the world, but the North American wild pigeon *Ectopistes migratorius)*, or passenger pigeon, was hunted to extinction in the 19th century. It was a migratory bird alternating between the Canadian woods and the Gulf of Mexico, and at certain times of the year it was present in such large numbers that the supply was deemed inexhaustible. At one point the total number was estimated at nine billion, but such was the slaughter that by 1900 that number had been reduced to zero in the wild. The last passenger pigeon died in the Cincinnati zoo in 1914.

PIGEON PEA

See **Congo Pea.**

PIGNOLIA

See **Pine Nut.**

PIGNUT

See **Hickory Nut.**

PIGWEED

See **Good King Henry.**

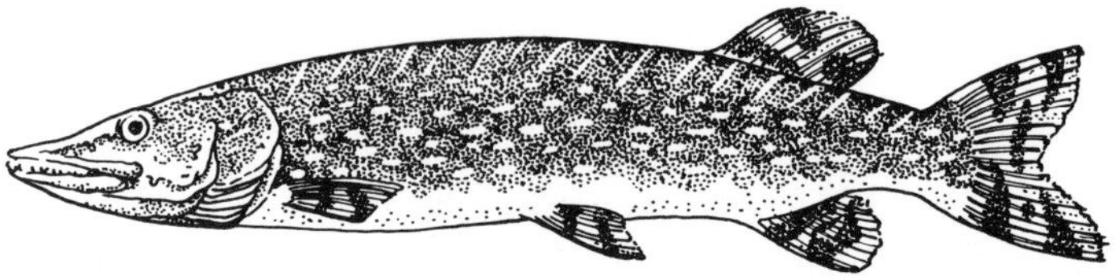

Pike

PIKE

Here is a family *(Esox)* of large, voracious freshwater fish, including the northern pike *(Esox lucius)*, which is found in northern Europe, Asia and North America. Europe has only the one species of *Esox*, but North America has several, most notably the giant muskellunge and the smaller pickerel. These will be discussed under separate headings. The pike's readiness to attack other fish, including its own species, and even small mammals, has earned it such names as the freshwater shark and the river wolf. It is highly regarded by anglers as a gamefish for its fighting qualities.

It is held in lesser regard as a food fish because, although its flesh is lean, firm and white, the taste is bland and sometimes muddy, due to the pike's feeding habits. Moreover, there is an abundance of small forked bones threaded through the flesh. This has not bothered its reputation in France, however, because pike rivals trout as the number-one freshwater food fish.

Northern pike is a fast-growing fish with a long thin body, flat head and pointed duckbill jaws. It has a green back that shades to yellow sides and a white belly. In its first two years of growth, it can reach 30 inches, and a mature pike of 20 pounds or more is not unusual. The largest recorded pike was taken from Lake Conn in Ireland. It weighed 53 pounds and measured 4½ feet.

PIKE-PERCH

See **Walleye.**

PILCHARD

This European sardine, *Sardinia pilchardus*, is common in large schools from the southern coast of Portugal north to the British Isles and Scandinavia. The pilchard has been an important food fish for centuries, and today supports a large industry in Portugal, where it is canned and preserved in oil. The French sardine is also a pilchard.

"Sardine" probably derives from the island of Sardinia, where the fish was first packed in olive oil. The "false pilchard" found in North American waters is actually a species of herring *(Harengula clupeola)* and is often called "sprat." The Spanish sardine *(Sardinella anchovia)* is related to the pilchard, which probably takes its name, in turn, from "pilcher," a short thin scabbard, which Shakespeare's Mercutio threatened to "have about" Tybalt's ears.

The pilchard may reach a length of 10 or 12 inches but is usually taken and canned when half this size. Pilchards are useful in the manufacture of fish oil, fish meal and for fertilizer, particularly in Japan, where a Pacific version of the fish, similar to the Spanish sardine, is abundant.

PILE PERCH

Also DUSKY SEA PERCH. A small food fish found along the West Coast of North America from Alaska to southern California, the pile perch *(Rhacochilus vacca)* prefers shallow, inshore waters and is popular with pier and surf anglers. It rarely exceeds 15 inches in length and is dark brown above with silver sides and dusky blotches running down its flanks. It is closely related to the **rubberlip seaperch.**

PILINUT

Good-tasting nut from a tree, *Canarium ovatum*, of the Philippines and other Pacific Islands, the pilinut has a smooth, hard shell and is generally light brown in color and triangular in shape. The nut is roasted before being eaten and is added to rice dishes or used to make confectionary. It is related to the **Java almond.**

PILOTFISH

Also RUDDERFISH. This cosmopolitan fish, *Naucrates ductor*, got its name through its habit of leading larger fish and following sailing ships. The pilotfish has an elongated and round body, reaching a length of about two feet. It seeks the company of larger creatures, such as sharks and turtles, apparently acting as a cleaner of parasites. Its flesh is described as white and delicious. It is often broiled with oil or butter, lemon juice and herbs, or it may be prepared like mackerel.

PILSENER BEER

A light, bright lager beer produced originally in Pilsen, Czechoslovakia, it continues to be produced there under the label "Pilsener Urquell." Brewers the world over, however, have appropriated this designation to describe their best, light, lager beers. Thus it appears on scores of labels that have nothing to do with Czechoslovakia and is meant to convey that the brewer's produce has the smooth delicious flavor of the original. Unlike bock beer, Pilsener is not a separate and distinct type.

PIMENTO

See **Allspice.**

PIMIENTO

See **Pepper, Green and Red.**

PIMM'S CUP

This is an alcoholic drink, the base for which is premixed and bottled under a proprietary label. Pimm's Cups are designated by numbers 1 to 6. The original Pimm's Cup No. 1 is based on gin and bitters. In the bottle it is heavy and bittersweet, but when mixed with soda water or sparkling lemonade, it makes a refreshing long drink. According to the authoritative *Grossman's Guide to Wines, Beers, and Spirits:*

> *A bartender in Pimm's restaurant in the London financial district invented the original gin sling many years ago, and the patrons liked it so much they used to ask that it be prepared for them in quantity so they could take it up to the country when they went on holiday. From the numerous requests of this nature, it was natural that the drink be prepared commercially.*

This success was followed by subsequent Pimm's Cups, namely, No. 2, based on Scotch whisky; No. 3, based on brandy; No. 4, based on rum; No. 5, based on rye whisky; and No. 6, based on vodka. The exact formulas for Pimm's Cups are trade secrets.

PIMP CHEESE

See **Mainzer Hand Cheese.**

PIMPRENELLE

See **Burnet.**

PINEAPPLE

A sweet, juicy, often tart fruit that originated in tropical America, the pineapple *(Ananas comosus)* is a multiple fruit consisting of the fusion of many blossoms around a central axis. The fresh pulp is a whitish yellow and contains about 15 percent sugar, plus malic and citric acids, and a ferment, bromeline, like pepsin.

It was first encountered by Columbus in Guadeloupe and brought to Europe in 1493. Its cylindrical shape and rough, spiky surface caused the Spaniards to name it *pina*, after the pinecone, although the pineapple is much larger by comparison. The English noted the same resemblance, hence our word "pineapple." The Portuguese, along with other Europeans, took their cue from the Carib appellation, *nana*, and called it *ananaz*.

To the Caribs, the pineapple symbolized hospitality, and the Spaniards soon learned they were welcome if a pineapple was placed by the entrance to a village. This symbolism spread to Europe, then to colonial North America, where it became the custom to carve the shape of a pineapple into the columns at the entrance of a plantation.

Pineapples do not travel well, losing much of their sweetness and flavor if not allowed to ripen at the source. They were still rare in Europe in 1688 when John Evelyn, in his *Diary*, recorded tasting his first pineapple at a reception the English king gave for the French ambassador Colbert:

> *It fell short of those ravishing varieties of deliciousness described in Captain Ligon's History, and others, but possibly it might be, or certainly was, much impaired in coming so far; it has yet a graceful acidity, but tastes more like the quince and melon than of any other.*

Cultivation spread to tropical areas around the world, including the Azores, Canary Islands, Brazil, Cuba, Formosa, Ceylon, Africa and Mexico. But because of the traveling problem, the industry did not really take off until a canning factory was built in Hawaii early in the 20th century. Hawaii now produces 75 percent of the world crop, 95 percent of which is canned.

The most popular varieties of the plant include Red Spanish, a red yellow fruit of fair quality grown mainly in Cuba, Florida and Puerto Rico; Smooth Cayenne, a large orange yellow fruit of very good quality grown extensively in Hawaii and the Azores; and the Cabezona or Bullhead, a large, good-quality fruit that is excellent for canning. Other varieties are Sugar Loaf, Antigua Black and Antigua White.

Eaten fresh, it is an excellent dessert and is sometimes enhanced by a sprinkling of **kirsch.** In Anglo-Saxon countries, pineapple is used as a garnish for roast meats, especially ham. Other ways of prepar-

Pineapple

ing include making candies or jellies, squeezing into juice and flavoring ice cream and sherbet. In the Philippines, it is made into vinegar and served with a national dish, chicken *adobo*.

PINEAPPLE CHEESE

An American cheddar-type cheese, first made in Litchfield, Connecticut, it is pressed into pineapple-shaped molds. The surface has the ridges and furrows typical of the fruit and is oiled or varnished. Pineapple cheese has a curd that is firmer than most cheddars and can weigh up to six pounds.

PINEAPPLE GUAVA

See **Feijoa.**

PINE-CONE FISH

This small Indo-Pacific fish is encased in heavy, uneven scales that constitute a kind of body armor. The scales, together with its plump, round shape, suggest the appearance of a pine cone. Although it only grows to five inches, the Japanese consider it delicious eating and fish it commercially. It is eaten fried or roasted and seasoned with vinegar. The species is *Monocentris japonicus.*

PINE MUSHROOM

See **Matsutake.**

PINE NUT

Also PIGNOLI, PIGNOLIA, PINE SEED, PINON. This is a type of nut or seed obtained from the cones of certain pine trees whose edible kernel is white, aromatic and rich in starch. The most important species for the harvesting of pine nuts are the Italian stone pine *(Pinus pinea);* the Swiss stone pine *(P. cenbra)*, which grows from the Swiss Alps eastward through Siberia to Mongolia, and the pinon pine *(p. cembroides* var. *edulis)*, a dwarf species of Colorado, New Mexico, Arizona and northern Mexico.

The economic importance of the stone pine was noted by several ancient authors, including Theocritus, Cato and Virgil. It remains so today in areas of heaviest concentration, principally for the harvesting of the nuts rather than as lumber. Much of the pine nut harvest is consumed locally and never reaches the market. Some of the cash crop, however, is exported to the United States and the Middle East.

The umbrella-like stone pines do not produce usable cones until their 15th year. At maturity, the cone is about six inches long and is composed of a number of scales containing two seeds each. More than 100 seeds may be recovered from a single cone, each measuring about three quarters of an inch long. The scales are removed by hand and cracked mechanically.

The cones of the pinon pine open up on the tree, allowing the nuts to fall to the ground. For the most part they are gathered by native Americans who extract the kernels and eat them or use them for trade. Three to five million pounds are gathered in this way annually.

Pine nuts are eaten raw or roasted as a snack. They do not store well raw because the fat they contain goes rancid. They are a regular ingredient in some Italian dishes, in Turkish and Balkan cooking and in Middle Eastern and Mexican cooking. Pine nuts are also used in candy and in decorating cakes and cookies, such as macaroons.

PINGA

See **Cachaca.**

PINTAIL

A wild duck of Europe, Asia and North America, distinguished by its long, slender neck and long, green black tail feathers, the pintail *(Anas acuta)* is a swift-flying bird (attaining speeds of up to 65 miles an hour) that is considered both good eating and a fine game bird.

See also: **Duck.**

PINTO BEAN

See **Kidney Bean.**

PIORA

A mild to medium-sharp cheese made in the canton of Ticino in the Swiss Alps, it is ripened with red cheese bacteria so that the curd is quite yellow and the flavor like a very mild Limburger.

There are three grades of *Piora: Piora vero*, which use only milk from cows of the Piora Alp; *tipo Piora*, which uses cow's milk from other Alps in the canton; and *tipo uso Piora*, which uses a mixture of cow and goat milk. Individual cheeses are round and flat (12 to 16 inches across by four inches thick) and weigh from 18 to 35 pounds. They are cured from three to six months.

PIQUANTE SAUCE

This classical French sauce is basically an **espagnol sauce,** flavored with shallots, capers and white wine, then put through a sieve and seasoned with pepper. Chopped chervil, parsley and tarragon are added with chopped gherkins, a little meat juice and maybe French mustard. Piquante sauce is used on small cuts of meat and various left-over meat dishes.

See also: **Sauce.**

PIRANHA

Also PIRAYA. A freshwater fish of South America, infamous for its attacks on humans and other large animals, the piranha has a formidable set of teeth, and a school of piranhas can strip the flesh off a large mammal, such as a horse, in a matter of minutes. Of the three piranha species, the largest, *Pygocentrys piraya*, is used as food by residents of the lower Amazon River basin in eastern Brazil.

The *piraya* reaches a length of up to two feet, and is very deep-bodied, having a high back and curved belly profile. It has a snappish disposition and must be handled with care even when apparently dead.

PISCO

Pisco is a brandy produced in Peru and Chile. The best Pisco is distilled from Muscat grapes in the Ica Valley near Pisco, a port in southern Peru. As a rule, Pisco is consumed quite young. It is drunk straight or, more usually, mixed into the Pisco sour, the most popular cocktail in both Peru and Chile. A mixture of Pisco and *chicha* (corn beer) is called *chicha de jora*.

PISTACHIO NUT

Pistachio nuts are the kernels of the pink, grape-sized fruit of the *Pistacio vera* tree. The nut is naturally green or ivory colored, but some Near Eastern varieties are dyed red in processing to hide blemishes. The pistachio has a characteristically delicate, sweet, oily taste that is esteemed as a flavoring for confectionary, sauces, cakes and ice cream. Although it is pistachio oil that is used as a flavoring ingredient, the vast majority of pistachio nuts, at least in the United States, are sold in the shell and eaten out of hand as a snack.

The tree originated in the Levant, and it is first mentioned historically in the Bible. But it was known in Persia by 6 B.C., and by the ancient Greeks. Arabs introduced it into Sicily, which has remained a substantial production center. The largest producers are Iran, Turkey and lately, with the introduction of the Kerman variety, California. This variety produces nuts that are larger and plumper than the Middle Eastern varieties and that mature uniformly and crack open of their own accord. This makes them more amenable to mechanical processing.

Pistachios are about 54 percent oil and have a high iron content. Apart from flavoring, the oil is used in some cosmetics as an emollient. Germans and Italians use it in curing pork sausage.

PIT

Also KERNEL, STONE. The hard center of such soft fruits as cherries, plums, peaches and apricots, it contains a seed which, when pressed, yields an essential oil containing the principle, amygdalin. The latter tastes of bitter almonds. Pits are often added to the mash in the making of such fruit brandies as kirsch and slivovitz precisely to add a soupcon of bitter almonds to the taste. The French liqueur, *noyau*, is based on fruit pits.

See also: **Noyau.**

PITAHAYA

Spiny, red fruit of a treelike cactus, *Acantheocereus pentagonus*, found in southern Texas and Mexico as

Pistachio nuts

well as Central America, it it three inches long with seeds. It is also known as *naranjada. Pitahaya de agosto* is the purplish fruit of a variety of strawberry cactus *(Echinocereus conglomeratus)* found in the southwestern United States and Mexico. It measures about an inch in diameter. Another variety, *E. stramineus*, yields the Mexican strawberry, also known as *pitahaya*. The *pitahaya oregona* is the fruit of the night-blooming cereus *(Hylocereus undatus)*, a cactus often cultivated in Mexico and Central America. This fruit attains a diameter of five to six inches; it is red and considered to be of excellent quality.

PITANGA

See **Surinam Cherry.**

PITOMBA

Egg-shaped fruit of a Brazilian shrub, *Eugenia luschnathiana*, cultivated in the Bahia area, it is orange yellow with a soft, juicy pulp whose aromatic, mildly acidic flavor makes a good jelly.

PIZZA

An Italian open-faced pie that has become a major fast-food item in the United States and elsewhere, the basic pizza consists of a layer of pasta dough, or yeast dough, spread with spiced tomato paste and topped with mozzarella cheese. Other toppings include pepperoni, Italian sausage, anchovy, green peppers and other savory items. There are no sweet pizzas in this sense of the word. In Italy a *pizza dolce* is a cheese cake, and a *pizza rustica* a savory pie like a *quiche*.

The pizza is said to have originated in Naples, but regional varieties abound in Italy, where they are sold in small cafes called *pizzerie*. The latest addition to the American canon is the so called Sicilian pizza, which employs yeast dough to produce a sort of deepdish effect. No small town in the United States is complete without its pizza parlor, and large cities have hundreds.

PLA BA

This river fish of Thailand, Sumatra and Borneo is popular among anglers for its fighting qualities. It is edible too, but must be approached with caution since it is said to be poisonous during certain seasons. The species is *Leptobarbus hoevenii*, a member of the carp family. The name *pla ba* means "mad fish" in Thai because the fish behave oddly after eating fruit of the chaulmoogra tree that falls into the water. The *pla ba* reaches a length of 20 inches and has beautiful, but varied, coloration.

PLAICE

A European flatfish, the plaice *(Pleuronectes platessa)* is known as "the poor man's sole," because, though palatable, it is placed lower on the gastronomic scale than turbot, brill, sole, flounder and halibut. It is a bottom dweller, with both eyes placed on its upper (right) side. It is easily recognizable by the orange red spots on its otherwise brown upper skin. In the market these spots should be bright; if not, the fish is stale.

A ten-pound plaice is considered large, the normal size encountered in the market averaging no more than two pounds. Smaller fish are usually fried or broiled, and larger ones filleted and baked in the oven, but the plaice may be prepared in any way suitable for sole. There are no true plaice in American waters, but the name is given to the American summer flounder or fluke *(Paralichthys dentatus)*.

See also: **Flounder.**

PLANCHONI

A tropical fruit related to the **mangosteen,** the *planchoni*, *(Garcinia planchoni)*, grows on a small tree native to Vietnam and adjacent countries. It is oval, about three inches long and yellow green. The taste is agreeably acidic. It is eaten fresh or dried.

PLANTAIN

A variety of banana, known also as the cooking banana, the plaintain, *(Musa paradisica)*, is starchy but not sweet and is much larger than the fruit, or dessert, **banana.** It is the staple starch in some tropical areas, such as the West Indies, tropical Africa and Malaysia, much as the potato is in temperate zones. Indeed, uncooked it has much the consistency of raw potato or turnip. However, it is never eaten raw. It is picked unripe and baked, fried or made into fritters.

Plantain needs salt, pepper or a certain amount of spice to make it palatable. In the tropics, plantain chips are often a substitute for potato chips as an accompaniment to drinks.

PLECTRONIA PLUM

Light brown fruit of a South African tree, *Plectronia lanciflora*, it is about the size of a plum and considered to be one of the best indigenous fruits.

PLECTROPOMUS

A good food fish, *Plectropomus maculatus* is of the grouper type found in ocean waters from East Africa to the central Pacific. It is a reef fish and reaches a length of four feet or more. It may be red or nearly white with brown bars.

PLEUROTE

See **Elm Tree Pleurotus.**

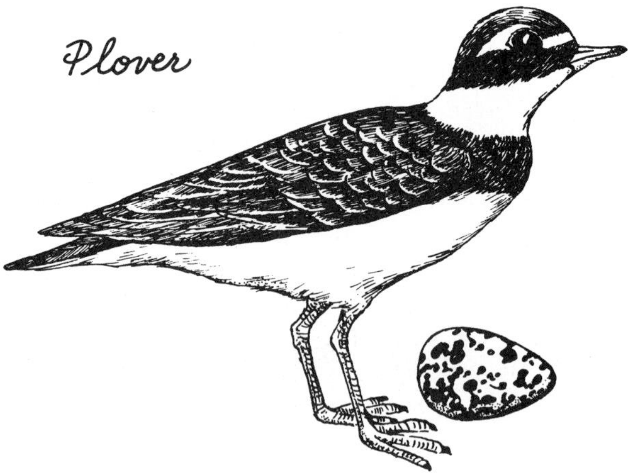

PLOVER

This is a family of small birds, *Charadriidae*, with about 60 species. Most frequent the shore or other watery areas, but some are found in inland meadows. Several species of plover have long been considered excellent game birds in Europe, but it is illegal to take them in the United States. These include the golden plover *(Pluvialis apricarius)*, a bird the size of a pigeon with golden speckled plumage; the gray plover *(P. squatarola)* with black and white plumage but no golden spots; and the green plover *(Vanellus vanellus)*, a smaller bird, also known as the lapwing or peewit. Plovers were popular fare in the Middle Ages and were usually roasted without being drawn first. Nowadays, they are prepared in any way suitable for **woodcock.**

Plover's eggs, specifically those of the green plover, are much beloved by gourmets but are increasingly hard to purchase because many countries have outlawed their collection. About the size of pigeon's eggs, they are black-spotted on an olive ground. Traditionally they are hard-boiled, producing an orange yolk acclaimed for its delicate flavor. Another method of preparation, said to be favored by the last tsarina of Russia, was scrambled with a garnish of sliced breast of hazel-hen, and slivers of black truffle, all topped with game sauce.

PLUCK

See **Heart.**

PLUM

This smooth-skinned fruit comes from trees of the *Prunus* genus and contains a single, flat stone. Plums may be deliciously sweet or quite bitter, depending on the variety. There are many varieties of plum, ranging in color from yellowish green to deep purple, and in size from that of a small cherry to a hen's egg. They are eaten fresh, dried to make **prunes,** made into pies, tarts, jams, jellies and preserves, used to make liqueurs and distilled to make brandy, such as the Yugoslavian **slivovitz.**

Our prehistoric ancestors gathered wild plum, as evidenced in Swiss lake dwellings where plum pits of a tart variety called the Bullace *(Prunus institia)* were found. Cultivated plums were introduced into ancient Rome, it is believed, from Damascus. Again, it was a tart variety, this one called the Damson *(Prunus damascena)*. It is sweeter than the Bullace, but sour enough to be recommended only for cooking, for which it is highly esteemed. It is not much cultivated except in England and the eastern United States. An English specialty, called Damson cheese, is a sort of plum paste boiled down to a cheeselike consistency.

A favorite French plum is the *Reine-Claude*, named for Claude, queen of Francis I. It was brought to England in 1725 by Sir Thomas Gage, and became known as the Greengage. The Greengage is small, round, green or yellow green and sweet. It is equally popular fresh, canned or in preserves.

The *Mirabelle*, another French plum, is small, golden yellow and highly aromatic. Though sweet, it has an underlying tartness that makes it especially good cooked, usually served stewed or in jams. The *mirabelle* tree is the nearest relative of the original form of *Prunus domestica* and is often used as stock upon which to graft other varieties.

These varieties are grown in the United States, but today most commercially grown U.S. plums are descendants of the Sino-Japanese plum, which was introduced into California in 1870. Many of the most prolific producers are hybrids of this plum and either the European plum or the wild American species. The Sino-Japanese varieties, while not as flavorful as the European and American, brought other virtues, i.e., they are showy, productive and long-keeping. Following are some commonly seen U.S. plums:

The *Burbank*, of American origin, is medium-sized and round, with thin, dark red skin and yellow flesh, which is sweet, juicy and firm. It matures about the end of July.

Santa Rosa is large and spherical, with dark red skin, pinkish yellow flesh, and a pleasant, slightly tart taste. It ripens around mid-July.

The *Stanley* is a large, oval plum of exceptional productivity. The skin is dark purple, and the flesh greenish yellow, juicy and sweet. It is good fresh and excellent when dried.

The sloe is a small, extremely bitter kind of plum used to make the liqueur sloe gin and jam.

Plums are shipped before they are fully mature, but they ripen quickly and turn overripe faster than any other fruit. In the market, they should be just soft enough to give to slight pressure and should not be sticky or too soft. They should be stored in a cool, dry place, or if fully ripe, in the refrigerator.

POCHARD

Also POKER BIRD, SEA DUCK. This wild duck (genus *Aythya)* known for its fine-tasting flesh is considered by some to be the equal of the mallard. It summers in arctic regions and winters on the coasts of North America (as far south as North Carolina), Europe and Asia. It is said that the bird tastes best when frequenting fresh water rather than salt.

The common pochard *(Aythya ferina)* has a red head and neck and a black and gray body. It is known under a variety of names, including the dunbird (England), the red-headed poker (U.S.A.) and the red-headed widgeon. It is avidly hunted in France, Germany and Holland during its migration. Its flesh is described as succulent and distinctively flavored. Any recipe for wild duck is suitable for the pochard.

POHA

See **Cape Gooseberry.**

POI

See **Taro.**

POITIERS

See **Goat's Milk Cheese.**

POIVRADE SAUCE

A famous and popular French sauce is based on **espagnole sauce** with the following ingredients added: red wine, wine vinegar, freshly ground black pepper, herbs, light stock and diced vegetables. It is sieved before serving and is used on meat, ragouts and game (when game essence is added). The same sauce in England, with the addition of a little red currant jelly, is called roebuck sauce.

See also: **Sauce.**

POKEWEED

This popular name for the native American *pocam*, is often used to designate any tall plant that yields a red or yellow dye. Pokeweed, or poke *(Phytolacca americana)*, is edible when the young shoots are properly cooked. It is a strong-smelling perennial herb, from six to eight feet high, with dark purple berries that contain a crimson juice used in pioneer days as ink. (Another name for poke is "Inkberry.") It is common in North America. The large white root is poisonous but can be used in small doses as an emetic.

The young leaves and shoots serve as a potherb or green in the making of poke salad. Euell Gibbons cautions that pokeweed greens should be first boiled, the juice then discarded and the greens reboiled. Cooked in this manner, and lightly salted and buttered, poke salad resembles spinach or turnip greens in taste. During the Civil War and in the Great Depression, pokeweed was a cheap and valuable survival food. It is cultivated and marketed today on a small scale in the southern United States but is more commonly collected in its wild or natural state.

POLAND WATER

A natural spring water from South Poland, Maine, it is bottled as a still water, its natural state, and as a sparkling water. Both versions have a very low mineral content (125 and 99 ppm total dissolved solids). A sensory panel sponsored by the Consumers Union in 1980 judged the taste of the still water to be very good, the only sensory defect being a mildly soapy flavor, and the taste of the sparkling water to be good, with the following comments: mildly bitter, mildly sour, mildly astringent and mildly salty.

See also: **Mineral Water.**

POLENTA

This is an Italian porridge or mush made usually from cornmeal (maize), but also occasionally from barley meal, and in certain areas, from chestnut meal. It is prepared by boiling the meal in salted water, then mixing in butter or olive oil, and topping it with grated cheese. Polenta may be served hot or cold. Often it is allowed to cool, then cooked in various other ways, such as baking or frying. Polenta is a specialty of northern Italy, especially the Piedmont region. The word is also used for an Italian version of **hominy grits.**

POLIOMINTHA

This is a wild shrub, *Poliomintha incana*, of the southwestern United States. Its flowers are used as a seasoning.

POLISH SAUSAGE

Also KIELBASA. Although the Poles make many kinds of sausage, this term has come to mean one that looks like a **frankfurter,** but is coarser in texture and flavored with garlic. Both pork and beef are used, and the casing varies from eight to 12 inches. The finest kind are smoked over juniper wood. Polish sausage can be eaten cold or poached. It is frequently accompanied by red cabbage.

See also: **Cabbage.**

POLLACK

Also POLLOCK, COALFISH. There are two nearly identical fish inhabiting the North Atlantic called "pollack," the *Pollachius pollachinus* of European waters, and the *Pollachius virens* of North American waters, the latter called coalfish in England. The main point of difference seems to be that, although both are green, the coalfish is much darker.

The pollack is a close relative of the **cod** but is considered much inferior as food. On the other hand, the pollack is popular with anglers, having good fighting qualities. Sometimes called green cod, the pollack, when freshly caught, has a back of striking olive green. It is distinguished from the cod by its undershot jaw, deep plump body and pointed snout. Maximum weight for the pollack is 36 pounds, but most are caught in the four to 15-pound range. They are eaten both fresh and salted.

The Alaska pollack, which inhabits Pacific waters from the Bering Sea south to the Puget Sound, is quite similar to the coalfish.

POLLAN

Also EUROPEAN CISCO, VENDACE. A species of whitefish, *Coregonus albula*, closely related to the **houting** and found in lakes in the British Isles and across Europe to western Russia, it reaches a length of 18 inches and can be recognized by its prominent lower jaw, upturned mouth and pointed head. Overall, it looks like a herring. The name "pollan" derives from the Irish word, *polag*, for whiting. At first, it was thought to exist only in certain Irish loughs, but then it was found to be identical to the Scottish vendace of Loch Maben. Like its cousins the other **whitefish,** the pollan is excellent to eat and may be prepared like trout. Commercially, it is a moderately valuable food fish in Scandinavia and parts of eastern Europe and Russia.

POLLOCK

See **Pollack.**

POLYPORE

A group of edible fungi that includes the sulphur shelf mushroom *(Polyporus sulphureus)*, the hen of the woods *(Polyporus frondosus)* and the many-capped polypore *(Polyporus umbellatus)*, these are unusually large mushrooms occurring in clusters of fan-shaped caps near or on hardwood trees in North America, the British Isles, Europe and, in some cases, the Far East. These fungi are commonly six inches across, but larger specimens may reach a width of two feet.

The sulphur shelf mushroom is popularly called the chicken of the woods, not only because its color and shape sometimes suggest a setting chicken, but because it tastes like chicken and the interior looks like white chicken meat when torn into strips. The term "polypore" refers to the many tiny openings or pores on the underside of the mushroom. Its caps are sulphur yellow with orange bands or borders. The sulphur shelf is best when young; when older, only the tender tips of the caps are eaten.

These fungi attacks the heartwood of trees. As an historical footnote, the *Speedwell* was a ship that was to accompany the *Mayflower*, bearing Pilgrims to the New World in 1620. The *Speedwell* was declared unseaworthy, however, because sulpher shelf mushroom, growing in the unventilated hold, had rotted the ship's planks.

The hen of the woods, about the same size as the sulphur shelf mushroom, grows on the ground near trees or stumps and, with its gray brown caps, resembles a setting hen. It is popular with Italians and Italo-Americans, who call it cauliflower mushroom. It recurs in the same spot year after year and is found in the fall after heavy rains. It is excellent sauteed in butter and served on toast or in casseroles. It may be substituted for chicken in many recipes.

The many capped polypore is somewhat smaller and appears earlier than the other two. Its color resembles that of the hen of the woods. Polypores maintain their flavor well when preserved by freezing.

POMBE

Pombe is a millet beer made in Africa. As in the malting process of traditional beer, the millet seed is allowed to sprout, which breaks down the starch and converts it to fermentable sugar. It is then allowed to ferment naturally.

POMEGRANATE

This is a fruit the size of a large orange, containing a red, juicy pulp that is divided into compartments and encloses myriad tiny seeds. Despite its delicious and refreshing flavor, it has limited appeal as a fresh fruit, since the seeds must be laboriously separated from the pulp or swallowed with it. More often the pulp is put through a sieve, and used to make cool summer drinks or employed in the manufacture of grenadine syrup. The seeds have an unpleasant taste, so it is best to avoid chewing them or crushing them in the pulp.

The pomegranate is a fruit of very ancient cultivation, antedating the arrival of the Hebrews in Egypt, for example. Perhaps because of its abundance of seeds, it was used in ancient rites as a symbol of fertility and figures importantly in several myths. In Greek mythology, it is the symbol of Persephone, goddess of Spring, who was kidnapped by Hades and carried to the underworld. Her mother Demeter, goddess of agriculture, appealed for her return but received only partial satisfaction because, while in the underworld, Persephone had partaken of six pomegranate seeds. According to legend, this obliged her to remain six months of each year in the underworld. This is interpreted as an allegory of the vegetative cycle, i.e., six months in the earth during winter, then appearing above ground in the spring.

The pomegranate grows on an attractive small tree, *Punica granatum*, which is believed to be native to Persia and which is often cultivated as an ornamental. There are several varieties of the fruit, with their outer skin varying in color from pale yellow to purple. The rind is leathery. The interior arrangement of pulp compartments is so pleasing to the eye that the design was carried over into woven fabrics of the Italian Renaissance.

Pomegranate flavor is unique, but the degree of acidity varies widely among species, ranging from astringent to pleasingly subacidic. Some Middle Eastern varieties lack acidity altogether and are cloyingly sweet. Countries that use pomegranate in the most versatile fashion are Iran and Jamaica, where in addition to being eaten raw, it goes into soups, sauces, jellies and other sweets.

In the United States, pomegranates grow well in California and in the Southeast, particularly in Georgia, Alabama and Florida, where they are especially popular in the autumn.

POMEGRANATE MELON

See **Mango Melon.**

POMELO

See **Grapefruit, Shaddock.**

POMEROL

This superior red wine comes from the district of Pomerol on the Dordogne near **Bordeaux** in western France. Like the fine red wine of nearby **St. Emilion,** Pomerol reds are darker, slower to mature and have a slightly stronger flavor than other Bordeaux red wine. Grown primarily from the Merlot and Bouchet grapes, Pomerol goes well with any red meat, game and cheese. Chateau Petrus is an outstanding wine from this district. The adjacent vineyards of Lalande de Pomerol yield a wine comparable in quality.

POMETIA

Edible fruit of a Polynesian tree, *Pometza pinnata*, it is round and smooth, about two inches in diameter, juicy, sweet and aromatic.

POMFRET

Also RAY'S BREAM, BULLEYE, SEA BREAM. This is a food fish commonly caught off the Atlantic and Mediterranean coasts of Spain, but occasionally as far north as Britain. In the Southern Hemisphere it is more widely distributed, appearing off South Africa, New Zealand, Australia and Chile. The pomfret is a deep-bodied, compressed fish with a high forehead. It reaches a length of up to 30 inches. Its flesh is described as very good, white, firm and flaky with very few bones. In Spain, it is sold fresh or canned. This fish has a dark brown back, coppery sides and a lighter belly. It is prepared like **bream.** The name "pomfret" is also applied sometimes to the **butterfish.**

POMMARD

This red wine comes from the commune of Pommard two miles south of **Beaune** in the Burgundian wine-growing area of the Cote d'Or ("the slopes of gold"). Unlike most of the vineyards along the Cote, the grapes here face south instead of southeast and receive the rays of the sun differently. Pommard wine is consequently lighter than the **Chambertin** and **Vougeot,** grown only a few miles farther north, and is ruddier in color.

POMPANO

A fish caught around Florida and the West Indies, the pompano has an excellent taste that Mark Twain thought "as delicious as the less criminal forms of sin."

The Florida pompano is but one of several members of the *carangidae* family that bear the name, though by far the most famous. A flat fish, oval in shape and silvery blue in color, it is caught year round but most plentifully in December, January

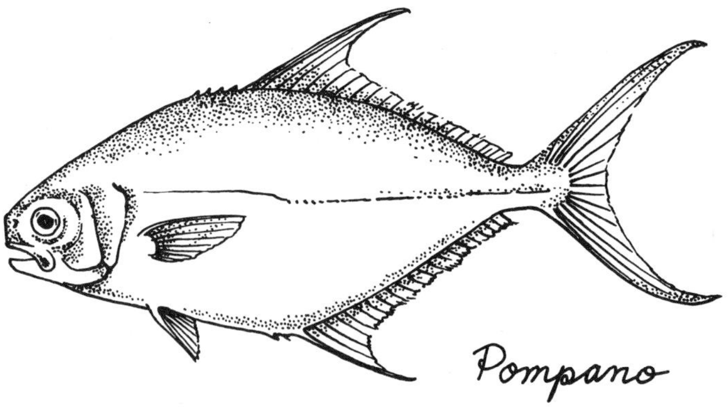

and February. An average pompano weighs three pounds, and larger ones rarely exceed eight pounds or 18 inches in length. The taste has been variously described as nutty, or somewhere between salmon and turbot. The California pompano is something else, a **butterfish,** and inferior in flavor.

Most flat-fish cooking methods are appropriate for pompano. A celebrated item of New Orleans creole cooking is pompano *en papillote*, i.e., baked in paper.

POND APPLE

Fruit of a small tree, *Annona glabra*, of the same genus as sweetsop, soursop and cherimoya, the pond apple grows to about four inches long and is smooth and yellow in color. Its taste is insipid, definitely inferior to other *Annonaceae*. The tree is grown in Florida, tropical America and West Africa, mainly for grafting stock. Its fruit is sometimes used to make jellies.

POND SMELT

A small, mainly freshwater fish of Asia, the pond smelt *(Hypomesus olidus)* is exploited throughout its range as a food fish. It is found from northern Japan to Siberia and on the coastline of the Arctic Ocean, extending into Canada and Alaska. Some varieties are migratory, living a major part of their lives in the sea. *H. olidus* is a true smelt, and like its European cousin, its flesh is delicious and redolent of cucumbers. The pond smelt rarely exceeds eight inches in length and has a green back with a prominent silver stripe along its sides.

PONT L'EVEQUE

A medium-firm, fermented cheese that ranks among the greatest French cheeses, it originated in a town of the same name in the Normandy region, where its history dates back well before the 13th century. Pont l'Eveque is small and mold ripened in the style of **Camembert,** but differs in that it has firmer body, a shorter curing period and less mold growth. Similar cheeses are *St. Remy*, which is French; and *Brioler*, *Steinbuscher* and *Woriener*, which are German.

Whole or partly skimmed cow's milk is used, and color is added during processing. A coating of fine salt is applied, and the cheeses are dried, then put in square molds for curing. The result is a plump cheese, with crosshatch markings from the straw matting in the molds. It has countless tiny holes and a pale yellow color. The ripening agent is *Monilia candida*, a growth peculiar to the locality, which gives it a distinctive flavor very difficult to imitate, though many try. Individual cheeses are crusty, about four and a half inches square and weigh 12 ounces. It is at its best in autumn and winter but is eaten in any month save August.

See also: **Steinbuscher, Westphalia Sour-Milk Cheese.**

POONA

A soft, fermented cheese developed in the 1940s in New York State, poona is fully flavored, and although it looks much like **Camembert,** the color and aroma are closer to mild **Limburger.** These cheeses are round and flat, weigh 12 ounces and are cured for six weeks.

POPCORN

Popcorn is a distinct variety of corn (maize), *Zea Mays* var. *praecox*. It has a small ear and grains that are pointed at the base and apex and contain a very hard endosperm that explodes or pops when heated. Its cultivation goes back to the ancient Incas who used the popped kernels as funeral decorations. It was known to the tribes of North America who introduced the Pilgrims to it. This occurred, according to legend, at the very meal commemorated each year at Thanksgiving Day. James Trager, in his well-written volume *The Food Book*, gives this account:

> *The first Thanksgiving dinner was really a breakfast. It ended with a surprise. When the Pilgrims and their 92 Indian guests had finished, Chief Massasoit's brother, a brave named Quadequina, disappeared into the woods and returned with a bushel of popped popcorn, a startling novelty to the colonists.*

It is easily made, either in a special popper or in an ordinary pan such as a saucepan or an iron skillet with a cover. Kernels are heated over a low flame until the layer of oil coating the bottom of the pan reaches a boiling point. The kernels explode, producing a white mass of starch several times the size of the kernel. Popcorn is customarily served with salt and melted butter, but may be combined with sugar or molasses to make a type of candy.

The United States dominates in the commercial production of popcorn. Popcorn is the mainstay of the U.S. movie-theatre industry in which film rental fees have risen so high that exhibitors depend on concession sales to survive. Popcorn is the highest-profit item.

POPE

Also RUFFE. A small, freshwater member of the perch family, the pope *(Gynocephalus cernua)* is found in Europe and Asia from Britain to Siberia and favors slow-flowing water. It has a delicate flesh somewhat like the U.S. walleye. Despite its edibility, and perhaps because of its small size, the pope is not an important food fish, nor is it very attractive to anglers. It may be prepared like **walleye.**

POPENOEI

Also JOYAPA. The purplish black berry of an evergreen shrub, *Macleania popenoei*, found from southern Mexico to Peru, the popenoei has a juicy pulp and an agreeable taste. It is considered a delicacy in Ecuador.

POPPY SEED

This is the edible seed of a poppy plant, which may be either the opium poppy *(Papaver somniferum)* or the common field poppy of Europe *(P. rhoeas)*. The seeds are very tiny (900,000 to the pound) and are either bluish black or white, in which case they are dyed to make them more attractive in the marketplace.

Poppy seeds have a distinctive flavor that is especially well liked in the Balkans where the seeds are used to flavor a number of dishes. In western Europe and the United States they are used mainly as a garnish on top of breads, pastries, cakes and the like. But they may be eaten by themselves, roasted or browned in butter, or used to flavor pickles, preserves and beverages. An oil is expressed from the seeds that is used for cooking in parts of Europe, especially in France. The young green leaves of the plant may be cooked and eaten like spinach.

PORBEAGLE

Also MACKEREL SHARK. This is a large shark, *Lamma nasus*, found on both sides of the Atlantic and in the Mediterranean. It is esteemed as a sportfish in British waters and is fished commercially in the North Atlantic for its good flavor and firm texture. Much of the catch taken by Norwegian fishermen is exported to Italy.

The porbeagle is considered unaggressive, but it is a vigorous swimmer that keeps to the open ocean. It reaches a maximum length of 10 feet. A related species, *L. whitleyi*, is found in Australian waters.

PORCUPINE

This is a large rodent, usually terrestrial, common throughout the world. Its rather fatty flesh is considered good eating by some. In North America the porcupine belongs to the genus *Erethizon* and differs from the European porcupine *(Hystrix cristata)* in being more plump, more heavily built, with long hairs that conceal detachable barbed spines. Many of the New World porcupines live in trees.

Like most small wild game, the porcupine should be skinned, gutted and soaked overnight in brine and vinegar. Its four waxy glands, two in the small of the back and one under each foreleg, should be removed before it is roasted or cooked, usually in a stew or meat pie.

PORGY

Also RED SEA BREAM, PARGO CRIOLLO. A food fish of the Mediterranean and the Atlantic coast of North Africa and Europe as far north as Great Britain, the porgy *(Pagellus bogaraveo)* may weigh up to nine pounds and reach a length of 20 inches. It is pink with silver sides, red fins and a black spot behind the head. The porgy is considered extremely good eating and is both fished commercially and taken by anglers. The Spanish, calling it *pargo criollo*, are particularly fond of its milky flavor. They poach, fry or bake it whole with sliced potatoes, onion, lemon slices, tomatoes and red peppers. They season it with coriander seeds. For U.S. "porgies" see **Jolthead Porgy** and **Scup.**

See also: Bream.

PORK

Pork is the fresh meat of pigs. A pig is usually slaughtered at the age of five to six months, and the best quality young pork meat is gray white or pale pink. This is partly due to the butcher's practice of draining the blood for black puddings, but older pork tends to be redder all the same. Pigs raised for pork tend to be leaner than those raised for ham, which needs a good deal of fat for flavor.

Pork meat is firm and fine-grained, and the fat is white. The names of the cuts vary from region to region and country to country. (See the accompanying illustration for the parts of a pig.) The most desirable

Pork Cuts

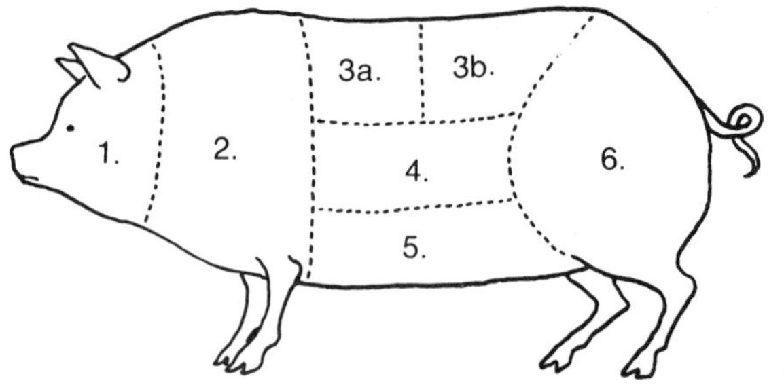

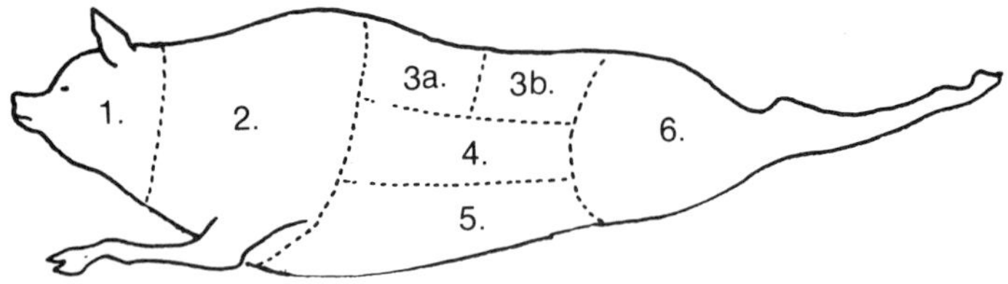

1. Head	3b. Loin (beneath Back Cut)
2. Shoulder	4. Middle Cut
3. Back Cut	5. Belly
3a. Ribs (beneath Back Cut)	6. Ham

cuts come from the loin, leg and shoulder. The back cut is almost entirely fat, but under it is the loin, which yields the fillet, or tenderloin, chops, cutlets and roasts, and the ribs, which yield spareribs. Leg of pork is fresh ham (i.e., not cured or smoked), which is roasted plain or stuffed and is especially delicious with the skin left on. The shoulder gives the most economical cuts, including pork shoulder, fresh shoulder butt, boneless shoulder butt, picnic pork and shoulder steaks. The belly is generally used for bacon.

The larger cuts of pork are usually roasted, and the smaller ones fried or broiled. Pork is a rich, fatty meat, and for this reason it is customarily accompanied by such sharp-flavored sauces as apple sauce, red currant jelly or cranberry sauce. The Chinese are the world's foremost eaters of pork, and many of their pork dishes have attained general popularity, including sweet-and-sour pork and spareribs.

Suckling pig is a piglet young enough to be still nursed by the mother. The usual method of preparation is to scald it, stuff it with sage and onion, sew it up and roast for 30 to 35 minutes per pound. Salt pork usually comes from the middle cut, and is often cubed and used in stews, or to flavor soups. Scraps from all parts of the hog, including fat, are used to stuff sausages.

Cured meats are discussed under **Ham** and **Bacon,** while organs and other odds and ends are discussed under **Pig,** or under the specific name, e.g., **Chitterling.**

PORK BRAIN SAUSAGE

Also GEHIRNWURST, SAUCISSES DE CERVELLE. This is a German specialty consisting of poached pig's brains ground up with pork meat (half fat, half lean) and seasoned with mace, salt and pepper. This mixture is stuffed into pork bungs, which are tied off in six-inch sections. This sausage is rare in the United States, but where found it is usually cooked by boiling or steaming for seven to eight minutes, then browning in fat or butter. It may be served with grits, cornbread or mashed potatoes. In Germany, it is often accompanied by sauerkraut and in France by beans.

See also: **Sausage.**

PORPOISE

This is a small sea mammal, *Phocaena phocaena,* of the *Cetacea* order, which also includes whales and dolphins. The porpoise reaches a maximum length of about six feet and rarely exceeds 165 pounds in weight. Its skin is smooth, shiny and hairless and is dark gray to black above, becoming white below. It has a blunt snout, a triangular dorsal fin (one species lacks this), and many teeth. The common porpoise may travel with a single companion, or in the company of up to 100 others. It frequents coastal waters and especially the mouths of large rivers.

Porpoise flesh is oily, but edible, and to some even palatable. It is said that the oiliness can be much reduced by stripping the meat away from the tissue that unites it to the blubber. Porpoise meat is eaten today in Scotland, Iceland and Newfoundland, and by certain native Americans living along the coasts of North and South America.

In former times, porpoise flesh was much appreciated in Great Britain. The Anglo-Saxons held it in high regard, and in the early 16th century it was considered a royal dish because King Henry VIII was fond of it. Porpoise was cooked in various ways and served at banquets. A sauce frequently served with it was made with vinegar, breadcrumbs and sugar. During the same epoch in France, according to Rabelais, it was eaten in Lent as an abstinence food.

Two species of Pacific porpoises, *P. dalli* and *P. truei*, are fished commercially by the Japanese for both meat and oil. These species are larger than the common porpoise, reaching a length of nearly eight feet and a weight of up to 275 pounds.

PORRIDGE

A gruel or mush obtained by boiling some type of meal or cereal in salted water, it most often refers to an oatmeal popular in Scotland, Ireland and parts of

England. Specially treated oats are added to boiling, salted water and simmered until the mixture reaches the desired thickness. It is served in individual bowls, called porringers, with cold milk, buttermilk or cream, and often with a pat of butter and a sweetener such as molasses, honey or sugar.

PORT

A wine from the ravines of the upper Douro Valley in northern Portugal, port is exported from Oporto (hence the name) and has an alcoholic strength of more than 16.5 percent. The original vines were perhaps brought from Burgundy by Henry, Count of Portugal, in the late 12th century.

The true history of port begins in 1703, with the Treaty of Methuen and the settling of English wine merchants at Oporto. Before the treaty, which forbade the importation of French wine into England and gave guarantees to Portuguese wine importers, shipments of wine from Oporto to England rarely exceeded 600 pipes annually (of 115 gallons each). By 1747, however, 17,000 pipes a year were exported. After the establishment of the wine monopoly company of Oporto (Real Companhia dos Vinhos) in 1756, the shipments rose to 33,000 pipes a year.

The British found the wine to be warm, comforting and tonic, "retaining the strength of youth with the wisdom of age." George Meredith describes an English lawyer in *The Ordeal of Richard Feverel* who, though inwardly warm with port, tries hard to preserve a dour, Anglo-Saxon semblance of decorum —to no avail:

> *Having slowly ingurgitated and meditated upon this precious draught, and turned its flavour over and over with an aspect of potent Judicial wisdom (one might have thought he was weighing mankind in the balance), the old lawyer heaved, and said, sharpening his lips over the admirable vintage, "The world is in a very sad state, I fear, Sir Austin!"*
>
> *His client gazed at him queerly.*
>
> *"But that," Mr. Thompson added immediately, ill-concealing by his gaze the glowing intestinal congratulations going on within him, "that is, I think you would say, Sir Austin—if I could but prevail upon you—a tolerably good character wine!"*

The demand for port and **Madeira** in England has declined sharply since 1939. France, which finds no equivalent among its own wines, has become a major customer.

The harvesting of port wine is hazardous. The soil is crumbled lava, the terrain stony and rugged. Winters are severe in the valleys, and the summers have an oven-like heat. The vines are grown in terraces. The grapes are picked by hand, and are carried in 165-pound baskets single-file down the steep ravines to the *quintas* (or cellars) of the cooperatives. Here the grapes are pressed, stored until spring, and "dosed" with an addition of wine alcohol.

The wine is then shipped down the river by means of *barcos rabelos*, flatbottom barges with large rudders, to Villa Nova da Gaia, across from Oporto, to become either a blend or a vintage port.

Most port wines are blends. These are aged in the wood. After two years the wine is sampled—to see what kind of port (full, tawny or dry) it "wants to be"—and other types of must (or wine) are added. This aging and blending process takes five or six years. Vintage port, when the harvest is extraordinarily good, is put straight into bottles with no blending. The bottles are hermetically sealed, and the wine stays for ten, twenty, thirty years or more. Most vintage ports tend to become "tawny" (light mahogany) or extra-dry.

Official colors of port are deep red, red, ruby (the full ports), light gold, onion peel (tawny ports), pale white, pale straw and golden. A good port has a strong aroma and "weeps" down the bottle or glass in a long tear when tilted and set back down. The sweet ports are red. The dry are white.

Dry white port is normally served as an aperitif and should be chilled. It is also appropriate as an afternoon refreshment, as is a tawny or a full port.

Dessert pastries and fruit call for a semidry or sweet port. Cheese and any kind of port always go together. The British put port into their **Stilton** cheese, allowing the wine to saturate the creamy mass. In private homes, port should be decanted a few hours before serving. A vintage port should never be uncorked. Special pliers are recommended, heated red-hot in a fire, to decapitate the bottle.

PORT DU SALUT

A famous, creamy yellow cheese made by Trappist monks in many parts of the world, but original to France, it was first made by monks of the Abby of Notre Dame de Port du Salut, near Laval, in the department of Mayennes. They began marketing it in 1854 under the trademark *Port du Salut*, but the same cheese made elsewhere, for example, in Austria, Germany, Canada and the United States, is usually marked Port Salut, dropping the *du*.

Monks have kept the exact process of making Port du Salut a secret, but it is known that whole cow's milk is used, that some surface ripening takes place and that the curing period is six to eight weeks. The curd is medium soft with a taste that has been compared to both Swiss and Gouda. The aroma at times approaches that of a mild Limburger. Cheeses are round and flat, weighing from three to five pounds. They are wrapped and boxed for market.

PORTER

Porter is a dark English beer with a strong, bittersweet flavor and an alcohol content of about 6 percent. Tradition has it that the name derives from the porters of London who had a predilection for this brew. Porter was the forerunner of stout, an even darker and stronger beer achieved through adding roasted barley to the mash. It was at first referred to as "extra stout" porter, which was shortened to "stout" as it became a recognized product.

PORT SALUT

See **Port Du Salut.**

POSH TE

Fruit of a small tree, *Annona scleroderma*, closely related to the **soursop,** it is found in Central America and is occasionally cultivated. The fruit has a richer flavor than soursop and is highly aromatic. The skin, however, is much thicker.

POSSET

A drink popular in medieval times, it consisted of hot milk or cream curdled by the addition of white wine, ale, sack or molasses. Spices were added for flavor. After the milk was boiled and the curdling substance added, the mixture was poured rapidly from vessel to vessel to give it a smooth texture. It was served hot and might be taken as a cure for a cold, as a before-dinner drink or, if rich enough, drunk *instead* of a meal.

POSSUM

See **Opossum.**

POTATO

Also IRISH POTATO. This is the edible, starchy tuber of the common plant, *Solanum tuberosum*, a member of the nightshade family. The tuber is neither the fruit nor the root of the potato plant, but a portion of the underground stem, growing slightly above the roots. Potatoes may be round, oval, irregularly oblong, or even kidney-shaped and vary in weight up to one pound. Each plant may yield a half-dozen or more of the tubers which, depending on the variety, will range in color from whitish brown through purple. The interior color is white or light yellow.

Potatoes

The potato is native to the Andean *altiplano* of South America. Potatoes had been domesticated by the native Americans as far back as 3000 B.C., but the first Europeans to run across them were Pizarro's men in about 1553. The Spaniards first thought they were truffles, partly because those cultivated by the Indians were much smaller than those we see in the market today. They were about the size of peanuts, or at the most, plums. Their small size was due mainly to the Indians' practice of eating the larger specimens and saving the smaller ones for planting. Since the eyes of the potato, and not the seeds, were used in planting, propagation of the least desirable specimens was guaranteed.

The Indians had a characteristic way of preparing potatoes that continues to this day. After being soaked in water, they were frozen, then dried in the sun. This primitive freeze-drying process was helped by great numbers of men, women and children who trod barefoot on the potatoes, squeezing out moisture and removing the skin. After four or five days of this treatment, the potatoes were black, hard as stones, and pretty much relieved of all moisture. They are called *chunos* today and are a staple part of the Indian diet, used to make soup and sometimes to make a kind of flour for bread.

Potatoes were called *papas* by the Indians, a word still in general use in Spanish Latin America. The Spaniards called them *patatas*, which is close to their word for sweet potato, *batata*, a vegetable they much preferred. The potato was brought to Spain and is believed to have been under cultivation in Galicia by the end of the 16th century. According to legend, Sir Francis Drake brought the potato to England in the 1580s. Since his last port of call had been Virginia before sailing home, the new vegetable was called the "Virginia potato," although none grew there. In those days, the word "potato," unmodified, meant sweet potato. The Virginia potato would not be cultivated in North America until 1719, brought there as an import from Ireland where, again according to legend, it was first cultivated by Sir Walter Raleigh.

In the 18th century, first botanists, then statesmen began to appreciate the advantages of the potato. It had a much higher yield per acre than cereal crops, was less exposed to the vagaries of the weather, and, being underground, was less vulnerable to being trampled by soldiers in that era of continual warfare. The upper classes regarded it as good food for animals and the common folk, a solution to the problem of famine.

The potato took hold in Germany, France, England and especially Ireland, where indeed it staved off famine in 1740. Ironically, a century later the Irish were so dependent on the potato that, when a blight caused crop failure, the disastrous "potato famine" occurred, with the resulting wholesale emigration of the Irish to America. (The crops also failed at about the same time in America, Russia and Germany, contributing significantly to widespread political unrest of the late 1840s.) Potatoes continued to gain in popularity in the latter half of the 19th century, despite a distinct lack of enthusiasm in certain circles. For example, the German philosopher, Friedrich Nietzsche wrote: "A diet that consists predominantly of rice leads to the use of opium, just as a diet which consists predominantly of potatoes leads to the use of liquor."

Although there are approximately 160 varieties of potato grown in the United States, they can be lumped into four basic categories: russets, round whites, round reds and long whites.

Russets or *Idahos* are a standard choice for baking, and often for french fries. They are rounded and oblong with heavy, netted brown skins.

Round whites are preferred for roasting alongside meat or for boiling, mashing and home-frying. They include Superiors and Katahdins from Maine and Long Island, and Triumphs from Nebraska.

Round reds are thin-skinned and ideal for boiling.

Long whites are the most versatile of the lot, can be fried, roasted, boiled or mashed. Developed in California, they have tiny eyes and pale, yellowish skin.

The potato is a superior food, with an undeserved reputation for being fattening, which stems from the custom of adding fat in the preparation. Four ounces of boiled potatoes contain a mere 45 calories, while one ounce of potato chips contains 150, 70 of which are fat. A medium-sized baked potato (minus butter, minus gravy, minus sour cream) contains about 100 calories. This compares favorably to two slices of bread (120 calories), or a medium-sized sweet potato (155 calories). The superiority of the potato lies in its nutritional excellence, high satiety value and generous crop yield.

Like most vegetables, the potato is mostly water, 77 to 80 percent. In terms of dry weight, however, the potato consists of an average of 66 percent starch, 9 percent protein, 4 percent sugars and about 0.5 percent potassium, phosphorus, fats, vitamins and other minerals. It also has significant roughage or fiber content. The high starch content accounts for most of the calories, the texture, and the potato's ability to satisfy the appetite quickly and inexpensively. It is both easily cooked and digested. In quantity, potato protein is on a par with rice and wheat, but qualitatively, it is generally superior, containing substantially more of all the essential amino acids, except histidine, than whole wheat does. Acre for acre, because of the higher potato yield, more potato protein is produced than either wheat or rice protein.

The potato is high in B vitamins, including niacin, thiamine, riboflavin and pyridoxine. In fact, one baked potato provides 10 percent of the niacin, 9 percent of the thiamin, and 2.5 percent of the riboflavin needed daily. Potatoes are an excellent source of vitamin C, contributing more of it to the U.S. food supply than any other major food. When freshly dug, a potato contains about 30 milligrams of vitamin C per 100 grams (3½ ounces). Much of this can be lost in aging or cooking, since both B and C vitamins are soluble in water. Much of the potato's nutritional value lies in or near the skin, so the best way to preserve it in cooking is to leave the potato unpeeled. It should be placed in a minimum of water, brought to a boil, then steamed until done, but not overcooked. Minerals found in the potato include, iron, magnesium, and calcium. Sodium content is low, which makes the potato ideal for those who need to limit their salt intake.

On the negative side, some potatoes contain solanine, a poisonous substance found in the green skin of certain varieties. Solanine is not a problem in modern commercial varieties, and new varieties are screened for it. When potatoes were introduced into Europe in the latter half of the 16th century, however, they gained the reputation of causing leprosy. Solanine was the villain, according to best authority, because if eaten, it causes a skin rash, a manifestation interpreted by 16th-century Europeans as the first sign of the dread disease. This drawback helped retard the general acceptance of the potato until the beginning of the 19th century.

Per capita potato consumption in the United States peaked around 1900 at 200 pounds a year and by 1960 had declined to 108.4. Since then the trend has been reversed, with consumption rising to 121.6 pounds in 1975. Whereas in 1900 Americans were eating fresh potatoes, the recent gain lies in the area of processed potatoes, especially chips, frozen and dehydrated potatoes. Unfortunately, the skin is usually discarded in the processing and with it many of the nutritional assets. Moreover, the delicate taste of the fresh potato, which authorities describe as "exquisite," frequently does not survive.

In the market, fresh potatoes should be selected carefully. Choose specimens that are smooth-skinned, clean and rot-free. Avoid green coloring (a sign of solanine), and look for shallow eyes.

Today potatoes are the world's fourth largest crop, after wheat, rice and corn. But as human food, they rank second only to rice. In the United States approximately 1,257,000 acres are cultivated in potatoes. The states leading in potato production are Idaho, Washington, Maine, Oregon and California.

See also: **Sweet Potato.**

POTATO CHEESE

This German cheese contains an admixture of mashed potatoes. It is generally made from cow's milk but also from sheep or goat's milk. After the curd has been formed, boiled potatoes that have been either mashed or put through a sieve are mixed together with salt and sometimes caraway seeds. After the cheeses are formed and dried, they are covered with beer or cream, and set to ripen in tubs for two weeks.

POTATO CHIP

Also POTATO CRISP. A snack food of American origin, it consists of a paper-thin slice of potato that is soaked in cold water, then deep-fried, usually in cottonseed oil. It is dried and salted before being served. In Great Britain, this is known as the potato crisp, or game chip. The original name in the United States was "Saratoga chip," owing to its place of origin, Saratoga Springs, N.Y., a popular spa in the 19th century. Potato chips are probably the most popular snack food in the United States. They come seasoned in various ways, e.g., flavored with onion salt, chili powder, etc.

POTATO FLOUR

A fine white flour is made from potatoes that have been cooked, dried and milled. It is used chiefly as a thickener in soups, sauces and stews. It may also be used to make bread when mixed with wheat or rye flours that have an adequate gluten content. Potato flour is used more in Europe for these purposes than in the United States where cornstarch is more popular.

POT CHEESE

See **Cottage Cheese.**

POTEEN

See **Moonshine.**

POTHERB

A term used rather loosely, it can mean any plant whose stem or leaves are boiled and eaten as a vegetable. It can also mean any plant used to flavor foods, but some writers use it to mean just the "strong" herbs, i.e., those whose flavor is so powerful that it can overpower any other flavor if used freely. These include bay leaf, basil, dill, marjoram, mint, oregano, rosemary, sage, tarragon and thyme.

POT MARJORAM

See **Marjoram.**

POTTED MEAT

Also DEVILED MEAT. The term includes any meat, such as ham, beef, pork or game that has been chopped or ground to the consistency of paste, mixed with seasonings and put up in cans or jars. The meat has been cooked before processing and once in the jar is usually covered with a layer of suet or butter to aid in preserving it. This process is also applied to fish.

Deviled meat is a similar preparation whose taste has been enhanced with chili peppers and other tasty spices. Originally a form of food for travelers, potted meats today are used as sandwich spreads and as picnic fare. A French version of this is the *terrine*, with the difference that the ingredients are cooked inside the container rather than before the canning process.

POUCHONG TEA

Pouchong is a type of semifermented tea similar to **oolong black dragon** but even less fermented. Main production areas are Foochow, in mainland China and Taiwan. It is often scented with jasmine and gardenia.

See also: **Tea.**

POUILLY-FUISSE

This is a white wine of Macon *(Cote Maconnais)* in southern **Burgundy.** This is the country of Alphonse de Lamartine, the famed Romantic lyricist, who called himself "a vintner rather than a poet." The *Cote Maconnais* is divided from the **Beaujolais** region to the south by a narrow creek. The wine itself comes from the communes, or towns, of Pouilly, Fuisse, Solutre (origin of the name "Solutrian" in paleontology, where skeletons of prehistoric humans and horses have been unearthed), Vergisson and Chaintre. Pouilly-Fuisse has a distinctive bouquet and has an aesthetically pleasing golden color with a faint emerald tinge. It is often kept in France until it has aged 10 or more years, but it is best drunk, with seafood, when it is from two to five years old.

POUILLY-FUME

This dry white wine of the **Loire** from the region Pouilly-sur-Loire, north of Nevers has a pronounced "smoky" quality and a delicate bouquet. An excellent wine with oysters, Pouilly-Fume is not to be confused with the **Pouilly-Fuisse** from **Burgundy,** which it resembles slightly.

POULETTE SAUCE

A French sauce for vegetables, variety meats, mussels, frogs' legs and ragout of veal, it is based on bechamel with the following additions: white stock, meat juice, thick cream, egg yolks, mushrooms and seasonings plus a few drops of lemon juice. It may be garnished with chopped parsley.

See also: **Sauce.**

POULTRY

The term "poultry" refers to any domestic fowl bred and reared to provide eggs or meat for the table. Included are chickens, ducks, geese, turkeys, pigeons and guineafowl, and by stretching it a bit, peafowl, quail, pheasants and swans. The **chicken** is far and away the most important poultry bird. It was domesticated more than 3,000 years ago, but only since 1930 has it become the center of an important meat-producing industry. In the 1920s important advances were made in poultry nutrition and control of epidemic diseases. This enabled chickens to be concentrated in huge numbers. A combination of genetic improvement and hormonal techniques halved the age and doubled the size of the average table bird. This has led to poultry's being the most economical source of animal protein, not only in the United States, but also in many other countries. In the chicken industry alone broiler production in the United States increased 100-fold between the mid-1930s and the mid-1970s, from 34 million to about 3 billion units. Americans eat about 60 pounds per capita annually as opposed to about 100 pounds of beef.

Yet, despite this boon to world nutrition, chicken remains taboo in some parts of the world, most notably in areas of Tibet, Sri Lanka and the Arabian Peninsula, and among Mongols, the Taureg of North Africa and the Walamo tribe of Africa who regard chicken-eating as a capital offense. Calvin Schwabe, in his delightful and well written book, *Unmentionable Cuisine*, pointed out that:

> *In some areas, a chicken-eating taboo applies only to women. In parts of rural Vietnam, for instance, pregnant women do not eat chicken meat because they believe it is poisonous, and among certain Philippine tribes it is thought that if a woman with a newborn child eats chicken she will die. Some other Filipinos believe that women must not eat chickens that "lay here and there in different places" or they will become unfaithful to their husbands. In fact, among the Kafa of Ethiopia, women who disobey a similar taboo are made slaves. Only men eat chicken meat among the aboriginal Kamar people of India, and in the Marquesas Islands of Polynesia.*

POULTRY SEASONING

This is a prepackaged mixture of seasoning herbs used in the cooking of chickens, turkeys, duck and the like and in stuffing. Usually included are parsley, sage, marjoram and thyme. It is easily obtainable at the market.

POUTARGUE

See **Botargo.**

PRAINIANA

Edible fruit of a Malaysian tree, *Garcinia prainiana*, it is related to the **mangosteen** and has an agreeable, subacidic flavor.

PRAIRIE CHICKEN

See **Grouse.**

PRAIRIE DOG

This is a small rodent *(Cynomys* species) plentiful in the southwestern United States but also found in the states of North and South Dakota, Nebraska, Kansas, Montana, Wyoming and in northern Mexico. The flesh of the prairie dog is edible and is said to have an "earthy" taste. It was a staple of native Americans and continues to be eaten by them to some extent. Prairie dog is cooked like rabbit or **squirrel.**

Prairie dogs reach a maximum length of about

12 inches and may weigh up to three pounds. They are highly organized socially, living together in "towns," which are themselves divided into clearly defined "wards." One such town in Texas at the turn of the century contained an estimated 400 million prairie dogs inhabiting a system of burrows that extended 100 miles in one direction and 250 miles in the other. The most prevalent species is *C. ludovicianus.*

PRALINE

This is a confection consisting of nuts and melted sugar. The original praline was French, invented by the cook of the Count Duplessis-Praslin (d. 1675). He used almonds, and a praline consisted usually of a single nut covered with cooked caramel or a hard icing. The American praline is a specialty of Louisiana. It is a cookie-sized mixture of almonds and brown sugar syrup. Coconut pralines are made with white sugar.

PRATO

Also QUEIJO PRATO. This firm Brazilian cheese is made from pasteurized cow's milk and is much like **Gouda** or **Edam.** The paste is yellow and has small eyes. Prato is similar to Cuban **Patagras** cheese.

PRATTIGAU

An aromatic cheese named for the Swiss valley where it originated, it is prepared from cow's skim milk. In taste, odor and texture it resembles **Limburger.** Prattigau is also made in France. These cheeses weigh from 20 to 25 pounds.

PRAWN

See **Shrimp.**

PREIGNAC

This is one of the five communes of the Bordeaux region of France that produces Sauternes, a rich, highly perfumed white wine. The other communes are Barsac, Bommes, Fargues and Sauternes. Wine from any of these communes is legally permitted to be called "Sauternes." This wine owes its richness to the practice of allowing the grapes to become overripe on the vine, a condition called *pourriture noble*, "noble rot." This reduces the water and acid content and increases the sugar and glycerine. Consequently, there is no such thing as a dry Sauternes.

PRESERVATION OF FOOD

Various techniques, including those of curing, canning, smoking, drying, salting, candying, pickling and freezing have been devised to store and preserve food for future use.

Salting of bacon and ham was practiced as early as 200 B.C. in England, and the process remained in effect and virtually unchanged until the mechanical refrigeration of food was introduced in 1877. Because of spoilage in hot weather, the salting and "curing" of domestic meat could only be managed in winter. The salting of meat and fish was carried out in Greek and Roman times, especially in communities that had ready access to salt from the sea. Fruit and vegetables, also, were commonly left to dry in the sun and could be stored following their dehydration. In Greece, bits of lamb and goat meat—after being partially cooked—were often sealed in clay pots whose narrow open tops were coated with a layer of congealed fat, like paraffin on jars of jams and jellies, and buried in the ground. So called robbers' stew, a favorite lamb dish among the Greek inhabitants of Cyprus, is still available today, a remnant of this early method of preservation. After storage in earthen pots, the meat is cooked below the ground. Originally this practice helped to conceal the fire from prospective vigilantes or police.

Canning (see **Canned Foods)** is today the most widely used process in food preservation. This consists of excluding as much oxygen as possible from food packed in cans or jars (as in home canning) to prevent or to inhibit **fermentation** and the consequent action of microorganisms which spoil the contents. This industry began in France in Napoleonic times, spread to England and eventually to the United States, where Thomas Kensett invented the modern tin can in 1823. The canning of fish, meat, milk, fruit and vegetables was a large and growing industry in the United States by the end of the Civil War. Ideally, commercial canneries should be located as close as possible to the source of the food to be packed and marketed. After the food is prepared (by slicing, paring, coring, husking, parboiling, etc.), the cans are filled and the air exhausted by the release of carbon dioxide and the pressure of the food itself. The cans are sealed, then boiled and sterilized, ready to be cooled and labeled for storage or shipment.

Curing is the preservation of food by any one of many special ways. Meat and fish are cured by soaking them in flavored brines, by rubbing them or packing them with salt or by drying them with heat or smoke. The curing of cheese is induced by inoculating or spraying the cheese with various molds, by wrapping them in flavor-imparting containers, by smoking them and generally by regulating the fermentation process in some manner. Smokehouses are still found in the rural United States, particularly in mountain areas of the South. Here the creosote and formaldehyde in the smoke of hickory and other hard woods coat ham, bacon, sausages, spareribs, beef brisket and turkey with a tasty preservative. Pine is not good for this purpose, or for outdoor cooking generally, since the resin tends to spoil the food's flavor. The freshly dressed meat should first be cured by being rubbed with a mixture of salt, saltpeter and sugar. Then it is wrapped or "canvassed" (often hung in flour sacks) in a dark but well-ventilated smokehouse or shed. Again, this process should not be attempted in hot weather, nor should the heat from the wood exceed 90° F (32.2° C) so that the fat will not melt. Herring, salmon, eels, and cheese are delectable foods when smoked, as are geese, a favorite in Europe.

Freezing simply reduces the temperature of food so that its liquid content, including oils, becomes solidified. This reduces spoilage from bacteria. The food should be prepared, wrapped and securely sealed, then subjected—commercially—to "flash freezing" (sudden freezing down to 0° F, − 17.8° C or below) to prevent the formation of ice crystals and subsequent cell destruction.

Some foods do not lend themselves to this method, including custards, cream sauces, creamy cheeses and some raw fruits and vegetables, especially lettuce, tomatoes, celery, onions and bananas. The ordinary freezing compartment in the modern refrigerator never reaches this low a temperature and, therefore, is not adequate for long-term preservation and storage.

In *freeze-drying* all but a small amount of the water content of the food is removed in a vacuum. The food becomes brittle, porous, light in weight and may be stored for long periods of time with no refrigeration. Fruit, particularly apple slices, pears, figs, and peaches, are typically preserved in this manner. Instant coffee crystals and fruit used in some breakfast cereals are good examples of this kind of preservation as well. Freeze-dried foods are easily reconstituted with the addition of liquid.

Candying preserves, jams, jellies and other sweet fruit through the addition of alcohol, sugar and syrup. Sugar is less effective than salt as a preservative, for its inclusion leads to rapid fermentation and, therefore, to chemical changes in the food. On the other hand, writes Mrs. Isabella Beeton in *The Book of Household Management* (London: 1861):

> *although sugar passes so readily into the state of fermentation, and is, in fact, the only substance capable of undergoing the vinous stage of that process, yet it will not ferment at all if the quantity be sufficient to constitute a very strong syrup; hence, syrups are used to preserve fruits and other vegetable substances from the changes they would undergo if left to themselves.*

Pickling is the preservation of certain foods in brine (water and salt) or a solution of vinegar, spices and other seasonings. Sauerkraut, raw, shredded cabbage that undergoes a slow fermentation process as well, is a good example of food prepared and preserved in this way.

PRESERVED EGG

Also HUNDRED-YEAR-OLD EGG. In Chinese cuisine, a duck egg coated with a pickling solution of lime, salt, tea and ashes is then buried and allowed to cure for three months. When mature, the egg is shelled, revealing a yellow green yolk and a white like dark green jelly. Preserved eggs are served as appetizers on a toothpick with a slice of ginger. Given the unusual taste and texture, it is considered a real delicacy. There are two kinds, the one just described, called *pay don*, and a second, *harm don*, which is cured with salt only.

PRETOST

Also SAALAND PFARR. This is a Swedish cow's-milk cheese that is flavored by the fiery national liquor, **aquavit,** but otherwise resembles the Dutch **Gouda.** Its history goes back to the 18th century. Individual cheeses are cylindrical and weigh from five to 30 pounds. Akuavit is mixed with the curd during processing and again used to wash the finished cheeses during ripening.

PRETZEL

A hard, brittle biscuit shaped into the form of a loose knot and customarily eaten with beer, the pretzel is an old food, its history traceable back to ancient Rome. In modern times it is most closely associated with Germany and Alsace. Its popularity has spread to both the United States and Great Britain.

Pretzels are made from dough consisting of flour, water and yeast. Once the dough has risen, it is rolled into pencillike lengths, which are fashioned into loose knots vaguely resembling the letter *B*. The knots are dropped into a boiling mixture of water, baking soda and carbonate of ammonia. The knots are removed when they rise to the surface. After being brushed with beaten egg, they are sprinkled with coarse salt, and sometimes crushed cumin seeds, then baked until hard. In the United States, special salt is mined on the Gulf of Mexico for pretzels. Salt from these rare deposits forms large, regular, flat flakes that are ideal for coating pretzels.

In former times, pretzels were associated with prayer and good luck. It is said that the word "pretzel" derives from a Latin term meaning "little reward," and that pretzels were given to children as a little reward for learning their prayers. Pretzels were once made large enough to pass over the head and be worn around the neck, a practice believed to be effective in warding off evil spirits. They might also be hung from fruit trees as a charm to improve the yield. Breaking a pretzel with someone else is supposed, like a wishbone, to make a wish come true.

See also: **Bread.**

PRICKLY PEAR

Also INDIAN FIG, BARBARY FIG, TUNA, NOPAL. The succulent berrylike fruit of the *Opuntia* cactus, a plant native to America, was transplanted and is now naturalized in many warm—mostly arid—parts of the world, including India, North Africa, Hawaii and Australia. The plant is called *nopal* in Mexico.

Although there are at least 12 different species, the two that produce the best fruit are *Opuntia ficus-indica* and *Opuntia tuna.* The former is a treelike plant, standing 10 to 15 feet high, which produces the largest and least spiny of all prickly pears. They are oval, with thick yellow skin and generally measure three to four inches long by two to three inches wide. The latter produces smaller, more spiny fruit but is sometimes preferred because it grows into a better hedge. The plant bears for five months of the year, the first fruit appearing in June or July.

The pulp is generally bright red, sweet, juicy and with a mealy consistency. To enjoy it, the skin must first be slit lengthwise and peeled away from the pulp. Mexicans also eat the fleshy, oval joints of the cactus branches, preparing them in a dish called *nopalitos.*

Mexico has adopted the *nopal* cactus as part of a national symbol. According to legend, the forebears of the Aztecs wandered across Mexico in search of a sign from the gods that would tell them where to settle. On an isalnd in the middle of Lake Texcoco, they spotted the divine omen: An eagle, perched on a *nopal* cactus, clutching a serpent. There they founded the ancient city of Tenochtitlan, which later became Mexico City. The eagle-cactus-serpent symbol appears on Mexican coins and the flag.

In North Africa, the prickly pear, which the French call "barbary fig," is so ubiquitous that it was dubbed "wife of the legionnaire." Although *Opuntia* cactus flourish in the American Southwest, prickly pears have never excited much dietary interest. They are an important cash crop in two places, Mexico and Sicily.

Another cactus fruit generally called prickly pear is that of the saguaro, or giant cactus *(Carnegiea gigantea).* It is also called "tuna." The saguaro is a tree that grows from 20 to 60 feet high, generally consisting of a single bole, but occasionally branching. It was a major part of the diet of pre-Columbian peoples who, by selective breeding, managed to produce a practically thornless fruit. It was oval, two to three inches long with sweet, red pulp, which they ate raw or made into preserves. They made the juice into a syrup, which could be fermented into an alcoholic drink, and ground the seeds into a butterlike paste. Parts of the young plants were cooked as a green vegetable. Nowadays, in northern Mexico, it becomes an important part of the diet of range cattle during times of drought.

PRICKLY SUNPLANT

Prickly sunplant is a Central American shrub, *Solanum diversifolium*, of the nightshade family. Its apple-shaped young fruits are eaten raw with salt and are often served with codfish. They are also eaten in the West Indies.

PRIMULA CHEESE

Primula is a very mild, white Norwegian cheese made from the caramelized whey of **Gammelost.** It is classed as a processed cheese.

PROCESS CHEESE

This very popular commercial product is obtained by grinding and blending huge lots of one, two or more types of cheese, then heating, stirring and emulsifying the mixture until it becomes a homogeneous mass. The result is poured into airtight packages, refrigerated and sent to market.

Many people think process cheese is synonomous with **American cheese.** This is not the case. Although it is ever present in American markets, alongside white bread, powdered coffee and packaged cakes, process cheese was a Swiss invention. Two Swiss chemists came up with it in 1910 when they sought to develop a cheese that would keep better than conventional Swiss cheese. Process cheese was a striking success in this regard, because the heating renders it practically sterile, which prevents further ripening. If stored properly, process cheese will keep much better than the original. On the other hand, the taste of process cheese bears little resemblance to the original.

More than 40 percent of the cheese consumed in the United States today is process cheese. Although the United States is the largest producer of such cheese, experts claim the Swiss product is superior in quality.

When a sharp, mature cheese is used as raw material the best flavor is obtained. Cheddar is the most popular type, but others include Colby, granular, Swiss, Gruyere, brick and Limburger. Kinds of cheeses not used are cream, Neufchatel, cottage,

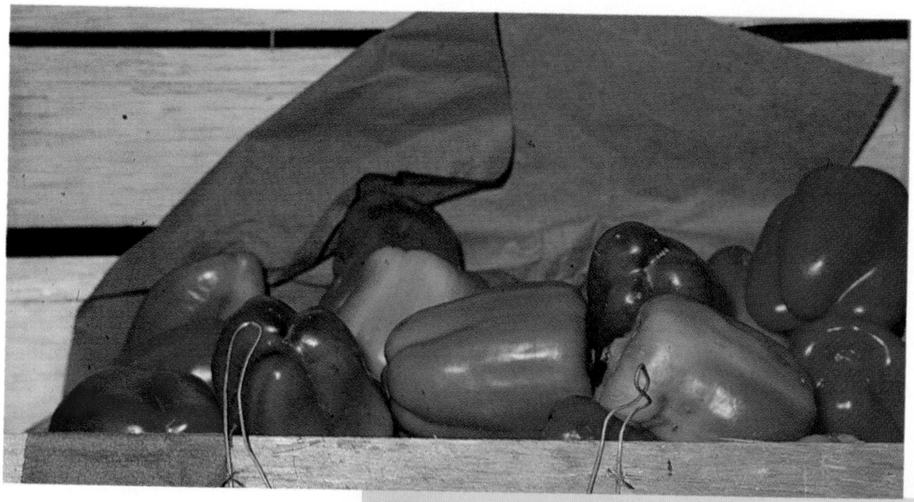

41 Red and green peppers

42 Chili peppers

43 Plums

44 Pomegranates

45 Prickly pears

47 Red radishes

48 Squash blossoms

49 A strawberry field

50 Sugarcane

51 Tamarillos

53 A vineyard in California

cooked, hard grating types, semisoft and skim milk.

In a variation called process blended cheese, cream or Neufchatel cheeses are mixed in, and the emulsifier left out. Sometimes fruits, vegetables and meats are added.

Subtypes of process cheese are process cheese food and process cheese spread. In these, the mixture usually contains only 51 percent cheese, the balance being made up by another dairy product, such as cream, milk, skim milk, whey or whey albumin. The spread contains more moisture and less fat, and must be spreadable at 70° F (21.1° C).

PRONGHORN

A small antelope native to western North America from southern Canada to northern Mexico, pronghorn *(Antilocapra americana)* is hunted for sport and meat. Early in the 20th century it seemed to be headed for extinction. Conservation measures proved successful, however, and the animal is now plentiful.

A large adult may weigh as much as 130 pounds, stand 40 inches at the shoulder and reach a length of five feet. The horns have a characteristic shape. They stand erect, and are backwardly curving at the tip. A small upwardly projecting branch grows out of each horn about halfway up its length.

PROTEIN

This is a component of food that is essential to human nutrition, as it provides amino acids, which are the chief constituents of soft body tissue. Proteins play other roles as well. The biochemical catalysts, enzymes, are proteins, as are many hormones. such as insulin and the growth hormone. Major sources of animal protein are meat, poultry, game, fish, eggs and dairy products, such as milk and cheese; good sources of vegetable protein are nuts, cereals, legumes and soy beans. To ascertain the protein content of more than 700 common foods, see **Nutritive Value of Foods.**

Of the more than 200 amino acids that have been identified, 20 are present in mammalian protein. Of the 20, eight are considered to be essential in the diet of the normal human, although this can change depending on age. They are: tryptophan, phenylalanine, lysine, threonine, valine, methionine, leucine and isoleucine. With these present, the remaining proteins can be formed from other materials found in the body.

As a rule, animal protein is considered superior to vegetable protein mainly because the latter tend to be lacking in two of the essential amino acids: lysine and tryptophan. Soy protein is an exception to this rule.

PROVATURA

A Italian soft cheese whose curd is heated and drawn much like that of **caciocavallo,** it is made in southern Italy, originally of buffalo milk, but more recently of cow's milk. It is eaten fresh like **mozzarella.**

See also: **Formaggio di Pasta Filata.**

PROVENCALE SAUCE

A French sauce served cold with cold roast beef, veal or fish, it consists of shallots and garlic browned in olive oil, sprinkled with flour, moistened with meat stock and white wine and seasoned with salt, pepper and bouquet garni. After simmering, mushrooms are added for further simmering, then the sauce is strained, given a squeeze of lemon juice and allowed to cool.

See also: **Sauce.**

PROVIDENCE CHEESE

This French cheese is made at the monastery at Bricquebec (Manche). Individual cheeses measure eight inches in diameter and are 1½ inches thick. They are quite like **Port du Salut** in taste, texture and color.

PROVOLE

This small, spherical Italian cheese from the southern province of Catania was made originally from buffalo milk. *Provole* is nowadays more generally produced from cow's milk. The curd has a plastic quality from being drawn and heated like that of **caciocavallo** and **scamorze.** Cheeses, which usually weigh two pounds, are often smoked over burning straw. They are eaten when a few days old.

See also: **Formaggio di Pasta Filata.**

PROVOLETTI

See **Provolone.**

PROVOLONCINI

See **Provolone.**

PROVOLONE

Also PROVOLETTI, PROVOLOTINI, PROVOLONCINI. This is a pale yellow, sharp Italian cheese of the drawn-curd type from the southern province of Catania. Like *provole*, it is made from

Prune plum (left) and dried prune

buffalo or cow's milk, but the size and shape vary widely, ranging from one to 350 pounds, and from pear-shaped to sausage-shaped. Provolone and **caciocavallo** are practically identical, with the former containing more fat, and usually being smoked after salting and drying. The curd is heated and drawn, like *caciocavallo*'s, to impart an elastic texture, which nevertheless is smooth and fairly soft for cutting. Though basically sharp in taste, provolone has two types, *dolce* and *piccante*. The latter is stronger owing to the goat rennet used in setting the curd.

Much provolone is eaten fresh, yet it is a good table cheese after six to nine months' curing. Cheeses are dipped in paraffin or rubbed with oil, then hung in string nets to cure. Provolone is also produced in Wisconsin and Michigan in the United States.

See also: **Formaggio di Pasta Filata.**

PROVOLOTINI

See **Provolone.**

PROWFISH

This is an edible but rare fish of the northern Pacific, found from northern California to Alaska and along the Siberian coast south to Kamchatka and Hokkaido. The prowfish *(Zaprora silenus)* resembles a sea catfish. It reaches a length of three feet and dwells on the bottom in moderately deep water. It has reddish flesh, which is described as mild and tasty. It is dark green or brown above, dotted with dark spots and a tan belly.

PRUNE

The name refers both to a dried plum, usually of a particularly sweet variety and to the trees that bear such plums. Prunes may be dried naturally in the sun, in an oven or in a combination of the two. The practice of drying plums is believed to have its origin in the Middle East, and in very ancient times. In any case, the ancient Gauls had mastered the art long before they came under Roman domination. The Romans had no prunes, but did pickle plums.

Perhaps this is why French prunes are considered the best in the world, particularly those from the region around *Agen*. The plums are of medium size, purple, and have especially firm flesh and high sugar content. These are the qualities that make superior and long-lasting prunes. Consequently, these plums have been transplanted in many other parts of the world. California is an example, since the Agen plum is virtually the only one used for its prune industry, and California supplies 90 percent of U.S. prunes. Oregon and Washington produce most of the rest. Within California, the Santa Clara valley is the largest source of prunes. Prunes in California are mainly sun-dried, but in other states specially built, artificially heated dehydrators are used.

Prunes are well known for their laxative properties. Nearly all prunes are dried with the pit in them. An exception is the French Brignolles, a small acidic prune which is pitted and peeled before drying. Prunes are eaten raw, or cooked, i.e., soaked and stewed, or used in puddings, jams and cakes. Bottled prune juice serves as an appetizer or health drink.

PTARMIGAN

Also ROCK PARTRIDGE. A game bird of the grouse family, it is found in the northern reaches of the Northern Hemisphere. The European common ptarmigan *(Lagopus mutus)* has gray brown plumage in the spring and summer that is replaced in the winter with nearly snow white feathers. It is distinguished from other grouse by having feathers down to its claws.

It feeds on berries, buds, mosses and lichens, a diet that promotes a good taste in its flesh. It is considered Norway's finest game bird, the breast meat being especially appreciated. In the British Isles, it is confined to Scotland. In North America, the willow ptarmigan *(L. saliceti)* is abundant in arctic regions from Alaska to Labrador. Ptarmigan is prepared in any way suitable for **grouse.**

PUDDING

The word is used to denote at least three different things. In the United States, it almost invariably means a sweet dish served as a dessert either cooked or uncooked, hot or cold. Bases for this dessert include fruit, rice, sago, semolina, tapioca, cornmeal, cream custard, cake, etc.

A second type is savory pudding, which is served with other foods and is quite popular in the British Isles. It often consists of diced beef, kidney, game, chicken or seafood baked in a sauce under a crust. Yorkshire pudding is another example of savory pudding. It is made of batter that is baked in the oven with roast-beef drippings and served as a potato substitute. Finally, black and white puddings are types of sausage.

See also: **Blood Sausage.**

PUDU

A small, South American deer, *Pudu pudu*, found on the west coast from Ecuador to the Straits of Magellan, it inhabits temperate rain forests at elevations ranging from sea level to 10,000 feet. The pudu is covered with long, coarse hair. A large adult weighs as much as 20 pounds. Pudu flesh is well regarded as food by native people, who often hunt them with dogs.

PUFFBALL

Here is a group of large, edible fungi, often round and white, ranging in size from that of a softball to a basketball and in rare cases larger. Puffballs are popular among mushroom gatherers because none are poisonous or easily mistaken for something else.

Puffballs appear in the late summer or early fall on lawns, in pastures and along the edges of woodlands. The taste is subtle, and simple preparations are best. It is enjoyed raw—cut into cubes and added to mixed green salads—or cooked. Slices are sauteed in butter or margarine or dipped in batter and deep fried, then served with sour cream.

One of the best is the giant white puffball *(Calvatia gigantea)*, which in the British Isles averages 11 to 12 inches in diameter and may reach twice that size in North America, weighing up to 30 pounds. It is best when young and appetizing. The skin is thin and downy, and the inside consists of billions of spores, which at an immature stage have the consistency of cream cheese. This is the edible stage, because later as the spores develop, the inside becomes mustard-yellow, brown or purple and turns powdery.

Other common puffballs are the western giant puffball *(Calvatia booniana)*, and the cup-shaped puffball *(Calvatia cyathiformis)*.

Nineteenth-century surgeons sometimes used dried puffballs to staunch the bleeding after amputations.

See also: **Mushroom.**

PULASAN

A popular oriental fruit, the pulasan *(Nephelium mutabile)* is native to Indonesia, but much cultivated in China. It grows on a small tree related to the **litchi.** The skin of the pulasan is thick and pebbly. When this is removed, the fruit resembles an unusually large peeled grape. The pulp is sweet, juicy and subacidic, with a delicate flavor resembling the **mangosteen.** The pulasan is eaten fresh or in a compote.

PULIGNY-MONTRACHET

See **Montrachet.**

PULQUE

This is a popular, mildly alcoholic, Mexican beverage that was sacred to the Aztecs. It is the result of fermenting the sweet juice of the **maguey** plant, also known as agave or century plant. Cloudy, thick and slightly foamy, pulque has a heavy taste somewhat like sour milk. Because of continuous fermentation, it must be consumed near the source. Consequently, it is neither bottled nor exported. Usually it is drunk in small bars, called *pulquerias*, with whimsical names like "My Office" and "Memories of the Future."

PULSE

See **Legume.**

PULTOST

Also KNAOST, RAMOST. This popular, soft Norwegian cheese is made from sour skim milk, often with buttermilk or thick cream added. It may be flavored with caraway seeds. This cheese may be eaten fresh, just a few days after being made or may be aged. When fresh the curd is pale yellow, but it darkens with age.

PUMPERNICKEL

Also SCHWARZBROT. This is a type of heavy, dark bread made from unsifted, whole rye flour, mixed with salt, molasses, shortening, yeast and water. It originated in Westfalia, Germany. To achieve a really dark color, caramel coloring is often added. Pumpernickel has an aromatic flavor, a slightly acidic aftertaste and a close, firm texture that makes it ideal for canapes and open sandwiches. It is also particularly good with a hearty cheese or sweet butter.

Pumpernickel is usually sold in delicatessens and is often imported in cans. Domestic varieties often contain wheat flour, and some are not much darker than ordinary rye bread. In England, pumpernickel is sometimes called "Brown George."

See also: **Bread.**

PUMPKIN

This is the gourd-shaped fruit of several herbaceous plants of the genus *Cucurbita*, which includes a number of squashes and gourds as well. The distinction between pumpkins and winter squashes is not crystal clear, since certain species produce both. But the fruit referred to as "pumpkin" most commonly comes from cultivars of the following four species: *C. Pepo*, *C. mixta*, *C. moschata* and *C. maxima*.

The typical pumpkin plant has rough, heart-shaped leaves and large, yellow, solitary flowers. Pumpkins generally vary in size from a diameter of eight to fourteen inches, although certain large specimens can weigh up to several hundred pounds. The shape is round, melonlike, depressed at both ends, and its color ranges through various shades of orange. The fruit has a hollow interior containing edible seeds. The rind is also orange and faintly sweet.

Pumpkin is prepared in a variety of ways: baked and eaten as a vegetable; baked into pie, which is a traditional Thanksgiving dessert in the United States; or used to make soup. The seeds are a popular snack in Latin American countries when dried and sometimes roasted and salted. They have a high phosphorous content.

In British usage, the term "pumpkin" has broader meaning, encompassing many of the cucurbits referred to as "squashes" in the United States.

PUNCH

Punch is a sweetened drink served hot or cold and composed of fruit juices, spices and often an alcoholic ingredient, such as wine or rum. The word supposedly derives from the Hindi word for five, *pauch*, because the original punch was an Indian drink made up of five ingredients: arrack, tea, lemon juice, water and sugar (or honey).

PUNGAS CATFISH

This is an Asian species, *Pangasius pangasius*, considered an important food fish in Java, Burma, India and Thailand. It is a night-feeder, scavenging on the bottom of large rivers, estuaries and still-water pools. Although it is avoided in some areas because of its feeding habits, its flesh is white, with a fine texture and usually good-flavored. The *pungas* has a slender body, deep belly, short barbels and a forked tail. The dominant color is dusky green.

A close relative, *P. sanitwongsei*, grows to an enormous size, sometimes measuring more than 9½ feet in length. It is found in the river system of Menam Chao Phya of Thailand and is widely eaten. The quality of its flesh is rated mediocre because of its scavenging habits.

PURSLANE

An edible, ground-hugging, fleshy-leaved plant common to both hemispheres, purslane grows to a height of only about two inches, but may extend to more than a foot across in a network of pinkish red rubbery stems. It is frequently uprooted by North American gardeners as a troublesome weed, but the entire plant is edible as a salad green, boiled and served with butter, or even when frozen or pickled. Its mild acidic taste and fatty quality make it a good addition to stews, gumbos and soups. It persists in gardens throughout the harshest weather, for it can retain moisture and can blossom and ripen seeds long after its removal from the soil.

Purslane seems to have originated in India or Persia, but spread quickly to Europe and to the New World. In 1819 William Cobbett spurned the commonness of purslane as "a mischievous weed that Frenchmen and pigs eat when they can get nothing else." But Thoreau made a steady diet of purslane at Walden Pond:

> *I learned from my two years' experience that it would cost incredibly little to obtain one's necessary food, even in this latitude; that a man may use as simple a diet as the animals, and yet retain health and strength. I have made a satisfactory dinner, satisfactory on several accounts, simply off a dish of purslane* (Portulaca oleracea) *which I gathered in my cornfield, boiled and salted. I give the Latin on account of the trivial name.*

Pumpkins

Pumpkin seeds

Q

QUACHEG

Also QUACHE. This sheep's milk cheese is made in Macedonia on the border of Greece and Yugoslavia. Whole milk is curdled with sour whey, then pressed. Quacheg may be eaten fresh or after aging.

QUADRO

See **Milano Cheese.**

QUAHOG

See **Clam.**

QUAIL

Also BOB WHITE, COLIN. The true quail is a small, migratory game bird, originating in India and Africa, but inhabiting Europe during certain months of the year. There are many species, the most prevalent being the European common quail *(Coturnix coturnix)* and the blue quail of Africa. They are ground-nesting birds that prefer to run from danger but are capable of rapid, short bursts of flight, usually following a straight line. Because of the latter, they are considered an "honest" bird to hunt and are a great favorite with hunters. Moreover, their flesh is firm, white and delicately flavored, a delight to eat.

The American quail *(Colinus virginianus)*, more familiarly known as the bob-white because of its characteristic call, is a different bird altogether. Larger than the European variety, it was called "quail" by early colonists in the Northeast because of similiarities in general size, appearance and habits. Although not migratory, it nests on the ground, prefers walking and is capable of only short bursts of flight. It is somewhat more confusing to hunt because a covey of quail nests in a circle, tails together, heads facing out, so that members have a 360° angle of view. If startled, the covey bursts into flight in all directions. In the southern United States, this bird is known as partridge. On the average, a dressed bird weighs six to seven ounces.

Other quails of the Western Hemisphere are the valley quail of California, which is the official state bird, and the mountain quail, also of California, reputed to be the best-tasting quail of all. In the Southwest and Mexico, the Messena quail is the most prevalent.

As noted, though migratory, the European quail is not a strong flyer, and on its way south customarily island-hops in the Mediterranean. It often arrives at its resting place so exhausted that it is easily captured by hand. The English author, Norman Douglas, a longtime resident of Capri, noted that 50 years ago there was wholesale slaughter of the birds when they stopped there during the migration to or from Egypt. Indeed, centuries earlier the bishop of Capri earned himself the nickname, "The Bishop of Quails," because he attempted to impose a tithe on the taking of birds there. According to more recent reports, quail no longer stop there on their migrations.

Although it is customary to hang some gamebirds for a few days to achieve a stronger flavor, this is not true of quail. Quail is eaten fresh, usually prepared simply, i.e., roasted or baked for a short period of time. Among the Japanese, quail eggs are considered a great delicacy. Their consistency is said to be creamy and velvety. A favorite way of serving them is as a variety of sushi, i.e., raw, with salmon eggs, on top of a rice ball wrapped in seaweed.

QUANDONG

Edible fruit of an Australian tree, *Fusanus acuminata*, it has a single stone and a peachlike pulp. It is also known as "native peach." The stone itself has an edible kernel known as the quandong nut.

QUARTIROLO

A soft Italian cheese made of cow's milk in Lombardy, it is prepared in the autumn. Some authorities claim it is simply **Milano** produced in September, October and November. Others say it is a form of **taleggio,** which is a surface-ripened cheese.

QUASS

See **Kvass.**

QUASSIA

Quassia is a shrub or small tree, *Quassia amara*, native to Mexico, the West Indies and northern South America, whose wood is the source of a bitters called quassin. Quassin is a pure and simple bitters that is soluble in alcohol. It is used as a flavoring agent in some *apperitifs* and as a drug. Formerly, some brewers used it in place of hops to flavor beer.

QUATRE-EPICES

This is a French mixture of spices used for flavoring meats and stews. The name means "four spices," and although the mixture contains more than four, it tastes like a mixture of nutmeg, clove, ginger and white pepper. Other spices (and herbs) that may also be included are allspice, mace, cinnamon, bay leaves, rosemary, marjoram and sage. The name *quatre-epices* is also used to denote herbs of the *Nigella* genus, such as black cumin *(N. sativa).*

QUEENFISH

Also TALANG, LARGEMOUTH LEATHER-SKIN. A popular gamefish of the Indo-Pacific area, the queenfish *(Chorinemus lysan)* is a member of the jack family. It attains a length of four feet and has a beautiful olive-green back and sides and a golden belly. It is sought by anglers in both South Africa and Australia and is fished commercially as well. A good specimen weighs 25 pounds. It is appreciated as a food fish, but the quality of the flesh varies.

QUEENSLAND APPLE

Edible fruit of a tree, *Timonius rumphii*, native to southern and eastern Australia, it is apple-shaped and much liked where it grows.

QUEENSLAND ARROWROOT

See **Tous-les-Mois.**

QUEENSLAND AVICENNIA

Edible fruit of an Australian tree, *Avicennia officinalis*, that grows in coastal regions, it is usually baked or steamed before being eaten.

QUEENSLAND NUT

See **Macadamia Nut.**

QUEENSLAND SPINY PLUM

This edible fruit of an Australian coniferous tree, *Podocarpus spinulosa*, is plumlike, one-seeded, with fleshy red or purple pulp. It is used to make preserves.

QUEENSLAND WILD LIME

This thick-skinned fruit of an Australian shrub, *Micocitrus inodora*, may be used as a substitute for ordinary lime. It is oval, up to 2 inches in diameter and has a juicy, acidic pulp.

QUEIJO PRATO

See **Prato.**

QUESO ANEJO

This is a Mexican skim-milk cheese with a dry, crumbly texture that is cured from six to eight months. This earns it the name *queso anejo*, meaning "aged cheese." These cheeses are round and weigh from 11 to 22 pounds. They are shipped to market in jute bags, which hold from six to eight cheeses. *Queso anejo* is quite popular, especially in the Mexico City area, where it is used in enchiladas and other typical dishes. Wholesalers often cover it with chili powder and market it as *queso enchilado.*

QUESO BLANCO

The main cheese of Latin America, *queso blanco* means "white cheese," and comes in many different forms, under many different names, depending on the country. It may be made from whole, skim or partly skimmed milk, often with cream added, and may turn out to be a cottage cheese, a fresh cheese, pressed or unpressed, or a ripened cheese. *Queso blanco* is made from cow's milk. If eaten fresh, the curd is fairly dry, soft and granular with a salty flavor. In the pressed variety, the curd has a hard, crumbly, open texture and, again, a salty flavor. If held for ripening, which could be anywhere from two weeks to two months, it develops a strong flavor and a dry, hard texture suitable for grating. Some skim-milk cheeses are smoked for two or three days. Following are some of the local names for various permutations of *queso blanco:*

Cottage cheese: *queso de puna*, *queso fresco*, *queso de llanero*, *queso de maracay*, and *queso de Perija.*

Fresh unpressed: *panela.*

Fresh, pressed: *queso de prensa*, *queso del pais*, *queso de la tierra*, and *queso estera.*

Skim milk, pressed: *queso descremado*, *queso huloso.*

Whole milk, pressed and cured: *queso de bagaces*, *queso de crema.*

See also: **Queso de Crema, Queso del Pais, Queso de Prensa, Queso de Puna, Queso Fresco.**

QUESO DE BOLA

This whole-milk cheese made in Spain, Latin America and the Philippines is shaped like a ball and most resembles red, Dutch **Edam.** The texture is firm, and, as a rule, cheeses are cured for three months.

QUESO DE CAVALLO

This is a Venezuelan, pear-shaped cheese.

QUESO DE CINCHO

Also QUESO DE PALMA METIDA. Here is a simple, Venezuelan sour-milk cheese that is ball-shaped and wrapped in palm leaves. Individual cheeses are firm, orange in color and weigh four pounds.

QUESO DE CREMA

Generally in Latin America, this is **cream cheese,** that is, a rich, perishable cheese made from cow's milk and enriched with cream. Often used as a substitute for butter, this cheese is especially popular in Cuba.

An exception is Costa Rica where queso de crema is a soft cheese, resembling **brick,** which is cured from two to eight weeks. It is a staple cheese of Costa Rica.

See also: **Queso Blanco.**

QUESO DE HOJA

This is a firm Puerto Rican cheese made of cow's milk. Its name means "leaf cheese." During processing, the curd is sliced in thin layers, salted, folded and wrapped in cloth to squeeze out the whey. When the finished cheese is cut, these layers of curd are visible, looking like leaves resting on top of one another. Individual cheeses are round and flat, measuring six inches in diameter by one to two inches thick.

QUESO DE LA TIERRA

See **Queso del Pais.**

QUESO DEL PAIS

Also QUESO DE LA TIERRA. This is a white, semisoft cheese produced by both farm and factory in Puerto Rico for local consumption. Much of it is eaten fresh, in which case it has the consistency of cottage cheese. The cured version is firmer and has a slightly bitter taste. These cheeses are round and flat, ranging in weight from one to five pounds, the larger ones usually being factory-made.

See also: **Queso Blanco.**

QUESO DE MANO

See **Hand Cheese.**

QUESO DE PALMA METIDA

See **Queso de Cincho.**

QUESO DE PRENSA

This hard, pressed cheese is made in Puerto Rico from whole cow's milk. Milk may be coagulated with rennet or acetic acid, depending on the custom in different localities. It is eaten fresh or after curing for two or three months. Cheeses are marketed in five-pound loaves.

See also: **Queso Blanco.**

QUESO DE PUNA

This is a Puerto Rican cottage cheese. After coagulation, the curd is salted, kneaded and drained, then held for a day or two until firm enough to retain a molded shape.

See also: **Queso Blanco.**

QUESO ENCHILADO

See **Queso Anejo.**

QUESO FRESCO

This dry cottage cheese is made in Latin America from skim milk.

See also: **Queso Blanco.**

QUETSCH

A dry, colorless brandy made from plums in Alsace, quetsch is distilled from the fermented juice of a particular plum, the plump, oblong quetsche, which is also used to make tarts and jam. It is bottled unaged and served ice cold as an after-dinner drink.

QUEYRAS

See **Champoleon.**

QUILLAJA

Also SOAPBARK. The dried bark of a Chilean tree, *Quillaja saponaria*, which has soaplike properties, it has been used as a foamer in soft drinks.

QUILLBACK

A member of the sucker family, the quillback *(Carpiodes cyprinus)* is a relatively large fish (up to 12 pounds) and is distinguished by a long, quill-like second ray on its dorsal fin. It is found in many rivers of the central United States and is fished commercially in Lake Erie.

QUINCE

A fruit cultivated since very early times, the quince *(Cydonia oblonga)* is too sour to be eaten unsweetened. Consequently, it is rarely eaten fresh but usually is cooked with sugar for use in jams, jellies, syrups, compotes and even liqueurs. It grows on a shrub or

Quince: fruit and jelly

small tree 12 to 20 feet high, which is native to Iran or the Caspian region. Quince leaves are large and hairy, and the fruit comes in two shapes, round and oblong, both covered with fine, resistant hair.

The fruit is golden yellow and resembles a **pear,** although its taste has been compared to the **guava.** In commercial orchards, pear trees are customarily grafted onto quince rootstock to hold down the height of the tree. But this grafting does not produce hybrids, nor does grafting quince with apple, of which the ancients believed quince to be a species. Hence, modern botanists have concluded that quince is a genus by itself.

Quince probably reached its apogee of popularity in the Middle Ages when a quince preserve, called in French *cotignac,* was regarded as a gift fit for royalty. When such honored a city with a visit, they were given *cotignac* to mark the occasion. It was a particular specialty of Orleans; and when Joan of Arc arrived to lift the siege there, she was presented with a gift of *cotignac.*

Portuguese quinces, called *marmelo,* were held in especially high esteem. The term "marmalade" was coined to describe the preserve most commonly made of Portuguese quince.

Since then quince has declined drastically in popularity. Although it was once common in New England, it is now the least grown of all fruit trees in the United States. In certain areas it has remained in favor, especially in Germany, South Africa and Latin America. In England, quince is often added to apple or strawberry jam because its mucilaginous and soothing properties add to their setting quality and improve the flavor. Neither **Bengal quince,** nor Japanese quince are true quinces. For information on the latter, see **Japonica.**

QUINCY

Quincy is a dry, golden yellow wine from the **Loire,** tributary of the Cher near the town of Bourges. The vine thrives in the rich soil between the two rivers and gives a mellow dry wine perfect with shellfish. Quincy, unlike other wines from the vicinity, is exported, particularly to the United States. The wine (pronounced "Kan-see") is best drunk young.

QUININE WATER

See **Tonic Water.**

QUINNAT

See **Salmon.**

QUINOA

An annual plant of the goosefoot family that has been cultivated since pre-Columbian times by Indians of the Andean region, quinoa *(Chenopodium quinoa)* reaches a height of five to six feet, has green woolly leaves and abundant seeds, which have been described as small, round, slightly flattened and glutinous.

The leaves make a nutritious green and are boiled like spinach or added to soups. The seeds are also added whole to soups, but more often ground to make a flour that is used for meal or porridge or baked into bread. An attractive feature of the quinoa is its ability to flourish at altitudes above 13,000 feet. It was cultivated by the Indians along with potatoes because it supplied some of the nutrients the potatoes lacked. Among the several varieties of quinoa, it is the white-seeded that has become the staple crop.

The Indians also used the seeds to make a type of beer called *chicha.* Ashes of the plant are used to season coca leaves, which the Indians chew as a daily stimulant.

Quinoa has been planted in England, and the leaves found to be occasionally useful in salads. The seeds are used there as fodder.

See also: **Coca.**

R

RAAB

Also BROCCOLI RAAB, RUVO KALE, TURNIP BROCCOLI, ITALIAN TURNIP. An annual leafy plant, *Brassica ra pa* var. *ruvo,* closely related to the turnip but tasting like **broccoli,** it is native to the southern United States, particularly Virginia and the Carolinas. The plant has a taproot, grows 2½ to 3½ feet high at maturity, and has large, lobed leaves. The stems are more slender than those of broccoli and do not end in a head. Raab is marketed in the spring and is cooked like spinach.

RABACAL

This is a mild, semisoft Portuguese cheese made from sheep or goat's milk in the Coimbra area. These cheeses have a creamy texture and are round, measuring five inches across by one inch thick.

RABBIT

A burrowing rodent that is abundant in the wild state and has been bred domestically for its meat and fur, the rabbit is often confused with the hare; indeed, the terms are sometimes used interchangeably. They are members of the same family, but different genera, hares *Lepus* and rabbits *Oryctolagus.* Hares are generally larger and have never been domesticated, refusing to reproduce in captivity. Among food snobs, the hare is respectable while the rabbit is not. For reasons unexplained, rabbit is tabu at the gourmet table.

Rabbits are best eaten when young, three months for frying; eight to nine months for stewing. They will weigh from three to eight pounds at those ages. The flesh is white, close-grained, high in protein and low in fat. Domestic rabbit meat is considered inferior in taste to that of the wild rabbit unless special care is taken with its fodder. The best tasting wild rabbits are those that feed on tree bark and wild herbs, such as thyme, rosemary and the like. In general, wild rabbit meat has a stronger flavor, and its sections of darker meat have a slightly gamey flavor. Because of its dryness, rabbit meat is usually marinated before cooking. Rabbit is also very gelatinous and makes good soup stock.

All domesticated rabbits are descended from the common rabbit of Europe *(O. cuniculus),* which is believed to be native to Spain and the Balearics or northwestern Africa. Wild rabbits were firmly established in prehistoric times in both the Eastern and Western Hemispheres. They are found world-wide today, but especially in temperate climates. There are historic references to them as early as the third century B.C., often as pests, and both Pliny and Varro reported on their undermining of the Spanish city of Tarragona, where 25 to 30 houses collapsed into soil honeycombed by their burrows. Romans raised rabbits in captivity and were especially fond of their feti, i.e., unborn offspring. It is believed that a similar predilection led to the rabbits' true domestication by monks in the Middle Ages who were subject to austere rules on the eating of meat. According to Reay Tannahill's *Food in History,* "It may have been medieval monks who first domesticated the rabbit—for the sake of its feti. Unborn or newly born rabbits, once a favorite delicacy of the Romans, were classified [by the church] (like eggs) as 'not meat.' "

Rabbits were widely eaten by pre-Columbian Indians, particularly the Aztecs, who even revered a rabbit god who, among other things, was the protector of *pulque,* the main alcoholic drink. The English settlers arriving in North America used the old word "cony" or "coney" for rabbit. One place they found thickly populated with rabbits they called "Coney Island." The main American wild rabbit is the cottontail *(Sylvillagus floridanus),* which seems to be midway between a rabbit and a hare. It exists in all 50 states and today is America's number one game animal. In certain states, however, it is subject to a disease called "tularemia" (rabbit fever), which can be passed on to humans. Cooking kills the bacteria in the meat, but rubber gloves should be used when handling uncooked wild rabbits.

The French are fondest of rabbits, consuming about 6.6 pounds a year per capita, which nearly equals their consumption of lamb. Americans consume about 50 million pounds a year (not counting wild rabbits) which works out to about 3.5 ounces per capita. Wild rabbit was once a popular dish in Great Britain and Australia, but the animal's rapid multiplication got to be such a problem that myxomatosis was introduced to abate them in the 1950s. It succeeded in eliminating much of the rabbit population, which only recently has begun to make a comeback.

See also: **Hare.**

RABBITFISH

Also SPINY. This is an Indian Ocean fish, *Siganus oramin*, so called because of its rounded blunt snout and rabbitlike jaws. It is found from East Africa to the East Indies and, since the opening of the Suez Canal, northward to the Mediterranean. The rabbit fish favors shallow water around reefs. It reaches a length of about 14 inches. This species has strong fin spines which are capable of inflicting painful wounds that can become infected with a venomous mucus that the fish secretes. It is, however, considered delicious eating and is consumed fresh or smoked.

RACAHOUT

Also RACACHOU. This powdered beverage base was made originally by Arabs from the ground acorns of the Barbary oak *(Quercus ilex* var. *rotundifolia)*, sugar and spices. More recently the name refers to a beverage taken in France like drinking chocolate and prepared from a more elaborate base including acorn flour, potato flour, **salep,** rice, sugar, cocoa and vanilla.

RACCOON

Also MAPACHE. The raccoon *(Procyon lotor)* is a small, furry mammal found in North, Central and South America. It is characterized by a broad head and narrow muzzle with a black "mask" across the eyes. Its body fur ranges from gray to almost black. The size of a raccoon matches that of a big housecat, but large specimens can weigh as much as 48 pounds and reach a length of two feet. Raccoons are usually nocturnal and inhabit timbered and brushy areas near water.

They are considered good game in several areas, but especially in the U.S. South. Raccoon meat is nutritious, consisting of up to 30 percent protein. It is said to have an agreeable flavor provided it is skinned as soon as possible, and the glands inside the front legs and on the back are removed intact. A traditional dish is roast raccoon stuffed with sweet potatoes. Raccoon may also be marinated and charcoal broiled, baked or used in a stew, such as the famous Calalou of the Gulf states.

RACCOON DOG

This small wild dog, *Nyctereutes procyonoides*, resembles a raccoon in its facial markings but has a foxlike body. It is found in eastern Siberia, Manchuria, Japan, parts of China and in northern Indochina. A well-fed specimen might weigh as much as 16 pounds. In some parts of Japan, the flesh of this dog is considered a delicacy.

RADENER

Also SKIM-MILK RUNDKASE. A hard, German cow's-milk cheese made in the Mecklenburg area, it is much like **Swiss cheese,** but given less pressing. These cheeses are cured from six to eight months and weigh from 30 to 35 pounds. A similar cheese, made in Switzerland, is called *magere schweizerkase.*

RADICCHIO

Also WILD CHICORY. Three kinds of well known *radicchio*, or wild chicory, grow in Italy's Veneto province: the red Verona, the red Treviso and the variegated of Castelfranco. These are all varieties of the same species, *Chicorium intybus.* Their leaves are highly prized as a salad vegetable, but the root, unless too stringy and tough, can be the best part. It is usually crisp, with a white, compact pith. The red Verona has short leaves and a roundish heart. The red Treviso has long leaves and a tapering heart, suggesting romaine lettuce in shape and having the same crisp texture. The color is generally bright red, but may show some dark green unless the plant is bleached. Bleaching produces leaves of uniform redness supported by white stalks. The taste of the Treviso is agreeably bitter, but bleaching makes the taste less sharp. The variegated Castlefranco is globe-shaped, with green leaves speckled with wine-red spots and streaks. It is less bitter than the Treviso variety.

These kinds of wild chicory are planted as a second crop, and are therefore classed as a winter salad. Local enthusiasts claim it is the best winter salad plant in all Italy. Outside of their region, they are combined in a Treviso salad. Closer to home, however, the varieties aren't mixed, but fennel is added instead if more flavor is desired.

RADISH

Also DAIKON. This small vegetable is commonly cultivated for its edible root, which, though of little nutritive value, has a peppery taste believed to stimulate the appetite. The nutlike root ranges in color from white, red and white, through yellow and purple and has a crunchy white flesh inside. The smaller varieties are invariably eaten raw as an appetizer or sliced into salads. They are spring vegetables, very fast growing, that are harvested young. Left in the

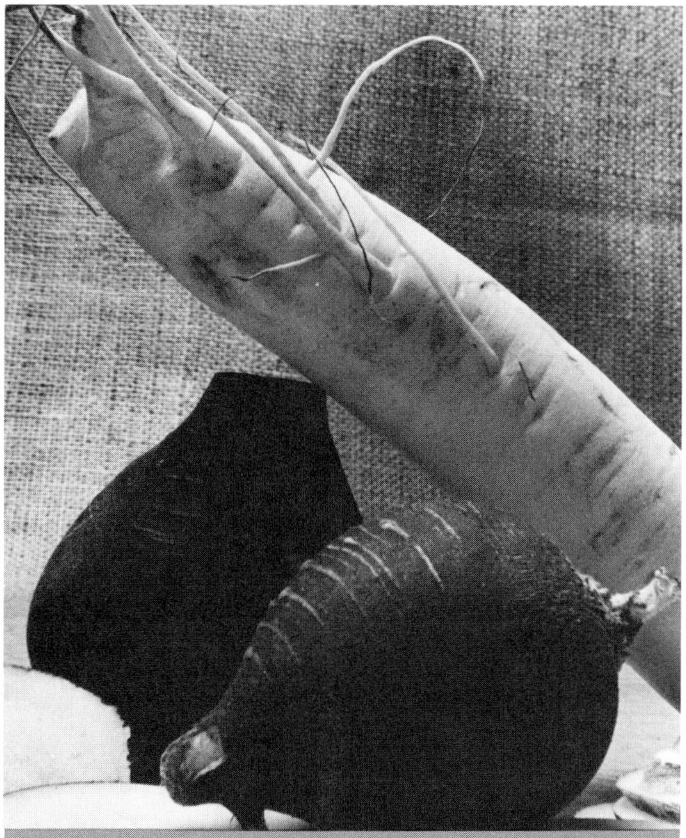
Black radishes and daikon, a larger, winter radish

ground, they become woody and often wormy or hollow in the center. Another, somewhat larger spring variety, is the Spanish or black radish, whose flavor is even more pronounced.

Winter radishes grow much larger, attaining lengths of three feet or more and weights of up to 50 pounds. The best known of these is the *daikon*, a Japanese specialty. They more resemble turnips in appearance and taste, although they are less sweet. They are more often cooked than eaten raw, and the Japanese also pickle them. Other varieties of radish are cultivated for their leaves; their pods, which have a peppery taste like the roots, and their seeds. The oil pressed from radish seeds had some importance in ancient Egypt and Rome as a cooking oil and retains some popularity in modern India.

Radishes are among the oldest cultivated plants. All the ones of gastronomic importance belong to the same species, *Raphanus sativus*. Its origin is unknown; it may be descended from the wild radish *(Raphanus raphanistrum)*, a weed common to Europe and North America. The earliest reference to cultivated radishes comes from China in the 7th century B.C. Both the spring and winter varieties were cultivated in ancient times. The large winter variety seemed to be especially popular in Europe up through the Renaissance, and then the taste for them died out. Now they are cultivated only in the Far East or by Asian immigrants in the Americas.

RADOLFZELLER CREAM CHEESE

This is a semisoft, fermented cheese made in the vicinity of Lake Constance, which is bounded by Germany, Austria and Switzerland. It is made from whole cow's milk and is similar in taste and texture to ***Mainauer*** and **Munster.** Individual cheeses are cured on straw mats for about one month. They are square or round in shape, measuring 6½ inches by four inches.

RAGNIT

See **Tilsiter.**

RAIL

Also MUDHEN. The name includes any of several small wading birds of the *Rallidae* family, which resemble quail somewhat. They are considered fine game in Europe, especially France, where the favorite is the landrail or **corncrake,** known as the *rale de genet* or *roi de cailles*. The French also eat the water rail, but deem it definitely inferior.

In the United States rails are eaten in the southeastern states, particularly Louisiana where they inhabit swamps and are consequently known as mudhens. The best known variety is the sora. In their thorough-going treatise, *Eating in America: A History*, Waverly Root and Richard de Rochemont noted:

> *Hardier, or hungrier, back-country Louisianians occasionally seek coot and rail (generally known as "mud hens") and cook them with special precautions to rid them of their strong taste, soaking them in lemon juice and necessarily skinning them since the skin contains an evil-smelling oil which protects the bird from the damp, but does nothing for gourmets.*

RAIPONCE

See **Rampion.**

RAISIN

This is a sweet, dried grape. Most raisins are dried naturally in the sun after being scalded and dipped into an alkaline solution, but at times artificial heat is used. The **grapes** are all of the *Vitis vinifera* species and are classed as seeded and seedless. Important seedless varieties are the Sultana and the Thompson; the White Muscat of Alexandria is the most important seeded variety.

California is the greatest raisin-producing area of the world, particularly in Fresno county. South Africa and Australia are substantial producers. They have now surpassed Spain, which was the 19th century's leading producer and which, in turn, had eclipsed the traditional leaders in the eastern Mediterranean, Greece and Turkey.

Raisins made from seeded grapes are said to have a better flavor than those made from seedless varieties. The California White Muscat is a thin-skinned, yellowish green grape that averages five-eighths of an inch in diameter and one inch in length. It is rich, fruity and only moderately juicy. It is not eaten fresh to any extent. The Thompson Seedless is an oval, yellow grape, rather small and low in acidity. A special device removes the seeds of the seeded varieties before packing.

Among Spanish raisin grapes, the best known are Malagas or Muscatels. Smyrna Sultanas are pale yellow, fine-flavored and seedless. A special, larger variety of Sultana is known as the Corinthian raisin. The small, seedless raisin known as the currant is grown chiefly in the Grecian islands of Zante, Cephalonia and Ithaca and in the vicinity of Patras. The word "currant" is a corruption of "Corinth."

Raisins have a very high sugar content and are rich in iron, potassium, calcium, magnesium and phosphorus, plus vitamins A and B. They are eaten plain as a snack or used in cookies, muffins, puddings, cakes and sauces for tongue and ham. *Raisin* is the French word for grape.

See also: **Grape.**

RAKI

This strong alcoholic drink is made from macerated (softened by steeping) figs, dates, plums, grapes or other fruit, flavored with **anise.** It is found in Turkey, Greece and other eastern Mediterranean countries. When based on grapes or plums, raki is a fiery, highly intoxicating eau-de-vie, colorless and deceptively smooth.

The pleasures of raki are amply (and ironically) described by the Greek writer, Nikos Kazantzakis, in his novel, *The Greek Passion:*

> *The Agha half shut his heavy eyelids and savored this world below. All that the good God has made is perfect, he thought: this world's a great success. Are you hungry? here's bread and minced meat or pilaff with cinnamon. Are you thirsty? here's that water of youthfulness, raki.*

See also: **Arrack, Ouzo.**

RALE

See **Rail.**

RAMBUTAN

A common fruit of Southeast Asia, the rambutan *(Nephelium lappaceum)* has a bright red skin covered with soft, curled hairlike spines. The pulp is juicy, translucent and sweet, somewhat like the litchi. It makes a good thirst quencher. The rambutan is eaten raw and, as it is much cultivated, there are many varieties in Hong Kong, Malaysia, Singapore, Indonesia and Thailand.

RAMOST

See **Pultost.**

RAMPION

A hardy European rootplant, formerly much cultivated, but now neglected. Rampion *(Campanula rapunculus)* is often compared to the radish or salsify in appearance. It has a large, white taproot that is eaten raw like radish or cooked and eaten like salsify. The root tastes a little like walnuts. The leaves are added raw to salads or cooked like spinach. Rampion is in season from November through the winter. It was transplanted in North America by the French, but is seldom seen except in the wild.

A North American plant, *Oenothera biennis*, is called German rampion or evening primrose. Its roots may be prepared and eaten like rampion's. The young shoots are eaten in salads.

RAMSONS

Also BEAR'S GARLIC, HOG'S GARLIC, GYPSY ONION, BUCKRAMS. A broad-leaved garlic plant, *Allium ursinum*, native to Europe and Asia, it has a pungent smell and bears bulbs on a short rhizome. The leaves are boiled and eaten as a green vegetable in parts of Europe. The roots are used in salads as well.

RAMTIL

See **Niger Seed.**

RANDIA

This yellow fruit of a spiny shrub, *Xeromphis spinosa*, native to tropical Asia, is round or oval, 1½ inches long and is eaten cooked. A tropical American species *(Randia formosa)* also produces edible fruit.

RANGIPORT CHEESE

This round French cow's milk cheese made in the Seine-et-Oise department is similar to **Port du Salut.** Each cheese weighs two and a half pounds.

RANGPUR

Also LEMANDARIN, MANDARIN LIME, OTAHEITE ORANGE. The rangpur is the strongly acidic fruit of a medium-sized tree, *Citrus x limonia*, which is a hybrid of the lemon and the tangerine (mandarin orange). It is about the size of a lemon, round but flattened on the ends and yellow to reddish orange in color. The pulp is divided into eight to 10 easily separated segments.

The *otaheite* orange is a sweet, or low acid, version of this hybrid. It is orange to deep yellow in color, round with flattened ends and averages about two inches in diameter. The *otaheite* orange grows on a small, thornless bush that is highly ornamental and is often sold as a potted plant. Its taste is sweet, but otherwise insipid.

RAPE

Also COLZA. The name refers to any of several plants used for making an oil similar to rape oil in India. Rape *(Brassica napus)* is an annual herb, closely related to the turnip. From the aerial portion come oil seeds, fodder and vegetable crops. The seeds are contained in long, slender pods, and are pressed to yield rape oil, which make up 10 to 12 percent of the world's total of vegetable oil. It is a cool season crop and can be grown in northern Canada, Europe and Asia. The leaves, which are gathered in the spring, can be used like spinach. The plant is used as forage for sheep in Europe and as food for hogs and sheep in America.

Colza *(Brassica rapa* var. *olifera)*, whose name comes from the German *Kohlsaat*, meaning cabbage seed, has been an important source of cooking oil in Europe since the 17th century. Its cultivation has diminished in this century because some studies have suggested its use in cooking may be harmful. It is still widely cultivated in India and Romania, however, because its oil yield is even higher than rape.

Likewise, some nutritionists have questioned the value of rape oil itself in human nutrition.

RAPER CHEESE

See **Rayon Cheese.**

RAPINI

This is a variety of foliage turnip, *Brassica rapa* var. *rapifera*, that forms no swollen root but has a cluster of leaves that are cooked and eaten as green vegetables.

Rapini

RASCASSE

See **Hogfish.**

RASPBERRY

This is a delicious berry of the world's temperate regions, belonging to the *Rubus* genus and growing wild in red and black varieties. The raspberry plant is a low, thorny shrub that grows profusely in wooded places, and has also been cultivated for many centuries. The roots are perennial, but the stalks, or canes, are biennial. The latter are erect in the case of red raspberries and arched in the case of black. The oldest cultivated raspberry is the European red raspberry *(Rubus idaeus)*, which in the wild prefers mountainous or hilly regions.

Raspberries

It takes its scientific name from Mount Ida in Turkey, where, according to legend, the Greek gods went berrying and returned with raspberries, to the everlasting delight of humankind. Each fruit consists of a cluster of tiny drupes, which are usually dark red, but in some hybrids are white, yellowish or pink. This berry spread all over Europe and Asia in prehistoric times, and archeological evidence suggests it was gathered wild by humans long before its existence was recorded in history. It was known by the Greeks and Romans, but so profuse and delicious was it wild that no thought was given to cultivating it until the 16th century.

Colonists arriving in North America found ample growths of indigenous raspberries, represented chiefly by the American red raspberry *(R. strigosus)* and the American black raspberry *(R. occidentalis).* They preferred, however, to transplant the familiar *R. idaeus*, and bias towards the latter persisted until after the American Civil War when it came to be recognized that American varieties were just as delicious as the European, and a lot hardier. The black raspberry closely resembles the blackberry, but can be distinguished pragmatically in the picking. When the black raspberry is picked, it comes easily away from the stem, leaving a small white core attached there, and a corresponding cuplike depression in the fruit. In the blackberry, the core remains firmly embedded in the fruit. *R. Occidentalis* is the eastern black raspberry. There are other varieties such as the western black *(R. leucodermis)*, the Rocky Mountain, or boulder raspberry *(R. deliciosus)*, the dwarf raspberry *(R. triflous)*, and the lowbush raspberry *(R. trivialis).* The purple raspberry is a hybrid between the red and black.

Raspberries are a popular dessert fruit and may be eaten fresh during the summer months where they are in season, either plain or with sugar and whipped cream. They are also used in jams, jellies, tarts, pies, puddings and sauces. They are available year round frozen, and much commercial production is dedicated to this segment of the market. Chief producing states are Michigan, Oregon, New York, Washington, Ohio, Pennsylvania, New Jersey and Minnesota. Raspberries are also used to make liqueurs (in France called *framboise)*, and a vinegar, consisting of raspberry juice, vinegar and sugar.

Besides being tasty and refreshing, the raspberry has about the same vitamin properties as oranges and lemons, plus carbohydrates to the extent of 12 to 15 percent of total constituents. It has laxative and diuretic properties and small quantities of calcium, magnesium and iron salts.

RAT

This common rodent is eaten regularly in certain parts of Africa and the Far East. The rat is viewed with repugnance in Western countries and has become an item of diet only during times of great deprivation, such as the siege of Paris in 1870. An exception to this rule, according to the *Larousse Gastronomique*, is the case of the alcoholic rats that inhabit wine cellars of the Gironde. There it used to be the custom for cellar workmen to prepare a dish called *entrecote a la bordelaise*, which consisted of grilled rats that had first been skinned, eviscerated and brushed with a thick sauce of olive oil and crushed shallots.

Ghanians are the most conspicuous consumers of rat meat. Calvin W. Schwabe made this comment in his absorbing discussion of taboo food, *Unmentionable Cuisine:*

> *In West Africa . . . rats are a major item of diet. The giant rat* (Cricetomys), *the cane rate* (Thryonomys), *the common house mouse, and all other species of rats and mice are all eaten. According to a United Nations Food and Agricultural Organization report, they now comprise over 50 percent of the locally produced meat eaten in some parts of Ghana. Between December 1968 and June 1970, 258,206 pounds of cane rat meat alone were sold in* one *market in Accra.*

The cane rat is discussed under **Marmat.** The giant rat, also known as the giant African pouched rat *(C. gambianus)*, can reach a length of 18 inches and weigh as much as 2¼ pounds. In Ghana it is fried, then stewed with tomatoes and hot peppers.

Thai farmers relish certain species of rice rat, which they can purchase in local markets, and whose price competes favorably with that of pork and chicken, and whose taste, according to some, beats chicken. Schwabe notes that the North American species most closely corresponding to the cane rat and the Thai rice rat in delectability are the southeastern rice rat *(Oryzomys* sp.) and the cotton rat *(Sigmodon hispidus)*.

Rats have been regular fare for centuries in China. Marco Polo was the first Westerner to comment on this. When he visited the Hangchow market in the 13th century, he noted rat meat selling under the name "household deer." In modern Canton, the rat carcass is gutted, heavily salted, then sun-dried in the open air. Rat meat is prepared in a wide variety of ways and is considered a good hair restorer.

RATA DEL MAR

See **Stargazer.**

RATAFIA

This Italian liqueur is made from black cherries. One way of preparing it is to soak ripe cherries together with their stones in alcohol for a number of days. The liquid is filtered, and syrup of water and sugar is added. Sometimes a few strawberries, raspberries and black currants are mixed in.

RATFISH

Also MOUSEFISH, BEAKED SALMON, SAND EEL. This is a long, thin-bodied fish, *Gonorhynchus gonorhynchus*, found throughout the Indo-Pacific area from East Africa to Hawaii. It shuns very warm waters, preferring temperate areas. Its flesh is said to be firm and to have a very good flavor. Perhaps because of its small size (up to 18 inches) and habit of burrowing into the sand, it is not fished commercially and is, therefore, rarely seen in markets. The ratfish's entire body is covered by rough-edged scales, and its general color is purplish blue shading to brown on top and red on the belly. It is no relation to the rat or rabbitfish of the family *Chimaeridae* found in the Atlantic and eastern Pacific Oceans.

RATTAN

This type of palm shrub, *Calamus rotang*, is a source of the rushlike rattan cane of commerce; but its shoots are edible, and its fruit is used in the Far East to make a spicy condiment.

RAVIGGIOLO

A soft Italian cheese made of sheep's milk in Tuscany, it is sweet and creamy, much like ***Crescenza.*** Cheeses are cured for two weeks and weigh from one-half to 3½ pounds.

RAVIGOTE SAUCE

There are two ravigote sauces, one hot, one cold. Hot ravigote is an important French sauce, based on **bechamel** with the addition of white wine, herbs (parsley, chives, chervil, tarragon, shallots and garlic), white stock, vinegar, plus pepper and nutmeg. It is used on poultry and variety meats (offal). Cold ravigote is served chilled with fish, calf's head, beef or chicken, and consists of mayonnaise seasoned with caper, chives, parsley, tarragon, gherkins, shallots and onions.

See also: **Sauce.**

RAVIOLI

This is a type of filled Italian pasta. In English it is a generic term for most *pasta ripiena*, i.e., small envelopes of dough—square or round in shape—stuffed with a mixture of chopped meat, cheese, egg, vegetables, etc. They are all forms of *pasta asciutta*, that is, the kind eaten "dry" with a sauce, rather than in a soup. The dough is made from the flour, or semolina, of hard, durum wheat and eggs.

Ravioli, specifically, are square (1½ to 2 inches), traditionally stuffed with spinach and **ricotta.** The same envelop containing a savory meat stuffing is called *agnolotti.* Other types of *pasta ripiena* are *cannelloni* (tubes with savory meat stuffing), *cappelletti* (small discs, filled, then twisted into the shape of a tricorn hat), *rotoli* (rare, giant *cannelloni)* and ***tortellini.*** They are put into boiling water until tender, usually about 10 minutes, then served with a savory sauce and grated cheese.

See also: **Pasta.**

RAY

See **Skate.**

RAYON CHEESE

Also RAPER CHEESE. This hard, very dry cheese of the **Swiss** type is made in Fribourg canton in Switzerland, especially for export to Italy. Partly skimmed cow's milk is used, and the curd is cooked to ensure firmness and to prevent eye formation. After curing, it is sent to Turin to be dried in caves. When thoroughly dry, it is called raper cheese and sold for grating.

RAZORBACK SUCKER

Also HUMPBACK SUCKER. An edible fish found only in the basins of the Colorado and Gila Rivers of North America, it resembles other members of the *Catostomidae* family (see also: **Sucker),** except for its high, sharp-edged back. At one time the razorback sucker *(Xyrauchen texanus)* was an important food fish for tribes living in the immediate vicinity of the Colorado and Gila Rivers. Large specimens reach a length of two feet and a weight of 10 pounds.

REBLOCHON

Soft French cheeses made of sheep or cow's milk in the Savoy region, reblochon are small, round and flat with a reddish rind and creamy texture. They are cured from four to five weeks and generally weigh between one and two pounds. They are in season from September to July. Brizecon is another, similar cheese from the same area.

RECUIT

See **Ricotta.**

RED BAY

See **Borbonia.**

RED BEAN

This variety of soybean, *Glycine max*, grown in China, is used to make red bean sauce. The sauce, which is usually served with meat, is made from a fermented mash of beans. Some find its odor slightly unpleasant.

See also: **Red Cheese.**

REDBUD

This is a small, deciduous tree, *Cercis canadensis*, of North America, whose rosy-pink flowers were used by French Canadians in salads and pickling solutions.

RED CHEESE

In Cantonese cuisine, fermented red soybeans are cooked, combined with salt and pressed into cakes. Canned red cheese is immersed in a red liquid that should be blended with the cheese before serving.

RED COTTON TREE

Also RED SILK-COTTON TREE. A large tree, *Bombax ceiba*, native to Malaysia and Burma but widely transplanted to other tropical areas, it has bright red flowers surrounded by fleshy calyces that are much esteemed locally as a curry vegetable.

RED-EAR SARDINE

A Caribbean variety of sardine, *Harengula humeralis*, it gets its name from a red spot at the edge of the gill opening. This is a schooling fish often found close inshore where West Indians catch them with beach seines and cast nets. In certain seasons it ranks as a local food fish of some consequence.

See also: **Pilchard, Sardine.**

REDFISH

Also NANNYGAI. This is the name given to several food fishes, most prominently the *Sebastes marinus* of the North Atlantic, and the nannygai *(Centroberyx affinis)* of Australian waters. *S. marinus* inhabits offshore banks, reaches a length of 32 inches and has white, well-flavored flesh. It is fished commercially by all North Atlantic countries of Europe and by Canada in the western Atlantic. It is prepared like **red snapper.**

The *nannygai* reaches a length of 18 inches and is found in waters off southern Australia and Tasmania. It has a deep, full-scaled body with reddish head and sides and orange belly. Its flesh is deemed to be of excellent quality and it has been subject to heavy commercial exploitation.

The name "redfish" is also applied to the red or blue-backed salmon *(Oncorhynchus nerka)*.

See also: **Salmon.**

RED MOMBIN

Also SPANISH PLUM, JOCOTE. Dark red fruit of a small tree of the American tropics, the red mombin *(Spondias purpurea)* is pear-shaped, with spicy, subacidic pulp surrounding a large seed. It is mainly eaten fresh and raw but also boiled or dried. It is widely cultivated in the West Indies, Mexico and Central America. The red mombin is also known as the *ciruela*.

RED SEA BREAM

See **Porgy.**

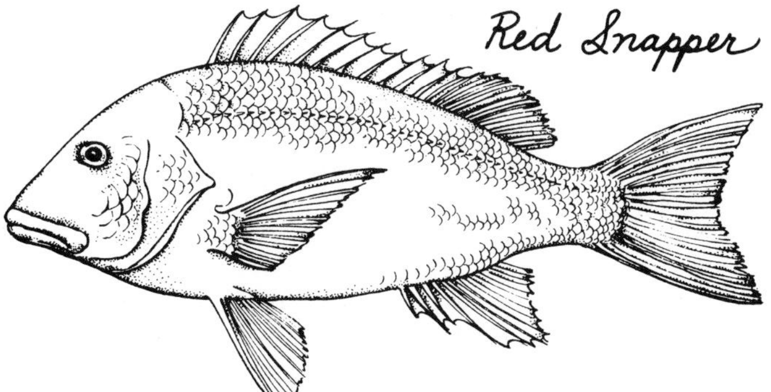

RED SNAPPER

This is an excellent food fish that inhabits warm marine waters, especially off the Atlantic and Gulf Coasts of the United States. The red snapper *(Lutjanus blackfordi)* is frequently marketed whole, or "in the round," when weighing from four to five pounds. The skin is a bright rose, somewhat paler on the underside, and the fins and eyes red. Larger fish (up to 30 pounds) are sold in the form of steaks and fillets. The meat is white and very firm, agreeably chewy, but with a faint "fishy" taste, reminding some of **swordfish.**

A choice way to prepare red snapper is to lightly fry the sliced fillets, and baste with melted butter, parsley and garlic. The flesh is particularly rich and delicate near the gill flaps, and a demand for "throats" is considerable in some localities. (A good idea, then, is not to throw the head away.) Red snapper is also a fine stock fish for chowders and bouillabaisse.

RED STAINING MUSHROOM

Also WOOD AGARIC. This edible mushroom of the British Isles and North America is found in coniferous forests and resembles the **field mushroom.** The red staining mushroom *(Agaricus silvaticus)* is delicious to eat, but when young has the disconcerting characteristic of turning pinkish red, or blood red if bruised or cut. Otherwise the flesh is white. It is a relatively small'mushroom (height up to four inches; cap up to three inches across) with a reddish brown cap, pink gills and white stem. Both the gills and stem turn reddish brown with age. This mushroom generally appears in autumn amidst stands of pine. It loses its red staining characteristic when older.

See also: **Mushroom.**

REDSTART

A common songbird, *Ruticilla pheonicura*, of Europe, Asia and North Africa, it is considered a fine game bird in France, where it is prepared like **lark.**

RED STEENBRAS

Also YELLOW STEENBRAS. A large sea bream, *Petrus rupestris*, of South African waters, it has a good reputation as a gamefish. The taste and texture of its flesh are rated excellent. The red steenbras can weigh as much as 150 pounds and reach a length of six feet. It is a long fish that has a pointed head and large jaws with prominent canine teeth. It must be handled with care and has been reported on occasion to attack swimmers. Its coloration includes a green brown back, orange sides and yellow belly. The liver of this fish is discarded as poisonous.

See also: **Musselcracker, White Steenbras.**

REDWARE

Also SEA GIRDLE, TANGLE. This is an edible seaweed, *Laminaria digitata*, that is large, brown and leathery. It is prepared like **dulse.**

REEDBIRD

Also BOBOLINK, RICE BIRD. This is a migratory songbird, *Dolichonyx oryzivorus*, of the United States, where it is now illegal to hunt it. In former times, it was considered fair game and rated a delicious table delicacy. The reedbird or ricebird was so called because during its migrations it feeds on wild rice or on the seedlings of commercial plantings in the southern states. It was prepared like **ortolan,** a similar bird of Europe.

REED GRASS

This is a tall, perennial reed, *Phragmites australis* var. *Berlandieri*, of cosmopolitan distribution whose rootstocks are dried and ground into flour. The rootstocks exude a sweet substance as a result of insect punctures, and the flour is made into an excellent, sweet-tasting porridge. Though not cultivated, reed grass is found in marshes and wet places on all continents. It reaches a height of 12 feet.

REFORME SAUCE

A sauce named after the Reform Club of London and created by its chef Alexis Soyer, it consists of **half-glaze** and ***poivrade* sauce** with gherkins, mushrooms, truffles, tongue and a julienne of egg whites. It was served there on mutton cutlets.

See also: **Sauce.**

REGGIANO

An Italian cheese of the Parmesan type, i.e., a variety of what the Italians call ***grana,*** or hard, grating cheeses such as *Parmigiano*, *Emiliano* and *Lodigiano*. Compared to ***Lodigiano,*** Reggiano is softer, finer-textured, contains more fat and cures faster. Curing generally takes from 14 months to two years. This cheese originated in Reggio, Emilia, but is made in many countries, including the United States. Cheeses weigh between 55 and 66 pounds. A similar hard cheese made in Uruguay is called *colonia* hard cheese and in Argentina, *treboliano*.

REINDEER

This is a large deer of the genus *Rangifer*, which inhabits arctic and subarctic regions of North America and Eurasia. The American species of reindeer is called caribou. It is generally larger than the European reindeer, lighter in color and has never successfully been domesticated.

In northern Europe and Asia, the reindeer has served for food (including milk) and hide, and has been a draft animal (in the absence of oxen) for more than 2000 years. The flesh of cows and steers (but especially that of a three-year-old steer) is considered a tasty venison, close to beef in flavor. In Alaska, a favorite meal among the Eskimos is *akutuq*, whipped caribou fat with bits of meat. Unlike other deer, both sexes are antlered. Reindeer tongues, imported from Russia, were thought a delicacy in the United States well into the 19th century.

REINDEER CHEESE

This is a hard salty rennet cheese made in limited quantities in Scandinavian countries from reindeer milk. Cheeses are rectangular, measuring five by four by 2½ inches.

REINWALD

See **Schamser.**

REMOULADE SAUCE

This is a sauce based on mayonnaise, served with cold eggs, fish, meat or poultry, includes mustard, anchovy essence (if served with fish), and chopped chervil, tarragon, parsley, shallots, gherkins and capers.

See also: **Sauces.**

RENNET

This is a substance used to curdle milk. There are two types, animal rennet and vegetable rennet. Animal rennet is obtained from the fourth stomach of a suckling mammal, preferably a calf, but it may also be taken from a lamb or a kid. The operative ingredient is an enzyme called rennin, which breaks milk down into two components, curds and whey. Curds are milk solids consisting of casein, fat and a little water and sugar. Whey is a yellowish liquid composed chiefly of water and milk sugar. Curds and whey was once a popular dish. Nowadays the ordinary person would encounter curds only in the following nursery rhyme:

Little Miss Muffet
Sat on a tuffet
Eating her curds and whey.
Along came a spider
And sat down beside her
And frightened Miss Muffet away.

Curds and whey are the raw materials for cheese, and cheesemakers are the big users of commercial rennet, which is of the animal type and comes in powder or paste form. Rennet works best at blood temperature and loses its effectiveness at temperatures above 140° F (60° C). Vegetable rennet is extracted from such common plants as thistle, yellow bedstraw and figs.

A common household use for rennet is to make the milk pudding called junket.

REPTONIA

Sweet, edible fruit of a small tree of eastern India, *Reptonia busifolia*, it is one-seeded, sold in local markets and is highly regarded as a fresh fruit.

REQUEIJAO

This is a Brazilian skim-milk cheese that is cooked several times, then enriched with butterfat or rich cream. It is marketed in parchment-lined boxes.

RESTAURANT

Cook-shops and eating-houses have been with us since the dawn of history, but the restaurant, so called, is a fairly recent innovation. According to most authorities, the first restaurant opened in Paris in 1765 under the proprietorship of a M. Boulanger. Until that time, there were only inns, which sold meals to their guests, and *traiteurs*, or caterers, who sold cooked meat to the public, but only in whole pieces. M. Boulanger set up business to sell soups, which he called "restoratives," or *restaurants*, a name he displayed over the door to his shop. His principal dish was sheep's feet in white sauce, a concoction the *traiteurs* claimed was meat that only they were licensed to sell. In a subsequent lawsuit, the Paris Parliament intervened and declared it not to be meat. Thus M. Boulanger had his way and began to serve stews to the public at his restaurant. A second restaurant was opened in 1783 by M. Beauvilliers, and then many others followed suit.

A flaw in this geneology is that the *Tour d'Argent*, one of the most famous Parisian restaurants, opened its doors in 1553. Because of its uniqueness, perhaps, it did not start a trend or establish a genre, and could only be classified a couple of centuries later when the name was created.

RETSINA

This Greek wine is usually white and flavored with pine resin during fermentation. The resin is collected from a tree, *Calitris quadrivalvis*, which grows throughout the land, although the retsina of Attica is the only version of this wine produced and shipped on a large scale. Retsina acquires its typical bitter taste after one year of aging.

Opinions differ as to why the Greeks would so tamper with their wine. One explanation is that some early vintner or merchant stored his product in pine barrels by mistake, and the pitch, or resin, accidentally blended with the wine. Another story has it that the Greeks deliberately tried to spoil their wine by dumping resin into it to upset the palates of the conquering Turks. Whatever the origin, the outcome is the same. A lot of people have grown accustomed to the taste of retsina, and like it that way.

RHINE WINES

The term usually refers to very fine German white wines that are smooth, not terribly dry, relatively low in alcohol content, often slightly effervescent and with a delicate fragrance. The Rhine begins in glacial Switzerland not far from the source of the **Rhone.** It forms the northern boundary of Switzerland, dividing that country from the German district of Baden-Wurttemberg, but turns north at Basel on its way through western Germany to the North Sea. Swiss Rhine wine is noteworthy for its reds, grown from the Pinot Noir grape. Swiss white wine from the Rhine basin is similar to that produced across the river, along the northern bank of Lake Constance, where the German Seewein and Weissherbst (a white Burgundy) are the best-known labels.

The great German Rhine vineyards, however, lie north of the Black Forest and Karlsruhe, in the historic wine-growing areas of the Palatinate, Rheinhesse and the Rheingau. Relatively weak sunlight over long periods of time is adequate—in this northernmost of all wine-growing countries—for the vintage familiarly known as Rhine Wine. The principal grapes are Rieseling (in the Rheingau), Sylvaner (in Rheinhesse and the Palatinate), and Muller-Thurgau (called Riesling-Sylvaner in Switzerland).

German Rhine wine is frequently labeled according to the vineyards that border the river and its tributaries—the Neckar, the Moselle and the Nahe. **Liebfrauenmilch** is one exception to this tradition, being a name for all the sweet white wine produced in Rheinhesse.

The practice of late picking *(spatlese)* is typical of the Rhine harvest. At times the grapes are picked as late as mid-November, when they have overripened, in order to bring out as much sweetness as possible. When the noble rot *(pourriture noble*, or, in German, *Edelfaule)* has thus occurred, the grapes picked are called *Beerenauslese*. *(Auslese* refers to wine made from carefully selected grapes.)

Wine has grown along the Rhine since before the time of Charlemagne (the *konig* of the most northern Rhine vineyards near Konigswinter). And it was along the Rhine ("the wine road") that the grape traveled for centuries—on its way from countries blessed with a warmer sun and a more bountiful yield—into northern Europe. In spite of two world wars and ever-encroaching industrialization, the German Rhine still vies with **Burgundy** and **Bordeaux** in producing possibly the greatest white wine in the world.

See also: **Wines, German; Wines, Swiss.**

RHINOCEROS

This massive, hoofed animal (family *Rhinocerotidae)* is found in Africa and, much more rarely, in parts of Asia. There are five species, the largest of which is the white rhino *(Ceratotherium simum)* of South Africa. It can reach a length of 16 feet and weigh eight tons. Much more plentiful is the smaller black rhino *(Diceros bicornis)*, which occurs in most parts of eastern and southern Africa. Asian species include the Indian rhino *(Rhinoceros unicornis)*, which is found today only in Java, and the two horned rhino *(Didermocerus sumatrensis)*, which is found throughout Southeast Asia and is the smallest, rarely exceeding nine feet in length and 2200 pounds.

Rhinos are hunted chiefly for their horns, which are believed to have medicinal and aphrodisiac qualities and are also used to make carvings. Most often hunted for food is the black rhino, whose flesh is rated as better than the elephant but not as good as hippopotamus. The black rhino is the only species rated dangerous to humans as its behavior is unpredictable. It may charge without warning if it detects a disturbing sound or smell.

RHONE WINES

This great river, which flows from Alpine Switzerland into Lake Geneva and south through France to the Mediterranean, is possibly the road by which the *vitis vinifera*, or "noble grape," came into Gaul—being cultivated there long before the Roman conquest. Wine from the banks of the Rhone in both Switzerland and France is of great appeal today, with dry whites predominating in Switzerland, and rich satiny reds the majority along the French Cotes (or "slopes") du Rhone.

Swiss Rhone wine is mainly grown in three cantons, those of Geneva, Valais and Vaud. The white wines—known by various local names—are almost all from the Fendant Vert, Chasselas, Sylvaner, Riesling-Sylvaner and Pinot Blanc grapes. In Valais, near the town of Sion, the harvest is particularly difficult and chancy—the vineyards bordering at times the very glaciers of the Alps. Near Geneva the white wines are lightly carbonated, bottled and sold without first being decanted. Charles Dickens, in *Little Dorrit*, found the Rhone wine of Switzerland unpleasant:

> *It was vintage time in the valleys on the Swiss side of the Pass of the Great Saint Bernard, and along the banks of the Lake of Geneva. The air there was charged with the scent of gathered grapes. . . . A pity that no ripe touch of this generous abundance could be given to the thin, hard, stony wine, which after all was made from the grapes!*

Tasters today, however, find the wine to be light, lively and refreshing.

From Geneva the Rhone flows southeast through Savoy to Lyons, where it turns due south on its ways to the sea. The white wines of Savoy are similar to the Swiss wines, from the Chasselas grape primarily, clear and semisparkling. Some outstanding wines are grown here (between Lyons and Geneva), among them Frangy, Marestel, Monthoux and **Seyssel.** But the best known of all Rhone wines are the reds from the Cote Rotie (or "roasted slopes," so named for the hot sun that warms the grapes) south of Lyons.

The French wine-growing district of the Rhone begins just below Lyons and plunges south about 140 miles to Avignon. Both banks of the Rhone abound in vineyards. The hearty red wines from this region include the famous **Hermitage,** and the better-known **Chateauneuf-du-Pape.** Hermitage (or Ermitage) is almost exclusively the product of the Syrah (or Sirah) grape, but the Chateauneuf-du-Pape comes from a blend of some 13 grapes, which include the Syrah, the Grenache and Muscadin. Chateauneuf-du-Pape is a highly-colored wine, ideal with roast meats and game. Hermitage is ruby-colored and is best drunk when aged for at least six years, when it becomes smooth and velvety. **Tavel** is a rose wine (some say it is the best rose in France), lightly pink, but very strong, from a village about eight miles north of Avignon.

See also: **Wines, Swiss.**

RHUBARB

Also PIE PLANT. Rhubarb *(Rheum rhaponticum)* is a wholesome plant with a uniquely tart flavor, much appreciated in compotes, pies and tarts, but always with lots of sugar. Perhaps because of the taste, many regard it as a fruit, but it is a vegetable, a large perennial cultivated for its thick, cylindrical stalks, which are pink to dark red in color. Typically, they run 12 to 18 inches in length. The stalks are topped by large green leaves, which should not be eaten, since they contain a toxic element, oxalic acid.

It is believed to have originated in northern Tibet. The Greeks knew about rhubarb; their name for it relates it to the country of Rha, i.e., the Volga, whence it was imported into England in the 16th century. It did not come into vogue as a food until the 19th century.

Both hothouse and field-grown varieties are marketed, the latter being much more robust, colorful and flavorful. Rhubarb appears in quantity in the early spring. Young rhubarb is tender and crisp. Older rhubarb will cook stringy and tough with poor flavor. Strawberries are often eaten with rhubarb in compotes, pies and tarts.

Medicinally, rhubarb is used for its laxative properties. It makes an unusual homemade wine. Rhubarb liqueur is made in Italy.

RIBEAUVILLE

A famous vineyard in the Haut-Rhin region of Alsace, it is known for producing excellent white wines that are described as firm and winey, yet fresh, flowery and delicate.

RIB GRASS

Also NARROW-LEAVED PLANTAIN. This is a small, weedy, European herb, *Plantago lanceolata*, whose strongly ribbed, lance-shaped leaves may be eaten when young as a spinach vegetable. When mature the leaves may be as much as nine inches long. The plant has been widely naturalized in temperate zones and is a common lawn weed. It is considered a good emergency greenfood.

RICE

A starchy cereal grain, rice *(Oryza sativa)* is probably the world's single most important food. It is the basic sustenance of about two billion people in Asia and Africa. In addition, rice is an important commercial crop in Europe and America. Rice grows best in a hot moist climate. Sufficient water must be available to immerse the crop in standing water during the main growing season. A few weeks before harvesting, however, the water is drained off and the crop reaches maturation in relatively dry conditions. In the major rice-growing states of the United States—Louisiana, Texas and Arkansas—this cycle is created through irrigation techniques. In Asia, these conditions are created naturally by the monsoons, a season of torrential rains followed by a dry spell.

Although the origin of rice cultivation is obscure, and much older than history, it is believed to have occurred in monsoon lands—India, Thailand, southern China, etc.—because the life cycle of rice fits so well into the monsoon rhythm. An exception is upland rice, which has a low water requirement but which constitutes a small part of total rice production.

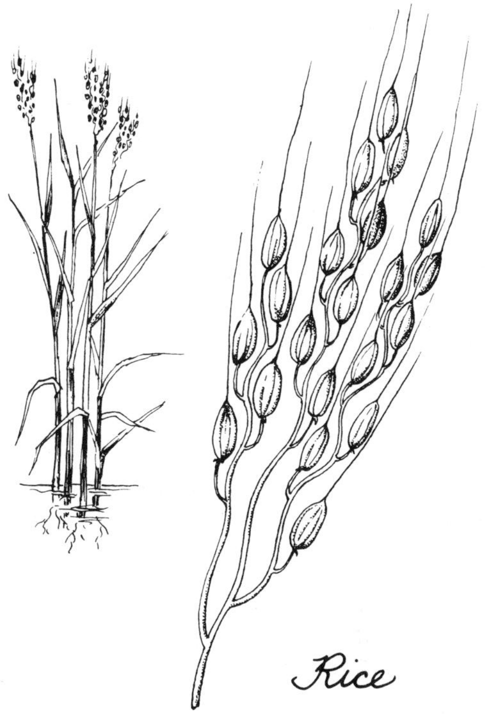

Although rice was cultivated in Asia as early as 3,500 B.C., this did not occur in Europe until about the 8th century A.D., when the Moors planted it in Andalusia, Spain. The best-known Spanish rice dish is *paella*. In the 10th century, rice cultivation began in Italy, which has become Europe's largest producer and consumer of rice. *Risotto*, which has innumerable varieties, is a favorite Italian rice dish. Rice was brought to the American colonies in 1695 and swiftly became the main crop of South Carolina, which attained a worldwide reputation for the quality of its product. Although rice was displaced there by cotton around 1850, "Carolina" has maintained its reputation as a fine long-grain variety, even when grown in Texas, Arkansas or California.

Rice is an annual grass of the *Gramineae* family, which also includes wheat, rice's only serious rival in importance as food. For more information on the relative importance of various grains, see **Cereal.** In contrast to wheat, which has a compact ear, rice sprouts a number of fine stalks, each bearing a single grain. The rice plant grows from three to six feet high, and due to the presence of silicon, has rough, coarse tissues.

Rice grains are classified as long, medium or short. Long means that the grain is four to five times longer than it is wide. In the United States, Carolina and Extra fine Honduras are the best long-grained varieties. In Asia, Patna is regarded as a fine long-grained strain. When cooked, long grains separate and the rice looks light and fluffy. These are desirable characteristics for pilaffs and side dishes eaten with curries, chicken, meat dishes or stews.

Shorter grains—Japan and Blue Rose are well known types—are plumper and when cooked are generally tender, moist and sticky. They are considered ideal for the everpresent steamed rice eaten with Japanese and Chinese food and are favored for risotto, croquettes, puddings and molds.

Rice grains are processed as follows: first they are threshed, which separates them from the stalk. At this stage, the grains are called paddy rice; they are then milled, which at the first stage removes only the tough outer husk, and yields what is called whole or brown rice. A second stage of milling removes most of the bran and the embryo to produce white rice. White rice is then washed, cleaned and polished. A further step is "coating," i.e., adding a layer of corn syrup and talc to give it a pearly luster.

Rice that proceeds beyond the first stage of milling loses many of its nutritional elements, including most of its vitamin B, fat and some of its protein. It is, however, more attractive to many consumers because it keeps better and cooks faster than brown, or unpolished, rice. In most forms, rice is extremely digestible, nourishing and palatable. Polished rice is about 88 percent solid residue, of which 6 percent is protein and 93 percent carbohydrate. Brown rice has about 2 percent fat, more than wheat. Caloric content is about 350 per 3½ ounces (100 grams.).

It is in Asia that rice assumes overwhelming importance, particularly in India, China, Japan, the Philippines and Indonesia. In wheat-growing areas, wheat is often only supplementary to other foods. In rice-producing areas, rice customarily provides 80 percent of food calories and is the *only* food for enormous numbers of people. The Japanese acknowledged the central position of rice by adopting the word for rice, *gohan*, as the name for the whole meal. Breakfast is *asa gohan*, "morning rice"; dinner is *hiru gohan*, "afternoon rice"; and supper is *yoru gohan*, "evening rice."

Rice bran, or rice meal, the first by-product of milling, contains most of the vitamins, fat and much of the protein of the original grain. It is used chiefly as livestock feed.

Puffed rice, which is used as a breakfast cereal, is created by putting grains of rice in a sealed cylinder, which is heated and rotated until the moisture in each grain is converted to steam. When the cylinder is unsealed, the steam "explodes," puffing the grain to several times its normal size.

Rice polish, a by-product of the polishing process, is high in fat and carbohydrates. It is like the bran, but somewhat finer and heavier. Rice polish is used in processed foods and as livestock feed.

Rice flour is ground from milled rice. It contains no gluten, so is not suitable for breadmaking, yet is excellent for puddings, pastries and cakes. It may often be substituted for wheat flour, where the latter might cause an allergic reaction. Ground rice is a similar product, but slightly coarser in texture.

Wild rice, an annual grass, is of a different genus, native to North America.

Converted rice is an intermediate stage of polished rice that still has some bran left on it. Although yellowish in color, it turns white on cooking.

Par-boiled rice is another that retains more vitamins and fat. It is subjected to a steam or water treatment before milling. Rice has had its share of detractors in the West, including the philosopher Friedrich Nietzsche, who claimed that rice-eating led to opium addiction; and Jean Brillat-Savarin, the French gastronome, who believed it sapped the moral fiber and even courage.

RICE BEAN

The seeds of this slender twining plant *(Vigna umbellata)* are used in soups or boiled and eaten whole. It is a native of southern Asia but is more commonly eaten now in tropical Africa. The pods of the rice bean are slender, curved and up to three inches long. They are so tender that a lot of the crop is lost in the picking.

RICEBIRD

See **Reedbird.**

RICE EEL

An Asian eel, *Monopterus alba*, found in rivers, ditches and rice paddies, it is an important food fish in some areas of northern China, Japan, Indochina, Thailand and Burma. The rice eel reaches a length of three feet and has an olive-brown back and pale underside. This fish estivates in the mud, which enables it to be dug up and transported live for long distances.

RICE WINE

See **Sake; Wines, Chinese.**

RICHEBOURG, LE

A famous Burgundy vineyard located in the commune of Vosne-Romanee, a few miles north of the city of Beaune, Le Richebourg produces great red wine noted for its beautiful color, excellent bouquet and flavor, elegance and fine breeding.

RICOTTA

Ricotta is a bland, white cheese of Italian origin that is usually made from the whey left over from the manufacture of other cheeses. Some varieties, though, are made from ewe's buttermilk. Ricotta is an important element in Italian cooking, figuring in sweet dishes and serving as a filling in ravioli, lasagne and cannelloni dishes. However, it is made in many European countries, and the United States, and is known under many different names, which include albumin cheese, *broccio*, *brocotte*, *ceracee*, *mejette*, *recuit*, *schottenziger*, *serac*, whey cheese and *ziger*.

The coagulable material in whey is mostly albumin. Whey does contain appreciable fat, and to bring this out in processing, 5 or 10 percent whole or skim milk is added to the whey. The resulting mixture of albumin and cheese improves the body, flavor and food value of the ricotta. To obtain ricotta, fresh whey is heated to 200° F. (93.3° C), then sour whey is added, causing the curds to form at the top. At this stage, the curd is moist and grainy, like cottage cheese. This is the form in which most ricotta is consumed. It is simply drained, pressed briefly, then packed into cartons.

Some is sold as dry ricotta, also called *ricotta salata*, in which case it is salted, pressed into forms and held until dry. The result is hard-textured and suitable for grating.

RIDGE CUCUMBER

This variety of **cucumber,** *Cucumis sativus*, is shorter and fatter than the ordinary kind most often sold fresh in the market. It is still many times larger than a gherkin. It grows better on ridges than on level ground. The ridge cucumber achieved popularity first in Russia, England and France and is now grown in the United States. It is used in the same way as other cucumbers, i.e., eaten raw, cooked or pickled. The ridge cucumber is known as *agoursi* in French.

RIESENGEBIRGE

This Czechoslovakian soft cheese has a sharp taste and is made from goat's milk in the mountains of Bohemia.

RIGOTTES

See **Goat's Milk Cheese.**

RING-NECKED DUCK

A wild duck of North America, the ring-necked duck *(Aythya collaris)* is so called because the adult male has a red ring around its neck. It frequents the interior of the Northeast and feeds mainly on water grasses and wild celery, which enhances the flavor of its flesh. As a table bird, it is rated second only to the canvasback duck.

See also: **Duck.**

RINNEN

This Polish sour-milk cheese is spiced with caraway seeds and named for the wooden trough used in processing it. Rinnen has been made in Pomerania since the 18th century. Curds are kneaded, shaped, pressed and salted, then ripened in wooden forms.

RIOJA

A wine district in northern Spain encompassing parts of the provinces of Logrono, Alava and Navarre, which lie in the basin of the Rio Oja, Rioja is best known for dry, red table wines that are consistently good but rarely great. They are sturdy, reliable and mostly inexpensive.

Production is tightly controlled by an official authority, and only wine from the designated region may be labeled Rioja. Riojas are aged in American oak barrels and are known for their oaky flavor which, in some cases, overwhelms the taste of the fruit. Recently, the regulatory agency halved the amount of time in the barrel necessary to garner the *Rioja* designation. Rioja white wines come from Malvasia and Viura grapes, the reds from Graciano, Mazuela, Grenache and preponderantly the Tempranillo.

Rioja designations include *crianza* ("with breeding"), which must be aged at least two years, one in oak barrels; *reserva*, whose aging must total four years, one in fermentation tanks and three years in barrels, and *gran reserva*, which requires even more aging in a combination of containers amounting in some cases to eight years.

See also: **Wines, Spanish.**

RIOLA

A strongly flavored, soft French cheese, usually made from sheep or goat's milk, it is made in the Normandy region and is practically identical to ***Mont d'Or*** except that it is aged for two or three months, instead of a week.

RIS DE VEAU

See **Sweetbreads.**

RIVEA

This edible flower of a woody climbing vine, *Rivea ornata*, found in tropical America and Africa, is quite fleshy and eaten as a vegetable. Another species, *Rivea corymbosa*, is known in Mexico as *ololiuqui* and is used by Indians as a hallucinogen in medicine and religious ceremonies.

RIVESALTES

This is sweet white wine, especially the Muscat de Rivesaltes, grown just north of Perpignan in southern France. Besides the Muscat grape, the vineyards of Rivesaltes flourish with the Grenache Blanc and the Malvoisie (malmsey), All three varieties make wine with a very pronounced bouquet, a light golden tint and high alcohol content.

ROACH

One of the most abundant freshwater fishes of Europe, the roach *(Rutilis rutilis)* is a member of the carp family. It is a silvery fish with orange fins and a small head. It reaches a length of about 18 inches. The roach is a popular fish with anglers, especially in Great Britain, and is fished commercially in Europe where it is marketed fresh, smoked and salted.

Roach has a good taste, but its many bones make eating difficult unless it is filleted. The roach's range extends from Britain to Russia and from Sweden to the Black and Caspian Sea basins.

ROB

This is fruit juice that has been thickened to the consistency of honey. This is accomplished by adding sugar to the juice and perhaps a stick of cinnamon, then boiling it until the desired consistency is achieved. In England, elderberries were often used to make rob.

ROBBIOLE

Also ROBBIOLINI, ROBIOLA. Here is a soft, fast-ripening Italian cheese that resembles **Brie** in flavor. Several versions are made in Lombardy and Piedmont. Usually they are made from skimmed cow's milk, but occasionally whole milk, and allowed to ripen for two weeks. The paste is yellow and creamy, sometimes runny, and the shape is round and flat. Individual cheeses weigh from eight to 12 ounces. Another version is made from goat's milk or a mixture of cow, sheep and goat's milk. The curd is kneaded into small rolls that weigh 3½ ounces and ripen in just a few days.

ROBERT SAUCE

A French brown sauce served with goose, pork and venison, it is rather spicy and is based on a roux of butter, flour and chopped onions, plus white wine and a strong bouillon. It is highly seasoned with mustard and pepper and sometimes chili. Reputed to be one of the oldest French sauces, dating from the early 17th century, *Robert* sauce is now available commercially.

See also: **Sauce.**

ROBIN

This is a small migratory bird of the thrush family. The European robin *(Erythacus rubecula)* is eaten in France, prepared like **lark** and served on a skewer. The North American variety, *Merula migratoria*, is twice the size of the European. Robin pie was a popular American dish at the beginning of the 19th century.

ROBIOLA

See **Robbiole.**

ROCAMADUR

Two cheeses go under this name. One is a small sheep's milk cheese (average weight: two ounces) made in the small pilgrimage town of Rocamadur in southwestern France. The second is a goat's milk cheese produced in Guyenne that is in season from April to November.

ROCAMBOLE

Also SAND LEEK, GIANT GARLIC, SERPENT GARLIC. The name is given to two plants of the *Allium* genus, both varieties of garlic. One is serpent garlic *(A. sativum* var. *ophioscorodon)* and the other is giant garlic *(A. scorodoprasum)*. They are used in the same way as ordinary garlic, but the flavor is milder. The second variety is especially popular in Denmark.

ROCK AND RYE

This is a liqueur prepared from rye whisky, rock-candy syrup, neutral spirits and fruit flavoring, usually lemon, orange or cherry. It is bottled at 60 to 70 proof. The same drink can be mixed at home by adding rock-candy syrup to rye whisky and adding a slice of lemon.

ROCK CANDY

This is clarified sugar syrup that has been crystallized, usually by boiling with a few drops of acetic acid, which facilitates the formation of crystals. The crystals are usually formed around string. Rock candy is said to be good for sore throats. The syrup is used in a liqueur called **rock and rye.** Slivers of rock candy are sometimes used as stirrers in mixed drinks.

ROCK COD

Also COWCOD. A sport and food fish found off the coast of California, the rock cod *(Sebastes levis)* is related to the **red snapper** and reaches a length of three feet. It can weigh as much as 28 pounds. The rock cod's body is light colored and marked by several broad dusky bars. It is found in shallow, rocky areas where it feeds on fish, crustaceans and squid. It may be prepared like red snapper.

ROCK CORNISH HEN

This small broiler chicken is produced by crossing a white Plymouth Rock hen with a Cornish or Bantam or small game cock. It is also known as a Cornish hen, Cornish game hen, Cornish Rock hen and Rock Cornish game hen. The typical bird weighs one to 1¼ pounds, which is right for an individual serving. A two-pound bird will serve two people. The Rock Cornish hen is usually sold frozen and has achieved wide popularity in the United States. It may be fried, broiled or roasted and is often served with wild rice.

ROCK DASSY

Also ROCK HYRAX, CONY. This African mammal, *Procavia capensis*, inhabits rocky and scrub-covered ranges and looks like a woodchuck. It is also found in parts of Syria, Sinai and Israel. The flesh of the rock dassy is highly prized by some people. A large dassy can reach a length of 22 inches and weigh up to 44 pounds. This animal is mentioned in the Bible, where it is referred to as a cony (in English translation).

ROCK EEL

See **Wolffish.**

ROCKET

Also ROCKET SALAD, ROQUETTE, RUGULA, GARDEN ROCKET, ROCKET CRESS. This is *Eruca Sativa*, a sort of colewort, from the Mediterranean region and now widely cultivated as a garden vegetable in Europe and America. It is a strong-smelling plant with smooth leaves, having a peppery flavor and pale yellow flowers. Leaves are gathered while still young as a salad seasoning in France and Italy. It is not quite as popular in America yet, possibly because the horseradish flavor requires some palate training.

See also: **Barbarea.**

ROCKFISH

The name includes any of several Pacific Ocean fish that inhabit rocky coasts and rocky sea bottoms, especially those of the *Sebastes* genus, such as the Pacific Ocean perch, the **rock cod,** the quillback rockfish, the **redfish,** the bocaccio and the yelloweye rockfish or **red snapper.** These are all foodfish of high quality. The quillback rockfish *(S. maliger)*, which reaches a length of two feet, is prized as a gamefish for its fighting qualities. Its range is from Southern California to the Gulf of Alaska, and it is fished commercially throughout. It is yellow to brown overall with orange spots, but its distinguishing feature is the high-spined first dorsal fin.

The bocaccio *(S. paucispinis)*, which inhabits the same range, reaches three feet in length. It is olive-brown and lacks dorsal spines. It is favored more by commercial fishermen than anglers.

The name "rockfish" is applied to other unrelated genera, such as the striped bass and the grouper.

ROCK LOBSTER

See **Spiny Lobster.**

ROCK MEDLAR

Also SAVOY MEDLAR, SWEET PEAR, GRAPE PEAR. Sweet, edible fruit of the European shad bush, *Amelanchier ovalis*, it is closely related to the **juneberry.** The blue black fruit is used to make jelly, often in combination with apples. In size and shape, it resembles a large black currant.

ROCK PARTRIDGE

See **Ptarmigan.**

ROCKWEED

Also SEA WRACK. Edible seaweed of the *Fucus* genus, which has large, flat fronds, rockweed has been eaten with some regularity in Scotland and as famine fare in Iceland, the Faroe Islands and Denmark. The Scots call it sea lettuce and use it in salads. Seaweed of this type is a major food source in Japan. For more on that, see **Kelp.**

ROCKY MOUNTAIN FLAX

Also PRAIRIE FLAX. A perennial herb of western North America, Rocky Mountain Flax *(Linum perenne* subsp. *lewisii)* has seeds that can be ground into flour and used for various culinary purposes. This plant is related to common flax *(L. usitatissimum)*, which furnishes commercial fiber (flax) and whose seeds are pressed for linseed oil used in oil paints, printer's ink, etc., but not as a food.

ROCKY MOUNTAIN WHITEFISH

Also MOUNTAIN HERRING. This freshwater fish, *Coregonus williamsonii*, found in the rivers and lakes of the Pacific Northwest from Vancouver to Colorado, is considered a great delicacy and may be prepared in any way suitable for trout.

See also: **Whitefish.**

ROE

This is the eggs or spawn of fish and crustaceans. "Hard roe" is eggs from the female fish; "soft roe" is the sperm or gonads of the male fish. It is also called **milt.** The best known, and most highly prized, of all roes is that of the female sturgeon, called **caviar.**

Other noted hard roes are taken from the shad, the salmon (sometimes called "red caviar"), and the gray mullet. The latter is made into a delicacy called ***botargo*** in Mediterranean countries. The roe is soaked in brine, pressed and dried in the sun. It is used to make a Greek specialty called *taramosalata.* Tuna roe may also be used to make *botargo.* Cod roe is eaten fresh or smoked.

As the sturgeon fisheries of the Caspian Sea decline, lumpfish roe is becoming an increasingly common substitute for caviar, and it is often dyed to simulate the real thing. Carp and herring roe are appreciated in the Far East, the latter being eaten raw in Japan after marinating for one to two days in a mixture of soy sauce, sweet rice wine and seasonings.

Among the soft roes, the best liked are those of carp, herring and mackerel, with catfish also considered good. Soft roes are cleaned of blood vessel membranes then gently poached before being ultimately prepared in a wide variety of ways.

ROGNON DE COQ

The word *rognon* generally means kidney in French, except in the case of the cock and certain other fowls. "Cock's kidneys" is a euphemism for cock's testicles, which are considered a great delicacy in France. They are used as an ingredient in certain garnishes and, like cockscombs, as a hot hors d'oeuvre.

ROLL

The term refers to an individual small loaf or cake of leavened bread that may take any of a number of round, oval or oblong shapes and be named accordingly. A French roll, for example, which is made from the same dough as **French bread,** is a pointed oval. White bread dough may be used to make plain rolls, but usually the recipe is enriched with eggs and milk. Additional butter or fat produces a softer crust and a roll that stays soft and fresh longer. A very crisp crust is achieved by eliminating the fat and brushing the crust with cold water at intervals during the baking.

Examples of classic rolls are the Parker House (a circle folded in half), the cloverleaf (ball-shaped), the crescent (see also **Croissant),** the fan tan (dough rolled thin, cut in strips that are piled six high, cut into one-inch lengths and baked cut-edges down), the knot (a loosely knotted strip), the snail, the butterfly, the pan roll, etc.

The dough may be further enriched with sugar, spices and fruit to make a variety of sweet and filled rolls.

See also: **Bread.**

ROLL CHEESE

This is a hard English cheese made from whole cow's milk. It is cylindrical in shape, measures nine inches in diameter by eight inches long and weighs 20 pounds.

ROLLINIA

This is a tropical fruit resembling the custard apple genus, several species of which are found in South America. These include the *caehiman (R. deliciosa)*, the *fructa da condessa (R. longifolia)* and the ***fructa de macaco.*** All are round or oval and borne on small trees that are cultivated like the **cherimoya.** The quality is considered good.

ROLLMOPS

See **Herring.**

ROLLOT

Also BIGOLOT. A soft, surface-ripened French cheese made from cow's milk in the Picardy region, it is similar to **Brie** and **Camembert** in taste and aroma but is smaller in size, averaging six ounces. Rollot has a red rind and is in season from October to June.

Preparing rolls in a small commercial bakery

ROMADUR

This is a soft, fermented cheese made in southern Germany, Austria and Switzerland from whole or partly skimmed cow's milk. It is similar to **Limburger,** but some experts rate it higher because of its milder taste and aroma. Indeed the whole-milk *Romadur* is closer to **Liederkranz.** Compared to **Limburger,** *Romadur* contains less salt and is cured less intensively and for a shorter time period.

Individual cheeses are produced in quarter-pound or one-pound cubes that are wrapped in tinfoil or parchment and packed in wooden boxes for shipment. Similar cheeses are *harracher*, *hochstrasser* and *kremstaler* made in Hungary.

See also: **Schlosskase, Schutzenkase.**

ROMAINE

See **Lettuce.**

ROMAN CORIANDER

See **Black Cumin.**

ROMANEE

See **Vosne.**

ROMANELLO

This very hard, grating cheese is made in Italy and the United States from partly skimmed or skim milk. Its name means little Romano, and it is made in much the same way; but cheeses are smaller, and the curd is white with many small openings. The surface of the cheese often has a crosshatch pattern left by wicker baskets used for draining the cheese. Cured cheeses have a very sharp flavor, suitable for use as a condiment, and weigh from nine to 12 pounds.

See also: **Romano.**

ROMANO

This popular, very hard Italian cheese can be eaten as table cheese when young or grated for cooking when it is aged for a year or more. Originally made from sheep's milk in the area around Rome, Romano is made all over southern Italy and in Sardinia from cow's, goat's or sheep's milk. In Sardinia, it is called *Sardo.* Romano made in the United States is exclusively from cow's milk.

The cheese is usually prepared from partly skimmed milk. The curd is heated, salted and pressed. The surface of the cheese is kept clean during ripening, which takes at least five months and may extend for a year or more. At the end of the ripening period the surface of the cheese may be blackened or oiled. Cheeses are round with flat ends and weigh from 15 to 25 pounds. The texture is granular with no holes or eyes. Romano is sometimes called *incanestrato* because of the surface pattern left by its draining in wicker baskets.

See also: **Parmesan.**

RONCAL

This is a hard, sharp-flavored Spanish cheese. Like Parmesan, it is used for grating. *Roncal* is popular in northern Spain, and it is named for the Roncal Valley in Navarre. Made from cow's milk, *Roncal* has a yellow, close-grained paste, which is both salted and smoked. After aging, the rind is sealed with a hot iron.

ROOK

This European crow, *Corvus frugilegus,* is eaten in pies and is sometimes added to other game dishes. Rooks are gregarious birds, and they gather in colonies called rookeries. Only the very young birds are used in rook pie, and then only the breast meat is taken from the bird. The rest is said to be bony and bitter-tasting.

ROOT BEER

This popular soft drink is sweet, carbonated and flavored by extracts from various roots and herbs, including sarsaparilla, sassafras, spruce, wild cherry, spikenard, wintergreen and ginger. The formula was changed perforce in 1960 to exclude safrole, a flavoring material extracted from the South American tree, *Ocetea cymbarus.* After experimental evidence showed that safrole tended to produce cancer in the small intestines of test rats, the Food and Drug Administration ruled it out.

In former times, root beer could be made at home using commercially produced packages of flavorings and extracts. The flavoring was put together with sugar and yeast and then fermented. The resulting beverage was naturally effervescent and contained a small amount of alcohol.

ROQUEFORT

This blue-veined, semisoft French cheese vies with **Brie** for the unofficial title of king among cheeses and is billed as "the cheese of kings and popes."

Roquefort is believed to be the oldest French cheese, and the only **blue cheese** to be made from ewe's milk. It comes from the village of Roquefort in the Cevennes Mountains of southeastern France, and by French law only blue, ewe's milk cheese from this region may be called "Roquefort." American Roquefort is made from cow's milk. There are many other blue cheeses made in France, for example, ***Gex*** and ***Septmoncel,*** but they do not equal the quality of Roquefort, which is made under conditions ideally suited for producing blue-mold cheese.

Chief among these conditions is a system of limestone caves whose temperature (50° F, 10° C) and humidity (95 percent) are perfect for curing mold ripened cheese. The mold in question, *Penicillium roqueforti*, is cultured in bread loaves, reduced to powder, then sprinkled between layers of curd as they are put into hoops. The mold produces a mottled, marbled appearance in the interior of the cheese and the sharp peppery flavor so treasured by consumers. Cheeses are matured from two to five months but are usually sold before the sharp taste develops and may be kept for as long as a year. A cured cheese has a gray rind and a yellowish, fatty paste. If the paste is white or chalky, it is not completely ripened. The season is from May to September.

Roquefort can be put to many uses. It complements a dry red wine and may be eaten as a hors d'oeuvre. It is the base for an excellent dressing or can be crumbled directly into a green salad. It is a fine accompaniment to fresh fruit.

ROQUETTE

See **Rocket.**

ROSE

The name includes any plant or flower of the genus *Rosa*, family *Rosaceae*, order *Rosales*. These are bushy, creeping or climbing shrubs with thorny stems, pinnate leaves and showy solitary or clustered flowers. Wild rose flowers have five petals, but cultivated species may have double that number. Repeated hybridization of about 30 wild species has now resulted in over 4,000 species. Horticulturists divide these into 43 classes.

Roses have a variety of food uses. The eglantine rose bears flowers that, with honey, produce a sweet called *gulangabin*, popular in Asia Minor and the punjab of India. The California rose's ripe fruits can be made into a pleasant syrup. *Pomifera* and *Rugosa* roses' leaves make an aromatic tea, rose wine and rose honey. The common dog rose has leaves that, when dried, can make delicious tea. Bulgarians make a sweet rose liqueur and the French have their *Parfait D'Amour*.

Roses are popular as emblems: England's floral emblem is the rose; the American Beauty rose has been adopted for the District of Columbia; the Cherokee rose represents the state of Georgia; and the wild rose has been chosen by the states of New York, North Dakota and Iowa.

The American poet Gertrude Stein made a very observant statement about this flower. She wrote, "A rose is a rose is a rose is a rose."

See also: **Attar of Roses, Rose Apple, Rose Hips.**

ROSE APPLE

This is the edible fruit of several very handsome tropical trees. *Eugenia jambos* bears fruit like a berry and grows all over Southeast Asia. Also called malabar plum, it has been naturalized extensively in Florida as an ornamental. *Eugenia malaccensis*, also called malay apple and pomerac jambos, bears pear-shaped fruit about two inches long that has one large seed and is brown. It is popular on the Malay peninsula. *Jambos Australis*, called also Australian brush cherry, bears berrylike, rose purple fruit that is ovoid and up to three-quarters of an inch across.

Fruit of all of these trees may be eaten raw and, though they smell like roses and taste like apples, they are rather dry and insipid. They find their best uses in jellies, jams and preserves.

Species noted here and others are widely grown as ornamentals. They reach 40 feet in height, have large, glossy, dark green leaves and showy white flowers.

See also: **Rose, Rose Hips.**

ROSE HIPS

Fruit of the dog rose, *(Rosa Canina* and *Rosa Rugosa)*, it is an urn-shaped receptacle, bright red, nearly closed at the top, with swollen torus and a fleshy calyx. Hips are rich in vitamin C. A commercial product, rose hip syrup, is taken for vitamin C deficiency. Hips make delicious, fragrant jams, jellies and preserves and a heart-warming tisane but are too tart to eat.

Canina and *Rugosa* are widely cultivated shrubs of the temperate zones. However, commercial hips are harvested mostly from plants growing wild. They come from states in the northwestern United States, England, Germany and Denmark, to name a few sources.

See also: **Rose.**

ROSELLE

Also JAMAICA SORREL, INDIAN SORREL. This highly useful type of annual hibiscus *(Hibiscus sabdariffa)* originated in tropical Africa or Asia but has been widely transplanted to other tropical areas. Both the seed pods and large, red calyxes are used to make jams, jellies, sauces and pleasantly acidic drinks. The nearest equivalent in taste would be the cranberry. There is a yellow calyx strain that is nearly as good. In addition, the stems yield fiber for cordage.

ROSEMARY

An evergreen shrub of the mint family, rosemary *(Rosmarinus officinalis)* is the herb of remembrance. In *Hamlet*, Shakespeare has Ophelia say, "There's rosemary, that's for remembrance; pray, love, remember."

Pliny called it *rosmarinus*, meaning sea dew. The name derived from the plant's ability to thrive in arid places that have a heavy dew, a phenomenon typically occurring near the sea. The plant is also associated with the Virgin Mary. Legend has it that she spread her cloak over a nearby white-blossomed rosemary. From then on, rosemary blossoms were blue like her cloak.

Rosemary is native to the Mediterranean and can grow as high as five feet. It has a strong piny flavor and is considered by some to be the ideal herb for all roasts and barbecued meats. The Italians use it freely with roast lamb and suckling pig. Discretion is the usual rule, though, when it is added to such things as duck, beef, salmon and dressings.

ROSE OF SHARON

See **Saint John's Wort.**

ROSEROOT

The leaves of this low-growing, succulent plant may be eaten fresh, salted or dressed with oil in a salad. Roseroot *(Sedum rosea)* is a perennial found in Europe and in western North America from Alaska to California and Colorado.

ROSETTE

A French sausage that takes its name from the casing used, which is fat and thick, the rosette is stuffed with shoulder of pork and is said to be of excellent quality. It is a specialty of the Lyons district and is eaten raw.

ROTENGLE

See **Rudd.**

ROUGERETS

See **Goat's Milk Cheese.**

ROUGERNIS

See **Goat's Milk Cheese.**

ROUND WHITEFISH

One of the more abundant and widespread of the **whitefish,** the round whitefish *(Prosopium cylindraceum)* is found in Siberia and northern North America. It inhabits streams, rivers and lakes, including the Great Lakes (except Erie). The round whitefish has a blue back, a slender, rounded body and a small mouth. It reaches a length of 20 inches. It is an important food fish in Siberia, and at one time large catches were taken from the Great Lakes.

See also: **Cisco, Fera, Houting.**

ROWANBERRY

Also EUROPEAN MOUNTAIN ASH. This is the scarlet, often bitter, fruit of the European mountain ash tree *(Sorbus aucuparia)*. Really a pome, the tiny clustered fruit is rarely eaten raw, except perhaps by children when it is overripe. Instead, it is heavily sweetened and made into rowanberry jelly or sometimes mixed with apples to make a jelly. The jelly is a popular accompaniment to meat dishes, roast lamb, mutton, game birds and especially venison. The tree is found in Asia Minor and Russia as far as western Siberia, where rowanberry preserves and sweetened compotes are enjoyed.

In Germany, the rowan fruit is used as the basis of a liqueur called *Sechsamtertrophen.* It is also used to flavor some Russian vodkas. The flavor has been described as tart and smoky.

ROYAL BRABANT

Here is a Belgian fermented cheese much like **Limburger,** which is made from whole, cow's milk.

RUBBERLIP SEAPERCH

This seaperch species, *Rhacochilus toxotes*, is found only off the coast of California, ranging from Mendocino County to Baja California. It is found inshore and is considered good sport by pier and surf anglers. The rubberlip seaperch is fished commercially as well, enjoying a good reputation as a food fish. It reaches a maximum length of about 18 inches and is deep-bodied, almost oval in shape. The largest member of the *Embiotocidae* family, it is recognized by its thick, fleshy lips.

RUDD

A popular angling fish in the British Isles, the rudd *(Scardinius erythrophthalmus)* resembles the **roach,** to which it is closely allied. It is widely distributed across Europe as far east as the Caspian basin and has been introduced into the United States, where it is known as the pearl roach. The rudd is a hardy fish that prefers deep, slow-moving rivers and shallow warm lakes. It has the large eyes, light coloring and slightly humped appearance of the roach. It may be prepared like roach.

RUDDY DUCK

This American wild duck, *Erismature rubida*, is distinguished by a band of red brown encircling the upper part of its body and a reddish neck in an otherwise black and white color scheme. Its flavor is rated good but below that of the canvasback, the mallard and the redhead.

See also: **Duck.**

RUE

A small shrub of the citrus family, *Ruta graveolens* enjoyed centuries of popularity as an holy herb, charm against witchcraft, panacea for ills ranging from poor eyesight to arthritis, and as a seasoner for food. Mithridates, ancient toxicologist and king of Pontus (120–63 B.C.), fearing assassination, trained himself to eat various poisons, along with an antidote based on rue. This tactic worked well, according to legend, so well in fact that when later, in disgrace, he attempted suicide by poisoning, the attempt failed. He was still immune and had to resort to the sword.

The leaves are highly aromatic, and the taste bitter, so that many people find it unpleasant. One of the few domestic uses that survives is a seasoning where the finely chopped leaves are added to green salad. Commercially, it is used to flavor **grappa,** a typical northern Italian liquor.

RUFF

Also AUSTRALIAN SALMON. The family *Arripidae* of Australia and New Zealand resembles salmon but is no relation to that of the Northern Hemisphere. The ruff *(Arripis georgianus)* reaches a length of only 16 inches and has a cylindrical body and large head. It is caught close to the seashore and, despite its small size, is considered an important food and game fish. Its flesh is described as extremely tasty and tender.

Its larger relative, the Australian salmon *(A. trutta)* reaches a length of three feet and a weight of 20 pounds. It is abundant on the southern shores of Australia from West Australia to New South Wales and in Tasmania and New Zealand. Although deemed a superb sport fish, its flesh is considerably poorer in quality than the ruff's. The commercial catch is large, and most is canned, a process that improves its palatability.

Both species are green above and light below. Young specimens of *A. trutta* have troutlike markings that earned it the name "salmon-trout."

RUFF

Also REEVE. This is a wild bird, *Machetes pugnax*, of Europe and Asia, which at one time was considered a table delicacy, but which in Europe is now protected by law. It resembles the **sandpiper.** During the mating season, the male grows a large ruff. The female is called a reeve. It used to be the custom to trap the birds and fatten them in captivity. They were prepared like **woodcock.**

RUFFE

See **Pope.**

RUKAM

This is the purplish green or dark red fruit of a small tree, *Flaucourtia rukam*, native to the Malay archipelago and the Philippines. Several varieties are cultivated, some sweet enough to eat raw. The more acidic varieties are used to make jams and pies. The roots, fruit and leaves are used medicinally as well.

RUM

This liquor is distilled from fermented molasses and other by-products of sugar production and, to a lesser extent, from sugarcane juice. Originating in the West Indies, rum is now made in most places where sugarcane is grown. It is bottled in various alcoholic strengths, from 80 to 151 proof, and its color ranges from a clear translucence (the natural color) to a deep mahogany, achieved by adding caramel.

Sugarcane was unknown in the New World until the arrival of Columbus, who brought with him cuttings from the Canary Islands. The plant grew easily in the West Indies, and sugar found a ready market in Europe. The planters soon noticed that molasses, the main by-product of sugar production, could be fermented with little difficulty. Indeed, for many it was the only practical way of recovering the 5 percent of sugar left in molasses that might otherwise go to waste.

They were soon distilling a crude liquor that they called Kill-Devil. British planters themselves preferred to drink brandy, but the new liquor, because of its warm qualities, caught on in England, and they were soon making a more refined grade. It was first known in England as the "comfortable waters of Barbados" or "rumbullion" (a Devonshire word meaning "great tumult"), which was soon shortened to "rum." When punch became a fad, rum was an indispensable ingredient. In 1745, the Royal Navy adopted the practice of issuing common seamen a daily rum ration as a protection against scurvy.

In the meantime, a rum-distilling industry had sprung up in New England as an adjunct to the slave trade. Yankee ship masters followed a regular circuit. They would take on a cargo of rum in their home port and sail for Africa where the rum would be exchanged for slaves. From Africa, they sailed to the West Indies where they traded the slaves for molasses, with which they returned home. They sold it to the distilleries and started on a new round.

Rum was also an important drink in 18th-century America, where colonists were downing an estimated 3¾ gallons of rum a year per person (counting men, women and children). It has been argued that the Molasses Act of 1733 did more to foment rebellion in the colonies than the later taxes on tea and stamps. This law placed a heavy tax on all sugar and molasses not coming from the British sugar islands of the Caribbean and thus interfered with the rum trade.

There are four categories of rum: the very dry, light-bodied and light-colored rums, made mostly in Spanish-speaking areas, such as Puerto Rico; medium-bodied rums, often made from sugarcane juice rather than molasses—prototypes are Haitian and Martinique rums; the heavy-bodied, rich, pungent, dark-colored rums characteristic of English-speaking areas. Jamaica rum is the best example. Finally, there is ***arak*** of Java, a light-bodied, but highly aromatic rum of the East Indies.

Distilling methods differ according to the category of rum. In Puerto Rico, molasses, water and a portion of a previous mash are fermented two to four days using special strains of yeast. Distilled in a column still, the mash yields a 160-proof spirit. The high proof is essential to light rum because it produces dryness, a light body, low congener content and a neutral flavor. These light rums are also produced in the Virgin Islands, Cuba, Santo Domingo, Venezuela, Mexico, Hawaii and the Philippines. The white or silver rum is usually bottled at 80 proof.

Demarara rum comes from Guyana on the northern coast of South America. It is darker and fuller-bodied and has a characteristic taste resulting from the type of sugarcane and the soil it is grown in. It is bottled at 80, 86 and 151 proof, the latter type often drunk as grog, a mixture of half rum and half very hot water.

For Jamaica rum, the mash contains not only molasses but skimmings from previous distillations and dunder, the residue of previous batches. The mash is allowed to ferment through the action of natural yeast from the air, which takes much longer to act, five to 20 days. The fermentation is twice distilled in a pot still at lower proof, which results in a stronger taste. Indeed, traditional Jamacian rum is believed to be the most pungent of all alcoholic beverages. It is bottled at 86, 97 and 151 proof.

Rum is drunk straight, mixed in highballs, such as a Cuba Libre (rum and cola) or in a variety of cocktails, of which the Daiquiri is the best known (rum, sugar and lime juice). Denatured rum is a favorite flavoring in the tobacco industry.

RUMBERRY

Also MURTA. Edible fruit of a small tree found in the West Indies, southern Mexico, Central America, Guyana and Brazil, the rumberry *(Myrciaria floribunda)* is roundish, about one-half inch across and yellow ranging to dark red and black. It is used to make jams or a liqueur.

RUNEALA PLUM

Edible fruit of a shrub, *Flaucourtia cataphracta*, native to India and Malaysia, the runeala plum has a russet purple color and a creamy white pulp, which has a pleasant, slightly acidic taste. It measures about three-quarters of an inch across. The fruit is much used in compotes. The shrub has been introduced into the Americas.

RUNESTEN

This hard cheese is originally from Denmark but is also made in Wyoming and Minnesota in the United States. It resembles the Swedish ***herrgardsost*** and **Swiss.** Compared to Swiss, Runesten has smaller eyes and is much smaller, averaging five pounds. Curing takes three months. Individual cheeses are wrapped in red cellophane.

RUNNER

Also PRODIGAL SON, RAINBOW RUNNER. An ocean gamefish, *Elagatis bipinnulata*, famous along the coast of East Africa and Madagascar, it is found in warm waters around the world and is plentiful in the tropical Atlantic. The runner reaches a maximum length of four feet and weighs up to 31 pounds.

The appellation "rainbow" derives from its beautiful coloring, which includes a bluish green back, two broad blue stripes on the sides separated by a yellow line, a second yellow line along the lower sides and a white belly. The runner is a slender, fast-swimming fish that fights well on the line. It prefers open ocean and is rarely seen inshore. Its flesh is deemed excellent eating.

RUNNER BEAN

Also SCARLET RUNNER. This is a variation of the kidney bean that is popular in northern Europe and Great Britain as a fresh string bean while still unripe. The best known runner is the scarlet runner *(Phaseolus multiflorus)*, a strong, large plant that can reach a height of 10 feet.

The runner bean is native to South America, but was brought to Europe in the 17th century from Mexico and appreciated first for its ornamental qualities. The pods, however, grow larger, longer and wider than the French string bean and soon came to be used for food.

The pods are picked when young and tender, averaging three to six inches in length. When mature they can measure a foot or more. Compared to the French bean, the flesh is more finely textured and the skin thinner and more tender. Other varieties of runners and semirunners include the blue coco bean, which turns green on cooking, and such dwarfs as the dwarf gem and the tenderpod. To prepare them as string beans, they are stringed, then thinly sliced and immersed in boiling salted water. The scarlet runner is used in soups or stewed with tomato sauce and meat. They are used in salads and go well with tuna fish and onions.

See also: **Bean, Kidney Bean.**

RUSCUS

Also BUTCHER'S BROOM. Butcher's broom *(Ruscus aculeatus)* is an evergreen shrub whose shoots may be cooked and eaten like asparagus or hop shoots. It is found from the Azores through western Europe to Asia and Japan. Butcher's broom has been naturalized in the United States where it is used as a florist's decoration. The name derives from the Latin *ruskum* for a butcher's broom, and the ancient Romans used to pickle the shoots, but the practice seems to have ended when they did.

RUSH NUT

See **Chufa.**

RUSK

This very light bread or cake is sliced after baking and rebaked in a slow oven until brown and crisp throughout. The dough may be plain or sweetened. Because of their easy digestibility, rusks are given to young children and invalids. Rusks are also marketed under various names—for example, "Zwiebach"—as low calorie, or low sodium, snacks for dieters.

RUSSIAN TEA

The name includes various blends of black Chinese teas akin to those brought overland by caravan from earliest times. The brew is very strong and dark. Russians customarily take tea in a glass with lemon.

See also: **Tea.**

Rutabaga

RUTABAGA

Also SWEDE, SWEDISH TURNIP, TURNIP-ROOTED CABBAGE. A root vegetable resembling the turnip but usually somewhat larger in size and coarser in flavor, the rutabaga *(Brassica napo-brassica)* is believed to be a mutant of the common turnip. According to one authority, it first appeared in Hungary in the 17th century. The flesh of the rutabaga is usually yellow, but there is also a white variety. It is a common vegetable in Great Britain, Ireland, Scandinavia and the United States, but in most of northern Europe it is considered more appropriate as animal fodder. A common way of preparing it is to boil and serve it mashed with butter, pepper and a pinch of cinnamon or mace.

RYE

A cereal grain, rye *(Secale cereale)* is used chiefly for making bread and whisky. It is a hardy, herbaceous plant native to northeastern Europe and contiguous parts of Asia. It grows well in harsh climates and on poor soil. Rye flour is brown gray and has a high gluten content like wheat. Used alone, it produces a black bread, like **pumpernickel,** which is characteristic of Central Europe. The lighter rye breads popular elsewhere in Europe and in the United States contain an admixture of wheat, barley or pea flour. Rye grains contain about 15 percent protein, 70 percent carbohydrate and 2 percent fat. The largest producers of rye are the Soviet Union, Poland and Germany.

A good deal of rye production in the United States and Canada goes into making whisky. Rye was especially important in the early history of North America because population was centered in Northeastern areas where rye does better than wheat. It gradually ceded first place to corn, which is the principal source of bourbon whisky. Straight rye whisky is distilled at a fairly low proof, and therefore has a distinctive taste of the grain and is sweeter than Scotch or Irish whisky. However, "rye" is a popular term for ordinary blended whisky in the northeastern United States, most of which has little or no rye content.

As a cereal, rye was known but not much appreciated by the ancient Romans. It came into its own between the 14th and 17th centuries when wheat and rye were commonly grown together in the same field. The grains were harvested and ground together, producing a flour called maslin. For three centuries, it was the staple bread flour of Europe.

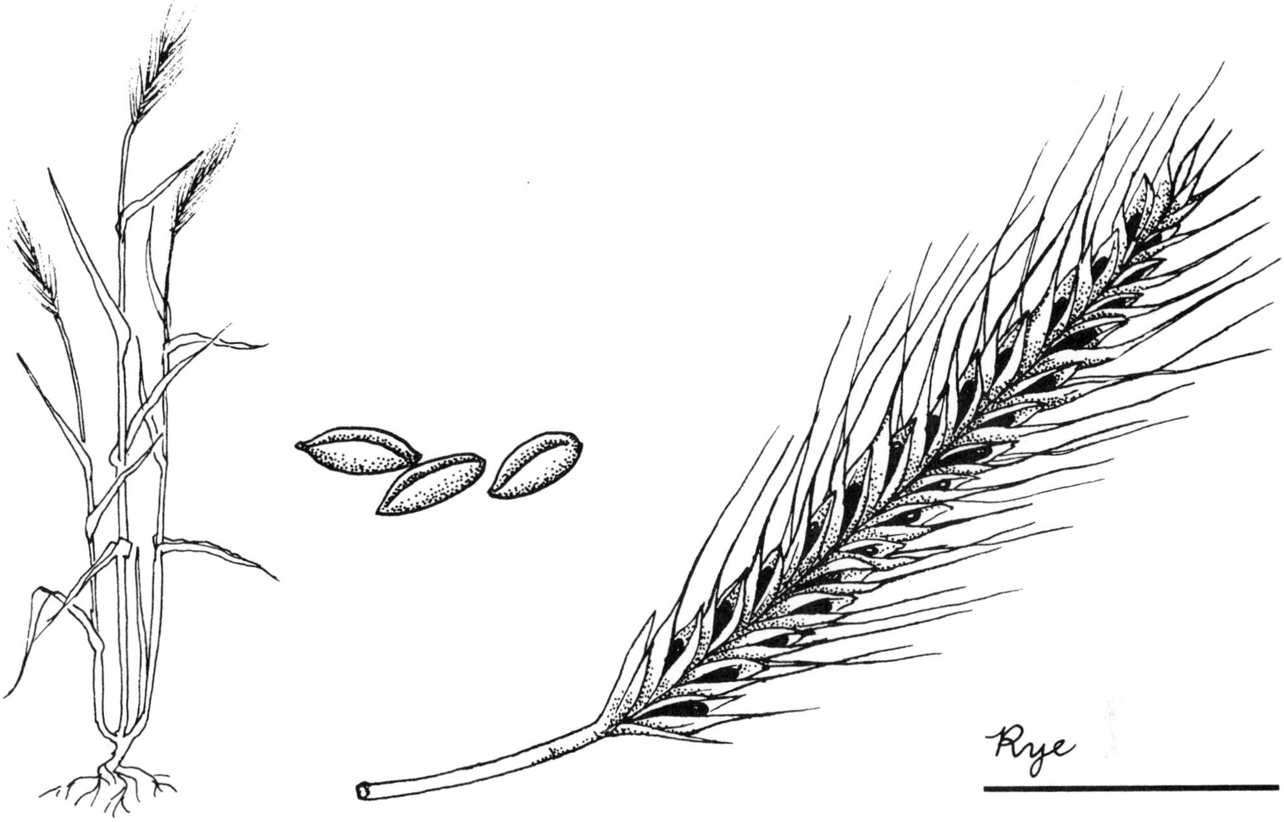

Rye is subject to contamination by ergot, a fungus called *Claviceps purpurea*, which turns the ears of grain purple and has a sweet, musty taste, and is poisonous to cattle and humans. In flour, the fungus produced ergotamine, which among other poisons, contains the hallocinigen, LSD. Those who eat the poisoned grain in bread or fodder are afflicted with a disease known as ergotism, or St. Anthony's Fire. Symptoms include burning sensations in the hands and feet, convulsions, foaming at the mouth, vertigo, blindness, hallucinations, madness and death. Although much of the bizarre behavior and hallucinating is explained by the fact that ergotamine contains LSD, these manifestations in earlier times were attributed to the work of the Devil.

In modern times ergotism has become very rare. The last outbreak occurred in France in 1951. In Pont-St.-Esprit, a town in the Rhone Valley, loaves of French rye bread, the solid, round *pain de seigle,* were made with infected flour. The results were described by John Fuller in his book, *The Day of St. Anthony's Fire:*

> *Hundreds of respectable townspeople went totally mad on a single night. Many of the most highly regarded citizens leaped from windows or jumped into the Rhone, screaming that their heads were made of copper, their bodies wrapped in snakes, their limbs swollen to gigantic size or shrunk to tiny appendages. Others ran through the streets, claiming to be chased by "bandits with donkey ears," by tigers, lions and other terrifying apparitions. Animals went berserk. Dogs ripped bark from trees until their teeth fell out. Cats dragged themselves along the floor in grotesque contortions. Ducks strutted like penguins. Villagers and animals died right and left.*

A recent study of the Salem witchcraft episode of 1692 suggests that the "witches"—19 of whom were hanged—suffered from ergotism rather than diabolic possession.

See also: **Bread.**

RYE WHISKY

Straight rye is a whisky that is distilled from a mash consisting of at least 51 percent rye grain. Other rules apply too, e.g., it may be distilled at a proof no higher than 160, matured at least two years in charred, white oak barrels and be diluted at bottling time by only distilled water to a proof no lower than 80. A whisky that meets these rules can be labeled "straight rye" in the United States. It will retain a distinctive flavor of the grain and will be sweeter and fuller bodied than an Irish or Scotch whisky.

The term "rye whisky" is used loosely in the northeastern United States to mean an inexpensive blended whisky. It has been theorized that the usage stems from a tradition of using rye to make whisky in that region. But blended whiskies usually have no more than 20 percent straight whisky (of any grain) in their makeup, the rest consisting of neutral spirits, light whiskies, etc. Blended whiskies have a much lighter body and flavor than straight whiskies.

S

SAALAND PFARR

See **Pretost.**

SAANEN

Also HARTKASE, REIBKASE, WALLISER, WALLISKASE. This very hard cheese, noted for its keeping qualities, is made in the cantons of Bern and Wallis in Switzerland from partly skimmed cow's milk. Its manufacture dates from the 16th century, and it is similar to **Swiss cheese.** However, it differs from Swiss in that during processing the curd receives more heat, which produces a firmer, drier paste with fewer, smaller eyes. These cheeses are smaller, ranging from 12 to 25 pounds in weight, and are cured for longer periods, i.e., three to seven years. The longer curing time assures that a cheese will last for 100 years or more, with some achieving 200 years. In the mature cheese, the curd is very firm, turning deep yellow and brittle as the age increases. According to local custom, a Saanen cheese may be acquired at the birth of a child and kept for his or her entire life, with portions being eaten at feast days and at his or her burial. What's left over may be passed on to descendents to keep his or her memory alive. Saanen is not exported.

SABALITO

A small but important food fish in the rivers of central South America, such as the Parana, Uruguay and Plata, the sabalito *(Pseudocruimata gilberti)* is closely related to the **sabalo,** but is much smaller, rarely exceeding eight inches in length. It is deep-bodied, prefers slow water and feeds on plant material.

SABALO

Also CURIMBATA. A freshwater fish of South America, the sabalo *(Prochilodus platensis)* is especially abundant in rivers in the central part of the continent, such as the Rio Parana, the Rio Uruguay and the Rio de la Plata. It is a popular commercial food fish, and, being migratory, it is most often caught in nets or traps set to take it during its migration upstream.

The sabalo reaches a maximum length of about 20 inches and has a deep body. It is greenish gray on the back with silver sides.

SABLEFISH

Also BLACK COD. A fish of moderate commercial importance in the North Pacific, the sablefish *(Anoplopoma fimbria)* has firm, white, flaky flesh that is too oily for some tastes. It is found from the Bering Sea to Baja California, but, except in the northern part of its range, it keeps well offshore in deep waters. The sablefish has a long, slender body (up to four feet), two dorsal fins, a broad mouth and blunt snout. It is slaty blue to black above, shading lighter on the sides. Because of its deepwater habits, it is of only minor importance as a sport fish. It reaches a top weight of 56 pounds and, due to its oiliness, is often sold smoked.

SABRE

Also CUCHILLA. A freshwater fish, the sabre *(Sternopygus macrurus)* has a tapered body and pointed tail that suggest the shape of a knife, and reaches a length of three feet. It is found in northeastern South America where it inhabits rivers, streams, trenches, ditches and backwaters. The sabre is a nightfeeder. Its flesh is firm and well flavored, and it is widely eaten throughout its range.

SACCHARIN

A coal tar derivative, saccharin is a sweetening agent about 500 to 700 times as sweet as cane sugar. It is a white, crystalline powder, but the form in which it is usually consumed is sodium saccharin, which is available in tiny tablets and in liquid solutions. A drawback of most saccharin is a metallic or bitter aftertaste, which is said not to be intrinsic, but a result of conventional synthesis.

The use of saccharin is indicated for the person, such as the diabetic or the dieter, who cannot tolerate normal sugar. The broad use of saccharin in low-calorie foods, soft drinks, etc. has been challenged, but no conclusive evidence has been presented to warrant its removal from the marketplace. Saccharin is not absorbed by the body, but passes through it relatively unchanged and is excreted in the urine.

SACK

Sack is any of several dry white wines imported to England from Jerez in southern Spain and from the Canary Islands. The name is a corruption of the Spanish word *sec*, or "dry." In Elizabethan times, sack was often heated (interestingly, like Japanese *sake)* and sometimes bolstered by the addition of raw eggs, although Falstaff, the most notorious literary connoisseur of sack, took his wine neat: "I'll no pullet-sperm in my brewage!"

See also: **Sherry.**

SAFEWAY BEL-AIR WATER

A mineral water carbonated and bottled in the United States, it has average mineral content when compared to 21 other brands. A 1980 Consumers Union sensory panel rated the taste of this water as fair, with the following qualifying comments: mildly sour; mild chemical flavor; stale, old flavor; mildly salty, mild salty aftertaste.

See also: **Mineral Water.**

SAFFLOWER

Also SAFFLOWER OIL. This is a thistlelike herb, *Carthamus tinctoria*, whose tender young shoots are edible, whose orange red flowers yield dyestuffs, and whose seeds yield an oil that is high in polyunsaturated constituents. The plant, which reaches a height of about three feet, is believed to have originated somewhere in Eurasia and has been used for centuries in India as a source of cooking oil. More recently it has become an important commercial crop in the western United States due to the quality of the oil extracted from the seeds.

Three-fourths of its makeup consists of either oleic or linoleic fatty acid, which makes it useful in the kitchen for cooking, salads, margarines, etc., and in industry for protective coatings, calks, putties, linoleums, etc.

Safflower coloring is a traditional adulterant/substitute for the more expensive seasoning, saffron, to which it owes its name. This use continues, but its importance as a dye for cloth and cosmetics has declined due to competition from synthetic products. In India, the leaves are occasionally used in salads.

See also: **Cholesterol, Fat, Oil.**

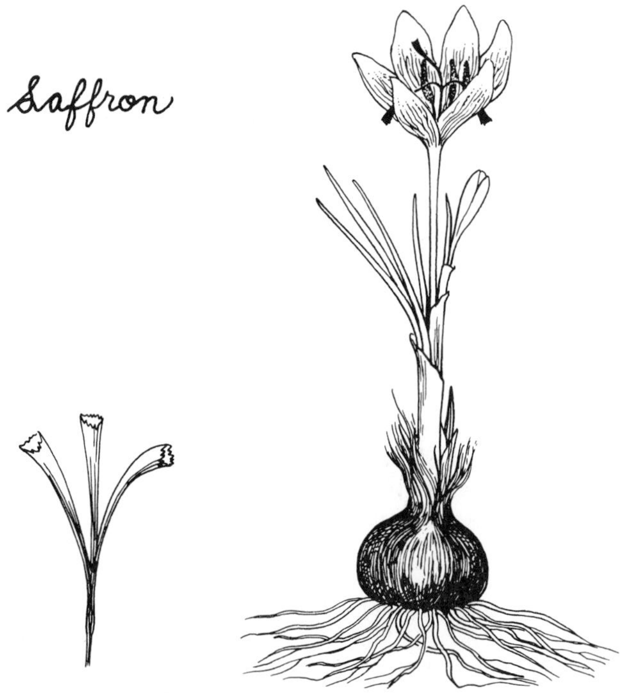

SAFFRON

Famous both as a spice and yellow dye, saffron is reputed to be the most expensive seasoning in the world. It is made from the bright orange stigmas in the flowers of the *crocus sativus*, a bulbous plant native to the Mediterranean but easily cultivated elsewhere. The difficulty and consequent expense stem from the harvesting, which must be done by hand, and the drying of the stigma to obtain the powder known as "saffron." Moreover, since there are but three stigmas per flower, it takes about 5,000 flowers to yield one ounce of powder.

The saffron crocus is an ornamental perennial that grows to a height of eight to 10 inches. It usually develops just one mauve blossom with a honey, spicy smell. The resulting powder is highly aromatic and pleasantly bitter. A single pinch is usually enough to color and flavor most dishes.

It was a product of the ancient world and well known to the Greeks, Romans and Egyptians. They used it in dyeing clothes and cosmetics as well as in food. It was recorded that the Emperor Nero caused the streets of Rome to be sprinkled with saffron at great expense for his entry into the city.

It was introduced into Spain by the Arabs in the 10th century, but did not come into wide use in Europe until it was reintroduced by Crusaders, pilgrims or traders returning from the Holy Land. Britain became an important producer of saffron, the major growing area centering on the town of Saffron Walden in Essex. Use declined drastically in the 18th century but survives to the present day in dyeing confectionary. Saffron cakes are a Cornish specialty.

Because of saffron's high cost, adulteration has always been a problem, traditionally with **turmeric,** or **safflower** *(Carthamus tinctorius).* It aroused such ire in the Middle Ages that merchants caught adulterating saffron were burnt at the stake.

It is widely used in Iranian, Arab and Indian cooking. In Europe it is the indispensable seasoning for such specialties of southern European cooking as *paella, bouillabaisse, arroz con pollo* and *risotto alla milanese.* In the United States, it is a noted feature of Pennsylvania Dutch cooking.

SAFFRON MILK CAP

Also ORANGE MILK LACTARIUS. This is a mild-flavored, edible mushroom of North America and the British Isles. If bruised or cut, it weeps orange tears that turn green on exposure to air. The saffron milk cap *(Lactarius deliciosus)* is particularly good when young, having a pleasant, sweet taste. The flesh is white, but the eater should be warned that it turns the urine red for a short time. The cap and stem are orange and the gills yellow, all turning green in patches with age.

The saffron milk cap appears in open conifer or hardwood forests in late summer and autumn. It achieves a height of about four inches, and the cap may be five inches in diameter.

See also: **Mushroom.**

SAFROLE

This natural flavoring ingredient has been banned since 1960 because, under experimental conditions, it was found to cause cancer in rats. Safrole is a colorless, oily liquid. It was extracted mostly from the bark of a South American tree, *Ocetea cymbarus,* and used to flavor root beer, among other food items. Later on, the FDA discovered that sassafras bark and roots contain safrole, and in 1976 it banned the sale of sassafras tea, an herbal tea often found in health-food stores.

SAGE

This potent seasoning herb is a member of the mint family and has several varieties, the best being garden sage *(Salvia officinalis).* The leaves are grayish green and powdery to the touch and are generally used in dried form. The aroma is pungent, suggesting

Sage

thyme, but with a tiny whiff of turpentine. It is a hardy perennial, native to the northern rim of the Mediterranean, that reaches two feet in height and has purplish blue flowers.

It has a venerable history, particularly as a medicinal herb among the ancient Greeks, Romans and Arabs, who considered it a general tonic. Besides being good for cleaning the teeth, it improved the memory and alleviated grief. They coined the proverb, "How can a man die who has sage in his garden?" At one point in time, sage tea was a highly popular drink, and the Dutch established a lucrative trade with the Chinese, who preferred it to their own, by exchanging sage for their finest tea at a ratio of one to three.

It is preeminently the seasoning herb for meat. It is the most widely used herb in the United States, perhaps because Americans are such hearty meat eaters. Sage's essential oil is believed to aid in digesting such rich fare as pork, duck and goose. It is a standard seasoning in poultry stuffings.

Italians too are sage lovers, but the English use it sparingly in stuffings and sausage, while the Germans and Belgians add it to certain eel dishes.

SAGE CHEESE

There are two cheese going by this name, one an American cheddar-type cheese flavored by sage extract. It has a mottled, green curd colored by the juice of green corn. The other is a British cream cheese, colored green, with sage leaves added. It is made from cow's milk and is also known as green cheese.

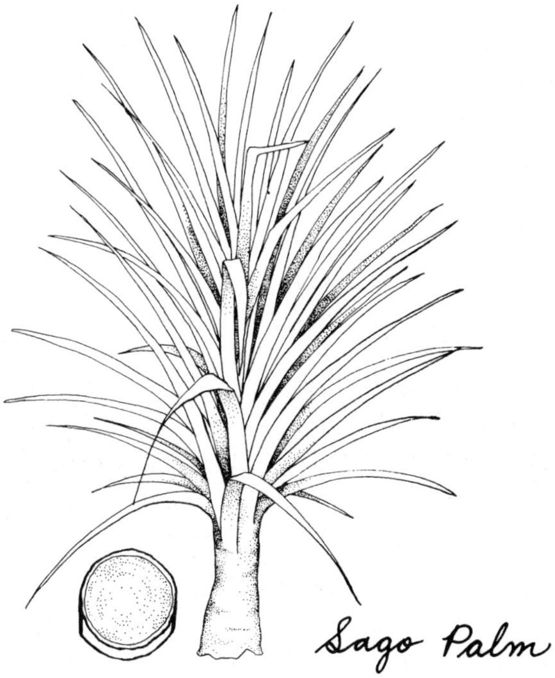

SAGO

This starchy food extracted from the soft core of the trunk of a palm tree, *Metroxylon sagu*, has several varieties, the best being the spineless sago *(Metroxylon laeva)* and the prickly sago *(Metroxylon rumphii)*. The sago palm grows wild in the freshwater marshes of Southeast Asia, particularly the East Indies, reaching heights of perhaps 30 feet at maturity. It flowers but once in its lifetime, at about age 15. Preparatory to this, it stores up starch in the pith of its trunk. Just before budding, the tree is cut down and the core scraped out. A single tree can yield as much as 600 to 800 pounds of starch. For local consumption, the starch is grated to powder and washed.

The resulting flour, after seasoning, is yellow shading to red or brown. It is a staple food in the East Indies, being made into paste dishes and cakes. For export, a further refinement is added. The flour is mixed with water, forming a paste, which is then put through a sieve. The resulting small pellets drop on a hot surface and form what is called pearl sago, the preferred form in Western countries. Sago is cheap, nutritious and cooks quickly. It is not unlike **tapioca** in its makeup and is used mostly in puddings. Sago globules can be made from any number of starches, and, in Germany, for example, what they call "sago" is made from potato flour.

Many other trees besides those of the *Metrosylon* genus produce true sago. The best of these is the cabbage palm *(Areca oleracea)* of the American tropics. Of lesser quality is sago from the jaggery and fishtail palms of India and Malaysia.

SAGUARO

See **Prickly Pear.**

SAILFISH

Distinguished by its high dorsal fin, the sailfish *(Istiophorus platypterus)* is popular among anglers for its fighting qualities and is also well regarded as food. It is considered somewhat inferior to the **marlin,** however, in both these respects. Perhaps due to its much smaller body weight (maximum 275 pounds), it is not exploited commercially to nearly the same degree.

The sailfish is cosmopolitan in its distribution and migrates according to weather, keeping to warmer waters. It is a surface swimmer and is often found close to shore. Its coloration tends toward dark, steel blue above, and white to silver below, often with pale vertical bars along the body. The sailfish can be up to 12 feet long, but the average commercially caught fish weighs only 70 pounds. More important to the angler, however, is its leaping abilities and its speed. The sailfish has been clocked at 70 mph.

ST. BENOIT

A soft, fermented French cheese made from cow's milk in the vicinity of Orleans, it is similar to **Olivet,** with charcoal and salt being rubbed into the rind, thus giving it an ashen color. Cheeses are six inches in diameter and are cured from 12 to 20 days depending on the season.

ST. CLAUDE

This is a small, square French cheese made from goat's milk in the Franche Comte in the vicinity of St. Claude. Individual cheeses are salted on the surface and weigh from four to six ounces. They may be eaten fresh or after aging in a cool, damp cellar.

SAINTE-MAURE

See **Goat's Milk Cheese.**

ST. EMILION

This is a historic wine-growing region in western France on the right bank of the Dordogne slightly east of **Bordeaux.** The red wines of St. Emilion and those of its neighbor, **Pomerol,** have held a high position among Bordeaux wines for centuries. They differ from the dry reds of **Medoc** and **Graves** farther north in being stronger and more "masculine," like some of the best red wine from **Burgundy.** A good St. Emilion should not be drunk until it is from six to ten years old, and at its peak it should have a dark, velvety color and a hint of bitterness. Among the most prized of St. Emilion red wines are those from the Chateau Ausone—named for the Roman poet Ausonius, who planted the vineyard over two thousand years ago—and those of the Chateau Cheval Blanc.

ST. GEORGE'S AGARIC

This is a smaller variety of the common field mushroom, *Agaricus campestris,* which grows wild in France. It is so named because it appears on or about April 23, St. George's Day. Opinions differ on its quality, some rating it only fair, others excellent. In France, it is used to flavor stews. In the south of France it is often dried for later use, in which case it must be soaked in water before cooking.

See also: **Mushroom.**

ST. JOHN'S BREAD

See **Carob.**

ST. JOHN'S WORT

Also HYPERICUM, ROSE OF SHARON. The name applies to any of several evergreen herbs or shrubs, but especially the rose of Sharon *(Hypericum calycinum).* Native to southeastern Europe and Asia Minor, the rose of Sharon is often planted as an ornamental and has attractive golden flowers. It is an aromatic plant, and the flowering tops have been infused to make herbal tea. They have also been used as a flavoring agent in liqueurs. The young leaves are said to be eaten sometimes in China.

ST. MARCELLIN

Also FROMAGE DE CHEVRE. This soft, creamy French cheese is made of goat's milk in the town of St. Marcellin of the Isere Department. Blue mold is cultivated on the surface as with **Brie** and **Coulommiers,** but not in the interior, so it is not considered a blue cheese. This cheese used to be made exclusively from goat's milk, but increasingly sheep and cow's milk are substituted in part. The season is from April to November.

ST. NECTAIRE

See **Senecterre.**

ST. PIERRE

See **John Dory.**

ST. STEPHANO

A German soft cheese made from whole cow's milk that is similar to **Bel Paese,** it is cured at temperatures below 40° F (4.4° C).

SAKE

Traditionally the national alcoholic beverage of Japan, sake is made from white rice, malt and water. Although usually described as a wine, sake is a kind of still beer produced by a double fermentation of the rice mash. It is either clear or pale amber in color. The flavor is mild and sweet, and for that reason, somewhat deceptive in that the alcoholic content is a potent 14 to 18 percent. It is taken with meals, sipped out of tiny porcelain cups, smaller than egg cups. There are various qualities of sake, but it is usually drunk warm, which makes the quality difficult to discern.

SALAD

This is, basically, a cold dish of raw or cooked vegetables anointed with a dressing, most commonly a mixture of oil and vinegar. A plain salad consists of a single vegetable (not counting herbs), usually a green such as lettuce; a mixed salad contains two or more vegetables.

Apart from lettuce, which holds uncontested first place, favorite ingredients for a raw salad include borage, celery, chicory, chives, cresses, cucumbers, dandelion, endive, escarole, mint, mustard greens, nasturtium leaves, chopped onion tops, parsley, petsai, sprouts and tomatoes. If the chief ingredient of the salad is a leafy green vegetable, the dish is called a green salad; otherwise it takes the name of the main ingredient, such as, for example, a cucumber salad.

The most commonly cooked vegetable for salad is the potato. Potato salads are particularly popular in Germany, where certain varieties are served hot. Other frequently cooked ingredients for salads are artichoke, asparagus, beet, carrot, cauliflower, celeriac, salsify, seakale, cheese, chicken, crab, crayfish, lobster, salmon, shrimp, tuna and various meats. These salads commonly take the name of the chief ingredient, e.g., crab salad, etc.

In the United States a green salad is often served before the main dish as an appetizer course. In Great Britain and Europe, the order is reversed with the salad coming after the main course. Occasionally, a plain green salad may accompany a cooked meat course, but many Europeans object to this, saying the vinegar in the dressing interferes with the taste of the wine, which is customarily taken with the meat. An exception to the continental practice is made for *Salade Nicoise*, which is served as a first (and sometimes sole) course. This is a hearty mixture of chopped tomatoes, green beans, capers, black olives, chopped potatoes, sliced sweet peppers, chopped garlic, anchovy fillets and tuna fish, all topped with oil and vinegar dressing.

Elaborations on the basic formula are numerous. Fruit salads, both savory and sweet, are served. Fancy concoctions, such as a chef's salad or luncheon salad, constitute a meal in themselves. They are huge mixtures of green vegetables, tomatoes and often fruit, a julienne of cheese and meat and even cottage cheese or sherbet. Jellied salads are popular in the United States and may be savory—cooked shellfish, meat, cream cheese etc., in aspic—or sweet—fruit in sweet jello—or a combination of sweet and savory.

The classic salad dressing is composed of three parts oil to one of vinegar (or lemon juice), plus salt and pepper. This is called *vinaigrette* in French, and the term is also used in English. The French admit certain additions, such as chopped herbs, shallot or a pinch of mustard. Wine vinegar is deemed to be the best vinegar and olive oil the best oil. Other salad dressings abound, many based on cream, mayonnaise and cheese. Some of these are covered under **Sauce.** Many are available commercially in bottled or in powdered form. In the Middle East taste in salad dressing runs to such sweet bases as honey or syrup. In Southeast Asia, soy sauce and **nuoc-mam** are popular bases for dressing.

Abraham Hayward, a 19th-century English essayist, made this comment on salads, "According to the Spanish proverb, four persons are wanted to make a good salad; a spendthrift for oil, a miser for vinegar, a counsellor for salt, and a madman to stir it all up."

Salad is often used as a symbol of youth, as in the following quotation from Shakespeare: "My salad days when I was green in judgement: cold in blood."

SALAD CHICORY

See **Endive.**

SALAK

Also ZALACCA. Edible fruit of a small palm tree indigenous to Malaysia but cultivated in other tropical areas, including America, the *salak (Salacca edulis)* is reddish brown, up to three inches long and top-shaped or pear-shaped. It has sweet, succulent flesh. It usually contains three seeds. When ripe, the *salak* is eaten fresh; immature fruits may be pickled. The *salak* is also canned in a brine solution and used as travel food by Moslem pilgrims to Mecca.

SALAMANA

This is a soft cheese made in southern Europe from ewe's milk. Put in a sausage like casing to ripen, it develops a sharp flavor. It is spread on bread or used in cooking, mixed with cornmeal.

SALAME CHEESE

This is usually **Provolone,** so called because cheeses sometimes are shaped like salame, but the name can also include *stracchino salame* and *formaggio salame*, which are soft cheeses of the **Bel Paese** type that are ripened in sausage-like casing.

SALAMI

Also SALAME. This is the best-known Italian sausage, with as many versions as there are provinces. It is widely imitated abroad, the German and Hungarian styles being the most prominent. As a generalization, Italian salamis contain both lean pork and beef (ratio 2:1) chopped fine, moistened with white wine and seasoned with garlic and pepper. It is salted, stuffed into natural casings and hung to dry for as long as four months, losing during this time up to 35 percent of its weight. Aged salamis are very firm and with proper storage will keep indefinitely without refrigeration. German and Hungarian salamis are smoked, rather than aged and are milder in taste than the Italian. Salamis made in the United States are quite mild, as a rule; kosher salamis contain no pork and are a little spicier than the other American varieties.

Italian salamis differ from province to province in such matters as the kinds and proportion of meats used, the shape and size of the sausage, the salting and the drying. Following is a description of a few of the better-known types:

Milan salami contains equal proportions of beef, pork and pork fat. It is a small sausage, weighing one-half pound on the average. It is seasoned with garlic, salt, pepper and white wine. It is the most widely exported salami.

Florentine salami, a large salami often flavored with fennel, contains only lean and fat pork, chopped relatively coarsely, which gives it a tender texture.

Felino salami, made near Parma, is delicately flavored and contains only pork, both fat and lean. It is lightly spiced with whole peppercorns, garlic and local white wine.

Varieties of salami

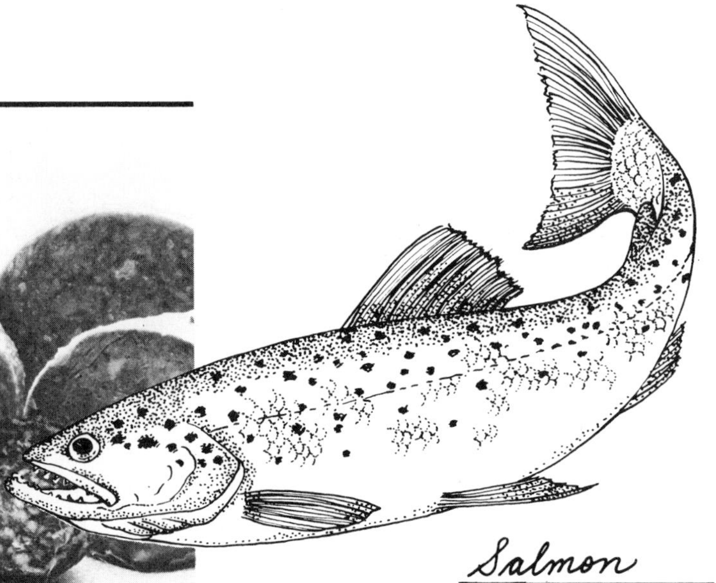

Genoa salami is strongly flavored and garlicky. This is true even of U.S. versions, which otherwise are mild. It contains pork, veal and pork fat (in the United States pork, beef and their hearts) and is dried from 90 to 130 days.

Napolitano salami is a strongly flavored mixture of beef and pork in equal parts, seasoned with black pepper, chili powder, garlic and white wine.

Sopresse salami uses equal parts of pork and young beef and originates in Verona, Padua and Venice.

Sardinian salami is made entirely from pork and flavored with red chili.

Sicilian salami comes in two or three versions. One made in the United States consists primarily of pork trimmings and whole boneless picnic trimmings, chopped coarsely and seasoned with white and black pepper. It is hung to dry for five to six weeks. Chili pepper is the favored seasoning in Sicilian salami.

Salami is a favorite sandwich filling, sliced cold and uncooked. It may be cubed and served as an hors d'oeuvre. It is a staple item of Italian antipasto.

See also: **Sausage.**

SALANGANE

A bird whose nest is used to make bird's nest soup, the salangane is a variety of swift *(Collocalia* spp.) that is found along the Chinese coast and among the islands of the Indian Ocean.

See also: **Bird's Nest.**

SALCHICHON

A Spanish sausage composed of pork fillet minced with fat bacon and seasoned with white pepper, it is salted and lightly smoked. Salchichon is eaten raw.

See also: **Sausage.**

SALEP

Also SALOP. This is a drink made from the dried tubers of certain orchids, most notably the *Orchis morio* and *O. latifolia.* The name is also applied to the tubers themselves. The tubers are ground into a powder, which when mixed with hot water becomes thick and gelatinous. Salep is a product of Iran and other countries of the Middle East. There it is used to make soups and jellies, as well as medicinal preparations.

Until the 19th century, salep was a popular drink in England. It was sold from street stalls in the early morning and evening as a hot drink for workers. Salep was often laced with alcohol or mixed with spices, syrup, lemon, cream or eggs. Its popularity was eclipsed by that of coffee.

Salepi remains a popular drink in Greece. It is essentially the same as the English salep, i.e., the powdered orchid tubers, sugar and boiling water. It is sold by street vendors, and its taste is described as insipid.

SALIOTA

A rock cod of southern South America, the saliota *(Saliota australis)* reaches a length of 15 inches and is sometimes taken by trawlers from deep waters (700 plus feet) off the Falkland Islands, Patagonia and southern Chile. It is well regarded as food but is not fished commercially to any extent. It is greenish brown above, lightening below.

SALMON

A fish revered both as game and food, the salmon comes in two distinct kinds, the Atlantic salmon *(Salmo salar)* and the Pacific salmon (genus *Oncorhyncus)*, which has five species. The Atlantic salmon is acknowledged to be the tastier of the two types, with those caught in Scotland and then Ireland given top honors.

The salmon is a migratory fish, spawned in fresh water, which goes down to the sea to reach sexual maturity and then returns to its river or stream of origin to spawn. The run upstream occurs in the spring. There are four stages in a salmon's growth. The baby salmon, called a parr, remains in its river or stream until it attains a length of five to six inches, which may take from one to four years. At this stage it is called a smolt. Smolts swim downstream to the sea and remain there for from one to eight years. Those that return after only one winter at sea are called grilse, which weigh an average of five pounds.

Adults are those that remain at sea for at least two winters before the run upstream to spawn. The longer they remain at sea, the larger they become, so that after six winters, a salmon may weigh between 35 and 45 pounds. The record Atlantic salmon was caught in Norway and weighed more than 79 pounds. A rule of thumb is the longer a salmon remains at sea and the farther the destination upstream, the better meal it makes. They must be caught before spawning, however, because after that their flesh becomes flabby and dull, and they soon die.

In former times, Atlantic salmon were plentiful in the northeastern rivers of the United States, but the number found there now are negligible due to the damming of the rivers and pollution. Given this example, dam builders on western rivers have provided fish ladders for the salmon. These are terraced waterfalls that enable the fish to mount the dammed portions in easy stages. Pacific salmon are now the mainstay of the U.S. salmon catch, most of which is canned.

The premier Pacific salmon is the chinook *(Oncorhynchus tshawytscha)* or king salmon. This largest of all salmon (record: 126 pounds) goes by many names, including Sacramento salmon, Columbia River salmon, quinnat and tyee. The chinook is the most sought-after by the sports angler and is excellent eating, but is not the most desirable salmon commercially. That honor goes to the sockeye *(O. nekra)* or blueback salmon, which, though much smaller, has rich red flesh, high oil content and outstanding flavor. Next comes the coho *(O. kisutch)* or silver salmon, which is also found in the Great Lakes. The pink salmon *(O. gorbuscha)* is the most frequently found in cans because it is the most plentiful. It is also the smallest, and has been nicknamed "humpback" because just before spawning a ridge of cartilage forms on its back. Least of all is the chum *(O. keta)* or dog salmon, so named by the Athabascans of the Yukon, who regarded it as fit only for their dogs. Although larger than the pink salmon, it is too sluggish to swim upstream and has unappetizing pale, pink flesh.

Salmon is served in a variety of ways. It may be poached in water and served cold or cut into steaks and grilled. Whole salmon is stuffed and baked.

Smoked salmon is a luxury food, made from the larger fish, which have generally been soaked in brine before smoking. A particularly salty variety called *lox* plays an important role in Jewish cuisine.

SALMONBERRY

A variety of raspberry, *Rubus specabilis*, found wild in the Pacific Northwest from Idaho and California to Alaska, it is now cultivated in Alaska and has been introduced into England. The berries are large, conical and salmon-colored. They are sweet and may be eaten raw or used in jams and jellies. Salmonberry is a favorite among native Americans of the area.

SALOIO

A Portuguese **hand cheese** made from cow's skim milk in the Lisbon area, it is a small, cylindrical cheese, weighing four ounces. It has a pronounced flavor. There is a milder variety made from goat or ewe's milk.

SALSAFY

See **Salsify.**

SALSICCIA DOLCE

See **Italian Sweet Sausage.**

SALSIFY

Also OYSTER PLANT, SALSAFY, VIPER GRASS. This carrot-shaped root vegetable native to southern Europe, though popular 100 to 200 years ago, today is considered rare and exotic. There are three main types: White *(Tragopogon porrisolius)*, black *(Scorzonera hispanica)* and Spanish *(Scolymus hispanicus)*. A fourth, wild type, *Tragopogon pratensis*, is gathered for its gray green leaves and tender shoots. For more information, see **Goat's Beard.**

White salsify has yellowish gray skin, white flesh, and attains a maximum length of about 12 inches. It has a mild, sweet flavor, similar to **parsnips.** When boiled, the root's taste reminds some people of oysters, hence the name. Salsify matures in autumn but is regarded as a good winter vegetable because it may be left in the ground to be pulled when needed. It is not harmed by freezing. Salsify is similar to the carrot in chemical composition

and is prepared for cooking by scraping the outer skin. At this stage, to avoid discoloration, the root should be soaked in a weak vinegar or lemon juice solution. It is frequently parboiled, then fried or prepared in any way appropriate for carrots or parsnips.

Black salsify, though dark skinned, has a shape similar to the white variety, but is usually smaller. It is better tasting than the white salsify. Native to Spain, it is also known as *scorzonera*, a name that is said to derive from the Catalan word *escorso*, meaning serpent. A century or two ago, black salsify was used as a snakebite remedy both in Spain and in England, where it earned the name "viper grass." Left in the ground through the winter, it produces tender young shoots in the spring. Their flavor is similar to that of asparagus or chard shoots. Black salsify is prepared like white salsify.

Spanish salsify, also known as golden thistle, is the largest of the three but has a less distinctive flavor. It is light in color and has prickly leaves that require careful handling.

Though not a popular vegetable, salsify is cultivated in the United States. The tender young leaves of the first two types, as well as the white part of the stalk, are used in green salads. In the mature plant, the stalk reaches two to four feet in height.

SALT

This is the crystal sodium chloride used as a condiment and in the preservation of certain animal products. Salt is made up of approximately 39 percent sodium and 61 percent chloride, but the common table variety usually contains additives, such as magnesium carbonate and calcium phosphate, to keep it dry and running easily, and iodine as a dietary supplement. Salt is essential to human health, the lack of it leading to serious malnutrition. The human body requires a minimum of 3½ ounces for optimal functioning, and one-third of an ounce per day is considered a normal intake. In some cultures, salt is not eaten as a separate item. Bedouins, for example, do not take salt. Eskimos are reported to have an aversion to it. The salt they require is supplied in the food they eat, such as the flesh of game animals, or milk, which contains 1.6 grams of salt per liter.

The use of salt as a condiment dates from Neolithic times. With the creation of agriculture and city-based civilization, hunting declined and, as a consequence, the amount of game flesh in the human diet was greatly reduced. This coincided with the adoption of moist methods of cooking, such as boiling, which leaches the natural salt out of the food. The craving for salt was a natural result, and by the Bronze Age, salt-making and salt-mining were important industries. The town of Salzburg, "salt city", Austria, was the center of a large, prehistoric salt-mining operation.

Salt played an important role in the rise of the Roman Republic. Around 800 B.C., Latin tribesmen were transformed from shepherds to merchants when they learned to extract more salt than they needed from the marshes at the mouth of the Tiber River. They sold this surplus salt to their neighbors, gradually creating a trade route that stretched eastward to the Adriatic Sea. It was called the *Via Salaria* (salt road), a route that still exists today. Trade in other goods flourished along this route, which eventually became a military road for Roman legions. The Romans acknowledged the importance of salt by naming their god of health *Salus*. From this we derive such English words as "salutary," "salvation" and "salute." As part of their rations, Roman soldiers were issued salt, or, in lieu of that, a sum of money to buy salt, a *salarium*, from which the word "salary" is derived.

Colorful phrases have come down to us from the history of salt. "Being sent to the salt mines," an early form of punishment, is still used to describe disagreeable and tedious work. The use of "below the salt" to convey low social status dates from medieval times when the custom was to place the salt in the center of the table. Persons of distinction were seated above the salt, and ordinary folk sat below the salt. Also, an unsuccessful person is said to be "not worth his salt."

Salt comes from several sources including the evaporation of brine from salt beds, sea water and natural brine springs and from mining. Salt mines are usually dug on the sites of ancient salt lakes that dried up and were then covered over by movements of the earth. A mine on Avery Island, Louisiana, which provided the Confederate States with much of its salt, has been worked for more than 150 years. The famous salt mines of Wieliczka, Poland, tunnel more than 65 miles underground. Underground shops and restaurants have been carved out of the rock salt at depths of 800 feet or more.

The salt obtained from mines and other sources is refined into various commercial grades, including topping flake, which is used for crackers; fine flake, which is for general purposes, table salt, baking, canning, and kosher salt, which has the largest crystals. A very fine salt is produced in Essex, England from the waters of the Maldon Sea. Celery salt is fine salt mixed with powdered celery seed, and garlic salt is powdered garlic with salt added. Spiced salt contains white pepper and other mixed spices.

See also: **Sodium.**

SALTPETER

Also POTASSIUM NITRATE. A mineral salt used in the preservation of certain meats, saltpeter is an antioxidant and is used very sparingly (in a ratio of about 1 to 40 with salt) in the curing of ham, bacon, corned beef and sausage. It also adds an attractive pink color to the meat. Overuse of saltpeter toughens the meat and can be harmful, or at least irritating, to the consumer of the meat. It used to be a common belief that saltpeter suppressed the sexual appetite, and that it was added liberally to the food in such institutions as the Army, prisons and boys' boarding schools to curb the erotic desires of the inmates. Neither belief had any foundation in fact.

SALT-RISING BREAD

Here is a bread leavened by spontaneous fermentation and made from a dough consisting of flour, cornmeal, sugar, salt, butter, water and milk. Portions of the cornmeal, milk and salt are mixed and set aside in a warm place to ferment through the action of wild yeast. It is, in fact, a starter, and the salt functions to prevent the growth of unwanted bacteria in it while it ferments. When the starter is bubbly, it is mixed with the rest of the ingredients, kneaded, allowed to rise and then baked. The result is not as light as bread produced by commercial yeast but instead has a moist, crumbly texture.

See also: **Bread.**

SALTWORT

The leaves of the small, perennial shrub, saltwort *(Batis maritima)* are slightly salty to the taste and are used to flavor salads. It is found in the West Indies, Hawaii and the tropical areas of Mexico and Florida. The young, tender shoots may also be eaten after being boiled. The plant grows in sandy, coastal areas and is considered a good standby food for emergencies.

SAMBUCA

An Italian liqueur based on the fruit of the elderbush, whose Latin name is *sambucus*, it is a clear, colorless liquid with a licorice flavor. Sambuca is bottled at from 70 to 84 proof and may be drunk as an aperitif or as an after-dinner cordial.

SAMOS WINE

See **Wines, Greek.**

SAMPHIRE

Also SEA FENNEL, PETER'S GRASS, CHRISTE MARINE. A European seaside plant, *Crithmum maritimum*, of the parsley family, it is used occasionally today as a salad plant, its succulent leaves adding a piquant sulphurlike aroma to the mix. It used to be pickled as well as eaten as a cooked vegetable. Samphire frequently grows on cliffs and was more popular formerly than it is now.

On the risks of gathering samphire, Shakespeare remarked in *King Lear:* "Half way down/Hangs one that gathers samphire, dreadful trade!" The name "samphire" is an allusion to Saint Peter, probably from the French *herbe de Saint Pierre.*

See also: **Marsh Samphire.**

SAMRONG

The seeds of this Southeast Asian tree are used to make a refreshing drink in Cambodia. The samrong, *Sterculia lychnophora*, belongs to the same botanical family as the **cola** tree.

SAMSHU

A Chinese rice beer of ancient origin, it is prepared from malted rice using a double or even triple fermentation in the manner of **sake.** Samshu, consequently, has a higher alcoholic content than western-style beers. It ranges from 14 to 16 percent.

SAMSOE

A popular Danish cheese with a firm texture, golden color, and a sweet but sharp taste, it is made from whole cow's milk on the island of Samsoe. The cheeses, which weigh about 30 pounds, reach maturity in about six months but are sometimes eaten younger. The paste has rather large holes in it, like Gruyere or Swiss, but the texture is different.

See also: **Tybo.**

SANDAL

See **Santol.**

SANDALWOOD

See **Santal Fruit.**

SAND CHERRY

Also DWARF CHERRY. The name refers to at least three species of American shrub: *Prunus pumila*, *P. depressa*, and *P. besseye*, that produce small, purple black fruits with a pleasantly sweet-acidic flavor. They are eaten raw or used in jams, pies and jellies. Sand cherries are hardy plants, cultivated in sandy areas, such as the shores of the Great Lakes, in the northern Midwest and south-central Canada.

SAND DAB

See **Dab.**

SAND DROPSEED

The seeds of this North American perennial grass, *Spirobolus flexuosus*, are used as food. It is seen mostly in the western United States and is also known as mesa dropseed.

SAND EEL

Also SAND LANCE. The name covers several species of marine fish, *Ammodytidae*, which are small and snakelike in appearance. The American sand lance *(Ammodytes americanus)* occurs on the East Coast from Labrador to Cape Hatteras. It reaches a length of nine inches and lives on sandy bottoms inshore and on off-shore banks. It is closely related to the European sand eel **(A. marinus).** Both are brown or blue green above and white on the belly. Another European species, *A. tobianus*, found from Iceland to Norway and south to the Mediterranean, is an important source of fish meal. Largest is the greater sand eel *(Hyperoplus lanceolatus)* which is found on the Atlantic coastlines of Europe. It measures up to 13 inches. Sand eels are very plentiful and fished commercially for meal, but they also make excellent eating. They are prepared like **smelt.**

SANDER

See **Zander.**

SANDPIPER

This is a common shorebird of Europe and North America. The most common American species is the spotted sandpiper *(Actilis macularius);* the European counterpart is *A. hypoleucus*. The sandpiper is a small bird with a long bill, flexible at the tip. It resembles the **snipe** and is prepared as such. The sandpiper is protected by conservation laws in the United States.

SANDWICH

In its simplest form, the sandwich consists of two slices of bread with some meat, cheese or other filler in between. The sandwich has been with us for millennia, yet the name is quite recent. It is attributed to John Montagu, the fourth Earl of Sandwich (1718–1792). According to Woody Allen, in *Getting Even*, "He freed mankind from the hot lunch. We owe him so much." The Earl of Sandwich was an avid gambler, the story goes, and disliked leaving the gaming tables for meals. The sandwich was the perfect solution because it left his hands disencumbered from knife and fork and free of grease during his card-playing sessions. His adoption of the sandwich, in addition to giving it a name, gave it social cachet. It became a staple of 18th-century buffets, and the French incorporated it into their gastronomic repertoire.

Long before then, however, the ancient Romans were known to enjoy eating meat between two slices of bread. Among Jews, a certain Rabbi Hillel, who lived during Herod's reign, is credited with inventing a form of the sandwich. He started the Passover custom of sandwiching a mixture of chopped nuts, apples, spices and wine between two matzos to eat with bitter herbs. This serves as a reminder of the suffering of the Jews before their deliverance from Egypt. For centuries, Arabs have been stuffing their envelopelike pita bread with barbecued lamb and other good things, surely a more efficient arrangement than two slices of bread. The tortilla had been developed in Mexico long before the Spaniards arrived, and with it the custom of rolling up various fillings in them, such as beans, eggs and meat. Medieval Europe saw the trencher come into use. The trencher was a hard-cooked rectangle of bread, which served as a plate. Food was piled on top of it, and the diner ate off it, having the option at the end of the meal of eating his or her plate or tossing it to the dogs. The trencher was not far from being an open-face sandwich, about which more later. In the fields, meanwhile, French peasant laborers were used to lunching off cheese sandwiched between two slices of bread.

Since the 18th century, the sandwich has come into its own. It flourishes in bewildering variety, from tiny crustless watercress sandwiches served with British tea, to foot-long hero sandwiches on

French bread and two-decker club sandwiches. The Danes have perfected the openface sandwich, called *smorrebrod*, which consists of filling placed on top of a single slice of dark rye bread or white toast. They range from the simple to the bizarre, with one Copenhagen restaurant listing 250 varieties.

The sandwich played a starring role in the fast-food boom that swept America in the 1960s and 1970s, and none was more prominent than the hamburger. Historically the hamburger has had nothing to do with ham, and authorities disagree on whether Hamburg figured in its genealogy. One account points out that many Europeans immigrated to America on the Hamburg-Amerika Line of boats, which served a famous type of Hamburg beef. It was salted and smoked and kept well but was hard of texture. Therefore, it was usually chopped up and mixed with onions and breadcrumbs before cooking. It was popular with Jewish immigrants during the 1850s, and they continued to make Hamburg steaks once they were established in America. Nobody knows how the chopped beef "Hamburg steak" got between two halves of a bun, but the concoction was an immediate hit at the St. Louis Fair of 1903. The hamburger has gained steadily in popularity ever since.

The hamburger is sometimes called a Wimpy, especially in the British Isles, after a character in the Popeye comic strip, who doted on hamburgers. The hamburger steak, without the bun, is also known as the Salisbury steak, after a Dr. J. H. Salisbury, who around the turn of the century recommended eating it three times a day as a remedy for a whole list of ailments.

SANDWICH NUT CHEESE

This is a soft, mild cheese, usually cream or Neufchatel, that has chopped nuts and sometimes raisins mixed in.

SANGRIA

This is a Spanish wine cup that can be purchased already prepared in the bottle or mixed at home. Typically sangria consists of red or white wine, sugar, water, sliced oranges and limes and soda water. As it is a refreshing summer drink, these ingredients are usually put into a pitcher with ice cubes and served when thoroughly chilled. The name means "bleeding" in Spanish, for the bright red color. Sangria is often made in the southwestern United States with very cheap wine (the fruit and sugar obscure the cheap flavor). In the words of Jerry Jeff Walker, a contemporary singer,

> *"Yeah I love that Sangria wine*
> *Just like I love them old friends of mine*
> *They tell the truth when they're mixed with the wine*
> *That's why I love them old lemons and wine."*

A variation of this from the American south is the sangaree, which consists of lemon juice, red wine, sugar, ice and water. The sangaree has come to mean any sweetened wine drink, or a cocktail with spirits, wine and sugar, such as the Barbados sangaree, which is made with Madeira wine, sugar, nutmeg mixed with brandy, gin or whisky.

SAN PELLEGRINO WATER

This is a natural sparkling mineral water from Italy. A sensory panel sponsored by the Consumers Union in 1980 judged its taste to be fair, and made the following additional comments: mildly sour, mildly astringent, mildly salty, distinctly bitter, distinctly soapy flavor.

See also: **Mineral Water.**

SANSAPOTE

Also ZAPOTE CABILLO, MONKEY APPLE. Edible fruit of a tree, *Licania platypus*, native to the Central and South American tropics, it has rough, brownish skin and reaches a length of six inches.

SANTAL FRUIT

Fleshy fruit of an Australian shrub, *Eucarya acummata*, whose seeds are also edible, it is eaten raw or made into preserves.

SANTOL

Edible fruit of a tropical Asian tree, *Sandoricum indicum*, found especially in the Philippines and in Malaysia, it is eaten fresh, dried or candied.

SAPODILLA

Also NASEBERRY. The name applies both to the tropical evergreen tree, *Achras zapota*, and to its fruit, which looks like a cross between a potato and a russet apple. The best known product of this tree is its sap, chicle, which is the raw material of most **chewing gum.** The sapodilla is native to Mexico and South America; its name derives from the Nahuatal word *tsapotl*. It is widely cultivated elsewhere, including the West Indies, Florida, Bermuda and the Far East, particularly in India, where it has made an excellent adaptation. The sapodilla is called the naseberry or naseberry plum in the West Indies, and *chickoo* in some parts of the Far East.

The fruit has a rough, grayish brown skin similar to the medlar; it may be round, lemon-shaped or oblong, averaging about three inches in diameter. Its pulp is yellowish red and very sweet when ripe. The texture is soft and yielding and usually contains one or two black seeds.

The sapodilla is usually eaten raw; it can be peeled, sliced and mixed in a fruit salad with other fruits, but it is equally good cooked. The flavor is described as delicious. The sapodilla does not travel well. It must ripen on the tree, and for this reason it is generally eaten near where it is grown.

Sapodilla

SAPSAGO

Also SWISS GREEN CHEESE. This small, very hard cheese is flavored with a variety of clover called blue melitot *(Melilotus coerulea)*, which gives it a pungent flavor, pleasant aroma and light green color. Sapsago has been made in the Swiss canton of Glaurus for the past 500 years, and it is also made in Germany.

Curd is obtained from slightly sour skim milk and ripened for at least five weeks under heavy pressure. It is sent to a cheese factory where it is ground and mixed with 5 percent salt and 2.5 percent powder prepared from clover leaves. The mixture is packed into cone-shaped forms called *stockli*. The resulting cheeses are four-inch cones weighing from one to 2½ pounds. When fully cured, they are used for grating. A powdered form is also sold that is usually mixed with butter and spread on bread. Sapsago is widely exported and is known under a variety of names, which include *glarnerkase*, *grunerkase*, *grunerkrauterkase*, *krauterkase* and *schabzieger*.

SARACEN CORN

See **Buckwheat.**

SARACHA

Edible fruit of a perennial wild plant, *Chamaesaracha caronopus*, of the western United States, it is a berry eaten locally by the Hopi and Navajo people.

SARATOGA WATER

A naturally sparkling mineral water bottled in Saratoga Springs, New York, it has a relatively low mineral content, less than 500 ppm of total dissolved solids. A sensory panel sponsored by the Consumers Union in 1980 judged the taste of Saratoga water to be good, but with the following "sensory defects": mildly bitter, mildly astringent, mildly salty flavor.

See also: **Mineral Water**

SARDELOWA

A horseshoe-shaped Polish sausage made chiefly of pork with small amounts of beef and veal, it is three to four inches thick. Sardelowa is heated, usually by steaming, and eaten hot with sauerkraut or potatoes.

See also: **Sausage.**

SARDINE

The name is given to several species of small, oily fish, usually immature pilchards or herrings. The European sardine *(Sardina pilchardus)* is a young pilchard, a migratory fish found in the Mediterranean Sea and in the Atlantic Ocean off the coast of Europe. It is especially plentiful around Sardinia, hence the name. Due to its high fat content, it is eaten fresh only in the neighborhood of fishing ports. It is delicious fried or broiled. Far better known are canned sardines, especially those of France, Portugal and Norway, although in Norway sprats are used rather than pilchards.

The European sardine is rushed to the cannery, if possible within an hour or two of being caught. Its processing for canning includes removing the head and viscera, salting and drying. It is usually preserved in olive oil and less often in cottonseed oil. Low sodium sardines are also packed in Norway and Portugal. They are not salted and may be packed in tomato sauce or water.

The pilchard is not found in American waters. Consequently, Atlantic coast canners pack young herring as sardines, while those on the Pacific coast

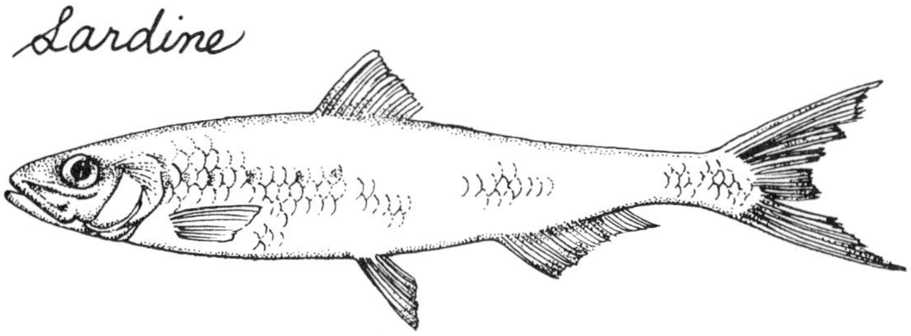

utilize the California sardine *(Clupanodon caeruleus)*, a fish that resembles the European pilchard but grows to a much larger size on maturity. Sardine canning boomed in California at the start of the 20th century and centered in Monterey Bay. Author John Steinbeck brought this area into the limelight in his popular novel, *Cannery Row* and its sequel, *Sweet Thursday*.

Collection of vintage canned sardines was explored by Vyvyan Holland in the 1964 edition of *The Compleat Imbiber*. Holland, the son of Oscar Wilde, ran across a collection of canned sardines dated back to 1906. He theorized that good vintage years for olive oil might coincide with good vintage years for wines. In a taste test he discovered that the best years for sardines were 1921, 1929, 1924 and 1914, a series that corresponded exactly with good sauternes. Armed with this knowledge, he began to lay down a sardine cellar, buying only the best French sardines, Rodel, Amieux or Peneau. He recommends this hobby only to young men "because it may be 20 years before he will reap the full benefit of his industry."

See also: **Herring, Pilchard, Sprat.**

SARDO

Also SARDO ROMANO. This hard, white cheese was made on Sardinia originally only from ewe's milk, but now with cow's milk mixed in. It is a **Romano**-type cheese that has a sharp, salty tang when fresh, and when fully cured is used for grating. Its spicy flavor makes it a popular condiment on pasta dishes. Sardo is also made in Argentina and the United States, and if from ewe's milk only, it is called *pecorino Sardo*.

SARGASSO

Also GULFWEED. A genus, *Sargassum*, of floating brown seaweed that is eaten in Spain as a salad. The Spanish word is *sargazo*.

SARGENT LILY

The bulbs of this western Chinese variety, *Lilium sargentiae*, are ground to make a flour for porridge or baking. Its rose purple flowers are also eaten.

SARGO

An abundant game fish of the U.S. Pacific Coast, found from Monterey Bay to Baja California, the sargo *(Anisotremus davidsoni)* is related to snappers and grunts and occurs on rocky and sandy bottoms and in kelp beds. It reaches a length of 17 inches and has a greenish blue back and silvery sides marked by a broad black bar extending vertically from the dorsal fin to the belly. The sargo is good to eat, and, although it is fished commercially, it is not an important market fish.

The sargo is related to the larger black margate *(A. surinamensis)* of the Caribbean and Gulf of Mexico. This reaches a length of two feet and is eaten locally.

SARRAZIN

This semisoft, blue-veined cheese, much like **Roquefort,** is made in the Swiss canton of Vaud.

SARSAPARILLA

This flavoring ingredient is extracted from the roots of several tropical plants of the genus *Smilax*, including *S. medica* of Mexico, *S. officinalis* of Honduras, *S. papyracea* of Brazil and *S. ornata* of Jamaica. It is used in medicines and as a flavoring agent for beverages, especially soft drinks. In England, sarsaparilla was used to make a wine tonic that became popular among Victorian ladies.

SASSAFRAS

This is a North American wayside shrub or tree possessing a strong, sweet-smelling root and broad trilobed or mitten-shaped leaves, used in making tea, **root beer,** sauces and to flavor certain medicines and candies.

Sassafras *(Sassafras albidum)* was one of the earliest exports from the New World and was highly regarded in Elizabethan England. Thomas Heriot in his *Briefe and True Report of The New Found Land of Virginia* (1590) described it as "a kind of wood of most pleasant and sweete smel, and of most rare vertues in physick for the cure of many diseases." Its name comes from the Spanish *sasafras*, an apparent confusion with the plant, **saxifrage.**

Sassafras grows abundantly in tight thickets throughout the eastern half of the United States and west to the Rocky Mountains. It is known by various local names, including ague tree, chewing stick, cinnamonwood and tea tree. A belief that sassafras twigs and bark, when brewed as a tea, thins the blood and the body is still common. Sassafras tea used to be one of the common herb teas found in health-food stores. But in 1976 the FDA determined that sassafras tea contained safrole, which produces liver cancer in rats. The tea was subsequently banned by the FDA.

A sauce called file, made of dried and powdered sassafras leaves, is used in the South, particularly in creole recipes, to flavor stews, soups and gumbos. Oil of sassafras *(Oleum sassafras)* is a major ingredient in some medicines, soft drinks and confections and in the manufacture of perfumes. Its root and bark give the distinctive taste to root beer.

See also: **File.**

SASSENAGE

This semihard, blue-veined cheese similar to *Gex* and *Septmoncel*, comes from Sassenage (Isere), France. It is made from cow's milk, plus a little sheep and goat's milk, in a mixture of whole and skim. Blue mold is allowed to grow on the surface during curing, which takes two months. The taste is salty and piquant. Individual cheeses are round, measuring 12 inches across by three inches thick. Their season is from November to May.

SATSUMA

See **Tangerine.**

SAUCE

Socrates is reputed to have said, "Hunger is the best sauce." Having acknowledged his wisdom, one is left with the question of what is second best, and here the field is practically limitless. A sauce is defined as a liquid, or semiliquid, seasoning poured over or served with a food to enhance its flavor and/or decorate its appearance. The French, who are the best saucemakers of the West, regard it as the soul of their cuisine, an element that can add greatness to a dish that otherwise might be merely excellent.

The basic French sauces—the "mother sauces" they are called—were developed in the 17th and 18th centuries. Authorities differ on how many of these mother sauces there are: some say two, others mention up to five. They all agree on two, i.e., white sauce (example, *bechamel)* and brown sauce (example, *espagnole).* Others considered basic by some are *veloute*, a white sauce; mayonnaise, a cold sauce; tomato sauce; Hollandaise sauce, a mixture of butter and egg yolks, and oil and vinegar. There are also sweet sauces for dessert and the like.

The basic sauces are considered building blocks for further elaboration, and are therefore quite simple in conception.

Bechamel, for example, is made by thickening milk or cream with **roux,** a previously prepared mixture of butter and flour.

Veloute is made the same way, except a stock or wine mixture is substituted for the milk. Gravy, in fact, is a form of *veloute* (which means velvety).

Espagnole is beef stock, thickened with a roux made of cornstarch and butter, reduced by boiling, with a few vegetables thrown in for flavoring. This is the basic brown sauce.

Add further ingredients to a basic sauce for flavoring—say, grated cheese—and you have a compound sauce *(sauce composee)* of which there are scores, many immortalized with specific names. Mornay, for example, is *bechamel* with the addition of grated cheese, usually Gruyere, Parmesan or Romano. Many of the more prominent French sauces are described elsewhere in the alphabet under their specific names.

The English have been maligned in the matter of sauces, viz., "In England there are sixty different religions, and only one sauce," a statement attributed to Prince Francesco Caraccoli. Actually, British sauces tend to fall into four categories: uncooked vinegar-based sauces (example, mint sauce); white sauces, such as discussed above (example, caper sauce); cooked sweet sauces, made with roux, or with eggs and milk and purees of cooked fruit, which are sweetened and served with meat or poultry (example, gooseberry sauce). German sauces are similar to French or English sauces.

The English word "sauce" derives from the Latin *salsus,* meaning salted, which gives a clue to the kind of sauce that the ancient Romans were fond of. Their basic sauce, in the sense described above, was a liquid called **garum** or *liquamen.* It might better be called a condiment, since it was used in place of salt. *Garum* was a clear, golden liquid, with a salty, slightly fishy, slightly cheesy flavor, made from small fish and the fermented entrails of larger fish, which were placed in a pot and allowed to ferment in the sun for two to three months. It has been called the Roman soy sauce. Yet, like the basic French sauces, it could be varied to suit the demands of a particular dish by the addition of vinegar, oil or pepper. The closest thing to it in modern terms is the Vietnamese **nuoc-mam,** a fermented fish sauce, which is labeled "fish soy" in Chinese grocery stores.

Sauces, as the term was understood in medieval times, tended to be closer to a relish, that is, a zesty, sharp-tasting mixture served on the side, and into which individuals dipped their food according to taste. From these medieval dishes comes our word "saucy" (sassy), meaning sharp or pert.

Our modern commercial preparations, such as Worcestershire sauce and Tabasco sauce are closer to *garum,* that is, they function more as a condiment than a French sauce, which with its careful blending attempts to exactly complement the taste of the dish it adorns. Many of the commercial sauces have soy as a basis, plus vinegar, garlic and extracts of other vegetables and spices. Some, like **ketchup,** are based on tomatoes; others, like **Tabasco,** are based on chili pepper. They are discussed under separate headings.

The function of a sauce was summed up by Auguste Escoffier, the father of modern cookery, as follows: "A sauce emphasizes flavor, provides contrast and makes perfection complete."

SAUCE-ALONE

See **Allaria.**

SAUCISSON

Here is a class of large French sausages, weighing 12 to 16 ounces minimum, that differ from region to region in detail, but are always composed chiefly of pork, both lean and fat, with admixtures of veal, beef and occasionally mutton. Introduction of a filler, such as flour or bread, must by law be disclosed on the label. The same is true if donkey or horsemeat is used. Some, like large **cervelats,** are cured; others like the **Lyons** and **Arles** sausages are smoked and air dried. The latter two are sliced and eaten raw, often as hors d'oeuvres. The cervelat is sometimes poached and eaten warm.

See also: **Sausage.**

SAUERKRAUT

This is pickled white cabbage. To prepare it cabbage is shredded finely and mixed with salt to a level of about 2.5 percent by weight. The mass is then pressed or pounded to squeeze out the cabbage juice, which, because it contains sugar, undergoes a natural lactic acid fermentation. The fermentation takes place in a large tub over a three-week period. Once a week the slime is skimmed off the top of the ferment, and a little salted water is added. Caraway seeds, and sometimes juniper berries are put in to enhance the flavor. The finished sauerkraut has an acid content of 1.7 to 1.8 percent. Fresh sauerkraut is usually washed briefly before cooking to remove excess acid; older sauerkraut may be soaked for several hours.

Sauerkraut is considered a German specialty, but according to tradition the Austrians were the first Europeans to learn how to make it, and they were taught by the Tartars, who brought it from China. The Chinese method of making it involved cooking cabbage in rice wine to preserve it for the winter months. The Tartars developed a taste for soured cabbage, but prepared it differently and passed that method on to the Europeans.

Germans eat sauerkraut hot or cold, and the French prefer to cook it with fatty meats, a dish they call *choucroute garni.* The Russians make a hearty sauerkraut soup called *shchi.* Sauerkraut is an ideal dish for dieters because it is low in calories, yet filling.

SAUREL

See **Scad.**

SAURY

Also SAURIE, SKIPPER. This is a small ocean fish with both Atlantic and Pacific varieties, the latter being more abundant and more important as food. The Atlantic saury or skipper *(Scomberesox saurus)* is a long, thin fish with beaklike jaws. It reaches a length of 18 inches and moves in large shoals. Of considerable importance in the food chain, its movements are too sporadic for commercial exploitation.

The Pacific saury *(Cololabis saira)* lacks the long snout of the Atlantic variety but is otherwise similar. It moves in large schools, and is fished extensively by the Japanese and Russians who sell it fresh and canned. The Pacific saury is practically unknown to anglers, since it keeps to open ocean.

SAUSAGE

This is meat (most often pork) that has been chopped fine, usually mixed with spices and filler, then stuffed into a cylindrical casing. The wall of the casing is a thin membrane, which may be natural material, such as the intestine of a steer, sheep or hog, or artificial material such as cloth or cellulose. The natural material is eaten along with the stuffing and in many

Varieties of sausage (left to right): kielbasa, Italian sweet sausage, chorizo, English link, knackwurst and (top) frankfurters

cases, adds greatly to the flavor of the sausage. In smaller sizes, the membrane is twisted into standard lengths, called links. The meat is treated in a variety of ways. It may be fresh, simply ground or chopped and mixed with other foodstuffs. It may be cured—salted, pickled, smoked or dried. It may also be cooked. Favorite flavorings are such herbs and spices as pepper, cumin, dill, fennel, mace and parsley, as well as orange peel and red wine. Fillers like flour, cereal, fat and bread round out the stuffing mixture. Given the possible variations in ingredients, preparation and casings, the varieties of sausage are practically endless.

Sausage making had its origin in prehistory. The *oryae*, or sausage of ancient Greece, figured in Homer's *Odyssey*, which dates back to 850 B.C. The Greek island, Salamis, is reputedly the birthplace of our modern sausage, *salami*. The ancient Romans enjoyed sausage, their favorite ingredients being ground pork and pine nuts, and our word "sausage" derives from *salsus*, the Latin term for salted or preserved meat.

In Rome, the sausage fell casualty to the pious disapproval of Constantine the Great, the first Christian emperor, who assumed office in the fourth century A.D. Shocked by public gluttony and drunkenness during the pagan feast days of *Lupercalia* and *Floralia*, he banned both the holidays and favorite food of the revelers, sausage. This did not end sausage eating in Rome, but it did drive it underground for a while.

Scholars reckon that ancient sausage was pretty tasteless fare, and that the modern sausage began to take shape in the Middle Ages, an era noted for its heavy use of herbs and spices. Local experimentation with various meats and spices led to the many kinds of sausage we have today, many named after the cities they originated in, such as bologna (from Bologna, Italy), romano (from Rome) and frankfurter (from Frankfurt).

The sausage was not exclusively European. The Chinese have *lop chong*, a sausage usually made of pork, and sometimes liver. Colonists in North America discovered the native Americans making cakes of chopped, dried meat and berries, much resembling sausage stuffing, which they smoked and stored for future use. It is generally conceded, however, that the art of sausage making reached its zenith in Germany, and that German sausages today are unrivaled for their variety and flavor.

Pork is the usual meat for sausage, but sausages are also made from beef, veal, liver and other interior organs and tongue, plus mixtures of some of them. The quality of the sausage depends greatly on the quality of the meat selected for it, and the proportion of meat to filler. It is not true that sausage meat always comes from the less desirable cuts and castoff scraps. Since the meat is to be ground, tastiness is a better criterion than tenderness. Pork rump and shoulder are favorite sources of sausage meat. And the beef meat often comes from bulls, rather than steers.

Sausages are divided into categories depending on how the meat is prepared:

Fresh uses meat that has not been cooked or cured, e.g., bockwurst, bratwurst or weisswurst.

Smoked uses meat that has been cured, then smoked over wood fires, and may be cooked as in frankfurters, bologna and mortadella, or uncooked, as in pork sausage and mettwurst.

Cooked employs fresh or cured meat, which is then cooked in the casing, as in liverwurst and blood sausage.

New conditioned uses ground meat mixed with spices and curing agents, which is then cured for several days and smoked. Examples are cooked salamis, cervelats and kosher salamis.

Dry contains fresh, spiced meat that has been cured, then dried under special conditions for lengthy periods, and includes Italian dry salamis, the German *holsteiner*, *langjaeger* and *gothaer* sausages, and the Spanish *chorizo*.

Cooked specialties is a final category for those that don't fit into the other categories, such as haggis.

The making of sausage involves the following steps. *Bratwurst* is used as an example. The name means "sausage for frying." Lean pork and veal are minced with a very sharp knife, or twice ground using the fine blade in a meat grinder. Marjoram, caraway seeds and nutmeg are mixed in a mortar and ground to a fine powder, then added to the meat with salt, pepper and water. The mixture is forced into casings (also called bungs) using a funnel and spoon or a sausage nozzle fitted to a grinder. The casings are twisted and tied off at three to four inch intervals.

For certain sausages a prefatory step would be to cook the meat (in head cheese, for example), and for others, after tying off, a final step of cooking or drying. For fresh sausage, immediate cold storage is essential to prevent spoilage. Sausages resist spoilage longer if smoked, the process being similar to smoking **ham,** but requiring less time.

Fresh sausages are usually grilled, fried or broiled. Italian sausage is made into a casserole with green peppers, cheese, tomato sauce and mashed potatoes. In the United States a favorite midwestern boiled dinner combines kielbasa (Polish sausage) with such vegetables as potatoes, carrots and asparagus. Dry sausages are eaten cold.

For information on specific sausages, look directly under the name, such as **Bologna, Cervelat, Haggis, Kielbasa, Mortadella, Salami, Thuringer, Vienna Sausage,** etc.

SAUTERNES

This sweet white wine is cultivated and harvested in the region of Sauternes and **Barsac** about six miles south of **Bordeaux** in western France. The harvest in this area is unique. The Semillon grapes are picked individually, rather than in bunches, when they are overripe, even when they have begun to shrivel and crack. (This is the condition known as the "noble rot," or *pourriture noble.)* The vine leaves, also, are pulled off by hand, so the sun can shine on the grapes directly. By these painstaking means the sugar concentration in each grape is vastly increased. But the chief aim of this process is to encourage the advent of a microscopic fungus, *botrytis cinerea*, which makes a powdery film on the grapes—essential to the wine's distinctive flavor and bouquet. The harvest in Sauternes-Barsac, then, can last for as long as two months past the regular time of yield, and may require half a dozen trips to the vineyard to select the appropriate grapes. In this region quality has precedence over quantity—at whatever cost.

The color of Sauternes should be, at its best, a brilliant gold. The wine has a high alcohol content (usually between 15 and 20 percent). Once the grapes have been picked and pressed, the process is still delicate. Excess air must not be in contact with the vintage, or the wine will darken. If the weather turns hot again in late fall, the grapes may ferment a second time and spoil the entire harvest. One "superior growth" of Sauternes-Barsac has held its place since it was first classified in 1855. This is the elegant **Chateau d'Yquem.** Gourmets will not drink a d'Yquem with a meal, but instead treat it as a liqueur, rarely drinking more than a few sips or a small glass at one time. The rich, smooth sweetness of this classic wine easily overwhelms any food flavor.

SAVANNAH FERN

This is a fern, *Gleichenia linearis*, found in Malaysia, Sumatra and Australia, whose roots are edible and can be dried, ground into flour and used to make bread or porridge.

SAVORY

Two varieties of this member of the mint family are useful as seasoning herbs, summer savory *(Satureia hortensis)* and winter savory *(Satureia montana)*. The summer variety is a delicate annual with light purple flowers, whose young leaves have a flavor similar to marjoram's. Winter savory, a perennial with white or pink flowers, is hardier and stronger to the taste.

Savory was once known as *the* bean herb because of its ability to enhance the flavor of beans, peas and lentils. Also, earlier writers on herbs claimed it relieved flatulence. Summer savory is a frequent constituent of the *bouquet garni*, while winter savory is often added to egg and potato dishes. Either may be used in stuffings or meat dishes, where **sage** is called for or when a milder alternative is desired.

SAVOY CABBAGE

An autumn/winter cabbage, which takes its name from the Savoy region of France, it has typically crimped and blistered leaves that form a compact, globelike head.

The Savoy is a hardy vegetable with many varieties including Dwarf Green Curled, Early Dwarf Ulm, Perfection, Best of All and Drumhead. It is short-stemmed and usually light green in color. It has a delicate, some say better, flavor than common **cabbage,** and is particularly suitable for stuffing because of its large leaves. But is also makes its appearance in cole slaw, in salads or alone as a green vegetable.

Savoy cabbage

SAVOY WINE

See **Rhone Wines.**

SAW SHARK

Here is a family of sharklike fish whose outstanding characteristic is a long snout with many sharply pointed teeth along its edges. Saw sharks use their toothy snouts to root around in muddy bottoms, and, handled with care, are not considered dangerous to humans. The saw shark is found only in the Indian and Pacific Oceans. The best known is probably the common saw shark *(Pristiophorus cirratus)*, which is found from South Africa to Australia. It reaches a length of four feet and is highly regarded as a food fish.

Its flesh is described as white, firm and excellently flavored. It is sold under the name "flake." Less well known are the southern saw shark *(P. nudipinnis)* and the saw shark *(Pliotrema warreni)*, the latter confined to South African coastal waters on the Indian Ocean side. It reaches a length of only three feet, but its flesh too is rated as excellent.

SAXIFRAGE

Herbs of the family *Saxifragaceae* are generally found in mountains and rocky places of temperate and subarctic regions. Various species are found in Europe, Asia, North Africa and in North and South America. Among the edible varieties are the golden saxifrage *(Chrysosplenium alternifolium)* of France's Vosges Mountains; meadow or pepper saxifrage *(Silaus flavescens)* first described by Pliny the Elder (23–79 A.D.), and mountain lettuce *(Saxifraga micranthidifolia)* of the high ground from Pennsylvania to Georgia. These plants have fleshy leaves and are eaten as cooked vegetables or added to soups.

SBRINZ

Also NIDWALDNER SPALENKASE, SBRINZA, SPALEN, STRINGER. A very hard cheese with a long history, *sbrinz* originated in the Swiss canton of Unterwalden, but is now made in other cantons, in the Italian Alps and in Argentina and Uruguay. It is a cooked-curd cheese, similar to Gruyere, produced from whole or partly skimmed cow's milk. It has a sharp, nutty flavor. It has small eyes, and when fully cured it is an excellent grating cheese. Argentine *sbrinz,* which is sold in the United States, is closer to **Parmesan** than the true sbrinz.

During processing, *sbrinz* is cooked to achieve the desired firmness of curd, which is then heavily pressed and salted over a three to four-week period. Cheeses are round, approximately 20 inches in diameter and four inches thick, weighing from 30 to 45 pounds. They are cured for as long as three years. Immature *sbrinz,* called *spalen,* is sold locally as table cheese. Mature cheeses are exported, mainly to France and Italy.

Grated *sbrinz* is a fine condiment and may be used as a substitute for Parmesan in pasta or risotto dishes. It does not become stringy when cooked.

SCABBARDFISH

Also BLACK SCABBARD FISH. Two species of long, eel like fish are known by this name. The black scabbardfish *(Aphanopus carbo)* is the favorite food fish of Madeira, but it is also found in the North Atlantic as far north as Iceland. It is a deepwater fish, preferring depths of at least 600 feet, and is caught on long, baited lines. The black scabbard fish has a long compressed body with a dorsal fin that runs from just behind its head all the way to its tail. It has the undershot jaw of a **barracuda,** and a beautiful iridescent copper color that turns black when it dies. In Portuguese, it is known as *pez espada.*

The scabbardfish of worldwide distribution, *Lepidopus caudatus*, is also known as the ribbonfish and the frost fish. It can reach a length of nearly seven feet, and like the black variety, it has a long dorsal fin, a big jaw and large teeth. This species has a brilliant silver color, with larger specimens being darker above. It is considered very good eating and is fished commercially in the North Atlantic. In the Southern hemisphere it is frequently caught in cool weather, hence the name "frostfish."

SCABWORT

See **Elecampane.**

SCAD

Scad is an alternative name for the **horse mackerel,** but it also designates other food fish including the goggle-eye, the yellowtail scad and the big-eye scad. The goggle-eye *(Priacanthus hamrur)* is a small (up to 16 inches) food fish of the Indian and Pacific Oceans. It is called *alalaua* in Hawaii. It lives on reefs and is red to purplish red. The yellowtail scad *(Trachurus mccullochi)*, a relative of the horse mackerel, is a small (up to 13 inches) fish of Australian waters. It is edible, well liked by anglers, but has no commercial value. The big-eye scad *(Selar crumenophthalmus)* is a schooling fish, reaching two feet in length. It is found worldwide in tropical waters and is commercially exploited as a food fish in both the Indian and Pacific Oceans. It is distinguished by its huge eyes, which are covered by adipose tissue.

SCAEVOLA

Also BEACH NAUPAKA. This white, fleshy fruit of a spreading shrub, *Scaevola frutescens*, is found on islands and coasts of the Indian and Pacific Oceans. The fruit is eaten in Australia. The plant is cultivated in Florida as a hedge and for soil binding on coastal sands.

SCALELESS TUNA

Also DOG-TOOTH TUNA. A little-known species, the scaleless tuna *(Orcynopsis unicolor)* is good to eat. It reaches a maximum length of five feet and has a steel-blue back, paler sides and a silver belly. It is characterized by minute corselet scales and conical "dog teeth" in its jaws. The scaleless tuna is found worldwide in tropical seas, but, because of its preference for offshore waters, it is not caught in significant numbers.

See also: **Tuna Fish.**

SCALLION

Also SPRING ONION, WELSH ONION. Although the term usually means the small, bulbless onion, *Allium fistolosum*, it is also popularly applied to seedlings of the common onion that are pulled before bulbing. To add confusion, the term is applied often to the **shallot,** which does not resemble the scallion at all. Scallions have green tops, hollow like chives, and should show white for two or three inches above the roots. A slight swelling does develop at the base of the stalk.

The flavor is characteristically of onion but milder than the common onion. Both the lower, white portion and the green upper portions are eaten cooked or raw. They may be added to flavorings or chopped like chives into salads. The French word for scallion is *ciboule.* The English word derives from Ashkelon, one of the royal cities of the ancient kingdom of Canaan, which, in antiquity, was renowned for its onions.

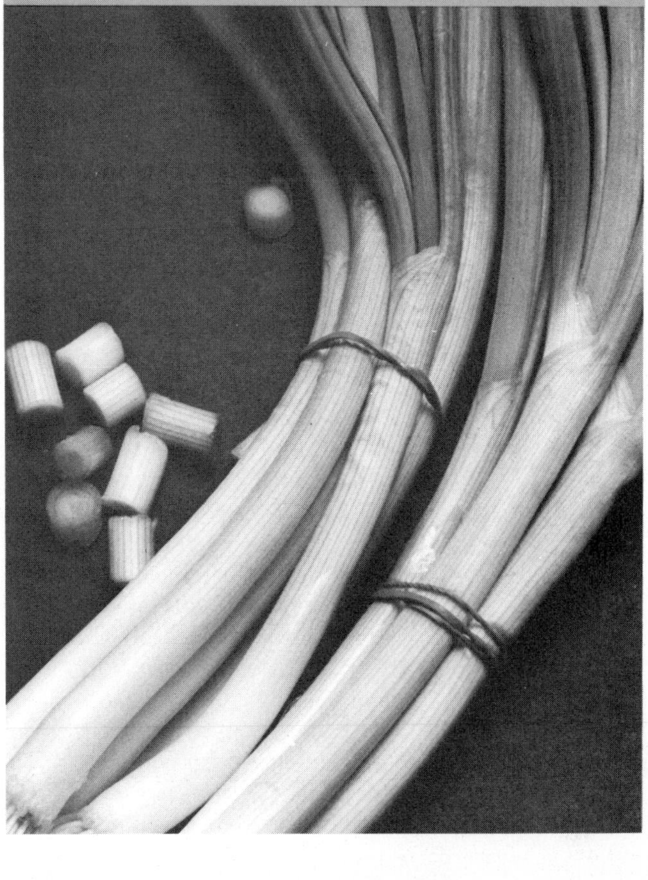

Scallions

SCALLOP

Also SCOLLOP. Scallops *(Pectinidae)* are a large family of bivalve, saltwater mollusks famous for their beautiful ridged shells and delicate flesh. There are more than 300 species worldwide, all of them edible. The edible part of a scallop consists of the "eye" or abductor muscle, and the coral, which is a pink segment attached to the eye. In Europe scallops tend to be larger than in America, and consumers prefer the coral, which is the reproductive gland or roe. In America, only the abductor muscle, which opens and closes the shell, is eaten; the rest is discarded. Scallops are usually purchased live in European markets, while in American markets they are already dead and cleaned for cooking.

The scallop is highly mobile, rocketing through the water by opening and closing its shell vigorously. Thus it has a singularly large and fleshy "eye," which is a round, almost translucent, creamy white morsel that suggests lobster, but has its own particular taste. It is eaten raw on the half shell in some places—most notably on the west coast of South America—but is usually fried, baked or poached. A well-known dish in English-speaking countries is scallops in mornay sauce, called *coquilles St. Jacques*, which is simply the French expression for scallops, meaning literally "St. James' shells."

According to legend, scallops acquired that name in the following manner:

The body of St. James the Greater was being brought by ship from Joppa to Compostela, a town in Galicia, a province in the northwest corner of Spain. Onshore a nobleman, described as Lord of the Maya, was proceeding to church on horseback to get married. His horse bolted, ran into the ocean and swam out towards the incoming ship, which slowed to meet him. The sailors explained the ship's mission to the nobleman, along with a few tenets of Christianity, whereupon, convinced he was witnessing a miracle, he immediately converted to Christianity. Swimming back to shore, horse and rider emerged covered with scallop shells, which were thenceforward associated with St. James.

In the Middle Ages, Compostela became an important shrine for pilgrims who, on returning home, brought back scallop shells as proof they had reached their destination, as Santiago de Compostela was the only place in Europe where scallops were fished. Pilgrims often wore a scallop-shell badge on their hats, and the latter came to be known as "cocked hats," because of the scallop shell's resemblance to the cockle shell, a more familiar item to the English.

The most common European scallop is the great scallop *(Pecten maximus)*, found on Atlantic and English Channel coasts, and the queen scallop *(Chlamys opercularis)* which seldom exceeds 1¼ inches. Although edible year round, they are best from January to June.

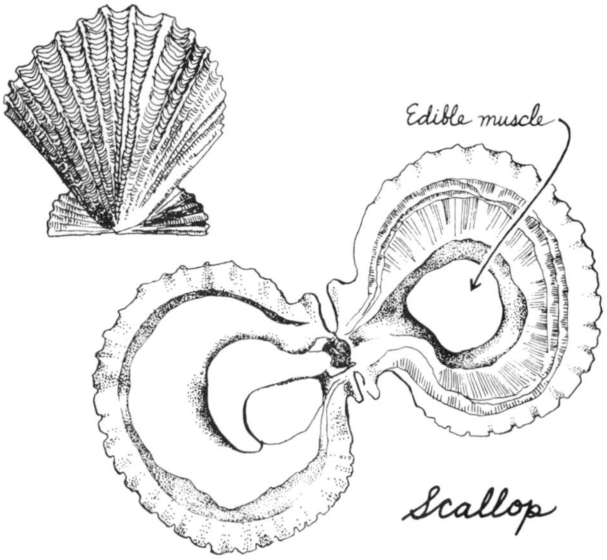

In the eastern United States, bay scallops *(Aequipecten irradians)* are fished from New England to Cape Hatteras. They are small (2½ to three inches) sweet and tender, while the sea scallop is much larger, though very scarce nowadays.

On the Pacific Coast, the thick scallop *(Aequipecten circularis)*, from Peru to Monterey, and the northern scallop *(Chlamys hindsii)*, from San Diego to the Bering Sea, are the most plentiful. The Alaskan scallop is the leading sea scallop and is so large that it takes only eight of the eyes to make a pound.

SCAMORZE

Also SCAMOZZA, SCARMORZE. This is a small, mild Italian cheese with a rubbery curd that is eaten fresh like **mozzarella.** Originally made from buffalo milk in the Abruzzi, *scamorze* is made from cow's and goat's milk too in several parts of the country. It is especially favored in Naples. The curd is formed from fresh milk with extra cream, then heated and kneaded until it is very compact and elastic. Cheeses are formed by hand, tied in pairs and immersed in brine. Sizes vary, averaging one-quarter to one-half pound but going as high as 2½ pounds. It is essentially a table cheese but can be used in cooking where mozzarella is indicated, incorporated into an omelet or toasted on bread.

SCAMOZZA

See **Scamorze.**

SCAMPI

See **Norway Lobster.**

SCANNO

This sheep's milk cheese with a buttery consistency is made in the Abruzzi region of southeastern Italy. It is of the **pecorino** type, and during processing it is repeatedly dipped into an iron oxide solution. Finished cheeses are black on the outside, deep yellow on the inside and have a burnt flavor. Scanno is often eaten with fruit.

SCARLET RUNNER

See **Runner Bean.**

SCARMORCE

See **Scarmorze.**

SCARUS

See **Parrotfish.**

SCAT

Also SPOTTED BUTTERFISH. Scat is a small, deepbodied fish, *Scatophagus argus*, of the Indian and Pacific Oceans, which some people regard a good food when fresh, but others reject because of its feeding habits. It belongs to a family of fish known as *Scatophagidae*, which literally means "dung-eaters." They prefer to feed on bottom trash and are found in great numbers at sewer outfalls. Nevertheless, the scat is eaten in many places and is a popular aquarium fish.

SCAUP

Also BLACK HEAD. This wild duck *(Nyroca* spp.) is found in the northern parts of Asia, Europe and North America. There are two types, the greater scaup *(N. marila)* and the lesser scaup *(N. affinis)*, the latter most frequently found in North America. The scaup is a diving bird, and the flavor of its flesh depends greatly on its diet. If it has been feeding on its namesake, i.e., scaup (broken shellfish), then its flavor is not relished.

SCHABZIEGER

See **Sapsago.**

SCHAMSER

Also REINWALD. This large skim-milk cheese is made in the Swiss canton of Graubunden. Individual cheeses are round, weighing 40 to 45 pounds and measuring 18 inches across by five deep.

SCHLESISCHE SAUERMILCHKASE

This German/Polish sour-milk cheese is surface ripened and very hard like **hand cheese.** It has a sharp taste and aroma. Individual cheeses are dried hard, then cured for three to eight weeks in a cellar. They are produced in Silesia.

SCHLESISCHE WEICHQUARG

See **Silesian Cheese.**

SCHLOSSKASE

Also CASTLE CHEESE. This German/Austrian cheese is small, soft and surface-ripened like ***Romadur***. It is similar to Limburger but milder. It is marketed in small cubes, 1½ inches square by four long, and also, more popularly, in the shape of a small castle, weighing less than two ounces.

SCHMEIRKASE

See **Cottage Cheese.**

SCHNAPPS

This is the German or Dutch word for hard liquors, especially clear, colorless spirits such as Dutch gin or aquavit, which are flavored with herbs. The similar word *snaps* is another word in Scandanavia for **aquavit.** It may also be spelled *schnaps*.

SCHOOLMASTER

A small, but well-flavored fish of the snapper family, the schoolmaster *(Lutjanus apodus)* is found on both sides of the tropical Atlantic and in the Caribbean and Gulf of Mexico. It is a slender, deep-bodied fish that reaches a high weight of eight pounds. It is grayish brown overall with light crossbars and orange yellow fins. It is found in shallow water and is deemed a good sportfish for angling.

SCHOTTENSEID

This is an Alpine whey cheese made by peasants for local consumption.

See also: **Ricotta.**

SCHOTTENZIGER

See **Ziger.**

SCHUTZENKASE

This Austrian cheese is soft and surface-ripened like **romadur,** itself a milder version of Limburger. Schutzenkase is marketed in small cubes, an inch square by four long, and individually wrapped in tinfoil.

SCHWARZENBERGER

This popular beer cheese of the **Limburger** type is made in Austria, Bohemia and Hungary from a mixture of skim and whole cow's milk. It is formed into cubes weighing less than one pound. Cheeses are cured in cellars for two to three weeks.

SCHWARZBROT

See **Pumpernickel.**

SCHWEPPES SPARKLING MINERAL WATER

A mineral water manufactured from filtered tap water by adding carbonation and minerals, it is relatively low in minerals and has a sodium content of 21 mg. per 8-ounce glass. A 1980 Consumers Union sensory panel rated the taste of this water as fair, with the following qualifying comments: mildly bitter, mild bitter aftertaste, mild chemical flavor, mild soapy flavor, soapy mouthfeel, mildly salty, mild salty aftertaste.

See also: **Mineral Water.**

SCLEROPAGES

A predatory Asian freshwater fish related to the **arapaima** of South America and the spotted barramundi of Australia, it inhabits streams, canals and swamps of Borneo, Malaya, Sumatra and Thailand. The *sclerpages (S. formosus)* is a fairly common fish, and its flesh is described as well-flavored. It can attain a length of up to three feet and weigh as much as 16 pounds.

SCOLLOP

See **Scallop.**

SCOLYMUS

See **Salsify.**

SCONE

A quickbread popular in the British Isles, it is usually triangular in shape. The custom is to form a circle of dough eight to nine inches in diameter, then cut it into four sections. The dough may be rolled, however, and cut into rounds, in which case the scone much resembles the American baking powder **biscuit.** White or brown wheat or barley flour may be used. In addition to baking powder, the dough may be enriched with cream or eggs or sweetened. Originally, the scone was baked on a griddle (and in Scotland was made of oatmeal), but now it is usual to bake scones in an oven. It is frequently eaten hot as a teacake.

See also: **Biscuit.**

SCORZONERA

See **Salsify.**

SCOTCH BONNET

See **Fairy ring.**

SCOTER DUCK

This is a black wild duck, *Melanitta nigra*, that breeds in the arctic regions of Europe and North America, then migrates south for the winter. Its flesh is very oily, and only the very young ducks are considered palatable, and even then they must be carefully prepared. Slow cooking is recommended, either braising, or wrapping in foil and baking in an oven.

SCREW BEAN

See **Mesquite.**

SCREWPINE

Also PANDANUS. This genus of shrublike trees is characterized by aerial prop roots and leaves arranged in spirals. Some varieties, e.g., *P. boulletii* and *P. utilis* bear edible fruit that have a soft texture and a pleasant, sweet taste resembling that of pineapple. The fruit is popular in the Asian tropics where the tree is native. Another species, *P. odoratissimus*, is valued for the essential oil that is extracted from the male flowers, and the leaves that are used for floor covering and thatching.

SCROD

See **Cod.**

SCULPIN

This marine fish is characterized by a broad, flat head, generally stout, scaleless body and an abundance of poisonous spines. Sculpins are edible, and have a good taste but are not commercially valuable. They are particularly plentiful in the North Pacific, where the prickly sculpin *(Cottus asper)* reaches a length of about 12 inches. The sculpin is closely related to the **miller's thumb.**

SCUP

Also PORGY. The name is applied to two species of **sea bream,** which are important food fish on the Atlantic coast of North America. They are the *Stenotomas argyrops* and *S. versicolor*. The scup is a lean fish that reaches an average length of 10 to 12 inches and three-quarters to one pound in weight. The name "scup" originated with the Naragansett word *mishcup*. The fish are also known as porgy, a term applied to other fish as well.

See also: **Porgy.**

SCUPPERNONG

A native American grape, *Vitis rotundifolia*, that grows prolifically from Delaware to Florida and west to Kansas and Mexico, it is the most important of the two **muscadine** grapes and usually grows in clusters of two to six berries. They are dull purple, thick-skinned and have a strong, musky flavor. They do not make particularly good table grapes but do make fine grape juice, jellies and syrups. They are also used to make **scuppernong wine.**

See also: **Muscadine.**

SCUPPERNONG WINE

This is both a white wine and a grape native to North America. The vine was found by a member of Sir Walter Raleigh's colony in 1554 on an island in the Scuppernong River in North Carolina. The original vine, supported by a tree, still stood at the end of the Civil War. The wine has an agreeably musky flavor and odor, and it is very delicate and sweet.

SCURVY GRASS

Also COCHLEARIA. The name "scurvy grass" is applied to two European herbs, the cochlearia *(Cochlearia officinalis)* and wintercress *(Barbarea verna)*, both of which have been naturalized in North America. They are so named because of their high vitamin C content, and hence antiscorbutic properties.

Cochlearia is a kind of wild horseradish whose leaves used to be added to salads for protection against scurvy, despite a very strong mustardy or tarry flavor. For this reason, it was sometimes cultivated in Ireland, England and Brittany. It is said that the explorer Vitus Jonassen Bering died of scurvy in 1744 amidst fields of scurvy grass on Bering Island, ignorant of the plant's effectiveness against the disease. Its leaves are spoonshaped, which is how it came to be called cochlearia, after the Latin for spoon, *cochlea*.

Wintercress, known also as upland cress, American cress and Belle-Isle cress, is sometimes cultivated today in the United States for its leaves, which are used in salads, as seasoning or as garnishing.

SEA ANEMONE

This is a marine polyp *(Actinozoa)* that attaches itself to rocks and has a mouth full of brightly colored tentacles, which, when open, give it the appearance of a flower. The French are fond of eating certain species that are abundant on the Mediterranean coast. Sea anemone are said to taste like shrimp.

SEA BASS

See **Bass.**

SEABEACH SANDWORT

This is a low-growing, perennial herb, *Arenaria peploides*, indigenous to arctic and northern temperate regions, which may be eaten as fresh salad.

SEA BREAM

See **Bream.**

SEA BUCKTHORN

Also SALLOW THORN. Bright orange yellow fruit of a hardy tree, *Hippophae rhamnoides*, of Europe, Asia and northern China, it persists through winter and is sometimes made into jelly. In Siberia, it is eaten with milk and cheese. The French make a sauce of sea buckthorn to accompany meat and fish dishes.

SEA CHUB

A small but delicious food fish, the sea chub *(Ditrema temmincki)* is found throughout Japanese waters, including the Yellow Sea, the Sea of Japan and the Okhotsk Sea. It is rarely longer than 10 inches and is taken in the surf. The sea chub is deep-bodied, with a spiny dorsal fin and variable coloration that usually includes stripes against a rusty blue or coppery red background. Its flesh is highly regarded in Japan.

SEA COCONUT

See **Coco de Mer.**

SEA COW

See **Manatee.**

SEA CRAYFISH

See **Spiny Lobster.**

SEA CUCUMBER

Also BECHE DE MER, SEA SLUG, TREPANG. Sea cucumbers are holothurians, sausage-shaped, shell-less, marine gastropods, prized as food in the Western Pacific and China. There are various species ranging in size from one-half foot to four feet long. The color range is wide too, including brown, black, red and white. In some species the skin is smooth and in others covered with tiny starfish-style feet. A curious thing about the sea cucumber is the tiny fish that live in its cloaca and can be seen darting in and out of its anus. Regarding this fish, Calvin Schwabe, in his delightful book, *Unmentionable Cuisine*, wrote:

> *When John Steinbeck and "Doc" Ricketts took their famous fishing and beer-drinking trip into the Gulf of Lower California (commemorated in their fascinating book* Sea of Cortez)*, they thought they had discovered a new species of this peculiar commensal fish which over a few drinks one afternoon they playfully decided to give the scientific name* Procotphilus winchelli. *Probably no other news columnist has been so honored in perpetuity.*

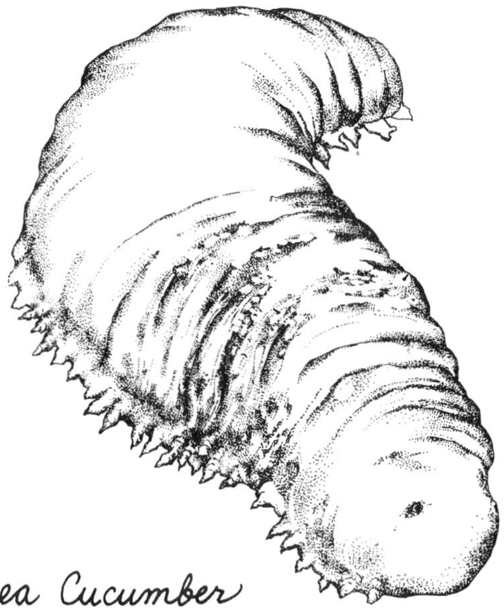

Sea Cucumber

By way of commercial preparation, the sea cucumber is slit up the back, eviscerated, then boiled and dried, both in the sun and in ovens. The end product of this treatment can be tough and leathery, or dry and hard as a rock. Before it can be used in a recipe, therefore, it must be soaked and repeatedly boiled over a 24-hour period with frequent changes of water. The Chinese commonly use sea cucumbers to make a stew and a soup which is thick and gelatinous.

A rare treat in Samoa are the ovaries of sea cucumber, which are marketed in cola bottles filled with sea water. The sea cucumber sheds these when attacked, along with portions of its respiratory tract and intestines. These organs are allowed to ferment a few days in the cola bottle to improve the flavor. Samoans also eat the sea cucumber raw after skinning it.

SEA EGG

See **Sea Urchin.**

SEA FIG

See **Chilean Fig.**

SEA GRAPE

Also KINO. This purplish fruit of a small tree, *Coccoloba uvifera*, grows along the seashore in Florida, the West Indies and other tropical areas. Though not a member of the grape family, the fruit grows in clusters like the grape and has a pleasing, subacidic flavor. It is used for making jelly and cold drinks.

The tree is also known as the platterleaf for its large, leathery leaves, which can be up to eight inches across. The leaves came in handy for Eliza Fraser, wife of the captain of the *Stirling Castle*, a ship wrecked on the coast of Australia in the 1880s. The aborigines stripped her of all clothing save her Easter hat, and she made do with a platterleaf in place of a fig leaf. Her story inspired the recent engrossing novel, *A Fringe of Leaves*, by Australian author Patrick White.

SEA HEDGEHOG

See **Sea Urchin.**

SEA HOLLY

A small coastal plant, *Eryngium maritimum*, found along the Mediterranean and on both sides of the Atlantic, it has pale blue flowers and spiny, bluish green leaves. The young root tops are eaten like asparagus. This perennial plant reaches a height of 12 inches.

SEA KALE

An herb of the mustard family that grows wild in Europe, sea kale *(Crambe maritima)* is now cultivated in France, England and the United States for its thick stalks with leafy crests. Several varieties have been developed of this hardy, winter vegetable. It has a delicate, nutty flavor. It is eaten raw in salads, like celery, which it slightly resembles, or cooked like asparagus and served with butter.

SEAL

Seal is a sea mammal (family *Phocidae)* whose flesh is eaten by Eskimos. Seals eat fish, other sealife and in some cases, birds. They are characterized by a torpedo-shaped body, a doglike head and webbed feet or flippers. They range in size from a minimum of 200 pounds (four feet long) to a maximum of about 7700 pounds (14 feet long). Some of the more popular varieties among Eskimos are the ringed seal *(Pusa hispida)*, the ribbon seal *(Histriophoca fisciata)* and the bearded seal *(Erignathus barbatus)*.

Seal flesh is dark but not strong to the taste. Eskimos consider the liver and kidneys to be particular delicacies. They are a good source of vitamin C. Eskimos also make sausage from these parts, plus the heart, brains and tongue. According to one source, seal meat enjoyed a vogue in aristocratic London circles during the 15th century.

SEA MILKWORT

Also BLACK SALTWORT. A common seashore plant, *Glaux maritima*, of Europe and Asia, its young shoots may be eaten in salads. It is a perennial plant and has been introduced into North America. It is considered useful in case of food scarcity.

SEA MOSS

See **Carageen.**

SEA NEEDLE

See **Gar.**

SEA PERCH

See **Bass.**

SEA SLUG

See **Sea Cucumber.**

SEA TROUT

See **Weakfish.**

SEA URCHIN

Also SEA HEDGEHOG, SEA EGG. This small marine mammal is shaped like a pincushion and is found abundantly off the coasts of Europe, America and Asia. Some have sharp, even poisonous spines and are a menace to bathers. Their gonads—minute orange colored eggs—are highly prized as food in France, other Mediterranean countries and in the Far East. They live in clusters in shallow water and are gathered using gloves or pincers. Many people enjoy them raw. They are simply cut in half, and the gonads eaten on the half-shell with a little lemon juice, a sort of "poor-man's caviar."

Although sea urchins are rarely eaten in the United States, two North American varieties are considered excellent eating: the green urchin *(Strongylocentrotus droebbachiensis)*, common to both coasts, and the big purple or red urchin *(S. franciscanus)* of the Pacific coast, which may reach a diameter of seven inches. They are fished commercially in California for export to the Orient.

The Japanese make a sauce from sea urchins, and eat the gonads raw on rice cakes (sushi). Likewise the French prepare a sea urchin sauce by mashing the gonads with some olive oil and blending them into a hollandaise sauce or mayonnaise. The sauce is served on fish or eels. In other Mediterranean countries, the gonads are boiled or roasted and served in the shell or added to omelets. The gonads have a distinctive, fishy, seafood flavor and are supposed to be a potent aphrodisiac.

SEAWEED

The term refers to marine plants, especially **algae,** of which several varieties are eaten in Scandinavia, Ireland and Scotland. Most notable among these are **dulse, laver** and **rock weed.** Other varieties are valuable for their yield of gelatin. **Agar-agar, carageen** and **kelp** are examples of these. In Japan, kelp is a highly popular food, serving not only as a soup base and a chewy snack, but as tasty wrappers for sushi and a flavoring agent in a wide variety of foods, including cookies.

Kelp is also a source of industrial iodine and gelatin. Kelp may also contain a high level of arsenic, exposure to which, according to the U.S. Public Health Service, is associated with a greater occurrence of cancer. Kelp tablets are a food supplement sold widely in U.S. health-food stores. Research studies have shown elevated levels of urinary arsenic in persons who took kelp tablets, the U.S. Public Health Service said.

SEA WOLF

See **Bass.**

SEA WRACK

See **Rockweed.**

SEBADAL

See **Gray Snapper.**

SELF-RAISING POWDER

See **Baking Powder.**

SELLU

Also ASSYRIAN PLUM. This is the edible fruit of a deciduous shrub, *Cordia myxa*, found from India to Australia and also in the American tropics. In Brazil, the fruits, which are oval, single-seeded and dark brown, are used in compotes. The *sellu* is highly mucilagenous and is used medicinally.

SEMILLON

This French wine grape is used along with the Sauvignon Blanc grape to produce some of the finest white wines of Bordeaux's Graves region. Finesse, velvetiness, color and aroma are the special qualities it brings to the mixture. It is also used in the making of **cognac.**

Semillon grapes are used to produce a fine California varietal wine called Dry Semillon; they are also one of the many types of grapes employed in making California champagne. A good dry white Semillon-Oreanda is produced in southern Russia. Semillon grapes have been transplanted the world over and are producing fine white wines in Argentina, Australia, Brazil, Chile, Hungary, Israel, Japan, Mexico, Tunisia, Uruguay and Yugoslavia.

SEMINOLE ASPARAGUS

Also LAUREL-LEAVED GREENBRIER. The young shoots of this high-climbing evergreen vine, *Smilax laurifolia*, are eaten like asparagus in Florida and Georgia.

SEMOLINA

This is the wheat middling, i.e., the larger, hard particle of the endosperm left in the bolting (sifting) machine after the finer particles have passed through into the flour. Semolina is unusually rich in gluten, the protein matter in wheat, and makes the best flour for **pasta** dough, especially if it comes from the very hard durum wheat. Semolina absorbs water readily and can be employed as a soup thickener and to make puddings. It may be used individually as a cereal, as in France, or as a dish of groats or **grits.** Indeed, the Russian *kasha* is a dish of buckwheat groats, which are obtained in much the same way as semolina.

SENCHA

A medium-priced green tea of Japan, probably the most common commercial type, it has a fresh, soothing flavor and is often served with **sushi.**

See also: **Tea.**

SENECTERRE

Also ST. NECTAIRE. This soft, surface-ripened French cheese was made originally around the village of St. Nectaire in the Mont Dore district of the Auvergne. It is produced from whole cow's milk and cured in cool, damp cellars where mold forms on the surface. These cheeses are cylindrical, weigh one and a half pounds and are eaten year round.

SEPTMONCEL

Also JURA BLEU. A hard, blue-veined French cheese made of a partly skimmed mixture of goat and cow's milk in the Jura Department around the village of Septmoncel, it is mainly a farmhouse cheese and its methods of manufacture, while necessarily crude, resemble those of **Roquefort.** After being formed, the curd is repeatedly salted, then cured from one to two months in a cold, damp atmosphere, encouraging the growth of mold. It is similar to **Gex** and **Sassenage**. It is considered a first-rate cheese.

SERGEANT BAKER

This ocean fish, found off the coast of Australia, is known for its beautiful coloring and firm, white, fine-flavored flesh. The sergeant baker *(Aulopus purpurissatus)* is so named, it is thought, after the British soldier who first caught one off the coast of New South Wales; or, alternatively, because its scarlet coloring is reminiscent of the British uniforms of that period. The sergeant baker reaches a length of two feet, and is distinguished by a dorsal fin with especially long second and third rays. It is not an important food fish, being difficult to catch. It favors rocky or coral areas and is only occasionally caught by an angler or netted by trawlers.

Its European cousin, *A. filamentosus*, favors the deep waters of the eastern Atlantic and Mediterranean. It lives on the bottom and is rarely brought to market.

SERRA DA ESTRELA

This excellent soft cheese is named for the Portuguese mountain range, Serra da Estrela, where it is made. Usually made from sheep's milk, *Serra da Estrela* often has an admixture of goat's or cow's milk. A thistle extract is used as rennet. During maturation, which takes several weeks, cheeses are repeatedly salted and washed with whey. The flavor is pleasant, but slightly acidic. Cheeses are round and come in various sizes, the largest measuring 10 inches across by two thick.

Castelo branco is a similar Portuguese ewe's milk cheese with a firmer paste.

SERVICE BERRY

See **Juneberry.**

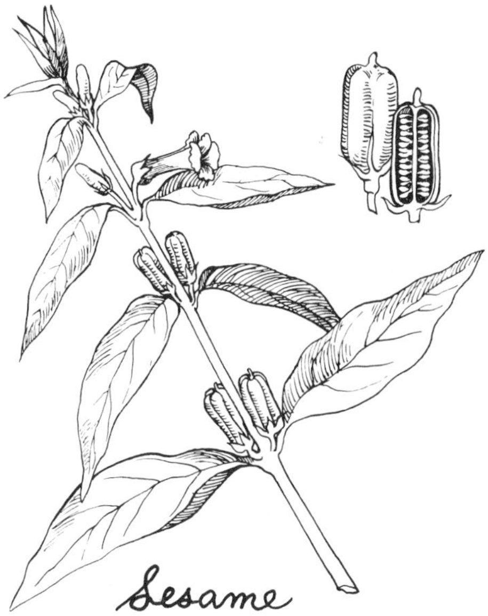

Sesame

SESAME

One of the oldest cultivated plants, sesame *(Sesanum indicum)* is grown for its seeds, which are a condiment in the United States and most of Europe but a primary source of cooking oil in Africa and Asia.

The plant is a native of India, but archeological evidence suggests that the earliest residents of the Tigris and Euphrates valley ate bread made from sesame dough. It remains a staple item of the Iraqi diet.

Sesame is a hardy annual plant partial to tropical climates but grows easily in temperate zones. The seeds range in color from white through orange to black. They are high in protein and consist of about 55 percent oil, which is famous for its resistance to rancidity. It is of enormous commercial importance in Africa and Asia, where it is used much like olive oil is in the West.

Sesame seeds are prepared in a variety of ways in Balkan and Middle Eastern cooking, but they make their appearance in the rest of Europe and the United States sprinkled on bread, rolls and pastry, to which they add a delicious toasted, nutlike flavor.

SESBANIA

See **Katuray.**

SEYSSEL

A white fruity French wine from Savoy, grown along the **Rhone** between Geneva and Lyons, Seyssel has a light and pleasing bouquet and is said to be the product of *Altesse*, a vine brought to France by the Count of Mareste returning from a Crusade. Seyssel Mousseux is the name of a semisparkling wine *(mousseux* means sparkling, or frothy).

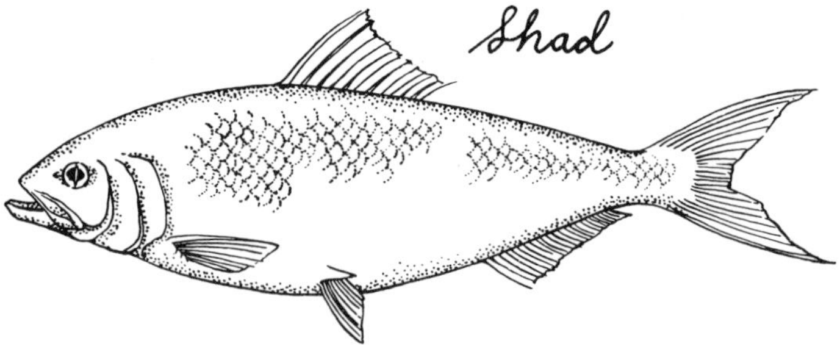

SHAD

Also WHITE SHAD, EASTERN SHAD, AMERICAN SHAD. Shad is a name given to several members of the **herring** family only one of which, the American shad *(Alosa sapidissima)* has any gastronomic or commercial importance in the United States. Two other shad are common in the North and Mediterranean Seas, the allis shad *(Alosa alosa)* and the twaite shad *(Alosa finta)* but only in France have they attained near the reputation of the shad in America. A fourth variety, the hickory shad *(Alosa mediocris)*, is esteemed as a game fish in some Southeastern rivers, but gastronomically its flesh is considered much inferior to the American shad.

The American shad is the largest fish of the entire herring family, averaging three to five pounds, although some as large as 13 pounds have been caught. Its body has a compressed appearance, with silvery sides and a rounded bluish back. Essentially an ocean fish, the shad, like the **salmon,** migrates up coastal rivers to spawn. The spawning season begins in January and lasts until June, the start being determined by the temperature of a particular river. They are best taken when they begin their journey upstream because then they are fat and succulent. After spawning, they tend to be thin and tasteless. At sea they remain far offshore and at depths below 400 feet.

The American shad is an Atlantic Ocean fish, but it was successfully transplanted to the Pacific Coast in the 1870s. Historically, it has thrived in the Delaware, Susquehanna, Hudson and Potomac Rivers on the East Coast, and the Sacramento and Columbia Rivers on the West Coast. About 100,000 pounds of shad are caught in a year. This is a precipitous decline from normal catches in the 19th century when, for example, 4,500,000 pounds were caught in 1869.

The Pilgrims were introduced to shad by native Americans who used it as both food and fertilizer. George Washington liked shad, as did Thomas Jefferson. It has maintained its popularity on the East Coast, the decline in catches being attributed to pollution in the rivers, rather than loss of interest on the part of consumers. Shad roe is considered the greatest delicacy. Rex Stout's famous gourmand/sleuth, Nero Wolfe, had a predilection for shad roe.

In the market, female shad with roe (hen) would be the first choice; then the female (usually the fattest) without roe (cut shad), and finally the male shad (buck). Shad is not much appreciated on the West Coast. Usually, the roe is removed, frozen and sent east. Then the flesh is sold as cat food.

A problem with eating shad, particularly the smaller varieties such as are available in Europe, is the profusion of small, curved and forked bones. Apart from the allis shad which is liked in Scotland, the shad has been pretty much ignored except in France. Experts speculate that this is because the French have devised a way of dealing with the bones. Before cooking, the fish is stuffed with a puree of sorrel, whose oxalic acid softens the bones, and all but dissolves them. Perhaps this is why praises of shad—particularly Bordeaux shad—have been appearing in French culinary writing since the 13th century. Some consider it the finest of all white fish, and Brillat-Savarin wrote, "It is one of the purest and suavest joys of Lent."

Shad may be prepared using any recipe suitable for herring or mackerel. A favorite American way of preparing it is stuffed with crab meat and baked on a wooden plank.

SHADBUSH

See **Juneberry.**

SHADDOCK

This large, yellow, pear-shaped citrus fruit, *Citrus maxima*, similar to the grapefruit in appearance and taste, was brought to the New World from the East Indies by a Captain Shaddock in 1696. The shaddock is grown commercially in Florida and to some extent

Shaddocks

in California. The pulp is either pallid, like grapefruit, or red. The rind is thicker and grainier than grapefruit.

The shaddock and its tree are sometimes called "pummelo" (or "pomelo"). A huge, red-fleshed variety is grown in India and was named "forbidden fruit" by the British. The tangelo is a hybrid of tangerine and the shaddock or pomelo.

SHAG BARK

See **Hickory Nut.**

SHAGGY INK CAP

See **Shaggy Mane.**

SHAGGY MANE

Also SHAGGY INK CAP. This is the best-tasting mushroom of the ink cap genus. Also called the horse tail, the shaggy mane *(Coprinus comatus)* is a tall, slender mushroom (up to 10 inches tall; up to three inches in diameter) whose cap when young resembles a guard's shako. It appears after heavy rain in spring and fall. With other ink cap mushrooms, it shares the unusual characteristic of melting into ink shortly after reaching maturity. This process is called "autodigestion" and causes the release of spores. It is a safe mushroom to gather because it is not easily confused with toxic varieties.

The ancient Romans were fond of this mushroom. Pliny recorded the existence of an edible "white fungus whose head stems are similar in form to the caps of the Flamens." Flamens were priests whose caps, as pictured on coins and wall paintings, do resemble shaggy manes.

Gastronomically, the shaggy mane is very choice and easily digested. The taste of its flesh is not bland, and when sauteed emits a heady aroma of wild mushroom. It is excellent in cream sauce, with eggs and as a garnish with meat. This mushroom must be cooked with a certain amount of dispatch because liquefaction occurs from four to six hours after picking.

See also: **Ink Cap, Mushroom.**

SHALLON

Also SALAL. This purple black fruit of a flowering shrub, *Gaultheria shallon*, of western North America, is found from Alaska to Southern California. The fruit ripens in spring and early summer and is dried to be eaten during winter months. Florists know the foliage of this plant as lemonleaf.

SHALLOT

Like the onion and garlic, the shallot *(Allium ascalonicum)* is a bulbous member of the lily family. Its taste is onionlike, but milder. Although generally larger in size, it resembles garlic in form, i.e., the bulb consists of several segments, which are easily separated. Some detect a slight taste of garlic in the shallot. In any case, it is considered easier to digest than either onion or garlic. The shallot is used chiefly as a flavoring agent in sauces, stews, soups and pickling solutions and often in dried or powdered form.

A shallot bulb is usually no larger than a walnut or a small fig and is covered by a thick outer skin, which varies in color from red to gray. The cloves themselves range from green in some parts to violet in others. The Jersey shallot is quite similar in appearance but larger. It is called the "false shallot" because it propagates like the onion, from seed, whereas the true shallot propagates by bulblets cast

Shallots

off from a mature plant. Popular usage promotes confusion between the shallot and the **scallion** by using the two terms interchangeably. Properly speaking, the scallion is a bulbless onion, also called spring onion or Welsh onion.

The shallot is believed to be native to Central Asia but takes its name from Ashkelon, one of the five royal cities of the ancient land of Canaan, as does the scallion. Although it is not certain what sort of onion Ashkelon produced 3,000 years ago—shallots, scallions, or common onions—the last kind is being produced in that area today. Pliny the Elder wrote about shallots in the first century A.D., noting that the ones from Megara in Greece were best. Ovid recommended the white shallots from Megara as an aphrodisiac. According to tradition, shallots were introduced into England by Crusaders returning from the Holy Land in the 13th century.

SHARK

This widely distributed family of predator fish ranges in size up to 30 feet long and inspires more fear than gastronomic interest in the ordinary person. Yet certain species are regularly eaten in Europe and the Far East. Apart from the **dogfish,** shark has never been popular fare in the United States, tabooed perhaps by its fearsome image as a mankiller, which is true for only a limited number of the larger species. A good case can be made for shark flesh. It is white, firm and has a mild taste, and is tender, especially steaks and fillets from the flesh along the backbone. Shark is economical in that, being cartilaginous rather than bony, 42 percent of its weight is recovered as steaks and fillets, as opposed to 20 percent for most bony fish. Moreover, it is high in protein (22.7 percent) and low in fat (0.5 percent) when compared to steak (14.7 percent and 32.1 percent) or even salmon (16.2 percent and 11.5 percent). This makes it low in calories. In addition, it contains generous amounts of minerals and vitamins A and B but is low in sodium.

Shark steak is most often compared to swordfish and halibut, and, indeed, masquerades as such in many restaurants. This is changing; shark is appearing on more and more menus under its own name, perhaps because of the growing scarcity and rising prices of other food fish. The bull shark is the most popular, accounting for a large proportion of commercially processed shark meat. Known as veal of the sea, it rarely exceeds 40 pounds in weight.

Other sharks frequently taken for food are the Atlantic sharpnose, the bonnetnose, the blacktip, the Pacific thresher, the tiger, hammerhead and the great white shark. In Australia, sharkmeat accounts for a large portion of fish sold in fish and chip stands. One of the more exotic ways of preparing shark is the *Hakarl*, or fermented shark of Iceland, which, after being gutted, is buried in the sand or kept in an open barrel for three years. *Harkarl* is rich in ammonia and has a taste that most resembles ripe cheese. Sharks are hunted for the oil in their liver, particularly the larger varieties such as the basking shark, which can yield as much as 1½ tons of oil per fish.

The shark's fin is a particular delicacy of China. It is salted and dried in the sun and yields a rich, high-quality gelatin when used to make shark-fin soup. Other ingredients in this example of Chinese *haute cuisine* are chicken stock, shreds of chicken meat, shredded crabmeat, minced smoked ham and minced scallions. A species prized for its fin is the soup-fin shark or gray tope *(Galeorhinus zyopterus)* of the Pacific Ocean.

SHARKSUCKER

Also SUCKERFISH. A long, slender fish that attaches itself to a larger fish by means of a sucker and feeds on the other parasites attached to the host, the sharksucker *(Echeneis naucrates)* is one of a family of such fish, but is larger than most, reaching a length of three feet. It has proven itself useful to humans in the following way. The Torres Strait islanders tie a line to its tail and release it near a large turtle. The sharksucker immediately attaches itself to the turtle, and the fishermen reel in the line and capture the turtle. The fish is itself edible, as is its cousin, the remora.

SHEA BUTTER

Also GALAM BUTTER. This is a solid fat obtained from the nuts of the shea tree *(Bassia parkii)*, which is native to Central Africa. It is also known as bambuck butter and galam butter. The shea nut is about the size and shape of a walnut but more resembles a chestnut. It is edible raw but is more often crushed and boiled to produce the butter, which is used in food preparations, chocolate manufacture, artificial butter, and in the manufacture of soap and candles. Africans make an edible oil cake from the butter as well. Other edible parts of the tree, which the Africans call *meepampa*, are the flower calyces, and the fruit pulp which surrounds the seeds.

SHEARWATER

Also MUTTON BIRD. This is a petrel *(Oestrelata lessoni)* of antarctic seas considered good eating in Australia when it is young and fat.

SHEEP

See **Lamb, Mutton.**

SHEEPBERRY

Also NANNYBERRY. This is the edible, blue black fruit of the shrubs *Vibernum lentago* and *V. prunifolium*, which are native to eastern North America. The berries are sweet and flavorful, but the *V. prunifolium* is usually not palatable until after the first frost. It is also used in jams and jellies.

SHEEPSHEAD

This valuable food fish, *Archosargus probatocephalus*, of the Atlantic Coast of the United States, is found from Massachusetts to Texas. Its name derives from the shape of its head and its broad incisor teeth, which it uses to detach shellfish from the bottom of the sea. The sheepshead reaches a length of 30 inches and weighs an average of seven to eight pounds, with very large specimens going as high as 20 pounds. Its flesh is white and flaky and tastes much like that of its favorite prey, shellfish, and for that reason it is sometimes slipped into crabmeat cocktails by unscrupulous restaurant owners. The sheepshead is a deep-bodied fish with several dark transverse bands across its body.

The California sheepshead *(Pimelometopon pulchrum)* is a similarly-sized fish, with curved incisor teeth and a rounded nape that gives it a bump-headed look. It is a member of the wrasse family and, though edible, is not nearly the table delicacy of the Atlantic sheepshead.

The freshwater drumfish of Texas and Louisiana is sometimes called "sheepshead." (See **Croaker).** "Sheepshead" is also a name the English give to the gray and red **breams** of the eastern Atlantic.

SHEFFIELD'S O_2 WATER

A mineral spring water, carbonated and bottled in the United States, it is relatively low in mineral content, i.e., just 73 ppm of total dissolved solids. A 1980 Consumers Union sensory panel rated the taste of this water as fair, with the following qualifying comments: mildly bitter, mild chemical flavor, mildly salty, distinctly sour, mild sour aftertaste.

See also: **Mineral Water.**

SHELDRAKE

A strikingly colored wild duck, *Tadorna vulpanser*, found all over Europe, it was a popular table bird in medieval France where an unsuccessful attempt was made to domesticate it. The sheldrake is larger than the **mallard,** but not nearly as good to eat. Both the duck and its eggs are popular fare in the Frisian Islands, however.

SHELLBARK

See **Hickory Nut.**

SHELLFISH

This is an aquatic animal whose external covering consists of a shell. Examples are clams, cockles, crabs, crayfish, limpets, lobsters, mussels, oysters, scallops, shrimps, whelks and winkles. They are rich in protein, vitamin B, iodine and mineral salts. See also under the names of individual shellfish.

SHEPHERD'S PURSE

See **Lamb's Lettuce.**

SHERBET

See **Ice Cream.**

SHERRY

This is the famous Spanish wine from Jerez de la Frontera, in the province of Cadiz. The name comes from the Phoenician *Xera*, "a town situated close to the Pillars of Hercules," renamed *Sherisch* by the Moors, from which comes the English "sherry." The wine known as sherry is legally protected and comes from grapes gathered within a restricted area of eight communes near Cadiz.

Two grape varieties, the Palomino and the Pedro Ximenez, and two white subvarieties of the Palomino—the Fino and the Jerez—make up more than 70 percent of the vines in the district. The grapes are gathered in September when fully ripe, when they change color from green to a dark tobacco brown, and when the stalks become woody. They are picked in stages, as only the ripest ones are chosen, placed in baskets of about 25 pounds each, transported to the *almijar* (a platform of beaten earth) where they are spread in the sun before pressing. A special feature in the production of sherry is "plastering," or the addition of a small, strictly regulated amount of gypsum (calcium sulphate) to the wine to induce the necessary amount of acidity.

Sherry is aged in cellars located within the three communes of Jerez, Puerto de Santa Maria and Sanlucar de Barrameda. The cellars are above ground. The casks are stacked lengthwise above each other in rows of three. Air is vital to the maturing process. The cellars are open to the southwest for the sea breeze. Here the wine is classified as *fino*, as fuller-bodied or as sweeter and sharper. It is then fortified, in March, with additional alcohol. Here too occurs the action of *flor*, (flower) which determines the aroma and the taste peculiar to sherry. Microorganisms that live in the wine and feed on its components form a weblike substance that "blossoms" over the surface of the wine. With the *amontillado* wine called *fino* (pale dry) the *flor* is allowed to proceed during the first years of aging until the wine is bottled. With the *olorosos* (sweet dark sherry), the development of the *flor* is muted by the addition of some wine alcohol.

Aging takes place in the cask lowest to the ground *(sole)*. Above the row of sole casks are the two *criaderas* (breeders). The wine to be marketed it drawn off from the *sole* casks. These are then filled with slightly younger wine from the *criadera* directly above, but with never more than 50 percent, so the remaining old wine "teaches" its virtues to the new, younger wine. There is no such thing, then, as a vintage sherry. The casks are continually and carefully blended. They are only partly-filled to give air access to the wine and to permit the formation of *flor*, which blossoms twice a year.

The major types of sherry are these:

Finos: light, dry, straw-colored, with an alcohol strength of from 15.5 to 17 percent. These include

Shiitake

the *amontillados*, which are very dry, strong (16 to 18 percent), amber in color, and have a nutty taste.

Olorosos: darker, heavier, stronger than the finos. Cream sherry is a blend of dry olorosos with some Pedro Ximenez wine.

Dulces: deep-colored, sweet wines. The Pedro Ximenez is a naturally sweet wine of this type, as is the Moscatel.

Some competent sherries are produced in California and in South Africa; but none of these has so far been able seriously to rival the strong, rich wine of Jerez de la Frontera. Perhaps the most fanatical of all sherry lovers was Falstaff. "If I had a thousand sons," he swore, "the first humane principle I would teach them should be to forswear thin potations and to addict themselves to sack."

SHIITAKE

Also HOANG ME. This edible mushroom is essential to Japanese and Chinese cuisines. As a cultivated mushroom, it is second only to the familiar common mushroom *(Agaricus bisporus)* of the West. The shiitake *(Lentinus edodes)* has a solid reputation in the Far East both as a taste treat and a health food. Research in Japan produced evidence that substances in the shiitake lower the cholesterol level in the blood, while creating antibodies that help ward off invading viruses such as the flu.

The name shiitake means "oak fungus" in Japanese, and, indeed, these mushrooms grow on oak trees or oak logs placed in shady areas. The plant has a brown cap, pure white gills and extends outward from the trunk on a thick stem. The Japanese use them in sukiyaki and tempura dishes, and the Chinese in soups, stews or with pork and beef. Fresh mushrooms, lightly sauteed, are said to have a meaty taste and texture reminiscent of the finest steak, plus overtones of mushroom flavor. In the market, shiitake are usually found dried, packed in small transparent bags labeled forest mushrooms, black mushrooms, black forest mushrooms, shiitake, or just dried mushrooms from Japan. The dried caps are one to two inches in diameter and just one imparts an impressive amount of flavor. The United States boasts commercial cultivation of shiitake on both coasts, such that fresh mushrooms are becoming increasingly available in the markets. They can be grown at home, too, from a kit.

Nutritionally, the shiitake is above average for mushrooms, having twice the protein of the cultivated mushroom *A. bisporus*, plus unusual amounts of calcium, phosphorus, iron and vitamin D.

See also: **Mushroom.**

SHINER PERCH

A very abundant surf perch, *Cymatogaster aggregata*, found along the Pacific coast of North America from Alaska to Southern California, it attains a maximum length of eight inches. Most of those caught are under four inches. The shiner perch is roundish, flat and silver with light yellow and greenish markings on the side. During the summer, it is found inshore in small schools and is most frequently taken from piers. The shiner perch is a small but tasty morsel.

SHIRAZ

This grape produces a sweet, full-bodied red wine known as Sirah or Syrah in France and California. The shiraz is a very popular grape in South Africa, where it gives a heady wine with a rich bouquet, although it is more frequently mixed with grapes from the Douro vines—imported from Portugal—to make a South African **port.** In Australia, the Shiraz is known as **Cabernet,** Cabernet Shiraz, or sometimes Hermitage. Here, as in South Africa, the shiraz grape makes a strong, fruity wine with a strong bouquet but requires long aging.

SHORE PODGRASS

A perennial herb, *Triglochin maritima*, found in salt and freshwater marshes of North America and Eurasia, whose very young leaves may be used in salads, it is considered a useful emergency food plant.

SHORT-NOSED GARFISH

A saltwater halfbeak, *Hemiramphus quoyi*, found in Australian and New Guinea waters, it is regarded as a high quality food fish. It is a schooling fish that reaches a maximum length of 14 inches. The schools move close inshore and are taken with beach seines. The lower jaw of this fish is prolonged into a beak, but one that is shorter than other halfbeaks, such as the **ballyhoo** and the **black-barred garfish.**

SHOVELER

A wild duck, *Spatula clypeata*, found in both Europe and North America, it is characterized by brilliant plumage and a very long, flattened bill. The flesh of this duck is succulent and highly prized by gourmets provided it has been feeding on the right sort of diet. It is prepared like other wild **duck.** The shoveler is also known as the spoonbill and the river duck.

SHOVELNOSE

Also SAND SHARK. The largest of the Indo-Pacific guitarfishes (family *Rhynchobatidae*), the shovelnose *(Rhynochobatus djeddensis)* is a coveted game fish in South Africa and Australia, where specimens have been landed weighing more than 500 pounds and reaching a length of 10 feet or more. It has a bluntly triangular snout and relatively slender body. The shovelnose is a deepwater fish and is not commercially exploited. Its flesh is more highly regarded than that of a similar species, the **shovel-nose ray,** being firm and white with a flavor reminiscent of prawns.

SHOVEL-NOSE RAY

An Australian species related to the guitarfish (family *Rhinobatidae)* of the Atlantic Ocean, it is a raylike fish with a slender body and a pointed snout that forms a triangle with the pectoral fins. The flesh of this fish is rated quite good when taken from young specimens, and it regularly appears in the fish markets of North Australia and Queensland. Mature fish can reach a length of seven feet. It frequents shallow water, and some fish are able to live in brackish and even fresh water.

See also: **Skate.**

SHRIKE

Also BUTCHERBIRD. This is a small, perching bird, *Lanius excubitor*, of Europe, which feeds on insects, frogs, small birds, etc. It is eaten in France much in the same way as the **lark.** The North American counterpart is the northern butcherbird *(Laneius borealis).*

SHRIMP

Also PRAWN. Shrimp are smaller, clawless crustaceans of the *Decapoda* (ten-legged) order whose larger members are **lobster** and **crayfish.** There are hundreds of species of shrimp worldwide, but most of them live in the Northern Hemisphere, inhabiting the muddy bottoms of oceans and rivers. Though small, shrimp are relatively long and slender, with a leathery shell. The brown, or gray, common shrimp *(Crangon crangon)* of Europe and the *Crangon vulgaris* of the Atlantic and Pacific Coasts of the United States are quite similar. They have greenish gray backs with brown dots, are two to three inches long and turn reddish brown when cooked.

In England, the term "prawn" means a shrimp more than two to three inches long, while in the

Arctic shrimp

United States it is applied to some shrimp without, apparently, conforming to any particular rule. Also in popular usage, the name "shrimp" is applied to other creatures, which, though they may resemble shrimp, are not related, such as the mantis shrimp, which is a **squill fish;** the Dublin Bay Prawn, or *scampi*, which is a **Norway lobster,** and the Peruvian *camaron* (Spanish for shrimp), which is a crayfish.

Gastronomically, shrimp is the most popular crustacean in the United States, followed, not very closely, by crab and lobster. American consumption runs 500 million pounds a year. Shrimp are priced by size, of which there are six categories: giant, 10 to 12 per pound; jumbo, 15 to 20; large, 20 to 25; medium, 25 to 35; small, 35 to 45, and tiny, 75 to 100.

Eighty-five percent of the American catch comes from the Gulf of Mexico, the giant Campeche Gulf shrimp being the most desirable species. It comes out of the water purplish blue and turns pink when cooked. In the same geographical area giant freshwater shrimp are also found, most notably the West Indian *(Macrobrachium jamaicense).* A shrimp of this type weighing three pounds was taken from the Devils River in Texas.

New Orleans is the premier shrimp-eating city in the United States, although by weight New York consumes more because of the sheer size of the market. In New Orleans, shrimp liver, or tomalley, is highly prized, but it is often mistakenly described as "brain" because of its location in the shrimp's head. A small, sweet white shrimp is found in Northeastern coastal waters, while the large (5 inches in length), striped California shrimp *(Crangon franciscorum)* is found from California to Alaska.

Shrimp are farmed commercially in Mexico along the Gulf of California in tanks constantly supplied with filtered seawater. Female shrimp lay more than 100,000 eggs at a time, and in the artificial atmosphere more than 30 percent survive to mature over a 20-week period, which is many times the number that would survive in a state of nature. The smallest shrimp to be fished commercially is the pygmy shrimp *(Artemia salina)*. It resembles a small worm and is fed to cultivated shrimp, a natural predator in the wild.

The ancient Greeks and Romans liked shrimp, preferring the larger ones to lobster. They were usually cooked in fig leaves. *Liquamen*, the finest grade Roman seasoner, was prepared from shrimp. In modern times, Americans are the biggest shrimp eaters, but Danes and Japanese are also passionately fond of shrimp. In Copenhagen, they are sold from pushcarts with a slice of buttered bread; in Japan they can be purchased live from street stands where, after a swift decapitation, they are eaten raw and wriggling.

In the West, fresh shrimp are usually shelled, then cooked for 10 minutes in boiling salt water, preferably seawater. They may also be purchased frozen or canned.

SHRUB

A drink that became popular in the 18th century, it usually has an alcoholic base, such as brandy or rum, but may be made of just fruit juices, sugar and water. The normal formula for shrub consists of the liquor, plus lemon juice, lemon and orange rind and sugar. All the ingredients but the sugar are mixed together and allowed to steep for a few months. The result is sweetened to taste, strained and bottled. It may be drunk straight as a liqueur or mixed with water or soda water and drunk as a refreshing iced drink.

SHUNGIKU

See **Chrysanthemum.**

SIAMESE CARP

Notable for being one of the largest members of the carp family, the Siamese carp *(Catlocarpio siamensis)* is an important food fish in Thailand. It reaches a length of about 10 feet and is found in the larger rivers of Thailand, Cambodia and Vietnam. It is netted or caught on lines baited with rice balls. The fisherman who hooks it may be taken for a ride in his boat for several hours before the fish tires.

SICKLEFISH

Also CONCERTINAFISH. An abundant food fish in tropical Africa and Madagascar, the sicklefish *(Drepane punctata)* is widely distributed in the Indo-Pacific area. The sicklefish has a very deep, almost diamond- shaped body with a bright silver gray color above and rows of dusky spots on its sides. It may be as long as 15 inches and lives in shallow water on sandy or muddy bottoms.

SIEVA BEAN

Also BUTTER BEAN, CIVET BEAN, SEWEE BEAN, CAROLINA BEAN. An edible bean, *Phaseolus lunatus*, which is very similar to the **lima bean,** it is native to tropical South America, and today is an important food crop in tropical Africa, especially Madagascar and Mauritius.

SIFAKA

A tree-dwelling mammal of Madagascar, the sifaka *(Propithecus diadema)* is closely related to the lemur and is similar in appearance, but generally larger. It reaches a length of about 42 inches and is covered by soft fur. The *sifaka* is rarely seen outside of Madagascar because it does not adapt well in captivity. In some areas of Madagascar, the *sifaka* is hunted for meat.

SILESIAN CHEESE

Also SCHLESICHE WEICHQUARG. This sour-milk cheese, frequently flavored with onions or caraway seeds, has a sharp taste and firm texture similar to **hand cheese.** The curd is cooked and kneaded for firmness, then milk or cream is added. This cheese is eaten fresh or after brief ripening.

SILK COTTON TREE

The name is applied to at least two species of trees, the *Ceiba petandra* and the *Cochlospermum religiosum. C. petandra* is also known as the white silk cotton tree and the kapok tree. It is cultivated in many tropical areas throughout the world for the commercial fiber, kapok, but also for its young leaves and buds, which are cooked as greens in Jamaica; its flower petals, which are eaten in China; and its calyces and seeds, which are eaten in Africa. An edible oil may also be extracted from the seeds. **C. religiosum** is cultivated in Burma and India as a source of an edible gum, which can be used as a substitute for gum **tragacanth.**

See also: **Kapok.**

SILKWORM

See **Caterpillar.**

SILKY SOPHORA

The roots of this woody, leguminous plant, *Sophora sericea*, are edible. Considered a delicacy in New Mexico, the roots are pleasant tasting, even sweet, and are cooked before being served.

SILLABUB

See **Syllabub.**

SILLERY WINE

Here is a "still" (not effervescent) red or white wine from **Champagne,** grown in the commune of Sillery near the Marne in north-central France. Like the better known red **Bouzy** from this region, sillery wine resembles good **Burgundy Wines** in robustness and flavor but has a slight fruitiness. It should be drunk when slightly chilled.

SILOND CATFISH

A large catfish of the Ganges River, the silond *(Silonia silonia)* is highly regarded as a food fish and is also popular with anglers. Specimens in the six-foot range have been landed but are now rare due to overfishing. For information on other huge Indian catfish, see **Pungas Catfish.**

SILPHIUM

An herb highly esteemed by ancient Romans as a flavoring agent, it went out of use during the time of the Emperor Nero (37–68 A.D.) and never reappeared. Its botanical identity has never been established. Modern writers have speculated that it was laserwort *(Laserpitium latifolium)*, a variety of **asafetida.** In any case, it was asafetida, from which is made a very pungent resin, that replaced silphium in the Roman kitchen.

The chief source of silphium was the former Greek colony of Cyrenaica. It was located in North Africa, near the modern city of Bengazi, Libya. Cyrenaica was famous for two exports: horses and silphium. Silphium was expensive, and the Roman cookbook of Apicius gives a tip on how to stretch the supply of silphium by storing it in a jar of pine nuts, which become impregnated with silphium's aroma and can be used in its place. The disappearance of silphium is attributed to overcropping.

See also: **Garum.**

SILVER CARP

Also TOLSTOL. This is a large carp, *Hypophthalmichthys molitrix*, of China and eastern Russia, which is a valuable commercial food fish throughout its range. It is native to the Amur basin but has been introduced into other rivers, and in China is raised on fish farms. The silver carp lives on plant plankton and reaches a maximum length of 3½ feet. Its flesh is described as very tasty. Despite its size, this fish, when disturbed, leaps clear out of the water, occasionally landing in the boat that caused the disturbance.

SILVERFISH

Also GREAT AMBERJACK, PEZ DE LIMON. A large game fish, *Seriola dumerili*, found on both sides of the Atlantic Ocean and in the Mediterranean, it can exceed six feet in length and weigh up to 175 pounds. The silverfish is especially plentiful off Spain and Morocco where it is highly thought of as food. The Spanish call it *pez de limon* and usually cut it into steaks for broiling or poaching.

The silverfish is green or blue above and silver or white below. Large specimens are taken in the West Indies, but are suspect as food, since the fish has been known to cause *ciguatera*, a fish poisoning passed on in the food chains of the reef. It is related to the yellowtail.

See also: **Amberfish.**

SILVER GRUNTER

Also GRUNTER BREAM, SPOTTED JAVELIN FISH. A moderately sized, slender-bodied food fish of the Indian and Pacific Oceans, the silver grunter *(Pomadasys hasta)* reaches a length of about two feet and has an olive-green back and silver sides. Its name derives from the grunting noises it makes when caught. The fish produces these noises by grinding its teeth together and amplifying the sound with its swim bladder.

The silver grunter is considered a valuable food fish from the Red Sea and the coast of East Africa all the way to the east coast of Australia.

SILVER PERCH

This Australian freshwater sportfish, *Bidyanus bidyanus*, is more akin to the sea bass than the perch. The silver perch reaches a length of 16 inches and is found in the Murray-Darling river system and a few coastal streams of New South Wales. The silver perch has a long and prominent dorsal fin and an overall silvery color with brown reticulations on the back. It is related to the ocean-dwelling **tigerfish** of Asian waters. It is popular with anglers, and its flesh is said to be firm and tasty.

SILVERSIDE

Also SAND SMELT. This is a family, *Atherinidae*, of small saltwater fish that typically have a brilliant silver line running along the side from head to tail. Common species are the atherine or sand smelt *(Atherina presbyter)* of the eastern Atlantic, the hardhead silverside *(Atherinomorus stipes)* of the middle Atlantic and Caribbean, and the Atlantic silverside *(Menidia menidia)*. In size, they measure five to six inches long and mass together in large schools. Some species spawn on sandy beaches at the low water mark, as does the **grunion.** Silversides are not commercially exploited but are delicious to eat. They are prepared like **smelt.**

See also: **Whitebait.**

SILVER VINE

A climbing shrub of temperate eastern Asia, *Actinidia polygama*, is related to the kiwi fruit vine. It produces a yellow, round fruit, averaging about one inch in diameter, which is eaten in Japan. The Japanese salt the fruit and eat it together with the decorative leaves.

SILVERWEED

Also GOOSE TANSY. The roots of this cosmopolitan herb are edible as a cooked vegetable. Silverweed *(Potentilla anserina)* grows in damp, grassy and waste places in temperate areas of North America, Europe and Asia. The leaves are silky white on both surfaces.

SIMAROUBA

Also ACEITUNO, BITTERWOOD, PARADISE TREE. Native to the American tropics, the simarouba *(Simarouba glauca)* is a large, leafy tree whose bark is the source of bitters, and whose seeds yield an edible oil. It is found in southern Florida, the West Indies, and from Mexico to Costa Rica. It is cultivated in El Salvador for its oil.

SIMCAMAS

See **Jicama.**

SING-KWA

Also ANGLED LOOFAH. The club-shaped fruit of this tropical vine, *Luffa acutangula*, is used for food in the Orient when it is young and tender. When ripe, the fruit is up to 12 inches long and has sharp ridges running its length.

SIRAZ

This semisoft cheese made in Serbia from whole cow's milk is formed by hand into round, flat cakes, which are dried in the sun and then cured in wooden containers. The mature cheese has a compact, eyeless body and a mellow taste.

SIRENE

This staple Bulgarian cheese made from sheep's milk has a good, mild taste that is slightly sour and salty. The paste is semisoft and creamy. Individual cheeses are matured for at least seven weeks and have an unusual, six-sided shape. They weigh between one and 2½ pounds.

SIR IZ MJESINE

This Yugoslavian cheese is made from ewe's skim milk in Dalmatia. After coagulation, the curd is heated to firm it up. The cheese is formed into eight-inch squares, two inches thick and is sometimes eaten fresh. If not, the cheese is dried, cubed, salted and aged in fresh goat or sheep skin.

SIR MASTNY

This Yugoslavian cheese is made of sheep's milk in Montenegro. Rennet is added to fresh, whole milk and the cheeses are molded in forms.

SIR POSNY

Also TORD, MRSAV. This hard, white Yugoslavian cheese is made of ewe's milk in Montenegro. Rennet is added to skim milk and the resulting curds are molded in forms. After aging, the paste has many small holes.

SKATE

Also RAY. This flat, saltwater fish is of the genus *Raia*, which has several edible species. Europeans appreciate skates as food far more than Americans, who have only recently come around to them. The common skate *(Raia batis)* is the kind most frequently eaten by the British and the French. It can weigh as much as 150 pounds, but the smaller specimens make better eating. The barn door skate *(R. laevis)* is found on both sides of the Atlantic and is the kind most commonly eaten on the United States East Coast. It averages four feet in length. Two other species often seen in markets are the sand rock skate and the buckled skate, both of which are small.

The skate is characterized by a pointed nose and large winglike pectoral fins, which contain the best muscle meat. The head may be flat or protuberant, depending on the species, with the eyes on top or at the side of the head. The mouth is on the ventral side, which is white. The skin, which is gray or mottled on top, is often stripped off because it tends to be tough. The meat is white and coarse, but has good flavor. Unlike most fish, the skate is sometimes aged for a day or two to improve its flavor, giving it a redolence of ammonia. This is a matter of individual preference, but it also makes it more tender.

In Europe the most popular way of preparing skate is to cut meat off the wings in thick strips six inches long, poach them in *court bouillon* and serve them with black butter sauce. They may also be deep-fried in batter fish-and-chips style. A small whole skate may be marinated in milk or lemon juice, dusted with flour and deep-fried. In the United States, unscrupulous fish dealers or restauranteurs punch disklike rounds of skate meat out of the pectoral areas and sell them as scallops. Skate meat consists of from 18.2 to 24.2 percent protein, far more than beefsteak, and with virtually no fat.

Many gourmets fancy skate liver and prepare it in a variety of ways, poached, jellied, in a crust or as fritters. It is obtainable only where the fish is landed. Skate, being very gelatinous, also makes a good soup.

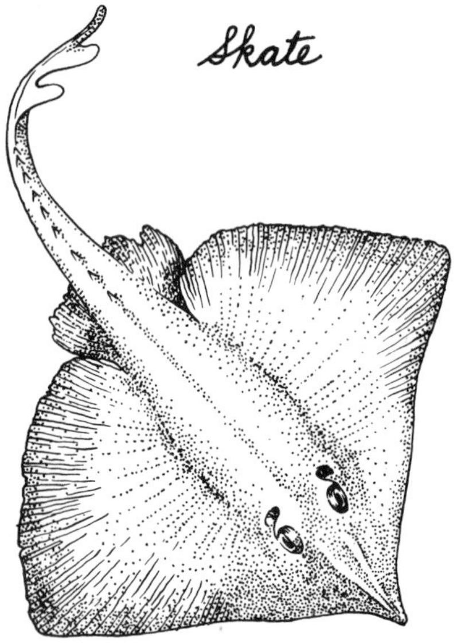

SKILFISH

A commercially important food fish in Japan, the skilfish *(Erilepis zonifer)* is found throughout the North Pacific Ocean, including the coastal waters of California. It is a large fish, often exceeding six feet in length and is closely related to the **sablefish.** Not much is known about this fish, but its flesh is quite oily, which the Japanese greatly appreciate during their cold, wet winter.

SKIM-MILK RUNDKASE

See **Radener.**

SKIRRET

Also CHERVIN. The clustered, tuberous roots of this aromatic herb, *Sium sisarum*, are edible and may be cooked like **salsify.** The plant originated in eastern Asia and is still popular there, but has been cultivated in Europe since Roman times. The Emperor Tiberius reportedly imported skirret roots from Germany. Skirret continued to be frequently cultivated in the West until the 20th century. It has now lapsed into obscurity.

Skirret roots are grayish white and irregularly shaped. They have a sweet taste and a woody core that is removed before cooking. The taste has been compared to that of sweet potato. The plant is a hardy perennial and may be sown in the autumn or the spring. It is hardy enough to remain in the ground during the winter months, and thus may be pulled from the ground when convenient. Skirret roots may also be dried, ground and used as a coffee substitute. The plant is closely related to the **water parsnip.**

SKUNK CABBAGE

Also POLECAT WEED, SWAMP CABBAGE. This plant gives off a disagreeable, skunklike odor when bruised, yet it yields an excellent, edible tuber. Skunk cabbage *(Symplocarpus foetidus)* is a hardy, perennial herb of swamps and wet woods of northeast Asia and North America. Its stout rhizomes, or tubers, are dried, and then baked for food. The leaf stalks are delicious too, but must be boiled with two or three changes of water to get rid of the smell.

SLAW

See **Cabbage.**

SLEEVE FISH

See **Squid.**

SLIMY

Also SOAPY. This fish of the Indian and Pacific Oceans is widely eaten despite the copious coating of slime on its skin. The slimy *(Leiognathus equula)* has a slender, deep body that seldom exceeds 12 inches in length. A marked characteristic is its ability to project its seemingly small mouth into a long, downward-pointing tube. It is an abundant, staple food fish throughout its range, which extends from East Africa to Australia and Japan.

SLIPCOTE

Also COLWICK. This soft English cheese has been made from whole cow's milk in Rutlandshire since the 18th century. The name derives from the condition of the cheese's surface when it is ripe and ready to eat. The surface becomes soft and loose and tends to slip off. Cheeses are laid between cabbage leaves to ripen, which takes only three days to a week. They are round or square, measuring at the most six inches wide by two thick.

SLIVOVITZ

This plum brandy is popular in such Central European countries as Hungary and Rumania, but especially in Yugoslavia where it is considered the national drink of the Bosnian and Serbian republics. It is amber in color from being aged in wood, dry and fiery in taste, with overtones of bitter almond.

To prepare slivovitz, ripe plums are mixed and mashed in a wooden tub and allowed to ferment, stones and all, for six weeks. The contents of the tub then constitute the mash, which is twice distilled in a pot still, emerging at about 100 proof. It is oil from the stones—distilled with the alcohol—that imparts the desired bitter flavor. Slivovitz is aged for at least a year before bottling. Other, similar plum brandies of Europe are known as *quetsch* (Germany), *mirabelle* and *prunelle* (France), and *Pfumli* (Switzerland).

SLOE

Also BLACKTHORN, SLOEBERRY. Sloe is the purplish fruit of a small shrub, *Prunus spinosa*, which grows wild in Europe, Great Britain and the United States. The sloe is a close relative of the plum; it is round in shape, and commonly reaches the size of a large pea. The fruit is not palatable raw, because it is very bitter. Its primary use is as a flavoring agent in liqueurs, such as **sloe gin,** and *eau de vie de prunelle des Vosges*. It is cultivated in two areas of France, near Aggers and at Haute-Saone, where, in addition to the liqueur, it is used to make jam. The United States variety is used to make jam only if it has been exposed to frost, which reduces the bitterness.

See also: **Sloe Gin.**

SLOE GIN

Here is a well-known and delicious liqueur flavored by the sloeberry, a small, bitter fruit closely related to the plum. Home recipes for making this liqueur call for steeping sloes in sweetened gin for three months to obtain the desired flavor. Commercial sloe gin is gin in name only because it does not contain juniper flavoring. Sloe gin is red and very sweet, with a slightly bitter aftertaste. It is bottled at 42 proof.

SLOKE

See **Laver.**

SMALLAGE

See **Celery Seed.**

SMELT

Also SPARLING. These small fish of the family *Osmeridae* are related to the salmon and, being migratory, are found in both fresh and salt water bodies of the Northern Hemisphere. The smelt *(O. eperlanus)* of Europe reaches a length of about 12 inches and is found from the Bay of Biscay to the Baltic and White Seas. It is a slender, silvery fish with an olive-green back whose flesh has a pleasant smell of cucumbers. It is known as *eperlan* in France and sparling in Scotland. A favorite way of preparing smelts is to gut them, roll them in flour, then quickly fry them and serve with lemon.

The Asiatic smelt *(O. dentex)* reaches a length of 16 inches and is common in the North Pacific and arctic areas of Russia and North America. A closely related species, the rainbow smelt *(O. mordax)*, is found in both the Atlantic and Pacific, and a landlocked variety thrives in the Great Lakes. The rainbow smelt supports commercial fisheries in both Russia and the United States.

SNAIL

Land snails have been an item in the human diet for millennia, despite strong disapproval in certain quarters, such as the Bible. According to Leviticus 11:29–30: "These also shall be unclean unto you among the creeping things that creep upon the earth; the weasel, and the mouse and the tortoise after his kind. And the ferret, and the chameleon, and the lizard, and the snail and the mole."

Snails

Archaeological evidence suggests prehistoric peoples ate snails, as did the ancient Franks, Chinese and Peruvians, perhaps more in times of scarcity than as regular fare.

The ancient Romans' special fondness for them is evident in the fact that one Fulvius Lupinus is credited by Pliny the Elder with running the first commercial snail farm near Pompeii in the first century B.C. He fed them on meal and boiled wine. The species farmed by the Romans was the Burgundy, or large white snail *(Helix pomatia)*, although they considered a great delicacy the giant snail, large as a man's fist, which they imported from Africa, and which is still eaten there today. The Burgundy snail has a grayish yellow to grayish red shell with irregular markings. It was introduced by the Romans into Britain, where it remained a traditional food through the 19th century in the west of England, especially around the Mendip Hills. It was known locally as "wallfish." Otherwise, the British, like the Americans, are generally not snail eaters.

France is today the leading consumer of snails, followed by Italy, Spain and Belgium. The Burgundy snail is favored in the north of France. They are raised on farms or gathered wild in the spring. Grape leaves or lettuce is the usual food, although they may be fed thyme or other herbs if a special flavor is desired. They are almost invariably served in the shell with a garlic butter sauce, but the method of preparation is complex and involves removing them from their shells, using two different cleaning solutions, boiling them, then returning them to their shells. The French name for them is *escargot*, and they are available canned, already cleaned.

A more popular species in the south of France is the small gray snail *(Helix aspera)*, which in California is known as the common garden snail. It is served in a variety of ways, often without the shell, but usually with a thick sauce, highly seasoned with aromatic herbs. In Italy, snails are boiled, sauteed and served with tomato and ginger sauce.

A gastropod mollusk, the snail has a delicate flavor somewhat like that of another mollusk, the oyster, although in the usual method of preparation the natural taste is overpowered by garlic. Snails gathered in the wild are customarily held for a few days without food, so that they may purge themselves before being cooked. Because of the complexity of preparing them, snails are most frequently eaten in restaurants, and then as an appetizer or snack, never the main course.

Rattlesnake

SNAKE

Many species of snake are edible, though not much eaten, except in China, Japan and other Far Eastern countries and in parts of Africa. The French do eat a grass snake, which they call "hedge eel" *(anguille des haies)*, and prepare using eel recipes.

Snake eating is not unheard of in the United States. As recently as 1979, a minor governmental flap was caused by rattlesnake meat's appearance on the menu of a Washington, D.C. restaurant. An official of the U.S. Department of the Interior wrote to the owner of the restaurant suggesting he take rattlesnake off the menu, because rattlesnake is an endangered species. As a result, the official, whose job it was to protect endangered species, got fired from his position. It was noted in the newspapers at the time that the secretary of the Interior was a patron of the restaurant, but no connection was suggested between that and the firing. Yet, after the matter was exposed in the press, the official was speedily rehired.

Alaskans make much of their fondness for rattlesnakes and coach whip snakes. Oklahomans conduct an annual rattlesnake hunt and auction off the catch of meat to the highest bidder. Perhaps the most imaginative preparation of rattlesnake was recorded by Calvin W. Schwabe in his delightful book *Unmentionable Cuisine:*

> *In 1971 I was introduced to a Chinese cafe owner in a little town in western Montana who also ran a thriving export business in rattlesnakes. Actually his product was a preparation of rattlesnakes in bourbon, marinated (aged?) for 4 to 5 years, filtered through a piece of bread, and then shipped to San Francisco's Chinatown, where it is in great demand as a remedy for rheumatism!*

There is no theoretical reason why snake meat should not make good eating. Indeed, its taste is most often compared to chicken. Even the flesh of many poisonous snakes is wholesome, provided the poison sacs are removed intact. Yet, most people in the West are put off by a repulsion for snakes. This stems from various causes: fear of poisonous snakes and constrictors, although this is a small minority of snakes: the slithery, writhing characteristics of snakes; protruding tongues, and even the role played by the snake in the biblical story of Adam and Eve.

In the Far East, on the other hand, these Western inhibitions don't seem to apply. The Chinese eat snakes with gusto, relishing the poisonous ones above all, such as the king cobra and the banded krait. They are marinated and cooked with rice, stir-fried or added to fish or chicken stock to make a snake soup. The Japanese enjoy snake grilled, much as they would eel. The heads and backbones of snake are boiled in fish stock, to which is added wine and soy sauce. This is used as a marinade for skewered strips of snake, which are then charcoal broiled.

SNAKEFISH

Also ATLANTIC CUTLASSFISH, HAIR-TAIL. This remarkably long, thin fish with strong jaws and large teeth is found throughout the Atlantic. Though sparse, the flesh of this fish is good to eat, and in tropical areas it is caught in large numbers for local consumption. The snakefish reaches a length of five feet and is silver with yellowish green fin tips. It prefers deep waters and is found close inshore only off South Africa.

SNAKE GOURD

Also CUCUMBER GOURD, SERPENT CUCUMBER. Fruit of a climbing vine, *Trichosanthes anguina*, native to tropical Asia and northern Australia, it grows wild but is cultivated in India and Africa for food. The fruits are skinny and cylindrical and light green when immature. They reach a length of from one to six feet and will grow in coils unless the vine is supported and weights hung from the ends of the fruit. Although it turns orange on maturity, the fruit is usually picked green, sliced down the middle and then boiled in water. The snake gourd is grown in the United States as a curiosity.

SNAKEHEAD

This genus of African and Asian freshwater fish is closely related to the **milkfish.** Many species are large, giving them considerable value as food fish, and they are characterized by a broad head, deeply angled mouth, and a body that is round at the front but compressed toward the rear. Largest is *Ophicephalus micropeltes* found in the larger rivers of India, Burma, Malaya, Vietnam, Thailand and Cambodia. It often exceeds three feet in length and can weigh as much as 44 pounds. Snake heads have accessory breathing organs that enable them to survive in oxygen-poor water, or even out of water for a considerable length of time. This enhances their market value, since they can be transported long distances and be sold alive.

O. striatus is the most common of all Asian snakeheads, being found from Sri Lanka and India to China and the Philippines. It is comparable in size to *O. micropeltes* and is particularly prized as food in Thailand. During times of drought, snakefish survive by burrowing deeply into the mud where they can live for as long as the mud remains moist. Thai fishermen swap their nets for shovels and simply dig the fish out of the mud.

SNAKE MELON

Also SNAKE CUCUMBER. Fruit of a running herb of the melon family *(Cucumis melo* var. *flexuosus)*, the snake melon is grown in France and the United States to be used in making preserves or simply as a curiosity. The snake melon generally reaches one to three feet in length and some three inches in diameter. It is cylindrical in shape and mostly curved or coiled. Egyptians consider it a delicacy.

SNAKEROOT

See **Bistort.**

SNAKEWEED

See **Bistort.**

SNAPPER

Also REDBREAM, SQUIRE, COCKNEY. A valuable food fish of the bream *(Sparidae)* family, the snapper *(Chrysophrys auratus)* is a Pacific Ocean fish, especially plentiful in Australian and New Zealand waters. Adults are red with pale blue spots and reach a length of up to 51 inches. Older fish develop a prominent bump on the forehead and fleshy lips, such that they are nicknamed, "old man snapper." The snapper has the fighting qualities valued by anglers, and larger specimens can weigh up to 43 pounds. The snapper is fished commercially throughout its range and is taken on long lines or captured in fishtraps and nets. It may be prepared like **bream.**

SNIPE

This is a small wading bird *(Gallinago* spp.) of the Northern Hemisphere whose delicate flavor has made it popular game. It has a long, flexible bill, with which it roots into the mud for worms and other small prey. The snipe resembles the **woodcock,** but is only half its size, weighing from two to 10 ounces, and has variegated color. The female is larger than the male, and both grow fat as winter approaches. They are best taken in the fall. They are in season from the middle of August to the middle of March.

The common snipe of the United States is *Gallinago wilsoni*, also known as Wilson's snipe and jacksnipe. In Great Britain and Europe the common snipe is *Capella gallinago*, but is reckoned to be nearly identical to the American species. Snipe is a favorite game in the Delta region of the Mississippi and is famous for the evasive zig-zag movements it makes on initiating flight. It is skinned before cooking and may be prepared in any way suitable for woodcock, but roasting is said to bring out the flavor best.

SNOEK

Also BARRACOUTA. A large schooling fish of the Southern Hemisphere that looks somewhat like a long, slender tuna, the snoek *(Thyrsites atun)*, as it is known in South Africa, constitutes a valuable fishery both there and in Australia where it is called barracouta. The flesh of this fish is eaten both fresh and smoked.

A large snoek can attain a length of 4½ feet, and its colors include a steel blue back, dark fins and silvery belly. Snoeks are migratory and travel in large schools close to the surface.

SNOOK

A popular gamefish of the Caribbean, the snook *(Centropomus undecimalis)* is also highly regarded as a food fish. A large snook can be nearly six feet long and weigh as much as 52 pounds. Snooks live close inshore and can tolerate brackish water. The fish has a tapering snout with an undershot jaw and an olive-green back shading into silvery sides. Its fighting qualities make it a prime quarry for sportfishers. Its flesh is white, flaky and delicately flavored.

SNOWBALL TREE

See **Cranberry Tree.**

SNOWBERRY

Also CREEPING SNOWBERRY. Two North American plants are known as snowberry for their edible white berries. They are *Symphoricarops albus* whose fruit was eaten by the native Americans of Oregon and is also known as the waxberry, and *Gaultheria hispidula*, the creeping snowberry, moxie plum or maidenhair berry, which was eaten by the native Americans of Maine.

SNOW FUNGUS

See **Black Tree Fungus.**

SNOW PARTRIDGE

See **Partridge.**

SOAKED-CURD CHEESE

See **Washed-curd Cheese.**

SOAPBARK

See **Quillaja.**

SOAPBERRY

See **Buffalo Berry.**

SOAP PLANT

This is a perennial herb of western North America whose edible bulbs yield a lather that can be used as a soap substitute. The species is *Cholorgalum pomeridianum.*

SOAVE

The name means suave in Italian. It is a light, dry, sophisticated, white wine, produced near Verona. Soave is made from two vines, the Garganega and the Trebbiano. Straw-yellow, it has a dry but harmonious flavor, a delicate bouquet and low alcoholic content.

SOBA

See **Noodle.**

SOCHU

Also SHOCHU. A distilled liquor made in Japan from grain or sweet potatoes, sochu is a neutral spirit, i.e., it retains nothing of the character of the grain or sweet potato.

SODA

See **Bicarbonate Of Soda.**

SODA CRACKER

See **Cracker.**

SODA POP

See **Carbonated Beverage.**

SODA WATER

See **Mineral Water.**

SODIUM

Sodium is a silver white metal found naturally only in combined form, as in sodium chloride, commonly known as table salt. The human body contains about 100 grams of sodium. It is essential to certain body functions, e.g., maintaining blood volume and cellular osmotic pressure and in transmitting nerve impulses. Yet many Americans consume more sodium than they need.

According to the Food and Nutrition Board of the National Academy of Sciences National Research Council, consuming 1,100 to 3,300 milligrams a day is considered safe and adequate for the healthy adult. The group estimates, however, that persons average between 2,300 and 6,900 milligrams a day. Most of this is in the form of table **salt,** which is approximately 40 percent sodium and 60 percent chloride. A teaspoon of salt contains about 2,000 milligrams of sodium. Thus, Americans average between one and 3½ teaspoons of salt a day.

The U.S. Department of Health and Human Resources has suggested that people should avoid eating too much sodium. The reason for this is that it is believed to contribute to high blood pressure or hypertension in some persons. One of the measures prescribed by physicians for control of hypertension is restriction of sodium intake from foods, drinks and drugs.

The following table will help the reader figure out how much sodium is in his or her diet. It should be remembered that many foods contain sodium as a part of their normal chemical composition. Moreover, household staples such as baking powder and baking soda are sodium compounds.

The values in the table were obtained from published reports of laboratory analyses that used flame photometry, atomic absorption or emission spectroscopy to find the sodium content. Because this content varies considerably in some products, the table gives representative values. Also, the values reflect current processing practices and typical product formulas. If these change, sodium values may change too.

Values given in the table are for unsalted products, unless specified. Cooked items have been prepared using unsalted water, even though the manufacturers' instructions may call for salt. Canned vegetable values are for total can contents of solids and liquids.

It should be noted that another source of sodium is drinking water. The sodium content of drinking water varies considerably throughout the country. This variation also affects the sodium content of soft drinks and beer produced and bottled at different locations. Water softeners raise the sodium content of water. In most states, the state department of public health can supply information on the sodium content of public water supplies.

It is worth noting that some popular flavoring agents are high in sodium, such as soy sauce, Worcestershire sauce, ketchup, pickles, olives and garlic, onion and celery salts. Many processed foods contain added sodium. Salted or brined meats and fish are obviously higher in salt content than the uncured forms. Many canned vegetables are packed in a salt solution or brine.

Finally, it is important to read the label to see which, if any, sodium compounds have been added in processing. These might include such things as **monosodium glutamate,** a flavor enhancer; sodium saccharin, a sweetener; sodium phosphates, emulsifiers, stabilizers, buffers; sodium caseinate, a thickener and binder, and sodium benzoate and sodium nitrite, preservatives.

The Sodium Content of Foods

Food	Portion	Weight (grams)	Sodium (Milligrams)
Alcoholic beverages:			
Beer	12 fl. oz.	360	25
Gin, rum, whisky	2 fl. oz.	60	1
Wine:			
Red			
Domestic	4 fl. oz.	120	12
Imported	4 fl. oz.	120	6
Sherry	4 fl. oz.	120	14
White:			
Domestic	4 fl. oz.	120	19
Imported	4 fl. oz.	120	2
Almonds:			
Salted, roasted	1 cup	157	311
Unsalted, slivered	1 cup	115	4
Apples:			
Raw or baked	1 apple	138	2
Frozen, slices	1 cup	200	28
Frozen, scalloped	8 oz.	227	45
Dried, sulfured	8 oz.	227	210
Applesauce, canned:			
Sweetened	1 cup	250	6
Unsweetened	1 cup	250	5
With added salt	1 cup	250	68
Apricots:			
Raw	3 apricots	114	1
Canned:			
Peeled	1 cup	258	27
Unpeeled	1 cup	258	10
Dried	1 cup	130	12
Artichokes:			
Cooked	1 medium	120	36
Hearts, frozen	3 oz.	85	40
Asparagus:			
Raw	1 spear	20	1
Frozen	4 spears	60	4
Canned:			
Regular	4 spears	80	298
Low sodium	1 cup	235	7
Avocado, raw	1 avocado	216	22
Baking powder	1 tsp.	3	339
Baking soda	1 tsp.	3	821
Banana, raw	1 banana	119	2
Barley, pearled, cooked	1 cup	200	6
Beans:			
Baked, canned:			
Boston style	1 cup	260	606
With or without pork	1 cup	260	928
Dry, cooked:			
Great northern	1 cup	179	5
Lima	1 cup	192	4
Kidney	1 cup	182	4
Navy	1 cup	195	3
Pinto	1 cup	207	4

Food	Portion	Weight (grams)	Sodium (Milligrams)
Italian:			
Frozen	3 oz.	85	4
Canned	1 cup	220	913
Kidney, Canned	1 cup	255	844
Lima:			
Cooked	1 cup	170	2
Frozen	1 cup	170	128
Canned	1 cup	170	456
Low sodium	1 cup	170	7
Snap:			
Cooked	1 cup	125	5
Frozen:			
Regular	3 oz.	85	3
With almonds	3 oz.	85	335
With mushrooms	3 oz.	85	145
With onions	3 oz.	85	360
Canned:			
Regular	1 cup	130	326
Low sodium	1 cup	135	3
Beansprouts, mung:			
Raw	1 cup	105	5
Canned	1 cup	125	71
Beets:			
Cooked	1 cup	170	73
Canned:			
Sliced	1 cup	170	479
Low sodium	1 cup	170	110
Harvard	1 cup	170	275
Pickled	1 cup	170	330
Beet greens, cooked	1 cup	145	110
Berries:			
Blackberries (Boysenberries)			
Raw	1 cup	144	1
Canned	1 cup	244	3
Blueberries:			
Raw	1 cup	145	1
Canned	1 cup	250	2
Raspberries:			
Raw	1 cup	123	1
Frozen	1 package	284	3
Strawberries:			
Raw	1 cup	149	2
Frozen, sliced	1 cup	255	6
Biscuits, baking powder:			
Regular flour	1 biscuit	28	175
Self rising flour	1 biscuit	28	185
With milk, from mix	1 biscuit	28	272
Low sodium	1 biscuit	28	1
Brazil nuts, shelled	1 cup	140	1
Bread:			
Boston brown bread	1 slice	45	120
Cornbread, homemade	1 oz.	28	176
Cracked wheat	1 slice	25	148

Food	Portion	Weight (grams)	Sodium (Milligrams)
French	1 slice	23	116
Mixed grain	1 slice	23	138
Pita	1 loaf	64	132
Rye:			
Regular	1 slice	25	139
Pumpernickel	1 slice	32	182
Salt rising	1 slice	26	66
White:			
Regular	1 slice	25	114
Thin	1 slice	16	79
Low sodium	1 slice	23	7
Whole wheat	1 slice	25	132
Breakfast cereals:			
Hot, cooked, in unsalted water:			
Corn (hominy) grits:			
Regular	1 cup	236	1
Instant	¾ cup	177	354
Cream of wheat:			
Regular	¾ cup	184	2
Instant	¾ cup	184	5
Quick	¾ cup	184	126
Mix 'n eat	¾ cup	184	350
Farina	¾ cup	184	1
Oatmeal:			
Regular or quick	¾ cup	180	1
Instant:			
No sodium added	¾ cup	180	1
Sodium added	¾ cup	180	283
With apples and cinnamon	¾ cup	180	220
With maple and brown sugar	¾ cup	180	277
With raisins and spice	¾ cup	180	223
Ready-to-eat:			
Bran cereals:			
All-bran	⅓ cup	28	160
Bran Chex	⅔ cup	28	262
40% Bran	⅔ cup	28	251
100% Bran	½ cup	28	221
Raisin Bran	½ cup	28	209
Cheerios	1¼ cup	28	304
Corn cereals:			
Corn Chex	1 cup	28	297
Corn Flakes:			
Low sodium	1¼ cup	28	10
Regular	1 cup	28	256
Sugar coated	¾ cup	28	274
Sugar Corn Pops	1 cup	28	105
Granola:			
Regular	¼ cup	34	61
No sodium added	¼ cup	34	16
Kix	1½ cup	28	261
Life	⅔ cup	28	146
Product 19	¾ cup	28	175
Rice Cereals:			
Low sodium	1 cup	28	10
Puffed rice	2 cups	28	2
Rice Chex	1⅛ cup	28	238
Rice Krispies	1 cup	28	340
Sugar coated	⅞ cup	28	149

Food	Portion	Weight (grams)	Sodium (Milligrams)
Special K	1¼ cup	28	265
Total	1 cup	28	359
Trix	1 cup	28	160
Wheat cereals:			
Puffed wheat	2 cups	28	2
Sugar coated	1 cup	28	46
Shredded wheat	1 biscuit	24	3
Wheat Chex	⅔ cup	28	190
Wheaties	1 cup	28	355
Wheat germ, toasted	¼ cup	28	1
Breakfast drink, instant:			
Grape	8 fl. oz.	240	0
Citrus fruits	8 fl. oz.	240	14
Breakfast sweets:			
Coffee cake:			
Almond	⅛ cake	42	167
Blueberry	⅛ cake	35	135
Honey nut	⅛ cake	55	110
Pecan	⅛ cake	40	172
Danish:			
Apple, frozen	1 roll	72	220
Cheese, frozen	1 roll	72	250
Cinnamon, frozen	1 roll	72	260
Orange, refrigerated dough	1 roll	39	329
Doughnut:			
Cake type	1 doughnut	32	160
Yeast leavened	1 doughnut	42	99
Sweet rolls:			
Apple crunch, frozen	1 roll	28	105
Caramel, frozen	1 roll	29	118
Cinnamon, frozen	1 roll	26	110
Honey	1 roll	28	119
Toaster pastry:			
Apple, frosted	1 pastry	52	324
Blueberry, frosted	1 pastry	52	242
Cinnamon, frosted	1 pastry	52	326
Strawberry	1 pastry	52	238
Broccoli:			
Raw	1 stalk	151	23
Frozen:			
Cooked	1 cup	188	35
With cheese sauce	3⅓ oz.	94	440
With hollandaise sauce	3⅓ oz.	94	115
Brussels sprouts:			
Raw	1 medium	18	1
Frozen:			
Cooked	1 cup	150	15
In Butter Sauce	3⅓ oz.	94	421
Butter:			
Regular	1 tbsp.	14	116
Unsalted	1 tbsp.	14	2
Whipped	1 tbsp.	9	74
Cabbage:			
Green:			
Raw	1 cup	70	8
Cooked	1 cup	144	16
Red, raw	1 cup	70	18

Food	Portion	Weight (grams)	Sodium (Milligrams)
Cakes, from mix:			
Angel food:			
Regular	1/12 cake	56	134
One Step	1/12 cake	57	250
Devils food	1/12 cake	67	402
Pound	1/12 cake	55	171
White	1/12 cake	68	238
Yellow	1/12 cake	69	242
Candy:			
Candy corn	1 oz.	28	60
Caramel	1 oz.	28	74
Chocolate:			
Bitter	1 oz.	28	4
Milk	1 oz.	28	28
Fudge, chocolate	1 oz.	28	54
Gum drops	1 oz.	28	10
Hard	1 oz.	28	9
Jelly beans	1 oz.	28	3
Licorice	1 oz.	28	28
Marshmallows	1 oz.	28	11
Mints, uncoated	1 oz.	28	56
Peanut brittle	1 oz.	28	145
Taffy	1 oz.	28	88
Toffee bar, almond	1 oz.	28	65
Cantaloup	½ melon	272	24
Carbonated beverages:			
Club soda	8 fl. oz.	240	39
Regular	8 fl. oz.	240	16
Low calorie	8 fl. oz.	240	21
Fruit flavored:			
Regular	8 fl. oz.	240	34
Low calorie	8 fl. oz.	240	46
Ginger ale	8 fl. oz.	240	13
Root beer	8 fl. oz.	240	24
Carrots:			
Raw	1 carrot	72	34
Frozen:			
Cut or whole	3⅓ oz.	94	43
In butter sauce	3⅓ oz.	94	350
With brown sugar glaze	3⅓ oz.	94	500
Canned:			
Regular	1 cup	155	386
Low sodium	1 cup	150	58
Casaba	⅕ melon	230	34
Cashews:			
Roasted in oil	1 cup	140	21
Dry roasted, salted	1 cup	140	1,200
Cauliflower:			
Raw	1 cup	115	17
Cooked	1 cup	125	13
Frozen:			
Cooked	1 cup	180	18
With cheese sauce	3 oz.	85	325
Celery, raw	1 stalk	20	25
Chard, cooked	1 cup	166	143

Food	Portion	Weight (grams)	Sodium (Milligrams)
Cheese:			
Natural:			
Blue	1 oz.	28	396
Brick	1 oz.	28	159
Brie	1 oz.	28	178
Camembert	1 oz.	28	239
Cheddar:			
Regular	1 oz.	28	176
Low sodium	1 oz.	28	6
Colby	1 oz.	28	171
Cottage:			
Regular and lowfat	4 oz.	113	457
Dry curd, unsalted	4 oz.	113	14
Cream	1 oz.	28	84
Edam	1 oz.	28	274
Feta	1 oz.	28	316
Gouda	1 oz.	28	232
Gruyere	1 oz.	28	95
Limburger	1 oz.	28	227
Monterey	1 oz.	28	152
Mozzarella, from:			
Whole milk	1 oz.	28	106
Part skim milk	1 oz.	28	132
Muenster	1 oz.	28	178
Neufchatel	1 oz.	28	113
Parmesan:			
Grated	1 oz.	28	528
Hard	1 oz.	28	454
Provolone	1 oz.	28	248
Ricotta, made with:			
Whole milk	½ cup	124	104
Part skim milk	½ cup	124	155
Roquefort	1 oz.	28	513
Swiss	1 oz.	28	74
Tilsit	1 oz.	28	213
Pasteurized processed cheese:			
American	1 oz.	28	406
Low sodium	1 oz.	28	2
Swiss	1 oz.	28	388
Cheese food:			
American	1 oz.	28	337
Swiss	1 oz.	28	440
Cheese spread:			
American	1 oz.	28	381
Cherries:			
Raw	1 cup	150	1
Frozen	8 oz.	227	3
Canned	1 cup	257	10
Chestnuts	1 cup	160	10
Chickpeas, cooked	1 cup	169	13
Chicory	1 cup	90	6
Chili powder	1 tsp.	3	26
Cocoa mix, water added	8 fl. oz.	240	232
Coffee:			
Brewed	8 fl. oz.	240	2
Instant:			
Regular	8 fl. oz.	240	1

Food	Portion	Weight (grams)	Sodium (Milligrams)
Decaffeinated	8 fl. oz.	240	1
With chicory	8 fl. oz.	240	7
With flavorings	8 fl. oz.	240	124
Substitute	8 fl. oz.	240	3
Collards:			
Cooked	1 cup	190	24
Frozen	3 oz.	85	41
Cookies:			
Brownies, Iced	1 brownie	32	69
Chocolate chip	2 cookies	21	69
Fig bars	2 bars	28	96
Ginger snaps	4 cookies	28	161
Macaroons	2 cookies	38	14
Oatmeal:			
Plain	1 cookie	18	77
With chocolate chips	2 cookies	26	54
With raisins	2 cookies	26	55
Sandwich type	2 cookies	20	96
Shortbread	4 cookies	30	116
Sugar	1 cookie	26	108
Sugar wafer	4 cookies	28	43
Vanilla wafer	6 cookies	24	53
Corn:			
Cooked	1 ear	140	1
Frozen	1 cup	166	7
Canned:			
Creamed style:			
Regular	1 cup	256	671
Low sodium	1 cup	256	5
Vacuum packed	1 cup	210	577
Whole kernel:			
Regular	1 cup	165	384
Low sodium	1 cup	166	2
Crackers:			
Graham	1 cracker	7	48
Low sodium	1 cracker	4	1
Rye	1 cracker	6	70
Saltine	2 crackers	6	70
Whole wheat	1 cracker	4	30
Cranberry, raw	1 cup	95	1
Cranberry sauce	1 cup	277	75
Cream products, imitation:			
Sweet:			
Coffee whitener:			
Liquid	1 tbsp.	15	12
Powdered	1 tbsp.	6	12
Whipped topping	1 tbsp.	4	2
Sour, cultured	1 oz.	28	29
Cream, sour, cultured	1 tbsp.	12	6
Cream, sweet:			
Fluid, all types	1 tbsp.	15	6
Whipped	1 tbsp.	3	4
Cucumber	7 slices	28	2
Currant:			
Raw	1 cup	133	3
Dried	1 cup	140	10

Food	Portion	Weight (grams)	Sodium (Milligrams)
Dandelion greens, cooked	1 cup	105	46
Dates, dried	10 dates	80	1
Eggplant, cooked	1 cup	200	2
Eggs:			
Whole	1 egg	50	59
White	1 white	33	50
Yolk	1 yolk	17	9
Substitute, frozen	¼ cup	60	120
Endive, raw	1 cup	50	7
Fast foods:			
Cheeseburger	1 each	111	709
Chicken dinner	1 portion	410	2,243
Fish sandwich	1 sandwich	164	882
French fries	2½ oz.	69	146
Hamburger:			
Regular	1 each	92	461
Jumbo	1 each	236	990
Frankfurter	1 frankfurter	93	728
Pizza, cheese	¼ pie	110	599
Shake	1 shake	308	266
Taco	1 taco	75	401
Figs:			
Raw	1 fig	50	2
Canned	1 cup	248	3
Dried	1 fig	20	2
Fish:			
Bass, black sea, raw	3 oz.	85	57
Bluefish:			
Baked with butter	3 oz.	85	87
Breaded, fried	3 oz.	85	123
Bonito, canned	3 oz.	85	437
Catfish, raw	3 oz.	85	50
Cod, broiled with butter	3 oz.	85	93
Eel, raw	3 oz.	85	67
Flounder (includes sole and other flat fish)			
Baked with butter	3 oz.	85	201
Haddock, breaded, fried	3 oz.	85	150
Halibut, broiled with butter	3 oz.	85	114
Herring, smoked	3 oz.	85	5,234
Lingcod, raw	3 oz.	85	50
Mackerel, raw	3 oz.	85	40
Mullet, breaded, fried	3 oz.	85	83
Ocean perch, fried	3 oz.	85	128
Pollock, creamed	3 oz.	85	94
Pompano, cooked	3 oz.	85	48
Rockfish, ovensteamed	3 oz.	85	57
Salmon:			
Broiled with butter	3 oz.	85	99
Canned:			
Salt added			
Pink	3 oz.	85	443
Red	3 oz.	85	329
Silver	3 oz.	85	298
Without salt added	3 oz.	85	41

Food	Portion	Weight (grams)	Sodium (Milligrams)
Sardines, canned:			
Drained	3 oz.	85	552
In tomato sauce	3 oz.	85	338
Shad, baked with butter	3 oz.	85	66
Snapper, raw	3 oz.	85	56
Trout, lake, raw	3 oz.	85	67
Tuna, canned:			
Light meat:			
Chunk:			
Oil pack	3 oz.	85	303
Water pack	3 oz.	85	288
Grated	3 oz.	85	246
White meat (Albacore)			
Chunk, low sodium	3 oz.	85	34
Solid:			
Oil pack	3 oz.	85	384
Water pack	3 oz.	85	309
Fruit cocktail, canned	1 cup	255	15
Fruit drinks, canned:			
Apple	8 fl. oz.	240	16
Cranberry juice cocktail	8 fl. oz.	240	4
Grape	8 fl. oz.	240	1
Lemonade	8 fl. oz.	240	60
Orange	8 fl. oz.	240	77
Pineapple-grapefruit	8 fl. oz.	240	80
Fruit drinks, dehydrated, reconstituted:			
Sweetened:			
Lemonade	8 fl. oz.	240	50
Orange	8 fl. oz.	240	35
Other fruit	8 fl. oz.	240	0
Unsweetened, all flavors	8 fl. oz.	240	0
Fruit juices:			
Apple cider or juice	1 cup	248	5
Apricot nectar	1 cup	251	9
Citrus:			
Grapefruit juice:			
Canned	1 cup	250	4
Frozen, diluted	1 cup	247	5
Lemon or lime juice:			
Canned	1 cup	244	2
Frozen, diluted	1 cup	248	4
Orange juice:			
Canned	1 cup	249	5
Frozen, diluted	1 cup	249	5
Tangerine juice	1 cup	249	2
Grape juice, bottled	1 cup	253	8
Peach nectar	1 cup	249	10
Pear nectar	1 cup	250	8
Pineapple juice	1 cup	250	5
Prune juice	1 cup	256	5
Garlic:			
Powder	1 tsp.	3	1
Salt	1 tsp.	6	1,850
Grapefruit:			
Raw	½ grapefruit	120	1
Frozen, unsweetened	1 cup	244	6
Canned, sweetened	1 cup	254	4

Food	Portion	Weight (grams)	Sodium (Milligrams)
Grapes, Thompson seedless	10 grapes	50	1
Hazelnuts (filberts)			
chopped	1 cup	115	2
Honeydew melon	⅕ melon	298	28
Horseradish, prepared	1 tbsp.	18	198
Jams and Jellies:			
Jam:			
Regular	1 tbsp.	20	2
Low calorie	1 tbsp.	20	19
Jelly:			
Regular	1 tbsp.	18	3
Low carlorie	1 tbsp.	18	21
Kale:			
Cooked	1 cup	110	47
Frozen	3 oz.	85	13
Ketchup:			
Regular	1 tbsp.	15	156
Low sodium	1 tbsp.	15	3
Kohlrabi, cooked	1 cup	165	9
Kumquat	1 kumquat	19	1
Leek	1 bulb	25	1
Lemon, raw	1 lemon	74	1
Lentils, cooked	1 cup	188	4
Lettuce	1 cup	55	4
Macaroni, cooked	1 cup	140	2
Mangos, raw	1 mango	200	1
Margarine:			
Regular	1 tbsp.	14	140
Unsalted	1 tbsp.	14	1
Meat:			
Beef:			
Cooked, lean	3 oz.	85	55
Corned:			
Cooked	3 oz.	85	802
Canned	3 oz.	85	893
Dried, chipped	1 oz.	28	1,219
Lamb, cooked, lean	3 oz.	85	58
Pork:			
Cured:			
Bacon:			
Cooked	2 slices	14	274
Canadian	1 slice	28	394
Ham	3 oz.	85	1,114
Salt pork, raw	1 oz.	28	399
Fresh, cooked, lean	3 oz.	85	59
Veal, cooked, lean	3 oz.	85	69
Meat tenderizer:			
Regular	1 tsp.	5	1,750
Low sodium	1 tsp.	5	1
Milk:			
Fluid:			
Whole and lowfat	1 cup	244	122
Whole, low sodium	1 cup	244	6
Buttermilk, cultured:			
Salted	1 cup	245	257
Unsalted	1 cup	245	122

Food	Portion	Weight (grams)	Sodium (Milligrams)
Canned:			
Evaporated:			
Whole	1 cup	252	266
Skim	1 cup	255	294
Sweetened, condensed	1 cup	306	389
Dry:			
Nonfat:			
Regular	½ cup	60	322
Instantized	1 cup	68	373
Buttermilk	½ cup	60	310
Milk beverages:			
Chocolate	1 cup	250	149
Cocoa, hot	1 cup	250	123
Eggnog	1 cup	254	138
Malted:			
Natural flavor	1 cup	265	215
Chocolate flavor	1 cup	265	168
Shakes, thick:			
Chocolate or vanilla	1 shake	306	317
Milk desserts, frozen:			
Ice cream:			
Chocolate	1 cup	133	75
Custard, French	1 cup	133	84
Strawberry	1 cup	133	77
Vanilla:			
French, softserve	1 cup	173	153
Hardened	1 cup	140	112
Ice milk:			
Vanilla:			
Hardened	1 cup	131	105
Soft serve	1 cup	175	163
Novelty products:			
Bars:			
Fudge	1 bar	73	54
Orange cream	1 bar	66	27
Vanilla, chocolate-coated:			
Ice cream	1 bar	47	24
Ice milk	1 bar	50	31
Cones, vanilla, Chocolate-coated	1 small	71	64
Sandwich	1 sandwich	62	92
Sherbet, orange	1 cup	193	89
Milk desserts, other:			
Custard, baked	1 cup	265	209
Puddings:			
Butterscotch:			
Regular, whole milk	½ cup	148	245
Instant, whole milk	½ cup	149	445
LoCal, skim milk	½ cup	130	130
Ready-to-serve	1 can	142	290
Chocolate:			
Home recipe	½ cup	130	73
Regular, whole milk	½ cup	148	195
Instant, whole milk	½ cup	149	470
LoCal, skim milk	½ cup	130	80
Ready-to-serve	1 can	142	262

Food	Portion	Weight (grams)	Sodium (Milligrams)
Vanilla:			
Home recipe	½ cup	128	83
Regular, whole milk	½ cup	148	200
Instant, whole milk	½ cup	149	400
LoCal, skim milk	½ cup	130	115
Ready-to-serve	1 can	142	279
Tapioca, cooked	½ cup	145	130
Mineral water, imported	8 fl. oz.	240	42
MSG (Monosodium glutamate)	1 tsp.	5	492
Muffin, English	1 medium	57	293
Mushrooms:			
Raw	1 cup	70	7
Canned	2 oz.	56	242
Mustard, prepared	1 tsp.	5	65
Mustard greens:			
Raw	1 cup	33	11
Cooked	1 cup	140	25
Frozen	3 oz.	85	25
Nectarines, raw	1 nectarine	138	1
Noodles, cooked	1 cup	140	2
Oranges, raw	1 orange	131	1
Organ meats:			
Brains, raw	1 oz.	28	35
Gizzard, poultry, simmered	1 oz.	28	17
Heart:			
Beef, braised	1 oz.	28	29
Calf, braised	1 oz.	28	32
Poultry, simmered	1 oz.	28	14
Kidney, beef, braised	1 oz.	28	71
Liver:			
Calf, fried	1 oz.	28	33
Pork, simmered	1 oz.	28	14
Poultry, simmered	1 oz.	28	16
Sweetbreads, calf cooked	1 oz.	28	32
Tongue beef, braised	1 oz.	28	17
Tripe:			
Commercial	1 oz.	28	13
Okra, cooked	10 pods	106	2
Olives:			
Green	4 olives	16	323
Ripe, mission	3 olives	15	96
Onion:			
Powder	1 tsp.	2	1
Salt	1 tsp.	5	1,620
Onions:			
Mature, dry	1 medium	100	10
Green	1 medium	30	2
Flaked	1 tbsp.	6	31
Pancake mix	1 cup	141	2,036
Pancakes, from mix	1 pancake	27	152
Papaya, raw	1 papaya	303	8
Parsley, raw	1 tbsp.	4	2
Parsley, dried	1 tbsp.	1	6
Parsnips, cooked	1 cup	155	19
Peaches:			
Raw	1 peach	100	1
Frozen	1 cup	250	10

Food	Portion	Weight (grams)	Sodium (Milligrams)
Canned	1 cup	256	15
Dried, uncooked	1 cup	160	10
Peanut butter:			
Smooth or crunchy	1 tbsp.	16	81
Low sodium	1 tbsp.	16	1
Peanuts:			
Dry roasted, salted	1 cup	144	986
Roasted, salted	1 cup	144	601
Spanish, salted	1 cup	144	823
Unsalted	1 cup	144	8
Pears:			
Raw	1 pear	168	1
Canned	1 cup	255	15
Dried	1 cup	180	10
Peas, green:			
Cooked	1 cup	160	2
Frozen:			
Regular	3 oz.	85	80
In butter sauce	3⅓ oz.	94	402
In cream sauce	2⅔ oz.	74	420
With mushrooms	3⅓ oz.	94	240
Canned:			
Regular	1 cup	170	493
Low sodium	1 cup	170	8
Pecans	1 cup	118	1
Pepper, black	1 tsp.	2	1
Peppers:			
Hot, raw	1 pod	28	7
Sweet, raw or cooked	1 pod	74	9
Pickles:			
Bread and butter	2 slices	15	101
Dill	1 pickle	65	928
Sweet	1 pickle	15	128
Pies, frozen:			
Apple	⅛ of pie	71	208
Banana cream	⅙ of pie	66	90
Bavarian Cream:			
Chocolate	⅛ of pie	80	78
Lemon	⅛ of pie	83	71
Blueberry	⅛ of pie	71	163
Cherry	⅛ of pie	71	169
Chocolate cream	⅙ of pie	66	107
Coconut:			
Cream	⅙ of pie	66	104
Custard	⅛ of pie	71	194
Lemon cream	⅙ of pie	66	92
Mince	⅛ of pie	71	258
Peach	⅛ of pie	71	169
Pecan	⅛ of pie	71	241
Pumpkin	⅛ of pie	71	169
Strawberry cream	⅙ of pie	66	101
Pilinuts	4 oz.	113	3
Pineapple:			
Raw	1 cup	135	1
Canned	1 cup	255	77
Pistachios	1 cup	125	6

Food	Portion	Weight (grams)	Sodium (Milligrams)
Plums:			
Raw	1 plum	66	1
Canned	1 cup	256	10
Potatoes:			
Baked or broiled	1 medium	156	5
Frozen:			
French fried	10 strips	50	15
Salted	2½ oz.	71	270
Canned	1 cup	250	753
Instant, reconstituted	1 cup	210	485
Mashed, milk and salt	1 cup	210	632
Au gratin	1 cup	245	1,095
Poultry and game:			
Chicken, roasted:			
Breast with skin	½ breast	98	69
Drumstick with skin	1 drumstick	52	47
Products:			
Canned	1 5-oz. can	142	714
Frankfurter	1 frankfurter	45	617
Duck, roasted flesh and skin	½ duck	382	227
Goose, roasted, flesh and skin	½ goose	774	543
Rabbit:			
Leg, raw	4 oz.	113	40
Flesh, cooked	4 oz.	113	70
Turkey, small, roasted:			
Breast with skin	½ breast	344	182
Leg with skin	1 leg	245	195
Prepared main dishes:			
Beef:			
And macaroni:			
Frozen	6 oz.	170	673
Canned	1 cup	227	1,185
Cabbage, stuffed			
Frozen	8 oz.	226	63
Chili con carne with beans, canned:			
Regular	1 cup	255	1,194
Low sodium	1 cup	335	100
Dinners, frozen:			
Beef	1 dinner	312	998
Meat loaf	1 dinner	312	1,304
Sirloin, chopped	1 dinner	284	978
Swiss steak	1 dinner	284	682
Enchiladas	1 pkg.	207	725
Goulash, canned	8 oz.	227	1,032
Hash, corned beef, canned	1 cup	220	1,520
Meatballs, Swedish	8 oz.	227	1,880
Peppers, stuffed, frozen	8 oz.	226	1,001
Pizza, frozen:			
With pepperoni	½ pie	195	813
With sausage	½ pie	189	967
Pot pie:			
Home baked	1 pie	227	644
Frozen	1 pie	227	1,093
Ravioli, canned	7½ oz.	213	1,065
Spaghetti, canned:			
And ground beef	7½ oz.	213	1,054
And meatballs	7½ oz.	213	942

Food	Portion	Weight (grams)	Sodium (Milligrams)
Sauce	4 oz.	114	856
Stew, canned	8 oz.	227	980
Chicken:			
And dumplings, frozen	12 oz.	340	1,506
and noodles, frozen	¾ cup	180	662
Chow mein, home recipe	1 cup	250	718
Dinner, frozen	1 dinner	312	1,153
Pot pie:			
Home recipe	1 pie	232	594
Frozen	1 pie	227	907
Fish and shellfish:			
Fish dinner, frozen	1 dinner	248	1,212
Shrimp:			
Dinner, frozen	1 dinner	223	758
Egg roll, frozen	1 roll	71	648
Tuna, pot pie, frozen	1 pie	227	715
Pork, sweet and sour canned	1 cup	275	1,968
Turkey:			
Dinner, frozen	1 dinner	333	1,228
Pot pie:			
Home recipe	1 pie	227	620
Frozen	1 pie	233	1,018
Veal parmigiana	7½ oz.	214	1,825
Without meat:			
Chow mein, vegetable, frozen	1 cup	240	1,273
Pizza, cheese	¼ 12-in. pie	90	447
Spanish rice, canned	1 cup	221	1,370
Prunes:			
Cooked	1 cup	213	8
Dried	5 large	43	2
Pumpkin, canned	1 cup	245	12
Radish	4 small	18	2
Raisins, seedless	1 cup	145	17
Relish, sweet	1 tbsp.	15	124
Rhubarb:			
Cooked, sugared	1 cup	270	5
Frozen	1 cup	270	5
Rice, cooked:			
Brown	1 cup	195	10
White:			
Regular	1 cup	205	6
Parboiled	1 cup	175	4
Quick	1 cup	165	13
Rolls:			
Brown and serve	1 roll	18	138
Refrigerated dough	1 roll	35	342
Rutabaga, cooked	1 cup	200	8
Salad dressing:			
Blue cheese	1 tbsp.	15	153
French:			
Home recipe	1 tbsp.	14	92
Bottled	1 tbsp.	14	214
Dry mix, prepared	1 tbsp.	14	253
Low sodium	1 tbsp.	15	3
Italian:			
Bottled	1 tbsp.	15	116

Food	Portion	Weight (grams)	Sodium (Milligrams)
Dry mix, prepared	1 tbsp.	14	172
Mayonnaise	1 tbsp.	15	78
Russian	1 tbsp.	15	133
Thousand Island:			
Regular	1 tbsp.	16	109
Low cal	1 tbsp.	14	153
Salads:			
Bean:			
Marinated	½ cup	130	104
Canned	½ cup	130	537
Carrot-raisin	½ cup	63	97
Cole slaw	½ cup	60	68
Macaroni	⅔ cup	127	676
Potato	½ cup	125	625
Salt	1 tsp.	5	1,938
Sauces:			
A-1	1 tbsp.	17	275
Barbecue	1 tbsp.	16	130
Chili:			
Regular	1 tbsp.	17	227
Low sodium	1 tbsp.	15	11
Soy	1 tbsp.	18	1,029
Tabasco	1 tsp.	5	24
Tartar	1 tbsp.	14	182
Teriyaki	1 tbsp.	18	690
Worcestershire	1 tbsp.	17	206
Sauerkraut, canned	1 cup	235	1,554
Sausages, luncheon meats, and spreads:			
Beer salami, beef	1 slice	6	56
Bologna:			
Beef	1 slice	22	220
Beef and pork	1 slice	22	224
Bratwurst, cooked	1 oz.	28	158
Braunschweiger	1 slice	28	324
Bratwurst	1 oz.	28	315
Chicken spread	1 oz.	28	115
Frankfurter	1 frankfurter	57	639
Ham:			
And cheese loaf	1 oz.	28	381
Chopped	1 slice	21	288
Deviled	1 oz.	28	253
Spread	1 oz.	28	258
Kielbasa	1 slice	26	280
Knockwurst	1 link	68	687
Lebanon bologna	1 slice	18	228
Liver cheese	1 slice	20	245
Old fashioned loaf	1 slice	22	275
Olive loaf	1 slice	21	312
Pepperoni	1 slice	6	122
Salami:			
Cooked:			
Beef	1 slice	22	255
Beef and pork	1 slice	22	234
Dry or hard, pork	1 slice	10	226
Sausage:			
Cooked:			
Pork	1 link	13	168

Food	Portion	Weight (grams)	Sodium (Milligrams)
Pork and beef	1 patty	27	217
Smoked	1 link	28	264
Thuringer	1 slice	22	320
Tuna spread	1 oz.	28	92
Turkey roll	1 oz.	28	166
Vienna sausage	1 link	16	152
Shallot	1 shallot	20	3
Shellfish:			
Clams, raw:			
Hard	3 oz.	85	174
Soft	3 oz.	85	30
Crab:			
Canned, drained	3 oz.	85	425
Steamed	3 oz.	85	314
Lobster, boiled	3 oz.	85	212
Mussels, raw	3 oz.	85	243
Oysters:			
Raw	3 oz.	85	113
Fried	3 oz.	85	174
Frozen	3 oz.	85	323
Scallops:			
Raw	3 oz.	85	217
Steamed	3 oz.	85	225
Shrimp:			
Raw	3 oz.	85	137
Fried	3 oz.	85	159
Canned	3 oz.	85	1,955
Squid, dried	1 serving	4	183
Snacks:			
Corn chips	1 oz.	28	231
Popcorn:			
Caramel coated	1 cup	35	262
Oil, salt	1 cup	9	175
Plain	1 cup	6	1
Potato chips	10 chips	20	200
Pretzels:			
Regular twist	1 pretzel	6	101
Small stick	3 sticks	1	17
Soups:			
Beef broth, cubed	1 cup	241	1,152
Beef noodle:			
Condensed, with water	1 cup	244	952
Dehydrated, with water	1 cup	251	1,041
Chicken noodle:			
Condensed, with water	1 cup	241	1,107
Dehydrated, with water	1 cup	252	1,284
Chicken rice:			
Condensed, with water	1 cup	241	841
Dehydrated, with water	1 cup	253	980
Clam chowder, Manhattan, condensed, with water	1 cup	244	1,808
Clam chowder, New England, condensed:			
With water	1 cup	244	914
With milk	1 cup	248	992
Minestrone, condensed, with water	1 cup	241	911
Mushroom:			
Condensed, with water	1 cup	244	1,031
Condensed, with milk	1 cup	248	1,076

Food	Portion	Weight (grams)	Sodium (Milligrams)
Dehydrated, with water	1 cup	253	1,019
Low sodium	1 cup	244	27
Pea, green:			
Condensed, with water	1 cup	250	987
Dehydrated, with water	1 cup	271	1,220
Tomato:			
Condensed, with water	1 cup	244	872
Condensed, with milk	1 cup	248	932
Dehydrated, with water	1 cup	265	943
Low sodium	1 cup	244	29
Vegetable:			
Condensed, with water	1 cup	241	823
Dehydrated, with water	1 cup	253	1,146
Vegetable beef:			
Condensed, with water	1 cup	244	957
Dehydrated, with water	1 cup	252	1,000
Low sodium	1 cup	244	51
Soybeans:			
Cooked	1 cup	180	4
Curd (tofu)	¼ block	130	9
Fermented (miso):			
Red	¼ cup	72	3,708
White	¼ cup	67	2,126
Spaghetti, cooked	1 cup	140	2
Spinach:			
Raw	1 cup	55	49
Cooked	1 cup	180	94
Frozen:			
Regular	3⅓ oz.	94	65
Creamed	3 oz.	85	280
Canned:			
Regular	1 cup	205	910
Low sodium	1 cup	205	148
Squash:			
Summer:			
Cooked	1 cup	210	5
Frozen, with curry	⅓ cup	71	228
Canned	1 cup	210	785
Winter:			
Baked, mashed	1 cup	205	2
Frozen	1 cup	200	4
Stuffing mix, cooked	1 cup	170	1,131
Sugar:			
Brown	1 cup	220	66
Granulated	1 cup	200	2
Powdered	1 cup	120	1
Sweet potatoes:			
Baked or boiled in skin	1 potato	132	20
Canned:			
Regular	1 potato	100	48
Low sodium	1 serving	113	27
Candied	1 potato	100	42
Syrup:			
Chocolate flavored:			
Thin	1 tbsp.	19	10
Fudge	1 tbsp.	19	17
Corn	1 tbsp.	20	14

Food	Portion	Weight (grams)	Sodium (Milligrams)
Maple:			
Regular	1 tbsp.	20	1
Imitation	1 tbsp.	20	20
Molasses:			
Light	1 tbsp.	20	3
Medium	1 tbsp.	20	7
Blackstrap	1 tbsp.	20	18
Tangelo	1 tangelo	95	1
Tangerine	1 tangerine	86	1
Tea:			
Hot:			
Brewed	8 fl. oz.	240	1
Instant	8 fl. oz.	240	2
Iced:			
Canned	8 fl. oz.	240	9
Powdered, lemon-flavored:			
Sugar sweetened	8 fl. oz.	240	1
Low calorie	8 fl. oz.	240	15
Thirst quencher	8 fl. oz.	240	140
Tomatoes:			
Raw	1 tomato	123	14
Cooked	1 cup	240	10
Canned:			
Whole	1 cup	240	390
Stewed	1 cup	240	584
Low sodium	1 cup	240	16
Tomato juice:			
Regular	1 cup	243	878
Low sodium	1 cup	243	9
Tomato paste	1 cup	258	77
Tomato sauce	1 cup	248	1,498
Turnip greens, cooked	1 cup	155	17
Vegetable juice cocktail	1 cup	243	887
Vegetables, mixed:			
Frozen	3⅓ oz.	94	45
Canned	1 cup	170	380
Vinegar	½ cup	120	1
Waffle, frozen	1 waffle	37	275
Walnuts, English	1 cup	120	3
Watermelon	1/16 melon	426	8
Yam, white, raw	1 cup	200	28
Yeast, baker's, dry	1 package	7	1
Yogurt:			
Plain:			
Regular	8 oz.	227	105
Lowfat	8 oz.	227	159
Skim milk	8 oz.	227	174
With fruit	8 oz.	227	133

Adapted from: U.S. Department of Agriculture. *Home and Garden Bulletin, No. 233*. Washington, D.C.: GPO, 1980.

SODIUM BENZOATE

See **Benzoate of Soda.**

SODIUM BICARBONATE

See **Bicarbonate Of Soda.**

SOFT ROE

See **Roe.**

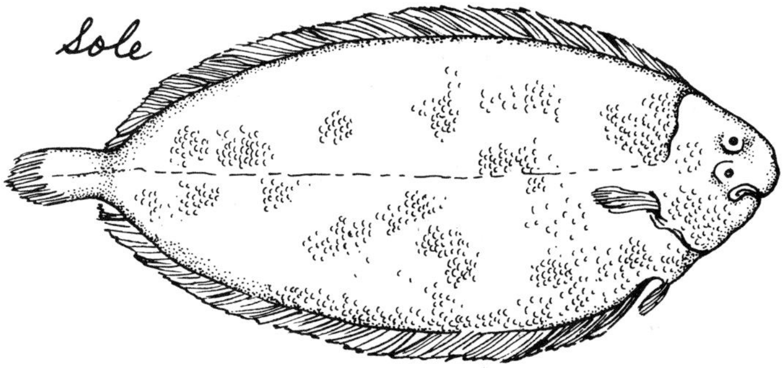

SOLE

A European flatfish, sole is highly esteemed for its firm, white flesh and its delicate flavor. There are several species of sole, including the lemon sole, the witch sole, the Torbay sole and the megrim, but this high esteem attaches mainly to the common sole *(Solea solea)*, also called English and Dover sole. Its territorial range stretches from Norway to the Mediterranean Sea, but the best common soles are caught in the English Channel.

In size, the common sole reaches a length of 10 to 20 inches and weighs on the average of one to 1½ pounds. It is a broad, thin fish adapted to living on the bottom of the sea, having both its eyes placed on the right or upper side, which is brown in color with black spots. The underside is white and equipped with sensors to detect its favorite food, bottom-dwelling organisms such as worms, small crustaceans and mollusks, brittle stars, sand eels and gobies. The sole derives its name from the Latin word for sandal, *solea*, supposedly from its resemblance to the sole of a shoe.

The sole has a wide popular reputation as a fine eating fish ("sole is the favorite fish of those who don't eat much fish because its flavor is not fishy"), yet among gourmets it ranks third in the company of flatfish, behind **turbot** and **brill.** Some recommend that it be aged for a day or two to intensify the flavor, which suggests that flavor is not the sole's forte. Concerning this point, food writer Waverley Root commented:

> *When the Larousse gastronomic encyclopedia reports that the sole is considered the best of flatfish, and then goes on to give 46 recipes for cooking sole whole, 75 for preparing fillets of sole and 31 for other concoctions, I am inclined to suspect that sole is one of those foods which can enter into an endless number of combinations because, being neutral in flavor itself, it serves admirably to carry the tastes of other foods without interjecting any pronounced savor of its own.*

True soles exist in North American waters, but they are too small and bony to be of commercial value. The petrale *(Eupsetta jordani)*, a brill, is sometimes sold as sole. The Pacific Coast "Dover sole" is actually the short-finned sole *(Microstomus pacificus)*, and not a true sole. The same goes for the Pacific "English sole," which is *Parophrys vetulus*, the California sole. Also mistakenly named is the Atlantic sand sole *(Pegusa lascaris)*, which has a number of aliases including rex sole, rex, petrale, flounder and even turbot. Of the above the *Eupsetta jordani* is probably the best food fish, surpassed among American soles only by the gray sole *(Glytocephalus cynoglossus)*, which is a **flounder.**

SOLOMON'S SEAL

See **Great Solomon's Seal.**

SONCOYA

The sweet, aromatic fruit of a small, Central American tree, *Annona purpurea*, it is a member of the same genus as the sweetsop, soursop and cherimoya. It looks somewhat like a mango and has an agreeable flavor. It is sometimes cultivated and sold in local markets.

SONORA MESQUITE

The seeds of this small tree, *Cercidium microphyllum*, are ground into flour or meal and cooked as porridge or cakes. This tree is closely related to the ***palo verde,*** and thrives in the dry conditions of its native habitat—southern California, Arizona and New Mexico.

SORB APPLE

Also SERVICE TREE. This sour-tasting fruit of the service tree *(Sorbus domestica)*, is native to the Mediterranean region and is closely related to the rowan tree (see **Rowanberry)** for which it is sometimes mistaken. It is larger, however, and its fruit comes in two distinct varieties, apple-shaped and pear-shaped. Neither type is much good fresh until after the first frost. Until touched by frost, they are hard and bitter.

Alternatively, sorb apples may be picked and set aside for post-ripening. They become sweet and palatable when on the point of spoiling.

Typically, sorb apples measure 1¼ inch across. They are not much cultivated, but when they are it is as a source of alcohol. They are used to make cider, wine and distilled liquor.

SORBITOL

This is a sugar alcohol derived from dextrose, which is used as a sweetener and a stabilizer in candies. Sorbitol is only about 60 percent as sweet as ordinary sugar and has the same number of calories, but it may be metabolized differently. It has an effect on the sugar crystal that keeps candies and shredded coconut from drying out over extended periods of time.

SORGHUM

A minor grain in most Western countries, used almost exclusively as animal fodder, sorghum is nevertheless a major food crop in Africa and Asia. Indeed, among cereals, it stands fourth behind wheat, rice and corn (maize) in worldwide production. The plant, *Sorghum vulgare*, is believed to be native to Africa. As food, there are two main types: grain sorghum and sweet sorghum.

Ancient Romans were acquainted with sorghum, although according to Pliny, it was a wild variety of black sorghum *(Sorghum nigrum)*. This variety of grain sorghum is still grown in Europe, particularly in Hungary, Yugoslavia, Portugal and Italy, where it is made into black bread. A bitter variety of red-grained sorghum is used to make beer.

Grain sorghum somewhat resembles the corn (maize) plant in its stalk and leaves, but it culminates in a head of small seeds, rather than bearing ears. There are hundreds of varieties of sorghum, some of the more common being durra, or Egyptian corn, negro corn, kaffir corn and rice corn. Three varieties, which are unusual elsewhere, are grown in the United States as animal food. They are Sudan grass *(Holcus sudanensis)*, Johnson or Aleppo grass *(Holcus halepensis)* and chicken corn *(Holcus sorghum* var. *drummondi)*. Sorghum yields less grain per acre than wheat, and authorities rate its nutritive value lower than other leading grains. It contains protein, but in most varieties the protein is not assimilable due to a lack of lysine, an amino acid.

Sweet sorghum *(Holcus sorghum* var. *saccara)*, also known as sugar sorghum and sorgo, enjoyed wide popularity as a sweetener in the United States between 1860 and 1900. The plant closely resembles grain sorghum, except that the stalk is much juicier. When crushed the stalk produces a golden syrup with a high sugar content that used to be poured over pancakes or employed in candymaking, baking, or preserves. Use of sorghum syrup went into a decline in competition with granulated sugar, a much handier product. Also, crystallizing sucrose from sorghum proved to be more difficult than from cane or beets. Considerable amounts of sweet sorghum are still grown in the southeastern United States.

A third variety of sorghum called broomcorn *(S. vulgare technicum)* is used to make brooms and brushes.

SOROCO

Red fruit of a treelike cactus, *Espostoa lanata*, native to Ecuador and Peru, it is sweet and eaten raw. The plant is also known as the cottonball or Peruvian snowball, because of the white, woolly hairs that grow from its stem.

SORREL

Also DOCK. This herb with many varieties—some called "sorrel," some called "dock"—has a pungent, acidic flavor due to the presence of oxalic acid in its leaves. A common variety is *Rumex acetosa*, called simply "sorrel," "garden sorrel" or "sour dock." It is a plant of northern Europe that also grows well in the United States.

Sorrel's history goes back to 3,000 B.C., but the ancient Greeks and Romans used it sparingly, gathering it wild rather than cultivating it. It was mentioned frequently by medieval sources in England and France. In the 18th and 19th centuries its popularity declined everywhere but France, where it soared.

It peaked at the turn of the century when market gardens around Paris were delivering 44 million pounds annually to city markets.

As a vegetable, it is largely ignored in English-speaking countries. It is still a popular salad green in France, an occasional green in Scandinavia, and a potherb in some parts of India. Other well-known varieties are round sorrel *(R. scutatus)*, slightly more bitter; French sorrel *(R. montanus)* milder; and patience, or spinach dock *(R. patientia)*, whose flavor is described as pleasingly acidic. This last plant has large, tender, fleshy leaves that are particularly good when mixed with spinach. Generally, leaves of the younger plants are used in salads, while the older ones are cooked like spinach. Creamed sorrel soup is a traditional dish.

Garden sorrel *(R. acetosa)*, though not so flavorful as the French, does better in the United States and is used much the same way. It is a rich source of vitamin C. Wood sorrel *(Oxalis viclacea)*, also called sourgrass, grows wild throughout North America. It is not much eaten anymore, but its tiny cloverlike leaves are used as a garnish. It is believed to be the true shamrock of ancient Ireland.

The French have a unique way of using sorrel. Shad is cooked with a stuffing of sorrel leaves whose oxalic acid dissolves the fish's many small bones, which otherwise would plague the diner.

SORREL BOUNCE

This is a once-popular drink prepared by soaking the flowers and leaves of the roselle or Jamaica sorrel *(Hibiscus sabdariffa)* in rum, then adding sugar to taste. It has a pleasantly acidic flavor.

SOUARI NUT

Also SUARI NUT. This oily nut, also known as the butternut of South America, grows on any of several species of large forest trees of the *Caryocar* genus, but most especially on the *Caryocar nucifera*. The nut is kidney-shaped and grows in a pod two or three at a time. The nutmeat is white and has an almondlike flavor. The trees are native to Brazil and Guyana but have been transplanted and cultivated in other regions.

SOUBISE SAUCE

A classic French sauce served with roast pork, eggs, chicken and mutton dishes, it is basically a bechamel sauce combined with a puree of onions and seasoned with salt, pepper and a little nutmeg. The sauce is strained and butter added just before serving.

See also: **Sauce.**

SOUCHET

See **Galingale.**

SOUDZOUKAKIA

A Turkish sausage containing minced veal or pork, garlic, eggs, parsley, cumin seeds, breadcrumbs, flour and seasonings, *soudzoukakia* is fried and served hot with tomato sauce. It is a feature of Smyrnan cuisine.

See also: **Sausage.**

SOUP

An ancient food, soup is prepared by cooking meat, fish or vegetables and the like in such fluids as water or milk; it is then consumed as a liquid. The varieties of soup number in the hundreds, but most fall into one of three categories: a thin, clear soup; a thin, cream soup; and a heavy, thick soup. The latter is often hard to distinguish from a close relative, the stew, except that in stew the solid food takes priority over the liquid part. A fourth, special category is the jellied soup, but these are rare.

Anthelme Brillat-Savarin, the authoritative French writer on gastronomy, wrote, "A rich soup; a small turbot; a saddle of venison; an apricot tart: this is a dinner fit for a king." His placing of soup first in the succession of dishes is no accident. Theory holds that soup (the thin ones, at least) is a stimulant to the appetite; it gets the salivary glands working and the gastric juices flowing. In the realm of fine cooking, the soup must also set the tone for the rest of the meal. Grimod de la Reyniere, another gastronomic writer, put it this way:

It is to a dinner what a portico or peristyle is to a building; that is to say, it is not only the first part of it, but it must be devised in such a manner as to set the tone of the whole banquet, in the same way as the overture of an opera announces the subject of the work.

These dicta apply to the thin soups, as a hearty soup is often a meal in itself. Of the thin, clear soups, the simplest is broth, which some experts regard as a little too thin to meet the definition of soup.

Broth is the unclarified liquid in which meat, poultry or vegetables have been cooked. It may be served unelaborated as a soup, or with vegetables or rice added.

Bouillon is a broth that has been clarified, i.e., had undesired matter removed, usually by the addition of egg white or egg shell, which is then strained out, bringing the other substances with them.

Consommee is a bouillon that has been reduced by boiling to perhaps half its original volume and seasoned with salt, pepper and often other spices.

These thin soups are the raw materials for stocks, liquid or jellylike substances that are the bases for other soups and sauces. They are simply the much-reduced and usually highly seasoned broths of beef, chicken, veal, fish, gravy and vegetables.

The second category is *cream* soup, which is always based on a standard cream, or **white sauce,** consisting of flour, butter, and milk or cream, plus seasoning and perhaps an egg yolk. This is enriched by cooked and pureed (or sieved) vegetables, meat, fish, crustacean or shellfish. Cream soups are most often named after their principal ingredient, which is often a single vegetable, such as cream of tomato, cream of asparagus, etc. Closely related to cream soup is the *puree,* which uses the same base but is always made from sieved vegetables and is usually thicker than a cream soup. Another variation of the cream soup is the *bisque,* which is generally based on a fish, crustacean or shellfish but occasionally on a vegetable as well. It too is thicker than the regular cream soup.

The third and final category of heavy, thick soups is a catch-all that includes chowders, thick vegetable soups, thick cream soups, plus such things as pepper pot, Scotch broth, minestrone, mulligatawny and gumbo.

Chowder is a rich soup containing solid ingredients, usually fish or shellfish, but vegetables as well. It has a milk base, except for the Manhattan variety, which is made with tomatoes.

Pepper pot, usually called Philadelphia pepper pot, is a highly spiced, thick soup containing tripe, meat and vegetables.

Scotch broth can be made either as a soup or a stew and is based on mutton or lamb to which is added mixed vegetables and barley.

Minestrone is a thick, Italian vegetable soup, seasoned with garlic and garnished with small pasta. It is usually topped with a sprinkling of Parmesan cheese.

Mulligatawny is Anglo-Indian, the name deriving from the Tamil words, *milagu tannir,* meaning pepper water. It is a chicken or lamb soup, spiced with curry powder and onions. A frequent side dish in India are cold bananas and tomatoes.

Gumbo is a rich soup of the American South containing mixed vegetables, herbs, meats, poultry, shellfish and especially okra, which adds considerably to the thickness of the liquid. A particular gumbo will be designated by its principal ingredient, e.g., shrimp gumbo. In former times, gumbo was thickened and seasoned with file powder, made of dried, pulverized sassafras leaves.

Over the years, certain soups have become associated with particular countries, and counted as part of the nation's culture. The *minestrone* of Italy has already been mentioned. Russians favor *borscht,* which is made from beets or cabbage, plus other ingredients and often served with sour cream. The classical French soup is *pot-au-feu,* which is really two dishes in one. Meat, vegetables and herbs are boiled in a large earthenware or copper pot. Then the liquid is drunk as soup, and the meat eaten separately. The Scandinavian countries are renowned for fruit soups, such as *frugtsuppe,* a Danish variety made of raspberries and red currants. The fruit is simmered, then strained and served cold as a first course with whipped cream. Alternatively, the fruit can be pureed, mixed with cream and served as a dessert. China has *shark's fin soup,* made of the dried cartilaginous part of the fin which, when powdered and added to water, becomes gelatinous and absorbs the flavors of the other ingredients, which include chicken, ham, garlic, onions and ginger. By the way, soup is not always served first in Chinese meals, but may be introduced midway or later. An English specialty is *Windsor* or *brown soup,* a rich beef consomme thickened with arrowroot and flavored with sherry and turtle herbs.

Jellied and chilled soups are a refreshing alternative in hot weather. A jellied soup may be based on a pure beef consomme which, through being much reduced, jells when cold. It may have gelatin added to a beef or chicken bouillon. Many common soups, including those mentioned above, such as borscht, can be served cold. Others, such as *vichyssoise,* a cream soup with leeks and potatoes, and *gazpacho,* a Basque puree of tomatoes, garlic, green peppers, onions, olive oil and vinegar, are always served cold.

SOURDOUGH BREAD

This bread is leavened by spontaneous fermentation encouraged by a starter, i.e., a piece of sour dough left over from the previous day's baking. It has a characteristic taste, which is subtly acidic and slightly biting.

Sourdough bread is so closely identified with prospecting for gold that the very word "sourdough" is a nickname for prospector, especially one who operated in California, Alaska or the Canadian Yukon. The prospector carried his starter in a pot that fitted conveniently in his pack. He was prepared to make bread anywhere by mixing a portion of his starter (yeast, flour, sugar and water) with flour and the other ingredients. Starters using the same strain of yeast have been kept going for decades.

But the sourdough starter long antedates the gold rushes of the 19th century; in fact, it may be our most ancient reliable method of leavening, a process discovered by the ancient Egyptians and passed on by them to the Greeks. Speaking of the ancient Greeks and Romans, Reay Tannahill wrote in *Food in History:*

> *But the commonest method [of leavening] was to keep a piece of dough from the previous day's baking and incorporate it in the new mix. The "sourdough starter," in fact, has continued to be used ever since, for despite the fact that it has now been generally superseded by commercially produced block or dried yeasts, it still makes the best leaven for really good bread.*

See also: **Bread.**

SOURSOP

This very large succulent fruit is widely cultivated in the West Indies. Ovoid, it has thick greenish skin with blunt fleshy spines. The soursop is borne by a small tree, *Annona muricata*, an evergreen about twenty feet high, native to tropical North and South America and the West Indies.

"A complete food," the soursop, or *guanabana*, contains some of almost all vitamins, minerals, carbohydrates, some fat, protein and calories. Its flesh is creamy, evenly cotton-white, aromatic but slightly tart. The skin should be peeled before eating. A delightful frozen dessert, resembling ice cream, is made of the sweetened soursop, but the fresh fruit, chilled and eaten raw, is perfect for a breakfast with rich black coffee. Its flavor is like that of the **mango** and **pineapple.** The soursop is found also in India, Laos, parts of Polynesia and along the west coast of Africa. With frost protection, this fruit can be grown successfully along the southern coast of Florida as well.

SOUTH AUSTRALIAN PLUM

Edible fruit of the shrub *Carissa ovata*, which is related to the karanda and the **natal plum,** the South Australian plum is an oval berry about the size of a small plum with a taste pleasant enough to eat raw, i.e., not as tart as other members of the genus. It is eaten locally.

SOUTHERN COMFORT

An American specialty, Southern Comfort is a mixture of bourbon whisky, freshly pitted and peeled peaches and peach liqueur. The addition of peaches and peach liqueur considerably mellows the robust bourbon flavor, but there is still a bite to it. The name of the creator is lost, but up until 1875 the concoction bore the name "Cuff and Buttons," which, at the time, meant white tie and tails. Then, according to tradition, Louis Herron, a bartender in St. Louis, Missouri, dubbed it, appropriately, "Southern Comfort." The method Herron developed of making it is still in use today. It is bottled at 100 proof.

SOUTHERNWOOD

See **Lad's Love.**

SOYBEAN

Also SOYA BEAN. An important factor in world nutrition, the soybean *(Glycine max)* is valued in the Far East for its high protein content and in the West for its abundance of oil. The plant is believed to have originated in Africa, to have been brought to the Far East in prehistory and to have been cultivated there for at least 4,000 years.

The soy plant is a small bush that stands erect, reaching a height of between two and six feet. It

Soybeans and their by-products (clockwise from top): soybean flour, soy sauce, white soybeans, black soybeans and miso

Tofu

annually bears velvety pods that contain from two to five beans or seeds. These are round or oval, somewhat flattened and, depending on the variety, may be yellow, black, white or brown. The seeds consist of as much as 41 percent protein and 20 percent oil, plus small amounts of lactose and other carbohydrates. Each bush may bear a hundred or more pods.

The soybean arrived in Europe at the end of the 17th century, and in the United States at the end of the 18th century. There, after a slow start, it has become the second most important agricultural product after corn (maize). The United States is the world's leading producer and exporter, followed by Brazil, the People's Republic of China, Mexico, Indonesia and Argentina. Fully half the United States crop is crushed for oil or otherwise processed, 35 percent exported as whole beans (mostly to Asia) and 5 percent replanted as seed.

The most important and popular soybean food in the Far East is soybean curd. This is prepared by first making soybean milk. The beans are soaked in water, then ground and filtered. The resulting liquid is similar in composition to cow's milk, but lower in fat and higher in protein. From this is made bean curd, the commonest form of which is *tou fu* or *tofu*. It is soft, cheeselike and has a bland taste. A fermented form of this, called stinking *tofu*, is a favorite snack of the Chinese. It has a pungent smell and is usually deepfried and seasoned with **soy sauce,** vinegar, mashed garlic or chili paste. The food value is high, consisting of 53 percent protein, 26 percent fat, 17 percent carboyhydrate, 4 percent minerals, plus vitamins and fiber.

Tofu is a staple of Japanese cooking along with *miso*, a product of fermenting soybeans and rice, using the bacterium *Aspergillus oryzae. Miso* has a pasty consistency, a distinctive taste, and keeps well in wooden vats, improving with age. It is versatile, appearing in soups as an ingredient in marinades for vegetables and fish and as part of a dressing in which foods are broiled. It can be used as a meat substitute in such a dish as meatloaf. A similar product is the Indonesia *tempeh*, made by fermenting soybeans with the mushroom *Rhizopus oryzae.* It turns brown and crisp in the process. All of these fermenting processes make soybeans more easily digestible.

A soybean cheese can be made by combining the bean curd with rennet. Soybean jam is a condiment made from the residue left over from the manufacture of soy sauce.

In the United States, by far the most important soybean product is oil. It is a popular cooking oil and a major raw material for shortening, margarines and salad dressings. The residue left from oil extraction is called soybean cake, 98 percent of which is used for animal fodder. The rest is processed for human consumption. A portion is ground coarsely into grits or finely into flour and used in processed meats, bakery mixes, cereals, breads and baby foods. A growing industry utilizes soy concentrates and isolates (which may be up to 90 percent protein) to create textured food items, such as imitation bacon bits. The latter are extruded, but soy protein may also be spun into fine filaments and woven to imitate ham, chicken or beef.

See also: **Bean.**

SOY SAUCE

This dark, salty sauce is used to flavor meat, fish, vegetables, marinades and other sauces, such as **Worcestershire Sauce.** It is the staple sauce of oriental cooking and, being salty, it has practically eliminated the use of ordinary table salt with Japanese and Chinese food. Soy sauce is made in various qualities by the Japanese and Chinese, and in both light and dark versions, the latter most commonly seen in the West. Apart from saltiness and a slight sweetness, soy sauce has a taste all its own. It is made from soy beans, which have been mashed and mixed with bruised, roasted wheat. This mixture is doubly fermented in a solution of salted water. The resulting liquid is strained and bottled as soy sauce. The residue may be eaten as a kind of cheese.

See also: **Sauce.**

SPACH'S PLUM

Edible, plumlike fruit of a West Indian tree, *Mouriria domingensis*, it has a pleasant taste and is consumed locally. The black-skinned Brazilian *pusa (M. pusa)* is a similar species.

SPADEFISH

A large, deep-bodied fish, *Chaetodipterus faber* of the warm waters of the western Atlantic, Caribbean and Gulf of Mexico, it can reach a length of three feet. Such large specimens weigh up to 20 pounds. Its color ranges from black to grayish silver with pronounced vertical bars on the body. The flesh of the spadefish has a good flavor and a firm texture. It is taken by anglers close in to shore. "Angelfish" and "porgy" are alternative names.

SPAGHETTI

Here is a type of Italian pasta consisting of long strings that are solid and not tubular, as in **macaroni.** It is cooked by boiling or steaming and usually served with a sauce. Of all pasta, it is the most popular in Italy and the best known around the world. The ingredients of spaghetti dough are a meal, or semolina, made from hard, very glutenous durum wheat and water. This is thoroughly mixed and kneaded by machine, then forced at great pressure through small holes in a perforated plate. There are spaghetti of various thicknesses.

The terminology runs as follows: *capellini* (very small, about one millimeter in diameter, named after hair), *fedeli or fedelini* (a size larger), *vermicelli* (meaning "little worms"), *spaghettini* (getting larger still) and *spaghetti* (the standard size, familiar to all).

The origin of spaghetti in Italy has been attributed variously to the Ostrogoths, a Teutonic tribe that invaded in 405 A.D. and set up headquarters in Ravenna;

the Chinese, whose noodles were brought west by Marco Polo in the 13th century; and to either Indians or Arabs who ate noodles before Marco Polo's time and probably brought them to Venice. The Indians called their noodles *sevika* ("thread"), the Arabs *richta* (also "thread"), while the Italians took a larger standard, spaghetti ("little strings").

Spaghetti are placed in boiling, salted water and cooked until they are *al dente*, i.e., still biteable, not mushy, but have lost any recognizable taste of flour. Spaghetti is served with a variety of sauces, including bechamel, tomato, bolognese and brown and usually seasoned with Parmesan or pecorino cheese.

See also: **Pasta.**

SPALEN

See **Sbrinz.**

SPANISH BAYONET

See **Yucca.**

SPANISH HOPS

The leaves of this southern European herb, *Origanum creitcum*, are used as a flavoring agent. It is a member of the marjoram genus and it tastes like thyme.

SPANISH LIME

See **Ginep.**

SPANISH MACKEREL

Also CHUB MACKEREL. This name usually refers to *Scomberomorus maculatus*, a fish found on both sides of the tropical Atlantic, but more plentiful in African waters. Its body shape is typical of the **mackerel,** and its coloring consists of a deep blue back, silvery sides and belly with yellow to orange spots. It reaches a length of four feet. Large specimens can weigh up to 20 pounds. Fish in the five-pound range are most common. The Spanish mackerel is considered a fine sport fish, and in areas where it is common, such as West Africa, it is an important food fish.

The smaller *Scomber japonicus* of the Pacific Ocean is also known as the Spanish or chub mackerel. It is found off California and Japan and in the Southern Hemisphere. The Atlantic species, *A. colias*, is thought to be identical. This is a schooling species and has been heavily fished off California and Japan for both canning and fresh fish markets. It is one of Japan's most important food fishes. *S. japonicus* reaches a length of no more than 16 inches and has a blue back marked by dark wavy lines and silver sides and belly.

See also: **Mackerel.**

SPANISH OYSTER PLANT

See **Salsify.**

SPANISH TAMARIND

See **Wild Medlar.**

SPARKLETTS WATER

A still water bottled in plastic containers in the United States for bulk drinking, it has a relatively low mineral content. A 1980 Consumers Union sensory panel rated the taste of Sparkletts Crystal Fresh Drinking Water as fair, with the following qualification: distinctly plastic flavor.

See also: **Mineral Water.**

SPARROW

This small bird, *Passer domesticus*, of the finch family, is plentiful in Europe, Asia and the United States. Sparrows were eaten by ancient Romans and the 16th-century English and continue to be eaten by modern Italians. Sparrow pie is a recognized delicacy in which the birds are baked under a crust after being plucked, drawn and decapitated.

In Japan, sparrows are skinned and charcoal-broiled or dipped in soybean paste *(miso)* and roasted in smoke oven. The bones of the sparrow are soft and may be eaten along with the flesh. Sparrows have become a costly agricultural pest in the United States but, despite a pre-20th century tradition of eating small birds, Americans generally avoid them.

SPEARMINT

Also GARDEN MINT, LAMB MINT. The mint most commonly used as a kitchen herb, spearmint *(Mentha spicata)* is also important commercially because its oil is used to flavor candy, chewing gum and toothpaste. It is a low-growing plant, rarely reaching more than two feet in height, with curly leaves and flowers of lilac pink. It is a native of Europe that has been naturalized in the United States.

Spearmint jelly is the traditional accompaniment of leg of lamb. Fresh leaves are added to green

salads, used to flavor iced drinks, such as the mint julep, and to garnish fruit cups. When dried, the leaves have tints of red and bronze that enhance their value as a garnish.

See also: **Mint.**

SPERRKASE

See **Dry Cheese.**

SPICE

The term refers to aromatic and often pungent vegetable substances used to flavor and to season food and—in earlier times—drink. True spices are normally prepared from seeds, berries, kernels, roots, rootstocks, bark, fruit or flowerbuds of a given plant. Ginger, for example, is made from the rootstock of its plant. Nutmegs are seeds. Black peppercorns are the whole fruits. Cinnamon is prepared from the inner bark of its tree. Capers and cloves are flowerbuds. Mace is the rind of an Indian root.

Herbal spices, such as basil, bay leaf, chervil, dill, marjoram, mint, parsley, sage, tarragon and thyme, are technically different from true spices. Here the young leaves from plants that have no woody tissue and that wither and die after flowering make up the "spice." A blend of spices, such as in curry powder, may be used as either a seasoning or a **condiment.**

In the Middle East, spices were used as currency, part of the tribute regularly accorded by oriental monarchs to Solomon, and were used in sacred temple rites. Europe discovered spice in the early Middle Ages, through military and commercial and political contact with the East. Spicery was an established trade in London by 1180, when the Pepperers' Guild is first officially mentioned. The British spicers or pepperers (forerunners of the modern grocer) dealt in pepper, cloves, nutmeg, mace, ginger, "painfully transported from India" often by way of Arabia or, from c. 1500, by ship around the Cape of Good Hope. Many bloody wars were fought to control the spice trade. The Portuguese and the Dutch, in particular, were notorious in their ruthless exploitation of native populations in Ceylon and the East Indies (The "Spice Islands") in order to protect their monopolies.

Spice was used in early Europe as a preservative and to heighten the monotonous local fare. Spices were thought to have curative powers and were alleged to stimulate sexual prowess and appetite. One of the most sumptuous resumes of spices occurs in Keats's "Eve of St. Agnes," traditionally the coldest evening of the year, when a chilly sleeping beauty is aroused through—in part—the profusion of delicacies heaped around her:

> *"With jellies smoother than the creamy curd,*
> *And lucent syrops, tinct with cinnamon;*
> *Manna and dates, in argosy transferred*
> *From Fez; and spiced dainties, every one,*
> *From silken Samarkand to cedared Lebanon.*

Herbs used as spices should be kept in a very dry place, for they readily absorb moisture and become moldy. Some foods are primed with spices beforehand, as in Greece where lives snails are gorged on branches of thyme before they are cooked. Spices are now at hand in any grocery store or market. Sage, dill, thyme, parsley, basil may be grown readily in most gardens.

SPICE BUSH

Also BENJAMIN BUSH, WILD ALLSPICE. This is a North American shrub, *Lindera benzoin*, whose twigs were once used to make an herb tea, and whose scarlet berries were dried and used as a substitute for allspice in such things as puddings, pastry and preserves.

SPICED CHEESE

The term applies to cheeses that have had spices added to them at some point in processing, usually at the salting stage, before hooping. Spices customarily used in cheese include caraway seeds, cumin seeds, pepper, cloves, anise and sage. To meet United States government standards spiced cheeses must contain at least 1½ ounces of spice for each 100 pounds of cheese.

Spiced cheeses are usually hard cheeses. Following are some examples: caraway, *kuminost*, *kommenost*, noekkelost, Frisian clove, Christian IX, *pepato* and sage. For further information, see under the specific name.

It is also the name of a type of Dutch cheese,

similar to **Frisian clove cheese,** but incorporating only cumin seed. Each cheese weighs from 12 to 18 pounds.

SPICE TREE

Also CALIFORNIA BAY, CALIFORNIA LAUREL, CALIFORNIA OLIVE, MYRTLE, OREGONMYRTLE, PEPPERWOOD. This is an aromatic evergreen tree, *Umbellularia californica*, of Oregon and California, whose leaves were used as a condiment by early Spanish Americans. The tree reaches a height of 80 feet, and its wood takes a high polish and is valued for fine woodworking.

SPICY CEDAR

The fragrant flowers of the African tree, *Tylostemon mannii*, are used to flavor rice and other foods.

SPIDER

Regular spider eating is a rare phenomenon and confined mainly to rural parts of Asia and to primitive tribes of Africa and Latin America. The giant orb-weaving spider *(Nephila maculata)* is eaten in Thailand, Burma, India and Indochina. The delectable part is the abdomen, which Thai peasants will sometimes bite off the living spider and consume raw. More commonly, the spider is roasted and dipped in salt. The flavor has been likened to raw potato, lettuce or raw cabbage. A second spider eaten in Thailand, as well as in Burma, Annam and Kampuchea, is the blue-legged "bird eater" *(Melopoeus albostriatus)*, a very large spider that can attain a length of 2½ inches and weigh up to 1½ ounces. It has a "jaw" that must first be removed. Then it is roasted on a skewer (thus singeing off the hair) and eaten whole. It may also be sliced and served with chilies. Two kinds of spider are eaten in Madagascar, the *Epeira nigra* and the *Nephila madagascariensis*. They are fried in oil or fat.

In Venezuela, the Yanomami are fond of the crow-foot spider or tarantula, and the horse-killer spider. The Diyuarua Indians of Venezuela eat the monkey spider after first passing it through flames to burn off the toxic hairs.

There have been isolated instances of spider eating in Western Europe. Ronald L. Taylor, in his fascinating treatise on insect eating, called *Butterflies in My Stomach*, cites the following:

> *When Alexander the Great reigned . . . it is reported that there was a very beautiful strumpet in Alexandria who had eaten spiders since her childhood. For that reason the King was admonished that he should be very careful not to embrace her, lest he should be poisoned by venom that might evaporate from her by sweat.*

Anna Maria Van Schurmann, a celebrated artist and religious fanatic of the 17th century, liked to eat spiders and compared their taste to nuts. The 18th-century astronomer, Joseph Jerome de Lalande, was fond of both spiders and caterpillars, comparing the taste of spiders to hazelnuts and that of caterpillars to stonefruits.

SPIDER LET TEA

A Japanese green tea with long, thin, twisted leaves of a dark olive color, it makes a delicate, mild brew the color of pale sherry. Spider let is basket-fired, that is, fired in bamboo baskets over a charcoal fire and handled with great care to maintain the leaf intact.

See also: **Tea.**

SPIDER MONKEY

The most agile of the New World apes, the spider monkey *(Ateles paniscus)* is found in tropical forests from southern Mexico south to central Bolivia and the Matto Grosso in Brazil. A large one can be up to 25 inches long and weigh 13 pounds. The flesh of this monkey is highly prized as food by native people.

SPIDERWISP

See **Gynandropsis.**

SPIKENARD

This is a North American plant, *Aralia racemosa*, whose roots and rhizomes are used to flavor root beer and other soft drinks. It has a pleasant fragrance and a bitter, aromatic flavor. The name also refers to an East Indian plant, *Nardostachys jatamansi*, whose roots were used to make a spice that was popular in the Middle Ages in Europe and is still used in Malayan cookery.

SPINACH

A garden vegetable cultivated for its broad, arrow-shaped leaves, spinach *(Spinacea oleracea)* has been incorporated into such a variety of dishes that it could appear in every part of a menu. Basically, of course, it can be eaten by itself as a separate dish, either raw or cooked. Cooked spinach is perhaps more common. Before cooking, it needs a thorough washing because, being a low lying plant, it collects a lot of sand and other soil particles. The leaves are gently cooked in a pot with very little water added, since they release a

lot of fluid naturally. After draining, they may be pureed, mixed with butter, pepper and salt, immersed in a vinegar solution or served with cream.

Spinach is exceptionally rich in vitamins, including A, B, C, E and K, plus iron and potassium of oxalate. Unfortunately, these vitamins are soluble in water or fat, so care must be taken to keep the cooking to a minimum if these values are to be maintained. Spinach is famous for its iron content, indeed suffered some unpopularity in the 1920s for its reputation as "children's food," but the iron is not in readily assimilable form. Moreover, the oxalic acid in spinach is not recommended for anyone suffering from liver ailments or kidney stones, as it hinders utilization of calcium.

Small, fresh spinach leaves are excellent eaten raw, with vinegar, salt, pepper and a little oil or bacon fat added. They may also be added to a green salad. The stems should be removed, however, before using the leaves raw; in cooked spinach, the stems are eaten right along with the leaves. Apart from these solo uses, spinach figures in dozens of recipes for such things as souffles, soups, green lasagna, ravioli, puddings, omelets, tarts, croquettes and *subricas.* In French cuisine, a dish containing spinach is often styled *al la florentine,* supposedly referring to Catherine de Medici, a native of Florence, Italy, who became Queen of France in the 16th century and who was reputedly fond of spinach.

Spinach is a member of the goosefoot family, and its many varieties are divided into two types: smooth-seeded and prickly seeded. The prickly seeded varieties, with their rougher, darker green leaves, are considered the hardier of the two. They are also called winter spinach and are planted in the fall and overwintered, to be harvested in the Lenten season. Smooth-seeded spinach (summer spinach) is planted in the spring and harvested 40 to 50 days later. Both are essentially cool-season crops and suffer from any intense heat or sunlight. Smooth-seeded spinach is generally preferred in Europe, while the prickly-seeded varieties are preferred in the United States. According to the noted food writer, Waverly Root, this is a mistake. He maintains the smooth-seeded varieties are much more palatable and adds:

> *"Italian spinach is as much better than French spinach as French spinach is better than American spinach," I wrote in the* Food of Italy *in 1971. It was a simple observation, tested at the table, which I did not attempt to follow up, except to note that Italians are exceptionally skillful market gardeners. But today I wonder if the reason for the mediocrity of American spinach is not simply that America plants the wrong seed.*

Spinach is believed to have originated in Persia, where a wild variety is still eaten. It was not known to the classical Mediterranean world, and the first European plantings are thought to have occurred in Moorish Spain in the 11th century. It was generally accepted in Great Britain and the continent in the 17th century and was a favorite Lenten food, since it ripened at just the right time. There is no record of its introduction into North America, but at least three varieties were growing there in the early 19th century. California, Texas and Oklahoma are the three most important producing states today.

For the wild spinach, *Chenopodium bonus-henricus,* see **Good King Henry.** New Zealand spinach is not a true spinach and is discussed under its own heading. For mountain spinach, see **Orach.**

SPINACH RHUBARB

A type of dock, *Rumex abyssinica,* native to Ethiopia but growing as far south in Africa as the Congo Basin, it can reach a height of nine feet. The stalks are eaten like rhubarb, and the leaves boiled and eaten like spinach.

SPINY ANTEATER

Also ECHIDNA. This is a family of anteaters found in Australia, Tasmania and New Guinea. The five species of this animal are characterized by a body covering consisting of fur intermixed with barbless spines and by a pointed snout. The short-nosed variety *(Tachyclossus aculeatus)* is relished as food by Australian aborigines. It reaches a length of about 24 inches and weighs up to 13 pounds. Its flesh is said to have an odor of crushed ants. The New Guinean long-nosed echidna *(Zaglossus bruijni)* is a larger animal, weighing as much as 22 pounds in the wild and reaching a length of 31 inches. Natives in certain areas of New Guinea greatly like its taste.

SPINY LOBSTER

Also CAVE LOBSTER, LANGOUSTE, ROCK LOBSTER, SEA CRAYFISH. The spiny lobster *(Palinuris vulgaris)* is a clawless crustacean with a spiny shell, two long antennae and a fan-shaped tail. It frequents warmer waters than does the true lobster (genus *Homarus)* and has a more barrel-shaped body. It is found on the Atlantic coasts of southern England and France, in the Mediterranean and in African waters south to the Cape of Good Hope. South Africa is a major exporter of frozen spiny lobster tail, and the crustacean is also known in England as the Cape lobster. On the other side of the Atlantic, its territory starts at North Carolina, continues down through the Gulf of Mexico and on as far south as Brazil. In Pacific waters, it is found from Santa Barbara south.

Some people call clawless lobsters "crayfish," but they are wrong because crayfish are freshwater crustaceans. Due to its long antennae, it has an insectlike appearance. Hence, its French name, *langouste*, comes from the Latin for locust, *locusta*. The shell has numerous sharp spines and spiny joints, and thus must be handled with care. The spiny lobster can weigh as much as 20 pounds, though seven to eight pounds is considered a good size, and the average market size is less. The color of the shell varies from bright red to green, to mottled green and blue, to almost black, depending on location, habitat and diet. The flesh is flavorful but has a less pronounced taste than that of the true lobster. It is dense, rather coarse and white, all of it lying in the tail and lower thorax.

The ancient Greeks and Romans ate this crustacean, but seem to have preferred shrimp, as do modern Americans. A large mosaic representing a spiny lobster was found in the floor of a dining room in the buried city of Pompeii. It is one of the most popular crustaceans on the European continent today. The United States imports about 20 million pounds of frozen tails from South Africa, South America, New Zealand, Australia and Mexico. It may be prepared in any way suitable to the true **lobster.**

SPINY RAT

A small Latin American rodent, *Proechimys trinitatis*, noted for its tasty flesh, it occurs in Central America, northern and central South America and on the island of Trinidad. The spiny rat attains a maximum length of about 12 inches and a weight of up to 14 ounces. It frequents coastal areas and lives near water in the forested foothills.

SPINY VITIS

A prickly climbing vine, *Vitis davidi* is cultivated in China. Its round, black, often harsh-flavored berries are appreciated in the area of cultivation.

SPIRITS

See **Liquor.**

SPITZKASE

This spiced German cheese made of cow's skim milk is similar to ***Backsteiner,*** except that caraway seeds are added to the curd. This is a flavorful, highly aromatic cheese that comes in two shapes, small cubes or cylinders 1½ inches across by four long.

SPONDIAS

This is a large tree, *Spondias mangifera*, of tropical Asia, whose flower clusters are eaten in salads or as a vegetable. It is cultivated in Indochina. Other trees of the same genus produce the *otaheite* apple, the hog plum and the Spanish plum or *jocote*.

SPONGE MUSHROOM

See **Morel.**

SPOOM

Also SPOGANDA. A type of Italian water ice that has a frothy consistency, it is made with light syrup and fruit juices or sweet wines. When it is half-frozen, meringue is beaten into the mixture. Spoom is served in chilled sherbet glasses.

SPOONBILL

Any of several heronlike wading birds, such as the white spoonbill *(Platalea leucorodia)* found in Europe, Asia and North Africa, the spoonbill has long legs, a crest and a long, flat bill with a spoon-shaped tip. It was much more popular as food in 15th century England than it is now. It may be prepared like heron.

SPOT

Spot is a marine food fish, *Liostomus xanthurus*, caught off the Atlantic Coast of North America. The name derives from a black spot behind the shoulders.

SPRAT

A small, schooling fish, *Sprattus sprattus*, of the north Atlantic, Mediterranean, Black and Baltic Seas, it is commercially exploited for fish meal and oil but is also quite good to eat smoked, salted or fresh. A member of the herring family, the sprat is commonly about five to six inches long and has a greenish back and silvery sides. Fresh sprat is often broiled and served with mustard sauce or dipped in batter and fried. Sprats are particularly abundant in Norwegian fjords. *Brislings*, which are young sprats canned in oil, are a Norwegian specialty.

SPRING BEAUTY

See **Fairy Spuds.**

SPRING ONION

See **Scallion.**

SPRUCE BEER

This fermented beverage is made from the twigs, cones and shoots of the spruce tree *(Picea* spp.). The spruce material is boiled with sugar, hops and yeast, then put into containers and allowed to ferment. The resulting beverage is mildly alcoholic. A spruce essence may be used instead of the raw material; a soft drink like root beer can also be made with spruce essence and water.

SPUR DOG

See **Dogfish.**

SQUAB

These are fledgling pigeons that are four weeks old or less. At this stage, the birds are just becoming old enough to leave the nest, after which they rapidly become so tough as to be inedible. Squabs are commercially raised from strains all believed to be descended from the rock pigeon *(Columba livia).* A squab generally weighs from eight to 14 ounces and has tender, dark and delicate flesh. Squabs are marketed frozen or fresh, and are available all year round. They may be broiled, stuffed, roasted, prepared in a casserole or split and fried in olive oil.

See also: **Pigeon.**

SQUASH

Also VEGETABLE MARROW. This general term for native American fruit of the gourd type includes a variety of pumpkins, gourds and marrow of the *Cucurbita* genus. A corresponding general term in England would be "vegetable marrow." The word "squash" derives from the Naragansett word, *askutasquash*, meaning "something eaten green." This description applies specifically to summer squash, one of the two major categories of squash. The other category, winter squash, is eaten ripe. Squashes assume a dazzling variety of shapes, and the sizes range from a pound or two to mammoth specimens weighing 40 pounds or more. Yellow is a typical color for squash, but again the possible range is very wide, including white, orange, red, purple, green and near-black.

Varieties of summer squash include the following: yellow or orange crookneck *(C. moschata)*, which is also called cushaw and is warty, large and clublike; chayote, or custard marrow *(Sechium edule)*, which in some varieties is spiny and resembles a huge pear; the pattypan, or scallop gourd *(C. pepo melopepo);* the cocozzelle, or bottle gourd *(Lagenaria vulgaris)*, which is long and tapering; and the popular zucchini, or courgette *(C. pepo)*, which is small, smooth and cylindrical and generally dark or light green. These squashes have a number of traits in common. They grow quickly and have a delicate flavor. They are picked unripe and are eaten without delay. If allowed to ripen, the rind and seeds become hard and the flesh fibrous. They are cooked whole and eaten without paring. Because their flavor is so delicate, it is frequently augmented with some sort of stuffing, such as cheese, tomatoes or meat.

Winter squashes are harvested late as they are much slower growing. They are harvested ripe and as a consequence have tough skins, but also a stronger flavor. They tend to be sweeter and more nutritious than the summer squashes. Winter varieties include the Hubbard, or Ohio squash *(C. Maximus ohioensis)*, the Canada or winter crookneck *(C. pepo)*, the Boston marrow, the butternut, the acorn squash and the sugar pumpkin *(C. pepo)*, which is the Halloween jack-o-lantern. The peel and seeds of the winter squashes must be removed before cooking. Then they are usually boiled and mashed and served with butter and seasonings. The Canada and the sugar pumpkin make good pie fillings.

Squashes typically contain almost 95 percent water, 3 to 4 percent carbohydrates, traces of protein and fat. They are inexpensive and very digestible.

See also: **Gourd** and **Pumpkin.**

Banana squash

Varieties of squash: butternut (front left), yellow (front center), summer (front right and left rear), and hubbard (right rear)

SQUASH BLOSSOMS

These golden, bell-shaped flowers of summer squash and pumpkin *(Cucurbita pepo)* are used in Italian, Mexican and, formerly, in English cuisines. In England, the blossoms used to be stuffed with sausage meat, dipped in batter and fried in deep oil. The dish was known as "golden pockets." In Mexico, pumpkin or squash blossom soup is made, incorporating about 40 large flowers, chicken broth, tomatoes and onions. It is seasoned with *epazote* (Mexican tea). They are also fried in oil with garlic and chilies, and used to stuff *quesadillas (tortillas* filled with cheese). Farther north Zuni women picked squash blossoms to use in soup or as appetizers, gathering only the large male flowers for this purpose.

SQUAWFISH

Also WHITE SALMON. This is the name of two large fish of North America. The Colorado squawfish *(Ptychocheilus lucius)* is thought to be the largest member of the carp family found in North America. It reaches a length of five feet and inhabits only the Colorado River Basin. This fish can weigh as much as 80 pounds, and at one time was an important food fish for indigeneous tribes and later on for white settlers. Its numbers are greatly diminished due to fishing and damming of the river. A related species is the northern squawfish *(P. oregonensis)* found in rivers and lakes from British Columbia to Nevada. It reaches a length of four feet and has a good reputation as a game fish. Large specimens weigh as much as 50 pounds. It was once an important food fish for native Americans but is now considered somewhat of a pest in waters where salmon are stocked, since the squawfish preys on the young salmon.

SQUAWROOT

See **Yampa.**

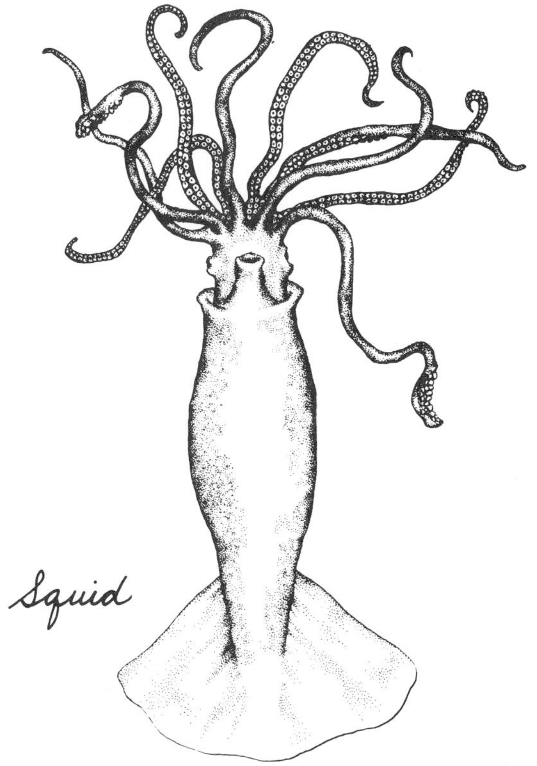

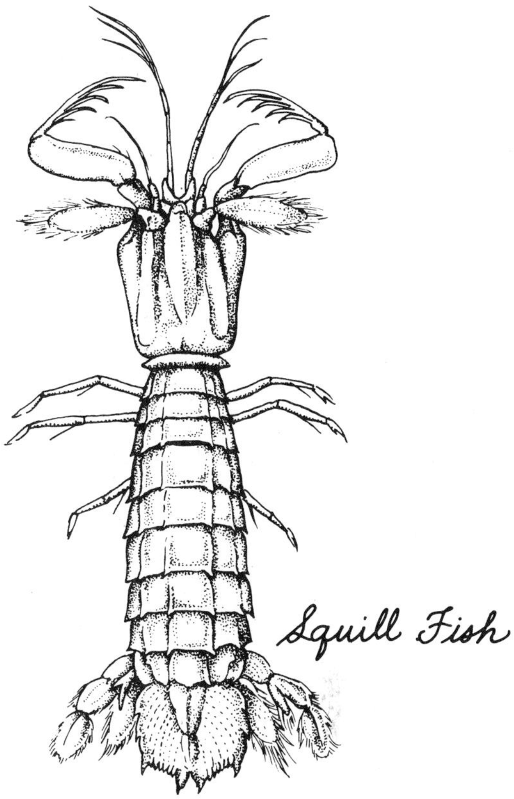

SQUID

Also CALAMARY. Among cephalopods, this is the most popular of all as human food, easily surpassing the cuttle fish and the octopus. The squid is a mollusk without an external shell and as such is closely related to oysters, snails and clams. It has ten arms as opposed to the octopus' eight, all equipped with suckers, a head which contains an ink sac, and a muscular mantle that varies in color from a milky translucence to hues of reddish brown. The squid has a transparent shell inside its body.

Among species of squid the size varies enormously. The giant squid *(Architeuthis princeps)* is a veritable sea monster, reaching a length of 48 feet and a body diameter of five feet. The one most frequently eaten, however, is the *Loligo vulgaris* of Atlantic and Mediterranean waters, which rarely exceeds two feet in length. When endangered, the squid shares the ability of the octopus and cuttlefish to squirt out a cloud of ink, called "sepia," to confuse its enemies and cover its retreat. It goes by a variety of names including "calamary" in England, *calmar* in France (or *tantonnet* in Provence), *calamar* in Spain (or *chiripua* in Basque country) and *calamaro* in Italy.

The squid is considered a delicacy among Mediterranean folk. It is prepared by removing the visceral organs and skeletal cartilage, then stripping away the pigmented skin and washing what remains very well. Usually the tentacles are eaten, and sometimes the head. It is cooked most simply by grilling or frying, but it is also served with a wide variety of accompaniments, such as mushroom sauce, Swiss chard, artichokes, or it may be stewed, stuffed or steamed.

Squid is an important foodstuff in Japan, amounting to about 8 percent of all seafood consumed, which in some years added up to more than 500,000 metric tons. Much of it is eaten fresh on sushi, or boiled, or made into squid rolls. A great deal is also dried, after which it may be pulverized, or left whole to be reconstituted by soaking in water for 24 hours. Dried squid is a favorite ingredient of soup. A special Japanese dish is fermented squid, which is prepared by mixing the raw muscles and liver of squid with salt, inoculating it with the rice mold *Aspergillus oryzae* and allowing it to ferment.

See also: **Cuttlefish, Octopus.**

SQUILL FISH

Also MANTIS SHRIMP. The name includes any of several species of small crustaceans (genus *Squillidae)* inhabiting the eastern Atlantic Ocean and Mediterranean Sea. Squill fish burrow along the seashore, and in body configuration resemble insects, such as the grasshopper. A flat-tailed Adriatic variety, *Squilla mantis*, called *cannochie* in Italian, has been described as the marine equivalent of the praying mantis because its pincers are a prolongation of its mouth. It is also called *cigala di mare*. The squill fish tastes like lobster or prawn and may be prepared in the same way. Usually, however, squill fish are put into fish stews, such as the Italian *bredo*, or the Spanish *zarzuela de pescado* or the French *bourride*.

SQUIRREL

This is a wild rodent (genus *Sciurus*, family *Sciuridae)* with a furry, slender body and a long bushy tail. There are many species of squirrel—both land-dwelling and tree-dwelling—and one or another of them is found in all parts of the world, except perhaps Oceania. There are about 55 species in the forested areas of Europe, Asia and North and South America. Common varieties are the gray squirrel, the red squirrel, the fox squirrel and the European squirrel.

The head and body of a large squirrel can be up to 12 to 13 inches in length and weigh as much as 2¼ pounds. The kind most often eaten is the gray squirrel *(Sciurus carolinensis)*. If a young animal, it may be fried or roasted. Its flesh should be pink or light red. Older animals are stewed.

There is, apparently, no tradition of squirrel-eating in Europe, but in both Great Britain and the United States until recent times squirrel was considered fair game for hunters and, if properly cooked, a gastronomic delicacy. The taste of squirrel meat is compared most often to hare, chicken or rabbit.

Most modern city dwellers would feel some repugnance to eating squirrels, since they most often see them in public parks where they are protected by law and even treated as pets. Our ancestors, on the other hand, encountered them as pests—particularly ground squirrels of the West who attacked grain and fruit crops—and thus felt little compunction about killing and eating them.

Some traditional American dishes, such as Brunswick stew, are based on squirrel. The Brunswick stew also includes tomatoes, okra, kernels of corn, lima beans and pimentos and is seasoned with parsley and thyme. The Appalachian version of this stew is called burgoo. Nowadays chicken is usually substituted. The Cajuns of Louisiana relish squirrel meat as a stuffing for ravioli. In England, young gray squirrels were (and sometimes still are) fried or grilled. Older animals were stewed, after soaking in a marinade for 24 hours.

It should be noted that squirrels from the Western states of the United States can be infested with ticks that transmit Rocky Mountain spotted fever (a form of typhus) and tularemia. Animals that behave oddly or lethargically should be avoided.

Calvin W. Schwabe, in his delightful book *Unmentionable Cuisine* (1979), gives the following quotation from the *Cambridge* (England) *News:*

> *. . . Grey squirrel is not unknown to British chefs and there is even the story of a well known professor of veterinary science who lunched at a London restaurant. When the headwaiter asked if he had enjoyed the chicken, the professor replied that the squirrel was very good. In answer to the waiter's protests, he picked up a small piece of bone, "You'll not find a bone like that in any animal other than a squirrel," he said.*

SQUIRRELFISH

Also CANDIL. Several species are called squirrelfish, one of which is an important food fish in Hawaii. The name derives from its large, squirrel-like eyes. Other squirrelfish are the *Diplectrum fasciculare* of the West Indies and the *Holocentrus ascensionis* of Florida waters.

SQUIRREL HAKE

Also RED HAKE. Here is a fish of the cod family found in the western Atlantic from southern Labrador to Virginia. While not a true **hake,** the squirrel hake *(Urophycis chuss)* is a moderately important food fish. It reaches a length of 28 inches and has rather soft flesh, which is, nevertheless, eaten fresh, salted and canned.

SQUIRTING CUCUMBER

See **Touch-me-not.**

STACHYS

See **Crosne.**

STAGBUSH

See **Black Haw.**

STANGENKASE

A German cheese made from partly skimmed cow's milk, similar to **Limburger** in taste and aroma, but milder, it is marketed in small rectangles weighing 1¾ pounds.

STAR ANISE

See **Anise.**

STAR APPLE

Fruit of a tropical evergreen tree native to the West Indies, the star apple *(Chyrsophyllum cainito)* is medium-sized with skin varying in color from green to purple,

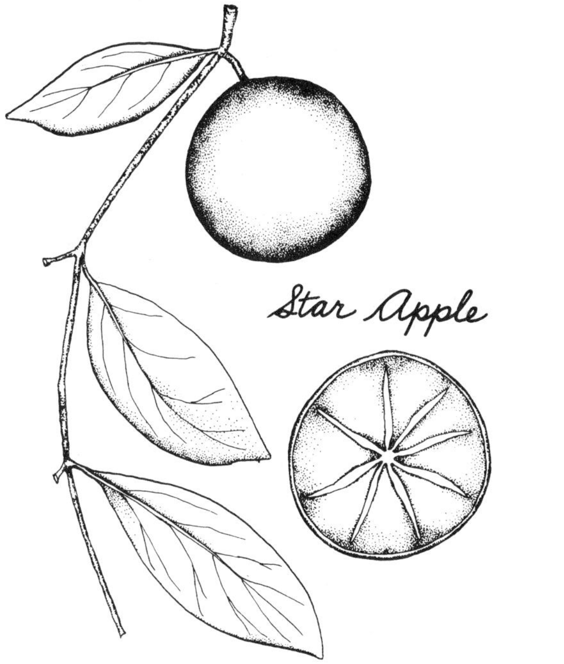

the latter variety looking like an eggplant. All varieties taste pretty much the same, but some say that the green is better. When cut crossways, the fruit reveals a pulp of translucent jelly that forms a starlike figure. Black seeds are embedded in the pulp, which has a texture like custard. The flavor is delicious, provided the fruit is tree-ripened. It is eaten raw.

STARCH

A white, tasteless carboyhydrate substance found in the seeds, roots or stems of plants, starch is widespread and abundant and for centuries has supplied much of the **carbohydrate** for human nutrition. There are only a few plants, however, with starch abundant enough to serve as a source for commercial extraction. These plants are corn (maize), tapioca, potato, sago, waxy maize, wheat, sorghum, rice and arrowroot. Material is extracted from these plants and ground, soaked, washed, sieved, filtered, dried in cake form and then reground. The result is a white powder, the source of which is impossible to detect with the naked eye.

Commercial starch is used for thickening soups and stews, in baking and for mixing batters and coating foods. It is also used in a water solution to stiffen cloth fabrics. Certain enzymes such as amylase and diastase convert starch to sugar and figure importantly in brewing and distilling alcoholic beverages.

STARGAZER

Also RATA DEL MAR. This is a family of ocean fish distributed worldwide, the most common European species of which is *Uranoscopus scaber*, called *rata del mar* in Spain. It is found throughout the Mediterranean and in the eastern Atlantic from Portugal to Senegal. The stargazer's eyes are placed on top of its head, and it habitually lies buried in the sand or mud with just the top of the head projecting. Small fish are lured into its mouth by means of a stalked flap that folds out from its head. The flesh of the stargazer is coarse, but it is eaten throughout the Mediterranean in soups and stews, such as bouillabaisse.

The stargazer favors warm seas and reaches a length of 15 inches. It is equipped with organs that generate electrical power and can deliver a shock of about 50 volts to the unwary hand.

STARLING

This small bird, *Sturnus vulgaris*, is native to Europe but is now plentiful in the United States where it is regarded as a serious pest. With its black, iridescent plumage, the starling resembles the blackbird. The ancient Romans were fond of starlings and prepared them in a variety of ways, including starling pie. Europeans have continued to eat starlings, less so nowadays than formerly, but especially in southern Europe where small birds are eagerly hunted. The birds are plucked and eviscerated, but not boned, often hung for a few days, then barded or larded before cooking. They may be roasted, grilled, made into a casserole or a pie, or prepared in any way suitable for **thrush.**

Although in the pre-20th century United States there was a strong tradition of eating small birds, starlings today are for the most part avoided by Americans. Starlings were introduced into the United States in 1890, reached California in 1940, and have developed into a costly consumer of feed grains and other crops.

STAR OF BETHLEHEM

Also NAP-AT-NOON, SUMMER SNOWFLAKE, PRUSSIAN ASPARAGUS. Two plants of the lily family are known by this name and have edible parts. *Ornithogalum pyrenaicum*, or Prussian asparagus, is found in southern Europe, Asia Minor and Morocco and has been naturalized in the United States. Its stalks are prepared and eaten like asparagus. *O. umbellatum*, also known as nap-at-noon, summer snowflake and dove's dung, has edible bulbs, which are eaten like salsify. It is native to Europe and North Africa but has also been naturalized in the United States. Both species are small, herbaceous plants with white or greenish white flowers.

STEAMERS

See **Clam.**

STEENBRAS

See **Musselcracker.**

STEINBUSCHER

This soft German cheese, made from whole or partly skimmed cow's milk, originated in Steinbusch in 1860. Steinbuscher is surface ripened and has a taste and aroma similar to ***Romadur.*** The surface is yellow, and the paste has a butterlike consistency. The flavor is pungent and mildly sour. Curing takes eight to 10 weeks, depending on the season, and finished cheeses are five inches square by two thick.

STEPPE

This rich, mellow cheese was first made in Russia by German colonists but also manufactured in Austria, Denmark and Germany. It is made of whole milk with color added, and has a flavor like ***Tilsiter*** but milder. Individual cheeses have small, irregular eyes and come in two shapes: flattened balls, weighing 14 to 25 pounds, and rectangular blocks, weighing 13 pounds.

STERLET

One of the smaller **sturgeons,** the sterlet *(Acipenser ruthenus)* has fine, delicately flavored flesh and also produces fine caviar. It is a migratory fish found in the Black and Caspian Seas as well as in rivers that feed into them, such as the Danube, Don and Volga. The sterlet has the typical long spindle-shaped body of the sturgeon, with bony ridges on the skin and a narrow, pointed, up-turned snout. It reaches a length of about 32 inches maximum. Flesh of the sterlet is broiled, baked or poached in white wine. It is also popular dried, smoked or salted.

See also: **Sturgeon.**

STICKLEBACK

Also EPINOCHE. This is a small fish of the family *Gasterosteidae*, many species of which can live in either fresh or salt water. A characteristic of the family is the presence of a series of separate sharp spines along the back and a sharp spine in the pelvic fins. Usually, they are elongate, torpedo-shaped and scaleless. In France, they are taken from rivers and, as a rule, deep-fried. They are considered to be of mediocre quality as a food fish.

Well-known species are the three-spined stickleback *(G. aculeatus)*, found in fresh water from the Mediterannean basin to the Arctic Circle and in the sea around northern Europe; the sea or 15-spined stickle back *(Spinachia spinachia)*, found from the Bay of Biscay to the Baltic; and the nine-spined stickleback *(Pungitius pungitius)*, found across the entire Northern Hemisphere.

STILTON

One of the finest and best-known English cheeses, Stilton has a semihard, white curd shot with blue green veins and a piquant but mellow flavor. Like its counterparts in France (Roquefort) and Italy (Gorgonzola), Stilton is ripened with the aid of *Penicillium roqueforti* mold, yet Stilton is milder than the other two. It is made from whole cow's milk, sometimes double-creamed. Stilton is distinguished by the narrow, blue green veins running throughout the curd, which has an open, flaky texture. The open texture obviates the punching of holes to facilitate mold growth, as is done to Roquefort and Gorgonzola. The rind is a dull brown, highly wrinkled, but not cracked.

Stilton's history is easily traced back to the early 18th century in Leicestershire where a Mrs. Orton, who resided in Little Dalby, reportedly first produced it. It acquired its name, and its first fame, through the activities of an innkeeper in Stilton, Huntingdonshire, a relative of Mrs. Orton, who served Stilton to his guests. It quickly became famous, and Alexander Pope alluded to it in his *Imitation of Horace* published in 1736:

> *Cheese such as men in Suffolk made*
> *But wished it Stilton for his sake.*

Cheeses are ripened for at least six months, but experts say they reach perfection in nine. A typical cheese weighs from 12 to 15 pounds and is round in shape, measuring eight inches in diameter by 12 deep.

Stilton goes well with port, and some people recommend pouring a glass of port or sherry onto the cheese after it has been cut and allowing the wine to soak in. Some experts recommend scooping cheese out from the center of a Stilton while others decry the practice as wasteful, saying a level cut should be made by drawing a knife straight across the face of the cheese.

STINGING NETTLE

See **Bigstring.**

STOCK

See **Soup.**

STOCKFISH

See **Cod.**

STONE CURLEW

Also NORFOLK PLOVER. A European shorebird, *Oedicnemus crepitans*, of the **plover** family, it is found in Europe in the summer, but is generally protected by laws. The stone curlew is also common in North Africa and India where it is regarded as fair game. The stone curlew is prepared in any way suitable for **woodcock.**

STOUT

See **Porter.**

STRACCHINO

This term originally described a condition of the milk used in cheesemaking, but has come to be a generic term for soft, rich, ripened cheeses made in the north of Italy. They are made from whole milk and include Gorgonzola, *Milano* (or *fresco*, or *quadro)*, *quartirolo*, *Crescenza* and *salame*. Check under the names of these cheese for more information.

STRACCHINO DE GORGONZOLA

See **Gorgonzola.**

STRACCHINO DI MILANO

See **Milano Cheese.**

STRACCHINO QUARTIROLO

See **Milano Cheese.**

STRACCHINO SALAME

See **Salame Cheese.**

STRAWBERRY

A small, reddish berry, whose flavor is best in the wild, it has been cultivated extensively and is one of the most popular fruits in the world.

The wild, or wood strawberry *(Fregaria vesca)*, a perennial trailing plant, grows wild throughout Europe and the British Isles. Its sweetly tart flavor is unequalled. Izaak Walton, in *The Compleat Angler*, quoted Dr. William Boteler in its praise, "Doubtless

Strawberries

God could have made a better berry, but doubtless God never did." But the wild fruit is smaller, sparser and does not travel or keep as well as the commercial varieties, which are hybrids of the Chilean and Virginia wild strawberries.

Native Americans were fond of the latter, which drew the attention of Roger Williams, founder of Providence, Rhode Island in 1636. Local berries were larger than the European type, he wrote, and are "the wonder of all the Fruits growing naturally in these parts. The Indians bruise them in a Morter, and mixe them with meale and make strawberry bread." It was but a short jump to the invention of strawberry shortcake. Commercial hybrids originated in France when, in the 18th century, the Chilean and Virginia varieties were planted side by side. The resulting cross-breed was called the pineapple strawberry.

Hybrid berries are larger than the wild varieties, some attaining four to five inches in length, and are hollow at the core. Larger berries do not have the intense flavor of the smaller ones and can have a somewhat woody texture.

Strawberries are grown in every state of the United States, but California alone accounts for ¼ of world production. They are rich in vitamins C, B1 and B2 and are usually eaten fresh, sometimes with sugar and cream, less often with salt, or even pepper. They are made into pies, tarts, jellies and preserves, but much of the vitamin content is lost in the cooking.

STRAWBERRY CACTUS

This edible fruit of a variety of hedgehog cactus *(Echinocereus enneacanthus)* is found in the southwestern United States and northern Mexico. The round, green or purplish fruit has a delicious strawberry taste. It is eaten raw or preserved.

STRAWBERRY PEAR

Also NIGHT-BLOOMING CEREUS, QUEEN-OF-THE-NIGHT, HONOLULU-QUEEN. The name refers to the fleshy, red fruit of several species of cactus native to tropical America, especially Mexico and the West Indies. Most familiar are *Hylocereus triangularus* and *H. undatus*, which are climbing plants with nocturnal white or red flowers. The fruit is pear-shaped, four to five inches in diameter. The pulp is white and resembles the strawberry in flavor. The strawberry pear is eaten fresh or added to such dishes as the West Indian pepper pot.

STRAWBERRY TOMATO

See **Ground Cherry.**

STRAWBERRY TREE

See **Arbutus.**

STRAW MUSHROOM

Also CHINESE MUSHROOM, PADI-STRAW MUSHROOM. This very tasty, edible mushroom has a status in China and Southeast Asia similar to that of the white cultivated mushroom in the United States and Europe. It has been cultivated by the Chinese since earliest times on beds of rice straw, hence the name.

The straw mushroom *(Volvariella volvacea)* has a gray to brown cap and a stem that grows out of a cuplike base. Under cultivation it fruits rapidly, and in a couple of weeks or so it is ready for canning, which is accomplished shortly after the cap emerges from the sheath at the base of the stem. Although it is enjoyed fresh in the Far East, it appears in the West only in canned or dried form. It has the reputation of retaining its excellent flavor when canned. It is ubiquitous in Chinese and Southeast Asian cuisines, especially in stir-fried foods and steaming dishes. Dried mushroom should be soaked for 15 minutes in warm water before cooking.

There are related species of *Volvariella* in Northern Europe, but they are rare. Incidentally, one of the oldest pictures of a mushroom extant is that of a *Volvariella* represented in a North African market of Roman times. It is not the straw mushroom, however.

See also: **Mushroom.**

STRAW WINES

This is wine made from grapes that have been stored through the winter on straw mats. The practice is common in the Jura region of eastern France near Arbois. After harvest, the grapes are left to dry until February. They are then pressed and put to age in small oak barrels. The resulting vintage *vin de paille*, is a rich golden amber dessert wine with a sweet bouquet.

STREGA

This is a famous Italian liqueur with a golden-yellow color and a spicy taste. A number of plants are used to produce its unique flavor, most notably citrus fruits. The name literally means "witch." It is bottled at 80 proof and served at room temperature.

STRING BEAN

See **Kidney Bean.**

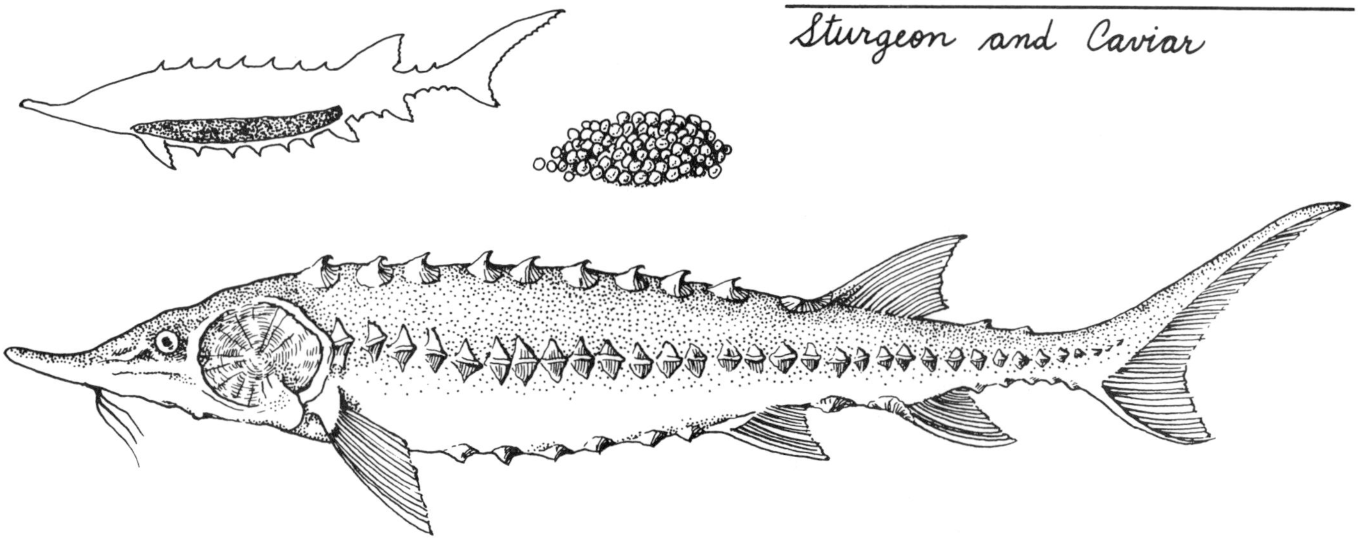

Sturgeon and Caviar

STRINGER CHEESE

See **Sbrinz.**

STROMATEUS

See **Butterfish.**

STURGEON

These fish of the *Acipenser* family are best known as producers of caviar but are also valued for their oily, white flesh. Some species of sturgeon are found in fresh water, others in salt water, and still others in both, i.e., they are migratory. They are fish of the Northern Hemisphere, inhabiting both sides of the Atlantic, the Black and Caspian Seas and such rivers as the Vistula, Rhine, Weser, Elbe, Odor and Garonne in Europe; the Volga, Ural and Danube in Russia and the Columbia River in the United States. Characteristically, they have a long, slender body with rows of shiny plates on the back and a projecting snout.

The great sturgeon, or beluga, *(Acipenser huro)*, is the largest sturgeon (one caught in 1912 tipped the scales at 2,250 pounds), and perhaps the largest fish found in fresh water. They live in the Black and Caspian Seas but migrate up the Danube and the Volga Rivers to spawn. Beluga roe is considered the finest caviar and may make up as much as one-third the weight of the fish. It is not unusual for the Beluga to be 20 feet long and weigh 1,000 pounds. The flesh of a fish this size, though white and oily, tends to be coarse and rubbery. It is often smoked, or if eaten fresh, hung for a couple of days to soften up before cooking. *Vesiga* is a sort of gelatin made from the spinal marrow of the sturgeon. Other Russian sturgeons include the sterlet (maximum three feet in length), the *sevruga* (six feet) and the *osseter* (12 feet).

The common sturgeon *(A. sturio)* of the Atlantic Ocean averages eight feet in length (although an 18-footer was caught off New England), but smaller sizes are preferred for eating. It is also plentiful in the Caspian and is believed to be the species highly prized by Roman emperors who imported it from there, kept alive in tubs on the decks of ships and carried live by relays of slaves from the port of Ostia into Rome. In England, traditionally, the sturgeon has been considered a royal fish, though not popular as a food fish, and sturgeons caught in British waters were customarily offered to the monarch. The common sturgeon is sauteed, roasted or baked whole (if small) with herbs. It may also be braised or poached in a champagne sauce.

Sturgeon has been extremely plentiful in American rivers, such that in 1900 the United States was the world's leading producer of caviar. Since then, overfishing has caused sturgeon to be an endangered species in some places, such as California, where they are protected by law. American sturgeons average five feet in length and have the characteristic snout, which they use to root out crustaceans and mollusks from the soft sea or river beds. Commercial supplies come mainly from Washington and Oregon where unrestricted fishing is permitted along the Columbia and other rivers. Sturgeon flesh is most popular smoked.

See also: **Caviar.**

STYRIA

This is a cylindrical Austrian cheese made from whole cow's milk in the province of Styria.

SUCKER

Also BARBIER. Several varieties of fish are called by this highly descriptive name, but not all for the

Sugar in various forms: Sugar cane and cubes appear in front. Displayed on the dishes are (left to right) turbinado, dark brown and powdered sugars.

same reason. Freshwater sucker fish, such as the blackhorse of the Mississippi Valley, are so called because of their big mouths and rubbery lips, which are used to suck up plants and tiny animals from river bottoms. This type of scavenger fish is common in the British Isles as well as in Europe. Its flesh is delicate, and is often broiled, pan-fried or cooked in any way suitable for catfish.

Members of the *Catostomidae* family are called "sucker" because of the way their pelvic fins come together to form a cup-shaped sucker. One of the best known is the **lumpfish** of the North Atlantic, much prized for its roe, which is dyed black and served as caviar. Other varieties of this saltwater type are the sucking fish, the hagfish, the northern sucker, the northern white and the Buffalo chub. *Barbier* is the French term for the Mediterranean sucker fish, which is best when lightly sauteed.

Finally, the term is applied to certain perches that have sharp spines in their dorsal fins.

SUDAN COFFEE

This is a drink made in Africa from roasted, ground kola nuts, which contain the stimulating principle, caffeine.

See also: **Cola.**

SUET

This is hard, white fat, especially that found around the kidneys and loins of beef and mutton. In cooking, it may be used to make stuffings, mincemeat and suet puddings, which are sweet or savory and usually steamed or boiled. In England, spotted dick is a suet pudding containing raisins or other fruit and sugar, bread crumbs, flour, milk, eggs and spices. It is shaped into a roll. Suet may be purchased in lump form from a butcher or shredded in packets in the market. It was formerly used to make tallow for candles.

SUGAR

Sugar is a class of carbohydrates present in many plants, but usually extracted from cane or beets for use as a food and a sweetening agent. Sugar ranks high in food value and is of great culinary and nutritional importance. Cane and beet sugar are sucrose crystals. Other forms of sugar will be discussed under such headings as corn sugar, fructose, glucose, invert sugar, maltose, palm sugar and sorghum.

Sugar cane *(Saccharum officinarum)* had its origin in Southeast Asia and was cultivated in India before the birth of Christ. Our word "sugar" comes from the Sanskrit *sarkara*, after being handed down and filtered through various languages, such as the Persian *shakar*, the Arabic *sukkar*, the Latin *saccharum* and the French *sucre*.

The Arabs first brought sugar from cane to the Mediterranean area during Classical Antiquity. It was a crude, sticky, semicrystallized paste, which was thought to have some medicinal value. Ways of purifying it were developed by the Persians and improved upon by the Arabs, who later introduced its cultivation into Sicily and Spain in the 8th and 9th centuries A.D. It was taken to the New World by Columbus. In the Caribbean area it found a more propitious climate for development and rapidly spread to other tropical areas. Production increased enormously over the next 300 years, and by 1800 sugar, which until then had been affordable only by the rich, was coming into general use. Beet sugar was introduced at about this time, an event that had a drastic effect on the cane industry, about which more below.

Sugar cane is a reed that accumulates sugar in its tissues to the extent of about 15 percent by weight. To do this it requires a suitable climate, i.e., an average temperature of 75° F (23.9° C), and a uniform rainfall of about 80 inches a year. Growing to a height of six to 10 feet, it is cut down between its 11th and 12th month. The cane is stripped of its leaves, either by trimming or burning, and taken to a refinery where the juice is extracted by pressing or by diffusion. The woody residue (called "bagasse") is composted to make fertilizer, used to make paper, or burnt as fuel. The juice (called "vesou") is boiled several times to concentrate the sucrose, purified with a lime water solution, then separated into sugar crystals and molasses by centrifugation. The raw sugar, which is about 96 percent sucrose, is further washed and refined. The molasses can be distilled to produce rum, used as animal or human food or made into vinegar. Sugar cane produces more calories per acre of human nourishment than any other plant. Leading producers are Cuba, Puerto Rico, Santo Domingo, Brazil, Hawaii and tropical countries of Africa.

The sugar beet *(Beta vulgaris)* is a variety of the common beet and could be eaten at table if anyone desired to. Although its juice was known to contain sugar as early as 1747, it remained for Napoleon, motivated by the English blockade of his country, to give impetus to large-scale production of sugar from beets. Using a process perfected by Francois Achard, a Berliner of French origin, Benjamin Delessert, head of the Bank of France, opened a huge refinery at Passy in 1810. France's supply of cane sugar had been cut off for some time, and the French were sugar-starved. Napoleon took one look at the factory and ordered 70,000 acres to be planted in sugar beets. Delessert was made a baron.

As with other innovations, there was resistance from the public to sugar from beets. It was alleged to have an unpleasant taste, to be less sweet than cane sugar and to be generally unhealthy. A caricature that appeared in the press summed up the public scorn for beet sugar. Napoleon is depicted as squeezing a beet into a cup of coffee. Nearby, his little son, the King of Rome, weeps as his nurse hands him a beet saying, "Suck this, child! Your father says it's sugar."

When the blockade ended, the market for beet sugar collapsed under the competition from cheaper cane sugar. It revived in 1878 with the advent of more efficient machinery for processing beets, and the development of a better beet, the white Silesian beet, from which all current strains of sugar beet are descended. Development of the sugar beet industry is of incalculable importance, since it freed countries in the temperate zone from dependence on tropical cane. Indeed, the Soviet Union, which grows about a third of the world's sugar beet crop, is the world's largest sugar producer. Beet sugar gradually won general acceptance after it was shown experimentally that beet sugar and cane sugar are identical chemically. Yet, to this day most gourmets prefer cane sugar.

At the sugar refinery, beets are cut into strips and put into diffusion cells with water at about 175° F (79.4° C). After the sugar diffuses into the water, the solution is evaporated to make a thick syrup. The beet strips are pulped and used for stock feed or treated chemically to extract commercial pectin. Sugar is crystallized from the syrup, then separated from the residual molasses in a centrifuge. Unlike raw cane sugar, raw beet sugar is not immediately usable, except as animal food. Because of its unpleasant smell, it must be further refined to be palatable for humans.

Following is a list of some of the various types of sugar that appear in the market:

Granulated sugar, with dry, white crystals, is the ordinary sugar of everyday use. Sugar of finer granulation is called "castor" or "superfine"; it dissolves quickly, and is popular for use on fruit, cereals, and in preparation of puddings and cakes. The finest granulation is *powdered* sugar.

Icing, confectioner's or Four X sugars are powdered and usually have an admixture of cornstarch to prevent lumping.

Cube or lump sugar has been moistened with sugar-cane liquor and pressed into molds. It is popular for hot drinks or situations when exact quantities are desired. It is sometimes called "loaf" sugar, a name that harks back to earlier centuries when sugar was molded in the shape of a cone, which was called a sugarloaf. Pieces were broken off of the loaf in convenient sizes using a sugar cutter (now a museum piece).

Confetti sugar consists of fairly large crystals dyed various hues to be used as decoration.

Brown sugar comes in several shades and degrees

of coarseness. The darker the color, the stronger the taste. It should be stored in a glass container with a tight cover.

Demerara sugar is raw sugar with large, light amber crystals. Only the grossest impurities have been removed.

Barbados is soft, moist, very dark brown and has about the same degree of refining as Demarara.

Foot sugar is the coarsest, most unrefined form of cane sugar available. It has a treacly consistency (due to a high proportion of molasses) and is almost black.

Sand or *soft* sugar is pale brown and has the texture of damp sand. It is called "light brown" in the United States, and is used chiefly in confectionary.

Sugar provides 1,794 calories per pound, and due to the ease of its digestion, is a quick supplier of energy to the human body.

SUGAR APPLE

See **Sweetsop.**

SUGARBERRY

See **Hackberry.**

SUGAR GRASS

Also MAMMA GRASS. The seeds of the North American plant, *Glyceria fruitans*, are used for food. A perennial, it is also found in Europe and Asia.

SUGAR PLUM

See **Juneberry.**

SUGEE

In India, white grain grown around Calcutta is ground to powder and used as an ingredient in bread and puddings. It is said to resemble semolina or tapioca in flavor.

SULPHER SHELF MUSHROOM

See **Polypore.**

SULTAN HEN

This is a game bird of the *Rallidae* family, which also includes rails, coots and water hens. The common European species is also known as the purple water-hen *(Porphyrio porphyrio)* and is found on both sides of the Mediterranean. A variety found in the West Indies and the southern United States is *Ionornis martinica*, also known as the purple gallinule. These birds frequent marshes and have webbed feet. They are prepared like **coot.**

SUMAC

This genus of vines, shrubs and trees *(Rhus* spp.) is found in temperate and subtropical regions around the world. Sumacs are best known as a source of tannin, but some varieties have culinary uses, including the following:

Fragrant sumac *(R. aromatica)* of eastern North America and the *dwarf sumac (R. copallina)* of Europe and the United States, both of which are shrubs and produce red berries. After soaking, the berries are made into a cooling drink.

Smooth or red sumac *(R. glabra)* of temperate North America bears red berries. The fruit of *Rhus glabra* is covered with fine hairs, which must be filtered out through several thicknesses of cloth. The strained liquid is slightly sour and tart, similar to cranberry juice, although thinner in flavor. Sumac juice is a good addition to **elderberries** in the making of elderberry jam. These also are used to make drinks and are often mixed with maple sugar.

Squawberry or lemonade sumach *(R. trilobata)*, is a shrub found from the Midwest to California, whose red fruits were used by the native Americans as food, fresh or dried, made into jam or used to make cooling drinks. They also smoked the leaves and used the stems for making baskets.

Staghorn sumac or lemonade tree *(R. typhina)* is a tree of eastern North America that yields crimson berries that are made into a drink known as Indian lemonade.

Care should be exercised with sumac, since there are six poisonous species that are known as poison ivies and poison oaks. A white-berried sumac is included in this group.

SUMATRA TEA

This Indonesian black tea from the islands of Java and Sumatra enjoys ample popularity in Asia but is used mainly for blending in Europe and the United States. It is similar in style to **Ceylon tea** and has a fairly good flavor.

See also: **Tea.**

SUN BERRY

This is a tropical species of ground cherry, *Physalis minima*, whose fruit is eaten as a vegetable.

SUNDAE

See **Ice Cream.**

SUNDEW

Also OILPLANT. This genus of bog plants, *Drosera* spp., is worldwide in its distribution, the most familiar of which is the round-leaved variety *(D. rotundifolia)*. This is common in the United States, the British Isles and France. The sundew has slender stems, small white to pink flowers and leaves fringed with green to reddish hairs that are capable of trapping and digesting insects. The leaves are covered with a dewlike secretion to which the plant owes its name.

In France, the sundew leaves are eaten both raw as a salad vegetable or cooked as greens. The French used to make a liqueur from it called *rossolis*. In former times, it was credited with aphrodisiac qualities to the extent that in the 16th century it was often mixed with ale or garden herbs or incorporated into potions containing variously sugar, mace, ginger, cinnamon, nutmeg and other spices.

SUNFISH

The name refers to several species of ocean fish *(Molidae)* that range up to eight feet in length and can weigh as much as two tons. They are distinguished by an odd looking, tail-less body that is very deep and looks truncated. It is rectangular in shape in some species, and in others nearly circular.

The ocean sunfish *(Mola mola)* is found worldwide in temperate and tropical seas and is often encountered floating inactively on the surface, apparently basking in the sun. Sunfish are edible, but are not deliberately fished because the flesh tends to be tough and is usually infested with parasitic worms. If eaten, they are generally put into soups, but some people consider them a delicacy.

Another huge species is the sharptail mola *(Masturus lanceolatus)*, which has a pronounced tail. Much smaller is the slender sunfish *(Ranzania laevis)*, which rarely exceeds 25 pounds.

"Sunfish" also refers to a genus of U.S. freshwater fish *(Lepomis)*, which includes the pumpkinseed *(L. gibbosus)* and most prominently, the **bluegill,** a renowned fighting fish. They range in size from eight to 14 inches, and several species are considered good eating.

SUNFLOWER

Sunflowers

This plant, *Helianthus annuus*, native to the Americas, is characterized by large yellow-petaled flowers whose seeds are edible and yield a valuable oil. There are many varieties of wild and cultivated sunflowers. The cultivated varieties have a single stem, broad leaves and flowers whose seed heads vary between six and 15 inches in diameter. The plant may grow as high as 20 feet under cultivation, while it rarely exceeds 12 in the wild.

The sunflower is closely related to the **Jerusalem artichoke** *(H. tuberosa)*, part of whose name is a corruption of the Spanish word for sunflower, *girasol*. *Girasol* means "turns to the sun," after the flower's purported ability to move its seed heads so that they always face the sun.

Sunflower seeds are usually the size of watermelon or pumpkin seeds. They are black or gray and occasionally dark-striped. Dried or roasted and salted, they are eaten as a snack, as in Greece, along with wines or liquor. There they are sold in the streets by a vendor called the *passa tempo* man. The oil pressed from sunflower seeds is of very high quality, pale yellow, nearly odorless, with a mild, pleasant flavor. In world commerce, it ranks third in importance behind soybean and peanut oils. It is used as a cooking oil, in salad dressings, margarine and soap. It is high in polyunsaturates, which makes it attractive to persons who wish to restrict their intake of saturated fats. The seed meal, a by-product of oil extraction, together with threshed sunflower heads, are used as cattle feed. Sunflower stalks were once an important silage in the United States.

Although sunflowers were an important crop in several places in the Americas when Europeans first arrived, it was more than 100 years before they were transplanted to Europe, first to Spain, then central Europe, Russia, the Middle East and India. Russia is the largest producer of sunflowers, followed by Argentina, India, South Africa and Canada. In the United States, the largest producing states are North Dakota, Minnesota and California.

The sunflower's supposed fidelity to the sun's movements has inspired many literary allusions of which the following by Moliere (from *La Malade*

Imaginaire) is typical. "The naturalists tell us that the flower called heliotrope turns without ceasing toward the star of the day, and just so will my heart hereafter turn toward the resplendent stars of your adorable eyes."

SUNTWOOD

Also BABUL, GUM-ARABIC TREE. This African tree, *Acacia nilotica*, produces a substitute **gum arabic.** It reaches heights of up to 75 feet and has been widely naturalized in India where it is also an important source of tanbark and timber.

SUOMUURIAN

See **Lakka.**

SUPREME SAUCE

This is a variation of the basic French **veloute sauce** in which fresh cream is added to a *veloute* sauce based on chicken stock. Butter is blended in just before serving. It is used with eggs, poultry, variety meats (offal) and vegetables.

See also: **Sauce.**

SURATI

Also PANIR. One of the better-known Indian cheeses made from buffalo's milk in the Gujarat area of Bombay province, *surati* is unusual in that it is transported and cured floating in its own whey. Cheeses weigh four ounces and are cured from 12 to 36 hours. Surati is believed to have some therapeutic properties.

SURINAM CHERRY

Also PITANGA, BRAZILIAN CHERRY. This is the yellow to deep red fruit of the shrubby tree, *Eugenia uniflora*, native to tropical Brazil, but widely transplanted in the tropics. It is a highly decorative tree that has been grown with success in Florida, California and Hawaii. The fruit is round to egg-shaped, about an inch in diameter, with a distinctive eight-ribbed configuration. There is a single, large stone surrounded by a juicy pulp. The taste is subacidic to acidic, often a little too tart for eating raw, though it goes well in a mixed fruit salad and makes an excellent jelly. It is often cooked, sweetened and used to make a fruit sauce, or as a filling for pie. Another species, *Eugenia pitanga* of Brazil and Argentina, produces a smaller fruit that is treated similarly.

See also: **West Indian Cherry.**

SUSHI

A Japanese food specialty, sushi consists of boiled rice accompanied by raw fish or other seafood, such as octopus, squid or cuttlefish, often seaweed, and sometimes vegetables. For some varieties, the rice is formed by hand into small balls or squares flavored with vinegar, then covered by a thin slice of seafood or vegetable. It makes a nice, bite-sized snack. In others, a layer of rice is spread over a sheet of kelp or purple seaweed, then both wrapped around a core of fish or vegetable and the roll sliced into bite-sized portions. The individual portion may then be topped with an exotic garnish, such as a quail egg.

Sushi is eaten as a snack, appetizer or as an accompaniment to other dishes. They are sometimes sold a dozen or so to a wooden box and eaten as a takeout lunch, as one would a box lunch in the West. Sushi bars are common today in many large American cities; there skillful chefs delight the eye as well as the palate as they create beautifully arranged platters of sushi.

SVECIAOST

A popular and typical Swedish cheese made for local consumption, sveciaost resembled **Gouda** except that its texture is more open and spices are often added to the curd. It is a rich cheese, with a fresh distinctive flavor, that is made in full cream, part-cream and skim versions. Cheeses are round and flat, 15 inches in diameter by six inches thick, and weigh from 26 to 33 pounds. They are aged from two to four months and are eaten soon after that because at six months the quality begins to deteriorate. Spices added are usually caraway seeds or cloves.

SWALLOW

The name includes any of several small songbirds of the family *Hirundinidae* that are noted for their punctual migrations. Swallows are swift-flying and have pointed wings and forked tails.

In former times the European swallow *(Hirundio rustica)* was trapped in great numbers to be spit-roasted. Nowadays they are protected by law in many countries—including Great Britain, France, and the United States—but are still eaten enthusiastically in Italy. A Far Eastern variety, the *salangane* swallow, makes gelatinous nests that are collected to make bird's nest soup, a dish much esteemed by Chinese gourmets.

See also: **Bird's Nest.**

SWALLOWTAIL

A common deepwater fish of Australian waters, the swallowtail *(Trachichthodes lineatus)* reaches a length of about 14 inches and has a striking, deep crimson coloring. It is good to eat and is marketed in small numbers in South and West Australia.

SWAMP CABBAGE

See **Skunk Cabbage.**

SWAN

Also CYGNET. This large, white aquatic bird of the genus *Cygnus* enjoyed equal popularity with the peacock as banquet fare in the Middle Ages. It has fallen into disfavor nowadays, because the flesh of the mature bird has a tendency to be oily and tough. Hunters occasionally take a young swan, or cygnet, whose flesh is tender and appetizing. It looks somewhat like a dark goose when dressed. Cygnets are also eaten at the annual Swan Banquet put on by the Swan Wardens of the Vintners' Company of the City of London. This takes place after the marking and counting of the Thames swans, which are possessions of the English Crown. Cygnet is usually roasted on a spit or stuffed and cooked in a pastry case. Swan breast is a great delicacy. Swan eggs are also eaten, usually hard boiled, but sometimes poached.

The swan has long been considered a royal bird in England, and in former times was an indispensable item at royal banquets. It was customary to remove the bird's skin and plumage intact, gild them, then slip the roasted bird back inside for presentation at the table with a small crown on its head. A swan was as costly as a pig. This was not true in France where they were raised in quantity for broader consumption.

SWEDE

See **Rutabaga.**

SWEDISH PUNSCH

This is a liqueur of great repute produced in Sweden from sugar syrup and Batavian arak, a brandylike rum of great pungency that is highly aromatic and very dry.

SWEDISH TURNIP

See **Rutabaga.**

SWEET BAY

See **Borbonia.**

SWEETBREADS

Also RIS DE VEAU. The term refers to the thymus gland, and to a lesser extent, the pancreas of a calf, primarily, but also of a lamb or a kid. Sweetbread terminology can lead to confusion. The thymus is known popularly as the "neck sweetbread." It is regarded as far superior in taste and texture to the pancreas, which is also called the "stomach sweetbread." The thymus, however, when dressed for sale by the butcher, comes in two parts: a round section called the "heart sweetbread," and an irregularly shaped section called the "throat sweetbread." So, there are three sweetbreads—the heart, the throat and the stomach sweetbread—in descending order of desirability.

For home consumption, though, one generally considers only the heart sweetbread, which is the choice cut. Throat and stomach sweetbreads are more often sold to restaurants, which include them in other dishes. Due to their bland taste, and their reputation as a luxury food, sweetbreads are often incorporated as background items in complex preparations involving expensive ingredients, such as **truffles.**

The function of the thymus gland is somewhat obscure, but it reaches peak size at puberty, then gradually shrinks to practically nothing at maturity. Thus, there are no neck sweetbreads to be obtained from adult mammals. Calf's sweetbreads are generally preferred because they are larger and tastier than lamb or kid sweetbreads. They are very perishable, and it is recommended that they be eaten within 24 hours of purchase. It is customary to blanch them before cooking to enhance tenderness. The taste of sweetbreads is delicate, so to appreciate their true flavor a simple method of cooking is needed, such as braising, broiling or sauteeing.

SWEET BROOM

The branches of this tropical American shrub, *Scoparia dulcis,* are placed in drinking water to improve its flavor, giving it a cool taste.

SWEET CICELY

Also CICELY. In Europe, "sweet cicely" is the name given to a fernlike member of the parsley family, *Myrrhis odorata,* which is an aromatic herb. In the United States it generally refers to *Osmorrhiza longistylis,* which is unrelated but similarly aromatic.

The European variety originated in the central and southern regions, the name coming from the

Greek *sesilis* and Latin *sesli*. Pliny and Dioscordes mentioned this herb, and it was extensively cultivated in France and England in the 16th and 17th centuries. The French call it musk chervil, and the Spanish aromatic chervil, although it is not related to chervil. Use as a potherb has declined drastically in the 20th century. This has been attributed to cicely's flavor and aroma, which are more assertive than chervil's. If crushed between the fingers, sweet cicely gives off an aroma much like aniseed. The root too is aromatic. Although the American version is widely distributed throughout eastern and central regions, it is not much used in the kitchen.

Sweet cicely, finely chopped, is occasionally used to flavor soups and stews. It is said to remove the acidity from rhubarb, if added during the cooking. The chief contemporary use of sweet cicely is in flavoring liqueurs, most notably Chartreuse.

SWEET CLOVER

See **Melilot.**

SWEET CURD CHEESE

In the United States this is a **cheddar-**type cheese that departs from the normal cheddar process in two ways: the milk is set with rennet before turning acidic, and the curd is unmilled. The result is a moister cheese with a texture that is less compact. **Brick, Munster, Edam** and **Gouda** are also sweet-curd cheeses.

SWEET GALE

Also BOG MYRTLE, MEADOW FERN. This is an evergreen shrub, *Myrica gale*, of Eurasia and northern North America, whose leaves have been used from very early times to flavor beer. Its yellowish, waxy fruit is used as a seasoning. Sweet gale is a member of the **myrtle** family.

SWEET GRANADILLA

See **Parcha.**

SWEET HEMP

The glucosid estevin is extracted from the South American plant, *Eupatorium rebaudianum*. Estevin is considered a good sweetening agent and is said to be 150 times sweeter than sugar. Paraguay is the main producer.

SWEET LEMON

This species of lemon, *Citrus limetta*, though yellow like the ordinary lemon, is sweet to the taste.

SWEET MASTIC

Also SWEET AFRICAN OLIVE. This is a tree, *Sideroxylon dulcificum*, of tropical Africa, whose ripe fruit imparts a sweet taste to anything eaten with it that is bitter, acidic or sour. This is true only if sweet mastic is very fresh and eaten immediately.

SWEET MILLET

A sweet, thick syrup is extracted from this grass plant, *Panicum stagnium*, of Central Africa and the Sudan. It is used to make candy.

SWEET POTATO

The tuberous root of the trailing vine, *Ipomoea batatas*, sweet potato is native to Central America but grown around the world in tropical and subtropical areas. Sweet potatoes are about the size of ordinary potatoes, although a bit closer to a turnip in shape. They are often prepared in much the same way as the potato, although they are not botanically related and contain a good deal more sugar. There are many varieties of sweet potato, but only two are generally seen in markets. They are the light yellow one *(I. batatas* var. *alba)*, whose flesh remains dry on cooking, and the deep orange one *(I. batatas* var. *rosa)*, which is heavier, sweeter, and whose flesh becomes very moist on cooking. The latter is very rich in vitamin

A, and is often confused with a **yam,** which is of African origin and unrelated botanically.

Along with discovering America on his first voyage, Christopher Columbus also discovered the sweet potato, which was a staple food among the Arawaks of the West Indies. It came to them, apparently, from South America because Peru is the site of achaeological digs containing the most ancient sweet potato seeds. The Arawaks called the sweet potato *batata*, which in English evolved into "potato." Indeed, the sweet potato was known simply as "potato" until the middle of the 18th century when the name was transferred to its present owner. Of the many foods brought from the New World to the Old, the sweet potato (along with the chili pepper) was one of the swiftest to be accepted by Europeans. It was cultivated in Spain as early as 1493, and the Spaniards liked them better than the white potato, itself a transplant from Peru. Within a decade or two England was importing them from Spain (first calling them "Spanish potatoes"). King Henry VIII (who ascended the throne of England in 1509) reportedly took gluttonous delight in heavily spiced sweet potato pies. The English sea dogs were bringing them directly to England by the 1560s, and two decades later Richard Hakluyt tried them and wrote in *The Principal Navigations, Voyages and Discoveries of the English Nation*, "These potatoes be the most delicate rootes that may be eaten, and doe farre exceed our passeneps or carets."

The success of the sweet potato in England was short-lived, and it never really took hold anywhere but Spain. Sweet potato's greatest success was achieved outside Europe, in Africa, India, Southeast Asia and the Pacific Islands, where today it remains a staple food of primary importance. They were taken by the Spaniards to Manila in the Philippines, and by 1616 the sweet potato had arrived in India where today it is widely cultivated. The Chinese adopted it and introduced it to the Japanese, who took to it with such ardor that today 10 percent of the arable land in Japan is devoted to sweet potato cultivation. The Maoris of New Zealand, the Tahitians and the Fijians consider it indispensable, but perhaps dependence on the sweet potato reaches its zenith in New Guinea where it is said to account for 90 percent of the total food intake.

In the United States, the southern states, particularly Louisiana, are the leading producers of sweet potatoes. With the development of new varieties and improved techniques, early breeding strains can be grown as far north as Canada. The light species is grown largely along the eastern shores of Virginia (which grew its first sweet potato in 1648), Maryland, Delaware and New Jersey as well as in Iowa and Kansas. New uses have been developed for the sweet potato, such as the sweet-potato chip (higher in vitamins and carbohydrates than the regular potato chip), sweet-potato flakes (like corn flakes) for use as cereal, in pie fillings and in casseroles, and dehydrated sweet potatoes for feeding hogs, poultry and dairy cattle.

As traditional fare, sweet potatoes may be boiled, glazed, baked or fried. A classic Thanksgiving dish is candied sweet potatoes, which are prepared with orange peel and juice. They can also be mashed in the same manner as white potatoes and are often used to make pie, much as the pumpkin is.

Sweet potatoes should be handled carefully to avoid bruising them, and in the market bruised ones should be rejected. At home, they require dry storage at about 55° F (12.8° C).

SWEET POTATO LEAVES

The leaves of the sweet potato *(Ipomea batatas)* make a tasty and nutritious spinach. They may be picked continuously as the plants grow, leaving enough to promote normal development.

Sweet potatoes

Varieties of Swiss cheese (clockwise from top center): Australian Jarlsberg, hot pepper, Finnish Swiss, Swiss Appenzeller, Jarlsberg and Switzerland

SWEETSOP

This sweet tropical fruit, native to the West Indies and southern Florida, is borne by a small tree, *Annona squamosa.* The sweetsop is round or heart-shaped, somewhat resembling a stubby pine cone with a thick, scaly green rind. Its pulp is a soft, creamy yellow, and tastes best when eaten raw or served frozen as a dessert (like ice cream) or as a chilled breakfast treat. It differs from its cousin the **soursop** in the color of its flesh, in having no spines on its skin and—as the name indicates—in being much less tart. Sweetsop is also known as "sugar-apple." The mature fruit is from three to four inches in diameter. Its yellow pulp reminds some of custard.

SWISS CHARD

See **Chard.**

SWISS CHEESE

Also EMMENTAL, EMMENTHAL. One of the best known and most widely copied of all, this cheese originated in the Emmenthal Valley of the canton of Bern in Switzerland. It is a hard, pale yellow cheese, distinguished by large holes, or eyes, in the paste. These eyes, caused by the proprionic acid bacteria, are an index of quality because, to a large extent, the bacteria determine the unique flavor of Swiss cheese. This has been described as mild, nutty and sweet. Swiss cheeses, called "wheels," are very large, ranging from 145 to 220 pounds. Gruyere, another famous cheese produced in Switzerland, is quite similar, except that its taste is stronger, its eyes smaller and its overall size about one-third of the Swiss.

Swiss cheese is made from fresh, clarified cow's milk, which usually has been standardized as to fat content. About 2,000 pounds of milk are placed in huge copper kettles and reduced by complex and precise methods to about 300 pounds of curd, which,

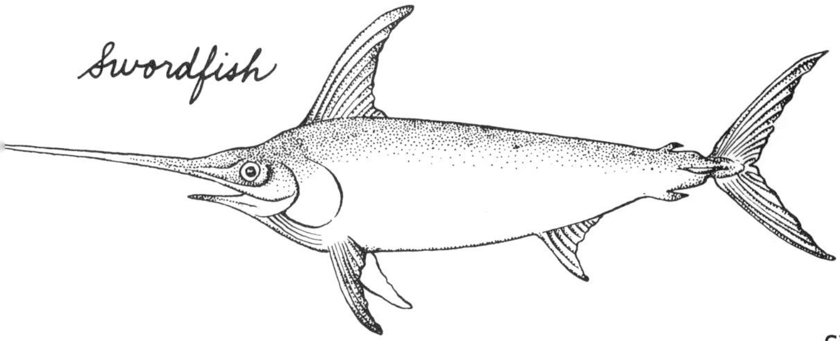

after draining, pressing and drying, yield about 200 pounds of cheese. Curing averages three to four months for Swiss cheese produced in the United States, but six to 10 months for cheese exported from Switzerland. The latter has a stronger flavor.

Swiss cheese production dates from the 15th century in the Emmenthal Valley, but was first produced in the United States in the 1850s by Swiss immigrants. Today it ranks third among hard cheeses produced in the United States, with Illinois and Wisconsin the major production centers. It is often called Schweizer, or Sweitzer, whereas the imported variety is called Switzerland.

Swiss cheese is also made in France, Denmark, Germany, Italy, Austria, Finland, Russia and Argentina under the following local names: **Allgaver**, Emmentaler, *Bellunese*, *formaggio dolce*, **Fontina**, *fontine d'Aosta*, *Traanen* and *Samsoe*.

SWISS GREEN CHEESE

See **Sapsago.**

SWORDFISH

This large marine fish, *Xiphias gladius*, is found in temperate waters all over the world. Its upper jaw protrudes in a long, flat, bony "sword." A peculiarity of the swordfish is that it breeds and spawns in only one place, in the Mediterranean near Messina, Sicily. The Sicilian fishermen claim that the best way to attract the fish is to mutter incantations in ancient Greek, for the swordfish flees at the sound of Italian.

The swordfish appears regularly off the coast of New England in late June and early July, stays for the summer, then moves south into deeper water. Its sword is used to slash and maim, rather than to pierce. In the 1960s both swordfish and tuna were though to contain dangerous concentrations of mercury. Health authorities no longer consider this to be so, except perhaps in the case of swordfish taken off Japan, where almost the entire catch is consumed locally.

Swordfish meat, broiled or fried as steaks, or, as is common in the eastern Mediterranean, grilled on skewers or *kabobs* is one of the finest seafoods known. The meat is firm, white, somewhat oily, unfishy in its taste but must be amply basted to prevent drying. Swordfish steak is a common summer dish in New England, lightly broiled and served with butter, parsley and lemon wedges. Swordfish also lends itself to being grilled over a hot charcoal or wood fire. When prepared in this manner, it should be heavily marinated for several hours beforehand, and basted continually while cooking. Swordfish quickly loses its flavor if even slightly overcooked.

SYCAMORE FIG

Also EGYPTIAN SYCAMORE, MULBERRY FIG. The sycamore of the Bible, this is a popular shade tree of Egypt, Palestine and Arabia whose small fruit (up to one inch in diameter) is popularly known as asses fig. It is, nevertheless, a true fig tree *(Ficus sycomorus)*; and the fruit, which is borne in loose clusters, is sweet and much liked locally. It was honored in ancient Egyptian mythology as the goddess Nepte's gift to the dead admitted to the regions of eternal happiness.

SYLLABUB

Also SILLABUB. This is a sweet beverage dating back to 16th-century England when sweetened wine or cider was mixed with fresh milk, preferably poured from a height to create froth or squirted in directly from the cow. The name derived from "sille," i.e., **Sillery wine** and "bub" a popular word for bubbling (frothy) drink.

More recently, syllabub developed into a thick dessert composed of brandy, rum or wine, spices, a fruit juice and sugar all beaten into a thick cream and served cold in an ice-cream glass. It is eaten with a spoon, or it may be used as a topping on another dessert.

SYRUP

See **Cooking, Menu and Canning terms.**

SZILVA

This dry plum brandy is made in Hungary.

See also: **Quetsch, Slivovitz.**

T

TABASCO

Tabasco is a variety of very hot chili pepper, *Capsicum*, but more familiarly a pepper sauce made and sold in the United States since 1868. Tabasco sauce is a proprietary brand originating in Avery Island, Louisiana. It consists of peppers, spirit vinegar and salt. Sold in small dropper bottles, Tabasco sauce is a concentrated extract of pepper and is extremely hot. Used sparingly, it is an excellent seasoning for soups, salads, seafood and other sauces.

TACCA

Also PIA, TAHITIAN ARROWROOT. This is a tropical herb, *Tacca leontopetaloides*, with a tuberous root and large, feather-shaped leaves. It is widely grown in Asia and the Pacific Islands for the roots which are used to make an arrowroot starch. The roots are dried and ground into flour, which can be used to make porridge or gruel or in baking. Tacca is known by a variety of local names including Fiji arrowroot, South Sea arrowroot, Polynesian arrowroot and salep.

See also: **Arrowroot.**

TAFFELOST

This is a variety of sharp-flavored, Scandinavian whey cheese.

See also: **Mysost.**

TAFFY

Also TOFFEE, TOFFY. This chewy candy is made by boiling down a mixture of sugar, brown sugar or molasses, water and butter, or its equivalent, until it reaches the ball stage, i.e., when a piece of it dropped into cold water hardens into a ball at once. When the mixture cools, it is often pulled and stretched to achieve a light, porous texture. There are many variations on this formula, including the addition of corn syrup or honey, or a variety of flavors, such as chocolate, peppermint, vanilla, etc.

The product may be treated in various ways. In the United States, it may be wrapped in twists of white paper and sold at seaside resorts and other amusement centers as taffy. If it is cut into squares, wrapped and boxed, it may be sold as butterscotch or toffee.

Toffee is a very popular candy in Great Britain, and its origin is said to date back to the days of the West Indian rum trade when it was made from blackstrap molasses (a by-product of rum manufacture) and called "tafia," which was a variety of rum made from molasses and used to flavor the candy. The name evolved into "taffy," then "toffee."

TAFIA

See **Ratafia.**

TAHITIAN ARROWROOT

See **Tacca.**

TAHR

Also KRAS, JAGLA. This Himalayan mountain goat is much valued as food by local inhabitants. In addition to food value, hill people consider the flesh a helpful medicine against fever and rheumatism. The Himalayan species is *Hemitragus jemlahicus.* A closely related species, *H. jayakari*, is found in the Oman district of Arabia, and another, *H. hylocrius*, in the Nilgiri hills south of Travancore in southern India.

TAKABE

A tasty food fish found in the Sea of Japan and in the Pacific from central Honshu to the Philippines, the takabe *(Labracoglossa argentiventris)* is a slender fish, seldom exceeding 10 inches in length. It has a bluish green back, gray belly and a clear yellow stripe running from eye to tail along the side. Despite its small size, it is heavily fished and is common in Tokyo's fish markets.

Tamarind

TALA

See **Targola.**

TALEGGIO

A variety of ***stracchino,*** Taleggio is a soft, surface-ripened Italian cheese made from whole cow's milk, originally in the Taleggio Valley of Lombardy. The paste is creamy and has a delicate flavor. Curing takes about two months. Cheeses are eight inches square by two inches thick and weigh about four pounds.

TALI

See **Eriwani.**

TALLOW TREE

Two African trees are known by this name. The first is the dattock *(Detarium senegalense)*, which reaches 100 feet in height and is found from Senegal to the Congo. Its fruit is a one-seeded pod, the flesh of which is edible, and the seed of which is pressed for edible oil. The butter tree *(Pentadesmae butyracea)* has fruit that produces a greasy, yellow juice that Africans find appetizing when mixed with other food despite its turpentinelike odor.

TALLOW WOOD

This is a tree of the American tropics, *Ximenia americana*, whose plum-sized fruit is widely eaten.

TAMARILLO

See **Tree Tomato.**

TAMARIND

The name is used for several different tropical fruits, the most prominent of which is the seed pod of the tree *Tamarindus indica.* The latter is native to India, and grows to a great height (80 feet or more) and age. The pods are brown, with a thin, shell-like skin, containing a number of seeds embedded in an aromatic, sweet-acrid pulp. The pods are sickle-shaped and reach a length of up to eight inches. Tamarinds are now grown in many tropical areas of the world; they do especially well in the West Indies. They are sold in Mexico under the name *tamarindo.* The name derives from the Arabic words, *tamr* (date) and *hind* (hind), although the resemblance is remote.

Tamarind pods come from the tree green and may be sold as they are. The pulp is white and crisp, containing a great deal of sugar and acid. For export, the pods are covered with a thin film and exposed for some time to the air, which turns them brown. They may be shipped as is, or, as a further refinement, the shell is removed and the seeds and pulp are placed in a keg with boiling syrup and shipped after solidifying. Retailers cut the dried mass into small squares of a size suitable for kitchen use. Or, the pulp may be reduced to a sticky, jellylike paste, sold in small jars as instant tamarind extract.

In India, tamarind is a favorite ingredient in chutneys, curries and in other sauces and pickling solutions. It is also used to make sweet preserves and is one flavoring ingredient of Worcestershire sauce. Tamarind syrup and water is drunk as an iced summer beverage. The fruit is said to have laxative properties. The hard, glossy seeds are ground into meal and baked as cakes.

The wild tamarind *(Leucaena glauca)* and horse tamarind *(Leucaena leucocephala)* both bear podlike fruits whose pulp and seeds are eaten. The white or violet tamarind, *(Dialium guineense)* of tropical Africa, has a pleasantly acidic pulp that is appreciated by many. The Spanish tamarind *(Vangueria madagascariensis)* is found in Africa, India and the West Indies. It bears an apple-sized fruit whose taste has been compared to that of the European medlar.

TAMARIND PLUM

Small, black fruit of a Malaysian tree, *Dialium indum*, it is considered a delicacy. A closely allied species is the *maingayi (D. maingayi)*, also of Malaysia, which bears edible fruit. Of the same genus is the Sierra Leone or velvet tamarind tree *(D. guienense)* which bears flat, oval fruit about one inch across with velvety skin and orange red pulp. It is eaten from Senegal to the Congo region of Africa.

TAMIE

A semihard French cheese made by Trappist monks in Savoy, it is produced from whole cow's milk, and resembles ***tomme** de Beaumont*.

TAMISAN

A lesser known species of citrus fruit, *Citrus longispina*, is mildly acid, very juicy and flavorful.

TAMPALA

Also JOSEPH'S COAT. This erect, many-branched herb, *Amaranthus tricolor*, is grown in the Orient as a green vegetable. It flourishes in the tropics.

TANGELO

This hybrid fruit crosses the grapefruit and the tangerine. The result varies greatly in appearance, depending on the variety of tangerine used: Dancy, Satsuma, etc. It is generally irregular in shape with green-orange skin and is about the size of an orange. Some varieties are yellow, yet all are juicy and sweet smelling. Despite an unprepossessing exterior, the tangelo is a delicious eating fruit. The flavor is sweet-tart and often blends the sweetness and bitterness of the parents in a distinctive flavor of its own. Best known variety is the Sampson tangelo, which was developed in Florida in 1897 by W. T. Swingle. It closely resembles the ***ugli,*** a similar fruit originating in Jamaica. Most tangelos appear in the markets during November, December and January.

TANGERINE

Also MANDARIN. This small, sweet orange arrived rather late in the West, not until the 18th century, and thus remained more closely identified with China than other varieties of orange. Hence it acquired the name "mandarin," and later, because it was distributed to Europe through the port of Tangiers, came to be known as tangerine. The names are interchangeable. The tangerine *(Citrus reticulata)* is smaller than its cousin the **orange** and its skin is more easily separable from the pulp. It has the shape of a flattened sphere and is deliciously sweet. Although generally eaten as a fresh fruit, it is sometimes candied, glazed or used to prepare a liqueur. Well-known varieties of tangerine are the Mikan of Japan, the Satsuma, the Dancy and the Temple, which some authorities believe to be a cross between a tangerine and an orange. For hybrids of tangerine, see **Clementine, Ortanique, Tangelo, Tangor** and **Ugli.**

TANGLEBERRY

See **Huckleberry.**

TANGOR

This hybrid citrus fruit crosses the sweet orange with the tangerine (mandarin). Unlike a similar hybrid, the tangelo, which is man-made, the tangor occurs spontaneously in nature. The Murcott Honey orange is a type of tangor.

See also: **Tangelo.**

TANNIA

See **Yautia.**

TANSY

A bitter, aromatic herb that is decorative and easily grown, tansy *(Tanacetum vulgare)* is seldom cultivated any more as a seasoning. The name derives from the Greek for immortality, *athanasia*, because its yellow, button flowers were so long lived. It has a long history of medicinal use. It was eaten in the spring to prevent summer sickness. Tansy tea was believed to relieve fever. Currently, it is believed to have no therapeutic value and might even prove injurious if taken internally in any quantity.

Tansy was declared a Holy Herb in the 17th century, and taken during Easter to commemorate the bitter herbs of the Jewish Passover. From this grew the custom of preparing tansy pudding and tansy cakes at Easter. Tansy is still used occasionally to flavor puddings and poultry stuffings, particularly in France.

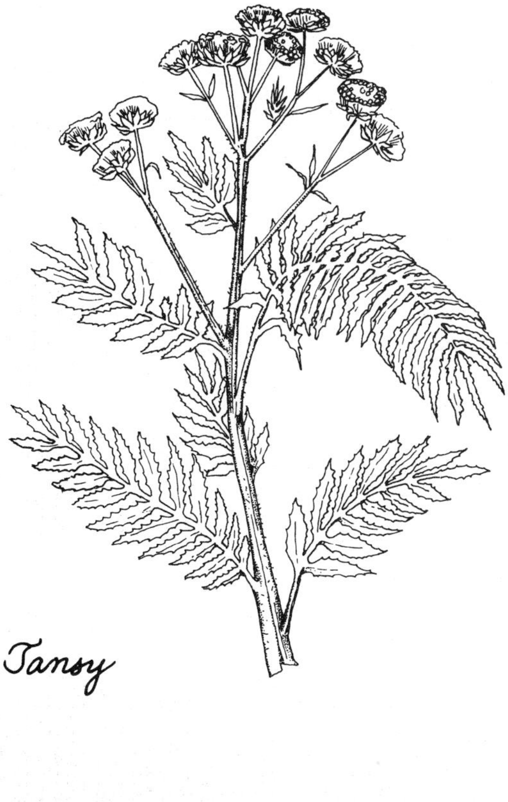

Tansy

TANZENBERGER

This soft, fermented Austrian cheese resembling **Limburger** is made in the southern state of Carinthia.

TAPIOCA

Tapioca is a food obtained from the root of the bitter cassava plant, *Manihot utilissima*, which is known also as manioc. To become edible the manioc must first be cooked to dissipate the prussic acid it contains in its raw form. The residue may then be put through a sieve to obtain white, yielding pellets called pearl tapioca; alternatively, the tapioca may be precipitated from the residue onto metal plates that have been heated to 300° F (148.9° C). When thoroughly dry, this is called flake tapioca. It may be sold in that form or ground to be sold as granulated tapioca. It is also pulverized and sold as tapioca flour.

Manioc is a Brazilian plant, and the word "tapioca" derives from the word, *typyoca*, of the Tupi language. Its three parts consist of *ty* (juice), *pya* (heart), and *oc*, *og* (to squeeze out).

In cooking, tapioca grains swell up to become a gelatinous mass that is very nutritious and easily digestible. Its composition is carbohydrates 85 percent, water 10 to 12 percent, plus small amounts of protein, minerals, salts and fat. Calories are 350 for each 3½ ounces (100 grams). Tapioca is used to thicken soups and puddings. As a dessert, tapioca pudding is easy to make in large amounts, and being acceptable to nearly everyone, is a favorite with the cooks in large institutions, such as hospitals, army mess halls, and college dormitories. It is reputedly an aid in the digestion of milk, and has been used effectively in the diet of nursing infants who have trouble assimilating milk.

TAPIR

Also DANTA. A four-legged mammal of the *Tapirus* species found in Central and South America and in parts of Asia, the tapir is about the size of a donkey, but more resembles a pig or wild boar. It has a rounded rump, tapering forequarters and a short, fleshy proboscis. Its flesh is highly regarded in some areas, and it is hunted for both food and sport. It is cooked in ways suitable for pork.

A large tapir can weigh as much as 660 pounds, stand 3½ feet at the shoulder and be as much as eight feet long. Tapirs are shy and docile beasts that eat vegetation and live in both open and closed terrain. They are good at both running and swimming.

The Asian tapir *(T. indicus)* is easily distinguished from other species by its coloring: black forequarters and hind legs, white elsewhere. The others are dark brown or reddish above, paler below. The number of tapir worldwide is shrinking due to the clearing of forest land. The name "tapir" derives from the Brazilian Tupi language.

TARA

Also YANG-TAO. This greenish yellow berry, *Actinidia arguta*, or *A. callosa*, of temperate eastern Asia, is related to **kiwi** fruit and much esteemed in Manchuria, North China and eastern Siberia. Taras are round, averaging one inch in diameter, but sometimes grow as large as plums. They may be eaten fresh, dried in a product called *kismis* or baked into bread, pastry or fruit cake.

TARAIRE TREE

An evergreen tree, *Beilschmiedia taraire*, of New Zealand, bears a dark purple fruit. The Maoris eat this fruit after boiling it to neutralize the poison contained in the seeds.

TAKE

See **Vetch.**

TARGOLA

Also TALA. This globular fruit of the Palmyra palm *(Borassus flabellifer)* is otherwise known as the toddy palm. The tree is best known as a source of toddy, a palm wine made of its fermented sap. The fruit is edible, however. When sliced open, it yields pleasant-tasting lumps of jellylike material, which are served with cream or eaten alone. They are about the size and shape of chestnuts and are contained in a yellowish skin that is peeled off before eating. The tree is also known as the *tar* or *tad* palm in India where it grows prolifically.

See also: **Palm Sugar, Palm Wine, Sago.**

TARO

A tropical root, known also as dasheen *(Colocasia esculenta)*, is valued when cooked for its edible starchy flesh and nutty flavor. Dasheen, taro, and the Egyptian *qolqas*, are all essentially the same plant, which has supplied a basic, readily accessible food for centuries. The dasheen, imported from Trinidad, is now grown in the southern United States as a potato substitute.

Its white meat, from large tubers called corms, is akin to the potato in food value, (although it contains more sugar) and in preparation. Smaller tubers, or cormels, grow laterally from the one to six pound corm and have a flavor resembling that of the common mushroom if boiled first with salt water, drained, and left to dry in a dark, airy place.

Taro

The plant is often called "elephant's ear," from its wide green fronds, and is sometimes grown as an ornamental. In Hawaii, the national dish, *poi*, is a slightly fermented concoction of ground and cooked taro roots, and is eaten either separately or in a sticky paste with meat or fish. The taste of the raw dasheen is slightly acidic. It should be cooked and then served immediately.

TARPON

A renowned game fish of the tropical Atlantic, the tarpon *(Tarpon atlanticus)* can reach a length of eight feet. It is better known for its fighting qualities than for its gastronomic merit, for its flesh tends to be dry and bony. The tarpon is found on both sides of the Atlantic and in U.S. waters from North Carolina south. It has a dark blue back but is silvery otherwise. It is distinguished by a jutting lower jaw and a long hind ray on its dorsal fin. Adult tarpons are coastal fish but tend to live near the open sea.

TARRAGON

A culinary herb with a mild licorice flavor, tarragon came into use fairly recently and is best known as a flavoring for vinegar. Two varieties are cultivated, Russian *(Artemisia dracunculoides)* and French *(Artemisia dracunculus)*, with the latter having the better flavor and the widest use. French tarragon, called *estragon* in French, is a hardy perennial plant, native to southern Europe, whose named means "little dragon," so called because it was once thought to be effective in curing venomous bites and stings, although it has no medicinal use in the present day.

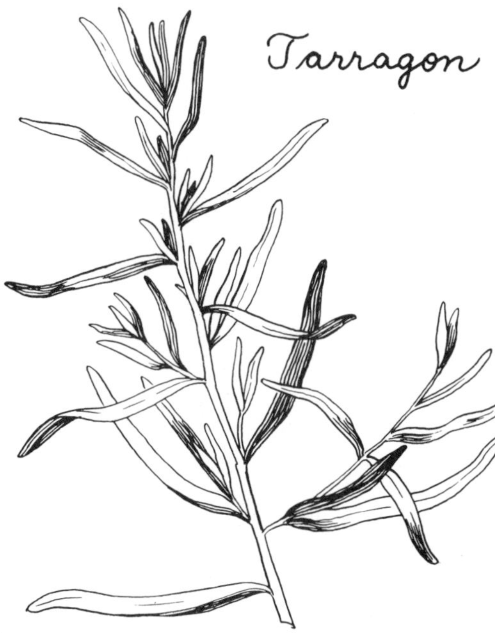

Tarragon leaves are used, but sparingly, with steaks, chops, in salads, fish sauce, preserves, pickles, mustard and mayonnaise. Tarragon is a close relative of wormwood and **absinthe,** and is one of the herbs used to flavor liqueurs where anise flavor is demanded.

The French add it to omelets and chicken dishes and it is essential to bearnaise sauce.

See also: **Sauce.**

TARTARIC ACID

This clear, colorless, crystalline acid is sometimes used as an acidulant in grape-flavored soft drinks, jellies and candies. It may also be used in effervescent powders, such as **baking powder** or **cream of tartar.** Tartaric acid is found in vegetable tissues and fruit juices. For commercial purposes it is often extracted from wine lees.

TARTAR SAUCE

A cold sauce used with fish, cold chicken and other cold meats, it is based on **mayonnaise** mixed with chopped olives, capers, gherkins and chives, moistened with a little white wine, lemon juice or vinegar.

See also: **Sauce.**

TASMANIAN GAULTHERIA

Edible fruit of a shrub, *Gaultheria antipoda*, native to New Zealand and Tasmania, it is red, capsule-shaped and has a good flavor.

TASMANIAN POTATO

The kidney-shaped tubers of this plant, *Gastrodia sesamoides*, are cooked and eaten like potatoes. Maoris relish the tubers of a related New Zealand species.

TASSEL HYACINTH

Also CIPOLLINO, MUSCARI. This is a perennial flowering herb, *Muscari comosum*, native to western Europe and North Africa, whose bulbs are sometimes eaten in Mediterranean countries. They are occasionally exported to the United States and sold under the name *cipollino*.

TAUTOG

See **Blackfish.**

TAVEL

This exceptional rose wine is grown near the village of Tavel, in France, about eight miles north of Avignon on the banks of the **Rhone.** The popes at Avignon much appreciated this wine, light to the taste but strongly alcoholic. Unlike other roses, Tavel is a fit companion to red meat and game. Tavel rivals the rose of Anjou and Saumur, grown along the **Loire,** as "the best rose in France."

TAWNY DAYLILY

Also ORANGE DAYLILY. The dried leaves of this perennial, flowering plant, *Hemerocallis fulva*, are used as a condiment in China and Japan. It is also found in Europe and the United States.

TAWOROG

See **Tworog.**

TEA

Tea is a beverage obtained by infusing in hot water the leaves of the tea plant *(Thea sinensis)*, an evergreen tree native to China and akin to the camellia. In the wild *Thea sinensis* may reach a height of 30 feet, but under cultivation it is kept low by pruning to facilitate picking the "flush," as the foliage that becomes the harvest is called. The leaves are dark green, elliptically shaped with serrated edges, and measure from 1½ to 10 inches long. Leaves and leaf nodes make the best tea but internodes and stems are collected as well and used in the lesser grades. A flush is normally produced every 40 days and may be picked at the end of the period, as is the practice in China and Japan. A different approach is used in India where leaves are picked every week or two to harvest each leaf at the optimal stage of maturation.

The origin of tea as a beverage is lost in prehistory, but according to Chinese legend, the Emperor Shennung brewed the first cup of tea after noticing the pleasant aroma coming from his campfire one evening when some scorched leaves fell into a pot of boiling water. This was supposed to have occurred in 2737 B.C., but it was not until the 8th century A.D. that tea drinking became popular in China and shortly thereafter in Japan. Tea was first imported into Europe in the 17th century by the Dutch East India Company, becoming important in England in the 18th century and overtaking coffee as the national drink only in the 19th century. Several things combined, apart from tea's intrinsic qualities, to make it the drink of choice. The government derived a great deal of revenue from a tax on tea; in 1839 production of tea started up in India, lowering the cost of bringing it from China; a pound of tea can yield up to 300 cups, while a pound of coffee yields only 30 or 40, and in the mid-19th century the Ceylon coffee crop failed due to a rust blight that cut off England's major source of supply. Ceylon quickly switched to tea production, and in 1878 Indonesia followed suit.

Next to water, tea is the most popular drink in the world. Three kinds of tea are marketed: black, green and oolong—all three coming from the same variety of tea plant. It is the processing that differs, the key element being fermentation. The tea harvest is rushed to the factory as quickly as possible and, if destined to become black tea, is set out to wither, i.e., dry under currents of hot air for 24 hours or until the leaves become flaccid. They are then rolled, a process that bruises the plant cells, releasing the juices that bear the typical tea aroma. The rolled tea is spread out in fermenting beds to allow both enzyme action and oxidation to take place. This is a carefully controlled stage, employing high heat and humidity, that determines the body or strength of the tea. During oxidation, the leaves turn copper color. Firing is the final stage that halts fermentation, dries the leaves and turns them black. A harvest destined to become green tea is first steamed, which makes the leaves soft and pliable and prevents fermentation. It is then rolled and dried for packing. The processing of oolong falls midway between the two extremes. It is briefly withered in the sun, rolled and then semifermented. It has a green brown finish.

Tea contains the stimulating substance, caffeine, as well as tannins, essential aromatic oils, proteins, gums and sugars. Fermentation affects the taste of tea, as well as the body and color. It frees the caffeine from the tannin, enhances the aromatic properties and has a general mellowing effect. Tannin adds bitterness to the taste of tea, and this effect is more pronounced in green teas. On the other hand, green tea leaves may be brewed two or three times.

The chief tea-producing countries are India, Sri Lanka, China, Japan, Indonesia and Taiwan. China produces about ½ the world supply, much of it green tea. The finest teas are produced at altitudes of 4,000 feet and above such as the Darjeeling tea of India, which is black. Taiwan is the major producer of oolong, followed by the southern coastal provinces of China—Amoy, Foochow and Canton.

Black tea leaves are graded in various ways, depending on the producing country, but the most familiar and ancient system is that developed by the Chinese according to size. It runs from small to large and includes the *flowery pekoe* (or *pekoe tip*), the *orange pekoe*, the *pekoe*, the *souchong* and the *congou*. *Pekoe* refers to the downiness of young leaves, but in India and Sri Lanka it has come to be the collective term for the smallest leaves and leaf buds, and is further subdivided into *broken orange pekoe*, *broken pekoe* and *broken pekoe-souchong*. The term "orange pekoe" appears on some brand labels in the market, and it is well to remember that it refers to appearance and size and not to quality.

Green tea classifications as to size run from *gunpowder* (so called because of its color and pelletlike leaves), through *imperial*, *young hyson* and *hyson*. "Hyson" refers to an East Indian merchant who first shipped this grade of tea.

Packaged teas are blends, combining as many as 25 to 30 teas of different grades and origins. The idea is to come up with a blend that will provide a consistent quality from year to year. Some examples of these are English Breakfast tea, Irish Breakfast tea and Russian tea. Certain blends are scented, incorporating the fragrance of flowers. Jasmine is probably the most important of these fragrances but others include gardenia, lavender, magnolia, orange and mint.

For better value, tea should be purchased loose in bulk because you get better flavor at lower cost. Tea bags, however, have proven a popular way of merchandising tea. In 1905 a wholesaler got the idea of sending out samples in little silk bags, which, his customers soon realized, could be dipped in hot water to brew a cup of tea. The idea caught on after the right bag was developed—a long fiber paper bag—and now more than half the tea sold in the United States comes in bags. In the 1960s and 1970s tea bags caught on in England and even Japan, although in a bag you never get the whole leaf, and generally a high proportion of dust and *fannings* (tiny fragments). In a tea bag, you purchase convenience at the expense of quality.

The British Isles are by far the greatest consumers of tea, if you take the English, Scots, Welsh and Irish together. The average is about eight pounds of tea per person each year, which is enough to make 2400 cups. Hot tea is Russia's national drink, and the Australians, New Zealanders and Americans are not far behind. In the green tea area, China and Japan are the largest consumers.

Black tea may be drunk hot or cold, iced tea being a standard summer refresher. Hot tea is drunk straight, sometimes with a squeeze of lemon; or, in some parts of the world, such as the British Isles and the New England states, it is drunk with milk and sugar added. Green tea is usually drunk hot, with no additives, and recently has become a base for ice cream.

In 19th-century England the Duchess of Bedford popularized afternoon tea as a social event, a focus of intellectual discussion and smart-set gossip. The English author Sydney Smith remarked, "Thank God for tea! What would I do without tea? How would I exist? I am glad I was not born before tea."

In a satirical vein, William Somerset Maugham, writing in the novel, *Cakes and Ale*, conjured up this image of the deceased Henry James, an American expatriate author: "Poor Henry, he's spending eternity wandering round and round a stately park and the fence is just too high for him to peep over and they're having tea just too far for him to hear what the countess is saying."

For articles on major tea varieties, check elsewhere in the alphabet under the specific name, e.g., **Assam, Ceylon, Darjeeling,** etc. See also the index.

TEA, INSTANT

This is a fine powder made in much the same way that powdered coffee is made, i.e., by first brewing the tea, then dehydrating it, leaving only the solids. It is reconstituted by adding water. Instant tea may contain additives such as preservatives, flower flavorings, sugar and lemon.

See also: **Coffee, Instant; Tea.**

TEAK

A large African tree, *Guibourtia coleosperma* bears edible fruit. The fruit is a flat, leathery legume about an inch long and a little wider. It is eaten in the area of southern Africa stretching from Angola and Southwest Africa to Zimbabwe.

TEAL

This small freshwater wild duck, *Querquedula* spp., is found in Europe, Asia and the Americas. Its flesh is said to be highly esteemed by gourmets, although some find it rather oily. It is not one of the popular table birds, perhaps because of its small size, one bird being adequate for one diner, or at the most two. Teals have beautiful coloring, which is variegated and differs from species to species. They are distinguished by descriptive names, such as green-winged teal, blue-winged teal, cinnamon teal, etc. The common European teal *(Q. crecca)* has a predominant grayish blue color and is considered best eating from October to January. Common North American varieties are *Q. carolinensis* and *Q. discors.*

See also: **Duck.**

TEA OIL PLANT

This is a small Chinese tree of the *Camellia* family *(C. oleifera)* whose seeds, when pressed, yield commercial tea oil. This is said to equal olive oil in quality and is used similarly.

TELEME

Also BRANZA DE BRAILA. Here is a salty ewe or goat's milk cheese popular in Greece, Rumania, Bulgaria and Turkey. It is a pickled cheese, i.e., it is cured for eight or 10 days in dry salt or brine. The curd is white and creamy, somewhat resembling **feta,** but is saltier and more quickly maturing than the latter. It is produced in squares weighing approximately two pounds.

TELOSMA

This is a climbing plant, *Telosma cordata*, of Java, whose fleshy roots are made into a popular candy.

TELPANIR

See **Tschil.**

TEMPETE

See **Canquillote.**

TENCH

A European freshwater fish of the carp family, the tench *(Tinca tinca)* has a thickset, heavy body and can be up to 25 inches long. It is found in lakes, slow-moving rivers and marshes from Great Britain to western Russia. The tench likes muddy bottoms, especially in cold weather, but is considered good eating nonetheless, and better still if caught in faster water. It is popular with anglers in Britain and is an important food fish in parts of eastern Europe. It has been introduced into Australia, New Zealand and the United States.

The tench is dark green or brown and very slimy. The latter characteristic earned it the nickname "Doctor fish," in Britain where in some parts it is believed that another fish can cure any ailment by rubbing against the tench and coating itself with the slime. In Europe the tench is used chiefly in fish stews, but is good broiled or *au bleu*.

TEN POUNDER

See **Ladyfish.**

TEPARY BEAN

A small bean peculiarly adapted to the dry conditions of the southwestern United States and northwest Mexico, it is shaped much like a kidney bean and ranges in color from white through yellow, brown and black, including flecked and spotted varieties. The tepary bean *(Phaseolus auctifolius)* withstands drought very well and can produce a quick crop after the slightest rain shower. A problem is that its skin is usually tougher than that of its close relatives of the genus *Phaseolus*, which necessitates long soaking before cooking. The flavor is stronger than that of the pinto bean, which is the standard *frijol* of Texas and Mexico.

See also: **Bean, Kidney Bean.**

TEPEJILOTE

Also PACAYA. A member of the *Chameadorea* genus of small, ornamental palm trees, the *tepejilote* is found in tropical areas from Mexico to Colombia. The spathes may be eaten like asparagus. In Guatemala the tree is cultivated for the unopened male flower clusters, which are cooked and eaten as vegetables.

TEQUILA

See **Mezcal.**

TERAGLIN

Also CAPE SALMON, GEELBEK. A croaker caught off the coasts of South Africa and northeastern Australia and highly esteemed as a food fish, the teraglin *(Atractoscion aequidens)* may be as much as 50 inches long and attains a weight of 20 pounds. Adult fish are blue above with silver sides and a white belly. It is an open ocean fish, preferring deep waters and is, therefore, rarely taken by anglers. The teraglin is brought to market by trawlers. It is eaten fresh or cured.

TERFAS

See **Truffle.**

TERFEZIA

See **Truffle.**

TERMITE

See **Ant.**

TERRAPIN

See **Turtle.**

TESTICLES

These are the sex glands of male mammals, consisting of two oval structures suspended in a sac, or scrotum. Many people consider them very good food. The ancients believed the testicles of donkeys to be an aphrodisiac. In the United States rural folk are said to prize "mountain oysters" or calf's testicles, which are harvested at round-up time on the ranch. They are somewhat like **sweetbreads** in flavor and texture, and are often prepared simply by being sliced and sauteed in butter.

Lamb and pig's testicles are enjoyed in many countries of the world, and they share the macho aura of calf's testicles which has fostered jokes and legends to the effect that they will grow hair on women's chests. They too may be simply sauteed, or more often parboiled, then breaded and fried. A little more unusual are turkey testicles which, when breaded and deep-fried, are about the size of jumbo olives and can be served as cocktail hors d'oeuvres. Cock's "kidneys," as the French delicately put it, have been served for centuries in France as a companion garnish with **cockcombs.**

TETE DE MAURE

See **Edam.**

TETE DE MOINE

See **Bellelay.**

TEXAS SOTOL

A dry-area plant of the agave family, the Texas sotol *(Dasylirion texanum)* is native to Texas, Arizona, New Mexico and northern Mexico. The trunk contains a sugary pulp that is made into a fermented, alcoholic beverage called sotol. The spoon flower *(D. wheeleri)*, a closely related plant, is treated similarly.

TEXEL

This Dutch green cheese is made from sheep's milk on the North Sea island of Texel, where production dates back to the 17th century. Individual cheeses weigh from three to four pounds.

THELESPERMA

The leaves of this annual herb, *Thelesperma gracile*, are infused to make a tisane. It is found in the southwestern United States.

THEMEDA

This is a grass plant, *Themeda triandra*, indigenous to Australia, Africa and India, whose seeds are used for food. In some places it is cultivated as grain.

THENAY

This soft French cheese is made of whole cow's milk in the vicinity of Thenay (Loire et Cher). Though of fairly recent origin, it resembles **Camembert** and ***Vendome,*** being ripened with the aid of surface molds. Curing takes a little more than a month.

THIMBLEBERRY

See **Raspberry, Salmonberry.**

THISTLE

Several plants of the *Cirsium* genus are edible, though usually not resorted to except in cases of emergency. They are better known as noxious weeds. Yet, in the northwestern United States, Drummond's thistle *(C. drummondii)* has roots that have been eaten as a vegetable. The soft, sweet stems of the Cheyenne thistle *(C. edule)* are peeled and eaten. The stems, which are guarded by spiny leaves, reach a height of six feet. It is found from northwestern Oregon to British Columbia.

Other American thistles with edible roots are the scopoli *(C. scopolorum)*, the wobby thistle *(C. undulatum)*, the western thistle *(C. virginianum)*. The young stems and leaves of the Siberian thistle *(C. oleraceum)* are cooked and eaten as greens. And the spindle-shaped roots of the European tuberous thistle *(C. tuberosum)* are palatable and well-flavored.

The creeping Canadian thistle *(C. arvense)* of temperate Europe, Asia and North America can be used to coagulate milk.

THISTLE SAGE

The seeds of the California plant, *Salvia carduacea*, are roasted and ground into flour. They are also used to make a cooling beverage.

THONINE

See **Tuna Fish.**

THREADFIN

Also GUCHHIA, SAWAL, GIANT THREADFIN. Threadfins are found in the Indo-Pacific area, and two species are important food fish in the coastal waters of India. The name "threadfin" derives from the long filaments trailing from their pectoral fins. Largest is the *guchbia* or giant threadfin *(Eleutheronena tetradactylum)*, which reaches a maximum length of 6½ feet. It favors inshore, brackish waters, estuaries and low salinity lakes. Commercial catches of *gucchia* from trawls and gill nets are substantial. A variety of traditional fishing methods is also used with success.

The smaller, bastard mullet or *dara (Polynemus indicus)* is a threadfin that seldom exceeds four feet in length. It dwells in the same habitat and is even more valuable as a commercial species. It is dark purple above with a yellowish belly. Both species are found as far east as Australia.

THRUSH

Thrush is the general name for the *Turdidae* family of medium-sized songbirds, usually brown-colored with speckled plumage. They are common in North America and Europe, but only in the latter are they eaten with regularity. American thrushes include robin, wood thrush, bluebird and hermit thrush. Among gastronomes, the European song thrush *(Turdus musicus)* is rated excellent eating.

It was considered a delicacy by the wealthier people of ancient Greece and Rome where the song thrush was trapped, then fattened for the table on millet. The tradition has been handed down to modern Italy where today the preferred fodder is juniper berries and grapes. Other game thrushes of Europe are the missal thrush, the redwing and the fieldfare.

Thrushes are most often roasted, then served on a crouton that has been fried in pan juices. But the birds may be boned, stuffed and baked, broiled on skewers, or made into pates. Appreciation of thrushes is pretty much confined to France, Italy, Corsica and Sardinia; they are protected by law in Great Britain.

THUNBERG'S HYDRANGEA

Also TEA-OF-HEAVEN. This is a subspecies of hortensia *(Hydrangea macrophylla* subsp. *serrata)* whose young leaves are steamed, rolled and dried in Japan, then used to make a sweet drink called *amacha* (sweet tea).

THUNBERG'S LILY

A much cultivated variety of lily, *Lilium thunbergii*, has flowers considered a table delicacy in China. They are generally yellow, orange or apricot in color. It is grown from a bulb.

THURINGER

This is a German sausage of the **cervelat** type, containing lean beef and pork, beef and pork hearts and seasoned with whole white peppers, German marjoram and other spices, but usually no garlic. American versions are smoked, but continental versions are often air-dried like salami.

See also: **Sausage.**

THYME

A culinary herb of the mint family, thyme has many varieties, the most common being garden, or black, thyme *(Thymus vulgaris)*. Garden thyme has a sharp, piny fragrance and flavor. Other varieties have distinctive scents, such as orange, caraway and lavender. As seasoning herbs, two other varieties are important, lemon-scented *(T. citriodorus)* and wild *(T. serpyllum)*.

It was a widely used seasoning and medicinal herb in the ancient world, being sought out at various times for its aphrodisiac qualities, ability to instill courage and therapeutic properties for whooping cough and sore throat. Thymol, its essential oil, is still commercially exploited as a base for medicines and perfumes. The ancient Greeks were aware of its value in perfume, since its name comes from the Greek *thymon*, or sacrifice, owing to its presence in temple incense.

Poets were quick to pick up on thyme, not just for its erotic reputation, but for its cushionlike feel when planted as a lawn. A. E. Houseman, author of *Shropshire Lad*, in his poem, "Here of a Sunday Morning/My love and I would lie," beds his lovers down "among the springing thyme."

The leaves, both fresh and dried, add zest to soups, stews and stuffings; the fresh tops make good garnish. Lemon thyme is considered by many to be the ideal seasoning for fish dishes, veal and chicken.

THYMUS

See **Sweetbreads.**

TI

Also DRACAENA. This treelike plant, *Cordyline australis*, is found on the Pacific Islands from Hawaii to New Zealand. It is referred to as the "sacred ti plant" in Hawaii, presumably because it was venerated by the original Polynesian inhabitants. Today ti roots, which are rich in levulose, constitute the main ingredient of the fermented mash used to make Okolehao, Hawaiian whisky. The plant has long sword-shaped leaves used to wrap food. It produces berries that, according to one source, are eaten in New Zealand.

See also: **Okolehao.**

TIA MARIA

This coffee flavored liqueur made in Jamaica is prepared with the famous local Blue Mountain coffee and has a rum base. It is bottled at 63 proof.

TIBET CHEESE

This hard grating cheese is made in Tibet from ewe's milk and hung up to dry in two-inch cubes that are strung together in bunches of 50 to 100.

TI-ES

See **Canistel.**

TIGERFISH

Also CRESCENT PERCH, ZEBRAFISH. The name is given to several fish, most notably *Therapon bidyanus*, a small ocean fish eaten in Japan, and an African freshwater gamefish, *Hydrocynus vittatus.* The tigerfish or zebra fish of the Indo-Pacific reaches a length of 12 inches and is marked by a pattern of dark, curved lines along the back and sides. The African tigerfish is one of the most famous sportfish in the world. It is plentiful in such rivers as the Nile, Niger, Volta, Congo, Zambezi and Limpopo, plus Lakes Albert and Tanganyika. Large specimens measure up to 40 inches long and can weigh up to 40 pounds, although anglers say smaller fish (five to 10 pounds) are better fighters.

The tigerfish has a long, heavily scaled body and fanglike teeth. Its larger cousin, the giant tigerfish *(H. goliath)* is restricted in its habitat to Lake Tanganyika and the Congo Basin. Its six-foot length and weight of up to 125 pounds make it a dangerous fish to handle while alive, and very few are taken by anglers. These fish are eaten by Africans throughout their range.

The tigerfish of South America *(Hoplias malabaricus)* is also known as the *tararira* and the *haimara.* It inhabits rivers from Venezuela to Argentina, and is fished commercially in many parts. It attains a length of 25 inches and has a dull green color. Its flesh is highly regarded.

TIGER MULLET

Also JUMPING MULLET, TYGUM. A valuable food fish of Australian and Samoan waters, this gray mullet *(Mugil argenteus)* reaches a length of about 18 inches. It has a steely blue color lightening to silver on the sides and white below. The tiger mullet frequents inshore waters and is taken in shore seines, which it is sometimes able to leap out of, hence the name, "jumping mullet." It is a difficult fish for anglers and is rarely taken on a line.

TIGNARD

A hard, blue-veined, French cheese made of ewe or goat's milk in the Tigne Valley of Savoy, it resembles ***Gex*** and ***Sassenage.***

TILAPIA

This is a small but important food fish of Africa. There are several species, all of the cichlid family, and they are found from Israel and Jordan south to South Africa in lakes and rivers including the Nile, Zambezi and Orange systems and in Lake Victoria. The southernmost species is the banded bream *(Tilapia sparmanii)*, which averages seven inches in length. Many of the significant food species are classed in the *Sarotherodon* genus. For information on these, see under **Galilee Cichlid.**

According to legend, during the biblical parting of the Red Sea, the tilapia was split into two distinct species, although this doesn't explain what a freshwater fish was doing in the sea.

TILEFISH

The name includes any of several ocean fish, the largest of which is the tilefish *(Lopholatilus chamaeleonticeps)* of the Atlantic seaboard of North America. It is a bottom-dweller and brilliantly colored, with a blue or green back and yellow or rose sides. A thick-meated fish, it may weigh as much as 50 pounds and reach 42 inches in length. The body is slender but very deep.

The tilefish was first caught off the Georges Bank and became an important food fish in the latter half of the 19th century. It then disappeared owing to some marine catastrophe and is only now regaining its former numbers. Its flesh is coarse but is good both fresh and smoked.

A Pacific tilefish is *Branchiostegus japonicus*, a smaller fish (up to 24 inches), but a popular food fish in Japan where it is known as *akaamadai* and is eaten fresh, canned and salted. The sand tilefish *(Malacanthus plumieri)* reaches a length of two feet and is found from North Carolina to Brazil.

TILSITER

Also RAGNIT. A semihard, yellow cheese with a piquant flavor that was first produced near Tilsit, East Prussia by Dutch immigrants, it is made from whole or skim cow's milk, has many small eyes and, like **Limburger,** is ripened with the aid of red cheese bacteria. Tilsiter is produced in Germany, Yugoslavia, Hungary, Denmark, Switzerland and the United States. American Tilsiter is milder than the original and is closer to **brick** cheese than to Limburger. Skim-milk Tilsiter is often flavored with caraway seeds. These cheeses are considered fully ripe in five or six months, although they may be wrapped and shipped after only two or three. Their shape is usually round and flat, nine to 10 inches in diameter by five inches thick, weighing about 10 pounds. Some producers favor the loaf shape.

TIMBIRI

A tropical Asian type of persimmon, which grows on a dense tree found from India to Indonesia, the timbiri *(Diospyros malabarica)* is one to two inches in diameter, round or oval, and has an astringent taste.

TINAMOU

This is a flightless game bird of Central and South America which resembles the partridge and quail. The largest species is the great tinamou *(Tinamus braziliensis)*, which inhabits the forests of Guiana. Tinamous are considered excellent eating and have been introduced into France and successfully bred there. The tinamou is cooked like pheasant.

TIPARI

See **Cape Gooseberry.**

TISANE

The word refers to any herb tea, but specifically an infusion of camomile, mint leaves, rose hips, etc. taken for its tonic or refreshing effect. The word derives from the Latin *ptisana* for barley water and is used the same way in English, French and Greek more in a medicinal than in a culinary sense. The herbs may be fresh or dried, and the parts used include leaves, stems, flowers or seeds.

TISTE

In Central America and Mexico, a beverage is made from toasted corn flour, cocoa, sugar and water. It is a favorite soft drink in Costa Rica.

TODDY

See **Palm Wine.**

TODDY PALM

See **Sago.**

TOFU

See **Soy Bean.**

TOHEROA

This mollusk, *Amphidesma ventricosum*, is found off the coast of New Zealand and is known by its Maori name, meaning "long-tongued," which refers to its roe. Typically, the toheroa is about the size of a person's hand. It has a hinged shell and has been likened to a "giant clam," a "large scallop" and the **ormer.** Its flesh is fat and pearly white and most often is used to make a bisque, which is a famous local delicacy and reputed to be one of the finest of its kind. Toheroa bisque has a pale green color.

The mollusk buries itself in intertidal sands off the northwest coast. Harvesting is strictly regulated: no more than 20 a day per person; no digging implements allowed other than the hands, and no specimens under three inches in diameter. These measures insure the species survival, but make the toheroa an expensive treat.

TOKAY WINE

A famous white wine from the vicinity of Tokaj, a town in northeastern Hungary, Tokay has long been associated with royalty and with poets. The word "imperial" is often applied to it ("He has had a smack of every sort of wine, from humble port to imperial Tokay . . ." remarked the Reverend James Townley in his *High Life Below Stairs.)* This is due, no doubt, to its popularity in the 18th and 19th centuries with the crowned heads of Europe. Louis XIV is said to have called it "The wine of kings and the king of wines."

Twenty-eight villages in the region have the right to call the vine they produce "tokay." The vineyard area of nearly 150 square miles lies in the volcanic foothills of the Hegyalja Mountains (which rise to about 2,700 feet above sea level), and in the valleys of the Bodrog and Tisza Rivers. The summers are hot, the autumns long and sunny, and the winters harsh.

The wine may have been introduced by Italian settlers in the 13th century, following the decimation of the land by the Tartars. But the word *Furmint*, the grape that produces the Tokay wines, is perhaps a corruption of the French word *froment*, meaning wheat—the color of the grape and the wine.

There are three main kinds of Tokay, the Furmint, the Szamarodni and—most famous—the Aszu. A special process is used in the making of Tokay Aszu. The grapes are picked very late, when the noble rot or *pourriture noble* has well set in. (This practice dates from a 17th-century local war, which caused a delay in the wine harvest. The grapes were picked after the snow had fallen, when they were overripe, already beginning to ferment.) The grapes are then crushed and stirred together until they form a thick crust. Then, from two to six basketsful (called *puttonos)* weighing 33 pounds each of the final mixture are added to every hogshead (30 gallons) of must or wine that is produced in the region.

The sugar and the aroma dissolve in the wine, and a second slow fermentation process takes place in the cask. Depending on the addition of these *puttonos* and the art of the winemaker, the final product can be sweet or semisweet. The label will say how many barrels of concentrated grapes have been added to the hogshead. Three *puttonos* is sweet, but not as sweet as six *puttonos*, the maximum.

TOMALLEY

See **Lobster.**

TOMATE VERDE

See **Tomatillo.**

TOMATILLO

This berry of the *Physalis ixocarpa* is a close relative of the **Cape gooseberry** and the **ground cherry.** It is also known as *alkekengi.* The fruit resembles a cherry-sized green tomato, contained in a straw-colored calyx, or husk. Indeed, other varieties of this berry are called the husk tomato. It has a slightly acidic flavor. In Mexico, where this variety is prevalent, it is used chiefly in the preparation of chili sauce or to dress meat.

Tomatilloes

Varieties of tomato (left to right): plum, beefsteak and cherry

TOMATO

A tender, succulent fruit native to Peru, the tomato *(Lycopersicum esculentum)* is generally regarded as a vegetable because of the way it is served. A ripe tomato is usually red, although there are yellow and green varieties. Conversely, redness is no assurance of ripeness, since a tomato may be picked green (usually a sign of unripeness) and stored in the presence of ethylene gas, which will change its color to red without affecting its maturity. It assumes various shapes and sizes. On the small side, it may resemble a large cherry. Others resemble plums or pears, and finally the largest are globeshaped, such as the beefsteak tomato, and weigh as much as two pounds. The taste of the ripe tomato is slightly acidic and refreshing.

The tomato originated in Peru and traveled as far north as Mexico before the arrival of Europeans. There is no evidence that the early Peruvians cultivated the tomato; rather, they gathered it wild. This early tomato was about the size of a large cherry. The Spaniards brought it to Spain in the first quarter of the 16th century, and from there it swiftly found its way to the kingdom of Naples, which was then a Spanish possession. Spaniards liked the tomato, but Italians took to it with a passion. The Italians called the tomato *pomodoro*, golden apple. Some sources say this is because the first tomatoes to arrive there were yellow. Other sources state that the tomato got to Italy via Morocco, and were first called *pomi di mori* (Moorish apples), which became corrupted to *pomodori* (golden apples). This theory would also account for the French appellation *pommes d'amour* (love apples) as a gallicized version of *pomi di mori*.

Tomatoes were regarded with suspicion in Northern Europe and the British Isles, since botanists recognized the plant as a member of the *Solanaceae* family, which includes such well-known poisons as belladonna, deadly nightshade and black henbane. Indeed, tomato leaves are toxic, and should not be eaten. At first the tomato was accepted as an ornamental plant, appropriate for covering outhouses and arbors, but not as food. It was not until the middle of the 19th century that gastronomes in Europe began to appreciate it, and not until the beginning of the 20th century that the general public accepted it as delicious and healthful. In the United States it was subject to similar prejudice. Specifically, many Americans believed that tomatoes caused cancer. Also, its seeds were thought to bring on an appendicitis attack.

The popularity of the tomato remained steady in Italy and gradually became so important that it is difficult to conceive of an Italian cuisine without the tomato. In the United States the popularity of the tomato grew by leaps and bounds reaching a peak in the 1950s and 1960s. Since then it has come to be regarded by many as a food that is losing its clientele. This is due to the perishability of the tomatoes and the difficulty of distributing them over a huge marketing area, such as the United States. As the demand for tomatoes increased, the quality declined. That is, new strains of tomato were introduced that have tougher skins and a higher yield. The tendency has increasingly been to pick most of the crop green, since the green fruit is less vulnerable to bruising and spoiling. Moreover, the unripe fruit can be turned red by exposure to ethylene gas. It seems the factor of taste was left out of account. The result has been in many cases a hard, grainy tomato with little taste or palatability.

The raw tomato consists of about 90 percent water. It has less than 1 percent protein, and 4 to 5 percent carbohydrate, but is rich in vitamin A, thiamine, riboflavin and vitamin C. Its calorie content is about 24 in 3½ ounces (100 grams).

Cherry tomatoes are often served as hors d'oeuvres, while the large varieties may be broiled, baked, stuffed or used in salads. They are canned in several forms: stewed, pureed and as paste. Tomato juice is a popular drink, with or without liquor. **Ketchup,** a tomato sauce, is an everpresent seasoner in Western countries.

TOMATO SAUCE

See **Ketchup.**

TOMCOD

This small member of the cod family *(Gadidae)* is found off both coasts of North America and rarely exceeds 10 inches in length. It has the three well-spaced dorsal fins typical of cods and prefers sandy or muddy bottoms or, sometimes, the surf zone. The Atlantic tomcod or frostfish *(Microgadus tomcod)* is excellent tasting and is usually taken by anglers from piers or in the surf. It is only occasionally fished commercially. The Pacific tomcod *(M. proximus)* is found from Washington south to the Mexican border and has similar gastronomic qualities. In California, a fish often mistakenly called "tomcod" is the white croaker *(Genyonemus lineatus)*, also caught off piers and beaches and also delicious to eat, especially when panfried in butter.

TOME

See **Tomme.**

TOMME

Also TOME, LA TOMME. Tomme is a broad category of small French cheeses, usually made from cow's milk, but often of goat or sheep's milk, in the Alps region, particularly around Savoy. Either whole or skim milk is used, the latter producing a faster maturing cheese.

Varieties made from cow's milk include *tomme de Beauges*, *de Beaumont*, *de Boudave*, *de fenouil* (flavored with fennel seed), *grise*, *de marc* (ripened in grape pulp after marc has been distilled), *de raisin* (matured in a dry mixture of grape skins, seeds and stalks) and *de Savoie*.

Goat's milk varieties include *tomme de Bellay*, *de chevre* and *de praslin*. *Tomme de Cantal*, which should not be confused with ***Cantal*** is a soft, unripened cheese made from cow's milk in the Auvergne.

TOMME DE MONTAGNE

See **Vacherin.**

TONG

A flatfish of the sole family, the tong *(Synaptura marginata)* is found in shallow waters along the eastern coast of Africa. It reaches a length of about 16 inches and is widely eaten on a local basis. A closely allied species is the black sole *(S. orientalis)* of Australian waters. It is very plentiful along the coasts of Queensland and New South Wales, and its flesh is rated very good eating.

TONGUE

One of the variety meats (offal), tongue is a relatively cheap source of lean meat, yet it has little popularity in the United States, perhaps because, as one author suggested, it is so readily identifiable for what it is. Tongues commonly eaten are those of the beef (ox), calf, lamb, pig, deer, elk and, in countries that have them, reindeer. Beef tongue weighs from three to six pounds when fresh and must be poached and skinned before it is prepared in a variety of ways, which include slicing it and serving hot with sweet and sour sauce, or in a stew, cold in salad, ground into a pate, or pressed and then sliced as luncheon meat. Beef tongues are often sold after some sort of processing, such as smoking, brining or pickling. These may be canned and ready-to-eat or may require soaking overnight before further preparation. Lamb's and pig's tongues, while being much smaller, are treated in much the same manner.

During the push westward after the American Civil War, the American bison was slaughtered by the thousands for its hide or for "sport." Although the plains tribes depended on the beast as their main source of meat, the only food item brought away by the white hunter was the tongue, the "red, rolling" tongue, which was considered a delicacy. In *Eating in America*, Waverly Root and Richard de Rochemont noted:

> *As a source of food the buffalo was, at that time, useless—the whole buffalo, that is; there were connoisseurs for parts of it. The choicest morsels were considered to be the humps and the tongues. Even the humps were too bulky to be consumed far from the place of killing, but tongues were not, and they could be smoked on the spot to preserve them until they reached a market. Bison were killed by the thousands, their tongues were cut out to be shipped to luxury restaurants in the East or even in Europe, and the carcasses were left lying on the prairie for the coyotes and the buzzards.*

TONGUE CRESS

See **Garden Cress.**

TONGUE-SOLE

This is a family of tropical flatfish *(Cynoglossidae)*, various species of which are exploited as food fish in Africa, Japan and Southeast Asia. The red tongue-sole *(Cynoglossus joyneri)* is a Japanese species that reaches a length of 12 inches. Its flesh is highly esteemed and deemed superior to all other local soles. The long tongue-sole *(C. lingua)* is widely distributed in the Indo-Pacific region. It is longer but thinner than *C. joyneri*, and as a food is of only local importance. *C. senegalensis* is a larger tongue-sole (up to 27 inches) found in estuaries and rivers of West Africa. It is rated the best of all tongue-soles and, in addition to being sold fresh in local markets, fresh frozen fillets are exported to Europe.

See also: **Sole.**

TONIC WATER

Also QUININE WATER. This carbonated beverage is used as a highball or cocktail mixer, usually with gin or vodka. It is flavored with quinine, citrus fruits and sweetened with sugar. It may be referred to as simply "tonic" as in "gin and tonic."

TONKA BEAN

Also COUMARIN. This aromatic seed of the South American tree, *Dipteryx odorata*, contains coumarin, an essential oil used in flavorings and perfume. The seed is embedded in the soft, pulpy flesh of an egg-shaped fruit. It resembles an almond. Coumarin is a white substance found in small crystals under the coating of the seed and between the lobes. Coumarin's aroma resembles that of vanilla, except it is stronger, sweeter and more pungent. Because of this, for 75 years coumarin was used to make imitation vanilla extract and to flavor chocolate. In 1954, however, it was banned for this purpose in the United States because it was found to cause liver damage in dogs and rats at high levels of use. Coumarin is still used in perfumes, and tonka bean oil in the manufacture of bitters.

TONKIN PLUM

A tropical fruit, *Spondias laoensis*, related to the ***ambarella,*** it is round, fleshy and single-seeded. It is borne on a large tree that is plentiful in Indochina.

TOPE

Also TOPER, SWEET WILLIAM. Tope is a shark plentiful in the eastern Atlantic, especially in British and Irish waters. Its firm, white flesh is considered very palatable and is especially suitable for baking, since it holds together well under slow cooking. The tope *(Galeorhinus galeus)* lives mainly on the bottom, has a slender, grayish body and reaches a length of 6½ feet. The name "toper" supposedly derives from its rather heavy snout, which is often flushed after capture.

The Australian species, *G. austalis,* has become a valuable food fish and is now protected from overfishing. A closely related Pacific shark, the soupfin or oil shark *(G. zyopterus)* formerly supported a rich fishery. Its liver oil is particularly rich in vitamin A. The soupfin remains a prized fish among Chinese for its dorsal and pectoral fin, which go to make sharkfin soup.

TOPFKASE

This sour-milk variety of German cooked cheese is poured into pots called *topfen*, hence the name. It has a pleasant flavor and buttery consistency.

See also: **Cooked Cheese.**

TOPI

Also BLESBOEK. This African antelope of the genus *Damaliscus* was formerly very plentiful in the grasslands, sparsely timbered regions and arid regions of the continent. Its flesh is considered excellent eating and its head a fine trophy. Consequently, *topi* herds have been much depleted by hunters.

The animal reaches a maximum length of six feet, may stand four feet high at the shoulder and weigh as much as 300 pounds. It is distinguished by a splendid set of angular, curved horns. The South African species, *D. lunatus*, known as the blesboek, has been domesticated and its meat is marketed on a regular basis.

TORCH GINGER

Also GREAT PHAEMORIA, PHILIPPINE WAX-FLOWER. This member of the ginger family *(Nicolaia elatior)* is native to the Celebes and Java and much cultivated in Hawaii and throughout the tropics. It may be used to season food, and the young flowering shoots are added to curries.

TORD

See **Sir Posny.**

TORPEDO

Also ELECTRIC RAY. The name refers to any of several rays which are capable of delivering electric shocks, but most especially *Torpedo torpedo*, a small Mediterranean species. It is eaten by the French who rate its flesh as mediocre and prepare it in the same way as skate. This torpedo reaches a length of two feet. Much larger is the Atlantic torpedo *(T. nobiliana)*, which measures up to six feet and can weigh 110 pounds. The shock is generated in kidneylike organs and is powerful enough in this species to knock a human to the ground. It varies from 170 to 220 volts, but is quickly exhausted by repeated discharges. Bathers rarely encounter this ray because it likes depths of 30 feet or so, but anglers and spearfishers have received shocks. The Pacific Coast species, *T. californica*, rarely exceeds three feet.

TORTELLINI

This type of filled Italian pasta is a specialty of Bologna. The dough for tortellini is always of the *pasta all'uovo* kind, i.e., consisting of flour from hard durum wheat, mixed with eggs, rather than flour and water. They are made as follows: the dough is rolled exceedingly thin, then cut into small circles. The filling is placed in the center, and the dough rolled into a bulgy tube. The ends of the tube are then twisted together to form a ring. Some sources compare the shape to a half moon, while others see in it the likeness of the feminine navel. According to the poet Tasso (1544-1595), tortellini are modeled on the navel of the goddess Venus, who, wandering Italy during the Middle Ages, sought a night's refuge in a Bolognese inn. The innkeeper, smitten with her beauty, peeked through the keyhole of her room. He was rewarded with a glimpse of her naked form, but his field of view was restricted to the midsection. The next day he recreated her stupendous navel in the form of tortellini.

Tortellini are stuffed with a paste of prosciutto (ham), mortadella, veal, Parmesan cheese and a dash of nutmeg. They are a favorite Christmas dish. They begin the meal and are either eaten in broth or served poached and drained with grated cheese and butter and sometimes sliced white truffles. The Bolognesi are passionate about tortellini, as expressed in the words of one writer, "Tortellini is more essential than the sun for Sunday or love for a woman."

See also: **Pasta.**

TORTILLA

An unleavened Mexican flatbread or pancake made either of corn or wheat flour, water and a little salt, the tortilla is the common bread of the Mexican peasant and is one of the pillars of Mexican cuisine. Use of the corn tortilla is ancient, dating back probably to Neolithic times. It is the Mexican counterpart of the Indian ***chupatty,*** the Scottish oatcake, and the native American johnnycake (see **Corn Bread).** When the Spanish conquerors arrived in Mexico City in the 1520s, they noted that the tortilla was the foundation of the Mexican diet.

Tortillas

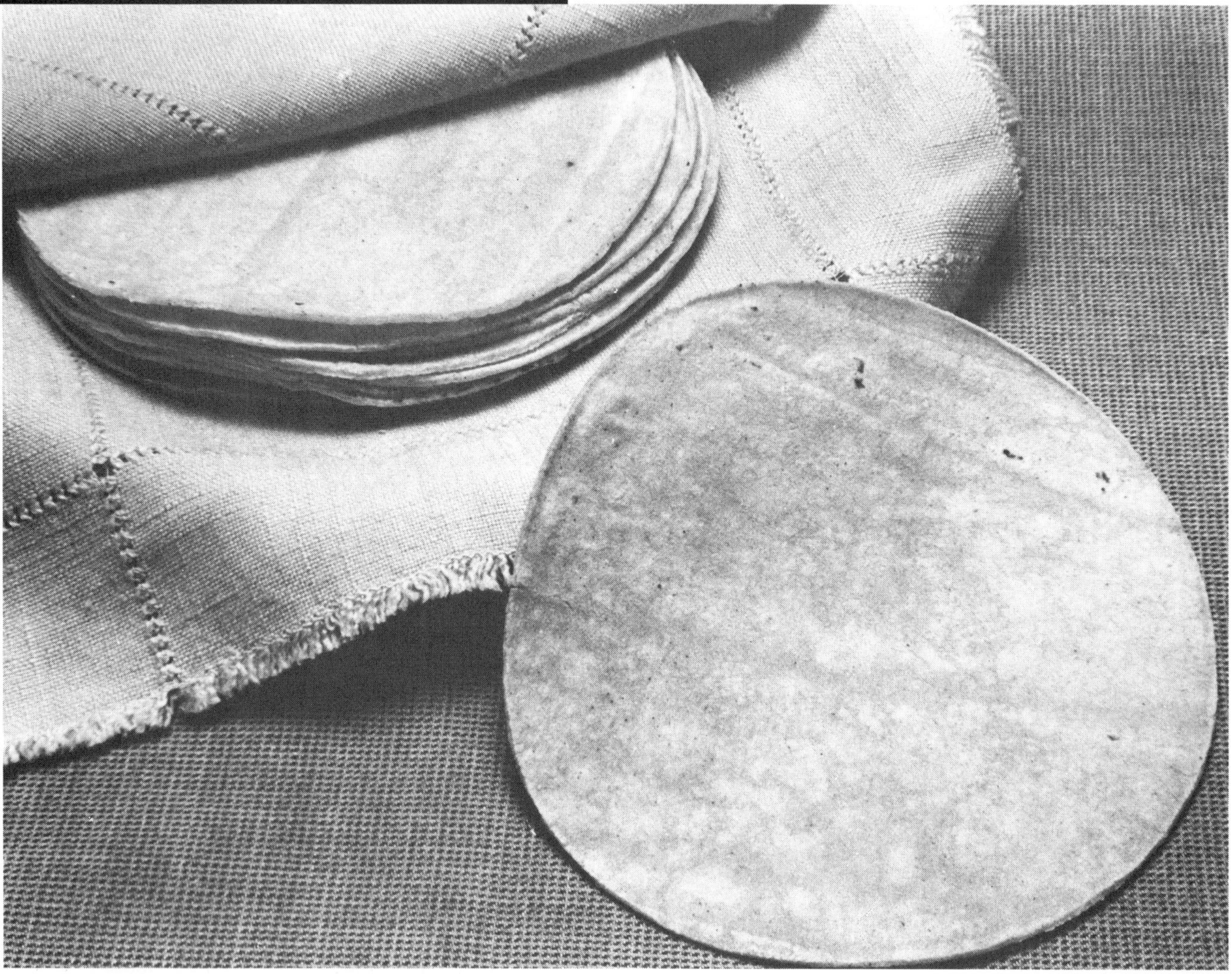

Following is the ancient method of making tortillas, which can still be observed in remote places in Mexico. Kernels of corn are heated in a mildly corrosive solution of lime until the skins come off. The Aztecs called these skinless kernels *mixtamal*, a word still in use. The dried *mixtamal* is placed on a concave grinding stone or saddle quern, called a *metate*, and mashed with a roller stone to a floury consistency. The flour, called *masa*, is mixed with water and salt and kneaded into a dough. Balls of this dough about the size of a walnut are patted by hand into flat disks five to six inches in diameter and one-eighth of an inch thick. They are cooked one by one on an ungreased griddle called the *comal*, usually two minutes to a side, or until lightly brown. At this point, the tortilla has developed a thin, tough skin on both sides, but it remains soft and flexible.

In cities and towns, the *masa* may be purchased by the bag in stores and the dough pressed into shape using a cast-iron tortilla press. Or, going a step further, the cook may purchase tortillas made by a machine which, through an ingenious system of cylinders, belts and burners, produces perfect tortillas either cooked or uncooked.

Freshly cooked tortillas eaten at table are usually torn into triangular strips and used to scoop or push food. They may be rolled around a filling, such as meat or chicken, or fried in a *V*-shape and stuffed with a filling, in which case they become *tacos*. Rolled around a filling, covered with sauce, and baked in a casserole, they become *enchiladas*. They are used in countless other dishes, but this versatility applies only to the corn tortilla. Use of those made from wheat flour is restricted pretty much to eating them as a bread-substitute at table, or filling them like tacos with beans, in which case they are called *burritos*.

See also: **Bread.**

TORTOISE

See **Turtle.**

TOSCANELLO

Also TOSCANO. This hard Italian grating cheese is made of ewe's milk in Tuscany.

See also: **Pecorino.**

TOSCANO

See **Toscanello.**

TOTUAVA

A large ocean fish found in the Gulf of California, the totuava *(Eriscion macdonaldi)* is related to the **weakfish** and the white sea bass. It is considered excellent eating and reaches a top weight of about 300 pounds.

TOUAREG CHEESE

This hard, dry, unsalted cheese is made from skim milk by Berber tribes that are scattered from the Barbary states to Lake Chad in Africa. The curd is sometimes formed with rennet and sometimes with an extract of the leaves of the *korourou* tree.

TOUCH-ME-NOT

Also SQUIRTING CUCUMBER. This is a trailing herb, *Ecballium elaterium*, whose small green fruit is edible but grown mainly as a curiosity. The fruit has a rough, hairy skin, an oblong shape and reaches a length of about two inches. On reaching maturity it squirts seeds explosively from the opening at its base. The touch-me-not is native to the Mediterranean region.

TOULOUMISIO

A white, crumbly Greek cheese made from sheep and goat's milk that has an astringent taste and firm texture, it is similar to **feta** in most respects, including the ways of making it. It is cured in brine and, therefore, qualifies as a pickled cheese.

TOULOUSE SAUSAGE

A specialty of southern France, the Toulouse is a large, fresh sausage containing coarsely chopped pork and veal seasoned with mace, nutmeg, salt, pepper and a dash of saltpeter. It is grilled or fried like smaller sausages or used in casseroles

See also: **Sausage.**

TOURAINE WINE

See **Loire Wines.**

TOUS-LES-MOIS

Also ACHIRA, EDIBLE CANNA, QUEENSLAND ARROWROOT. This is a starch resembling **arrowroot** obtained from the rhizomes of the *Canna edulis*, an herb of the West Indies and South America whose purple stalks reach a height of 10 feet. The rhizomes themselves are used for food in Andean South America, but they are cultivated in Queensland for the starch. *Tous-les-mois* is sometimes used in France as a substitute for arrowroot.

TRAGACANTH

Also GUM DRAGON, GUM TRAGACANTH. This tasteless, odorless gum is obtained from several species of plants of the *Astragalus* genus, such as milk vetch and goat's thorn. These are mountain plants of Asia Minor, commonly found in Iran, Turkey and Greece. The gum is reddish or white, and exudes through natural fissures in the plant or through incisions made by gatherers. It is marketed in powdered form, and when put in water, it swells up, not dissolving, but absorbing all the water into a viscous, adhesive mass. It is used by pastry cooks to bind oils, firm up pastries and to thicken sauces and gelatinous desserts. It also makes a good stabilizer for **ice cream.**

See also: **Gum.**

TRAPA NUT

See **Water Chestnut.**

TRAPPIST CHEESE

This semisoft, mild cheese originally was made in a Trappist monastery in Yugoslavia but now is made in many parts of Europe including Hungary, Czechoslovakia, Germany and Austria. It is very similar to **Port du Salut** and ***Oka.***

It is made from fresh cow's milk, with sheep or goat's milk sometimes added, and has a pale yellow paste. Its curing resembles that of hard cheese in that washing is frequent, a practice that curbs mold growth. Thus it ripens evenly throughout, not just on the surface. Ripening takes five to six weeks, and cheeses range from two pounds on up to 10 pounds.

TRAVELER'S TREE

Also TRAVELER'S PALM. This is a treelike plant, *Ravenala madagascariensis*, of Madagascar, whose seeds and terminal buds are edible. This plant has several palmlike stems that grow in clumps; and the leaves resemble those of the banana plant. It is cultivated in various tropical areas, and its name derives from the fact that rainwater collects in hollow places at the base of the leaf stalks and is useful for emergency drinking.

TRAVNIK

Also ARNAUTEN, VLASIC. This is a soft, white cheese whose production originated in Albania, but now centers in Yugoslavia around the town of Travnik. Curds are pressed by hand, dried in the open air, then packed in kegs between layers of salt for curing. The result is mild and pleasing to the taste. These cheeses are eaten fresh or after aging anywhere from two weeks to several months. Travnik is also made in Russia.

TREACLE

Also GOLDEN SYRUP. This term is used in Great Britain for **molasses.** The darkest and crudest molasses is known as black treacle, and the more refined and light brown in color is known simply as treacle. The term is also used for golden syrup, a fluid obtained in the making of refined, crystallized sugar. It has the texture and color of corn syrup and is used for sauces, cakes and puddings.

TREBOLIANO

See **Reggiano.**

TRECCIA

This is a small, drawn-curd Italian cheese, originally made from buffalo milk like mozzarella, that is braided or interlaced. It is eaten fresh and is popular in Naples.

See also: **Caciocavallo, Formaggio di Pasta Filata, Scamorze.**

TREE EAR

See **Black Tree Fungus.**

TREE ONION

Also CATAWISSA ONION, EGYPTIAN ONION, TOP ONION. This onion plant, *Allium cepa* var. *proliferum*, produces bulblets at the top of its stalks as well as large bulbs at the roots. Both may be used in cooking.

See also: **Onion.**

TREE TOMATO

This is the orange red, or sometimes violet, fruit of a small tree, *Cyphomandra betacea*, native to tropical Peru, but grown in subtropical areas such as northern New Zealand. The tree is short-lived and reaches a height of only 10 feet. This is not the true tomato, although it is of the same botanical family, the *Solanaceae*, but it is a pleasant fruit nonetheless. It is egg-shaped, reaching a length of three to 3½ inches and is 1¼ inches in diatmeter. The fruit is known as tamarillo in New Zealand, where it has become a valuable cash crop.

The tree tomato is eaten raw, cut in half, sprinkled with sugar and the pulp scooped out with a spoon, or more frequently stewed. The fruit is rich in pectin and makes a good jelly. It is prepared in other ways like a vegetable.

TREFOIL

Also BIRD'S FOOT TREFOIL, MARSH TREFOIL. Bird's foot trefoil *(Lotus corniculatus)* is a leguminous plant, native to Europe and Asia, whose narrow, inch-long pods are edible. It is eaten in Iceland and Crete, and has some claim to be the **lotus** of Greek legend.

Marsh trefoil *(Menyanthes trifoliata)*, a plant of the gentian family, is found in temperate regions. Its large, dark green leaves have a bitter taste and have been used as a hop substitute, and its starchy rhizomes may be cooked and eaten like carrots, or, as in Lapland and Finland, ground as flour and used to make bread. The leaves of another variety, Shanghai trefoil, are cooked and eaten as a vegetable in China.

TRENCHER BREAD

A medieval forerunner of the dinner plate, the trencher was a slice of coarse, dark bread made of wholewheat flour mixed with a quantity of rye or barley flour. The trencher measured from four by six to 10 inches square. It was oven-baked, browned evenly on both sides, and allowed to age for four days before being used at table. Diners at the table of a medieval lord ate in pairs (except for the lord himself and other high-ranking nobles), so that two persons shared a table setting. Each, however, was provided a trencher, which served as his or her dinner plate. The two guests would be served a single bowl of meat, for example, from which each would have to remove his or her portion by hand, transferring it to the trencher before eating it. The trencher was designed to absorb gravy and juices from the meat.

On rare occasions, a guest might eat the trencher; more often it was eaten by the servants, the dogs or the poor. In time, a hearty eater came to be known as a good trencherman. Following is *Advice to a Child*, dated 1500, concerning the trencher:

> *Lay a clean trencher before you, and when your pottage is brought, take your spoon and eat quietly; and do not leave your spoon in the dish, I pray you. Lay salt honestly on your trencher, for that is courtesy.*
>
> *Do not put the meat off your trencher into the dish, but get a voider and empty it into that. Do not play with the spoon, or your trencher, or your knife; but lead your life in cleanliness and honest manners. Heap not thy trencher with many morsels, and from blackness always keep thy nails.*

TRIGGERFISH

This name is applied to many species of warmwater sea fish (family *Balistidae)*, few of which are edible, and some of which are suspected of being poisonous. One distinctive species, the queen triggerfish, or oldwife *(Balistes vetula)* is eaten regularly in the Bahamas, where it is sometimes called "turbot" in the markets. It has unusual long streamers on the tail and dorsal fins but otherwise has a typical triggerfish look: deep compressed body and the dorsal spine that occasions the name "triggerfish," i.e., the first, stout dorsal spine, when erected, is locked into place by a small second spine. The latter acts as a trigger that must be released before the other spine can come down. This fish is yellowish brown to deep brown with a blue ring around its mouth. It can be as much as 22 inches long.

TRIPE

Tripe is the stomach lining of ruminating animals, such as cattle and sheep, when dressed and prepared as food. Tripe dishes usually consist of the first two stomachs of beef cattle, the rumen (blanket tripe) and the reticulum (honeycomb tripe). But the term also covers the third stomach, the omasum (the many-plies or book tripe) and the fourth stomach, the abomasum (true glandular stomach). In France the term also includes pig's stomach and sometimes intestines. The French nomenclature runs as follows: rumen, *gras double* or *panse;* the reticulum, *reseau* or *millet* or *cailette;* the omasum, *feuillet* or *bonnet*, and the abomasum, *franche mule. Gras double* is sometimes used to cover all of the first three stomachs.

Beef tripe is usually sold already cleaned, and partly cooked (parboiled). Boiling turns the abundant connective tissue gelatinous, which gives tripe the rubbery, slithery consistency that many people find objectionable. Yet this consistency makes tripe an easily digestible food. It has virtually no flavor of its own, but is enjoyed for its texture and the abundance of herbs, spices and condiments that usually accompany it. Sheep's stomach is used to make **haggis.**

Tripe is much appreciated in Europe, particularly France, but generally ignored in the United States, except in French or Mexican restaurants. In the latter tripe is typically served in a soup called *menudo.* Americans of the Old West did enjoy tripe, however, as one of the main ingredients of a cowboy dish called son-of-a-bitch stew. The milk-filled abomasum, or fourth stomach, was used, which lent a distinctive flavor of renin-curdled milk to the concoction. Other ingredients were calf's tongue, liver, heart and sweetbreads, onions, chilis, salt and pepper. The classic French dish is *tripe a la mode de Caen*, a casserole flavored with Norman cider and applejack. Other methods of preparation include stewed (Spain and Italy), sauteed (Lyon, Provence), roasted (Hungary), simmered (Provence, England), fried (France, England) and soup (Poland, Mexico). Canned tripe has been cooked in milk and salt. For tripe as a sausage casing, see **Sausage.**

See also: **Stomach.**

TRIPLE SEC

This is a white or colorless orange-flavored liqueur, consumed as an **aperitif** or as an after-dinner drink. Triple Sec may contain up to 40 percent alcohol (80 proof). In the United States and Mexico, Triple Sec is an essential ingredient in a Margarita, a strong cocktail based on tequila and served ice-cold in salt-rimmed glasses.

TROCKENKASE

See **Dry Cheese.**

TROUT

This fish of the salmon family, usually inhabiting fresh water exclusively, is popular for its fighting qualities as well as its delicate flavor. Trout are members of the *Salmo* genus. Although many **char** are commonly called trout, e.g., American brook trout, they are members of the *Salvelinus* genus. Trout are native to both Europe and North America. Adults vary in size from one to two pounds, caught in fast moving streams, to lake varieties that weigh 45 pounds and more.

The European brown trout *(Salmo trutta fario)* has brook, river, lake and sea (migratory) varieties. The kind inhabiting brooks and rivers are often known as common trout. Common trout can weigh as much as 18 pounds. Their flesh is white and fine-grained. The lake variety *(Salmo trutta fario* var. *lacustris)* becomes much larger, as much as 45 pounds in Swiss lakes. Their flesh is also white, but according to some sources, they are not nearly as tasty as the smaller brook and river trout. The sea trout *(Salmo trutta fario* var. *marina)*, or salmon trout, is a migratory fish, rising from the sea to spawn in rivers at the beginning of winter. It too is a larger fish, topping out at about 30 pounds and reaching a length of 4½ feet. It is called "salmon trout" because its flesh is pink much like the salmon's. This is not due, however, to a closer relationship to the salmon, but to the type of crustaceans the trout feed on. Remove these from the fish's diet and its flesh turns white like that of other trout.

The rainbow trout *(Salmo irideus)* is the only native United States species, and it originated in California. Fish called trout that are native to the United States east of the Rocky Mountains are not true trout. The Eastern brook trout is a char. The American sea trout is a **weakfish.** And the lake trout of the Great Lakes is also a char. The rainbow trout has come to be the most famous and widely eaten trout in the world. It is a beautiful fish, and its gameness surpasses that of the European brown trout. Adults average about two pounds in weight but run as high as six.

The many varieties of West Coast trout are considered subvarieties of the rainbow. These include the steelhead, which is larger (six to 18 pounds) and migratory; the cutthroat, which is smaller (1½ to five pounds); the golden trout, which is the state fish of California, and the Kern Plateau rainbow trout. Rainbows have been transplanted to the Eastern Seaboard and to many other parts of the world including Europe, South America, Asia, Africa, Australia and New Zealand. It is the trout most frequently raised on fish farms. The flavor of those raised in captivity does not come near to matching that of the wild variety. The artificially raised trout industry is most developed in Japan and France. French food critics have likened the tame trout to "a wet bandage," and called it, "a cotton-fleshed substitute."

Another well-known American trout, the Dolly Varden, is not a trout at all, but a char. It received its name, apparently, because its red spots are reminiscent of the red ribbons worn by a Charles Dickens character of the same name. The green trout of the northwestern United States is a large-mouthed bass.

Ancient Romans were fond of trout, and there is some evidence to suggest that they raised them artificially. The trout they preferred, however, came from the Vosges mountains in what was then Gaul. They were convinced that the colder northern water produced better fish. Indeed, trout thrive in cold water of a sort that is fast moving, and never exceeds 60° F (16° C.). Both of these qualities promote a high oxygen saturation of the water, a condition necessary for the trout. One reason for the widespread transplantation of the rainbow is its easier adaptation to poor water conditions.

Trout is usually prepared simply, by grilling, poaching or frying. Smoked trout is excellent; white and moist, with a subtle flavor.

TROUT-PERCH

A small, edible fish, *Percopsis omiscomaycus*, native to North America but naturalized in Europe, it reaches a length of eight inches and frequents large muddy rivers and shallow lakes. It is more important as forage for larger fish than as human food but may be prepared like **perch.**

TROUVILLE

A soft, ripened French cheese made from whole cow's milk in the Normandy region, it resembles a top quality **Pont l'Eveque,** which is also made in the region and in ways that differ very little from Trouville. Unlike Pont l'Eveque, Trouville is never made from skim milk, and the action of surface molds and smears is controlled a little more carefully during ripening.

TROYES

See **Barberey, Ervy.**

TRUCKLES

See **Wiltshire Cheese.**

TRUFFLE

The truffle is an edible fungus that usually grows a foot or two underground. The average size has been likened to that of a small potato or tangerine, although the range is considerable on both ends of the scale,

with giant truffles becoming increasingly rare. The shape is roundish or irregular. The best truffles are highly aromatic and have a unique flavor, often described as peppery, which has excited extravagant praise from gastronomes beginning in Classical Antiquity and continuing to the present. At various times writers have proclaimed the truffle "the black diamond of the kitchen," the "black pearl," the "fairy apple," the "divine tuber," the "fragrant nugget," and the "underground nugget."

As a rule, truffles are temperate growths, the desert truffle of North Africa being the most notable exception. They need warmth and plenty of rain, they prefer chalky or clayey soil and almost always grow in the vicinity of a tree, usually an oak. Truffles draw in all the nutrients from the surrounding soil, leaving none for other plants, hence the characteristically barren appearance of a truffle ground, which may stretch for 150 feet around a host tree. Truffles do not propagate directly but require the services of the truffle fly and host tree for that purpose. The fly burrows into the soil and lays its eggs in the truffle, carrying away truffle spores when it exits. The fly lands on the leaves of the tree, depositing some of the spores there. Later, the leaves fall off, returning the spores to the earth. It is these spores that grow into truffles.

The finest truffles come from France and Italy, with Spain and North Africa a distant third and fourth. More than 30 species grow in North America, but none is of much gastronomic interest. Great Britain has one edible variety, which will be discussed below. In France, the world's most important supplier of truffles, production reached a peak in 1892 with 2,000 tons. It has declined precipitously since then, with the annual crop ranging somewhere between 25 and 150 tons. Nevertheless, demand has increased steadily even as the supply has diminished, with the result that truffles have become one of the world's most expensive foods, outdistancing other luxury items, such as **caviar** and **foie gras.** The chief factor restricting the supply is the failure of the truffle to respond to cultivation, which means it must be found in the wild.

Truffle hunting is a sizeable occupation in France, and in other truffle producing areas. Finding a truffle ground is fairly easy, owing to its characteristic appearance as mentioned above. But the exact location of a truffle is a mystery. Giant truffles may cause a break in the surface of the soil, which the trained eye easily spots. Or a swarm of truffle flies may be seen hovering over a certain spot. Usually, however, a truffle must be detected by its aroma. Although some hunters claim to have a sense of smell keen enough to detect a truffle, most employ the services of a dog, or sow, or in some areas goats or even bear cubs, as in Russia. Dowsing rods have also been tried with indifferent success. After detection, the truffle must be dug up with care, to avoid breaking the mycelium, or vegetative part made up of threadlike tubes. Then for some species, such as the Perigord, or black truffle, cleaning presents a problem because it has an irregular, warty surface. All this hand labor contributes to the high cost.

Following are the most important varieties of truffle:

The *black*, or *Perigord truffle (Tuber melanosperm):* Named for the old French province that was once a center of production, the Perigord truffle now comes chiefly from the regions of Quercy and Vaucluse in the southwest of France. It is black or very dark brown on the outside with an irregular, warty surface. The inside is white, turning gray or brown as the truffle ripens and is marbled with fine white veins. The consistency is more like a meat than a vegetable. This is acknowledged to be the finest of all truffles and is a major ingredient of pate de foie gras. It is often cooked, and black truffles sauteed in champagne have long been a symbol of sybaritic living.

The *Italian*, or *white truffle (Tuber magnatum):* This second best of truffles grows especially well in the region of Alba in northern Italy. It is yellowish or rosy white on the outside and marbled on the inside, much like the black truffle. It has a peppery, garlicky aroma and taste and is rarely, if ever, cooked. Usually, it is cut into extremely thin slices and sprinkled over rice dishes.

The *Bath* or *summer truffle (Tuber aestivus):* The only edible English truffle, it is dark brown or black, with a spicy aroma but little taste. Terriers are used to hunt this truffle on the South Downs in the Epping Forest, where it is associated with beech rather than oak trees.

The *desert truffle (Terfezia leonis):* This is found in North Africa, particularly Libya, and experts differ on whether it is a genuine truffle. Nevertheless, ancient writers gave it high praise. It was eaten as early as 1800 B.C., and Juvenal, a Roman satiric poet, who was writing around the first century

A.D., made this declaration: "Lybians, unyoke your oxen! Keep your grain, but send us your truffles." These are large truffles, usually pear-shaped, with a flavor closer to mushrooms. They are whitish and grow beneath the surface but are often left exposed on the surface by strong desert winds.

The *violet truffle (Tuber brumale):* This is of good but lesser quality than the black and white truffles and is found in Switzerland, Northern Italy and Southern Germany.

Much to the dismay of gourmets who claim that to enjoy truffles one must have plenty of them at one sitting, truffles are increasingly present only in tiny portions, serving more as a garnish or condiment than anything else. They are principally used to lard chicken, flavor pate and omelets and sprinkle over rice dishes.

TRUMPETER

This is a delicious food fish of the cooler waters of the Southern Hemisphere. Two species are prominent, the bastard trumpeter *(Latridopsis forsteri)* and the Tasmanian trumpeter *(Latris lineata)*. Both are similarly shaped, having slender, oval bodies and long, many-rayed dorsal fins. The bastard trumpeter reaches a length of two feet and is found along the coasts of South Australia, Victoria, New South Wales and Tasmania. It has a dark olive-green back, silvery sides and belly and lateral yellow stripes. It is not a very abundant fish, although its flesh is rated as top quality.

The Tasmanian trumpeter, a larger fish (up to 40 inches long), ranges over the same territory and is found as far east as New Zealand. It supports extensive commercial fishing and is deemed one of Australia's finest food fishes. A large specimen can weigh as much as 60 pounds. This fish is silver with lateral dark stripes.

TRUNKFISH

Also BOXFISH. Trunkfish belong to the *Ostraciontidae* family, which includes boxfish and **cowfish.** Fish of this family are characterized by a heavy "shell" that encloses their body and by some members' ability to exude a poisonous slime when alarmed. The trunkfish *(Lactophrys trigonus)* of the western Atlantic, also known as the buffalo trunkfish, is regarded as an excellent food fish throughout its range, which extends from Massachusetts to Brazil, including the Gulf of Mexico. It is a grunter and has the typical carapace of the family, but it does not emit toxins. Large specimens may be 17 inches long. Some Pacific varieties, despite their toxic slime, are considered not only edible but a delicacy in certain South Pacific islands.

TSCHIL

Also LEAF CHEESE, TELPANIR, ZWIRN. Tschil is an Armenian sour, skim-milk cheese made chiefly in eastern Europe from the milk of sheep and cows. The curd is worked by hand until it is fairly firm and dry, then pressed into cakes that are put in wooden troughs for five to eight days of ripening.

TUBA

This word is used in the Philippines for palm tree sap, or toddy, which is used to make a wine or distilled to make a stronger liquor. For more information, see **Palm Wine.**

TUBEROUS RUSH

Also BATEIFUN. The rhizomes of this Far Eastern species, *Scirpus tuberosus*, are used to produce starch or flour for cakes. It is cultivated under very moist conditions in China and Japan.

TUBERROOT

Also BUTTERFLY WEED, PLEURISY ROOT, INDIAN PAINTBRUSH. This perennial herb, *Asclepias tuberosa*, of the milkweed family was a valuable source of food for several native American tribes. The plant is native to North America and is found from New England to North Dakota and south to Florida, Arizona and northern Mexico. Its roots and seed pods were boiled and eaten as vegetables; its shoots were eaten like asparagus. Sugar was extracted from its flowers as well.

TUCKAHOE

Also INDIAN BREAD, VIRGINIA TRUFFLE. This is an edible fungus gathered by native Americans in what is now the state of Virginia and used to make a kind of bread. Tuckahoes were found in marshy areas. They are thought to have been hard, enlarged mycelia of mushrooms growing near the roots of pine trees. A plant growing in similar areas, *Peltandra virginica*, called Virginian wake-robin, or arrow arum, is also known as tuckahoe, and it is speculated that its roots were used in the same way as the mycelia.

TUCUMA

The name refers to several species of palm trees *(Astrocaryum* spp.) found in the American tropics, which produce edible fruit. The species *A. vulgare* is especially important to Brazilian Indians who not only eat the fruit, but also use fiber taken from the leaves to make cordage, bowstrings, fishing nets, hats, fans, hammocks, etc. The species *A. aculeatum* is cultivated in Trinidad for its edible palm oil.

TUHU

The berries of this small New Zealand tree, *Coriaria sarmentosa*, are made into a drink. Its shoots, however, should not be eaten. Other species of this plant are found in South America, southern Europe, eastern Asia and the Pacific islands, and their fruits are all considered more or less poisonous.

TULIP

See **Edible Tulip.**

TULLIBEE

This is a kind of whitefish, *Coregonus tullibee*, found in the Great Lakes of North America.

See also: **Whitefish.**

TULSI

Also TOOLSI, HOLY BASIL. Tulsi is a variety of basil, *Ocimum sanctum*, found in India and held sacred by the Hindus. Its tiny black seeds are used in Indian cookery.

See also: **Basil.**

TUNA

See **Prickly Pear.**

TUNA FISH

Also TUNNY. The flesh of this large, fat fish has been compared in taste to raw beef, chicken and veal, depending on the species under discussion. Generally bullet-shaped, tuna *(Thunnidae)* are the largest members of the mackerel family, ranging in size up to 1,800 pounds. The most highly prized eating varieties are, in order of size, bluefin, yellowfin, albacore, little tunny and skipjack. They are common to the Mediterranean Sea and the warmer waters of the Atlantic, Pacific and Indian Oceans. They travel in schools and spend the winter at the bottom of the sea, rising to the surface in the spring near shore to spawn.

Archaeological remains attest to the importance of tuna to prehistoric people. In salted form, it was the mainstay for the poor in ancient Greece. Indeed,

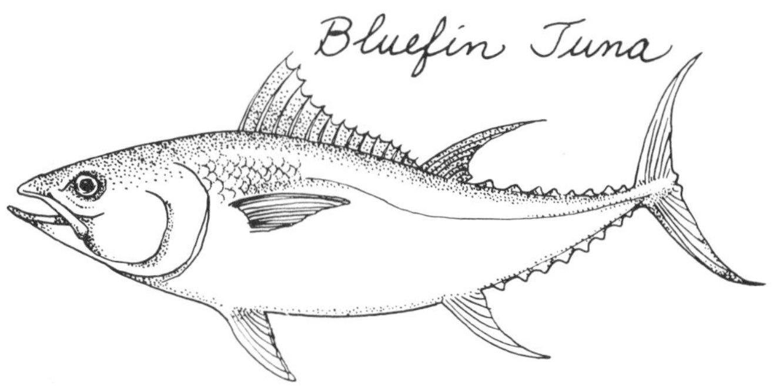

tuna was probably the main food fish of the classical world. Romans created their all-purpose seasoner, *garum*, from the fermented intestines of tuna.

Currently, white or light meat tuna are preferred by Westerners, and this means albacore, yellowfin or skipjack. Only albacore may legally be called "white meat tuna" in the United States, yellowfin and skipjack being classed a light meat. The Japanese, on the other hand, prefer the dark, red meat of the bluefin.

Bluefin *(Thunnus thynnus)* is the monarch of tuna with specimens commonly weighing in at 700 to 1000 pounds. It is one of the strongest swimmers in the ocean and, unlike other fish, is warmblooded. These factors account for the dark red color of its flesh. Because of the color, most Americans are reluctant to eat it, but more of it is eaten than any other species because the Japanese love it, eating it raw. They liken its flavor variously to refrigerated beef and something midway between cold raw beef and raw shellfish. They call it *maguro*, and in Japan it fetches from eight to 20 times the American price.

In the Pacific, bluefin are caught in large purse seine nets, but in the Mediterranean they are trapped, using an age-old method, which is both an ancient sacrificial rite and a good tourist attraction. Schools of fish are herded into an enclosure consisting of miles of anchored netting. They are driven through a narrowing series of funnel shaped nets, arriving eventually at the shallow killing chamber. They are then gaffed and killed on boats lying parallel to the nets, or stabbed to death in the water.

Albacore *(T. alalunga)*, also called long-finned, white tuna and germon, is a much smaller fish, the largest specimens weighing 65 pounds and attaining four feet in length. Americans prefer its bland, white flesh, which some call "chicken of the sea." It is delicious fresh, but hard to find that way because most is purchased for canning even before it reaches the dock. Albacore are taken with a pole and line, an inefficient method that adds to the already high cost.

Yellowfin *(T. albaceres)* is less migratory, confining its movements to certain areas in the Pacific, so that its fishing has had to be limited by international agreement. Yellowfin has light tender flesh and is generally caught in the 20 to 30 pound range.

Little tunny *(T. thunina)*, also called horse mackerel, whose flesh has been compared to veal, is preferred in Mediterranean countries over the more common bluefin. Its popular name in Italy is *letterato*, which refers to the markings on its back. They look as if someone had been scribbling in an unknown language. Alexandre Dumas commented, "You might say that it is neither meat nor fish."

The skipjack *(Katsuwomus palamis)*, which fishermen refer to as the fastest and most beautiful of all tuna, also called ocean bonito, is often confused with the California bonito *(Sarda chilensis)*. It is the smallest of the main tuna, usually being taken at from six to 15 pounds, and has darker flesh than the yellowfin. But the meat is tender, with a soft texture, and is highly prized in Hawaii, where it is called *aku*.

Most people encounter tuna in canned form, but the fresh steaks are good, though oily. They should be marinated in lemon juice and oil before broiling or sauteeing.

TURBOT

This large European food fish resembles the **halibut** but is not found in American waters. Although the average market weight is 10 pounds, it may run as high as 60.

The turbot *(Scophthalmus maximus)* is a flat fish that holds to the bottom, both eyes being placed on the left, or up side. Its scales are so minute as to seem merely rough skin. The main fishing grounds are the Atlantic coast of France, the English Channel and the Baltic Sea. The ones favoring rocky, rather than muddy shores, have a superior flavor.

"American turbot" is a name applied to a large flounder or, sometimes, a chicken halibut.

Called the "pheasant of the sea," the turbot has flesh that is white and firm and so delicate and delicious that the simplest cooking methods suffice. Traditionally, it was a favorite main dish for feast days, particularly in Lent. The Roman author Martial wrote, "However great the dish that holds the turbot, the turbot is still greater than the dish."

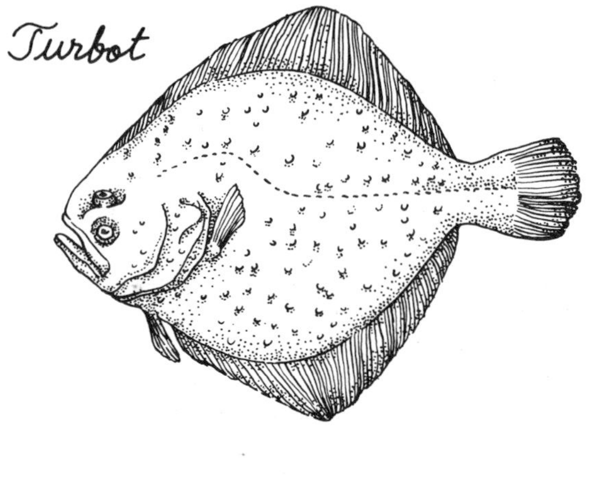

TURKEY

This bird is native to North America, although the English word, "turkey," suggests an Eastern provenance. By the time the Spaniards arrived in Mexico, it had long been domesticated by the Pueblos and the Aztecs, who called it *uaxolote*, a name that persists in Mexico today. Of course, the land was teeming with wild turkeys too. The chief types were the common turkey *(Meleagris galloporo)*, of northeastern and central areas, and the Mexican and ocellated turkeys, of the southwest, Mexico and Central America. It was the southwestern varieties that got domesticated first and that the explorers brought back to Spain in 1498. Unlike potatoes and beans, the turkey was an instant gastronomic hit. Within a few years, it was distributed throughout Europe. Its arrival in England was marked by this popular jingle:

Turkeys, carps, hops, pickerel and beer
Came to England all in one year.

That year is said to be 1520. All new things were popularly believed to come from the East. The guinea fowl of West Africa was already called "turkey," but the name was quickly switched to the new bird.

Although native to North America, the turkey had been well established in Europe as a domestic fowl long before it became the centerpiece of American Thanksgiving in 1621. The birds consumed by the Pilgrim Fathers were wild, of course, but many authorities claim that the wild American turkey was not the progenitor of today's commercial birds. Instead, domesticated turkeys were reintroduced from Europe to start commercial strains. Paradoxically, American commercial birds are much larger than their European cousins.

The turkey was America's largest game bird (and continues to be on a limited basis in some 21 states). It is also the largest domesticated bird. It is characterized by a small, bare head, wattled neck and handsome feathers. Indeed, turkey-breeding in the United States was begun for the feathers, and it was not until the 1920s that meat surpassed feathers in economic importance. The male is called a tom, the female a hen, and the immature bird, a poult.

Opinion is divided over which is better for eating, the tom or the hen. Although the tom is said to have a better flavor, it yields less meat per pound because of its heavier bone structure. In the market, the average weight for young toms is 12 pounds, for hens eight.

The most popular breed in America is the Bronze turkey, which can weigh as much as 35 to 40 pounds, but averages 25 for the tom and 16 for the hen. The Bronze turkey is broadbreasted, heavily fleshed, and its plumage is a copperish red on a background of black and brown, with white tips to the feathers. Other standard breeds, and top weights,

Turkey

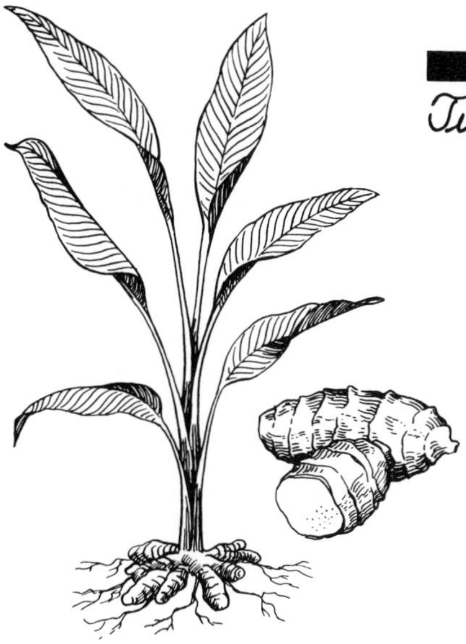

Turmeric

are the Bourbon red, black and slate (30), the White Holland (28) and the Narragansett (25 to 30). A smaller breed of white turkey, developed by the United States government, averages 12 to 14 pounds.

In Europe, birds are smaller. In Spain and Italy, turkeys from six to 10 pounds are preferred, while in England the popular breeds, Norfolk black and the Cambridge, rarely exceed 20 pounds.

The turkey industry in the United States is huge, averaging 100 million birds a year, which is an estimated 170 times the wild population when Europeans landed in the New World. For centuries tradition demanded that turkey be eaten on Christmas and Thanksgiving and rarely otherwise. This has broken down to such an extent that more than 50 percent are eaten at other times of the year. Turkeys are usually stuffed and roasted in the oven. They need plenty of basting to keep the breast meat moist, although self-basting birds are available in the markets. They should be cooked slowly for maximum tenderness. In the United States smoked turkey is popular. Turkey eggs are larger than hen's eggs and have a delicate flavor but are used in the same way as hen's.

TURKISH SAGE

This variety of sage, *Salvia fruitcosa*, is found from Sicily to Syria. Its leaves are infused to make an herbal tea in Turkey and Greece.

TURK'S CAP

See **Melon Thistle.**

TURK'S HEAD

See **Leon Lemon.**

TURMERIC

A member of the ginger family, turmeric *(Curcuma longa)* is cultivated for its spicy, fleshy root. Native to China and Indonesia, it was mentioned in the Bible as a spice and food coloring, and later was one of the chief commodities in the European spice trade that led to so much exploration and colonization.

Turmeric root is a principal ingredient of curry powder and is under vast cultivation in India, as well as in Haiti, Jamaica and Peru. Although similar to ginger root in size, turmeric root is sweeter, more delicate and more fragrant. It has a pleasantly bitter taste. The root varies in shade from orange to reddish brown, but when dried and powdered it is yellow and, indeed, is added to prepared mustards to give them their characteristic hue.

At times turmeric has been used illegally to adulterate **saffron** but, in cooking, may legitimately be substituted for it when just a pinch is required to add color.

Curcuma oil is extracted from turmeric and marketed as a dyestuff.

TURNIP

This is a vegetable of the cabbage family, cultivated usually for its tuberous root, but sometimes for its green tops. It comes in various shapes and sizes depending on the variety. The common turnip *(Brassica rapa)* of England and the United States can weigh 40 to 50 pounds or be as small as an orange. It may be conical in shape, twice as long as it is wide; nearly round, or broader than it is long and slightly flattened. The flesh is most often white—it is also known as the white turnip—but sometimes yellow. The upper part of the root bulges up from the earth, and it can have a wide range of colors, including white, yellow, green, red, purple and black. The taste is tangy,

Turnip

peppery, stronger in the yellow varieties than in the white, which tends to be sweeter and more delicate.

The French turnip *(Brassica napa)* or *navet* is typically carrot-shaped. The flesh is most often white, but there are yellow and black varieties too. The taste of this turnip is known for its delicacy and sweetness, and is used in soups, stews or to accompany meat dishes, rather than as a separate dish. Both the common turnip and the French turnip are fall vegetables. The French also produce a spring turnip, which is small and round and whose spicy flavor goes particularly well in soups.

The food value of turnips is modest. It is mostly water, but contains 1 percent protein, 6 to 7 percent carbohydrates and a trace amount of fat. The turnip also contains minute amounts of arsenic—the only common vegetable to do so along with cabbage—which in trace amounts is essential to human nutrition. The pungent taste is due to its sulpher content. As a separate vegetable, turnips are usually peeled and boiled and served with butter, salt and pepper.

Turnip tops or greens are rich in vitamins and minerals. They are popular in Portugal and the U.S. South where they are boiled for 15 to 20 minutes with diced salt pork and a pinch of pepper or chili.

Throughout its long history, the turnip has been considered a vegetable for the humble. There is good reason for this. It grows well in poor soil. It ripens quickly. It keeps relatively well. Consequently, it has usually been very cheap. Native to Asia Minor, the turnip was well known to the ancient Greeks and Romans who, though they ate it copiously, thought of it as food for the poor or for countryfolk. It was a common vegetable in Europe during the Middle Ages, and its cultivation spread to England in the 17th century. Popularity there did not come until the 18th century when Lord Townshend—nicknamed Turnip Townshend—introduced improved varieties from Holland. Both French and English colonists cultivated turnips in the New World. They were enthusiastically adopted there by native Americans.

Turnips do best in cold or temperate-cold climates in soil near the seashore. Some authorities believe **sea kale** to be the ancestor of the turnip.

See also: **Rutabaga.**

TURNIP-ROOTED CABBAGE

See **Rutabaga.**

TURTLE

Also TERRAPIN, TORTOISE. For convenience, edible reptiles of the order *Testudines* or *Chelonia* will be discussed here, whether they be freshwater, saltwater or land varieties. They have these characteristics in common: a horny, toothless beak, a soft body encased in a hard or leathery shell (into which the head, tail, and legs may be withdrawn), and partly webbed feet. Of the order's approximately 300 species, virtually all are edible. Two exceptions, for example, are the common musk turtle, and the yellow mud turtle of the United States whose odoriferous glands make them unsuitable for food.

Sea turtles are distributed worldwide in tropical and subtropical waters, but most exported turtle meat comes from South America, Africa, Australia and particularly the West Indies. The most common species of sea turtle are the loggerhead *(Caretta caretta);* the hawksbill *(Eretmochelys imbricata)*, which, though the smallest, is highly valued as a source of tortoise shell; the flatback *(Chelonia depressa);* the olive or Pacific ridley *(Lepidochelys olivacea);* Kemp's ridley *(Lepidochelys kempi);* the leathery turtle *(Dermochelys coriacea)*, and the green turtle *(Chelonia mydas)*, which is the largest, and, gastronomically, the most important of all.

The green turtle is usually green brown in color, and may weigh as much as 850 pounds, though most vary between 50 and 300 pounds. It swims near the surface of the water and, being vegetarian, prefers shallow seas where the algae and sea grasses are plentiful. The Caribbean area is the famous source of green turtles, but ruthless commercial exploitation has greatly reduced their numbers.

Turtle meat may be prepared in a number of ways including baking, broiling, sauteeing and deep-frying. Turtle flippers are considered a true delicacy. These turtles are celebrated, however, for providing calipash and calipee, ingredients of the renowned green turtle soup. Calipash is the cartilaginous outer circumference of the upper shell, which, though solid and tough in its natural state, turns gelatinous when cooked. The green color it acquires on being cooked accounts for the name "green turtle." Calipee

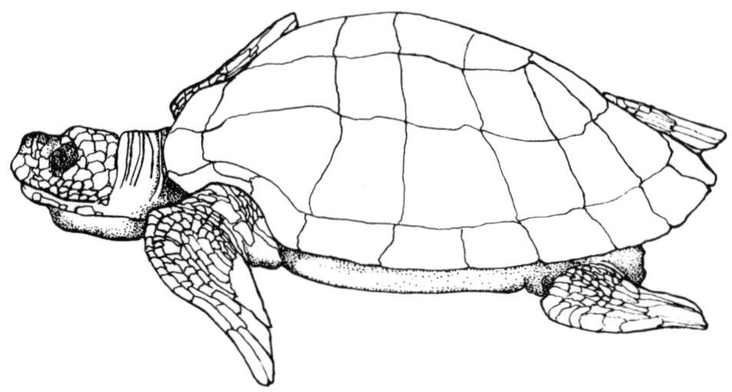

Turtle

is corresponding material from the lower shell, which has a lighter yellow color. Calipash and calipee are believed to be corruptions of the word "carapace." Lean meat from under the top shell is regarded as the best for steaks, and in the raw state resembles veal. Only the female is sought for its meat, the male being thought too tough, but both yield turtle oil for the cosmetics industry, and skin for the leather trade. Green turtles are still plentiful in the waters off northern Australia, Malaysia and Borneo. Their numbers have begun to decline in the last area due to the collection of their eggs, which are soft shelled and highly prized as food.

The loggerhead is another large species (reaching 900 pounds) whose dark red flesh is considered inferior and not much eaten, but whose eggs are relished by coastal people everywhere. Both ridleys are exploited for oil and leather as well as their eggs. The harvesting of the eggs of the leathery turtle have made it a critically endangered species worldwide.

Of the nonmarine turtles, the principal food species in the United States are the alligator snapping turtle *(Macroclemys temminckii)*, of the southeastern states, which can weigh as much as 200 pounds; and the common snapping turtle *(Chelydra serpentina)*, which occurs throughout the eastern states and reaches 50 pounds. Lesser known, but delicious varieties, are the ornate box turtle *(Terrapene ornata)*, the map and false map turtles *(Graptemys geographica* and *G. Pseudogeographic)*, the painted turtle *(Chrysemys picta)*, and several sliders, which are smooth soft-shelled and spiny soft-shelled turtles.

Best known of all is the diamond-back terrapin (Genus *Malaclemys)*, whose succulent flesh, when properly prepared, rates high on the gourmets' list. Several species of diamond back (named for the markings of their shells) inhabit the salt marshes of the Atlantic coast of the United States. They are small turtles (nine inches at most). Females from the mouth of the Chesapeake River and from Louisiana are the most prized. They were nearly made extinct by the great demand for Philadelphia terrapin stew and Maryland terrapin soup. The demand peaked before 1920 due to soaring prices, and the genus has made a comeback since then. Its flesh, like that of the green turtle, is known for its gelatinous quality when cooked.

In French cuisine, interest has centered on turtle flippers, which are usually braised in a wine sauce. In England, turtle soup is made from either fresh or dried turtle meat.

TURTLE DOVE

This is an edible wild bird, *Turtur turtur*, of the pigeon family. The name derives from the Latin *turtur*, a sound imitative of the bird's plaintive cooing. It has a marked devotion to its mate. The turtle dove may be prepared like **pigeon.**

TUSCHKINSK

See **Ossetin.**

TVOROG

See **Tworog.**

TWDR SIR

This is a sharply flavored Serbian cheese made from sheep's skim milk. Individual cheeses are round and flat, measuring 10 inches across by two thick. It generally resembles **brick** cheese, but the paste has many small holes and is less fatty.

TWIST

See **Challah.**

TWOROG

Also TVOROG, TAWOROG. A Russian farmhouse cheese made from sour milk, much like cottage cheese, it is often used to flavor a bread called *notrushki.*

TYBO

This Danish cheese is made from skimmed cow's milk and generally weighs between 4½ and 6½ pounds. It is similar to ***Samsoe*** and has a golden color and red skin.

U

UBRINI

See **Buttiri.**

UDO

This tall, herbaceous plant, *Aralia crodata*, is much cultivated in Japan for its edible stalks and shoots. These may be eaten raw with a little salt and in their crispness are reminiscent of celery. They may also be boiled and eaten like asparagus. Like asparagus, the shoots are often blanched. Udo has been planted in California but has never gained favor with the general public.

UGLI

This hybrid citrus fruit originating in Jamaica, as its name suggests, is not good to look at. It resembles a large tangerine, with loose, wrinkled, yellowish red skin. It has a greenish tinge even when ripe, yet the taste and juice are excellent. The pulp is orangelike and almost seedless. Some experts believe it to be a variety of tangelo, i.e., a cross between a tangerine and a grapefruit. Others theorize that it has three parents: the tangerine, the grapefruit and the bitter orange. It is not manmade, but was discovered in 1915 or 1916 by F. G. Sharp, owner of Jamaica's Trout Hall estates. The *ugli* is generally eaten raw, but in the West Indies it is often baked in hot cinders and eaten sprinkled with sugar.

See also: **Tangelo.**

ULLUCO

See **Oca.**

ULVA

Also SEA LETTUCE. Ulva is an edible seaweed, *Ulvaceae*, that has flat, greenish fronds. The two best known species are *U. latissium* and *U. lactuca*. Japan is the main country of consumption, where it is used in salads, soups and stews.

UMBLES

Also HUMBLE PIE. "Umbles" is an old English term for the entrails of deer, heart, liver, kidneys, etc. By extension, it was used for the entrails of other animals as well. After a hunt, the English gentry reserved the better cuts of venison for themselves and allotted the entrails to the servants who often made them into a pie. This is the origin of the phrase, "to eat [h]umble pie," i.e., the lot of social underlings.

UMBRA

Also MUDMINNOW. These small, freshwater, bottom-living fish are represented by species in Europe and North America. The European mudminnow *(Umbra karameri)* seldom exceeds five inches in length, while the central midminnow *(U. limi)* of North America is a little larger. Both burrow into mud and silt at the bottom of slow-moving rivers or still bywaters. They are edible but are not marketed.

UMKOKOLO

See **Kei Apple.**

UNICORN PLANT

See **Martynia.**

URANOSCOPUS

See **Stargazer.**

URD BEAN

See **Black Gram.**

URI CHEESE

This tangy, hard cheese is made of cow's milk in the canton of Uri, Switzerland. Weighing between 20 and 40 pounds, individual cheeses measure eight-12 inches in diameter by eight inches thick.

URSEREN

Also ORSERA. This is a mild, fermented cheese made in Switzerland.

UTAH JUNIPER

This small, bushy tree, *Juniperus osteosperma*, is found in western North America from Montana to New Mexico and California. The female cones are berrylike and are eaten fresh or dried. They may be ground and pressed into cakes.

UVALHA

Uvalha is the aromatic, pear-shaped fruit of a small Brazilian tree, *Eugenia uvalha*, which grows in the southern part of the country. The color of the fruit ranges from yellow to orange; the pulp is pleasant-tasting and very juicy. It is eaten raw and used to make drinks.

V

VACHELIN

See **Gruyere.**

VACHERIN

The name applies to several different cow's milk cheeses made in eastern France and western Switzerland. They are usually soft and ripened, but not always. *Vacherin* is a soft cheese made in the Swiss canton of Fribourg. *Vacherin du Mont d'Or* is a French cheese much like ***Livarot,*** while *vacherin fondu* is a hard cheese much like **Swiss.**

Vacherin a la main, known also as *tomme de montagne*, is made both in Switzerland and the Savoy region of France. It has a hard rind, but a paste soft enough to eat with a spoon or spread on bread.

VALDEPENAS

This rich red wine high in alcoholic content (at least 14 percent) comes from south-central Spain. The wine is ruby colored, made from the Cencibel grape and is the staple of the better *tinto* wine sold in Madrid *bodegas* accompanied by olives and sardines. It is exported, too, as a bona fide, quality wine.

VALENCIAS

See **Raisin.**

VALERIAN

This is a family of herbs, *Valerianaceae*, some species of which are eaten as salad vegetables, namely the red valerian *(Centranthus ruber)* in Italy, long-spurred valerian *(C. macrosiphon)* in France, and African valerian *(Fedes cornucopiae)*, also known as the horn-of-plenty, in the Mediterranean region. The drug valerian is extracted from the roots of the common valerian *(Valeriana officinalis)* a plant known for its strong odor. Valerian is used as a sedative and antispasmodic.

VAN DER HUM

A South African liqueur similar to Curacao, it has a sharp, spicy flavor and is a mixture of **Cape brandy,** sugar, spices, herbs and especially essence from the peel of the *naartje*, or South African tangerine, known also as the **king orange.**

VANILLA

True vanilla, a flavoring essence, is the product of a tropical vine, of which there are some 20 species, the best producer being *Vanilla planifolia.* The vine is a member of the orchid family whose climbing growth requires the support of a tree or a trellis. It is native to Central America and was first noted by Europeans in Mexico, where it was used by Aztecs to flavor their drink, *chocolatl.* William Prescott, in his *Conquest of Mexico*, wrote:

> *The emperor (Montezuma) took no other beverage than* chocolatl, *a potation of chocolate, flavored with vanilla and other spices, and so prepared as to be reduced to froth the consistency of honey, which gradually dissolved in the mouth.*

In recent times, it is best known as a flavoring in ice cream, particularly in the United States, and in cakes, sweet dishes and candy. The flavor has been described as sweet, permeating and unique. However, the world annual production of true vanilla would be barely adequate to supply the needs of the American ice-cream industry, with the result that most vanilla flavoring marketed today is artificial, produced from wood pulp or synthesized chemically.

The word "vanilla" comes from the Spanish, *vainilla*, meaning "little sheath," which describes the appearance of the pod produced by the vanilla plant. Its looks have also been likened to a cross between a string bean and a thin banana. The pods are picked just before reaching maturity and submitted to a process of fermentation, which causes a coating to form on the outside of the pod. The technical term for this coating is *givre*, the French word for frost. *Givre*, which sometimes takes crystalline form, is the flavoring essence. Its major constituent is vanillin, but it has a host of minor ingredients that contribute to natural vanilla's unique flavor. Although vanillin has been synthesized chemically, no artificial vanilla flavoring approaches the subtle mixture of aromas achieved in a state of nature. On the other hand, production of natural vanilla is an expensive process, requiring such time-consuming hand labor as inspecting each vanilla pod daily to see whether it is ready for plucking. The industry could never satisfy world demand at a reasonable price.

The trade distinguishes three grades of vanilla. At the top is fine, or legitimate vanilla, with pods measuring eight-12 inches that are thin, nearly black and completely covered with a shiny coating of *givre.* Second comes "woody," or *cimarron* (Spanish for wild) vanilla, with reddish brown pods, five to eight inches long, which have a dull surface and little *givre.* Last is vanillon with pods four to five inches long that are thick, flat and usually show no *givre* at all, although they give off the strongest odor of vanilla.

The leading producers of natural vanilla are Madagascar, Reunion Island, Mexico, Guinea, Mauritius, the Seychelles Islands, Tahiti, Java and several other Latin American countries. The United States imports 100,000 pounds annually from Mexico, but most European vanilla is supplied by Madagascar, which produces 65 percent of the world output.

Germany was the first to produce a vanilla substitute in 1876. It was obtained from eugenol, a substance derived from essence of clove. Vanilla extract as a home remedy for toothache probably originated from this substitute because oil of clove is commonly used in dental preparations for this purpose. Coumarin, another vanilla substitute, apparently contains no vanillin but has a taste near enough to fool most people. It is obtained from tonka beans, sweet clover and woodruff. Vanillin is also found in conferin and lingnin, substances removed from wood pulp in paper manufacturing.

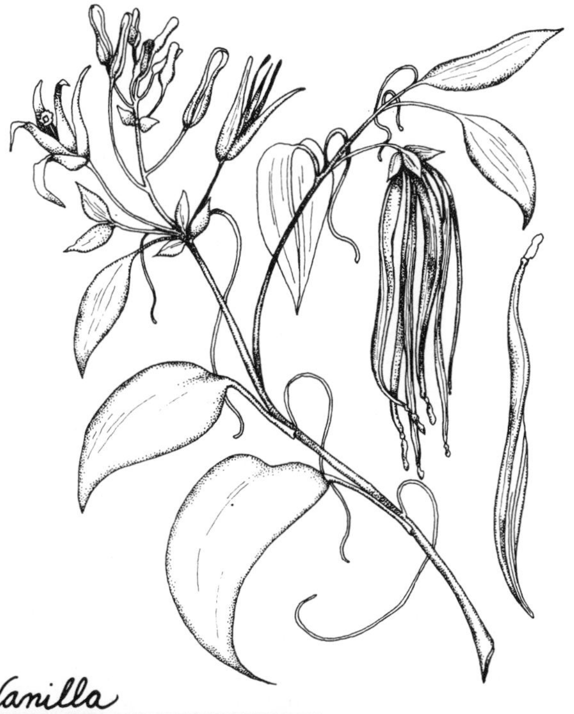

Vanilla

VANILLA EXTRACT

Also VANILLA ESSENCE. This flavoring liquid is obtained by soaking sweated vanilla beans in a solution of grain alcohol and water. Beans are usually submitted to three extractions with progressively lower proportions of alcohol in the solutions. Extracts are often aged before bottling to improve the aroma, and commonly contain additives such as sugar, dextrose and glycerol. To satisfy United States labeling requirements, vanilla extract must contain the soluble matter from 13.35 ounces of beans per gallon; the bottled extract needs to contain at least 35 percent alcohol to keep the vanilla soluble in solution.

Vanillin, the principal flavoring element, can be obtained from many other sources, although the quality is inferior to that obtained from vanilla beans. Over the years, tonka beans and oil of cloves have been major sources, but most now comes from wood pulp. The bulk of vanilla flavoring today is obtained from sources other than the vanilla bean. Vanilla extract is widely used to flavor such food items as beverages, ice cream, candy, toppings, baked goods, syrups and icings.

VANILLIN

See **Vanilla, Vanilla Extract.**

VARIETY MEATS

Also OFFAL. The term is used in the United States for the interior organs of beef, mutton, lamb, pork and veal. The term in England is offal, from "off-fall," i.e., the parts that fall out when the butcher

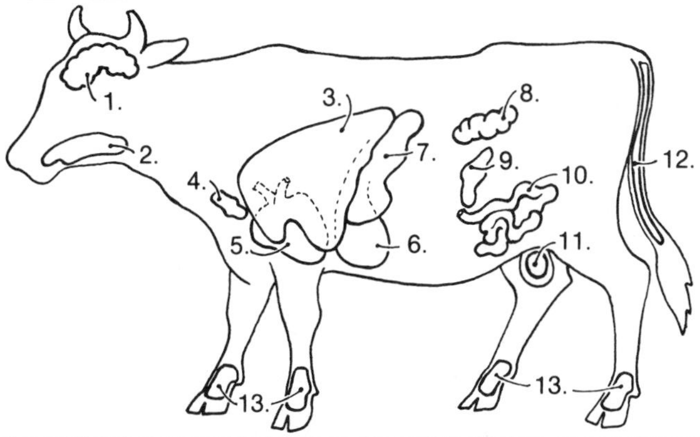

Variety Meats

1. Brain
2. Tongue
3. Lung
4. Thymus
5. Heart
6. Tripe
7. Liver
8. Kidney
9. Pancreas
10. Small Intestine
11. Testicle
12. Tail
13. Feet

opens the carcass. The principal variety meats are liver, heart, kidneys and sweetbreads, but the term is extended to include a wide range of odds and ends such as tongue, brains, tripe, lungs, feet, tail, mesentery (of veal), head (of veal), intestines (called chitterlings in pigs) and testicles. While very nutritious, variety meats are not popular fare in the United States and are often less expensive than regular cuts of lean meat. Synonyms for variety meats are side meats and organ meats. For more information see under the names of specific items and check the index.

VASTBOTTNESOST

Also WEST BOTHIAN CHEESE. This hard Swedish cheese is made from cow's milk in the northern province of Vasterbotten. Weighing from 35 to 45 pounds, cheeses have a highly pungent flavor. They are ripened for a year or more.

VASTGOTAOST

Also WEST GOTHLAND CHEESE. A semihard Swedish cheese made from partly skimmed cow's milk in the province of Vastergotland, it has a pungent taste, but in other ways is similar to ***herrgardsost,*** except that the texture is looser due to being unpressed. Ripening takes from four to six months, and cheeses weigh from 20 to 30 pounds.

VEAL

Veal is the meat of a calf that, at its best, comes from an animal slaughtered between the ages of six weeks and 14 weeks. Meat from an animal younger than six weeks is called "bob" veal, and from one older than 14 weeks, "baby beef." Both are considered less desirable. The best veal is creamy white, or, at the most, greenish pink. This indicates that the calf has been fed entirely on mother's milk or a combination of that and eggs. A reddish tinge means either the animal has been fed solid food or that it was older, i.e., it is baby beef.

The best veal comes from Italy, France or Holland. A lot of American veal is baby beef, which is tougher and stringier than prime veal. Veal is most abundant in late winter or spring and carries little, if any, fat. Popular cuts of veal are the leg, loin, shoulder, breast, rib and roast. Veal is often larded with fat or bacon because, being so lean, it has a tendency to dry out in the cooking.

Veal was popular with ancient Romans and has maintained its reputation with modern Italians, who eat more than 15 pounds annually per capita, as compared to Americans, who consume only four. Waverly Root, who wrote *The Food of Italy*, explains this predilection as follows:

> *Most persons think of the French as the great sauce makers, but it was the Italians who first developed this art . . . It is a giveaway that in large French kitchens making the sauces is a job entrusted to a specialist, the* saucier. *In Italy every cook must be able to concoct sauces or he could hardly cook at all. In France, a sauce is an adornment, even a disguise, added to the dish more or less as an afterthought. In Italy, it is the dish, its soul, its* raison d'etre, *the element that gives it character and flavor. The most widespread Italian foods are bland, neutral; they would produce little impact on the taste buds unassisted . . . Even the favorite meat of Italy is the most neutral of all—veal . . . The charm of veal for the Italians is the opportunity it gives them to utilize their culinary artistry to the full.*

Some scholars believe that the very name of the country, Italy, comes from the Italian word for veal, *vitello,* though there is no way of verifying this contention. The favorite Italian veal dishes bear out Root's opinion, e.g., *vitello tonnato* (with tuna fish sauce), *parmigiana* (with a coating of melted Parmesan cheese), and *scaloppe farcite* (thin slices of veal sandwiched with a slice of ham, mushrooms or truffles, and grated cheese). See the accompanying chart for standard cuts of veal.

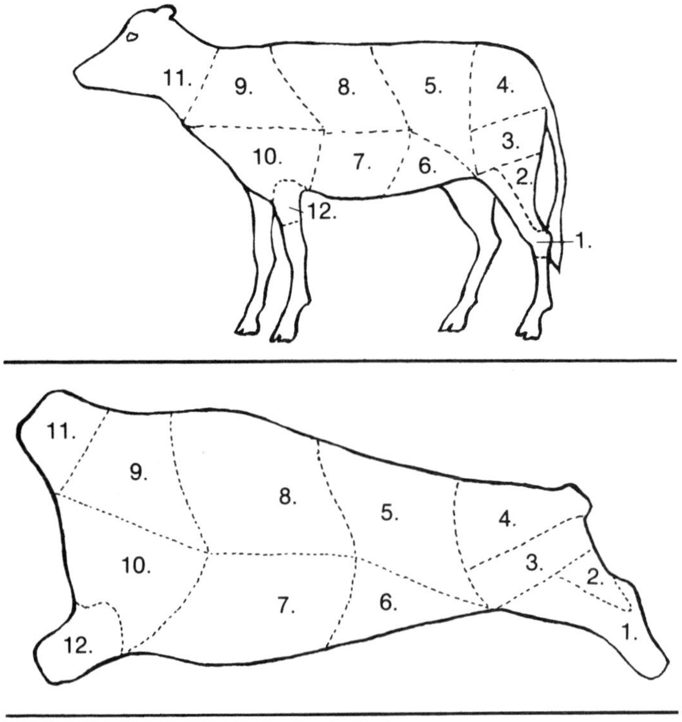

Veal Cuts

1. Hindshank
2. Heel of Round
3. Leg
4. Rump
5. Loin
6. Flank
7. Breast
8. Rib
9. Shoulder
10. Arm
11. Neck
12. Foreshank

Some typical vegetables found in an American market

VEGETABLE

In the broad sense, all plants are vegetable, but we are concerned here with a narrower class of plants that are edible. A further distinction is made among vegetables, fruits and nuts, although, of course, they are all vegetable matter. The definitions are discussed fully under **Fruit.** Suffice it to say here that certain fruits in the botanical sense are considered vegetables by the layperson (tomatoes, eggplant, squash) because of their taste (savory, not sweet) and the way they are used, i.e., served in the main part of the meal to accompany other savory dishes.

One way of classifying vegetables is by the part of the plant that is eaten (although in some cases, the entire plant is eaten), as follows:

Leaves: Examples are cabbage, lettuce, chard, spinach, parsley, artichokes, Brussels sprouts.

Flowers: Examples are cauliflower and broccoli.

Seeds or seed pods: Examples are peas, beans, sweet corn and lentils.

Fruits: Examples are cucumbers, eggplants, pumpkins, squashes and tomatoes.

Stalks or stems: Examples are asparagus and rhubarb.

Roots: Examples are carrots, beets, parsnips, sweet potatoes, turnips and radishes.

Tubers or rhizomes: Examples are potato, Jerusalem artichoke, arrowroot.

Bulbs: Examples are onions, garlic, shallots.

What is considered an edible vegetable varies widely from place to place in the world. One person's vegetable is another's weed. Or, putting it another way, George Washington Carver remarked, "A weed is only a vegetable growing in the wrong place." For a full description of various vegetables, where they grow and what they taste like, see generally the main alphabet and index under the name of a specific vegetable.

The growing application of science to vegetable farming has led to great refinement in developing new strains of vegetables to meet specific marketing needs, e.g., blunt carrots that will not perforate the plastic wrapping; square tomatoes that make packing easier; others of startling size and vivid color, and vegetables of a predictable size that is evenly divisible into pounds or kilos. Yields have been greatly increased by new fertilizers and pest controls.

One area of apparent neglect is taste. That is, the rule seems to be the prettier and handier a vegetable becomes the blander it tastes. This led one wag to remark, "Vegetables have been improved until they're downright poisonous." A reaction to this trend has been the growth of the "natural-foods" industry, which purports to grow food using no pesticides or inorganic fertilizers.

In literature, the vegetable is an image of dullness. "To vegetate" is a bleak fate, according to Alexander Pope in his *Essay on Man:* "Fixed like a plant on his peculiar spot,/To draw nutrition, propagate and rot." Commenting on the life of the rural parson in England, Sydney Smith wrote, "And, from long residence upon your living, are become a kind of holy vegetable." Cecelia, a Fanny Burney character, uttered this plaint, "One really lives nowhere; and does but vegetate and wish it all at an end."

VEGETABLE BUTTER

This fatty substance is present in some vegetables and is solid at room temperatures but melts easily. Common vegetable butters are **cocoa butter, shea butter,** nutmeg butter and **coconut butter.**

VEGETABLE MARROW

See **Squash.**

VELOUTE

See **Sauce.**

VELVET BEAN

Also FLORIDA BEAN, LYON BEAN, MUCUNA BEAN, MAURITIUS BEAN. Several species of closely related legumes are called velvet bean because of the dense, dark velvety hairs that cover the pods. The hair is irritating to the touch and can be mildly poisonous in some varieties. Nevertheless, a species of velvet bean, *Mucuna nivea*, is grown in tropical Asia and Africa for food. It is a strong, quick-growing, twining plant whose pods reach three to five inches in length and whose seeds are dark brown or mottled in color. The outer skin of the seeds is removed before cooking. The young pods and leaves are edible as well. The seeds are round.

Another variety *(M. deeringiana)*, called the Florida velvet bean, is grown in the United States as green manure.

VENDACE

See **Pollan.**

VENDOME

Three French cheeses are called *Vendome*. One is a soft, surface-ripened cheese like **Camembert** made from whole cow's milk in the vicinity of Vendome in the Loire et Cher Departments. A second, *Vendome bleu*, is a blue-veined cheese made in the Touraine. A third, called *Vendome cendre*, is a hard, sheep's milk cheese that is ripened under ashes.

See also: **Goat's Milk Cheese.**

VENETO

Also VENEZZA. This is an Italian cheese of the **Parmesan** type, with a sharp, sometimes bitter flavor, and hard texture. It is usually cured from one to two years, with the younger suitable for the table and the mature cheese for grating. The surface of the cheese is dark and oily, while the paste is greenish yellow with no eyes. Individual cheeses are round, and size vary from eight to 16 inches in diameter and from 25 to 60 pounds in weight.

VENEZZA

See **Veneto.**

VENISON

The term refers to the flesh of any sort of deer—including elk, moose and reindeer—that is used as food. The word comes from the Latin *venatio*, meaning the chase or hunt, through the French *venaison*. Formerly the term "venison" was applied to any game killed through hunting, but it is now restricted to **deer.**

VENUS

See **Cockle.**

VENUS COMB

The stem tops of this annual plant, *Scandix pecten-veneris*, may be eaten in salads. It may be found in both Europe and North America.

VERBENA

See **Lemon Verbena.**

VERJUICE

This is the sour, green juice of certain unripe fruits, most commonly crabapples and/or grapes, but sometimes sorrel, green wheat or oranges. Verjuice was used most often in cooking when an acidic element was needed, much as today vinegar or a squeeze of lemon juice is used; but it was also used to make stale meat palatable and, in fermented form, as a drink to ward off scurvy. Verjuice was widely employed from Classical Antiquity up to the end of the 18th century when citrus fruit and vinegar became more readily available. Today it is still used occasionally in game pies, in the preparation of mustard and in some oriental cuisines, such as Iran's.

VERMICELLI

See **Spaghetti.**

VERMOUTH

Vermouth is essentially a white wine that has been steeped with a complex infusion of herbs, plants, roots, leaves, peels, seeds and flowers, which give it a special aroma and taste aimed at stimulating the appetite. It is also sweetened and fortified with enough brandy to bring it up to 19 percent alcohol. The resulting flavor is pleasant, with a slightly bitter aftertaste, which is supposed to stimulate the flow of saliva and prepare the diner to enjoy his or her meal. It can be purchased dry, medium or sweet.

Although the word "vermouth" coms from the German, *vermut*, meaning wormwood, the wine was first produced in northern Italy in the 18th century, employing white Piedmont wines. About 20 years later, a drier version began to be produced in France by Louis Noilly of Lyon. The base wines of the French Midi were naturally somewhat drier and lighter in color than their Italian counterparts, so the dry vermouth came to be known as the French type, while the sweet vermouth became known as Italian. These distinctions no longer have much meaning since most wine-making countries produce their own vermouth in any color and in any degree of sweetness desired.

The exact bouquet of each vermouth differs according to the recipe for the infusion, which varies from maker to maker and is a closely guarded trade secret. The infusion usually includes such ingredients as alder, aniseed, centaury, cinnamon, clove, colombine, coriander, elder, galanga, nutmeg, orange peel, quassia, quinine, tansy and wormwood. The inclusion of quinine, apart from contributing to the bitter aftertaste, originally had the function of protecting European troops from malaria during colonial campaigns.

Sweet vermouth is generally a larger seller worldwide, except in the United States where dry vermouth maintains equality due to the popularity of the Martini cocktail, which requires dry vermouth. Argentina is believed to have the highest per capita consumption of vermouth, which is all produced domestically.

Vermouth, especially in Europe, may be drunk straight, and, if as an appetizer, slightly chilled. It is also taken in long drinks, with water or soda, or mixed with syrups such as grenadine, cassis or lemon. It is meant to be sipped slowly and savored.

VESIGA

In Russia, marrow and cartilage from the backbone of the sturgeon is dried for sale, but when used in such dishes as the traditional Russian meat pie, it has a gelatinous consistency.

VETCH

Vetch is a genus of legumes *(Vicia spp.)* grown in the United States almost exclusively as green manure, cover crops, hay and pasture, but cultivated as a food plant in South America, India, North Africa and the Near East. The vetch best known as human food is *V. faba*, the fava or **broad bean,** which is the bean of Classical Antiquity.

Vetches, as a rule, are trailing plants, and they are often planted interspersed in a taller crop so as to have its stalks for support. Their seeds are eaten as beans. Among the more important vetches are the bard vetch *(V. monantha)* of southern Europe and western Asia; the Hungarian vetch *(V. pannonica)* of central Europe; the common vetch *(V. sativa)* or tare, of Europe and North America; the hairy or Russian vetch *(V. villosa)* of Europe and Asia; the kidney vetch *(Anthyllus vulnearia)*; the Narbonne vetch *(V. narbonensis)* of southern Europe, and the one-flowered vetch *(V. articulata)* also of southern Europe.

Vetches are characterized by weak viny stems terminating in tendrils. Each pod segment contains a seed. Vetch seeds should be soaked in water before use.

VICHY CELESTINS WATER

This naturally sparkling, bottled mineral water from the warm springs at Vichy, France, has a relatively high mineral content (3,400 ppm of total dissolved solids) and is also very high in sodium, 309 mg. per eight-ounce glass. A sensory panel sponsored by the Consumers Union in 1980 judged the taste of Vichy Celestins water to be only fair in comparison to 23 other bottled waters, and made the following comments on its flavor: mildly bitter, mildly sour, mildly astringent, mild soapy flavor, distinctly salty.

See also: **Mineral Water.**

VICUNA

A graceful cameloid, *Vicugna vicugna*, of the Andean highlands of South America, the vicuna is closely related to the **llama** but, unlike the llama, has not been domesticated. It is a highly valued animal nonetheless, especially for its exquisite wool. Vicuna meat, particularly that of young males, is also well regarded by the native population. Legal protection has been extended to the vicuna, but it has not proven effective due to poor enforcement.

A large adult attains a maximum weight of about 140 pounds, stands up to three feet high at the shoulder and may be up to 5½ feet long.

VIENNA SAUSAGE

Also WIENERWURST. This tiny Austrian sausage is like a frankfurter in ingredients and texture, but blander in taste. The ends are cut off this sausage, and it is often marketed in canned form.

See also: **Sausage.**

VILLIERS

This soft French cheese produced in one-pound squares in the department of Haute Marne is wrapped in vine leaves and brought to maturity in ashes.

VINAIGRETTE

See **Sauce.**

VINEGAR

This is a weak solution of acetic acid (4 to 6 percent) in water with minor amounts of other substances, such as tartaric acid and albumin. Vinegar is obtained through the action of the *Mycoderma aceti* bacteria on alcohol. White or distilled vinegar is made from a base of straight alcohol to which distilled water is added after fermentation. From a gastronomic point of view, it is more desirable to start from a base of wine, or other weak alcoholic mixture, such as fermented apple or currant juice. That way the number of other minor substances is increased, giving the vinegar special characteristics that enhance its taste and, consequently, its value in cooking.

Vinegar is an ancient substance. The name comes from *vin aigre*, i.e., sour wine, and so has been around as long as wine has. Throughout history vinegar has been put to various uses. Roman legions used it to purify drinking water. To spite Mark Antony, Cleopatra dissolved a flawless pearl in vinegar. In 17th and 18th-century England, a sponge soaked in vinegar was used to protect the nose from the noxious odors then prevalent in cities.

The vinegar bacterium is everpresent, and wine can be turned to vinegar by simply exposing it to the air and waiting a certain amount of time. The process can be speeded up by adding vinegar plant, the so-called mother of vinegar, to the mixture. This is a living mat of *Mycoderma aceti* and other microorganisms formed in previous vinegar-making operations. In some places, such as Modena, Italy, where vinegar-making is an ancient and traditional art, the mother of vinegar may be a decade or more old. *Aceto balsamico* or herb-flavored vinegar, is the specialty there. It is the product of an herb-flavored base and a mother that has been moved in the previous year through a series of 12 barrels of oak, chestnut, mulberry and juniper wood, blending at each move with part of the contents of each barrel. The resulting vinegar may be aged for as long as 70 years.

On a more prosaic level, the major types of vinegar are white, or distilled vinegar; vinegar from fermented fruit juices; malt vinegar and sugar vinegar.

Wine is the major source of vinegar from fermented juice. Vinegar from white wine has a pale golden color, and from red wine, a rose color. Orleans, France, produces the finest wine vinegar. Malt vinegar is made from a malt infusion, or malt beverage, such as beer, and is more popular in England than elsewhere. Sugar vinegar is obtained from a dilute sugar solution, using a mother that contains yeast bacteria, so that it is possible to skip the fermentation step.

It is an essential ingredient in salad dressings, marinades and some pickling solutions. To avoid deterioration, vinegar should be protected from exposure to air, strong light or severe cold.

VINEGAR JAMBOSA

Edible fruit of a small tree, *Myrciaria edulis*, found in Brazil and Argentina, the vinegar jambosa is pear-shaped, orange yellow in color, downy-skinned, and reaches a length of about two inches. Though edible, it has a bad smell and is used mostly to make vinegar.

VINE MESQUITE

This is a variety of millet, *Panicum obtusum*, found in the western United States and Mexico whose seeds are ground into meal for bread or porridge.

VINHOS VERDES

These are the "green wines" of northern Portugal. The wine can be actually either red or white. The name comes from the grapes being picked early, before maturity. *Vinhos verdes* are very popular with the Portuguese and make up about one-third of the wine consumed in their country.

The grapes are grown in the Minho region, in harsh, granitelike soil. Because of the dense population and the scarcity of arable land, the vines are by law cultivated only on waste ground or along fields and roadways. So the farmer uses trees as natural supports, as well as hedges and trellises. Each inch of available land is used, and bunches of grapes hang from almost every tree. Racked at the end of the year, a scant six weeks after they have been bottled, *vinhos verdes* are already sparkling wines. The whites are thirst-quenchers, light, airy, with only six to nine percent alcohol content. The reds are really dark purple, with a crimson foam that stains the glass.

VIOLET

Violet is the flowery plant of many species, but especially *Viola odorata*, the florist's or English violet whose petals are a deep purple color and, rarely, rose or white. In France, there is a tradition of sugar-coating violet petals and using them to decorate cakes, confections, pastries and ices. The fresh petals are used in salads and added to soups as flavoring. The dried leaves are infused to make an herbal tea that is thought to be helpful in cases of bronchitis. They are also used to flavor a liqueur called *creme de violettes* and as a basis for violet vinegar.

VIPER GRASS

See **Salsify.**

VIRGINIA MOUNTAIN MINT

This perennial herb, *Pynnanthemum virginianum*, of the eastern United States has a mintlike aroma and taste. The dried buds and flowers are used for seasoning meat and soups.

VISCACHA

Also MOUNTAIN VISCACHA, PERUVIAN HARE. A furry rodent, *Lagidium pervanum*, inhabiting the rugged mountainous country of Peru, Bolivia, Chile, Argentina and Patagonia, it is hunted by native people for food and fur, the latter being mixed with wool and spun into yarn. The mountain viscacha resembles a long-tailed rabbit. It attains a maximum length of about 12 inches and weight of about 3½ pounds.

VITAMINS

Organic compounds needed by the human body for normal growth and functioning, vitamins are obtained from food through the diet. The average eater, provided he or she has a reasonably varied diet, should never need vitamin supplements under normal circumstances.

Vitamins do not provide energy; rather they help transform food for energy and body maintenance. The amounts needed are minute. For example, the recommended daily allowance (RDA) of Vitamin B_{12} for an adult is just six micrograms. (A microgram amounts to 1/1000 of a milligram, which equals 1/1000 of a gram, which is 35/1000 of an ounce.) Nevertheless, should any of the essential vitamins be lacking over time, a deficiency disease results.

Most knowledge about vitamins has been obtained since 1900 from the study of nutritional diseases, such as beriberi, rickets and pellagra, and the feeding of special diets to experimental animals. It was thought at first that all vitamins were amines, hence the name: *vita*, the Latin for "life," and "amine." The "e" was dropped when it was discovered that not all vitamins were amines. Since their chemical composition was unknown at first, it was customary to identify them by letters of the alphabet, A, B, C, D, etc. This has given way to specific names as they were analyzed. Certain vitamins, such as B, have turned out to be several, necessitating the use of numbers.

For nutritional labeling, the United States Food and Drug Administration has specified recommended daily allowances (RDAs), which represent the amount of a particular vitamin that a person should absorb each day to stay healthy. (See table below.) Exceeding the allowances on certain "fat soluble" vitamins, such as A and D, can be unhealthy, as they are stored by the body and can cause alarming symptoms (see below). An excess of "water soluble" vitamins, such as B and C, on the other hand, is simply excreted by the system. Following are popular misconceptions about vitamins:

- Natural vitamins found in food are superior to vitamins manufactured in the laboratory. The fact is that they are identical.
- Vitamins provide extra pep, vitality or an unusual level of well-being. There is no scientific evidence to support this.
- Getting enough vitamins is essential, so taking more is better, like taking out insurance. The fact is that excess vitamins are a waste in both money and effect.

The most common vitamins are listed below with some descriptive comment:

Vitamin A (Retinol): A fat-soluble vitamin, stored in the liver, and necessary for new cell growth and healthy tissues and essential for vision in dim light. Deficiency causes night blindness, other eye injuries and dry, rough skin, which may become easily infected. Too much vitamin A causes headache, nausea, irritability, and in severe cases, growth retardation in children, enlargement of the liver and spleen, loss of hair and rheumatic pain. Foods containing abundant vitamin A are liver, fortified margarine, eggs, butter and whole milk. Carotene, a red or orange-colored compound found in carrots, green and yellow vegetables and yellow fruits, is converted by the body into vitamin A.

Vitamin B_1 (Thiamine): A water-soluble vitamin necessary for the normal functioning of nerve tissue and digestion, and for growth, fertility and lactation. A deficiency causes nervous system dysfunction, loss of appetite, body swelling, growth retardation, cardiac problems, nausea, vomiting, spastic colon, and pain in the calf and thigh muscles. Foods containing abundant thiamine are pork, beans, peas, nuts and enriched or whole grain breads and cereals.

Vitamin B_2 (Riboflavin): A water-soluble vitamin that assists the body in obtaining energy from protein and carbohydrates. A deficiency causes lip sores and cracks and dimness of vision. Foods containing abundant riboflavin are leafy vegetables, enriched and whole-grain bread, liver, cheese, lean meat, milk and eggs.

Vitamin B_3 (Pantothenic acid): A water-soluble vitamin that supports a variety of body functions, including proper growth and maintenance. A deficiency causes headaches, fatigue, poor muscle coordination, nausea and cramps. Foods containing abundant pantothenic acid are liver, eggs, white potatoes, sweet potatoes, peas and peanuts.

Vitamin B_5 (Niacin): A water-soluble vitamin needed to maintain the health of all tissue cells. Severe deficiency causes pellagra, a disease characterized by rough skin, mouth sores, diarrhea and mental disorders. Foods containing abundant niacin are liver, lean meat, peas, beans, whole-grain cereal products and fish.

Vitamin B_6 (Pyridoxine-Pyridoxal-Pyridoxamine): A water-soluble vitamin that helps the body utilize protein and that is essential for proper growth and maintenance. A deficiency causes mouth soreness, dizziness, nausea, weight loss and sometimes severe nervous disturbances. Foods with abundant B_6 are liver, whole-grain cereals, potatoes, red meat, green vegetables and yellow corn (maize).

Vitamin B_{12} (Cyanocobalamin): A water-soluble vitamin needed for normal development of red blood cells and the functioning of other cells as well, especially those in the bone marrow, nervous system and intestines. Deficiency causes pernicious anemia, and if prolonged, a degeneration of the spinal cord. Foods containing abundant vitamin B_{12} are organ meats, lean meats, fish, milk and shellfish. Since it is lacking in plants, a strict vegetarian would have to supplement this vitamin in his or her diet.

Biotin: A water-soluble vitamin important in the metabolism of carbohydrates, proteins and fats. A deficiency causes mild skin disorders, anemia, depression, sleeplessness and muscle pain. Foods with abundant biotin are eggs, milk and meat.

Vitamin C (Ascorbic acid): A water-soluble vitamin that promotes growth, tissue repair and the healing of wounds. A deficiency of vitamin C causes scurvy, the symptoms of which are lassitude, weakness, bleeding of the gums, loss of weight and irritability. Bleeding of the gums is an early sign. Foods containing abundant vitamin C are citrus and tomato juices, strawberries, currants, green vegetables and potatoes. Nobel laureate Linus Pauling, a biochemist, has

Vitamins
United States Recommended Daily Allowances*

	Unit	Infants (0–12 mo.)	Children under 4 years	Adults and children 4 years or more	Pregnant or lactating women
Vitamin A (Retinol)	IU	1,500.0	2,500.0	5,000.0	8,000.0
Vitamin B_1 (Thiamine)	mg	0.5	0.7	1.5	1.7
Vitamin B_2 (Riboflavin)	mg	0.6	0.8	1.7	2.0
Vitamin B_3 (Panthothenic acid)	mg	3.0	5.0	10.0	10.0
Vitamin B_5 (Niacin)	mg	8.0	9.0	20.0	20.0
Vitamin B_6 (Pyridoxine-Pyridozal-Pyridoxamine)	mg	0.4	0.7	2.0	2.5
Vitamin B_{12} (Cyanocobalamin)	mcg	2.0	3.0	6.0	8.0
Biotin	mg	0.05	0.15	0.3	0.3
Vitamin C (Ascorbic acid)	mg	35.0	40.0	60.0	60.0
Vitamin D (Calciferol)	IU	400.0	400.0	400.0	400.0
Vitamin E (The tocopherols)	IU	5.0	10.0	30.0	30.0
Folic acid	mg	0.1	0.2	0.4	0.8

IU = International Unit
mg = milligram
mcg = microgram

*Source: *FDA Consumer*, May, 1974

advocated taking very large doses of vitamin C as a preventive of the common cold or as a palliative for its symptoms. Many claims have been made about the efficacy of this therapy, and it is a matter of scientific controversy. In any case, the action of vitamin C in such large doses would seem to be pharmacological, rather than nutritional in character.

Vitamin D (Calciferol): A fat-soluble vitamin that helps in the absorption of calcium and phosphorus in bone formation. A deficiency causes rickets, the symptoms of which are skeletal deformations such as bowed legs, deformed spine, stunted growth, flat feet and a "potbelly" appearance.

An excess of vitamin D causes nausea, weight loss, weakness and excessive urination. Severe cases result in hypertension, calcification of soft tissues, bone deformities and multiple fractures.

Vitamin D is formed in the skin by the action of the sun's ultraviolet rays. Foods with abundant vitamin D include canned fish, such as herring, salmon and tuna, egg yolk and vitamin D fortified milk. The body needs very little vitamin D, and any excess is stored in the body.

Vitamin E (The tocopherols): A fat-soluble vitamin that helps prevent oxygen from destroying other substances. It is essentially a preservative, and no clinical symptoms are associated with low intake in humans. Foods containing abundant vitamin E are vegetable oils, beans, eggs, whole grains, liver, fruits and vegetables. Extravagant claims have been made for vitamin E therapy for reproductive problems and heart disease based on studies with experimental animals. The National Academy of Sciences deflated these claims saying attempts to apply the results of those studies to human beings have been unproductive, and that self-medication may be dangerous if it postpones medical diagnosis and treatment of serious conditions.

Folic Acid (Folacin): A water-soluble vitamin essential to metabolism, i.e., converting food to energy. A deficiency results in a type of anemia. Foods containing abundant folic acid are liver, navy beans, dark green leafy vegetables, nuts, fresh oranges and whole wheat products.

Vitamin K: A fat-soluble vitamin that is essential for the clotting of blood. A deficiency causes hemorrhage and liver damage. Foods with abundant vitamin K are spinach, lettuce, kale, cabbage, cauliflower, liver and egg yolk. Another type is produced in the intestinal tract.

Following is a table showing the United States Food and Drug Administration's recommended daily allowances of essential vitamins. An International Unit (IU) represents a given amount of activity that can be measured.

VITELLOISE WATER

This is a natural spring water that is carbonated and bottled in France. Its mineral content is a fairly low 465 ppm of total dissolved solids, which under California law would be too low to qualify as a mineral water (500 being the standard). A 1980 Consumers Union sensory panel rated the taste of this water as fair, with the following additional comments: mildly bitter, mildly sour, mild salty aftertaste.

See also: **Mineral Water.**

VIVE

See **Weeverfish.**

VIZE

Vize is a hard, Greek sheep's milk cheese that resembles **Romano** and is suitable for grating.

VLASIC

See **Travnik.**

VLATTERO

This currant-flavored liqueur is made in Greece.

VODKA

This distilled liquor originated in Russia or eastern Poland and is generally considered to be the national drink of those countries. Vodka is a neutral spirit, i.e., it is clear and colorless, odorless and nearly tasteless. It may be made from grain, potatoes or any other fermentable material, but it is distilled at such a high proof that nothing of the original character of the raw materials remains. In this respect it is like gin, except that gin is later flavored with juniper berries and other aromatics, while vodka is charcoal-filtered to remove all congeners and any hint of flavoring. There are, however, certain flavored vodkas, which will be discussed below.

The word *vodka* is a diminutive of the Russian word for water, *vod*, i.e., "little water," which comes pretty close to the original meaning of whiskey and aquavit, our "waters of life." It is believed to have appeared first in 14th-century Russia and remained a Russian/East European thing until after World War II. At that time, practically the only vodka made in the United States was Smirnoff, a name associated with vodka distilling in Russia from 1818 to 1917 when the distilleries passed out of the Smirnoff family's control. Vodka went from being an exotic drink in 1948 to being the largest-selling individual type of spirits in the United States by 1976. This success is attributed to the popularity of vodka high-balls beginning in the forties with the Moscow Mule (vodka and ginger ale), continuing in the fifties with the screwdriver (vodka and orange juice), and more recently the Bloody Mary (vodka and tomato juice). In the 1970s some Western vodka drinkers came the full circle, that is, drinking vodka in the traditional Russian/East European way: a straight shot, drunk ice cold.

Vodka is bottled in the United States at from 80 to 100 proof. It is distilled all over the world, but the prestige vodkas come from the motherlands, Russia and Poland, and to a lesser extent, Finland. Fruit-flavored vodkas are made in the United States, but again the prestige flavored vodkas come from Russia and Poland. Flavored vodkas are bottled at 70 proof or higher. Following are some of the best-known types:

Okhotnichya ("hunter's vodka"): flavored with many herbs and sweetened with heather honey.

Pertsovka ("pepper vodka"): its biting flavor comes from an infusion of capsicum, cayenne and cubeb. It has a dark brown color and a pleasant aroma.

Starka ("old vodka"): mellowed for 10 years in oak casks previously used for wines, it has an amber color and brandylike flavor.

Yubileyneya osobaya ("jubilee vodka"): flavored with brandy, honey and other elements.

Zubrowka ("bison grass vodka"): a soft, smooth drink with a yellowish color, flavored by a type of grass found only in eastern Poland.

There seems to be no limit to vodka's popularity, perhaps because of its neutral character. Its lack of individual taste makes it a versatile—perhaps the ideal—liquor for mixing.

VOID

This soft, fermented French cheese, made of cow's milk in the Meuse Department, is similar to **Pont l'Eveque.** Cheeses weigh about 1¼ pounds.

VOLNAY

This light red wine comes from the commune of Volnay, south of **Beaune** in central Burgundy. During the Crusades the Knights of Malta were responsible for publicizing Volnay as the true heart of the Burgundy wine region, since they owned several vineyards here. Grown slightly south of **Pommard,** the wine of Volnay differs from that red wine in being a touch lighter and more velvety in its quality. The typical Volnay red has a "berry" taste evocative of raspberries and a similarly delicate bouquet.

See also: **Burgundy Wines.**

VORALBERG SOUR-MILK CHEESE

Here is a hard, aromatic cheese made from whole or skim cow's milk. The curd is heavily salted and matured in a cool, moist cellar. A greasy, strongly flavored cheese results.

VOSNE

Vosne is a rich, full-bodied, ruby-colored wine from northern Burgundy, which many experts claim to be the best red wine in the world. The name *Vosne* is usually linked wth *Romanee*, which evokes the ancient Roman origin of these vineyards. The wine is similar to that of nearby **Vougeot** but boasts an even more prestigious lineage and popularity. It is delicate as well as strong, with a satiny texture, a wine to drink for its own sake.

See also: **Burgundy Wines.**

VOUGEOT

A superior dry, red wine from the *clos* (or vineyard) of Vougeot in northern Burgundy. The *clos*, which is large (about 125 acres) by Burgundian standards, is traditionally honored by the French army. A battalion of Napoleon's troops, on its way to join the army on the Rhine, was halted before the vineyard by the commander, Colonel Bisson, and was ordered to present arms to the accompaniment of drums and bugles. The vineyard was developed by the monks of Citeaux in the twelfth century and produces an officially designated *grand cru* (or "great growth") of red wine to this day.

See also: **Burgundy Wines.**

VOUVRAY

This is a popular white wine from the **Loire,** grown near the village of Vouvray in Touraine. The wine is aromatic, typically fruity and dry, but in certain harvests it asserts a delightful sweetness. Often, Vouvray whites are semisparkling, or *petillant*, which adds to their charm. Connoisseurs claim that when a Vouvray is sweet it should be cherished at least three to five years before it is experienced.

W

WAFFLE

This is a batter cake made with baking powder or yeast and cooked in a special two-part hinged iron that leaves a regular pattern of indentations. The batter is similar to that of pancakes, but a little stiffer. Egg whites are well beaten before being folded into the rest of the ingredients.

Waffles are considered a breakfast treat in the United States. They are eaten with melted butter and a sweet, such as maple syrup or jam. Waffles have a long history, dating back at least to the 12th century when the French *gaufre* was hawked in the streets of Paris. The English word comes from the Dutch *wafel*, and it is believed to be the Dutch who introduced this delicacy into America during the early days of New Amsterdam.

WAGTAIL

Here is a type of small European bird, especially the common or pied wagtail *(Motacilla yarrelli)*, which is considered good eating and is prepared like **lark.**

WAHOO

Also PETO. This large game fish, *Acanthocybium solanderi*, of the mackerel family, is found in tropical seas around the world. Top size for the wahoo is seven feet long and 140 pounds. It has a long, tubular body, deep blue on the back and silver below with dusky bands running vertically on the back and sides. The wahoo is a fast-swimming, hard-fighting, high-leaping fish that is considered prime sport by anglers. Its flesh is good to eat, but the fish is rather too scarce to support a commercial fishery.

WALLABY

This is a type of small kangaroo, several species of which are found in Australia, Tasmania, New Guinea and in the Bismarck Archipelago. Wallabies rarely exceed three feet in height or 50 pounds in weight. Most are much smaller. Several varieties are avidly sought by Australian aborigines as meat, including the hare wallaby *(Lagorchestes hirsutus)*, also known as the *wurrup* or *wodgi worra*, which might weigh as much as 6½ pounds; the banded hare wallaby *(L. fasciatus)* of Shark Bay and Western Australia, and the scrub wallaby *(Thylogale* species). The New Guinean forest wallaby *(Dorcopsis* species) is considered a valuable food animal by the native population.

See also: **Kangaroo.**

WALLEYE

Also PIKE PERCH. A large freshwater fish of the perch family found in eastern and central North America, the walleye *(Stizostedion vitreum)* is highly prized as a food fish. It has white, flaky flesh and a good flavor. Because of its size, it is considered good game as well. It can reach a length of up to three feet and weigh as much as 25 pounds, although the average is in the five to 10 pound range. The walleye is found from Georgia to Hudson Bay, with two closely related species distinguished from the main one. They are the yellow walleye *(S. vitrium vitreum)* and the blue pike *(S. vitreum glaucum)* of the Great Lakes.

See also: **Zander.**

WALLEYE POLLOCK

A valuable food fish of the northern Pacific, the walleye pollock *(Theragra chalcogramma)* is a member of the cod family. It reaches a length of three feet, has a slender body, a large head and a prolonged lower jaw with a chin barbel. The walleye pollock is used mainly for fish meal and industrial purposes in the United States but is widely eaten in Japan, Korea and the eastern USSR.

Walnuts

Wapiti

WALNUT

This is the fruit of the walnut tree *(Juglans regia)*. It is native to Persia but was introduced into Europe at least 1,000 years before Christ and was well known to the Greeks and Romans who dedicated it to Diana and Jupiter, respectively. In the Mediterranean area the walnut is the classic nut, taking over the definition of the general word for nut in several languages. For example, *nuez* in Spanish first means walnut, then any nut.

The tree is an elegant hardwood, typical of mild and temperate climates, that grows as high as 60 feet with a spreading head and a trunk three to four feet thick. It is longlived—200 years not being unusual. The nutmeat is enclosed in a hard shell, which in turn is covered by a thick, green husk. When the fruit ripens, the husk splits to reveal the shell, which consists of two valves. The kernel is large, wrinkled, and has a creamy texture. The tree flowers in May, and in July bears fruit, which reaches maturity in the fall. Ripe walnuts may be eaten right after picking, or after being dried. Apart from reducing water content, the process raises the proportion of proteins and oil. Walnuts are sometimes picked green for pickling whole, or preserving in heavy syrup.

The Romans brought the walnut to England, and the English later took it to many other countries of the world in their trading ships. Thus the best known species is called the English walnut. The Spanish introduced the English walnut into California, where it flourished alongside two native varieties, the black walnut and the white walnut, or **butternut.** The black walnut is generally larger than the English and has an extremely hard shell.

Walnut leaves are extremely aromatic, and in former times it was customary to plant a walnut tree in the stable area to keep flies away from the horses. Also, legend has it that beating a walnut tree with a stick increased its yield of nuts.

In France, walnut oil is preferred to olive oil for some purposes, because it is heavier, sweet and highly aromatic. However, it quickly turns rancid and jellylike.

Walnuts are sold in the shell, or shelled with the nutmeats broken or chopped. They may be eaten alone or used in confections, ice cream or baked goods. In England, pickled walnuts are eaten with cold meat and cheese. Walnuts are considered a classic accompaniment to port wine.

Walnut liqueurs abound. They go by various names—*nocino* (Italy), *brou*, *ratafia* and *eau-de-noix* (France).

See also: **Nut.**

WALRUS

This huge member of the seal family, *Odobenus rosmarus*, is characterized by large tusks, a thick mustache, small, piglike eyes, tough wrinkled skin and a heavy layer of blubber. It is found in arctic regions, mainly on the northeastern coast of Siberia, the northwestern coast of Alaska, and in north to northwestern Greenland and Ellsmere Island. The walrus is the favorite quarry of many Eskimos who put every part of it to use as food, or material for boats, shelter, oil or charms. It has been called "the Eskimo's grocery store."

A large bull walrus can attain a length of 12 feet and a weight of up to 2800 pounds. Cows are one-third smaller. Walrus have tusks that project from the upper jaw. They grow continuously, reaching lengths of up to three feet and weights of up to 12 pounds. The tusks are solid ivory, and Eskimos hunting ivory have seriously depleted walrus populations.

WAMPI

The very small citrus fruit of a Chinese tree, *Clausena lansium*, cultivated widely in the tropics and subtropics of Asia, Australia and South Africa, the wampi is yellow and has the size and taste of a grape. The tree can be grafted on to other citrus species.

WAPATOO

Also ARROWHEAD, ARROWLEAF, DUCK POTATO, SWAMP POTATO. This is an aquatic plant of North America, Europe and the Far East whose edible tubers are similar to potatoes. The leading North American variety, *Sagittaria latifolia*, was once a great favorite with native Americans who gathered it by wading through marshes and searching out the tubers with their toes. The Lewis and Clark Expedition had to subsist largely on wapatoo and other root vegetables during the winter of 1805–1806. The explorers liked the wapatoo best of all, according to Meriwether Lewis, who wrote, "They are nearly equal in flavor to the Irish potato and afford a very good substitute for bread." The corms are large and starchy and are eaten like potatoes after boiling or roasting.

In China, the variety *Sagittaria sagittifolia* is cultivated in paddies. In the 19th century, Chinese immigrants imported arrowhead into the United States and planted it in the area around San Francisco. Their descendents are the main consumers of arrowhead today. They slice it thinly, sautee it and use it in the preparation of various dishes.

In Europe, the arrowhead is used only as an ornamental plant. The word *wapatoo* is from the Chinook language derived from the Cree *wapatowa*, meaning "white mushroom." The name "arrowhead" derives from the shape of the leaves.

WAPITI

Also AMERICAN ELK. Next to the moose, the wapiti *(Cervus canadensis)* is the largest North American member of the deer family. The wapiti is often called elk but more resembles the European red deer than the European elk, which is related to the **Moose.** Its distinctive name is derived from the native American word, *wapitik*. The animal grows to enormous size and has long branching antlers.

Wapiti meat has a high reputation for excellence but is usually only available to hunters, although it occasionally appears in meat markets in states bordering on Canada. The meat is classified as game and is generally high priced. It does not have much of a gamy flavor however, unless hung for more than 48 hours. It is juicy and tender, and the texture is fine-grained. The leg and buttock are considered the best parts; the flesh is light, digestible and nearly tendon-free. It may be prepared in any manner appropriate to deer or beef. It is very lean, however, and to avoid excessive drying out during cooking, it should be larded with pork fat. Wapiti meat is customarily marinated for 24 hours, then cooked very slowly.

See also: **Moose.**

WAREHOU

Also SEA BREAM. A food fish of the temperate waters of the Southern Hemisphere, the *warehou (Seriolella brama)* is common around Australia and New Zealand. *Warehou* is the Maori name for the fish, but it resembles the sea **bream.** The warehou reaches a length of 30 inches and has a compressed, elongated body with a deep purple back and silver sides. It may be prepared like bream.

WASABI

The roots of this perennial plant, *Eutrema wasabi*, are ground up or grated and used as a condiment. It has an agreeably sharp taste often compared to that of horseradish. *Wasabi* is cultivated in Japan.

WASHED-CURD CHEESE

Also SOAKED-CURD CHEESE. This is basically a cheddar cheese with a variation in the standard process that provides for stirring the curds in water for a few minutes between milling and salting. The resulting cheese has more moisture, less acidity and a softer, more open texture than regular cheddar. It does not keep as well, however, and is cured for only a month or two. Washed-curd is popular in Canada.

WATER

The most important nutrient in the human diet is water. The human body is more than 50 percent water by weight, and can survive only five days without water under moderate climatic conditions, fewer under hot, dry conditions. Putting it another way, experts say the loss of 10 percent of body water will cause severe symptoms of dehydration, while the loss of 20 percent is fatal. In contrast, the human body can survive about five weeks without food (other than water). That is, it can lose all its carbohydrate reserve (glycogen), all its fat, and half of the lean protein tissues—up to 50 percent of body weight—before it is in danger of starving to death.

The adult male carries about 20 quarts of water inside him, the adult female somewhat less because of her smaller size and higher proportion of fat. Water is the basis of the "internal sea" of fluids that bathe all the body's cells and, indeed, make up their major component. Its importance to the system cannot be overrated. The elasticity or pliability of muscles, cartilages, tendons and even of bones, is in large part due to the water in these tissues. Sodium is the principal mineral element in the "internal sea," while potassium predominates in the fluid inside cells.

Although the body has a fairly efficient system for recirculating body fluids, a certain amount is lost each day. Of the total lost, about 50 percent is eliminated through urine, 28 percent through the skin via perspiration, 20 percent through the lungs and 2 percent through other secretions and solid waste. These proportions vary greatly under extreme conditions. As a result of this loss, the human body needs to take in a certain amount of water each day, approximately three quarts under normal circumstances.

One hears the dictum: drink six glasses of water a day. But this amounts to only half the recommended amount. The rest must come from solid food and other liquids. In addition, the body itself creates about two cups a day through breaking down foods. It is called metabolic water. Much water can be obtained from juicy fruits and vegetables, such as tomatoes, lettuce, watermelon, eggplant, cauliflower and strawberries, all of which are about 90 percent water. Bread is about 35 percent water by weight, and even dry foods like uncooked oatmeal and crackers contain about 5 percent water. Milk is 87 percent water, and other liquids that go to make up the total, such as coffee, tea and soup, are almost all water. Water contains no calories and, contrary to popular belief, is not fattening. It should not cause weight gain, unless salt intake is excessive.

Pure drinking water is that which is uncontaminated by sewage or other pollutants, but is not necessarily chemically pure. A certain amount of minerals in drinking water is beneficial. Water is classified as *hard* or *soft* depending on the mineral content, the former having eight grains or more to the gallon. Some hard water may be better for you, but soft water generally tastes better. Natural soft water comes from rainwater at the close of a shower (after atmospheric pollutants have been cleared), melting snow and mountain lakes receiving their water therefrom, provided they rest on impermeable rocks. Hard water comes from artesian wells and especially springs.

Spring water is exceptionally pure, and often contains enough minerals to be thought of as having medicinal value. For more on this, see **Mineral Water.**

Distilled water is ordinary water that has been filtered and boiled to convert it to steam and then condensed. This gives it a flat or metallic taste due to the absence of air and salts. This is remedied by aeration. Ocean-going naval and passenger vessels usually distill their water from the sea.

Boiled water will be free of any organic impurities, and in some cases free of certain salts, thereby softening the taste. Boiling water leaves it with a flat taste, but it may be aerated by pouring it from one container to another.

Most of the world's water supply is obtained from the ocean. Although it averages about 3.5 percent salt, this is left behind as the water is drawn up into the atmosphere as vapor, to return to earth later as rain and snow.

Despite the essential and innocent character of water, certain persons have taken exception to its exclusive use. For example, the Roman poet Horace opined that, "No verses can please long, or live, which are written by water drinkers." *(Epistles,* I, 19, 2). An anonymous contributor to the London magazine, *Spectator*, wrote:

> *Pure water is the best of gifts that man to man can bring,*
> *But who am I that I should have the best of anything?*
> *Let princes revel at the pump, let peers with ponds make free,*
> *Whiskey, or wine, or even* beer *is good enough for me.*

WATERBUCK

Also KOB. This is a water-loving genus of African antelope, *Kobus lechee*, found south of the Sahara and in the Nile Valley. A large waterbuck might reach 4½ feet at the shoulder and weigh up to 600 pounds. Its curved horns are valuable trophies, but its flesh is said to be coarse and strong to the taste.

WATER BUFFALO

Also CARABAO. This domesticated beast of burden, *Bubalus bubalis*, is found from Egypt to the Philippines. Wild water buffalo are also found in Nepal, Bengal and Assam. The water buffalo is a large, clumsy animal with heavy, curving, triangularly shaped horns. It can be as much as 10 feet long and weigh up to 1800 pounds. Water buffalo provide meat that is edible, though not considered especially good, and they are valuable for milk and hides as well. It is as draft animals that they excel, however.

WATER CHEESE

See **Asin.**

Raw and canned water chestnuts

Watercress

WATER CHESTNUT

The name refers to the nutlike tuber of several aquatic plants of the genus *Trapa.* These plants are plentiful in several parts of the world, but the fruit is a staple item only in the cuisines of Japan, China and Thailand. The plant grows in lakes or ponds, anchored to the bottom, but sends its leaves to the surface. The tuber is three or four-sided, shaped somewhat like a chestnut, with a diameter of one to two inches. Beneath a tough brown skin, the pulp is white, delicately sweet and crunchy. It is rich in starch and mineral salts.

T. natans is the most common variety. It grows prolifically in southern Europe and in the eastern United States, particularly in the Potomac River where its thick growth sometimes hinders navigation. In former times, it was a popular food in northern Italy, around Mantua and Bologna. Now the best known variety is the Chinese *ling kio (T. bicornis)*, used in a wide range of Chinese dishes. It is eaten fresh, dried and canned, and may be sliced, diced or eaten whole. In Southeast Asia, India and Africa, *T. bispinosa* is known as *singhara.* It is usually boiled or made into a flour and used for confections with sugar and honey. The flour is also used as a binder in many dishes, much like cornstarch in Western cookery.

At one time, the water chestnut was known as the "Jesuit's nut," because the seeds were often used in making rosaries.

WATERCRESS

A popular salad green and garnish, watercress *(Nasturtium officinalis)* has a mild but peppery flavor. It is a small, perennial aquatic herb, which is cultivated in Europe and the United States but also grows wild in many parts. The whole leaves and stems may be eaten raw, or cooked as greens, but they are sometimes chopped finely and used as seasoning. It is a well-known sandwich filling and base for cream soup.

WATER ICE

See **Ice Cream.**

WATERLEAF

This is a genus of herbs, *Hydrophyllum* spp., indigenous to both the eastern and western United States and adjacent areas of Canada, whose young shoots were eaten by native Americans. The *H. virginianum* was known to early settlers as Shawnee salad and was much used by them in salads. Another species, *H. appendiculatum*, is also valuable.

WATERLILY ROOT

See **Lotus.**

WATER MAIZE

Also AMAZON GIANT WATER LILY, VICTORIA WATER LILY. These edible seeds of a very large aquatic herb, *Victoria regia*, are found in the Amazon and Guyana regions. They are pea-sized and green or black. Water maize is eaten locally by the Indian population.

WATERMELON

This is a large melon, round or oblong in shape, with a sweet, juicy, red pulp and a thick, green rind. It is the fruit of a ground-hugging vine, *Citrullus vulgaris*, which generally reaches a length of 10 to 15 feet. In commercial stands, one mature melon per vine is considered an average yield. Watermelon is believed to be native to Africa, where it grows wild and is enjoyed by animals as well as humans. The most favorable climate for watermelon is subtropical, but varieties have adapted well to both tropical and temperate climates.

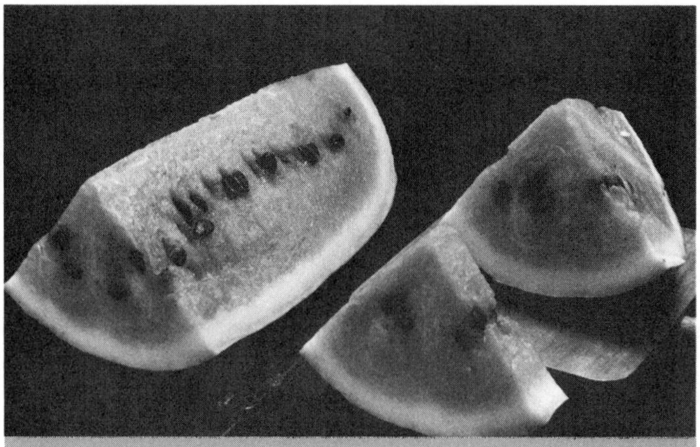

Watermelon

Watermelon was naturalized in the Middle East and in Russia long before recorded history. The Moors brought watermelon to southern Europe after the fall of the Roman Empire, and European colonists in turn brought it to the Western Hemisphere and the Pacific islands. The Chinese began to cultivate watermelon apparently in the 10th century A.D.

Plant science has been applied to watermelon, and current offerings in the market fall generally into three groups: a small, spherical melon, weighing between six and 10 pounds, with dark green rind and a red pulp that is very sweet. This variety was developed in response to the demand for a melon that fit easily into a refrigerator. A larger type runs 20 to 25 pounds but is also spherical. Its rind is also green and covered with a soft bloom. A third, very large, oblong fruit averages 40 pounds or more and has a lighter green, often striped rind. These last two have a sweet pulp of a strawberry red. Seedless varieties have also been developed, which are especially popular in Japan. They are smaller and more expensive, however.

Its sweet taste and thirst-quenching properties are watermelon's most attractive qualities. About this fruit, Mark Twain wrote, "Chief of the world's luxuries . . . . When one has tasted it, he knows what angels eat." The melon consists of 91 percent water by weight, with a modest 8 percent carbohydrates, which makes it fairly low in calories. A low-sugar variety, called the citron melon *(C. vulgaris* var. *citroides)* is grown in some localities, mainly for animal feed. However, in Greece its rind is used to make preserves. Watermelon juice is bottled commercially and it can be drunk fresh or reduced to a sugar or syrup. The rinds of some varieties are used to make pickles. Roasted or salted preserved watermelon seeds are a popular snack in Iran and China. They are said to be beneficial in controlling hypertension.

In the United States the chief watermelon-producing states are California, Indiana and Texas.

See also: **Muskmelon.**

WATER PARSLEY

The black-skinned tubers of this perennial herb, *Oenanthe sarmentosa*, make an excellent cooked vegetable. The taste is sweet and creamy. Water parsley is native to the West Coast of North America from British Columbia to central California.

WATER PARSNIP

This aquatic plant, *Sium latifolium* or *S. suave*, is related to the **skirret.** Unlike the skirret, the leaves of the plant are eaten rather than the root. They taste like celery and are added to salads. The root is said to be poisonous.

WATER PEPPER

This perennial herb, *Polygonum hydropiper*, found in damp or boggy places, is used in salads in the southern United States. It is a variety of smartweed.

WATER ROSE APPLE

Edible fruit of a tropical evergreen tree, *Syzygium aqueum*, found in Malaysia, Sri Lanka, Indonesia and Borneo, it is a berry, light red or white in color, with many seeds and a rather insipid flavor. The fruit is cultivated and sold in Java where it is eaten raw or used to make a syrup called *roedjak*. It has been cultivated successfully in Florida too.

WAX BEAN

Here is a variety of kidney bean, *Phaseolus vulgaris*, eaten as a string bean when immature. At this stage the beans are yellow, waxy looking and crisp enough to snap when broken. They are available fresh, canned or frozen.

See also: **Bean** and **Kidney Bean.**

WAX GOURD

See **Chinese Watermelon.**

WAXWING

These small birds of the Northern Hemisphere, of the genus *Ampedis*, are considered a delicacy in France. Waxwings are crested birds with silky-brown plumage and scarlet spines that resemble sealing wax. They are prepared like lark.

WEAKFISH

Also SEA TROUT. A popular food fish on the East Coast of the United States from Florida to Massachusetts, the weakfish *(Cynoscion regalis)* has a long (up to four feet) slender body, a pointed head, dark olive-green coloring on the back and silver sides. A large specimen can weigh as much as 30 pounds. The weakfish is so called because of its extremely tender mouth. Nevertheless, it is a sought-after sportfish. This fish was highly regarded by native Americans who called it *squeteague.* It may be prepared in any way suitable for trout. The weakfish is closely related to the California white sea bass *(C. nobilis).*

See also: **Bass.**

WEEVERFISH

Also DRAGONFISH. The name refers to any of several species of the family *Trachinidae*, small, poisonously spined fish of the eastern Atlantic and Mediterranean. These fish are prized as food, especially the greater weever or dragonfish *(Trachinus draco)*, which burrows into the sand in moderately deep water. Its venomous spines are placed at the top of its dorsal fin, but are a menace only to fishermen. The lesser weever *(T. vipera)*, of English and Mediterranean waters, comes closer in and is frequently stepped on by bathers. The result is an extremely painful wound, at least in the short run. A third species, the spotted weever *(T. araneus)* is found exclusively in the Mediterranean.

Flesh of the greater weever is firm and white; it is especially popular in Belgium and the Mediterranean countries. It is prepared like **whiting.** The other species are usually put into fish stews such as bouillabaisse, or soups.

WEIHEN STEPHAN

See **Box Cheese.**

WEISSLACKER

This is a soft, ripened German cheese produced from cow's milk in Bavaria whose white, lustrous, smeary surface earned it the sobriquet, "white lacquer." Its production methods resemble Limburger's, and it has a similarly strong flavor and aroma. Some well-ripened versions of this cheese are called *bierkase.* Cheeses are four to five inches square, and weigh two to three pounds. It generally takes four months' curing to develop the spicy flavor, but cheeses are wrapped and shipped at three months.

WEISSWURST

This popular white veal sausage is a German specialty from the Munich area. It is light and delicate in both flavor and texture and is eaten fresh. Ingredients include minced lean pork, veal, white bread, nutmeg, lemon peel, salt and white pepper. Sausages are four to five inches long and are broiled, baked or steamed and served hot or cold with sauerkraut and potato salad.

See also: **Sausage.**

WELS

Also EUROPEAN CATFISH. A freshwater species of central and eastern Europe, the wels *(Silurus glanis)* can grow to enormous size. The largest on record measured 16 feet long and weighed more than 670 pounds. The flesh of smaller specimens makes better eating, having finer texture and taste. It is an important commercial species in the basins of the Black, Caspian and Aral Seas, and it has been introduced into England. It inhabits large rivers and lakes.

The wels may be prepared in a variety of ways. It may be cut into steaks and broiled or fried. Alternatively, it may be poached and served with caper sauce. The wels is also known as the silure.

See also: **Catfish.**

WELSH ONION

See **Cibol, Scallion.**

WENSLEYDALE CHEESE

This is a fine old English cheese whose tradition reputedly goes back more than 1,000 years in the Ure River Valley, Yorkshire. It is marketed almost exclusively as a white cheese nowadays, although before World War II, an excellent blue Wensleydale was produced. Made from whole cow's milk, white Wensleydale, a very popular cheese, has a soft, creamy texture and a good flavor. It is packaged when less than a month old to be eaten when between one and two months old. Cheeses come in many convenient sizes, one being small and cylindrical, measuring four inches across by five long.

If Wensleydale is allowed to ripen under the right conditions, it becomes a medium hard, blue-veined cheese that rivals **Stilton** in quality. The paste is rich, creamy and white, with blue veins widely distributed. Unlike Stilton's crumbly texture, Wensleydale's is smooth and spreadable. The flavor, though somewhat stronger than Stilton's, is without acidity or bitterness. Cheeses average between 10 and 12 pounds.

WERDER

Also ELBINGER, NIEDERUNGSKASE. This semi-soft German cheese is made from whole or partly skimmed cow's milk in West Prussia. *Werder*, like **Tilsiter,** is ripened by both white mold and red smear bacteria, and thus has a mildly acidic, piquant flavor, though not so strong as Tilsiter. Cheeses are fairly moist, and ball-shaped like **Gouda,** ranging in weight from 11 to 26 pounds. Full ripening takes about 10 weeks.

WEST BOTHIAN CHEESE

See **Vastbottensost.**

WEST FRISIAN CHEESE

This Dutch cheese is made from cow's milk and is best eaten when only a week old.

WEST GOTHLAND CHEESE

See **Vastgotaost.**

WEST INDIAN CHERRY

This is the red, edible fruit of two species of shrubs or trees, the *Cordia nitida* of the West Indies and the *Malpighia punicifolia*, found in the West Indies and from Mexico south to Venezuela and Peru. The fruit is juicy and is used to make jellies and preserves. The second species is closely related to the **Barbados Cherry.**

WESTPHALIA SOUR-MILK CHEESE

Also BRIOLER. This is a German **hand cheese** made from sour milk and named for the province of its origin. The texture is soft and fatty, and the usual sharp flavor of hand cheese is further enhanced by the addition of pepper and caraway seeds to the curd.

WHALE

This large, warm-blooded marine mammal is of the order *Cetacea*, which also includes dolphins and porpoises. The whale looks like a fish, but it is air-breathing. Very large whales (up to 95 feet long, 300,000 pounds in weight) are hunted for oil and whalebone but not meat because the latter is very tough-fibered. The flesh of smaller whales is more palatable, especially that of the finback *(Balaenoptera physalus)* and the humpback *(Megaptera novaeangliae)* whales. These reach lengths of 65 and 50 feet respectively, and weigh 30 to 50 tons. The best cuts of meat are taken from along the spine toward the tail, and are red in color, resembling coarse beef. The average humpbacked whale yields one to two tons of meat.

If eaten very fresh, it tastes somewhat like beef. If aged at all, it is said to develop a taste described by some as fishy, and by others as "sour and tangy," which, nevertheless, is much appreciated by some people. It is best cooked using a moist method, such as potroasting or braising.

Very small cetaceans, such as the white whale or beluga *(Delphinapterus leucas)* and the narwhal *(Monodon monoceros)*, are highly valued by Eskimos as sources of meat and hides. These mammals inhabit arctic seas of both North America and Eurasia. Large specimens may be up to 15 feet long and weigh as much as 1500 pounds. The narwhal is distinguished by a single tusk that projects forward out of its upper jaw, reaching a length of up to nine feet. It has a spiral twist, and in medieval times it was sold as a unicorn horn, fetching a high price for its supposed medicinal properties.

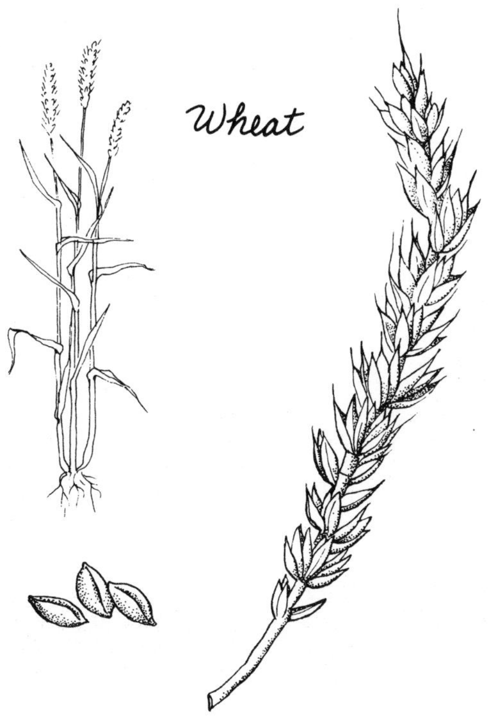

WHEAT

Wheat may have been the first food plant to be cultivated. Today it is the major cereal grain of the world's temperate regions. Wheat, rice and corn (maize) make up 66 percent of the annual supply of all cereals, which in turn constitute 80 percent of all calories consumed by humans. As a human food, wheat is rivaled by **rice** in the hot, moist areas, but worldwide it leads rice in the amount produced and the acreage sown with it. Corn runs a poor third in human nutrition, since much of it is fed to livestock (though, eventually, much of that may end up as human food).

Wheat has played a major role in human history. Its cultivation in Neolithic times led to the abandonment of nomadism in many areas and fostered the rise of urban civilization. This was the beginning of agriculture, as opposed to the mere gathering of wild crops, and is thought to have occurred about 7,000 B.C. The oldest written reference to it occurs in the Sumerian language, dated about 3,100 B.C. It notes that in addition to breadmaking, wheat was used to make eight different types of beer. Wheat was the economic mainstay of ancient Egypt. Its overwhelming importance is made clear in the story of Joseph from the Bible. Joseph, who foresaw a catastrophic drought, averted famine and achieved power second only to the Pharaoh's by storing up enough grain during the seven fat years to see the population through the seven lean years. According to one authority, yields of wheat in ancient Egypt are comparable to those attained today on the same land using the best improved seed and modern methods and machinery.

Egyptian wheat was one of Imperial Rome's major imports and by the first century A.D. formed one cornerstone of its domestic policy. This has been summed up in the phrase, "Bread and circuses." The emperors of Rome maintained domestic peace through the *annona*, or dole, which issued free grain (later loaves of bread) to all citizens of the city. During the reign of Augustus (27 B.C.–14 A.D.), it is estimated that 320,000 people were on the dole, i.e., approximately one-third of the city's population. Wheat was introduced into the New World by Spaniards in the early 16th Century, and today wheat thrives best in many countries to which it was originally foreign, namely, Australia, the United States, Canada and Argentina.

Although wheat grows best in temperate regions, it is adaptable to almost any climate but the tropical. The combination of high heat and humidity do not inhibit its growth. Quite the opposite: it grows quickly and luxuriently, but bears no ears of grain.

Wheat is a grass of the genus *Triticum*—annual or biennial depending on the variety—which possesses a distinct advantage over other cereal grasses. Its grain contains large amounts of gluten. Gluten is a gray, sticky, nutritious substance which gives dough it tough, elastic quality. Consequently, wheat makes better bread than other grains, with the possible exception of **rye,** which also contains appreciable amounts of gluten. Wheat varieties are lumped into categories according to the texture of their kernels: hard and soft.

Hard wheats *(T. durum, T. aestivum, T. turgidum)* as a class contain more gluten and are thus more suitable for breadmaking. Durum, the hardest of hard wheat, is used mainly in macaroni and other forms of **pasta.** Other types are English wheat and the hard red winter and spring wheats of Minnesota and the remaining states of the west north central area of the United States. These grains, which are believed to have originated in the north and east of Russia, are hardy and resistant to drought and rust. They yield a creamy colored flour. The heads of hard wheat are so heavily bearded that they resemble barley.

Soft wheat *(T. vulgare)* is a less hardy plant, contains less gluten and yields a whiter flour. It is more appropriate for pastries and breakfast foods. The head is usually beardless. Major grain producers are the USSR, Canada, the United States, Argentina, China, France, India and Italy.

A grain of wheat has the following composition: 14 percent water, 12 percent protein, 70 percent carbohydrates, one to two percent fat, one to two percent of cellulose and ash. A grain of wheat has at its center the endosperm or kernel, which makes up most of its weight. It is a floury mass of starch and gluten encased in a layer of aleurone, which is rich in protein and mineral salts, such as phosphate of calcium, magnesium and potassium. On top of the aleurone layer are three layers of bran, which are mainly cellulose. The final constituent is the embryo or germ, the living part of the grain. It contains a high proportion of fat, proteins and vitamins. In the production of white flour, the germ and bran are eliminated. Whole wheat, or graham flour, which contains the whole grain, is a far more nutritious product, but spoils more rapidly than the white and makes a heavier bread.

Wheat germ, a by-product of milling white flour, is marketed as a separate product. Its major food values are vitamins B1 and E, protein, minerals and natural fiber. It may be purchased toasted and vacuum-packed in jars or cans or in some stores, raw. After being opened, wheat germ must be stored in the refrigerator. It has a pleasant, nutty flavor. It may be added to white flour for breadmaking or sprinkled over soups, stews and cereals, or even over such desserts as ice cream.

WHEATEAR

The name refers to any member of the *Saxicola* genus, small migrating birds of the Northern Hemisphere, which the French find to be tasty morsels. They prepare them like **lark.**

WHELK

A marine mollusk with a single, convoluted shell, the whelk is a popular seafood in Great Britain and other parts of Europe, such as Italy. It is not well known in the United States, except for one type, the **conch,** which enjoys a following in the West Indies, Florida and Texas. Most widely eaten is the common whelk *(Buccinum undatum)*, which for a century at least has been a popular treat sold at roadside stands in British seaside resorts, such as Brighton. It is cooked in boiling salted water for 15 minutes, then served on a small saucer with lemon juice or vinegar. *Buccinum*, as well as other edible genera including *Thais* and *Busycon*, are found in North America.

WHEY

When milk separates, the solid portion is known as curds and the liquid portion as whey. Whey is a straw-colored liquid, consisting of 95 percent water plus some milk sugar and traces of casein and fat. In former times, whey—especially buttermilk whey—was considered a refreshing drink and was often improved by the addition of nutmeg and sugar.

The 16th-century nursery rhyme, *Little Miss Muffet*, is a sort of testimonial to its popularity. Little Miss (Patience) Muffet is an historical figure. She was the daughter of Dr. Thomas Muffet (1533–1604), who was the author of an early book on food and health and an expert on spiders.

Goat's milk whey, because of its diuretic properties, achieved a reputation in the 19th century as a cure for renal ailments. Today a fermented version of whey, called *blaand*, is drunk in the Shetland Islands. In most cheese-making whey is disposed of and sold as pig food, but certain cheeses are based on whey, most notably ***gjetost*** and ***mysost.***

WHISKY

Also WHISKEY. Whisky is a strong liquor distilled from the fermented mash of a grain, such as barley, rye or corn (maize) and aged in wooden casks. The word "whisky" is the English approximation of the Gaelic words *uisgebeatha* (Scottish) and *uisgebaugh* (Irish), which mean "water of life." *Whisky* is the standard spelling, except in the United Kingdom where the "e" is retained when referring to Irish whisky.

Whisky is usually identified by national origin, as in Scotch, Irish, Canadian, American and Japanese. A number of factors come into play in determining their characteristics, including the type of grain used, the distilling process, the character of the water, how the grain is cured and the kind of storage casks used. The major types are discussed below.

Scotch whisky: Malted barley is the principal source grain for Scotch and, in the curing, it is permeated by peat smoke whose distinctive flavor is carried over into the distilled spirit. It is said that the Scots have been distilling whisky for 600 years, yet it wasn't until 1853 that a distiller hit upon an idea that led to popular acceptance of Scotch whisky, first in England, then throughout the world. Up until then, Scotch was always a straight malt whisky, heavy-bodied and strong-tasting. Its popularity has been confined to Scotland. Then, a distiller began blending malt whiskies with grain whiskies (mainly to cut costs), which were made primarily from corn (maize). They lightened the finished product, which increased its appeal. Nowadays, most Scotch whiskies are blends, and may be composed of as many as 40 different whiskies, which are balanced by the master blender to produce a consistent taste year after year. About 1 percent of bottled Scotch is straight malt whisky, usually from the Highland region, which has a fuller body and much higher price.

By law Scotch must be aged in wooden casks (often recycled sherry casks) for at least three years, but in practice they are customarily aged seven to eight years before bottling. It is marketed at 86 proof.

Irish whisky: Barley is also the principal source grain for Irish whisky, but the peaty flavor is absent because the grain is cured with smokeless anthracite. This gives Irish whisky a lighter flavor, which has been described as smooth, clean and unique. It has a medium body and must be aged at least four years, although, again, in actual practice it is aged seven to eight years before shipping. Before Prohibition became law in 1919, Irish whisky was America's favorite imported whisky. After repeal in 1933, Scotch whisky was established as the new favorite. Scotch's popularity has risen steadily to a point where the United States accounts for more than 50 percent of all Scotch whisky sold each year in the world. Irish whisky is bottled at 86 proof.

Canadian whisky: Canadian whisky is believed to have rye as its main grain source, although corn (maize), wheat and barley are also used. The exact proportions are a trade secret. Canadian whisky is always blended, and is characterized by a light body and delicate taste. It is customarily bottled at six years old (three years is the legal minimum), and at 86.8 proof.

American whisky: Whisky-making has a venerable history in the United States. A memorable chapter is the Whisky Rebellion of 1791. Since early colonial days, given the difficulties of transportation, the farmers of western Pennsylvania had found it economical to convert their surplus grain to whisky, which was less bulky and easy to store and sell. This had always been done without government interference. In George Washington's first administration the foundling republic levied a tax on whisky to shore up its finances. The Pennsylvania distillers rebelled. There were riots, and a few tax collectors were tarred and feathered. President Washington was obliged to send an armed force to quell the insurrection, which was accomplished without bloodshed. But the federal government established its point, and has been profiting from the whisky business ever since. Moreover, the incident drove some independent types farther west to Kentucky, where they found the proper water for whisky-making. Since then Kentucky has been the traditional home of fine whisky. American whisky is made from a number of different grains, corn and rye being the most prominent.

Important marketing categories of whisky are straight, blended and light. A *straight whisky*, to deserve the name, must be distilled at 160 proof or lower, be aged for at least two years in charred white oak barrels, be diluted only by distilled water and be bottled at at least 80 proof. The proportion of grain in the mash determines how a whisky is labeled, e.g., a mash of 51 percent corn (maize) makes Bourbon (a mash of 80 percent corn, however, makes straight corn whisky), a mash of 51 percent rye makes rye whisky, a mash of 51 percent wheat makes wheat whisky, and so on. Tennessee whisky may have a majority of any grain, but must be distilled in Tennessee. Straight whiskies may be mixed with other, very similar, straight whiskies, but not with anything else or they lose their designation. They are on the average aged for six years, and bottled at 80, 86 and 100 proof.

Sweet mash and *sour* mash refer to the yeasting process. Sweet mash utilizes freshly developed yeast, while sour mash takes at least one-fourth its volume of yeast from the spent beer of a previous fermentation.

Blended whisky represents about half of the whisky consumed in the United States, and usually consists of about 20 percent straight whisky, and the rest neutral grain spirits, (those that are distilled at 190 proof, which have no appreciable aroma or flavor) or light whisky. Flavoring agents used in the blending include sherry and prune or peach juice. Blended whisky is lighter-bodied and lighter-flavored than straight and is usually bottled at 80 proof.

Light whisky is a recent innovation and a response to the "trend to lightness" that has been observed in consumer taste patterns. It may be distilled from practically any grain, although corn (maize) is used mostly, but it is finished at a higher proof than straight whisky, i.e., between 161 and 189 proof, which considerably reduces the body and the amount of congeners that contribute to taste. An attempt to market light whisky as a separate, uncolored product met with little success in the 1970s, and it is chiefly used for blending.

Japanese whiskies are primarily blends produced from millet, corn, Indian corn and rice. Malted barley is used for some fuller-bodied whiskies, but wheat and rye are used only rarely. Originally, Japanese distillers sought to approximate Scotch, and succeeded very well in their more expensive lines, aided in some cases by the addition of real Highland Malt whiskey. But they have since developed a line of whiskies with a distinct flavor of their own.

WHITEBAIT

This is the name given to immature sprat, herring and smelt which are caught in their first year and usually fried crisp. At that age, they are less than two inches long and have a silver white color. They are washed, rolled in flour and deep fried. The fish may be eaten whole, head, bones, tail and all. Whitebait are probably the smallest fish eaten by humans and are certainly one of the most delicious.

See also: **Herring, Smelt** and **Sprat.**

WHITE CHEESE

Also FROMAGE BLANC, FROMAGE A LA PIE. This simple French cheese is made from whole cow's milk, usually during the summer months, and eaten fresh. Milk may be set with rennet or allowed to sour, then put in a muslin bag to drain off the whey.

It can be eaten immediately, customarily with salt and pepper sprinkled on top. If mixed with cream, it is called ***fromage a la creme.*** A popular variation of the latter is *coeur a la creme*, where the curd is drained in a heart-shaped, wicker basket, then served with sugar, cream and often wild strawberries.

WHITEFISH

This is a family of fish, the *Coregonidae*, which are closely related to the salmons and look rather like herrings. Whitefish inhabit fresh water, preferably cold lakes and rivers of the Northern Hemisphere. Most species are exclusively freshwater types, but some are migratory. Best known whitefish include the cisco, the houting, also known as the gwyniad or skelly, the fera, the pollan, the arctic cisco, the humback whitefish, and the least cisco. All are good to eat, and some are important food fishes. For more information, see under the names of specific whitefish.

WHITE HAKE

A fairly large fish of the cod family found in the western Atlantic from the Gulf of St. Lawrence to North Carolina, the white hake *(Urophycis tenuis)* is not a true **hake,** but it is good to eat nonetheless. It reaches a maximum length of about four feet and can weigh up to 40 pounds. The white hake is closely related to the **squirrel hake,** and is eaten fresh, salted and canned.

WHITE MENTZEL

This is a perennial shrub, *Mentzelia albicaulis*, of the western and southeastern United States, whose seeds are made into a parched meal that is consumed locally.

WHITE SAPOTE

Also MEXICAN APPLE. This is a yellow green subtropical fruit native to Mexico and Central America. The white sapote tree *(Casimiroa edulis)* does best at altitudes above 3,000 feet and is also cultivated in subtropical Florida and in California. The fruit is generally round, multi-seeded, three to four inches across and has a soft, melting pulp, which is divided into several cells. The taste is aromatic and ranges from very sweet to bittersweet. The fruit is eaten fresh or used to make drinks.

WHITE SHAD

See **Shad.**

WHITE STEENBRAS

Also PIGNOSE GRUNTER, WHITEFISH. A variety of sea bream found in South Africa, the white steenbras *(Lithognathus lithognathus)* reaches a length of six feet or more and is considered a fine food fish. It has a slender, silvery body, and a long snout with thick lips. A sportfish prized for its fighting qualities, the white steenbras can weigh 30 pounds or more.

WHITE STONECROP

Also WALL PEPPER. This succulent, mat-forming plant, *Sedum album*, is found in Europe, western Asia and North Africa and is eaten in salads. Many varieties are commonly cultivated. It ripens in early summer.

WHITE STUMPNOSE

Also GO-HOME FISH. A type of sea bream found in South African waters, the white stumpnose *(Rhabdosargus globiceps)* is moderately sized (up to 20 inches long) but is well flavored and is highly regarded as a sport fish. It is a night feeder and prefers shallow, sandy areas. The fish has a blue back and silver sides and belly with dark crossbars on the upper sides. It is called the "go-home fish" because of a belief that other fish disappear when it is present in an area.

WHITE WINE SAUCE

This is a sauce for fish based on French *veloute* which has been prepared from fish stock. White wine is added to the *veloute* and the mixture is reduced, then thickened with egg yolks and finished with butter.

See also: **Sauce.**

WHITING

The name is given to several species of fish, the most common being the European sea fish, *Merlangius merlangus*. A member of the cod family, this fish is found in the North Atlantic and in the Mediterranean and Black Seas. It is slender bodied, reaching a length of 28 inches and has a small barbel at its mouth. The flesh of the whiting is white and wholesome, insipid to the taste, but easily digestible. It is prepared in a variety of ways, including frying, poaching and broiling.

A related species is the blue whiting *(Micromesistius poutassou)*, also of the North Atlantic, which rarely exceeds 16 inches in length. Blue whiting swim together in huge shoals, usually far out at sea, but from February to April they appear off the coasts of Ireland, Scotland and Norway where they are fished commercially and turned into frozen fish fingers and fish cakes.

The Indo-Pacific whiting belongs to the family *Sillaginidae* and includes the spotted whiting *(S. punctatus)*, the northern whiting or *pescadinha (S. sihama)* and the sand whiting *(S. ciliata)*. The spotted whiting can exceed two feet in length and is an important food and game fish in Australian waters. The northern whiting, which is also called smelt, is a delicious food fish and is important locally throughout its range.

WHORTLEBERRY

See **Huckleberry, Cranberry.**

WIDGEON

See **Baldpate.**

WIENER

See **Frankfurter.**

WIENERWURST

See **Vienna Sausage.**

WILD BEAN

See **Bean Vine, Ground Nut.**

WILD BEET

Also GREEN AMARANTH. This is a coarse herb, *Amaranthus hybirdus*, of North America, whose seeds were ground into flour by pre-Columbian people but are neglected today, though still considered edible. The leaves are occasionally gathered by wild-food enthusiasts and added to salads.

WILD BOAR

See **Wild Pig.**

WILD CHERIMOYA

A wild Mexican shrub, *Annona longiflora*, found chiefly in the state of Jalisco, it produces edible fruit that are boiled to make sweetmeats.

WILD CHERRY

This is the edible fruit of at least three species of shrubby trees of North America. These are the *Prunus ilicifolia* of California and Baja California whose red or yellow fruit is thin but sweetish; the *P. pennsylvanica* or wild red cherry, found from Labrador to British Columbia and south to Colorado, Iowa and North Carolina, whose round, bright red fruit has a thin, acidic flesh; and *P. serotina*, the wild black cherry, found in eastern and southeastern sections, whose purplish black fruit may be sweet or bitter. Wild cherries are used in making jelly and homemade wines and in flavoring candy and coughdrops.

WILD CHICORY

See **Radicchio.**

WILD CINNAMON

See **Canella.**

WILD CUMIN

This is a European plant, *Lagaecia cuminoides*, of the parsley family, whose flower clusters produce a kind of cumin seeds.

WILD GARLIC

See **Wild Onion.**

WILD GOURD

Also CALABAZILLA, MISSOURI GOURD. Orange-sized fruit of a long-running vine, *Cucurbita foetidissima*, found from Nebraska to California and areas of northern Mexico, it is not edible, but its seeds are sometimes used as food.

WILD MEDLAR

Also MATUGUNGO. This is a genus of small African fruits, which includes the small wild medlar *(Vangueria infausta)*, or *matugongo*, and the Spanish tamarind *(Vangueria madagascariensis)*. Like medlars, the skin of the fruit is brown, its flavor is acidic but sweet, and the pulp contains pits, which are sometimes also eaten.

WILD OLIVE

This yellow or black fruit of a tropical tree, *Masticho-*

dendron foetidissimum, is common in East Bengal, the Himalaya Mountains and Malaysia, but grows equally well in tropical Florida, the West Indies and Mexico. In India, the fruit is used in curry dishes or is pickled like an olive. It has one seed, and in the Western Hemisphere it attains a length of about 1¼ inches.

WILD ONION

Also MEADOW LEEK, ROSE LEEK, WILD GARLIC. This is a plant, *Allium canadense*, native to North America, whose bulbs have a pungent, onionlike taste. It is found in the eastern United States as far south as Florida and Texas. It can be used as a substitute for domestic onion, boiled or pickled.

WILD PIG

Also BUSH PIG, WILD HOG, WILD BOAR, PECCARY, JAVELINA. This wild member of the *Suidae* family tends to medium size and has a larger head and shorter body than the domestic pig and, with one exception, a hairy hide. Several species of wild pig are native to the Old World, including Eurasia, Africa, Madagascar, Japan, Formosa, the Philippines and Indonesia. A large boar can weigh as much as 600 pounds and be up to 6¼ feet long. Long tusks are a striking characteristic of boars, most especially in the *babirusa (Babyrousa babyrussa)* a species native to the North Celebes, Tongian and Sula Islands and Buru Island of the North Moluccas. Its tusks grow from both the upper and lower jaw and are long enough to invite comparison with deer antlers. The name *babirusa* means "pig-deer." This pig is almost hairless, and has been hunted to near extinction by native people for its meat, which is most palatable in younger animals.

The European wild boar *(Sus scrofa)* grows formidable tusks as well and is a courageous fighter when aroused. This is the wild ancestor of domestic pigs. It has been hunted for hundreds of years for sport and as a source of meat, although only animals less than a year old are considered good to eat. The flesh of older animals is too tough and strong-tasting. An exception is made of the head. Boar's head is a classic French dish. It is an elaborate concoction containing, among other ingredients, stuffings of pork and chicken meat, fresh pork tongue, fat bacon, truffles and pistachios. The wild boar is extinct in Great Britain, but plentiful in France. It is also found in North Africa, Asia, Japan and the Malayan Archipelago. It has been introduced and established in the Great Smoky Mountains of North Carolina and in the coastal range of California. Feral domestic swine (e.g. razorbacks) are found in other states, most notably Florida, Arkansas and Hawaii.

The peccary, or javelina *(Tayassu tajacu* and *T. pecari)* are piglike animals native to South and Central America and extend up to the American Southwest. They are smaller than the wild boar, rarely exceeding 66 pounds in weight, but are hunted for their meat and hides. Peccary meat tends to be dry and should be barded with fat. It is prepared like suckling pig.

There are at least three African species, the bush pig, the wart hog and the giant forest hog. The heavily tusked wart hog *(Phacochoerus aethiopicus)* is found in the east and the south, preferring savannah and light forests. Its flesh is considered the tastiest of the three and it is widely hunted by native people.

The ancient Romans associated wild boar with great feasting. The poet Juvenal, in his *Satires*, wrote, "O what gluttony is his who has whole boars served up for himself, an animal born for banquets."

Wild Pig

Wild Rice

WILD POTATO

Also WILD RUE. The roots of this herb, *Solanum fendleri*, may be cooked and eaten like potatoes. It is native to eastern North America and especially plentiful in the mountains of Pennsylvania.

WILD RICE

A wild grass, *Zizania aquatica*, of North America whose seeds are cooked and eaten like rice, it has a distinctive flavor and is highly regarded among gourmets. Wild rice is found in most states east of the Rocky Mountains, growing in fresh water or brackish swamps. It is most plentiful in Michigan, Wisconsin and Minnesota, which provides about two-thirds of the world's supply. Another species, *Z. caducifolia*, grows in the Far East. It is not certain whether it is native to the area or was brought there from America in the 18th or 19th centuries.

The wild rice stalk may be from three to 12 feet high depending on soil and climatic conditions. Certain native American tribes—most notably the Chippewa—were fond of wild rice. They harvested the grain from canoes, bending the stalks and knocking the heads with a stick, so that the grains fell in the bottom of the canoe. Only the ripest grains were dislodged by this practice, and the Chippewa had to make several passes during a season to get the entire crop. The grains were dried in the sun or over a fire, threshed and winnowed. The Menominee of Wisconsin take their name from the Indians' word for wild rice, *menomin*.

The European settlers learned to eat wild rice following the native Americans' example but at first did not regard it so highly. They called it by a variety of names, including blackbird oats, fool oats, Indian oats, Indian rice, duck rice and wild oats. Later, wild rice became so popular that overharvesting threatened it with extinction. Conservation measures were taken to regulate the harvesting.

Wild rice grains are gray and brown and about twice as long as grains of ordinary rice. They require longer cooking than ordinary rice. They are often served with game or used to stuff poultry. Sauteed mushrooms or slivered almonds are a frequent accompaniment to wild rice. Wild rice is said to enhance the flavor of ducks and other game birds that feed on it.

WILD SERVICE TREE

See **Checker Tree.**

WILD SPINACH

See **Good King Henry.**

WILD THYME

See **Lemon Thyme.**

WILD TOBACCO

This is an American shrub, *Acnistus arborescens*, of the nightshade family whose fruits are edible. It is found in warm regions. The fruit is often made into jellies.

WILLUGHBEIA

This edible fruit of a woody vine, *Willughbeia edulis*, is found in the Himalayan region, Malaysia and Indochina. It is yellow, egg-shaped and about the size of a lemon.

WILSTERMARSCH

Also HOLSTEINER MARSCH. This semihard German cheese is made from cow's milk in Schleswig-Holstein. There are several varieties, based on the condition of the milk and what mixtures are used. These include *rahm*, *sussmilch*, *zweizeitige*, *dreizeitige* and *herbst*. *Zweizeitige* is more commonly marketed and is made from evening skim milk and morning whole milk. *Wilstermarsch* is similar to **Tilsiter** but is cured for a shorter period of time, usually three to four weeks, and thus is considerably milder though slightly acidic in flavor. Cheeses weigh from nine to 12 pounds.

WILTSHIRE CHEESE

Also TRUCKLES. This hard, sweet-curd English cheese of the cheddar type is similar to Derby or **Gloucester.** Cheeses are aged from one to four months, the flavor improving with age.

WINDSOR BEAN

See **Broad Bean.**

WINE

Wine is the fermented juice of the grape, especially of the species *vinifera* of the grape genus *vitis*, although one other wine-producing species of grape, *vitis labrusca*, is cultivated in North America. Particular wines have long been associated with specific foods. (See **Wine and Food Affinities.**) Wine production has accompanied the growth of Western civilization from the Middle East through the Mediterranean and Western Europe to the New World.

In ancient Greece wine was stored and shipped in casks, goatskins, and earthenware *amphorae* and was stoppered with rags, olive oil and pitch. The wine was dark (Homer's "wine-dark sea") and was usually cut with water. In Rome an elaborate connoisseurship was in full swing by the time of the poet Horace (65–8 B.C.). The Romans planted vines wherever they established colonies—in Gaul, Iberia, Carthage and Great Britain.

Later, Charlemagne is said to have built vineyards in the Rhineland and in Burgundy. In the Middle Ages the production of wine—because of its liturgical use—was almost exclusively the pursuit of the clergy. Dom Pierre Perignon, the father of **champagne,** for example, was a Benedictine monk. By the end of the 12th century the wine trade was a major industry. Most vineyards were placed along rivers, such as the Rhine, the Loire and the Garonne, for easy transportation.

In the 17th century the bottle and cork (resulting also from earlier experiments by Dom Perignon) revolutionalized the wine industry, making possible a much longer preservation of the vintage. The planting of vineyards followed the European conquests—those of France, Spain, and England—into the New World, and of the Dutch into South Africa. The French occupation of Algeria, in 1830, led eventually to that country's emergence as a major source of wine, particularly of *vin ordinaire.*

Vitis vinifera, or "the noble grape," almost disappeared in the "disaster of 1863," when virtually all the vineyards in France—then as now a world leader in wine production and consumption—were threatened with failure because of the accidental importation from North America of the wine louse, *phylloxera,* which feeds upon the roots of the vines. Only a last-ditch grafting of New World *(vitis labrusca)* root stocks onto the remaining French vines saved the day. All French wines today are the fruit of vines with North American roots.

The various colors of wine—red, rose and white—are caused by the length of time the grape skins stay in contact with the fermented matter, or "must." Red wines are those from black grapes only, the skins remaining in contact with the must until a desired result is attained. White wine is the product of greenish or black grapes, but the must is separated immediately from the skins. Rose wine occurs when the skins are left in contact with the must for a short time only.

Wines are further classified as natural, fortified or sparkling. A natural or "table" wine, such as **Bordeaux Wine** or **Chablis,** is produced by a natural fermentation with but a slight addition of yeast and sugar. A fortified wine, such as **sherry** or **port,** is given a dose of alcohol, usually in the form of grape brandy, in the fermentation process and is consequently stronger with a higher percentage (15 to 22) of alcohol per volume. Sparkling wine, such as champagne, has a double fermentation, the second taking place in the bottle.

What takes place in fermentation is the conversion of the sugars glucose and fructose into alcohol and carbon dioxide. To enhance the process, an injection is made of true wine yeast, *Saccharomyces ellipsoideus,* to supplement the work of wild yeasts. Sulfur dioxide is also usually added to suppress other organisms that cover the surface of the ripe grapes. Other innovations, the result of centuries of experimentation, contribute to the production of particular wines, such as the *pourriture noble* ("noble rot") that goes into the making of **Sauternes,** allowing the grapes to rot in order to develop a sweetness, a bouquet and a higher sugar content that characterize this and similar wines. The addition and encouragement of *flor*, a mildewlike growth, is essential to the making of Spanish sherry.

The climate, the soil, the topography and the specific techniques of each maker all play a major part in the production of wine. No beverage varies so much—from year to year and from place to place. Wine, then, has become an intricate gastronomic art with experts, fans and a vocabulary all its own. Even the word "vignette," which meant originally a small design of vine leaves and tendrils, is an example of our long and close contact with wine.

The Romans allowed their grape vines to grow as high as they could climb, a practice which is no longer commercially feasible. But keeping them near the ground contributes to other problems.

Higher off the ground, the vines are less affected by mildew and black rot—chief enemies of commercial vineyards today—though easily controlled by frequent spraying with "Bordeaux mixture," a solution of copper sulphate and hydrated lime.

Only in North America are wines produced from the strain of *vitis labrusca,* such as **Catawba, Delaware,** and **Scuppernong.** Only in Chile are the vine roots still those of the original *vitis vinifera.*

Wines have long been synonymous with comfort, hospitality, graceful living and with divine inspiration. In Horace's second Epode, "The Praises of a Country Life," the poet advocates the peaceful contemplation of "vines wedding lofty poplars" and the happy person who has nothing to do but "lop off useless branches with his pruning hook."

WINE AND FOOD AFFINITIES

The relationship between specific wines and specific foods is ancient and time-tested. This has evolved from purely local practice, depending on the availability of particular foods and types of wine grapes, into an art, even into a kind of dogma. White wines are served with fish and white meats. Red wines, especially of the dry and "robust" kinds, are served with red meats or with dark-fleshed fowl, such as ducks and geese, with wild game and pasta. A dry port, sherry or Madeira, goes well with cheeses before dessert. Sweet "fortified" wines (Madeira, sherry, port, Sauternes) complement desserts. A chilled dry sherry or Madeira or a semisweet Sauternes may accompany soup (if this is not too hot and spicy). Champagne is the one wine that can be served with any kind of food, during any portion of the meal.

The ruling principle in wine selection is to enhance and not to obliterate the taste of the food. The delicate flavor of most fish, for example, should never be overwhelmed by a "hearty" wine, obviously. Hence, a dry white wine is suitable. The same holds true for chicken—although a light rose often agrees with roast turkey and red Beaujolais with roast duck. Some fish—such as swordfish and salmon, which have a more "meaty" taste—may also be accompanied by a light rose or red wine. Shellfish, with their delicate rich flavor, are agreeably companioned by a white wine with a more "smoky" taste and effect, such as Graves, Chablis or Pouilly-Fume. A dry, almost sparkling Muscadet is excellent here as well. German and Alsatian wines, which are lighter and fruitier than the great French white wines, relate ideally to cold meats, fish and to salads.

The wild, gamy taste of fowl and venison call for a dry and robust red wine, such as a good Burgundy or Barolo. Beaujolais is agreeable with any light red meat (as meat loaf) and with meat pies and casseroles. Steak and roast beef are highly complemented by a dry red Medoc or St. Emilion (from Bordeaux) and with any dry red wine from Burgundy. A red Lambrusca is typically served with pork dishes, which are the main fare of Bologna, the culinary capital of Italy. Chianti and spaghetti is also a well-known combination.

Individual taste and preference will always determine which wines to serve with meals. But the rule holds: dry or semidry white wine with white meats, including fish and shellfish; dry or hearty red wines with roast meats and game; rose wines with luncheon meats and with some fowl and fish; sweet wines with or following desserts; chilled fortified wines as aperitifs, with soups, and with first courses; dry white, red, or fortified wine with cheeses; red wine with pasta, especially when served in tomato or meat sauce. Hot spicy meals urge pungent "drinkable" red wines, although few vintages can hold their own with curried or heavily peppered dishes.

Although the British do not produce wine grapes of their own, they have long had particular theories about the affinity between wine and food. Here is a typical 19-century menu for "a picnic for 40 persons," with the main fare being:

> *"a joint of cold roast beef, a joint of cold boiled beef, two ribs of lamb, two shoulders of lamb, four roast fowls, two roast ducks, one ham, one tongue, two veal-and-ham pies, two pigeon pies, six medium-sized lobsters, one piece of collared calf's head, 18 lettuces, six baskets of salad, and six cucumbers,*

Among other necessities it called for the following wines: "six bottles of sherry, six bottles of claret, champagne *a discretion*, and any other light wine that may be preferred." The menu also notes that "water can usually be obtained, so it is useless to take it."

The key here is "preferred." To explore cookbooks, recipes and wine shops for oneself—and to experiment—is the best way to discover which wines to serve with specific meals. The red wine-red meat, white wine-white meat guideline is merely a rule of thumb (or palate). It should be followed, but never slavishly. In Greece, for example, a heavily flavored white retsina is drunk with all meals, no matter what their chief ingredients may be. In Germany, where white wine is the dominant harvest, a semidry Rhine or Moselle wine may be served with even the heartiest of meats.

WINE AND LIQUOR TERMS

Following is a list of words that frequently crop up in discussions of wine or liquor. Not included are relevant terms that have been explained elsewhere in the text. Check the index to locate a term if it does not appear below.

abbocato (Italian): Semisweet; equivalent to the French *moelleux*.

Abfullung (German): Bottling.

Abstich (German): Racking; drawing off of young wine from one barrel to another, leaving the sediment behind.

acerbe (French): Green or acidic wine with a sour, unpleasant taste.

acetic: The type of acid formed in wine vinegar by the action of a particular fungus. Wine affected by this fungus has a thin, white film on the surface.

acid, acidity: Substance occuring in all wines that provide a tartness in the taste. Normally these are fruit acids such as tartaric and malic. Acetic acid, however, causes a distinctly sour taste and renders the wine unfit to drink.

adega: (Portuguese) A wine warehouse, equivalent of *bodega* in Spanish and *chai* in French.

aftertaste: The lingering taste in the back of the throat after swallowing; a test of a wine's complexity.

aging: The time needed to bring a particular wine to its prime for drinking. Depending on the type of wine, this may vary anywhere from six months to 50 years. It is said that 75 percent of all wines are ready to be drunk at one year, and begin to deteriorate at the end of three years.

aigre (French): An acidic taste or undertone.

albariza (Spanish): White soil typical of the sherry vineyards at Jerez, Spain.

aldehyde: A colorless, pungent, volatile liquid, produced as a by-product of alcohol fermentation.

alembic, alambic (French), *alambique* (Spanish): A still.

amabile (Italian): Sweet or semisweet; said of a wine that is normally dry, but in a specific instance is appearing in sweeter form.

amaro (Italian): Very dry; bitter.

ameliore (French): Improved; this usually means that sugar has been added to the juice or must before fermentation. Its purpose is to bring the wine up to the normal minimum alcohol content.

amertume (French): Bitter.

anada (Spanish): Said of wine of a specific vintage, and at least one year old.

ansprechend (German): Appealing; attractive.

apagado (Spanish): Fresh grape juice to which alcohol has been added to the proportion of 16 to 18 percent, which guarantees that no fermentation will take place. The French equivalent is called *mistelle*, or vin *mute*. It is used in Spain to sweeten the cheaper grades of sherry.

appellation d'origine controlee (French): A labeling term that serves notice that the name the wine bears is officially recognized, and that to be legal the contents must come from the particular district, town or vineyard named on the label. The law specifies many other restrictions too, as to variety of grape, ripeness, etc.

apre (French): Harsh, rough; usually said of a young wine with high tannin content.

arena (Spanish): Sandy type of soil found in some sherry vineyards of Jerez, Spain.

aroma, arome (French): The scent of a wine, as distinguished from its bouquet (See below). It tends to diminish as a wine ages, to be replaced by bouquet.

arroba (Spanish): A wine measure of just over four gallons, or 16 2/3 liters.

arrope (Spanish): Sweetened, concentrated grape juice that has been boiled down to one-fifth its original volume; used to sweeten and color lesser sherries.

artig (German): Smooth; rounded.

asciutto (Italian): Dry.

*astringence:*Mouth-puckering quality of wine that has an excess of tannin.

Aszu (Hungarian): A superior type of sweet Tokay.

Auslese (German): Superior sort of wine made from selected grapes.

austere: Said of an undeveloped wine that may become big or full-bodied.

balance: In wine tasting, a harmonious quality of wine present when no particular component of taste predominates, and there are no pronounced deficiencies.

Balthazar: An outsize champagne bottle with a capacity of 16 regular bottles, or 2.8 gallons.

banvin (French): Ancient custom of fixing the date for the gathering of the grapes.

barrique (French), *barrica* (Spanish): A cask or hogshead holding 225 liters (about 60 U.S. gallons).

barro (Spanish): Clay soil of the sherry vineyards of Jerez, Spain. See also *albariza* and *arena*. Of the three types *albariza* is the best, *barro* is second and *arena* is third.

basto (Spanish): Coarse, as applied to poor quality sherry.

B.A.T.F. Bureau of Alcohol, Tobacco and Firearms of the U.S. Treasury Department.

baume (French): Sweetness measure in wines and spirits invented by the French chemist Antoine Baume.

Beerenauslese (German): A rare and special wine made from individually selected grapes, cut from bunches with tiny scissors, only in good or great years.

beeswing: A light, filmy crust on the surface of some old ports; said to resemble a bee's wing.

beste (German): Best.

beverage wines: Denotes wines suitable for everyday use, as distinct from vintage wines.

bianco (Italian): White.

binning: Wines stored for development are placed in bins, usually in a cellar, hence "binning."

bite: The taste sensation imparted by tannin and acid in wine.

black rot: A grapevine fungus disease.

blanc de noirs (French): A white wine made from the juice of black grapes, especially from the Champagne region.

blanco (Spanish): White.

blending: The mixing of two or more wines which have similar qualities but differ as to age, origin or a particular characteristic, with a view to improving the product. Some wines, such as sherries and champagnes, are virtually all blends; others, such as vintage table wines, are rarely blended.

Blume (German): Aroma; bouquet.

blumig (German): Good bouquet.

Bocksbeutel (German): The squat, flat-sided green flask used to bottle wines from Franconia and many Chilean wines. The word means literally "goat's scrotum."

bocoy (Spanish): A wine cask holding approximately 162 gallons.

bodega (Spanish): A wine storage room, usually at ground level.

body: In winetasting, body refers to the thickness of a wine, e.g., light-bodied is thin or watery when compared to full-bodied. The latter is weightier, more substantial.

bond: "In bond" refers to alcoholic beverages stored in government-supervised warehouses awaiting payment of duty.

bon gout (French): Good taste.

bor (Hungarian): Wine.

bota (Spanish): Sherry cask holding 132 gallons; butt.

bottle, bouteille (French), *botella* (Spanish): Standard wine bottle holding approximately one-fifth of a gallon, i.e., from 23 to 26 ounces.

bottled in bond: Refers to whisky bottled under government supervision before taxes have been paid. In the United States, it is straight whisky, at least four years old, and 100 proof. In Canada, it is blended whisky, at least three years old, and 100 proof.

bottle sickness: A condition of recently bottled wine, which may last for several months. Because of the rough handling, filtration, etc., immediately before bottling the wine deteriorates and is practically undrinkable for 90 days or so.

bouchonne (French): Said of a wine that tastes unpleasantly of cork which is defective or diseased; corky.

bouquet: The odor or perfume a mature wine gives off especially just after opening. Some experts make a distinction between aroma and bouquet, the former referring to young wines, and affecting the sense of taste rather than smell.

brandwijn (Dutch), *Branntwein* (German): Brandy.

breed: A wine's character or degree of excellence; use of this word is often restricted to wines of the highest caliber.

brouilli (French): In the manufacture of cognac, the middle distillate (24 to 32 percent alcohol) collected for the second distillation.

browning: A process affecting some red wine with old age. Its color changes from red to brown, which is noticeable around the edges of the glass.

brut (French): The driest of champagnes to which little or no sugar has been added, i.e., less than 2 percent.

Bukettreich (German): Rich bouquet.

butt: A wine cask, usually with a 132-gallon capacity, but in Hungary only 13.7 liters.

Cabinettwein (German): Finest quality Rhine wine, pre-1971, so stated on the label.

cantina (Italian): Cellar; bar; winery.

cantina sociale (Italian): Wine growers' cooperative.

capiteux (French): Heady, high in alcohol content.

capsule: Metal or plastic covering for a bottle cork.

caque (French): Grape basket used in harvesting.

casco (Spanish): Large barrel used for aging or shipping wines and liquors; most often made of oak.

cask: A large container for wines or liquor; often made of oak.

casse (French): A disease in wine caused by an excess of metallic salts, particularly iron. Symptoms are a persistent cloudiness and an off-taste.

cave, celler, cellier (French): Cellar; a storage place for wines, often underground.

cep, cepage (French): Vinestock; wine-grape plant.

chai, chaix (French): Building for storing wine or liquor. In theory, it is above ground, as distinct from a *cave*, which is below ground, but in practice the terms are used interchangeably.

chambrer (French): To bring a red wine up from cellar temperature to room temperature, usually by letting it stand for an hour or so in the room before serving.

chaptalization: The adding of sweetened grape juice to wine must before fermentation for the purpose of assuring a minimum alcohol content in the wine. It is often necessary in cool climates, or poor years, cases where the grapes do not produce enough natural sugar. Named for Chaptal, Napoleon's minister of agriculture, who invented or introduced the practice into France.

character: Said of a wine with definite and unmistakable qualities, usually of its grape variety of place of origin.

charnu (French): Full-bodied.

chateau-bottled: Bottled on the property that produced the grapes. This phrase is used mostly for Bordeaux wines. An equivalent phrase is "estate bottled." In French it reads, *mise du chateau*, or *mise en bouteilles au chateau*, and appears on the label.

chiaretto (Italian): Rose wine; light red wine.

clarete (Spanish): A red wine that is light both in body and color.

classic: Said of an exceptionally fine wine from one of the classic regions, e.g., Medoc.

classified growths: French wines officially classified first in 1855 for the *Exposition Universelle*, then again in 1955 and 1959, and listed according to merit. Wines designated are from specific vineyards, estates or "growths" *(crus)*, all of which are considered great.

clean: In winetasting, the term refers to a wine that is palatable, agreeable, refreshing and without defects.

climat (French): A specific, named vineyard, especially one in the Burgundy region.

clos (French): A vineyard, originally one that was walled or otherwise enclosed.

cochylis: A grapevine disease.

collage (French): Fining; clarifying a wine.

commune (French): Parish; township; a village and its surrounding land.

concentrated: Said of a wine with a strong bouquet or aroma.

confreries (French): Wine or gastronomic fraternities or brotherhoods. Example: *Confrerie des Chevaliers du Tastevin* (Brotherhood of the Gentlemen of the Tasting Cup).

consejo regulator (Spanish): Governing body for the *denominacion de origin*, or designation of origin and authenticity of Spanish wines.

consorzio (Italian): Growers' association.

consumo (Spanish and Portuguese): Ordinary wine.

cordial: A sweet, alcoholic, after-dinner drink; a liqueur.

cork: Bottle stopper made of the elastic bark of the cork oak, of which Portugal is the leading producer. By extension, plastic stoppers in the shape of a cork.

corkage: Fee collected by a restaurant for serving a wine brought in by a patron, who purchased it elsewhere. It may run as high as 40 percent of the value of the wine.

corky: Said of a wine with a disagreeable odor and flavor caused by a defective or diseased cork.

corps (French): Body.

corse (French): Full-bodied.

cosecha (Spanish): Harvest; crop; vintage.

cote (French): A hill or slope covered with vineyards.

coulant (French): In winetasting, a term applied to a pleasant wine that is easy to drink and usually low in tannin and alcohol.

couleur (French), *color* (Spanish): Color; in a good wine, it should be clear and brilliant.

coupage (French): The blending of wines.

coupe (French): A blended wine.

courtier (French), *corredor* (Spanish): Broker.

cremant (French): Slightly sparkling; crackling.

criadera (Spanish): A stage in the *solera* system used in Jerez, Spain, for making sherries.

criado y embotellado por (Spanish): Grown and bottled by.

cru (French): Growth, i.e., a specific vineyard and the wine it produces.

cru classe (French): Classified growth (See above).

crudite (French): A raw, unfinished wine.

crust: A deposit cast up by aged wines, particularly ports, which forms a film on the inner surface of the bottle.

cuit (French), *cotto* (Italian): Heated, or "cooked."

cup: An iced wine drink, usually containing fruit, sugar and soda water.

cuvaison (French): In making red wine, the practice of allowing the juice and grape skins to ferment together in the early stages to obtain the desired color.

cuvee (French): A specific batch of wine from a particular vineyard, or wine press; a vintage; literally, a tub or vatful.

decant: To transfer wine from its bottle to another container, so as to separate clear wine from any sediment. This is necessary as a rule only for red wines more than five years old.

decanter: A glass bottle, or carafe, into which wine is transferred for serving.

degorgement (French): A technique for removing sediment from champagne bottles while they are in storage.

delicat (French), *delicate:* Said of a wine that is light, fine or elegant rather than big, full or coarse.

demi (French): Half.

demijohn: A fat-bodied jug, usually covered in wicker, which may vary in capacity from two to 10 gallons. The French term is *Dame Jeanne* or *bonbonne.*

demi-muid (French): A cask of the Cognac region which holds 157 gallons.

demi-queue (French): A cask used in the Burgundy region holding 228 liters.

demi-sec (French): Half-dry, meaning sweet when applied to champagne. A bottle labeled *demi-sec* contains six to eight percent sugar, which is about the maximum on the market.

denominacion de origen (Spanish): Spanish system of controlling the use of place names in the labeling of wines, and hence their authenticity.

density: The body or thickness of a wine, a property measured by specific gravity (See below).

depart (French): Aftertaste.

deposit: Sediment released by wine while aging in the bottle.

depot (French): Deposit, sediment.

dextrin: A gummy carbohydrate substance obtained from starch and converted to grape sugar by the action of hot acid or malt.

diastase: The enzyme in malted barley that converts dextrin to sugar.

dolce (Italian): Sweet.

domaine (French): Estate; in wine terms, it may refer to all vineyard holdings of a particular estate, even though they are widely separated geographically, and the product bottled under different appellations. The name of the *domaine* then appears as the producer.

domane (German): A vineyard owned or managed by the state.

dosage (French): A syrup added to champagnes after the *degorgement.* It usually consists of cane sugar plus old wine, or, less often, brandy. The amount varies from a teaspoonful to two ounces, and determines whether a champagne will be labeled as *brut, extra dry, sec* or *demi-sec.*

douil (French): An open cask used to transport grapes from the fields to the pressing house.

doux (French): Sweet; not a term applied to good wines, which, if naturally sweet, are usually described as *moelleux;* also, the sweetest type of champagne.

dry: In wine terms, the opposite of sweet is not sour, but dry, i.e., a dry wine is one lacking in sugar. In California wine parlance, dry sometimes implies "unfortified."

drying: The stage at which fruit and sugar lose predominance in the young wine, yielding to tannin.

duftig (German): Fragrant.

dulce (Spanish): Sweet.

dulce apagado (Spanish): Fortified, unfermented

grape juice used as a sweetener in other wines, particularly sherries. See *apagado.*

dunder: The leftover part of sugarcane juice, used in making heavier rums.

dur (French): Hard; harsh; austere.

earthy: In French, *gout de terroir.* In winetasting, a taste quality reminiscent of the soil in which the wine was produced. Highly valued in some areas, such as Burgundy, but disagreeable if too pronounced.

echt (German): Real; genuine; also, unsugared.

edel (German): Noble; superior; fine.

Edelbeerenauslese (German): A pre-1971 term for a particularly fine *Beernauslese* (See above).

Edelfaule (German): Noble rot; see *pourriture noble.*

Edelsusse (German): Natural sweetness from the noble rot.

edes (Hungarian): Sweet.

egrappage (French): The removing of the stems from the grapes before pressing.

Ehrwein (German): Very fine wine.

Eigene abfullung (German): Producer-bottled.

Eiswein (German): Wine produced from frozen or partially frozen grapes, literally "ice wine." The grapes are gathered from certain Rhine and Moselle vineyards after a severe night frost. The frost is less able to penetrate the best grapes (most heavily sugared), hence an unusually fine wine is produced, which has been compared to Auslese and Edelbeerenauslese. Eiswein, however, is produced but rarely, and then in limited quantities.

elegance (French): In winetasting, a term applied to a small, light wine. It is faint praise, however, being a good deal less flattering than "distinguished." The wine in question is usually from a great vineyard in an off-year and does not promise longevity.

elixir (French): Early term for liqueur.

enology, oenology: The knowledge or study of wines.

enzyme: An organic substance that acts as a catalyst in fermentation.

epluchage (French): The sorting of grapes before pressing to remove less desirable specimens.

Erben (German): Heirs.

erdig (German): Earthy.

espumoso (Spanish): Sparkling.

Essenz, Eszencia (Hungarian): A fine Tokay of extreme rarity, which, according to legend, could revive the dying when all doctoring had failed.

estate-bottled: Bottled by the producer-owner of the vineyard. A term much used in Burgundy, and virtually synonomous with *chateau-bottled* and *Original-abfullung.* The practice is desirable since it is a pretty good guarantee of authenticity, and sometimes an indicator of superior quality.

esters: Organic compounds formed by the reaction of acid and alcohol, which give bouquet to a wine or liquor.

estufa (Portuguese): Hothouse; in the manufacture of Madeira, a heated room where recently made Madeira is held until it acquires the distinctive Madeira taste.

ether: An aromatic substance found in mature wines and liquors formed by the dehydration of alcohol molecules. It contributes a sweet smell to the bouquet.

ethyl alcohol: See **Alcohol.**

extra dry, extra sec (French): In champagnes, the next step up from *brut* in sweetness.

fade (German): Insipid; stale; flat.

faible (French): Thin; weak; feeble.

Fass (German): Barrel; a 600-liter wine cask used for Rhine wines; also called *halbstuck.*

feine (German): Fine.

feints: The first and last parts of a distillation from a pot still and also the least desirable parts. Nicknamed "head and tails."

ferme (French): A strong, full wine; may indicate too much body.

fett (German): Fat; in wine terms, full-bodied, big.

fiasco (Italian): Flask; a round-bottomed bottle, covered in woven straw, used for Italian wines such as Chianti, Orvieto, etc.

filter: To clarify a wine before bottling by passing it through any of several different types of filters.

finage (French): The bounds or limits of a parish or district, hence all the vineyards contained therein.

fine: In winetasting, a term used to describe a wine of unmistakable superiority.

fine, fine maison (French): Brandy; a restaurant's house brandy whose origin is unknown, or, at least unrevealed.

finesse (French): Said of a wine that is out of the ordinary, usually indicating a degree of delicacy and pleasantness.

fining: A method of clarifying wine by adding substances to it which gradually settle out, bringing with them suspended particles.

flagon: Bulbous container for wine or liquor. Antiquated term for flask.

flask: A squat, flat-sided bottle for wine or liquor with a capacity ranging from eight to 32 ounces; a flattened container for liquid, small enough to be carried in the pocket.

flinty: Term applied to a white wine such as Chablis which has a dry, clean, hard taste and a special bouquet reminiscent of flint struck by steel; in French, *pierre a fusil.*

fliers: Whitish, fluffy particles which sometimes appear in a white wine that has been transported to a colder climate. They do not affect the taste and disappear if the wine is rested in a warm temperature.

flor (Spanish): Flower; regarding sherry, a property of the yeast native to Jerez, in Spain, and now used in California and elsewhere. It forms a film, or flower, on the surface of the wine. It may attain a thickness of ½ inch and look a little like cottage cheese. It contributes a special flavor and bouquet to the drier sherries, such as *fino* and *amontillado.*

flowery: In winetasting, a term of high praise applied to wines, especially whites, whose aroma recalls the fragrance of flowers.

fort (French): Strong; highly alcoholic.

fortified wines: Wines whose alcoholic content has been boosted by the addition of brandy or other spirits at some point in the manufacture. This is customary with such wines as port, sherry, muscatel, Madeira and Marsala, yet in the United States the term is banned from the label.

foudre (French): A large cask used to store wines.

foxiness: A unique taste quality of native American wines and grapes. It is immediately noticeable, and has been described as "very grapey."

franc de gout (French): Tasting of the natural grape; clean-tasting.

frappe (French): Iced; a liqueur poured over cracked ice.

frisch (German): Fresh.

frizzante (Italian): Slightly sparkling; crackling.

fruity, fruite (French), *fruchtig* (German): Said of a wine that has a definite flavor of fresh fruit. It is a pleasant characteristic of many young wines.

Fuder (German): An oak cask used to store wine in the Moselle region. Its usual capacity is 1,000 liters (264 United States gallons).

full: A winetaster's term related to body and vaguely connected with alcohol content, specific gravity and the presence of mineral salts.

fulle (German): Fullness; richness.

fumet (French): Bouquet.

fumeux (French): Spirited; heady.

fusel oil: A mixture of acids, higher alcohols, aldehydes and esters found in all spirits in low concentration. It imparts a special flavor to liquor once it matures.

Gay-Lussac: A French scientist who invented the alcoholometer and certain standard measures of alcohol strength.

gefallig (German): Pleasing; obliging.

Gemarkung (German): Wine growing district boundary.

genereux (French): In winetasting, a hearty, warming wine.

gewachs (German): Growth or vineyard, and on a label is usually followed by the producer's name.

gezuckert (German): Improved; sugared.

glatt (German): Smooth.

gout (French): Taste.

gout americain (French): Among champagnes, means fairly sweet, prepared for the South American market.

gout anglais (French): Among champagnes, quite dry, i.e., appropriate for the English market.

gout de bois (French): Woody taste.

gout de bouchon (French): Corky.

gout de paille (French): Musty.

gout de pique (French): Vinegary.

gout de terroir (French): Earthy.

gout d'event (French): Flat.

gradi (Italian): Degree; *gradi alcool* means percentage of alcohol when followed by a number.

grain spirits: Spirits distilled from malted and unmalted grain in a patent still.

grand vin (French): Great wine; not a reliable indicator of quality.

green: In winetasting, said of a wine that is raw, harsh, or disagreeably acidic; also, a young, light wine such as the *vinho verde* (green wine) of Portugal.

gros producteur (French): Said of a vine that is a prolific producer of grapes, but whose wine is of less than fine quality.

grossier (French): Rough; harsh.

growth cru, (French): A vineyard and the wine it produces.

grun (German): Green; immature.

gut (German): Good.

habzo (Hungarian): Sparkling.

Halb-fuder (German): A Moselle wine cask whose capacity is half a *Fuder* (See above), i.e., 500 liters.

Halb-stuck (German): A 600-liter winecask used in the Rhinegau; also called *Fass.*

hard: In winetasting, said of a wine that is austere, excessively tannic; an excellent wine may be hard in its youth, and then mellow with age.

harmonisch (German): Well balanced; harmonious.

harsh: Extremely hard and usually astringent to boot.

hart (German): Hard; acidic; vinegary.

heads: See *feints,* above.

hecho (Spanish): Made; a completed wine.

herb (German): Bitter.

high wines: The middle distillate, i.e., the useful product of a pot still when the heads and tails have been discarded.

Hochgewachs (German): Superior growth.

hock: Any Rhine wine, but used only in English. Short for Hochheimer.

hogshead: A large barrel or cask. The capacity varies anywhere from 66 (as in sherry) to 140 gallons.

honigartig (German): Honeylike.

Hospices de Beaune (French): A charity hospital whose endowment consists almost entirely of vineyards. It is located in Beaune, Burgundy, and its annual revenue is provided by a yearly wine auction. The wines are generally of superior quality.

hot: Said of a wine with a peppery taste.

hubsch (German): Nice.

hydrometer: An instrument used to measure the specific gravity of a liquid.

imbottigliato (Italian): Bottled.

imperiale: A large Bordeaux bottle holding six liters; in champagne terms, a Methuselah.

I.N.A.O (French): *Institut National des Appellations d'Origine des Vins et Eaux-de-Vie.*

informing grape: The grape operative in establishing a wine's varietal character.

isinglass: A fish gelatin, used to fine a wine.

jarra (Spanish): A jar used in sherry blending that serves as a standard measuring unit. Its capacity varies from 11½ to 12½ liters.

Jeroboam: An outsize champagne or Bordeaux bottle with a capacity of 104 ounces, i.e., four bottles.

jigger: A shot-glass with a 1½ ounce capacity.

jung (German): Young.

Kabinett (German): *Qualitatswein mit Pradikat* of the driest sort.

keg: A small barrel, usually holding less than 10 gallons.

Keller (German): Cellar.

Kellerabfullung (German): Estate-bottled.

klein (German): Small.

Korper (German): Body.

kraftig (German): Robust; strong (in the alcoholic sense).

krausen (German): A way of carbonating beer.

lagar (Spanish, Portuguese): A trough for pressing or treading grapes.

Lage (German): A named vineyard. Compare *climat, cru.*

lager: In beermaking, to store beer for aging and sedimentation, hence any beer so treated. All American beers are lagers. The process originated in Germany.

legendig (German): Lively; fresh.

lees: Coarse sediment left in the barrel by young wines before bottling.

leger (French): Light; also, a wine that may be lacking in body or alcoholic content.

legs: In winetasting, a rough measure of a wine's body or density, as in "thick legs." This is judged by how quickly a wine runs back down after being swirled around the inside of a glass.

length: The attribute of a wine with a lingering aftertaste.

levante (Spanish): A hot wind from the Sahara Desert that blows across Spain's sherry region.

lias (Spanish): Wine lees.

licoroso (Spanish): Heady; fortified.

Limousin (French): A type of oak used to make cognac casks.

liqueur: A distilled spirit, sweetened and flavored. An after-dinner drink; a cordial.

liqueur de tirage (French): A solution of sugar and yeast culture added to a young champagne to insure a second fermentation inside the bottle.

liqueur d'expedition (French): See *dosage.*

liquoreux (French): Sweet; said of an unfortified white wine that is rich in natural grape sugar.

lodge: In Portugal, a warehouse where Porto wine is stored in Vila Nova de Gaia. In Madeira, a warehouse where Madeira wine is stored in Funchal.

low wine: In whisky-making, the bulk distillate obtained from the first operation in a pot still.

mache (French): Chewed; said of a thick wine, i.e., almost of a consistency to be chewed.

maderise (French): maderized. The term means to become like Madeira wine and is applied especially to whites and roses that darken and take on the characteristic aroma and taste due to oxidation and exposure to heat.

mager (German): Thin; lacking in body.

magnum: An outsize bottle, double the normal capacity, used for champagnes, clarets and burgundies.

maigre (French): Thin; weak.

malts: Scotch whisky distilled from a mash of malted barley.

mashing: In whisky making, the mixing of ground meal and malt with water to create the mash, the raw material for fermentation. In the mash, starches are liquified and turned into sugar by diastase, then converted to alcohol by yeast.

master of wine (M.W.): In the English wine trade, a professional title requiring years of study and rigorous examination.

metallic: Akin to flinty (See above), but more an acrid, unpleasant taste in a wine—usually white but occasionally a red—that recalls the tang of metal.

Methuselah: An outsize bottle used for champagnes with a capacity of 179 to 208 ounces, i.e., seven to eight regular bottles.

mildew: A grapevine disease caused by a virus or fungus.

millesime (French): Date; vintage year.

mise d'origine (French): Bottled by the shipper.

mise en bouteille a la propriete (French): Bottled by the shipper.

mise en bouteille au chateau (French): In the Bordeaux region, estate-bottled (See above).

mise en bouteille au domaine (French): In the Burgundy region, estate-bottled.

mistelle (French): The French version of *apagado* (See above), used to sweeten vermouths and other aperitif wines.

moelle, moelleux (French): In winetasting, a term used to describe white wines that are smooth and mellow, i.e., not bone dry, but not precisely sweet either.

Monimpex (Hungarian): An acronym used as the title of the Hungarian state wine export monopoly.

mou (French): In winetasting, a term meaning soft, or lacking in character.

monopole (French): Monopoly; sometimes used on wine labels in connection with a trademarked name, but has no particular meaning as to origin or quality.

mousseux (French): Sparkling.

mur (French): Mature; balanced; fruity.

must, mout (French), *Moot* (German), *mosto* (Spanish): Unfermented grape juice in the process of becoming wine.

mustimeter: A device to measure the sugar content of must.

musty: Said of a wine with an unpleasant odor and flavor, due usually to unhygienic conditions in the cellar and casks.

mute (French): See *apagado.*

Mycodermae aceti: Vinegar yeast.

Mycodermai vine: Wine yeast.

Natur, Naturrein, Naturwein (German): Wine label terms meaning no sugar has been added either before or after fermentation.

nature (French): Champagne label term synonymous with *brut;* in former times, it meant still champagne.

Nebuchadnezzar: An outsize champagne bottle with a capacity of 520 ounces, i.e., 20 regular bottles.

negociant-eleveur (French): In the wine trade, a wholesale merchant. He buys wine from the grower, bottles it and markets it.

nerf (French): Strong; said of a wine with high alcohol content.

nero (Italian): Black; in the wine sense, very dark red.

nerveux (French): Well balanced; vigorous; possessing good keeping qualities.

nervig (German): Vigorous; full-bodied.

neutral spirits: Liquors distilled at a proof of 190 or more. The term is used even after they are reduced in proof.

Nicolauswein (German): Wine made from grapes gathered on St. Nicholas Day, December 6.

nip: Miniature bottle of liquor.

nose: Bouquet or aroma.

nu (French): Bare; said of a wine price quote that excludes the cost of the cask.

nube (Spanish): Cloudiness in wine.

Ochsle (German): Scale for measuring the sugar content of must.

octave, octavilla (Spanish): In the sherry trade, an eighth of a cask, or 16½ gallons.

oeil de perdrix (French): Partridge eye; pale pink/bronze color of certain sparkling wines made from black grapes.

oenology: See enology, above.

oidium: Powdery mildew, a fungus that attacks grape vines.

olig (German): Oily; said of a wine with a thick consistency.

organoleptic examination: An evaluation of the quality of alcoholic beverages through the human senses (sight, taste, smell), as opposed to laboratory analysis.

Original-Abfullung (German): Estate-bottling.

overproof: Said of a liquor whose proof exceeds 100 (50 percent alcohol).

oxidized: A condition resulting from a wine's being exposed too much to air. Freshness is lost, and the color darkens. The first stage of maderization (See *maderise*, above), an undesirable state.

palma (Spanish): A special chalk mark, resembling a Y, used to designate a superior *fino* sherry.

palo cortado (Spanish): Chalk mark used to designate *dos rayas*, sherries that have developed *fino* characteristics: Resembles a cross.

passito (Italian): A wine made from partially raisined grapes—generally a dessert wine, but sometimes a dry wine.

pasteurization: The sterilizing of wine by heating it to between 130°–170° F (54.4°–76.7° C) and holding it there for a short time. Named for Louis Pasteur, the French scientist who developed the process. Fine wines are never pasteurized because it forecloses further development and possible improvement in the bottle.

patent still: A still invented by Aeneas Coffey and patented in 1839. It operates continuously and produces a purer alcohol than the traditional pot still, which must be refilled after each distillation.

pateaux (French): Said of a wine with a thick consistency that is unpleasant and sometimes cloying.

pelure d'oignon (French): Onion skin; but when referring to wine, a russet tinge acquired by certain red wines on aging, or by other light reds or roses.

perfume: In winetasting, a synonym for fragrance or aroma, the attributes of a young wine, rather than bouquet, which is acquired with age.

Perlwein (German): Crackling wine; slightly sparkling.

petillant (French): Crackling; slightly sparkling.

petit (French): Small; thin.

Pfarrgut (German): Parochial estate. A vineyard that contributes to the support of a parsonage.

Phylloxera vastatrix: An insect, the grapevine louse, which is native to the eastern United States. In the 1860s it was accidentally imported into Europe where it laid waste to the European grapevines of the *vitis vinifera* species. European viticulture did not recover until *vitis vinifera* plants were grafted onto American roots, which are resistant to the insect.

piece (French): An oak barrel used for storing wine in the Burgundy and Beaujolais areas. Its capacity varies, being either 56 or 60 U.S. gallons.

pierre a fusil (French): Gun flint; in wine, a flinty taste (See above).

pikant (German): Piquant; a fresh, rather tart wine.

pipe: A large oak barrel used for storing and shipping port and Madeira wines. Capacities vary, being 138 United States gallons for port, and 110 for Madeira.

piquant (French): A tart white wine, but pleasantly so. *Pikant* in German.

pique (French): Said of a wine that has begun to turn to vinegar.

piquette (French): Originally, a mixture of marc, pomace or grape pressings, plus sugar and water. A sort of subwine given away free to cellar workers. More recently a derogatory term for any thin, acidic wine.

pisador (Spanish): In Jerez, one who treads the juice out of grapes.

plastering: In making sherry, the addition of gypsum or plaster to the grapes before fermentation, a legitimate procedure that improves the color and clarity of the resulting wine.

plat (French): Flat; lifeless.

plein (French): Well-balanced; full-bodied; fairly alcoholic.

pomace: The residue of skins, seeds and stems left in the wine press or fermenting vat after the wine has been drawn off. The French term is *marc*.

pony: A brandy or liqueur glass with a one-ounce capacity.

portes-greffes (French): The rootstock of American grapevines resistant to the plant louse, *Phylloxera vastatrix*. Grafting the *vitis vinifera* scion onto it revived the European wine industry in the 19th century.

pot: A wine measure equivalent to 2/3 of the regular bottle.

pot still: A still of the old-fashioned sort used for such liquors as cognac, malt whisky and Irish whisky. It has a fat belly and a tapering neck like an alchemist's alembic, and needs refilling after each distillation. Compare *patent still* (See above).

pourriture noble (French): The mold, *Botrytis cinerea*, dubbed "noble rot" because the grapes it afflicts do a better job of concentrating sugar and flavor, thus improving the quality of the wine. It most frequently occurs in the Rhine area and Sauterne country. It is called *Edelfaule* in German.

precoce (French): Precocious; early maturing; can refer to grapes, wine or both.

pressoir (French), *prensa* (Spanish): Wine press.

proof: A measure of the alcoholic strength of a liquid derived from an old way of "proving" or testing. In America, proof is expressed in a number which is exactly twice the percentage of alcohol contained in the liquid, e.g., 86 proof whisky is 43 percent alcohol, 100 proof vodka is 50 percent alcohol, and so on. "Proof spirits" are those containing 50 percent alcohol by volume at a temperature of 60° F (15.6° C). Those that vary are said to be "overproof" or "underproof."

puncheon: A wine cask with a capacity of about 600 liters (160 United States gallons). This is the expected yield of one ton of grapes.

punt: The hump in the bottom of some wine and champagne bottles.

puttony (Hungarian): A basket or hod used in the harvest of Tokay grapes. Also a measure of quality in some Tokays, going from one puttony to six. That is, quality is judged by how many baskets of overripe grapes (*Auslese* type) were added to the cask. This high quality Tokay is called *aszu*.

Qualitatswein (German): Wine of superior quality (according to specified criteria) from any of 11 declared regions.

Qualitatswein mit Pradikat (German): *Qualitatswein* of special distinction.

quarter bottle: A wine bottle with a capacity of one-fourth that of a regular bottle, i.e., six to 6½ ounces. In champagne terms, a split.

quarter cask: A cask with a capacity one-fourth of the normal-sized cask, whatever that may be for a given region.

queue (French): An antiquated measure of volume or capacity equivalent to 456 liters or two standard Burgundy *pieces*.

quinquina (French): Quinine, an ingredient of most French aperitif wines.

quinta (Portuguese): Vineyard; winery estate.

race (French): Breed.

racking: The practice of drawing off clear wine from one cask to another, leaving behind the lees. An indispensable procedure in wine making that is done to some fine wines several times before bottling.

rancio (Spanish): A special taste imparted to certain wines during aging in the wood, especially to such fortified wines as Madeira, port, Marsala, and Banyuls. Unlike maderization, it is desirable.

rassig (German): Characterized by good breeding.

rauh (German): Harsh; raw.

raya (Spanish): In the sherry region, a chalk mark used to designate wines that will develop into *finos* and *amontillados*.

recemment degorge (French): Said of a champagne that recently has had the sediment removed, i.e., "disgorged."

recolte (French): Vintage.

recorking: The replacing of a rotten cork. This is routine for some wines that remain in the bottle for 20 to 25 years, such as Madeira. It is usually acknowledged on the label.

rectification: Redistillation of a liquor with any of a number of objects in view: to obtain a purer alcohol (as in vodka), to flavor with herbs, such as juniper (in gin), etc. Adding sweetening and coloring matter may also be construed as rectifying.

redondo (Spanish): Round; in wines, rounded, well-balanced.

reduce: Adding water to a liquor to lower its alcoholic strength.

refresh: To rejuvenate an old wine by adding a young wine to it in the cask. It may also be done to spirits, such as brandies.

Rehoboam: An outsize champagne bottle with a capacity of 156 ounces, i.e., six regular bottles.

reif (German): Ripe; mature; sweet.

rein (German): Pure.

reintonig (German): Well-balanced.

remuage (French): The shaking and turning of champagne bottles in their racks during aging. This essential operation brings the sediment down to the cork for later disgorging. In California, the process is called *riddling.*

Rentamt (German): Revenue office.

reserve: A word frequently seen on wine labels. It has no agreed meaning in that context, but usually manages to suggest a wine of special or mature quality. It means whatever the bottler chooses it to mean.

riche (French): Rich; full-bodied; good bouquet.

rick: In liquor warehouses, the rack or framework in which storage barrels are placed. As a verb, it means to place or rack barrels.

riddling: See *remuage*, above.

robe: The film of color a highly pigmented red wine leaves on the inside of a glass. See *legs*, above.

rociar (Spanish): To sprinkle; in sherry making, to refresh.

rondeur (French): Roundness.

rose (French and English), *rosado* (Spanish), *rosato* (Italian): Pink wine.

rosso (Italian): Red.

rotwein (German): Red wine.

roundness: Balance; completeness; lack of major defects; drinkability; low acidity; substantial alcoholic strength.

rund (German): Round; see above.

saccharometer: A device to measure the sugar content of must, wines or liqueurs.

saftig (German): Juicy; succulent.

Salmanazar: An outsize champagne bottle with a capacity of from 270 to 312 ounces, i.e., 10 to 12 regular bottles.

sancocho (Spanish): A syrup used to sweeten and color sherry wine. It is obtained by boiling must until it is reduced by two-thirds.

sauber (German): Clean; elegant.

scantling: A beam used to support casks in wine cellars.

schal (German): Musty; stale; flat.

Schaumwein (German): Sparkling wine made either by the champagne process or the bulk fermentation (Charmat) process.

Schloss (German): Castle; in wine terms, the equivalent of the French *chateau*, i.e., the entire property including the vineyards, the buildings and the wine.

Schlossabzug (German): Estate-bottled.

schnapps (Dutch and German): Liquor, spirits.

Schwefel (German): Sulfur; the smell of sulfur in a wine's bouquet.

sec (French): Dry; among champagnes, a fairly sweet type.

secco (Italian), *seco* (Spanish): Dry.

sediment: A deposit released by wine as it ages in the bottle, normally containing bitartrates, tannins, pigments and mineral salts.

Sekt (German): Sparkling wine; champagne; by treaty with France, the word *champagne* (on a label) can be used only to denote the French product.

self whiskies: A straight, or unblended, Scotch malt whisky.

seve (French): Sap; said of a wine that is vigorous or aromatic.

Sikes: Refers to the hydrometer and tables for measuring alcoholic strengths invented by Bartholomew Sikes; used in England.

skunky: Said of beer that has gone off due to excessive exposure to heat and light.

slatko (Yugoslavian): Sweet.

solear (Spanish): Sunning, a practice in the sherry regions of Spain of exposing the grapes to the sun for 24 to 48 hours.

solera (Spanish): A set of tiered casks, and a system of maturing and blending fortified wines, especially sherries. It tends to produce consistent quality year after year.

sophistiquer (French): To adulterate or falsify a wine in an attempt to cover up defects.

souche (French): Vine rootstock; *cep.*

sour mash: A method of fermenting whisky mash in which a portion of the yeast is taken from a previous mash and mixed with fresh yeast to produce the desired results. The other method is called *sweet* mash.

soutirer (French): Racking (See above).

soyeux (French): Silky; absence of rough qualities.

Spatlese (German): Late harvest; a type of wine made from grapes picked after the general harvest and, therefore, riper and possessing of more natural sugar than the ordinary grape. Such a wine is richer, fuller-bodied and a little sweeter than other wines from the same vineyard, and a lot more expensive.

specific gravity: For liquids, a measure of density expressed as a ratio of the weight of the liquid to the weight of an equal volume of water.

spirits: Distilled alcoholic beverage; liquor.

split: A quarter bottle, i.e., six to 6½ ounces.

spritzig (German): Crackling; slightly effervescent.

spumante (Italian): Sparkling.

stahlig (German): Steely; austere.

stalky: Said of a wine that is harsh due to

excessive pressure on the pulp.

steely: Very hard; austere; some tartness.

still: Distilling apparatus.

still wine: Nonsparkling; also, no additional alcohol or flavoring.

stirrup cup: One for the road. Name is derived from the old custom of having a drink with a guest after he had mounted his horse.

stolno vino (Yugoslavian): Table wine.

Stuck, *Stuckfasser* (German): A wine measure of the Rhineland equalling 1200 liters; a wine cask of that capacity.

subtle: Said of a wine whose flavor represents a delicate blend, with no particular element dominating.

sugaring: Adding sugar to grape-must before fermentation.

suho (Yugoslavian): Dry.

sulfur: Used to treat the insides of casks as a sterilizing agent that prevents the refermentation of sweet wines. It can be overdone and affect the taste of the wine.

suss (German): Sweet.

sweet mash: Compare *sour mash* (See above). The other method of adding yeast to whisky mash to induce fermentation, using only fresh yeast.

Tafelwein (German): Dinner wine; ordinary wine from any of the five *Tafelwein* regions.

tannin: An astringent element in the taste of wine due to organic compounds drawn from the skin and stems of the grapes. It puckers the mouth, and is more evident in younger wines, particularly those with the ability to age well. During aging, much of the tannin drops out as sediment, mellowing the taste.

teinturier (French): Dyer; grape varieties with red or red purple juice, cultivated for their ability to add color to the must.

tendre (French): A light and delicate quality of a wine. Usually said of young wines that are fresh, charming and easy to drink.

tete de cuvee (French): Superior growth.

tierce (French), *terzo* (Italian), *tercero* (Spanish): A third; a cask whose capacity is one-third that of a butt or pipe.

tilts: In wine storage, bars used to lever casks or scantlings into the desired positions.

tinto (Spanish): Red wine.

tirage (French): The drawing off of a wine from cask to bottle; in the Champagne region, the term refers to the first bottling when the wine is still and includes the *liqueur de tirage* (See above) that induces the second fermentation inside the bottle.

tonelero (Spanish): Barrel maker.

tonneau (French): Same as *tonne*, i.e., tun or cask. Specifically, in Burgundy, a wine measure equal to four *barriques*, each containing 225 liters, for a total of 900 liters.

Traube (German): Bunch of grapes.

Traubenkelter (German): Hydraulic wine press.

Trockenbeerenauslese (German): The highest category of fine German wines. It is made from selected, individually picked grapes that have been left on the vine so long they are nearly as dry as raisins. The result is a remarkable wine that is very sweet, and very expensive.

uisgebeatha, *uisgebaugh* (Celtic): Water of life; origin of the English word "whisky."

ullage: Loss of liquor from a container due to evaporation or spillage; also, the amount by which it falls short of being full; also, the air space between the surface of the liquor and the cork, or top of the cask. "To ullage" is to fill up the space by topping off the cask or bottle. If ullage is due to a bad cork, the wine may be spoiled. The term comes to English through French from the Latin *ad oculum*, i.e., (fill) to the eye, or bunghole.

underproof: Said of a spiritous liquor containing less than 50 percent alcohol by volume. See *proof*, above.

ungezuckert (German): Unsugared; pure.

use (French): Worn out; a wine past its prime and on the decline.

uva (Spanish): Grape.

varietal: An American wine term denoting a wine named for a variety of grape rather than a town, district, or vineyard. Legally, a varietal wine must be made from at least 51 percent of the juice of the named variety.

vats: Containers for fermenting or blending alcoholic beverages.

vatting: Mixing or blending in a vat.

veloute (French): Velvety; said of wines that are mature, mellow and soft. Compare *soyeux*, above.

vendange (French), *vendemmia* (Italian), *vendimia* (Spanish): Grape harvest; not used in the sense of vintage as referring to a specific year.

vendange tardif (French): Late harvest; compare *Spatlese*.

venencia (Spanish): Special cup used to draw samples through the bunghole of a sherry cask. It may be of silver and attached to a pliable whalebone handle, or simply a length of bamboo with the bottom section forming the cup.

viejo (Spanish): Old.

vif (French): In winetasting, said of a young wine that is lively and fresh, with a tartness somewhere between ***tendre*** (See above) and ***vivace*** (See below).

vigne (French): Vine; also, a small parcel in a vineyard, or an individual holding within a named vineyard whose ownership may be split among several interests.

vigneron (French): Wine grower; vineyardist.

vignoble (French): Vineyard; often a vineyard area, or a collection of vineyards of a district, that possesses an appellation of its own.

vin (French): Wine.

vina (Spanish): Vineyard.

vin blanc (French): White wine.

vin cuit (French): A concentrate used to improve thin wines; also, in winetasting, said of a wine whose taste smacks of concentrate, or suggests it has been reduced before fermentation to increase alcoholic strength and body.

vin de garde: A wine with good aging qualities, i.e., worth laying down in a wine cellar.

vin de goutte (French): Wine from the end of a pressing, which is generally of poor quality.

vin de messe (French): Altar wine.

vin de paille (French): Straw wine; a sweet, rich wine made from grapes that have been spread out on straw to dry.

vin de pays (French): Small wine of a particular region, consumed locally.

vin doux (French): Sweet wine.

vinedo (Spanish): Vineyard.

vineux (French): Vinous; winy.

vin gris (French): Very pale rose wine made usually in Lorraine and Alsace.

vinho (Portuguese): Wine.

vinho claro (Portuguese): Natural wine.

vinho estufado (Portuguese): Wine baked in an *estufa*, a process to which Madeira is submitted.

vinho generoso (Portuguese): Fortified wine of superior quality and specific origin.

vinho surdo (Portuguese): Fortified wine.

vinho verde (Portuguese): Green wine in the sense of youth, not color. It is a name given to light white, red, or rose wines grown in northern Portugal, near the Spanish province of Galicia. They are pleasant, and some are lightly sparkling.

viniculture: The whole science and business of producing wine, from cultivation of the vine through marketing the finished product.

vini tipici (Italian): Typical wines.

vin mousseux (French): Sparkling wine.

vin nature (French): Unfortified, unsweetened wine.

vino (Spanish): Wine.

vino corriente (Spanish): Ordinary wine.

vino crudo (Spanish): Immature wine.

vino de anada (Spanish): In sherry making, a young wine of a particular vintage, which is ready for the *criadera*.

vino de color (Spanish): In sherry making, a concentrate used to give color and sweetness to the final product.

vino de crianza (Spanish): A wine suitable to be made into sherry.

vino de mesa (Spanish): Table wine.

vino frizzante (Italian): Crackling wine; lightly sparkling.

vino liquoroso (Italian): Very sweet wine.

vino maestro (Spanish): Master wine. In blending, a sweet, full-bodied wine added to weaker, thinner wines to give them body and character.

vin ordinaire (French): Ordinary wine for everyday use; wine of unknown or unstated origin, sold as white, red or rose.

vinosite (French), *Vinosity.* State or quality of being vinous, winy; also said of a wine with a strong grapey bouquet, or high alcoholic strength.

vino spumante (Italian): Sparkling wine.

vinous: Pertaining to wine; having the nature or characteristic of wine; addicted to wine drinking.

vin rose (French): Pink wine.

vin rouge (French): Red wine.

vin santo (Italian): Also *vino santo:* A white wine made usually in Tuscany from partly raisined grapes. It is sweet and has a golden color.

vin sec (French): Dry wine.

vintage: The grape harvest and the wine made from the grapes of that year. By extension, the year the grapes were harvested for a particular wine, so stated on the label, e.g., *vintage 1970.*

vintage wine: Wine dated as to year of vintage. Some wines, e.g., champagne, are dated only in exceptionally good years, hence the term is used to imply a fine wine. Some wines are dated each year, however, whether exceptional or not.

virgin brandy: Unblended cognac.

viticulture: Grape growing, and the science thereof. Compare *viniculture.*

vitis (Latin): Vine.

vivace (French): In winetasting, a term applied to fresh, lively young wines, with a tartness that suggests they will keep well and mellow with age.

vornehm (German): High-ranking; noble; aristocratic.

voros (Hungarian): Red.

Wachstum (German): Growth; appears on a label followed by the name of the producer; must be unsugared.

wash: In whisky distilling, the fermented mash that is ready to go to the still.

weeper: A wine bottle that leaks around the cork.

Wein (German): Wine.

Weinbau (German): Cultivation of grapevines; winegrowing.

Weinberg (German): Vineyard.

Weingut (German): Vineyard or winery estate, including the vines, the buildings, cellars, etc.

Weinkeller (German): Wine cellar.

Weisswein (German): White wine.

weinig (German): Vinous.

wine broker: Middleman between grower and buyer.

Winzer (German): Wine grower; wine producer.

Winzergenossenschaft (German): Wine producers' association or cooperative.

Winzerverein (German): Wine producers' association or cooperative, usually at the peasant level.

woody: In winetasting, a term applied to table wine that tastes of wood from too much time in the cask; said also of spirits.

worn: The term refers to brandy kept too long in the cask, or wine kept too long in the bottle; past its prime; on the decline. Compare *use.*

wurzig (German): Spicy; fragrant; fruity.

Xeres: Old name for the Sherry region of Spain and the wine. It is still used in France as in *vin de Xeres.*

yayin: Wine in biblical Hebrew.

yema (Spanish): Yolk of an egg; in wine terms, the must after treading but before pressing.

yeso (Spanish): Powdered gypsum. See *plastering.*

yield: The number of tons of grapes or gallons of wine produced from a given acreage of vines. A way of judging the productivity of grapes by variety or method of culture.

zapatos de pisar (Spanish): Treading shoes used in the *lagar* of the sherry region; nail-studded.

zwicker: Alsatian white wine, usually a blend.

zymase: An enzyme of yeast that catalyzes fermentation.

1978 Wine Production Figures

Country	Hectoliters	Gallons
Italy	66,500,000	1,756,797,000
France	58,799,000	1,553,351,000
USSR	30,700,000	811,032,600
Spain	29,031,000	766,940,958
Argentina	21,080,000	556,891,440
U.S.A.	15,349,000	405,489,882
Romania	10,430,000	275,539,740
Germany	6,714,000	177,370,452
South Africa	6,000,000	158,508,000
Portugal	5,567,000	147,069,006
Yugoslavia	5,200,000	137,373,600
Chile	5,200,000	137,373,600
Hungary	4,800,000	126,806,400
Greece	4,520,000	119,409,360
Australia	3,930,000	103,822,740
Bulgaria	3,801,000	100,414,818
Brazil	2,850,000	75,291,300
Austria	2,740,000	72,385,320
Algeria	2,549,000	67,500,000
Czechoslovakia	1,400,000	36,985,200
Switzerland	1,226,000	32,388,468
Turkey	622,000	16,431,996
Uruguay	440,000	11,623,920
Israel	366,000	9,668,988
Peru	94,000	2,483,292
Bolivia	16,000	422,688

Source: *U.N. Statistical Yearbook*, 1978.

WINEBERRY

This small, bright red berry, *Rubus phoenicolasius*, is cultivated in China and Japan. Wineberry is a type of raspberry with a mediocre taste. It is used to make sweetened, iced drinks.

New Zealand wineberry *(Aristotelia racemosa)* is the pea-sized, dark red or nearly black fruit of a tree native to New Zealand. It is closely related to the **Chilean wineberry** or maqui.

WINE GRAPES

The vast majority of grapes in the following list belong to the species *Vitis vinifera*, which is the wine grape par excellence throughout the world. Some native American varieties are included, however, of the species *Vitis lambrusca*, *Vitis aestivalis* and *Vitis rotundifolia.* For a full discussion of their role in wine making, see the articles on **Wine** and the wines of various countries. This list serves to identify them briefly. Where fuller treatment is needed, the reader is referred to articles in the main alphabet.

Aglianico: An Italian grape grown chiefly in the regions of Basilicata and Campania; used to produce red wines such as Aglianico del Vulture and Taurasi.

Albana: An Italian grape grown in the Emilia region, and used to produce a semisweet white wine of the same name.

Albanello: A Sicilian grape cultivated in Syracuse province that produces a white wine, high in alcohol, which is at times dry and coarse and sometimes quite sweet.

Aleatico: A grape of the Muscat family, grown on the island of Elba and in northern Italy, which produces a sweet red wine of the same name.

Alicante-bouschet: A red-wine grape used to produce cheap, bulk wine in southern France, Algeria, Spain and Southern California.

Aligote: A highly productive grape that produces an undistinguished, shortlived white wine. It is widely grown in Burgundy, and the wine is used locally.

Ansonica: A white-wine grape of Sicily used to produce Corvo and Marsala.

Aramon: A very productive grape of the French Midi and California. It makes a low-grade red wine used for blending with other wines.

Baco: Hybrid grapes named for the French scientist Baco. His No. 1 is cultivated in some eastern U.S. vineyards for red wine; Baco No. 22 is used to make **Armagnac.**

Barbera: A dark red Italian grape, planted chiefly in the Piedmont region and in California, which produces a deep red, full-bodied wine that is agreeable but lacking in distinction.

Biancolella: An Italian white-wine grape of the Campania region used to produce Ischia Bianco.

Black Hamburg: Known chiefly as a table fruit, this black grape is occasionally used in Germany to produce wine, which has poor color and taste.

Blaue Spatburgunder: A German red-wine grape of the Baden-Wurttemberg region, which produces the best red wine of the area.

Bombino Bianco: An Italian white-wine grape grown chiefly in Abruzzo and Apulia; used to produce Trebbiano d'Abruzzo and San Severo Bianco.

Bombino Nero: An Italian red-wine grape of the Apulia region, used to produce Castel del Monte.

Boal Madeira: Also *bual.* One of the principal wine grapes of the island of Madeira. It has a greenish color, but produces the fine, golden wine for which Madeira is famous.

Bonarda: An Italian red-wine grape of the Piedmont region, used to make Boca, Fara, Ghemme and Sizzano wines.

Brunello di Montalcino: An Italian red-wine grape of the Tuscany region, used to produce a wine of the same name.

Burger: A Hungarian grape used to produce a white wine that is rather dull and low in acid. It is widely planted in Germany, Alsace and California, where it is very productive. It is used to make cheap grades of California "chablis" and "sauterne."

Cabernet-Sauvignon: A superior red-wine grape widely cultivated in France (Bordeaux) and California (North Coast counties). It is a small, thin-skinned black grape. It produces the fine clarets of France and Cabernets of California.

Cabernet Franc: A more productive variety of the Cabernet grape, the leading variety of the St. Emilion, where it produces Chinon, Bourgeuil and Champigny. It is also used to produce roses in the Loire Valley.

Canaiolo Nero: An Italian red-wine grape of Tuscany, used to produce Chianti and Vino Nobile de Montepulciano.

Carignane: A red-wine grape that is highly productive of ordinary table wine, and which is also used for blending. It is planted chiefly in southern France, Algeria and California, where its acreage is second only to Zinfandel.

Catarratto: A Sicilian grape, yellow, with a tough consistency, that produces wine used for blending in Alcamo, Corvo, Etna Bianco and Marsala.

Catawba: See **Catawba.**

Charbono: A red-wine grape that produces a rough, full-bodied, mediocre wine. Of Italian or French origin, it is well represented in California's Napa Valley.

Chardonnay: A very fine white-wine grape and a variety of the famous Pinot grape. The great white Burgundies come from this grape, including Chablis, Montrachet, Pouilly-Fuisse and champagnes too. Although not extensively planted in California, due to its relatively small yield, it produces a fine table wine marketed there as Pinot Chardonnay.

Chasselas: A well-known French table grape. Certain varieties are used to produce both red and white wines, none of superior quality. It tends to be low in acid, flat and shortlived, yet, in Switzerland, under the name Fendant, it is the leading wine grape.

Chenin Blanc: A grape of French origin that produces white wines of excellent quality, including Vouvray, Saumur, Coteaux du Layon and Savennieres. It has proved highly productive in California and is represented in Sonoma, Napa and Santa Clara counties where it produces a dry, pale wine of considerable finesse that is marketed under the varietal name.

Clairette Blanche: A white-wine grape that produces a good quality, rather neutral wine which is well-balanced and pleasant. In France, it is used in Chateauneuf-du-Pape and in Tavel rose, despite its color; alone, it has produced two wines that merit the *appellation controllee*, the Clairette du Languedoc (from Montpellier) and the Clairette de Bellegarde (from Nimes).

Colombard: A productive French grape that yields white wine of good quality. In France, it is grown mainly in the Cognac region, and the wine is dry and full-bodied. In California's North Coast counties, it produces a tart, well-balanced wine, marketed as French Colombard or "Chablis." It is also used in lesser-quality California champagnes.

Concord: See **Concord Wine.**

Corinth: An Italian grape, almost seedless and thick-skinned, which yields an inferior wine.

Cornichon: Despite its good reputation as a table grape, the varieties used for wine-making produce an inferior wine with poor color and aroma. It is grown both in France and California.

Cortese: An Italian grape, grown in Lombardy, that yields superior quality white wine. It is fresh, light and pale, and is sold under such names as Gavi and Oltrepo Pavese Cortese.

Corvino, also *Corvina Veronese:* An Italian red-wine grape grown in the Veneto region, used to produce Bardoline and Valpolicella.

Degoutant: A French grape that yields an ordinary red wine. It is medium-sized and black.

Delaware: A hybrid American grape, pink in color, that yields a white wine that is fresh, pale, well-balanced and fairly high in acid. The grape is small and sweet, and believed to be a cross between the *lambrusca* and either the *vinifera* or *aestivalis* species. It has a definite but not too strong "foxy" flavor, and is used for many eastern champagnes.

Diana: An American grape similar to the **Catawba,** which produces a wine lighter in color and higher in yield.

Dolcetto: An Italian red-wine grape grown mainly

e grapes from a California vineyard

Harvesting wine grapes in California

in the Piedmont region. It produces a soft, red wine that matures quickly and is marketed under the varietal name as in Dolcetto d'Acqui and Dolcetto di Ovada.

Dutchess: A hybrid of the native American Concord and Delaware. It has a higher yield than its parents, and the wine has little aroma but good taste.

Elbling: The German version of the burger grape (see above), which yields a flat, dull wine of poor quality. It goes into cheap, sparkling wine, or *sekt.*

Elvira: A native American hybrid grape of the *Lambrusca* type that produces a fresh and attractive white wine which, nevertheless, has a "foxy" aroma. It is cultivated in the Finger Lakes district of New York and to some extent in California.

Emerald Riesling: Not a true Riesling, but a grape originated in a California breeding program designed to develop new grape varieties that yield good table wines in the warm interior valley. It produces a dry, white wine.

Erbaluce: An Italian grape grown in the Piedmont region that is used to produce *passito* of Caluso. See *passito* in **Wine and Liquor Terms.**

Feher Szagos: A grape used in making California sherry. It originated in Hungary.

Flame Tokay: An eminent table grape, some varieties of which are used in California to make sweet wines, both red and white.

Folle Blanche: A white grape that in France has traditionally been used to make cognac, but which is gradually being supplanted by other varieties. Some are grown in California and the clean, highly acidic wine produced is marketed under the varietal name, or as "Chablis." In Armagnac, this grape is known as Piquepoul.

Freisa: An Italian red-wine grape grown chiefly in Piedmont, used to make a dry fruity wine bottled under the varietal name, e.g., Freisa d'Asti and Freisa di Chiere. It also is used in a slightly sweet, slightly sparkling wine that is rarely exported.

Fresia: American misspelling of the name for the Italian Freisa grape. Often seen in California where there are some plantings.

Furmint: The celebrated white-wine grape of Hungary used in making Tokay, and several other well-known wines. There are also plantings in California and Germany. The grape is high in sugar and yields a wine high in alcohol.

Gamay: See **Gamay.**

Gargenega: An Italian white-wine grape of the Veneto region used to produce Gambellara and **Soave.**

Gewurztraminer: An excellent white-wine grape, pink in color, grown in Germany, Alsace and California. It yields a spicy, soft wine that is heavily perfumed. It fetches a higher price than most Rieslings and other traminers. *Gewurz* means spice in German.

Giro: A Sardinian red-wine grape that yields a dessert wine like a light port called Giro di Cagliari.

Gray Riesling: A white-wine grape that produces a California varietal wine of the same name. It is not, however, a true Riesling grape but a Chauche Gris from the Poitier region. It is widely planted in the Livermore Valley where it yields a mild, soft wine with little character.

Greco: An Italian white-wine grape cultivated in the provinces of Latium, Campania and Calabria near the toe of the Italian peninsula. It is used to produce wines of some reputation, such as Frascati, Ciro Bianco and Greco di Tufo.

Green Hungarian: A California white-wine grape believed to be of Hungarian origin. It is very productive, yielding an agreeable, but rather neutral, wine, which is often used to blend into sweet, dessert types.

Grenache: A black, sweet grape put to a variety of uses in France, Spain and California. One variety is used in Chateauneuf-du-Pape, another in the sweet Banyuls, and still another in California port. It is best known, perhaps, for producing roses such as Tavel and the Grenache Rose of California.

Grignolino: An Italian red-wine grape of the Piedmont region used to produce the Grignolino d'Asti, an unusual wine with a hint of orange in its crimson color, light body, but 12 to 14 percent alcohol. California plantings of this grape are used to produce *vin rose.*

Grillo: A Sicilian white-wine grape used in the production of Marsala.

Gropello: An Italian red-wine grape, cultivated in Lombardy and used in Gropello Amarone and Riviera del Garda.

Gutedel: German name for the grape Chasselas Fendant (see above).Principal plantings are in southern Baden,where it is used to produce an ordinary table wine.

Iona: A native American red-purple grape that, nevertheless, produces a white wine. In the Finger Lakes area of New York it is used to make champagne.

Ives: A native American grape yielding a red wine of pronounced "foxy" flavor, which is heavy and coarse. It is also used in New York State Burgundies and sparkling wines.

Lagrein: A grape of the Italian Tyrol used to produce red (Trentino Lagrein) and rose (Lagrain Rosato) wines.

Lambrusco: See **Lambrusco.**

Malbec: An excellent French red-wine grape and also an abundant producer, mostly in the Bordeaux country. The wine is well-balanced and often used for blending.

Malvasia: A very ancient and very sweet white-wine grape, originally grown in Greece, but now also in Spain, Madeira, southern France, northern Italy, South Africa and California. It is used in such sweet dessert wines as malmsey and Madeira, and in some California table wines.

Malvoisie: French for *Malvasia* (see above), a grape widely planted in southern France and used in such dessert wines as Banyuls, Rivesaltes and Maury.

Marsanne: A French grape of the Rhone Valley used for blending in such wines as Chateauneuf-du-Pape and Hermitage. By itself, it produces a coarse, badly balanced white wine, inferior to even that of the Burger.

Mataro: A black Spanish grape that is also extensively planted in California. It yields a coarse red wine suitable for blending.

Merlot: A blue black grape of great importance in the Bordeaux country of France. It is productive and yields a less astringent wine used to blend with well-known wines to add softness and a fruity quality.

Mission: A European grape introduced into California in the 19th century by the Mission Fathers and used by them to produce very sweet wines. It is still widely cultivated in California and used to make port and Angelica.

Montepulciano: A good red-wine grape of southern Italy used to produce Rosso Conero, Rosso Piceno and San Severo. Montepulciano, a wine of the same name made in Tuscany, is only of passable quality.

Moursetel, also *mourastel:* A red-wine grape grown chiefly in California of undistinguished quality. In the Livermore Valley it yields a pleasant, soft but common wine.

Muller-Thurgau: A German grape variety that is a cross between the Riesling and the Sylvaner. It is widely grown and productive, yielding a pleasing, low-acid white wine.

Muscadel, also *Muscadelle:* A French white-wine grape, much used in the Bordeaux country, whose wine is used to blend with the sweeter whites at a proportion of five to 10 percent.

Muscadine: See **Muscadine.**

Muscat: See **Muscat.**

Nebbiolo: See **Nebbiolo.**

Palomino: The classic and finest grape variety for producing sherry. Practically all of the Jerez vineyards are planted in palomino, and it is extensively cultivated in California too.

Pedro Ximenez: A very sweet Spanish grape that yields a fine, dry white wine of high alcohol content (15 to 16 percent). In Sherry country, the grapes are placed in the sun to raisin, then pressed and fermented to produce a very sweet wine used as a sweetening agent in sherry.

Perricone: A Sicilian red-wine grape used to produce the wine, Corvo Rosso.

Petit Syrah: A California red-wine grape believed related to the Syrah (see below) of the Rhone Valley. It yields a full-bodied, deep-colored ordinary wine often marketed as "California Burgundy." It does not approach the quality of the French grape. Also known as *Petite Sirah.*

Picolit: An Italian white-wine grape grown in the Friuli-Venezia-Giulia region that yields a wine bottled as Colli Orientale del Friuli-Picolit.

Pinot Blanc: A distinguished white-wine grape widely planted in Burgundy vineyards and in California. Fine white Burgundies are a product of this grape and, in California, *pinot* on the label is a reliable sign of good quality.

Pinot Chardonnay: An American designation for the Chardonnay (see above) grape, which is probably not related to the Pinot group, although it produces some of the finest California white wines.

Pinot Gris, also *pinot grigio:* A grayish rose grape related to the other Pinots and planted extensively in Germany, Alsace and Italy where it goes by a number of names including Rulander and Tokay. It yields some distinguished wines, and others that are low in acid and rather flat.

Pinot Noir: A black grape of the same variety as the pinot blanc, and, though less productive, yields all of the great Burgundy reds.

Pinot St. George: An inferior California grape, not a true Pinot, which yields an ordinary red wine often labeled "Red Pinot."

Piquepoul: The Folle Blanche (See above) grape, as it is known in the Armagnac country of France where, though it makes a thin, acidic wine, yields an outstanding brandy. Used also in the Cognac district.

Portugieser: A German red-wine grape cultivated in the Rheinpfalz, Ahr Valley, Baden and Rheinhessen.

Prosecco: An Italian white-wine grape of the Veneto region which yields the fine Prosecco di Cognegliano-Valdobbiadene.

Refosco: An Italian red-wine grape of mediocre quality that has been transplanted to California's Napa valley. It yields an ordinary California burgundy.

Riesling: The classic white-wine grape of Germany, believed native to the Rhine Valley and grown there since Roman times. It is a small, yellow, round grape which turns red brown at maturity. It produces the best German wines and has been successfully transplanted to California, Chile, Austria and Italy. California whites from this grape are called "White Riesling" or "Johannesberg Riesling."

Rondinella: An Italian red-wine grape of the second rank, cultivated in the Veneto region and used to produce Bardolino and Valpolicella.

Ruby Cabernet: A red-wine grape related to the Cabernet Sauvignon, but yielding a fairly good, light wine of lesser quality.

Rulander: German designation of the Pinot Gris grape, extensively cultivated in Baden.

Salvador: A California red-wine grape used to produce port.

San Gioveto: An Italian red-wine grape of excellent quality, which predominates in Chianti country and is extensively planted in Tuscany. Apart from Chianti, it is used to produce such wines as Sangiovese (from several areas), Elba Rosso, Torgiano Rosso, Riviera del Garda.

Sauvignon Blanc: A first-rate white-wine grape, rivaled only by the Chardonnay (See above) and the Riesling (See above). In the Bordeaux region, it is the leading variety in producing Graves and Sauternes; in the Loire, it yields Pouilly Fume, Sancerre and Quincy; in California it yields a similar but fuller-bodied wine that is marketed under the varietal name.

Sauvignon Vert: A California white-wine grape.

Scheurebe: A German white-wine grape chiefly planted in the Rheinhessen area.

Schiava: An excellent red-wine grape of Lombardy and the Italian Tyrol (Trention-Alto Adige), which is a good table-grape as well. It yields early maturing wines that are light in color and low in tannin, e.g., Botticino, Cellatica, Caldaro and Santa Maddalena.

Schwarzriesling: A German white-wine grape planted chiefly in the Wurttemberg area.

Scuppernong: See **Muscadine, Scuppernong.**

Semillon: See **Semillon.**

Syrah, also *Sirrah.* A black grape of the Rhone Valley in France that produces excellent red wine, notably red Hermitage and Chateauneuf-du-Pape. The wine is deeply colored and slow to mature. This is not the "Petite Syrah" of California, which is more productive but yields lesser quality wine.

Sylvaner: A superior white-wine grape of German or Austrian origin, which is second in quality only to the Riesling but easily first in total acreage in Germany. It does well in Alsace and northern Italy and has been successfully transplanted to California and Chile. The wine it yields is lighter, softer and shorter-lived than that of the Riesling.

Thompson Seedless: A renowned table grape, which, in California, is also used to make sherry.

Tinta Cao: A Portuguese red-wine grape used to produce table wines such as Dao, and in California, port, which is sometimes called "Tinta Port."

Tinta Madeira: A member of the same group of red wine grapes as the Tinta Cao, but grown chiefly in Madeira; used to produce red table wines and sweet dessert wines.

Traminer: A white-wine grape of Alsace that grows well in the Rhine Valley, the Tyrol and in California. It yields a soft white with a distinctive aroma and a trace of sweetness. The best of the traminers is the Gewurztraminer (See above).

Trebbiano: An Italian white-wine grape extensively cultivated in Emilia-Romagna, Latium, Lombardy, Tuscany, Umbria and Veneto that produces a good but not distinguished wine. It is grown in France, where it is known as the Ugni Blanc, and in California. It is the grape of white Chianti, plus a host of other well known labels, such as Est, Est, Est!, Frascati and Soave.

Trollinger: A German red-wine grape, particularly important in the Wurttemberg area, which yields a rather light wine.

Trousseau: A productive red-wine grape, identical to the Bastardo of Portugal, which, in California, is used to produce port. In France, it yields a dry red table wine, but, in the hot conditions of California the wine has a tawny color and low acid content.

Ugni Blanc: A white-wine grape called Trebbiano in another context. It is widely planted in southern France where it gives a well-balanced, sound wine. It is used to make Cassis and, in California, Chianti.

Uva di Troia: An Italian white-wine grape of the Apulia region used to produce Castel del Monte.

Valdepenas: A red-wine grape of Spanish origin that yields red table wines of moderately good quality. It is also planted in California, where it yields a wine of similar quality.

Veltliner: A white-wine grape, seemingly of Austrian origin, which produces a wine similar to Traminer but with a less marked bouquet and flavor. It is cultivated in the cooler counties of California too.

Verdicchio: An Italian white-wine grape of superior quality, used to produce such wines as Verdicchio dei Castelli di Jesi and Verdicchio di Matelica.

Verdot: A small, black grape of superior quality, especially important in Bordeaux country, where it is combined with Cabernets, Merlots and Malbecs to produce full-bodied, deep-bodied, slow-maturing wines.

Verduzzo Friulano: An Italian white-wine grape of the Friuli-Venezia-Giulia and Veneto regions, used to produce Colli Orientale del Friuli Verduzzo, Grave del Friuli Verduzzo and Piave Verduzzo.

Vernaccia: A white-wine grape of Sardinia that produces an unusual wine that is dry, rather aromatic and higher in alcoholic content (17 percent or more) than other natural wines.

Vespaiolo: An Italian white-wine grape cultivated in the Veneto region, which yields a wine called Breganze Vespaiolo.

Vespolina: An Italian red-wine grape of the Piedmont region used to produce such well-known labels as Boca, Fara, Ghemme and Sizzano.

White Muscat: A California white-wine grape used to produce White Muscat wine. This is the White Muscat of Alexandria and has the distinctive Muscat fragrance.

Zibibbo: A Sicilian designation of the Muscat of Alexandria, a white-wine grape, used there to produce Marsala, Moscato di Pantelleria and Moscato Passito di Pantelleria.

Zinfandel: California's most widely planted red-wine grape. It yields a fruity red wine of ordinary character. Zinfandel is a mass production grape which, nevertheless, has an easily recognizable, varietal personality. It does not age well and is best drunk young.

WINES, ALSATIAN

These white wines, with the exception of a few roses, are grown in Alsace in the northeastern corner of France near the German border. Some of the earliest French vineyards were located here, and, in spite of the German occupation from 1870 to 1918—when Alsatian wines were downgraded by the conquerors in favor of their own wines from the Moselle and the **Rhine**—Alsace today produces several fine wines from a wide variety of grapes. Alsatian vineyards are customarily planted between 500 and 1200 feet high in the foothills of the Vosges, above the icy fogs that regularly blanket the area in winter and early spring. In a northern climate wines are apt to be drier, more acidic and weaker in alcohol content. Alsatian wines are usually on the dry side, with between 11 and 14 percent alcohol. But, like the wines of the Moselle, they are fruity, youthful, well-balanced, and are excellent with the rich and ample cuisine of the region.

Labels in Alsace commonly list the type of grape from which the wine is made, and only occasionally add the name of a specific vineyard or town where the wine is marketed. The noblest of Alsatian wine is, then, the Gewurztraminer, served with rich food, such as lobster, strong cheese, foie gras and pheasant *a la Strasbourg.* Riesling is a wine of high reputation also. Along with the Pinot and Sylvaner, a good Riesling well suits not very highly seasoned dishes, such as shellfish, trout and white meat. A **Muscat** and a **Tokay** are produced, the latter from Hungarian vines introduced to the area in the 16th century. These have more sweetness and should accompany highly seasoned foods and desserts. Zwicker is a dry white table wine from the more ordinary Chasselas grape, usually served in carafes. It is ideal with cold cuts, picnics and light luncheons. Alsatian wines have made a strong comeback since the end of World War II and—though they are not yet in a class with the Moselles—are gradually gaining more ground and favor with French and other consumers.

WINES, AUSTRALAIN

The European wine grape was introduced into Australia north of Sydney in the early 1790s. Within two decades the first commercial vineyards were created in the Hunter Valley about a hundred miles farther north. Today, however, about 70 percent of all Australian wine comes from South Australia, especially from the Barossa Valley, northeast of Adelaide. The climate in this area is like that of the famed Coastal Belt in South Africa—temperate, unvaried, cool and moist. The same grape varieties that do well in South Africa also flourish here, notably those of cabernet, sauvignon, hermitage, **shiraz,** riesling, frontignan, **muscat** and **semillon.**

Another important area of grape cultivation is along the Murray River, which rises in the Australian Alps and runs inland from the eastern coast before turning south in a wide bend to empty in the Southern Ocean—1,609 miles from its source—about 60 miles east of Adelaide. Vineyards are planted on both banks of this long river, the work largely of two Canadian brothers and irrigation experts, George and William Chaffey, who came to Australia from California in 1886. Grapes from the Murray Valley are typically varieties of muscat, which make sweet dessert wines and brandy. A *flor*-type **sherry** is also produced along the Murray, from a blend of Muscat grapes.

The best Australian wine is that from the Barossa Valley. Here are produced several excellent dry red table wines, notably the Kaiser-Stuhl cabernet-sauvignon and a good Australian shiraz, as well as delicate dry white rieslings and a "musky" semisweet frontignan. The Barossa Valley plantings were initiated by a group of Lutheran immigrants who fled to Australia from Silesia in the 1840s to escape religious persecution. German is still widely spoken in this area, the home (near Nuriootpa) of an annual European-style Vintage Festival. The Barossa rises 80 miles north of Adelaide and ascends south to a plateau around Tanunda, Nuriootpa and Angaston to the high districts of Springton, Eden Valley and Pewsey Vale. Wines from this great region have labels that designate the variety of grape used, such as shiraz, **grenache,** riesling, semillon, cabernet-sauvignon, but also proudly proclaim "from the Barossa Valley."

Australia does not yet produce a great quantity of wine. In 1978 its production was 103,822,740 gallons, slightly less than that of Greece, but more than that of Bulgaria, Brazil and Austria. Australian wine is gradually being exported in larger volume, however, to Great Britain and to the United States.

WINES, AUSTRIAN

Austrians drink more beer than wine. Though Austrian vineyards are ancient, planted first along the Danube in the days of the Roman Empire, wine is produced today on a relatively small scale, in mostly the eastern part of the country. In fact, Austria produces much less wine than it did in the heyday of the Austro-Hungarian Empire. Its production in 1978 was 72,385,320 gallons, smaller than that of Hungary and of Greece.

The vine was introduced by the Romans over 2,000 years ago. After the barbarian incursions, the vineyards were replanted in 955 by Otto I. The Turkish occupation of Hungary in 1526 ended the competition in wines between Austria and Hungary, and the land under cultivation for the vine increased still more.

Today only 1/10 of that former acreage is still under cultivation. Most of the Austrian wine production, about 85 percent, is of white wine, from the Riesling, Sylvaner and Gruner Velthiner grapes. In the Mur Valley, near Graz, some very good white wines are grown. In the area known as the Sudbahn, south of Vienna, superior wines are found near the town of Gumpoldskirchen. But the best Austrian wines are grown in the region of Krems and Wachau on the Danube. The best of these are comparable to the tasty Rieslings of the Moselle.

Austrian wine is grown largely for home consumption. A delightful custom in the spring and summer is the *Heurigen*, when Viennese and tourists alike visit the neighboring countryside and its wineries to sample the milky, slightly effervescent, local white wine outdoors in shady arbors.

WINES, CHINESE

Cultivation of the vine *(Vitis vinifera)* in China dates from the second century B.C. According to tradition, it was introduced by Arab traders, and its cultivation flourished in Turkestan, in the far west of China. Today many of China's best eating grapes come from the Turfan area of Turkestan. Production of wine from grapes is documented from the seventh century A.D., yet it was and has remained a drink of the elite. Courtiers and artists partook and sang its praises. The most famous of the early period was the poet Li Po (d. 762) who, full of wine one night, attempted to embrace the reflection of the moon on the surface of the river. He fell in and drowned.

Chinese wine production today is pretty much confined to five provinces along the Yellow River in the center of the eastern seaboard: Shantung, Hopeh, Shansi, Honan and Kiangsu. Grapes used include *lambruscana, and vinifera*, as well as native varieties. Wine from grapes is called *p'u t'ao chiu*, as distinguished from *Shaoxing*, or rice wine, which will be discussed further on. Riesling and Pinot grapes produce reds, whites and roses. Perhaps the best known are the reds and whites of Tsingtao. They contain between 12 and 16 percent alcohol and are described as tasting like natural sherries, except for a more pronounced acidity. A prominent sweet wine is *Chefoo*, which is available in both red and white types. Both are strong and aromatic, the red being more often compared to **port.** A sparkling wine called *Ta-xiang-pih-chiu* is also produced. China is currently exporting to the United States a white wine called *Tai Shan*, which contains 12 percent alcohol. It is most comparable to Gray Riesling and comes from Hopeh Province.

A more popular drink is rice wine, called *Shaoxing*. It is named for the town in Chekiang Province where it originated 2,000 years ago, and where the best rice wine is still made. Production is centralized under the Communist regime and amounts to about 30,000 tons a year, valued at 12 million dollars. About a third of the production is the basic wine. *Shaoxing* is made of glutinous rice plus some millet. It is soaked in water from the nearby Lake Jian, then steamed and fermented for nearly 90 days. It is drawn off, filtered, pasteurized, then aged in sealed stone jars for three to six years minimum. Better grades are aged up to 10 years. It has an alcohol content of about 16 percent. Better grades are sweetened and contain up to 20 percent alcohol. *Shaoxing* has a golden color and a rich, mellow flavor. Similar rice wines are made from yellow rice in Shantung Province. Fine *Shaoxing* is also made in Taiwan by the Republic of China state monopoly. Put up in rectangular whisky bottles, it has a dark amber color, 13 to 14 percent alcohol and costs about $5 a fifth.

WINES, CYPRIAN

Viticulture in Cyprus has declined seriously in the past 10 years because of civil unrest and the repartitioning of the island. The dominant (almost 80 percent) Greek community has been responsible for almost all Cyprian wine. A dry but full-bodied red, named Otello—from the legendary Moor who served the Venetians against the Turks—it is grown near Famagusta. Another dry wine, Aphrodite, is clearly among the best of the whites (the goddess of love traditionally was born on the sea near Paphos). Kokkinelli is the best-known Cyprian rose, semisweet but darker than most roses (*Kokkinos* means "red" in Greek) and is perhaps the finest of all Aegean roses, including those of Greece. But the best Cyprian vintage is the Commandaria, a sweet dessert wine that can be made from either red or white grapes dried in the sun to increase their sugar content.

The Greek white **Retsina** is not normally tolerated on Cyprus. Instead, ordinary whites and reds are often served in hollowed-out, hand-painted gourds, which adds to the light gardeny taste of the wine. Historically, Cyprus supplied the vine-shoots that first were planted by the Portuguese on **Madeira.**

WINES, FRENCH

France, the nation most renowned for its fine wines, annually rivals Italy in world wine production. In 1978 France produced 1,553,351,000 gallons of wine, second to Italy by about 200,000 gallons in output. But the wines of France are almost universally considered finer than those of Italy though perhaps not as varied. Historically, too, French cuisine has always held the edge over that of Italy (and of any other European country, for that matter) even though the grape in its early stages was cultivated and improved by Roman methods of viticulture.

Vitis vinifera grew native in Gaul well before the Roman occupation. Fossilized traces of the grape have been found in ancient chalk beds as far north as Champagne and in limestone and other deposits throughout France. Surely the Rhone, which enters the Mediterranean Sea south of Arles, was a major highway for the spread of the vine—brought by Phoenician and Greek sailors—up the picturesque valley of this great waterway into Burgundy, and westward into Languedoc and up the Garonne to Bordeaux.

A serious blow to the existence of *vitis vinifera*—the European wine-grape—occurred in the mid-19th century, when the wine louse, *Phylloxera*, entered France from North America. Only the grafting of French vine stock onto native North American roots saved the day. Now all French wine, and those of other European countries, owe their very existence—not to mention their prestige—to these hardy New World foundations.

To safeguard its national product from fraudulent practices (for example, *coupage*, or "cutting" a superior wine with inferior blends), the French government has over the years devised elaborate regulatory machinery. These are the laws of the *Appellation d'Origine*. The codification of French wine under this system ensures that only wine from a specific region, district or vineyard may be so labeled, and classified further with an *appellation controlee*, or *A.O.C.* The rules pertain to quality, the percentage of alcohol, types of grapes used, methods of fermentation, whether or not the wine is a "blend" (blended wine can be composed of the same wine but from different years, or of wine from the same year but from different vineyards), bouquet, the amount of tannin (or tannic acid) present, the time of harvest and even to the hours of sunlight in a particular growing season. The result is a legalized aristocracy of wine from that classified through the years as *Grands Crus* ("great growths"), such as the **Chambertin** and **Montrachet** from Burgundy or much of the wine from the large chateaux, or estates, in Bordeaux, (e.g., *Chateau Lafite-Rothschild*, *Chateau Latour*, *Chateau d'Yquem)*, down almost to the plebeian *vin ordinaire* (most of this being supplied by Algeria).

The great wine-growing regions of France are easily named. Bordeaux has from Roman times produced some of the world's best wine. With the English annexation of the province of Aquitaine in 1152, the Bordeaux wine trade with Great Britain began, and the English language gained a new word, **"claret."** In the off-and-on political rivalry with France throughout the centuries—when French wine was at times prohibited—England still enjoyed its smuggled Bordeaux along with **port** and **sherry** "to disperse," said Robert Louis Stevenson, "the fogs of London." From Bordeaux come the sweet white **Sauternes,** the red and white **Graves** and the red **Medoc,** the name of a rich tidewater plain east of this venerable city.

Burgundy is of an equal reputation with Bordeaux as a wine-growing region, giving to the world the dry white **Chablis** and the red silky **Beaujolais** as well as red, white, and sparkling burgundies. In Burgundy the great dry reds (synonymous with the name of the region) are produced, north of Lyons. One thinks, too, of the white wine of **Beaune** and that from the splendid Cote d'Or (or "slopes of gold"). The popes of Avignon cherished the red **Chateauneuf-du-Pape** grown along the Rhone, and the lusty rose of **Tavel.**

Champagne, an area east of Paris, yields the internationally known aristocratic sparkling wine, thanks largely to the efforts of Dom Perignon, a 17th-century Benedictine monk, for toasts and for all special occasions. The wines of the **Rhone** and the **Loire** are of almost equal fame with these other three districts for the gentle and sumptuous reds, whites and beautifully colored roses. Finally, the wine of Alsace—an area so often beset by war—produces wine that, if given a chance, competes well with that of the German Moselle.

The roses of Anjou, the gentle reds of Touraine—so admired by Rabelais—testify also to the skill of the French in making wine. The western coast of France is warmed by the Gulf Stream. In the south, along the Mediterranean, and in the Rhone valley, the land is fortunate in long hours of unbroken sunlight. The vast chalk beds of Champagne give to the wine there its subtle "flinty" taste. The nation as a whole is freshened by a network of cool lovely rivers. The lively *Esprit Gallois*—so pronounced in literature and the visual arts—when turned to viticulture offers the genius of Dom Perignon and Louis Pasteur. One falters at superlatives, but perhaps these words by Rabelais describe well the Gallic love of excellent wine and indicate the role of the French in producing it:

> *So we maintain that not laughter but drinking is the proper lot of man. I do not mean simply and badly drinking, for beasts also drink. I mean drinking good cool wine. Note, my friends, that by wine one grows divine; there is no surer argument, no art of divination less fallacious.*

See also: **Bordeaux Wines** and **Burgundy Wines.**

WINES, GERMAN

Germany is the northernmost wine-growing country in the world. Comparatively weak sunlight over long periods of time, however, provide ideal conditions for exceptionally smooth white wines with low alcoholic content. Germany is world famous for its dry and semidry whites—especially those along the Rhine and its tributaries the Neckar, the Moselle and the Nahe. In total production, Germany ranks eighth among wine-producing nations, after the United States and Romania, with a figure of 177,370,452 gallons in 1978.

The vine has grown in Germany from Roman times. In the Middle Ages the Rhine was a literal "Wine Road" in the shipment of vintages to the northern countries. The Thirty Years War (1618–1648) was fatal to some formerly great wine-producing areas. In Wurttemberg today, for example, the wine-growing area is less than half of what it was in 1550. Industrialization, too, is a serious threat to German viticulture, especially in the factory areas of the Saar. Nevertheless, German white wine continues to be the best in the world.

Rhine wine is a product largely of riesling, sylvaner, traminer and rulander grapes. These require good years and very sunny exposures. Other white grapes like the muller-thurgau (a blend of riesling and sylvaner vines) ripen quickly and produce good wine even without much sun. Germany does not produce much red wine, although a good light Burgundy, the Portugieser, is grown in many of the Rhine vineyards. In exceptional years this wine turns a dark red color and is very warm and velvety.

On the northern slopes of Lake Constance (where the Rhine forms a natural barrier between Germany and Switzerland), good white wines called Seewein and Weissherbst are produced, the latter a white Burgundy with a full body and rich bouquet. The best German rose wine is grown in Wurttemberg, near Stuttgart. This is the Schillerwein, said to be named for the family of the great dramatist and poet, Friedrich Schiller. This wine is made by mixing white and red grapes in the press, or by leaving the skins of the red grapes in contact with the must for a short time.

The Palatinate, on the right bank of the Rhine across from Alsace, is the largest wine-growing area in Germany. Sylvaner is the principal grape grown here, although the traminer and riesling grapes also prosper. This area also produces a fine Gewurztraminer, a wine of great maturity and gentleness.

Rheinhesse, farther north, is the land of Charlemagne, though there is evidence that wine was grown there well before his time. Rheinhesse is the second largest wine-growing area in Germany. Sylvaner leads here among the whites, followed by muller-thurgau and riesling. **Liebfrauenmilch** is from this area. This is a name applied to all the sweet, white wines of Rheinhesse and to some neighboring wines from the Palatinate.

Mainz and Worms have long been capitals of the German wine trade. But other names, such as Bingen, Nierstein, and Oppenheim are almost as famous. Oppenhein still produces good Auslese (wines from carefully selected bunches of grapes) and beerenauslese (selected berries, picked after the noble rot—or *Edelfaule*—has set in). At Nierstein (on the Rhine between Mainz and Worms) is made some of the best white wine in Germany.

The Nahe flows into the Rhine at Bingen, from the east. Here the Sylvaner is the dominant grape. It makes an exceptional wine near Bad Kreuznach. To the east, in Franconia, the typical beverage is Steinwein, a Riesling, sharp and perfumed. Franconian wines are dry, with a steely taste and a bright greenish glitter. They are typically, and colorfully, bottled in special flagons called *Bocksbeutel.*

North towards Koblenz in the "elbow" of the Rhine—where the river flows east in a long bend before again turning north—the vines have a full southern exposure. This is the land of the Rheingau—from Hochheim to Rudesheim. In quality, the wines here are among the best in the world. Hochheim wines were so prized by the British in the 18th and 19th centuries that the English word "hock" came to mean *any* good Rhine wine. "A good hock keeps the doctor away" was, in fact, for many years, a household saying in England. Riesling accounts for almost 80 percent of the grapes grown in the Rheingau. The vineyards are mostly small, and the grapes are picked when the *Edelfaule*, ("noble rot") has well begun. This practice is called *Spatlese*, or "late-picking." The ripest grapes are carefully picked when the autumn mist, known as the *Traubendrucker*, or "grape-presser," rises from the Rhine and brings the fruit to repletion. This can occur as late as mid-November. Rilke, the great German poet, perhaps has this activity in mind in his beautiful lyric, "Autumn Day":

> *Tell the last fruits to ripen;*
> *Give them two more southern days,*
> *Press them on to fulness and drive*
> *Sweetness into the heavy wine.*

The practice of *Spatlese* makes for full-bodied, fruity but, at the same time, very elegant wines.

Along the Moselle, which enters the Rhine at Koblenz, the vineyards are extremely steep. All farming is done by hand. The earth, in fact, must be replaced, carried back in hods, when it is washed down by rains. This is the oldest wine-growing region in Germany. It produces only white wines, light, dry, soft green in color, which go well with fish and hors d'oeuvres. When young, Moselle wines contain some carbonic acid gas, and so are slightly sparkling. Moselblumchen ("little flower of the Moselle") is a general name for these young wines. "Nowhere else," wrote the French poet, Charles Baudelaire, after a visit to the Moselle vineyards, "is so much hard work, so much sweat, and so much ardent sun needed to bring the grapes to life and to imbue the wine with soul."

See also: **Burgundy Wines.**

WINES, GREEK

The emergence of the religion of Dionysus in the seventh century B.C. helped promote the vine as a major crop in Greece and led to the cultivation of vineyards throughout the land and in Greek colonies around the Mediterranean and the Black Sea. The wines of the Rhone Valley, the wine of **Malaga,** of Sicily, and even Spanish **sherry** are of Greek origin. Dionysus was the protector of the vine, of vineyards and of wine drinkers. And wine grapes were better suited to the dry and arid Greek soil than were the grains and cereals previously grown there.

Greece was the first country in Europe to produce and to export wine, and was second only to Rome in wine production until the division of the Roman Empire in 395 A.D. Wine production continued in Greece, despite the occupation of the land by various outsiders, until the Turkish invasion in the 14th century. Since gaining a measure of freedom from the Turks in 1830 (though full independence did not occur until the beginning of the 20th century), Greece has steadily increased its production of wine—tenfold since World War I, and the acreage under cultivation by 15 times. In 1978 Greece produced about 120,000 gallons of wine, slightly less than Hungary.

Probably the most well-known Greek wine is **Retsina** from Attica, a white wine flavored with pine resin. This is drunk with every kind of meal (and simply for its own sake) in every part of the land, in the many *tavernas*, some of which have their own vineyards and their own methods of cultivation. *Retsina* varies from place to place, even within the city limits of Athens, according to the amount of pine resin added to the wine. Superior white and red table wines without the resin flavor are produced in the Peloponnesus and on some of the islands, particularly on Crete, Samos, Chios and Rhodes. A good sweet red dessert wine, Mavrodaphne *(mavro* means "dark") comes from the western Peloponnesus near Patras, as does the dry white and red Demestika.

From Nemea, near Corinth, also in the Peloponnesus, comes perhaps the best red table wine of Greece—hearty, tangy and strong. Red Nemean wine is sold under various labels, the most intriguing of which is "Sang d'Hercule," the blood of Hercules. Samos still produces a good dry white wine, excellent with salted fish and octopus, which Byron justly "loved and sung." In *Don Juan*, completed shortly before his death at Missolonghi, Byron exclaims:

Fill high the cup with Samian wine!
Leave battles to the Turkish hordes,
And shed the blood of Scio's vine!

Greek food is simpler and less varied than the cuisine of Italy and Turkey, its neighbors. Lamb, veal and fish are the staples. But what it lacks in variety, Greek cooking supplies with seasoning, especially with thyme, cumin, basil (a Greek word meaning "king"), oregano and cinnamon. Greek wine is simple, unpretentious, and balances this food well.

WINES, HUNGARIAN

Hungary is tenth among the wine-producing countries of Europe, with a 1978 production figure of 126,806,400 gallons. The wine of this country is overshadowed by the production of **Tokay,** *the* Hungarian wine since the early 18th century.

Wine came with the Roman colonization of the upper Danube, and was cultivated by the Magyars until the Tartars ravaged the country in 1241. Later, settlers from the west—presumably Italians—brought the Tokay vine, the Furmint, to Hungary. Following the Turkish conquest of 1526–1699, Tokay became one of the most coveted vintages in Europe. Thanks to the efforts of Count Istvan Szecheny, an enlightened statesman of the early 19th century, Hungarian wine cellars became amply stocked.

Production in Hungary now is about 60 percent white wine (dominated by Tokay), 25 percent rose, and 15 percent red. Sopron, near the Austrian border, south of Lake Balaton, is famous for its red wines. Most reds in Hungary come from an original Balkan grape, the Kadarka. Egri Bikaver ("Bull's Blood of Eger") is a red wine from between Budapest and the Tokay region (in the northeastern part of the country). Dark rich in color, with a slightly bitter taste, "Bull's Blood" is made from a mixture of several vines, including Kadarka, Medoc Noir and Bourguinon.

The western bank of Lake Balaton is particularly suited to wine grapes. The Mor region, farther to the north, is one of Hungary's oldest viticultural areas. Dry wine is produced here with a very lovely light green color and a sharp tang. Tokay is grown at the confluence of two rivers—the Bodrog and the Tisza—in the foothills of the Hegalja Mountains. The best Tokay is a sweet dessert wine, but others can be dry or semisweet.

WINES, ISRAELI

In 1978 Israel produced 9,668,988 gallons of wine, over five times the amount of neighboring Jordan, Syria and Lebanon combined. Wine was produced in Canaan from earliest times, according to the Old Testament. Modern wine production in Israel, however, began with the Rothschilds, who introduced French vines into Palestine in the late 19th century. Today almost 30,000 acres of vineyards exist in Israel, sown predominantly with **Carignane** and Alicante Grenache grapes.

Israel makes every kind of wine, chief among which are the avdat and carmel hock dry white wines, the binyamina rose, and white **Muscatel** and "Independence" (red) dessert wines. Carmel hock is widely exported to the United States. Chateau Latrun, made by Christian missionaries, is one of the best dry red wines grown in the Middle East.

WINES, ITALIAN

Italy rivals France as the world's largest producer of wine. In 1978, 1,756,797 gallons of wine were produced in Italy, compared to 1,553,351 gallons in France. Second to France in winegrowing area, Italy boasts the largest variety of wines—ranging from the numerous excellent dry reds and whites of the North to the syrupy white **Marsala,** the famous dessert wine of Sicily.

A controversy still rages whether the vine was first brought to Italy from Greece in ancient times or whether it grew native. It is certain that the Greek colonists in Sicily, Sardinia and along the mainland planted vines along with their pantheon. But Homer tells that the cyclops Polyphemus was drunk on homegrown Sicilian wine when Odysseus blinded him. The vine Nuragos, known to the most ancient inhabitants, is still cultivated in Sardinia.

By the time of Pliny the Elder (23–79 A.D.), Roman wine production was the largest in the known world, outdoing even that of Greece. "*In vino veritas*," wrote Pliny. "In wine there is truth." He listed in his *Natural History* over 195 kinds of wine, half of which were grown in Italy. The mountainous peninsula was a naturally fertile area for wine production. "*Bacchus amat colles*," wrote Virgil. "Bacchus loves the hills." And today the Apennines, the volcanic slopes of Vesuvius and Etna and the foothills of the Italian Alps abound with vines under culture. As for the variety of Italian wines, Virgil claims in the *Georgics*, "He who would know the numberless kinds of vines would just as well count the Libyan sands."

Vineyards are planted in all parts of modern Italy. Major wine-production centers, however, tend to be grouped in the far north, and in the south, particularly Sicily. Certain central provinces, such as Tuscany and Latium, are justly famous for some single varieties. Italy is unique in wine production in that over half of its acreage is of a mixed culture, the vines growing alongside other crops—as they did in ancient times. In central Italy wine production is relatively small, though the famous red **Chianti** from Tuscany is one of the largest single wines produced in the country. Good white wines, including the agreeable Frascati and Orvieto, come from the area around Rome.

But from the North, in Piedmont, Lombardy, and from Verona and Venice, come "the king of Italian wines," the red **Barolo,** as well as **Barbera,** Bardolino, Valpolicella, and the dry white **Soave.** Traminers and Rieslings are grown near the Alps, and the thick hearty red **Lambrusca** is the wine of Bologna.

Farther south, along the Bay of Naples, come the dry white Vesuvio, the white **Lacrima Cristi,** and the strong heavy red Falerno, beloved of Virgil and Horace. Apulia, on the Adriatic, produces the largest quantity of Italian wine by region—superior whites, reds, and roses, but notably the fragrant white Sansevero.

The wines of Italy, though not so prized among connoisseurs as are French wines, are excellent with pasta, veal, chicken and roasts. They are wines designed to accompany rich, hearty and savory meals. For Italian cooking, the wise eater will order Italian wine.

WINES, JAPANESE

Wine production in Japan is concentrated in three or four areas, all on Honshu Island—the Kofu Valley and Katsunuma district in Yamanashi prefecture, which is 75 miles west of Tokyo, and in Osaka and Yamagata provinces. Annual production amounts to about six million gallons, most of it consumed locally. Certain *vinifera* grape varieties, such as the Koshu and Jaraku, have been planted since the 12th century but are believed to be of European origin. *Lambrusca* varieties do equally well in Japan, and recently European Semillon, Chardonnay and Riesling grapes have produced good results with white wines and Cabernet Sauvignon and Merlot with reds. Another important grape is the Muscat Baily A, an American hybrid.

Four large companies dominate the market: Sanraku Ocean, Manns Wine, Godo Shusei and Suntory. Wine labeling is modeled after Western types, e.g., Sanraku Ocean's Chateau Mercian, which is labelled *grand cru classe* and *mis en bouteille au chateau* and Mann's Wine's Koshu, a varietal, which is labelled *premier grand cru classe mis en bouteille dan nos caves*.

Humidity is the main threat to Japanese wines and renders much of the production astringent and unbalanced. The best are light and dry and would be considered respectable table wines by Western standards.

See also: **Sake.**

WINES, LUXEMBOURG

These are dry white wines from the Moselle and Sure (Sauer) Valleys that form the eastern boundary of Luxembourg. Vines have been cultivated on both banks of the Moselle, in steep terraces, since Roman times. The poet Ausonius celebrated these vineyards in his poem "Mosella": . . . the pleasant stream . . . whose hills are overgrown with Bacchus' fragrant vines."

Moselle wines from Luxembourg rival those of Germany in quality. They are made from green grapes, mostly Rieslings and those from a very ancient vinestock called "Elbling." Like the neighboring wines of Germany, Luxembourg wine is typically fruity, relatively low in alcohol and sometimes sparkling. Perhaps the best wine in this tiny country comes from the village of Grevenmacher, on the Moselle. Luxembourg is among the smallest of the world's wine-producing countries, and is—along with Germany—the most northern.

WINES, MEXICAN

Until very recently, Mexico has not been an important wine-producing nation. Competition from beer and from superior California wine, a climate that is hot and arid in the north and tropical in the south and a widespread belief that wine does not go well with spicy food, have all played a major part in inhibiting wine consumption in Mexico. Large-scale plantings of wine grapes were not initiated until the 1920s, although the European grape *(Vitis vinifera)* had been introduced into North America through Mexico by Spanish missionaries in the mid-18th century. Until now, Mexico has been known, if at all, for sweet fortified wines, prticularly those from the grapes of the **Muscat** variety grown near Ensenada in Baja California.

Today, with better training for wine-makers and a nation-wide publicity campaign, Mexican wine is better known and even respected. Over 150,000 acres are now planted in vineyards—some of which yield table grapes and raisins. The best wine-growing areas are in the north, in Sonora, Aguascalientes, Zacatecas, Coahuila, Durango and Baja California Norte. Many of the vines are grown on dry mountain slopes just under 6,000 feet and must be irrigated. Perhaps the best potential area under wine cultivation is Zacatecas, which has a relatively cool climate and adequate rainfall. Superior grapes that make both red and white dry wines—including the cabernet sauvignon, ruby cabernet, chenin blanc, **carignane,** malbec and **zinfandel—**are now regularly cultivated. A good dry white **hock** or riesling is made by Vergel in Aguascalientes.

Annual wine consumption in Mexico is only about 300 cubic centimeters per capita (or about 2/3 of a pint). The price of wine is also rather high—in relation to that of tequila and beer. But the future holds much promise. With the help of foreign enologists and with growing skill Mexican wine growers now project a thriving industry and the exportation of quality wine to the United States.

WINES, NORTH AFRICAN

Until Algeria's independence from France in 1962, this large colonial nation ranked high in wine production, supplying most of the red table wine, or *vin ordinaire*, found throughout its mother country. Today only about half of the vineyards cultivated under French rule remain intact, the others having been converted to pastures and fields. Algerian wine, mostly red and for use in blending, is exported now mainly to Russia and Poland in glass-lined fermentation tanks built for special tankers. In 1978, Algeria produced 67,500,000 gallons of wine, a figure slightly less than that reported by Austria.

Wine was grown in North Africa in Roman times, but came into its own with the importation of European vines—mostly from southern France—in the late 19th century, when *Phylloxera*, the wine louse, threatened to destroy all the French vineyards. Only a few native vines (Hasseroum, Grilla, Fahana) are cultivated today. French planters introduced the **alicante-bouschet** along with cinsault, **carignane,** clairette, **grenache, gamay,** pinot noir and **cabernet.** White wines are full-bodied, perfumed, rather strong, and come mostly from clairette, grenache, ugni blanc, macabeo, farignan and other European plantings.

North African red wine is better known than the white. It is generally thick and heavy and makes a good blend with lighter and more acidic French wines. Once the holdings of single families, vineyards in North Africa are usually farmed now on a cooperative basis. Algeria still produces a surplus of wine—since Moslems generally are not wine drinkers—although sheep graze in abandoned vineyards and many ancient stumps have been uprooted for firewood.

In Algeria, as in Tunisia and Morocco, the vines are planted basically along the coastal mountains. Wines from the higher elevations are hearty, rich in tannin and alcohol. Wines from the mountain slopes nearer the sea are finer, more lively and with a delicate bouquet. About two-thirds of all Algerian wine is grown near the port of Oran in western Algeria. The notable red and white Coteaux de Mascara is from this vicinity.

Tunisia grows and exports wine, though on a much smaller scale than that in Algeria. French colonists planted vineyards near ancient Carthage, on the coast just north of Tunis. Here again the major varieties are those of the grenache, carignane, alicante-bouschet and pinot noir for red wines; with Pedro Ximenez, **semillon,** sauvignon, muscat d'Alexandrie, clairette and ugni blanc providing most of the whites. *Phylloxera* reached Tunisia only in 1936, several decades after it had ravaged the French vineyards, and was not checked by the grafting of American root-stalk until slightly after Tunisia's independence from France in 1956. Today, France is still Tunisia's main customer. "Vin Superieur de Tunisie," a red, white or rose wine with an alcohol content of from 11 to 13 percent, is widely exported, and a sweet Muscat de Tunisie dessert wine is also deserving of praise.

Morocco produces the least amount of wine in North Africa. Most Moroccan wines are either reds or roses. The reds are hearty, well-balanced and rich, with an alcohol content of from 12 to 14 percent. The roses are very clear, lively and fruity. Some white wine is produced, especially from the muscat d'Alexandrie, Pedro Ximenez, clairette and grenache varieties. For the reds, cinsault, carignane, grenache and alicante-bouschet here yield some very good wine, which is lighter than that grown in Algeria, from near Fez and Meknes in north-central Morocco on the slopes of the Atlas Mountains.

WINES, PORTUGUESE

Portugal is tenth in world wine production, reporting a figure of 147,069,006 gallons in 1978. The land is blessed by sunlight and ocean winds and so is not excessively dry. The vines are very old, perhaps originating with the Romans in their descent from Gaul or else from Greek sailors. The word for "Orange" in Greek is still "Portokali," or "Portugal." In any case, the vine had so flourished by Domitian's time that the emperor forbade its cultivation in provinces under Roman sway and even uprooted existing vines.

The barbarians and the Moors were tolerant of viticulture. The capture of Lisbon in 1147 by Alfonso Henriques (who had fought with the Cid), marked the birth of modern Portugal and a new prominence for the vine. By the time of Sancho I, at the beginning of the 13th century, an edict was in force that "whomsoever shall destroy with premeditation a vine plant shall be brought in judgment as it were for the death of a man."

In 1703, however, came the halcyon days of Portuguese wine. In this year, with the Treaty of Methuen, the English prohibited the importation of French wine—and virtually assured Portugal a monopoly in wine imports. So began the long love affair of the British with the wine they called **port.** English wine merchants established themselves at Oporto to ensure a high quality (and profit) in port wine. The following dialogue, from George Meredith's novel, *The Egoist*, is a good example of this rapport:

> ". . . . *Have you anything great?*"
> "*A wine aged ninety.*"
> "*Is it associated with your pedigree, that you pronounce the age with such assurance?*"
> "*My grandfather inherited it.*"
> "*Your grandfather, Sir Willoughby, had meritorious offspring, not to speak of generous progenitors. What would have happened had it fallen into the female line! I shall be glad to accompany you. Port? Hermitage?*"
> "*Port.*"
> "*Ah! We are in England!*"

The British trade in wool for the wine of Oporto stood fast for over two centuries.

Vineyards in Portugal are still dependent on the family unit, on small holdings, although the majority of winegrowers belong to cooperatives. Most of the wine comes from the northern third of the country and is produced under very difficult conditions. From the Dao come strong, full-bodied table wines. The grapes are grown on steep, terraced, rocky slopes and in deep valleys, with a varying mixture of sun. In Colares, on the Atlantic, the vineyards are on the beach or in silted-up rivers. These are among the oldest in Portugal, the only ones that survived the outbreak of *Phylloxera* that swept over the European vineyards in the 19th century. In Setubal, on the southern bank of the Tagus River, a very amiable rose, Faisca, is produced. A thirst-quencher, this is usually served chilled or with ice cubes. It is sold in the United States under the trade name "Lancers."

Vinhos verdes are red and white wines from northern Portugal. The grapes are pruned early before they reach maturity and the wine is bottled "green." Refreshing and sparkling, with a low alcoholic content, Vinhos verdes make up about one-third of the home consumption of Portuguese wine. Port wine comes from the valley of the Douro—with its steep, rugged banks and treacherous rapids. The other great Portuguese wine, **Madeira,** is grown and cultivated in much the same manner as port, on a volcanic island in the mid-Atlantic.

WINES, SOUTH AFRICAN

European wine grapes were planted in South Africa in the mid-17th century by Johan Van Riebeeck, governor of the Dutch colony at Capetown. Van Riebeeck, who was a medical doctor, knew that red wine and brandy could be used effectively to combat scurvy—on Dutch ships bound to and from the Indies—and might prove in time to be a useful export. Growing conditions on Table Mountain were ideal for wine. Despite raids from the Hottentots, and aided by a large influx of French Huguenots near the end of the 17th century, Van Riebeeck's original vineyard flourished. Today, South Africa is ninth in world wine production, making 158,508,000 gallons in 1978—more than Portugal, and only slightly less than West Germany.

South African wine has enjoyed a particularly high reputation in Great Britain—still its best customer—since the time of the Napoleonic Wars. It is commonly said that Napoleon himself, exiled on St. Helena, died calling for a glass of Constantia, a

muscat, the most famous early South African wine. Certainly, dozens of cases of this unusual beverage (fortified with the blood of sheep and goats) were shipped to him in his later years. At present, the only danger to the reputation of South African wine seems to be that of overproduction, since the climate near the Cape is so unvaryingly temperate. In 1919 a Cooperative—*Kooperatieve Wijnbouwers Vereniging* or K.W.V.—was formed to regulate the quantity and quality of wine grown. Today no one can cultivate wine for sale without the approval of the K.W.V.

Vineyards in South Africa occur in two zones, in the Coastal Belt around Capetown, which includes the wine-growing areas of Stellenbosch, Paarl, the Constantia Valley, Cape Peninsula and Tulbagh, and farther inland in the Little Karoo, where irrigation is needed as well as refrigeration in storage. Good, dry table wines, both white and red, are grown in the Coastal Belt, whites and reds from Stellenbosch and Paarl, whites from Tulbagh and red wine from the Cape Peninsula. Delicate pale sherries are made at Stellenbosch, Paarl and Tulbagh. In the Little Karoo the yield is mostly robust table wines and fortified dessert wines, including **sherry, port** and **muscatel.**

Chief among the white grape varieties in the Coastal Belt are white French or palomino (for sherry), steen or chenin blanc, "the Green Grape" (actually a semillon), and riesling and clairette blanche for sparkling wines. The coastal reds are made from Hermitage (or cinsault), cabernet sauvignon, **shiraz, gamay,** and the South African hybrid pinotage—perhaps the best of the reds—a combination of pinot noir and hermitage. Pinotage resembles a **beaujolais,** fruity, rich, and full-bodied. Like all South African red wines, which closely compare to those grown in Europe, pinotage should be drunk when aged from three to five years.

Wines made from the cabernet, gamay, pinot noir and hermitage grapes tend to resemble good light **bordeaux wines.** The shiraz vine does especially well in South Africa, and makes a hearty red wine with a rich bouquet. Unlike the reds, coastal white wines are usually bottled and drunk when young, sometimes after a mere six months. They are consequently fresh, slightly sparkling and fruity, especially the Riesling, which is stronger and sweeter than the German variety. Common grape varieties in the Little Karoo include the muscat d'Alexandrie (or "Hanepoot"), white french and steen for white wines, hermitage for reds and various muscats for the dessert wines.

Among the best-known South African wine is sherry, both the *fino* or very pale and dry, and the *amontillado* or medium dry. These great vintages, which are the closest in the world to Spanish sherry, are made from white palomino and chenin blanc grapes and are processed by the classic solera method. A South African strain of *flor*, the yeast film necessary to Spanish sherry, is introduced to the wine before it is fortified with brandy and coats the mixture—as it ferments a second time—with a weblike fungus. After a year or two the *flor* turns brown and sinks through the clear wine—carefully racked in casks with loose-fitting bungs to allow air to enter—and forms a sediment at the bottom. The action of the *flor*, plus an addition of gypsum to the freshly pressed liquid, gives the wine its distinctive sherry taste and color.

South African port is made from the hermitage grape and with grapes imported from the Douro Valley in Portugal. Is is carefully blended and is aged from five to 10 years before consumption. It too is a fortified wine (with an addition of brandy). Muscat is still the base of a Constantia dessert wine, matured in oak up to four years, and for a South African **Marsala.**

A feature of South African viticulture (as well as for that in Australia) is that the summer occurs from December to February, with the grapes ripening fully between February and April, precisely the reverse of the seasonal yield in the Northern Hemisphere.

WINES, SOUTH AMERICAN

The majority of wine from South America is grown along both sides of the Andes in Chile and Argentina. The vine arrived in South America with the conquistadores, but the industry really developed when French, Italian and German immigrants brought their own wine-making techniques and knowledge to the continent. The major wine-producing countries in South America are, in order of their production, Argentina, Chile, Brazil, Uruguay, Peru, Bolivia and Colombia.

Argentina is the fifth-largest wine-producing country in the world, after Spain and ahead of the United States, with 556,891,440 gallons in 1978. Wine is grown in Argentina solely for domestic consumption, however, and not for world markets. The vine was introduced by the Spanish in the 16th century. Italian immigrants devised a method of using lime-rich water, which poured down in torrents from the Andes, for irrigation. Later this same water brought the wine-louse, *phylloxera*, which practically destroyed the Argentine vineyards—until the growers flooded the fields and drowned the pest.

Criollo was the first vine plant cultivated in Argentina. This came from Mexico and Peru. It still produces a good white wine. Other Argentine white wines are made from grapes brought by the Italians and French: the Pedro Ximenez, Semillon, Pinot Blanc, Malvoisie (malmsey) and Riesling. Two-thirds of the Argentine red wine is made from the Malbec grape variety.

The most important wine-growing provinces in Argentina are Mendoza, San Juan and Rio Negro—all on the eastern slopes of the Andes and in the northern and central part of the Cordillera Range. These three provinces make up about 96 percent of Argentina's total annual wine harvest. Mendoza has the largest total South American acreage given to the cultivation of the vine, almost 40 percent. Most wine produced here is red. From Rio Negro, farther south, comes the country's best red wines (which are very light) and sparkling wines.

Chile produces the best of South American wines, having a 1978 production figure of 137,373,600 gallons, slightly less than that of Portugal. But it exports very little. The Europeans planted *Vitis vinifera* here, and modern European techniques brought by immigrants have helped create a major industry. In Chile's central valley, especially in Linares, imported French vines—especially the Cabernet, the Sauvignon, and the Pinot—produce the best of Chilean wines.

Brazil is South America's third-largest wine producer (75,291,300 gallons in 1978) but is still well behind Chile in its annual production. As in Chile and Argentina, the techniques brought by immigrants —especially by the Italians—firmly established the wine industry in this country. The average Brazilian drinks only about four pints of wine a year, however, so most of the wine is exported to the United States, Argentina and Germany. The Isabella grape, a North American hybrid, is used to produce a good red table wine. Other *labrusca* hybrids from North America—the **Concord, Delaware** and Niagara—are blended with *vinifera* (European) grapes to produce some interesting quality wines. The largest area of production in Brazil is in the southernmost part of the country, the Rio Grande do Sul, just north of Uruguay, on the Atlantic.

Uruguay became a wine-producing country only at the end of the last century. Today, in spite of its small size and the competition from *mate*, the national drink, it ranks fourth in South American wine production, with 11,623,920 gallons listed in 1978. Uruguay is blessed with a temperate climate and ample rainfall. The most common wine in Uruguay, a good quality red, is rarely found elsewhere. This is the Harriague, a vine from the Haute-Pyrenees in France where it is known as Tannat.

Wine was brought to *Peru* by Francisco Carabantes in the middle of the 16th century. Although the climate is not favorable to the grape, some very pleasant white wines are grown near Lima along the Pacific coast south of the capital. *Bolivia* and *Colombia* produce small quantities of wine—mostly heavy, strong and sweet.

WINES, SPANISH

Spain is fourth in wine production among the nations of the world, with a total of 776,940,958 gallons produced in 1978. The Romans brought the vine to Spain, and today grapes are grown all over the peninsula, side by side with olives, in numerous small holdings.

A region of quality wines is that of the Rioja, in north central Spain. In the upper Rioja region, good red wines are made from the Tempranillo, Mazuela, Graciano and Garnacha grapes. These, mostly from the Tempranillo, are well-balanced and robust, with from 10½ to 12 percent alcoholic strength. Rioja wine is aged in small oak casks (about 50 gallons) in underground cellars, or *calados.* They make good table wines, called *corrientes,* which are stabilized and bottled during the first year. Wines of a light red color, darker than roses but lighter than reds called Riojas Claretes, reach many foreign markets and the better Spanish restaurants. White Rioja wines, produced in smaller quantities, are from the Viura and Malvasia vines.

In the province of Zaragoza, the district of Carinena produces classic Aragon Claretes—red table wines of high alcoholic content. Good white table wines are the strongpoint of the east coast from Barcelona to Valencia. Wines from central Spain (Castile and La Mancha) account for about 35 percent of the total Spanish wine production. Most of the grape varieties are white. La Mancha produces *corrientes.* Most of the La Mancha wines are still vinified in tinajas, large vats of baked clay. Valdepenas wine, from La Mancha, is ruby-colored, hearty and strong (up to 14 percent in alcohol strength). Most Castilian white wines are made from the Airen grape. Their alcoholic content is from 12 to 14 percent. The wine is golden, clear but not very bright, and the acidity is low.

In southern Spain, near Malaga, the area abounds with Moscatel and Pedro Ximenez grapes (one of the important grapes in the making of sherry). Moscatel makes raisins. Pedro Ximenez produces sweet and semisweet wines, old gold in color, with an alcohol content of from 14 to 23 percent. A good **Lacrima Cristi** is produced here. From Jerez de la Frontera comes **Manzanilla** and the great **sherry,** from Palomino and Pedro Ximenez grapes gathered within a restricted area in the northwest corner of the province of Cadiz.

> *A good sherris sack hath a twofold operation in it. It ascends me into the brain, dries me there all the foolish and dull and crudy vapours which environ it, makes it apprehensive, quick, forgetive, full of nimble, fiery, and delectable shapes, which, delivered o'er to the voice, the tongue, which is the birth, becomes excellent wit. The second property of your excellent sherris is the warming of the blood, which, before cold*

and settled, left the liver white and pale, which is the badge of pusillanimity and cowardice. But the sherris warms it and makes it course from the inwards to the parts extremes.
—Falstaff, Henry IV Part II.

"Sherry" is a British corruption of the Spanish *Jerez.* The British have long been enamoured of this superb Spanish wine.

WINES, SWISS

Two great rivers define the shape of this mountainous country and give their banks to the production of wine. Vineyards along the Rhine and the Rhone date from ancient times. The Rhone flows east through French-speaking Switzerland, becomes Lake Leman (or Lake Geneva), and finally cuts south into France on its way to the Mediterranean. The Rhine forms the northern boundary of the country, and turns abruptly north at Basel on its way through Germany to the North Sea.

French-speaking Switzerland produces more wine than any other viticultural region in the country. White wine is harvested on both sides of the Rhone, though the production of red—about 25 percent of the total—is gradually increasing. Three regions lead all others in the Rhone wine area of Switzerland: the cantons of Geneva, Valais and Vaud.

Land in Valais has been improved patiently over the years by tremendous and dangerous effort. Almost 90 percent of the Valais wine is grown on terraced mountainsides, mostly on the right bank of the Rhone to catch the sun. Artificial canals, or *bisses,* bring water down from the high glaciers for irrigation. White wines from Valais are known by the name Fendant, from the Chasselas Roux and Fendant Vert grapes. Dole is the name given here for red wines, from the Pinot Noir and Gamay vines. Valais wine should be drunk young and on the spot.

Vaud also produces mostly white wines—under the name Dorin, while reds carry the name Salvagnin. Vaud white wines are said to be less tender than those of Valais, but less lively than those of Geneva. The red wines have their name from an old vine stock but are essentially from the Pinot and Gamay grapes.

In Geneva, one-fifth of the wine-growing area is planted with red wines, with Gamay being the major grape. Geneva white wine is from the Chasselas, Riesling-Sylvaner, Sylvaner and Pinot Blanc vines. The vineyards here date back to the Roman conquest. Wines produced from Chasselas are called Perlan, and are generally light and sparkling with a natural carbonic acid gas.

The vineyards along the Rhine are not as prolific as those of the Rhone, but the wine-making tradition is just as old. Reds predominate today, except in vineyards along the lakes of Biel and Neuchatel. Industrialization, particularly in the vicinity of St. Gallen and Zurich, is a problem for Swiss Rhine wine, as is the competition from superior German vintages.

Riesling-Sylvaner is the main white grape variety here. This is a cross between the Riesling, a late ripening grape with a high acid content, and the green Sylvaner (or Johannisberg), also a late ripener. In Germany this grape retains the name of its inventor, Muller-Thurgau. Riesling-Sylvaner has a fine bouquet, is light, fresh, with a slight muscat flavor.

A common red wine is the Pinot Noir, known here as the Blauburgunder (or Blue Burgundy). It was brought to the region in the 1630s by the French Duc de Rohan. The *fohn,* the strong south wind that brings unseasonable heat in the fall, is unpleasant to people but amiable to the grapes of the upper Rhine.

Other Swiss vineyards are along the Aare, a tributary of the Rhine, and around Lake Neuchatel in northwestern Switzerland. These wine-growing areas go back at least to the 10th century. The vineyards are high, between 1300 and 1600 feet, on the banks of Lake Neuchatel, north of Geneva. Neuchatel reds are among the finest in Switzerland. One of the very best is the Cortaillod. All are derived from the Pinot Noir (Burgundy) grape. Oeil de Perdrix ("Partridge Eye") is a wine made from this grape but is fermented slightly in the vat. Neuchatel produces almost three times as many whites as it does reds, all from the Chasselas vine. These are bottled while still on the lees to retain an amount of carbonic acid, which makes them slightly sparkling. Whites from the Sylvaner grape are light, go well with fish, and are sold under the name Bonvillars.

Except for the more select wines of Neuchatel, Swiss wine is made almost totally for home consumption. Switzerland produced 32,388,468 gallons of wine in 1978, smallest of the European wine-growing nations.

WINES, TURKISH

In spite of its Moslem population, Turkey produced 16,431,996 gallons of wine in 1978, almost twice as much as Israel. Although the Turks favor sweet, even syrupy wine (labeled *sarap),* some good dry reds and whites are grown and exported, among them the fine dry red Buzbag (pronounced "boozbah") and a semi-dry white wine, Beyaz, from Thrace in European Turkey. Most Turkish vineyards are located in Thrace and in Anatolia near Smyrna, where many believe the vine originated before it migrated into Europe.

WINES, UNITED STATES

The United States was sixth in world wine production in 1978, behind fifth-ranked Argentina, with a total of 405,489,882 gallons reported. Most of the wine in the United States is grown in California, the only area where the European species of wine grape, *Vitis vinifera*, has so far managed to thrive. *Vinifera* grapes were brought to North America (New Spain) in the 16th century. In 1769, Spanish missionaries planted the first vines (probably of Spanish origin) in the San Diego area. Later, in the 1830s, a Frenchman, Jean-Louis Vignes, introduced French vines to California. A Hungarian nobleman, Agoston Haraszthy ("the father of California viticulture"), followed Vignes' example, and in 1851 imported over 100,000 cuttings from 300 foreign varieties.

In 1919 Prohibition dealt a heavy blow to the American wine industry. The making of wine was declared unlawful, and this remained the case until 1933. Wine could be used, in these years, for medicinal purposes, and each householder could make up to 200 gallons of wine per year for family consumption.

In California the most adaptable wine grapes of European origin have proved to be Cabernet-Sauvignon, Barbera and Pinot Noir for the reds, and Pinot Chardonnay and Sauvignon Blanc for the whites. In the warm, sunny San Joaquin Valley, the Palomino and Tinta grapes from Portugal do very well. Most of the select California wines are grown in the northern coastal region, where the foggy ocean breezes alternate with long hours of unbroken sunlight, with a year-round mild temperature. Some excellent white wines are found in this area in the Napa Valley:Rieslings, the Gewurztraminer and Chenin Blanc. Good dry red wines, from the Barbera, Gamay and Zinfandel grapes also come from Napa.

Charles Krug founded Napa's first commercial winery in 1861 in St. Helena, about 75 miles north of San Francisco. Now the Napa Valley is one of the most famous wine-producing regions in the world. Good northern California wines are also to be found in Sonoma (south of Napa) and in the Livermore area around Alameda and the hills to the east and south of Oakland. Presentable dessert and table wines are produced in southern California, in the area around Los Angeles, though industrialization there is a constant menace to space and sunlight.

In other states, notably in Arkansas where Swiss and German immigrants in the 1880s brought their wine-making expertise, in New York in the Finger Lakes region in the northwestern part of the state, in Ohio, in Pennsylvania (near Lake Erie), in Washington and Oregon, the majority of the wines produced are of the *Vitis labrusca* (native) species, although experimentation does go on with French hybrids and with *vinifera* grapes. Most wine drinkers find the *labrusca* wines to have a strong, "foxy" taste (caused by the presence of methyl anthrenilate). Another drawback to *labrusca* is that it must be heavily sweetened before it is palatable. But it is a hardy plant in most varieties and is very resistant to diseases that kill *vinifera*.

Good, honest *labrusca* or hybrid grapes that make up some of the better North American table wines are the **Concord, Catawba, Delaware,** Elvira and Niagara. Valuable work with *Vitis labrusca* was initiated by T. V. Munson in the late 19th century. In poetry, Munson described the growth and spread of the grape from mythological times to the present bountiful years in North America:

> *Thus on and on, through old, ten thousand years,*
> *Have come adown to all mankind the twining vines*
> *Of Ararat, in Muscats, Flame Tokays and Cornichons.*
> *The sons of men still hand them on with loving care,*
> *Well mingled with those from our free American hills.*

In the Fall of 1873 Munson began his task of cataloging all the grape varieties to be found in the United States "before they forever perish by browsing cattle and the woodman's ax." His experiments with grapes in the 1870s led to the establishment of wineries, experimental stations and laboratories in many of the central and southern states.

For thirty years Munson traveled the North American continent, "never neglecting any opportunity to hunt and study the wild plants, especially the grapes and other wild fruits." He believed that the future of the American wine industry lay in the cultivation and hybridization of native *Vitis labrusca* varieties, which could resist the diseases that crippled *Vitis vinifera*. Today, some *labrusca* grapes are used in the growing wine industry in Brazil. From Munson's work, experiments with *labrusca* still show promise for a new, "ideal" American wine—healthy, prolific and tasty.

See also: **California Wines.**

WINES, USSR

Russia is the world's third-largest producer of wine, with over 811,032,600 gallons reported in 1978. The area given to wine production forms a large semicircle in the south of European Russia and extends from the Romanian frontier to the borders of Iran and India. The most important wine-growing areas are Moldavia, the Ukraine, Crimea, the lower waters of the Don, Krasnodar, Georgia and Uzbekistan.

The vine has existed in a wild state from ancient times. Russian botanists have discovered at least 60 varieties of wild vine—the earliest dating from the Stone Age. With Russia's emergence into modern Europe in the 19th century the snobbery of a francophile aristocracy demanded vineyards. Wines were grown and cultivated from imported French stock and were given famous names, such as **"Sauternes"** and "Vougeot." In 1914, vineyards in

Russia spread over 526 acres. Today the acreage is about 2½ million.

Moldavia (formerly part of Romania) produces mostly table wines. Good Ukrainian white wines are made from Riesling and Aligote grapes. An excellent dry red Ukrainian Bordo is made from the Cabernet-Sauvignon grape. Crimea has a wide range of wines—dry whites, dry reds, desserts. Georgia, with its subtropical climate, is an ideal area for vine cultivation and produces mostly sweet wines. Armenia and Uzbekistan (in Asia, south of the Aral Sea) make **Tokay** and dessert wines. Donski is a sparkling and popular wine (red and white) grown along the banks of the Don.

The Soviet Union produces six times more sweet and dessert wine than it does dry wines, partly because in Russia wine is considered to be a drink for special occasions. The average Russian, also, prefers sparkling to still wine. Consumption runs about twenty bottles a year per 1000 inhabitants.

WINKLE

See **Periwinkle.**

WINTERBERRY

See **Checkerberry.**

WINTER CHERRY

See **Ground Cherry.**

WINTER CRESS

See **Barbarea.**

WINTERGREEN

Oil of wintergreen is a flavoring agent originally obtained from the creeping shrub *Gaultheria procumbens*, which is native to the United States Midwest. The main source is now the tree *Betula lenta*, which is known as the cherry birch, sweet birch, black birch, mahogany birch and mountain mahogany. The oil is extracted from the twigs and bark. It is used to flavor candies, chewing gum and medicinal preparations.

Leaves of *G. procumbens* are infused to make an herbal tea. Its red berries, known as winterberries, have a spicy flavor and are used for pies, puddings and sauces.

WINTER MELON

See **Muskmelon.**

WINTER PURSLANE

Also MINER'S LETTUCE. Here is a small, soft, annual herb, *Montia perfoliata*, with bright green stems and leaves and white flowers. The leaves and stems are eaten in salads or boiled as spinach. It is sometimes cultivated but is found wild in North America from British Columbia to Mexico. Winter purslane has also been introduced into Europe.

WISKERED ANCHOVY

An Indo-Pacific species, *Thrissocles setirostris*, plentiful from East Africa to Australia, it reaches a length of about eight inches and is said to be excellent eating. Greenish yellow above, and silver below, it lacks the silver sideline of other anchovies.

See also: **Anchovy.**

WISNIAK

A liqueur flavored with wild cherries, it is bottled at from 48 to 60 proof. The best wisniak comes from Poland, but is also made in Russia and Czechoslovakia. The bottle often contains whole cherries.

WITCHETY GRUB

A class of insect larvae, including caterpillars and beetle grubs, these are highly prized as food by Australian aborigines. Witchey grubs have never been scientifically identified and classified, yet most observers agree that the caterpillar of the giant ghost moth is one of them, as are the larvae of the big longicorn beetle.

The grubs are found in the roots of shrubs, such as the cassia and acacia, and in the trunk of a certain species of eucalyptus tree. The hunter tests the roots with a special stick, and if the root snaps, he digs out the grub. He must climb the eucalyptus tree for the trunk-boring larvae but is rewarded for his effort with a much larger, greener caterpillar. The grubs are put in the hot ashes of a fire for a few moments to singe off the hair, and are then eaten without further cooking. Europeans describe the taste as delicate and nutty, comparing it to slightly sweetened scrambled eggs, roast pork or bone marrow.

See also: **Beetles.**

WITHANIA CHEESE

This is a ripened cheese made in India and so named because the milk is coagulated with rennet obtained from withania berries rather than from animal sources, which are considered undesirable from a religious point of view. Aged properly the cheese has a pleasant flavor but, if left too long, it becomes acrid.

WITLOOF

See **Chicory.**

WOANDZEIA

See **Bambara Groundnut.**

WODKA

See **Vodka.**

WOLFFISH

Also SPOTTED CATFISH, WOLF-EEL. The wolffish *(Anarhichas lupus)* is found on both sides of the Atlantic and is recognized by its large, doglike teeth. It is edible and is of some local importance as food in Iceland and Greenland and other North Atlantic areas. An ocean catfish, the wolffish attains a maximum length of about 50 inches and is closely related to the spotted catfish *(A. minor)* also of the North Atlantic as well as the Arctic Ocean. The latter exceeds six feet in length and is a moderately important commercial fish in northern waters. A related species is the wolfel *(Anarhichthys ocellatus)* of the Northern Pacific, a slender, long (up to eight feet) fish that can weigh as much as 100 pounds. It is edible but not commercially exploited.

WONG BOK

Also CHIHLI. Wong bok and chihli are varieties of Chinese cabbage *(Brassica chinensis)* similar to *pet-sai.* Each differs to a minor degree in color, hairiness and serration of leaf edges. Wong bok is eaten more like lettuce in autumn and winter. Otherwise they are used like ***petsai.***

WOOD AGARIC

See **Red Staining Mushroom.**

WOOD APPLE

See **Elephant Apple.**

WOODCHUCK

See **Marmot.**

Woodcock

WOODCOCK

Also BECASSE. This is a small, long-billed game bird of Europe and America that is renowned for its dark, tender and fine-tasting flesh. The European woodcook *(Scolopax rusticula)* inhabits marshes, shores or other muddy areas that permit it to root around with its beak for shoots, insects, earthworms or berries. The bird is migratory, arriving in Great Britain and the Continent in September and staying through the winter. It is in season from September to February.

A woodcock is about the size of a grouse and it yields an unusual amount of meat for a bird of that size. One 12-ounce woodcock is a good serving for a person of normal appetite. The French are very fond of woodcock and have dozens of recipes for it. But many game fanciers prefer the simplest methods of preparation, such as roasting or sauteeing. The bird is plucked with the head intact (but with eyes removed), and of the innards, only the gizzard is removed. It is cooked and served on toast.

The American woodcock *(Philohela minor)* is a smaller bird, but just as delicious. It is found in many parts of eastern North America from Canada to the Gulf of Mexico. The plumage is varied in color including gray, buff, brown and black. The female averages one-half pound in weight and the male less. Among American game bird fanciers, the woodcock is second in the culinary hierarchy only to the canvas-back duck. John James Audubon, the American naturalist, wrote:

> *When a jug of sparkling Newark cider stands nigh, and you, without knife or fork, quarter a woodcock, ah reader!—but alas! I am not in the Jerseys just now . . . I am . . . without any expectation of Woodcocks for my dinner, either today or tomorrow, or indeed for some months to come. So tender and savory is its flesh that I would quickly put the merits of the widely celebrated Canvass-Backed Duck in the shade . . . I myself saw a friend kill 84 by pulling together the triggers of his double-barreled gun.*

WOOD EAR

See **Black Tree Fungus.**

WOOD GROUSE

See **Capercaillie.**

WOOD LILY

The bulbs of this flowering plant, *Lilium philadelphicum*, can be eaten like potatoes. This species is native to the northern states of the Midwest. The wood lily is characterized by vivid orange red flowers.

WOODRUFF

See **Asperula.**

WOOLLY BUCKTHORN

Also CHITTAMWOOD, BLACK HAW. This is the small, black fruit of a deciduous tree, *Bumelia lanuginosa*, found in southeastern United States and as far west as Arkansas and Texas. The fruits are gathered wild and eaten. A closely allied species, the Mexican buckthorn, has similar fruit that is gathered unripe and pickled in salt or vinegar.

WORCESTERSHIRE SAUCE

This is a proprietary sauce used as a condiment on a wide variety of dishes, but especially meat and fish. It is thin, dark and piquant, and is said to contain more than 100 ingredients, including soy sauce, vinegar, molasses, chili, anchovies, garlic, shallots, tamarinds, limes and many spices.

Worcestershire sauce is said to be of ancient origin, starting with the Phoenicians and continuing with the ancient Romans. It may have been an offshoot of ***garum.***

The story goes that it came to its present proprietor, Lea and Perrins, by way of India. Many years ago the company was asked to prepare a batch of sauce by a former governor of Bengal from a formula in his possession. He rejected their efforts, however, and the sauce was put away and forgotten about. Years later the sauce was rediscovered during a cleaning session, tasted and pronounced excellent. Since they still had the formula, Lea and Perrins began to manufacture it. It is produced under license now in many countries of the world, including India.

WORMWOOD

This very bitter woody herb, *Artemisia absinthium*, is used to flavor **absinthe** and **vermouth.** "Wormwood" is a name applied to several species of bitter plants, including Alpine Yarrow—used to prepare medicinal herb teas—and Musk Milfoil, the main ingredient of a liqueur (*Liqueur d'Ira* or *Irabitter)* made in Italy and Switzerland from several Alpine herbs and originally distilled at the Grande Chartreuse.

Etymologically, "wormwood" is the same as "vermouth," from the Germanic *wer* or man, and *mut*, spirit or courage. As an aphrodisiac, wormwood was thought to stimulate virility. But the name has come to mean anything bitter or grievous. Anne Bradstreet, the New England Puritan poet, points to the use of wormwood in weaning children and symbolically bringing healthy bitterness to lazy Christians: "Some children are hardly weaned: although the teat be rubbed with wormwood or mustard, they will either wipe it off or else suck down sweet and bitter together. So it is with some Christians . . ." The star "Wormwood" in the Book of the Revelation, which poisoned one-third of the fresh waters of the world, is translated directly from the Greek *Absinthos*, or absinthe.

See also: **Absinthe.**

WRASSE

Here is a large family of fish, *Labridae*, found in all but polar waters the world over. Most are small, and many act as cleanerfish, i.e., picking parasites off other fish. The ones most commonly eaten in Europe are the ***girella*** or rainbow wrasse; the ballan wrasse *(Labrus bergylta)*, which seldom exceeds 20 inches and has coarse, rather sweet flesh; and the cuckoo wrasse *(L. mixtus)*, which averages less than 13 inches in length. The latter two wrasses are eaten mostly in fish stews, such as bouillabaisse.

The largest wrasse in the world is the hump-headed maori or giant wrasse *(Cheilinus undulatus)* of tropical Indo-Pacific waters. A specimen was caught off the Queensland, Australia, coast that measured more than seven feet long and weighed 420 pounds. The giant wrasse is remarkable for a big fleshy crest or bump on its forehead and for its beautiful yellow head, dark blue throat, greenish overall color and blue-centered scales.

WURSTE VAN KALBSGEKROSE

This is a sausage whose chief ingredient is calf's mesentery, a ventral membrane that surrounds the stomach. The mesentery is blanched, cooked, chopped and mixed with salt, pepper, nutmeg and heavy cream. The mixture is put in pork casings, which are usually tied off at 10-inch lengths. This is a German specialty and it is best poached, then drained and fried in butter until brown.

See also: **Sausage.**

X–Y

XIMENIA

See **Tallow Wood.**

YAGE

Also AYAHUASCA. Yage is a south American climbing vine, *Banisteria caapi*, *B. mettalicolor*, whose leaves and twigs are used to make a narcotic drink. Large amounts of this drink, itself called *ayahuasca*, are said to cause delirium, hallucinations and telepathic effects. Yage is especially plentiful in Brazil.

YAK

Also GRUNTING OX. An ox, *Bos grunniens*, inhabiting the higher elevations of Asia, it has been domesticated for centuries in Tibet, where it is the major source of milk and meat. Wild yaks, especially bulls, are huge, and are twice the size of the domesticated variety, standing up to 6½ feet at the shoulder and weighing up to 1200 pounds. They have large upward and forward-curving horns, blackish brown coats (in the wild), or red, mottled, brown or black coats (domesticated), and a fringe around the lower parts of the shoulders and sides that reaches almost to the ground. They are agile climbers despite an awkward appearance, and, when domesticated, are quite docile beasts of burden.

YAM

Here is a climbing plant, *Discorea* spp.,the tuberous root of which, although botanically unrelated, much resembles the **sweet potato.** Root size ranges from very small to more than 100 pounds, with specimens of 40 to 50 pounds not unusual. There are several species so that skin color can vary from dirty white to reddish brown, and flesh from greenish yellow to orange. The flesh of the yam is moist and sweet.

Native to the tropics of both hemispheres, the yam is greatly relished in the West Indies and the American South, where it is a staple item of soul food. There the terms "yam" and "sweet potato" are often used interchangeably. Yams are usually boiled or baked until tender and sometimes candied.

YAM BEAN

See **Jicama.**

YAMPA

Also SQUAWROOT, INDIAN CARAWAY. The tubers of this perennial herb, *Perideridia gairdneri*, were eaten by native Americans and early European settlers. It is native to western North America and was a favorite food because of the pleasant nutty flavor of the roots. They could be eaten fresh or preserved for winter consumption. Two closely related species are Kellogg's yampa and Oregon yampa, all considered excellent vegetables.

YANGONA

See **Kava.**

YANG-TAO

See **Tara.**

YAUPON

See **Cassina.**

YARD-LONG BEAN

See **Asparagus Bean.**

YARROW

See **Achillea.**

Yams

YAUTIA

Also **OCUMO, TANNIA.** This is a genus of large-leaved plants *(Xanthosoma* spp.) widely grown in the tropics for its yamlike tubers. Two important species are the yellow yautia *(X. sagittifolium)* and the blue taro *(X. violaceum)*. Yautias are of the same family as the **taro** and are as important a food crop in the American tropics and West Africa, as taro is in eastern Asia and the Pacific islands. Yautias may be the world's oldest cultivated root vegetable.

The yellow yautia is practically stemless, has a milky sap and arrow-shaped leaves that reach a length of three feet. These leaves make an excellent boiled green when young. The stems remain underground as thick tubers, or cormels, which have an acrid taste when raw. Cooking dispels this acridity and produces a palatable, potatolike, starchy vegetable. Its nutritive value is much like the potato's, but some varieties have a greater carbohydrate content and less water. The tubers range in color from white to orange and rose to purple.

Yautia is grown in the United States mainly as an ornamental plant, but some commercial crops are cultivated in the southeastern region. They need a tropical climate and grow well in moist soils that would not support other starchy vegetables.

YEAST

Yeast is a living organism—minute and generally transparent—which is used, through fermentation, to produce alcohol, leavening for bread, and vitamins. It is a type of fungus with many varieties, but the kinds most useful to humans are strains of *Saccharomyces cerevisiae*. Under the right conditions, these strains, which are generally unicellular, multiply rapidly in a sugar solution, converting the sugar to alcohol and carbon dioxide gas. This process is called fermentation and upon it depends the manufacture of beer, wine and distilled spirits. The alcohol in these beverages is ethanol, produced by yeast. The other product of fermentation, carbon dioxide gas, is released by yeast in bread dough and captured there by the gluten in the wheat flour, which causes the bread to swell up and become lighter. The alcohol in the dough is vaporized during the baking. Commenting on temperance reformers, Ralph Waldo Emerson wrote, "God made yeast, as well as dough, and loves fermentation just as dearly as he loves vegetation."

The ancient Egyptians would have agreed with Emerson since, according to archaeologists, they were the first people to harness yeast as leavening for their bread. Their bread often incorporated both wheat and barley, which they often sprouted before grinding. This made the flour more digestible and gave it better keeping qualities. This was, in effect, barley-malt, the raw material for beer making, and, indeed, Egyptians began making beer from this type of bread by soaking half-baked loaves in water, then leaving the mixture to ferment for a day. By 3000 B.C. Egyptians had a number of "bear-breads" to choose from, some of which were spiced and flavored. The alcohol content ranged as high as 12 percent. Reay Tannihill, author of *Food in History*, wrote:

> *Brewers in the early world were usually women, who sold the beer from their homes. The Code of Hammurabi, dated at just before 1750 B.C., strikes a very familiar note in its condemnation of ale houses and their under-strength, overpriced beer, while an Egyptian papyrus of about 1400 B.C. gave advice to drinkers which has remained good ever since. "Do not get drunk," it recommended, "in the taverns in which they drink beer, for fear that people repeat words which may have gone out of your mouth, without you being aware of having uttered them."*

Yeast spores are present everywhere, but down through the centuries certain strains have been isolated and propagated commercially. Two of these are brewer's yeast and baker's yeast. Predictably enough, brewer's yeast produces more alcohol than carbon dioxide, while baker's yeast does the reverse. Brewer's yeast is also slower-acting than baker's yeast. It is the latter that is readily available in stores in compressed or dried form.

Compressed yeast, sold in cakes, consists of fresh yeast cells in a culture medium (often molasses and oil) that have been compressed to one-tenth normal volume. When absolutely fresh, this type is better and quicker to use in baking than the dried form. The latter, however, will keep for six months under refrigeration if the packaging is intact.

Yeast works best at between 70° and 90° F (21.1°–32.2°C). Most strains will die at temperatures above 132° F (55.5° C) or below approximately 40° F (4.4° C). At breadmaking time both types of yeast are set working in a warm sugar solution some time before they are incorporated into the dough. Many factors go into determining the amount of yeast appropriate to a given bread, including quantity and quality of the flour, the liquid and fat content of the dough, the general temperature and time to be allowed for rising. Coarse flour, such as whole wheat, requires more yeast than white flour.

Regarding the yeast plant, the biochemist George Wald is said to have remarked:

> *as living creatures we are more like yeast than unlike it. Yeast and man had a common ancestor. Some of the ancestor's progeny became yeasts and some went another way and became men, and these two journeys resulted in a change of only 53 nucleotides out of 312.*

See also: **Alcohol, Bread.**

YELLOW-FIN BREAM

Also SILVER BREAM, TARWHINE. An important food fish of the Indo-Pacific area from East Africa to Japan, the yellow-fin bream *(Rhabdosargus sarba)* seldom exceeds 16 inches in length, except in South African waters where it can weigh as much as 25 pounds and be much longer. It is a favorite with anglers there. Like other sea breams, it favors inshore waters with sandy bottoms. It has a deep, relatively thick body with a bluish back, deep yellow belly and lower fins and yellow horizontal lines.

YELLOW MOMBIN

Also HOG PLUM, IMBU, JOBO. This edible fruit of a tropical American tree, *Spondias mombin*, plentiful in northeastern Brazil, is bright yellow, oval, with a soft, juicy subacidic pulp surrounding a large seed. It averages about one inch long.

The yellow mombin is often eaten fresh, but it has a fine flavor when boiled in sweetened milk and served as a dessert called *imbuzada*. It is also made into jelly or used to make a cooling beverage.

YELLOWTAIL

This substantial food and game fish, *Seriola dorsalis*, of the Pacific Ocean, is found from California to northern South America and in Australian waters. The yellowtail is one of the **amber fish,** and it reaches a length of five feet and a weight of 100 pounds. It is a favorite with anglers and can be taken in inshore waters as well as offshore. The yellowtail is significant commercially, being fished by large purse seiners and marketed fresh, canned and smoked.

Its Australian counterpart, *S. grandis*, is a larger fish, reaching weights of 150 pounds or more. The flesh of the large specimens tends to be coarse and tough, but young fish are considered a gastronomic delicacy. They are plentiful off the coasts of Queensland, New South Wales and South Australia.

See also: **Amber Fish, Kingfish.**

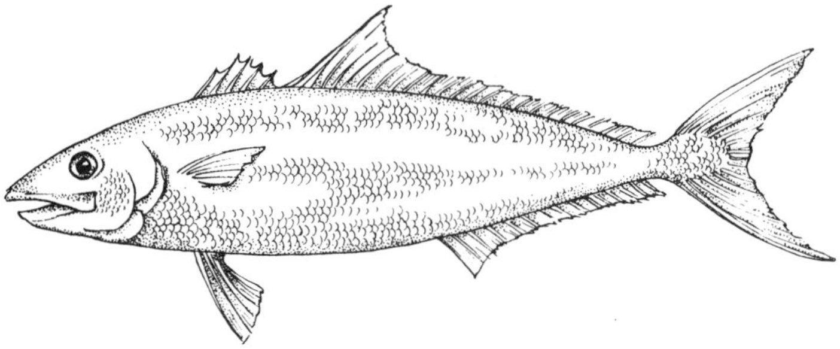

Yellowtail

YELLOWTAIL SNAPPER

A slender-bodied member of the snapper family *(Lutjanidae)*, the yellowtail snapper is considered a fine food fish. It is found on both sides of the Atlantic, in the east in waters near the Cape Verde Islands, and in the west in coastal waters from New England to southern Brazil.

The yellowtail snapper *(Ocyurus chrysurus)* is popular with anglers. It reaches a length of up to 30 inches and typically weighs about five pounds. It prefers open water near a reef. It has a grayish blue back and a silver belly, but it is distinguished by a deep yellow stripe extending from snout to tail.

YELLOW TANG

See **Knotted Wrack.**

YERBA BUENA

This flavoring herb, *Saturja douglasii*, of the mint family, is native to western North America. It is highly aromatic and is used sparingly to season vegetables, especially potatoes.

YERBA MATE

See **Mate.**

YEW

Also PLUM-FRUITED YEW. Yew is an evergreen shrub or tree, *Cephalotaxus harringtonia* var. *drupacea*, native to Japan, whose fleshy seeds resemble plums and have a sweet piney taste.

YOGURT

This is cultured milk, which has been turned into a thick creamy curd by the action of two bacteria: *Lactobacillus bulgaricus* and *Streptococcus thermophilus.* Except for the difference in bacteria, yogurt and sour milk are brought about through much the same process. Like other fermented milks, yogurt is digestible by persons who cannot tolerate fresh milk because of its lactose content. (Many adults, having stopped drinking fresh milk at weaning, fail to secrete the enzyme lactase, which is essential to the digestion of milk sugar, or lactose). In yogurt, the latter is changed into lactic acid. Claims are made as to yogurt's healthy qualities, mainly that it is good for the digestive tract and that it promotes longevity. Yogurt is known by a variety of names including *mast* (Iran), *matzoon* (Armenian), *laban* (Arabs) and *kumiss* and *kefir* in Russia.

According to legend, the biblical patriarch Abraham was the first to make yogurt, after an angel whispered the secret in his ear. It seems to have originated in Bulgaria, however, and for thousands of years has been a staple food in Balkan countries and among Mongolians, Arabs, Armenians, Persians and Turks. The two operative bacteria in yogurt were first isolated by a Russian doctor, Elie Metchnikoff of the Pasteur Institute, at the beginning of this century. Metchnikoff was a Nobel Laureate in 1908.

It is only in the past 20 years that yogurt has attained much acceptance in the United States, and then only after being sweetened by the addition of fruit. Commercial yogurt is made from whole or low-fat cow's milk with milk solids added. The milk is scalded, allowed to cool, then inoculated with the proper bacteria. During the incubation period, it must be kept between 77° and 115° F (25° and 46.1° C). When the proper acidity is reached (0.09 percent) the yogurt is cooled to stop bacterial action. Much of the incubation is completed in the final container (usually a paper cup) to which fruit has been added. The latter may be mixed throughout, settled on the bottom, or (if the container has been inverted) settled on the top. Stabilizers, such as gelatin, are often added to guarantee a custardlike consistency.

Many people make yogurt at home by simply scalding a quantity of milk, letting it cool, then adding a spoonful of commercial yogurt as a starter. It is incubated in a glass container and must be kept at the proper temperature, either in an oven or in a store-bought yogurt maker for between eight and 14 hours. Typically the homemade product has a milder taste than that purchased in a store because the latter tends to increase in acidity as it sits on the shelf. Plain yogurt of the commercial variety have about 125 calories per cup, while the sweetened varieties have much more.

Stories about yogurt's healing and rejuvenating properties have circulated for centuries. In 16th-century France, it was recommended by the Turkish ambassador to King Francis I who suffered from intestinal disorders. An aged Jewish doctor was dispatched from Constantinople to the French court on foot, herding a flock of sheep and goats through Bulgaria, Serbia, Hungary, Austria and Germany. Although he refused to tell the secret of making yogurt, he gave the king a fresh supply every day. The king's health was restored whereupon the doctor trudged back to Turkey with his flock and his secret intact. Later, the king relapsed, and died "sorely lamenting the loss of the daily yogurt which had so alleviated his suffering."

Bulgarians claim that only *true* yogurt is able to prolong life, that is, yogurt made with bacilli from the mountains of Bulgaria. Moreover, the milk, to meet their standards, must be a combination of goat's and water buffalo's milk, both of which are much richer in butterfat than cow's milk. It is not unusual for a Bulgarian to eat as much as six pounds of yogurt a day.

There is a wealth of scientific literature about the nutritional and therapeutic benefits of eating yogurt, but none that bears out the claim that it significantly lengthens human life.

See also: **Acidophilus Milk, Buttermilk, Kefir, Kumiss, Laban.**

YOGURT CHEESE

Also ACIDOPHILUS CHEESE. Practically any style of cheese—hard or soft—can be a yogurt cheese, provided the proper bacterial starters are added to the milk before renneting. In order for these to operate properly the milk must be pasteurized. For yogurt the starters are *Streptococcus thermophilus*, *Thermobacterium bulgaricus* and *Thermobacterium joghurt*. The starters for acidophilus are *Streptococcus thermophilus* and *Thermobacterium acidophilum*. These starters contribute a characteristic acidic flavor to the resulting cheese, which otherwise might be conventional cream, Camembert or Gouda.

YOPON

See **Cassina.**

YOUNGBERRY

A hybrid of the Pacific dewberry *(Rubus ursinus* Cv. *Young)* much resembling the **loganberry** and the **boysenberry,** it ripens earlier than the boysenberry and is dark red to black, juicy, soft and tart in flavor. It measures up to two inches in length and an inch in diameter. Though native to the West Coast of North America, the youngberry is more popular in Africa, where it is cultivated in both the north and the south. Youngberries may be eaten fresh or used in jams and pies. The dewberry is a variety of blackberry or bramble.

YORK CHEESE

See **Cambridge Cheese.**

YOUNG HYSON TEA

Here is a type of Chinese green tea that utilizes young to medium-age leaves, as opposed to **Hyson,** which uses older leaves. In Young Hyson the leaves are thin and twisted, and the brew fragrant, mellow and lighter than that produced by Hyson. The name "Hyson" derives from that of an East Indian merchant who first imported this grade of tea.

See also: **Tea.**

YSANO

Also ANYU, PERUVIAN POTATO. Ysano is a tuberous-rooted climbing plant, *Tropaelum tuberosum*, of Andean South America. The tubers are eaten as vegetables and have been grown experimentally in France and Great Britain. Somewhat resembling sweet potatoes, the tubers are yellow or greenish with purple markings. They are washed, peeled and cooked like potatoes, yet are said to have a disagreeable taste if eaten after simple boiling. The people of Peru, Chile and Bolivia remedy this by leaving them out to freeze after boiling or by allowing them to dry partially. Ysano is also used in salads.

YUCATAN CHESTNUT

The seeds of a medium to large tree, *Ceiba aesculifolia*, of tropical Mexico and Guatemala, are contained in a woody capsule and are eaten only when young. This tree is closely related to the kapok tree *(C. pentandra)*, which has a cotton-like fiber surrounding the seeds that becomes commercial kapok.

YUCCA

Also SPANISH BAYONET, SPANISH DAGGER. A plant of the southwestern United States and of Mexico, the yucca is characterized by stiff, sword-shaped leaves and white flowers in a single cluster on a stalk rising from the center of the plant. Several species of yucca have edible flowers, stalks or fruit.

Among them are the datil or Spanish bayonet *(Y. baccata)*, which has bell-shaped fruit varying in color from yellow to dark purple. It has a sweet taste and, when peeled, may be eaten raw or roasted as was the general custom among native Americans of the Southwest. The flowers were boiled and eaten as vegetables.

The same can be said of the Mohave yucca *(Y. schidigera)*, the ozote or spineless yucca *(Y. elephantipes)* and the Our Lord's candle *(Y. whipplei)*. The fruit of the Adam's needle or needle palm *(Y. filamentosa)* and the soapweed *(Y. glauca)* are less common but still edible. Stalks of young yucca may be prepared and eaten like asparagus.

YULAN

This large, spreading tree, *Magnolia heptapeta*, of China, has large, snow-white flowers that are pickled in the bud stage and used to flavor rice.

Z

ZAHRTE

A freshwater bream of Central Europe, the *zahrte (Vimba vimba)* is found in the Danube Basin in rivers emptying into the Black and Caspian Seas and in the rivers of northern Germany, but not in the Rhine. The *zahrte* reaches a length of about 20 inches and has reddish brown coloring above, paling below to rosy yellow. It is fished commercially in eastern Europe and is especially popular in Poland, where it is canned extensively. Zahrte is prepared like **bream.**

ZAMANG

Also MONKEYPOD, RAIN TREE, SAMAN, SAMAN TREE. This is a large, ornamental shade tree, *Samanea saman*, of tropical America, whose pods are edible. These pods are a curved legume with seeds embedded in pulp. The zamang is found in parks and large gardens throughout the tropics.

ZAMIA

See **Coontie.**

ZANDER

Also PIKE-PERCH. This giant perch or pike-perch *(Stizostedion lucioperca)* is native to the Danube and Elbe Rivers but is now widely distributed in Europe. It is fished commercially in Central Europe and Russia (called *sudak* there) and is well liked by anglers in western Europe and England. The zander is deemed a gastronomic delicacy and is served in a variety of ways including baked, broiled, stuffed and simmered in wine. It reaches up to 3½ feet in length.

ZANTHOXYLUM

This is a genus of aromatic shrubs or small trees, three species of which yield seeds that are used as condiments in eastern Asia. Two are known as Chinese pepper, namely, *Z. bunger* and *Z. nitidum*, and a third is known as Japan pepper *(Z. piperatum)*. These trees are cultivated in China, Japan, India and Indochina.

This genus is known as prickly ash in the United States and it is represented by the northern prickly ash or toothache tree *(Z. americanum)* whose dried bark is used medicinally.

ZAPALLITO DE TRONCO

Also AVOCADELLA. A small bush squash or pumpkin, *Cucurbita melopepo*, of South America, especially Argentina, it is of the summer squash (vegetable marrow) type. It takes its alternative name, *avocadella*, from its resemblance to the **avocado,** though it has pink flesh and does not have a pit. The *zapallito de tronco* is usually grapefruit-sized and is also known as Argentine or South American squash. It is grown under glass in France, Great Britain and Iceland.

ZARA

See **Maraschino.**

ZEBRAFISH

See **Tigerfish.**

ZEBU

The "sacred cattle" of India, the zebu *(Bos indicus)* has a characteristic large hump over its shoulders, drooping ears and large dewlaps. It is the main draft animal of India and is highly valued in other tropical areas because of its ability to resist heat, ticks and other insects. The zebu is eaten all over Africa and has been used to develop valuable hybrids in the United States, such as the Santa Gertrudis breed, which was recognized in 1940.

ZEDOARY

See **Curcuma.**

ZEUS CARROT

See **Ammodaucus.**

ZIEGE

A freshwater, schooling fish, *Pelecus cultratus*, of the Baltic States, it is fished commercially in the estuaries of rivers emptying into the Black and Caspian Seas. The ziege reaches a maximum length of about 20 inches. It has a greenish back and brilliant silver sides. It is generally eaten smoked. The scales of the ziege are valuable as a raw material for the artificial pearl industry.

ZIEGEL

A semihard cheese made in Germany and Austria from whole cow's milk, sometimes with 15 percent cream added, it is cured for two months.

ZIEGENKASE

See **Goat's Milk Cheese.**

ZIGER

Also SCHOTTENZIGER. These are German-language terms for whey cheese, i.e., cheese consisting largely of albumin, which is the protein left in whey after the curd has coagulated. It was first made in Italy and called *ricotta.*

See also: **Ricotta.**

ZINFANDEL

A dry red wine made from a native California grape variety of the same name, Zinfandel has a fruity flavor, which some have compared to that of raspberries. Similar to the French **beaujolais,** although darker in color, it often can be aged up to 10 years and especially complements pasta and roast meats.

ZINGEL

This long, slender fish, *Aspro zingel*, of the perch family, is found in the Danube, Prut and Dneister rivers of Central Europe. Although the zingel prefers rapidly running water, it is an inactive, bottom-living fish whose flesh is liable to have a slightly muddy taste. It reaches a length of about 14 inches.

ZOMMA

This is a Turkish cheese of the drawn curd type, much resembling ***caciocavallo.***

See also: **Formaggio di Pasta Filata, Katschkawalj.**

Zucchini

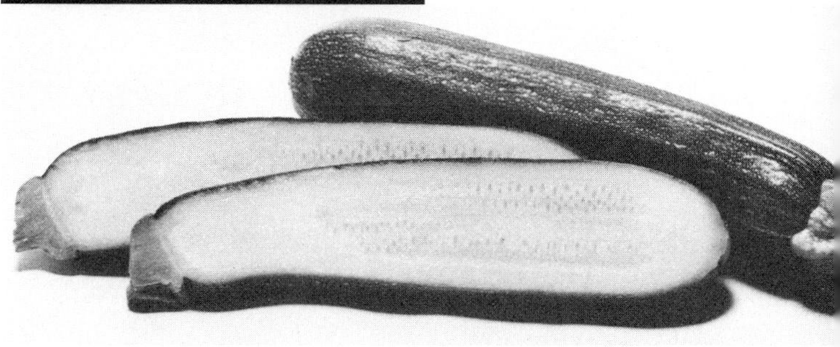

ZUCCHINI

Also BABY MARROW, COURGETTE. This small, usually cylindrical, variety of summer squash, *Cucurbita pepo*, is believed to have originated in South Africa. It is identified with Italy, however, and is often referred to as Italian marrow or Italian squash. Zucchini is dark green or variegated in color and measures four to six inches in length. There is one variety which is globular. Zucchini is picked when unripe, to assure a soft rind (which is not removed for cooking), and good flavor. Some specimens are picked so young that they still bear the corolla, that is, the flower petals.

The zucchini fruits grow out of the female flowers. These flowers themselves are sold in bunches in Mexican and European markets as food. They may be prepared by dipping them into a batter of flour and milk and then frying them. See also **Squash Blossom.**

Zucchini are prepared in a variety of ways. They may be simply boiled and served with a little oil and lemon juice. The flavor is delicate and easily overwhelmed by strong seasoning. Yet, they are frequently stuffed, stewed with other vegetables or dipped into breadcrumb and egg batter and fried.

Zucchini is very low in calories (approximately eight per 3½ ounces [100 grams]) and consists of about 95 percent water. The rest is carbohydrates and ash, plus a few vitamins and minerals.

ZUNI APPLE

Edible fruit of an American shrub, *Solanum triflorum*, found from British Columbia to Mexico, zuni apples are eaten raw when ripe. They are also boiled or ground up and mixed with red pepper and salt.

ZWIEBACH

See **Rusk.**

ZWIRN

See **Tschil.**

Selected Bibliography

Allen, Woody. *Getting Even.* New York: Warner, 1976.

Arens, W. *The Man-Eating Myth: Anthropology & Anthropophagy.* New York: Oxford University Press, 1979.

Bailey, Adrian. *The Blessings of Bread.* New York: Paddington Press, 1975.

Bailey, Liberty H.; and Bailey, Ethel Z. *Hortus Third: A Concise Dictionary of Plants Cultivated in the United States and Canada.* New York: Macmillan, 1976.

Bianchini, F., and Corbetta, F. *The Complete Book of Fruits and Vegetables.* New York: Crown, 1975.

Bodenheimer, F. S. *Insects as Human Food.* The Hague: W. Junk, 1951.

Brothwell, Don; and Brothwell, Patricia. *Food in Antiquity.* New York: Praeger, 1969.

Carper, Jean. "Wonder Milk." *American Home Magazine,* January 1977, p. 24.

Castenada, Carlos. *The Teachings of Don Juan: A Yaqui Way of Knowledge.* Berkeley: Univeristy of California Press, 1968.

Damon, G. Edward. "A Primer on Vitamins." *FDA Consumer,* May 1974.

DeGouy, Louis P. *The Bread Tray.* New York: Dover, 1944.

Dictionary of the English Language. New York: Random House, 1967.

Douglas, James S. *Alternative Foods: A World Guide to Lesser-Known Edible Plants.* London: Pelham Books, 1978.

Encyclopedia Britannica, 15th Edition. 1974.

Fitzgibbon, Theodora. *The Food of the Western World.* New York: Quadrangle, 1976.

Fuller, John. *The Day of St. Anthony's Fire.* New York: Macmillan, 1968.

Funk & Wagnalls Cook's and Diner's Dictionary: A Lexicon of Food, Wine and Culinary Terms. New York: Funk & Wagnalls, 1968.

Gehman, Richard. *The Sausage Book.* New York: Weathervane, 1969.

Gibbons, Euell. *Stalking the Wild Asparagus.* New York: David McKay, 1971.

Glassco, John. *Memoirs of Montparnasse.* New York: Viking, 1970.

Goode's World Atlas, 14th Edition. Chicago: Rand McNally, 1974.

Grigson, Jane. *The Mushroom Feast.* New York: Alfred A. Knopf, 1975.

Grigson, Jane and Mitchell Beazley. *World Atlas of Food.* New York: Mitchell Beazley, 1974.

Grossman, Harold J. *Grossman's Guide to Wines, Beers, and Spirits.* 6th Edition. New York: Charles Scribner's Sons, 1977.

Gurdjieff, Georges. *Meetings with Remarkable Men.* New York: E.P. Dutton, 1969.

Hansen, Barbara J. *Good Bread.* New York: Macmillan, 1976.

Hauser, Gaylord. *The Dictionary of Foods.* Greenwich, Conn.: Lust, Benedict, 1971.

Hervey, George F. *Encyclopedia of Freshwater Fish.* New York: Doubleday, 1973.

Jeffs, Julian. *The Dictionary of World Wines, Liqueurs, and Other Drinks.* Toronto, Pangurian Press, 1973.

Johnson, Hugh. *World Atlas of Wine.* New York: Simon & Schuster, 1971.

Jones, Evan. *A Food Lover's Companion.* New York: Harper & Row, 1979.

Kavaler, Lucy. *Mushrooms, Molds, and Miracles: The Strange Realm of the Fungi.* New York: John Day, 1965.

Kazantzakis, Nikos. *The Last Temptation of Christ.* New York: Simon & Schuster, 1960.

Kennedy, Diana. *Cuisines of Mexico.* New York: Harper & Row, 1972.

Kolpas, Norman. *The Coffee Lover's Companion.* New York: Quick Fox, 1977.

LaGorce, John O., ed. *Book of Fishes.* Washington, D.C.: National Geographic Society, 1939.

Lampert, Lincoln M. *Modern Dairy Products.* 3rd edition. New York: Chemical Publishing, no date.

Lapedes, Daniel N., ed. *McGraw-Hill Encyclopedia of Food, Agriculture & Nutrition.* New York: McGraw-Hill, 1977.

Lichine, Alexis. *New Encyclopedia of Wines and Spirits.* New York: Alfred A. Knopf, 1974.

Loewenfeld, Claire; and Back, Philippa. *Complete Book of Herbs and Spices.* New York: G.P. Putnam's Sons, 1974.

Major, Alan. *Collecting and Studying Mushrooms, Toadstools, and Fungi.* New York: Arco, 1974.

Martin, Ruth. *International Dictionary of Food and Cooking.* New York: Hastings House, 1973.

Marteka, Vincent. *Mushrooms: Wild and Edible.* New York: Norton, 1980.

Miller, Henry. *The Colossus of Maroussi.* New York: New Directions, 1941.

Montagne, Prosper. *The Larousse Gastronomique.* New York: Crown, 1960.

Nash, Ogden. *Parents Keep Out.* Boston: Little, Brown, 1951.

Nash, Ogden. *Verses from 1929 On.* Boston: Little, Brown, 1942.

Nicholson, B. E. et al. *The Oxford Book of Food Plants.* London: Oxford University Press, 1969.

Ogilvy, David. *Confessions of an Advertising Man.* Boston: Atheneum, 1963.

Payson, Herb. "Laid Back in Lau." *Sail,* vol 11, no. 3 (March 1980): 97–101.

Root, Waverley. "Barberry: The Jekyll and Hyde of the World of Fruits." *Los Angeles Times,* January 29, 1981, Part VIII, p. 19.

———. *Food: An Authoritative and Visual History and Dictionary of the Foods of the World.* New York: Simon & Schuster, 1980.

———. "Beaver," *Los Angeles Times,* June 8, 1972, Part VI, p. 10.

———. "History of HERBS: A Fondness Even in Folk Songs," *Los Angeles Times*, February 26, 1982, Part VIII, p. 29.

———. "The Legacy of Lewis and Clark: The Roots of North America." *Los Angeles Times*, March 12, 1981, Part VIII, p. 34.

———; and de Rochemont, Richard. *Eating in America: A History*. New York: William Morrow, 1976.

Schafer, Charles; and Schafer, Violet. *Teacraft*. San Francisco: Yerba Buena, 1975.

Schoonmaker, Frank. *Frank Schoonmaker's Encyclopedia of Wine*. New York: Hastings House, 1968.

Schwabe, Calvin W. *Unmentionable Cuisine*. Charlottesville: University Press of Virginia, 1979.

"The Selling of H_2O." *Consumer Reports*, Vol. 45, no. 9 (September 1980): 531–38.

Simon, Andre; and Howe, Robin. *Dictionary of Gastronomy*. New York: Overlook Press, 1970.

Small, Arnold. *The Birds of California*. New York: Winchester Press, 1974.

Stevenson, Burton, ed. *The Home Book of Quotations, Classical and Modern*, 9th Edition. New York: Dodd, Mead, 1958.

Tannahill, Reay. *Flesh and Blood: A History of the Cannibal Complex*. New York: Stein & Day, 1975.

———. *Food in History*. New York: Stein & Day, 1973.

Taylor, Ronald L. *Butterflies in My Stomach: or Insects in Human Nutrition*. Santa Barbara: Woodbridge Press, 1975.

"Taste Treat or Digestive Treatment." *Chemistry Magazine*, April 1977, p. 5.

Trager, James. *The Foodbook*. New York: Grossman, 1970.

U.S. Department of Agriculture. *Cheeses of the World*. New York: Dover, 1972.

Villiard, Paul. *The Practical Candymaking Cookbook*. New York: Abelard-Schuman, 1970.

Waldo, Myra. *The International Encyclopedia of Cooking*, Volume 2: *Glossary*. New York: Macmillan, 1967.

Walker, Ernest P. et al. *Mammals of the World*, Vols. 1 & 2. Baltimore: Johns Hopkins University Press, 1964.

Ward, Artemus. *Encyclopedia of Food*. New York: Peter Ward, 1923.

Webster's New Twentieth Century Dictionary of the English Language, Unabridged. New York: Publishers Guild, 1959.

Wheeler, Alwyne C. *Fishes of the World: An Illustrated Dictionary*. New York: Macmillan, 1975.

The Wise Encyclopedia of Cookery. New York: Grosset & Dunlap, 1971.

Index

B

D

H

P

U

V